Understanding **Business**

Understanding

Business

ELEVENTH EDITION

William G. Nickels
University of Maryland

James M. McHugh
St. Louis Community College at Forest Park

Susan M. McHugh
Applied Learning Systems

Mc
Graw
Hill
Education

UNDERSTANDING BUSINESS, ELEVENTH EDITION

Published by McGraw-Hill Education, 2 Penn Plaza, New York, NY 10121. Copyright © 2016 by McGraw-Hill Education. All rights reserved. Printed in the United States of America. Previous edition © 2013, 2010, and 2008. No part of this publication may be reproduced or distributed in any form or by any means, or stored in a database or retrieval system, without the prior written consent of McGraw-Hill Education, including, but not limited to, in any network or other electronic storage or transmission, or broadcast for distance learning.

Some ancillaries, including electronic and print components, may not be available to customers outside the United States.

This book is printed on acid-free paper.

6 7 8 9 0 DOW 21 20 19 18 17 16

ISBN 978-0-07-802316-3
MHID 0-07-802316-5

Senior Vice President, Products & Markets: *Kurt L. Strand*
Vice President, General Manager, Products & Markets: *Michael Ryan*
Vice President, Content Design & Delivery: *Kimberly Meriwether David*
Managing Director: *Susan Gouijnstook*
Brand Manager: *Anke Weekes*
Director, Product Development: *Meghan Campbell*
Marketing Manager: *Michael Gedatus*
Marketing Specialist: *Liz Steiner*
Associate Market Development Manager: *Andrea Scheive*
Product Developer: *Kelly Delso*
Digital Product Analyst: *Kerry Shanahan*
Director, Content Design & Delivery: *Terri Schiesl*
Program Manager: *Mary Conzachi*
Content Project Managers: *Christine Vaughan, Danielle Clement,* and *Judi David*
Buyer: *Carol A. Bielski*
Design: *Srdjan Savanovic*
Content Licensing Specialist: *Carrie Burger*
Cover Image: *© Maureen McCutcheon*
Compositor: *Laserwords Private Limited*
Typeface: *10/12 New Aster*
Printer: *R. R. Donnelley*

All credits appearing on page or at the end of the book are considered to be an extension of the copyright page.

Library of Congress Cataloging-in-Publication Data

Nickels, William G.
    Understanding business / William G. Nickels, James M. McHugh, Susan M.
McHugh. —Eleventh edition.
        pages cm
    ISBN 978-0-07-802316-3 (alk. paper)
    1. Industrial management. 2. Business. 3. Business—Vocational guidance.
I. McHugh, James M. II. McHugh, Susan M. III. Title.
HD31.N4897 2016
658—dc23

2014030245

The Internet addresses listed in the text were accurate at the time of publication. The inclusion of a website does not indicate an endorsement by the authors or McGraw-Hill Education, and McGraw-Hill Education does not guarantee the accuracy of the information presented at these sites.

www.mhhe.com

dedication

To our families—Marsha, Joel, Carrie, Claire, Casey, Dan, Molly, Michael, Patrick, and Quinn. Thank you for making everything worth doing and giving us the support to do it well!

and

To the team that made this edition possible, especially the instructors and students who gave us such valuable guidance as we developed the text and package.

Bill Nickels is emeritus professor of business at the University of Maryland, College Park. He has over 30 years' experience teaching graduate and undergraduate business courses, including introduction to business, marketing, and promotion. He has won the Outstanding Teacher on Campus Award four times and was nominated for the award many other times. He received his M.B.A. degree from Western Reserve University and his Ph.D. from The Ohio State University. He has written a marketing communications text and two marketing principles texts in addition to many articles in business publications. He has taught many seminars to businesspeople on subjects such as power communications, marketing, non-business marketing, and stress and life management. His son, Joel, is a professor of English at the University of Miami (Florida).

Jim McHugh holds an M.B.A. degree from Lindenwood University and has had broad experience in education, business, and government. As chairman of the Business and Economics Department of St. Louis Community College–Forest Park, Jim coordinated and directed the development of the business curriculum. In addition to teaching several sections of Introduction to Business each semester for nearly 30 years, Jim taught in the marketing and management areas at both the undergraduate and graduate levels. Jim enjoys conducting business seminars and consulting with small and large businesses. He is actively involved in the public service sector and served as chief of staff to the St. Louis County Executive.

Susan McHugh is a learning specialist with extensive training and experience in adult learning and curriculum development. She holds an M.Ed. degree from the University of Missouri and completed her course work for a Ph.D. in education administration with a specialty in adult learning theory. As a professional curriculum developer, she has directed numerous curriculum projects and educator training programs. She has worked in the public and private sectors as a consultant in training and employee development. While Jim and Susan treasure their participation in writing projects, their greatest accomplishment is their collaboration on their three children. Casey is carrying on the family's teaching tradition as an adjunct professor at Washington University. Molly and Michael are carrying on the family writing tradition by contributing to the development of several supplementary materials for this text.

The Platinum Experience

Understanding Business has long been the MARKET LEADER. We've listened to you and your students and that's helped us offer you:

Resources that were developed based directly on *your* feedback—all geared to make the most of your time and to help students succeed in this course. All the supplemental resources for *Understanding Business* are carefully reviewed by Bill, Jim, and Susan to ensure cohesion with the text.

Technology that leads the way and is consistently being updated to keep up with you and your students. Connect Business offers students a truly interactive and adaptive study arena. Interactive Presentations, Interactive Applications, SmartBook, and LearnSmart are designed to engage students and have been proven to increase grades by a full letter.

Support that is always available to help you in planning your course, working with technology, and meeting the needs of you and your students.

KEEPING UP WITH WHAT'S NEW

Users of *Understanding Business* have always appreciated the currency of the material and the large number of examples from companies of all sizes and industries (e.g., service, manufacturing, nonprofit, and profit) in the United States and around the world. A glance at the Chapter Notes will show you that almost all of them are from 2013 or 2014. Accordingly, this edition features the latest business practices and other developments affecting business including:

- U.S. economic status post-financial crisis and recession
- Growing income inequality
- Gross output (GO)
- Core inflation
- Trans-Pacific Partnership
- Types of social commerce
- JOBS Act of 2012
- Crowdinvesting vs. crowdfunding
- Big data
- Nanomanufacturing
- Generation Z
- Alpha Generation
- Affordable Care Act (Obamacare)
- Ethnographic segmentation
- Mobile/social/on-demand marketing
- Bitcoin and other cryptocurrencies
- Net neutrality
- Internet of Things (IoT)
- And much, much more

RESULTS-DRIVEN TECHNOLOGY FOR STUDENTS

Across the country, instructors and students continue to raise an important question: How can introduction to business courses further support students throughout the learning process to shape future business leaders? While there is no one solution, we see the impact of new learning technologies and innovative study tools that not only fully engage students in course material but also inform instructors of the students' skill and comprehension levels.

Interactive learning tools, including those offered through McGraw-Hill Connect, are being implemented to increase teaching effectiveness and learning efficiency in thousands of colleges and universities. By facilitating a stronger connection with the course and incorporating the latest technologies—such as McGraw-Hill LearnSmart, an adaptive learning program—these tools enable students to succeed in their college careers, which will ultimately increase the percentage of students completing their postsecondary degrees and create the business leaders of the future.

Connect

 McGraw-Hill Connect is the leading online assignment and assessment solution that connects students with the tools and resources they need to achieve success while providing instructors with tools to quickly pick content and assignments according to the learning objectives they want to emphasize.

Connect improves student learning and retention by adapting to the individual student, reinforcing concepts with engaging presentations and activities that prepare students for class, help them master concepts, and review for exams. You can learn more about what is in Connect on the next page.

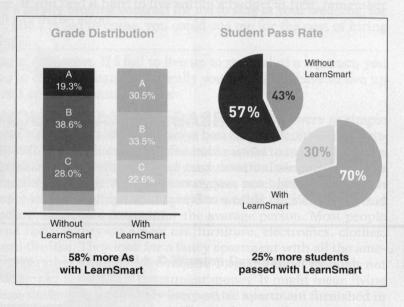

Grade Distribution

Without LearnSmart: A 19.3%, B 38.6%, C 28.0%

With LearnSmart: A 30.5%, B 33.5%, C 22.6%

58% more As with LearnSmart

Student Pass Rate

Without LearnSmart 43%

57%

With LearnSmart 70%

30%

25% more students passed with LearnSmart

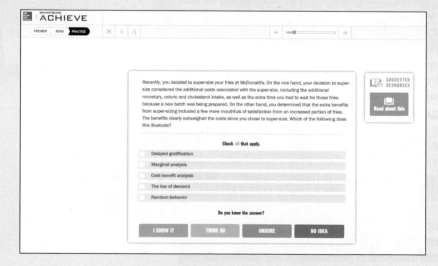

SmartBook Achieve

A revolution in reading Fueled by LearnSmart, SmartBook Achieve is the first and only adaptive reading experience available today. SmartBook personalizes content for each student in a continuously adapting reading experience. Reading is no longer a passive and linear experience, but an engaging and dynamic one where students are more likely to master and retain important concepts, coming to class better prepared.

Leveraging a continuously adaptive learning path, the program adjusts to each student individually as he or she progresses through the program, creating just-in-time learning experiences by presenting interactive content that is tailored to each student's needs. This model is proven to accelerate learning and strengthen memory recall. A convenient time-management feature and turnkey reports for instructors also ensure student's stay on track.

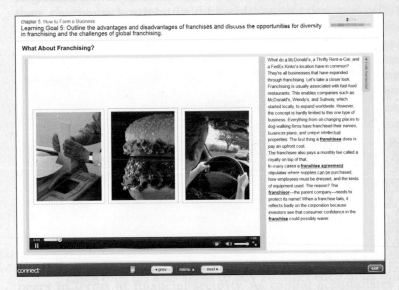

Interactive Presentations

Aid for Visual Learners These visual presentations within Connect are designed to reinforce learning by offering a visual presentation of the learning objectives highlighted in every chapter of the text. Interactive presentations are engaging, online, professional presentations (fully Section 508 compliant) covering the same core concepts directly from the chapter, while offering additional examples and graphics. Interactive Presentations teach students learning objectives in a multimedia format, bringing the course and the book to life. Interactive Presentations are a great prep tool for students—when the students are better prepared, they are more engaged and better able to participate in class.

Interactive Applications

A higher level of learning These exercises require students to APPLY what they have learned in a real-world scenario. These online exercises will help students assess their understanding of the concepts.

Click and Drag exercises allow students to reinforce key models/processes by requiring students to label key illustrations and models from the text or build a process, and then demonstrate application-level knowledge.

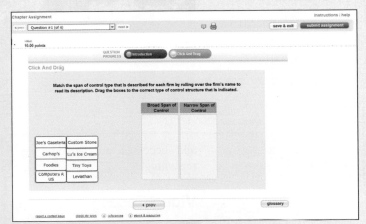

Video cases give students the opportunity to watch case videos and apply chapter concepts to a real-world business scenario as the scenario unfolds.

Decision generators require students to make real business decisions based on specific real-world scenarios and cases.

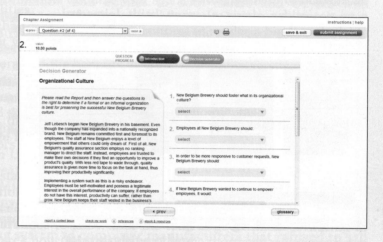

Comprehensive Cases encourage students to read a case and answer open-ended discussion questions to demonstrate writing and critical-thinking skills.

Manager's Hotseat (Connect Library)— short video cases that show 15 real managers applying their years of experience in confronting certain management and organizational behavior issues. Students assume the role of the manager as they watch the video and answer multiple-choice questions that pop up during the segment, forcing them to make decisions on the spot. Students learn from the managers' unscripted mistakes and successes, and then do a report critiquing the managers' approach by defending their reasoning.

Video Cases

Real-world assignments Industry-leading video support helps students understand concepts and see how real companies and professionals implement business principles in the workplace. The video cases highlight companies from a broad range of industries, sizes, and geographic locations, giving students a perspective from a variety of businesses.

Media-Rich E-Book

Connect provides students with a cost-saving alternative to the traditional textbook. A seamless integration of a media-rich e-book features the following:

- A web-optimized e-book, allowing for anytime, anywhere online access to the textbook.
- Our iSee It! animated video explanations of the most often confused topics can be accessed within this e-book.
- Highlighting and note-taking capabilities.

PLATINUM EXPERIENCE STUDENT-FRIENDLY FEATURES

Learning Objectives Everything in the text and supplements package ties back to the chapter learning objectives. The learning objectives listed throughout the chapter help students preview what they should know after reading the chapter. Chapter summaries test students' knowledge by asking questions related to the learning objectives. The Test Bank, Instructor's Manual, PowerPoints, Online Course, and Connect are all organized according to the learning objectives.

Getting to Know Business Professionals Every chapter in the text opens with the profile of a business professional whose career relates closely to the material in the chapter. These business professionals work for a variety of businesses from small businesses and nonprofit organizations to large corporations. These career profiles are an engaging way to open the chapter and to introduce students to a variety of business career paths.

Name That Company Every text chapter opens with a Name That Company challenge. The answer for the challenge can be found somewhere in the chapter.

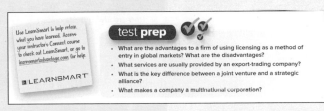

name that **company**

This Swiss-based company has many foreign subsidiaries including Jenny Craig (weight management), Ralston Purina, Chef America (maker of Hot Pockets), and Dreyer's Ice Cream in the United States, as well as Perrier in France. The company employs over 328,000 people and has operations in almost every country in the world. Name that company. (Find the answer in the chapter.)

www.rickshawbags.com

seeking **sustainability**

Sustainability's in the Bag

When it comes to sustainable products, making sure an item is environmentally sound is just the first step. After all, the word "sustainability" implies that something will last for a long time. A shoddy product that needs to be replaced often takes a hefty toll on resources, which can cancel out the environmental benefits of even the greenest production methods.

That's why Rickshaw Bagworks in San Francisco makes sustainable accessories designed to last for the long term. For instance, at first the company began producing bags using expensive Italian wool herringbone tweed. Although the fabric was beautiful and environmentally friendly, the prototypes wore out in a manner of weeks. So Rickshaw teamed up with an upholstery mill to create its own fabric, Rickshaw Performance Tweed. Made from recycled plastic bottles, this synthetic fabric ended up being stronger and more eco-friendly while still looking gorgeous as a handbag.

Rickshaw employees and executives abide by the company's "three Fs" of sustainable design: form, function and footprint. Not only must a product make as small a carbon footprint as possible, it must also serve a long-term practical function and look great doing it. That's why Rickshaw's messenger bags are designed in a way that ensures every piece of fabric cut by the company makes it into the bag.

The company's dedication to sustainability is even incorporated in its name, which means "human powered vehicle" in Japanese. Do you think more companies should be as dedicated to sustainability as Rickshaw?

Sources: Mark Dwight, "How to Build a Sustainable Business," *Inc.*, November 2013; and http://blog.rickshawbags.com/the-rickshaw-story/, accessed February 2014.

Seeking Sustainability boxes highlight corporate responsibility and help students understand the various ways business activities affect the environment.

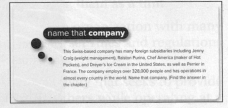

Use LearnSmart to help retain what you have learned. Access your instructor's Connect course to check out LearnSmart, or go to learnsmartadvantage.com for help.

LEARNSMART

test **prep**

- What are the advantages to a firm of using licensing as a method of entry in global markets? What are the disadvantages?
- What services are usually provided by an export-trading company?
- What is the key difference between a joint venture and a strategic alliance?
- What makes a company a multinational corporation?

Test Prep Questions help students understand and retain the material in the chapters. These questions stop them at important points in the chapter to assess what they've learned before they continue reading and help them prep for exams.

PLATINUM EXPERIENCE INSTRUCTOR RESOURCES

Connect offers instructors autogradable material in an effort to facilitate learning and to save time.

Student Progress Tracking

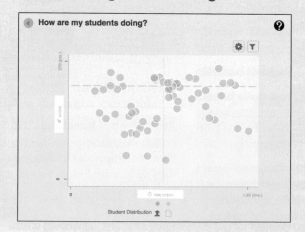

Connect Insight is a powerful data analytics tool that allows instructors to leverage aggregated information about their courses and students to provide a more personalized teaching and learning experience.

Connect's Instructor Library

Connect's Instructor Library serves as a one-stop, secure site for essential course materials, allowing you to save prep time before class. The instructor site resources found in the library include:

- Instructor's Manual
- PowerPoint Presentations
- Test Bank/EZ Test
- Monthly Bonus Activities
- Videos
- Video Guide
- Connect Instructor's Manual

Instructor's Manual: The authors have carefully reviewed all resources provided in the Instructor's Manual to ensure cohesion with the text. It includes everything an instructor needs to prepare a lecture, including lecture outlines, discussion questions, and teaching notes. More than 900 PowerPoint slides offer material from the text, as well as expanded coverage to supplement discussion.

PowerPoint Presentations: More than 900 PowerPoint slides offer material from the text, as well as expanded coverage to supplement discussion.

Test Bank and EZ Test Online: The Test Bank and Computerized Test Bank offer over 8,000 multiple-choice, true/false, short answer, essay, and application questions. ISBN: 0077474376

Monthly Bonus Activities: Monthly Bonus Activities contain a variety of tools to help freshen your classes: (1) links to interesting new videos; (2) abstracts of recent articles with accompanying critical-thinking questions to spark class discussion (sample answers included); and (3) a PowerPoint file that integrates these elements in an easy-to-use package. If you're a current adopter of the text, then we are already sending you the Monthly Bonus Activities. If you are not receiving them and would like to, please contact your McGraw-Hill Sales Representative.

Videos: Chapter-specific videos are provided to complement each chapter of the text. Eleven of the 20 videos have been updated to include interesting companies that students will identify with such as SXSW, Sonic, and Whole Foods.

Video Guide: The Video Guide offers additional detailed teaching notes to accompany the chapter videos, and provides essay-style and multiple-choice questions.

Connect Instructor's Manual: This Instructor's Manual offers instructors what they need to set up Connect for their courses. It explains everything from how to get started to suggestions of what to assign and ideas about assigning credit. This tool was developed by instructors who have used and continue to use Connect successfully in their course.

PLATINUM EXPERIENCE TEACHING OPTIONS AND SOLUTIONS

Blackboard Partnership

McGraw-Hill Education and Blackboard have teamed up to simplify your life. Now you and your students can access Connect and Create right from within your Blackboard course—all with one single sign-on. The grade books are seamless, so when a student completes an integrated Connect assignment, the grade for that assignment automatically (and instantly) feeds your Blackboard grade center. Learn more at www.domorenow.com.

Create

Instructors can now tailor their teaching resources to match the way they teach! With McGraw-Hill Create, www.mcgrawhillcreate.com, instructors can easily rearrange chapters, combine material from other content sources, and quickly upload and integrate their own content, like course syllabi or teaching notes. Find the right content in Create by searching through thousands of leading McGraw-Hill textbooks. Arrange the material to fit your teaching style. Order a Create book and receive a complimentary print review copy in three to five business days or a complimentary electronic review copy via e-mail within one hour. Go to www.mcgrawhillcreate.com today and register.

Tegrity Campus

Tegrity makes class time available 24/7 by automatically capturing every lecture in a searchable format for students to review when they study and complete assignments. With a simple one-click start-and-stop process, you capture all computer screens and corresponding audio. Students can replay any part of any class with easy-to-use browser-based viewing on a PC or Mac. Educators know that the more students can see, hear, and experience class resources, the better they learn. In fact, studies prove it. With patented Tegrity "search anything" technology, students instantly recall key class moments for replay online or on iPods and mobile devices. Instructors can help turn all their students' study time into learning moments immediately supported by their lecture. To learn more about Tegrity, watch a two-minute Flash demo at http://tegritycampus.mhhe.com.

McGraw-Hill Campus

McGraw-Hill Campus is a new one-stop teaching and learning experience available to users of any learning management system. This institutional service allows faculty and students to enjoy single sign-on (SSO) access to all McGraw-Hill Higher Education materials, including the award-winning McGraw-Hill Connect platform, from directly within the institution's website. With McGraw-Hill Campus, faculty receive instant access to teaching materials (e.g., eTextbooks, test banks, Power Point slides, animations, learning objects, etc.), allowing them to browse, search, and use any instructor ancillary content in our vast library at no additional cost to instructor or students.

COURSE DESIGN AND DELIVERY

In addition, students enjoy SSO access to a variety of free content (e.g., quizzes, flash cards, narrated presentations, etc.) and subscription-based products (e.g., McGraw-Hill Connect). With McGraw-Hill Campus enabled, faculty and students will never need to create another account to access McGraw-Hill products and services. Learn more at www.mhcampus.com.

Assurance of Learning Ready

Many educational institutions today focus on the notion of *assurance of learning,* an important element of some accreditation standards. *Understanding Business* is designed specifically to support instructors' assurance of learning initiatives with a simple yet powerful solution. Each test bank question for *Understanding Business* maps to a specific chapter learning objective listed in the text. Instructors can use our test bank software, EZ Test and EZ Test Online, to easily query for learning objectives that directly relate to the learning outcomes for their course. Instructors can then use the reporting features of EZ Test to aggregate student results in similar fashion, making the collection and presentation of assurance of learning data simple and easy.

AACSB Tagging

McGraw-Hill Education is a proud corporate member of AACSB International. Understanding the importance and value of AACSB accreditation, *Understanding Business* recognizes the curricula guidelines detailed in the AACSB standards for business accreditation by connecting selected questions in the text and the test bank to the six general knowledge and skill guidelines in the AACSB standards. The statements contained in *Understanding Business* are provided only as a guide for the users of this textbook. The AACSB leaves content coverage and assessment within the purview of individual schools, the mission of the school, and the faculty. While the *Understanding Business* teaching package makes no claim of any specific AACSB qualification or evaluation, we have within *Understanding Business* labeled selected questions according to the six general knowledge and skills areas.

McGraw-Hill Customer Experience Group Contact Information

At McGraw-Hill Education, we understand that getting the most from new technology can be challenging. That's why our services don't stop after you purchase our products. You can e-mail our Product Specialists 24 hours a day to get product training online. Or you can search our knowledge bank of Frequently Asked Questions on our support website. For Customer Support, call **800-331-5094** or visit www.mhhe.com/support. One of our Technical Support Analysts will be able to assist you in a timely fashion.

Our Senior Brand Manager, Anke Weekes, led the talented team at McGraw-Hill Education. We appreciate her dedication to the success of the project and her responsiveness to the demands of the market. Kelly Delso served as our product developer and kept everyone on task and on schedule. Molly and Michael McHugh contributed the new boxes and profiles. Srdjan Savanovic created the new fresh, open interior design and extraordinary cover. Carrie Burger and Jen Blankenship carried out the extensive research for photos that was necessary to effectively reflect the concepts presented in the text. Lead project manager, Christine Vaughan, did a splendid job of keeping the production of the text on schedule. Danielle Clement expertly supervised Connect production.

Many dedicated educators made extraordinary contributions to the quality and utility of this text and package. For this edition, Molly McHugh did an exceptional job in preparing the Test Bank and creating the quizzes for Connect. Molly also did a superb job of creating the PowerPoint slides and a useful and current Instructor's Resource Manual. We also recognize the efforts of those who contributed to the creation of Connect materials, and to our LearnSmart "team" at Monroe Community College; Judy Bulin, John Striebich, and Donna Haeger who tirelessly worked to review and perfect LearnSmart content. Thank you to Chris Cole, Dayna Brown, Dan Mack, and the crew of Cole Creative Productions for the fabulous new videos they produced. Thank you to the Digital Faculty Consultants who have helped train and support so many instructors in the Introduction to Business course, as well as assist them in successfully implementing Connect into their courses: Chris Finnin, Drexel University; Todd Korol, Monroe Community College; John Striebich, Monroe Community College; and Marie Lapidus, Oakton Community College.

Our outstanding marketing manager, Michael Gedatus, was up to the challenge of once again guiding the text to market leadership. With the assistance of the market's finest sales professionals, he led the text to record highs. We appreciate his commitment and the renowned product knowledge, service, and dedication of the McGraw-Hill Education sales reps. We want to thank the many instructors who contributed to the development of *Understanding Business*.

REVIEWERS

We would like to thank the following instructors for sharing their opinions with us in an effort to improve this and previous editions:

Ashraf Almurdaah, *Los Angeles City College*

Lydia Anderson, *Fresno City College*

Chi Anyasi-Archibong, *North Carolina A&T*

Maria Aria, *Camden County College*

Michael Aubry, *Cuyamaca College*

Frank Barber, *Cuyahoga Community College*

Richard Bartlett, *Columbus State Community College*

Lorraine P. Bassette, *Prince George's Community College*

Jim Beard, *University of Arkansas–Fort Smith*

Amy Beattie, *Champlain College*

Charles Beem, *Bucks County Community College*

Robert Bennett, *Delaware County Community College*

Michael Bento, *Owens Community College*

George H. Bernard, *Seminole State College of Florida*

Marilyn Besich, *Montana State University–Great Falls*

Dennis Brode, *Sinclair Community College*

Kathy Broneck, *Pima Community College*

Harvey Bronstein, *Oakland Community College*

Jerri Buiting, *Baker College–Flint*

Bonnie Chavez, *Santa Barbara City College*

Savannah Clay, *Central Piedmont Community College*

Paul Coakley, *Community College of Baltimore County*

Patrick Conroy, *Delgado Community College*

James Darling, *Central New Mexico Community College*

Joseph Dutka, *Ivy Tech Community College of Indiana*

MaryBeth Furst, *Howard Community College*

Wayne Gawlik, *Joliet Junior College*

Ross Gittell, *University of New Hampshire*

Constance Golden, *Lakeland Community College*

Doug Greiner, *University of Toledo–Scott Park*

John Guess, *Delgado Community College*

Lisa E. Hadley, *Southwest Tennessee Community College*

Nancy Hernandez, *Howard College*

Maryanne Holcomb, *Oakland Community College*

Russell E. Holmes, *Des Moines Area Community College*

Janice Karlen, *La Guardia Community College*

James W. Marco, *Wake Technical Community College*

Theresa Mastrianni, *Kingsborough Community College*

Michelle Meyer, *Joliet Junior College*

Catherine Milburn, *University of Colorado–Denver*

Mihai Nica, *University of Central Oklahoma*

David Oliver, *Edison Community College*

Dyan Pease, *Sacramento City College*

Vincent Quan, *Fashion Institute of Technology*

David Robinson, *University of California–Berkeley*

Rieann Spence-Gale, *Nova Community College*

Kurt Stanberry, *University of Houston*

Marguerite Teubner, *Nassau Community College*

Rod Thirion, *Pikes Peak Community College*

William J. Wardrope, *University of Central Oklahoma*

David Washington, *North Carolina State University*

We would like to thank the following instructors and students who generously provided the input and advice that contributed to the development of this text.

Nikolas Adamou, *Borough of Manhattan Community College*

Cathy Adamson, *Southern Union State Community College*

Gary Amundson, *Montana State University–Billings*

Kenneth Anderson, *Borough of Manhattan Community College*

Kenneth Anderson, *Mott Community College*

Lydia Anderson, *Fresno City College*

Narita Anderson, *University of Central Oklahoma*

Roanne Angiello, *Bergen Community College*

Chi Anyansi-Archibong, *North Carolina A&T University*

Michael Atchison, *University of Virginia–Charlottesville*

Andrea Bailey, *Moraine Valley Community College*

Sandra Bailey, *Ivy Tech Community College of Indiana*

Scott Bailey, *Troy University*

Wayne Ballantine, *Prairie View A&M University*

Ruby Barker, *Tarleton State University*

Rosalia (Lia) Barone, *Norwalk Community College*

Barbara Barrett, *St. Louis Community College–Meramec*

Barry Barrett, *University of Wisconsin–Milwaukee*

Lorraine Bassette, *Prince George's Community College*

Robb Bay, *College of Southern Nevada–West Charle*

Charles Beavin, *Miami Dade College North*

Charles Beem, *Bucks County Community College*

Cathleen Behan, *Northern Virginia Community College*

Lori Bennett, *Moorpark College*

Ellen Benowitz, *Mercer Community College*

Patricia Bernson, *County College of Morris*

William Bettencourt, *Edmonds Community College*

Robert Blanchard, *Salem State College*

Mary Jo Boehms, *Jackson State Community College*

James Borden, *Villanova University*

Michael Bravo, *Bentley College*

Dennis Brode, *Sinclair Community College*

Harvey Bronstein, *Oakland Community College–Farmington Hills*

Deborah Brown, *North Carolina State University–Raleigh*

Aaron A. Buchko, *Bradley University*

Laura Bulas, *Central Community College–Hastings*

Judy Bulin, *Monroe Community College*

Barry Bunn, *Valencia Community College–West Campus*

Bill Burton, *Indiana Wesleyan University*

Paul Callahan, *Cincinnati State Technical and Community College*

William Candley, *Lemoyne Owen College*

Nancy Carr, *Community College of Philadelphia*

Ron Cereola, *James Madison University*

Bonnie Chavez, *Santa Barbara City College*

Susan Cisco, *Oakton Community College*

Margaret (Meg) Clark, *Cincinnati State Technical and Community College*

David Clifton, *Ivy Tech Community College of Indiana*

C. Cloud, *Phoenix College*

Doug Cobbs, *JS Reynolds Community College*

Brooks Colin, *University of New Orleans*

Debbie Collins, *Anne Arundel Community College*

Andrew Cook, *Limestone College*

Bob Cox, *Salt Lake Community College*

Susan Cremins, *Westchester Community College*

Julie Cross, *Chippewa Valley Tech College*

Geoffrey Crosslin, *Kalamazoo Valley Community College*

Douglas Crowe, *Bradley University*

John David, *Stark State College of Technology*

Peter Dawson, *Collin County Community College*

Joseph Defilippe, *Suffolk County Community College–Brentwood*

Tim DeGroot, *Midwestern State University*

Len Denault, *Bentley College*

Frances Depaul, *Westmoreland County Community College*

Donna Devault, *Fayetteville Tech Community College*

Sharon Dexter, *Southeast Community College–Beatrice*

John Dilyard, *St. Francis College*

Barbara Dinardo, *Owens Community College*

George Dollar, *St. Petersburg College*

Glenn Doolittle, *Santa Ana College*

Ron Dougherty, *Ivy Tech Community College of Indiana*

Michael Drafke, *College of DuPage*

Karen Eboch, *Bowling Green State University*

Brenda Eichelberger, *Portland State University*

Kelvin Elston, *Nashville State Tech Community College*

Robert Ettl, *Stony Brook University*

Nancy Evans, *Heartland Community College*

Michael Ewens, *Ventura College*

Hyacinth Ezeka, *Coppin State University*

Bob Farris, *Mt. San Antonio College*

Karen Faulkner, *Long Beach City College*

Gil Feiertag, *Columbus State Community College*

Joseph Flack, *Washtenaw Community College*

Lucinda Fleming, *Orange County Community College*

Jackie Flom, *University of Toledo*

Andrea Foster, *John Tyler Community College*

Michael Foster, *Bentley College*

Leatrice Freer, *Pitt Community College*

Alan Friedenthal, *Kingsborough Community College*

Charles Gaiser, *Brunswick Community College*

Ashley Geisewite, *Southwest Tennessee Community College*

Katie Ghahramani, *Johnson County Community College*

Debora Gilliard, *Metropolitan State College–Denver*

James Glover, *Community College of Baltimore County–Essex*

Constance Golden, *Lakeland Community College*

Toby Grodner, *Union County College*

Clark Hallpike, *Elgin Community College*

Geri Harper, *Western Illinois University*

Frank Hatstat, *Bellevue Community College*

Spedden Hause, *University of Maryland–University College*

Karen Hawkins, *Miami-Dade College–Kendall*

Travis Hayes, *Chattanooga State Technical Community College*

Jack Heinsius, *Modesto Junior College*

Charlane Held, *Onondaga Community College*

James Hess, *Ivy Tech Community College of Indiana*

Steve Hester, *Southwest Tennessee Community College–Macon Campus*

William Hill, *Mississippi State University*

Nathan Himelstein, *Essex County College*

Paula Hladik, *Waubonsee Community College*

David Ho, *Metropolitan Community College*

Douglas Hobbs, *Sussex County Community College*

Maryanne Holcomb, *Antelope Valley College*

Mary Carole Hollingsworth, *Georgia Perimeter College*

Russell Holmes, *Des Moines Area Community College*

Scott Homan, *Purdue University–West Lafayette*

Stacy Horner, *Southwestern Michigan College*

Dennis Hudson, *University of Tulsa*

Jo Ann Hunter, *Community College Allegheny County in Pittsburgh*

Kimberly Hurns, *Washtenaw Community College*

Victor Isbell, *University of Nevada–Las Vegas*

Deloris James, *University of Maryland–University College*

Pam Janson, *Stark State College of Technology*

William Jedlicka, *Harper College*

Carol Johnson, *University of Denver*

Gwendolyn Jones, *University of Akron*

Kenneth Jones, *Ivy Tech Community College of Indiana*

Marilyn Jones, *Friends University*

Michael Jones, *Delgado Community College*

Dmitriy Kalyagin, *Chabot College*

Jack Kant, *San Juan College*

Jimmy Kelsey, *Seattle Central Community College*

Robert Kemp, *University of Virginia–Charlottesville*

David Kendall, *Fashion Institute of Technology*

Kristine Kinard, *Shelton State Community College*

Sandra King, *Minnesota State University–Mankato*

John Kurnik, *Saint Petersburg College*

Jeff LaVake, *University of Wisconsin–Oshkosh*

Robert Lewis, *Davenport University*

Byron Lilly, *DeAnza College*

Beverly Loach, *Central Piedmont Community College*

Boone Londrigan, *Mott Community College*

Ladonna Love, *Fashion Institute of Technology*

Ivan Lowe, *York Technical College*

Yvonne Lucas, *Southwestern College*

Robert Lupton, *Central Washington University*

Megan Luttenton, *Grand Valley State University*

Elaine Madden, *Anne Arundel Community College*

Lawrence Maes, *Davenport University*

Niki Maglaris, *Northwestern College*

James Maniki, *Northwestern College*

Martin Markowitz, *College of Charleston*

Fred Mayerson, *Kingsborough Community College*

Stacy McCaskill, *Rock Valley College*

Vershun L. McClain, *Jackson State University*

Gina McConoughey, *Illinois Central College*

Patricia McDaniel, *Central Piedmont Community College*

Pam McElligott, *St. Louis Community College–Meramec*

Tom McFarland, *Mt. San Antonio College*

Bill McPherson, *Indiana University of Pennsylvania*

Ginger Moore, *York Technical College*

Sandy Moore, *Ivy Tech Community College of Indiana*

Jennifer Morton, *Ivy Tech Community College of Indiana*

Peter Moutsatson, *Central Michigan University*

Rachna Nagi-Condos, *American River College*

Darrell Neron, *Pierce College*

Mihia Nica, *University of Central Oklahoma*

Charles Nichols, *Sullivan University*

Frank Novakowski, *Davenport University*

Mark Nygren, *Brigham Young University–Idaho*

Paul Okello, *Tarrant County College*

Faviana Olivier, *Bentley College*

John Olivo, *Bloomsburg University of Pennsylvania*

Teresa O'Neill, *International Institute of the Americas*

Cathy Onion, *Western Illinois University*

Susan Ontko, *Schoolcraft College*

Glenda Orosco, *Oklahoma State University Institute of Technology*

Christopher O'Suanah, *J. S. Reynolds Community College*

Daniel Pacheco, *Kansas City Kansas Community College*

Esther Page-Wood, *Western Michigan University*

Lauren Paisley, *Genesee Community College*

John Pappalardo, *Keene State College*

Ron Pardee, *Riverside Community College*

Jack Partlow, *Northern Virginia Community College*

Jeff Pepper, *Chippewa Valley Tech College*

Sheila Petcavage, *Cuyahoga Community College Western–Parma*

Roy Pipitone, *Erie Community College*

Lana Powell, *Valencia Community College–West Campus*

Dan Powroznik, *Chesapeake College*

Litsa Press, *College of Lake County*

Sally Proffitt, *Tarrant County College–Northeast*

Michael Quinn, *James Madison University*

Anthony Racka, *Oakland Community College*

Larry Ramos, *Miami-Dade Community College*

Greg Rapp, *Portland Community College–Sylvania*

Robert Reese, *Illinois Valley Community College*

David Reiman, *Monroe County Community College*

Gloria Rembert, *Mitchell Community College*

Levi Richard, *Citrus College*

Clinton Richards, *University of Nevada–Las Vegas*

Patricia Richards, *Westchester Community College*

Susan Roach, *Georgia Southern University*

Sandra Robertson, *Thomas Nelson Community College*

Catherine Roche, *Rockland Community College*

Tim Rogers, *Ozark Technical College*

Sam Rohr, *University of Northwestern Ohio*

Pamela Rouse, *Butler University*

Carol Rowey, *Community College of Rhode Island*

Jeri Rubin, *University of Alaska–Anchorage*

Storm Russo, *Valencia Community College*

Mark Ryan, *Hawkeye Community College*

Richard Sarkisian, *Camden County College*

Andy Saucedo, *Dona Ana Community College–Las Cruces*

James Scott, *Central Michigan University*

Janet Seggern, *Lehigh Carbon Community College*

Sashi Sekhar, *Purdue University–Calumet-Hammond*

Pat Setlik, *Harper College*

Swannee Sexton, *University of Tennessee–Knoxville*

Phyllis Shafer, *Brookdale Community College*

Richard Shortridge, *Glendale Community College*

Louise Stephens, *Volunteer State Community College*

Desiree Stephens, *Norwalk Community College*

Clifford Stalter, *Chattanooga State Technical Community College*

Kurt Stanberry, *University of Houston–Downtown*

Martin St. John, *Westmoreland County Community College*

John Striebich, *Monroe Community College*

David Stringer, *DeAnza College*

Ron Surmacz, *Duquesne University*

William Syvertsen, *Fresno City College*

Scott Taylor, *Moberly Area Community College*

Jim Thomas, *Indiana University Northwest*

Deborah Thompson, *Bentley College*

Evelyn Thrasher, *University of Massachusetts–Dartmouth*

Jon Tomlinson, *University of Northwestern Ohio*

Bob Trewartha, *Minnesota School of Business*

Bob Urell, *Irvine Valley College*

Dan Vetter, *Central Michigan University*

Andrea Vidrine, *Baton Rouge Community College*

Daniel Viveiros, *Johnson & Wales University*

Joann Warren, *Community College of Rhode Island–Warwick*

R. Patrick Wehner, *Everest University*

Sally Wells, *Columbia College*

Mildred Wilson, *Georgia Southern University*

Karen Wisniewski, *County College of Morris*

Greg Witkowski, *Northwestern College*

Colette Wolfson, *Ivy Tech Community College of Indiana*

Deborah Yancey, *Virginia Western Community College*

Mark Zarycki, *Hillsborough Community College*

Lisa Zingaro, *Oakton Community College*

Mark Zorn, *Butler County Community College*

This edition continues to be the market's gold standard due to the involvement of these committed instructors and students. We thank them all for their help, support, and friendship.

Bill Nickels   **Jim McHugh**   **Susan McHugh**

BRIEF CONTENTS

CONTENTS

PART 2

Business Ownership: Starting a Small Business 118

CHAPTER 5
How to Form a Business 118

PART 4

Management of Human Resources: Motivating Employees to Produce Quality Goods and Services   268

CHAPTER 10
Motivating Employees   268

CHAPTER 11
Human Resource Management: Finding and Keeping the Best Employees   298

PART 6

Managing Financial Resources 472

CHAPTER 17

Understanding Accounting and Financial Information 472

EPILOGUE
Getting the Job You Want   E

Getting Ready for This Course and Your Career

Top 10 Reasons to Read This Introduction

(EVEN IF IT ISN'T ASSIGNED)

10 What the heck—you already bought the book, so you might as well get your money's worth.

9 You don't want the only reason you get a raise to be that the government has increased the minimum wage.

8 Getting off to a good start in the course can improve your chances of getting a higher grade, and your Uncle Ernie will send you a dollar for every A you get.

7 Your friends say that you've got the manners of a troll and you want to find out what the heck they're talking about.

6 How else would you find out a spork isn't usually one of the utensils used at a business dinner?

5 You don't want to experience the irony of frantically reading the "time management" section at 3:00 a.m.

4 Like the Boy Scouts, you want to be prepared.

3 It must be important because the authors spent so much time writing it.

2 You want to run with the big dogs someday.

AND THE NUMBER ONE REASON FOR READING THIS INTRODUCTORY SECTION IS . . .

1 It could be on a test.

LEARNING THE SKILLS YOU NEED TO SUCCEED TODAY AND TOMORROW

Your life is full. You're starting a new semester, perhaps even beginning your college career, and you're feeling pulled in many directions. Why take time to read this introduction? We have lightheartedly offered our top 10 reasons on the previous page, but the real importance of this section is no joking matter.

Its purpose, and that of the entire text, is to help you learn principles, strategies, and skills for success that will serve you not only in this course but also in your career and your life. Whether you learn them is up to you. Learning them won't guarantee success, but not learning them—well, you get the picture.

This is an exciting and challenging time. Success in any venture comes from understanding basic principles and knowing how to apply them effectively. What you learn now could help you be a success—for the rest of your life. Begin applying these skills now to gain an edge on the competition. READ THIS SECTION BEFORE YOUR FIRST CLASS and make a great first impression! Good luck. We wish you the best.

Bill Nickels   **Jim McHugh**   **Susan McHugh**

USING THIS COURSE TO PREPARE FOR YOUR CAREER

Since you've signed up for this course, we're guessing you already know the value of a college education. The holders of bachelor's degrees make an average of about $46,000 per year compared to less than $30,000 for high school graduates.[1] That's greater than 50 percent more for college graduates than those with just a high school diploma. Compounded over the course of a 30-year career, the average college grad will make nearly a half-million dollars more than the high school grad! Thus, what you invest in a college education is likely to pay you back many times. See Figure P.1 for more of an idea of how much salary difference a college degree makes by the end of a 30-year career. That doesn't mean there aren't good careers available to non–college graduates. It just means those with an education are more likely to have higher earnings over their lifetime.

The value of a college education is more than just a larger paycheck. Other benefits include increasing your ability to think critically and communicate your ideas to others, improving your ability to use technology, and preparing yourself to live in a diverse and competitive world. Knowing you've met your goals and earned a college degree also gives you the self-confidence to work toward future goals.

Experts say today's college graduates will likely hold seven or eight different jobs (often in several different careers) in their lifetime. Many returning students are changing their careers and their plans for life. In fact, in recent years the percentage increase of students age 25 or older enrolling in college has been larger than the percentage of younger students.[2] In addition, over 50 percent of all part-time college students are 25 or older.[3]

You too may want to change careers someday. It can be the path to long-term happiness and success. That means you'll have to be flexible and adjust your strengths and talents to new opportunities. Learning has become a lifelong job. You'll need to constantly update your skills to achieve high competence and remain competitive.

If you're typical of many college students, you may not have any idea what career you'd like to pursue. That isn't necessarily a big disadvantage in today's fast-changing job market. After all, many of the best jobs of the future don't even exist today. Figure P.2 lists 10 careers that didn't exist 10 years ago. There are no perfect or certain ways to prepare for the most interesting and challenging jobs of tomorrow. Rather, you should continue your college education, develop strong technology and Internet skills, improve your verbal and written communication skills, and remain flexible and forward thinking while you explore the job market.

The rewards of college are well worth the effort for graduates, who can expect to earn over 60 percent more than high school graduates over the course of their careers. Businesses like graduates too, because the growing needs of a global workplace require knowledgeable workers to fill the jobs of the future. What other benefits do you see from earning a college degree?

FIGURE P.1 SALARY COMPARISON OF HIGH SCHOOL VERSUS COLLEGE GRADUATES

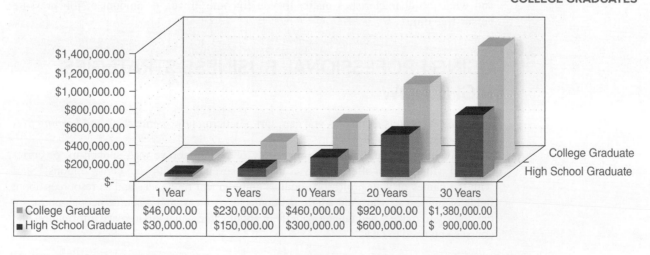

	1 Year	5 Years	10 Years	20 Years	30 Years
College Graduate	$46,000.00	$230,000.00	$460,000.00	$920,000.00	$1,380,000.00
High School Graduate	$30,000.00	$150,000.00	$300,000.00	$600,000.00	$ 900,000.00

FIGURE P.2 NEW
CAREERS

These careers didn't exist 10 years ago:

- IOS Developer
- Android Developer
- Zumba Instructor
- Social Media Intern
- Data Scientist
- UI/UX Designer
- Big Data Architect
- Beachbody Coach
- Cloud Services Specialist
- Digital Marketing Specialist

Source: LinkedIn, www.linkedin.com, accessed May 2014.

One of the objectives of this class, and this book, is to help you choose an area in which you might enjoy working and have a good chance to succeed. You'll learn about economics, global business, ethics, entrepreneurship, management, marketing, accounting, finance, and more. At the end of the course, you should have a much better idea which careers would be best for you and which you would not enjoy.

But you don't have to be in business to use business principles. You can use marketing principles to get a job and to sell your ideas to others. You can use your knowledge of investments to make money in the stock market. You'll use your management skills and general business knowledge wherever you go and in whatever career you pursue— including government agencies, charities, and social causes.

ASSESSING YOUR SKILLS AND PERSONALITY

The earlier you can do a personal assessment of your interests, skills, and values, the better it can help you find career direction. Hundreds of schools use software exercises like the System for Interactive Guidance and Information (SIGI) and DISCOVER to offer self-assessment exercises, personalized lists of occupations based on your interests and skills, and information about different careers and the preparation each requires. Visit your college's placement center, career lab, or library soon and learn what programs are available for you. Even if you're a returning student with work experience, an assessment of your skills will help you choose the right courses and career path to follow next.

Self-assessment will help you determine the kind of work environment you'd prefer (technical, social service, or business); what values you seek to fulfill in a career (security, variety, or independence); what abilities you have (creative/artistic, numerical, or sales); and what job characteristics matter to you (income, travel, or amount of job pressure versus free time).

USING PROFESSIONAL BUSINESS STRATEGIES RIGHT NOW

Here are two secrets to success you can start practicing now: *networking* and *keeping files on subjects important to you.*

Networking is building a personal array of people you've met, spoken to, or corresponded with who can offer you advice about and even help with your career options.[4] Start with the names of your professors, both as employment references and as resources about fields of interest to you. Add additional contacts, mentors, and resource people, and keep the notes you make when talking with them about careers including salary information and courses you need to take.

All students need a way to retain what they learn. An effective way to become an expert on almost any business subject is to set up your own information system. You can store data on your computer, tablet, and cell phone (back up these files!), or you can establish a comprehensive filing system on paper, or you can use a combination of the two. Few college students take the time to make this effort; those who don't lose much of the information they read in college or thereafter.

Keep as many of your textbooks and other assigned readings as you can, as well as your course notes. Read a national newspaper such as *The Wall Street Journal, The New York Times,* or *USA Today.* Read your local newspaper. Each time you read a story that interests you, save a paper copy or add a link to the story online in your electronic file, under a topic heading like *careers, small business, marketing, economics,* or *management.* You'll easily find the latest data on almost any subject on the Internet. Don't rely on just one site for information (and be wary of Wikipedia)! Get familiar with a variety of sources and use them.

Networking provides you with an array of personal contacts on whom you can call for career advice and help. Have you begun creating your network yet? Are you part of someone else's?

Start a file for your résumé. In it, keep a copy of your current résumé along with reference letters and other information about jobs you may have held, including projects accomplished and additions to your responsibilities over time, plus any awards or special recognition you may have received. Soon you'll have a tremendous amount of information to help you prepare a polished résumé and answer challenging job interview questions with ease.

Watching television shows about business, such as *Nightly Business Report* and Jim Cramer's *Mad Money,* helps you learn the language of business and become more informed about current happenings in business and the economy. Try viewing some of these shows or listening to similar ones on the radio, and see which ones you like best. Take notes and put them in your files. Keep up with business news in your area so that you know what jobs are available and where. You may also want to join a local business group to begin networking with people and learning the secrets of the local business scene. Many business groups and professional business societies accept student members.

LEARNING TO BEHAVE LIKE A PROFESSIONAL

There's a reason good manners never go out of style. As the world becomes increasingly competitive, the gold goes to teams and individuals with that extra bit of polish. The person who makes a good impression will be the one who gets the job, wins the promotion, or clinches the deal. Good manners and professionalism are not difficult to acquire; they're second nature to those who achieve and maintain a competitive edge.

Not even a great résumé or designer suit can substitute for poor behavior, including verbal behavior, in an interview. Say "please" and "thank you" when you ask for something. Certainly make it a point to arrive on time, open doors for others, stand when an older person enters the room, and use a polite tone of voice. You may want to take a class in etiquette or read a book on etiquette to learn the proper way to eat in a nice restaurant, what to do at a formal party, and so on.[5] Of course, it's also critical to be honest, reliable, dependable, and ethical at all times.

Some rules are not formally written anywhere; instead, every successful businessperson learns them through experience. If you follow these rules in college, you'll have the skills for success when you start your career. Here are the basics:

1. **Making a good first impression.** An old saying goes, "You never get a second chance to make a good first impression." You have just a few seconds to make an impression. Therefore, how you dress and how you look are important. Take your cue as to what is appropriate at any specific company by studying the people there who are most successful. What do they wear? How do they act?

Many businesses have adopted business casual as the proper work attire, but others still require traditional clothing styles. How does your appearance at work affect both you and your company?

2. **Focusing on good grooming.** Be aware of your appearance and its impact. Wear appropriate, clean clothing and a few simple accessories. Revealing shirts, nose rings, and tattoos may not be appropriate in a work setting. Be consistent, too; you can't project a good image by dressing well a few times a week and then showing up looking like you're getting ready to mow a lawn.

   Many organizations have adopted "business casual" guidelines, but others still require traditional attire, so ask what the organization's policies are and choose your wardrobe accordingly. Casual doesn't mean sloppy or shabby. Wrinkled clothing, shirttails hanging out, and hats worn indoors are not usually appropriate. For women, business casual attire includes simple skirts and slacks (no jeans), cotton shirts, sweaters (not too tight), blazers, and low-heeled shoes or boots. Men may wear khaki trousers, sport shirts with collars, sweaters or sport jackets, and casual loafers or lace-up shoes.

3. **Being on time.** When you don't come to class or work on time, you're sending this message to your teacher or boss: "My time is more important than your time. I have more important things to do than be here." In addition to showing a lack of respect to your teacher or boss, lateness rudely disrupts the work of your colleagues.

   Pay attention to the corporate culture. Sometimes you have to come in earlier than others and leave later to get that promotion you desire. To develop good work habits and get good grades, arrive in class on time and avoid leaving (or packing up to leave) early.

4. **Practicing considerate behavior.** Listen when others are talking—for example, don't check your cell phone for messages, read the newspaper, or eat in class. Don't interrupt others when they are speaking; wait your turn. Eliminate profanity from your vocabulary. Use appropriate body language by sitting up attentively and not slouching. Sitting up has the added bonus of helping you stay awake! Professors and managers alike get a favorable impression from those who look and act alert.

5. **Practicing good e-mail etiquette.** The basic rules of courtesy in face-to-face communication also apply to e-mail exchanges. Introduce yourself at the beginning of your first e-mail message. Next, let your recipients know how you got their names and e-mail addresses. Then proceed with your clear but succinct message, and always be sure to type full words (*ur* is not the same thing as *your*). Finally, close the e-mail with a signature. Do not send an attachment unless your correspondent has indicated he or she will accept it. Ask first! You can find much more information about proper Internet etiquette, or netiquette, online—for example, at NetManners.com.

6. **Practicing good cell phone manners.** Your Introduction to Business class is not the place to be arranging a date for tonight. Turn off the phone during class or in a business meeting unless you are expecting a critical call. If you are expecting such a call, let your professor know before class. Turn off your ringer and put the phone on vibrate. Sit by the aisle and near the door. If you do receive a critical call, leave the room before answering it. Apologize to the professor after class and explain the situation.

7. **Practicing safe posting on social media.** Be careful what you post on your Facebook page or any other social media. While it may be fun to share your latest adventures with your friends, your boss or future boss may not appreciate your latest party pictures. Be aware that those pictures may not go away even if you delete them from your page. If anyone else downloaded them, they are still out there waiting for a recruiter to discover. Make sure to update your privacy settings frequently. It's a good idea to separate your list of work friends and limit what that group can view. Also be aware that some work colleagues aren't interested in becoming your Facebook friends. To avoid awkwardness, wait for work associates

to reach out to you first. Make sure you know your employer's policy on using social media on company time.[6] Obviously, they will probably frown on using it for personal use on company time, but there may be rules about sharing technical matter, company information, etc. Be mindful that social media accounts time-stamp your comments.

8. **Being prepared.** A businessperson would never show up for a meeting without having read the appropriate materials and being prepared to discuss the topics on the agenda. For students, acting like a professional means reading assigned materials before class, having written assignments ready to be turned in, asking and responding to questions in class, and discussing the material with fellow students.

Behavior that's taken for granted in other countries might be unusual in the United States. In some cultures bowing is a form of greeting to show respect. How can you learn the appropriate business etiquette for the countries in which you do business?

Just as traffic laws enable people to drive more safely, business etiquette allows people to conduct business with the appropriate amount of consideration. Sharpen your competitive edge by becoming familiar with its rules. If your job or career requires you to travel internationally, learn the proper business etiquette for each country you visit.[7] Customs differ widely for such everyday activities as greeting people, eating, giving gifts, presenting and receiving business cards, and conducting business in general. In Japan, businesspeople typically bow instead of shaking hands, and in some Arab countries it is insulting to sit so as to show the soles of your shoes. Honesty, high ethical standards, and reliability and trustworthiness are important for success in any country.

Having a reputation for integrity will enable you to be proud of who you are and contribute a great deal to your business success. Unethical behavior can ruin your reputation; so think carefully before you act. When in doubt, don't! Ethics is so important to success that we include discussions about it throughout the text.

DOING YOUR BEST IN COLLEGE

The skills you need to succeed in life after college are the same ones that will serve you well in your studies. Career, family, and hobbies all benefit from organizational and time management skills you can apply right now. Here are some tips for improving your study habits, taking tests, and managing your time.

Study Hints

For the remainder of your college career, consider studying to be your business. Though you may hold another job while enrolled in this class, you're in school because you want to advance yourself. So until you get out of school and into your desired occupation, studying is your business. And like any good businessperson, you aim for success. Follow these strategies:

1. **Go to class.** It's tempting to cut a class on a nice day or when there are other things to do. But nothing is more important to doing well in school than going to class every time. If possible, sit in the front near the instructor. This will help you focus better and avoid distractions in the room.

2. **Listen well.** It's not enough to show up for class if you use the time for a nap. Make eye contact with the instructor. In your mind, form a picture of what he or she is discussing. Include your existing knowledge and past experiences in your picture. This ties new knowledge to what you already know.

3. **Take careful notes.** Make two columns in your notebook, laptop, or tablet. On one side write down important concepts, and on the other examples or more detailed explanations. Use abbreviations and symbols whenever possible and wide spacing to make the notes easier to read. Edit your notes after class to make sure you fully understand what was discussed in class. Rereading and rewriting help store the information in your long-term memory. Learn the concepts in your courses the same way you learn the words to your favorite song: through repetition and review.

4. **Find a good place to study.** Find a place with good lighting and a quiet atmosphere. Some students do well with classical music or other music without lyrics playing in the background. Keep your study place equipped with extra supplies such as pens, pencils, calculator, folders, and paper so you don't have to interrupt studying to hunt for them.

5. **Read the text using a strategy such as "survey, question, read, recite, review" (SQ3R).**

   a. *Survey* or scan the chapter first to see what it is all about. This means looking over the table of contents, learning objectives, headings, photo essays, and charts so you get a broad idea of the content. The summaries at the end of each chapter in this text provide a great overview of the concepts in the chapter. Scanning will provide an introduction and help get your mind in a learning mode.

   b. Write *questions,* first by changing the headings into questions. For example, you could change the heading of this section to "What hints can I use to study better?" Read the questions that appear throughout each chapter in the Test Prep sections to give yourself a chance to recall what you've read.

   c. *Read* the chapter to find the answers to your questions. Be sure to read the boxes in the chapter as well. They offer extended examples or discussions of the concepts in the text. You've probably asked, "Will the material in the boxes be on the tests?" Even if your instructor chooses not to test over them directly, they are often the most interesting parts of the chapter and will help you retain the chapter concepts better.

   d. *Recite* your answers to yourself or to others in a study group. Make sure you say the answers in your own words so that you clearly understand the concepts. Research has shown that saying things is a more effective way to learn them than seeing, hearing, or reading about them. While often used in study groups, recitation is also good practice for working in teams in the work world.

   e. *Review* by rereading and recapping the information. The chapter summaries are written in a question-and-answer form, much like a classroom dialogue. They're also tied directly to the learning objectives so that you can see whether you've accomplished the chapter's objectives. Cover the written answers and see whether you can answer the questions yourself first.

6. **Use flash cards.** You'll master the course more easily if you know the language of business. To review the key terms in the book, write any terms you don't know on index cards and go through your cards between classes and when you have other free time.

7. **Use** Connect **Introduction to Business** (if your professor has recommended it for your course). Connect's online features include interactive presentations, LearnSmart (adaptive learning technology that identifies what you know and don't know, and personalizes your learning experience, ensuring that every minute spent studying with LearnSmart is the most efficient and productive study time possible), SmartBook (creates a personalized reading

The SQ3R study system recommends that you "survey, question, read, recite, and review" to stay up-to-date with assignments and shine in class every day. Have you adopted this system?

experience by highlighting the most impactful concepts you need to learn at that moment in time), and interactive applications.

8. **Go over old exams, if possible.** If old exams are not available from your professor, ask how many multiple-choice, true/false, and essay questions will be on your test. It's acceptable to ask your professor's former students what kind of questions are given and what material is usually emphasized. It is unethical, though, to go over exams you obtain illegally.

9. **Use as many of your senses in learning as possible.** If you're an auditory learner—that is, if you learn best by hearing—record yourself reading your notes and answering the questions you've written. Listen to the tape while you're dressing in the morning. You can also benefit from reading or studying aloud. If you're a visual learner, use pictures, charts, colors, and graphs. Your professor has a set of videos that illustrate the concepts in this text. If you're a kinesthetic learner, you remember best by doing, touching, and experiencing. Doing the Developing Workplace Skills exercises at the end of each chapter will be a big help.

Test-Taking Hints

Often students will say, "I know this stuff, but I'm just not good at taking multiple-choice (or essay) tests." Other students find test taking relatively easy. Here are a few test-taking hints:

1. **Get plenty of sleep and have a good meal.** It's better to be alert and awake during an exam than to study all night and be groggy. If you keep up with your reading and your reviews on a regular basis, you won't need to pull an all-nighter. Proper nutrition also plays an important part in your brain's ability to function.

2. **Bring all you need for the exam.** Sometimes you'll need No. 2 pencils, erasers, and a calculator. Ask beforehand.

3. **Relax.** At home before the test, take deep, slow breaths. Picture yourself in the testing session, relaxed and confident. Reread the chapter summaries. Get to class early to settle down. If you start to get nervous during the test, stop and take a few deep breaths. Turn the test over and write down information you remember. Sometimes this helps you connect the information you know to the questions on the test.

4. **Read the directions on the exam carefully.** You don't want to miss anything or do something you're not supposed to do.

5. **Read all the answers in multiple-choice questions.** Even if there is more than one correct-sounding answer to a multiple-choice question, one is clearly better. Read them all to be sure you pick the best. Try covering up the choices while reading the question. If the answer you think of is one of the choices, it is probably correct. If you are still unsure of the answer, start eliminating options you know are wrong. Narrowing the choices to two or three improves your odds.

6. **Answer all the questions.** Unless your instructor takes off more for an incorrect answer than for no answer, you have nothing to lose by guessing. Also, skipping a question can lead to inadvertently misaligning your answers on a scan sheet. You could end up with all your subsequent answers scored wrong!

7. **Read true/false questions carefully.** All parts of the statement must be true or else the entire statement is false. Watch out for absolutes such as *never, always,* and *none.* These often make a statement false.

8. **Organize your thoughts before answering essay questions.** Think about the sequence in which to present what you want to say. Use complete sentences with correct grammar and punctuation. Explain or defend your answers.

9. **Go over the test at the end.** Make sure you've answered all the questions, put your name on the exam, and followed all directions.

Keeping a daily schedule is only one of the many strategies that will help you manage your time. You should also keep a running list of goals and things you need to do each week. In what other ways can you defend your study time?

Time Management Hints

The most important management skill you can learn is how to manage your time. Now is as good an opportunity to practice as any. Here are some hints other students have learned—often the hard way:

1. **Write weekly goals for yourself.** Make certain your goals are realistic and attainable. Write the steps you'll use to achieve each goal. Reward yourself when you reach a goal.

2. **Keep a "to do" list.** It's easy to forget things unless you write them down. Jot tasks down as soon as you know of them. That gives you one less thing to do: remembering what you have to do.

3. **Prepare a daily schedule.** Use a commercial printed or electronic daily planner or create your own. Write the days of the week across the top of the page. Write the hours of the day from the time you get up until the time you go to bed down the left side. Draw lines to form columns and rows and fill in all the activities you have planned in each hour. Hopefully, you will be surprised to see how many slots of time you have available for studying.

4. **Prepare for the next day the night before.** Having everything ready to go will help you make a quick, stress-free start in the morning.

5. **Prepare weekly and monthly schedules.** Use a calendar to fill in activities and upcoming assignments. Include both academic and social activities so that you can balance your work and fun.

6. **Space out your work.** Don't wait until the last week of the course to write all your papers and study for your exams. If you do a few pages a day, you can write a 20-page paper in a couple of weeks with little effort. It is really difficult to push out 20 pages in a day or two.

7. **Defend your study time.** Study every day. Use the time between classes to go over your flash cards and read the next day's assignments. Make it a habit to defend your study time so you don't slip.

8. **Take time for fun.** If you have some fun every day, life will be full. Schedule your fun times along with your studying so that you have balance.

"Time is money," the saying goes. Some, however, would argue that time is more valuable than money. If your bank account balance falls, you might be able to build it back up by finding a better-paying job, taking a second job, or even selling something you own. But you have only a limited amount of time and there is no way to make more. Learn to manage your time well, because you can never get it back.

MAKING THE MOST OF THE RESOURCES FOR THIS COURSE

College courses and textbooks are best at teaching you concepts and ways of thinking about business. However, to learn firsthand how to apply those ideas to real business situations, you need to explore and interact with other resources. Here are seven basic resources for the class in addition to the text:

1. **The professor.** One of the most valuable facets of college is the chance to study with experienced professors. Your instructor is a resource who's there to answer some questions and guide you to answers for others. Many professors get job leads they can pass on to you and can provide letters of recommendation too. Thus it's important to develop a friendly relationship with your professors.

2. **The supplements that come with this text.** Connect Introduction to Business online course material (if your professor has recommended it for your course) will help you review and interpret key material and give you practice answering test questions. Even if your professor does not assign these materials, you may want to use them anyhow. Doing so will improve your test scores and help you compete successfully with the other students.

3. **Outside readings.** One secret to success in business is staying current. Review and become familiar with the following magazines and newspapers during the course and throughout your career: *The Wall Street Journal, Forbes, Barron's, Bloomberg Businessweek, Fortune, Money, The Economist, Hispanic Business, Harvard Business Review, Black Enterprise, Fast Company, Inc.,* and *Entrepreneur.* You may also want to read your local newspaper's business section and national news magazines such as *Time* and *Newsweek.* You can find them in your school's learning resource center or the local public library. Some are also available online free.

4. **Your own experience and that of your classmates.** Many college students have had experience working in business or nonprofit organizations. Hearing and talking about those experiences exposes you to many real-life examples that are invaluable for understanding business. Don't rely exclusively on the professor for all the answers and other exercises in this book. Often there is no single "right" answer, and your classmates may open up new ways of looking at things for you.

    Part of being a successful businessperson is learning how to work with others. Some professors encourage their students to work together and build teamwork as well as presentation and analytical skills. Students from other countries can help you learn about different cultures and different approaches to handling business problems. There is strength in diversity, so seek out people different from you to work with on teams.

Your college professors are among the most valuable resources and contacts you'll encounter as you develop your career path. How many of your professors have you gotten to know so far?

5. **Outside contacts.** Who can tell you more about what it's like to start a career in accounting than someone who's doing it now? One of the best ways to learn about different businesses is to visit them in person. The world can be your classroom.

   When you go shopping, think about whether you would enjoy working in and managing a store. Think about owning or managing a restaurant, an auto body shop, a health club, or any other establishment you visit. If something looks interesting, talk to the employees and learn more about their jobs and the industry. Be constantly on the alert to find career possibilities, and don't hesitate to talk with people about their careers. Many will be pleased to give you their time and honest opinions.

6. **The Internet.** The Internet offers more material than you could use in a lifetime. Throughout this text we present information and exercises that require you to use the Internet. Information changes rapidly, and it is up to you to stay current.

7. **The library or learning resource center.** The library is a great complement to the Internet and a valuable resource. Work with your librarian to learn how to best access the information you need.

Getting the Most from This Text

Many learning aids appear throughout this text to help you understand the concepts:

1. **List of Learning Objectives at the beginning of each chapter.** Reading through these objectives will help you set the framework and focus for the chapter material. Since every student at one time or other has found it difficult to get into studying, the Learning Objectives are there to provide an introduction and to get your mind into a learning mode.

2. **Getting to Know and Name That Company features.** The opening stories will help you *get to know* professionals who successfully use the concepts presented in the chapters. The Name That Company feature at the beginning of each chapter challenges you to identify a company discussed in the chapter.

3. **Photo essays.** The photos offer examples of the concepts in the chapter. Looking at the photos and reading the photo essays (captions) before you read the chapter will give you a good idea of what the chapter is all about.

4. **Self-test questions.** Periodically, within each chapter, you'll encounter set-off lists of questions called Test Prep. These questions give you a chance to pause, think carefully about, and recall what you've just read.

5. **Key terms.** Developing a strong business vocabulary is one of the most important and useful aspects of this course. To assist you, all key terms in the book are highlighted in boldface type. Key terms are also defined in the margins, and page references to these terms are given at the end of each chapter. A full glossary is located in the back of the book. You should rely heavily on these learning aids in adding new terms to your vocabulary.

6. **Boxes.** Each chapter contains a number of boxed extended examples or discussions that cover major themes of the book: (a) ethics (Making Ethical Decisions); (b) small business (Spotlight on Small Business); (c) global business (Reaching Beyond Our Borders); (d) environmental issues (Seeking Sustainability); and (e) contemporary business issues (Adapting to Change). They're interesting to read and provide key insights into important business issues; we hope you enjoy and learn from them.

7. **End-of-chapter summaries.** The chapter summaries are directly tied to the chapter Learning Objectives so that you can see whether you've accomplished the chapter's objectives.

8. **Critical Thinking questions.** The end-of-chapter questions help you relate the material to your own experiences.

9. **Developing Workplace Skills exercises.** To really remember something, it's best to do it. That's why Developing Workplace Skills sections at the end of each chapter suggest small projects that help you use resources, develop interpersonal skills, manage information, understand systems, and sharpen technology skills.

10. **Taking It to the Net exercises.** These exercises direct you to dynamic outside resources that reinforce the concepts introduced in the text. You might want to bookmark some of the websites you'll discover.

11. **Video Cases.** These cases feature companies, processes, practices, and managers that bring to life the key concepts in the chapter and give you real-world information to think over and discuss.

If you use the suggestions we've presented here, you'll actively participate in a learning experience that will help you greatly in this course and your chosen career. The most important secret to success may be to enjoy what you're doing and do your best in everything. To do your best, take advantage of all the learning aids available to you.

notes

1. Danielle Kurtzleben, "Study: Income Gap Between Young College and High School Grads Widens," *U.S. New & World Report,* February 11, 2014.
2. National Center for Education Studies, www.nces.ed.gov, accessed May 2014.
3. U.S. Census Bureau, www.census.gov, accessed May 2014.
4. David Lavenda and Susan Fisher, "15 Tips to Master the Awkward Networking Waltz," *Fast Company,* October 31, 2013; and Elaine Wherry, "Networking Tips for Wallflowers," *The Wall Street Journal,* March 13, 2014.
5. Barbara Pachter, *The Essentials of Business Etiquette—How to Greet, Eat, and Tweet Your Way to Success* (New York, McGraw-Hill, 2013); and Susan Adams, "A Guide to Business Etiquette: What's New?" *Forbes,* May 14, 2014.
6. Jeanne Meister, "To Do: Update Company's Social Media Policy ASAP," *Forbes,* February 7, 2013; and Erik Sherman, "You Tweeted What about My Company?" *Inc.,* January 31, 2014.
7. Andy Molinsky, "When Crossing Cultures, Use Global Dexterity," *Harvard Business Review,* March 12, 2013; and Christina Larson, "Office Cultures: A Global Guide," *Bloomberg Businessweek,* June 13, 2013.

photo credits

1

Taking Risks and Making Profits within the Dynamic Business Environment

Learning Objectives

AFTER YOU HAVE READ AND STUDIED THIS CHAPTER, YOU SHOULD BE ABLE TO

LO 1-1 Describe the relationship between profit and risk, and show how businesses and nonprofit organizations can raise the standard of living for all.

LO 1-2 Compare and contrast being an entrepreneur and working for others.

LO 1-3 Analyze the effects of the economic environment and taxes on businesses.

LO 1-4 Describe the effects of technology on businesses.

LO 1-5 Demonstrate how businesses can meet and beat competition.

LO 1-6 Analyze the social changes affecting businesses.

LO 1-7 Identify what businesses must do to meet global challenges, including war and terrorism.

LO 1-8 Review how past trends are being repeated in the present and what those trends mean for tomorrow's college graduates.

Getting to know **Sammy Hagar**

Most 1980s hard rockers are known for their big hair and wild lifestyles rather than their business expertise. But unlike many of his colleagues, Sammy Hagar has juggled a decades-long music career with a lucrative business portfolio that has earned him tens of millions of dollars over the years. From humble beginnings to the heights of international stardom, the Red Rocker's careful money management skills and immense entrepreneurial enthusiasm have helped him become one of the richest musicians in the world.

Born to a poor family in Fontana, California, Hagar credits his mother as his first business advisor. "She convinced me, 'If you're going to be in the music business, then you have to save your money and invest it properly, because all those guys end up alcoholic, drug addicts, and broke,'" says Hagar. After first finding success with the band Montrose, Hagar partnered with his brother-in-law and invested his earnings in some apartment complexes. Then as the band began to tour more, he started his own travel agency so they wouldn't have to pay anyone to book travel arrangements.

When his stint with Montrose ended, Hagar focused on his solo career. The early 1980s found him packing stadiums across the country and earning $3 million annually. However, Hagar was always careful not to depend solely on his music to earn money. In 1987 he bought and expanded a specialty mountain bike store called Sausalito Cyclery that soon grew into one of the highest-rated bike shops in California.

But just as Hagar's business interests were progressing steadily, his music career took a sudden shot upward. After the band Van Halen fired its fitful front-man David Lee Roth, lead guitarist Eddie Van Halen hired Hagar for the job. Although Hagar was certainly well known before, Van Halen's position as one of the biggest bands in the world launched Hagar's fame to enormous heights. The band's relentless touring and recording schedule took a toll on the hardworking rocker. Whenever Hagar got a free moment in his hectic schedule, he would unwind at his condo in Cabo San Lucas, Mexico. The small resort hideaway ended up giving Hagar his biggest business idea yet. "[The town had] three hotels,

and none of the restaurants had air conditioning, telephones, or TV," says Hagar. "But I fell in love with the place. I wanted a place to hang out down there, so I said, 'I'm going to build a tequila bar.'"

With his bandmates as partners, Hagar opened the Cabo Wabo Cantina in 1990. However, his responsibilities with Van Halen prevented him from taking an active role in the business. The failing restaurant added to the tension within the band, and by 1996 Hagar and Van Halen parted ways. Hagar bought out his bandmates and hired new management at Cabo Wabo. As the revamped restaurant became a hot destination both for locals and tourists, Hagar looked to expand his brand. Along with opening Sammy's Beach Bar restaurants in cities and airports across the country, in the late 1990s he launched Cabo Wabo Tequila as a national brand. By 2010 the liquor had become so popular that Hagar sold it for $91 million. All told, Hagar's holdings have grown the Red Rocker's net worth to $120 million.

Although Hagar has come a long way from his youthful days on welfare and food stamps, he hasn't forgotten those who continue to struggle to put food on the table. In addition to contributing all of the profits from his airport restaurants to charity, Hagar contributes $2,500 to food banks in each of the cities he visits and brings awareness to food banks by featuring information about them on video screens during his live performances.

The business environment is constantly changing, and along with those changes come opportunities. The purpose of this chapter, and this text, is to introduce you to the dynamic world of business and to some of the people who thrive in it. Entrepreneurs like Sammy Hagar contribute much to the communities they serve, and they also make a good living doing so. That's what business is all about.

Sammy Hagar

- Entrepreneur and Rock Star
- Van Halen frontman
- Entrepreneur
- Philanthropist

www.redrocker.com

@sammyhagar

Sources: Liz Welsh, "How I Did It: Sammy Hagar," *Inc.*, November 2013; Mike Burr, "Paul McCartney Heads List of World's Richest Singers," *Prefix*, September 13, 2012; and Mitchell Peters, "Banking on Sammy Hagar: Red Rocker Is Serious about Helping Local Food Banks", *Billboard*, August 13, 2013.

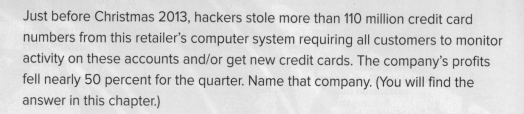

LO 1–1 Describe the relationship between profit and risk, and show how businesses and nonprofit organizations can raise the standard of living for all.

ENTREPRENEURSHIP AND WEALTH BUILDING

One thing you can learn from the chapter-opening Getting to Know feature is that success in business is based on constantly adapting to the market. A **business** is any activity that seeks to provide goods and services to others while operating at a profit. To earn that profit, you provide desired goods, jobs, and services to people in the area. **Goods** are *tangible* products such as computers, food, clothing, cars, and appliances. **Services** are *intangible* products (i.e., products that can't be held in your hand) such as education, health care, insurance, recreation, and travel and tourism.[1] Once you have developed the right goods and services, based on consumer wants and needs, you need to reach those consumers using whatever media they prefer, including blogs, tweets, Facebook, TV advertising, and more.[2]

Although you don't need to have wealth as a primary goal, one result of successfully filling a market need is that you can make money for yourself, sometimes a great deal, by giving customers what they want. Sam Walton of Walmart began by opening one store in Arkansas and, over time, became one of the richest people in the United States. Now his heirs are some of the richest people in the United States.[3]

There are about 9 million millionaires in the United States.[4] Maybe you will be one of them someday if you start your own business. An **entrepreneur** is a person who risks time and money to start and manage a business.

Revenues, Profits, and Losses

Revenue is the total amount of money a business takes in during a given period by selling goods and services. **Profit** is the amount of money a business earns above and beyond what it spends for salaries and other expenses needed to run the operation. A **loss** occurs when a business's expenses are more than its revenues. If a business loses money over time, it will likely have to close, putting its employees out of work. About 80,000 businesses in the United States close each year. Even more close during a recession like the recession of 2007–2009.[5]

As noted above, the business environment is constantly changing. What seems like a great opportunity one day may become a huge failure when the economy changes. Starting a business may thus come with huge risks.[6] But huge risks often result in huge profits. We'll explore that concept next.

business
Any activity that seeks to provide goods and services to others while operating at a profit.

goods
Tangible products such as computers, food, clothing, cars, and appliances.

services
Intangible products (i.e., products that can't be held in your hand) such as education, health care, insurance, recreation, and travel and tourism.

entrepreneur
A person who risks time and money to start and manage a business.

revenue
The total amount of money a business takes in during a given period by selling goods and services.

profit
The amount of money a business earns above and beyond what it spends for salaries and other expenses.

loss
When a business's expenses are more than its revenues.

Matching Risk with Profit

Risk is the chance an entrepreneur takes of losing time and money on a business that may not prove profitable. Profit, remember, is the amount of money a business earns *above and beyond* what it pays out for salaries and other expenses. For example, if you were to start a business selling hot dogs from a cart in the summer, you would have to pay for the cart rental. You would also have to pay for the hot dogs and other materials, and for someone to run the cart while you were away. After you paid your employee and yourself, paid for the food and materials you used, paid the rent on the cart, and paid your taxes, any money left over would be profit.

Keep in mind that profit is over and above the money you pay yourself in salary. You could use any profit to rent or buy a second cart and hire other employees. After a few summers, you might have a dozen carts employing dozens of workers.

Not all enterprises make the same amount of profit. Those that take the most risk may make the most profit. There is high risk, for example, in making a new kind of automobile.[7] It's also risky to open a business in an inner city, because insurance and rent are usually higher than in suburban areas, but reduced competition makes substantial profit possible. Irish entrepreneur Denis O'Brien, of Digicel, made billions of dollars selling cell phones in the poorest, most violent countries in the world. Big risk can mean big profits.

Standard of Living and Quality of Life

Entrepreneurs such as Sam Walton (Walmart) and Bill Gates (Microsoft) not only became wealthy themselves; they also provided employment for many other people. Walmart is currently the nation's largest private employer.

Businesses and their employees pay taxes that the federal government and local communities use to build hospitals, schools, libraries, playgrounds, roads, and other public facilities. Taxes also help to keep the environment clean, support people in need, and provide police and fire protection. Thus, the wealth businesses generate, and the taxes they pay, help everyone in their communities. A nation's businesses are part of an economic system that contributes to the standard of living and quality of life for everyone in the country (and, potentially, the world). How has the recent economic slowdown affected the standard of living and quality of life in your part of the world?

The term **standard of living** refers to the amount of goods and services people can buy with the money they have. For example, the United States has one of the highest standards of living in the world, even though workers in some other countries, such as Germany and Japan, may on average make more money per hour. How can that be? Prices for goods and services in Germany and Japan are higher than in the United States, so a person in those countries can buy less than what a person in the United States can buy with the same amount of money. For example, a bottle of beer may cost $7 in Japan and $3 in the United States.

Often, goods cost more in one country than in another because of higher taxes and stricter government regulations. Finding the right level of taxes and regulation is important in making a country or city prosperous.[8] We'll explore those issues in more depth in Chapter 2. At this point, it is enough to understand that the United States enjoys a high standard of living largely because of the wealth created by its businesses.

risk
The chance an entrepreneur takes of losing time and money on a business that may not prove profitable.

standard of living
The amount of goods and services people can buy with the money they have.

connect

▶ **iSee It!** Need help understanding standard of living vs. quality of life? Visit your Connect e-book video tab for a brief animated explanation.

When Nick Woodman wanted to show off videos of his stunts to other surfers, he used rubber bands and a surfboard leash to attach cameras to his wrist. His early attempts didn't work, but after a lot of work and a $235,000 investment, his GoPro cameras are now the gold standard for self-documenting extreme sports. Today Woodman's company brings in $526 million in annual revenue. What risks and rewards did Woodman face when starting his business?

quality of life
The general well-being of a society in terms of its political freedom, natural environment, education, health care, safety, amount of leisure, and rewards that add to the satisfaction and joy that other goods and services provide.

stakeholders
All the people who stand to gain or lose by the policies and activities of a business and whose concerns the business needs to address.

outsourcing
Contracting with other companies (often in other countries) to do some or all of the functions of a firm, like its production or accounting tasks.

The term **quality of life** refers to the general well-being of a society in terms of its political freedom, natural environment, education, health care, safety, amount of leisure, and rewards that add to the satisfaction and joy that other goods and services provide. Maintaining a high quality of life requires the combined efforts of businesses, nonprofit organizations, and government agencies. Remember, there is more to quality of life than simply making money.

Responding to the Various Business Stakeholders

Stakeholders are all the people who stand to gain or lose by the policies and activities of a business and whose concerns the business needs to address. They include customers, employees, stockholders, suppliers, dealers (retailers), bankers, people in the surrounding community, the media, environmentalists, competitors, unions, critics, and elected government leaders (see Figure 1.1).[9]

A primary challenge for organizations of the 21st century will be to recognize and respond to the needs of their stakeholders. For example, the need for the business to make profits may be balanced against the needs of employees to earn sufficient income or the need to protect the environment.[10] Ignore the media, and they might attack your business with articles that hurt sales. Oppose the local community, and it may stop you from expanding.

Staying competitive may call for outsourcing. **Outsourcing** means contracting with other companies (often in other countries) to do some or all of the functions of a firm, like its production or accounting tasks. Outsourcing has had serious consequences in some states where jobs have been lost to overseas competitors. We discuss outsourcing in more detail in Chapter 3.

FIGURE 1.1 A BUSINESS AND ITS STAKEHOLDERS
Often the needs of a firm's various stakeholders will conflict. For example, paying employees more may cut into stockholders' profits. Balancing such demands is a major role of business managers.

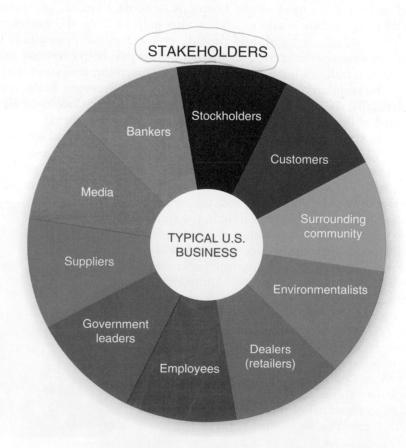

The other side of the outsourcing coin is *insourcing.*[11] Many foreign companies are setting up design and production facilities here in the United States. For example, Korea-based Hyundai operates design and engineering headquarters in Detroit, Michigan, and produces cars in Montgomery, Alabama. Japanese automakers Honda and Toyota have been producing cars in the United States for years. Hon Hai Precision Industry Company assembles gadgets for Apple and other global technology companies. It is evaluating a plan to build an advanced display-manufacturing plant in the United States.[12] Insourcing creates many new U.S. jobs and helps offset those jobs being outsourced.

It may be legal and profitable to outsource, but is it best for all the stakeholders? Business leaders must make outsourcing decisions based on all factors. Pleasing stakeholders is not easy and often calls for trade-offs.

Using Business Principles in Nonprofit Organizations

Despite their efforts to satisfy their stakeholders, businesses cannot do everything needed to make a community all it can be. Nonprofit organizations—such as public schools, civic associations, charities like the United Way and the Salvation Army, and groups devoted to social causes—also make a major contribution to the welfare of society. A **nonprofit organization** is an organization whose goals do not include making a personal profit for its owners or organizers. Nonprofit organizations often do strive for financial gains, but they use them to meet their social or educational goals rather than for personal profit.

Your interests may lead you to work for a nonprofit organization. That doesn't mean, however, that you shouldn't study business in college. You'll still need to learn business skills such as information management, leadership, marketing, and financial management. The knowledge and skills you acquire in this and other business courses are useful for careers in any organization, including nonprofits. We'll explore entrepreneurship in more detail right after the Test Prep.

nonprofit organization
An organization whose goals do not include making a personal profit for its owners or organizers.

The goals of nonprofit organizations are social and educational, not profit-oriented. The Red Cross, for example, provides assistance to around 30 million people annually, from refugees to victims of natural disasters. Why do good management principles apply equally to businesses and nonprofit organizations?

test prep

- What is the difference between *revenue* and *profit*?
- What is the difference between *standard of living* and *quality of life*?
- What is *risk*, and how is it related to *profit*?
- What do the terms *stakeholders*, *outsourcing*, and *insourcing* mean?

LO 1–2   Compare and contrast being an entrepreneur and working for others.

ENTREPRENEURSHIP VERSUS WORKING FOR OTHERS

There are two ways to succeed in business. One is to rise through the ranks of a large company. The advantage of working for others is that somebody else assumes the company's entrepreneurial risk and provides you with benefits like paid vacation time and health insurance. It's a good option, and many people choose it.

The other, riskier, but often more exciting, path is to become an entrepreneur.[13] The national anthem, "The Star Spangled Banner," says that the United States is the "land of the free and the home of the brave." Part of being free is being able to own your own business and reap the profits from it. That includes older people who have some experience and are looking for new opportunities.[14] In 2013, for example, over 23 percent of companies were started by people aged 55 to 64.[15] But freedom to succeed also means freedom to fail, and many small businesses fail each year. It takes a brave person to start one. As an entrepreneur, you don't receive any benefits such as paid vacation time, day care, a company car, or health insurance. You have to provide them for yourself! But what you gain—freedom to make your own decisions, opportunity, and possible wealth—is often worth the effort. Before you take on the challenge, you should study successful entrepreneurs to learn the process.[16] You can talk to them personally and read about them in Chapter 6, as well as in other books and magazines. Read the nearby Spotlight on Small Business box to learn about an example of entrepreneurship helping those in a devastated community and how a natural disaster was turned into an opportunity.

To create wealth for its citizens, a country requires more than natural resources. It needs the efforts of entrepreneurs and the skill and knowledge to produce goods and services. How can government support entrepreneurship and the spread of knowledge?

Opportunities for Entrepreneurs

Millions of people from all over the world have taken the entrepreneurial challenge and succeeded.[17] For example, the number of Hispanic-owned businesses in the United States has grown dramatically (Hispanics are now the largest ethnic group in the United States). Both Hispanic men and women are doing particularly well. Similar successes are true of businesses owned by Asians, Pacific Islanders, Native Americans, and Alaska Natives. Young people today have many choices—including working for others for a while and then entrepreneurship—to find the right fit.[18]

How a Food Truck Helped Rebuild a Storm-Struck Community

Although Hurricane Sandy devastated hundreds of communities along the East Coast in 2012, few places experienced a worse "superstorm" than Rockaway Beach in the New York City borough of Queens. An especially powerful storm surge flooded the whole neighborhood, while fires simultaneously consumed residential as well as commercial districts. By the time the winds had settled, thousands of Rockaway residents found themselves without access to electricity, food, or clean water.

After witnessing the destruction firsthand, Mike Diamond of the hip-hop group the Beastie Boys knew he had to do something. A native New Yorker and dedicated activist, Diamond teamed up with some friends in the restaurant industry and started the Rockaway Plate Lunch Truck. Just days after the storm cleared, Diamond's food truck began serving more than 500 free lunches of chicken, rice, and beans every day to residents. The venture continued even after Rockaway Beach began to rebuild, but Diamond noticed major changes within the community during its recovery. "One of the main things that has not returned is prosperity," says Diamond. "[Rockaway Beach] wasn't a thriving economy before Sandy, and it was really set back post-Sandy. You have all these businesses that won't reopen."

In an effort to provide entrepreneurial experience to the residents of Rockaway, Diamond and his partners decided to shift the food truck from a charity to a business. But instead of hiring professionals to do the cooking, the team brought in local high school students to staff the truck. The idea was to bring valuable work experience to young adults in the community that will lead to careers in food service and perhaps beyond. "It's really about opportunity and access," says Diamond. "We can find the people who are leaders and give them a chance at learning from our restaurant partners."

Sources: Melinda Newman, "How a Beastie Boy's Food Truck Helped the Rockaways Rebuild after Hurricane Sandy," *Entrepreneur*, September 19, 2013; and Stacey Anderson, "Beastie Boys' Mike D Feeds Hurricane Sandy Victims with Free Food Truck," *Rolling Stone*, April 2, 2013.

Women now own over a third of all businesses. Businesses owned by minority women are growing faster than those owned by men or nonminority women. Women of color are establishing businesses at twice the rate of their male counterparts and more than four times that of nonminority entrepreneurs. As one woman put it in a recent article, "Today, women have choices that their grandmothers could not have imagined. The challenge lies in recognizing that having choices carries the responsibility to make them wisely."[19] For many, that choice is entrepreneurship.

The Importance of Entrepreneurs to the Creation of Wealth

Have you ever wondered why some countries are relatively wealthy and others poor? Economists have been studying the issue of wealth creation for many

factors of production
The resources used to create wealth: land, labor, capital, entrepreneurship, and knowledge.

years. They began by identifying five **factors of production** that seemed to contribute to wealth (see Figure 1.2):

1. *Land* (or natural resources). Land and other natural resources are used to make homes, cars, and other products.
2. *Labor* (workers). People have always been an important resource in producing goods and services, but many people are now being replaced by technology.
3. *Capital.* (This includes machines, tools, buildings, or whatever else is used in the production of goods. It may not include money; money is used to buy factors of production but is not always considered a factor by itself.)
4. *Entrepreneurship.* All the resources in the world have little value unless entrepreneurs are willing to take the risk of starting businesses to use those resources.
5. *Knowledge.* Information technology has revolutionized business, making it possible to quickly determine wants and needs and to respond with desired goods and services.

Traditionally, business and economics textbooks emphasized only four factors of production: land, labor, capital, and entrepreneurship. But the late management expert and business consultant Peter Drucker said the most important factor of production in our economy is and always will be *knowledge.*

What do we find when we compare the factors of production in rich and poor countries? Some poor countries have plenty of land and natural resources. Russia, for example, has vast areas of land with many resources such as timber and oil, but it is not considered a rich country (yet). Therefore, land isn't the critical element for wealth creation.

Most poor countries, such as Mexico, have many laborers, so it's not labor that's the primary source of wealth today. Laborers need to find work to make a contribution; that is, they need entrepreneurs to create jobs for them. Furthermore, capital—machinery and tools—is now fairly easy for firms to find in

FIGURE 1.2 THE FIVE FACTORS OF PRODUCTION

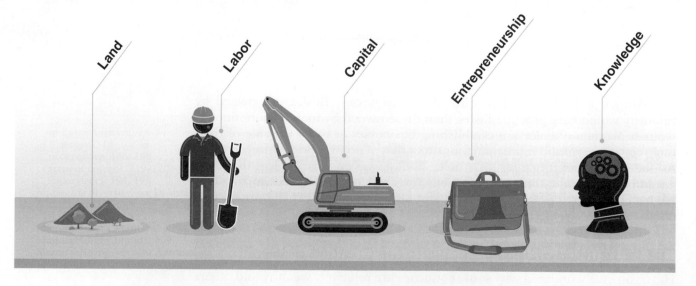

world markets, so capital isn't the missing ingredient either. Capital is not productive without entrepreneurs to put it to use.

What makes rich countries rich today is a combination of *entrepreneurship* and the effective use of *knowledge*.[20] Entrepreneurs use what they've learned (knowledge) to grow their businesses and increase wealth. Economic and political freedom also matter.

The business environment either encourages or discourages entrepreneurship. That helps explain why some states and cities in the United States grow rich while others remain relatively poor. In the following section, we'll explore what makes up the business environment and how to build an environment that encourages growth and job creation.

test prep

- What are some of the advantages of working for others?
- What benefits do you lose by being an entrepreneur, and what do you gain?
- What are the five factors of production? Which ones seem to be the most important for creating wealth?

Use LearnSmart to help retain what you have learned. Access your instructor's Connect course to check out LearnSmart, or go to learnsmartadvantage.com for help.

LEARNSMART

THE BUSINESS ENVIRONMENT

The **business environment** consists of the surrounding factors that either help or hinder the development of businesses. Figure 1.3 shows the five elements in the business environment:

1. The economic and legal environment.
2. The technological environment.
3. The competitive environment.
4. The social environment.
5. The global business environment.

Businesses that create wealth and jobs grow and prosper in a healthy environment. Thus, creating the right business environment is the foundation for social benefits of all kinds, including good schools, clean air and water, good health care, and low rates of crime. Businesses normally can't control their environment, but they need to monitor it carefully and do what they can to adapt as it changes.

business environment
The surrounding factors that either help or hinder the development of businesses.

LO 1–3   Analyze the effects of the economic environment and taxes on businesses.

The Economic and Legal Environment

People are willing to start new businesses if they believe the risk of losing their money isn't too great. The economic system and the way government works with or against businesses can have a strong impact on that level of risk. For example, a government can minimize spending and keep taxes and regulations to a minimum—policies that tend to favor business. Much of the debate

FIGURE 1.3 TODAY'S
DYNAMIC BUSINESS
ENVIRONMENT

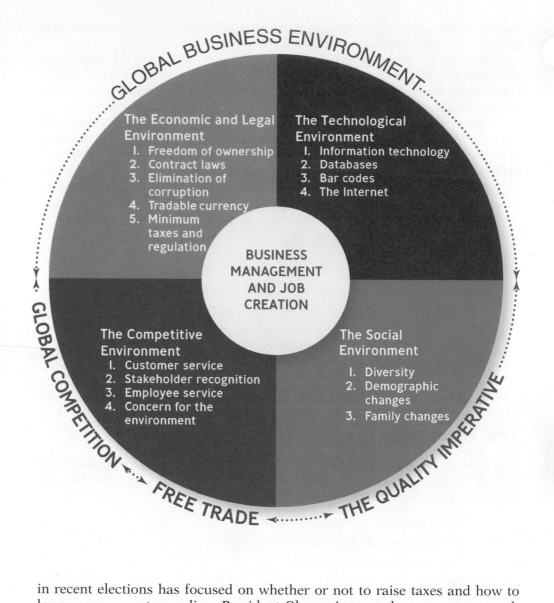

in recent elections has focused on whether or not to raise taxes and how to lower government spending. President Obama increased government spending with the idea of getting the economy moving faster. Some economists agreed with such a stimulus, but some did not.[21]

One way for government to actively promote entrepreneurship is to allow private ownership of businesses. In some countries, the government owns most businesses, and there's little incentive for people to work hard or create profit. Around the world today, however, some governments are selling those businesses to private individuals to create more wealth. One of the best things the governments of developing countries can do is to minimize interference with the free exchange of goods and services.

The government can further lessen the risks of entrepreneurship by passing laws that enable businesspeople to write enforceable contracts. In the United States, the Uniform Commercial Code, for example, regulates business agreements such as contracts and warranties so that firms know they can rely on one another. In countries that don't yet have such laws, the risks of starting a business are that much greater.

The government can also establish a currency that's tradable in world markets. That is, the currency lets you buy and sell goods and services anywhere in the world when it is easily exchanged for that of the other countries where you do business. If the Chinese did not want to trade their yuan for the U.S. dollar, for instance, it's hard to imagine how Coca-Cola or Disney would have been able to sell their products and services there.

Finally, the government can help minimize corruption in business and in its own ranks.[22] Where governments are corrupt, it's difficult to build a factory or open a store without a government permit, which is obtained largely through bribery of public officials. Among businesses themselves, unscrupulous leaders can threaten their competitors and unlawfully minimize competition.[23]

Many laws in the United States attempt to minimize corruption. Nonetheless, corrupt and illegal activities at some companies do negatively affect the business community and the economy as a whole. The news media widely report these scandals. Ethics is so important to the success of businesses and the economy as a whole that we feature stories about ethics in most chapters and devote Chapter 4 to the subject.

The capitalist system relies heavily on honesty, integrity, and high ethical standards. Failure of those fundamentals can weaken the whole system. The faltering economy that began in 2008 was caused in large part to such failure. Some mortgage lenders, for instance, failed to do the research necessary to ensure their borrowers' creditworthiness. Many subprime borrowers (people with low credit ratings) forfeited their loans. The ripple effects of these unpaid debts not only cost many people their homes but also reduced the value of housing across the world and made it difficult even for business borrowers to get new loans. Part of the blame for this economic disaster can be placed on the borrowers who didn't tell the truth about their income or who otherwise deceived the lenders.

It is easy to see the damage caused by the poor moral and ethical behavior of some businesspeople. What is not so obvious is the damage caused by the moral and ethical lapses of the everyday consumer—that is, you and me. The Making Ethical Decisions box discusses that issue in more depth.

Starting a business is more difficult in some countries than in others. In India, for example, it takes a time-consuming and bureaucratic process to obtain government permission. Nonetheless, new businesses can become a major source of wealth and employment. This sari shop is one small example. What do you think would be the effect of a little more freedom to create business opportunities in this country of over a billion people?

making **ethical decisions**

Ethics Begins with You

It is easy to criticize the ethics of people whose names appear in the headlines. It is more difficult to see the moral and ethical misbehavior of your own social group. Do you find some of the behaviors of your friends morally or ethically questionable?

A survey found that the number of employees calling in sick had reached a five-year high, and three-fifths were not sick at all. Other employees have been caught conducting personal business at work, such as doing their taxes. And others play video games on their work computers. We're sure you can add many more examples.

Many companies today are creating ethics codes to guide their employees' behavior. We believe the trend toward improving ethical behavior is so important that we've made it a major theme of this book. Throughout the text you'll see boxes like this one, called Making Ethical Decisions, that pose ethical dilemmas and ask what you would do to resolve them. The idea is for you to think about the moral and ethical dimensions of every decision you make.

Here is your first one: You have become addicted to your electronic gadgets. Some days at work you spend most of the time playing games, watching TV, texting, sending e-mails to friends, or reading a book or magazine on your devices. What is the problem in this situation? What are your alternatives? What are the consequences of each alternative? Which alternative will you choose? Is your choice ethical?

LO 1–4   Describe the effects of technology on businesses.

The Technological Environment

Since prehistoric times, humans have felt the need to create tools that make work easier. Few technological changes have had a more comprehensive and lasting impact on businesses, however, than the emergence of information technology (IT): computers, networks, smartphones, and the Internet. Read the nearby Reaching Beyond Our Borders box to learn more about how technology makes it possible for freelance employees to find good, lucrative work even though they don't even need to live in the same country as their employers.

Smartphones and other mobile devices, as well as social media like Facebook and Twitter, have completely changed the way people communicate with one another. Advertisers and other businesspeople have created ways of using these tools to reach their suppliers and customers. Even politicians have harnessed the power of the Internet to advance their causes. IT is such a major force in business today that we discuss its impact on businesses throughout the entire text.

technology

Everything from phones and copiers to computers, mobile devices, medical imaging machines, and the various software programs and apps that make business processes more effective, efficient, and productive.

productivity

The amount of output you generate given the amount of input (e.g., hours worked).

How Technology Benefits Workers and You   One of the advantages of working for others is that the company often provides the tools and technology to make your job more productive. **Technology** means everything from phones and copiers to computers, mobile devices, medical imaging machines, and the various software programs and apps that make business processes more effective, efficient, and productive. *Effectiveness* means producing the desired result. *Efficiency* means producing goods and services using the least amount of resources

Productivity is the amount of output you generate given the amount of input, such as the number of hours you work. The more you can produce in any given period, the more money you are worth to companies. The problem with productivity today is that workers are so productive that fewer are needed, and that is contributing to the high unemployment rate we are now experiencing.[24]

Connecting Companies with Global Freelancers

In the years since the recession of 2007–2009, freelancers have become more important to the business world than ever before. Rather than spend money on recruiting and retaining full-time employees, many companies prefer to hire temporary workers in order to cut costs. In fact, thanks to the Internet, freelance employees don't even need to live in the same country as their employers to do good, lucrative work.

The company Elance acts as an online marketplace that connects freelancers with companies looking for contractors. For instance, if a Silicon Valley startup is looking for an affordable engineer, Elance can introduce the company to a qualified candidate from Eastern Europe or India. Elance then collects an 8.75 percent transaction fee from the company. With more than 8 million registered individuals, in 2013 Elance saw its revenues grow to $300 million. Following a merger with its former rival ODesk, Elance expects billings to increase by more than $1 billion annually as businesses become more dependent on freelance labor, and workers adapt to its flexible structure. "Millennials want to work independently and control their careers," says Elance founder Fabio Rosati. "If I had to give advice to anybody about their careers, I would say your number one priority should be to remain employable as opposed to remaining employed."

Sources: Laura Weber, "Elance Taps Growing Demand for Freelancers," *The Wall Street Journal*, February 4, 2014; Ari Levy, "Elance Merges with ODesk to Enlarge Service for Freelancers," *Bloomberg Businessweek*, December 18, 2013; and Patrick Clark, "What Elance-ODesk Merger Means for Freelancers," *Bloomberg Businessweek*, December 19, 2013.

Technology affects people in all industries. For example, Don Glenn, a farmer in Decatur, Alabama, uses his computer to compare data from the previous year's harvest with infrared satellite photos of his farm that show which crops are flourishing. He can check the latest grain prices and use website AgTalk to converse with other farmers from all over the world. He also bids for bulk fertilizer on XSAg.com, an online agricultural exchange. High-tech equipment tells Glenn how and where to spread fertilizer and seed, tracks yields yard by yard, and allows him to maintain high profit margins. More tech often means fewer workers. Is that a good or bad thing for farmers?

The Growth of E-Commerce **E-commerce** is the buying and selling of goods online. There are two major types of e-commerce transactions: business-to-consumer (B2C) and business-to-business (B2B). As important as the Internet has been to retailers like Amazon in the consumer market, it has become even more important in the B2B market, where businesses sell goods and services to one another, such as IBM selling consulting services to a local bank. Websites have become the new stores.

e-commerce
The buying and selling of goods over the Internet.

Traditional businesses must deal with the competition from B2B and B2C firms, and vice versa. Many new parents would just as soon buy used items posted on Craigslist than shop in a baby-goods store. Starting a business on eBay has never been easier. E-commerce has become so important that we will discuss it throughout the text.

Using Technology to Be Responsive to Customers A major theme of this text is that those businesses most responsive to customer wants and needs will succeed. That realization points to one way in which brick-and-mortar (traditional) retailers also use technology. For example, businesses use bar codes to identify products you buy and their size, quantity, and color. The scanner at the checkout counter identifies the price but can also put all your purchase information into a **database**, an electronic storage file for information.

database
An electronic storage file for information.

Walt Disney World introduced MyMagic+, a convenient way for guests to create their ideal vacation experience. The key element is the MagicBand, providing an all-in-one way to effortlessly connect all the vacation choices guests make online with MyDisneyExperience.com. The MagicBand uses RF technology and serves as park ticket, hotel room key, access to FastPass+ advance reservation of attraction times, and Disney's PhotoPass. Disneyhotel guests may use the Bands to charge meals and merchandise to their hotel account.

identity theft
The obtaining of individuals' personal information, such as Social Security and credit card numbers, for illegal purposes.

empowerment
Giving frontline workers the responsibility, authority, freedom, training, and equipment they need to respond quickly to customer requests.

Databases enable stores to carry only the merchandise their local population wants. But because companies routinely trade database information, many retailers know what you buy and from whom you buy it. Thus they can send you catalogs and other direct mail advertising offering the kind of products you might want, as indicated by your past purchases.[25] We discuss other ways businesses use technology to be responsive to consumers throughout the text.

Unfortunately, the legitimate collection of personal customer information also opens the door to identity theft. **Identity theft** is the obtaining of individuals' personal information, such as Social Security and credit card numbers, for illegal purposes. Just before Christmas 2013, hackers stole more than 110 million credit card numbers from Target's computer system, requiring all customers to monitor activity on these accounts and/or get new credit cards. The company's profits fell nearly 50 percent for the quarter.[26]

The Federal Trade Commission says millions of U.S. consumers are victims of identity theft each year. What you should learn from these examples is to limit those to whom you give personal information.[27] You also need antivirus software on your computer as well as a firewall and antispyware software. You may also want to monitor your credit report. It is important for you to understand identity theft, security, privacy, stability, and other important IT issues. Many people today are concerned about the government listening in on their phone conversations and e-mails.[28]

LO 1–5   Demonstrate how businesses can meet and beat competition.

The Competitive Environment

Competition among businesses has never been greater. Some have found a competitive edge by focusing on *quality*. The goal for many companies is zero defects—no mistakes in making the product. However, even achieving a rate of zero defects isn't enough to stay competitive in world markets. Companies now have to offer both high-quality products and good value—that is, outstanding service at competitive prices.

Competing by Exceeding Customer Expectations   Today's customers want not only good quality at low prices but great service as well. Every manufacturing and service organization in the world should have a sign over its door telling its workers that the customer is king. Business is becoming customer-driven, not management-driven as often occurred in the past. Successful organizations must now listen more closely to customers to determine their wants and needs, and then adjust the firm's products, policies, and practices accordingly. We will explore these ideas in more depth in Chapter 13.

Competing by Restructuring and Empowerment   To meet the needs of customers, firms must give their frontline workers—for example, office clerks, front-desk people at hotels, and salespeople—the responsibility, authority, freedom, training, and equipment they need to respond quickly to customer requests. They also must allow workers to make other decisions essential to producing high-quality goods and services. The process is called **empowerment**, and we'll be talking about it throughout this book.

As many companies have discovered, it sometimes takes years to restructure an organization so that managers can and will give up some of their authority and employees will assume more responsibility. We'll discuss such organizational changes in Chapter 8.

LO 1–6 **Analyze the social changes affecting businesses.**

The Social Environment

Demography is the statistical study of the human population with regard to its size, density, and other characteristics such as age, race, gender, and income. In this text, we're particularly interested in the demographic trends that most affect businesses and career choices. The U.S. population is going through major changes that are dramatically affecting how people live, where they live, what they buy, and how they spend their time. Furthermore, tremendous population shifts are leading to new opportunities for some firms and to declining opportunities for others. For example, there are many more retired workers than in the past, creating new markets for all kinds of goods and services.

demography
The statistical study of the human population with regard to its size, density, and other characteristics such as age, race, gender, and income.

Managing Diversity   *Diversity* has come to mean much more than recruiting and keeping minority and female employees. Diversity efforts now include seniors, people with disabilities, people with different sexual orientations, atheists, extroverts, introverts, married people, singles, and the devout. It also means dealing sensitively with workers and cultures around the world.

Legal and illegal immigrants have had a dramatic effect on many cities. Schools and hospitals have been especially affected. Some local governments are making every effort to adapt, including changing signs, brochures, websites, and forms to include other languages. Has your city experienced such changes? What are some of the impacts you've noticed?

The Increase in the Number of Older Citizens   People ages 65 to 74 are currently the richest demographic group in the United States. They thus represent a lucrative market for companies involved with food service, transportation, entertainment, education, lodging, and so on. By 2020, the percentage of the population over 60 will be 22.8 percent (versus 16 percent in 2000). What do these changes mean for you and for businesses in the future? Think of the products and services that middle-aged and elderly people will need—medicine, nursing homes, assisted-living facilities, adult day care, home health care, recreation, and the like—and you'll see opportunities for successful businesses of the 21st century. Don't rule out computer games and online services, even Wii. Businesses that cater to older consumers will have the opportunity for exceptional growth in the near future. The market is huge.

On the other hand, retired people will be draining the economy of wealth. Social Security has become a major issue. The pay-as-you-go system (in which workers today pay the retirement benefits for today's retirees) operated just fine in 1940, when 42 workers supported each retiree; but by 1960, there were only 5 workers per retiree, and today, as the baby-boom generation (born between 1946 and 1964) begins to retire, that number is under 3 and dropping. In addition, the government has been spending the accumulated Social Security money instead of leaving it in a Social Security account.

Soon, less money will be coming into Social Security than will be going out. The government will have to do something to make up for the shortfall: raise taxes, reduce Social Security benefits (e.g., raise the retirement age at which people qualify for payments), reduce spending elsewhere

The United States boasts enormous ethnic and racial diversity. Its workforce is also widely diverse in terms of age, which means that managers must adapt to the generational demographics of the workplace. What are some challenges of working with someone much younger or much older than you?

(e.g., in other social programs like Medicare or Medicaid), or borrow on the world market.

In short, paying Social Security to senior citizens in the future will draw huge amounts of money from the working population. That is why there is so much discussion in the media today about what to do with Social Security.

The Increase in the Number of Single-Parent Families   It is a tremendous task to work full-time and raise a family. Thus, the rapid growth of single-parent households has also had a major effect on businesses. Single parents, including those forced by welfare rules to return to work after a certain benefit period, have encouraged businesses to implement programs such as family leave (giving workers time off to attend to a sick child or elder relative) and flextime (allowing workers to arrive or leave at selected times). You will read about such programs in more detail in Chapter 11.

More and more working families consist of single parents who must juggle the demands of a job and the responsibilities of raising children. What can managers do to try to retain valued employees who face such challenges?

LO 1–7   Identify what businesses must do to meet global challenges, including war and terrorism.

The Global Environment

The global environment of business is so important that we show it as surrounding all other environmental influences (see again Figure 1.3). Two important changes here are the growth of global competition and the increase of free trade among nations.[29]

World trade, or *globalization,* has grown thanks to the development of efficient distribution systems (we'll talk about these in Chapter 15) and communication advances such as the Internet. Globalization has greatly improved living standards around the world. China and India have become major U.S. competitors. Shop at Walmart and most other U.S. retail stores, and you can't help but notice the number of "Made in China" stickers you see. Call for computer help, and you are as likely to be talking with someone in India as someone in the United States.

World trade has its benefits and costs. You'll read much more about its importance in Chapter 3 and in the Reaching Beyond Our Borders boxes throughout the text.

War and Terrorism   War and terrorism have drained billions of dollars from the U.S. economy. Some companies—like those that make bullets, tanks, and uniforms—have benefited greatly. Others, however, lost workers to the armed forces, and still others (e.g., tourism) have grown more slowly as money was diverted to the war effort. The threat of more wars and terrorism leads the government to spend even more money on spying and the military. Such expenditures are subject to much debate, especially as the United States strives for economic recovery. Note the increased unrest in the world as people in other nations are demanding more freedom, which adds uncertainty.

The threat of terrorism also adds greatly to organizational costs, including the cost of insurance. In fact, some firms are finding it difficult to get insurance against terrorist attacks. Security, too, is costly. Airlines, for example, have had to install stronger cockpit doors and add more passenger screening devices. Read the nearby Adapting to Change box to learn more about how the threat of terrorism affects even airport restaurants, which must adapt to increasing security regulations.

Like all citizens, businesspeople benefit from a peaceful and prosperous world. One way to lessen international tensions is to foster global economic growth among both profit-making and nonprofit organizations.

Gourmet Airport Eateries Take Flight

Although the poor quality of airline food has been an easy punch line for decades, often the food served inside the airport itself isn't much better. That's because airport restaurants are especially difficult to operate on account of a number of security regulations. For example, open-flame grills aren't allowed, and kitchen knives must be tethered to a counter. On top of that, cooking spaces are typically tiny and the time-crunched clientele demands speedy service.

But airport diners are more than just cranky people in a hurry: they also tend to be more affluent than average consumers. As a result, more gourmet restaurants are setting up shop in airports in order to cash in on vacationing diners. For instance,

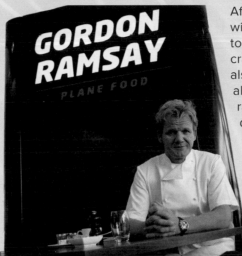

chief executive of Boston Legal Sea Foods Roger Berkowitz opened a location at Logan International Airport once he learned people were willing to spend more while traveling.

After stocking the bar with pricey wines, he edited the menu down to a few simple favorites like crab cakes and tuna burgers. He also tweaked his recipes so that all fish fillets would be griddled rather than grilled. Not only does the restaurant earn a lot of money for Berkowitz, but the airport also gets to show off a bit of local flavor to passing travelers. However, Berkowitz has one piece of advice about operating an airport eatery that many air carriers won't appreciate: "You want to be near airlines with more delays and cancellations."

Sources: Scott McCartney, "The Best Airport Food in the U.S. and Beyond," *The Wall Street Journal*, January 15, 2014; and Will Yakowicz, "Comfort Food: The Best U.S. Airport Restaurants," *Inc.*, January 16, 2014.

How Global Changes Affect You   As businesses expand to serve global markets, new jobs will be created in both manufacturing and service industries. Global trade also means global competition. The students who will prosper will be those prepared for the markets of tomorrow. Rapid changes create a need for continuous learning, so be prepared to continue your education throughout your career. You'll have every reason to be optimistic about job opportunities in the future if you prepare yourself well.

The Ecological Environment   Few issues have captured the attention of the international business community more than climate change. **Climate change** is the movement of the temperature of the planet up or down over time. Some of the world's largest firms—including General Electric, Coca-Cola, Shell, Nestlé, DuPont, Johnson & Johnson, British Airways, and Shanghai Electric—say the evidence for climate change is overwhelming. Saving energy and producing products that cause less harm to the environment is a trend called **greening**. We shall discuss these issues in the Seeking Sustainability boxes throughout the text.

climate change
The movement of the temperature of the planet up or down over time.

greening
The trend toward saving energy and producing products that cause less harm to the environment.

test prep ✓✓

- What are four ways the government can foster entrepreneurship?
- What's the difference between effectiveness, efficiency, and productivity?
- What is *empowerment*?
- What are some of the major issues affecting the economy today?

Use LearnSmart to help retain what you have learned. Access your instructor's Connect course to check out LearnSmart, or go to learnsmartadvantage.com for help.

▦ LEARNSMART

LO 1–8   Review how past trends are being repeated in the present and what those trends mean for tomorrow's college graduates.

THE EVOLUTION OF U.S. BUSINESS

Businesses in the United States have become so productive that they need fewer workers than ever before to produce goods.[30] If global competition and improved technology are putting skilled people out of work, should we be concerned about the prospect of high unemployment rates and low incomes? Where will the jobs be when you graduate? These important questions force us all to look briefly at the U.S. economy and its future.

Progress in the Agricultural and Manufacturing Industries

The United States has experienced strong economic development since the 1800s. The agricultural industry led the way, providing food for the United States and much of the world. Cyrus McCormick's invention of the harvester in 1834, other inventions such as Eli Whitney's cotton gin, and modern improvements on such equipment did much to make large-scale farming successful. Technology has made modern farming so efficient that the number of farmers has dropped from about 33 percent of the population to about 1 percent today. However, average farm size is now about 450 acres versus 160 acres in the past.

Agriculture is still a major industry in the United States. What has changed is that the millions of small farms that existed previously have been replaced by some huge farms, some merely large farms, and some small but highly specialized farms. The loss of farm workers over the past century is not a negative sign. It is instead an indication that U.S. agricultural workers are the most productive in the world.

Most farmers who lost their jobs during the 19th and 20th centuries went to work in factories springing up around the country. Manufacturers, like farms, began using new technology, new tools and machines, to become more productive. Eventually the consequence in manufacturing, as in farming, was the elimination of many jobs.

Again, the loss to society is minimized if the wealth created by increased productivity and efficiency creates new jobs elsewhere—and that's exactly what has happened over the past 50 years. Many workers in the industrial sector found jobs in the growing service sector. Most of those who can't find work today are people who need retraining and education to become qualified for jobs that now exist or will exist in the near future, such as building wind farms or making electric automobiles. We'll discuss the manufacturing sector and production in more detail in Chapter 9.

Agriculture is one of the largest and most important industries in the United States. Technology has increased productivity and made farmers more efficient, allowing for larger farms. This trend has helped to reduce the increase in price of some foods for consumers, but has also reduced the number of small, family-run farms. Does the new technology also help smaller farms compete? How?

Progress in Service Industries

In the past, the fastest-growing industries in the United States produced goods like steel, automobiles, and machine tools. Today, the fastest-growing firms provide services in areas such as law, health, telecommunications, entertainment, and finance.

Together, services make up over 70 percent of the value of the U.S. economy. Since the mid-1980s, the service industry has generated almost all the increases in employment. Although service-sector growth has slowed, it remains the largest area of growth. Chances are very high that you'll work in a service job at some point in your career. Figure 1.4 lists many service-sector jobs; look it over to see where the careers of the future are likely to be. Retailers like American Eagle are part of the service sector. Each new retail store can create managerial jobs for college graduates.

FIGURE 1.4　WHAT IS THE SERVICE SECTOR?

There's much talk about the service sector, but few discussions actually list what it includes. Here's a representative list of services as classified by the government:

Lodging Services

Hotels, rooming houses, and other lodging places
Sporting and recreation camps
Trailer parks and campsites for transients

Personal Services

Laundries	Child care
Linen supply	Shoe repair
Diaper service	Funeral homes
Carpet cleaning	Tax preparation
Photographic studios	Beauty shops
Health clubs	

Business Services

Accounting	Exterminating
Ad agencies	Employment agencies
Collection agencies	Computer programming
Commercial photography	Research & development labs
Commercial art	Management services
Stenographic services	Public relations
Window cleaning	Detective agencies
Consulting	Interior design
Equipment rental	Web design
Tax preparation	Trash collection

Automotive Repair Services and Garages

Auto rental	Tire retreading
Truck rental	Exhaust system shops
Parking lots	Car washes
Paint shops	Transmission repair

Miscellaneous Repair Services

Radio and television	Welding
Watch	Sharpening
Reupholstery	Septic tank cleaning

Motion Picture Industry

Production	Theaters
Distribution	Drive-ins

Amusement and Recreation Services

Restaurants	Racetracks
Symphony orchestras	Golf courses
Pool halls	Amusement parks
Bowling alleys	Carnivals
Fairs	Ice skating rinks
Botanical gardens	Circuses
Video rentals	Infotainment

Health Services

Physicians	Nursery care
Dentists	Medical labs
Chiropractors	Dental labs

Legal Services

Educational Services

Libraries	Computer schools
Schools	Online schools

Social Services

Child care	Family services
Job training	Elder care

Noncommercial Museums, Art Galleries, and Botanical and Zoological Gardens

Selected Membership Organizations

Business associations	Civic associations

Financial Services

Banking	Real estate agencies
Insurance	Investment firms (brokers)

Miscellaneous Services

Architectural	Surveying
Engineering	Utilities
Telecommunications	Lawn care
Vending	Delivery

Another bit of good news is that there are *more* high-paying jobs in the service sector than in the goods-producing sector. High-paying service-sector jobs abound in health care, accounting, finance, entertainment, telecommunications, architecture, law, software engineering, and more. Projections are that some areas of the service sector will grow rapidly, while others may have much slower growth. The strategy for college graduates is to remain flexible, find out where jobs are being created, and move when appropriate.[31]

Your Future in Business

Despite the growth in the service sector we've described above, the service era now seems to be coming to a close as a new era is beginning. We're in the midst of an information-based global and technical revolution that will alter all sectors of the economy: agricultural, industrial, and service. It's exciting to think about the role you'll play in that revolution. You may be a leader who will implement the changes and accept the challenges of world competition based on world quality standards. This book will introduce you to some of the concepts that make such leadership possible, not just in business but also in government agencies and nonprofit organizations. Business can't prosper in the future without the cooperation of government and social leaders throughout the world.

Use LearnSmart to help retain what you have learned. Access your instructor's Connect course to check out LearnSmart, or go to learnsmartadvantage.com for help.

LEARNSMART

test **prep**

- What major factor caused people to move from farming to manufacturing and from manufacturing to the service sector?
- What does the future look like for tomorrow's college graduates?

Summary

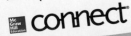
Access your instructor's Connect course to check out LearnSmart or go to learnsmartadvantage.com for help.

Mc Graw Hill Education connect

LO 1–1   Describe the relationship between profit and risk, and show how businesses and nonprofit organizations can raise the standard of living for all.

- **What is the relationship of businesses' profit to risk assumption?**
  Profit is money a business earns above and beyond the money that it spends for salaries and other expenses. Businesspeople make profits by taking risks. *Risk* is the chance an entrepreneur takes of losing time and money on a business that may not prove profitable. A loss occurs when a business's costs and expenses are higher than its revenues.

- **Who are stakeholders, and which stakeholders are most important to a business?**
  Stakeholders include customers, employees, stockholders, suppliers, dealers, bankers, the media, people in the local community, environmentalists, and elected government leaders. The goal of business leaders is to try to recognize and respond to the needs of these stakeholders and still make a profit.

LO 1–2   Compare and contrast being an entrepreneur and working for others.

- **What are the advantages and disadvantages of entrepreneurship?**
Working for others means getting benefits like paid vacations and health insurance. Entrepreneurs take more risks and lose those benefits. They gain the freedom to make their own decisions, more opportunity, and possible wealth.

- **What are the five factors of production?**
The five factors of production are land, labor, capital, entrepreneurship, and knowledge. Of these, the most important are entrepreneurship and knowledge. Entrepreneurs are people who risk time and money to start and manage a business. What makes rich countries rich today is a combination of *entrepreneurship* and the effective use of *knowledge*.

LO 1–3   Analyze the effects of the economic environment and taxes on businesses.

- **What can governments in developing countries do to reduce the risk of starting businesses and thus help entrepreneurs?**
The government may allow private ownership of businesses, pass laws that enable businesspeople to write contracts that are enforceable in court, establish a currency that's tradable in world markets, help to lessen corruption in business and government, and keep taxes and regulations to a minimum. From a business perspective, lower taxes mean lower risks, more growth, and thus more money for workers and the government.

LO 1–4   Describe the effects of technology on businesses.

- **How has technology benefited workers, businesses, and consumers?**
Technology enables workers to be more effective, efficient, and productive. *Effectiveness* means doing the right thing in the right way. *Efficiency* means producing items using the least amount of resources. *Productivity* is the amount of output you generate given the amount of input (e.g., hours worked).

LO 1–5   Demonstrate how businesses can meet and beat competition.

- **What are some ways in which businesses meet and beat competition?**
Some companies have found a competitive edge by focusing on making high-quality products, all the way to zero defects. Companies also aim to exceed customer expectations. Often that means *empowering* frontline workers by giving them more training and more responsibility and authority.

LO 1–6   Analyze the social changes affecting businesses.

- **How have social changes affected businesses?**
Diversity has come to mean much more than recruiting and keeping minority and female employees. Diversity efforts now include seniors, people with disabilities, people with different sexual orientations, atheists, extroverts, introverts, married people, singles, and the devout. Managing diversity means dealing sensitively with workers and cultures around the world. Providing Social Security benefits to senior citizens in the future will draw huge amounts of money from the working population. That is why there is so much discussion about Social Security in the media today.

LO 1–7   Identify what businesses must do to meet global challenges, including war and terrorism.

- **Which countries are creating the greatest challenges?**
  China and India are two major competitors.

- **What will be the impacts of future wars and terrorism?**
  Some businesses, such as those in the defense industry, may prosper. Others, such as tourism, may suffer. One way to minimize world tensions is to help less developed countries to become more prosperous.

LO 1–8   Review how past trends are being repeated in the present and what those trends mean for tomorrow's college graduates.

- **What is the history of our economic development in the United States, and what does it tell us about the future?**
  Agricultural workers displaced by improved farm technology went to work in factories. Improved manufacturing productivity and increased competition from foreign firms contributed to the development of a service economy in the United States. The service era is now giving way to an information-based global revolution that will affect all sectors of the economy. The secret to long-term success in such an economy is flexibility and continuing education to be prepared for the opportunities that are sure to arise.

- **What job opportunities for college graduates exist in the service sector?**
  Check over Figure 1.4, which outlines the service sector. That is where you are most likely to find the fast-growing firms of the future.

key terms

business 4	**factors of production** 10	**profit** 4
business environment 11	**goods** 4	**quality of life** 6
climate change 19	**greening** 19	**revenue** 4
database 15	**identity theft** 16	**risk** 5
demography 17	**loss** 4	**services** 4
e-commerce 15	**nonprofit organization** 7	**stakeholders** 6
empowerment 16	**outsourcing** 6	**standard of living** 5
entrepreneur 4	**productivity** 14	**technology** 14

critical thinking

Imagine you are thinking of starting a restaurant in your community. Answer the following questions:

1. Who will be the various stakeholders of your business?

2. What are some of the things you can do to benefit your community other than providing jobs and tax revenue?

3. How will you establish good relationships with your suppliers? With your employees?

4. Do you see any conflict between your desire to be as profitable as possible and your desire to pay employees a living wage?

5. Which of the environmental factors outlined in this chapter might have the biggest impact on your business? How?

developing workplace skills

Key: ● Team   ★ Analytic   ▲ Communication   ▣ Technology

1. Poll the class and determine which students believe that climate change is primarily caused by humans and which believe that other factors, such as climate cycles or sun spots, are the primary cause. Discuss what students can do to minimize human effects on the environment regardless of the primary causes of climate change. Are there any negative consequences to trying to minimize humans' impact on the environment? ● ▲ ★

2. Imagine you are a local businessperson who has to deal with the issue of outsourcing. You want to begin with the facts. How many, if any, jobs have been lost to outsourcing in your area? Are there any foreign firms in your area that are creating jobs (insourcing)? You will need to go online to find the data you need. ▣ ★

3. What indicates that you and other people in the United States have a high standard of living? What are some signs that maintaining such a high standard of living may have a negative impact on quality of life? Does everyone in the United States enjoy a high standard of living? If not, how does this impact their quality of life? ★

4. Use Yelp to find five businesses that provide services in your area. List those businesses and, for each, describe how social trends might affect them in both positive and negative ways. Be prepared to explain your descriptions to your team or the whole class, as your instructor directs. ● ▣ ▲ ★

5. Form into teams of four or five and discuss the technological and e-commerce revolutions. How many students now shop for goods and services online? What have been their experiences? What other high-tech equipment do they use (smartphones, tablets, laptops, etc.)? ● ▣ ▲

taking it to the net

PURPOSE

To learn what changes are occurring in the business environment today and how those changes are affecting businesses.

EXERCISE

1. Go to the National Taxpayers Union website (www.ntu.org). Search for "Who Pays Income Taxes? See Who Pays What." Study the tables showing what percentage of taxes the various income groups pay. Do you think that businesspeople pay their fair share? What percentage of taxes does the top 1 percent of earners pay? What about the top 5 percent? The lowest 50 percent? How do such tax rates affect incentives to become a successful entrepreneur?

2. Go to the Census Bureau's website (www.census.gov) and learn what the population of the United States is at this moment. While at the site, you may want to look up the population in your town or city. Explore what other data are available at this site. What trends seem most important to you and to businesspeople in general?

3. Do a Google search for "business blogs" and check out some of the available results. Go to one of the blogs that seems interesting to you and write a brief paragraph about it—including such things as who sponsors it, who contributes the posts, and what other features it has—and how it may help a student in an introductory business course.

THOMAS LENNON, ACTOR AND ENTREPRENEUR

Although comedy may look like all fun and games, making movies in Hollywood is serious business. Few people understand this as well as Thomas Lennon. Although best known for his starring role in the Comedy Central series *Reno 911*, Lennon does his most lucrative work off-screen. He and his writing partner, Robert Ben Garant, have penned the screenplays to a number of blockbuster movies, including the *Night at the Museum* series.

Staying successful in the writing business is a tough task. There's lots of competition, and few writers ever sell enough work to make a living. Some movie and TV writers work on teams for big studios. For instance, late night talk show hosts like Jimmy Fallon have writing staffs to pen jokes and sketches for each episode. While these writers receive a steady paycheck, there are also limitations to their work. After all, if one writer comes up with something especially brilliant, she doesn't receive anything more than her standard salary.

The most successful players in entertainment take control of their work so that they can reap the most benefit from their efforts. Lennon set off on this particular path at a young age. While a student at New York University, he joined a comedy troupe that quickly gathered a dedicated following. Within a few years the team had struck a deal with MTV to create their own show. Called *The State*, this short-lived but critically acclaimed series taught Lennon the value of creating his own projects.

This entrepreneurial outlook allows Lennon almost total freedom in his work, but it presents a number of risks as well. He launched a few failed TV projects before he managed to find the right formula with *Reno 911*. Moviemaking presents even more challenges than TV. In fact, Lennon had to shut down production on a film for nearly two years due to the writers' union strike of 2007–2008. As a result, that movie has never been released. Being an entrepreneur means not only taking risks, but enduring setbacks as well.

For those who work in Hollywood, creators must also be able to respond to changing tastes, technological advances, and drastic budget cuts. They must also know how to appeal to global audiences. Writers like Lennon have to be mindful not to focus jokes or characters on very limited cultural ideas. Instead, making characters broad and themes universal makes their film accessible to a wider audience. And that makes it more profitable to a studio. Lennon proved he could do that. In fact, the original *Night at the Museum* played in over 70 countries, earning huge box office numbers from the Americas to Australia, from Europe to Southeast Asia.

The film was so successful that it spawned a sequel, *Night at the Museum: Battle of the Smithsonian*, which did even more business. The two films combined brought in nearly $1 billion at the box office, to say nothing of DVD sales and merchandising revenue. In fact, a third film is likely to push Tom's career box office haul to more than $2 billion, making him only the sixth writer to achieve that feat. With his relentlessly creative mind and entrepreneurial drive, Lennon stands to be a major force in the entertainment industry for some time to come.

THINKING IT OVER

1. What are the risks and benefits of becoming an entrepreneur as opposed to working for others?

2. Why is the writing profession especially risky for entrepreneurs like Tom Lennon?

3. Does the entertainment industry seem like a stable option for aspiring entrepreneurs to pursue?

notes

1. Abram Brown, "Fred Smith Flies High," *Forbes,* February 10, 2014.
2. Farhad Manjoo, "Deal with It: Mobile Ads Are Here to Stay," *The Wall Street Journal,* December 19, 2013.
3. "The Definitive Ranking of the Richest People in the United States," *Forbes,* October 7, 2013.
4. "The Numbers," *Barron's,* March 25, 2013.
5. Richard Vedder, "The Wages of Unemployment," *The Wall Street Journal,* January 16, 2013.
6. Jeffrey McKinney, "Before Disaster Strikes," *Black Enterprise,* April/May 2013.
7. Craig Giammona, "Smooth Handling," *Fortune,* December 23, 2013.
8. Nina Easton, "Time to Get Creative about Helping the Unemployed Back into the Job Market," *Fortune,* February 3, 2014.
9. John Mackey and Raj Sisodia, *Conscious Capitalism* (Boston, MA: Harvard Business Review Press, 2013).
10. Michael R. Strain, "Back to Work," *The Weekly Standard,* December 16, 2013.
11. James R. Hagerty, "Flextronics Warms to U.S.," *The Wall Street Journal,* January 5–6, 2013.
12. Lorraine Luk, "Hon Hai Weighs Plant in U.S.," *The Wall Street Journal,* January 27, 2014.
13. Elaine Glusac, "No Permanent Address," *Entrepreneur,* February 2014.
14. James R. Hagerty, "Entrepreneur Let No Impediment Stop Him," *The Wall Street Journal,* January 16, 2014.
15. Steve Matthews, "For Many, the Age of Entrepreneurship Starts at 55," *The Washington Post,* January 12, 2014.
16. Ed Feulner, "Entrepreneurs: Spark Plugs in a Free-Market Economy," *The Washington Times,* September 3, 2013.
17. John Dearie and Courtney Geduldig, "More Immigration Means More Jobs for Americans," *The Wall Street Journal,* December 30, 2013.
18. Sue Shellenbarger, "Love and Work on a Strict Timetable," *The Wall Street Journal,* January 22, 2014.
19. Debora Spar, "American Women Have It Wrong," *Newsweek,* October 8, 2012.
20. Janel Martinez, "Atlanta's Tech Stars," *Black Enterprise,* November 2013.
21. Christopher S. Rugaber and Ken Sweet, "Explaining the Disconnect in the U.S. Economy," *St. Louis Post-Dispatch,* November 8, 2013.
22. Andrew Feinberg, "Swimming in a Cesspool," *Kiplinger's Personal Finance,* March 2014.
23. Paul M. Healy and Karthik Ramanna, "When the Crowd Fights Corruption," *Harvard Business Review,* January–February 2013.
24. Richard Stengel, "Made in America, Again," *Time,* April 22, 2013.
25. Jack Neff, "Marketers Become Big Data Hoarders," *Advertising Age,* March 18, 2013.
26. Maggie McGrath, "Target Profit Falls 46% on Credit Card Breach and the Hits Could Keep On Coming," *Forbes,* February 26, 2014.
27. Lisa Gerstner, "What You Need to Know about Identity Theft," *Kiplinger's Personal Finance,* June 2013.
28. "Snowden's Damage," editorial, *The Wall Street Journal,* January 11–12, 2014.
29. David Malpass, "Five Big Steps toward Faster Global Growth," *Forbes,* February 10, 2014.
30. David Von Drehle, "The Robot Economy," *Time,* September 9, 2013.
31. Parmy Olson, "Crowdsourcing Capitalists," *Forbes,* February 10, 2014.

2

Understanding Economics and How It Affects Business

Learning Objectives

AFTER YOU HAVE READ AND STUDIED THIS CHAPTER, YOU SHOULD BE ABLE TO

LO 2-1   Explain basic economics.

LO 2-2   Explain what capitalism is and how free markets work.

LO 2-3   Compare socialism and communism.

LO 2-4   Analyze the trend toward mixed economies.

LO 2-5   Describe the economic system of the United States, including the significance of key economic indicators (especially GDP), productivity, and the business cycle.

LO 2-6   Contrast fiscal policy and monetary policy, and explain how each affects the economy.

People talk about the state of "*the* economy" so much that it can seem as if economics deals only with big, world-shaking financial issues. In reality, though, economics can be found all around us in daily life. From a family saving money for the future to a major corporation measuring its revenue, the world is full of economies both large and small.

It's these small economies that are the major concern of Matt Flannery, co-founder and CEO of the microlending company Kiva.org. His company offers small loans to entrepreneurs working in developing countries in Africa, Asia and South America. Unlike businesspeople operating in the U.S., these entrepreneurs don't need thousands upon thousands of dollars to see their dreams become reality. Instead, many loans issued by Kiva are little more than a few hundred dollars.

But it's not the size of the loans that makes Flannery's work notable. In fact, microlending has been a common source of financing for the developing world since the early 1980s. What sets Kiva apart from the rest is the company's approach. Kiva operates in a similar way to crowdfunding sites like Kickstarter or Indiegogo. These companies rely on small donations from many people in order to fund a larger goal. At Kiva, users first go to the site to select the person or family they'd like to fund. Next, they lend $25 to the entrepreneur of their choice. If the borrowers reach their funding goal, then Kiva grants the loans. The borrowers gradually make repayments that are sent back to Kiva, which then distributes the money back to the lenders. Although lenders don't earn any interest, the satisfaction of helping another human being thousands of miles away is enough to ensure that 70 percent of all lenders make another loan.

Flannery took a winding road to reach this point in his career. Interestingly enough, other than Kiva, he doesn't have any previous background in either financing or the nonprofit sector. After getting a degree from Stanford University, Flannery got a job developing software at Tivo, but he really wanted a business of his own. "I tried to start maybe ten companies," says Flannery. "It was like I had a midlife crisis at 22." For example, Flannery attempted to start a DVD-rental machine business years before Redbox existed. He also tried his hand at starting an online luxury clothes rental company. "A lot of those other ideas for me were a little empty . . . they weren't proactive movements towards something I loved. This idea is different. The actual content of the idea I enjoy every day . . . this is my dream job."

The inspiration for Kiva didn't hit him until he spent a few months working in rural communities throughout Africa. The impact of small businesses on the communities Flannery visited made a profound impression on him. Kiva launched in 2005, after he spent a year researching the aid industry and talking with experts. Today Kiva has distributed more than $500 million in loans to entrepreneurs throughout the world. "Small loans used for business growth encourage self-respect, accountability, and hope among loan recipients," says Flannery. "Primarily, the challenges they [entrepreneurs in Africa] face are very similar to the challenges we face . . . a story about a woman selling fish on the side of the street in Uganda, you can get into profit margins, inventory management, the same things that businesses here think about. There's a commonality that can unify people. Which is exciting."

Many people don't realize the importance of the economic environment to the success of business. That is what this chapter is all about. You will learn to compare different economic systems to see the benefits and the drawbacks of each. You will learn how the free-market system of the United States works. And you will learn more about what makes some countries rich and other countries poor. By the end of the chapter, you should understand the direct effect economic systems have on the wealth and happiness of communities throughout the world.

Sources: Mohana Ravindranath, "Microfinance Nonprofit Kiva Launches in D.C.," *The Washington Post,* January 8, 2013; Interview, "Why Purpose Matters For Matt Flannery of Kiva.org," *Yscouts,* September 11, 2013; Charles Blass, "Matt Flannery: Co-Founder and CEO, Kiva Microfunds," *Thefuturemakers.net,* May 2, 2013; and www.kiva.org, accessed January 2014.

Matt Flannery

Co-Founder and CEO of Kiva.org

- From software developer to microlender
- Provides small loans to build businesses

www.kiva.org

twitter.com/kiva

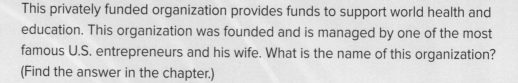

name that **company**

This privately funded organization provides funds to support world health and education. This organization was founded and is managed by one of the most famous U.S. entrepreneurs and his wife. What is the name of this organization? (Find the answer in the chapter.)

LO 2–1 Explain basic economics.

HOW ECONOMIC CONDITIONS AFFECT BUSINESSES

Compared to, say, Mexico, the United States is a relatively wealthy country. Why? Why is South Korea comparatively wealthy and North Korea suffering economically, with many of its people starving? Such questions are part of the subject of economics. In this chapter, we explore the various economic systems of the world and how they either promote or hinder business growth, the creation of wealth, and a higher quality of life for all.

A major part of the United States' business success in the past was due to an economic and social climate that allowed most businesses to operate freely. People were free to start a business anywhere, and just as free to fail and start again. That freedom motivated people to try until they succeeded because the rewards were often so great.[1]

Any change in the U.S. economic or political system has a major influence on the success of the business system.[2] For example, the recent increase in government involvement in business will have an economic effect. What that effect will be in the long run, however, remains to be seen.

Global economics and global politics also have a major influence on businesses in the United States. For example, there is even some talk today about having a one-time global wealth tax.[3] This is a tax that was proposed by the International Monetary Fund (IMF). The idea is to tax the wealth of individuals around the world by 10 percent to bring the debt of nations closer to the pre-recession levels. Think of how such a tax would affect businesses and workers in the United States. Clearly, to understand business, you must also understand basic economics and politics. This is especially true of new college graduates looking for jobs.

What Is Economics?

Economics is the study of how society chooses to employ resources to produce goods and services and distribute them for consumption among various competing groups and individuals. There are two major branches of economics: **macroeconomics** looks at the operation of a nation's economy as a whole (the whole United States), and **microeconomics** looks at the behavior of people and organizations in markets for particular products or services.[4] A question in macroeconomics might be: What should the United States do to lower its national debt?[5] Macroeconomic topics in this chapter include gross domestic product (GDP), the unemployment rate, and price indexes. Recently, there has been some question about macroeconomic policies and how effective they really are.[6] A question in microeconomics might be: Why do people buy smaller cars when gas prices go up? Such questions seem easier to answer.

economics
The study of how society chooses to employ resources to produce goods and services and distribute them for consumption among various competing groups and individuals.

macroeconomics
The part of economics study that looks at the operation of a nation's economy as a whole.

microeconomics
The part of economics study that looks at the behavior of people and organizations in particular markets.

The economic contrast is remarkable. Business is booming in Seoul, South Korea (as shown in the top photo). But North Korea, a communist country, is not doing well, as the picture on the bottom shows. What do you think accounts for the dramatic differences in the economies of these two neighboring countries?

Some economists define economics as the study of the allocation of *scarce* resources. They believe resources need to be carefully divided among people, usually by the government. However, there's no way to maintain peace and prosperity in the world by merely dividing the resources we have today among the existing nations. There aren't enough known resources to do that. **Resource development** is the study of how to increase resources (say, by getting oil and gas from shale and tar sands) and create conditions that will make better use of them (like recycling and conservation).[7]

Businesses can contribute to an economic system by inventing products that greatly increase available resources. For example, they can discover new energy sources (natural gas for autos), new ways of growing food (hydroponics), and new ways of creating needed goods and services such as nanotechnology

resource development
The study of how to increase resources and to create the conditions that will make better use of those resources.

and 4D technology (moving 3D, with time as the fourth dimension). Maricul-ture, or raising fish in pens out in the ocean, could lead to more food for every-one and more employment. It is believed that the United States could monopolize the shrimp industry using aquaculture. Now we import about a billion pounds of shrimp a year.

The Secret to Creating a Wealthy Economy

Imagine the world when kings and other rich landowners had most of the wealth, and the majority of the people were peasants. The peasants had many children, and it may have seemed a natural conclusion that if things went on as usual there would soon be too many people and not enough food and other

New ways of producing goods and services add resources to the economy and create more employment. Fish farms, for instance, create both food and jobs. Can you think of other innovations that can help increase economic development?

resources. Economist Thomas Malthus made this argument in the late 1700s and early 1800s, lead-ing the writer Thomas Carlyle to call economics "the dismal science."

Followers of Malthus today (who are called neo-Malthusians) still believe there are too many people in the world and that the solution to pov-erty is radical birth control, including forced abor-tions and sterilization.[8] The latest world statistics, however, show population growing more slowly than expected. In some industrial countries—such as Japan, Germany, Italy, Russia, and the United States—population growth may be so slow that eventually there will be too many old people and too few young people to care for them.[9] In the developing world, on the other hand, population will climb relatively quickly and may lead to greater poverty and more unrest. Studies about the effects of population growth on the economy are part of macroeconomics.

Some macroeconomists believe that a large population, especially an edu-cated one, can be a valuable resource. You've probably heard the saying "Give a man a fish and you feed him for a day, but teach a man to fish and you feed him for a lifetime." You can add to that: "Teach a person to start a fish farm, and he or she will be able to feed a village for a lifetime." *The secret to economic develop-ment is contained in this last statement.* Business owners provide jobs and eco-nomic growth for their employees and communities as well as for themselves.[10]

The challenge for macroeconomists is to determine what makes some countries relatively wealthy and other countries relatively poor, and then to implement policies and programs that lead to increased prosperity for every-one in all countries. One way to begin understanding this challenge is to con-sider the theories of Adam Smith.

Adam Smith and the Creation of Wealth

Rather than believing fixed resources had to be divided among competing groups and individuals, Scottish economist Adam Smith envisioned creating more resources so that everyone could become wealthier. Smith's book *An Inquiry into the Nature and Causes of the Wealth of Nations* (often called simply *The Wealth of Nations*) was published in 1776.

Smith believed *freedom* was vital to the survival of any economy, especially the freedom to own land or property and to keep the profits from working the land or running a business.[11] He believed people will work long and hard if they have incentives for doing so—that is, if they know they'll be rewarded. As a result of those efforts, the economy will prosper, with plenty of food and all kinds of products available to everyone. Smith's ideas were later challenged by Malthus and others who believed economic conditions would only get worse, but Smith, not Malthus, is considered the father of modern economics.

How Businesses Benefit the Community

In Adam Smith's view, businesspeople don't necessarily deliberately set out to help others. They work primarily for their own prosperity and growth. Yet as people try to improve their own situation in life, Smith said, their efforts serve as an "invisible hand" that helps the economy grow and prosper through the production of needed goods, services, and ideas. Thus, the phrase **invisible hand** is used to describe the process that turns self-directed gain into social and economic benefits for *all*.

How do people working in their own self-interest produce goods, services, and wealth for others? The only way farmers can become wealthy is to sell some of their crops to others. To become even wealthier, they have to hire workers to produce more food. So the farmers' self-centered efforts to become wealthy lead to jobs for some and food for almost all. Think about that process for a minute, because it is critical to understanding economic growth in the United States and other free countries. The same principles apply to everything from clothing to houses to iPhones.

Smith assumed that as people became wealthier, they would naturally reach out to help the less fortunate in the community. That has not always happened. In fact, today the poverty rate in the United States is quite high and there is a great disparity between the amount of money the wealthy have and the amount of money poor people have.[12] This is called "inequality" and is the central concern of many political, religious, and social leaders today.[13] Many businesspeople are becoming more concerned about social issues and their obligation to return to society some of what they've earned.[14] The economic question is: What can and should we do about poverty and unemployment in the United States and around the world?

As we mentioned in Chapter 1, it is important for businesses to be ethical as well as generous. Unethical practices undermine the whole economic system. The Making Ethical Decisions box explores the effects of corruption.

invisible hand
A phrase coined by Adam Smith to describe the process that turns self-directed gain into social and economic benefits for all.

According to Adam Smith's theory, business owners are motivated to work hard because they know they will earn, and keep, the rewards of their labor. When they prosper, as the owner of this restaurant has, they are able to add employees and grow, indirectly helping the community and the larger economy grow in the process. What might motivate you to start your own business?

making **ethical decisions**

How Corruption Harms the Economy

There are numerous forces in poor countries that hinder economic growth and development. One of those forces is corruption. In many countries, a businessperson must bribe government officials to get permission to own land, build on it, and conduct normal business operations. The United States has seen much corruption among businesspeople, such as use of prostitutes, illegal drug use, alcohol addiction, and gambling. Imagine you need a permit to add liquor to your restaurant menu to increase your profit. You have tried for years to get one, with no results. You have a friend in the government who offers to help you if you make a large contribution to his or her reelection campaign. Would you be tempted to make a campaign contribution? What are your alternatives? What are the consequences of each?

test **prep**

- What is the difference between macroeconomics and microeconomics?
- What is better for an economy than teaching a man to fish?
- What does Adam Smith's term *invisible hand* mean? How does the invisible hand create wealth for a country?

LO 2–2 Explain what capitalism is and how free markets work.

UNDERSTANDING FREE-MARKET CAPITALISM

Basing their ideas on free-market principles such as those of Adam Smith, businesspeople in the United States, Europe, Japan, Canada, and other countries began to create more wealth than ever before. They hired others to work on their farms and in their factories, and their nations began to prosper as a result. Businesspeople soon became the wealthiest people in society.

However, great disparities in wealth remained or even increased. Many businesspeople owned large homes and fancy carriages while most workers lived in humble surroundings. Nonetheless, there was always the promise of better times. One way to be really wealthy was to start a successful business of your own. Of course, it wasn't that easy—it never has been. Then and now, you have to accumulate some money to buy or start a business, and you have to work long hours to make it grow. But the opportunities are there.[15]

The economic system that has led to wealth creation in much of the world is known as capitalism. Under **capitalism** all or most of the factors of production and distribution—such as land, factories, railroads, and stores—are owned by individuals. They are operated for profit, and businesspeople, not government officials, decide what to produce and how much, what to charge, and how much to pay workers. They also decide whether to produce goods in their own countries or have them made in other countries. No country is purely capitalist, however. Often the government gets involved in issues such as determining minimum wages, setting farm prices, and lending money to some failing businesses—as it does in the United States. But capitalism is the *foundation* of the U.S. economic system, and of the economies of England, Australia, Canada, and most other industrialized nations.

Capitalism, liked all economic systems has its faults. For example, income inequality is a major issue that concerns many today. However, John Mackey,

capitalism
An economic system in which all or most of the factors of production and distribution are privately owned and operated for profit.

CEO of Whole Foods, believes that "conscious capitalism," that is, capitalism based on businesses that serve all major stakeholders, is the best system in the world.[16] Here is what he says about capitalism: "In the long arc of history, no human creation has had a greater positive impact on more people more rapidly than free-enterprise capitalism. . . . This system has afforded billions of us the opportunity to join in the great enterprise of earning our sustenance and finding meaning by creating value for each other."[17]

Some countries have noticed the advantages of capitalism and have instituted what has become known as state capitalism.[18] **State capitalism** is a combination of freer markets and some government control. China, for example, has had rapid growth over the last few years as a result of state capitalism—that is, freer markets and less government control.[19] We shall discuss the Chinese system in more detail when we look at communism.

state capitalism
A combination of freer markets and some government control.

The Foundations of Capitalism

Under free-market capitalism people have four basic rights:

1. *The right to own private property.* This is the most fundamental of all rights under capitalism. Private ownership means that individuals can buy, sell, and use land, buildings, machinery, inventions, and other forms of property. They can also pass property on to their children. Would farmers work as hard if they didn't own the land and couldn't keep the profits from what they earned?

2. *The right to own a business and keep all that business's profits.* Recall from Chapter 1 that profits equal revenues minus expenses (salaries, materials, taxes). Profits act as important incentives for business owners.

3. *The right to freedom of competition.* Within certain guidelines established by the government, individuals are free to compete with other individuals or businesses in selling and promoting goods and services.

4. *The right to freedom of choice.* People are free to choose where they want to work and what career they want to follow. Other choices people are free to make include where to live and what to buy or sell.

The right to own private property and the right to own a business and keep its profits are two of the fundamental rights that exist in the economic system called free-market capitalism. Would either of these rights be viable without the other?

One benefit of the four basic rights of capitalism is that people are willing to take more risks than they might otherwise. President Franklin Roosevelt believed four additional freedoms were essential to economic success: freedom of speech and expression, freedom to worship in your own way, freedom from want, and freedom from fear. Do you see the benefits of these additional freedoms?

Now let's explore how the free market works. What role do consumers play in the process? How do businesses learn what consumers need and want? These questions and more are answered next.

How Free Markets Work

A free market is one in which decisions about what and how much to produce are made by the market—by buyers and sellers negotiating prices for goods and services. You and I and other consumers send signals to tell producers what to make, how many, in what color, and so on. We do that by choosing to buy (or not to buy) certain products and services.

For example, if all of us decided we wanted T-shirts supporting our favorite baseball team, the clothing industry would respond in certain ways. Manufacturers and retailers would increase the price of those T-shirts, because they know people are willing to pay more for the shirts they want. They would also realize they could make more money by making more of those T-shirts. Thus, they have an incentive to pay workers to start earlier and end later. Further, the number of companies making T-shirts would increase. How many T-shirts they make depends on how many we request or buy in the stores. Prices and quantities will continue to change as the number of T-shirts we buy changes.

The same process occurs with most other products. The *price* tells producers how much to produce. If something is wanted but isn't available, the price tends to go up until someone begins making more of that product, sells the ones already on hand, or makes a substitute. As a consequence, there's rarely a long-term shortage of goods in the United States.

The economic concept of demand measures the quantities of goods and services that people are willing to buy at a given price. All else equal, the lower the price, the higher the demand will be. Do you think there would be this many customers rushing to shop on Black Friday if it wasn't for those low-price/low-quantity deals?

How Prices Are Determined

In a free market, *prices are not determined by sellers;* they are determined by buyers and sellers negotiating in the marketplace. A seller may want to receive $50 for a T-shirt, but the quantity buyers demand at that high price may be quite low. If the seller lowers the price, the quantity demanded is likely to increase. How is a price determined that is acceptable to both buyers and sellers? The answer is found in the microeconomic concepts of supply and demand. We shall explore both next.

The Economic Concept of Supply

Supply refers to the quantities of products manufacturers or owners are willing to sell at different prices at a specific time. Generally speaking, the amount supplied will increase as the price increases, because sellers can make more money with a higher price.

Economists show this relationship between quantity supplied and price on a graph. Figure 2.1 shows a simple supply curve for T-shirts. The price of the shirts in dollars is shown vertically on the left of the graph. The quantity of shirts sellers are willing to supply is shown horizontally at the bottom of the graph. The various points on the curve indicate how many T-shirts sellers would provide at different prices. For example, at a price of $5 a shirt, a T-shirt vendor would provide only 5 shirts, but at $50 a shirt the vendor would supply 50 shirts. The supply curve indicates the relationship between the price and the quantity supplied. All things being equal, the higher the price, the more the vendor will be willing to supply.

The Economic Concept of Demand

Demand refers to the quantity of products that people are willing to buy at different prices at a specific time. Generally speaking, the quantity demanded will increase as the price decreases. Again, we can show the relationship between price and quantity demanded in a graph. Figure 2.2 shows a simple demand curve for T-shirts. The various points on the graph indicate the quantity demanded at various prices. For example, at $45, buyers demand just 5 shirts, but at $5, the quantity demanded would increase to 35 shirts. All things being equal, the lower the price, the more buyers are willing to buy.

The Equilibrium Point, or Market Price

You might realize from Figures 2.1 and 2.2 that the key factor in determining the quantities supplied and demanded is *price*. If you were to lay the two graphs one on top of the other, the supply curve and the demand curve would cross where quantity demanded and quantity supplied are equal. Figure 2.3 illustrates that point. At a price of $15, the quantity of T-shirts demanded and the quantity supplied are equal (25 shirts). That crossing point is known as the *equilibrium point* or *equilibrium price*. In the long run, that price will become the market price. **Market price**, then, is determined by supply and demand. It is the price toward which the market will trend.

Proponents of a free market argue that, because supply and demand interactions determine prices, there is no need for the government to set prices. If quantity supplied exceeds quantity demanded, the resulting surplus

iSee It! Need help understanding supply and demand? Visit your Connect e-book video tab for a brief animated explanation.

supply
The quantity of products that manufacturers or owners are willing to sell at different prices at a specific time.

demand
The quantity of products that people are willing to buy at different prices at a specific time.

market price
The price determined by supply and demand.

FIGURE 2.1 THE SUPPLY CURVE AT VARIOUS PRICES

The supply curve rises from left to right. Think it through. The higher the price of T-shirts goes (the vertical axis), the more sellers will be willing to supply.

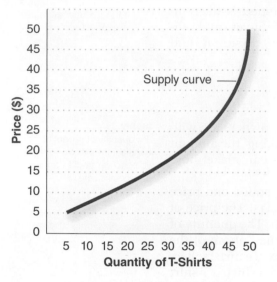

FIGURE 2.2 THE DEMAND CURVE AT VARIOUS PRICES

This is a simple demand curve showing the quantity of T-shirts demanded at different prices. The demand curve falls from left to right. It is easy to understand why. The lower the price of T-shirts, the higher the quantity demanded.

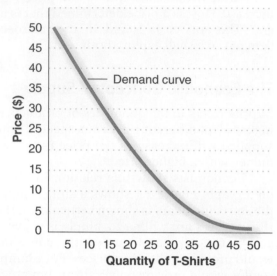

FIGURE 2.3 THE EQUILIBRIUM POINT

The place where quantity demanded and quantity supplied meet is called the equilibrium point. When we put both the supply and demand curves on the same graph, we find that they intersect at a price where the quantity supplied and the quantity demanded are equal. In the long run, the market price will tend toward the equilibrium point.

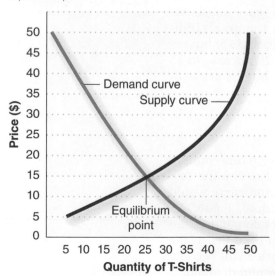

perfect competition

The degree of competition in which there are many sellers in a market and none is large enough to dictate the price of a product.

signals sellers to lower the price. If shortages develop because the quantity supplied is less than quantity demanded, it signals sellers to increase the price. Eventually, supply will again equal demand if nothing interferes with market forces. The Spotlight on Small Business box shows how environmental forces can influence supply and demand.

In countries without a free market, there is no mechanism to reveal to businesses (via price) what to produce and in what amounts, so there are often shortages (not enough products) or surpluses (too many products). In such countries, the government decides what to produce and in what quantity, but without price signals it has no way of knowing what the proper quantities are. Furthermore, when the government interferes in otherwise free markets, such as when it subsidizes farm goods, surpluses and shortages may develop. Competition differs in free markets, too. We shall explore that concept next.

Competition within Free Markets

Economists generally agree there are four different degrees of competition: (1) perfect competition, (2) monopolistic competition, (3) oligopoly, and (4) monopoly.

Perfect competition exists when there are many sellers in a market and none is large enough to dictate the price of a product. Sellers' products appear to be identical, such as agricultural products like apples, corn, and potatoes. There are no true examples of perfect competition. Today, government price supports and drastic reductions in the number of farms make it hard to argue that even farming represents perfect competition.

Bugs Bug Orange Farmers and Drive Prices Up

Normally, it takes a large force to significantly affect a product's supply and demand. However, in the case of 2013's Florida orange crop, the supply of this commodity experienced a major disruption due to tiny invaders. The state experienced its worst crop since 1990, thanks to an orange-killing disease brought on by gnat-sized insects called Asian citrus psyllids. As a result, orange prices rose by as much as 16 percent throughout 2014.

An unusually dry spell brought the wrath of the gnats swarming on Florida's orange groves. For small farmers throughout the state, the next step to take is unclear. "We're in uncharted territory," says John Ortelle, an expert who's been following the citrus industry for more than 30 years. "Whatever producers have tried to tackle the disease has had a minimal effect so far. Growers took out trees and added extra nutrients. You just don't know when and if the effects will be positive." With immediate solutions to the problem still out of reach, Florida's farmers can only hope that no other circumstances beyond their control harm crops and drive prices up further. In fact, the state's orange growers dodged a bullet during the harsh 2013/2014 winter season as temperatures often hovered around freezing. Thankfully for Florida's citrus farmers (as well as the nation's frugal OJ drinkers), oranges aren't damaged by cold unless the temperature drops below 28 degrees Fahrenheit.

Sources: Marvin G. Perez, "Bug Bites Cut Florida Orange Crop to Lowest in 2 Decades," *Bloomberg*, December 26, 2013; and Claudia Carpenter, Luzi Ann Javier, and Jeff Wilson, "Florida Oranges to U.S. Wheat Seen Escaping Freeze Damage," *Bloomberg*, January 7, 2014.

Under **monopolistic competition** a large number of sellers produce very similar products that buyers nevertheless perceive as different, such as hot dogs, sodas, personal computers, and T-shirts. Product differentiation—the attempt to make buyers think similar products are different in some way—is a key to success. Think about what that means. Through advertising, branding, and packaging, sellers try to convince buyers that their products are different from competitors', though they may be very similar or even interchangeable. The fast-food industry, with its pricing battles among hamburger offerings and the like, offers a good example of monopolistic competition.

An **oligopoly** is a degree of competition in which just a few sellers dominate a market, as we see in tobacco, gasoline, automobiles, aluminum, and aircraft. One reason some industries remain in the hands of a few sellers is that the initial investment required to enter the business often is tremendous. Think, for example, of how much it would cost to start a new airplane manufacturing facility.

In an oligopoly, products from different companies tend to be priced about the same. The reason is simple: Intense price competition would lower profits for everyone, since a price cut by one producer would most likely be matched by the others. As in monopolistic competition, product differentiation, rather than price, is usually the major factor in market success in an oligopoly. Note, for example, that most cereals are priced about the same, as are soft drinks. Thus, advertising is a major factor determining which of the few available brands consumers buy, because often it is advertising that creates the perceived differences.

A **monopoly** occurs when one seller controls the total supply of a product or service, and sets the price. In the United States, laws prohibit the creation of monopolies. Nonetheless, the U.S. legal system has permitted monopolies

monopolistic competition
The degree of competition in which a large number of sellers produce very similar products that buyers nevertheless perceive as different.

oligopoly
A degree of competition in which just a few sellers dominate the market.

monopoly
A degree of competition in which only one seller controls the total supply of a product or service, and sets the price.

in the markets for public utilities that sell natural gas, water, and electric power. These companies' prices and profits are usually controlled by public service commissions to protect the interest of buyers. For example, the Florida Public Service Commission is the administering agency over the Florida Power and Light utility company. Legislation ended the monopoly status of utilities in some areas, letting consumers choose among providers. The intention of such *deregulation* is to increase competition among utility companies and, ultimately, lower prices for consumers.

Benefits and Limitations of Free Markets

One benefit of the free market is that it allows open competition among companies. Businesses must provide customers with high-quality products at fair prices with good service. If they don't, they lose customers to businesses that do. Do government services have the same incentives?

The free market—with its competition and incentives—was a major factor in creating the wealth that industrialized countries now enjoy. Some people even talk of the free market as an economic miracle. Free-market capitalism, more than any other economic system, provides opportunities for poor people to work their way out of poverty. Capitalism also encourages businesses to be more efficient so they can successfully compete on price and quality. Would you say that the United States is increasing or decreasing the emphasis on capitalism? Why?

Yet, even as free-market capitalism has brought prosperity to the United States and to much of the rest of the world, it has brought inequality as well. Business owners and managers usually make more money and have more wealth than lower-level workers. Yet people who are old, disabled, or sick may not be able to start and manage a business, and others may not have the talent or the drive. What should society do about such inequality?[20]

One of the dangers of free markets is that some people let greed dictate how they act. Criminal charges brought against some big businesses in banking, oil, accounting, telecommunications, insurance, and pharmaceuticals indicate the scope of the potential problem. Some businesspeople have deceived the public about their products; others have deceived stockholders about the value of their stock, all in order to increase executives' personal assets.

Clearly, some government laws and regulations are necessary to protect businesses' stakeholders and make sure people who cannot work get the basic care they need. To overcome some of capitalism's limitations, some countries have adopted an economic system called socialism. It, too, has its good and bad points. We explore these after you review the following Test Prep questions.

test prep

- What are the four basic rights that people have under free-market capitalism?
- How do businesspeople know what to produce and in what quantity?
- How are prices determined?
- What are the four degrees of competition, and what are some examples of each?

LO 2–3   Compare socialism and communism.

UNDERSTANDING SOCIALISM

Socialism is an economic system based on the premise that some, if not most, basic businesses (e.g., steel mills, coal mines, and utilities) should be owned by the government so that profits can be more evenly distributed among the people. Entrepreneurs often own and run smaller businesses, and individuals are often taxed relatively steeply to pay for social programs. The top federal personal income tax rate in the United States, for example, was 39.6 percent recently, but in some socialist countries the top proposed rate can be as much as 75 percent.[21] While U.S. shoppers pay sales taxes ranging from over 10 percent in Chicago to zero in Delaware, some socialist countries charge a similar value-added tax of 15 to 20 percent or more. Socialists acknowledge the major benefit of capitalism—wealth creation—but believe that wealth should be more evenly distributed than occurs in free-market capitalism. They believe the government should carry out the distribution and be much more involved in protecting the environment and providing for the poor. Do you see evidence of that happening in the United States today?

socialism
An economic system based on the premise that some, if not most, basic businesses should be owned by the government so that profits can be more evenly distributed among the people.

brain drain
The loss of the best and brightest people to other countries.

The Benefits of Socialism

The major benefit of socialism is supposed to be social equality. Ideally it comes about because the government takes income from wealthier people, in the form of taxes, and redistributes it to poorer people through various government programs. Free education through college, free health care, and free child care are some of the benefits socialist governments, using the money from taxes, may provide to their people. Workers in socialist countries usually get longer vacations, work fewer hours per week, and have more employee benefits (e.g., generous sick leave) than those in countries where free-market capitalism prevails.

The Negative Consequences of Socialism

Socialism may create more equality than capitalism, but it takes away some of businesspeople's incentives. For example, tax rates in some socialist nations once reached 83 percent. Today, doctors, lawyers, business owners, and others who earn a lot of money pay very high tax rates. As a consequence, many of them leave socialist countries for capitalistic countries with lower taxes, such as the United States. This loss of the best and brightest people to other countries is called a **brain drain**.

Imagine an experiment in socialism in your own class. Imagine that after the first exam, those with grades of 90 and above have to give some of their points to those who make 70 and below so that everyone ends up with grades in the 80s. Would those who got 90s study as hard for the second exam? What about those who got 70s? Can you see why workers may not work as hard or as well if they all get the same benefits regardless of how hard they work?

Socialism has been more successful in some countries than in others. This photo shows Denmark's clean and modern public transportation system. In Greece, overspending caused a debt crisis that forced the government to impose austerity measures that many Greeks oppose. What other factors might lead to slower growth in socialist countries?

Socialism also tends to result in fewer inventions and less innovation, because those who come up with new ideas usually don't receive as much reward as they would in a capitalist system. Communism may be considered a more intensive version of socialism. We shall explore that system next.

UNDERSTANDING COMMUNISM

communism
An economic and political system in which the government makes almost all economic decisions and owns almost all the major factors of production.

Communism is an economic and political system in which the government makes almost all economic decisions and owns almost all the major factors of production. It intrudes further into the lives of people than socialism does. For example, some communist countries have not allowed their citizens to practice certain religions, change jobs, or move to the town of their choice.

One problem with communism is that the government has no way of knowing what to produce, because prices don't reflect supply and demand as they do in free markets. The government must guess what the people need. As a result, shortages of many items, including food and clothing, may develop. Another problem is that communism doesn't inspire businesspeople to work hard because the incentives are not there. Therefore, communism is slowly disappearing as an economic form.

Most communist countries today are suffering severe economic depression. In North Korea, many people are starving. In Cuba, people suffer a lack of goods and services readily available in most other countries, and some fear the government.

While some parts of the former Soviet Union remain influenced by communist ideals, Russia itself now has a flat tax of only 13 percent. Yet this low rate increased the government's tax revenues by nearly 30 percent, because more people were willing to pay.

LO 2–4   Analyze the trend toward mixed economies.

THE TREND TOWARD MIXED ECONOMIES

The nations of the world have largely been divided between those that followed the concepts of capitalism and those that adopted the concepts of communism or socialism. We can now contrast the two major economic systems as follows:

free-market economies
Economic systems in which the market largely determines what goods and services get produced, who gets them, and how the economy grows.

1. **Free-market economies** exist when the market largely determines what goods and services get produced, who gets them, and how the economy grows. *Capitalism* is the popular term for this economic system.

command economies
Economic systems in which the government largely decides what goods and services will be produced, who will get them, and how the economy will grow.

2. **Command economies** exist when the government largely decides what goods and services will be produced, who gets them, and how the economy will grow. *Socialism* and *communism* are variations on this economic system.

Although all countries actually have some mix of the two systems, neither free-market nor command economies have resulted in optimal economic conditions. Free-market mechanisms don't seem to respond enough to the needs of those who are poor, elderly, or disabled. Some people also believe that businesses in free-market economies have not done enough to protect the environment. Over time, voters in mostly free-market countries, such as the United States, have elected officials who have adopted many social and environmental programs such as Social Security, welfare, unemployment compensation, and various clean air and water acts. What new or enhanced social policies do you know of that have been enacted or are being considered today?

Socialism and communism haven't always created enough jobs or wealth to keep economies growing fast enough. Thus, communist governments are disappearing, and some socialist governments have been cutting back on social programs and lowering taxes on businesses and workers to generate more business growth and more revenue.

The trend, then, has been for mostly capitalist countries (like the United States) to move toward socialism (e.g., more government involvement in health care), and for some socialist countries to move toward capitalism (more private businesses, lower taxes). All countries have some mix of the two systems. Thus, the long-term global trend is toward a blend of capitalism and socialism. This trend likely will increase with the opening of global markets made easier by the Internet. The net effect is the emergence throughout the world of mixed economies (see the Reaching Beyond Our Borders box).

Mixed economies exist where some allocation of resources is made by the market and some by the government. Most countries don't have a name for such a system. If free-market mechanisms allocate most resources, the leaders call their system capitalism. If the government allocates most resources, the leaders call it socialism. Figure 2.4 compares the various economic systems.

mixed economies
Economic systems in which some allocation of resources is made by the market and some by the government.

Like most other nations of the world, the United States has a mixed economy. The U.S. government has now become the largest employer in the country, which means there are more workers in the public sector (government) than in any of the major businesses in the United States. Do you see the government growing or declining in the coming years?

Economic Expansion in Africa

For much of the 20th century, stories about Africa's economy inevitably focused on the continent's rampant poverty. The end of colonial rule in Africa brought military dictatorships and other oppressive forces to power in many countries. Coupled with disease and an almost nonexistent infrastructure, Africa's economy and its people suffered horribly.

Thankfully, so far the 21st century has been brighter for many Africans. A booming commodities market along with expanding manufacturing and service economies are leading to unprecedented growth. Over the last decade, six of the world's 10 fastest-growing countries have been African. In eight of those years, Africa has even outpaced the growth of East Asia, including

Japan. Looking to the future, experts expect the continent's GDP to grow 6 percent annually over the next 10 years.

Many Africans have seen their lives change radically as economies on the continent have expanded. Income per person has shot up 30 percent over the last decade, while life expectancy has increased by 10 percent. Even small, formerly war-torn nations are seeing improvements. For instance, in the 1990s Rwanda suffered a horrific civil war and genocide that claimed the lives of hundreds of thousands of citizens. Subsequent years of peace and a relatively stable government have since turned the country around significantly. Although many on the continent still experience major

hardships, improving economic conditions are allowing more and more people to enter the middle class. Goods and services that used to be scarce are now becoming commonplace. There are now three mobile phones for every four people in Africa, and by 2017 nearly 30 percent of households are expected to own a television. School enrollment has also skyrocketed in the last few years. Experts hope that this younger generation will take advantage of improving educational opportunities and ensure Africa's place on the global economic stage.

Sources: "A Hopeful Continent," *The Economist*, March 2, 2013; "Business in Rwanda: Africa's Singapore?" *The Economist*, February 25, 2012; and John O'Sullivan, "Middle East and Africa: Digging Deeper," *The Economist*, November 18, 2013.

Use LearnSmart to help retain what you have learned. Access your instructor's Connect course to check out LearnSmart, or go to learnsmartadvantage.com for help.

LEARNSMART

Test **prep**

- What led to the emergence of socialism?
- What are the benefits and drawbacks of socialism?
- What countries still practice communism?
- What are the characteristics of a mixed economy?

LO 2–5 Describe the economic system of the United States, including the significance of key economic indicators (especially GDP), productivity, and the business cycle.

UNDERSTANDING THE U.S. ECONOMIC SYSTEM

The following sections will introduce the terms and concepts that you, as an informed citizen, will need to understand in order to grasp the issues facing government and business leaders in the United States.

connect

iSee It! Need help understanding basic economic systems? Visit your Connect e-book video tab for a brief animated explanation.

Key Economic Indicators

Three major indicators of economic conditions are (1) the gross domestic product (GDP), (2) the unemployment rate, and (3) price indexes. Another important statistic is the increase or decrease in productivity. When you read

FIGURE 2.4 COMPARISONS OF KEY ECONOMIC SYSTEMS

	CAPITALISM* (United States)	SOCIALISM (Sweden)	COMMUNISM (North Korea)	MIXED ECONOMY (Germany)
Social and Economic Goals	Private ownership of land and business. Liberty and the pursuit of happiness. Free trade. Emphasis on freedom and the profit motive for economic growth.	Public ownership of major businesses. Some private ownership of smaller businesses and shops. Government control of education, health care, utilities, mining, transportation, and media. Very high taxation. Emphasis on equality.	Public ownership of all businesses. Government-run education and health care. Emphasis on equality. Many limitations on freedom, including freedom to own businesses and to assemble to protest government actions.	Private ownership of land and business with government regulation. Government control of some institutions (e.g., mail). High taxation for defense and the common welfare. Emphasis on a balance between freedom and equality.
Motivation of Workers	Much incentive to work efficiently and hard because profits are retained by owners. Workers are rewarded for high productivity.	Capitalist incentives exist in private businesses. Government control of wages in public institutions limits incentives.	Very little incentive to work hard or to produce quality goods or services.	Incentives are similar to capitalism except in government-owned enterprises, which may have fewer incentives.
Control over Markets	Complete freedom of trade within and among nations. Some government control of markets.	Some markets are controlled by the government and some are free. Trade restrictions among nations vary and include some free-trade agreements.	Total government control over markets except for illegal transactions.	Some government control of trade within and among nations (trade protectionism).
Choices in the Market	A wide variety of goods and services is available. Almost no scarcity or over-supply exists for long because supply and demand control the market.	Variety in the marketplace varies considerably from country to country. Choice is directly related to government involvement in markets.	Very little choice among competing goods.	Similar to capitalism, but scarcity and oversupply may be caused by government involvement in the market (e.g., subsidies for farms).
Social Freedoms	Freedom of speech, press, assembly, religion, job choice, movement, and elections.	Similar to mixed economy. Governments may restrict job choice, movement among countries, and who may attend upper-level schools (i.e., college).	Very limited freedom to protest the government, practice religion, or change houses or jobs.	Some restrictions on freedoms of assembly and speech. Separation of church and state may limit religious practices in schools.

*The United States is a mixed economy based on a foundation of capitalism.

business literature, you'll see these terms used again and again. Let's explore what they mean.

Gross Domestic Product

Gross domestic product (GDP), which we mentioned briefly in Chapter 1, is the total value of final goods and services produced in a country in a given year. Both domestic and foreign-owned companies can produce the goods and services included in GDP, as long as the companies are located within the country's boundaries. For example, production values from Japanese automaker Honda's factory in Ohio are included in U.S. GDP. Revenue generated by Ford's factory in Mexico is included in Mexico's GDP, even though Ford is a U.S. company. Although the country relies on such data, the accuracy of the data (at least in the short run) is questionable.[22]

Starting in the spring of 2014, the United States Bureau of Economic Analysis at the Commerce Department will report a statistic called gross output (GO). **Gross output (GO)** is a measure of total sales volume at all stages of production. GO is almost twice the size of GDP and is considered a better indicator of the business cycle and more consistent with economic growth theory. It shows that consumer spending is the effect, not the cause, of prosperity.[23]

Almost every discussion about a nation's economy is based on GDP. If growth in GDP slows or declines, businesses may feel many negative effects. A major influence on the growth of GDP is the productivity of the workforce—that is, how much output workers create with a given amount of input. The level of U.S. economic activity is actually larger than the GDP figures show, because those figures don't take into account illicit activities such as sales of illegal drugs. The high GDP in the United States is what enables its citizens to enjoy a high standard of living.

The Unemployment Rate

The **unemployment rate** refers to the percentage of civilians at least 16 years old who are unemployed *and tried to find a job within the prior four weeks.* The unemployment rate was over 7 percent in 2013 and went down below 6.5 percent in 2014 (see Figure 2.5). However, many people had given up looking for jobs (people who are not actively looking for work are not included in the unemployment figures).[24] Some people feel that the unemployment statistics don't accurately measure the pain being felt by those who have been unemployed for a long time or those who have

gross domestic product (GDP)
The total value of final goods and services produced in a country in a given year.

gross output (GO)
A measure of total sales volume at all stages of production.

unemployment rate
The number of civilians at least 16 years old who are unemployed and tried to find a job within the prior four weeks.

The overall unemployment rate in the United States fluctuates. Over the last decade, it has been as low as less than 5 percent and as high as more than 10 percent. Unemployment insurance goes only so far to relieve the loss of income caused by losing your job. How high is the unemployment rate in your area today?

FIGURE 2.5 U.S. UNEMPLOYMENT RATE 1989–2014

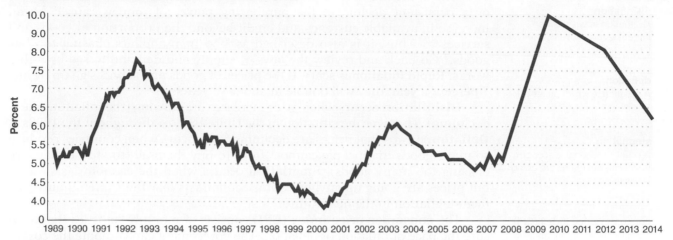

simply given up looking for a job.[25] Some believe that government benefits may lead to more unemployment.[26] Do you agree?

Figure 2.6 describes the four types of unemployment: frictional, structural, cyclical, and seasonal. The United States tries to protect those who are unemployed because of recessions (defined later in the chapter), industry shifts, and other cyclical factors. Nonetheless, the *underemployment* figure in 2014 was about 13.1 percent (this includes those who are working part time and want to work full time and those who have stopped looking for work).[27] Such high numbers raise the question of what the U.S. can do to increase employment.[28]

Inflation and Price Indexes   Price indexes help gauge the health of the economy by measuring the levels of inflation, disinflation, deflation, and stagflation. **Inflation** is a general rise in the prices of goods and services over time.

inflation
A general rise in the prices of goods and services over time.

FIGURE 2.6 FOUR TYPES OF UNEMPLOYMENT

Frictional unemployment

Frictional unemployment refers to those people who have quit work because they didn't like the job, the boss, or the working conditions and who haven't yet found a new job. It also refers to those people who are entering the labor force for the first time (e.g., new graduates) or are returning to the labor force after significant time away (e.g., parents who reared children). There will always be some frictional unemployment because it takes some time to find a first job or a new job.

Structural unemployment

Structural unemployment refers to unemployment caused by the restructuring of firms or by a mismatch between the skills (or location) of job seekers and the requirements (or location) of available jobs (e.g., coal miners in an area where mines have been closed).

Cyclical unemployment

Cyclical unemployment occurs because of a recession or a similar downturn in the business cycle (the ups and downs of business growth and decline over time). This type of unemployment is the most serious.

Seasonal unemployment

Seasonal unemployment occurs where demand for labor varies over the year, as with the harvesting of crops.

The official definition is "a persistent increase in the level of consumer prices or a persistent decline in the purchasing power of money, caused by an increase in available currency and credit beyond the proportion of goods and services."[29] Thus, it is also described as "too many dollars chasing too few goods." Go back and review the laws of supply and demand to see how that works. Rapid inflation is scary. If the prices of goods and services go up by just 7 percent a year, they will double in about 10 years.

Disinflation occurs when price increases are slowing (the inflation rate is declining). That was the situation in the United States throughout the 1990s.[30] **Deflation** means that prices are declining.[31] It occurs when countries produce so many goods that people cannot afford to buy them all (too few dollars are chasing too many goods). **Stagflation** occurs when the economy is slowing but prices are going up anyhow. Some economists fear the United States may face stagflation in the near future.

The **consumer price index (CPI)** consists of monthly statistics that measure the pace of inflation or deflation. The government can compute the cost of goods and services, including housing, food, apparel, and medical care, to see whether or not they are going up or down. Today, however, the government is relying more on the measure of **core inflation**. That means the CPI minus food and energy costs. Since the costs of food and energy have been going up rapidly, the inflation measures reported (core inflation) are actually lower than real costs. This is important to you because some wages and salaries, rents and leases, tax brackets, government benefits, and interest rates are based on these data.

The **producer price index (PPI)** measures prices at the wholesale level. Other indicators of the economy's condition include housing starts, retail sales, and changes in personal income. You can learn more about such indicators by reading business periodicals, listening to business broadcasts on radio and television, and exploring business sites on the Internet.

Productivity in the United States

An increase in productivity means a worker can produce more goods and services than before in the same time period, usually thanks to machinery or other equipment. Productivity in the United States has risen because computers and other technology have made production faster and easier. The higher productivity is, the lower the costs are of producing goods and services, and the lower prices can be. Therefore, businesspeople are eager to increase productivity. Remember, however, that high productivity can lead to high unemployment. Certainly, that is what the United States in now experiencing.[32]

Now that the U.S. economy is a service economy, productivity is an issue because service firms are so labor-intensive. Spurred by foreign competition, productivity in the manufacturing sector is rising rapidly. In the service sector, productivity is growing more slowly because service workers—like teachers, clerks, lawyers, and barbers—have fewer new technologies available than there are for factory workers.

Productivity in the Service Sector

One problem with the service industry is that an influx of machinery may add to the quality of the service provided but not to the output per worker. For example, you've probably noticed how many computers there are on college campuses. They add to the quality of education but don't necessarily boost professors' productivity. The same is true of some equipment in hospitals, such as CAT scanners, PET scanners, and MRI scanners. They improve patient care but don't necessarily increase the number of patients doctors can see. In other words, today's productivity measures in the service industry fail to capture the increase in quality caused by new technology.

Clearly, the United States and other countries need to develop new measures of productivity for the service economy that include quality as well as quantity of output. Despite productivity improvement, the economy is likely to go through a series of ups and downs, much as it has over the past few years. We'll explore that process next.

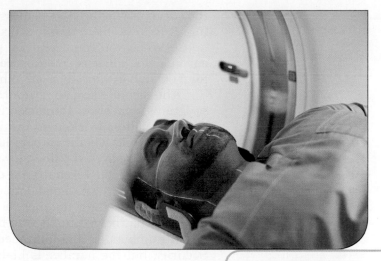

The Business Cycle

Business cycles are the periodic rises and falls that occur in economies over time. Economists look at a number of business cycles, from seasonal cycles that occur within a year to cycles that occur every 48–60 years.

Economist Joseph Schumpeter identified the four phases of long-term business cycles as boom–recession–depression–recovery:

1. An *economic boom* is just what it sounds like—business is booming.

2. **Recession** is two or more consecutive quarters of decline in the GDP. In a recession prices fall, people purchase fewer products, and businesses fail. A recession brings high unemployment, increased business failures, and an overall drop in living standards.

3. A **depression** is a severe recession, usually accompanied by deflation. Business cycles rarely go through a depression phase. In fact, while there were many business cycles during the 20th century, there was only one severe depression (1930s).

4. A *recovery* occurs when the economy stabilizes and starts to grow. This eventually leads to an economic boom, starting the cycle all over again.

One goal of some economists is to predict such ups and downs. That is very difficult to do. Business cycles are identified according to facts, but we can explain those facts only by using theories. Therefore, we cannot predict with certainty. But one thing is certain: over time, the economy will rise and fall as it has done lately.

Since dramatic swings up and down in the economy cause all kinds of disruptions to businesses, the government tries to minimize such changes. It uses fiscal policy and monetary policy to try to keep the economy from slowing too much or growing too rapidly.

LO 2–6   Contrast fiscal policy and monetary policy, and explain how each affects the economy.

Stabilizing the Economy through Fiscal Policy

Fiscal policy refers to the federal government's efforts to keep the economy stable by increasing or decreasing taxes or government spending. The first fiscal policy tool is taxation. Theoretically, high tax rates tend to slow the economy because they draw money away from the private sector and put it into the government. High tax rates may discourage small-business ownership because

It can be difficult to measure productivity in the service sector. New technology can improve the quality of services without necessarily increasing the number of people served. A doctor can make more-accurate diagnoses with scans, for instance, but still can see only so many patients in a day. How can productivity measures capture improvements in the quality of service?

business cycles
The periodic rises and falls that occur in economies over time.

recession
Two or more consecutive quarters of decline in the GDP.

depression
A severe recession, usually accompanied by deflation.

fiscal policy
The federal government's efforts to keep the economy stable by increasing or decreasing taxes or government spending.

they decrease the profits businesses can earn and make the effort less rewarding. It follows, then, that low tax rates will theoretically give the economy a boost. When you count all fees, sales taxes, and more, taxes on the highest-earning U.S. citizens could exceed 50 percent. Is that figure too high or not high enough in your opinion? Why?

The second fiscal policy tool is government spending on highways, social programs, education, infrastructure (e.g., roads and utilities), defense, and so on. The national deficit is the amount of money the federal government spends beyond what it gathers in taxes for a given fiscal year. The deficit is expected to be over $1 trillion for the next several years. Such deficits increase the national debt. The **national debt** is the sum of government deficits over time. Recently, the national debt was over $17 trillion (see Figure 2.7). That is a rather misleading number, however, since the unfunded obligation for Medicare has been estimated to be over $70 trillion (Various sources cite different numbers for the unfunded obligations for both Medicare and Social Security, but the number is high enough to be of concern, no matter how high it is.) If the government takes in more revenue than it spends (i.e., tax revenues exceed expenditures), there is a national *surplus*. That is not likely to happen soon.

One way to lessen deficits is to cut government spending. Many presidents and those in Congress have promised to make the government "smaller," that is, to reduce government spending—but that doesn't happen very often. There always seems to be a need for more social programs each year, and thus the deficits continue and add to the national debt. Some people believe that government spending helps the economy grow.

national debt

The sum of government deficits over time.

FIGURE 2.7 THE NATIONAL DEBT

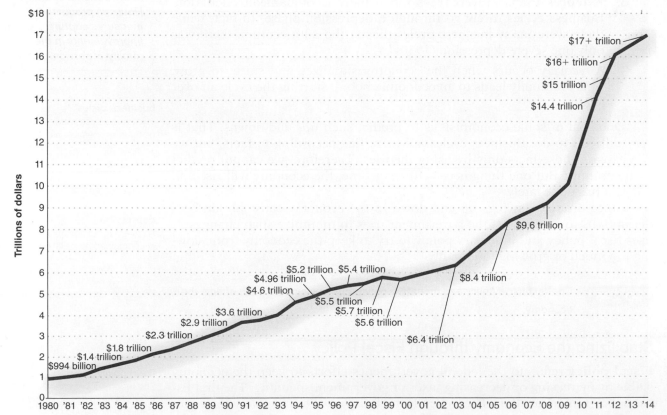

Others believe that the money the government spends comes out of the pockets of consumers and businesspeople, and thus slows growth. What do you think?

Fiscal Policy in Action during an Economic Crisis

During much of the early 2000s, the U.S. federal government followed the basic economic principles of free markets. By 2008, however, the economy was facing a dire economic crisis and the government spent more than $1 trillion of taxpayer money in an effort to revive the failing economy (including helping out banks, the auto industry, and others). ($1 trillion is about $3,272 per person in the United States.) The government was then following the basic economic theory of John Maynard Keynes. **Keynesian economic theory** is the theory that a government policy of increasing spending could stimulate the economy in a recession. The Federal Reserve has continued to pump trillions of dollars into the economy over the last few years. Recently, the Fed cut back on dollar generation from $85 billion to $65 billion per month. What do you expect the result of that cut will be?

Using Monetary Policy to Keep the Economy Growing

Have you ever wondered what organization adds money to or subtracts money from the economy? As noted above, the answer is the Federal Reserve Bank (the Fed). The Fed is a semiprivate organization that is not under the direct control of the government but does have members appointed by the president. We will discuss the Fed in detail when we look at banking in Chapter 20. Now we simply introduce monetary policy and the role of the Fed in controlling the economy. **Monetary policy** is the management of the money supply and interest rates by the Federal Reserve Bank. The Fed's most visible role is the raising and lowering of interest rates. When the economy is booming, the Fed tends to raise interest rates. This makes money more expensive to borrow. Businesses thus borrow less, and the economy slows as businesspeople spend less money on everything they need to grow, including labor and machinery. The opposite is true when the Fed lowers interest rates. Businesses tend to borrow more, and the economy is expected to grow. Raising and lowering interest rates should help control the rapid ups and downs of the economy. In 2010–2014, the Fed kept interest rates near zero, but the economy remained sluggish. You can imagine the pressure that puts on Janet Yellen, the new head of the Federal Reserve. Again, we shall discuss her later in the text.

The Fed also controls the money supply. A simple explanation of this function is that the more money the Fed makes available to businesspeople and others, the faster the economy is supposed to grow. To slow the economy (and prevent inflation), the Fed lowers the money supply. The Fed poured money into the economy in 2008–2014. What would you expect the result to be?

To sum up, there are two major tools for managing the economy of the United States: fiscal policy (government taxes and spending) and monetary policy (the Fed's control over interest rates and the money supply). The goal is to keep the economy growing so that more people can rise up the economic ladder and enjoy a higher standard of living and quality of life.

The financial crisis beginning in 2008 caused much anguish among Wall Street workers and people in general. How effective was the government's response?

Keynesian economic theory
The theory that a government policy of increasing spending could stimulate the economy in a recession.

monetary policy
The management of the money supply and interest rates by the Federal Reserve.

test prep

- Name the three economic indicators and describe how well the United States is doing based on each indicator.
- What's the difference between a recession and a depression?
- How does the government manage the economy using fiscal policy?
- What does the term *monetary policy* mean? What organization is responsible for monetary policy?

Summary

LO 1–1   Explain basic economics.

- **What is economics?**
  Economics is the study of how society chooses to employ resources to produce goods and services and distribute them for consumption among various competing groups and individuals.

- **What are the two branches of economics?**
  There are two major branches of economics: macroeconomics studies the operation of a nation's economy as a whole, and microeconomics studies the behavior of people and organizations in particular markets (e.g., why people buy smaller cars when gas prices go up).

- **How can we be assured of having enough resources?**
  Resource development is the study of how to increase resources and create the conditions that will make better use of them.

- **How does capitalism create a climate for economic growth?**
  Under capitalism, businesspeople don't often deliberately set out to help others; they work mostly for their own prosperity and growth. Yet people's efforts to improve their own situation in life act like an *invisible hand* to help the economy grow and prosper through the production of needed goods, services, and ideas.

LO 1–2   Explain what capitalism is and how free markets work.

- **What is capitalism?**
  Capitalism is an economic system in which all or most of the means of production and distribution are privately owned and operated for profit.

- **Who decides what to produce under capitalism?**
  In capitalist countries, businesspeople decide what to produce, how much to pay workers, and how much to charge for goods and services. They also decide whether to produce certain goods in their own countries, import those goods, or have them made in other countries.

- **What is state capitalism?**
  State capitalism is a combination of freer markets and some government control.

- **What are the basic rights people have under capitalism?**
  The four basic rights under capitalism are (1) the right to own private property, (2) the right to own a business and to keep all of that business's

profits after taxes, (3) the right to freedom of competition, and (4) the right to freedom of choice. President Franklin D. Roosevelt felt that other freedoms were also important: the right to freedom of speech and expression, the right to worship in your own way, and freedom from want and fear.

- **How does the free market work?**
The free market is one in which buyers and sellers negotiating prices for goods and services influence the decisions about what gets produced and in what quantities. Buyers' decisions in the marketplace tell sellers what to produce and in what quantity. When buyers demand more goods, the price goes up, signaling suppliers to produce more. The higher the price, the more goods and services suppliers are willing to produce. Price is the mechanism that allows free markets to work.

LO 1–3   Compare socialism and communism.

- **What is socialism?**
Socialism is an economic system based on the premise that some businesses should be owned by the government.

- **What are the advantages and disadvantages of socialism?**
Socialism intends to create more social equity. Workers in socialist countries usually receive more education, health care, and other benefits and also work fewer hours, with longer vacations. The major disadvantage of socialism is that it lowers the incentive to start a business or to work hard. Socialist economies tend to have a higher unemployment rate and a slower growth rate than capitalist economies.

- **How does socialism differ from communism?**
Under communism, the government owns almost all major production facilities and dictates what gets produced and by whom. Communism is also more restrictive when it comes to personal freedoms, such as religious freedom.

LO 1–4   Analyze the trend toward mixed economies.

- **What is a mixed economy?**
A mixed economy is part capitalist and part socialist. Some businesses are privately owned, but taxes tend to be high to distribute income more evenly among the population.

- **What countries have mixed economies?**
The United States has a mixed economy, as do most other industrialized countries.

- **What are the benefits of mixed economies?**
A mixed economy has most of the benefits of wealth creation that free markets bring plus the benefits of greater social equality and concern for the environment that socialism promises.

LO 1–5   Describe the economic system of the United States, including the significance of key economic indicators (especially GDP), productivity, and the business cycle.

- **What are the key economic indicators in the United States?**
Gross domestic product (GDP) is the total value of final goods and services produced in a country in a given year. The *unemployment rate* refers to the percentage of civilians at least 16 years old who are unemployed and tried

to find a job within the most recent four weeks. The *consumer price index (CPI)* measures changes in the prices of about 400 goods and services that consumers buy.

- **What is gross output?**
  Gross output (GO) is a measure of total sales volume at all stages of production.

- **What are the four phases of business cycles?**
  In an *economic boom*, businesses do well. A *recession* occurs when two or more quarters show declines in the GDP, prices fall, people purchase fewer products, and businesses fail. A *depression* is a severe recession. *Recovery* occurs when the economy stabilizes and starts to grow.

LO 1–6 Contrast fiscal policy and monetary policy, and explain how each affects the economy.

- **What is fiscal policy?**
  Fiscal policy consists of government efforts to keep the economy stable by increasing or decreasing taxes or government spending.

- **What is the importance of monetary policy to the economy?**
  Monetary policy is the management of the money supply and interest rates. When unemployment gets too high, the Federal Reserve Bank (the Fed) may put more money into the economy and lower interest rates. That is supposed to provide a boost to the economy as businesses borrow and spend more money and hire more people.

Access your instructor's Connect course to check out LearnSmart or go to learnsmartadvantage.com for help.

key terms

brain drain 41
business cycles 49
capitalism 34
command economies 42
communism 42
consumer price index (CPI) 48
core inflation 48
deflation 48
demand 37
depression 49
disinflation 48
economics 30
fiscal policy 49

free-market economies 42
gross domestic product (GDP) 46
gross output (GO) 46
inflation 47
invisible hand 33
Keynesian economic theory 51
macroeconomics 30
market price 37
microeconomics 30
mixed economies 43
monetary policy 51

monopolistic competition 39
monopoly 39
national debt 50
oligopoly 39
perfect competition 38
producer price index (PPI) 48
recession 49
resource development 31
socialism 41
stagflation 48
state capitalism 35
supply 37
unemployment rate 46

critical thinking

The U.S. Supreme Court ruled that cities could have school voucher programs that give money directly to parents, who could then choose among competing schools, public or private. The idea was to create competition among schools. Like businesses, schools were expected to improve their services (how effectively they teach) to win students from competitors. The result would be improvement in all schools, private and public, to benefit many students.

1 Do you believe economic principles, like competition, apply in both private and public organizations? Be prepared to defend your answer.

2. Are there other public functions that might benefit from more competition, including competition from private firms?

3. Many people say that businesspeople do not do enough for society. Some students choose to go into the public sector instead of business because they want to help others. However, businesspeople say that they do more to help others than nonprofit groups do because they provide jobs for people rather than giving them charity. Furthermore, they believe businesses create all the wealth that nonprofit groups distribute.

   a. How can you find some middle ground in this debate to show that both businesspeople and those who work for nonprofit organizations contribute to society and need to work together more closely to help people?

   b. How could you use the concepts of Adam Smith to help illustrate your position?

developing **workplace skills**

Key: ● Team   ★ Analytic   ▲ Communication   ▣ Technology

1. In teams, develop a list of the advantages of living in a capitalist society. Then develop lists headed "What are the disadvantages?" and "How could such disadvantages be minimized?" Describe why a poor person in a socialist country might reject capitalism and prefer a socialist state. ● ▲ ★

2. Show your understanding of the principles of supply and demand by looking at the oil market today. Go online and search for a chart of oil prices for the last few years. Why does the price of oil fluctuate so greatly? What will happen as more and more people in China and India decide to buy automobiles? What would happen if most U.S consumers decided to drive electric cars? ▣ ★

3. This exercise will help you understand socialism from different perspectives. Form three groups. Each group should adopt a different role in a socialist economy: one group will be the business owners, another group will be workers, and another will be government leaders. Within your group discuss and list the advantages and disadvantages to you of lowering taxes on businesses. Then have each group choose a representative to go to the front of the class and debate the tax issue with the representatives from the other groups. ● ▲ ★

4. Draw a line and mark one end "Free-Market Capitalism" and the other end "Central Planning." Mark where on the line the United States is now. Explain why you marked the spot you chose. Students from other countries may want to do this exercise for their own countries and explain the differences to the class. ▲ ★

5. Break into small groups. In your group discuss how the following changes have affected people's purchasing behavior and attitudes toward the United States and its economy: the wars in Iraq and Afghanistan, the increased amount spent on homeland security, the government involvement in banking and other industries, and the growth of the Internet. Have a group member prepare a short summary for the class. ● ▲ ★

taking it to the **net**

PURPOSE

To familiarize you with the sources of economic information that are important to business decision makers.

EXERCISE

Imagine that your boss asked you to help her to prepare the company's sales forecast for the coming two years. In the past, she felt that trends in the nation's GDP, U.S. manufacturing, and manufacturing in Illinois were especially helpful in forecasting sales. She would like you to do the following:

1. Go to the Bureau of Economic Analysis's website (www.bea.gov) and locate the gross domestic product data. Compare the annual figure for the last four years. What do the figures indicate for the next couple of years?

2. At the Bureau of Labor Statistics' website (www.bls.gov) under Industries, click on Industries at a Glance to find the information about the manufacturing industry. What is the employment trend in manufacturing over the last four years (percentage change from preceding period)?

3. Return to the Bureau of Labor Statistics' home page and use the Search feature to find trends in employment for the state of Illinois. Look around the website to see what other information is available. Plot the trend in manufacturing employment in Illinois over the last four years. On your own, discuss what economic changes may have influenced that trend.

4. Based on the information you have gathered, write a brief summary of what may happen to company sales over the next couple of years.

video case   Mc Graw Hill Education connect®

OPPORTUNITY INTERNATIONAL: GIVING THE POOR A WORKING CHANCE

Billions of people in the world make $2 a day or less. In fact, a billion people make less than $1 a day. In such places, a loan of $100 or $200 makes a huge difference. That's where microloans from organizations such as Opportunity International come in.

Opportunity International is an organization that grants microloans to people, mostly women, in developing countries so they can invest in a business. Those investments often lead to community growth and employment, and help the owners themselves to prosper on a moderate scale. The borrowers must pay back the money with interest—when they do, they can borrow more and keep growing. Opportunity International, unlike some other microlending organizations, also provides a banking function where entrepreneurs can safely

put their money. They can also buy some insurance to protect themselves against loss.

Opportunity International helps over a million people in over 28 countries, giving them the opportunity to change their lives for the better. This video introduces you to some of those people, but primarily explains how freedom and a little money can combine to create huge differences in people's lives.

Adam Smith was one of the first people to point out that wealth comes from freedom, the ability to own land, and the ability to keep the profits from what you do on that land. When people try to maximize profits, they have to hire other people to help them do the work. This provides jobs for others and wealth for the entrepreneur. And, like an invisible hand, the whole community benefits from the entrepreneurs' desire to earn a profit. In the video, you can see a woman in Uganda who has applied those principles to benefit her family, provide employment, and help her community.

Free-market capitalism is the system where people can own their own land and businesses and keep the profits they earn. Such a system demands that people can (1) own their own property (not a reality in many developing nations); (2) keep the profits from any business they start; (3) compete with other businesses (it is difficult to compete with the government); and (4) work wherever and whenever they want. The key word in capitalism is *freedom*—freedom of religion, freedom to own land, and freedom to prosper and grow. Opportunity International is making an attempt to show people how freedom plus a few dollars can make a huge difference in an economy.

In a free-market economy, price is determined by buyers and sellers negotiating over the price of a good or service. The equilibrium point is the place where buyers and sellers agree to an exchange; it is also called the market price. Without free markets, there is no way of knowing what buyers need and what sellers need to produce. Thus, in command economies, where there is no supply-and-demand mechanism in operation, there can be shortages or surpluses in food, clothing, and other necessities.

Socialism and communism are alternatives to a free-market economy. Under such systems, people are more likely to have a bit of equality, but there are fewer incentives to work hard, and entrepreneurs are often lured to countries where they can make more money by working harder. The result is called a brain drain, where the best and the brightest often move to free-market countries. There are advantages to socialism and communism, such as free schools, free health care, free day care, etc. But the taxes are higher, and there is usually less innovation and higher unemployment.

The trend in the world is toward mixed economies, where most of the economy is based on free-market principles, but the government gets involved in things such as education, health care, and welfare. The United States has been basically a free-market economy, but it is clear that there is a movement toward more government involvement. On the other hand, some countries are reducing the role of government in society and moving toward freer markets. Thus the world is moving toward mixed economies.

The United States government tries to control the money supply through the Federal Reserve and fiscal policy. Fiscal policy has to do with taxes and spending. The less the government spends, the more that is available for businesses to invest. And the lower the tax rates on entrepreneurs, the more they will invest in businesses and the faster the economy will grow.

Opportunity International shows the poorest of the poor how important entrepreneurs, freedom, opportunity, and a little bit of money are to economic growth and prosperity. You are encouraged in this video to participate in helping poor people around the world. You can do this by contributing time and money to organizations like Opportunity International. You can join the Peace Corps or other groups designed to assist less-developed countries.

THINKING IT OVER

1. Why is there a need for organizations like Opportunity International? Can't poor people get loans from banks and other sources?

2. Identify the four major requirements necessary for a free-market system to operate.

3. What is the main difference between capitalism and a mixed economy? Which model is used in the United States?

notes

1. Terry Miller, "America's Dwindling Economic Freedom," *The Wall Street Journal,* January 14, 2014.
2. Randall Stephenson, "A Business Short List for Growth," *The Wall Street Journal,* January 15, 2014.
3. Romain Hatchuel, "The Coming Global Wealth Tax," *The Wall Street Journal,* December 4, 2013.
4. Roger Lowenstein, "Macro Master," *The Wall Street Journal,* January 18–19, 2014.
5. Janet Hook and Kristina Peterson, "Congress Passes a Debt Bill," *The Wall Street Journal,* October 13, 2013.
6. Robert J. Samuelson, "Macroeconomics Loses Its Magic," *The Washington Post,* April 22, 2013.
7. Nidaa Bakhsh, "Shale Goes Global," *Bloomberg Businessweek,* November 18, 2013–January 2, 2014.
8. Nicholas Eberstadt, "China's Coming One-Child Crisis," *The Wall Street Journal,* November 27, 2013.
9. Charles Kenny, "The Reproductive Recession," *Bloomberg Businessweek,* February 11–February 17, 2013.
10. Stephenson, "A Business Short List for Growth."
11. Ed Feulner, "The Slow Fade of Economic Freedom," *The Washington Times,* January 14, 2014.
12. Donald Lambro, "Dickensian Poverty in 2013," *The Washington Times,* December 25, 2013.
13. Charles Lane, "The Politics of Inequality," *The Washington Post,* December 10, 2013.

14. "The Philanthropic," special feature, *Forbes,* December 2, 2013.

15. Steve Matthews, "For Many, the Age of Entrepreneurship Starts at 55," *The Washington Post,* January 12, 2014.

16. John Mackey and Raj Sisodia, *Conscious Capitalism* (Boston, MA: Harvard Business Review Press, 2013).

17. Ibid., p. 11.

18. "What Kind of Capitalism?" editorial, *The Economist,* October 12, 2013.

19. Charles Wolf Jr., "A Truly Great Leap Forward: How China Became Capitalist," *The Wall Street Journal,* May 1, 2013.

20. Peter Coy, "The Sting of Long-Term Unemployment," *Bloomberg Businessweek,* February 11–February 17, 2013.

21. Romain Hatchuel, "What's French for Economic Nonsense?" *The Wall Street Journal,* March 29, 2013.

22. Samuel Rines, "Monthly Economic Data Aren't Reliable," *The Wall Street Journal,* June 28, 2013.

23. Mark Skousen, "A New Way to Measure the Economy," *Forbes,* December 16, 2013.

24. John Cassidy, "Meet the 'Missing Millions' Who've Vanished from the Economy," *Fortune,* April 8, 2013.

25. Peter Coy, "The Sting of Long-Term Unemployment," *Bloomberg Businessweek,* February 11–February 17, 2013.

26. Richard Vedder, "The Wages of Unemployment," *The Wall Street Journal,* January 16, 2013; Brenda Cronin, "Jobless Benefits Set to Expire," *The Wall Street Journal,* December 28–29, 2013; and Arthur Laffer, "Work Disincentives, Still Crazy after All These Years," *The Wall Street Journal,* February 9–10, 2013.

27. "The Latest Jobs Miss," editorial, *The Wall Street Journal,* January 11–12, 2014.

28. Brenda Cronin and Jonathan House, "Hiring Slowdown Blurs Growth View," *The Wall Street Journal,* January 11–12, 2014.

29. www.thefreedictionary.com, accessed September 2014.

30. Gene Epstein, "More Disinflation Lies Ahead," *Barron's,* January 20, 2014.

31. Paul Hannon, "Economist Warns Europe on Deflation," *The Wall Street Journal,* January 18–19, 2014.

32. "Does More Work Lead to a Healthier Economy?" HBR Reprint, *Harvard Business Review,* December 2013.

photo credits

3

Doing Business in Global Markets

Learning Objectives

AFTER YOU HAVE READ AND STUDIED THIS CHAPTER, YOU SHOULD BE ABLE TO

LO 3-1 Discuss the importance of the global market and the roles of comparative advantage and absolute advantage in global trade.

LO 3-2 Explain the importance of importing and exporting, and understand key terms used in global business.

LO 3-3 Illustrate the strategies used in reaching global markets and explain the role of multinational corporations.

LO 3-4 Evaluate the forces that affect trading in global markets.

LO 3-5 Debate the advantages and disadvantages of trade protectionism.

LO 3-6 Discuss the changing landscape of the global market and the issue of offshore outsourcing.

Getting to Know **Leila Janah**

For decades U.S. companies have outsourced work overseas to countries known for providing cheap labor. The practice is controversial. While it saves businesses money, that's often the only benefit. Not only may it hurt job creation domestically, outsourcing can also overload foreign job markets with underpaid work that often offers little chance for advancement.

Leila Janah saw this problem firsthand when she befriended a call center employee working in India. The young man took a long commute to his job from one of Mumbai's worst slums, which was the only place he could afford. "I knew there were more people like him capable of doing quality work," says Janah. She then came up with the idea for Samasource, a nonprofit "microwork" company that helps young men and women in developing countries earn extra income in order to rise out of poverty.

The bulk of the work provided by Samasource involves simple, computer-related tasks—such as tagging images, moderating comments on websites, and transcribing interviews. These jobs normally end up in countries like India and the Philippines through large outsourcing corporations. Unlike these companies, however, Samasource carefully selects potential employees based on the skills they lack, not the ones they have already. "The criteria for selecting agents is that they must be between the ages of 18 and 30, have no formal work experience, and are currently earning less than a living wage," says Janah. "Agents are then provided free, specialized technology training, soft skills training, and project-specific training before beginning work." Samasource's contracts with companies like Google, Microsoft and eBay have helped more than 4,000 people and their families rise above the poverty line. In fact, a recent study projected that by 2020 more than 2.9 million people will be employed through "impact sourcing" companies like Samasource.

Janah's commitment to combating world poverty has been her driving force since her teenage years. She earned a $10,000 scholarship, which funded a trip to Ghana to teach English. Janah continued to travel the world while also studying at Harvard University. After graduating with a degree in economic development, she took a job with the World Bank that made her question traditional methods of providing aid. "The more time I spent in developing countries, and the more time I spent talking to poor people, I realized what they want more than anything is a good job," says Janah. "We spend billions on international aid annually, but we don't find ways to connect people to dignified work."

Janah hopes that Samasource will change that. The nonprofit currently operates 16 centers in nine countries and is always expanding. One of Samasource's most ambitious projects is SamaUSA, a pilot program the company recently launched in San Francisco. This 80-hour training program teaches marketable computer skills to community-college students from low-income neighborhoods and helps them find online work. In the end, though, much of the nonprofit's future success depends on outside companies choosing to work with Samasource instead of other outsourcing services. "We tell [clients], 'You're going to spend this money on an outsourcing company anyway—why not end poverty and save the world without spending more money than you already spend?'" says Janah.

Leila Janah is an example of an emerging global businessperson. She has learned to speak other languages, understands cultural and economic differences, and knows how to adapt to changes successfully. This chapter explains the opportunities and challenges businesspeople like Janah face every day in dealing with the dynamic environment of global business.

Sources: Jason Ankeny, "The 7 Most Powerful Women to Watch in 2014: The Humanitarian," *Entrepreneur*, January 3, 2014; Catherine Dunn, "40 Under 40: Leila Janah," *Forbes*, September 19, 2013; Visi R. Talik, "'Rising Star' Leila Janah on Fighting Poverty," *The Wall Street Journal*, November 29, 2012; and "A Letter from Leila Janah, Founder and CEO," www.samasource.org, accessed February 2014.

Leila Janah

- Founder and CEO of Samasource
- Fights world poverty and trains unskilled workers
- Finds jobs for newly trained workers

www.samasource.org

@samasource

This Swiss-based company has many foreign subsidiaries including Jenny Craig (weight management), Ralston Purina, Chef America (maker of Hot Pockets), and Dreyer's Ice Cream in the United States, as well as Perrier in France. The company employs over 328,000 people and has operations in almost every country in the world. Name that company. (Find the answer in the chapter.)

LO 3–1 Discuss the importance of the global market and the roles of comparative advantage and absolute advantage in global trade.

THE DYNAMIC GLOBAL MARKET

Have you dreamed of traveling to cities like Paris, London, Rio de Janeiro, or Moscow? Today, over 90 percent of the companies doing business globally believe it's important for their employees to have experience working in other countries.[1] The reason is not surprising—although the United States is a market of over 317 *million* people, there are over 7.1 *billion* potential customers in the 194 countries that make up the global market.[2] That's too many people to ignore! (See Figure 3.1 for a map of the world and important statistics about world population.)

Today U.S. consumers buy billions of dollars' worth of goods from China.[3] United Parcel Service (UPS) has experienced double-digit market growth in its global operations and Walmart operates more than 350 stores in Africa.[4] The National Basketball Association (NBA) played eight preseason games in Europe, Asia, and South America in 2013 and the National Football League (NFL) plans to play three games in London's Wembley Stadium in 2014.

FIGURE 3.1 WORLD POPULATION BY CONTINENT

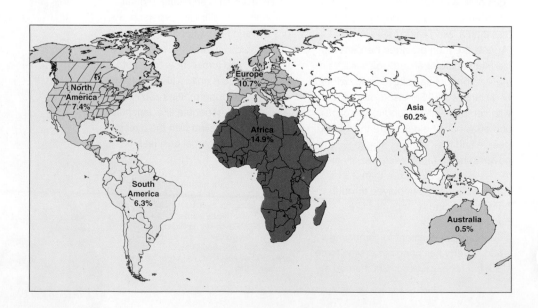

It may not be what the rest of the world calls "football," but American football is attracting an audience outside the United States. London's Wembley Stadium has been home to the NFL's International Series since 2007. What cultural factors must U.S. sports franchises overcome in order to increase popularity abroad?

NBC paid $250 million to telecast three full seasons of England's Barclays Premier Soccer League in the United States.[5] U.S. film stars Matt Damon, Tom Cruise, and Meryl Streep draw crowds to movie theaters around the globe.[6]

Because the global market is so large, it is important to understand the language used in global trade. For example, **importing** is buying products from another country. **Exporting** is selling products to another country. As you might suspect, competition among exporting nations is intense. The United States is the largest importing nation in the world and is the second-largest exporting nation, behind China.[7]

This chapter will familiarize you with global business and its many challenges. As competition in global markets intensifies, the demand for students with training in global business is almost certain to grow.

importing
Buying products from another country.

exporting
Selling products to another country.

WHY TRADE WITH OTHER NATIONS?

No nation, not even a technologically advanced one, can produce all the products its people want and need. Even if a country did become self-sufficient, other nations would seek to trade with it to meet the needs of their own people. Some nations, like Venezuela and Russia, have an abundance of natural resources but limited technological know-how. Other countries, such as Japan and Switzerland, have sophisticated technology but few natural resources. Global trade enables a nation to produce what it is most capable of producing and buy what it needs from others in a mutually beneficial exchange relationship. This happens through the process called free trade.[8]

Free trade is the movement of goods and services among nations without political or economic barriers. It has become a hotly debated concept.[9] In fact, many in the United States take the position "fair trade, not free trade."[10] Figure 3.2 offers some of the pros and cons of free trade.

free trade
The movement of goods and services among nations without political or economic barriers.

FIGURE 3.2 THE PROS AND CONS OF FREE TRADE

PROS	CONS
• The global market contains over 7 billion potential customers for goods and services. • Productivity grows when countries produce goods and services in which they have a comparative advantage. • Global competition and less-costly imports keep prices down, so inflation does not curtail economic growth. • Free trade inspires innovation for new products and keeps firms competitively challenged. • Uninterrupted flow of capital gives countries access to foreign investments, which help keep interest rates low.	• Domestic workers (particularly in manufacturing-based jobs) can lose their jobs due to increased imports or production shifts to low-wage global markets. • Workers may be forced to accept pay cuts from employers, who can threaten to move their jobs to lower-cost global markets. • Moving operations overseas because of intense competitive pressure often means the loss of service jobs and growing numbers of white-collar jobs. • Domestic companies can lose their comparative advantage when competitors build advanced production operations in low-wage countries.

The Theories of Comparative and Absolute Advantage

comparative advantage theory
Theory that states that a country should sell to other countries those products that it produces most effectively and efficiently, and buy from other countries those products that it cannot produce as effectively or efficiently.

absolute advantage
The advantage that exists when a country produces a specific product more efficiently than all other countries.

Countries exchange more than goods and services, however. They also exchange art, sports, cultural events, medical advances, space exploration, and labor. Comparative advantage theory, suggested in the early 19th century by English economist David Ricardo, was the guiding principle that supported the idea of free economic exchange.[11] **Comparative advantage theory** states that a country should sell to other countries those products it produces most effectively and efficiently, and buy from other countries those products it cannot produce as effectively or efficiently. The United States has a comparative advantage in producing goods and services, such as software and engineering services.[12] In contrast, it lacks a comparative advantage in growing coffee or making shoes; thus, we import most of the shoes and coffee we consume. By specializing and trading, the United States and its trading partners can realize mutually beneficial exchanges.

A country has an **absolute advantage** if it can produce a specific product more efficiently than all other countries. Absolute advantage does not last forever; global competition causes absolute advantages to fade. Today there are very few instances of absolute advantage in global markets.

 LO 3–2   Explain the importance of importing and exporting, and understand key terms used in global business.

GETTING INVOLVED IN GLOBAL TRADE

People interested in a job in global business often think they are limited to firms like Boeing, Caterpillar, or IBM, which have large multinational accounts. However, real global job potential may be with small businesses. In the United States, only 1 percent of the 30 million small businesses export yet they account for about 30 percent of the total U.S. exports.[13] In 2010,

President Obama challenged small businesses to think big and help double exports by 2015. With the support of the U.S. Department of Commerce, U.S. exports increased significantly but not quite at the level the president requested.[14]

Getting started globally is often a matter of observing, being determined, and taking risks. In a classic story, several years ago a U.S. traveler in an African country noticed there was no ice available for drinks or for keeping foods fresh. Research showed there was no ice factory for hundreds of miles, yet the market seemed huge. The man returned to the United States, found some investors, and returned to Africa to build an ice-making plant. The job was tough; much negotiation was necessary with local authorities (much of which was done by local citizens and businesspeople who knew the system). But the plant was built, and this forward-thinking entrepreneur gained a considerable return on his idea, while the people gained a needed product.

Importing Goods and Services

Students attending colleges and universities abroad often notice that some products widely available in their countries are unavailable or more expensive elsewhere. By working with producers in their native country, finding some start-up financing, and putting in long hours of hard work, many have become major importers while still in school.

Howard Schultz, CEO of Starbucks, found his opportunity while traveling in Milan, Italy. Schultz was enthralled with the ambience, the aroma, and especially the sense of community in the Italian neighborhood coffee and espresso bars that stretched across the country. He felt such gathering places would be great in the United States. Schultz bought the original Starbucks coffee shop in Seattle and transformed it according to his vision.[15] Because the Italian coffee bars caught his attention, U.S. coffee lovers now know what a grande latte is.

Exporting Goods and Services

Who would think U.S. firms could sell beer in Germany, home of so many good beers? Well, some of Munich's most famous beer halls now have American outposts where you can buy U.S. beers like Samuel Adams Boston Lager.[16] If this surprises you, imagine selling sand in the Middle East. Meridan Group exports a special kind of sand used in swimming pool filters that sells well there.

The fact is, you can sell just about any good or service used in the United States to other countries—and sometimes the competition is not nearly so intense as it is at home. For example, you can sell snowplows to Saudi Arabians, who use them to clear sand off their driveways. As Chinese women develop more sophisticated beauty routines, companies like Mary Kay are increasing their presence in China.[17] Exporting also provides a terrific boost to the U.S. economy. C. Fred Bergsten, founding director of the Peterson Institute for International Economics, states that U.S. exports of $1.5 trillion goods and services create approximately 10 million well-paid jobs in our economy. He also estimates that every $1 billion in additional U.S. exports generates over 7,000 jobs at home.[18] But selling in global markets and adapting products to global customers are by no means easy tasks. We discuss key forces that affect global trading later in this chapter.

Things may not have started off "pretty" for Ugly Dolls, a venture founded almost by accident, but the two-person company has grown into a global business selling its products in over 1,000 stores around the world. The original dolls have been joined by accessories, books, calendars, action figures, and T-shirts. Does a career in exporting or importing sound appealing to you?

If you are interested in exporting, send for "The Basic Guide to Exporting," a brochure from the U.S. Government Printing Office, Superintendent of Documents, Washington, DC 20402. More advice is available at websites such as those sponsored by the U.S. Department of Commerce (www.doc.gov), the Bureau of Export Administration (www.bea.gov), the Small Business Administration (www.sba.gov), and the Small Business Exporters Association (www.sbea.org).

Measuring Global Trade

In measuring global trade, nations rely on two key indicators: balance of trade and balance of payments. The **balance of trade** is the total value of a nation's exports compared to its imports measured over a particular period. A *favorable* balance of trade, or **trade surplus**, occurs when the value of a country's exports exceeds that of its imports. An *unfavorable* balance of trade, or **trade deficit**, occurs when the value of a country's exports is less than its imports. It's easy to understand why countries prefer to export more than they import. If I sell you $200 worth of goods and buy only $100 worth, I have an extra $100 available to buy other things. However, I'm in an unfavorable position if I buy $200 worth of goods from you and sell you only $100.

The **balance of payments** is the difference between money coming into a country (from exports) and money leaving the country (for imports) plus money flows coming into or leaving a country from other factors such as tourism, foreign aid, military expenditures, and foreign investment. The goal is to have more money flowing into the country than out—a *favorable* balance of payments. Conversely, an *unfavorable* balance of payments exists when more money is flowing out of a country than coming in.

In the past, the United States exported more goods and services than it imported. However, since 1975 it has bought more goods from other nations than it has sold and thus has a trade deficit. Today, the United States runs its highest trade deficit with China.[19] Nonetheless the United States remains one of the world's largest *exporting* nations even though the U.S. exports a much lower *percentage* of its products than other countries, such as China, Germany, and Japan. (Figure 3.3 lists the major trading countries in the world and the leading U.S. trading partners.)

balance of trade
The total value of a nation's exports compared to its imports measured over a particular period.

trade surplus
A favorable balance of trade; occurs when the value of a country's exports exceeds that of its imports.

trade deficit
An unfavorable balance of trade; occurs when the value of a country's imports exceeds that of its exports.

balance of payments
The difference between money coming into a country (from exports) and money leaving the country (for imports) plus money flows from other factors such as tourism, foreign aid, military expenditures, and foreign investment.

 connect

▶ **iSee It!** Need help understanding balance of trade? Visit your Connect e-book video tab for a brief animated explanation.

FIGURE 3.3 THE LARGEST EXPORTING NATIONS IN THE WORLD AND THE LARGEST U.S. TRADE PARTNERS

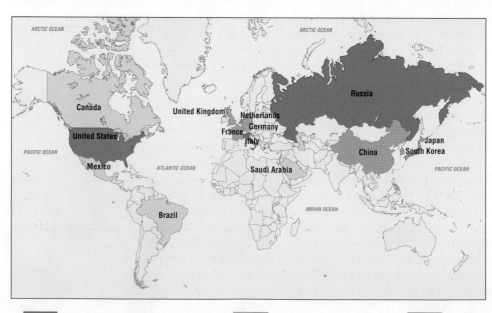

World's Largest Exporting Nations   Top U.S. Trading Partners   Both

In supporting free trade, the United States, like other nations, wants to make certain global trade is conducted fairly. To ensure a level playing field, countries prohibit unfair trade practices such as dumping. **Dumping** is selling products in a foreign country at lower prices than those charged in the producing country. This predatory pricing tactic is sometimes used to reduce surplus products in foreign markets or to gain a foothold in a new market. Some governments may even offer financial incentives to certain industries to sell goods in global markets for less than they sell them at home. China, Brazil, and Russia, for example, have been penalized for dumping steel in the United States. U.S. laws against dumping are specific and require foreign firms to price their products to include 10 percent overhead costs plus an 8 percent profit margin. Now that you understand some of the basic terms used in global business, we can look at different strategies for entering global markets. First, let's assess your progress so far.

dumping
Selling products in a foreign country at lower prices than those charged in the producing country.

test prep

- What are two of the main arguments favoring the expansion of U.S. businesses into global markets?
- What is comparative advantage, and what are some examples of this concept at work in the United States?
- How are a nation's balance of trade and balance of payments determined?
- What is meant by the term *dumping* in global trade?

Use LearnSmart to help retain what you have learned. Access your instructor's Connect course to check out LearnSmart, or go to learnsmartadvantage.com for help.

LEARNSMART

LO 3–3 Illustrate the strategies used in reaching global markets and explain the role of multinational corporations.

STRATEGIES FOR REACHING GLOBAL MARKETS

Businesses use different strategies to compete in global markets. The key strategies include licensing, exporting, franchising, contract manufacturing, international joint ventures and strategic alliances, foreign subsidiaries, and foreign direct investment. Each provides different economic opportunities, along with specific commitments and risks. Figure 3.4 places the strategies on

FIGURE 3.4 STRATEGIES FOR REACHING GLOBAL MARKETS

| Licensing | Exporting | Franchising | Contract manufacturing | International joint ventures and strategic alliances | Foreign direct investment |

LEAST ← Amount of commitment, control, risk, and profit potential → MOST

a continuum showing the amount of commitment, control, risk, and profit potential associated with each strategy. Take some time to look over the information in Figure 3.4 before you continue.

Licensing

A firm (the licensor) may decide to compete in a global market by **licensing** the right to manufacture its product or use its trademark to a foreign company (the licensee) for a fee (a royalty). A company with an interest in licensing generally sends company representatives to the foreign company to help set up operations. The licensor may also assist or work with a licensee in such areas as distribution, promotion, and consulting.

A licensing agreement can benefit a firm in several ways. First, the firm can gain revenues it would not otherwise have generated in its home market. Also, foreign licensees often must purchase start-up supplies, materials, and consulting services from the licensing firm. Coca-Cola has entered into global licensing agreements with over 300 licensees that have extended into long-term service contracts that sell over $1 billion of the company's products each year.[20] Service-based companies are also active in licensing. For example, retailer Frederick's of Hollywood recently entered into a licensing agreement with Emirates Associated Business Group to build and operate Frederick's of Hollywood stores in the Middle East.

A final advantage of licensing is that licensors spend little or no money to produce and market their products. These costs come from the licensee's pocket. Therefore, licensees generally work hard to succeed. However, licensors may also experience problems. Often a firm must grant licensing rights to its product for an extended period, 20 years or longer. If a product experiences remarkable growth in the foreign market, the bulk of the revenues belong to the licensee. Perhaps even more threatening is that the licensing firm is actually selling its expertise. If a foreign licensee learns the company's technology or product secrets, it may break the agreement and begin to produce a similar product on its own. If legal remedies are not available, the licensing firm may lose its trade secrets, not to mention promised royalties.

Warner Bros. has licensed many companies to make products related to successful film franchises like The Hobbit. *Do you think* Hobbit-*licensed products will maintain their global popularity with new generations of viewers?*

Exporting

To meet increasing global competition, the U.S. Department of Commerce created Export Assistance Centers (EACs). EACs provide hands-on exporting assistance and trade-finance support for small and medium-sized businesses that wish to directly export goods and services. An EAC network exists in more than 100 U.S. cities and 80 countries, with further expansion planned.[21]

U.S. firms that are still hesitant can engage in *indirect* exporting through specialists called export-trading companies (or export-management companies) that assist in negotiating and establishing trading relationships. An export-trading company not only matches buyers and sellers from different countries but also deals with foreign customs offices, documentation,

and even weights and measures conversions to ease the process of entering global markets. It also can assist exporters with warehousing, billing, and insuring. If you are considering a career in global business, export-trading companies often provide internships or part-time opportunities for students.

Franchising

Franchising is a contractual agreement whereby someone with a good idea for a business sells others the rights to use the business name and sell a product or service in a given territory in a specified manner. Franchising is popular domestically and globally. (We discuss it in depth in Chapter 5.) Major U.S. franchisors such as Subway, Holiday Inn, and Dunkin' Donuts have many global units operated by foreign franchisees, but global franchising isn't limited to large franchisors. For example, Rocky Mountain Chocolate Factory, a Colorado-based producer of premium chocolates, has agreements with the Al Muhairy Group of the United Arab Emirates and plans to open two stores in Saudi Arabia in 2015. In the Middle East, chocolate is considered a gourmet luxury much like caviar in the United States.[22] Foreign franchisors also may look to expand to the U.S. market. Guatemala-based Pollo Campara opened its first restaurant franchise in the U.S. in 2002, and Vietnamese entrepreneur Ly Qui Trung introduced his Pho24 franchises to the United States in 2012.

Franchisors have to be careful to adapt their product or service to the countries they serve. Yum! Brands has 40,000 of its KFC, Taco Bell, and Pizza Hut restaurants in 130 countries around the world.[23] It learned quickly that preferences in pizza toppings differ globally. Japanese customers, for example, enjoy squid and sweet mayonnaise pizza. In the company's KFC restaurants in China, the menu is chicken with Sichuan spicy sauce and rice, egg soup, and a "dragon twister" (KFC's version of a traditional Beijing duck wrap).[24] Read the nearby Reaching Beyond Our Borders box that highlights another global franchise champion, McDonald's.

Tired of studying and want a quick snack? How about a piping hot Domino's pizza with potatoes and corn topped with mayo? Domino's serves pizzas around the globe that appeal to different tastes (the mayo pizza is a hit in Japan). How can franchises ensure their products are appropriate for global markets?

Contract Manufacturing

In **contract manufacturing** a foreign company produces private-label goods to which a domestic company then attaches its own brand name or trademark. For example, contract manufacturers make circuit boards and components used in computers, printers, smartphones, medical products, airplanes, and consumer electronics for companies such as Dell, Xerox, and IBM. Nike has more than 800 contract factories around the world that manufacture all its footwear and apparel. The worldwide contract manufacturing business is estimated to be a $250 billion industry that's expected to grow to $325 billion soon.[25]

Contract manufacturing enables a company to experiment in a new market without incurring heavy start-up costs such as building a manufacturing plant. If the brand name becomes a success, the company has penetrated a new market with relatively low risk. A firm can also use contract manufacturing temporarily to meet an unexpected increase in orders, and, of course, labor costs are often very low. Contract manufacturing falls under the broad category of *outsourcing*, which we defined in Chapter 1 and will discuss in more depth later in this chapter.

contract manufacturing
A foreign company's production of private-label goods to which a domestic company then attaches its brand name or trademark; part of the broad category of outsourcing.

McDonald's: Over 100 Cultures Served

МакЭкспресс

For decades McDonald's has been the undisputed king of global food franchising. With more than 34,000 restaurants in over 118 countries, Mickey D's serves more than 69 million customers every day.

So how did McDonald's become such a global powerhouse? It certainly didn't get there through hamburgers alone. Since it first began expanding overseas, McDonald's has been careful to include regional tastes on its menus along with the usual Big Mac and French fries. For instance, in Thailand patrons can order the Samurai Burger, a pork-patty sandwich marinated in teriyaki sauce and topped with mayonnaise and a pickle. If fish is more your taste, try the Ebi Filet-o shrimp sandwich from Japan.

McDonald's is also careful to adapt its menus to local customs and culture. In Israel, all meat served in the chain's restaurants is 100 percent kosher beef. The company also closes many of its restaurants on the Sabbath and religious holidays. McDonald's pays respect to religious sentiments in India as well by not including any beef or pork on its menu. For more examples, go to www.mcdonalds.com and explore the various McDonald's international franchises websites. Notice how the company blends the culture of each country into the restaurant's image.

McDonald's main global market concern as of late has been Asia. So far McDonald's strategy seems to be working. In Shanghai the company's Hamburger University attracts top-level college graduates to be trained for management positions. Only about eight out of every 1,000 applicants makes it into the program, an acceptance rate even lower than Harvard's! McDonald's is reaching out further in Asia and in 2014 opened its first store in Vietnam. The Vietnamese location in Ho Chi Minh City is the country's very first drive-thru restaurant. Bringing McDonald's to Vietnam is a dream come true for Henry Nguyen, founder of Good Day Hospitality, who has been wanting to introduce the brand to Vietnam for over a decade. Nguyen brought in 20 top McDonald's employees from Australia to help aid in the opening while also sending prospective Vietnamese employees to Queensland to learn the ropes in a real-life restaurant setting. In the end, one can only hope that McDonald's remains dedicated to quality as it continues adapting and expanding into the global market.

Sources: Erin Smith, "Some McSkills to Share," *The Warwick Daily News,* February 4, 2014; Kate Taylor, "New Year, New Expansion: McDonald's to Open First Restaurant in Vietnam," *Entrepreneur,* December 23, 2013; Vivian Giang, "McDonald's Hamburger University: Step inside the Most Exclusive School in the World," *Business Insider,* April 7, 2012; and McDonald's, www.mcdonalds.com, accessed February 2014.

International Joint Ventures and Strategic Alliances

joint venture
A partnership in which two or more companies (often from different countries) join to undertake a major project.

A **joint venture** is a partnership in which two or more companies (often from different countries) join to undertake a major project. Joint ventures are often mandated by governments such as China as a condition of doing business in their country. For example, Disney and state-owned Shanghai Shendi Group entered a joint venture to create a Disneyland theme park in Shanghai that is expected to open in 2015.[26]

Joint ventures are developed for many different reasons. Marriott International and AC Hotels in Spain entered a joint venture to create AC Hotels by Marriott to increase their global footprint and future growth.[27] PepsiCo, as part of its Performance with Purpose global vision, agreed to joint ventures with Tata Global Beverages of India to develop packaged health and wellness beverages for the mass consumer market in India and the Strauss Group in Mexico to provide fresh dips and spreads.[28] Joint ventures can also be truly unique, such as the University of Pittsburgh's Medical Center and the Italian government's joint venture that brought a new medical transplant center to Sicily. The transplant center in Palermo called ISMETT recently celebrated its fifteenth year of operation.[29] The benefits of international joint ventures are clear:

1. Shared technology and risk.
2. Shared marketing and management expertise.
3. Entry into markets where foreign companies are often not allowed unless goods are produced locally.

The drawbacks of joint ventures are not so obvious but are important. One partner can learn the other's technology and business practices and then use what it has learned to its own advantage. Also, a shared technology may become obsolete, or the joint venture may become too large to be as flexible as needed.

The global market has also fueled the growth of strategic alliances. A **strategic alliance** is a long-term partnership between two or more companies established to help each company build competitive market advantages. Unlike joint ventures, strategic alliances don't share costs, risks, management, or even profits. Such alliances provide broad access to markets, capital, and technical expertise. Thanks to their flexibility, strategic alliances can effectively link firms from different countries and firms of vastly different sizes. Hewlett-Packard has strategic alliances with Hitachi and Samsung, and Coca-Cola and Nestlé have had an alliance since early 1990 to distribute ready-to-drink tea and coffee.

Foreign Direct Investment

Foreign direct investment (FDI) is the buying of permanent property and businesses in foreign nations. The most common form of FDI is a **foreign subsidiary**, a company owned in a foreign country by another company, called the *parent company*. The subsidiary operates like a domestic firm, with production, distribution, promotion, pricing, and other business functions under the control of the subsidiary's management. The subsidiary also must observe the legal requirements of both the country where the parent firm is located (called the *home country*) and the foreign country where the subsidiary is located (called the *host country*).

The primary advantage of a subsidiary is that the company maintains complete control over any technology or expertise it may possess. The major shortcoming is the need to commit funds and technology within foreign boundaries. Should relationships with a host country falter, the firm's assets could be *expropriated* (taken over by the foreign government). Swiss-based Nestlé has many foreign subsidiaries. The consumer-products giant spent billions of dollars acquiring foreign subsidiaries such as Jenny Craig (weight management), Ralston Purina, Chef America (maker of Hot Pockets), and Dreyer's Ice Cream in the United States as well as Perrier in France. Nestlé employs over 328,000 people and has operations in almost every country in the world.[30]

Nestlé is a **multinational corporation**, one that manufactures and markets products in many different countries and has multinational stock

strategic alliance
A long-term partnership between two or more companies established to help each company build competitive market advantages.

foreign direct investment (FDI)
The buying of permanent property and businesses in foreign nations.

foreign subsidiary
A company owned in a foreign country by another company, called the *parent company*.

multinational corporation
An organization that manufactures and markets products in many different countries and has multinational stock ownership and multinational management.

The United States has been and remains a popular global spot for foreign direct investment. Global automobile manufacturers like Toyota, Honda, and Mercedes have spent millions of dollars building facilities in the United States, like the Mercedes plant in Tuscaloosa, Alabama, pictured here. Do you consider a Mercedes made in Alabama to be an American car or a German car?

FIGURE 3.5 THE LARGEST MULTINATIONAL CORPORATIONS IN THE WORLD

COMPANY	COUNTRY	WEBSITE
1. Royal Dutch Shell	Netherlands	shell.com
2. Wal-Mart Stores	United States	walmart.com
3. ExxonMobil	United States	exxonmobil.com
4. Sinopec Group	China	Sinopecgroup.com
5. China National Petroleum	China	cnpc.com.cn
6. BP	Britain	bp.com
7. State Grid	China	sgcc.com.cn
8. Toyota Motor	Japan	toyota.co.jp
9. Japan Post Holdings	Japan	japanpost.jp
10. Chevron	United States	chevron.com

Source: *Fortune*, July 25, 2013.

ownership and management. Multinational corporations are typically extremely large corporations like Nestlé, but not all large global businesses are multinationals. For example, a corporation could export everything it produces, deriving 100 percent of its sales and profits globally, and still not be a multinational corporation. Only firms that have *manufacturing capacity* or some other physical presence in different nations can truly be called multinational. Figure 3.5 lists the 10 largest multinational corporations in the world.

A growing form of foreign direct investment is the use of **sovereign wealth funds (SWFs)**, investment funds controlled by governments holding investment stakes in foreign companies. SWFs from the United Arab Emirates, Singapore, and China have purchased interests in many U.S. companies. Norway, with a population of 5 million people, is the world's richest SWF with assets of approximately $830 billion.[31] The size of SWFs ($6 trillion globally) and government ownership make some fear they might be used for achieving geopolitical objectives, gaining control of strategic natural resources, or obtaining sensitive technologies. Thus far this has not been a problem. In fact during the Great Recession, SWFs injected billions of dollars into struggling U.S. companies.[32] Many economists argue that foreign investment through SWFs is a vote of confidence in the U.S. economy and a way to create thousands of U.S. jobs.

Entering global business requires selecting an entry strategy that best fits your business goals. The different strategies we've discussed reflect different levels of ownership, financial commitment, and risk. However, this is just the beginning. You should also be aware of market forces that affect a business's ability to thrive in global markets. After the Test Prep, we'll discuss them.

sovereign wealth funds (SWFs)

Investment funds controlled by governments holding investment stakes in foreign companies.

Use LearnSmart to help retain what you have learned. Access your instructor's Connect course to check out LearnSmart, or go to learnsmartadvantage.com for help.

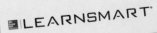

test prep

- What are the advantages to a firm of using licensing as a method of entry in global markets? What are the disadvantages?
- What services are usually provided by an export-trading company?
- What is the key difference between a joint venture and a strategic alliance?
- What makes a company a multinational corporation?

LO 3–4   Evaluate the forces that affect trading in global markets.

FORCES AFFECTING TRADING IN GLOBAL MARKETS

The hurdles to success are higher and more complex in global markets than in domestic markets. Such hurdles include dealing with differences in sociocultural forces, economic and financial forces, legal and regulatory forces, and physical and environmental forces. Let's analyze each of these market forces to see how they challenge even the most established and experienced global businesses.

Sociocultural Forces

The word *culture* refers to the set of values, beliefs, rules, and institutions held by a specific group of people. Culture can include social structures, religion, manners and customs, values and attitudes, language, and personal communication. (See the Spotlight on Small Business box for a story about how one entrepreneur is attempting to appeal to the changing values in China as newly affluent consumers desire luxury U.S. products.) If you hope to get involved in global trade, it's critical to be aware of the cultural differences among nations. Unfortunately, while the United States is a multicultural nation, U.S. business-people are often accused of *ethnocentricity*, an attitude that your own culture is superior to other cultures.

In contrast, many foreign companies are very good at adapting to U.S. culture. Think how effectively German, Japanese, and Korean carmakers adapted to U.S. drivers' wants and needs in the auto industry. In contrast, for many years U.S. auto producers didn't adapt automobiles to drive on the left side of the road and printed owner's manuals only in English. Liberia, Myanmar, and the United States are the only nations in the world that have not conformed to the metric system of measurement. Let's look at other hurdles U.S. businesses face in adapting to social and cultural differences in global markets.

Religion is an important part of any society's culture and can have a significant impact on business operations. Consider the violent clashes between religious communities in India, Pakistan, and the Middle East—clashes that have wounded these areas' economies. Even successful global companies can be affected by ignoring religious implications in making business decisions. For example, in honor of nations competing in the World Cup in 1994, both McDonald's and Coca-Cola reprinted the flags of the participating countries on their packaging. Muslims were offended when the Saudi Arabian flag was put on their packaging because the flag's design contained the Muslim Sha-hada (the Muslim declaration of faith), and Muslims believe their holy writ should never be wadded up and thrown away. Both companies learned from this experience that understanding religious implications in the global market is important.

In a similar classic story, a U.S. manager in Islamic Pakistan toured a new plant under his control. While the plant was in full operation, he went to his office to make some preliminary production forecasts. Suddenly all the machinery in the plant stopped. The manager rushed out, suspecting a power failure, only to find his production workers on their prayer rugs. Upon learning that Muslims are required to pray five times a day, he returned to his office and lowered his production estimates.

Understanding sociocultural differences is also important in managing employees. In some Latin American countries, workers believe managers are in positions of authority to make decisions concerning the well-being of the

From Setting Picks to Picking Grapes

Although Americans love to watch sports, professional athletes often receive criticism for collecting enormous paychecks. After all, some sports stars make more money in a single season than many educators or nurses would see in a lifetime. But matters can change drastically for athletes once their playing days end. Suddenly skills that you've spent your entire life honing are obsolete, often leading to confusion over what to do next.

When faced with this problem, the groundbreaking former NBA center Yao Ming opted to use his resources to start a business. Although this is a common post-retirement tactic for many athletes, Yao didn't unveil a line of

athletic wear or open a chain of sports bars. Instead, he established a high-end winery in California's famous Napa Valley. Although many wealthy Chinese celebrities have bought vineyards, Yao has set himself apart by building a brand from scratch

rather than investing in an existing operation. A national hero in China, Yao Family Wines uses the name recognition of its seven-and-half-foot founder to appeal to the nation's growing consumer class. Yao's wines are intentionally expensive: the cheapest vintage goes for about $87 while the priciest bottle, Yao Ming Family Reserve, lists for more than $1,000. With premium brands still a rarity in China, Yao could end up being just as influential in the Chinese business world as he was on the basketball court.

Sources: Jason Chow, "Yao Ming's Napa Winery Stoops to Conquer China's Middle Class," *The Wall Street Journal,* September 5, 2013; and Michelle FlorCruz, "Yao Ming's Wine Company Sets Sights on China's Growing Middle Class," *International Business Times,* September 6, 2013.

workers under their control. Consider the U.S. manager in Peru who was unaware of this cultural characteristic and believed workers should participate in managerial functions. He was convinced he could motivate his workers to higher levels of productivity by instituting a more democratic decision-making style. Workers instead began quitting in droves. When asked why, they said the new manager did not know his job and was asking the workers what to do. All stated they wanted to find new jobs, since this company was doomed due to its incompetent management.

Even today, many U.S. companies still fail to think globally, not understanding that something like the color of flowers can have different meanings in different cultures. A sound philosophy is: *Never assume what works in one country will work in another.* Intel, Nike, IBM, Apple, KFC, and Walmart have developed brand names with widespread global appeal and recognition, but even they often face difficulties.[33] To get an idea of the problems companies have faced with translations of advertising globally, take a look at Figure 3.6.

Economic and Financial Forces

Economic differences can muddy the water in global markets. In Qatar, annual per capita income is over $100,000, the highest in the world. In economically strapped Ethiopia and Haiti, per capita income is barely over $1,200. It's difficult for us to imagine buying chewing gum by the stick. Yet this behavior is commonplace in economically depressed nations like Haiti, where customers can afford only small quantities. You might suspect with over 1.2 billion potential customers, India would be a dream market for a company like Coca-Cola. Unfortunately, Indians consume only 12 eight-ounce bottles of Coke per person a year due to low per-capita income.[34] Financially, Mexicans shop with pesos, Chinese with yuan (also known as renminbi), South Koreans with won,

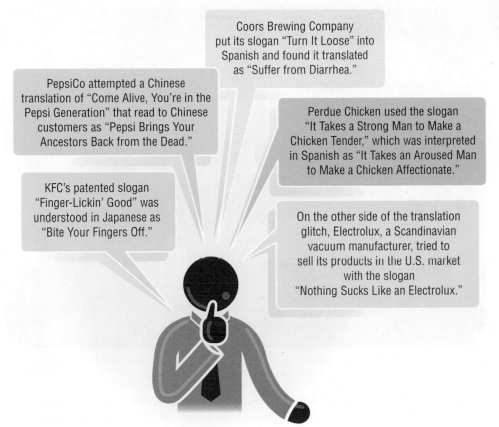

FIGURE 3.6 OOPS, DID WE SAY THAT?
A global marketing strategy can be very difficult to implement. Look at the problems these well-known companies encountered in global markets.

Japanese with yen, and U.S. consumers with dollars. Among currencies, globally, the U.S. dollar is considered a dominant and stable currency.[35] However, it doesn't always retain the same market value. In a global transaction today, a dollar may be exchanged for eight pesos; tomorrow you may get seven. The **exchange rate** is the value of one nation's currency relative to the currencies of other countries.

Changes in a nation's exchange rates have effects in global markets. A *high value of the dollar* means a dollar is trading for more foreign currency than previously. Therefore, foreign products become cheaper because it takes fewer dollars to buy them. However, U.S.-produced goods become more expensive because of the dollar's high value. Conversely, a *low value of the dollar* means a dollar is traded for less foreign currency—foreign goods become more expensive because it takes more dollars to buy them, but U.S. goods become cheaper to foreign buyers because it takes less foreign currency to buy them.

Global financial markets operate under a system called *floating exchange rates,* which means that currencies "float" in value according to the supply and demand for them in the global market for currency. This supply and demand is created by global currency traders who develop a market for a nation's currency based on the country's perceived trade and investment potential.

Changes in currency values can cause many problems globally.[36] For instance, labor costs for multinational corporations like Nestlé, General Electric, and Sony can vary considerably as currency values shift, causing them to juggle production from one country to another. The same is true for

exchange rate
The value of one nation's currency relative to the currencies of other countries.

When the dollar is "up," foreign goods and travel are a bargain for U.S. consumers. When the dollar trades for less foreign currency, however, foreign tourists like these often flock to U.S. cities to enjoy relatively cheaper vacations and shopping trips. Do U.S. exporters profit more when the dollar is up or when it is down?

medium-sized companies like H.B. Fuller, a global industrial adhesives provider from St. Paul, Minnesota, which has 4,000 employees in 43 countries. Like its larger counterparts, H.B. Fuller uses currency fluctuations to its advantage in dealing with its global markets.[37]

 Currency valuation problems can be especially harsh on developing economies. At times a nation's government will intervene and readjust the value of its currency, often to increase the export potential of its products. **Devaluation** lowers the value of a nation's currency relative to others. Argentina and Venezuela both devalued their currencies in 2014 to try to alleviate severe economic problems in both countries.[38] Sometimes, due to a nation's weak currency, the only way to trade is *bartering*, the exchange of merchandise for merchandise or service for service with no money traded.[39]

 Countertrading is a complex form of bartering in which several countries each trade goods or services for other goods or services. Let's say a developing country such as Jamaica wants to buy vehicles from Ford Motor Company in exchange for bauxite, a mineral compound that is a source of aluminum ore. Ford does not need Jamaican bauxite, but it does need compressors. In a countertrade, Ford may trade vehicles to Jamaica, which trades bauxite to another country, say India, which exchanges compressors with Ford. All three parties benefit and avoid some of the financial problems and currency constraints in global markets. Estimates are that countertrading accounts for over 20 percent of all global exchanges, especially with developing countries.[40]

Legal and Regulatory Forces

In any economy, the conduct and the direction of business are firmly tied to the legal and regulatory environment. In global markets, no central system of law exists, so different systems of laws and regulations may apply in different places. This makes conducting global business difficult as businesspeople navigate a

devaluation
Lowering the value of a nation's currency relative to other currencies.

countertrading
A complex form of bartering in which several countries may be involved, each trading goods for goods or services for services.

sea of laws and regulations that are often inconsistent. Antitrust rules, labor relations, patents, copyrights, trade practices, taxes, product liability, child labor, prison labor, and other issues are governed differently country by country.

U.S. businesses must follow U.S. laws and regulations in conducting business globally, although legislation such as the Foreign Corrupt Practices Act of 1978 can create competitive disadvantages. This law prohibits "questionable" or "dubious" payments to foreign officials to secure business contracts.[41] That runs contrary to practices in some countries, where corporate or government bribery is not merely acceptable but perhaps the only way to secure a lucrative contract. The Organization for Economic Cooperation and Development (OECD) and Transparency International have led a global effort to fight corruption and bribery in global business, with limited success.[42] Figure 3.7 shows a partial list of countries where bribery or other unethical business practices are most common.

The cooperation and sponsorship of local businesspeople can help a company penetrate the market and deal with laws, regulations, and bureaucratic barriers in their country.

Physical and Environmental Forces

Physical and environmental forces certainly affect a company's ability to conduct global business. Some developing countries have such primitive transportation and storage systems that international distribution is ineffective, if not impossible, especially for perishable food. Add unclean water and lack of effective sewer systems, and you can see the intensity of the problem.

Technological differences also influence the features of exportable products. For example, residential electrical systems in most developing countries do not match those of U.S. homes, in kind or capacity. Computer and Internet use in many developing countries is thin or nonexistent. These facts make for a tough environment for business in general and for e-commerce in particular. After the Test Prep, we'll explore how another force, trade protectionism, affects global business.

test prep

- What are four major hurdles to successful global trade?
- What does *ethnocentricity* mean, and how can it affect global success?
- How would a low value of the dollar affect U.S. exports?
- What does the Foreign Corrupt Practices Act prohibit?

LO 3–5 Debate the advantages and disadvantages of trade protectionism.

TRADE PROTECTIONISM

As we discussed in the previous section, sociocultural, economic and financial, legal and regulatory, and physical and environmental forces are all challenges to global trade. What is often a much greater barrier to global trade, however, is trade protectionism. **Trade protectionism** is the use of

FIGURE 3.7 COUNTRIES RATED HIGHEST ON CORRUPT BUSINESS

1. Somalia
2. North Korea
3. Afghanistan
4. Sudan
5. South Sudan
6. Libya
7. Iraq
8. Uzbekistan
9. Turkmenistan
10. Syria

Source: Transparency International, 2014.

Use LearnSmart to help retain what you have learned. Access your instructor's Connect course to check out LearnSmart, or go to learnsmartadvantage.com for help.

LEARNSMART

trade protectionism
The use of government regulations to limit the import of goods and services.

Some workers believe that too many U.S. jobs have been lost due to the growing number of imported products. Should governments protect their industries by placing tariffs on imported products? Why or why not?

tariff
A tax imposed on imports.

import quota
A limit on the number of products in certain categories that a nation can import.

embargo
A complete ban on the import or export of a certain product, or the stopping of all trade with a particular country.

government regulations to limit the import of goods and services. Advocates of protectionism believe it allows domestic producers to survive and grow, producing more jobs. Other countries use protectionist measures because they are wary of foreign competition in general. To understand how protectionism affects global business, let's briefly review a bit of global economic history.

Business, economics, and politics have always been closely linked. Economics was once referred to as *political economy*, indicating the close ties between politics (government) and economics. In the 17th and 18th centuries, businesspeople and government leaders endorsed an economic policy called *mercantilism*.[43] The idea was for a nation to sell more goods to other nations than it bought from them, that is, to have a favorable balance of trade. According to mercantilists, this resulted in a flow of money to the country that sold the most globally. The philosophy led governments to implement **tariffs**, taxes on imports, making imported goods more expensive to buy.

There are two kinds of tariffs: protective and revenue. *Protective tariffs* (import taxes) raise the retail price of imported products so that domestic goods are more competitively priced. These tariffs are meant to save jobs for domestic workers and keep industries—especially infant industries that have companies in the early stages of growth—from closing down because of foreign competition. *Revenue tariffs* are designed to raise money for the government.

An **import quota** limits the number of products in certain categories a nation can import. The United States has import quotas on a number of products, including sugar and shrimp, to protect U.S. companies and preserve jobs. Nations also prohibit the export of specific products. Antiterrorism laws and the U.S. Export Administration Act of 1979 prohibit exporting goods such as high-tech weapons that could endanger national security. An **embargo** is a complete ban on the import or export of a certain product, or the stopping of all trade with a particular country. Political disagreements have caused many countries to establish embargoes, such as the U.S. embargo against Cuba, in effect since 1962.

Nontariff barriers are not as specific or formal as tariffs, import quotas, and embargoes but can be as detrimental to free trade.[44] For example, India imposes a number of restrictive standards like import licensing, burdensome product testing requirements, and lengthy customs procedures that inhibit the sale of imported products. China omits many American-made products from its government catalogs that specify what products may be purchased by its huge government sector. Other trade barriers detail exactly how a product must be sold in a country or may insist on local content requirements that require that some part of a product be produced domestically. For example, even though we have a free-trade agreement with South Korea, nontariff barriers still restrict the import of U.S. cars there. Barriers such as the size of the engine and strict emission standards limit the number of U.S. cars that can be sold in the country. South Korea on the other hand sells almost 1.3 million cars to the United States.

Would-be exporters might view such trade barriers as good reasons to avoid global trade, but overcoming constraints creates business opportunities. Next, we'll look at organizations and agreements that attempt to eliminate trade barriers.

The World Trade Organization

In 1948, government leaders from 23 nations formed the **General Agreement on Tariffs and Trade (GATT)**, a global forum for reducing trade restrictions on goods, services, ideas, and cultural programs. In 1986, the Uruguay Round of the GATT convened to renegotiate trade agreements. After eight years of meetings, 124 nations voted to lower tariffs an average of 38 percent worldwide and to expand new trade rules to areas such as agriculture, services, and the protection of patents.

The Uruguay Round also established the **World Trade Organization (WTO)** to mediate trade disputes among nations. The WTO, headquartered in Geneva, is an independent entity of 159 member nations whose purpose is to oversee cross-border trade issues and global business practices.[45] Trade disputes are presented by member nations with decisions made within a year, rather than languishing for years as in the past; member nations can appeal a decision.

The WTO has not solved all global trade problems. Legal and regulatory differences (discussed above) often impede trade expansion. Also a wide gap persists between developing nations (80 percent of the WTO membership) and industrialized nations like the United States. The WTO meetings in Doha, Qatar, begun in 2001 to address dismantling protection of manufactured goods, eliminating subsidies on agricultural products, and overturning temporary protectionist measures, have still not resulted in any significant agreements.[46]

This Indian family used to use bullocks to pull their plow, but had to sell them because the cost to maintain the animals is now too high. Do you think a Doha resolution regarding tariff protection would help families like these?

Common Markets

An issue not resolved by the GATT or the WTO is whether common markets create regional alliances at the expense of global expansion. A **common market** (also called a *trading bloc*) is a regional group of countries with a common external tariff, no internal tariffs, and coordinated laws to facilitate exchange among members. The European Union (EU), Mercosur, the Association of Southeast Asian Nations (ASEAN) Economic Community, and the Common Market for Eastern and Southern Africa (COMESA) are common markets.

The EU began in the late 1950s as an alliance of six trading partners (then known as the Common Market and later the European Economic Community). Today it is a group of 28 nations (see Figure 3.8) with a population of over 500 million and a GDP of $17.2 trillion. Though the EU is represented as a unified body in the WTO, the economies of six members (Germany, France, United Kingdom, Italy, Spain, and the Netherlands) account for over three-fourths of the EU's GDP.

European unification was not easy, but in 1999 the EU took a significant step by adopting the euro as a common currency. The euro has helped EU businesses save billions by eliminating currency conversions and has challenged the U.S. dollar's dominance in global markets. Eighteen member nations now use the euro as their common currency. In 2013, the EU faced debt, deficit, and growth problems due to financial difficulties in member nations Greece, Italy, Portugal, and Spain that required bailout assistance.[47] EU officials moved forward with broad economic policies to ensure the financial stability of the union. Even though the EU faces challenges going

General Agreement on Tariffs and Trade (GATT)
A 1948 agreement that established an international forum for negotiating mutual reductions in trade restrictions.

World Trade Organization (WTO)
The international organization that replaced the General Agreement on Tariffs and Trade and was assigned the duty to mediate trade disputes among nations.

common market
A regional group of countries that have a common external tariff, no internal tariffs, and a coordination of laws to facilitate exchange; also called a *trading bloc*. An example is the European Union.

FIGURE 3.8 MEMBERS OF THE EUROPEAN UNION
Current EU members are highlighted in yellow. Countries that have applied for membership are in orange. Iceland (not shown) is also an EU candidate.

forward, it still considers economic integration among member nations as the way to compete globally against major competitors like the United States and China.

Mercosur unites Brazil, Argentina, Paraguay, Uruguay, Venezuela and associate members Bolivia, Chile, Colombia, Ecuador, and Peru in a trading bloc that encompasses more than 275 million people. The EU and Mercosur have hopes of finalizing a trade agreement in 2014 that would expand the movement of goods and services between the two trading blocs.[48]

The ASEAN Economic Community was established in 1967 in Thailand to create economic cooperation among its five original members (Indonesia, Malaysia, the Philippines, Singapore, and Thailand). ASEAN has expanded to include Brunei, Cambodia, the Lao People's Democratic Republic, Myanmar, and Vietnam, creating a trade association with a population of approximately 620 million and a GDP of $2.2 trillion.[49] COMESA is a 19-member African trading bloc. In 2008, COMESA joined with the Southern African Development Community (SADC) and the East Africa Community (EAC) to form an expanded free-trade zone that has a GDP of $624 billion and a population of 527 million.[50]

The North American and Central American Free Trade Agreements

A widely debated issue of the early 1990s was the **North American Free Trade Agreement (NAFTA)**, which created a free-trade area among the United States, Canada, and Mexico. Opponents warned of the loss of U.S. jobs and capital. Supporters predicted NAFTA would open a vast new market for U.S. exports and create jobs and market opportunities in the long term. In reality,

North American Free Trade Agreement (NAFTA)
Agreement that created a free-trade area among the United States, Canada, and Mexico.

NAFTA did not cause the huge job losses feared by many nor did it achieve the large economic gains predicted.[51]

NAFTA's objectives were to (1) eliminate trade barriers and facilitate cross-border movement of goods and services, (2) promote conditions of fair competition, (3) increase investment opportunities, (4) provide effective protection and enforcement of intellectual property rights (patents and copyrights), (5) establish a framework for further regional trade cooperation, and (6) improve working conditions in North America. Today, the three NAFTA countries have a combined population of over 460 million and a gross domestic product (GDP) of over $18 trillion.

After 20 years in existence, NAFTA remains a debated issue.[52] On the positive side, trade volume in goods and services among the three partners expanded from $289 billion in 1994 to over $1.2 trillion today. However, the major gains in trade were in the early years of the agreement.[53] On the negative side, in the United States, of the 680,000 manufacturing jobs that have been lost since enacting NAFTA in 1994, many were lost to Mexico. In Mexico, promises to close the wage gap with the U.S., boost job growth, fight poverty, and improve environmental controls have largely failed.[54] Illegal immigration remains a major problem between the two nations. Still, NAFTA controversies have not changed the U.S. commitment to free-trade agreements.

In 2005 the Central American Free Trade Agreement (CAFTA) was signed into law, creating a free-trade zone with Costa Rica, the Dominican Republic, El Salvador, Guatemala, Honduras, and Nicaragua. The United States is also considering an agreement with eleven Pacific-Rim nations called the Trans-Pacific Partnership and a massive free-trade deal with the EU called the Transatlantic Trade and Investment Partnership.[55]

Common markets and free-trade areas will be debated far into the future. While some economists resoundingly praise such efforts, others are concerned the world is dividing into major trading blocs (EU, NAFTA, etc.) that will exclude poor and developing nations. After the Test Prep, we'll look at the future of global trade and address the issue of outsourcing.

test prep

- What are the advantages and disadvantages of trade protectionism and of tariffs?
- What is the primary purpose of the WTO?
- What is the key objective of a common market like the EU?
- What three nations comprise NAFTA?

Use LearnSmart to help retain what you have learned. Access your instructor's Connect course to check out LearnSmart, or go to learnsmartadvantage.com for help.

≣ILEARNSMART

LO 3–6   Discuss the changing landscape of the global market and the issue of offshore outsourcing.

THE FUTURE OF GLOBAL TRADE

Global trade opportunities grow more interesting and more challenging each day. After all, over 7 billion potential customers are attractive. However, terrorism, nuclear proliferation, rogue states, income inequality, and other issues cast a dark shadow on global markets. Let's conclude this chapter by looking at issues certain to influence global markets, and perhaps your business career.

With more than 1.3 billion people and incredible exporting prowess, China has transformed the world economic map. China is the world's largest exporter and the second largest economy. Its rise has happened over a relatively short period of time, with the value of Chinese trade roughly doubling every four years over the last three decades.[56] Not long ago, foreign direct investment in China was considered risky and not worth the risk. In 2013, China attracted $117 billion in foreign direct investment.[57] Today, over 400 of the Fortune 500 companies (the world's largest companies) have invested in China. According to Goldman Sachs Group and the London Center for Economic and Business Research, China could overtake the United States as the world's largest economy by 2028.[58]

Since 2009 China has been the largest motor vehicle market in the world with sales and production topping nearly 22 million vehicles in 2013.[59] It's estimated that by 2030, there could be more cars on the road in China than all the cars in the world today. Walmart began operations in China in 1996 and now has over 390 stores with plans to open more. Even newcomers like IMAX Corporation are expanding in this fast-growing market. IMAX currently has 150 movie theaters with plans to grow to 400 by 2018.

Many view China as a free trader's dream, where global investment and entrepreneurship will lead to wealth. However, concerns remain about China's one-party political system, human rights abuses, currency issues, and increasing urban population growth. China's underground economy also generates significant product piracy and counterfeiting, although the country has been more responsive to these problems since its admission to the WTO. With the global economy continuing to grow, China will be a key driver of the world economy along with the United States, the EU, and Japan.

While China attracts most of the attention in Asia, India's population of 1.2 billion presents a tremendous opportunity. With nearly 575 million of its population under 25, India's working-age population will continue to grow while the United States, China, and the EU expect a decline in the 2020s. Already India has seen huge growth in information technology and biotechnology, and its pharmaceutical business is expected to grow to $30 billion, a jump of over 150 percent by 2020. Still, it remains a nation with difficult trade laws and an inflexible bureaucracy.[60]

China's economy is booming, and a highly educated middle class with money to spend is emerging, especially in the cities. Many observers believe China will continue its growth and play a major role in the global economy. Are U.S. firms prepared to compete?

Russia is an industrialized nation with large reserves of oil, gas, and gold that became a member of the WTO in 2012. Multinationals like Chevron, ExxonMobil, and BP have invested heavily in developing Russia's oil reserves. However, Russia's economy slowed when world oil prices declined and the government admitted that growth prospects for the economy were not strong for the next two decades.[61] Unfortunately, Russia is plagued by political, currency, and social problems and is considered by Transparency International as the world's most corrupt major economy.

Brazil is an emerging nation that along with China, India, and Russia was projected to be one of the wealthier global economies by 2030. In fact, the term *BRIC* has been used as an acronym for the economies of Brazil, Russia, India, and China. Today, Brazil is the largest economy in South America and the seventh-largest economy in the world with well-developed agriculture, mining, manufacturing, and service sectors. Along with Russia, Brazil was expected to dominate the global market as a supplier of raw materials. China and India were predicted to be leading global suppliers of manufactured goods and services. Unfortunately, the past few years have been tough times for Brazil's economy with growing inflation and slow growth. Still, its growing consumer market of over 200 million people is a target for major exporters like the United States and China.

The *BRIC* economies are certainly not the only areas of opportunity in the global market. The developing nations of Asia, including Indonesia, Thailand, Singapore, the Philippines, Korea, Malaysia, and Vietnam, also offer great potential for U.S. businesses. Africa, especially South Africa, has only begun to emerge as a center for global economic growth. Business today is truly global and your role in it is up to you.

The Challenge of Offshore Outsourcing

Outsourcing, as noted in Chapter 1, is the process whereby one firm contracts with other companies, often in other countries, to do some or all of its functions. In the United States, companies have outsourced payroll functions, accounting, and some manufacturing operations for many years. However, the shift to primarily low-wage global markets, called *offshore outsourcing*, remains a major issue in the United States. This is especially true as the growth in U.S. jobs has lagged since the financial crisis began in 2008. Take a look at the pros and cons of offshore outsourcing in Figure 3.9.

As lower-level manufacturing became more simplified, U.S. companies such as Levi Strauss and Nike outsourced manufacturing offshore. Today, economists suggest, we have moved into the "second wave" of offshore outsourcing, shifting from product assembly to design and architecture. This process has proved more disruptive to the U.S. job market than the first, which primarily affected manufacturing jobs. Today, increasing numbers of skilled, educated, middle-income workers in service-sector jobs such as accounting, law, finance, risk management, health care, and information technology have seen their jobs outsourced offshore. While loss of jobs is a major concern, it's not the only worry. Nations such as China have a spotty safety record in manufacturing toys, food, and drugs. Today, concerns are mounting about companies like Medtronic and Siemens shifting production of sensitive medical devices such as MRI and CT machines to China. IBM is setting up research facilities in offshore locations. U.S. airlines have even outsourced airline maintenance to countries such as El Salvador. India at one time was the center for telemarketing, data entry, call centers, billing, and low-end software development. Today—with its well-educated, deep pool of scientists, software engineers, chemists, accountants, lawyers, and physicians—India is providing more sophisticated services. For

FIGURE 3.9 THE PROS AND CONS OF OFFSHORE OUTSOURCING

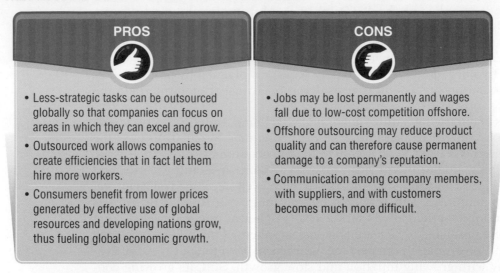

example, radiologists from Wipro Health Science read CAT scans and MRIs for many U.S. hospitals. Some medical providers are shifting surgical procedures to India and other nations. The nearby Making Ethical Decisions box offers an interesting ethical question about this process.

As technical talent grows around the globe, offshore outsourcing will increase. To stay competitive, education and training will be critical for U.S. workers to preserve the skill premium they possess today and to stay ahead in the future.

Globalization and Your Future

Whether you aspire to be an entrepreneur, a manager, or some other type of business leader, think globally in planning your career. By studying foreign languages, learning about foreign cultures, and taking business courses (including a global business course), you can develop a global perspective on your future. As you progress through this text, keep two things in mind: globalization is real, and economic competition promises to intensify.

Also keep in mind that global market potential does not belong only to large, multinational corporations. Small and medium-sized businesses have a world of opportunity in front of them. In fact, these firms are often better prepared to leap into global markets and react quickly to opportunities than are large businesses. Finally, don't forget the potential of franchising, which we examine in more detail in Chapter 5.

Use LearnSmart to help retain what you have learned. Access your instructor's Connect course to check out LearnSmart, or go to learnsmartadvantage.com for help.

test prep

- What are the major threats to doing business in global markets?
- What key challenges must India and Russia face before becoming global economic leaders?
- What does the acronym *BRIC* stand for?
- What are the two primary concerns associated with offshore outsourcing?

making **ethical decisions**

Making Your Operation Your Vacation

The Affordable Care Act (ACA) may bring some relief to astronomical insurance costs. But as premiums continue to rise at home, overseas in countries like Thailand, Colombia, and India, health care is not only affordable, it's also high quality. For instance, in the United States it would cost Patrick Follett, an avid skier, at least $65,000 for his hip replacement surgery. Unlike some Americans, Follett had medical insurance and would have part of the procedure covered. However, it would have still cost him at least $10,000 out-of-pocket. Follett, like 1.6 million other Americans, started looking for treatment elsewhere. In March of 2012, he underwent surgery in Mexico and was back on the California ski slopes in March of 2013. His total bill: $10,000, all of which was covered by his company.

Right now, few American companies include medical tourism in their health care plans, but some of the larger companies like Aetna and WellPoint are working with companies to include international coverage. It's even expected to become a booming industry with worldwide annual growth estimated between 20 and 30 percent. Would it be ethical to force patients to travel thousands of miles and be separated from friends and family in a time of crisis in order to save money?

Sources: Medical Tourism Association, "Medical Tourism Sample Surgery Cost Chart," www.medicaltourismassociation.com/en/for-patients.html, accessed March 2014; Kevin Gray, "Medical Tourism: Overseas and Under the Knife," *Men's Journal,* November 2013; and Elisabeth Rosenthal "The Growing Popularity of Having Surgery Overseas," *The New York Times,* August 6, 2013.

summary

LO 3–1 Discuss the importance of the global market and the roles of comparative advantage and absolute advantage in global trade.

- **Why should nations trade with other nations?**
  (1) No country is self-sufficient, (2) other countries need products that prosperous countries produce, and (3) natural resources and technological skills are not distributed evenly around the world.

- **What is the theory of comparative advantage?**
  The theory of comparative advantage contends that a country should make and then sell those products it produces most efficiently but buy those it cannot produce as efficiently.

- **What is absolute advantage?**
  Absolute advantage exists if a country produces a specific product more efficiently than any other country. There are few examples of absolute advantage in the global market today.

LO 3–2 Explain the importance of importing and exporting, and understand key terms used in global business.

- **What kinds of products can be imported and exported?**
  Though it is not necessarily easy, just about any product can be imported or exported.

- **What terms are important in understanding world trade?**
  Exporting is selling products to other countries. *Importing* is buying products from other countries. The *balance of trade* is the relationship of exports to imports. The *balance of payments* is the balance of trade plus

other money flows such as tourism and foreign aid. *Dumping* is selling products for less in a foreign country than in your own country. See the Key Terms list after this Summary to be sure you know the other important terms.

LO 3–3   Illustrate the strategies used in reaching global markets and explain the role of multinational corporations.

- **What are some ways in which a company can engage in global business?**
  Ways of entering world trade include licensing, exporting, franchising, contract manufacturing, joint ventures and strategic alliances, and direct foreign investment.

- **How do multinational corporations differ from other companies that participate in global business?**
  Unlike companies that only export or import, multinational corporations also have manufacturing facilities or other physical presence abroad.

LO 3–4   Evaluate the forces that affect trading in global markets.

- **What are some of the forces that can discourage participation in global business?**
  Potential stumbling blocks to global trade include sociocultural forces, economic and financial forces, legal and regulatory forces, and physical and environmental forces.

LO 3–5   Debate the advantages and disadvantages of trade protectionism.

- **What is trade protectionism?**
  Trade protectionism is the use of government regulations to limit the import of goods and services. Advocates believe it allows domestic producers to grow, producing more jobs. The key tools of protectionism are tariffs, import quotas, and embargoes.

- **What are tariffs?**
  Tariffs are taxes on foreign products. Protective tariffs raise the price of foreign products and protect domestic industries; revenue tariffs raise money for the government.

- **What is an embargo?**
  An embargo prohibits the importing or exporting of certain products.

- **Is trade protectionism good for domestic producers?**
  That is debatable. Trade protectionism offers pluses and minuses.

- **Why do governments continue such practices?**
  The theory of mercantilism started the practice of trade protectionism and it has persisted, though in a weaker form, ever since.

LO 3–6   Discuss the changing landscape of the global market and the issue of offshore outsourcing.

- **What is offshore outsourcing? Why is it a major concern for the future?**
  Outsourcing is the purchase of goods and services from outside a firm rather than providing them inside the company. Today, more businesses are outsourcing manufacturing and services offshore. Many fear that growing numbers of jobs in the United States will be lost due to offshore outsourcing and that the quality of products produced could be inferior.

Access your instructor's Connect course to check out LearnSmart or go to learnsmartadvantage.com for help.

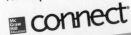

critical thinking

1. About 95 percent of the world's population lives outside the United States, but many U.S. companies, especially small businesses, still do not engage in global trade. Why not? Do you think more small businesses will participate in global trade in the future? Why or why not?

2. Countries like the United States that have a high standard of living are referred to as *industrialized nations.* Countries with a lower standard of living and quality of life are called *developing countries* (or *underdeveloped* or *less developed countries*). What factors prevent developing nations from becoming industrialized nations?

3. What can businesses do to prevent unexpected problems in dealing with sociocultural, economic and financial, legal and regulatory, and physical and environmental forces in global markets?

4. How would you justify the use of revenue or protective tariffs in today's global market?

developing **workplace skills**

Key: ● **Team**   ★ **Analytic**   ▲ **Communication**   ▣ **Technology**

1. Find out firsthand the global impact on your life. How many different ▲ countries' names appear on the labels in your clothes? How many languages do your classmates speak? List the ethnic restaurants in your community. Are they family-owned or corporate chains?

2. Call, e-mail, or visit a local business that imports foreign goods (perhaps a ▲★ wine or specialty foods importer). Ask the owner or manager about the business's participation in global trade, and compile a list of the advantages and disadvantages he or she cites. Compare notes with your classmates about their research.

3. Visit four or five public locations in your community such as schools, hospitals, city/county buildings, or airports. See how many signs are posted in ★ different languages (don't forget the restrooms) and look for other multilingual information, such as brochures or handouts. Do any of the locations fly flags from different nations? In what other ways do they recognize

the diversity of employees or students? What does your search tell you about your community?

 4. Suppose Representative I. M. Wright delivers a passionate speech at your college on tariffs. He argues tariffs are needed to
   a. Protect our young industries.
   b. Encourage consumers to buy U.S.-made products because it's patriotic.
   c. Protect U.S. jobs and wages.
   d. Achieve a favorable balance of trade and balance of payments.

   Do you agree with Representative Wright? Evaluate each of his major points and decide whether you consider it valid. Be sure to justify your position.

5. Form an imaginary joint venture with three classmates and select a product, service, or idea to market to a specific country. Have each team member select a key global market force in that country (sociocultural, economic and financial, legal and regulatory, or physical and environmental) to research. Have each report his or her findings. Then, as a group, prepare a short explanation of whether the market is worth pursuing.

taking it to the net

PURPOSE

To compare the shifting exchange rates of various countries and to predict the effects of such exchange shifts on global trade.

EXERCISE

One of the difficulties of engaging in global trade is the constant shift in exchange rates. How much do exchange rates change over a 30-day period? Research this by choosing five currencies (say, the euro, the British pound, the Japanese yen, the Mexican peso, the Saudi Arabian riyal) and recording their exchange rates relative to the U.S. dollar for 30 days. The rates are available on the Internet at Yahoo Finance's Currency Center (http://finance.yahoo.com/currency). At the end of the tracking period, choose a company and describe what effects the currency shifts you noted might have on this company's trade with each of the countries or areas whose currency you chose.

video case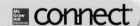

ELECTRA BICYCLE COMPANY

Doing business in global markets can be tricky, but the benefits that come from overseas success justify much of the risk. That's what Electra Bicycle Company's founders discovered after their business's growth suddenly halted. Throughout the early 2000s, many bicycle manufacturers concentrated on producing mountain and speed bikes while discontinuing casual models. Benno Baziger and Jeano Erforth of Electra didn't follow the fad, though, choosing instead to stick with cool, upright bikes perfect for cruising city streets.

The company thrived for years thanks to their unique "comfort bikes." However, major competitors like Schwinn eventually took notice and began making their own sleek street bikes. Electra's explosive growth halted, and the company's two founders searched for a solution. To grow further, the pair knew they would have to enter the global marketplace. They went on a search for places where their vintage sense of style and up-to-date technology would give them a comparative advantage against their bigger competitors.

Electra eventually settled on Taiwan as the site for its overseas manufacturing site. From Taiwan, the California-based company can simply export bikes to neighboring Asian countries like China where bikes are most popular. They can in turn feed their domestic demand by importing bikes into the U.S., a practice that is actually cheaper for Electra than producing bikes on their home soil. This outsourcing of production to a foreign manufacturing plant helps Electra keep its costs down. If labor costs increase or instability flares up between Taiwan and China, Electra could move its production to a less turbulent location.

Such unexpected problems represent just a few of the hurdles companies can face when they go global. For example, laws against motorized bikes forced Electra to tweak the design for its Townie Go model in order to make the bike acceptable in some foreign markets. Despite these issues, global commerce puts companies on the radar of millions of new customers. This immense access can make all the additional effort needed for going global worth it. In fact, Electra now sells more than 100,000 bikes each year.

Electra's success eventually brought it to the attention of Trek, a multinational corporation with offices in Wisconsin, the UK, and Germany. The conglomerate bought Electra, which can now use Trek's established distribution network to reach new markets more quickly and effectively. Letting their parent company worry about matters like capitalization and manufacturing infrastructure allows Electra to focus on other things, such as designing stylish bikes that are easy to ride and fun to own by people all over the world.

THINKING IT OVER

1. What major advantages did Electra gain by using a contract manufacturer in Taiwan to produce its bikes?

2. When Electra produced its bikes in Taiwan, did the company have to follow the laws of Taiwan or the laws of the United States?

3. What major forces impact Electra (or any global producer) in trading in global markets?

notes

1. Robert J. Thomas, Joshua Bellin, Claudy Jules, and Nandani Lynton, "Developing Tomorrow's Global Leaders," *Sloan Management Review,* Fall 2013; and Gregory C. Unruh and Angel Cabera, "Join the Global Elite," *Harvard Business Review,* May 2013.

2. "World Population Clock," U.S. Census Bureau, www.census.gov/ipc/www/popclockworld.html, accessed April 2014; and WorldAtlas.com, accessed April 2014.

3. Russell Flannery, "What Can be Done about the Big U.S. Trade Deficit with China?" *Forbes,* August 3, 2013; and Paul Davidson, "U.S. Trade Deficit Drops to 4-Year Low," *USA Today,* January 7, 2014.

4. *UPS.com,* accessed April 23, 2014; *Walmart.com,* accessed April 23, 2014; and Janice Kew, "Walmart Brand Favored in Massmarts Africa Growth," *Bloomberg Personal Finance,* April 16, 2013.

5. Ira Boudway, "Soccer Will Not Stop Arriving," *Bloomberg Businessweek,* January 2, 2014.

6. Pamela McClintock and Stuart Kemp, "The 21 Surprising Hollywood Actors Whose Names Sell Movies Overseas," *The Hollywood Reporter,* September 12, 2013.

7. World Bank, www.worldbank.org, accessed April 2014; World Trade Organization, www.wto.org, accessed April 2014; and Gordon Chang, "Is China Really the World's No. 1 Trader?" *Forbes,* January 12, 2014.

8. Matthew J. Slaughter, "Exports Sagging? Try Some Free Trade," *The Wall Street Journal,* January 23, 2013.

9. "Free Trade and Secrecy Don't Mix," *Bloomberg Businessweek,* December 1, 2013.

10. Joshua Kurlantzick, "Farewell to the Age of Free Trade," *Bloomberg Businessweek,* December 22, 2013.

11. Robert Skidelsky, "In a World Based on Free Trade, Love Will Cost You," *Global Times,* January 23, 2014.

12. Donald Lessard, Rafael Lucea, and Luis Vives, "Building Your Company's Capabilities Through Global Expansion," *MIT Sloan Management Review,* Winter 2013.

13. International Trade Administration, www.trade.gov, accessed April 2014.

14. Bryan Lowry, Tanvi Misra, and Katie Peralta, "U.S. Exports Rise but Are Likely to Fall Short of Obama's Goal," *McClatchy DC,* December 30, 2013.

15. Alexandra Wolfe, "Howard Schultz: What Next Starbucks?" *The Wall Street Journal,* September 27, 2013.

16. Greg Kitsock, "Beer: Brewers Find It Can Be Bright in Helles," *The Washington Post,* January 7, 2014.

17. Carolyn Berg, "Holding a Mirror to China's Economy Through Cosmetics," *China Daily USA,* October 15, 2013.

18. C. Fred Bergston, "How Best to Boost U.S. Exports," *The Washington Post,* February 3, 2010; and Barry Wood, "An Interview with C. Fred Bergsten, Evangelist for the Open Economy," *The Washington Post,* April 19, 2013.

19. Paul Davidson, "U.S. Trade Deficit Drops to 4-Year Low," *USA Today,* January 7, 2014; and Rob Hotakainen, "U.S. Exports on Record Pace but So Is Trade Deficit with China," *Miami Herald,* January 7, 2014.

20. www.goldmarks.com, accessed April 2014.

21. www.Export.gov, accessed April 2014; and www.sba.gov, accessed April 2014.

22. "Rocky Mountain Chocolate Factory, Inc. Reports Improved Third Quarter Operating Results," *The Wall Street Journal,* January 21, 2014.

23. "Yum Brands' World Hunger Relief Efforts Result in Record-Breaking $37 Million in Cash and Food Donations," *The Wall Street Journal,* January 9, 2014.

24. AnnaLisa Kraft, "Crazy Food You Can't Get Here," *The Motley Fool,* January 4, 2014.

25. Flextronics, www.flextronics.com, accessed May 2012.
26. Zhou Wenting, "Full Steam Ahead for Shanghai Disney in 2015," *China Daily USA,* January 24, 2014.
27. Alby Gallum, "European Hotel Chain Coming to River North," *Crain Chicago Business,* January 24, 2014.
28. "Pepsi Announces Plans for $5 Billion Investment in Mexico," *The Wall Street Journal,* January 24, 2014.
29. Sean D. Hamill, "How UPMC's Overseas Operation Blossomed in 14 Years," *Pittsburgh Post-Gazette,* May 30, 2010; and University of Pittsburgh Medical Center, www.upmc.com, accessed April 2014.
30. *CNNMoney,* www.cnnmoney.com, accessed April 2014; and Nestlé, www.nestle.com, accessed 2014.
3 1. Vivienne Walt, "Norway's Trillion Dollar Oil Problem," *Fortune Magazine,* January 16, 2014.
32. Ashley Stahl, "The Promise and Perils of Sovereign Wealth Funds," *Forbes,* December 19, 2013; and "More Money than Thor," *The Economist,* September 14, 2013.
33. Susan Bergfield, "4 Countries Walmart Can't Conquer," *MSN Money,* October 15, 2013; Walter Loeb, "Walmart: What Happened in India?" *Forbes,* October 16, 2013; and Agustino Fontevecchia, "IBM Falls Off Cliff as Q3 Sales Fall on Services and Hardware Weakness," *Forbes,* October 16, 2013.
34. Nikhul Gulati and Rumman Ahmed, "India Has 1.2 Billion People but Not Enough Drink Coke," *The Wall Street Journal,* July 13, 2012; and Coca-Cola, www.cocacola.com, accessed April 2014.
35. "In Dollars They Trust," *The Economist,* April 27, 2013.
36. Simon Kennedy, "Developed Economies Seen Fighting Off Emerging Market Contagion," *Bloomberg Businessweek,* January 27, 2014.
37. H.B. Fuller, www.hbfuller.com, accessed April 2014.
38. Taos Turner, Ken Parks, and Juan Foreno, "Crisis Squeeze Two Latin Leaders," *The Wall Street Journal,* January 26, 2014; and Jonathan Gilbert, Simon Romero, and William Neuman, "Erosian of Argentine Peso Sends a Shudder Through Latin America," *The New York Times,* January 24, 2014.
39. Christina LeBeau, "Rules of the Trade," *Entrepreneur,* February 2014.
40. www.wto.com, accessed April 2014.
4 1. Crayton Harrison, "Hewlett-Packard in Advanced Talks to Resolve U.S. Bribery Probes," *Bloomberg Businessweek,* December 30, 2013; and Chris Isidore, "SEC Expands Probe into Overseas Hiring by U.S. Banks," *CNN Money,* November 27, 2013.
42. Alexandra Wrage, "What Companies Can't Do about Corruption," *Forbes,* January 24, 2014.
43. "What Was Mercantilism?" *The Economist,* August 23, 2013; and Nathan Lewis, "Keynes and Rottbard Agreed: Today's Economics Is Mercantilism," *Forbes,* January 23, 2014.
44. "The Hidden Persuaders: Protectionism Can Take Many Forms, Not All of Them Obvious," *The Economist,* October 12, 2013.

45. www.wto.org, accessed April 2014; and "Unaccustomed Victory," *The Economist,* December 14, 2013.
46. David Nicklaus, "WTO Talks Could Boost Trade by $1 Trillion," *St. Louis Post Dispatch,* December 8, 2013; and "Life After Doha," *The Economist,* December 14, 2013.
47. Emma Ross Thomas,"EU Says Spain Should Improve Bank Monitoring as Bailout Ends," *Bloomberg Businessweek,* January 29, 2014; and Juergen Baetz, "EU Seeks to Make Mega-Banks Less Risky," *Bloomberg Businessweek,* January 29, 2014.
48. "EU-Mercosur Trade Talks: Strategic Patience Runs Out," *The Economist,* December 14, 2013; and Uruguay: CFK Must Improve EU Trade Offer," *Buenos Aires Herald,* January 22, 2014.
49. Association of Southeast Asian Nations, www.aseansec.org, accessed April 2014.
50. Common Market for Eastern and Southern Africa, www.comesa.int, accessed April 2014.
5 1. "Briefing NAFTA at 20: Ready to Take Off Again?" *The Economist,* January 4, 2014; and Mark Glassman, "NAFTA 20 Years After: Neither Miracle nor Disaster," *Bloomberg Businessweek,* December 30, 2013.
52. "Deeper, Better, NAFTA," *The Economist,* January 4, 2014.
53. www.uschamber.com, accessed April 2014; and "Deeper, Better, NAFTA."
54. Mark Stevenson, "20 Years after NAFTA, a Changed Mexico," *The Boston Globe,* January 3, 2014; and Alfredo Conchado, "20 Years after NAFTA, Mexico Has Transformed," *The Dallas Morning News,* January 1, 2014.
55. "Free Trade Deals such as the Trans-Pacific Partnership Help the United States," *The Washington Post,* January 16, 2014; and Christian Oliver and Shawn Donnan, "Brussels Wants Finance Rules Back in the U.S. Trade Pact," *Financial Times,* January 27, 2014.
56. Jamil Anderlini and Lucy Hornby, "China Overtakes U.S. as World's Largest Goods Trader," *Financial Times,* January 10, 2014.
57. Liyan Qi and Grace Zhu, "China's Capital Inflows, Foreign Direct Investment Rose in 2013," *The Wall Street Journal,* January 16, 2014.
58. www.goldmansachs.com, accessed April 2014; and Morris Beschloss, "Will China Overtake U.S. GDP World Leadership by 2028?" *The Desert Sun (Gannett),* January 23, 2014.
59. Samuel Shen and Norihiko Shirozu, "China Auto Market Seen Cruising to Another Strong Year," *Reuters,* January 12, 2014.
60. "Can India Become a Great Power?" *The Economist,* March 30, 2013; and Philip Stephens, "India Still a Contender in the Asian Race," *Financial Times,* January 30, 2014.
61. Paul Hannon, "EBRD Reduces Investment in Russia," *The Wall Street Journal,* January 15, 2014; and Mark Adomanis, "Russia's Economic Performance Is Actually Very Similar to Other East European Countries," *Forbes,* January 20, 2014.

Page 61: Postcode Lottery Green Challenge/Creative Commons, https://www.flickr.com/photos/post-codelotterygreenchallenge/8202992042; p. 63: © Sang Tan/AP Images; p. 65: Peter Rivera/Creative Commons, https://www.flickr.com/photos/riverap1/3258668503; p. 68: © Rex Features/AP Images; p.69: Courtesy of Domino's Pizza;

p. 70: © Andrey Rudakov/Bloomberg/Getty Images; p. 71: © imago stock&people/Newscom; p. 74: Courtesy of Yao Family Winery, © George Rose Photography; p. 76: © Eyecandy Images/age fotostock RF; p. 78: © Tom Williams/Roll Call/Getty Images; p. 79: © Sam Panthaky/AFP/Getty Images; p. 82: © Imaginechina/Corbis.

4

Demanding Ethical and Socially Responsible Behavior

Learning Objectives

AFTER YOU HAVE READ AND STUDIED THIS CHAPTER, YOU SHOULD BE ABLE TO

LO 4-1   Explain why obeying the law is only the first step in behaving ethically.

LO 4-2   Ask the three questions you need to answer when faced with a potentially unethical action.

LO 4-3   Describe management's role in setting ethical standards.

LO 4-4   Distinguish between compliance-based and integrity-based ethics codes, and list the six steps in setting up a corporate ethics code.

LO 4-5   Define *corporate social responsibility* and compare corporations' responsibilities to various stakeholders.

LO 4-6   Analyze the role of U.S. businesses in influencing ethical behavior and social responsibility in global markets.

Getting to Know **Patty Stonesifer**

Figuring out the next step to take after leaving a long-held job can be difficult for anyone. But what if your previous position had been leading the largest charitable organization in human history? That's the situation Patty Stonesifer found herself in after stepping down as CEO of the Bill & Melinda Gates Foundation.

For more than 10 years Stonesifer stood at the head of 500 employees and a $39 billion endowment. She used those resources to tackle some of the world's biggest problems, such as eliminating diseases like malaria and polio as well as reducing the U.S. high school dropout rate. Stonesifer played a major part in establishing the foundation's lofty goals. "When we were starting up the Gates Foundation, it meant envisioning the world as we thought it should be and setting our own vision accordingly. Everyone should have the opportunity for a healthy and productive life," says Stonesifer. "Big moves ahead start with big visions." Before taking charge of the foundation, Stonesifer spent more than 20 years at Gates's company Microsoft, rising to the position of vice president in charge of consumer products.

But two decades working for the same company followed by 10 years of trying to solve the most complicated issues on the planet eventually wore Stonesifer down. She left the Gates Foundation in 2008 to become an independent consultant for businesses and nonprofits interested in strategies for reducing inequality. In 2010 President Obama appointed her as the chair of the White House Council for Community Solutions. In fact, at the time there was even talk that she would be appointed as the president's domestic policy advisor. After years of high-level dealing, however, Stonesifer was looking for more hands-on work. "I would love to call my mother and tell her, 'Mom, I'm president of such-and-such,' a university or a great NGO [nongovernmental organization] or a corporation," says Stonesifer. "But when I sat and really thought about what I wanted to do, I realized that the only job I was interested in would be one

that would put me very close to the front lines, to go beyond white papers and PowerPoint presentations and get my boots dirty."

In 2013 Stonesifer shocked the business world by accepting the CEO position at Martha's Table, a Washington, DC–based nonprofit. The organization focuses on empowering local residents by providing healthy food, affordable clothing, and quality education. In the eyes of many businesspeople, for a person with Stonesifer's experience to join a small nonprofit would be as if Lebron James quit the NBA to coach basketball at his old high school. "If you just look at my résumé, I find that I have to explain this," says Stonesifer. "But if you know me, I don't have to explain it at all." As the sixth of nine children in a religious family, Stonesifer understands the importance of placing the needs of others before her own. "Our family didn't talk about volunteerism. It was just baked in," says Stonesifer. "We went down and put the new missals in the church pews, and we volunteered at the Sunday soup kitchen, and we went with my dad to pick up the deaf children for church." Stonesifer's good works have won her many awards, including two honorary doctorates to go with her bachelor's degree from Indiana University.

Although they may not receive as much media attention as fraudulent businesspeople, ethical entrepreneurs like Patty Stonesifer are the backbone of the business world. In this chapter, we explore the responsibility of businesses to their stakeholders, including customers, investors, employees, and society.

We look at the responsibilities of individuals as well. After all, responsible business behavior depends on the integrity of each person in the business.

Sources: Steve Hendrix, "Patty Stonesifer, Former CEO of Gates Foundation, to Lead D.C. Food Pantry," *The Washington Post,* January 29, 2013; Maureen Dowd, "She's Getting Her Boots Dirty," *The New York Times,* June 1, 2013; and "A Q&A with Patty Stonesifer, President and CEO, Martha's Table," *Washington Business Journal,* June 6, 2013.

Patty Stonesifer
- CEO of Martha's Table
- Washington, DC, nonprofit
- Provides food, clothes, and education to those in need

www.marthastable.org

@MarthasTableorg

93

The wage and benefit packages offered by this company are among the best in hourly retail. Even part-time workers are covered by its health plan. Increased benefits reduce employee turnover to less than a third of the industry average. Name that company. (Find the answer in the chapter.)

LO 4–1   Explain why obeying the law is only the first step in behaving ethically.

ETHICS IS MORE THAN LEGALITY

In the early 2000s, the U.S. public was shocked to learn that Enron, the giant energy trading company, had created off-the-books partnerships to unlawfully hide its debts and losses. The Enron disgrace was soon followed by more scandals at major companies such as WorldCom, Tyco International, ImClone, HealthSouth, and Boeing. (See the nearby Making Ethical Decisions box for a brief summary of one of the more notorious corruption cases.) In recent years, greedy borrowers and lenders alike were among those who brought the real estate, mortgage, and banking industries to the edge of a financial crisis that threatened the entire U.S. and world economies.[1]

Given the ethical lapses prevalent today, how can we restore trust in the free-market system and in leaders in general? First, those who have broken the law should be punished accordingly. New laws making accounting records more transparent (easy to read and understand) and businesspeople and others more accountable for their actions may also help. But laws alone don't make people honest, reliable, or truthful. If they did, crime would disappear.

Mortgage giant Fannie Mae paid the SEC $400 million to settle charges of misstating financial statements. The SEC filed a civil suit in 2011 charging three former top executives with securities fraud for misleading investors about the volume of higher-risk mortgage loans it held during the financial crisis.

Bernie Madoff's Ponzi Scheme

News stories of corporate fraud and corruption are all too common. White-collar criminals often assume the complexity of the financial system will hide their crimes, leaving them free to embezzle to their heart's content. But people tend to notice when a few billion dollars suddenly go missing. Eventually, even the most careful corporate criminals get caught.

When the credit crisis hit in 2008, it unexpectedly exposed one of history's most shameful financial felons. For many years, Bernie Madoff ran his exclusive wealth management firm as a gigantic Ponzi scheme. Legitimate money managers invest their clients' money in various ventures and pay them back on their returns, minus a commission. With a Ponzi scheme, however, the fraudsters don't invest the money. They simply pass money contributed by new investors on to early investors (minus a healthy sum held back for their own personal use, of course), claiming the money as profits from the existing clients' "investments." The steady income fools the investors into thinking their wealth is growing when in reality it is being siphoned off from other people. Obviously the scheme depends upon being able to continuously attract new "investors."

Once the bubble burst on Wall Street, everything fell apart for Madoff. He confessed his crimes to his sons, who then contacted the police. Though exact estimates are still uncertain, Madoff swindled approximately $65 billion from his investors, including $20 billion in cash losses that can never be recovered. A judge sentenced Madoff to 150 years behind bars with no chance of parole. Do you think the punishment fit the crime in this case?

Sources: James Sterngold, "Unraveling the Lies Madoff Told," *The Wall Street Journal*, December 10, 2013; Diana B. Henriques, "Madoff Victims, Five Years the Wiser," *The New York Times*, December 7, 2013; and Erik Larson, "Madoff Ex-Aide Knew of Scheme to Pay His Son, Jury Told," *Bloomberg Businessweek*, January 22, 2014.

While the number of accounting fraud cases pursued by the Securities and Exchange Commission (SEC) fell from its typical level of more than 25 percent of the SEC's enforcement efforts before the Great Recession to just 11 percent in 2013, experts predict this number will rise in the near future. Why? One reason is that new data mining technology will allow the SEC to more easily identify companies that may be making earnings misstatements.[2]

One danger in writing new laws to correct behavior is that people may begin to think that any behavior that is within the law is also acceptable. The measure of behavior then becomes "Is it legal?" A society gets into trouble when people consider only what is illegal and not also what is unethical. Ethics and legality are two very different things. Although following the law is an important first step, behaving ethically requires more than that. Ethics reflects people's proper relationships with one another: How should we treat others? What responsibility should we feel for others? Legality is narrower. It refers to laws we have written to protect ourselves from fraud, theft, and violence. Many immoral and unethical acts fall well within our laws. For example, gossiping about your neighbor or sharing something told to you in confidence is unethical, but not illegal.

Ethical Standards Are Fundamental

ethics
Standards of moral behavior, that is, behavior accepted by society as right versus wrong.

We define **ethics** as society's accepted standards of moral behavior, that is, behaviors accepted by society as right rather than wrong. Many Americans today have few moral absolutes. Many decide situationally whether it's OK to steal, lie, or text and drive. They seem to think that what is right is whatever works best for the individual—that each person has to work out for himself or herself the difference between right and wrong. Such thinking may be part of the behavior that has led to scandals in government and business.

This isn't the way it always was. When Thomas Jefferson wrote that all men have the right to life, liberty, and the pursuit of happiness, he declared it to be a self-evident truth. Going back even further in time, the Ten Commandments were not called the "Ten Highly Tentative Suggestions."

In the United States, with so many diverse cultures, you might think it is impossible to identify common standards of ethical behavior. However, among sources from many different times and places—such as the Bible, Aristotle's *Ethics*, the Koran, and the *Analects* of Confucius—you'll find the following common statements of basic moral values: Integrity, respect for human life, self-control, honesty, courage, and self-sacrifice are right. Cheating, cowardice, and cruelty are wrong. Furthermore, all the world's major religions support a version of what some call the Golden Rule: Do unto others as you would have them do unto you.[3]

LO 4–2   Ask the three questions you need to answer when faced with a potentially unethical action.

Ethics Begins with Each of Us

It is easy to criticize business and political leaders for moral and ethical shortcomings. Both managers and workers often cite low managerial ethics as a major cause of U.S. businesses' competitive woes. But employees also frequently violate safety standards and goof off during the work week. U.S. adults in general are not always as honest or honorable as they should be.

Even though volunteerism is at an all-time high according to the U.S. Census Bureau, three of every four citizens do not give any time to the community in which they live because they think it will take too much time or they don't think they are qualified.[4]

Plagiarizing material from the Internet, including cutting and pasting information from websites without giving credit, is the most common form of cheating in schools today. To fight this problem, many instructors now use services like TurnItIn.com, which scans students' papers against more than 40 billion online sources to provide evidence of copying in seconds.[5]

In a recent study, most teens said they were prepared to make ethical decisions in the workforce, but an alarming 51 percent of high school students admit that they have cheated on tests in the last year. Studies have found a strong relationship between academic dishonesty among undergraduates and dishonesty at work.[6] In response, many schools are establishing heavier

Plagiarizing from the Internet is one of the most common forms of cheating in colleges today. Have you ever been tempted to plagiarize a paper or project? What are the possible consequences of copying someone else's material?

"I don't know what plagiarizing is, so I'm gonna take the easy way out and just copy something off the internet."

Turning Ex-Convicts into Entrepreneurs

While starting a business from scratch is difficult for anybody, it can be an almost impossible task for someone with a criminal record. Most former convicts come from poor backgrounds with limited opportunities and only see their opportunities dwindle further once they've done time. With few options available, many return to their lives of crime and eventually end up back in jail.

That's why entrepreneur and activist Catherine Rohr began Defy Ventures, a New York–based nonprofit that helps newly released prisoners launch their own businesses. Rohr came up with the idea after a tour through a Texas prison shattered her previous thoughts on incarcerated people. "Most prison rehabilitation advocates talk about 'second chances,' but I recognized that those I met behind bars were never given a legitimate first chance," says Rohr. She also noticed that many inmates shared the same characteristics as most successful businesspeople: "Relentless drive, charisma that turns a 'no' into a 'yes,' and creative problem solving."

In 2004 Rohr founded the Prison Entrepreneurship Program (PEP) in Texas after investing her entire savings and 401(k). The nonprofit soon grew into a $2.5 million organization that had helped launch 60 startups. Of the 600 students Rohr graduated through the program, 98 percent found employment and less than 5 percent returned to prison. In 2010 Rohr established Defy in New York City where she continues to fight for the advancement of ex-convicts. "We break generational legacies of violence, poverty, and incarceration by coaching students to become successful entrepreneurs, employers, parents, and community leaders," says Rohr.

Sources: Riane Menardi, "Catherine Rohr Helps Former Felons Defy Odds, Start Businesses," *Silicon Prairie News*, May 9, 2013; and Ashoka, "Legalize IT: Met New Ashoka Fellow Catherine Rohr," *Forbes*, March 28, 2013.

consequences for cheating and requiring students to perform a certain number of hours of community service to graduate. Do you think such policies make a difference in student behavior?

Choices are not always easy, and the obvious ethical solution may have personal or professional drawbacks. Imagine that your supervisor has asked you to do something you feel is unethical. You've just taken out a mortgage on a new house to make room for your first baby, due in two months. Not carrying out your supervisor's request may get you fired. What should you do? Sometimes there is no easy alternative in such *ethical dilemmas* because you must choose between equally unsatisfactory alternatives.

It can be difficult to balance ethics and other goals, such as pleasing stakeholders or advancing in your career. According to management writer Ken Blanchard and religious leader Norman Vincent Peale, it helps to ask yourself the following questions when facing an ethical dilemma.[7]

1. *Is my proposed action legal?* Am I violating any law or company policy? Whether you're thinking about having a drink and driving home, gathering marketing intelligence, designing a product, hiring or firing employees, getting rid of industrial waste, or using a questionable

nickname for an employee, think about the legal implications. This is the most basic question in business ethics, but it is only the first.

2. *Is it balanced?* Am I acting fairly? Would I want to be treated this way? Will I win everything at the expense of another? Win–lose situations often become lose–lose situations and generate retaliation from the loser. Not every situation can be completely balanced, but the health of our relationships requires us to avoid major imbalances over time. An ethical businessperson has a win–win attitude and tries to make decisions that benefit all.

3. *How will it make me feel about myself?* Would I feel proud if my family learned of my decision? My friends? Could I discuss the proposed situation or action with my supervisor? The company's clients? Will I have to hide my actions? Has someone warned me not to disclose them? What if my decision were announced on the evening news? Am I feeling unusually nervous? Decisions that go against our sense of right and wrong make us feel bad—they erode our self-esteem. That is why an ethical businessperson does what is proper as well as what is profitable.

Individuals and companies that develop a strong ethics code and use the three questions above have a better chance than most of behaving ethically. The Spotlight on Small Business box features a story about how one woman chose to help others. If you would like to know which style of recognizing and resolving ethical dilemmas you favor, fill out the ethical orientation questionnaire in Figure 4.1.

test prep

- What are ethics?
- How do ethics differ from legality?
- When faced with ethical dilemmas, what questions can you ask yourself that might help you make ethical decisions?

LO 4–3   Describe management's role in setting ethical standards.

MANAGING BUSINESSES ETHICALLY AND RESPONSIBLY

Ethics is caught more than it is taught. That is, people learn their standards and values from observing what others do, not from hearing what they say. This is as true in business as it is at home. Organizational ethics begins at the top, and the leadership and example of strong managers can help instill corporate values in employees.

Trust and cooperation between workers and managers must be based on fairness, honesty, openness, and moral integrity. The same applies to relationships among businesses and between nations. A business should be managed ethically for many reasons: to maintain a good reputation; to keep existing customers and attract new ones; to avoid lawsuits; to reduce employee turnover; to avoid government intervention in the form of new laws and regulations controlling business activities; to please customers, employees, and society; and simply to do the right thing.

FIGURE 4.1 ETHICAL ORIENTATION QUESTIONNAIRE

Please answer the following questions.

1. Which is worse?

   A. Hurting someone's feelings by telling the truth.
   B. Telling a lie and protecting someone's feelings.

2. Which is the worse mistake?

   A. To make exceptions too freely.
   B. To apply rules too rigidly.

3. Which is it worse to be?

   A. Unmerciful.
   B. Unfair.

4. Which is worse?

   A. Stealing something valuable from someone for no good reason.
   B. Breaking a promise to a friend for no good reason.

5. Which is it better to be?

   A. Just and fair.
   B. Sympathetic and feeling.

6. Which is worse?

   A. Not helping someone in trouble.
   B. Being unfair to someone by playing favorites.

7. In making a decision you rely more on

   A. Hard facts.
   B. Personal feelings and intuition.

8. Your boss orders you to do something that will hurt someone. If you carry out the order, have you actually done anything wrong?

   A. Yes.
   B. No.

9. Which is more important in determining whether an action is right or wrong?

   A. Whether anyone actually gets hurt.
   B. Whether a rule, law, commandment, or moral principle is broken.

To score: The answers fall in one of two categories, J or C. Count your number of J and C answers using this key: 1. A = C; B = J; 2. A = J; B = C; 3. A = C; B = J; 4. A = J; B = C; 5. A = J; B = C; 6. A = C; B = J; 7. A = J; B = C; 8. A = C; B = J; 9. A = C; B = J

What your score means: The higher your J score, the more you rely on an ethic of *justice*. The higher your C score, the more you prefer an ethic of *care*. Neither style is better than the other, but they are different. Because they appear so different, they may seem opposed to one another, but they're actually complementary. In fact, your score probably shows you rely on each style to a greater or lesser degree. (Few people end up with a score of 9 to 0.) The more you can appreciate both approaches, the better you'll be able to resolve ethical dilemmas and to understand and communicate with people who prefer the other style.

An ethic of justice is based on principles like justice, fairness, equality, or authority. People who prefer this style see ethical dilemmas as conflicts of rights that can be solved by the impartial application of some general principle. The advantage of this approach is that it looks at a problem logically and impartially. People with this style try to be objective and fair, hoping to make a decision according to some standard that's higher than any specific individual's interests. The disadvantage of this approach is that people who rely on it might lose sight of the immediate interests of particular individuals. They may unintentionally ride roughshod over the people around them in favor of some abstract ideal or policy. This style is more common for men than women.

An ethic of care is based on a sense of responsibility to reduce actual harm or suffering. People who prefer this style see moral dilemmas as conflicts of duties or responsibilities. They believe that solutions must be tailored to the special details of individual circumstances. They tend to feel constrained by policies that are supposed to be enforced without exception. The advantage of this approach is that it is responsive to immediate suffering and harm. The disadvantage is that, when carried to an extreme, this style can produce decisions that seem not simply subjective, but arbitrary. This style is more common for women than men.

To learn more about these styles and how they might relate to gender, go to www.ethicsandbusiness.org/kgl.htm.

Source: Thomas I. White, *Discovering Philosophy—Brief Edition*, 1e, © Copyright 1996. Adapted by permission of Pearson Education, Inc., Upper Saddle River, NJ.

Some managers think ethics is a personal matter—either individuals have ethical principles or they don't. These managers believe that they are not responsible for an individual's misdeeds and that ethics has nothing to do with management. But a growing number of people think ethics has everything to do with management. Individuals do not usually act alone; they need the implied, if not the direct, cooperation of others to behave unethically in a corporation.

For example, there have been reports of cell phone service sales representatives who actually lie to get customers to extend their contracts—or even extend their contracts without the customers' knowledge. Some phone reps intentionally hang up on callers to prevent them from canceling their contracts. Why do these sales reps sometimes resort to overly aggressive tactics? Because poorly designed incentive programs reward them for meeting certain goals, sometimes doubling or tripling their salaries with incentives. Do their managers say directly, "Deceive the customers"? No, but the message is clear. Overly ambitious goals and incentives can create an environment in which unethical actions like this can occur.

compliance-based ethics codes
Ethical standards that emphasize preventing unlawful behavior by increasing control and by penalizing wrongdoers.

integrity-based ethics codes
Ethical standards that define the organization's guiding values, create an environment that supports ethically sound behavior, and stress a shared accountability among employees.

LO 4–4   Distinguish between compliance-based and integrity-based ethics codes, and list the six steps in setting up a corporate ethics code.

Setting Corporate Ethical Standards

More and more companies have adopted written codes of ethics. Figure 4.2 offers Johnson & Johnson's as a sample. Although these codes vary greatly, they can be placed into two categories: compliance-based and integrity-based (see Figure 4.3). **Compliance-based ethics codes** emphasize preventing unlawful behavior by increasing control and penalizing wrongdoers. **Integrity-based ethics codes** define the organization's guiding values, create an environment that supports ethically sound behavior, and stress shared accountability.

FIGURE 4.2 OVERVIEW OF JOHNSON & JOHNSON'S CODE OF ETHICS

Note: This is an overview of Johnson & Johnson's code of ethics, which it calls its Credo. To see the company's complete Credo, go to www.jnj.com, then under the "Our Company" tab click on "Our Credo Values."

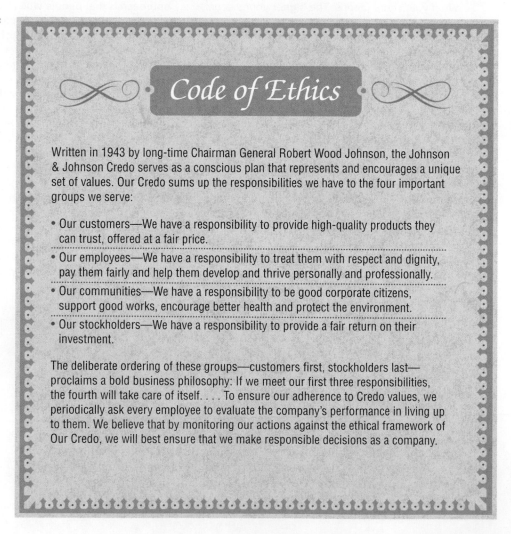

Code of Ethics

Written in 1943 by long-time Chairman General Robert Wood Johnson, the Johnson & Johnson Credo serves as a conscious plan that represents and encourages a unique set of values. Our Credo sums up the responsibilities we have to the four important groups we serve:

- Our customers—We have a responsibility to provide high-quality products they can trust, offered at a fair price.
- Our employees—We have a responsibility to treat them with respect and dignity, pay them fairly and help them develop and thrive personally and professionally.
- Our communities—We have a responsibility to be good corporate citizens, support good works, encourage better health and protect the environment.
- Our stockholders—We have a responsibility to provide a fair return on their investment.

The deliberate ordering of these groups—customers first, stockholders last—proclaims a bold business philosophy: If we meet our first three responsibilities, the fourth will take care of itself. . . . To ensure our adherence to Credo values, we periodically ask every employee to evaluate the company's performance in living up to them. We believe that by monitoring our actions against the ethical framework of Our Credo, we will best ensure that we make responsible decisions as a company.

FEATURES OF COMPLIANCE-BASED ETHICS CODES		FEATURES OF INTEGRITY-BASED ETHICS CODES	
Ideal:	Conform to outside standards (laws and regulations)	Ideal:	Conform to outside standards (laws and regulations) and chosen internal standards
Objective:	Avoid criminal misconduct	Objective:	Enable responsible employee conduct
Leaders:	Lawyers	Leaders:	Managers with aid of lawyers and others
Methods:	Education, reduced employee discretion, controls, penalties	Methods:	Education, leadership, accountability, decision processes, controls, and penalties

FIGURE 4.3 STRATEGIES FOR ETHICS MANAGEMENT

Integrity-based ethics codes move beyond legal compliance to create a "do-it-right" climate that emphasizes core values such as honesty, fair play, good service to customers, a commitment to diversity, and involvement in the community. These values are ethically desirable, but not necessarily legally mandatory.

Here are six steps many believe can improve U.S. business ethics:[8]

1. Top management must adopt and unconditionally support an explicit corporate code of conduct.

2. Employees must understand that expectations for ethical behavior begin at the top and that senior management expects all employees to act accordingly.

3. Managers and others must be trained to consider the ethical implications of all business decisions.

4. An ethics office must be set up with which employees can communicate anonymously. **Whistleblowers** (insiders who report illegal or unethical behavior) must feel protected from retaliation. The Sarbanes-Oxley Act protects whistleblowers by requiring all public corporations to allow employee concerns about accounting and auditing to be submitted confidentially and anonymously. The act also requires

whistleblowers
Insiders who report illegal or unethical behavior.

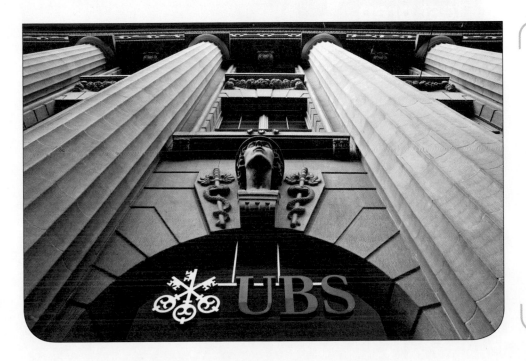

The Internal Revenue Service awarded $104 million to Bradley Birkenfeld, a banker-turned-whistleblower who gave the agency the information it needed to uncover a massive tax evasion scheme pulled off by Swiss bank UBS. Switzerland's largest bank helped thousands of its American clients dodge taxes. Birkenfeld also received 31 months in prison for his role in the scheme. What motivates whistleblowers?

reinstatement and back pay to people who were punished by their employers for passing information about fraud on to authorities. (We cover Sarbanes-Oxley in more detail in Chapter 17.) In 2010 the Dodd-Frank Wall Street Reform and Consumer Protection Act was signed into law. The law includes a "bounty" provision that allows corporate whistleblowers who provide information that leads to a successful enforcement action to collect 10–30 percent of the total penalty for violations that exceed $1 million. A whistleblower in the Enron case received a $1 million reward from the IRS (and, yes, it is taxable).

5. Outsiders such as suppliers, subcontractors, distributors, and customers must be told about the ethics program. Pressure to put aside ethical considerations often comes from the outside, and it helps employees resist such pressure when everyone knows what the ethical standards are.

6. The ethics code must be enforced with timely action if any rules are broken. That is the most forceful way to communicate to all employees that the code is serious.

This last step is perhaps the most critical. No matter how well intended a company's ethics code, it is worthless if not enforced. Enron had a written code of ethics. By ignoring it, Enron's board and management sent employees the message that rules could be shelved when inconvenient. In contrast, Johnson & Johnson's response to a cyanide poisoning crisis in the 1980s shows that enforcing ethics codes can enhance profit. Although not legally required to do so, the company recalled its Tylenol products and won great praise and a reputation for corporate integrity.

An important factor in enforcing an ethics code is selecting an ethics officer. The most effective ethics officers set a positive tone, communicate effectively, and relate well to employees at every level. They are equally comfortable as counselors and investigators and can be trusted to maintain confidentiality, conduct objective investigations, and ensure fairness. They can demonstrate to stakeholders that ethics are important in everything the company does.[9]

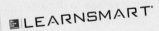

Use LearnSmart to help retain what you have learned. Access your instructor's Connect course to check out LearnSmart, or go to learnsmartadvantage.com for help.

LEARNSMART

test prep

- What are compliance-based and integrity-based ethics codes?
- What are the six steps to follow in establishing an effective ethics program in a business?

LO 4–5   Define *corporate social responsibility* and compare corporations' responsibilities to various stakeholders.

CORPORATE SOCIAL RESPONSIBILITY

corporate social responsibility (CSR)
A business's concern for the welfare of society.

Just as you and I need to be good citizens, contributing what we can to society, corporations need to be good citizens as well. **Corporate social responsibility (CSR)** is the concern businesses have for the welfare of society, not just for their owners. CSR goes well beyond being ethical. It is based on a commitment to integrity, fairness, and respect.

You may be surprised to know that not everyone thinks that CSR is a good thing. Some critics of CSR believe that a manager's sole role is to compete and win in the marketplace. The late U.S. economist Milton Friedman made the famous statement that the only social responsibility of business is to make money for stockholders. He thought doing anything else was moving dangerously toward socialism. Other CSR critics believe that managers who pursue CSR are doing so with other people's money—which they invested to make more money, not to improve society. In this view spending money on CSR activities is stealing from investors.[10]

CSR defenders, in contrast, believe that businesses owe their existence to the societies they serve and cannot succeed in societies that fail.[11] Firms have access to society's labor pool and its natural resources, in which every member of society has a stake. Even Adam Smith, the father of capitalism, believed that self-interested pursuit of profit was wrong and that benevolence was the highest virtue. CSR defenders acknowledge that businesses have deep obligations to investors and should not attempt government-type social responsibility projects. However, they also argue that CSR makes more money for investors in the long run. Studies show that companies with good ethical reputations attract and retain better employees, draw more customers, and enjoy greater employee loyalty.[12]

The social performance of a company has several dimensions:

- **Corporate philanthropy** includes charitable donations to nonprofit groups of all kinds. Eighty percent of the business leaders surveyed in a recent study said that their companies participate in philanthropic activities. Some make long-term commitments to one cause, such as McDonald's Ronald McDonald Houses for families whose critically ill

corporate philanthropy
The dimension of social responsibility that includes charitable donations.

More than 1,300 Florida Light & Power Company employees volunteer in their communities during the company's Power to Care Week. Here FLP volunteers work to beautify a school in Rivera Beach through painting, cleanups, landscaping, and rebuilding a volleyball court. Do companies have responsibilities to the communities in which they operate beyond obeying the laws?

children require treatment away from home. The Bill & Melinda Gates Foundation is by far the nation's largest philanthropic foundation, with assets of approximately $40 billion.[13]

- **Corporate social initiatives** include enhanced forms of corporate philanthropy. Corporate social initiatives differ from traditional philanthropy in that they are more directly related to the company's competencies.[14] For example, logistics giant TNT keeps a 50-person emergency response team on standby to go anywhere in the world at 48 hours' notice to provide support in aviation, warehousing, transportation, reporting, and communications. Over the years, 225 TNT employees have been involved in 30 emergency response activities.[15]

- **Corporate responsibility** includes everything from hiring minority workers to making safe products, minimizing pollution, using energy wisely, and providing a safe work environment—essentially everything that has to do with acting responsibly within society.

- **Corporate policy** refers to the position a firm takes on social and political issues. For example, Patagonia's corporate policy includes this statement: "A love of wild and beautiful places demands participation in the fight to save them, and to help reverse the steep decline in the overall environmental health of our planet. We donate our time, services and at least 1% of our sales to hundreds of grassroots environmental groups all over the world who work to help reverse the tide."[16]

The problems corporations cause get so much news coverage that people tend to get a negative view of their impact on society. But businesses make positive contributions too. Few people know, for example, that a Xerox program called Social Service Leave allows employees to take up to a year to work for a nonprofit organization while earning their full Xerox salary and benefits, including job security.[17] IBM and Wells Fargo Bank have similar programs.

In fact, many companies allow employees to give part-time help to social agencies of all kinds. The recent recession has changed the way that many corporations approach corporate philanthropy.[18] Now they are often likely to give time and goods rather than money. Many companies are now encouraging employees to volunteer more—on company time.[19] For example, Mars Incorporated encourages community involvement by offering paid time off to clean parks, aid medical clinic, and plant gardens. Nearly 10,000 Mars employees volunteer 37,000 hours a year.[20] NetworkforGood.org, 1-800-Volunteer.org, and VolunteerMatch.org are web-based services that link volunteers with non-profit and public sector organizations around the country. Volunteers enter a zip code or indicate the geographic area in which they'd like to work, and the programs list organizations that could use their help.

The majority of the MBA students surveyed by a group called Students for Responsible Business said they would take a reduced salary to work for a socially responsible company.[21] But when the same students were asked to define *socially responsible*, things got complicated. Even those who support the idea of social responsibility can't agree on what it is. Let's look at the concept through the eyes of the stakeholders to whom businesses are responsible: customers, investors, employees, and society in general.

Responsibility to Customers

President John F. Kennedy proposed four basic rights of consumers: (1) the right to safety, (2) the right to be informed, (3) the right to choose, and (4) the right to be heard. These rights will be achieved only if businesses and consumers recognize them and take action in the marketplace.

---

corporate social initiatives
Enhanced forms of corporate philanthropy directly related to the company's competencies.

corporate responsibility
The dimension of social responsibility that includes everything from hiring minority workers to making safe products.

corporate policy
The dimension of social responsibility that refers to the position a firm takes on social and political issues.

A recurring theme of this book is the importance of pleasing customers by offering them real value. Since three of five new businesses fail, we know this responsibility is not as easy to meet as it seems. One sure way of failing to please customers is to be less than honest with them. The payoff for socially conscious behavior, however, can be new customers who admire the company's social efforts—a powerful competitive edge. Consumer behavior studies show that, all else being equal, a socially conscious company is likely to be viewed more favorably than others. In fact, a recent Nielsen survey showed that 50 percent of the consumers surveyed were willing to pay more for goods from socially responsible companies.[22]

Given the value customers place on social efforts, how do companies make customers aware of such efforts? One tool many companies use to raise awareness of their social responsibility efforts is social media. The primary value of using social media to communicate CSR efforts is that it allows companies to reach broad and diverse groups, allows them to connect directly with customers in a low-cost, efficient way, and enables them to interact with specific groups more easily than through more traditional efforts.

It's not enough for companies to brag about their social responsibility efforts; they must live up to the expectations they raise or face the consequences. When herbal tea maker Celestial Seasonings ignored its advertised image of environmental stewardship by poisoning prairie dogs on its property, it incurred customers' wrath. Customers prefer to do business with companies they trust and, even more important, don't want to do business with those they don't trust. Companies earn customers' trust by demonstrating credibility over time; they can lose it at any point.

Responsibility to Investors

Ethical behavior doesn't subtract from the bottom line; it adds to it. In contrast, unethical behavior, even if it seems to work in the short term, does financial damage. Those cheated are the shareholders themselves. For example, in just 11 business days in June 2002, 44 CEOs left U.S. corporations amid accusations of wrongdoing, and the stock prices of their companies plummeted.

Many investors believe that it makes financial as well as moral sense to invest in companies that plan ahead to create a better environment. By choosing to put their money into companies whose goods and services benefit the community and the environment, investors can improve their own financial health while improving society's.[23]

A few investors, however, have chosen unethical means to improve their financial health. For example, **insider trading** uses private company information to further insiders' own fortunes or those of their family and friends. In 2011, one of the biggest insider trading cases in history went to trial in New York. Billionaire Raj Rajaratnam was convicted of masterminding an insider trading ring that made his Galleon Group hedge fund $64 million richer. Of course, he didn't do this all by himself. More than three dozen former traders, executives, and lawyers have pled guilty or faced charges that they helped Rajaratnam trade illegally on more than 35 stocks, including Intel, Hilton, IBM, and eBay. Rajaratnam was sentenced to 11 years in prison and lost an appeal in 2013.[24]

Insider trading isn't limited to company executives and their friends. Before it was publicly known that IBM was going to take over Lotus Development, an IBM secretary told her husband, who told

insider trading
An unethical activity in which insiders use private company information to further their own fortunes or those of their family and friends.

Billionaire hedge-fund manager Steven Cohen, head of SAC Capital Advisors, agreed to settle an insider-trading investigation against the firm by paying a record $1.8 billion fine. Six former SAC employees pled guilty to securities fraud. A seventh was found guilty in December 2013 of five counts of securities fraud and conspiracy. The trial of an eighth is ongoing. So far Cohen has somehow managed to avoid jail himself.

two co-workers, who told friends, relatives, business associates, and even a pizza delivery man. A total of 25 people traded illegally on the insider tip within a six-hour period. When the deal was announced publicly, Lotus stock soared 89 percent. One of the inside traders, a stockbroker who passed the information to a few customers, made $468,000 in profits. The U.S. Securities and Exchange Commission (SEC) filed charges against the secretary, her husband, and 23 others. Four defendants settled out of court by paying penalties of twice their profits. Prosecutors are increasingly pursuing insider trading cases to ensure that the securities market remains fair and equally accessible to all.[25]

After the deluge of insider trader cases was made public in the early 2000s, the SEC adopted a new rule called Regulation FD (for "fair disclosure"). The rule doesn't specify what information can and cannot be disclosed. It simply requires companies that release any information to share it with everybody, not just a few select people. In other words, if companies tell anyone, they must tell everyone—at the same time.

Some companies have misused information for their own benefit at investors' expense. When WorldCom admitted to accounting irregularities misrepresenting its profitability, investors who had purchased its stock on the basis of the false financial reports saw share prices free-fall from the mid-teens in January 2002 to less than a dime the following July. The pain was even greater for long-term investors, who had bought the stock at around $60 in 1999.

Responsibility to Employees

It's been said that the best social program in the world is a job. Businesses have a responsibility to create jobs if they want to grow. Once they've done so, they must see to it that hard work and talent are fairly rewarded. Employees need realistic hope of a better future, which comes only through a chance for upward mobility. One of the most powerful influences on a company's effectiveness and financial performance is responsible human resource management. We'll discuss this in Chapter 11.

If a company treats employees with respect, those employees usually will respect the company as well. Mutual respect can make a huge difference to a company's profit. In their book *Contented Cows Still Give Better Milk*, Bill Catlette and Richard Hadden compared "contented cow" companies with "common cow" companies. The companies with contented employees outgrew their counterparts by four to one for more than 10 years. They also outearned the "common cow" companies by nearly $40 billion and generated 800,000 more jobs. Catlette and Hadden attribute this difference in performance to the commitment and caring the outstanding companies demonstrated for their employees.[26]

The wage and benefit packages offered by warehouse retailer Costco are among the best in hourly retail. Even part-time workers are covered by Costco's health plan. Increased benefits reduce Costco employee turnover to less than a third of the industry average. Why do you think Costco is so successful at keeping its employees?

One way a company can demonstrate commitment and caring is to give employees salaries and benefits that help them reach their personal goals. The wage and benefit packages offered by warehouse retailer Costco are among the best in hourly retail. Even part-time workers are covered by Costco's health plan, and the workers pay less for their coverage than at other retailers such as Walmart. Increased benefits reduce employee turnover, which at Costco is less than a third of the industry average.[27] The U.S. Department of Labor estimates that replacing employees costs between 150 and 250 percent of their annual salaries, so retaining workers is good for business as well as morale.[28]

Getting even is one of the most powerful incentives for good people to do bad things. Few disgruntled workers are desperate enough to commit violence in the workplace, but a great number relieve their frustrations in subtle ways: blaming mistakes on others, not accepting responsibility, manipulating budgets and expenses, making commitments they intend to ignore, hoarding resources, doing the minimum needed to get by, and making results look better than they are.

The loss of employee commitment, confidence, and trust in the company and its management can be costly indeed. Employee fraud costs U.S. businesses approximately 5 percent of annual revenue and causes 30 percent of all business failures, according to the Association of Certified Fraud Examiners.[29] You'll read more about employee–management issues like pay equity, sexual harassment, child and elder care, drug testing, and violence in the workplace in Chapter 12.

Responsibility to Society and the Environment

More than a third of U.S. workers receive salaries from nonprofit organizations that receive funding from others, that in turn receive their money from businesses. Foundations, universities, and other nonprofit organizations own billions of shares in publicly held companies. As stock prices of those firms increase, businesses create more wealth to benefit society.

Businesses are also partly responsible for promoting social justice. Many companies believe they have a role in building communities that goes well beyond simply "giving back." To them, charity is not enough. Their social contributions include cleaning up the environment, building community toilets, providing computer lessons, caring for elderly people, and supporting children from low-income families.

As concern about climate change increased, the green movement emerged in nearly every aspect of daily life. What makes a product green? Some believe that a product's carbon footprint (the amount of carbon released during production, distribution, consumption, and disposal) defines how green it is. Many variables contribute to a product's carbon footprint. The carbon footprint of a package of, say, frozen corn includes not only the carbon released by the fertilizer to grow the corn but also the carbon in the fertilizer itself, the gas used to run the farm equipment and transport the corn to market, the electricity to make

Driving a Prius with a big banana on the roof is an eye-catching way for Mason Arnold of Greenling to attract the attention of potential customers while delivering fresh, nutritious food to local customers. Greenling believes that supporting local organic growers is a good way of supporting sustainable, healthy environments. What do you think?

the plastic packages and power the freezers, and so on. (See the Seeking Sustainability box for a story of how one company strives to reduce its carbon footprint by using recycled plastic bottles to make the fabric for its messenger bags.)

No specific guidelines define the carbon footprints of products, businesses, or individuals or outline how to communicate them to consumers. PepsiCo presents carbon information with a label on bags of cheese-and-onion potato chips, for example, that says "75 grams of CO_2." Simple enough, but what does it mean? (We don't know either.)

The green movement has provided consumers with lots of product choices. However, making those choices means sorting through the many and confusing claims made by manufacturers. The noise in the marketplace challenges even the most dedicated green activists, but taking the easy route of buying what's most readily available violates the principles of the green movement.

Environmental efforts may increase a company's costs, but they also allow the company to charge higher prices, increase market share, or both. Ciba Specialty Chemicals, a Swiss textile-dye manufacturer, developed dyes that require less salt than traditional dyes. Since used dye solutions must be treated before being released into rivers or streams, less salt means lower water treatment costs. Patents protect Ciba's low-salt dyes, so the company can charge more for its dyes than other companies can charge for theirs. Ciba's experience illustrates that, just as a new machine enhances labor productivity, lowering environmental costs can add value to a business.

Not all environmental strategies are as financially beneficial as Ciba's, however. In the early 1990s, tuna producer StarKist responded to consumer concerns about dolphins in the eastern Pacific dying in nets set out for yellow fin tuna. The company announced it would sell only skipjack tuna from the western Pacific, which do not swim near dolphins. Unfortunately, customers were unwilling to pay a premium for dolphin-safe tuna and considered the taste of skipjack inferior. Nor was there a clear environmental gain: for every dolphin saved in the eastern Pacific, thousands of immature tuna and dozens of sharks, turtles, and other marine animals died in the western Pacific fishing process.

The green movement can have a positive impact on the U.S. labor force. Emerging renewable-energy and energy-efficiency industries currently account for 9 million jobs and by 2030 may create as many as 40 million more in engineering, manufacturing, construction, accounting, and management, according to a green-collar job report by the American Solar Energy Society.[30]

Environmental quality is a public good; that is, everyone gets to enjoy it regardless of who pays for it. The challenge for companies is to find the public goods that will appeal to their customers. Many corporations are publishing reports that document their net social contribution. To do that, a company must measure its positive social contributions and subtract its negative social impacts. We discuss that process next.

Social Auditing

Can we measure whether organizations are making social responsibility an integral part of top management's decision making? The answer is yes, and the term that represents that measurement is *social auditing*.

social audit
A systematic evaluation of an organization's progress toward implementing socially responsible and responsive programs.

A **social audit** is a systematic evaluation of an organization's progress toward implementing socially responsible and responsive programs. One of the major problems of conducting a social audit is establishing procedures for measuring a firm's activities and their effects on society. What should a social audit measure? Many consider workplace issues, the environment, product safety, community relations, military weapons contracting, international operations and human rights, and respect for the rights of local people.

Sustainability's in the Bag

When it comes to sustainable products, making sure an item is environmentally sound is just the first step. After all, the word "sustainability" implies that something will last for a long time. A shoddy product that needs to be replaced often takes a hefty toll on resources, which can cancel out the environmental benefits of even the greenest production methods.

That's why Rickshaw Bagworks in San Francisco makes sustainable accessories designed to last for the long term. For instance, at first the company began producing bags using expensive Italian wool herringbone tweed. Although the fabric was beautiful and environmentally friendly, the prototypes wore out in a manner of weeks. So Rickshaw teamed up with an upholstery mill to create its own fabric, Rickshaw Performance Tweed. Made from recycled plastic bottles, this synthetic fabric ended up being stronger and more eco-friendly while still looking gorgeous as a handbag.

Rickshaw employees and executives abide by the company's "three Fs" of sustainable design: form, function and footprint. Not only must a product make as small a carbon footprint as possible, it must also serve a long-term practical function and look great doing it. That's why Rickshaw's messenger bags are designed in a way that ensures every piece of fabric cut by the company makes it into the bag.

The company's dedication to sustainability is even incorporated in its name, which means "human powered vehicle" in Japanese. Do you think more companies should be as dedicated to sustainability as Rickshaw?

Sources: Mark Dwight, "How to Build a Sustainable Business," *Inc.*, November 2013; and http://blog.rickshawbags.com/the-rickshaw-story/, accessed February 2014.

It remains a question whether organizations should add up positive actions like charitable donations and pollution control efforts, and then subtract negative effects like layoffs and overall pollution created, to get a net social contribution. Or should they just record positive actions? What do you think? However they are conducted, social audits force organizations to consider their social responsibility beyond the level of just feeling good or managing public relations.

In addition to social audits conducted by companies themselves, five types of groups serve as watchdogs to monitor how well companies enforce their ethical and social responsibility policies:

1. *Socially conscious investors* insist that a company extend its own high standards to its suppliers. Social responsibility investing (SRI) is on the rise, with nearly $3.7 trillion invested in SRI funds in the United States already.[31]

2. *Socially conscious research organizations,* such as Ethisphere, analyze and report on corporate social responsibility efforts.[32]

3. *Environmentalists* apply pressure by naming companies that don't abide by environmentalists' standards. After months of protests coordinated by the San Francisco–based Rainforest Action Network (RAN), JPMorgan Chase & Co. adopted guidelines that restrict its lending and underwriting practices for industrial projects likely to have a negative impact on the environment. RAN activists first go after an industry leader, like JPMorgan, then tackle smaller companies. "We call it, 'Rank'em and spank'em,'" says RAN's executive director.[33]

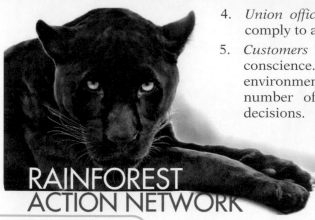

4. *Union officials* hunt down violations and force companies to comply to avoid negative publicity.

5. *Customers* make buying decisions based on their social conscience. Many companies surveyed are adjusting their environmental and social responsibility strategies because of the number of customers that factor these into their buying decisions.

As you can see, it isn't enough for a company to be right when it comes to ethics and social responsibility—it also has to convince its customers and society that it's right.

The goal of the Rainforest Action Network, an environmental activist group, is to show companies that it is possible to do well by doing good. It conducts public campaigns designed to put consumer pressure on companies that refuse to adopt responsible environmental policies. RAN has helped convince dozens of corporations including Home Depot, Citigroup, Boise Cascade, and Goldman Sachs to change their practices.

test **prep**

- What is corporate social responsibility, and how does it relate to each of a business's major stakeholders?
- What is a social audit, and what kinds of activities does it monitor?

LO 4–6   Analyze the role of U.S. businesses in influencing ethical behavior and social responsibility in global markets.

INTERNATIONAL ETHICS AND SOCIAL RESPONSIBILITY

Ethical problems and issues of social responsibility are not unique to the United States. Influence-peddling or bribery charges have been brought against top officials in Japan, South Korea, China, Italy, Brazil, Pakistan, and Zaire. What is new about the moral and ethical standards by which government leaders are being judged? They are much stricter than in the past. Top leaders are now being held to higher standards.

Many U.S. businesses also demand socially responsible behavior from their international suppliers, making sure they don't violate U.S. human rights and environmental standards. Sears will not import products made by Chinese prison labor. Clothing manufacturer PVH (makers of such brands as Calvin Klein and Tommy Hilfiger) will cancel orders from suppliers that violate its ethical, environmental, and human rights code. Dow Chemical expects suppliers to conform to tough U.S. pollution and safety laws rather than just to local laws of their respective countries. McDonald's denied rumors that one of its suppliers grazes cattle on cleared rain-forest land but wrote a ban on the practice anyway.

In contrast are companies criticized for exploiting workers in less developed countries. Nike, the world's largest athletic shoe company, has been accused by human rights and labor groups of treating its workers poorly while lavishing millions of dollars on star athletes to endorse its products. Cartoonist Garry Trudeau featured an anti-Nike campaign in his popular syndicated series *Doonesbury*.

Nike worked hard to improve its reputation. Nike monitors efforts to improve labor conditions in its 700 contract factories that are subject to local culture and economic conditions. The company released the names and locations of its factories, both as a show of transparency and to encourage its competitors to work on improving conditions as well. The company shared its audit data with a professor at MIT's Sloan School of Management. He concluded that despite "significant efforts and investments by Nike . . . workplace conditions in almost 80% of its suppliers have either remained the same or worsened over time." In 2014, a Nike supplier shut down a factory after four people were shot during a strike over higher wages.[34] This followed the 2013 collapse of a factory in Bangladesh that killed more than 1,000 workers.[35]

Why has Nike's monitoring program not been as successful as the company hoped? One reason is that in emerging economies, government regulations tend to be weak, which leaves companies to police their suppliers. That's a major task for a company like Nike, which produces 98 percent of its shoes in hundreds of factories in many different countries. Another reason is that as a buyer, Nike has different degrees of leverage. This leverage is based on how long Nike has worked with a supplier or how much of the factory's revenue depends on Nike alone.

The fairness of requiring international suppliers to adhere to U.S. ethical standards is not as clear-cut as you might think. For example, a gift in one culture can be a bribe in another. Is it always ethical for companies to demand compliance with the standards of their own countries? What about countries where child labor is accepted and families depend on children's salaries for survival? Should foreign companies doing business in the United States expect U.S. companies to comply with their ethical standards? Since multinational corporations span different societies, should they conform to any society's standards? Why is Sears applauded for not importing goods made in Chinese

Nike has outsourced the manufacture of its products to plants in other countries and has weathered much criticism for operating in low-wage countries where child labor is common. The company has taken many corrective measures, including working with other companies and advocacy groups on a set of common labor standards and factory guidelines. Can a successful firm overcome past ethical errors?

Going by a Different Standard

The extension of corporations' reach into communities across the globe has led to many questions: For which communities are the companies responsible? Are domestic operations more important than foreign ones? Should the interests of employees be put first, or is the company's image the main priority?

Here's an example of how corporate ethics can clash with cultural ethics. Joe, the oldest son of a poor South American cloth peddler, managed to move to the United States, earn an engineering degree, and get a job with a large telecommunications company. After five years, Joe seemed to have bought into the company culture and was happy to be granted a transfer back to his home country. He was told that the company expected him to live there in a safe and presentable home of his choice. To help him afford such a residence, his employer agreed to reimburse him a maximum of $2,000 a month for the cost of his rent and servants. Each month Joe submitted rental receipts for exactly $2,000. The company later found out that Joe was living in what was, by Western standards, a shack in a dangerous area of town. Such a humble home could not have cost more than $200 a month. The company was concerned for Joe's safety as well as

for the effect his residence would have on its image. The human resource manager was also worried about Joe's lack of integrity, given he had submitted false receipts for reimbursement.

Joe was upset with what he considered the company's invasion of his privacy. He argued he should receive the full $2,000 monthly reimbursement all employees received. He explained his choice of housing by saying he was making sacrifices so he could send the extra money to his family and put his younger siblings through school. This was especially important since his father had died and his family had no

one else to depend on. "Look, my family is poor," Joe said. "So poor that most Westerners wouldn't believe our poverty even if they saw it. This money means the difference between hope and despair for all of us. For me to do anything less for my family would be to defile the honor of my late father. Can't you understand?"

Often it is difficult to understand what others perceive as ethical. Different situations often turn the clear waters of "rightness" downright muddy. Joe was trying to do the honorable thing for his family. Yet the company's wish to have its higher-level people live in safe housing is not unreasonable, given the dangerous conditions of the city in which Joe lived. The policy of housing reimbursement supports the company's intent to make its employees' stay in the country reasonably comfortable and safe, not to increase their salaries. If Joe worked in the United States, where he would not receive a housing supplement, it would be unethical for him to falsify expense reports in order to receive more money to send to his family. In South America, though, the issue is not so clear.

Sources: Shirley Engelmeir, "Engage a Diverse Work Force to Capture Foreign Markets," *American Banker*, November 13, 2012; and Meghan M. Biro, "Happy Employees = Hefty Profits," *Forbes*, January 19, 2014.

prisons when there are many prison-based enterprises in the United States? None of these questions are easy to answer, but they suggest the complexity of social responsibility in international markets. (See the nearby Reaching Beyond Our Borders box for an example of an ethical culture clash.)

In the 1970s, the Foreign Corrupt Practices Act (discussed in Chapter 3) sent a chill throughout the U.S. business community by criminalizing the act of paying foreign business or government leaders to get business. Many U.S. executives complained that this law put their businesses at a competitive disadvantage when bidding against non-U.S. companies, since foreign companies don't have to abide by it.

To identify some form of common global ethics and fight corruption in global markets, partners in the Organization of American States signed the Inter-American Convention Against Corruption.[36] The United Nations adopted a formal condemnation of corporate bribery, as did the European Union and the Organization for Economic Cooperation and Development. The International Organization for Standardization (ISO) published a standard on social responsibility called ISO 26000, with guidelines on product manufacturing, fair pay rates, appropriate employee treatment, and hiring practices. These standards are advisory only and will not be used for certification purposes. The formation of a single set of international rules governing multinational corporations is unlikely in the near future. In many places "Fight corruption" remains just a slogan, but even a slogan is a start.

test prep

- How are U.S. businesses demanding socially responsible behavior from their international suppliers?
- Why is it unlikely that there will be a single set of international rules governing multinational companies soon?

Use LearnSmart to help retain what you have learned. Access your instructor's Connect course to check out LearnSmart, or go to learnsmartadvantage.com for help.

LEARNSMART

summary

LO 4–1   Explain why obeying the law is only the first step in behaving ethically.

- **How is legality different from ethics?**
  Ethics goes beyond obeying laws to include abiding by the moral standards accepted by society. Ethics reflects people's proper relationships with one another. Legality is more limiting; it refers only to laws written to protect people from fraud, theft, and violence.

LO 4–2   Ask the three questions you need to answer when faced with a potentially unethical action.

- **How can we tell if our business decisions are ethical?**
  We can put our business decisions through an ethics check by asking three questions: (1) Is it legal? (2) Is it balanced? and (3) How will it make me feel?

LO 4–3   Describe management's role in setting ethical standards.

- **What is management's role in setting ethical standards?**
  Managers often set formal ethical standards, but more important are the messages they send through their actions. Management's tolerance or intolerance of ethical misconduct influences employees more than any written ethics codes.

LO 4–4   Distinguish between compliance-based and integrity-based ethics codes, and list the six steps in setting up a corporate ethics code.

- **What's the difference between compliance-based and integrity-based ethics codes?**
  Whereas compliance-based ethics codes are concerned with avoiding legal punishment, integrity-based ethics codes define the organization's guiding values, create an environment that supports ethically sound behavior, and stress a shared accountability among employees.

LO 4–5   Define *corporate social responsibility* and compare corporations' responsibilities to various stakeholders

- **What is corporate social responsibility?**
  Corporate social responsibility is the concern businesses have for society.

- **How do businesses demonstrate corporate responsibility toward stakeholders?**
  Businesses demonstrate responsibility to stakeholders by (1) satisfying *customers* with goods and services of real value; (2) making money for *investors;* (3) creating jobs for *employees*, maintaining job security, and seeing that hard work and talent are fairly rewarded; and (4) creating new wealth for *society,* promoting social justice, and contributing to making the businesses' own environment a better place.

- **How are a company's social responsibility efforts measured?**
  A corporate social audit measures an organization's progress toward social responsibility. Some people believe the audit should add together the organization's positive actions and then subtract the negative effects to get a net social benefit.

LO 4–6   Analyze the role of U.S. businesses in influencing ethical behavior and social responsibility in global markets.

- **How can U.S. companies influence ethical behavior and social responsibility in global markets?**
  Many U.S. businesses are demanding socially responsible behavior from their international suppliers by making sure their suppliers do not violate U.S. human rights and environmental standards. Companies such as Sears, PVH, and Dow Chemical will not import products from companies that do not meet their ethical and social responsibility standards.

Access your instructor's Connect course to check out LearnSmart or go to learnsmartadvantage.com for help.

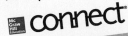

key terms

critical thinking

Think of a situation that tested your ethical behavior. For example, maybe your best friend forgot about a term paper due the next day and asked if he could copy a paper you wrote for another instructor last semester.

1. What are your alternatives, and what are the consequences of each?

2. Would it have been easier to resolve the dilemma if you had asked yourself the three questions listed in the chapter? Try answering them now and see whether you would have made a different choice.

developing **workplace skills**

Key: ● **Team**   ★ **Analytic**   ▲ **Communication**   ▣ **Technology**

1. What sources have helped shape your personal code of ethics and morality? What influences, if any, have ever pressured you to compromise those standards? Think of an experience you had at work or school that tested your ethical standards. How did you resolve your dilemma? Now that time has passed, are you comfortable with the decision you made? If not, explain what you would do differently.   ★ ▲

2. Do a little investigative reporting of your own. Go online and search for a public interest group in your community. Identify its officers, objectives, sources and amount of financial support, and size and characteristics of membership. List some examples of its recent actions and/or accomplishments. You should be able to choose from environmental groups, animal protection groups, political action committees, and so on. Visit the website of the local chamber of commerce, the Better Business Bureau, or local government agencies for help.

3. You're the manager of a coffeehouse called the Morning Cup. One of your best employees desires to be promoted to a managerial position; however, the owner is grooming his slow-thinking son for the job. The owner's nepotism may hurt a valuable employee's chances for advancement, but complaining may hurt your own chances for promotion. What do you do?   ★

4. Go to the website of a local corporation and search for its written ethics code. Would you classify its code as compliance-based or integrity-based? Explain.   ▣ ★ ▲

5. What effects have the new laws protecting whistleblowers had on the business environment? Go online or to the library to research individuals who reported their employers' illegal and/or unethical behavior. Did the companies change their policies? If so, what effect have these policies had on the companies' stakeholders? What effect did reporting the problems have on the whistleblowers themselves?   ▣ ★

taking it to the **net**

PURPOSE

To demonstrate the level of commitment one business has to social responsibility.

EXERCISE

According to household products and personal-care company Seventh Generation, corporate responsibility is in its DNA as it considers the effects of its actions on the next seven generations. It strives to limit the effect of all aspects of its products on the environment from development to their production, purchase, use, and disposal. Visit the company's website at www.seventhgeneration.com. Then answer the following questions:

1. What is the social mission of Seventh Generation?

2. What are Seventh Generation's four sustainability goals?

3. How is Seventh Generation involved in improving the Vermont community?

4. How does Seventh Generation communicate the company's social mission to its customers?

video case   Mc Graw Hill Education connect

WARBY PARKER/VISIONSPRING

Warby Parker is a relatively new player in the eyewear industry, but it's managed to make a big impact in a short amount of time. Neil Blumenthal and his three partners founded the company in 2010 in order to sell sophisticated and affordable glasses frames. But the team also wants the brand to stand for more than just profits, as evidenced by its commitment to keeping prices low and its relationship with its charitable partner, VisionSpring.

Unlike other start-ups that face competition from many established companies, Warby Parker only has one major competitor. However, it just so happens that this rival owns almost all of the best-selling eyewear and eyecare brands in the world. Since this large conglomerate doesn't create any barriers to upstarts like Warby Parker from entering the market, it is technically not a monopoly and can operate legally. Still, Warby's founders see this business model as unethical since it allows one huge company to set prices over an entire industry for maximum profit.

Blumenthal and his partners didn't want to contribute to the imbalance of power between consumers and manufacturers, so they set out to form a different kind of company. From the outset, Warby Parker developed an ethical standard that focused on its most important stakeholder—its customers. Since the company saves money by selling exclusively online and designing and manufacturing its own frames, it is able to fix the price of every pair at a modest $95. Considering that its competitor's frames can be as costly as a new iPhone, Warby immediately caught the interest of many stylish but budget-minded consumers.

An organization operates in a larger world, and there are more stakeholders than just customers. Warby Parker felt it had a mission to bring affordable eyewear to the masses, and nobody needed that tool more than impoverished people in developing nations. It was a natural thing, then, for the company to join forces with VisionSpring, a charity that gives quality eyeglasses to people struggling with vision problems in some of the poorest countries in the world. Warby donates a pair of glasses to the nonprofit for every pair that its customers buy. Together, they have put over a half-million pairs of glasses into the hands of people whose livelihoods depend on them.

VisionSpring hopes this model will inspire other American companies to get more involved in impacting global markets at the local level. For all its efforts, VisionSpring estimates that there are still over 700 million people worldwide who struggle to earn a living on account of lacking quality glasses. The folks at Warby Parker and VisionSpring believe that once you see that figure clearly, it's hard to look the other way.

THINKING IT OVER

1. Is Warby Parker is a good example of corporate social responsibility. What dimensions stand out in measuring the company's social performance?

2. What is a social audit and why do companies perform them? What factors would you consider in your social audit of Warby Parker?

3. Do you believe most businesses in the United States follow strict ethical standards? Make sure to offer some defense in support of your answer.

notes

1. Justin Baer and Julie Steinberg, "Volcker Rule Challenges Wall Street," *The Wall Street Journal,* December 10, 2013.

2. Christopher M. Matthews, "Law 2014: In White Collar Crime, It's Deja Vu All Over Again," *The Wall Street Journal,"* December 31, 2013.

3. Jahnabi Barooah, "The Golden Rule in World Religions (Quotes)," *Huffington Post,* www.huffingtonpost.com, accessed April 2014.

4. Kari Henley, "Why Don't We Volunteer," *Huffington Post,* www.huffingtonpost.com, accessed April 2014.

5. *Turnitin,* www.turnitin.com, accessed April 2014; and "Turnitin for iPad Surpasses 100,000 Downloads," *The Sacramento Bee,* January 14, 2014.

6. Thomas Ehrlich and Ernestine Fu, "Cheating in Schools and Colleges," *Forbes,* August 22, 2013.

7. Kenneth Blanchard and Norman Vincent Peale, *The Power of Ethical Management* (New York: William Morrow, 1996).

8. Will Yakowicz, "A New Website That Helps CEOs Lead More Ethically," *Inc.,* January 22, 2014; "Integrity in the Boardroom," www.wsj.com, accessed April 2014; Donna Boehme, "5 New Year's Compliance Resolutions for Boards in 2014," *Connecticut Law Tribune,* January 2, 2014; Victor Lipman, "New Study Shows Transparency Isn't Just Good Ethics—It's Good Business," *Forbes,* December 11, 2013; Rachel Louis Ensign, "Whistleblowers Coming from Compliance Departments," *The Wall Street Journal,* November 6, 2013; Venessa Wong, "So You Want to Be a Whistle-Blower . . . ," *Bloomberg Businessweek,* June 11, 2013; and Paul J. H. Schoemaker, "How to Defuse an Ethical Time-Bomb in Your Company," *Inc.,* June 10, 2014.

9. Gregory J. Millman and Ben Dipietro, "More Compliance Chiefs Get a Direct Line to the Boss," *The Wall Street Journal,* January 15, 2014; and Gregory J. Millman and Samuel Rubenfeld, "Compliance Officer: Dream Career?" *The Wall Street Journal,* January 15, 2014.

10. Doug Guthrie, "A Conversation on Corporate Social Responsibility," *Forbes,* January 9, 2014.

11. Aoltan J. Acs, "A Buffett Rule Worth Following," *The Wall Street Journal,* March 28, 2013.

12. Michael Cohn, "Investors Swayed by Corporate Social Responsibility Reputation," *Accounting Today,* January 10, 2014.

13. Gates Foundation, www.gatesfoundation.org, accessed April 2014; and Howard Husock, "Lessons from Zuckerberg and Bloomberg: As Giving Goes Up, Philanthropy under Fire," *Forbes,* January 11, 2014.

14. Annie Gasparro, "A New Test for Panera's Pay-What-You-Can," *The Wall Street Journal,* June 5, 2013.

15. TNT, www.tnt.com, accessed April 2014.

16. Patagonia, www.patagonia.com, accessed April 2014.

17. Xerox, www.xerox.com, accessed April 2014.

18. Ann Eigeman, "Giving in the Midst of a Polarized Economy," www.nonprofitquarterly.org, accessed April 2014; "The Philanthropic," *Forbes,* December 2, 2013; "Giving USA 2013: Giving Coming Back Slowly and Different After Recession," *Nonprofit Quarterly,* www.nonprofitquarterly.org, accessed April 2014.

19. Sarah Halzack, "Paid Time Off for Volunteering Gains Traction as Way to Retain Employees," *The Washington Post,* August 11, 2013.

20. David A. Kaplan, "Inside Mars," *Fortune,* February 4, 2013.

21. Debbie Haski-Leventhal, *MBA Students Around the World and Their Attitudes Towards Responsible Management, Second Annual Study* (Macquarie Graduate School of Management, 2013).

22. "50 Percent of Global Consumers Surveyed Willing to Pay More for Goods, Services from Socially Responsible Companies, Up From 2011," Nielsen, www.nielsen.com, accessed March 2014.

23. Eric Gneckow, "'Socially Responsible Investing Steps Toward Mainstream," *North Bay Business Journal,* January 6, 2014.

24. Chad Bray, "Court Upholds Conviction of Ex-Fund Manager Raj Rajaratnam," *The Wall Street Journal,* June 24, 2013.

25. Seth Stern, "FBI Fraud Probes Increase as 'Insider Trading' Widespread," *Bloomberg,* www.bloomberg.com, accessed March 2014.

26. Bill Catlette and Richard Hadden, *Contented Cows Still Give Better Milk* (Contented Cow Partners, 2012); and Contented Cow Partners, www.contentedcows.com, accessed March 2014.

27. Costco, www.costco.com, accessed March 2014.

28. Heather Boushey and Sarah Jane Glenn, "There Are Significant Business Costs to Replacing Employees," Center for American Progress, www.centerforamericanprogress.org, accessed March 2014; and Suzanne Lucas, "How Much Employee Turnover Really Costs You," *Inc.,* August 13, 2013.

29. Douglas M. Boyle, Brian W. Carpenter, and Dana R. Hermanson, "CEOs, CFOs, and Accounting Fraud," *The CPA Journal,* January 1, 2012; and Association of Certified Fraud Examiners, www.acfe.com, accessed March 2014.

30. American Solar Energy Society, www.ases.org, accessed March 2014.

31. USSIF, The Forum for Sustainable and Responsible Investment, www.ussif.org, accessed April 2014.

32. Ethisphere, www.ethisphere.com, accessed March 2014.

33. Rainforest Action Network, www.ran.org, accessed March 2014.

34. Russell Flannery, "Cambodia Factory Shootings Underscore Shifts, Openings in the Global Apparel Business," *Forbes,* January 16, 2014.

35. Jim Yardley, "Report on Deadly Factory Collapse in Bangladesh Finds Widespread Blame," *The New York Times,* May 22, 2013.

36. Organization of American States, www.oas.org, accessed March 2014.

photo credits

5

How to Form a Business

Learning Objectives

AFTER YOU HAVE READ AND STUDIED THIS CHAPTER, YOU SHOULD BE ABLE TO

LO 5-1   Compare the advantages and disadvantages of sole proprietorships.

LO 5-2   Describe the differences between general and limited partners, and compare the advantages and disadvantages of partnerships.

LO 5-3   Compare the advantages and disadvantages of corporations, and summarize the differences between C corporations, S corporations, and limited liability companies.

LO 5-4   Define and give examples of three types of corporate mergers, and explain the role of leveraged buyouts and taking a firm private.

LO 5-5   Outline the advantages and disadvantages of franchises, and discuss the opportunities for diversity in franchising and the challenges of global franchising.

LO 5-6   Explain the role of cooperatives.

Getting to Know **Anne Beiler**

Some people start businesses in order to fulfill a lifelong dream or to capitalize on a unique idea. But many other entrepreneurs simply need to earn money. That's the reason why Anne Beiler began rolling pretzels at a local farmer's market in the early 1980s. At the time her family was living paycheck to paycheck as her husband tried to get a nonprofit crisis counseling service off the ground. After earning $875 their first weekend, the Beilers were thrilled at their new venture's potential. However, neither could have imagined that their little pretzel stand would grow into Auntie Anne's, a mall-based chain with more than 1,200 locations worldwide and $410 million in annual sales.

As a child Beiler made her first entrepreneurial effort baking cakes and pies for her Amish-Mennonite family to sell. She married young and planned to live a quiet life on the farm raising her children. But Beiler's plans turned upside down in 1975 when her daughter Angela lost her life in a tractor accident. Although it took years for the family to recover, Beiler's husband came out of the tragedy wanting to start his own free counseling service for people in their Pennsylvania town. Beiler supported her husband's decision but realized that she would need to figure out a way to fund this nonprofit without the aid of his mechanic's salary.

Beiler soon discovered that a pretzel and pizza store was up for sale in an Amish farmer's market. After borrowing $6,000 to purchase the space, Beiler began to tweak the previous owner's pretzel recipe to fit her own tastes. Customers immediately responded to the changes. "The morning we launched the new recipe, the first customer to take a bite looked at us and said, 'This is amazing,'" says Beiler. "From that point on, we had to bring in more help and buy more ovens. We got rid of the pizza and sold only the pretzels." She renamed the store Auntie Anne's Soft Pretzels, a nod to her 30 nieces and nephews. Within a few months she launched a second location in Harrisburg, Pennsylvania. Operating a booming business in the state capital put her in contact with many people who wanted to help expand her brand. Although she refused at first, eventually Beiler decided to let family and friends open 10 stores under a licensing agreement.

For the next year Auntie Anne's continued to grow by licensing its name for a $2,500 upfront fee and 4 percent of gross sales. However, a licensee pointed out that the company was actually franchising, not licensing. "It was an honest mistake," says Beiler. "By then, we had 75 locations in several states. If you franchise without the proper documentation, you could be fined thousands of dollars a day per store." Luckily, Beiler managed to avoid any fines by immediately contacting her partners as well as state legislators about the issue. Auntie Anne's ran into more problems as its national expansion required more and more money. Although Beiler had incorporated the company by that point, she didn't want to risk putting financial benchmarks ahead of the needs of employees or franchisees by going public. Instead, good fortune found her again in the form of a Mennonite pig farmer who provided a $1.5 million loan on a handshake.

By 2005, though, the company had grown to such an enormous size that Beiler felt it was time to move on. She sold Auntie Anne's to her second cousin in order to focus more on the company's charitable organizations, such as the Angela Foundation, named in honor of her daughter. Beiler attributes her success to what she calls "the three small P's": purpose, product, and people. "We started with a *purpose*—counseling and helping people," says Beiler. "We had a *product* that supported our purpose. Then we got the *people* to do it. The three small P's, in that order, result in the big P—*profit.*"

Just like Anne Beiler, all business owners must decide for themselves which form of business is best for them. Whether you dream of starting a business for yourself, going into business with a partner, forming a corporation, or someday being a leading franchisor, it's important to know that each form of ownership has its advantages and disadvantages. You will learn about them all in this chapter.

Sources: "Franchise Players: An Auntie Anne's Franchisee on the Importance of Seeking Advice," *Entrepreneur,* January 28, 2014; Dinah Eng, "Soft Pretzels Out of Hard Times," *Fortune,* July 10, 2013; and www. auntieannebeiler.com, accessed June 2014.

Anne Beiler

- Founder of Auntie Anne's
- Twisted a small pretzel stand into a successful snack franchise

www.auntieannes.com

@AuntieAnnes

connect

 iSee It! Need help understanding forms of business ownership? Visit your Connect e-book video tab for a brief animated explanation.

sole proprietorship
A business that is owned, and usually managed, by one person.

partnership
A legal form of business with two or more owners.

corporation
A legal entity with authority to act and have liability apart from its owners.

BASIC FORMS OF BUSINESS OWNERSHIP

Hundreds of thousands of people have started new businesses in the United States. In fact, more than 600,000 are started each year.[1] Chances are, you've thought of owning your own business or know someone who has.

How you form your business can make a tremendous difference in your long-term success. The three major forms of business ownership are (1) sole proprietorships, (2) partnerships, and (3) corporations. Each has advantages and disadvantages that we'll discuss.

It can be easy to get started in your own business. You can begin a lawn mowing service, develop a website, or go about meeting other wants and needs of your community. A business owned, and usually managed, by one person is called a **sole proprietorship**. That is the most common form of business ownership.

Many people do not have the money, time, or desire to run a business on their own. When two or more people legally agree to become co-owners of a business, the organization is called a **partnership**.

Sole proprietorships and partnerships are relatively easy to form, but there are advantages to creating a business that is separate and distinct from the owners. This is a **corporation**, a legal entity with authority to act and have liability apart from its owners. The almost 5 million corporations in the United States make up only 20 percent of all businesses, but they earn 81 percent of total U.S. business receipts (see Figure 5.1).[2]

Keep in mind that just because a business starts in one form of ownership, it doesn't have to stay in that form. Many companies start out in one

FIGURE 5.1 FORMS OF BUSINESS OWNERSHIP
Although corporations make up only 20 percent of the total number of businesses, they make 81 percent of the total receipts. Sole proprietorships are the most common form (72 percent), but they earn only 6 percent of the receipts.
Source: U.S. Census Bureau.

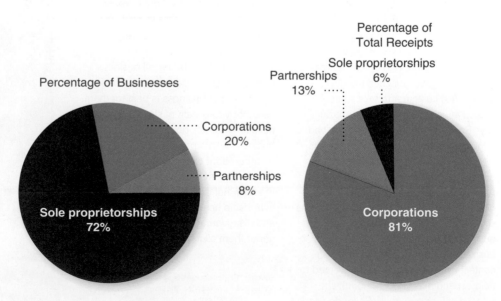

Percentage of Businesses
Sole proprietorships 72%
Corporations 20%
Partnerships 8%

Percentage of Total Receipts
Sole proprietorships 6%
Partnerships 13%
Corporations 81%

form, then add (or drop) a partner or two, and eventually become corporations, limited liability companies, or franchisors.[3] Let's begin our discussion by looking at the most basic form of ownership—the sole proprietorship.

LO 5–1   Compare the advantages and disadvantages of sole proprietorships.

SOLE PROPRIETORSHIPS

Advantages of Sole Proprietorships

Sole proprietorships are the easiest kind of businesses to explore in your quest for an interesting career. Every town has sole proprietors you can visit and talk with about the joys and frustrations of being in business on their own. Most will mention the benefits of being their own boss and setting their own hours. Other advantages include:

1. *Ease of starting and ending the business.* All you have to do to start a sole proprietorship is buy or lease the needed equipment (a saw, a laptop, a tractor, a lawn mower) and put up some announcements saying you are in business. You may have to get a permit or license from the local government, but often that is no problem. It is just as easy to get out of business; you simply stop. There is no one to consult or disagree with about such decisions.

2. *Being your own boss.* Working for others simply does not have the same excitement as working for yourself—at least, that's the way sole proprietors feel. You may make mistakes, but they are your mistakes—and so are the many small victories each day.

3. *Pride of ownership.* People who own and manage their own businesses are rightfully proud of their work. They deserve all the credit for taking the risks and providing needed goods or services.

4. *Leaving a legacy.* Owners can leave an ongoing business for future generations.

5. *Retention of company profits.* Owners not only keep the profits earned but also benefit from the increasing value as the business grows.

6. *No special taxes.* All the profits of a sole proprietorship are taxed as the personal income of the owner, and the owner pays the normal income tax on that money. However, owners do have to pay the self-employment tax (for Social Security and Medicare). They also have to estimate their taxes and make quarterly payments to the government or suffer penalties for nonpayment.

unlimited liability
The responsibility of business owners for all of the debts of the business.

In college, Jerry Swain earned a reputation for making delicious chocolate candies. Even after graduation and landing a job at IBM, he still loved to make chocolate and decided to take the risk of starting his own confection company. Swain now offers his awarding-winning candies in his Solana Beach store as well as supplying Barney's in New York and Costco around the country. Do you have a passion you would like to pursue as a business?

Disadvantages of Sole Proprietorships

Not everyone is equipped to own and manage a business. Often it is difficult to save enough money to start a business and keep it going. The costs of inventory, supplies, insurance, advertising, rent, computers, utilities, and so on may be too much to cover alone. There are other disadvantages:

1. *Unlimited liability—the risk of personal losses.* When you work for others, it is their problem if the business is not profitable. When you own your own business, you and the business are considered one. You have **unlimited liability**;

Being the sole proprietor of a company, like a dog-walking service, means making a major time commitment to run the business, including constantly seeking out new customers and looking for reliable employees when the time comes to grow. If you were a sole proprietor, what would you need to do if you wanted to take a week's vacation?

that is, any debts or damages incurred by the business are your debts and you must pay them, even if it means selling your home, your car, or whatever else you own. This is a serious risk, and undertaking it requires not only thought but also discussion with a lawyer, an insurance agent, an accountant, and others.

2. *Limited financial resources.* Funds available to the business are limited to what the one owner can gather. Since there are serious limits to how much money one person can raise, partnerships and corporations have a greater probability of obtaining the financial backing needed to start and equip a business and keep it going.

3. *Management difficulties.* All businesses need management; someone must keep inventory, accounting, and tax records. Many people skilled at selling things or providing a service are not so skilled at keeping records. Sole proprietors often find it difficult to attract qualified employees to help run the business because often they cannot compete with the salary and benefits offered by larger companies.

4. *Overwhelming time commitment.* Though sole proprietors say they set their own hours, it's hard to own a business, manage it, train people, and have time for anything else in life when there is no one with whom to share the burden. The owner of a store, for example, may put in 12 hours a day at least six days a week—almost twice the hours worked by a nonsupervisory employee in a large company. Imagine how this time commitment affects the sole proprietor's family life. Many sole proprietors will tell you, "It's not a job, it's not a career, it's a way of life."[4]

5. *Few fringe benefits.* If you are your own boss, you lose the fringe benefits that often come with working for others. You have no paid health insurance, no paid disability insurance, no pension plan, no sick leave, and no vacation pay. These and other benefits may add up to 30 percent or more of a worker's compensation.

6. *Limited growth.* Expansion is often slow since a sole proprietorship relies on its owner for most of its creativity, business know-how, and funding.

7. *Limited life span.* If the sole proprietor dies, is incapacitated, or retires, the business no longer exists (unless it is sold or taken over by the sole proprietor's heirs).

Talk with a few local sole proprietors about the problems they've faced in being on their own. They are likely to have many interesting stories about problems getting loans from the bank, problems with theft, and problems simply keeping up with the business. These are reasons why many sole proprietors choose to find partners to share the load.

test **prep**

- Most people who start businesses in the United States are sole proprietors. What are the advantages and disadvantages of sole proprietorships?
- Why would unlimited liability be considered a major drawback to sole proprietorships?

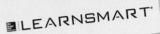

LO 5–2   Describe the differences between general and limited partners, and compare the advantages and disadvantages of partnerships.

PARTNERSHIPS

A partnership is a legal form of business with two or more owners. There are several types: (1) general partnerships, (2) limited partnerships, and (3) master limited partnerships. In a **general partnership** all owners share in operating the business and in assuming liability for the business's debts. A **limited partnership** has one or more general partners and one or more limited partners. A **general partner** is an owner (partner) who has unlimited liability and is active in managing the firm. Every partnership must have at least one general partner. A **limited partner** is an owner who invests money in the business but does not have any management responsibility or liability for losses beyond his or her investment. **Limited liability** means that the limited partners' liability for the debts of the business is *limited* to the amount they put into the company; their personal assets are not at risk.

One form of partnership, the **master limited partnership (MLP)**, looks much like a corporation (which we discuss next) in that it acts like a corporation and is traded on the stock exchanges like a corporation, but is taxed like a partnership and thus avoids the corporate income tax.[5] Master limited partnerships are normally found in the oil and gas industry. For example, Sunoco Inc. formed the MLP Sunoco Logistics Partners (SXL) to acquire, own, and operate a group of crude oil and refined-product pipelines and storage facilities. Income received by SXL is not taxed before it is passed on to investors as dividends as it would be if SXL were a corporation.[6]

Another type of partnership was created to limit the disadvantage of unlimited liability. A **limited liability partnership (LLP)** limits partners' risk of losing their personal assets to the outcomes of only their own acts and omissions and those of people under their supervision. If you are a limited partner in an LLP, you can operate without the fear that one of your partners might commit an act of malpractice resulting in a judgment that takes away your house, car, retirement plan, even your collection of vintage Star Wars action figures, as would be the case in a general partnership. However, in many states this personal protection does not extend to contract liabilities such as bank loans, leases, and business debt the partnership takes on; loss of personal

general partnership
A partnership in which all owners share in operating the business and in assuming liability for the business's debts.

limited partnership
A partnership with one or more general partners and one or more limited partners.

general partner
An owner (partner) who has unlimited liability and is active in managing the firm.

limited partner
An owner who invests money in the business but does not have any management responsibility or liability for losses beyond the investment.

limited liability
The responsibility of a business's owners for losses only up to the amount they invest; limited partners and shareholders (stockholders) have limited liability.

master limited partnership (MLP)
A partnership that looks much like a corporation (in that it acts like a corporation and is traded on a stock exchange) but is taxed like a partnership and thus avoids the corporate income tax.

limited liability partnership (LLP)
A partnership that limits partners' risk of losing their personal assets to only their own acts and omissions and to the acts and omissions of people under their supervision.

Eventbrite, an online ticketing service, boasts having processed more than $1.5 billion in ticket sales. Married partners Julia and Kevin Hartz say their secret to success is to "'Divide and conquer'... while we both operate the business on a day-to-day basis, we are diligent about not treading on each other's turf." What problems might partners who share both business and home encounter that other partners might not?

assets is still a risk if these are not paid. In states without additional contract liability protections for LLPs, the LLP is in many ways similar to an LLC (discussed later in the chapter).

All states except Louisiana have adopted the Uniform Partnership Act (UPA) to replace earlier laws governing partnerships. The UPA defines the three key elements of any general partnership as (1) common ownership, (2) shared profits and losses, and (3) the right to participate in managing the operations of the business.

Advantages of Partnerships

Often, it is much easier to own and manage a business with one or more partners. Your partner may be skilled at inventory control and accounting, while you do the selling or servicing. A partner can also provide additional money, support, and expertise as well as cover for you when you are sick or on vacation. Figure 5.2 suggests several questions to ask yourself when choosing a partner.

Partnerships usually have the following advantages:

1. *More financial resources.* When two or more people pool their money and credit, it is easier to pay the rent, utilities, and other bills incurred by a business. A limited partnership is specially designed to help raise money. As mentioned earlier, a limited partner invests money in the business but cannot legally have management responsibility and has limited liability.

2. *Shared management and pooled/complementary skills and knowledge.* It is simply much easier to manage the day-to-day activities of a business with carefully chosen partners. Partners give each other free time from the business and provide different skills and perspectives. Some people

FIGURE 5.2 QUESTIONS TO ASK WHEN CHOOSING A BUSINESS PARTNER

There's no such thing as a perfect partner, but you should share some common thoughts on the business. Ask yourself:

Do you share the same goals?

Do you share the same vision for the company's future?

What skills does the person have?

Are those skills the same as yours, or do they complement your skills?

What contacts, resources, or special attributes will the person bring to the business?

What type of decision maker is the person?

Is this someone with whom you could happily share authority for all major business decisions?

Do you trust each other?

How does the person respond to adversity?

Does he or she try to solve the problem or try to defend his or her ego?

Can the person accept constructive criticism without getting defensive?

To what extent can you build fun and excitement into the partnership?

find that the best partner is a spouse. Many husband-and-wife teams manage restaurants, service shops, and other businesses.[7]

3. *Longer survival.* Partnerships are more likely to succeed than sole proprietorships because being watched by a partner can help a businessperson become more disciplined.[8]

4. *No special taxes.* As with sole proprietorships, all profits of partnerships are taxed as the personal income of the owners, who pay the normal income tax on that money. Similarly, partners must estimate their taxes and make quarterly payments or suffer penalties for nonpayment.

Disadvantages of Partnerships

Anytime two people must agree, conflict and tension are possible. Partnerships have caused splits between relatives, friends, and spouses. Let's explore the disadvantages of partnerships:

1. *Unlimited liability.* Each *general* partner is liable for the debts of the firm, no matter who was responsible for causing them. You are liable for your partners' mistakes as well as your own. Like sole proprietors, general partners can lose their homes, cars, and everything else they own if the business loses a lawsuit or goes bankrupt.

2. *Division of profits.* Sharing risk means sharing profits, and that can cause conflicts. There is no set system for dividing profits in a partnership, and they are not always divided evenly. For example, if one partner puts in more money and the other puts in more hours, each may feel justified in asking for a bigger share of the profits.

3. *Disagreements among partners.* Disagreements over money are just one example of potential conflict in a partnership. Who has final authority over employees? Who hires and fires employees? Who works what hours? What if one partner wants to buy expensive equipment for the firm and the other partner disagrees? All terms of the partnership should be spelled out in writing to protect all parties and minimize misunderstandings.[9] The Making Ethical Decisions box offers an example of a difference of opinions between partners.

4. *Difficulty of termination.* Once you have committed yourself to a partnership, it is not easy to get out of it. Sure, you can just quit. However, questions about who gets what and what happens next are often difficult to resolve when the partnership ends. Surprisingly, law firms often have faulty partnership agreements and find that breaking up is hard to do. How do you get rid of a partner you don't like? It is best to decide such questions up front in the partnership agreement. Figure 5.3 gives you ideas about what to include in partnership agreements.

The best way to learn about the advantages and disadvantages of partnerships is to interview several people who have experience with them. They will give you insights and hints on how to avoid problems.

One fear of owning your own business or having a partner is the fear of losing everything you own if someone sues the business or it loses a lot of money. Many businesspeople try to avoid this and the other disadvantages of sole proprietorships and partnerships by forming corporations. We discuss this basic form of business ownership in the following section.

FIGURE 5.3 HOW TO FORM A PARTNERSHIP

It's not hard to form a partnership, but it's wise for each prospective partner to get the counsel of a lawyer experienced with such agreements. Lawyers' services are usually expensive, so would-be partners should read all about partnerships and reach some basic agreements before calling a lawyer.

For your protection, be sure to put your partnership agreement in writing. The Model Business Corporation Act recommends including the following in a written partnership agreement:

1. The name of the business. Many states require the firm's name to be registered with state and/or county officials if the firm's name is different from the name of any of the partners.

2. The names and addresses of all partners.

3. The purpose and nature of the business, the location of the principal offices, and any other locations where business will be conducted.

4. The date the partnership will start and how long it will last. Will it exist for a specific length of time, or will it stop when one of the partners dies or when the partners agree to discontinue?

5. The contributions made by each partner. Will some partners contribute money, while others provide real estate, personal property, expertise, or labor? When are the contributions due?

6. The management responsibilities. Will all partners have equal voices in management, or will there be senior and junior partners?

7. The duties of each partner.

8. The salaries and drawing accounts of each partner.

9. Provision for sharing of profits or losses.

10. Provision for accounting procedures. Who'll keep the accounts? What bookkeeping and accounting methods will be used? Where will the books be kept?

11. The requirements for taking in new partners.

12. Any special restrictions, rights, or duties of any partner.

13. Provision for a retiring partner.

14. Provision for the purchase of a deceased or retiring partner's share of the business.

15. Provision for how grievances will be handled.

16. Provision for how to dissolve the partnership and distribute the assets to the partners.

Good Business, Bad Karma?

Imagine that you and your partner own a construction company. You receive a bid from a subcontractor that you know is 20 percent too low. Such a loss to the subcontractor could put him out of business. Accepting the bid will certainly improve your chances of winning the contract for a big shopping center project. Your partner wants to take the bid and let the subcontractor suffer the consequences of his bad estimate. What do you think you should do? What will be the consequences of your decision?

test **prep**

- What is the difference between a limited partner and a general partner?
- What are some of the advantages and disadvantages of partnerships?

LO 5–3   Compare the advantages and disadvantages of corporations, and summarize the differences between C corporations, S corporations, and limited liability companies.

CORPORATIONS

Many corporations—like General Electric, Microsoft, and Walmart—are big and contribute substantially to the U.S. economy. However, it's not necessary to be big to incorporate. Incorporating may be beneficial for small businesses as well.

A **conventional (C) corporation** is a state-chartered legal entity with authority to act and have liability separate from its owners—its *stockholders*. Stockholders are not liable for the debts or other problems of the corporation beyond the money they invest in it by buying ownership shares, or stock, in the company. They don't have to worry about losing their house, car, or other property because of some business problem—a significant benefit. A corporation not only limits the liability of owners but often enables many people to share in the ownership (and profits) of a business without working there or having other commitments to it. Corporations may choose whether to offer ownership to outside investors or remain privately held. (We discuss stock ownership in Chapter 19.) Figure 5.4 describes various types of corporations.

conventional (C) corporation
A state-chartered legal entity with authority to act and have liability separate from its owners.

Advantages of Corporations

Most people are not willing to risk everything to go into business. Yet for a business to grow, prosper, and create economic opportunity, many people have to be willing to invest money in it. One way to solve this problem is to create an artificial being, an entity that exists only in the eyes of the law—a corporation. Let's explore some of the advantages of corporations:

1. *Limited liability.* A major advantage of corporations is the limited liability of their owners. Remember, limited liability means that the owners of a business are responsible for its losses only up to the amount they invest in it.

2. *Ability to raise more money for investment.* To raise money, a corporation can sell shares of its stock to anyone who is interested. This means that millions of people can own part of major companies like IBM, Apple, and Coca-Cola, and smaller corporations as well. If a company sells 10 million shares of stock for $50 a share, it will have $500 million available to build plants, buy materials, hire people, manufacture products, and so on. Such a large amount of money would be difficult to raise any other way.

Corporations can also borrow money by obtaining loans from financial institutions like banks. They can also borrow from individual investors by issuing bonds, which involve paying investors interest until the bonds are repaid sometime in the future.[10] You can read about how corporations raise funds through the sale of stocks and bonds in Chapter 19.

3. *Size.* "Size" summarizes many of the advantages of some corporations. Because they can raise large amounts of money to work with, big corporations can build modern factories or software development facilities with the latest equipment. They can hire experts or specialists in all areas of operation. They can buy other corporations in different fields to diversify their business risks. In short, a large corporation with numerous resources can take advantage of opportunities anywhere in the world.

But corporations do not have to be large to enjoy the benefits of incorporating. Many doctors, lawyers, and individuals, as well as partners in a variety of businesses, have incorporated. The vast majority of corporations in the United States are small businesses.

FIGURE 5.4 CORPORATE TYPES
Corporations can fit in more than one category.

You may find some confusing types of corporations when reading about them. Here are a few of the more widely used terms:

An *alien corporation* does business in the United States but is chartered (incorporated) in another country.

A *domestic corporation* does business in the state in which it's chartered (incorporated).

A *foreign corporation* does business in one state but is chartered in another. About one-third of all corporations are chartered in Delaware because of its relatively attractive rules for incorporation. A foreign corporation must register in states where it operates.

A *closed (private) corporation* is one whose stock is held by a few people and isn't available to the general public.

An *open (public) corporation* sells stock to the general public. General Motors and ExxonMobil are examples of public corporations.

A *quasi-public corporation* is a corporation chartered by the government as an approved monopoly to perform services to the general public. Public utilities are examples of quasi-public corporations.

A *professional corporation* is one whose owners offer professional services (doctors, lawyers, etc.). Shares in professional corporations aren't publicly traded.

A *nonprofit (or not-for-profit) corporation* is one that doesn't seek personal profit for its owners.

A *multinational corporation* is a firm that operates in several countries.

4. *Perpetual life.* Because corporations are separate from those who own them, the death of one or more owners does not terminate the corporation.

5. *Ease of ownership change.* It is easy to change the owners of a corporation. All that is necessary is to sell the stock to someone else.

6. *Ease of attracting talented employees.* Corporations can attract skilled employees by offering such benefits as stock options (the right to purchase shares of the corporation for a fixed price).

7. *Separation of ownership from management.* Corporations are able to raise money from many different owners/stockholders without getting them involved in management. The corporate hierarchy in Figure 5.5 shows how the owners/stockholders are separate from the managers and employees. The owners/stockholders elect a board of directors, who hire the officers of the corporation and oversee major policy issues. The owners/stockholders thus have some say in who runs the corporation but have no real control over the daily operations.[11]

Disadvantages of Corporations

There are so many sole proprietorships and partnerships in the United States that there must be some disadvantages to incorporating. Otherwise, everyone would do it. The following are a few of the disadvantages:

1. *Initial cost.* Incorporation may cost thousands of dollars and require expensive lawyers and accountants. There are less expensive ways of incorporating in certain states (see the following subsection), but

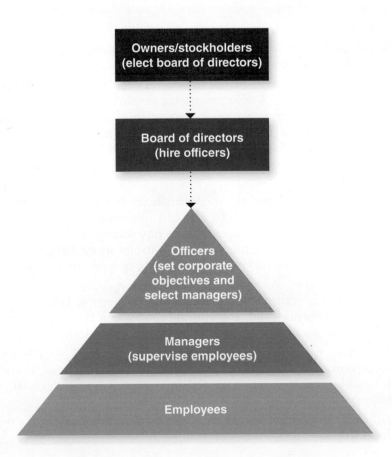

FIGURE 5.5 HOW OWNERS AFFECT MANAGEMENT
Owners have an influence on how a business is managed by electing a board of directors. The board hires the top officers (and fires them if necessary). It also sets the pay for those officers. The officers then select managers and employees with the help of the human resources department.

B Corporations Let Sustainability Set Sail

While vacationing on the small island of Tobago, Michael Dimin and his sons saw a nasty sight as their boat headed to dock after a day of fishing. Tons of rotting fish littered the water, left there by fishermen who caught too much to sell locally. That gave Dimin an idea: what if they sold the surplus fish directly to New York restaurants? After all, demand for fresh seafood would always be high at the city's many upscale eateries. Plus, with an outside market to sell to, fishermen in Tobago wouldn't need to waste so much of their catch.

Dimin knew this venture was likely to be profitable, but more than that he wanted ocean conservation and sustainability to be

the driving force of the business. That's why he registered his company Sea2Table as a benefit corporation, or B corporation. With this new sort of business structure, companies are judged by how well they meet their own set of socially or environmentally beneficial goals. For Sea2Table,

that means developing relationships with local fishermen rather than costly and wasteful middlemen. This allows the company to keep their supply lines transparent while still shipping the freshest fish possible to their clients in New York. Not only do business models like this help society, their compassionate goals tend to lure in some of the most talented people in the job market. It just goes to show that profits aren't the only way to measure success in the business world.

Sources: "Our Story," www.sea2table.com, accessed February 2014; "Sean and Michael Dimin," www.futureoffish.org, accessed February 2014; and Lindsay Gellman and Rachel Feintzeig, "Social Seal of Approval Lures Talent," *The Wall Street Journal*, November 12, 2013.

many people do not have the time or confidence to go through this procedure without the help of a potentially expensive lawyer.

2. *Extensive paperwork.* The paperwork needed to start a corporation is just the beginning. A sole proprietor or partnership may keep rather broad accounting records. A corporation, in contrast, must keep detailed financial records, the minutes of meetings, and more. As noted in Figure 5.4, many firms incorporate in Delaware or Nevada because these states' business-oriented laws make the process easier than it is in other states.

3. *Double taxation.* Corporate income is taxed twice. First the corporation pays tax on its income before it can distribute any, as *dividends,* to stockholders. Then the stockholders pay income tax on the dividends they receive. States often tax corporations more heavily than other enterprises, and some special taxes apply only to corporations.[12]

4. *Two tax returns.* An individual who incorporates must file both a corporate tax return and an individual tax return. Depending on the size of the corporation, a corporate return can be quite complex and require the assistance of a certified public accountant (CPA).

5. *Size.* Size may be one advantage of corporations, but it can be a disadvantage as well. Large corporations sometimes become too inflexible and tied down in red tape to respond quickly to market changes, and their profitability can suffer.

6. *Difficulty of termination.* Once a corporation has started, it's relatively hard to end.

7. *Possible conflict with stockholders and board of directors.* Conflict may brew if the stockholders elect a board of directors who disagree with management.[13] Since the board of directors chooses the company's officers, entrepreneurs serving as managers can find themselves forced out of the very company they founded. This happened to Tom Freston, one of the founders of MTV, and Steve Jobs, a founder of Apple Computer (Jobs of course returned to the company later).

Many businesspeople are discouraged by the costs, paperwork, and special taxes corporations must pay. However, many others believe the advantages of incorporation outweigh the hassles. See the Seeking Sustainability box for an example of a benefit corporation, a new type of nonprofit corporation.

Individuals Can Incorporate

Not all corporations are large organizations with hundreds of employees and thousands of stockholders. Truckers, doctors, lawyers, plumbers, athletes, and small-business owners of all kinds can also incorporate. Normally, individuals who incorporate do not issue stock to outsiders; therefore, they do not share all the advantages and disadvantages of large corporations (such as size and more money for investment). Their major advantages are limited liability and possible tax benefits. Although you are not required to file for incorporation through a lawyer, it is usually wise to consult one. In addition to lawyers' fees, the secretary of state's office charges a fee for incorporating a business, varying by state from a low of $50 (in Colorado, Iowa, Kentucky, Mississippi, and Oklahoma) to a high of $300 (in Texas).[14] Like the fee, the length of time it will take to actually have your business incorporated will vary by state. The average time is approximately 30 days from the date of application. Figure 5.6 outlines how to incorporate.

FIGURE 5.6 HOW TO INCORPORATE

The process of forming a corporation varies somewhat from state to state. The articles of incorporation are usually filed with the secretary of state's office in the state in which the company incorporates. The articles contain:

- The corporation's name.
- The names of the people who incorporated it.
- Its purposes.
- Its duration (usually perpetual).
- The number of shares that can be issued, their voting rights, and any other rights the shareholders have.
- The corporation's minimum capital.
- The address of the corporation's office.
- The name and address of the person responsible for the corporation's legal service.
- The names and addresses of the first directors.
- Any other public information the incorporators wish to include.

Before a business can so much as open a bank account or hire employees, it needs a federal tax identification number. To apply for one, get an SS-4 form from the IRS.

In addition to the articles of incorporation listed, a corporation has bylaws. These describe how the firm is to be operated from both legal and managerial points of view. The bylaws include:

- How, when, and where shareholders' and directors' meetings are held, and how long directors are to serve.
- Directors' authority.
- Duties and responsibilities of officers, and the length of their service.
- How stock is issued.
- Other matters, including employment contracts.

S Corporations

An **S corporation** is a unique government creation that looks like a corporation but is taxed like sole proprietorships and partnerships. (The name comes from the fact that the rules governing them are in Subchapter S of Chapter 1 of the Internal Revenue Code.) The paperwork and details of S corporations are similar to those of conventional (C) corporations. S corporations have shareholders, directors, and employees, and the benefit of limited liability, but their profits are taxed only as the personal income of the shareholders—thus avoiding the double taxation of C corporations.

Avoiding double taxation is reason enough for approximately 3 million U.S. companies to operate as S corporations. Yet not all businesses can become S corporations. In order to qualify, a company must:[15]

1. Have no more than 100 shareholders. (All members of a family count as one shareholder.)

2. Have shareholders that are individuals or estates, and who (as individuals) are citizens or permanent residents of the United States.

3. Have only one class of stock. (You can read more about the various classes of stock in Chapter 19.)

4. Derive no more than 25 percent of income from passive sources (rents, royalties, interest).

An S corporation that loses its S status may not operate under it again for at least five years. The tax structure of S corporations isn't attractive to all businesses.[16] For one thing, the benefits change every time the tax rules change. The best way to learn all the benefits or shortcomings for a specific business is to go over the tax advantages and liability differences with a lawyer, an accountant, or both.

Limited Liability Companies

A **limited liability company (LLC)** is similar to an S corporation, but without the special eligibility requirements. LLCs were introduced in Wyoming in 1977, and were recognized by the Internal Revenue Service as a partnership for federal income tax purposes in 1988. By 1996, all 50 states and the District of Columbia recognized LLCs.

The number of LLCs has risen dramatically since 1988, when there were fewer than 100 filings to operate them. Today more than half of new business registrations in some states are LLCs.

Why the drive toward forming LLCs? Advantages include:

1. *Limited liability.* Personal assets are protected. Limited liability was previously available only to limited partners and shareholders of corporations.

2. *Choice of taxation.* LLCs can choose to be taxed as partnerships or as corporations. Partnership-level taxation was previously a benefit normally reserved for partners or S corporation owners.

PetZen Products LLC offers doggie treadmills to help the nation's overweight pets get back their puppy figures. What are the advantages and disadvantages of LLCs?

3. *Flexible ownership rules.* LLCs do not have to comply with ownership restrictions as S corporations do. Owners can be a person, partnership, or corporation.

4. *Flexible distribution of profits and losses.* Profits and losses don't have to be distributed in proportion to the money each person invests, as in corporations. LLC members agree on the percentage to be distributed to each member.

5. *Operating flexibility.* LLCs do have to submit articles of organization, which are similar to articles of incorporation, but they are not required to keep minutes, file written resolutions, or hold annual meetings. An LLC also submits a written operating agreement, similar to a partnership agreement, describing how the company is to be operated.

Of course, LLCs have their disadvantages as well. These include:

1. *No stock.* LLC ownership is nontransferable. LLC members need the approval of the other members in order to sell their interests in the company. In contrast, regular and S corporation stockholders can sell their shares as they wish.

2. *Limited life span.* LLCs are required to identify dissolution dates in the articles of organization (no more than 30 years in some states). The death of a member can cause LLCs to dissolve automatically. Members may choose to reconstitute the LLC after it dissolves.

3. *Fewer incentives.* Unlike corporations, LLCs can't deduct the cost of fringe benefits for members owning 2 percent or more of the company. And since there's no stock, they can't use stock options as incentives to employees.

4. *Taxes.* LLC members must pay self-employment taxes—the Medicare/Social Security taxes paid by sole proprietors and partnerships—on their profits. In contrast, S corporations pay self-employment tax on owners' salaries but not on the entire profits.

5. *Paperwork.* While the paperwork required of LLCs is not as great as that required of corporations, it is more than required of sole proprietors.

The start-up cost for an LLC varies. Online legal services such as Legal Zoom (www.legalzoom.com) can file the necessary paperwork for as little as $99 plus the state filing fee.[17] Figure 5.7 summarizes the advantages and disadvantages of the major forms of business ownership.

test **prep**

- What are the major advantages and disadvantages of incorporating a business?
- What is the role of owners (stockholders) in the corporate hierarchy?
- If you buy stock in a corporation and someone gets injured by one of the corporation's products, can you be sued? Why or why not?
- Why are so many new businesses choosing a limited liability company (LLC) form of ownership?

FIGURE 5.7 COMPARISON OF FORMS OF BUSINESS OWNERSHIP

| | SOLE PROPRIETOR-SHIP | PARTNERSHIPS | | CORPORATIONS | | |
		GENERAL PARTNERSHIP	LIMITED PARTNERSHIP	CONVENTIONAL CORPORATION	S CORPORATION	LIMITED LIABILITY COMPANY
Documents Needed to Start Business	None; may need permit or license	Partnership agreement (oral or written)	Written agreement; must file certificate of limited partnership	Articles of incorporation, bylaws	Articles of incorporation, bylaws, must meet criteria	Articles of organization and operating agreement; no eligibility require-ments
Ease of Termination	Easy to terminate: just pay debts and quit	May be hard to terminate, depending on the partnership agreement	Same as general partnership	Hard and expensive to terminate	Same as conventional corporation	May be difficult, depending upon operating agreement
Length of Life	Terminates on the death of owner	Terminates on the death or withdrawal of partner	Same as general partnership	Perpetual life	Same as conventional corporation	Varies according to dissolution dates in arti-cles of organization
Transfer of Ownership	Business can be sold to qualified buyer	Must have other partner(s)' agreement	Same as general partnership	Easy to change owners; just sell stock	Can sell stock, but with restrictions	Can't sell stock
Financial Resources	Limited to owner's capital and loans	Limited to partners' capital and loans	Same as general partnership	More money to start and operate; may sell stocks and bonds	Same as conventional corporation	Same as partnership
Risk of Losses	Unlimited liability	Unlimited liability	Limited liability	Limited liability	Limited liability	Limited liability
Taxes	Taxed as personal income	Taxed as per-sonal income	Same as general partnership	Corporate, double taxation	Taxed as personal income	Varies
Management Responsibilities	Owner manages *all* areas of the business	Partners share management	Can't participate in management	Separate management from ownership	Same as conventional corporation	Varies
Employee Benefits	Usually fewer benefits and lower wages	Often fewer benefits and lower wages; promising employee could become a partner	Same as general partnership	Usually better benefits and wages, advancement opportunities	Same as conventional corporation	Varies, but are not tax deductible

LO 5–4 Define and give examples of three types of corporate mergers, and explain the role of leveraged buyouts and taking a firm private.

CORPORATE EXPANSION: MERGERS AND ACQUISITIONS

What's the difference between mergers and acquisitions? A **merger** is the result of two firms joining to form one company. It is similar to a marriage, joining two individuals as one family. An **acquisition** is one company's purchase of the property and obligations of another company. It is more like buying a house than entering a marriage.

There are three major types of corporate mergers: vertical, horizontal, and conglomerate. A **vertical merger** joins two firms operating in different stages of related businesses.[18] A merger between a soft drink company and an artificial sweetener maker would ensure the merged firm a constant supply of an ingredient the soft drink manufacturer needs. It could also help ensure quality control of the soft drink company's products.

A **horizontal merger** joins two firms in the same industry and allows them to diversify or expand their products. A soft drink company and a mineral water company that merge can now supply a variety of beverage products.

A **conglomerate merger** unites firms in completely unrelated industries in order to diversify business operations and investments. A soft drink company and a snack food company would form a conglomerate merger. Figure 5.8 illustrates the differences among the three types of mergers.

merger
The result of two firms forming one company.

acquisition
One company's purchase of the property and obligations of another company.

vertical merger
The joining of two companies involved in different stages of related businesses.

horizontal merger
The joining of two firms in the same industry.

conglomerate merger
The joining of firms in completely unrelated industries.

FIGURE 5.8 TYPES OF MERGERS

Soft drink company   Buys   Mineral water company   =   Horizontal merger (companies in same industry)

Soft drink company

+

Buys

Artificial sweetener company

=

Vertical merger (companies in different stages in related industries)

Soft drink company

+

Buys

Snack food company

=

Conglomerate merger (companies in unrelated industries)

leveraged buyout (LBO)
An attempt by employees, management, or a group of investors to purchase an organization primarily through borrowing.

Rather than merge or sell to another company, some corporations decide to maintain, or in some cases regain, control of a firm internally. By *taking a firm private,* management or a group of stockholders obtain all the firm's stock for themselves by buying it back from the other stockholders. Burger King and Gymboree are firms that have been taken private.

Suppose employees believe they may lose their jobs, or managers believe they could improve corporate performance if they owned the company. Does either group have an opportunity of taking ownership of the company? Yes—they might attempt a leveraged buyout. A **leveraged buyout (LBO)** is an attempt by employees, management, or a group of private investors to buy out the stockholders in a company, primarily by borrowing the necessary funds. The employees, managers, or investors now become the owners of the firm. LBOs have ranged in size from $50 million to $34 billion and have involved everything from small family businesses to giant corporations like Hertz Corporation, Toys "R" Us, Chrysler, and the former RJR Nabisco. In 2013, Dell became the largest company in terms of revenue to be taken private through a leveraged buyout. After closing the $25 billion deal (with $19.4 billion of the total coming from a group of lenders), Michael Dell now controls a 75 percent stake in the company he founded in his dorm room.[19]

Today, business acquisitions are not limited to U.S. buyers. Foreign companies have found the fastest way to grow is often to buy an established operation that can enhance their technology or expand the number of brands they offer. Swiss drugmaker Roche paid $43 billion to take control of biotechnology giant Genentech. Belgium's InBev purchased the largest U.S. brewer, Anheuser-Busch and its Budweiser and Bud Light brands, for $52 billion. Number two brewer Miller Brewing Company was acquired by London-based SAB. In 2012, foreign investors poured over $166 billion into U.S. companies.[20]

However, such deals are not always welcomed. U.S. lawmakers feared the proposed purchase of U.S. oil company Unocal by a Chinese oil company might threaten American economic and national security interests. CNOOC, the Chinese company, eventually withdrew its bid.

LO 5–5   Outline the advantages and disadvantages of franchises, and discuss the opportunities for diversity in franchising and the challenges of global franchising.

franchise agreement
An arrangement whereby someone with a good idea for a business sells the rights to use the business name and sell a product or service to others in a given territory.

franchisor
A company that develops a product concept and sells others the rights to make and sell the products.

franchise
The right to use a specific business's name and sell its products or services in a given territory.

franchisee
A person who buys a franchise.

FRANCHISES

In addition to the three basic forms of business ownership, there are two special forms: franchises and cooperatives. Let's look at franchises first. A **franchise agreement** is an arrangement whereby someone with a good idea for a business (the **franchisor**) sells the rights to use the business name and sell a product or service (the **franchise**) to others (the **franchisees**) in a given territory.

Some people, uncomfortable with the idea of starting their own business from scratch, would rather join a business with a proven track record through a franchise agreement. A franchise can be formed as a sole proprietorship, a partnership, or a corporation. The U.S. Census Bureau estimates that one out of every 10 businesses in the United States is a franchise.[21] Some of the best-known franchises are McDonald's, Jiffy Lube, 7-Eleven, Weight Watchers, and Holiday Inn.

According to the International Franchise Association, the more than 770,000 franchised businesses operating in the United States create approximately

8.5 million jobs that produce a direct and indirect economic impact of $839 billion in the U.S. economy.[22] The most popular businesses for franchising are restaurants (fast food and full service) and gas stations with convenience stores. McDonald's, the largest restaurant chain in the United States in terms of sales, is often considered the gold standard of franchising. Retail stores, financial services, health clubs, hotels and motels, and automotive parts and service centers are also popular franchised businesses. Today a fast-growing franchise sector is senior care. In fact, *Entrepreneur* magazine's 2013 list of 100 fastest-growing franchises included nine senior care concepts.[23] With roughly 40 million seniors in the United States today and projections the number will double in the next 20 years, it's a market that is not going to disappear.[24] See Figure 5.9 for some tips on evaluating franchises.

Advantages of Franchises

Franchising has penetrated every aspect of U.S. and global business life by offering products and services that are reliable, convenient, and competitively priced. Franchising clearly has some advantages:

1. *Management and marketing assistance.* Compared with someone who starts a business from scratch, a franchisee usually has a much greater chance of succeeding because he or she has an established product to sell, help choosing a location, and assistance in all phases of promotion and operation. It's like having your own store but with full-time consultants when you need them. Franchisors usually provide intensive training. For example, McDonald's sends all new franchisees and managers to Hamburger University in Oak Brook, Illinois.[25]

   Some franchisors help their franchisees with local marketing efforts rather than having them depend solely on national advertising. Franchisees also have a network of fellow franchisees facing similar problems who can share their experiences. The UPS Store provides its more than 4,700 franchisees with a software program that helps them build customer databases along with quick and personal one-on-one phone and e-mail support.[26]

2. *Personal ownership.* A franchise operation is still your business, and you enjoy as much of the incentives and profit as any sole proprietor would. You are still your own boss, although you must follow more rules, regulations, and procedures than with your own privately owned business. The Spotlight on Small Business box features an example of a growing franchise that is attracting new franchisees.

3. *Nationally recognized name.* It is one thing to open a gift shop or an ice cream store. It is quite another to open a new Hallmark store or a Baskin-Robbins. With an established franchise, you get instant recognition and support from a product group with established customers around the world.

Door-to-Door Dry Cleaning franchises are the brainchild of John Dame and his wife Joey. All franchisees need is get started is a truck to make pickups and deliveries, and a contract with a local dry cleaner. Start-up costs can be as low as $40,000 and profits as high as 26 percent. The Dames provide two weeks of training and plenty of online support. What type of service franchise might appeal to you as a business owner?

FIGURE 5.9 BUYING A FRANCHISE

Since buying a franchise is a major investment, be sure to check out a company's financial strength before you get involved. Watch out for scams too. Scams called *bust-outs* usually involve people coming to town, renting nice offices, taking out ads, and persuading people to invest. Then they disappear with the investors' money. For example, in San Francisco a company called T.B.S. Inc. sold distributorships for in-home AIDS tests. It promised an enormous market and potential profits of $3,000 for an investment of less than $200. The "test" turned out to be nothing more than a mail-order questionnaire about lifestyle.

A good source of information about evaluating a franchise deal is the handbook *Investigate before Investing*, available from International Franchise Association Publications.

Checklist for Evaluating a Franchise

The Franchise

Did your lawyer approve the franchise contract you're considering after he or she studied it paragraph by paragraph?

Does the franchise give you an exclusive territory for the length of the franchise?

Under what circumstances can you terminate the franchise contract and at what cost to you?

If you sell your franchise, will you be compensated for your goodwill (the value of your business's reputation and other intangibles)?

If the franchisor sells the company, will your investment be protected?

The Franchisor

How many years has the firm offering you a franchise been in operation?

Does it have a reputation for honesty and fair dealing among the local firms holding its franchise?

Has the franchisor shown you any certified figures indicating exact net profits of one or more going firms that you personally checked yourself with the franchisee? Ask for the company's disclosure statement.

Will the firm assist you with
   A management training program?
   An employee training program?
   A public relations program?
   Capital?
   Credit?
   Merchandising ideas?

Will the firm help you find a good location for your new business?

Has the franchisor investigated you carefully enough to assure itself that you can successfully operate one of its franchises at a profit both to itself and to you?

You, the Franchisee

How much equity capital will you need to purchase the franchise and operate it until your income equals your expenses?

Does the franchisor offer financing for a portion of the franchising fees? On what terms?

Are you prepared to give up some independence of action to secure the advantages offered by the franchise? Do you have your family's support?

Does the industry appeal to you? Are you ready to spend much or all of the remainder of your business life with this franchisor, offering its product or service to the public?

Your Market

Have you made any study to determine whether the product or service that you propose to sell under the franchise has a market in your territory at the prices you'll have to charge?

Will the population in the territory given to you increase, remain static, or decrease over the next five years?

Will demand for the product or service you're considering be greater, about the same, or less five years from now than it is today?

What competition already exists in your territory for the product or service you contemplate selling?

Sources: U.S. Department of Commerce, *Franchise Opportunities Handbook*; and Steve Adams, "Buying a Brand," *Patriot Ledger* (Quincy, MA), March 1, 2008.

4. *Financial advice and assistance.* Two major problems for small-business owners are arranging financing and learning to keep good records. Franchisees often get valuable assistance and periodic advice from people with expertise in these areas. In fact, some franchisors, including Meinike, Gold's Gym, and UPS Stores, provide financing to potential franchisees they feel will be valuable parts of the franchise system.[27]

5. *Lower failure rate.* Historically, the failure rate for franchises has been lower than that of other business ventures. However, franchising has grown so rapidly that many weak franchises have entered the field, so you need to be careful and invest wisely.[28]

The Building Blocks of Franchising

After work at Michelle Cote's architectural firm stopped due to the Great Recession, she found inspiration for her next venture in an unlikely place: her children's Lego toys. In 2008 she took a stash of the building blocks to an elementary school where she used them to teach kids about engineering and construction. Of course, the children didn't realize that they were learning. They thought the amusement parks and inventions they created were just another part of playtime. The class was a hit with both kids and parents, leading Cote to organize more events under the name Bricks 4 Kidz at other schools as well as summer camps and birthday parties.

However, Cote's company didn't hit its stride until she met Brian Pappas, a franchise developer with more than 30 years of experience in the industry. Pappas knew that such a low-cost business plan would be appealing to many potential franchisees. After all, a few boxes of Legos costs a lot less than opening a chain restaurant or retail store. Within five years, Bricks 4 Kidz expanded into more than 200 franchises in the U.S. and 11 other countries. The company's cheap and easily reproducible model could make it an even greater success in the years to come.

Sources: "Franchise Spotlight: Bricks 4 Kidz," *Entrepreneur*, March 2013; Jacklyn Corley, "Sickles Students Get a Hands-on Lesson in Engineering, Architecture," *Rumson-FairHaven Patch*, February 4, 2014; and http://www.bricks4kidz.com/, accessed February 2014.

Disadvantages of Franchises

There are, however, some potential pitfalls to franchising. Check out any franchise arrangement with present franchisees and discuss the idea with an attorney and an accountant. Disadvantages of franchises include the following:

1. *Large start-up costs.* Most franchises demand a fee for the rights to the franchise. Start-up costs for a Jazzercise franchise range from $4,200, but if it's Dunkin' Donuts you're after, you'd better have a lot more dough—-approximately $1.5 million.[29]

2. *Shared profit.* The franchisor often demands either a large share of the profits in addition to the start-up fees or a percentage commission based on sales, not profit. This share is called a *royalty*. For example, if a franchisor demands a 10 percent royalty on a franchise's net sales, 10 cents of every dollar the franchisee collects (before taxes and other expenses) must be paid to the franchisor.[30]

3. *Management regulation.* Management "assistance" has a way of becoming managerial orders, directives, and limitations. Franchisees feeling burdened by the company's rules and regulations may lose the drive to run their own business. Often franchisees will band together to resolve their grievances with franchisors rather than fighting their battles alone.[31] For example, the KFC National Council & Advertising Cooperative, which represents all U.S. franchisees, sued KFC to gain control of advertising strategies. The franchisees were angry over Yum! Brands' (owners of KFC) decision to implement an ad strategy that emphasized a shift to grilled chicken rather than fried chicken. The campaign centered around the slogan "Unthink KFC," which was exactly what customers did. Sales plummeted 7 percent that quarter and franchisees had to throw away up to 50 percent of their grilled chicken supplies.

4. *Coattail effects.* What happens to your franchise if fellow franchisees fail? The actions of other franchises have an impact on your future growth and profitability. Due to this *coattail effect,* you could be forced out of business even if your particular franchise has been profitable. For example, the customer passion for high-flying franchisor Krispy Kreme sank as the market became flooded with new stores and the availability of the product at retail locations caused overexposure. McDonald's and Subway franchisees complain that due to the company's relentless growth, some new stores have taken business away from existing locations, squeezing franchisees' profits per outlet.

5. *Restrictions on selling.* Unlike owners of private businesses, who can sell their companies to whomever they choose on their own terms, many franchisees face restrictions on the resale of their franchises. To control quality, franchisors often insist on approving the new owner, who must meet their standards.

6. *Fraudulent franchisors.* Most franchisors are not large systems like McDonald's and Subway. Many are small, rather obscure companies that prospective franchisees may know little about. Most are honest, but complaints to the Federal Trade Commission have increased about franchisors that delivered little or nothing of what they promised. Before you buy a franchise, make certain you check out the facts fully and remember the old adage "You get what you pay for."

Diversity in Franchising

A lingering issue in franchising is the number of women who own franchises. While women own about half of all U.S. companies and are opening businesses at double the rate of men, their ownership of franchises is only about 21 percent. However, that statistic doesn't tell the whole story; 45 percent of franchises are co-owned by male and female partners. "Because women in general are collaborative and want to create win-win relationships, we make wonderful franchisors," says Stephanie Allen, co-founder of Dream Dinners, a meal-preparation service.[32]

Women aren't just franchisees anymore; they're becoming franchisors as well. Women are finding if they face difficulty getting financing for growing their business, turning to franchisees to help carry expansion costs can help. For example, top-rated franchise companies Auntie Anne's, Decorating Den, and Jazzercise were started by women.

Minority-owned businesses are growing at more than six times the national rate. Franchisors are becoming more focused on recruiting minority franchisees. DiversityFran is an initiative by the International Franchise Association to build awareness of franchising opportunities within minority communities. The U.S. Commerce Department's Federal Minority Business Development Agency provides aspiring minority business owners with training in how to run franchises. Domino's Pizza launched a minority franchisee recruitment program called Delivering the Dream. The company provides financial support and a financing partner to help budding franchisees "realize their dream."

Today over 20 percent of franchises are owned by African Americans, Latinos, Asians, and Native Americans. Franchising opportunities seem perfectly attuned to the needs of aspiring minority businesspeople. For example, Junior Bridgeman was a basketball star in college and enjoyed a stellar career with the Milwaukee Bucks and Los Angeles Clippers in the NBA. He transferred his dedication on the court to dedication to building Bridgeman Foods.

His company now owns 125 Chili's and 155 Wendy's restaurants and plans to open 30 Blaze Pizza stores. Bridgeman is the fifth largest franchise owner in the country.[33]

Home-Based Franchises

Home-based businesses offer many obvious advantages, including relief from the stress of commuting, extra time for family activities, and low overhead expenses. One disadvantage is the feeling of isolation. Compared to home-based entrepreneurs, home-based franchisees feel less isolated. Experienced franchisors often share their knowledge of building a profitable enterprise with other franchisees.

Home-based franchises can be started for as little as $5,000. Today you can be a franchisee in areas ranging from cleaning services to tax preparation, child care, pet care, cruise planning, or direct mail services.[34] Before investing in a home-based franchise it is helpful to ask yourself the following questions: Are you willing to put in long hours? Can you work in a solitary environment? Are you motivated and well organized? Does your home have the space you need for the business? Can your home also be the place you work? It's also important to check out the franchisor carefully.

E-Commerce in Franchising

The Internet has changed franchising in many ways. Most brick-and-mortar franchises have expanded their businesses online and created virtual storefronts to deliver increased value to customers. Franchisees like Carole Shutts, a Rocky Mountain Chocolate Factory franchisee in Galena, Illinois, increased her sales by setting up her own website. Many franchisors, however, prohibit franchisee-sponsored websites because conflicts can erupt if the franchisor creates its own website. Sometimes franchisors send "reverse royalties" to franchisees who believe their sales were hurt by the franchisor's online sales, but that doesn't always bring about peace. Before buying a franchise, read the small print regarding online sales.

Today potential franchisees can make a choice between starting an online business or a business requiring an office or storefront outside the home. Quite often the decision comes down to financing. Traditional brick-and-mortar franchises require finding real estate and often require a high franchise fee. Online franchises like Printinginabox.com charge no up-front franchise fee and require little training to start a business. Franchisees pay only a set monthly fee. Online franchises also do not set exclusive territories limiting where the franchisee can compete. An online franchisee can literally compete against the world. See the Adapting to Change box for an example of a company using the power of the Internet to start a new digital franchise.

Using Technology in Franchising

Franchisors often use technology, including social media, to extend their brands, to meet the needs of both their customers and their franchisees, and even to expand their businesses. For example, Candy Bouquet International, Inc., of Little Rock, Arkansas, offers franchises that sell candies in flowerlike arrangements. Franchisees have brick-and-mortar locations to serve walk-in

Judi Sheppard Missett started a dance-fitness program called Jazzercise in 1969. The worldwide franchise company now takes fitness-minded adults and kids in 32 countries through weekly classes blending jazz dance, resistance training, Pilates, yoga, and kickboxing moves choreographed to the latest popular music. Jazzercise is consistently listed among Entrepreneur magazine's top 20 franchises. What accounts for its appeal?

Giving Entrepreneurs Options with Digital Franchising

Chris Jeffrey noticed something strange about the restaurants in his college town: few of them posted their menus online. And when an eatery did have a website, ordering food through it was usually out of the question. Sensing an opportunity, Jeffrey developed his own online restaurant ordering service after graduation. Called OrderUp, the site lets users scroll through various restaurants located in their area. Once they've decided what they'd like to eat, customers can place their order and either pick it up or have it delivered. OrderUp then sends the payment to the restaurant, minus a small commission.

Jeffrey's early success with the concept made him eager to expand. But potential investors wanted too large a stake in the business, leaving Jeffrey afraid that he could be forced out of his own company. So instead, he offered to franchise OrderUp digitally, something that had never been done before in the business world. Although investors weren't interested in such a risky venture, Jeffrey carried on and developed a tempting offer for potential franchisees. For a start-up fee of $42,000, franchisees receive software and training to launch an

OrderUp operation in their area. The franchisee maintains exclusive rights to sell the service within their territory while the company itself handles order processing and customer service. This digital franchising model keeps costs low while giving franchisees the time to focus on convincing restaurants to join OrderUp. So far Jeffrey's 20 digital franchisees have generated more than $30 million in food orders annually. Expect to see them in your town soon, or if you're prepared to take the risk, bring them there yourself by becoming an OrderUp franchisee!

Sources: Minda Zetlin, "Digital Franchises: New Spin on an Old Business Model," *Inc.*, March 7, 2013; "Business Opportunities: OrderUp," www.entrepreneur.com, accessed February 2014; and www.franchise.orderup.com, accessed February 2014.

customers, but they also are provided leads from the company's main website. All franchisees are kept up-to-date daily on company news via e-mail, and they use a chat room to discuss issues and product ideas with each other. The company has found the Internet a great way of disseminating information that is revolutionizing franchisor support and franchisee communications. Candy Bouquet International now has 300 locations around the globe.[35]

Franchising in Global Markets

Franchising today is truly a global effort. U.S. franchisors are counting their profits in euros, yuan, pesos, won, krona, baht, yen, and many other currencies. McDonald's has more than 34,000 restaurants in 118 countries serving over 69 million customers each day.[36]

Because of its proximity and shared language, Canada is the most popular target for U.S.-based franchises. Franchisors are finding it surprisingly easier now to move into China, South Africa, the Philippines, and the Middle East. Plus it's not just the large franchises like Subway and Marriott Hotels making the move. Newer, smaller franchises are going global as well. Auntie Anne's sells hand-rolled pretzels in 25 different countries including Indonesia, Malaysia, the Philippines, Singapore, Venezuela, and Thailand.[37] Build-A-Bear Workshops has 79 franchisees in 12 countries including South Africa and the United Arab Emirates.[38] In 2005, 29-year-old Matthew Corrin launched Freshii, a sandwich, salad, and soup restaurant with fresh affordable food in trendy locations. He already has 45 locations in eight countries.[39]

What makes franchising successful in global markets is what makes it successful in the United States: convenience and a predictable level of service and quality. Franchisors, though, must be careful and do their homework before entering into global franchise agreements. Three questions to ask before forming a global franchise are: Will your intellectual property be protected? Can you give proper support to global partners? Are you able to adapt to franchise regulations in other countries? If the answer is yes to all three questions, global franchising creates great opportunities. It's also important to remember that adapting products and brand names to different countries creates challenges. In France, people thought a furniture-stripping franchise called Dip 'N' Strip was a bar that featured strippers.

Just as McDonald's and Subway have exported golden arches and sub sandwiches worldwide, foreign franchises see the United States as a popular target. Japanese franchises like Kumon Learning Centers and Canadian franchises like tax preparer H&R Block are very active in the United States. Kumon was ranked as the number one tutoring franchise by *Entrepreneur* magazine 13 years in a row, and H&R Block even has its headquarters in Kansas City, Missouri.[40] Other franchises are hoping to change our tastes here. Ly Qui Trung would like to see his Pho24 noodle bars become a part of the American landscape, and Canada's Yogen Früz frozen yogurt wants us to eat healthier desserts.

Holiday Inn's InterContinental Amstel hotel in Amsterdam has been celebrated as the Netherlands' most beautiful and luxurious hotel. Holiday Inn franchises try to complement the environment of the area they serve. This hotel is on the crossroads of Amsterdam's financial and exclusive shopping districts. What do you think would have been the reaction if Holiday Inn had built the typical U.S.-style Holiday Inn in this area?

LO 5–6   Explain the role of cooperatives.

COOPERATIVES

Some people dislike the notion of owners, managers, workers, and buyers being separate individuals with separate goals, so they have formed cooperatives, a different kind of organization to meet their needs for electricity, child care, housing, health care, food, and financial services. A **cooperative**, or co-op, is owned and controlled by the people who use it—producers, consumers, or workers with similar needs who pool their resources for mutual gain. In many rural parts of the country, for example, the government sells wholesale power to electric cooperatives at rates 40 to 50 percent below the rates nonfederal utilities charge. Electric cooperatives serve 42 million U.S. consumer-members in 47 states—or 12 percent of the population.[41]

Worldwide, more than 1 billion people are members of cooperatives.[42] Members democratically control these businesses by electing a board of directors that hires professional management. Some co-ops ask members/customers to work for a number of hours a month as part of their membership duties. You may have one of the country's 4,000 food co-ops near you. If so, stop by and chat to learn more about this growing aspect of the U.S. economy. If you are interested in knowing more about cooperatives, contact the National Cooperative Business Association at 202-638-6222 or visit its website at www .ncba.coop.

Another kind of cooperative in the United States is formed to give members more economic power as a group than they have as individuals. The best example is a farm cooperative. The goal at first was for farmers to join together to get

cooperative
A business owned and controlled by the people who use it—producers, consumers, or workers with similar needs who pool their resources for mutual gain.

better prices for their food products. Eventually the idea expanded, and farm cooperatives now buy and sell fertilizer, farm equipment, seed, and other products in a multibillion-dollar industry. Cooperatives have an advantage in the marketplace because they don't pay the same kind of taxes corporations pay.

Cooperatives are still a major force in agriculture and other industries today. Some top co-ops have familiar names such as Land O' Lakes, Sunkist, Ocean Spray, Blue Diamond, Associated Press, Ace Hardware, True Value Hardware, Riceland Foods, and Welch's.

WHICH FORM OF OWNERSHIP IS FOR YOU?

You can build your own business in a variety of ways. You can start your own sole proprietorship, partnership, corporation, LLC, or cooperative—or you can buy a franchise and be part of a larger corporation. There are advantages and disadvantages to each. Before you decide which form is for you, evaluate all the alternatives carefully.

The miracle of free enterprise is that the freedom and incentives of capitalism make risks acceptable to many people who go on to create the great corporations of America. You know many of their names and companies: James Cash Penney (JCPenney), Steve Jobs (Apple Computer), Sam Walton (Walmart), Levi Strauss (Levi Strauss), Henry Ford (Ford Motor Company), Thomas Edison (General Electric), Bill Gates (Microsoft), and so on. They started small, accumulated capital, grew, and became industrial leaders. Could you do the same?

Use LearnSmart to help retain what you have learned. Access your instructor's Connect course to check out LearnSmart, or go to learnsmartadvantage.com for help.

LEARNSMART

test prep

- What are some of the factors to consider before buying a franchise?
- What opportunities are available for starting a global franchise?
- What is a cooperative?

summary

LO 5–1   Compare the advantages and disadvantages of sole proprietorships.

- **What are the advantages and disadvantages of sole proprietorships?**
  The advantages of sole proprietorships include ease of starting and ending, ability to be your own boss, pride of ownership, retention of profit, and no special taxes. The disadvantages include unlimited liability, limited financial resources, difficulty in management, overwhelming time commitment, few fringe benefits, limited growth, and limited life span.

LO 5–2   Describe the differences between general and limited partners, and compare the advantages and disadvantages of partnerships.

- **What are the three key elements of a general partnership?**
  The three key elements of a general partnership are common ownership, shared profits and losses, and the right to participate in managing the operations of the business.

- **What are the main differences between general and limited partners?**
  General partners are owners (partners) who have unlimited liability and are active in managing the company. Limited partners are owners (partners) who have limited liability and are not active in the company.

- **What does *unlimited liability* mean?**
  Unlimited liability means that sole proprietors and general partners must pay all debts and damages caused by their business. They may have to sell their houses, cars, or other personal possessions to pay business debts.

- **What does *limited liability* mean?**
  Limited liability means that corporate owners (stockholders) and limited partners are responsible for losses only up to the amount they invest. Their other personal property is not at risk.

- **What is a master limited partnership?**
  A master limited partnership is a partnership that acts like a corporation but is taxed like a partnership.

- **What are the advantages and disadvantages of partnerships?**
  The advantages include more financial resources, shared management and pooled knowledge, and longer survival. The disadvantages include unlimited liability, division of profits, disagreements among partners, and difficulty of termination.

LO 5–3   Compare the advantages and disadvantages of corporations, and summarize the differences between C corporations, S corporations, and limited liability companies.

- **What is the definition of a corporation?**
  A corporation is a state-chartered legal entity with authority to act and have liability separate from its owners.

- **What are the advantages and disadvantages of corporations?**
  The advantages include more money for investment, limited liability, size, perpetual life, ease of ownership change, ease of drawing talented employees, and separation of ownership from management. The disadvantages include initial cost, paperwork, size, difficulty in termination, double taxation, and possible conflict with a board of directors.

- **Why do people incorporate?**
  Two important reasons for incorporating are special tax advantages and limited liability.

- **What are the advantages of S corporations?**
  S corporations have the advantages of limited liability (like a corporation) and simpler taxes (like a partnership). To qualify for S corporation status, a company must have fewer than 100 stockholders (members of a family count as one shareholder), its stockholders must be individuals or estates and U.S. citizens or permanent residents, and the company cannot derive more than 25 percent of its income from passive sources.

- **What are the advantages of limited liability companies?**
  Limited liability companies have the advantage of limited liability without the hassles of forming a corporation or the limitations imposed by S corporations. LLCs may choose whether to be taxed as partnerships or corporations.

LO 5–4 Define and give examples of three types of corporate mergers, and explain the role of leveraged buyouts and taking a firm private.

- **What is a merger?**
  A merger is the result of two firms forming one company. The three major types are vertical mergers, horizontal mergers, and conglomerate mergers.

- **What are leveraged buyouts, and what does it mean to take a company private?**
  Leveraged buyouts are attempts by managers and employees to borrow money and purchase the company. Individuals who, together or alone, buy all the stock for themselves are said to take the company private.

LO 5–5 Outline the advantages and disadvantages of franchises, and discuss the opportunities for diversity in franchising and the challenges of global franchising.

- **What is a franchise?**
  An arrangement to buy the rights to use the business name and sell its products or services in a given territory is called a franchise.

- **What is a franchisee?**
  A franchisee is a person who buys a franchise.

- **What are the benefits and drawbacks of being a franchisee?**
  The benefits include getting a nationally recognized name and reputation, a proven management system, promotional assistance, and pride of ownership. Drawbacks include high franchise fees, managerial regulation, shared profits, and transfer of adverse effects if other franchisees fail.

- **What is the major challenge to global franchises?**
  It is often difficult to transfer an idea or product that worked well in the United States to another culture. It is essential to adapt to the region.

Access your instructor's Connect course to check out LearnSmart or go to learnsmartadvantage.com for help.

Mc Graw Hill Education connect®

LO 5–6 Explain the role of cooperatives.

- **What is the role of a cooperative?**
  Cooperatives are organizations owned by members/customers. Some people form cooperatives to acquire more economic power than they would have as individuals. Small businesses often form cooperatives to gain more purchasing, marketing, or product development strength.

key terms

acquisition 135
conglomerate merger 135
conventional (C) corporation 127
cooperative 143
corporation 120
franchise 136
franchise agreement 136
franchisee 136
franchisor 136

general partner 123
general partnership 123
horizontal merger 135
leveraged buyout (LBO) 136
limited liability 123
limited liability company (LLC) 132
limited liability partnership (LLP) 123

limited partner 123
limited partnership 123
master limited partnership (MLP) 123
merger 135
partnership 120
S corporation 132
sole proprietorship 120
unlimited liability 121
vertical merger 135

critical thinking

Imagine you are considering starting your own business.

1. What kinds of products or services will you offer?

2. What talents or skills do you need to run the business?

3. Do you have all the skills and resources to start the business, or will you need to find one or more partners? If so, what skills would your partners need to have?

4. What form of business ownership would you choose—sole proprietorship, partnership, C corporation, S corporation, or LLC? Why?

developing workplace skills

Key: ● **Team**   ★ **Analytic**   ▲ **Communication**   ▣ **Technology**

1. Research businesses in your area and identify sole proprietorships, partnerships, corporations, and franchises. Arrange interviews with managers using each form of ownership and get their impressions, hints, and warnings. (If you are able to work with a team of fellow students, divide the interviews among team members.) How much does it cost to start? How many hours do they work? What are the specific benefits? Share the results with your class. ● ▣ ▲ ★

2. Have you thought about starting your own business? What opportunities seem attractive? Choose someone in the class whom you might want for a partner or partners in the business. List all the financial resources and personal skills you will need to launch the business. Then make separate lists of the personal skills and the financial resources that you and your partner(s) might bring to your new venture. How much capital and what personal skills will be needed beyond those you already have? Develop an action plan for needed capital. ● ▲ ★

3. Let's assume you want to open one of the following new businesses. What form of business ownership would you choose for each? Why? Explain your choices to the rest of the class. ▲ ★
   a. Video game rental store.
   b. Wedding planning service.
   c. Software development firm.
   d. Online bookstore.

4. Successful businesses continually change hands. Methods of change discussed in this chapter include mergers, acquisitions, taking a firm private, and using leveraged buyouts. Search for an article online that illustrates how one of these methods changed an organization. What led to the change? How did this change affect the company's stakeholders? What benefits did the change provide? What new challenges were created? ▣ ★

5. Find information online about a business cooperative (e.g., Welch's, Land O' Lakes, Sunkist). Research how it was formed, who can belong to it, and how it operates. ▣ ★

taking it to the **net**

PURPOSE

To explore franchising opportunities and to evaluate the strengths and weaknesses of a selected franchise.

EXERCISE

Go to Franchise Expo (www.franchiseexpo.com).

1. Use the search tool to find a franchise that has the potential of fulfilling your entrepreneurial dreams. Navigate to the profile of the franchise you selected. Explore the franchise's website if a link is available. Refer to the questions listed in Figure 5.9 in this chapter and assess the strengths and weaknesses of your selected franchise.

2. Did your search give you enough information to answer most of the questions in Figure 5.9? If not, what other information do you need, and where can you obtain it?

video case   Mc Graw Hill Education **connect**

SONIC

With more than 3,500 locations in 44 states, Sonic is the largest chain of drive-in fast-food restaurants in the United States. Unlike other chains, many of Sonic's locations are individually owned and operated. That's because Sonic knows the value of motivated entrepreneurs who are willing to put everything they've got into their businesses.

Sonic has stuck to this go-getter attitude thanks to the leadership of founder Troy Smith. After coming back from World War II, Smith took a job as a milkman until he realized that he wanted to run a business of his own. Over the next few years he opened several restaurants in his hometown of Shawnee, Oklahoma, ranging from a diner to his own fried chicken chain to see what worked best for him. Since he ran these businesses by himself as sole proprietorships, that meant he could make all the major decisions himself, but he had no one to help him make the restaurants great. As a result, most of Smith's early ventures failed.

He didn't let those initial disappointments set him back, however. Eventually Smith bought a five-acre gravel lot that contained a little root beer stand and a big log cabin. While he planned to turn the latter into a steakhouse, Smith nearly tore down the root beer stand to make room for more parking. As time went by, though, he realized that the soda stand was actually doing better business than the steakhouse. After visiting a drive-in burger place in Louisiana, Smith thought that was just the thing his small soda shop needed to become a big success. He commissioned a speaker system, added a

canopy to the parking lot, and hired servers to bring food directly to customers' cars. Soon enough, revenue at the Top Hat Drive-In had tripled.

As Smith's burger-and-soda stand continued to grow, a local grocer named Charles Pappe approached him about investing in the business. The two ended up forming a partnership where Pappe would concentrate on sales while Smith improved the business. Things continued to run smoothly until the pair found out that the Top Hat name had already been trademarked by another company. Although Smith and Pappe's personal assets were protected by their limited partnership agreement, they stood to lose their entire business if they were successfully sued over the Top Hat name. So, deciding that it was better to be safe than sorry, they agreed to change the name of the business to Sonic Drive-In.

Business continued to boom as the years went by, leading Smith and Pappe to think bigger. More people expressed interest in becoming involved in the business, but Smith didn't want to take on any more partners. Instead, they decided to expand the Sonic brand by franchising. This allowed other entrepreneurs to open up their own locations throughout the country with the help of the Sonic home office. Today, Sonic has thousands of franchisees from all walks of life operating in every corner of America. The flexibility of their ownership system allows franchisees to focus on building their business, rather than on the brand itself. Maybe that's why Sonic continues growing at the speed of sound.

THINKING IT OVER

1. Like many entrepreneurs, Troy Smith started Sonic as a sole proprietorship, then took on a partner, and eventually offered franchises. What advantages did he enjoy at each stage of Sonic's development? What disadvantages did he face?

2. How is a franchise different from a partnership?

3. What important questions should you ask before becoming a franchisee in a company like Sonic?

notes

1. Small Business Administration, www.sba.gov, accessed March 2014; and SCORE, www.score.org, accessed March 2014.
2. U.S. Census Bureau, www.census.gov, accessed March 2014.
3. *My Own Business,* www.myownbusiness.org, accessed March 2014.
4. Elaine Pofeldt, "Going It Alone," *Inc.,* February 2014.
5. "Subterranean Capitalist Blues," *The Economist,* October 26, 2013; and "Rise of the Distorporation," *The Economist,* October 26, 2014.
6. Sunoco, www.sunoco.com, accessed March 2014.
7. Molly Wright, "Married to the Job," *Columbia Business Times,* January 30, 2014.
8. Bureau of Labor Statistics, www.bls.gov, accessed March 2014.
9. Paula Andruss, "Divide & Conquer," *Entrepreneur,* April 2013.
10. Nellie Akalp, "Top Reasons to Incorporate Your Business," *Small Business Trends,* February 3, 2014.
11. Carol Hymowitz, "Not Going Anywhere," *Bloomberg Businessweek,* May 27–June 2, 2013.
12. Nellie Akalp, "Is the Wrong Company Structure Hurting You at Tax Time?" *Forbes,* February 3, 2014.
13. Geoff Colvin, "Inside the Boardroom," *Fortune,* May 29, 2013.
14. Incorporate 101, www.incorporate101.com, accessed March 2014.
15. United States Internal Revenue Service, www.irs.gov, accessed March 2014.
16. Tony Nitti, "Tax Geek Tuesday: Reasonable Compensation in the S Corporation Arena," *Forbes,* February 4, 2014.
17. LegalZoom, www.legalzoom.com, accessed March 2014.
18. Gabrielle Karol, "V-Commerce Could Be the Next Big Trend for Startups," *Entrepreneur,* January 30, 2014.
19. Connie Guglielmo, "You Won't Have Michael Dell to Kick Around Anymore," *Forbes,* November 18, 2013.
20. The Whitehouse, www.whitehouse.gov, accessed March 2014.
21. U.S. Census Bureau, www.census.gov, accessed March 2014.
22. International Franchise Association, www.franchise.org, accessed March 2014.
23. *Entrepreneur,* www.entrepreneur.com, accessed March 2014.
24. U.S. Census Bureau, www.census.gov, accessed March 2014.
25. McDonald's, www.aboutmcdonald's.com, accessed March 2014.
26. United Parcel Service, www.ups.com, accessed March 2014.
27. Michelle Goodman, "Franchisors Offer Their Own Financing Programs," *Entrepreneur,* January 14, 2014.
28. Jason Daly, "What Is the Real Survival Rate of a Franchised Business?" *Entrepreneur,* September 13, 2013.
29. *Entrepreneur,* www.entrepreneur.com, accessed March 2014.
30. Leslie Patton, McDonald's Aiming for Better Bottom Line, Shifts More of the Burden to Its Franchisees," *St. Louis Post-Dispatch,* August 11, 2013.
31. Carol Coultas, "Jim Cohen Launches Franchise Owners Lobbying Efforts," *MaineBiz,* January 27, 2014; and J. Craig Anderson, "Maine Bill Aims to Protect Franchise Owners," *Press Herald,* January 28, 2014.
32. Kate Taylor, "Women in Franchising," *Entrepreneur,* October 31, 2013.
33. Caitlin Bowling, "Junior Bridgeman, Jim Patterson Backing New Franchise," *Business First,* January 31 2014.
34. Arlene Satchell, "Cruise Planners Expect Growth in 2014," *Sun Sentinel,* January 23, 2014.
35. CandyBouqet, www.candybouqet.com, accessed March 2014.
36. McDonald's, www.mcdonalds.com, accessed March 2014.
37. Auntie Annes, www.auntieannes.com, accessed March 2014; and Matthew D'Ippolito, "Auntie Anne Beiler Attributes Success to Giving, Finding Purpose at Ursinus Talk," *The Mercury Business,* January 30, 2014.
38. Build-a-Bear, www.buildabear.com, accessed March 2014; and Kavita Kumar, "New Build-a-Bear CEO Upbeat about Turnaround, Future," *St. Louis Post-Dispatch,* January 19, 2014.
39. Freshii, www.freshii.com, accessed March 2014; and Patti Woods, "An Appetite for Health Eating in the New Year," *Fairfield Citizen,* January 21, 2014.
40. *Entrepreneur,* www.entrepreneur.com, accessed March 2014; and "Entrepreneur Magazine Ranks Kumon No. 1 Education Franchise for 13th Consecutive Year," *BusinessWire,* January 7, 2014.
41. Nation Rural Electric Cooperative Association, www.nreca.coop, accessed March 2014.
42. National Cooperative Business Association, www.ncba.coop, accessed March 2014.

photo credits

6

Entrepreneurship and Starting a Small Business

Learning Objectives

AFTER YOU HAVE READ AND STUDIED THIS CHAPTER, YOU SHOULD BE ABLE TO

LO 6-1 Explain why people take the risks of entrepreneurship; list the attributes of successful entrepreneurs; and describe entrepreneurial teams, intrapreneurs, and home- and web-based businesses.

LO 6-2 Discuss the importance of small business to the American economy and summarize the major causes of small-business failure.

LO 6-3 Summarize ways to learn about how small businesses operate.

LO 6-4 Analyze what it takes to start and run a small business.

LO 6-5 Outline the advantages and disadvantages small businesses have in entering global markets.

Getting to Know **Prudencio Unanue**

For more than 75 years, Goya Foods has provided a little taste of home for millions of Hispanic immigrants. That commitment goes all the way back to the company's founder Prudencio Unanue, who moved from his native Spain to Puerto Rico before ultimately heading for New York. But as the years passed and tastes changed, Goya's business changed as well. Under the leadership of Unanue's sons and grandsons, Goya's products grew popular with non-Latinos as well, leading to current sales revenues of more than $1 billion.

After settling in Lower Manhattan in 1936, Unanue opened a small grocery store in his neighborhood. He catered to the area's large Spanish community by selling items like olives, olive oil, and sardines. Soon after Unanue set up shop, he purchased the Goya name for a dollar from one of his sardine importers. Not only was "Goya" easier to pronounce than "Unanue," but he also liked the association with the famous Spanish painter Francisco Goya. The store continued to grow even as the population of the neighborhood changed. After the end of World War II brought a wave of Puerto Rican immigrants, Unanue stocked up on local staples like yucca, plantains, and pigeon peas. Black beans, guava paste, and coconut were the next products to be added, after many Cubans and Dominicans moved to the city in the 1950s. Around that same time, Unanue moved the company headquarters to New Jersey and started distributing his products along the East Coast. By 1973 the company was harvesting and exporting its own olives from Spain. Prudencio Unanue died a few years later, leaving his son Joseph Unanue in charge.

Despite the loss to the family as well as the change in leadership, Goya grew steadily over the next few decades by sticking to its slogan, "If it's Goya, it has to be good." By the 1980s this motto rang true for millions of second-generation Hispanics who had grown up eating Goya products. While this core market continued to fuel sales, more non-Hispanic Americans were expanding their diets to include foods from other cultures.

Goya took advantage of this change in taste, and began appealing more to consumers outside of its traditional markets. After Joseph Unanue stepped down as president in 2004, his successor and nephew, Bob Unanue, went one step further and hired a marketing firm to help the company specifically target non-Hispanics. Still, the company strives to serve all customers regardless of their demographic. "We like to say we don't market *to* Latinos, we market *as* Latinos," says Bob Unanue. "We sell to the masses, food that is good for you and not expensive. We pretty much stick to that." This simple philosophy has grown Goya from a small neighborhood grocery store, with one man selling olives and sardines, into a large company with more than 3,500 employees selling more than 1,500 products across the U.S. and Caribbean. In fact, today Goya enjoys a 25 percent market share among authentic Hispanic food brands. And none of it would have been possible without the entrepreneurial spirit of the company's immigrant founder, Prudencio Unanue.

Stories about people who take risks, like Unanue, are commonplace in this age of the entrepreneur. As you read about such risk takers in this chapter, maybe you'll be inspired to become an entrepreneur yourself.

Sources: Bernadette R. Giacomazzo, "The Story of Goya Foods: How a Latino-Owned Specialty Company Became a Mainstream Monolith," *Latin Post,* February 7, 2014; Lisa Fickenscher, "Goya Grows Beyond Hispanics," *Crain's New York Business,* June 9, 2013; Erin Carlyle, "How Goya Became One of America's Fastest-Growing Food Companies," *Forbes,* May 8, 2013; and Kristina Puga, "Former President of Goya Foods Dead at 88, Remembered for His Philanthropy," *NBC Latino,* June 14, 2013.

Prudencio Unanue

- Founder of Goya Foods
- Grew a $1 billion business from a small New York City grocery store

www.goya.com

@GoyaFoods

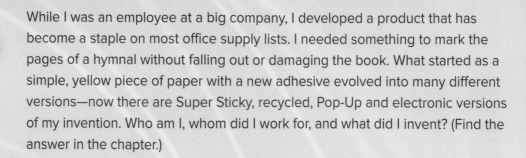
entrepreneurship
Accepting the risk of starting and running a business.

THE AGE OF THE ENTREPRENEUR

Today most young people know it's unlikely they will get a job in a large corporation and stay 30 years. For those who want more control over their destiny, working in or starting a small business makes sense. **Entrepreneurship** is accepting the risk of starting and running a business. Explore this chapter and think about the possibility of entrepreneurship in your future.

THE JOB-CREATING POWER OF ENTREPRENEURS IN THE UNITED STATES

Wacky grocer Jim Bonaminio may put on his wizard suit and roller-skate through his Jungle Jim's International Market, but he's serious when it comes to his business. Instead of competing on price against Walmart, Jungle Jim's competes on product variety. A case holding 1,200 kinds of hot sauce rests beneath an antique fire engine. Why do you think customers might remain loyal to Jungle Jim's?

Well before the recent economic turmoil, one of the major issues in the United States was the need to create more jobs. With the current high unemployment rate, job creation is even more critical. You can begin to understand the job-creating power of entrepreneurs when you look at some of the great U.S. entrepreneurs from the past and the present. The history of the United States is the history of its entrepreneurs. Consider just a few of the many who have helped shape the U.S. economy:[1]

- DuPont, which manufactures thousands of products under such brand names as Teflon and Lycra, was started in 1802 by French immigrant Éleuthère Irénée du Pont de Nemours. Some 18 shareholders provided $36,000 in start-up money.

- Avon, the familiar beauty products retailer, started in 1886 with $500 David McConnell borrowed from a friend.

- George Eastman launched photographic giant Kodak in 1880 with a $3,000 investment.

- Procter & Gamble, now a multinational marketer of household products, was formed in 1837 by William Procter, James Gamble, and a total of $7,000 in capital.

- Ford Motor Company began with an investment of $28,000 by Henry Ford and 11 associates.

- Amazon.com began with investments by founder Jeff Bezos's family and friends. Bezos's parents invested $300,000, a huge portion of their retirement account. Today they are billionaires.

Earning while Learning

Although most entrepreneurs wait until they finish their education to make the jump into their own businesses, some aspiring entrepreneurs choose to buck the trend. Here are just a few examples of young entrepreneurs who found success in their college years:

Jeremy Young enrolled in college to major in art history. During his sophomore year he attended a meeting of the entrepreneurship club on campus and shortly afterward pitched an idea he had for a prepaid laundry service for students. After developing a business plan and getting permission from the college, he negotiated an agreement with a local Laundromat that provided wash/dry/fold services and became a "laundry broker" for students.

Jessica Mah sold her first company (that rented server space to small businesses) at the ripe old age of 14. As a student at the University of California at Berkeley she came up with an idea for a new venture, InternshipIN, which helps students identify high-quality internships. Her service has built up increasing traffic through a partnership with SimplyHired, a job search engine. She plans to charge employers a fee to post listings on her site.

Zach Workman searched for an energy drink that did not contain heavy doses of sugar or caffeine. When he was unable to find an energy drink with only natural ingredients, he decided to develop his own from a family recipe for fruit-punch. With start-up capital from his parents he launched Punch, an all-natural energy drink that tasted good and had all the necessary dietary requirements. After a short while, three major distributorships decided to carry the product. While still a student at the University of Indiana, his business had hopes of reaching sales of $1 million.

Whitney Williams displayed a fine sense for design and business at an early age. During her first year at Texas Christian University, she started her own company named Tramonti (the Italian word for sunset), where she produced one-of-a-kind handcrafted jewelry. After two years of primarily selling her products through trunk shows, she set up an e-commerce site to expand distribution. You can view her products today at www.tramontibywhitney.com.

Sources: Dave Lerner, "4 Reasons Why Student Entrepreneurs Are Poised for Success," *Inc.*, February 24, 2014; Jason Ma, "Student Entrepreneurship Is Humming at Elite Universities," *Forbes*, May 14, 2014; and Nathan Resnick, "Student Raises $15 on Kickstarter Without Spending a Dime," *Entrepreneur*, February 12, 2014.

These stories have much in common. One or a couple of entrepreneurs had a good idea, borrowed some money from friends and family, and started a business. That business now employs thousands of people and helps the country prosper.

The United States has plenty of entrepreneurial talent. Names such as Mark Zuckerberg (Facebook), Michael Dell (Dell Inc.), Bill Gates (Microsoft), Howard Schultz (Starbucks), Jack Dorsey (Twitter), and Chad Hurley and Steve Chen (YouTube) have become as familiar as those of the great entrepreneurs of the past. The Spotlight on Small Business box highlights several young entrepreneurs who started businesses while still in school.

LO 6–1 Explain why people take the risks of entrepreneurship; list the attributes of successful entrepreneurs; and describe entrepreneurial teams, intrapreneurs, and home- and web-based businesses.

WHY PEOPLE TAKE THE ENTREPRENEURIAL CHALLENGE

Taking the risks of starting a business can be scary and thrilling at the same time. One entrepreneur described it as almost like bungee jumping. You might be scared, but if you watch six other people do it and they survive, then you're more likely to do it yourself. Here are some reasons people are willing to take the entrepreneurial risk:[2]

- *Opportunity.* The opportunity to share in the American dream is a tremendous lure. Many people, including those new to this country, may not have the skills for today's complex organizations, but they do have the initiative and drive to work the long hours demanded by entrepreneurship. The same is true of many corporate managers who leave corporate life (by choice or after downsizing) to run businesses of their own. Others, including an increasing number of women, minorities, older people, and people with disabilities, find that starting their own businesses offers them more opportunities than working for others.

- *Profit.* Profit is another important reason to become an entrepreneur. Bill Gates, who co-founded Microsoft, is the richest man in the United States and one of the richest people in the world.

- *Independence.* Many entrepreneurs simply do not enjoy working for someone else. Melissa Harvey, whose company Will n' Rose's LLC, produces all-natural nut and whole-grain Kizo bars, says one of the best things about being an entrepreneur is the freedom to pursue your passion: "It's about independence. You can take something that motivates you, that inspires you and act on it without roadblocks."[3]

- *Challenge.* Some people believe that entrepreneurs are excitement junkies who thrive on risk. Entrepreneurs take moderate, calculated risks; they don't just gamble. In general, though, entrepreneurs seek achievement more than power.

What Does It Take to Be an Entrepreneur?

Would you succeed as an entrepreneur? You can learn about the managerial and leadership skills needed to run a firm. However, you may not have the personality to assume the risks, take the initiative, create the vision, and rally others to follow your lead. Such personality traits are harder to learn or acquire than academic skills are. A list of entrepreneurial attributes to look for in yourself includes:[4]

- *Self-directed.* You should be self-disciplined and thoroughly comfortable being your own boss. You alone will be responsible for your success or failure.

- *Self-nurturing.* You must believe in your idea even when no one else does, and be able to replenish your own enthusiasm. When Walt Disney suggested the possibility of a full-length animated feature film, *Snow White*, the industry laughed. His personal commitment and enthusiasm caused the Bank of America to back his venture. The rest is history.

- *Action-oriented.* Great business ideas are not enough. Most important is a burning desire to realize, actualize, and build your dream into reality.

- *Highly energetic.* It's your business, and you must be emotionally, mentally, and physically able to work long and hard. Employees have weekends and vacations; entrepreneurs often work seven days a week and don't take vacations for years. Working 18-hour days in your own business can be exhausting, but most entrepreneurs think it is better than working long hours for someone else.

- *Tolerant of uncertainty.* Successful entrepreneurs take only calculated risks (if they can help it). Still, they must be able to take *some* risks. Remember, entrepreneurship is not for the squeamish or those bent on security. You can't be afraid to fail. Many well-known entrepreneurs failed several times before achieving success. The late football coach Vince Lombardi summarized the entrepreneurial philosophy when he said, "We didn't lose any games this season, we just ran out of time twice." New entrepreneurs must be prepared to run out of time a few times before they succeed.

Their love of bacon inspired Dave Lefkow and Justin Esch to create J&D Bacon Salt, a seasoning that adds the flavor of bacon to anything. With a start-up budget of just $5,000, they promoted their product with strategies like crazy antics, a Facebook page, blog, and free samples. Without food-industry connections, Lefkow and Esch created their own network of support the hard way—by picking up the phone and asking for it. Check out their story at www.baconsalt.com.

Turning Your Passions and Problems into Opportunities

As a young man in Queens, a borough of New York City, Russell Simmons channeled his passion for hip-hop culture into Def Jam Records. Today, his multimillion-dollar empire also includes Phat Farm clothing and Rush Management. Simmons used his time, money, and energy to turn his passion into a sustainable business.[5]

While many entrepreneurs' business ideas are inspired by their passions, many see business opportunities where others only see problems. For example, while Celtel's founder Mo Ibrahim saw the opportunity to bring mobile phones to the over 1 billion people in Africa who had never even used a phone much less owned one, large telecommunication companies saw only poor peasants and logistical hurdles. Celtel is now Africa's largest cell phone provider.[6]

Most entrepreneurs don't get ideas for products and services from some flash of inspiration. The source of innovation is more like a *flashlight*. Imagine a search party walking in the dark, shining lights, looking around, asking questions, and looking some more. "That's how most creativity happens," says business author Dale Dauten. "Calling around, asking questions, saying 'What if?' till you get blisters on your tongue."

To look at problems and/or passions and see opportunities in them, ask yourself these questions: What do I want, but can never find? What product or service would improve my life? What really irritates me, and what product or service would help?

Keep in mind, however, that not all ideas are opportunities. If your idea doesn't meet anyone else's needs, the business won't succeed. You may have a business idea that is a good opportunity if:[7]

- It fills customers' needs.
- You have the skills and resources to start a business.
- You can sell the product or service at a price customers are willing and able to pay—and still make a profit.
- You can get your product or service to customers before your window of opportunity closes (before competitors with similar solutions beat you to the marketplace).
- You can keep the business going.

If you think you may have the entrepreneurial spirit in your blood, complete the Entrepreneurial Readiness Questionnaire on the next page.

ENTREPRENEUR READINESS QUESTIONNAIRE

Each of the following items describes something that you may or may not feel represents your personality or other characteristics about you. Read each item and then circle the response (1, 2, 3, 4, or 5) that most nearly reflects the extent to which you agree or disagree that the item seems to fit you.

Looking at My Overall Philosophy of Life and Typical Behavior, I Would Say That . . .	RESPONSE				
	AGREE COMPLETELY (1)	MOSTLY AGREE (2)	PARTIALLY AGREE (3)	MOSTLY DISAGREE (4)	DISAGREE COMPLETELY (5)
1. I am generally optimistic.	1	2	3	4	5
2. I enjoy competing and doing things better than someone else.	1	2	3	4	5
3. When solving a problem, I try to arrive at the best solution first without worrying about other possibilities.	1	2	3	4	5
4. I enjoy associating with co-workers after working hours.	1	2	3	4	5
5. If betting on a horse race, I would prefer to take a chance on a high-payoff "long shot."	1	2	3	4	5
6. I like setting my own goals and working hard to achieve them.	1	2	3	4	5
7. I am generally casual and easygoing with others.	1	2	3	4	5
8. I like to know what is going on and take action to find out.	1	2	3	4	5
9. I work best when someone else is guiding me along the way.	1	2	3	4	5
10. When I am right I can convince others.					
11. I find that other people frequently waste my valuable time.	1	2	3	4	5
12. I enjoy watching football, baseball, and similar sports events.	1	2	3	4	5
13. I tend to communicate about myself very openly with other people.	1	2	3	4	5
14. I don't mind following orders from superiors who have legitimate authority.	1	2	3	4	5
15. I enjoy planning things more than actually carrying out the plans.	1	2	3	4	5
16. I don't think it's much fun to bet on a "sure thing."	1	2	3	4	5
17. If faced with failure, I would shift quickly to something else rather than sticking to my guns.	1	2	3	4	5
18. Part of being successful in business is reserving adequate time for family.	1	2	3	4	5
19. Once I have earned something, I feel that keeping it secure is important.	1	2	3	4	5
20. Making a lot of money is largely a matter of getting the right breaks.	1	2	3	4	5
21. Problem solving is usually more effective when a number of alternatives are considered.	1	2	3	4	5
22. I enjoy impressing others with the things I can do.	1	2	3	4	5
23. I enjoy playing games like tennis and handball with someone who is slightly better than I am.	1	2	3	4	5
24. Sometimes moral ethics must be bent a little in business dealings.	1	2	3	4	5
25. I think that good friends would make the best subordinates in an organization.	1	2	3	4	5

(continued)

Scoring:

Give yourself one point for each 1 or 2 response you circled for questions 1, 2, 6, 8, 10, 11, 16, 17, 21, 22, 23.

Give yourself one point for each 4 or 5 response you circled for questions 3, 4, 5, 7, 9, 12, 13, 14, 15, 18, 19, 20, 24, 25.

Add your points and see how you rate in the following categories:

21–25   Your entrepreneurial potential looks great if you have a suitable opportunity to use it. What are you waiting for?

16–20   This is close to the high entrepreneurial range. You could be quite successful if your other talents and resources are right.

11–15   Your score is in the transitional range. With some serious work you can probably develop the outlook you need for running your own business.

6–10   Things look pretty doubtful for you as an entrepreneur. It would take considerable rearranging of your life philosophy and behavior to make it.

0–5   Let's face it. Entrepreneurship isn't really for you. Still, learning what it's all about won't hurt anything.

Source: Kenneth R. Van Voorhis, *Entrepreneurship and Small Business Management* (New York: Allyn & Bacon, 1980).

Entrepreneurial Teams

An **entrepreneurial team** is a group of experienced people from different areas of business who join to form a managerial team with the skills to develop, make, and market a new product. A team may be better than an individual entrepreneur because team members can combine creative skills with production and marketing skills right from the start. Having a team also can ensure more cooperation and coordination later among functions in the business.

entrepreneurial team
A group of experienced people from different areas of business who join together to form a managerial team with the skills needed to develop, make, and market a new product.

While Steve Jobs was the charismatic folk hero and visionary of Apple Computers, it was Steve Wozniak who invented the first personal computer model and Mike Markkula who offered business expertise and access to venture capital. The key to Apple's early success was that it was built around this "smart team" of entrepreneurs. The team wanted to combine the discipline of a big company with an environment in which people could feel they were participating in a successful venture. The trio of entrepreneurs recruited seasoned managers with similar desires. Everyone worked together to conceive, develop, and market products.[8]

Micropreneurs and Home-Based Businesses

Not everyone who starts a business wants to grow a mammoth corporation. Some are interested in maintaining a balanced lifestyle while doing the kind of work they want to do. Such business owners are called **micropreneurs**. While other entrepreneurs are committed to the quest for growth, micropreneurs know they can be happy even if their companies never appear on a list of top-ranked businesses.

micropreneurs
Entrepreneurs willing to accept the risk of starting and managing the type of business that remains small, lets them do the kind of work they want to do, and offers them a balanced lifestyle.

Many micropreneurs are home-based business owners. More than half of all small businesses are run from owners' homes.[9] Micropreneurs include consultants, video producers, architects, and bookkeepers. Many with professional skills such as graphic design, writing, and translating have found that one way of starting a freelance business is through websites such as Elance (www.elance.com) and oDesk (www.odesk.com) that link clients and freelancers. The sites post job openings and client feedback and serve as secure intermediaries for clients' payments.

Many home-based businesses are owned by people combining career and family. Don't picture just moms with young children; nearly 60 percent are men.[10] Here are more reasons for the growth of home-based businesses:[11]

- Computer technology has leveled the competitive playing field, allowing home-based businesses to look and act as big as their corporate competitors. Broadband Internet connections, smartphones, and other technologies are so affordable that setting up a business takes a much smaller initial investment than it once did.

- Corporate downsizing has led many to venture out on their own. Meanwhile, the work of the downsized employees still needs to be done, and corporations are outsourcing much of it to smaller companies.
- Social attitudes have changed. Whereas home-based entrepreneurs used to be asked when they were going to get a "real" job, they are now likely to be asked for how-to-do-it advice.
- New tax laws have loosened restrictions on deducting expenses for home offices.

Working at home has its challenges, of course. Here are a few:[12]

- *Getting new customers.* Getting the word out can be difficult because you don't have a retail storefront.
- *Managing time.* You save time by not commuting, but it takes self-discipline to use that time wisely.
- *Keeping work and family tasks separate.* It's great to be able to throw a load of laundry in the washer in the middle of the workday if you need to, but you have to keep such distractions to a minimum. It also takes self-discipline to leave your work at the office if the office is at home.
- *Abiding by city ordinances.* Government ordinances restrict the types of businesses allowed in certain parts of the community and how much traffic a home-based business can attract to the neighborhood.
- *Managing risk.* Home-based entrepreneurs should review their homeowner's insurance policy, since not all policies cover business-related claims. Some even void the coverage if there is a business in the home.

Home-based entrepreneurs should focus on finding opportunity instead of accepting security, getting results instead of following routines, earning a profit instead of earning a paycheck, trying new ideas instead of avoiding mistakes, and creating a long-term vision instead of seeking a short-term payoff. Figure 6.1 lists 10 ideas for potentially successful home-based businesses, and Figure 6.2 highlights clues for avoiding home-based business scams. You can find a wealth of online information about starting a home-based business at *Entrepreneur* magazine's website (www.entrepreneur.com).

FIGURE 6.1 POTENTIAL HOME-BASED BUSINESSES

Many businesses can be started at home. Listed below are 10 businesses that have low start-up costs, don't require an abundance of administrative tasks, and are in relatively high demand:

1. Cleaning service.
2. Gift-basket business.
3. Web merchant.
4. Mailing list service.
5. Microfarming (small plots of land for such high-value crops as mushrooms, edible flowers, or sprouts).
6. Tutoring.
7. Résumé service.
8. Web design.
9. Medical claims assistance.
10. Personal coaching.

Look for a business that meets these important criteria: (1) The job is something you truly enjoy doing; (2) you know enough to do the job well or you are willing to spend time learning it while you have another job; and (3) you can identify a market for your product or service.

Web-Based Businesses

The Internet has sprouted a world of small web-based businesses selling everything from staplers to refrigerator magnets to wedding dresses. In 2013, online retail sales reached $262 billion, or approximately 8 percent of all retail sales. Online retail sales were up 13 percent in 2013, compared to just 2.5 percent for all retail sales. Forrester Research predicts that online retail sales will reach $370 billion by 2017.[13]

Web-based businesses have to offer more than the same merchandise customers can buy at stores—they must offer unique products or services. For example, Marc Resnik started his web-based distribution company after waking up one morning laughing about his business idea. Now Throw Things.com makes money for him—he's shipped products to more than 44 countries. Although the company's offerings seem like a random collection of unrelated items, everything it sells can be thrown. You can buy promotional products in the "Throw Your Name Around!" section, ventriloquist dummies in the "Throw Your Voice!" section, and sporting equipment in the "Things to Throw!" section. Stranger products include fake vomit ("Throw Up!") and a $3.50 certificate that says you wasted your money ("Throw Your Money Away!"). Resnik doesn't sell very many of those certificates, but he does sell more dummies than anyone else in the United States. About two-thirds of the company's revenue comes from the promotional products section, which allows customers to add a logo to thousands of products. Why is Resnik's business so successful? As one frequent customer said, it's because of Resnik's exceptional service and quick turnaround time.[14]

One of the easiest ways to start a web-based business is through affiliate marketing. **Affiliate marketing** is an online marketing strategy in which a business rewards individuals or other businesses (affiliates) for each visitor or

Jennifer Burnham operates her business, Pure and Simple Organizing, from her apartment. Burnham helps people organize their lives, homes, businesses, and more. Can you see why Burnham is considered a micropreneur?

affiliate marketing
An online marketing strategy in which a business rewards individuals or other businesses (affiliates) for each visitor or customer the affiliate sends to its website.

FIGURE 6.2 WATCH OUT FOR SCAMS

You've probably read many newspaper and magazine ads selling home-based businesses. You may have even received unsolicited e-mail messages touting the glory of particular work-at-home opportunities. Beware of work-at-home scams! Here are a few clues that tell you a home business opportunity is a scam:

1. The ad promises that you can earn hundreds or even thousands of dollars a week working at home.
2. No experience is needed.
3. You need to work only a few hours a week.
4. There are loads of CAPITAL LETTERS and exclamation points!!!!!
5. You need to call a 900 number for more information.
6. You're asked to send in some money to receive a list of home-based business opportunities.
7. You're pressured to make a decision NOW!!!!

Do your homework before investing in a business opportunity. Call and ask for references. Contact the Better Business Bureau (www.bbb.org), county and state departments of consumer affairs, and the state attorney general's office. Conduct an Internet search and ask people in forums or on social networking sites if they've dealt with the company. Visit websites such as Friends In Business (www.friendsinbusiness.com) to find advice on specific online scams. Most important, don't pay a great deal of money for a business opportunity until you've talked to an attorney.

There are more than 70,000 diamonds for sale on BlueNile.com, a Seattle-based company that took in $10.9 million in net income in 2013. Customers buy directly from the website or through a toll-free number staffed by helpful reps (who don't work on commission). What does Blue Nile offer that other jewelry retailers don't?

intrapreneurs
Creative people who work as entrepreneurs within corporations.

customer the affiliate sends to its website. For example, imagine you discovered a backpack online made of an extremely lightweight, amazingly strong fabric that holds everything you need for the day, is easy to carry, and looks great. You want to tell all your friends about it, so you register as an affiliate on the seller's website and post an affiliate link to the product on your Facebook page. Whenever anyone clicks on the link and buys a backpack, the seller pays you a commission.[15]

If you can make a little money in commissions from sales of a single backpack, imagine if you want to recommend products from many different e-tailers. Building such relationships has become easier with the advent of social commerce services such as SkimLinks (www.skimlinks.com). Once registered with SkimLinks, any links to participating e-tailers that you've posted to your website, Facebook page, or blog are automatically converted to affiliate links with those e-tailers. You then get commissions on sales generated through your visitors clicking on the links. While you do have to share a portion of your commissions with SkimLinks, the social commerce service saves you from the time-consuming task of researching and registering as an affiliate with multiple sellers. Such services are allowing users to become what amounts to peer-to-peer affiliates for e-retailers where the users can make money.[16]

A web-based business isn't always a fast road to success. It can sometimes be a shortcut to failure. Hundreds of high-flying dot-coms crashed after promising to revolutionize the way we shop. That's the bad news. The good news is that you can learn from someone else's failure and spare yourself some pain.

Entrepreneurship within Firms

Entrepreneurship in a large organization is often reflected in the efforts and achievements of **intrapreneurs**, creative people who work as entrepreneurs within corporations. The idea is to use a company's existing resources—human, financial, and physical—to launch new products and generate new profits. At 3M, which produces a wide array of products from adhesives like Scotch tape to nonwoven materials for industrial use, managers are expected to devote 15 percent of their work time to thinking up new products or services.[17] You know those bright-colored Post-it Notes people use to write messages on just about everything? That product was developed by Art Fry, a 3M employee. He needed to mark the pages of his hymnal with something that wouldn't damage the book or fall out. He came up with the idea of the self-stick, repositionable paper slips. The labs at 3M produced a sample, but distributors were unimpressed, and market surveys were inconclusive. Nonetheless, 3M kept sending samples to secretaries of top executives. Eventually, after a major sales and marketing program, the orders began pouring in, and Post-it Notes became a big winner. The company continues to update the product; making it from recycled paper is one of many innovations. Post-it Notes have gone international as well—the notepads sent to Japan are long and narrow to accommodate vertical writing. You can even use Post-it Notes electronically—the Post-it Software Notes program allows you to type messages onto brightly colored notes and store them on memo boards, embed them in documents, or send them through e-mail.

A classic intrapreneurial venture is Lockheed Martin Corporation's Skunkworks, a research and development center that turned out such monumental products as the United States' first fighter jet in 1943 and the Stealth fighter in 1991.[18]

Encouraging Entrepreneurship: What Government Can Do

Part of the Immigration Act passed by Congress in 1990 was intended to encourage more entrepreneurs to come to the United States. The act created a category of "investor visas" that allows 10,000 people to come to the United States each year if they invest $1 million in an enterprise that creates or preserves 10 jobs. Some people are promoting the idea of increasing the allowed number of such immigrants. They believe the more entrepreneurs that can be drawn to the United States, the more jobs will be created and the more the economy will grow.[19]

Another way to encourage entrepreneurship is **enterprise zones**, specific geographic areas to which governments attract private business investment by offering lower taxes and other government support. These are also sometimes called *empowerment zones* or *enterprise communities*. In 2014, President Obama announced the creation of the first 5 of 20 "promise zones." The promise zone plan calls on federal agencies to help business owners cut through bureaucracy to win federal grants and bring schools, companies, and nonprofits together to support literacy programs and job training.[20]

The government could have a significant effect on entrepreneurship by offering tax breaks to businesses that make investments to create jobs. The Jumpstart Our Business Startups (JOBS) Act of 2012 was enacted in an effort to make it easier for small business to raise funds and hopefully create new jobs.[21] We talk more about the JOBS Act later in this chapter and in Chapter 19.

States are becoming stronger supporters of entrepreneurs, and are creating programs that invest directly in new businesses. Often, state commerce departments serve as clearinghouses for such programs. States are also creating incubators and technology centers to reduce start-up capital needs. **Incubators** offer new businesses in the critical stage of early development low-cost offices with basic services such as accounting, legal advice, and secretarial help. According to a recent study conducted by the National Business Incubator Association (NBIA), 87 percent of incubator graduates remain in business.[22] Approximately 32 percent of all business incubators have ties to a university.[23] To learn more about what incubators offer and to find links to incubators in your area, visit the NBIA's website (www.nbia.org).

There are a few states that offer assistance to qualified candidates under the Self-Employment Assistance (SEA) program. The program allows participants to collect unemployment checks while they build their businesses. Participants often get training and counseling as well. Unemployment checks may not seem like much, but many business owners say they are enough to help them launch their companies without depleting savings to pay for living expenses until their businesses are strong enough to support them.[24]

enterprise zones
Specific geographic areas to which governments try to attract private business investment by offering lower taxes and other government support.

incubators
Centers that offer new businesses low-cost offices with basic business services.

When you come up with a winning idea, stick with it. That's certainly been the motto of 3M, the maker of Post-it Notes. The company encourages intrapreneurship among its employees by requiring them to devote at least 15 percent of their time to think about new products. How has this commitment to innovation paid off for 3M and its employees?

Incubators, such as this one in Washington DC, offer new businesses low-cost offices with basic business services such as accounting, legal advice, and secretarial help. Do you have such incubators in your area?

The government can also join with private entities to promote entrepreneurship. For example, Startup America is a White House initiative to "celebrate, inspire, and accelerate high-growth entrepreneurship throughout the nation."[25] It is a public and private effort to bring together the country's most innovative entrepreneurs, corporations, universities, foundations, and other leaders, to work with federal agencies to increase the number and success of U.S. entrepreneurs. One of the core goals is to empower more Americans not just to get a job, but also to create jobs. Learn more about the resources offered by Startup America at www.startupamericapartnership.org.

test prep

- Why are people willing to take the risks of entrepreneurship?
- What are the advantages of entrepreneurial teams?
- How do micropreneurs differ from other entrepreneurs?
- What does the government do to promote entrepreneurship?

Use LearnSmart to help retain what you have learned. Access your instructor's Connect course to check out LearnSmart, or go to learnsmartadvantage.com for help.

LEARNSMART

LO 6–2 Discuss the importance of small business to the American economy and summarize the major causes of small-business failure.

GETTING STARTED IN SMALL BUSINESS

Let's suppose you have a great idea for a new business, you have the attributes of an entrepreneur, and you're ready to take the leap into business for yourself. How do you start? That's what the rest of this chapter is about.

It may be easier to identify with a small neighborhood business than with a giant global firm, yet the principles of management are similar for each. The management of charities, government agencies, churches, schools, and unions is much the same as the management of small and large businesses. So, as you learn about small-business management, you will take a giant step toward understanding management in general. All organizations demand capital, good ideas, planning, information management, budgets (and financial management in general), accounting, marketing, good employee relations, and good overall managerial know-how. We shall explore these areas as they relate to small businesses and then, later in the book, apply the concepts to large firms and even global organizations.

Small versus Big Business

small business
A business that is independently owned and operated, is not dominant in its field of operation, and meets certain standards of size (set by the Small Business Administration) in terms of employees or annual receipts.

The Small Business Administration (SBA) defines a **small business** as one that is independently owned and operated, is not dominant in its field of operation, and meets certain standards of size in terms of employees or annual receipts (such as under $2.5 million a year for service businesses). A small business is considered "small" only in relationship to other businesses in its industry. A wholesaler may sell up to $22 million and still be considered a small business by the SBA. In manufacturing, a plant can have 1,500 employees and still be considered small. Let's look at some interesting statistics about small businesses:[26]

- There are 28 million small businesses in the United States.
- Of all nonfarm businesses in the United States, almost 97 percent are considered small by SBA standards.
- Small businesses account for more than 50 percent of the gross domestic product (GDP).
- Nearly 600,000 tax-paying, employee-hiring businesses are started every year.
- Small businesses have generated 65 percent of the new jobs since 1995.
- Small businesses employ about half of all private-sector employees.
- About 80 percent of U.S. workers find their first jobs in small businesses.

As you can see, small business is really a big part of the U.S. economy. How big? Let's find out.

Importance of Small Businesses

Since 60–80 percent of the nation's new jobs are in small businesses, there's a very good chance you'll either work in a small business someday or start one. In addition to providing employment opportunities, small firms believe they offer other advantages over larger companies—more personal customer service and the ability to respond quickly to opportunities.

Bigger is not always better. Picture a hole in the ground. If you fill it with boulders, there are many empty spaces between them. If you fill it with sand, there is no space between the grains. That's how it is in business. Big businesses don't serve all the needs of the market. There is plenty of room for small companies to make a profit filling those niches.

When Roni Di Lulla's dog Midnight had trouble squinting at a flying Frisbee, Roni retrofitted sports goggles to fit him. Midnight became the hit of the dog park and owners asked if she could make the eyewear for their dogs too. They became so popular, Di Lulla contracted with a Taiwanese company to make goggles with wide nose bridges and deep lens cups. Today Doggles brings in $3 million a year and are used by doggie fashionistas, veterinary ophthalmologists, and even military canines.

Small-Business Success and Failure

You can't be naïve about business practices, or you'll go broke. According to the SBA half of new businesses don't last five years.[27] Some people argue that the failure rate is actually much lower than that statistic suggests. When small-business owners closed down one business to start another, for instance, they were included in the "failure" category—even though they hadn't failed at all. Similarly, when a business changed its form of ownership or a sole proprietor retired, it was counted as a failure. The good news for entrepreneurs is that business failures are much lower than traditionally reported.

Figure 6.3 lists reasons for small-business failures, among them managerial incompetence and inadequate financial planning. Keep in mind that when a business fails, it is important that the owners learn from their mistakes. Some entrepreneurs

FIGURE 6.3 CAUSES OF SMALL-BUSINESS FAILURE

The following are some of the causes of small-business failure:

- Plunging in without first testing the waters on a small scale.
- Underpricing or overpricing goods or services.
- Underestimating how much time it will take to build a market.
- Starting with too little capital.
- Starting with too much capital and being careless in its use.
- Going into business with little or no experience and without first learning something about the industry or market.
- Borrowing money without planning just how and when to pay it back.
- Attempting to do too much business with too little capital.
- Not allowing for setbacks and unexpected expenses.
- Buying too much on credit.
- Extending credit too freely.
- Expanding credit too rapidly.
- Failing to keep complete, accurate records, so that the owners drift into trouble without realizing it.
- Carrying habits of personal extravagance into the business.
- Not understanding business cycles.
- Forgetting about taxes, insurance, and other costs of doing business.
- Mistaking the freedom of being in business for oneself for the liberty to work or not, according to whim.

who have suffered flops are more realistic than novice entrepreneurs. Because of the lessons they've learned, they may be more successful in their future ventures.[28] Milton Hershey, for example, tried starting candy businesses in Chicago and New York and failed both times. He could have followed in the footsteps of his father, a dreamer who lacked the perseverance and work ethic to stick to an idea long enough to make it work. Instead Hershey kept trying and eventually built not only the world's largest candy company, but also schools, churches, and housing for his employees.

Arianna Huffington, cofounder of the Huffington Post, put learning from failure this way: "I failed, many times in my life...but my mother used to tell me, 'failure is not the opposite of success, it's a stepping stone to success.' So at some point, I learned not to dread failure. I strongly believe that we are not put on this Earth just to accumulate victories and trophies and avoid failures; but rather to be whittled and sandpapered down until what's left is who we truly are."[29]

Choosing the right type of business is critical. Many businesses with low failure rates require advanced training to start—veterinary services, dental practices, medical practices, and so on. While training and degrees may buy security, they do not tend to produce much growth—one dentist can fill only so many cavities. If you want to be both independent and rich, you need to go after growth. Often high-growth businesses, such as technology firms, are not easy to start and are even more difficult to keep going.

The easiest businesses to start have the least growth and greatest failure rate (like restaurants). The easiest to keep alive are difficult to get started (like manufacturing). And the ones that can make you rich are both hard to start and hard to keep going (like automobile assembly). See Figure 6.4 to get an idea of the business situations most likely to lead to success.

When you decide to start your own business, think carefully. You're unlikely to find everything you want—easy entry, security, and reward—in one business. Choose those characteristics that matter most to you; accept the absence of the others; plan, plan, plan; and then go for it!

FIGURE 6.4 SITUATIONS FOR SMALL-BUSINESS SUCCESS

The following factors increase the chances of small-business success:

- The customer requires a lot of personal attention, as in a salon.
- The product is not easily made by mass-production techniques (e.g., custom-tailored clothes or custom auto-body work).
- Sales are not large enough to appeal to a large firm (e.g., a novelty shop).
- The neighborhood is not attractive because of crime or poverty. This provides a unique opportunity for small grocery stores and laundries.
- A large business sells a franchise operation to local buyers. (Don't forget franchising as an excellent way to enter the world of small business.)
- The owner pays attention to new competitors.
- The business is in a growth industry (e.g., computer services or web design).

LO 6–3 Summarize ways to learn about how small businesses operate.

LEARNING ABOUT SMALL-BUSINESS OPERATIONS

Hundreds of would-be entrepreneurs ask the same question: "How can I learn to run my own business?" Here are some hints.

Learn from Others

Investigate your local community college for classes on small business and entrepreneurship; there are thousands of such programs throughout the United States. Many bring together entrepreneurs from diverse backgrounds who form helpful support networks. Talk to others who have already done it. They'll tell you that location is critical and caution you not to be undercapitalized, that is, not to start without enough money. They'll warn you about the problems of finding and retaining good workers. And, most of all, they'll tell you to keep good records and hire a good accountant and lawyer before you start. Free advice like this is invaluable.

Get Some Experience

There is no better way to learn small-business management than by becoming an apprentice or working for a successful entrepreneur. Many small-business owners got the idea for their businesses from their prior jobs. The rule of thumb is: Have three years' experience in a comparable business first.

Back in 1818, Cornelius Vanderbilt sold his own sailing vessels and went to work for a steamboat company so that he could learn the rules of the new game of steam. After learning what he needed to know, he quit, started his own steamship company, and became the first U.S. business owner to accumulate $100 million.

When Luke Holden and Ben Conniff opened their first lobster shack in 2009, they depended on Holden's experience as a lobster fisherman and financial experience as an investment banker, and Conniff's background in food media and culinary experience. With the help of Holden's father, who spent 25 years fishing, cooking, packing, and shipping lobster, Luke's Lobster is now an $8.5 million business with 11 locations. How do you think this team's experience helped the business succeed?

Should You Stay or Should You Go?

Suppose you've worked for two years in a company and you see signs that it is beginning to falter. You and a co-worker have ideas about how to make a company like your boss's succeed. Rather than share your ideas with your boss, you and your friend are considering quitting your jobs and starting your own company together. Should you approach other co-workers about working for your new venture? Will you try to lure your old boss's customers to your own business? What are your alternatives? What are the consequences of each alternative? What's the most ethical choice?

Running a small business part-time, during your off hours or on weekends, can bring the rewards of working for yourself while still enjoying a regular paycheck at another job. It may save you money too, because you're then less likely to make "rookie mistakes" when you start your own business. The Making Ethical Decisions box presents ethical questions about using the knowledge you've gained as an employee to start your own business.

Take Over a Successful Firm

Small-business owners work long hours and rarely take vacations. After many years, they may feel stuck and think they can't get out because they have too much time and effort invested. Thus millions of small-business owners are eager to get away, at least for a long vacation.

This is where you come in. Find a successful businessperson who owns a small business. Tell him or her you are eager to learn the business and would like to serve an apprenticeship, that is, a training period. Say that at the end of the training period (one year or so), you would like to help the owner or manager by becoming assistant manager. Thus you can free the owner to take off weekends and holidays and have a long vacation—a good deal for him or her. For another year or so, work very hard to learn all about the business—suppliers, inventory, bookkeeping, customers, promotion. At the end of two years, make this offer: The owner can retire or work only part-time, and you will take over management of the business. You can establish a profit-sharing plan with the owner plus pay yourself a salary. Be generous with yourself; you'll earn it if you manage the business. You can even ask for 40 percent or more of the profits.

The owner benefits by keeping ownership in the business and making 60 percent of what he or she earned before—without having to work. You benefit by making 40 percent of the profits of a successful firm. This is an excellent deal for an owner about to retire—he or she is able to keep the firm and a healthy profit flow. It is also a clever and successful way to share in the profits of a successful small business without making any personal monetary investment.

If profit sharing doesn't appeal to the owner, you may want to buy the business outright. How do you determine a fair price for a business? Value is based on (1) what the business owns, (2) what it earns, and (3) what makes it unique. Naturally, an accountant will need to help you determine the business's value.[30]

If you fail at your efforts to take over the business through either profit sharing or buying, you can quit and start your own business fully trained.

MANAGING A SMALL BUSINESS

According to the Small Business Administration, one of the major causes of small business failures is poor management. Keep in mind, though, that *poor management* covers a number of faults. It could mean poor planning, record-keeping, inventory control, promotion, or employee relations. Most likely it includes poor capitalization. To help you succeed as a business owner, in the following sections we explore the functions of business in a small-business setting:

- Planning your business.
- Financing your business.
- Knowing your customers (marketing).
- Managing your employees (human resource development).
- Keeping records (accounting).

Although all the functions are important in both the start-up and management phases of the business, the first two—planning and financing—are the primary concerns when you start your business. The others are the heart of your operations once the business is under way.

Begin with Planning

Many people eager to start a small business come up with an idea and begin discussing it with professors, friends, and other businesspeople. At this stage the entrepreneur needs a business plan. A **business plan** is a detailed written statement that describes the nature of the business, the target market, the advantages the business will have over competition, and the resources and qualifications of the owner(s). A business plan forces potential small-business owners to be quite specific about the products or services they intend to offer. They must analyze the competition, calculate how much money they need to start, and cover other details of operation. A business plan is also mandatory for talking with bankers or other investors.

Lenders want to know everything about an aspiring business. First, pick a bank that serves businesses the size of yours. Have a good accountant prepare a complete set of financial statements and a personal balance sheet. Make an appointment before going to the bank, and go to the bank with an accountant and all the necessary financial information. Demonstrate to the banker that you're a person of good character, civic-minded and respected in business and community circles. Finally, ask for *all* the money you need, be specific, and be prepared to personally guarantee the loan.

Writing a Business Plan   A good business plan takes a long time to write, but you've got only five minutes, in the *executive summary*, to convince

business plan
A detailed written statement that describes the nature of the business, the target market, the advantages the business will have in relation to competition, and the resources and qualifications of the owner(s).

ModCloth co-founders Susan and Eric Koger started selling vintage clothes when they were in college. They entered a hastily written business plan in a school competition—and lost. While discouraging at first, the loss taught them that they needed to refocus and create a solid business plan if they were going to attract investors. Today their company has more than 400 employees and revenue over $100 million.

connect

▶ **iSee It!** Need help understanding how an entrepreneur can secure financing for a small business? Visit your Connect e-book video tab for a brief animated explanation.

Wouldn't it be great if money grew on trees? Unfortunately it doesn't, so prospective entrepreneurs must find other sources of capital such as personal savings, relatives, former employers, banks, finance companies, venture capitalists, and government agencies. What is the most common source of funding after personal savings?

readers not to throw it away. Since bankers receive many business plans every day, the summary has to catch their interest quickly. An outline of a comprehensive business plan is shown on the next page. There's no such thing as a perfect business plan; even the most comprehensive business plan changes as the new business evolves.[31]

Many software programs can help you get organized. One highly rated business-plan program is Business Plan Pro by Palo Alto Software. For a simplified business plan, you may want to check out Fortune 500 executive Jim Horan's book *The One Page Business Plan*. The book includes a CD with interactive exercises, forms and templates.[32] To see samples of successful business plans for a variety of businesses go to www.bplans.com/sample_business_plans. You can also learn more about writing business plans on the Small Business Administration website at www.sba.gov/starting.

Getting the completed business plan into the right hands is almost as important as getting the right information into the plan. Finding funding requires research. Next we discuss sources of money available to new business ventures. All require a comprehensive business plan. The time and effort you invest before starting a business will pay off many times later. The big payoff is survival.

Getting Money to Fund a Small Business

An entrepreneur has several potential sources of capital: personal savings; family and business associates; banks and finance institutions; angels and venture capitalists; and government agencies such as the Small Business Administration (SBA), the Farmers Home Administration, the Economic Development Authority, and the Minority Business Development Agency.

Family and business associates The most common source of funding after personal savings is friends and family.[33] You may even want to consider borrowing from a potential supplier to your future business. Helping you get started may be in the supplier's interest if there is a chance you will be a big customer later. This is what Ray Kroc did in the early years of McDonald's. When Kroc didn't have the funds available to keep the company going, he asked his suppliers to help him with the necessary funds. These suppliers grew along with McDonald's. It's usually not a good idea to ask such an investor for money at the outset. Begin by asking for advice; if the supplier likes your plan, he or she may be willing to help you with funding too.

Banks and finance institutions The credit crunch spurred by the recent financial crisis made it necessary for small-business owners to do a little extra shopping to find a friendly lender. Many found that smaller community banks were more likely to grant loans than larger regional banks. Since small banks do business in a single town or cluster of towns, they know their customers better. They have more flexibility to make lending decisions based on everything they know about their customers, rather than on a more automated basis as larger banks must.

Community development financial institutions (CDFIs) may be a source of funding for businesses in lower-income communities. Today CDFIs are playing a big role in the economic recovery.

OUTLINE OF A COMPREHENSIVE BUSINESS PLAN

A good business plan is between 25 and 50 pages long and takes at least six months to write.

Cover Letter

Only one thing is certain when you go hunting for money to start a business: You won't be the only hunter out there. You need to make potential funders want to read *your* business plan instead of the hundreds of others on their desks. Your cover letter should summarize the most attractive points of your project in as few words as possible. Be sure to address the letter to the potential investor by name. "To whom it may concern" or "Dear Sir" is not the best way to win an investor's support.

Section 1—Executive Summary

Begin with a two-page or three-page management summary of the proposed venture. Include a short description of the business, and discuss major goals and objectives.

Section 2—Company Background

Describe company operations to date (if any), potential legal considerations, and areas of risk and opportunity. Summarize the firm's financial condition, and include past and current balance sheets, income and cash flow statements, and other relevant financial records (you will read about these financial statements in Chapter 17). It is also wise to include a description of insurance coverage. Investors want to be assured that death or other mishaps do not pose major threats to the company.

Section 3—Management Team

Include an organization chart, job descriptions of listed positions, and detailed résumés of the current and proposed executives. A mediocre idea with a proven management team is funded more often than a great idea with an inexperienced team. Managers should have expertise in all disciplines necessary to start and run a business. If not, mention outside consultants who will serve in these roles and describe their qualifications.

Section 4—Financial Plan

Provide five-year projections for income, expenses, and funding sources. Don't assume the business will grow in a straight line. Adjust your planning to allow for funding at various stages of the company's growth. Explain the rationale and assumptions used to determine the estimates. Assumptions should be reasonable and based on industry/historical trends. Make sure all totals add up and are consistent throughout the plan. If necessary, hire a professional accountant or financial analyst to prepare these statements.

Stay clear of excessively ambitious sales projections; rather, offer best-case, expected, and worst-case scenarios. These not only reveal how sensitive the bottom line is to sales fluctuations but also serve as good management guides.

Section 5—Capital Required

Indicate the amount of capital needed to commence or continue operations, and describe how these funds are to be used. Make sure the totals are the same as the ones on the cash-flow statement. This area will receive a great deal of review from potential investors, so it must be clear and concise.

Section 6—Marketing Plan

Don't underestimate the competition. Review industry size, trends, and the target market segment. Sources like the *Rand McNally Commercial Atlas and Marketing Guide* can help you put a plan together. Discuss strengths and weaknesses of the product or service. The most important things investors want to know are what makes the product more desirable than what's already available and whether the product can be patented. Compare pricing to the competition's. Forecast sales in dollars and units. Outline sales, advertising, promotion, and public relations programs. Make sure the costs agree with those projected in the financial statements.

Section 7—Location Analysis

In retailing and certain other industries, the location of the business is one of the most important factors. Provide a comprehensive demographic analysis of consumers in the area of the proposed business as well as a traffic-pattern analysis and vehicular and pedestrian counts.

Section 8—Manufacturing Plan

Describe minimum plant size, machinery required, production capacity, inventory and inventory-control methods, quality control, plant personnel requirements, and so on. Estimates of product costs should be based on primary research.

Section 9—Appendix

Include all marketing research on the product or service (off-the-shelf reports, article reprints, etc.) and other information about the product concept or market size. Provide a bibliography of all the reference materials you consulted. This section should demonstrate that the proposed company won't be entering a declining industry or market segment.

If you would like to see sample business plans that successfully secured funding, go to Bplans.com (www.bplans.com). You can also learn more about writing business plans on the Small Business Administration website at www.sba.gov/starting.

CDFIs succeeded even after the credit bubble because they maintained the financial discipline other lenders lacked. They have the incentive to make sure their clients succeed because, if borrowers don't repay their loans, the CDFIs take the hit, not investors. Only 1 percent of their loans were not paid back in the last three decades.[34] CDFIs don't just loan money. More importantly, they provide business counseling such as helping owners learn how to develop marketing strategies, manage inventory, and improve cash flow.

Angels and venture capitalists　Individual investors are also a frequent source of capital for most entrepreneurs. *Angel investors* are private individuals who invest their own money in potentially hot new companies before they go public. A number of websites match people who want money with those willing to lend it. They include donation-based services like Kickstarter, equity-investment sites like Early Shares, and debt-investment sites like Prosper Marketplace. Other sites, such as GreenNote and People Capital, specialize in lending to students. This form of individual investing is called peer-to-peer (P2P) lending or crowdfunding.[35] A creditworthy borrower often gets such money faster and more easily than going to the bank. And the cost is often less than a bank loan. With so many crowdfunding sites (there more than 1,000 so far), it can be confusing to know which one is the best fit for you and your prospective business. Reviewing services like CrowdsUnite and Crowdfunding Websites Reviews offer feedback from users of lending sites to help you better understand your options.[36]

The **JOBS** Act of 2012 allows businesses to raise up to $1 million a year from private investors without making an initial public offering (discussed in Chapter 19). Unlike many crowdfunding options that accept small donations in exchange for perks like T-shirts and other memorabilia, the **JOBS** Act allows businesses to solicit larger investments in exchange for either ownership shares in the business or a commitment to repay the loan.[37] Many prefer the terms *crowdinvesting* or *equity crowdfunding* for this form of fund raising. The Adapting to Change box offers a couple of examples of companies seeking crowdinvested funds. You can read more about how the JOBS Act is changing how businesses can attract investors in Chapter 19.

venture capitalists
Individuals or companies that invest in new businesses in exchange for partial ownership of those businesses.

Venture capitalists may finance your project—for a price. Venture capitalists may ask for a hefty stake in your company (as much as 60 percent) in exchange for the cash to start your business. If the venture capitalist takes too large a stake, you could lose control of the business. Since the widespread failure of early web start-ups, venture capitalists have been willing to invest less and expect more return on their investment if the new company is sold.[38] Therefore, if you're a very small company, you don't have a very good chance of getting venture capital. You'd have a better chance finding an angel investor.

If your proposed venture does require millions of dollars to start, experts recommend that you talk with at least five investment firms and their clients in order to find the right venture capitalist.[39] You may be able to connect with potential investors through AngelList, an online nonprofit service that helps entrepreneurs and venture capitalists get to know each other.[40] To learn more about how to find venture capitalists, visit the National Venture Capital Association's website (www.nvca.org).

States Test New Crowdinvesting Rules

Crowdfunding websites like Kickstarter and Indiegogo have allowed thousands to receive the capital they need to realize their entrepreneurial dreams. However, these sites tend to work out best for people whose ideas play to an Internet audience, such as artists or video game designers who reward contributors with T-shirts or products. That's why U.S. lawmakers passed the Jumpstart Our Business Startups (JOBS) Act in 2012. The legislation is meant to make crowdfunding more accessible to small businesses that hope to attract investors.

However, the Securities and Exchange Commission (SEC) has yet to enact all the crowdinvesting (also known as *equity* crowdfunding) clauses laid out in the JOBS Act. Instead, portions of it are being given a test run in states like Georgia, Kansas, and Wisconsin, as legislators continue to modify the law. For instance, after failing to secure a bank loan, two brothers from Georgia used crowdinvesting to raise $126,000 for their oilcan guitar business. Not only did the

brothers spend six weeks explaining their business model to potential investors, but they also had to educate people in depth about the new law. "It's not just throwing up a profile on a website and investors swarm at you. It's a lot of effort," says one of the brothers.

Even with all that effort, though, there's no guarantee that a crowdinvesting campaign will work. For Daniel Popovic, another Georgia entrepreneur, three months of searching wasn't enough time to secure the $400,000 he needed to launch his fitness website. He says that scrounging for capital became a full-time job, something that didn't fit in with his skill set as a web designer. What's more, even if a company raises enough crowdinvested cash to meet its current goals, there's a good chance that other investors down the line wouldn't want to fund a company with 40 or more stockholders. As a result, crowdinvesting is recommended primarily for small, local shops and restaurants that won't need venture capital investment going forward. Still, circumstances could change once the revised federal bill finally gets enacted into law. Stay tuned.

Sources: Ruth Simon and Angus Loten, "Crowdfunding Gets State-Level Test Run," *The Wall Street Journal,* December 4, 2013; J. Craig Andersen, "Maine 'Crowd Investing' Bill Becomes Law," *Portland Press Herald,* March 6, 2014; and Nicole Fallon, "Equity Crowdfunding: 3 Facts Entrepreneurs Should Know," *Business News Daily,* March 21, 2014.

The Small Business Administration (SBA)

The **Small Business Administration (SBA)** is a U.S. government agency that advises and assists small businesses by providing management training and financial advice and loans (see Figure 6.5). The SBA started a microloan demonstration program in 1991. The program provides very small loans (up to $50,000) and technical assistance to small-business owners. It is administered through a nationwide network of nonprofit organizations chosen by the SBA. Rather than award loans based on collateral, credit history, or previous business success, the program judges worthiness on belief in the borrowers' integrity and the soundness of their business ideas.[41]

The SBA reduced the size of its application from 150 pages to 1 page for loans under $50,000. Since government regulations are constantly changing, you may want to go to the SBA's website (www.sba.gov) for the latest information about SBA programs and other business services.

Small Business Administration (SBA)
A U.S. government agency that advises and assists small businesses by providing management training and financial advice and loans.

FIGURE 6.5 TYPES OF SBA FINANCIAL ASSISTANCE

The SBA may provide the following types of financial assistance:

- *Guaranteed loans*—loans made by a financial institution that the government will repay if the borrower stops making payments. The maximum individual loan guarantee is capped at $5 million.

- *Microloans*—amounts ranging from $100 to $50,000 to people such as single mothers and public housing tenants.

- *Export Express*—loans made to small businesses wishing to export. The maximum guaranteed loan amount is $500,000.

- *Community Adjustment and Investment Program (CAIP)*—loans to businesses to create new, sustainable jobs or to preserve existing jobs in eligible communities that have lost jobs due to changing trade patterns with Mexico and Canada following the adoption of NAFTA.

- *Pollution control loans*—loans to eligible small businesses for the financing of the planning, design, or installation of a pollution control facility. This facility must prevent, reduce, abate, or control any form of pollution, including recycling.

- *504 certified development company (CDC) loans*—loans for purchasing major fixed assets, such as land and buildings for businesses in eligible communities, typically rural communities or urban areas needing revitalization. The maximum guaranteed loan amount is $5 million for meeting the job creation criteria or a community development goal. The business must create or retain one job for every $65,000 ($100,000 for small manufacturers) provided by the SBA.

- *CAPLine loans*—loans to help small businesses meet their short-term and cyclical working capital needs. The maximum CAPLine loan is $5 million.

Small Business Investment Company (SBIC) Program
A program through which private investment companies licensed by the Small Business Administration lend money to small businesses.

You may also want to consider requesting funds from the **Small Business Investment Company (SBIC) Program**. SBICs are private investment companies licensed by the SBA to lend money to small businesses. An SBIC must have a minimum of $5 million in capital and can borrow up to $2 from the SBA for each $1 of capital it has. It lends to or invests in small businesses that meet its criteria. Often SBICs are able to keep defaults to a minimum by identifying a business's trouble spots early, giving entrepreneurs advice, and in some cases rescheduling loan payments.

Perhaps the best place for young entrepreneurs to start shopping for an SBA loan is a Small Business Development Center (SBDC). SBDCs are funded jointly by the federal government and individual states, and are usually associated with state and community colleges and universities. SBDCs can help you evaluate the feasibility of your idea, develop your business plan, and complete your funding application—all for no charge.

Obtaining money from banks, venture capitalists, and government sources is very difficult for most small businesses. (You will learn more about financing in Chapter 18.) Those who do survive the planning and financing of their new ventures are eager to get their businesses up and running. Your success in running a business depends on many factors, especially knowing your customers, managing your employees, and keeping good records.

Knowing Your Customers

market
People with unsatisfied wants and needs who have both the resources and the willingness to buy.

One of the most important elements of small-business success is knowing the **market**, which consists of consumers with unsatisfied wants and needs who have both resources and willingness to buy. Most of our students have the willingness to own a brand-new Maserati sports car. However, few have the resources necessary to satisfy this want. Would they be a good market for a luxury car dealer?

Once you have identified your market and its needs, you must set out to fill those needs. How? Offer top quality at a fair price with great service. Remember, it isn't enough to get customers—you have to *keep* them. As Victoria Jackson, founder of the $50 million company Victoria Jackson Cosmetics, says of the stars who push her products on television infomercials, "All the glamorous faces in the world wouldn't mean a thing if my customers weren't happy with the product and didn't come back for more." Everything must be geared to bring customers the satisfaction they deserve.[42]

One of the greatest advantages small businesses have is the ability to know their customers better and adapt quickly to their ever-changing needs. The only way to know what your customers' needs are is to listen, listen, listen. Don't let your passion and ego get in the way of changing your products or services to fit what customers really want. The Reaching Beyond Our Borders box discusses how you can use crowdsourcing to let customers and others from around the world help you design your products. You will gain more insights about markets in Chapters 13–16. Now let's consider effectively managing the employees who help you serve your market.

Managing Employees

As a business grows, it becomes impossible for an entrepreneur to oversee every detail, even by putting in 60 hours per week. This means that hiring, training, and motivating employees are critical.[43]

It is not easy to find good help when you offer less money, skimpier benefits, and less room for advancement than larger firms do. That's one reason employee relations is important for small-business management. Employees of small companies are often more satisfied with their jobs than are their counterparts in big business. Why? Quite often they find their jobs more challenging, their ideas more accepted, and their bosses more respectful.

Often entrepreneurs are reluctant to recognize that to keep growing, they must delegate authority to others. Who should have this delegated authority, and how much? This can be a particularly touchy issue in small businesses with long-term employees and in family businesses. As you might expect, entrepreneurs who have built their companies from scratch often feel compelled to promote employees who have been with them from the start—even when they aren't qualified to serve as managers. Common sense tells you this could hurt the business. The idea that you must promote or can't fire people because "they're family" can also hinder growth. Entrepreneurs best serve themselves and the business if they gradually recruit and groom employees for management positions, enhancing trust and support between them. You'll learn more about managing employees in Chapters 7–12.

Keeping Records

Small-business owners often say the most important assistance they received in starting and managing their business was in accounting. A businessperson who sets up an effective accounting system early will save much grief later. Accurate recordkeeping enables a small-business owner to follow daily sales, expenses, and profits, as well as help owners with inventory control, customer records, and payroll.

Many business failures are caused by poor accounting practices that lead to costly mistakes. A good accountant can

Not all small businesses stay small; some become business superstars. Take Mattel, for example. Mattel founders Ruth and Elliot Handler started their business in their garage—making picture frames. When they found that the dollhouse furniture they made with the wood scraps sold better than the frames, they changed their business. Today toys like Barbie helped Mattel grow into a $14.4 billion business.

Beyond Knowing What Your Customers Need

What's better than knowing what your customers need and then designing products to meet those needs? Getting your customers to design the products themselves. That's what Quirky has done. You probably are familiar with Quirky's most successful product, Pivot Power, the pivoting power strip that allows you to bend the strip in order to fit large adapters in every outlet.

Pivot Power's creator, Jake Zien, will be the first Quirky inventor to earn $1 million in royalty a year. When Zien was a college junior, he joined the Quirky community and submitted his idea as a simple, basic drawing. A week later, it was selected for development. A year after that, it was on sale at Bed Bath & Beyond. Zien just submitted an idea; everything else was done by the Quirky community (i.e., all inventors, influencers, staff, and customers from around the globe). Anyone in the community who contributes their ideas regarding design, style, enhancing, packaging, naming, taglines, or pricing are called influencers. The influencers don't just get a pat on the back for helping out; if their ideas are used, they are paid a portion of the royalty as well. Once a product is ready for production, Quirky decides which of its 21 suppliers and factories (mostly in Asia) will make the product.

Quirky founder and CEO Ben Kaufman knew Quirky would work two years ago when he saw a tweet of a Target advertisement for Quirky products. The tweeter wrote, "I made that." Actually, the person hadn't made that. But he was part of the community that helped create it, an experience that gave him a sense of ownership. Can't build a customer relationship stronger than that!

Sources: Josh Dean, "Is This the World's Most Creative Manufacturer?" *Inc.*, October 2013; Stephanie Mlot, "Quirky, GE Unveil Aros Smart Air Conditioner," *PC Magazine*, March 19, 2014; and "Quirky's Ben Kaufman Gets GE to Share Its Patents," *Bloomberg Businessweek*, March 20, 2014.

help you decide whether to buy or lease equipment and whether to own or rent a building. He or she may also help you with tax planning, financial forecasting, choosing sources of financing, and writing requests for funds.

Other small-business owners may tell you where to find an accountant experienced in small business. It pays to shop around for advice. You'll learn more about accounting in Chapter 17.

Looking for Help

Small-business owners have learned, sometimes the hard way, that they need outside consulting advice early in the process. This is especially true of legal, tax, and accounting advice but also of marketing, finance, and other areas. Most small and medium-sized firms cannot afford to hire such experts as employees, so they must turn to outside assistance.

A necessary and invaluable aide is a competent, experienced lawyer who knows and understands small businesses. Lawyers can help with leases, contracts, partnership agreements, and protection against liabilities. They don't have to be expensive. In fact, several prepaid legal plans offer services such as drafting legal documents for a low annual rate. Of course, you can find plenty of legal services online. The SBA offers plain-English guides and mini-tutorials that will help you gain a basic understanding of the laws that affect each phase of the life of a small business. FindForms.com offers a search tool that helps you find free legal forms from all over the web as well as advice, links, books, and more. Remember, "free" isn't a bargain if the information isn't correct, so check the sources carefully and double-check any legal actions with an attorney.

Make your marketing decisions long before you introduce a product or open a store. An inexpensive marketing research study may help you determine where to locate, whom to select as your target market, and what is an effective strategy for reaching it. Thus a marketing consultant with small-business experience can be of great help to you, especially one who has had experience with building websites and using social media.

Two other invaluable experts are a commercial loan officer and an insurance agent. The commercial loan officer can help you design an acceptable business plan and give you valuable financial advice as well as lend you money when you need it. An insurance agent will explain all the risks associated with a small business and how to cover them most efficiently with insurance and other means like safety devices and sprinkler systems.

An important source of information for small businesses is the **Service Corps of Retired Executives (SCORE)**. This SBA office has more than 11,000 volunteers from industry, trade associations, and education who counsel small businesses at no cost (except for expenses).[44] You can find a SCORE counselor by logging on to www.score.org. The SBA also offers a free, comprehensive online entrepreneurship course for aspiring entrepreneurs.

Often business professors from local colleges will advise small-business owners free or for a small fee. Some universities have clubs or programs that provide consulting services by master of business administration (MBA) candidates for a nominal fee. The University of Maryland and Virginia Tech have internship programs that pair MBA students with budding companies in local incubator programs. The incubator companies pay half the intern's salary, which is around $20 an hour.

It is also wise to seek the counsel of other small-business owners. The website YoungEntrepreneur.com offers experienced entrepreneurs and young start-ups an open forum to exchange advice and ideas. Visitors have access to articles on marketing, business planning, incorporation, and financial management. Peer groups within specific industries can give you better insights into the challenges and solutions encountered by other business owners in your field. Peer advisory organizations that could help you connect with a peer group in your industry include the American Small Business Coalition and Entrepreneurs Organization.[45]

Other sources of counsel include local chambers of commerce, the Better Business Bureau, national and local trade associations, the business reference section of your library, and many small-business-related websites.

Dianne Harrison and Cynthia Clarke, founders and owners of Copioisty, worked with a SCORE mentor to develop the business side of their greeting cards and paper products company. The mentor advised them about financing, investor relations, sales and marketing, human resources, operations, and organizational planning. What was the price tag for all of this valuable advice? $0!

Service Corps of Retired Executives (SCORE)
An SBA office with volunteers from industry, trade associations, and education who counsel small businesses at no cost (except for expenses).

- A business plan is probably the most important document a small-business owner will ever create. There are nine sections in the business plan outline shown in the chapter. Can you describe at least five of those sections now?

Use LearnSmart to help retain what you have learned. Access your instructor's Connect course to check out LearnSmart, or go to learnsmartadvantage.com for help.

LEARNSMART

LO 6–5   Outline the advantages and disadvantages small businesses have in entering global markets.

GOING GLOBAL: SMALL-BUSINESS PROSPECTS

As we noted in Chapter 3, there are over 317 million people in the United States but more than 7.1 billion people in the world.[46] Obviously, the world market is a much larger, more lucrative market for small businesses than the United States alone. Small and medium-sized business accounted for 99 percent of the growth in exporting firms in recent years. All this exporting is paying off. According to the International Trade Commission small exporting firms averaged 37 percent revenue growth during a recent five-year period compared to the decline of 7 percent for nonexporting firms.[47]

Technological advances have helped increase small business exporting. PayPal makes it possible for small businesses to get paid automatically when they conduct global business online. The Internet also helps small businesses find customers without the expense of international travel. As people acquire more wealth, they often demand specialized products that are not mass-produced and are willing to pay more for niche goods that small businesses offer. Dave Hammond, inventor and founder of Wizard Vending, began to push his gumball machines into the global market via a website. In the site's first year, he sold machines in Austria, Belgium, and Germany.

Still, many small businesses have difficulty getting started in global business. Why are so many missing the boat to the huge global markets? Primarily because the voyage includes a few major hurdles: (1) financing is often difficult to find, (2) would-be exporters don't know how to get started and do not understand the cultural differences between markets, and (3) the bureaucratic paperwork can threaten to bury a small business.

Beside the fact that most of the world's market lies outside the United States, there are other good reasons for going global. Exporting can absorb excess inventory, soften downturns in the domestic market, and extend product lives. It can also spice up dull routines.

Small businesses have several advantages over large businesses in international trade:

- Overseas buyers often enjoy dealing with individuals rather than with large corporate bureaucracies.
- Small companies can usually begin shipping much faster.
- Small companies can provide a wide variety of suppliers.
- Small companies can give customers personal service and undivided attention, because each overseas account is a major source of business to them.

A good place to start finding information about exporting is the Department of Commerce's Bureau of Industry and Security (www.bis.doc.gov). Other sources include the SBA's Office of International Trade. The SBA's Export Express loan program provides export financing opportunities for small businesses. The program is designed to finance a variety of needs of small-business exporters, including participation in foreign trade shows, catalog translations for use in foreign markets, lines of credit for export purposes, and real estate and equipment for the production of goods or services to be exported.

test prep

- Why do many small businesses avoid doing business globally?
- What are some of the advantages small businesses have over large businesses in selling in global markets?

summary

LO 6–1 Explain why people take the risks of entrepreneurship; list the attributes of successful entrepreneurs; and describe entrepreneurial teams, intrapreneurs, and home- and web-based businesses.

- **What are a few of the reasons people start their own businesses?**
  Reasons include profit, independence, opportunity, and challenge.

- **What are the attributes of successful entrepreneurs?**
  Successful entrepreneurs are self-directed, self-nurturing, action-oriented, highly energetic, and tolerant of uncertainty.

- **What have modern entrepreneurs done to ensure longer terms of management?**
  They have formed entrepreneurial teams with expertise in the many skills needed to start and manage a business.

- **What is a micropreneur?**
  Micropreneurs are people willing to accept the risk of starting and managing the type of business that remains small, lets them do the kind of work they want to do, and offers them a balanced lifestyle.

- **What is intrapreneuring?**
  Intrapreneuring is the establishment of entrepreneurial centers within a larger firm where people can innovate and develop new product ideas internally.

- **Why has there been such an increase in the number of home-based and web-based businesses in the last few years?**
  The increase in power and decrease in price of computer technology have leveled the field and made it possible for small businesses to compete against larger companies—regardless of location.

LO 6–2 Discuss the importance of small business to the American economy and summarize the major causes of small-business failure.

- **Why are small businesses important to the U.S. economy?**
  Small business accounts for almost 50 percent of gross domestic product (GDP). Perhaps more important to tomorrow's graduates, 80 percent of U.S. workers' first jobs are in small businesses.

- **What does the *small* in small business mean?**
  The Small Business Administration defines a small business as one that is independently owned and operated and not dominant in its field of

operation, and that meets certain standards of size in terms of employees or sales (depending on the size of others in the industry).

- **Why do many small businesses fail?**
  Many small businesses fail because of managerial incompetence and inadequate financial planning. See Figure 6.3 for a list of causes of small-business failure.

LO 6–3   Summarize ways to learn about how small businesses operate.

- **What hints would you give someone who wants to learn about starting a small business?**
  First, learn from others. Take courses and talk with some small-business owners. Second, get some experience working for others. Third, take over a successful firm. Finally, study the latest in small-business management techniques.

LO 6–4   Analyze what it takes to start and run a small business.

- **What goes into a business plan?**
  See the outline of a business plan in the chapter.

- **What sources of funds should someone wanting to start a new business consider investigating?**
  A new entrepreneur has several potential sources of capital: personal savings; family and business associates; banks and finance institutions; angels and venture capitalists; and government agencies and more.

- **What are some of the special problems that small-business owners have in dealing with employees?**
  Small-business owners often have difficulty finding competent employees and grooming employees for management responsibilities.

- **Where can budding entrepreneurs find help in starting their businesses?**
  Help can come from many sources: accountants, lawyers, marketing researchers, loan officers, insurance agents, the SBA, SBDCs, SBICs, peer groups, and even college professors.

LO 6–5   Outline the advantages and disadvantages small businesses have in entering global markets.

- **What are some advantages small businesses have over large businesses in global markets?**
  Foreign buyers enjoy dealing with individuals rather than large corporations because (1) small companies provide a wider variety of suppliers and can ship products more quickly and (2) small companies give more personal service.

- **Why don't more small businesses start trading globally?**
  There are several reasons: (1) financing is often difficult to find, (2) many people don't know how to get started and do not understand the cultural differences in foreign markets, and (3) the bureaucratic red tape is often overwhelming.

Access your instructor's Connect course to check out LearnSmart or go to learnsmartadvantage.com for help.

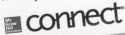

critical thinking

1. Do you have the entrepreneurial spirit? What makes you think that?

2. Are there any similarities between the characteristics demanded of an entrepreneur and those of a professional athlete? Would an athlete be a good prospect for entrepreneurship? Why or why not? Could teamwork be important in an entrepreneurial effort? Why or why not?

3. Imagine yourself starting a small business. What kind of business would it be? How much competition is there? What could you do to make your business more attractive than those of competitors? Would you be willing to work 60 to 70 hours a week to make the business successful?

developing workplace skills

Key: ● **Team**   ★ **Analytic**   ▲ **Communication**   ◙ **Technology**

1. Find issues of *Entrepreneur, Black Enterprise,* and *Inc.* magazines online. Read about the entrepreneurs who are heading today's dynamic new businesses. Write a profile about one.   ◙ ▲

2. Select a small business that looks attractive as a career possibility for you. Talk to at least one person who manages such a business. Ask how he or she started it. Ask about financing; human resource management (hiring, firing, training, scheduling); accounting issues; and other managerial matters. Prepare a summary of your findings, including whether the person's job was rewarding, interesting, and challenging—and why or why not.   ▲ ★

3. Contact the Small Business Administration by visiting a local office or the organization's website at www.sba.gov. Write a brief summary of the services the SBA offers.   ◙ ▲

4. Select a small business in your area or a surrounding area that has failed. List the factors you think led to its failure. Compile a list of actions the business owners might have taken to keep the company in business.   ▲ ★

5. Choose a partner from among your classmates and put together a list of factors that might mean the difference between success and failure of a new company entering the business technology industry. Can small start-ups realistically hope to compete with companies such as Microsoft and Intel? Discuss the list and your conclusions in class.   ● ▲ ★

taking it to the **net**

PURPOSE

To assess your potential to succeed as an entrepreneur and to evaluate a sample business plan.

EXERCISE

1. Go to www.bizmove.com/other/quiz.htm and take the interactive entrepreneurial quiz to find out whether you have the qualities to be a successful entrepreneur.

2. If you have entrepreneurial traits and decide you would like to start your own business, you'll need to develop a business plan. Go to www.bplans.com/sample_business_plans.cfm and click on Coffee Shops. Review the sample business plan for Internet Café. Although the plan may not follow the same format as the business plan outline in the chapter, does it contain all the necessary information listed in the outline? If not, what is missing?

video case   Mc Graw Hill Education connect

LAUNCHING A BUSINESS: PILLOW PETS

"If you like what you do, then life is a whole lot easier for you and for those around you." According to Jennifer and Clint Telfer, this is the key to success as an entrepreneur. Beginning with an idea and using $50,000 from credit cards, the Telfers launched the company CJ Products with the featured line of Pillow Pets. The idea began as Jennifer watched her son patting down his stuffed animal to use it as a pillow. Since that humble beginning, the company has grown tremendously; that growth includes a successful website and licensing agreements with Major League Baseball, the National College Athletic Association, and Disney.

Jennifer cites two mistakes they made early on as entrepreneurs: (1) they tried to grow the business too quickly; and (2) they used a less than quality manufacturer. These two errors were costly, and it took the Telfers a year and a half to recover their losses. Since those early setbacks, the Telfers and Pillow Pets have never looked back. Today, the company sells over 15 million units a year.

Part of the Telfers' success stems from their many years as salespeople in retail markets. Success as an entrepreneur requires a passion for what you do, action orientation, self-discipline, and high energy levels.

Small businesses are the backbone of the U.S. economy, with more than 2 million currently operating and over 750,000 new businesses starting up each year. Small businesses are responsible for over 75 percent of all jobs in the United States. In fact, small businesses generate over 50 percent of the U.S. GDP annually. And over 80 percent of all Americans began their first job with a small business. Many of today's large businesses, such as Avon, Ford, DuPont, Walmart, and Amazon.com, all started as small entrepreneurial ventures.

Do you have what it takes to be a successful entrepreneur? While self-discipline and high energy are essential, you must have a passion for what you want to do.

THINKING IT OVER

1. How does the notion of taking an existing idea and making it better relate to the successful launch of Pillow Pets?

2. What personal characteristics helped Jennifer and Clint Telfer succeed as entrepreneurs and build C.J. Products into the multimillion-dollar business it is today?

3. How did the Telfers finance their start-up? Why is it difficult for budding entrepreneurs to secure bank financing or venture capital?

1. Philipp Harper, "History's 10 Greatest Entrepreneurs," *NBC News,* www.nbcnews.com, accessed March 2014; and Lisa Ocker "The 50 Greatest Entrepreneurs of All Time," www.success.com, accessed March 2014.

2. Jane Bryant Quinn, "Start Your Own Business," *AARP Bulletin,* January–February 2013; Kerry Hannon, "Psst . . . Want to Start a Side-Gig? Here's What You Need to Know Now," *Forbes,* January 22, 2014; Julia Chang, "6 Successful Leaders On What It Takes to be Fearless," *Fast Company,* www.fastcompany.com, accessed March 2014; "The Forbes 400," *Forbes,* www.forbes.com, accessed March 2014; and Martin Zwilling, "How to Balance Business Risk versus Opportunity," *Forbes,* January 16, 2014.

3. Will n' Rose's, www.willnroses.com, accessed March 2014.

4. Jason Daley, "Born or Made," *Entrepreneur,* October 2013; James Stephenson, "25 Common Characteristics of Successful Entrepreneurs," *Entrepreneur,* www.entrepreneur.com, accessed March 2014; Ed Feulner, "Entrepreneurs: Spark Plugs in a Free-Market Economy," *The Washington Times,* September 3, 2013; Hanny Lerner, "Do You Have What It Takes to Be an Entrepreneur?" *Forbes,* March 18, 2013; and Joe Robinson, "The 7 Traits of Successful Entrepreneurs," *Entrepreneur,* January 10, 2014.

5. Rush Communications, www.rushcommunications.com, accessed March 2014.

6. "Crazy Diamonds," *The Economist,* July 20, 2014.

7. Chuck Green, "When Entrepreneurs Don't Take No for an Answer," *The Wall Street Journal,* April 29, 2013; Lizette Chapman "Extreme Sports Get a Camera," *The Wall Street Journal,* Jane 20, 2013; Lisa Quast, "Turning Your Passion into Business," *Forbes,* September 2, 2013; and Gautam Gupta, "How to Transform Your Passion into a Successful Business," *Entrepreneur,* November 20, 2013.

8. Cadie Thompson, "Is Apple Still the King of Consumer Design?" *Entrepreneur,* July 17, 2013.

9. U.S. Census Bureau, www.census.gov, accessed March 2014.

10. Ibid.

11. Lauren Folino, "Recession Feeds Increase of Home-based Businesses," *Inc.,* www.inc.com, accessed March 2014; and Rebecca Reeve, "Snapchat, Rdio, And Other Unlikely Workplace Engagement-Boosting Tools," *Fast Company,* October 28, 2013.

12. Paul Tassi, "11 Ways to Stay Motivated While Working from Home," *Forbes,* January 22, 2014; Jacquelyn Smith, "How to Succeed at Working from Home," *Forbes,* August 12, 2013; and Ruth Blatt, "What Musicians Teach Us about the Challenges of Being Your Own Boss," *Forbes,* January 17, 2014.

13. Forrester Research, "US Online Retail Sales to Reach $370B by 2017," *Forbes,* March 14, 2013; and Forrester Research, www.forrester.com, accessed March 2014.

14. Throw Things, www.throwthings.com, accessed March 2014.

15. Mark Cohen, "Surviving the Dark Side of Affiliate Marketing," *The New York Times,* December 4, 2014; Francine Hardaway, "10 Tips for Small Business Marketing From Infusioncon," *Fast Company,* March 29, 2013; and HBS Working Knowledge, "The Tricky Business of Managing Web Advertising Affiliates," *Forbes,* February 3, 2014.

16. Anthony Ho, "Skimlinks Says Its Affiliate Linking Technology Drove $500M+in E-Commerce Sales Last Year," *TechCrunch,* www.techcrunch.com, accessed March 2014.

17. www.3m.com, accessed March 2014.

18. www.lockheedmartin.com, accessed March 2014.

19. Catherine Rampell, "Immigration and Entrepreneurship," *The New York Times,* January 29, 2014.

20. Tom Moroney, "Putting a New Name on an Old Idea to Fix Inner Cities," *Bloomberg Businessweek,* January 27–February 2, 2014.

21. Kate Harrison, "What You Really Need to Know about the Jobs Act General Solicitation Rule," *Forbes,* October 21, 2013.

22. National Business Incubator Association, www.nbia.org, accessed March 2014.

23. "Give It the Old College Try," *Inc.,* June 2013.

24. "Laid Off and Want to Start a Business? Self-Employment Assistance Programs May Help," Small Business Administration, www.sba.gov, accessed March 2014.

25. Startup America, www.whitehouse.gov/issues/startup-america, accessed March 2014.

26. Small Business Administration, www.sba.gov, accessed March 2014; U.S. Census Bureau, www.census.gov, accessed March 2014; and Jason Nazar, "16 Surprising Statistics about Small Businesses," *Forbes,* September 9, 2013.

27. Small Business Administration, www.sba.gov, accessed March 2014; and Brian Headd, Alfred Nucci and Richard Boden, "What Matters More: Business Exit Rates or Business Survival Rates?" U.S. Census Bureau, www.census.gov, accessed March 2014.

28. Kathy Caprino, "The 7 Worst Marketing Blunders Small Businesses Make," *Forbes,* January 24, 2014; Eric T. Wagner, "Five Reasons 8 out of 10 Businesses Fail," *Forbes,* September 12, 2013; Steve Tobak, "It's a Marathon, Not a Sprint: The Real Reason Start-ups Fail," *Inc.,* March 6, 2013; and Norm Brodsky, "Everyone Fails. What's Key Is to Learn the Right Lessons," *Inc.,* July/August 2013.

29. Vivian Giang, "11 Famous Entrepreneurs Share How They Overcame Their Biggest Failures," Fast Company, May 1, 2014.

30. George Anders, "Takeover University," *Forbes,* October 28, 2013.

31. Steve Blank, "Why the Lean Start-Up Changes Everything," *Harvard Business Review,* May 2013.

32. Mindy Charski, "Front-Page Success," *The Costco Connection,* June 2013.

33. Karen E. Klein, "Funding a New Small Business? Don't Bother with Banks," *Bloomberg Businessweek,* February 13, 2014.

34. Michael Swack, Jack Northrup, and Eric Hangen, "CDFI Industry Analysis," *Community Investments,* Summer 2012; and "A Guide to Community Development Financial Institutions," *Entrepreneur,* www.entrepreneur.com, accessed March 2014.

35. Micahel Lev-Ram, "Crowdfunding Tries to Grow Up," *Fortune,* May 20, 2013; Vanessa Richardson," Funds and Feedback," *Entrepreneur,* August 2013; Ellen Gamerman, "The Trouble with Kickstarter," *The Wall Street Journal,* June 21, 2013; Michelle Goodman, "Seed Money," *Entrepreneur,* March 2013; Mat Honan, "Beyond Kickstarter," *Wired,* March 2013; Todd Woody, "Own a Piece of the Sun," *Forbes,* February 11, 2013; and Sheila Bair, "P2P Lending," *CNN Money,* December 2013.

36. Michelle Goodman, "Rating the Platforms," *Entrepreneur,* January 2014.

37. Chris Brummer and Daniel Gorfine, "The JOBS Act Isn't All 'Crowdfunding,'" *Forbes,* October 8, 2013; and Darren Dahl,

"Want Funding from the Crowd? Get Ready to Bare Your Soul," *Inc.,* February 2014.

38. Mahendra Ramsinghani, "Venture Capital 2013 Recap—Oh What a Year It Was," *Forbes,* December 26, 2013.

39. Deepak Malhotra, "How to Negotiate with VCs," *Harvard Business Review,* May 2013.

40. AngelList, www.angel.co, accessed March 2014.

41. "A Simple Guide to Microloans," *Entreprenuer,* www.entrepreneur.com, accessed March 2014.

42. "Testing, Testing," *The Economist,* January 18, 2014; Matt Villano, "That's My Motto," *Entrepreneur,* May 2013; Joann Muller, "Tough Clothes, Tough Company," *Forbes,* November 18, 2013; Kevin J. Boudreau and Karim R. Lakhani, "Using the Crowd as an Innovation Partner," *Harvard Business Review,* April 2013; Vincent Onyemah, Martha Rivera, and Abdul Ali,"

Harvard Business Review, May 2013; and Gladys Edmunds, "Refocus on Customers for Small Business Success," *USA Today,* January 1, 2014.

43. "Not Open for Business," *The Economist,* October 12, 2013; and Eric Paley, "Go Beyond Visionary; Be a Leader," *Inc.,* February 2014.

44. www.score.org, accessed May 2012; and Small Business Administration, www.sba.gov, accessed March 2014.

45. Susan Hirshorn, "Sharing Secrets," *The Costco Connection,* March 2013.

46. "World Population Clock," U.S. Census Bureau, www.census.gov/ipc/www/popclockworld.html, accessed March 2014; and WorldAtlas.com, accessed March 2014.

47. National Small Business Association, "2013 Small Business Exporting Survey," www.nsba.biz, accessed March 2014.

photo credits

PART 3

7

Management and Leadership

Learning Objectives

AFTER YOU HAVE READ AND STUDIED THIS CHAPTER, YOU SHOULD BE ABLE TO

LO 7-1 Describe the changes occurring today in the management function.

LO 7-2 Describe the four functions of management.

LO 7-3 Relate the planning process and decision making to the accomplishment of company goals.

LO 7-4 Describe the organizing function of management.

LO 7-5 Explain the differences between leaders and managers, and describe the various leadership styles.

LO 7-6 Summarize the five steps of the control function of management.

Although women have made great strides in the workplace over the last few decades, in many ways business remains a man's world at the top of the career chain. Women lead only 21 of the Fortune 500 companies.

As chief operating officer of Facebook, Sheryl Sandberg knows more than most about the struggles faced by high-powered women. But her fame isn't just because of her reputation as an all-star corporate manager. Sandberg is also the author of *Lean In: Women, Work and the Will to Lead,* the 2013 best seller about the ways she thinks women's roles in the workplace should change. While the book's runaway success turned her into a celebrity, people in the business world have known about Sandberg's seemingly superhuman ability to succeed for a long time.

The daughter of an eye doctor dad and PhD-holding mom, Sandberg's first management gig involved looking after her two younger siblings. Even in those early days she displayed an ability to be an assertive leader. In *Lean In* she writes that she taught her brother and sister to "follow me around, listen to my monologues, and scream the word 'Right!' when I concluded." Sandberg's confident attitude and intelligence set her apart even among the bright minds of her Harvard undergraduate class. Her talents caught the eye of the prominent economist and professor Larry Summers, who became Sandberg's mentor. When she moved on to Harvard Business School to earn an MBA, Summers volunteered to be her thesis advisor. His loyalty didn't stop there. When he received an appointment at the Treasury Department from President Clinton, Summers brought on his protégé as chief of staff. Still only in her 20s, Sandberg began to build a reputation in Washington as a tough go-getter who still made time for the people who operated below her.

Once the Clinton presidency ended, though, Sandberg left the capital to try her hand in Silicon Valley. She joined Google in 2001, years before the search engine became the worldwide force it is today. As an executive in charge of global sales and advertising, Sandberg struck a deal with AOL that set Google on the path to profitability. After playing a key role in the search engine's rise to dominance, Sandberg moved to Facebook in 2008. At the time the social network shared the same problem that Sandberg had faced at Google: the service was popular with millions but profits were hard to come by. To push Facebook into the black, CEO and founder Mark Zuckerberg granted Sandberg total freedom to revitalize the company's earnings structure. Along with her easygoing but dedicated management style, Sandberg also employed her army of high-level business contacts to ink important deals for Facebook. By 2010 the company was profitable. Two years later she helped launch the company's initial public offering, which, after a rocky start, grew into a well-performing stock.

But for all her accomplishments in the business world, Sandberg is still most famous for writing *Lean In.* In it, she argues that women should not have to choose between holding a career and having a family. According to Sandberg, this decision to "pull back" leaves too many women unfulfilled professionally as well as personally. But by "leaning in" to your career with passion and intensity, she claims that women can make the workplace more accessible. Sandberg's message inspired thousands to form their own "*Lean In* circles" to discuss the book as well as ways to advocate for change. However, others criticized Sandberg for offering advice that was aimed mainly at rich women. But despite how well her strategy works for others, there's certainly no denying that "leaning in" has paid off handsomely for Sheryl Sandberg.

This chapter is all about leadership and management. You will learn that shared leadership is more widespread than you might have imagined. You will also learn about the functions of management and how management differs from leadership. All in all, you should get a better idea of what leaders and managers do and how they do it.

Sources: David de Jong, "Sheryl Sandberg Becomes One of Youngest U.S. Billionaires," *Bloomberg,* January 21, 2014; Miguel Helft, "Sheryl Sandberg: The Real Story," *Fortune,* October 10, 2013; Paul Harris, "Sheryl Sandberg: The Facebook Boss on a Self-Help Mission," *The Guardian,* February 23, 2013; and Nina Bahaudur, "Lean In Quotes: 11 of the Best Quotations from Sheryl Sandberg's New Book," *The Huffington Post,* March 6, 2013.

Sheryl Sandberg
- COO of Facebook
- Wants to change women's roles in business
- Led Facebook to profitability

www.facebook.com

@facebook

name that **company**

This company knows that finding the right people and keeping them happy is the key to long-term business success. So it has its own gourmet chefs prepare delicious lunches, dinners, and snacks for its employees. What is the name of this company? (The answer can be found in this chapter.)

LO 7–1 Describe the changes occurring today in the management function.

MANAGERS' ROLES ARE EVOLVING

Managers must practice the art of getting things done through organizational resources, which include workers, financial resources, information, and equipment. At one time, managers were called "bosses" and their job consisted of telling people what to do, watching over them to be sure they did it, and reprimanding those who didn't. Many managers still behave that way. Perhaps you've witnessed such behavior; some coaches use this style.

Today, however, most managers tend to be more progressive. For example, they emphasize teams and team building; they create drop-in centers, team spaces, and open work areas. They may change the definition of *work* from a task you do for a specified period in a specific place to something you do anywhere, anytime. They tend to guide, train, support, motivate, and coach employees rather than tell them what to do.[1] Thus most modern managers emphasize teamwork and cooperation rather than discipline and order giving.[2] They may also open their books to employees to share the company's financials.

Managers of high-tech firms, like Google and Apple, realize that many workers often know more about technology than they do. At first, Google tried to get by with no managers. Soon, however, it found that managers were necessary for communicating strategy, helping employees prioritize projects, facilitating cooperation, and ensuring that processes and systems aligned with company goals.[3]

Rather than telling employees exactly what to do, managers today tend to give their employees enough independence to make their own informed decisions about how best to please customers. How do you think most employees respond to this empowerment on the job?

186

The recent financial crisis forced many leading firms to fire managers and lower-level workers. Managers tended to be cautious in starting new ventures as they waited to see what the economy would do. That hesitancy contributed to high unemployment in the United States.[4]

The people entering management today are different from those who entered in the past. Leaders of Fortune 100 companies tend to be younger, more of them are female, and fewer of them were educated at elite universities.[5] Managers in the future are more likely to be working in teams and assuming completely new roles in the firm. For one thing, they'll be doing more expansion overseas.[6] Further, they may be taking a leadership role in adapting to climate change.[7]

What these changes mean for you is that management will demand a new kind of person: a skilled communicator and team player as well as a planner, organizer, motivator, and leader.[8] Future managers will need to be more globally prepared; that is, they need skills such as adaptability, foreign language skills, and ease in other cultures.[9] We'll address these trends in the next few chapters to help you decide whether management is the kind of career you would like. In the following sections, we shall discuss management in general and the functions managers perform.

LO 7–2   Describe the four functions of management.

THE FOUR FUNCTIONS OF MANAGEMENT

The following definition of management provides the outline of this chapter: **Management** is the process used to accomplish organizational goals through planning, organizing, leading, and controlling people and other organizational resources (see Figure 7.1).

management
The process used to accomplish organizational goals through planning, organizing, leading, and controlling people and other organizational resources.

Planning
- Setting organizational goals.
- Developing strategies to reach those goals.
- Determining resources needed.
- Setting precise standards.

Leading
- Guiding and motivating employees to work effectively to accomplish organizational goals and objectives.
- Giving assignments.
- Explaining routines.
- Clarifying policies.
- Providing feedback on performance.

Organizing
- Allocating resources, assigning tasks, and establishing procedures for accomplishing goals.
- Preparing a structure (organization chart) showing lines of authority and responsibility.
- Recruiting, selecting, training, and developing employees.
- Placing employees where they'll be most effective.

Controlling
- Measuring results against corporate objectives.
- Monitoring performance relative to standards.
- Rewarding outstanding performance.
- Taking corrective action when necessary.

FIGURE 7.1 WHAT MANAGERS DO
Some modern managers perform all of these tasks with the full cooperation and participation of workers. Empowering employees means allowing them to participate more fully in decision making.

Planning is what helps managers understand the environment in which their businesses must operate. When people's tastes and preferences for restaurant meals change, food service managers need to be ready to respond with menu alternatives. What changes have occurred in your own preferences?

planning
A management function that includes anticipating trends and determining the best strategies and tactics to achieve organizational goals and objectives.

organizing
A management function that includes designing the structure of the organization and creating conditions and systems in which everyone and everything work together to achieve the organization's goals and objectives.

leading
Creating a vision for the organization and guiding, training, coaching, and motivating others to work effectively to achieve the organization's goals and objectives.

Planning includes anticipating trends and determining the best strategies and tactics to achieve organizational goals and objectives. One of the major objectives of organizations is to please customers. The trend today is to have *planning teams* to help monitor the environment, find business opportunities, and watch for challenges. *Planning* is a key management function because accomplishing the other functions depends heavily on having a good plan.

Organizing includes designing the structure of the organization and creating conditions and systems in which everyone and everything work together to achieve the organization's goals and objectives. Many of today's organizations are being designed around pleasing the customer at a profit. Thus they must remain flexible and adaptable, because when customer needs change, firms must change with them.[10] Whole Foods Market, for example, is known for its high-quality, high-priced food items. But it has introduced many lower-cost items to adjust to the financial losses of its customer base. General Motors lost much of its customer base to manufacturers of more fuel-efficient cars. It hopes to win back market share by offering hydrogen-powered or electric vehicles that cost less to run. GM has had some success in doing that.[11]

Leading means creating a vision for the organization and communicating, guiding, training, coaching, and motivating others to achieve goals and objectives in a timely manner. The trend is to empower employees, giving them as much freedom as possible to become self-directed and self-motivated. This function was once known as *directing;* that is, telling employees exactly what to do. In many smaller firms, that is still the manager's role. In most large firms, however, managers no longer tell people exactly what to do because knowledge workers and others often know how to do their jobs better than the manager does.[12] Nonetheless, leadership is still necessary to keep employees focused on the right tasks at the right time.[13]

Controlling establishes clear standards to determine whether an organization is progressing toward its goals and objectives, rewarding people for doing a good job, and taking corrective action if they are not. Basically, it means measuring whether what actually occurs meets the organization's goals.

Planning, organizing, leading, and controlling are the heart of management, so let's explore them in more detail. The process begins with planning; we'll look at that right after the Test Prep questions.

Use LearnSmart to help retain what you have learned. Access your instructor's Connect course to check out LearnSmart, or go to learnsmartadvantage.com for help.

LEARNSMART®

test prep

- What are some of the changes happening in management today?
- What's the definition of *management* used in this chapter?
- What are the four functions of management?

LO 7–3   Relate the planning process and decision making to the accomplishment of company goals.

PLANNING AND DECISION MAKING

Planning, the first managerial function, is setting the organization's vision, goals, and objectives. Executives find planning to be their most valuable tool. A **vision** is more than a goal; it's a broad explanation of why the organization exists and where it's trying to go.[14] It gives the organization a sense of purpose and a set of values that unite workers in a common destiny.[15] Managing an organization without first establishing a vision is like getting everyone in a rowboat excited about going somewhere, but not telling them exactly where. The boat will just keep changing directions rather than speeding toward an agreed-on goal.

Top management usually sets the vision for the organization and then often works with others in the firm to establish a mission statement. A **mission statement** outlines the organization's fundamental purposes. It should address:

- The organization's self-concept.
- Its philosophy.
- Long-term survival needs.
- Customer needs.
- Social responsibility.
- Nature of the product or service.

The mission statement becomes the foundation for setting specific goals and objectives. **Goals** are the broad, long-term accomplishments an organization wishes to attain. Because workers and management need to agree on them, setting goals is often a team process. **Objectives** are specific, short-term statements detailing *how to achieve* the organization's goals. One of your goals for reading this chapter, for example, may be to learn basic concepts of management. An objective you could use to achieve this goal is to answer the chapter's Test Prep questions.

Planning is a continuous process. A plan that worked yesterday may not be successful in today's market. Most planning also follows a pattern. The procedure you'll follow in planning your life and career is basically the same as the one businesses use. It answers several fundamental questions:

1. *What is the situation now?* What are the success factors affecting the industry participants and how do we compare? What is the state of the economy and other environments? What opportunities exist for meeting people's needs? What products and customers are most profitable? Who are our major competitors? What threats are there to our business? These questions are part of **SWOT analysis**, which analyzes the organization's **s**trengths and **w**eaknesses, and the **o**pportunities and **t**hreats it faces, usually in that order.[16] Opportunities and threats are often *external* to the firm and cannot always be anticipated.

   Weaknesses and strengths are more often *internal* and therefore more within reach of being measured and fixed. Figure 7.2 lists some of the general issues companies consider when conducting a SWOT analysis: What external success factors affect the industry? How does our firm measure up to other firms? What are our social objectives? What are our personal development objectives? What can we do to survive and prosper during a recession? For more on SWOT analysis, see the Taking It to the Net exercise at the end of this chapter.

controlling
A management function that involves establishing clear standards to determine whether or not an organization is progressing toward its goals and objectives, rewarding people for doing a good job, and taking corrective action if they are not.

vision
An encompassing explanation of why the organization exists and where it's trying to head.

mission statement
An outline of the fundamental purposes of an organization.

goals
The broad, long-term accomplishments an organization wishes to attain.

objectives
Specific, short-term statements detailing how to achieve the organization's goals.

SWOT analysis
A planning tool used to analyze an organization's strengths, weaknesses, opportunities, and threats.

FIGURE 7.2 SWOT
MATRIX

This matrix identifies potential
strengths, weaknesses,
opportunities, and threats
organizations may consider in
a SWOT analysis.

Potential Internal STRENGTHS	Potential Internal WEAKNESSES
• Core competencies in key areas • An acknowledged market leader • Well-conceived functional area strategies • Proven management • Cost advantages • Better advertising campaigns	• No clear strategic direction • Obsolete facilities • Subpar profitability • Lack of managerial depth and talent • Weak market image • Too narrow a product line
Potential External OPPORTUNITIES	Potential External THREATS
• Ability to serve additional customer groups • Expand product lines • Ability to transfer skills/technology to new products • Falling trade barriers in attractive foreign markets • Complacency among rival firms • Ability to grow due to increases in market demand	• Entry of lower-cost foreign competitors • Rising sales of substitute products • Slower market growth • Costly regulatory requirements • Vulnerability to recession and business cycles • Changing buyer needs and tastes

FIGURE 7.2 SWOT
MATRIX

This matrix identifies potential
strengths, weaknesses,
opportunities, and threats
organizations may consider in
a SWOT analysis.

2. *How can we get to our goal from here?* Answering this question is often the most important part of planning. It takes four forms: strategic, tactical, operational, and contingency (see Figure 7.3).

strategic planning

The process of determining the major goals of the organization and the policies and strategies for obtaining and using resources to achieve those goals.

Strategic planning is done by top management and determines the major goals of the organization and the policies, procedures, strategies, and resources it will need to achieve them.[17] *Policies* are broad guidelines for action, and *strategies* determine the best way to use resources. At the strategic planning stage, top managers of the company decide which customers to serve, when to serve them, what products or services to sell, and the geographic areas in which to compete. Take Taco Bell, for example. Recognizing the economic slump, the company introduced a "value menu" of items like cheese roll-ups and bean burritos with low prices. It also went after the "fourth-meal" (late-night) crowd and introduced several low-calorie, low-fat Fresco items. Blockbuster was not as successful in fighting off the introduction of new technology offered by Netflix and Hulu, making its brick-and-mortar stores obsolete.

In today's rapidly changing environment, strategic planning is becoming more difficult because changes are occurring so fast that plans—even those set for just months into the future—may soon be obsolete. Think of how the amusement park company Six Flags had to change its plans when the price of gas went from a couple of dollars per gallon to over four dollars and then dropped back to the three-dollar range again.

Clearly, some companies are making shorter-term plans that allow for quick responses to customer needs and requests. The goal is to be flexible and responsive to the market.[18]

tactical planning

The process of developing detailed, short-term statements about what is to be done, who is to do it, and how it is to be done.

Tactical planning is the process of developing detailed, short-term statements about what is to be done, who is to do it, and how. Managers or teams of managers at lower levels of the organization normally make tactical plans. Such plans can include setting annual budgets and deciding on other activities necessary to meet strategic objectives. If the strategic plan of a truck manufacturer, for example, is to sell more trucks in the South, the tactical plan might be to fund more research of southern truck drivers' wants and needs, and to plan advertising to reach them.

operational planning

The process of setting work standards and schedules necessary to implement the company's tactical objectives.

Operational planning is the process of setting work standards and schedules necessary to implement the company's tactical objectives. Whereas strategic planning looks at the organization as a whole, operational planning focuses on

FORMS OF PLANNING

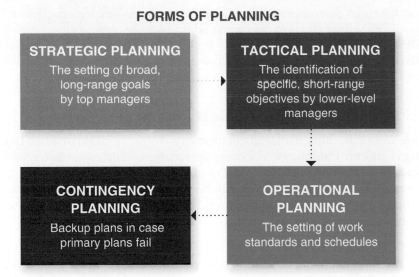

STRATEGIC PLANNING
The setting of broad, long-range goals by top managers

TACTICAL PLANNING
The identification of specific, short-range objectives by lower-level managers

CONTINGENCY PLANNING
Backup plans in case primary plans fail

OPERATIONAL PLANNING
The setting of work standards and schedules

FIGURE 7.3 PLANNING FUNCTIONS
Very few firms bother to make contingency plans. If something changes the market, such companies may be slow to respond. Most organizations do strategic, tactical, and operational planning.

specific supervisors, department managers, and individual employees. The operational plan is the department manager's tool for daily and weekly operations. An operational plan may include, for example, the specific dates for certain truck parts to be completed and the quality specifications they must meet.

Contingency planning is the process of preparing alternative courses of action the firm can use if its primary plans don't work out. The economic and competitive environments change so rapidly that it's wise to have alternative plans of action ready in anticipation of such changes. For example, if an organization doesn't meet its sales goals by a certain date, the contingency plan may call for more advertising or a cut in prices at that time. *Crisis planning* is a part of contingency planning that anticipates sudden changes in the environment.[19] For example, many cities and businesses have developed plans to respond to terrorist attacks. You can imagine how important such plans would be to hospitals, airlines, the police, and public transportation authorities.

Instead of creating detailed strategic plans, the leaders of market-based companies (companies that respond quickly to changes in competition or to other environmental changes) often simply set direction. They want to stay

contingency planning
The process of preparing alternative courses of action that may be used if the primary plans don't achieve the organization's objectives.

Organizations of all kinds need contingency plans for unexpected events. Here first responders at Washington's Reagan National Airport participate in a drill with volunteers who are pretending to be victims in a simulated airplane crash. What contingency plans are you aware of on your campus or at work?

flexible, listen to customers, and seize opportunities—expected or not. Think of how stores selling to teenagers must adapt to style changes.[20]

The opportunities, however, must fit into the company's overall goals and objectives; if not, the company could lose its focus. Clearly, then, much of management and planning requires decision making.

Decision Making: Finding the Best Alternative

decision making
Choosing among two or more alternatives.

Planning and all the other management functions require decision making. **Decision making** is choosing among two or more alternatives, which sounds easier than it is. In fact, decision making is the heart of all the management functions.

The *rational decision-making model* is a series of steps managers often follow to make logical, intelligent, and well-founded decisions. Think of the steps as the six Ds of decision making:

1. Define the situation.
2. Describe and collect needed information.
3. Develop alternatives.
4. Decide which alternative is best.
5. Do what is indicated (begin implementation).
6. Determine whether the decision was a good one, and follow up.

problem solving
The process of solving the everyday problems that occur. Problem solving is less formal than decision making and usually calls for quicker action.

Managers don't always go through this six-step process. Sometimes they have to make decisions *on the spot*—with little information available. They still must make good decisions in all such circumstances. **Problem solving** is less formal than decision making and usually calls for quicker action to resolve everyday issues. Both decision making and problem solving call for a lot of judgment.

brainstorming
Coming up with as many solutions to a problem as possible in a short period of time with no censoring of ideas.

Problem-solving teams are two or more workers assigned to solve a specific problem (e.g., Why aren't customers buying our service contracts?). Problem-solving techniques include **brainstorming**, that is, coming up with as many solutions as possible in a short period of time with no censoring of ideas. Another technique is called **PMI**, or listing all the **p**luses for a solution in one column, all the **m**inuses in another, and the **i**mplications in a third. The idea is to make sure the pluses exceed the minuses.

PMI
Listing all the pluses for a solution in one column, all the minuses in another, and the implications in a third column.

You can try using the PMI system on some of your personal decisions to get some practice. For example, should you stay home and study tonight? List all the pluses in one column: better grades, more self-esteem, more responsible behavior, and so on. In the other column, put the minuses: boredom, less fun, and so on. We hope the pluses outweigh the minuses most of the time and that you study often. But sometimes it's best to go out and have some fun, as long as doing so won't hurt your grades or job prospects.

test prep

- What's the difference between goals and objectives?
- What does a company analyze when it does a SWOT analysis?
- What are the differences among strategic, tactical, and operational planning?
- What are the six Ds of decision making?

Describe the organizing function of management.

ORGANIZING: CREATING A UNIFIED SYSTEM

After managers have planned a course of action, they must organize the firm to accomplish their goals. That means allocating resources (such as funds for various departments), assigning tasks, and establishing procedures. A managerial pyramid shows the levels of management (see Figure 7.4). **Top management**, the highest level, consists of the president and other key company executives who develop strategic plans. Job titles and abbreviations you're likely to see often are chief executive officer (CEO), chief operating officer (COO), chief financial officer (CFO), and chief information officer (CIO) or in some companies chief knowledge officer (CKO). The CEO is often also the president of the firm and is responsible for all top-level decisions. The CEO and president are the same person in over half of the S&P 500 companies, including big companies such as United Parcel Service, John Deere, and General Electric.

CEOs are responsible for introducing change into an organization. The COO is responsible for putting those changes into effect. His or her tasks include structuring work, controlling operations, and rewarding people to ensure that everyone strives to carry out the leader's vision. Many companies today are eliminating the COO function as a cost-cutting measure and assigning that role to the CEO. Often, the CFO participates in the decision to cut the COO position. The CFO is responsible for obtaining funds, planning budgets, collecting funds, and so on. The CIO or CKO is responsible for getting the right information to other managers so they can make correct decisions. CIOs are more important than ever to the success of their companies given the

top management
The highest level of management, consisting of the president and other key company executives who develop strategic plans.

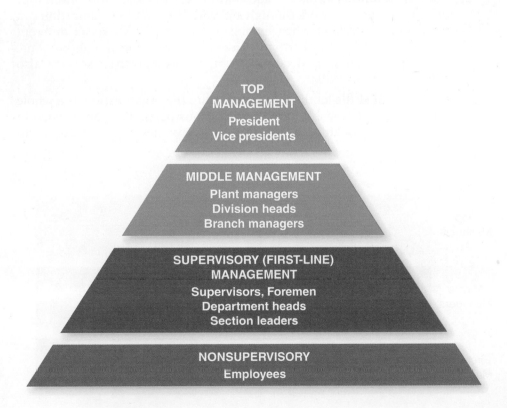

FIGURE 7.4 LEVELS OF MANAGEMENT
This figure shows the three levels of management. In many firms, there are several levels of middle management. However, firms have eliminated many middle-level managers because fewer are needed to oversee self-managed teams and higher-skilled employees.

TOP MANAGEMENT
President
Vice presidents

MIDDLE MANAGEMENT
Plant managers
Division heads
Branch managers

SUPERVISORY (FIRST-LINE) MANAGEMENT
Supervisors, Foremen
Department heads
Section leaders

NONSUPERVISORY
Employees

crucial role that information technology has come to play in every aspect of business.

middle management
The level of management that includes general managers, division managers, and branch and plant managers who are responsible for tactical planning and controlling.

Middle management includes general managers, division managers, and branch and plant managers (in colleges, deans and department heads) who are responsible for tactical planning and controlling. Many firms have eliminated some middle managers through downsizing and have given their remaining managers more employees to supervise. Nonetheless, middle managers are still considered very important to most firms.

supervisory management
Managers who are directly responsible for supervising workers and evaluating their daily performance.

Supervisory management includes those directly responsible for supervising workers and evaluating their daily performance; they're often known as first-line managers (or supervisors) because they're the first level above workers. This is the first management position you are most likely to acquire after college.

Tasks and Skills at Different Levels of Management

Few people are trained to be good managers. Usually a person learns how to be a skilled accountant or sales representative or production-line worker, and then—because of her or his skill—is selected to be a manager. Such managers tend to become deeply involved in showing others how to do things, helping them, supervising them, and generally being active in the operating task.

The further up the managerial ladder a person moves, the less important his or her original job skills become. At the top of the ladder, the need is for people who are visionaries, planners, organizers, coordinators, communicators, morale builders, and motivators. Figure 7.5 shows that a manager must have three categories of skills:

technical skills
Skills that involve the ability to perform tasks in a specific discipline or department.

1. **Technical skills** are the ability to perform tasks in a specific discipline (such as selling a product or developing software) or department (such as marketing or information systems).

human relations skills
Skills that involve communication and motivation; they enable managers to work through and with people.

2. **Human relations skills** include communication and motivation; they enable managers to work through and with people. Communication can be especially difficult when managers and employees speak different languages. Skills associated with leadership—coaching, morale building, delegating, training and development, and supportiveness—are also human relations skills.

conceptual skills
Skills that involve the ability to picture the organization as a whole and the relationships among its various parts.

3. **Conceptual skills** let the manager picture the organization as a whole and see the relationships among its various parts. They are needed in planning, organizing, controlling, systems development, problem

FIGURE 7.5 SKILLS NEEDED AT VARIOUS LEVELS OF MANAGEMENT
All managers need human relations skills. At the top, managers need strong conceptual skills and rely less on technical skills. First-line managers need strong technical skills and rely less on conceptual skills. Middle managers need to have a balance between technical and conceptual skills.

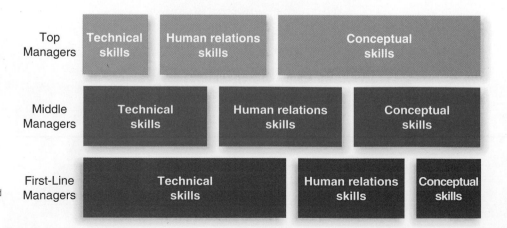

Back to School for Top Managers

As the overseer of an organization's "big picture," CEOs need to have strong conceptual skills. In today's global market, the scope of those skills is expanding rapidly as businesses increasingly focus on globalization in their long-term planning.

The shift from being a country-focused company to a global-focused company increases the CEO "to-do" list. Business leaders need to study a country's political, legal, and regulatory systems and the impact they have on important business functions such as supply chains, capital markets, and the productivity of human resources. It's also critical to thoroughly understand a nation's culture and respect its strengths and challenges.

There isn't a single global market, but rather a complex network of globally connected "local markets." Such "local markets" require their own set of global standards that require local training, development, and assessment. Aligning a company's business applications across such diverse networks is no simple task. However, leaders at companies such as Coca-Cola, Nestlé, and IBM have done a noteworthy job.

Samuel Palmisano, former CEO of IBM, perhaps summed up the global management challenge best in his book *Adapting from Re-Think: A Path to the Future*. In it he states, "The fundamental question for companies is not whether to compete globally, but how to compete globally." That's the challenge CEOs will have to answer company-by-company as they refine their conceptual skills.

Sources: Josh Bersin, "The World Is Not Global, It's Local," *Forbes*, April 23, 2013; Samuel J. Palmisano, "The New Era for Global Enterprise," *Bloomberg Businessweek*, March 28, 2014; and Rana Foroohar, "Globalization in Reverse," *Time*, April 7, 2014.

analysis, decision making, coordinating, and delegating (see the Reaching Beyond Our Borders box).

Looking at Figure 7.5, you'll notice that first-line managers need to be skilled in all three areas. However, they spend most of their time on technical and human relations tasks, like assisting operating personnel and giving directions, and less time on conceptual tasks. Top managers, in contrast, need to use few technical skills. Instead, they spend almost all their time on human relations and conceptual tasks. A person who is competent at a low level of management may not be competent at higher levels, and vice versa. Different skills are needed at different levels.

Staffing: Getting and Keeping the Right People

To get the right kind of people to staff an organization, the firm has to offer the right kind of incentives. For example, Google's gourmet chefs cook up free lunches, dinners, and snacks for employees. Would such an incentive appeal to you? How important to you is pay relative to other incentives?

Staffing is recruiting, hiring, motivating, and retaining the best people available to accomplish the company's objectives. Today, staffing is critical, especially in the Internet and high-tech areas. At most high-tech companies, like Google, Sony, and Microsoft, the primary capital equipment is brainpower. A firm with innovative and creative workers can go from start-up to major competitor in just a few years.

Many people are not willing to work at companies unless they are treated well and get fair pay. They may leave to find a better balance between work and home.[21] Staffing is becoming a greater part of each manager's assignment, and all managers need to cooperate with human resource management to win and keep good workers. Chapter 11 is devoted to human resource issues, including staffing.

staffing
A management function that includes hiring, motivating, and retaining the best people available to accomplish the company's objectives.

LEADING: PROVIDING CONTINUOUS VISION AND VALUES

One person might be a good manager but not a good leader. Another might be a good leader without being a good manager. Managers strive to produce order and stability, whereas leaders embrace and manage change. Leadership is creating a vision for others to follow, establishing corporate values and ethics, and transforming the way the organization does business in order to improve its effectiveness and efficiency. Good leaders motivate workers and create the environment for them to motivate themselves. Management is carrying out the leader's vision.[22]

Leaders must therefore:

- *Communicate a vision and rally others around that vision.* The leader should be openly sensitive to the concerns of followers, give them responsibility, and win their trust. A successful leader must influence the actions of others. Ellen Kullman took the reins at DuPont in the middle of a crisis. Nonetheless, she set the tone for growth and prosperity in the future.

- *Establish corporate values.* These include concern for employees, for customers, for the environment, and for the quality of the company's products. When companies set their business goals, they're defining the company's values as well. The number one trait that others look for in a leader is honesty. The second requirement is that the leader be forward looking.

- *Promote corporate ethics.* Ethical behavior includes an unfailing demand for honesty and an insistence that everyone in the company gets treated fairly (see the Making Ethical Decisions box). That's why we stress ethical decision making throughout this text. Many businesspeople have made the news by giving away huge amounts to charity, thus setting a model of social concern for their employees and others.[23]

- *Embrace change.* A leader's most important job may be to transform the way the company does business so that it's more effective (does things better) and more efficient (uses fewer resources to accomplish the same objectives).[24]

- *Stress accountability and responsibility.* If there is anything we have learned from the failures of banking managers and other industry and government managers, it is that leaders need to be held accountable and need to feel responsible for their actions. A key word that has emerged from the recent financial crisis is *transparency*.

    Transparency is the presentation of a company's facts and figures in a way that is clear and apparent to all stakeholders. Clearly it is time to make businesses and the government more transparent so that everyone is more aware of what is happening to the economy and to specific businesses and government agencies.[25]

All organizations need leaders, and all employees can help lead. You don't have to be a manager to perform a leadership function. That is, any employee can motivate others to work well, add to a company's ethical environment, and report ethical lapses when they occur.

transparency
The presentation of a company's facts and figures in a way that is clear and apparent to all stakeholders.

Jim Koch, founder and Chairman of Boston Beer Company, believes that culture and values can often substitute for money and resources. When he started his company, he had a very tight budget and his staff needed to be creative in figuring out how to use the limited resources wisely. Koch found that workers are motivated to do their best in a corporate culture of innovation and creativity.

What Do You Tell the Team?

First-line managers assist in the decisions made by their department heads. The department heads retain full responsibility for the decisions—if a plan succeeds, it's their success; if a plan fails, it's their failure. Now imagine this: As a first-line manager, you have new information that your department head hasn't seen yet. The findings in this report indicate that your manager's recent plans are sure to fail. If the plans do fail, the manager will probably be demoted and you're the most likely candidate to fill the vacancy. Will you give your department head the report? What is the ethical thing to do? What might be the consequences of your decision?

Leadership Styles

Nothing has challenged management researchers more than the search for the best leadership traits, behaviors, or styles. Thousands of studies have tried to identify characteristics that make leaders different from other people. Intuitively, you might conclude the same thing they did: leadership traits are hard to pin down. Some leaders are well groomed and tactful, while others are unkempt and abrasive—yet both may be just as effective.

Just as no one set of traits describes a leader, no one style of leadership works best in all situations. Even so, we can look at a few of the most commonly recognized leadership styles and see how they may be effective (see Figure 7.6):

1. **Autocratic leadership** means making managerial decisions without consulting others. This style is effective in emergencies and when absolute followership is needed—for example, when fighting fires. Autocratic leadership is also effective sometimes with new, relatively unskilled workers who need clear direction and guidance. Former Los Angeles Lakers Coach Phil Jackson used an autocratic leadership style

autocratic leadership

Leadership style that involves making managerial decisions without consulting others.

FIGURE 7.6 VARIOUS LEADERSHIP STYLES

Source: Reprinted by permission of the *Harvard Business Review*. An exhibit from "How to Choose a Leadership Pattern" by Robert Tannenbaum and Warren Schmidt (May/June 1973). Copyright © 1973 by the Harvard Business School Publishing Corporation. All rights reserved.

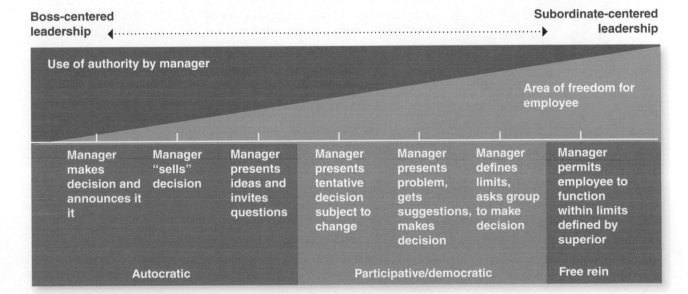

to take the team to three consecutive National Basketball Association championships in his first three seasons. By following his leadership, a group of highly skilled individuals became a winning team. Today Jackson is president of the New York Knicks. Do you think he is using the same leadership style as president as he did as coach? What kind of leadership do you see being used most successfully in baseball, football, and other areas?

participative (democratic) leadership
Leadership style that consists of managers and employees working together to make decisions.

free-rein leadership
Leadership style that involves managers setting objectives and employees being relatively free to do whatever it takes to accomplish those objectives.

Alan Mulally, former CEO of Ford Motor Company, managed to lead the U.S. auto giant back into the black after the recession—without a government bailout. The reason for this success was the leadership style of the most authoritarian CEO that Ford has seen since Henry Ford. When an organization is under extreme pressure, why might autocratic leadership be necessary?

2. **Participative (democratic) leadership** involves managers and employees working together to make decisions. Research has found that employee participation in decisions may not always increase effectiveness, but it usually does increase job satisfaction.[26] Many large organizations like Google, Apple, IBM, Cisco, and AT&T, and most smaller firms have been highly successful using a democratic style of leadership that values traits such as flexibility, good listening skills, and empathy. Employees meet to discuss and resolve management issues by giving everyone some opportunity to contribute to decisions.

3. In **free-rein leadership** managers set objectives and employees are free to do whatever is appropriate to accomplish those objectives. Free-rein leadership is often the most successful leadership style in certain organizations, such as those in which managers supervise doctors, professors, engineers, or other professionals. The traits managers need in such organizations include warmth, friendliness, and understanding. More and more firms are adopting this style of leadership with at least some of their employees.

Individual leaders rarely fit neatly into just one of these categories. We can think of leadership as a continuum along which employee participation varies, from purely boss-centered leadership to subordinate-centered leadership.

Which leadership style is best? Research tells us that it depends largely on what the goals and values of the firm are, who's being led, and in what situations. A manager may be autocratic but friendly with a new trainee, democratic with an experienced employee, and free-rein with a trusted long-term supervisor.

There's no such thing as a leadership trait that is effective in all situations, or a leadership style that always works best. A successful leader in one organization may not be successful in another organization. A truly successful leader has the ability to adopt the leadership style most appropriate to the situation and the employees.

Empowering Workers

Many leaders in the past gave explicit instructions to workers, telling them what to do to meet the goals and objectives of the organization. The term for this process is *directing*. In traditional organizations, directing includes giving assignments, explaining routines, clarifying policies, and providing feedback on performance. Many organizations still follow this model, especially fast-food restaurants and small retail establishments where the employees don't have the skill and experience needed to work on their own, at least at first.

Progressive leaders, such as those in some high-tech firms and Internet companies, empower employees to make decisions on their own. *Empowerment* means giving employees the authority to make a decision without consulting the manager and the responsibility to respond quickly to customer requests. Managers are often reluctant to give up their decision-making power and often resist empowerment. In firms that implement the concept, however, the manager's role is less that of a boss and director and more that of a coach, assistant, counselor, or team member.

Enabling means giving workers the education and tools they need to make decisions. Clearly, it's the key to the success of empowerment. Without the right education, training, coaching, and tools, workers cannot assume the responsibilities and decision-making roles that make empowerment work.[27]

enabling
Giving workers the education and tools they need to make decisions.

Managing Knowledge

"Knowledge is power." Empowering employees means giving them knowledge—that is, the information they need to do the best job they can. Finding the right information, keeping it in a readily accessible place, and making it known to everyone in the firm together constitute the tasks of **knowledge management**.

knowledge management
Finding the right information, keeping the information in a readily accessible place, and making the information known to everyone in the firm.

Today there is no shortage of information to manage. In fact, the amount of data gathered has grown so much that the term *big data* has become a popular term to describe the vast collection of available information. These data are collected from both traditional sources like sales transactions and digital sources like social media from both inside and outside the company.[28]

The first step to developing a knowledge management system is determining what knowledge is most important. Do you want to know more about your customers? Do you want to know more about competitors? What kind of information would make your company more effective or more efficient or more responsive to the marketplace? Once you've decided what you need to know, you set out to find answers to those questions.

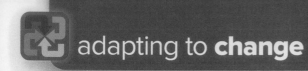
Using Social Media during the Worst of Times

When a company struggles with a recall of 1.6 million of its products that are linked to 13 deaths, managers naturally expect a harsh backlash from consumers. This was the situation Mary Barra faced, just a few short weeks after being named CEO of General Motors (GM). GM was forced to recall 2006 Saturn Ions and five other models because of a defective ignition switch that, if bumped or weighed down by a heavy key ring, could turn off, shutting down the engine and disabling the car's air bags.

To make matters worse for the company, investigations indicated that there were employees within the company who knew about the defective switch years ago; yet the problem was not corrected. At the time of this writing, the matter is still under investigation.

Barra knew it was impossible to undo the damage already done. She decided the best path was to try to redefine GM as an open, transparent, listening organization customers could trust. One of her first moves was appointing a vehicle-safety czar whose job is to quickly identify and resolve any safety issues facing the company. She

also wanted worried owners of recalled vehicles to know that GM was listening and ready to address their concerns. To achieve this, GM's social media group was deployed to reach out to impacted customers and explain their cars were drivable while they waited for repairs so long as extra items are not attached on their key rings. Despite such assurances, GM provided more than 6,000 loaner cars to customers who were skeptical about their car's safety. The company's social media staffers also set up dealership appointments with frustrated owners to have the problem fixed.

CEO Barra's overriding concern was that the recall not permanently

tarnish GM's image going forward. The company had made strong financial progress since emerging from bankruptcy and the government bailout. She knew on social media like Facebook and Twitter, a customer's perception of a brand is influenced by what a firm does and other people's opinion of it. Therefore, GM's social media commitment was to search for complaints, respond quickly, and solve the problems. Professor Roland Rust, an expert in managing brand crises from the University of Maryland, believed GM's responsiveness online was "absolutely the right thing to do." According to Rust, "If they didn't respond to customers, then those customers are going to continue to flame them." Mary Barra certainly hopes he is right and GM's response was right on. For right now, it remains to be seen whether GM can repair its internal quality control issues and whether consumers will trust its products again.

Sources: Vince Bond Jr., "GM Uses Social Media to Respond to Customer Gripes," *Automotive News*, March 8, 2014; Lindsay Gellman, "Companies Turn to Social-Media Coaches," *The Wall Street Journal*, March 26, 2014; and Vindu Goel, "G.M. Uses Social Media to Manage Customers and Its Reputation," *The New York Times*, March 23, 2014.

Knowledge management tries to keep people from reinventing the wheel—that is, duplicating the work of gathering information—every time a decision must be made. A company really progresses when each person continually asks, "What do I still not know?" and "Whom should I be asking?" It's as important to know what's *not* working as it is to know what *is* working. Employees and managers now have texting, tweeting, and other means of keeping in touch with one another, with customers, and with other stakeholders. The key to success is learning how to process information effectively and turn it into knowledge that everyone can use to improve processes and procedures. The benefits are obvious. See Bonus Chapter B for a more detailed discussion about using technology to manage information. See the Adapting to Change box for an example of how GM used social media to manage information customers needed during a time of crisis for the company.

CONTROLLING: MAKING SURE IT WORKS

The control function measures performance relative to the planned objectives and standards, rewards people for work well done, and takes corrective action when necessary. Thus the control process (see Figure 7.7) provides the feedback that lets managers and workers adjust to deviations from plans and to changes in the environment that have affected performance.

Controlling consists of five steps:

1. Establishing clear performance standards. This ties the planning function to the control function. Without clear standards, control is impossible.
2. Monitoring and recording actual performance or results.
3. Comparing results against plans and standards.
4. Communicating results and deviations to the appropriate employees.
5. Taking corrective action when needed and providing positive feedback for work well done.

For managers to measure results, the standards must be specific, attainable, and measurable. Setting such clear standards is part of the planning function. Vague goals and standards such as "better quality," "more efficiency," and "improved performance" aren't sufficient because they don't describe in enough detail what you're trying to achieve. For example, let's say you're a runner and you have made the following statement: "My goal is to improve my distance." When you started your improvement plan last year, you ran 2.0 miles a day; now you run 2.1 miles a day. Did you meet your goal? Well, you did increase your distance, but certainly not by very much.

A more appropriate statement would be "My goal is to increase my running distance from two miles a day to four miles a day by January 1." It's important

FIGURE 7.7 THE CONTROL PROCESS
The whole control process is based on clear standards. Without such standards, the other steps are difficult, if not impossible. With clear standards, performance measurement is relatively easy and the proper action can be taken.

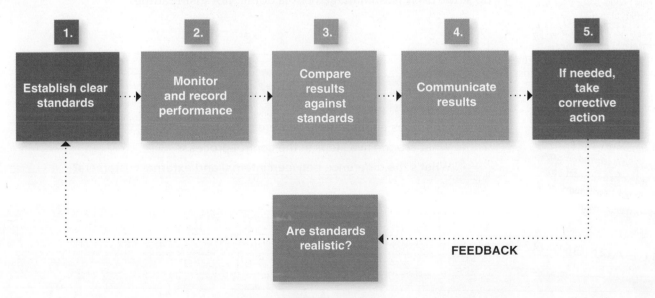

1. Establish clear standards
2. Monitor and record performance
3. Compare results against standards
4. Communicate results
5. If needed, take corrective action

Are standards realistic?

FEEDBACK

to establish a time period for reaching goals. The following examples of goals and standards meet these criteria:

- Cutting the number of finished product rejects from 10 per 1,000 to 5 per 1,000 by March 31.
- Increasing the number of times managers praise employees from 3 per week to 12 per week by the end of the quarter.
- Increasing sales of product X from 10,000 per month to 12,000 per month by July.

One way to make control systems work is to establish clear procedures for monitoring performance. Accounting and finance are often the foundations for control systems because they provide the numbers management needs to evaluate progress.

A Key Criterion for Measurement: Customer Satisfaction

Traditional measures of success are usually financial; that is, they define success in terms of profits or return on investment. Certainly these measures are still important, but they're not the whole purpose of the firm. Other purposes may include pleasing employees, stakeholders, and customers—including both external and internal customers.

External customers include dealers, who buy products to sell to others, and ultimate customers (also known as end users) such as you and me, who buy products for their own personal use. **Internal customers** are individuals and units within the firm that receive services from other individuals or units. For example, the field salespeople are the internal customers of the marketing research people who prepare market reports for them.

One goal today is to go beyond simply satisfying customers to "delighting" them with unexpectedly good products and services. We'll discuss management in more detail in the next few chapters. Let's pause now, review, and do some exercises. Management is doing, not just reading.

external customers
Dealers, who buy products to sell to others, and ultimate customers (or end users), who buy products for their own personal use.

internal customers
Individuals and units within the firm that receive services from other individuals or units.

test prep

- How does enabling help achieve empowerment?
- What are the five steps in the control process?
- What's the difference between internal and external customers?

summary

LO 7–1 Describe the changes occurring today in the management function.

- **What does management look like today?**
At one time, managers were called bosses, and their job consisted of telling people what to do, watching over them to be sure they did it, and reprimanding those who didn't. Many, if not most, managers still behave that way. Today, however, some managers tend to be more progressive. For example, they emphasize teams and team building; they create drop-in centers, team spaces, and open work areas. They tend to guide, train, support, motivate, and coach employees rather than tell them what to do.

- **What reasons can you give to account for changes in management?**
Leaders of Fortune 100 companies today tend to be younger, more of them are female, and fewer of them were educated at elite universities. They know that many of their employees know more about technology and other practices than they do. Therefore, they tend to put more emphasis on motivation, teamwork, and cooperation. Managers in the future are likely to be assuming completely new roles in the firm. For one thing, they will be taking a leadership role in adapting to climate change. Further, they'll be doing more expansion overseas.

LO 7–2 Describe the four functions of management.

- **What are the primary functions of management?**
The four primary functions are (1) planning, (2) organizing, (3) leading, and (4) controlling.

- **How do you define each of these functions?**
Planning includes anticipating trends and determining the best strategies and tactics to achieve organizational goals and objectives. Organizing includes designing the structure of the organization and creating conditions and systems in which everyone and everything works together to achieve the organization's goals and objectives. Leading means creating a vision for the organization, and communicating, guiding, training, coaching, and motivating others to achieve goals and objectives. Controlling means measuring whether what actually occurs meets the organization's goals.

LO 7–3 Relate the planning process and decision making to the accomplishment of company goals.

- **What's the difference between goals and objectives?**
Goals are broad, long-term achievements that organizations aim to accomplish, whereas objectives are specific, short-term plans made to help reach the goals.

- **What is a SWOT analysis?**
Managers look at the **s**trengths and **w**eaknesses of the firm and the **o**pportunities and **t**hreats facing it.

- **What are the four types of planning, and how are they related to the organization's goals and objectives?**
Strategic planning is broad, long-range planning that outlines the goals of the organization. *Tactical planning* is specific, short-term planning that lists organizational objectives. *Operational planning* is part of tactical planning and sets specific timetables and standards. *Contingency planning* is developing an alternative set of plans in case the first set doesn't work out.

- **What are the steps involved in decision making?**
  The six Ds of decision making are (1) define the situation; (2) describe and collect needed information; (3) develop alternatives; (4) decide which alternative is best; (5) do what is indicated (begin implementation); and (6) determine whether the decision was a good one, and follow up.

LO 7–4   Describe the organizing function of management.

- **What are the three levels of management in the corporate hierarchy?**
  The three levels of management are (1) top management (highest level consisting of the president and other key company executives who develop strategic plans); (2) middle management (general managers, division managers, and plant managers who are responsible for tactical planning and controlling); and (3) supervisory management (first-line managers/supervisors who evaluate workers' daily performance).

- **What skills do managers need?**
  Managers must have three categories of skills: (1) technical skills (ability to perform specific tasks such as selling products or developing software), (2) human relations skills (ability to communicate and motivate), and (3) conceptual skills (ability to see organizations as a whole and how all the parts fit together).

- **Are these skills equally important at all management levels?**
  Managers at different levels need different skills. Top managers rely heavily on human relations and conceptual skills and rarely use technical skills, while first-line supervisors need strong technical and human relations skills but use conceptual skills less often. Middle managers need to have a balance of all three skills (see Figure 7.5).

LO 7–5   Explain the differences between leaders and managers, and describe the various leadership styles.

- **What's the difference between a manager and a leader?**
  A manager plans, organizes, and controls functions within an organization. A leader has vision and inspires others to grasp that vision, establishes corporate values, emphasizes corporate ethics, and doesn't fear change.

- **Describe the various leadership styles.**
  Figure 7.6 shows a continuum of leadership styles ranging from boss-centered to subordinate-centered leadership.

- **Which leadership style is best?**
  The most effective leadership style depends on the people being led and the situation. The challenge of the future will be to empower self-managed teams.

- **What does empowerment mean?**
  Empowerment means giving employees the authority and responsibility to respond quickly to customer requests. Enabling is giving workers the education and tools they need to assume their new decision-making powers.

- **What is knowledge management?**
  Knowledge management is finding the right information, keeping the information in a readily accessible place, and making the information known to everyone in the firm.

LO 7–6 Summarize the five steps of the control function of management.

- **What are the five steps of the control function?**
Controlling incorporates (1) setting clear standards, (2) monitoring and recording performance, (3) comparing performance with plans and standards, (4) communicating results and deviations to employees, and (5) providing positive feedback for a job well done and taking corrective action if necessary.

- **What qualities must standards possess to measure performance results?**
Standards must be specific, attainable, and measurable.

Access your instructor's Connect course to check out LearnSmart or go to learnsmartadvantage.com for help.

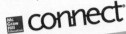

key terms

autocratic leadership 197
brainstorming 192
conceptual skills 194
contingency
 planning 191
controlling 188
decision making 192
enabling 199
external customers 202
free-rein leadership 198
goals 189
human relations
 skills 194

internal customers 202
knowledge
 management 199
leading 188
management 187
middle management 194
mission statement 189
objectives 189
operational planning 190
organizing 188
participative (democratic)
 leadership 198
planning 188

PMI 192
problem solving 192
staffing 195
strategic planning 190
supervisory
 management 194
SWOT
 analysis 189
tactical planning 190
technical skills 194
top management 193
transparency 196
vision 189

critical thinking

Many students say they would like to be a manager someday. Here are some questions to get you started thinking like a manager:

1. Would you like to work for a large firm or a small business? Private or public? In an office or out in the field? Give your reasons for each answer.

2. What kind of leader would you be? Do you have evidence to show that?

3. Do you see any problems with a participative (democratic) leadership style? Can you see a manager getting frustrated when he or she can't control others?

4. Can someone who's trained to give orders (like a military sergeant) be retrained to be a participative leader? How? What problems may emerge?

developing **workplace skills**

Key: Team   ★ Analytic   ▲ Communication   □ Technology

1. Allocate time to do some career planning with a SWOT analysis of your present situation. Choose one career you are interested in and answer the following questions: What does the marketplace for your chosen career   ★ ▲

look like today? What skills do you have that will make you a winner in that type of career? What weaknesses might you target to correct? What are the threats to your career choice? What are the opportunities? Prepare a two-minute presentation to the class.

● ★ ▲   2. Bring several decks of cards to class and have the class break up into teams of four or so members. Each team should then elect a leader. Each leader should be assigned a leadership style and learn how to perform that style: autocratic, participative (democratic), or free rein. Have each team try to build a house of cards by stacking them on top of each other. The team with the tallest house wins. Each team member should report his or her experience under the selected style of leadership.

★ ▲   3. In class, discuss the advantages and disadvantages of becoming a manager. Does the size of the business make a difference? What are the advantages of a career in a profit-seeking business versus a career in a nonprofit organization?

★ ▲   4. Review Figure 7.6 and discuss managers you have known, worked for, or read about who have practiced each management style. Students from other countries may have interesting experiences to add. Which managerial style did you like best? Why? Which was or were most effective? Why?

★ ▲   5. Because of the illegal and unethical behavior of a few managers, managers in general are under suspicion for being greedy and dishonest. Discuss the fairness of such charges, and suggest what could be done to improve the opinion of managers among the students in your class.

taking it to the **net**

PURPOSE

To perform a simple SWOT analysis.

EXERCISE

Go to www.marketingteacher.com, locate the list of SWOT analyses, and click the link to go to the SWOT for Toys "R" Us.

1. What are Toys "R" Us's strengths, weaknesses, opportunities, and threats?

2. Analyze Toys "R" Us's weaknesses. How do you think the company's strengths might be used to overcome some of its weaknesses?

3. Analyze Toys "R" Us's opportunities and threats. What additional opportunities can you suggest? What additional threats can you identify?

video case

ZAPPOS'S TEAM APPROACH

Located in Las Vegas, Nevada, with its fulfillment center situated next to the UPS hub, Zappos.com has $1 billion in annual revenue. In 2010, Zappos.com was ranked #6 by *Fortune* magazine as one of the best places to work in America. The origin of Zappos was an entrepreneurial effort by Nick Swinmurn called ShoeSite.com. Swinmurn launched this company during the dot-com boom. The concept emerged as a result of Swinmurn's inability to locate shoes that he was looking for in malls. Swinmurn took photos of the shoes from various shoe stores and uploaded them onto his website. He would take orders, go to the shoe store and purchase the shoes for the customer, and ship the shoes the next day. At the time, there was no single place online to purchase shoes in that way.

Today, Zappos is owned by Amazon.com, which purchased the company for $1.2 billion in 2010. Zappos CEO Tony Hsieh remains at the helm of the company, and the culture of the firm remains intact. In short, Amazon.com has allowed Zappos to continue to operate as it had in the past.

The emphasis on customer satisfaction and employee happiness permeates the culture of Zappos. The name "Zappos" is a derivative of the Spanish word for shoes, "zapatos." Its culture is driven by 10 core values, the first being to "wow" the customer. Two important core values influence the planning, organizing, leading, and controlling functions at the firm. They are (1) to pursue growth and learning; and (2) to have passion and determination. These and the other core values emphasize teams and employee empowerment, so much so that team leaders (management) are required to spend at least 20 percent of their time off the job with their team members.

Relationship building helps drive a management approach that focuses on the primary goal of the company—to provide the best possible experience for the customer. The four functions of management are discussed in the video, and members of the Zappos team indicate how these functions are practiced at Zappos.

THINKING IT OVER

1. What does the vision statement for a company like Zappos include?

2. How does the employee satisfaction and empowerment at Zappos help support the primary goals of the company?

3. Why do you think team leaders at Zappos are required to spend 20 percent of their time with their teams outside the work environment?

notes

1. Katherine Duncan, "Command Performance," *Entrepreneur*, March 2013.
2. Christian Stadler and Davis Dyer, "Why Good Leaders Don't Need Charisma," *Sloan Management Review*, Spring 2013.
3. David A. Garvin, "How Google Sold Its Engineers on Management," *Harvard Business Review*, December 2013.
4. "The Latest Job Miss," editorial, *The Wall Street Journal*, January 11–12, 2014.
5. "The 23 Female CEOs Running Fortune 500 Companies," *San Jose Mercury News*, December 10, 2013.
6. David Malpass, "Five Big Steps Toward Global Growth," *Forbes*, February 10, 2014.
7. Steven Overly, "Going Green, Bit by Bit," *The Washington Post*, April 22, 2013.
8. Alan Bird and James Root, "Making Star Teams Out of Star Players," *Harvard Business Review*, January–February, 2013.
9. Daniel Goleman, "The Focused Leader," *Harvard Business Review*, December 2013.
10. Leigh Buchanan, "The Essential Management Book You're Not Reading," *Inc.*, December 2013–January 2014.
11. Jeff Bennett and John Kell, "GM Restores Annual Dividend as Sales Shine," *The Wall Street Journal*, January 15, 2014.
12. Roger L. Martin, "Rethinking the Decision Factory," *Harvard Business Review*, October 2013.
13. "What Is the Difference Between Management and Leadership?" *The Wall Street Journal*, accessed March 2014.
14. Interesting contrasts among purpose, mission, and vision can be found in John Mackey and Raj Sisodia, *Conscious Capitalism* (Boston, MA: Harvard Business Review Press, 2013).
15. Eric Paley, "Go Beyond Visionary; Be a Leader," *Inc.*, February 2014.
16. "SWOT Analysis," www.MindTools.com, accessed January 2014.
17. Roger L. Martin, "The Big Lie of Strategic Planning," *Harvard Business Review*, February 2014.
18. Greg Bensinger, "Amazon Plans to Compete with PayPal and Square in Retail Stores," *The Wall Street Journal*, January 30, 2014.

19. Gregory J. Millman and Samuel Rubenfeld, "For Corporate America, Risk Is Big Business," *The Wall Street Journal,* January 16, 2014.

20. Miriam Gottfried, "This Eagle Must Hunt Elsewhere," *The Wall Street Journal,* January 24, 2014.

21. "The 10 Best Companies to Work For in 2014," www.forbes.com, accessed March 2014.

22. Amy C. Cooper, "Unite and Conquer," *Entrepreneur,* March 2013.

23. Kerry Dolan, "Billionaires, Led by Zuckerberg, Dig a Bit Deeper with 10 Biggest Charitable Gifts of 2013," www.forbes.com, January 1, 2014.

24. Dorrie Clark, "How the Best Leaders Embrace Change," www.forbes, November 5, 2013.

25. Barry Glassman, "In Business, Transparency Wins," *Forbes,* January 15, 2014.

26. Jim Pawlak, "Treating Employees as Assets, Not Expenses Boosts Profits," *Hartford Business Journal,* February 24, 2014.

27. Dino Signore. "Why Kicking It Old-School Could Kill Your Business," www.inc.com, accessed March 2014.

28. Lisa Arthur, "What Is Big Data?" *Forbes,* August 15, 2013.

photo credits

8

Structuring Organizations for Today's Challenges

Learning Objectives

AFTER YOU HAVE READ AND STUDIED THIS CHAPTER, YOU SHOULD BE ABLE TO

LO 8-1 Outline the basic principles of organization management.

LO 8-2 Compare the organizational theories of Fayol and Weber.

LO 8-3 Evaluate the choices managers make in structuring organizations.

LO 8-4 Contrast the various organizational models.

LO 8-5 Identify the benefits of interfirm cooperation and coordination.

LO 8-6 Explain how organizational culture can help businesses adapt to change.

Getting to know **Jenna Lyons**

In today's fast-paced business environment, companies need to keep current with trends if they want to succeed. But in the fashion industry, it's not enough for brands to simply know what customers want now. Garment designers and manufacturers must also define the trends that consumers will be following in the years to come. That's what Jenna Lyons does at J. Crew. As president and creative director of the respected fashion label, she must manage the design of clothes that are fashion-forward, but are also likely to sell well.

Striking this balance has been Lyons's top priority since she took over as president in 2010. Her history with J. Crew goes back much further than that. In 1990 she joined the company as a junior designer after graduating with a degree from the Parsons School of Design. In those days, J. Crew was a successful brand with a reputation for making "preppy" clothes that would look appropriate at a country club or yacht party. While catering to this upscale market proved lucrative at first, both sales and ideas started to decline as the 1990s drew to a close. Despite the drop in sales, executives ordered employees to continue making garments in step with J. Crew's stale branding. According to Lyons, this led to an uninspired atmosphere that stifled creativity. "We were lost soldiers, working away, following orders," said Lyons. "I was shell-shocked . . . fried."

All that changed in 2003 with the arrival of chair and CEO Mickey Drexler. As the architect of Gap's rise to retail dominance, Drexler was known throughout the industry as a tough boss who could get the most out of an ailing operation. He lived up to this reputation on his first day at J. Crew. "He sat down, pushed his chair back, put his foot up on the table, and he looked around, and he's like, 'You're all interviewing for your jobs,'" said Lyons. At a meeting with staff the next day, he asked Lyons to give her opinion on three different pairs of women's stretch pants that the company sold. "At that point I was like, I have to be honest," said Lyons. "I can't lie to him because this is sort of a do-or-die situation." She told him that only one pair fit the brand. After Drexler threw the other two on the floor, he and Lyons began sorting through the entire women's collection, tossing the items that Lyons deemed unfashionable. He then ordered Lyons to board a plane to Hong Kong and start designing clothes for all the new holes in J. Crew's collection.

Lyons soon proved that she was just as committed to quality as Drexler. While many of her colleagues lost their jobs, she implemented a new company structure that made J. Crew fashionable again. Before Drexler cleaned house, management consultants nitpicked designers' work so that no item strayed too far from the company's established branding. Lyons, on the other hand, employed a compassionate and understanding management style that guided designers to make clothes that were stylish, but still appealing on a wide scale.

Designing fashionable clothing was only the first step in turning J. Crew around. Lyons believed that in order for the company to create a coherent brand that would drive the business forward, every part of the organization had to be unified. She was frustrated that the aesthetics of the products were not reflected in either the stores or catalog, both run by merchandising. "There were a lot of really talented people, but they were all doing their own thing, and it looked like it." She told her teams that from that point on they should always consider how the brand appears to everyone who comes into contact with it. Lyons started by rehabbing the stores. She then moved on to completely overhauling the catalog and website, which now look more like fashion magazines than boring catalogs.

When asked how going private in 2011 helped the company, Lyons cited the freedom to invest more in information technology. "It's hard to make those kinds of capital expenditures when you're public," she says.

With sales of J. Crew clothes tripling since 2003, Lyons has shown that she understands all the organization's moving parts and how they connect. This chapter is about changing and adapting organizations to today's markets, as Jenna Lyons did at J. Crew. There are plenty of opportunities in every firm to use the principles of organizing to manage—and benefit from—change.

Sources: David Colman, "Jenna Lyons, The Woman Who Dresses America," *The New York Times*, January 18, 2013; Danielle Sacks, "How Jenna Lyons Turned J. Crew into a Cult Brand," *Fast Company*, May 2013; and Barbara McMahon, "Jenna Lyons: Fashion Queen of America," *The Guardian*, May 25, 2013.

Jenna Lyons
- President and Creative Director for J. Crew
- Used teams to unify the company's brand
- Tripled sales

www.jcrew.com

@jcrewProfile

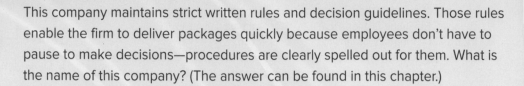
This company maintains strict written rules and decision guidelines. Those rules enable the firm to deliver packages quickly because employees don't have to pause to make decisions—procedures are clearly spelled out for them. What is the name of this company? (The answer can be found in this chapter.)

LO 8–1   Outline the basic principles of organization management.

EVERYONE'S REORGANIZING

You don't have to look far to find examples of companies reorganizing.[1] A. G. Lafley, CEO of legendary Procter & Gamble, transformed the company into one of the most innovative firms in the United States. Some entrepreneurial companies are organizing globally from the start, and succeeding. Other organizations have been declining, including some homebuilders, and banks.[2] Clearly the challenge to reorganize is strong.[3]

Few firms have established as strong an image in the United States as Starbucks, but even that company had to restructure to keep its customer base. As the company expanded its menu to include more sandwiches, one of the unexpected results was a change in the smell of the stores (the odor of burning cheese was overwhelming the smell of coffee). The company restored the stores' aroma by cutting back on sandwiches for a while. Many stores had to be closed and other stores were remodeled to recapture the feel of a Milan coffee bar. In the end, Starbucks regained its market image and is prospering again.

You may be wondering what has happened to U.S. producers—so many seem to be failing. But adjusting to changing markets is a normal function in a capitalist economy. There will be big winners, like Amazon, Google and Facebook, and big losers as well.[4] The key to success is remaining flexible enough to adapt to the changing times.[5] Often that means going back to basic organizational principles and rebuilding the firm on a sound foundation.[6] This chapter will begin by discussing such basic principles.

The principles of organization apply to businesses of all sizes. Structuring the business, making an appropriate division of labor using job specialization and departmentalization, establishing procedures, and assigning authority are tasks found in most firms. How do these principles operate at your current or most recent job?

Building an Organization from the Bottom Up

No matter the size of the business, the principles of organization are much the same. Let's say you and two friends plan to start a lawn-mowing business. One of the first steps is to organize your business. *Organizing*, or structuring, begins with determining what work needs to be done (mowing, edging, trimming) and then dividing up the tasks among the three of you; this is called a *division of labor*. One of you might have a special talent for trimming bushes, while another is better at mowing. The success of a firm often depends on management's ability to identify each worker's strengths and assign the right tasks to the right person. Many jobs can be done quickly and well when each

Would You Sacrifice Safety for Profits?

Imagine you have begun a successful lawn-mowing service in your neighborhood. Other lawn-mowing services in the area seem to hire untrained workers, many from other countries. They pay only the minimum wage or slightly more. Most obviously, however, they often provide no safety equipment. Workers don't have ear protection against the loud mowers and blowers. Most don't wear goggles when operating the shredder. Very few wear masks when spraying potentially harmful fertilizers.

You are aware there are many hazards connected with yard work, but safety gear can be expensive and workers often prefer to work without it. You are interested in making as much money as possible, but you also are concerned about the safety and welfare of your workers. You know yard maintenance equipment creates noise pollution, but quiet equipment is expensive.

The corporate culture you create as you begin your service will last a long time. If you emphasize safety and environmental concern from the start, your workers will adopt your values. On the other hand, you can see the potential for making faster profits by ignoring safety rules and paying little attention to the environment as your competitors seem to do. What are the consequences?

person specializes. Dividing tasks into smaller jobs is called *job specialization*. For example, you might divide the mowing task into mowing, trimming, and raking.

If your business is successful, you'll probably hire more workers to help. You might organize them into teams or departments to do the various tasks. One team might mow while another uses blowers to clean up leaves and debris. If you're really successful over time, you might hire an accountant to keep records, various people to handle advertising, and a crew to maintain the equipment.

You can see how your business might evolve into a company with several departments: production (mowing and everything related to that), marketing, accounting, and maintenance. The process of setting up individual departments to do specialized tasks is called *departmentalization*. Finally, you'll assign authority and responsibility to people so that you can control the whole process. If something went wrong in the accounting department, for example, you would know who was responsible.

Structuring an organization, then, consists of devising a division of labor (sometimes resulting in specialization); setting up teams or departments to do specific tasks (like production and accounting); and assigning responsibility and authority to people. It also includes allocating resources (such as funds for various departments), assigning specific tasks, and establishing procedures for accomplishing the organizational objectives. From the start, you have to make ethical decisions about how you'll treat your workers and how you will benefit the community (see the Making Ethical Decisions box).

You may develop an *organization chart* (discussed later in this chapter) that shows relationships among people: who is accountable for the completion of specific work, and who reports to whom. Finally, you'll monitor the environment to see what competitors are doing and what customers are demanding. Then you must adjust to the new realities. For example, a major lawn care company may begin promoting itself in your area. You might have to make some organizational changes to offer even better service at competitive prices. What would you do first if you began losing business to competitors?

LO 8–2   Compare the organizational theories of Fayol and Weber.

THE CHANGING ORGANIZATION

Never before in the history of business has so much change been introduced so quickly—sometimes too quickly, as we saw with the 2011 earthquake and tsunami in Japan. Think of the effects these disasters have had on the nuclear power industry. As we noted in earlier chapters, much change is due to the evolving business environment—more global competition, a declining economy, faster technological change, and pressure to preserve the natural environment.[7]

Equally important to many businesses is the change in customer expectations. Consumers today expect high-quality products and fast, friendly service—at a reasonable cost. Doug Rauch, former President of Trader Joe's, views employees and customers as two wings of a bird: you need both of them to fly. They go together—if you take care of your employees, they'll take care of your customers. When your customers are happier and they enjoy shopping, it also makes your employees' lives happier, so it's a virtuous cycle.[8]

Managing change, then, has become a critical managerial function. That sometimes includes changing the whole organization structure. Such change may occur in nonprofit and government organizations as well as businesses. Many organizations in the past were designed more to facilitate management than to please the customer. Companies designed many rules and regulations to give managers control over employees. As you'll learn later in this chapter, this reliance on rules is called *bureaucracy*. The government has to wrestle with bureaucracy just as businesses do.[9]

To understand where we are in organization design, it helps to know where we've been. We'll look at that subject next.

The Development of Organization Design

Until the 20th century, most businesses were rather small, the processes for producing goods were relatively simple, and organizing workers was fairly easy. Organizing workers is still not too hard in most small firms, such as a lawn-mowing service or a small shop that produces custom-made boats. Not until the 1900s and the introduction of *mass production* (methods for efficiently producing large quantities of goods) did production processes and business organization become so complex. Usually, the bigger the plant, the more efficient production became.

Business growth led to **economies of scale**. This term refers to the fact that companies can reduce their production costs by purchasing raw materials in bulk. Thus, the average cost of goods decreases as production levels rise. The cost of building a car, for example, declined sharply when automobile companies adopted mass production, and GM, Ford, and others introduced their huge factories.[10] Over time, such innovations became less meaningful as other companies copied the processes. You may have noticed the benefits of mass production in housing and computers.[11]

During the era of mass production, organization theorists emerged. Two influential thinkers were Henri Fayol and Max Weber. Many of their principles are still being used in businesses throughout the world. Let's explore these principles.

Fayol's Principles of Organization   In France, economic theoretician Henri Fayol published his book *Administration industrielle et générale* in

economies of scale
The situation in which companies can reduce their production costs if they can purchase raw materials in bulk; the average cost of goods goes down as production levels increase.

Henri Fayol introduced several management principles still followed today, including the idea that each worker should report to only one manager and that managers, in turn, should have the right to give orders for others to follow and the power to enforce them. Which of Fayol's principles have you observed?

1919. It was popularized in the United States in 1949 under the title *General and Industrial Management*. Fayol introduced such principles as the following:

- *Unity of command.* Each worker is to report to one, and only one, boss. The benefits of this principle are obvious. What happens if two different bosses give you two different assignments? Which one should you follow? To prevent such confusion, each person should report to only one manager. (Later we'll discuss an organizational plan that seems to violate this principle.)

- *Hierarchy of authority.* All workers should know to whom they report. Managers should have the right to give orders and expect others to follow. (As we discussed in Chapter 7, this concept has changed over time, and empowerment is often more important now.)

- *Division of labor.* Functions are to be divided into areas of specialization such as production, marketing, and finance. (This principle too is being modified, as you'll read later, and cross-functional teamwork is getting more emphasis.)

- *Subordination of individual interests to the general interest.* Workers are to think of themselves as a coordinated team. The goals of the team are more important than the goals of individual workers. (This concept is still very much in use.) Have you heard this concept being applied to football and basketball teams? Did you see this principle at work in the latest Super Bowl?

- *Authority.* Managers have the right to give orders and the power to enforce obedience. Authority and responsibility are related: whenever authority is exercised, responsibility arises. (This principle is also being modified as managers are beginning to empower employees.)

- *Degree of centralization.* The amount of decision-making power vested in top management should vary by circumstances. In a small organization, it's possible to centralize all decision-making power in the top manager. In a larger organization, however, some decision-making power, for both major and minor issues, should be delegated to lower-level managers and employees.

- *Clear communication channels.* All workers should be able to reach others in the firm quickly and easily.

- *Order.* Materials and people should be placed and maintained in the proper location.

- *Equity.* A manager should treat employees and peers with respect and justice.

- *Esprit de corps.* A spirit of pride and loyalty should be created among people in the firm.

Management courses in colleges throughout the world taught Fayol's principles for years, and they became synonymous with the concept of management. Organizations were designed so that no person had more than one boss, lines of authority were clear, and everyone knew to whom to report. Naturally, these principles tended to be written down as rules, policies, and regulations as organizations grew larger.

That process of rule making has often led to rather rigid organizations that haven't always responded quickly to consumer requests. For example, in various cities, the Department of Motor Vehicles (DMV) and auto repair facilities have been slow to adapt to the needs of their customers. So where did the idea of *bureaucracy* come from? We talk about that next.

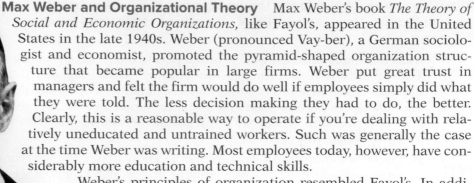

Max Weber and Organizational Theory   Max Weber's book *The Theory of Social and Economic Organizations*, like Fayol's, appeared in the United States in the late 1940s. Weber (pronounced Vay-ber), a German sociologist and economist, promoted the pyramid-shaped organization structure that became popular in large firms. Weber put great trust in managers and felt the firm would do well if employees simply did what they were told. The less decision making they had to do, the better. Clearly, this is a reasonable way to operate if you're dealing with relatively uneducated and untrained workers. Such was generally the case at the time Weber was writing. Most employees today, however, have considerably more education and technical skills.

Weber's principles of organization resembled Fayol's. In addition, Weber emphasized:

- Job descriptions.
- Written rules, decision guidelines, and detailed records.
- Consistent procedures, regulations, and policies.
- Staffing and promotion based on qualifications.

Max Weber promoted an organizational structure composed of middle managers who implement the orders of top managers. He believed less-educated workers were best managed if managers or supervisors gave them strict rules and regulations to follow and monitored their performance. What industries or businesses today would benefit by using such controls?

Weber believed that large organizations demanded clearly established rules and guidelines to be followed precisely. In other words, he was in favor of *bureaucracy*. Although his principles made sense at the time, rules and procedures became so rigid in some companies that they grew counterproductive. Some organizations today still thrive on Weber's theories.[12] United Parcel Service (UPS), for example, maintains strict written rules and decision guidelines. Those rules enable the firm to deliver packages quickly because employees don't have to pause to make decisions—procedures are clearly spelled out for them.

Some organizations that follow Weber's principles are less effective than UPS because they don't allow employees to respond quickly to new challenges. That has clearly been the case with disaster relief agencies in many areas. Later, we explore how to make organizations more responsive. First, let's look at some basic terms and concepts.

Turning Principles into Organization Design

Following theories like Fayol's and Weber's, managers in the latter 1900s began designing organizations so that managers could *control* workers. Many companies are still organized that way, with everything set up in a hierarchy. A **hierarchy** is a system in which one person is at the top of the organization and there is a ranked or sequential ordering from the top down of managers and others who are responsible to that person. Since one person can't keep track of thousands of workers, the top manager needs many lower-level managers to help. The **chain of command** is the line of authority that moves from the top of the hierarchy to the lowest level. Figure 8.1 shows a typical hierarchy on an organization chart. An **organization chart** is a visual device that shows relationships among people and divides the organization's work; it shows who reports to whom.

Some organizations have a dozen or more layers of management between the chief executive officer (CEO) and the lowest-level employees. If employees want to introduce work changes, they ask a supervisor (the first level of management), who asks his or her manager, who asks a manager at the next level up, and so on. It can take weeks or months for a decision to be made and passed from manager to manager until it reaches employees. At pharmaceutical

hierarchy
A system in which one person is at the top of the organization and there is a ranked or sequential ordering from the top down of managers who are responsible to that person.

chain of command
The line of authority that moves from the top of a hierarchy to the lowest level.

organization chart
A visual device that shows relationships among people and divides the organization's work; it shows who reports to whom.

FIGURE 8.1 TYPICAL ORGANIZATION CHART
This is a rather standard chart with managers for major functions and supervisors reporting to the managers. Each supervisor manages three employees.

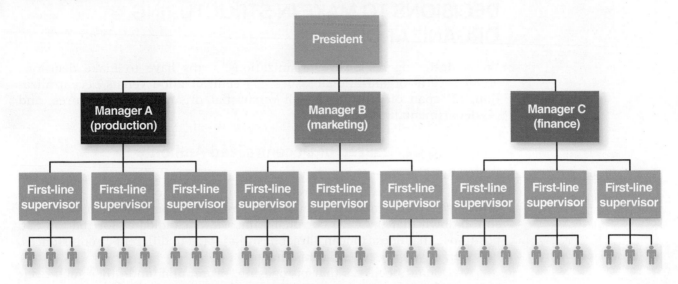

company Pfizer, for example, there were once 17 layers between the chief executive and the lowest employee.

Max Weber used the word *bureaucrat* to describe a middle manager whose function was to implement top management's orders. Thus, **bureaucracy** came to be the term for an organization with many layers of managers.

When employees in a bureaucracy of any size have to ask managers for permission to make a change, the process may take so long that customers become annoyed. Has this happened to you in a department store or other organization? Since customers want efficient service—and they want it *now*—slow service is simply not acceptable in today's competitive firms.

Some companies are therefore reorganizing to let employees make decisions in order to please customers no matter what. Home Depot has adopted this approach to win more customers from competitors. Nordstrom employees can accept a return from a customer without managerial approval, even if the item was not originally sold at that store. As you read earlier in this book, giving employees such authority is called *empowerment*. Remember that empowerment works only when employees are given the proper training and resources to respond. Can you see how such training would help first responders in crisis conditions?

bureaucracy
An organization with many layers of managers who set rules and regulations and oversee all decisions.

test prep

- What do the terms *division of labor* and *job specialization* mean?
- What are the principles of management outlined by Fayol?
- What did Weber add to the principles of Fayol?

Use LearnSmart to help retain what you have learned. Access your instructor's Connect course to check out LearnSmart, or go to learnsmartadvantage.com for help.

LEARNSMART

LO 8–3   Evaluate the choices managers make in structuring organizations.

DECISIONS TO MAKE IN STRUCTURING ORGANIZATIONS

When designing responsive organizations, firms have to make decisions about several organizational issues: (1) centralization versus decentralization, (2) span of control, (3) tall versus flat organization structures, and (4) departmentalization.

Choosing Centralized or Decentralized Authority

centralized authority
An organization structure in which decision-making authority is maintained at the top level of management.

Centralized authority occurs when decision making is concentrated at the top level of management. The retailing giant Target, for example, has a very centralized form of management. *Fortune* magazine commented that Target is so top-down that the CEO personally interviews candidates for the top 600 positions. That doesn't mean Target hasn't adapted to different circumstances, however, as you'll see later in this chapter.

McDonald's believes that purchasing, promotion, and other such decisions are best handled centrally. There's usually little need for each McDonald's restaurant in the United States to carry different items, although, as you have read, the restaurants' menus are often quite different in other countries. In the United States, McDonald's leans toward centralized authority. However, today's rapidly changing markets, added to global differences in consumer tastes, tend to favor some decentralization and thus more delegation of authority, even at McDonald's. Its restaurants in England offer tea, those in France offer a Croque McDo (a hot ham-and-cheese sandwich), those in Japan sell rice, and Chinese McDonald's offer taro and red bean desserts.

decentralized authority
An organization structure in which decision-making authority is delegated to lower-level managers more familiar with local conditions than headquarters management could be.

Decentralized authority occurs when decision making is delegated to lower-level managers and employees more familiar with local conditions than headquarters management could be. Macy's customers in California, for example, demand clothing styles different from what customers in Minnesota or Maine like. It makes sense to delegate to store managers in various cities the authority to buy, price, and promote merchandise appropriate for each area. Both Home Depot and Lowe's are doing more to cater to local markets. Figure 8.2 lists some advantages and disadvantages of centralized and decentralized authority.

FIGURE 8.2
ADVANTAGES AND DISADVANTAGES OF CENTRALIZED VERSUS DECENTRALIZED AUTHORITY

	Centralized	Decentralized
Advantages	• Greater top-management control • More efficiency • Simpler distribution system • Stronger brand/corporate image	• Better adaptation to customer wants • More empowerment of workers • Faster decision making • Higher morale
Disadvantages	• Less responsiveness to customers • Less empowerment • Interorganizational conflict • Lower morale away from headquarters	• Less efficiency • Complex distribution system • Less top-management control • Weakened corporate image

Choosing the Appropriate Span of Control

Span of control describes the optimal number of subordinates a manager supervises or should supervise. What is the "right" span of control? At lower levels, where work is standardized, it's possible to implement a broad span of control (15 to 40 workers). For example, one supervisor can be responsible for 20 or more workers assembling computers or cleaning movie theaters. The appropriate span gradually narrows at higher levels of the organization, because work becomes less standardized and managers need more face-to-face communication.

The trend today is to expand the span of control as organizations adopt empowerment, reduce the number of middle managers, and hire more talented and better educated lower-level employees. Information technology also allows managers to handle more information, so the span can be broader still.[13]

Choosing between Tall and Flat Organization Structures

In the early 20th century, organizations grew even bigger, adding layer after layer of management to create **tall organization structures**. As noted earlier, some had as many as 17 levels, and the span of control was small (few people reported to each manager).

Imagine how a message might be distorted as it moved up the organization and back down through managers, management assistants, secretaries, assistant secretaries, supervisors, trainers, and so on. The cost of all these managers and support people was high, the paperwork they generated was enormous, and the inefficiencies in communication and decision making were often intolerable.

More recently, organizations have adopted **flat organization structures** with fewer layers of management (see Figure 8.3) and a broad span of control (many people report to each manager). Flat structures can respond readily to customer demands because lower-level employees have authority and responsibility for making decisions, and managers can be spared some day-to-day tasks. In a bookstore with a flat organization structure, employees may have authority to arrange shelves by category, process special orders for customers, and so on.

Large organizations use flat structures to try to match the friendliness of small firms, whose workers often know customers by name. The flatter organizations become, the broader their spans of control, which means some managers lose their jobs. Figure 8.4 lists advantages and disadvantages of narrow and broad spans of control.

A broad span of control allows one supervisor to be responsible for many workers whose work tasks are predictable and standardized. In addition to assembly lines, can you think of other management situations that might benefit from a broad span of control? What about in a service industry?

span of control
The optimal number of subordinates a manager supervises or should supervise.

tall organization structure
An organizational structure in which the pyramidal organization chart would be quite tall because of the various levels of management.

flat organization structure
An organization structure that has few layers of management and a broad span of control.

FIGURE 8.3 A FLAT ORGANIZATION STRUCTURE

FIGURE 8.4
ADVANTAGES AND
DISADVANTAGES OF
A NARROW VERSUS
A BROAD SPAN OF
CONTROL
The flatter the organization, the
broader the span of control.

	Narrow	Broad
Advantages	• More control by top management • More chances for advancement • Greater specialization • Closer supervision	• Less empowerment • Higher costs • Delayed decision making • Less responsiveness to customers
Disadvantages	• Reduced costs • More responsiveness to customers • Faster decision making • More empowerment	• Fewer chances for advancement • Overworked managers • Loss of control • Less management expertise

Weighing the Advantages and Disadvantages of Departmentalization

departmentalization

The dividing of organizational functions into separate units.

Departmentalization divides organizations into separate units. The traditional way to departmentalize is by *function*—such as design, production, marketing, and accounting. Departmentalization groups workers according to their skills, expertise, or resource use so that they can specialize and work together more effectively. It may also save costs and thus improve efficiency. Other advantages include the following:

1. Employees can develop skills in depth and progress within a department as they master more skills.

2. The company can achieve economies of scale by centralizing all the resources it needs and locate various experts in that area.

3. Employees can coordinate work within the function, and top management can easily direct and control various departments' activities.

Disadvantages of departmentalization by function include the following:

1. Departments may not communicate well. For example, production may be so isolated from marketing that it does not get needed feedback from customers.

2. Employees may identify with their department's goals rather than the organization's. The purchasing department may find a good value somewhere and buy a huge volume of goods. That makes purchasing look good, but the high cost of storing the goods hurts overall profitability.

3. The company's response to external changes may be slow.

4. People may not be trained to take different managerial responsibilities; rather, they tend to become narrow specialists.

5. Department members may engage in groupthink (they think alike) and may need input from outside to become more creative.

Looking at Alternative Ways to Departmentalize   Functional separation isn't always the most responsive form of organization. So what are the alternatives? Figure 8.5 shows five ways a firm can departmentalize. One way is by product. A book publisher might have a trade book department (for books sold to the general public), a textbook department, and a technical book department, each with separate development and marketing processes. Such product-focused departmentalization usually results in good customer relations.

Some organizations departmentalize by customer group. A pharmaceutical company might have one department for the consumer market, another

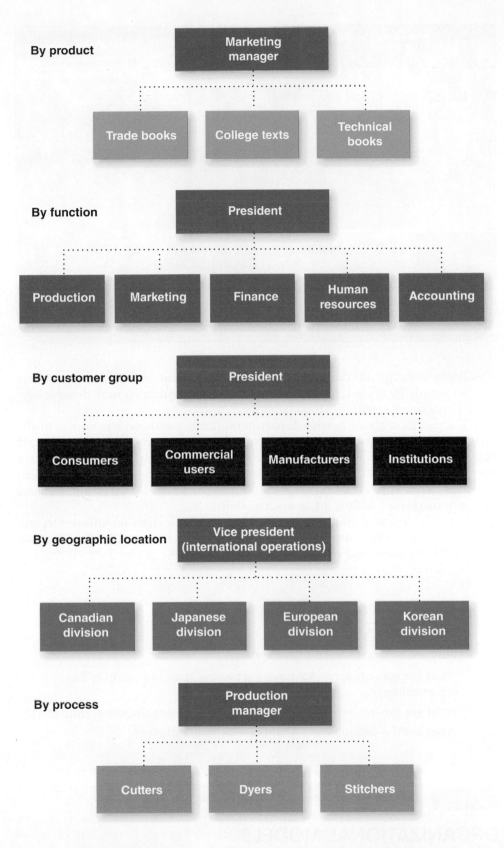

By product

By function

By customer group

By geographic location

By process

FIGURE 8.5 WAYS TO DEPARTMENTALIZE
A computer company may want to departmentalize by geographic location (countries), a manufacturer by function, a pharmaceutical company by customer group, a leather manufacturer by process, and a publisher by product. In each case the structure must fit the firm's goals.

that calls on hospitals (the institutional market), and another that targets doctors. You can see how customer groups can benefit from having specialists satisfying their needs.

After the material for footballs has been cut and sewn in the Wilson Sporting Goods factory, it moves on to the lacing department where workers like this one open up the deflated balls and prepare them for lacing. What are the advantages and disadvantages of departmentalizing by processes like this?

Some firms group their units by geographic location because customers vary so greatly by region. Japan, Europe, and South America may deserve separate departments, with obvious benefits.

The decision about how to departmentalize depends on the nature of the product and the customers. A few firms find that it's most efficient to separate activities by process. For example, a firm that makes leather coats may have one department cut the leather, another dye it, and a third sew the coat together. Such specialization enables employees to do a better job because they can focus on learning a few critical skills.

Some firms use a combination of departmentalization techniques to create *hybrid forms*. For example, a company could departmentalize by function, geographic location, *and* customer groups.

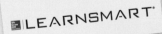

Use LearnSmart to help retain what you have learned. Access your instructor's Connect course to check out LearnSmart, or go to learnsmartadvantage.com for help.

LEARNSMART®

 test **prep**

- Why are organizations becoming flatter?
- What are some reasons for having a narrow span of control in an organization?
- What are the advantages and disadvantages of departmentalization?
- What are the various ways a firm can departmentalize?

LO 8–4   Contrast the various organizational models.

ORGANIZATIONAL MODELS

Now that we've explored the basic choices in organization design, let's look in depth at four ways to structure an organization: (1) line organizations, (2) line-and-staff organizations, (3) matrix-style organizations, and (4) cross-functional self-managed teams. You'll see that some of these models violate traditional management principles. The business community is in a period of transition, with some traditional organizational models giving way to new structures. Such transitions can be not only unsettling to employees and managers but also fraught with problems and errors.

Line Organizations

A **line organization** has direct two-way lines of responsibility, authority, and communication running from the top to the bottom of the organization, with everyone reporting to only one supervisor. Many small businesses are organized this way. For example, a locally owned pizza parlor might have a general manager and a shift manager. All the general employees report to the shift manager, and he or she reports to the general manager or owner.

A line organization does not have any specialists who provide managerial support. There is no legal department, accounting department, human resources department, or information technology (IT) department. Line organizations follow all of Fayol's traditional management rules. Line managers can issue orders, enforce discipline, and adjust the organization as conditions change.

In large businesses, a line organization may have the disadvantages of being too inflexible, of having few specialists or experts to advise people along the line, and of having lengthy lines of communication. Thus a line organization may be unable to handle complex decisions relating to thousands of products and tons of paperwork. Such organizations usually turn to a line-and-staff form of organization.

Line-and-Staff Organizations

To minimize the disadvantages of simple line organizations, many organizations today have both line and staff personnel. **Line personnel** are responsible for directly achieving organizational goals, and include production workers, distribution people, and marketing personnel. **Staff personnel** advise and assist line personnel in meeting their goals, and include those in marketing research, legal advising, information technology, and human resource management.

See Figure 8.6 for a diagram of a line-and-staff organization. One important difference between line and staff personnel is authority. Line personnel have formal authority to make policy decisions. Staff personnel have authority to advise line personnel and influence their decisions, but they can't make policy changes themselves. The line manager may seek or ignore the advice from staff personnel.

Many organizations benefit from expert staff advice on safety, legal issues, quality control, database management, motivation, and investing. Staff personnel strengthen the line positions and are like well-paid consultants on the organization's payroll.

Matrix-Style Organizations

Both line and line-and-staff organization structures may suffer from inflexibility. Both allow for established lines of authority and communication and work well in organizations with stable environments and slow product development (such as firms selling household appliances). In such firms, clear lines of authority and relatively fixed organization structures are assets that ensure efficient operations.

FIGURE 8.6 A SAMPLE LINE-AND-STAFF ORGANIZATION

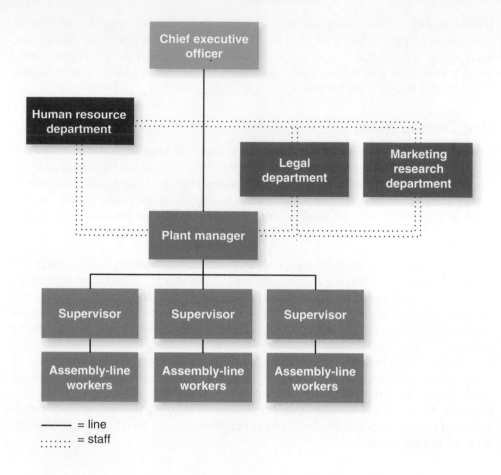

——— = line
······· = staff

matrix organization
An organization in which specialists from different parts of the organization are brought together to work on specific projects but still remain part of a line-and-staff structure.

Today's economy, however, is dominated by high-growth industries like telecommunications, nanotechnology, robotics, biotechnology, and aerospace, where competition is stiff and the life cycle of new ideas is short. Emphasis is on product development, creativity, special projects, rapid communication, and interdepartmental teamwork. From those changes grew the popularity of the **matrix organization**, in which specialists from different parts of the organization work together temporarily on specific projects, but still remain part of a line-and-staff structure (see Figure 8.7). In other words, a project manager can borrow people from different departments to help design and market new product ideas.[14]

The matrix structure was developed in the aerospace industry and is now familiar in areas such as banking, management consulting firms, accounting firms, ad agencies, and school systems. Among its advantages:

- It gives managers flexibility in assigning people to projects.
- It encourages interorganizational cooperation and teamwork.
- It can produce creative solutions to product development problems.
- It makes efficient use of organizational resources.

As for disadvantages:

- It's costly and complex.
- It can confuse employees about where their loyalty belongs—with the project manager or with their functional unit.
- It requires good interpersonal skills as well as cooperative employees and managers to avoid communication problems.
- It may be only a temporary solution to a long-term problem.

FIGURE 8.7 A MATRIX ORGANIZATION

In a matrix organization, project managers are in charge of teams made up of members of several departments. In this case, project manager 2 supervises employees A, B, C, and D. These employees are accountable not only to project manager 2 but also to the head of their individual departments. For example, employee B, a market researcher, reports to project manager 2 *and* to the vice president of marketing.

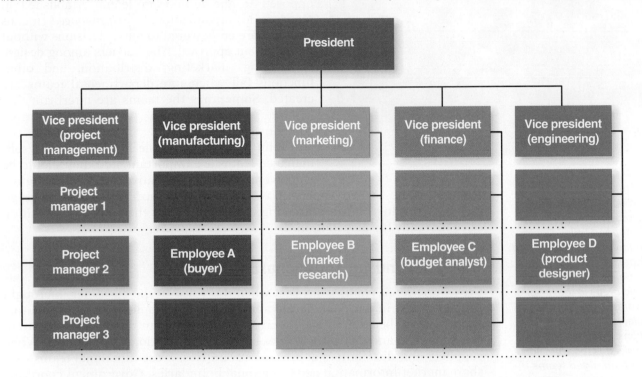

If you're thinking that matrix organizations violate some traditional managerial principles, you're right. Normally a person can't work effectively for two bosses. Who has the real authority? Whose directive has first priority?

In reality, however, the system functions more effectively than you might imagine. To develop a new product, a project manager may be given temporary authority to "borrow" line personnel from production, marketing, and other line functions. The employees work together to complete the project and then return to their regular positions. Thus, no one actually reports to more than one manager at a time.

A potential real problem with matrix management, however, is that the project teams are not permanent. They form to solve a problem and then break up. There is little chance for cross-functional learning, because teams work together so briefly.

Decision making in the future will be distributed throughout the organization so that people can respond rapidly to change, says the *Harvard Business Review*. Global teams will collaborate on the Internet for a single project and then disband. Young people who play online games will feel quite comfortable working in such groups.

Cross-Functional Self-Managed Teams

One solution to the temporary nature of matrix teams is to establish *long-lived teams* and empower them to work closely with suppliers, customers, and others to quickly and efficiently bring out new, high-quality products while giving great service.

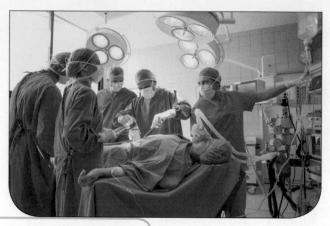

You can think of a team of medical specialists in an operating room as a cross-functional, self-managed team. Doctors, nurses, technicians, and anesthesiologists from different departments and areas in the hospital work together to complete successful operations. What kinds of tasks do cross-functional, self-managed teams complete in an office or retail environment?

cross-functional self-managed teams
Groups of employees from different departments who work together on a long-term basis.

Cross-functional self-managed teams are groups of employees from different departments who work together on a long-term basis (as opposed to the temporary teams established in matrix-style organizations). *Self-managed* means that they are empowered to make decisions without management approval. The barriers among design, engineering, marketing, distribution, and other functions fall when interdepartmental teams are created. Sometimes the teams are interfirm; that is, the members come from two or more companies.

John Mackey of Whole Foods says that self-managed teams are important, and they should be empowered and collaborative.[15] Cross-functional teams work best when leadership is shared. An engineer may lead the design of a new product, but a marketing expert may take the leadership position once it's ready for distribution.

Going Beyond Organizational Boundaries

Cross-functional teams work best when the voice of the customer is brought in, especially in product development tasks.[16] Suppliers and distributors should be on the team as well. A cross-functional team that includes customers, suppliers, and distributors goes beyond organizational boundaries. When suppliers and distributors are in other countries, cross-functional teams may share market information across national boundaries. Government coordinators may assist such projects, letting cross-functional teams break the barriers between government and business.

Cross-functional teams are only one way businesses can interact with other companies. Next we look at others.

test prep

- What is the difference between line and staff personnel?
- What management principle does a matrix-style organization challenge?
- What is the main difference between a matrix-style organization's structure and the use of cross-functional teams?

Use LearnSmart to help retain what you have learned. Access your instructor's Connect course to check out LearnSmart, or go to learnsmartadvantage.com for help.

LEARNSMART

LO 8–5   Identify the benefits of interfirm cooperation and coordination.

networking
Using communications technology and other means to link organizations and allow them to work together on common objectives.

MANAGING THE INTERACTIONS AMONG FIRMS

Whether it involves customers, suppliers, distributors, or the government, **networking** uses communications technology and other means to link organizations and allow them to work together on common objectives. Let's explore this concept further.

Transparency and Virtual Organizations

Networked organizations are so closely linked by the Internet that each can find out what the others are doing in real time. **Real time** simply means the present moment or the actual time in which an event takes place. The Internet has allowed companies to send real-time data to organizational partners as they are developed or collected.[17] The result is transparency (see Chapter 7), which occurs when a company is so open to other companies that electronic information is shared as if the companies were one. With this integration, two companies can work as closely as two departments in traditional firms.

Can you see the implications for organizational design? Most organizations are no longer self-sufficient or self-contained. Rather, they are part of a vast network of global businesses that work closely together. An organization chart showing what people do within any one organization is simply not complete, because the organization is part of a much larger system of firms. A modern chart would show people in different organizations and indicate how they are networked. This is a relatively new concept, however, so few such charts are yet available. The Spotlight on Small Business box offers an example of how small businesses outsource work rather than hire full-time workers.

Networked organization structures tend to be flexible. A company may work with a design expert from another company in Italy for a year and then not need that person anymore. It may hire an expert from a company in another country for the next project. Such a temporary network, made of replaceable firms that join and leave as needed, is a **virtual corporation** (see Figure 8.8). This is quite different from a traditional organization structure; in fact, traditional managers sometimes have trouble adapting to the speed of change and the impermanence of relationships in networking.[18] We discuss adaptation to change below; first, we describe how organizations use benchmarking and outsourcing to manage their interactions with other firms.

real time
The present moment or the actual time in which something takes place.

virtual corporation
A temporary networked organization made up of replaceable firms that join and leave as needed.

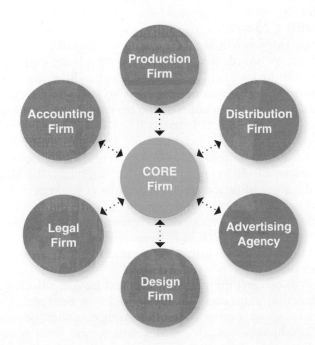

FIGURE 8.8 A VIRTUAL CORPORATION
A virtual corporation has no permanent ties to the firms that do its production, distribution, legal, and other work. Such firms are flexible enough to adapt to changes in the market quickly.

spotlight on **small business**

Cutting Back While Cutting Costs

When you look for your next job, it's likely you'll find it in a small business. In fact, over the past 20 years, almost two-thirds of the net new jobs have been created by small businesses. Unfortunately, keeping costs low is the name of the game for small businesses and hiring workers is a major expense. That's why many small businesses are asking: "Why hire here in the U.S. if someone in another country can do the job for less?" For example, when Mike Scanlin, CEO of Born to Sell, an online investment service, was looking for programming help for his company, he found that programmers from nearby Silicon Valley said it would cost $600,000. So he hired programmers from eastern Europe for

only $37,000. While language problems were an issue at times, quality was not sacrificed. The programmers from Romania and Russia were seasoned software developers with Master's degrees in computer science.

Today, outsourcing jobs is not just for big businesses anymore. Small businesses can grow without hiring additional full-time workers. They also do not need to pay high-priced local companies to handle projects such as website design, software development, and customer service since there are so many lower-cost global options available. This increase in small business outsourcing can be partly attributed to the presence of online job

marketplaces such as ODesk. At ODesk, workers' skills and portfolios, along with reviews of their work, are posted for businesses to review. ODesk handles payment to the contractors; it does require a fee for its services.

With growing numbers of reliable contractors available globally, the trend is not good for U.S. job seekers and freelancers, especially in basic tech positions. It's difficult for a U.S. worker to compete with a contractor in the Philippines who bids $5 per hour for a tech-related job.

Sources: Jose Pagliery, "Even Small Companies Are Outsourcing," *CNNMoney,* March 28, 2013; Adam Callinan, "To Outsource or Not? That Is the Question," *Entrepreneur,* February 7, 2014; and Phyllis Korkki, "Small Business, Joining a Parade of Outsourcing," *The New York Times,* February 15, 2014.

Benchmarking and Core Competencies

Organizations historically tried to do all functions themselves. Each had its own department for accounting, finance, marketing, production, and so on. As we've noted, today's organizations look to other organizations for help in areas where they do not generate world-class quality.

benchmarking

Comparing an organization's practices, processes, and products against the world's best.

Benchmarking compares an organization's practices, processes, and products against the world's best. As one example, K2 Skis is a company that makes skis, snowboards, in-line skates, and related products. It studied the compact-disc industry and learned to use ultraviolet inks to print graphics on skis. It went to the aerospace industry to get piezoelectric technology to reduce vibration in its snowboards (the aerospace industry uses the technology for wings on planes). It learned from the cable television industry how to braid layers of fiberglass and carbon, and adapted that knowledge to make skis. As another example, Wyeth, a pharmaceutical company, benchmarked the aerospace industry for project management, the shipping industry for standardization of processes, and computer makers to learn the most efficient way to make prescription drugs.

Benchmarking also has a more directly competitive purpose. In retailing, Target may compare itself to Walmart to see what, if anything, Walmart does better. Target will then try to improve its practices or processes to become even better than Walmart.

If an organization can't do as well as the best in, say, shipping, it will try to outsource the function to an organization like UPS or FedEx that specializes in shipping. Outsourcing, remember, means assigning one or more functions—such as accounting, production, security, maintenance, and legal work—to outside organizations. Even small firms are getting involved in outsourcing. We've already discussed some problems with outsourcing, especially when companies outsource to other countries. Some functions, such as information management and marketing, may be too important to assign to outside firms. In that case, the organization should benchmark the best firms and restructure its departments to try to be equally good. It is important to remember that companies in other countries often outsource their functions to companies in the United States. We call that *insourcing* and it is the source of many jobs.[19]

When a firm has completed its outsourcing process, the remaining functions are its **core competencies**, those functions it can do as well as or better than any other organization in the world. For example, Nike

is great at designing and marketing athletic shoes. Those are its core competencies. It outsources manufacturing, however, to other companies that assemble shoes better and less expensively than Nike can. Similarly, Dell is best at marketing computers and may outsource most other functions, including manufacturing and distribution.

After you have structured an organization, you must keep monitoring the environment (including customers) to learn what changes are needed. Dell, for example, reversed its practice of outsourcing customer support and now offers a premium service that allows U.S. customers to reach tech support in North America. The following section discusses organizational change in more detail.

ADAPTING TO CHANGE

Once you have formed an organization, you must be prepared to adapt the structure to changes in the market. That's not always easy to do.[20] Over time, an organization can get stuck in its ways. Employees have a tendency to say, "That's the way we've always done things. If it isn't broken, don't fix it." Managers also get complacent. They may say they have 20 years' experience when in fact they've had one year's experience 20 times. Do you think that slow adaptation to change was a factor in the decline of the manufacturing sector in the United States?

Introducing change is thus one of the hardest challenges facing any manager. Nonetheless, change is what's happening at General Motors (GM), Ford, Facebook, and other companies eager to become more competitive. If you have old facilities that are no longer efficient, you have to get rid of them. That's exactly what GM and other companies did. In fact, they asked the government to lend them billions of dollars to help. You may have to cut your labor force to lower costs.

The Internet has created whole new opportunities, not only to sell to customers directly but also to ask them questions and provide them with any information they want. To win market share, companies must coordinate the efforts of their traditional departments and their information technology staff to create friendly, easy-to-manage interactions. Young people today are called **digital natives** because they grew up with the Internet and cell phones; using high-tech devices is second nature to them. On the other hand, companies often need to retrain older employees to be more tech-savvy. While the ease and immediacy of communication created by technology may be powerful, being constantly connected to work does have its downsides (see Adapting to Change box).

Nike's core competencies are designing and marketing athletic shoes. The company outsources other functions (i.e., manufacturing) to other companies that assemble shoes better and cheaper than Nike could do on its own. What are the advantages of focusing on the company's core competencies? What are the disadvantages?

core competencies
Those functions that the organization can do as well as or better than any other organization in the world.

digital natives
Young people who have grown up using the Internet and social networking.

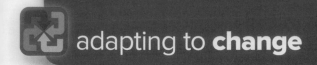
When Open Communication Should Not Be So Open

People today use technology to text, tweet, surf the web, and run apps as they go about their personal lives and, in many cases, their business lives. Many companies, in fact, provide work-issued smartphones, tablets, and other mobile technology to their employees. This blending of mobile technology and work has been a boon to employees and businesses in many ways, particularly in terms of speed, reach, and efficiency. Unfortunately, it has also encroached on the traditional boundaries between work and home.

According to a recent survey conducted by Right Management, a career and outplacement service, more than one-third of employees receive work-related e-mails after work hours. According to Monika Morrow, senior vice president at Right Management, "The boundaries of the workplace are expanding and now reach deeper into employees' lives. Workers can no longer leave the office at the office."

While no one disputes the value of technology, many believe its use has gone overboard and is affecting employees' quality of life. Companies such as Volkswagen, PricewaterhouseCoopers, and shipping company PBD have heard the complaints and created both formal and informal rules regarding e-mail.

The e-mail encroachment problem is not just in the United States. France is considering legislation that would block work e-mails and phone calls, and legally give employees at least 11 hours of daily rest free from mobile technology.

Sources: Cecilia Kang, "Firms Tell Employees: Avoid After-Hours E-Mail," *The Washington Post*, September 21, 2012; Chris Baysden, "Why You're Never Safe from More Work—Even After Hours," *CGMA Magazine*, July 4, 2013; and Scott Sayare, "In France, a Move to Limit Off-the-Clock Work Emails," *The New York Times*, April 11, 2014.

We've seen that Target is highly centralized. Nonetheless, the company reacts effectively to changes in consumer preferences throughout the country, in part by keeping in touch with an enormous web of people of all ages, interests, and nationalities—its "creative cabinet"—via the Internet. The members of the "cabinet," who never meet so they cannot influence each other, evaluate various new initiatives and recommend new programs to help Target figure out what belongs on store shelves.

Restructuring for Empowerment

restructuring
Redesigning an organization so that it can more effectively and efficiently serve its customers.

To empower employees, firms often must reorganize dramatically to make frontline workers their most important people. **Restructuring** is redesigning an organization so it can more effectively and efficiently serve its customers.

Until recently, department store clerks, and front-desk staff in hotels weren't considered key employees. Instead, managers were considered more important, and they were responsible for directing the work of the frontline people. The organization chart in a typical firm looked much like a pyramid.

inverted organization
An organization that has contact people at the top and the chief executive officer at the bottom of the organization chart.

A few service-oriented organizations have turned the traditional organization structure upside down. An **inverted organization** has contact people (like nurses) at the top and the chief executive officer at the bottom.

FIGURE 8.8 COMPARISON OF AN INVERTED ORGANIZATIONAL STRUCTURE AND A TRADITIONAL ORGANIZATIONAL STRUCTURE

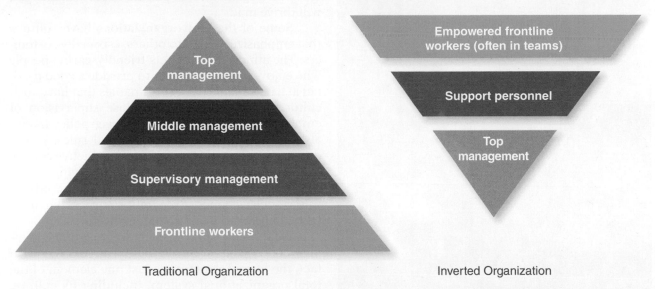

Traditional Organization   Inverted Organization

Management layers are few, and the manager's job is to *assist and support* frontline people, not boss them around. Figure 8.9 illustrates the difference between an inverted and a traditional organizational structure.

Companies based on this organization structure support frontline personnel with internal and external databases, advanced communication systems, and professional assistance. Naturally, this means frontline people have to be better educated, better trained, and better paid than in the past. It takes a lot of trust for top managers to implement such a system—but when they do, the payoff in customer satisfaction and profits is often well worth the effort.[21]

In the past, managers controlled information—and that gave them power. In more progressive organizations today, everyone shares information, often through an elaborate database system, and *among* firms as well as *within* them. No matter what organizational model you choose or how much you empower your employees, the secret to successful organization change is to focus on customers and give them what they want.

LO 8–6   Explain how organizational culture can help businesses adapt to change.

Creating a Change-Oriented Organizational Culture

Any organizational change is bound to cause some stress and resistance among members. Firms adapt best when their culture is already change-oriented. **Organizational (or corporate) culture** is the widely shared values within an organization that foster unity and cooperation to achieve common goals. Usually the culture of an organization is reflected in its stories, traditions, and myths.

Each McDonald's restaurant has the same feel, look, and atmosphere; in short, each has a similar organizational culture. It's obvious from visiting many McDonald's restaurants that the culture emphasizes quality, service, cleanliness, and value.

An organizational culture can also be negative. Have you ever been in an organization where you feel no one cares about service or quality? The clerks may seem uniformly glum, indifferent, and testy. Their mood pervades the atmosphere, and patrons become unhappy or upset. It may be hard to believe an organization, especially a profit-making one, can be run so badly and still

organizational (or corporate) culture
Widely shared values within an organization that provide unity and cooperation to achieve common goals.

survive. Clearly then, when you search for a job, study the organizational culture to see whether you will thrive in it.

Some of the best organizations have cultures that emphasize service to others, especially customers. The atmosphere reflects friendly, caring people who enjoy working together to provide a good product at a reasonable price. Companies that have such cultures have less need for close supervision of employees. That usually means fewer policy manuals; organization charts; and formal rules, procedures, and controls. The key to a productive culture is mutual trust. You get such trust by giving it. The very best companies stress high moral and ethical values such as honesty, reliability, fairness, environmental protection, and social involvement.

We've been talking as if organizational matters were mostly controllable by management. In fact, the formal structure is just one element of the total organizational system, including its culture. The informal organization is of equal or even greater importance. Let's explore this notion next.

Managing the Informal Organization

All organizations have two organizational systems. The **formal organization** details lines of responsibility, authority, and position. It's the structure shown on organization charts. The other system is the **informal organization**, the system that develops spontaneously as employees meet and form cliques, relationships, and lines of authority outside the formal organization. It's the human side of the organization that doesn't show on any organization chart.

No organization can operate effectively without both types of organization. The formal system is often too slow and bureaucratic to let the organization adapt quickly, although it does provide helpful guides and lines of authority for routine situations.

The informal organization is often too unstructured and emotional to allow careful, reasoned decision making on critical matters. It's extremely effective, however, in generating creative solutions to short-term problems and creating camaraderie and teamwork among employees.[22]

In any organization, it's wise to learn quickly who is important in the informal organization. Following formal rules and procedures can take days. Who in the organization knows how to obtain supplies immediately without the normal procedures? Which administrative assistants should you see if you want your work given first priority? Answers to these questions help people work effectively in many organizations.

The informal organization's nerve center is the *grapevine*, the system through which unofficial information flows between and among managers and employees. Key people in the grapevine usually have considerable influence.

In the old "us-versus-them" system of organizations, where managers and employees were often at odds, the informal system hindered effective management. In more open organizations, managers and employees work together to set objectives and design procedures. The informal organization is an invaluable managerial asset that can promote harmony among workers and establish the corporate culture.[23]

Empowering employees who deal directly with customers to solve problems without needing a manager's approval makes a higher level of customer service possible and helps employees grow as well. What kind of guest issues do you think a frontline hotel employee should be allowed to solve on his or her own?

formal organization
The structure that details lines of responsibility, authority, and position; that is, the structure shown on organization charts.

informal organization
The system that develops spontaneously as employees meet and form cliques, relationships, and lines of authority outside the formal organization.

The informal organization is the system that develops as employees meet and form relationships. The grapevine, the unofficial flow of information among employees, is the nerve center of the informal organization. How does the informal organization affect the work environment?

As effective as the informal organization may be in creating group cooperation, it can still be equally powerful in resisting management directives. Employees may form unions, go on strike together, and generally disrupt operations. Learning to create the right corporate culture and work within the informal organization is thus a key to managerial success.[24]

Use LearnSmart to help retain what you have learned. Access your instructor's Connect course to check out LearnSmart, or go to learnsmartadvantage.com for help.

LEARNSMART

test prep

- What is an inverted organization?
- Why do organizations outsource functions?
- What is organizational culture?

summary

LO 8–1   Outline the basic principles of organization management.

- **What is happening today to American businesses?**
  They are adjusting to changing markets. That is a normal function in a capitalist economy. There will be big winners, like Google and Facebook, and big losers as well. The key to success is remaining flexible and adapting to the changing times.

- **What are the principles of organization management?**
  Structuring an organization means devising a division of labor (sometimes resulting in specialization), setting up teams or departments, and assigning responsibility and authority. It includes allocating resources (such as funds), assigning specific tasks, and establishing procedures for accomplishing the organizational objectives. Managers also have to make ethical decisions about how to treat workers.

Access your instructor's Connect course to check out LearnSmart or go to learnsmartadvantage.com for help.

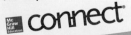
connect

LO 8–2   Compare the organizational theories of Fayol and Weber.

- **What were Fayol's basic principles?**
  Fayol introduced principles such as unity of command, hierarchy of authority, division of labor, subordination of individual interests to the general interest, authority, clear communication channels, order, and equity.

- **What principles did Weber add?**
  Weber added principles of bureaucracy such as job descriptions, written rules and decision guidelines, consistent procedures, and staffing and promotions based on qualifications.

LO 8–3   Evaluate the choices managers make in structuring organizations.

- **What are the four major choices in structuring organizations?**
  Choices to make in structuring and restructuring organizations cover (1) centralization versus decentralization, (2) breadth of span of control, (3) tall versus flat organization structures, and (4) type of departmentalization.

- **What are the latest trends in structuring?**
  Departments are often replaced or supplemented by matrix organizations and cross-functional teams that decentralize authority. The span of control becomes larger as employees become self-directed. Another trend is to eliminate managers and flatten organizations.

LO 8–4   Contrast the various organizational models.

- **What are the two major organizational models?**
  Two traditional forms of organization are (1) line organizations and (2) line-and-staff organizations. A line organization has clearly defined responsibility and authority, is easy to understand, and provides each worker with only one supervisor. The expert advice of staff assistants in a line-and-staff organization helps in areas such as safety, quality control, computer technology, human resource management, and investing.

- **What are the key alternatives to the major organizational models?**
  Matrix organizations assign people to projects temporarily and encourage interorganizational cooperation and teamwork. Cross-functional self-managed teams have all the benefits of the matrix style and are long term.

LO 8–5   Identify the benefits of interfirm cooperation and coordination.

- **What are the major concepts involved in interfirm communications?**
  Networking uses communications technology and other means to link organizations and allow them to work together on common objectives. A virtual corporation is a networked organization of replaceable firms that join and leave as needed. Benchmarking tells firms how their performance measures up to that of their competitors in specific functions. The company may then *outsource* to companies that perform its weaker functions more effectively and efficiently. The functions that are left are the firm's *core competencies*.

- **What is an inverted organization?**
  An inverted organization places employees at the top of the hierarchy; managers are at the bottom to train and assist employees.

LO 8–6   Explain how organizational culture can help businesses adapt to change.

- **What is organizational culture?**
  Organizational (or corporate) culture consists of the widely shared values within an organization that foster unity and cooperation to achieve common goals.

- **What is the difference between the formal and informal organization of a firm?**
  The formal organization details lines of responsibility, authority, and position. It's the structure shown on organization charts. The informal organization is the system that develops spontaneously as employees meet and form cliques, relationships, and lines of authority outside the formal organization. It's the human side of the organization. The informal organization is an invaluable managerial asset that often promotes harmony among workers and establishes the corporate culture. As effective as the informal organization may be in creating group cooperation, it can still be equally powerful in resisting management directives.

key terms

benchmarking 228
bureaucracy 217
centralized authority 218
chain of command 216
core competencies 229
cross-functional self-managed teams 226
decentralized authority 218
departmentalization 220
digital natives 229

economies of scale 214
flat organization structure 219
formal organization 232
hierarchy 216
informal organization 232
inverted organization 230
line organization 223
line personnel 223
matrix organization 224

networking 226
organization (or corporate) culture 231
organizational chart 216
real time 227
restructuring 230
span of control 219
staff personnel 223
tall organization structure 219
virtual corporation 227

critical thinking

Now that you have learned some of the basic principles of organization, pause and think about where you have already applied such concepts yourself or when you have been part of an organization that did.

1. Did you find a division of labor necessary and helpful?

2. Were you assigned specific tasks or left on your own to decide what to do?

3. Were promotions based strictly on qualifications, as Weber suggested? What other factors may have been considered?

4. What problems seem to emerge when an organization gets larger?

5. What organizational changes might you recommend to the auto companies? The airline industry?

developing **workplace skills**

Key: ● **Team**   ★ **Analytic**   ▲ **Communication**   ▣ **Technology**

● ▲   1. There is no better way to understand the effects of having many layers of management on communication accuracy than the game of Message Relay. Choose seven or more members of the class and have them leave the classroom. Then choose one person to read the following paragraph and another student to listen. Call in one of the students from outside and have the "listener" tell him or her what information was in the paragraph. Then bring in another student and have the new listener repeat the information to him or her. Continue the process with all those who left the room. Do not allow anyone in the class to offer corrections as each listener becomes the storyteller in turn. In this way, all the students can hear how the facts become distorted over time. The distortions and mistakes are often quite humorous, but they are not so funny in organizations such as Ford, which once had 22 layers of management.

Here's the paragraph:

Dealers in the midwest region have received over 130 complaints about steering on the new Commander and Roadhandler models of our minivans. Apparently, the front suspension system is weak and the ball joints are wearing too fast. This causes slippage in the linkage and results in oversteering. Mr. Berenstein has been notified, but so far only 213 of 4,300 dealers have received repair kits.

★   2. Describe some informal groups within an organization with which you are familiar at school or work. What have you noticed about how those groups help or hinder progress in the organization?

▲   3. Imagine you are working for Kitchen Magic, an appliance manufacturer that produces dishwashers. A competitor introduces a new dishwasher that uses sound waves not only to clean even the worst burned-on food but also to sterilize dishes and silverware. You need to develop a similar offering fast, or your company will lose market share. Write an e-mail to management outlining the problem and explaining your rationale for recommending use of a cross-functional team to respond quickly.

● ★ ▲   4. Divide the class into teams of five. Each team should imagine your firm, a producer of athletic shoes, has been asked to join a virtual network. How might you minimize the potential problems of joining? Begin by defining a virtual corporation and listing its advantages and disadvantages. Each team should report its solutions to the class.

● ★ ▲   5. A growing number of work groups, including management, are cross-functional and self-managed. To practice working in such an organization, break into groups of five or so students, preferably with different backgrounds and interests. Each group must work together to prepare a report on the advantages and disadvantages of working in teams. Many of the problems and advantages of cross-functional, self-managed teams should emerge in your group as you try to complete this assignment. Each group should report to the class how it handled the problems and benefited from the advantages.

taking it to the **net**

PURPOSE

To learn more about the process of organizational change.

EXERCISE

Xerox is a very familiar corporate name in the United States. There was a time, however, when the company was faltering and needed to adapt to foreign competition. This exercise will help you see how complex such change can be.

1. Do an online search for "Xerox Corporation."

2. Read through the history of the company and describe its current strengths, weaknesses, opportunities, and threats (a SWOT analysis; see Chapter 7).

3. Describe Xerox's reasons for success.

video case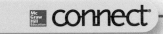

WHOLE FOODS

Whole Foods Market is a supermarket chain that specializes in fresh, organic produce from local sources. As an international company with locations around the world, it has a large operation to watch over and a very specific mission to uphold: to sell the highest-quality natural and organic products available.

Sticking to this goal and keeping up with the demands of a rapidly expanding business aren't always easy, though. In order to stay committed to stocking sustainable goods, Whole Foods relies on an organizational structure that combines aspects of a mom-and-pop operation with a traditional corporate hierarchy. Thanks to this unique organizational structure, the company has been able to expand to 360 stores and hire more than 58,000 employees without sacrificing its core principles.

Whole Foods got its start when John Mackey and Rene Lawson borrowed money from friends and family to open a small natural food store in Austin, Texas. The couple soon ended up living in the market after they were evicted from their apartment for storing some of their grocery stock there. Fortunately, business began to boom once the pair took on a couple of partners and merged with another store. But they quickly faced another huge setback when the most destructive flood Austin had experienced in 70 years took its toll on the market. Along with incurring damage to their building, the store also lost all of its produce and inventory. Thanks to a massive community cleanup effort, however, the market was soon back in business.

Whole Foods has never forgotten that lesson—that having a local, grass-roots structure sensitive to drastic and sudden changes in the business environment can keep an organization nimble and responsive. In the company's early days, the staff was small enough so that everyone could do every job. While this kept things running smoothly at first, the situation had to change as the company grew and opened more stores. They divided the labor between the four partners, with each specializing in one or more of the tasks critical to the business. After designating the leaders for departments like finance, human resources, and sales, Whole Foods began to look like a big company.

But John Mackey and his partners still wanted their stores to appear like small local markets, not corporate mega-grocers. That meant they had to make tough choices, like whether they should centralize supply in warehouses or depend on separate, local suppliers in each region they had stores. Whole Foods ultimately opted for the latter option. To stay responsive to market changes, each region received its own manager and the autonomy to make certain decisions about supply sources and pricing based on the needs of that region, without being slowed down waiting for responses from the home office. This decentralized structure gives Whole Foods the flexibility to adapt to important changes without involving needless bureaucracy.

Whole Foods Market continues to expand into new markets around the world. Despite that fact, it's managed to keep what's unique about its culture and pure about its mission: focusing on great, natural sources at the local level.

THINKING IT OVER

1. Organizations like Whole Foods need to follow the principles of Henri Fayol, such as the "unity of command." What is unity of command?

2. Whole Foods structures its organization in a decentralized manner. What does that mean for the company's operations?

3. Do you think the corporate culture at Whole Foods is somewhat resistant to change or accepting of change? Why?

notes

1. John Jullens, "How Emerging Giants Can Take On the World," *Harvard Business Review,* December 2013.
2. Jonathan House and Kathleen Madigan, "U.S. Factories Bounce Back in February," *The Wall Street Journal,* March 2, 2014.
3. Ann Hadley, "What Not to Do," *Entrepreneur,* September 2013.
4. Amol Sharma, Shalini Ramachandran, and Don Clark, "Amazon Joins the TV Crush," *The Wall Street Journal,* January 22, 2014.
5. Natalie Kaddas, "Being Flexible," www.huffingtonpost.com, November 23, 2013.
6. Mary Jordan, "The Promise of a 'Made in America' Era," *The Washington Post,* May 1, 2013.
7. Fredrik Eliasson, "Emphasizing the Management in 'Change Management,'" *The Wall Street Journal,* January 24, 2014.
8. John Mackey and Raj Sisodia, *Conscious Capitalism* (Boston, MA: Harvard Business Review Press, 2013).
9. Clint Boulton, "Government Must Boost Pay, Change Culture to Hire Top Tech Talent," *The Wall Street Journal,* January 6, 2014.
10. Jeff Bennett and John Kell, "GM Restores Annual Dividend as Sales Shine," *The Wall Street Journal,* January 15, 2014.
11. Rashik Parmar, Ian Mackenzie, David Cohn, and David Gann, "The New Patterns of Innovation," *Harvard Business Review,* January–February 2014.
12. Raymond Fisman and Tim Sullivan, "The Unsung Beauty of Bureaucracy," *The Wall Street Journal,* Mary 16–17, 2014.
13. Gary L. Neilson and Julie Wulf, "How Many Direct Reports?" *Harvard Business Review,* April 2012.
14. David Gann, Ammon Salter, Mark Dodgson, and Nelson Phillips, "Inside the World of the Project Baron," *Sloan Management Review,* Spring 2012.
15. Mackey and Sisodia, *Conscious Capitalism.*
16. Braden Kowitz, "Why You Should Listen to the Customer," *The Wall Street Journal,* February 19, 2014.
17. Mary C. Lacity and Leslie P. Willcocks," Outsourcing Business Processes for Innovation," *Sloan Management Review,* Spring 2013.
18. Tammy Johns and Lynda Gratton, "The Third Wave of Virtual Work," *Harvard Business Review,* January–February 2013.
19. Kasia Klimasinska, "Obama Budget Predicts Strongest U.S. Growth since 2005," *Bloomberg Businessweek,* March 4, 2014.
20. Robert I. Sutton and Huggy Rao, "Before You Make Any Changes, Ask These Questions," *Bloomberg Businessweek,* March 4, 2014.
21. Michael E. Raynor and Mumtaz Ahmed, "Three Rules for Making a Company Truly Great," *Harvard Business Review,* April 2013.
22. Alex (Sandy) Pentland, "The New Science of Building Great Teams," *Harvard Business Review,* April 2012.
23. Jay Rao and Joseph Weintraub, "How Innovative Is Your Company's Culture?" *Sloan Management Review,* Spring 2013.
24. Christopher Hann, "Good Vibes," *Entrepreneur,* February 2014.

photo credits

9

Production and Operations Management

Learning Objectives

AFTER YOU HAVE READ AND STUDIED THIS CHAPTER, YOU SHOULD BE ABLE TO

LO 9-1   Describe the current state of U.S. manufacturing and what manufacturers have done to become more competitive.

LO 9-2   Describe the evolution from production to operations management.

LO 9-3   Identify various production processes and describe techniques that improve productivity, including computer-aided design and manufacturing, flexible manufacturing, lean manufacturing, mass customization, and robotics.

LO 9-4   Describe operations management planning issues including facility location, facility layout, materials requirement planning, purchasing, just-in-time inventory control, and quality control.

LO 9-5   Explain the use of PERT and Gantt charts to control manufacturing processes.

Getting to know **Shahid Khan**

When Shahid Khan came to the U.S. at age 16, it didn't take him long to feel the power of the American Dream in spite of a shaky beginning. He moved to Champaign, Illinois, from his home country of Pakistan in order to earn a degree in engineering. Not only was a blizzard bombarding the midwestern town upon his arrival, but also the dorms at the University of Illinois hadn't opened yet. Reluctantly, Khan paid $3 for a room and a meal at the local YMCA. With precious little money to his name, Khan began to worry about how he would survive for the next four years.

But his fears subsided the next morning when he discovered a notice about an opening for a dishwashing job in the YMCA kitchen. With a starting salary of $1.20 per hour, Khan was shocked that he could recoup his losses from the previous night so quickly. "It's like, wow," said Khan. "If you put the $1.20 per hour in terms of Pakistan, you're making more than 99% of the people over there. I'm breathing oxygen for the first time." The opportunities offered by the U.S. fueled Khan's enthusiasm for his work in college and beyond. After graduating, he landed a job overseeing production for a local aftermarket auto parts company called Flex-N-Gate. At first Khan couldn't believe the inefficient manufacturing methods the company used to make its bumpers, which sometimes involved welding together as many as 15 different parts. Using his engineering expertise, Khan refined the process to make it less complicated. His hard work paid off in the form of a revolutionary new product: a bumper stamped from a single piece of steel that managed to slim down the rear end of a truck.

After seven years in the aftermarket business, Khan realized that the value-focused industry didn't provide much room for innovation. If Khan wanted his product to succeed, he knew he had to sell directly to automakers instead of to consumers. So armed with little more than a post office box and a small business loan, Khan started his own company. Within two years he earned enough money to buy the failing Flex-N-Gate from his old boss, giving him additional revenue streams as well as an established brand name. While business boomed at first, sales eventually ground to a halt when its biggest client, General Motors, simply passed off Khan's bumper design to its large-scale suppliers instead.

Other entrepreneurs would have reacted angrily to such a slight, but Khan kept on the bright side. "It really was the right thing for them," he says. "We had no business going from making 200 bumpers a day to making 40,000." Plus, his dealings with GM put him in contact with executives at Isuzu, one of Japan's biggest auto companies. Khan traveled to Japan in the early 1980s in a last-ditch effort to woo clients. His timing couldn't have been better. Japanese car companies had been preparing to enter the American market, but needed more domestic suppliers to fuel their growth. Not only did Khan's company fill this need, but he also brought his game-changing bumper design to the table. Soon Flex-N-Gate was manufacturing parts for Isuzu, Mazda, and Toyota. As those brands grew into some of the biggest names on the American market, Khan's company grew right along with them. Today Flex-N-Gate auto parts are in two-thirds of the cars and trucks sold in the U.S. Flex-N-Gate enjoys over $3 billion in sales a year. And since Kahn is the sole shareholder, the profit on those sales goes to him, making Kahn one of the richest men in the world.

In 2012 Kahn used some of that immense wealth to purchase the Jacksonville Jaguars, and in the process realized a personal dream to own an NFL franchise. Although the Jaguars aren't exactly Super Bowl contenders now, Khan is confident that the team will become another one of his patented comeback stories.

By setting Flex-N-Gate on the path to productivity, Shahid Khan made a fortune while also creating thousands of jobs. It has also earned him great respect in the auto industry. In this chapter you'll learn about how other company leaders thrive and survive in the production and operations sector. You'll also find out why the United States is generally moving from a production-based economy to a service economy.

Sources: Brian Solomon, "Shahid Khan: I Felt The American Dream in My First 24 Hours Here," *Forbes*, March 27, 2014; Henry Winter, "Fulham Owner Shahid Khan Preaches American Sensibilities, with Respect to English Traditions," *The Telegraph*, October 25, 2013; and Brian Solomon, "Shahid Khan: The New Face of the NFL and the American Dream," *Forbes*, September 5, 2012.

Shahid Khan

- CEO of Flex-N-Gate
- Former dishwasher built an auto parts empire
- Now one of the richest men in the world

www.flex-n-gate.com

@flexngate

241

LO 9–1 Describe the current state of U.S. manufacturing and what manufacturers have done to become more competitive.

MANUFACTURING AND SERVICES IN PERSPECTIVE

Let's begin with a little history of manufacturing news in the United States. On January 28, 2009, *The Wall Street Journal* reported, "Joblessness was worst in the West and Midwest, indicating that the industries hit first by the recession—housing and manufacturing—continue to lose jobs."[1] Another *Wall Street Journal* article went on to say that unemployment could reach double-digit levels, home values could plunge a total of 36 percent, and stocks could fall a total of 55 percent.[2] Such events led President Obama and Congress to propose a stimulus package to "create or save" millions of jobs and get the economy moving again—including manufacturing. Much of this chapter is devoted to showing you what manufacturers and service providers can and are doing to revive the U.S. economy to become world-class competitors.[3]

Sure, there has been lots of bad news about the manufacturing sector, but the story may not be as bad as you think.[4] How can we reconcile the fact that so many workers in manufacturing are unemployed while manufacturing output continues to increase? The answer is that today's workers are so productive that the United States needs fewer workers to produce more goods.[5] The Seeking Sustainability box discusses how one company is providing a more efficient and sustainable way of producing organic food with very few workers. Many manufacturing jobs are coming back to the United States as wages increase dramatically in other countries.[6]

Some areas of the country are enjoying economic growth from manufacturing while others are experiencing declines.[7] One key to ending such declines is to adapt to the new realities and attract new manufacturers. Boston did that when it attracted many high-tech firms and became another Silicon Valley. Another key is to train new workers in the new production processes.[8] It is important at this point to note that many U.S. firms are thinking more about producing in the United States (versus Japan) since the 2011 earthquake, tsunami, and resulting nuclear industry problems in Japan made it a less reliable source for auto parts.

Volkswagen is just one of many auto manufacturers that have insourced jobs to the United States like this one in the VW Chattanooga, Tennessee, plant. Why do you suppose so many news reports emphasize outsourcing when thousands of jobs are created by insourcing?

Your Own Farm in a Box

Imagine sitting in your favorite restaurant in Chicago in the middle of winter with a 12-inch snowfall coming your way. You crave some of the fresh, locally grown produce you enjoy so much in the warmer months. Unfortunately, it's winter so it probably won't be on the menu. Well, crave no more. Help is on the way thanks to a couple of Boston entrepreneurs.

Brad McNamara and Jon Friedman could not get the results they wanted growing produce in a rooftop greenhouse. Frustrated, Jon came up with the idea that using a shipping container to grow produce might be more appropriate. Thanks to his insight, Freight Farms' customers can now grow leafy greens, vine crops, and mushrooms hydroponically in insulated, climate-controlled containers. The company uses 320-square-foot shipping containers that are retrofitted and

converted into modular, stackable farms that can produce 900 heads of leafy greens per container each week. The entire hydroponic system is simple enough that it can be digitally monitored and controlled from a smartphone. The weekly output from one of Freight Farms containers is approximately equivalent to the annual yield of a one-acre farm.

The immediate goal of Freight Farms is to create an appropriate infrastructure that fosters local food economies. The company targets small and medium-sized food distributors such as wholesalers and restaurants with

revenues between $3 million and $75 million. However, it also wants to attract nonprofit groups involved in food distribution in depressed or disaster-relief areas as buyers for its $60,000 farms-in-a-box. But Friedman and McNamara do not want to stop here. While attracting enough customers to make local farming a cost-effective option is the key goal of Freight Farms today, the founders have a much broader objective for the future. Predicting a global food shortage in 2050, they believe Freight Farms is the first step in the redesign of the global food system. Bon appetit!

Sources: Jeremy Quittner, "A One-Acre Farm in a 320-Square-Foot Box," *Inc.,* March 2013; Peter Cohan, "Grow Produce Anywhere in Freight Farms' $60,000 Shipping Container," *Forbes,* June 27, 2013; and Leon Neyfakh, "If Urban Farming Took Off, What Would Boston Look Like?" *The Boston Globe,* January 19, 2014.

American industry is doing what it can to rebuild.[9] The construction industry is ready to build homes that are easier to heat and cool, and U.S. automakers are scrambling to stage a comeback with more competitive vehicles (e.g., driverless cars).[10] The boom in fracking (a process that uses a high-pressure mixture of water, sand, and chemicals to fracture rock in order to release gas) in the United States is lowering natural gas and electric prices so much that the U.S. is becoming one of the lowest-cost countries for manufacturing.[11]

Don't expect a comeback to result in the same number of jobs as were available before the recession. Just as U.S. productivity gains in agriculture lowered the number of farmers needed, today's productivity gains in manufacturing have lowered the number of manufacturing workers companies require. *The U.S. economy is no longer manufacturing-based.* Over 70 percent of U.S. GDP and over 80 percent of U.S. jobs now are in the *service sector.* In fact, the majority of college graduates are likely to be employed in the service sector. Top-paying jobs already exist in legal services; medical services; entertainment; broadcasting; and business services such as accounting, finance, and management consulting. In fact, the service sector in general has suffered along with manufacturing as a result of the economic slowdown, but not nearly as much.

Nobody Does It Better

As the European Union (EU) faced what seemed like a new financial crisis every week, one nation stayed above the problems facing the continent. Germany clearly established itself as the most powerful and respected economy in the EU.

Germany's economic success is mainly attributed to the strength of its industrial sector, consisting of a longstanding group of small manufacturers, many of which have been in business for centuries. At the core of this manufacturing juggernaut is the Mittelstand, consisting of family-owned, small to midsized companies that account for 52 percent of the country's economic output and supply almost two-thirds of the nation's jobs. Many feel Germany could be poised to overtake the United States as the world's second largest exporter primarily based on the strength of the Mittelstand.

Mittelstand companies compete in very narrow market segments where they work closely with their customers that stretch across the globe. These companies design their own machines

and production processes by following the philosophy that it's easier to maintain and ensure product quality with equipment you designed yourself. Employees are generally very loyal and

competent. In fact, many come from Germany's vocational colleges and stay with a particular company for their entire working careers.

The success of the Mittlestand has not gone unnoticed. Companies from China purchased 25 German firms this past year. The Chinese are attracted by the German companies' attitudes and know-how. They plan to learn a great deal from these German acquisitions about high-quality production techniques. While most of the world has never heard of PWM (the world market leader in electronic gas-station price signs) or BSW, a 400-employee company that uses recycled rubber to make products like synthetic surfaces for running tracks, the Germans don't care. They intend to let their 1,300 "hidden champions" in specialized products keep doing what they have been doing for centuries.

Sources: Leigh Buchanan, "How to Build a Company That Lasts Forever," *Inc.*, February 2014; Wei Gu, "China Finds New Investment Opportunities in Germany," *The Wall Street Journal*, March 27, 2014; and "Mittlestand and Middle Kingdom," *The Economist*, April 5, 2014.

Manufacturers and Service Organizations Become More Competitive

U.S. producers no longer strike fear in the heart of foreign competitors. In fact, they have much to learn from them, although one reason foreign producers have become so competitive is that they are using U.S. technology and concepts to increase effectiveness and efficiency. Overall, that's a good thing because it helps reduce poverty and hunger in developing countries and opens new markets to the developed world.

Foreign producers are also streaming to the United States to take advantage of its labor force and opportunities. The United States is still the leader in building big trucks, and in nanotechnology, biotechnology, and other areas.[12] Its workforce is creative and dynamic. Nonetheless, U.S. business cannot stand still; it must keep up with the latest production techniques and processes. The Reaching Beyond Our Borders box looks at Germany and how some companies there have found a competitive advantage that could be applied in the United States.

As the U.S. service sector becomes a larger part of the overall economy, managers will be more occupied with service productivity, and with blending services and manufacturing through the Internet. How can U.S. manufacturers and service organizations maintain a competitive edge? Most of them are:

- Focusing more on customers.
- Maintaining closer relationships with suppliers and other companies to satisfy customer needs.
- Practicing continuous improvement.[13]
- Focusing on quality.
- Saving on costs through site selection.
- Relying on the Internet to unite companies that work together.
- Adopting production techniques such as enterprise resource planning, computer-integrated manufacturing, flexible manufacturing, lean manufacturing, and robotics.

This chapter explores these and other operations management techniques in both the service and the manufacturing sectors. We'll begin by going over a few key terms.

LO 9–2   Describe the evolution from production to operations management.

FROM PRODUCTION TO OPERATIONS MANAGEMENT

Production is the creation of finished goods and services using the factors of production: land, labor, capital, entrepreneurship, and knowledge (see Chapter 1). Production has historically meant *manufacturing,* and the term **production management** has described the management activities that helped firms create *goods.* But the nature of business has changed significantly over the last 20 years as the service sector, including Internet services, has grown dramatically. *The United States has become a service economy—that is, one dominated by the service sector.*

Operations management is a term that is used in both manufacturing and service organizations. **Operations management** is a specialized area in management that converts or transforms resources, including human resources like technical skills and innovation, into goods and services. It includes inventory management, quality control, production scheduling, follow-up services, and more. In an automobile plant, operations management transforms raw materials, human resources, parts, supplies, paints, tools, and other resources into automobiles. It does this through the processes of fabrication and assembly.

In a college or university, operations management takes inputs—such as information, professors, supplies, buildings, offices, and computer systems—and creates services that transform students into educated people. It does this through a process called education. For a more extensive discussion, see the Free Management Library's entry on operations management (www.managementhelp.org/ops_mgnt/ops_mgnt.htm).

Some organizations—such as factories, farms, and mines—produce mostly goods. Others—such as hospitals, schools, and government agencies—produce mostly services. Still others produce a combination of goods

production
The creation of finished goods and services using the factors of production: land, labor, capital, entrepreneurship, and knowledge.

production management
The term used to describe all the activities managers do to help their firms create goods.

operations management
A specialized area in management that converts or transforms resources (including human resources) into goods and services.

Each year companies discover new ways of automating that eliminate the need for human labor. This robot demonstrates its ability to cook Okonomiyaki, a Japanese pancake. The robot can take verbal orders from customers and use standard kitchen utensils. Do you think there's a better chance the robot will get your order right than a human would?

and services. For example, an automobile manufacturer not only makes cars but also provides services such as repairs, financing, and insurance. At Wendy's you get goods such as hamburgers and fries, but you also get services such as order taking, order filling, food preparation, and cleanup.

Operations Management in the Service Sector

Operations management in the service industry is all about creating a good experience for those who use the service.[14] In a Ritz-Carlton hotel, for example, operations management includes restaurants that offer the finest in service, elevators that run smoothly, and a front desk that processes people quickly. It may include fresh-cut flowers in the lobbies and dishes of fruit in every room. More important, it may mean spending thousands of dollars to provide training in quality management for every new employee.

Ritz-Carlton's commitment to quality is apparent in the many innovations and changes the company has initiated over the years. These innovations included installation of a sophisticated computerized guest-recognition program and a quality management program designed to ensure that all employees are "certified" in their positions.

Hotel customers today want in-room Internet access and a help center with toll-free telephone service. Executives traveling on business may need video equipment and a host of computer hardware and other aids. At the International House in New Orleans, 16 rooms have Apple TV boxes so that mobile device-dependent clients can easily stream live video.[15]

Foreign visitors would like multilingual customer-support services. Hotel shops need to carry more than souvenirs, newspapers, and some drugstore and food items to serve today's high-tech travelers: the shops may also carry smartphone and laptop computer supplies, electrical adapters, and the like. Operations management is responsible for locating and providing such amenities to make customers happy. Ritz-Carlton uses an internal measurement system to assess the performance results of its service delivery system.

In short, delighting customers by anticipating their needs has become the quality standard for luxury hotels, as it has for most other service businesses.[16] But knowing customer needs and satisfying them are two different things. That's why operations management is so important: it is the implementation phase of management. Can you see the need for better operations management in airports, hospitals, government agencies, schools, and nonprofits like the Red Cross? The opportunities seem almost unlimited. Much of the future of U.S. growth is in these service areas, but growth is also needed in manufacturing. Next we'll explore production processes and what companies are doing to keep the United States competitive in that area.

test prep

- **What have U.S. manufacturers done to regain a competitive edge?**
- **What must U.S. companies do to continue to strengthen the country's manufacturing base?**
- **What led companies to focus on operations management rather than production?**

LO 9–3 Identify various production processes and describe techniques that improve productivity, including computer-aided design and manufacturing, flexible manufacturing, lean manufacturing, mass customization, and robotics.

PRODUCTION PROCESSES

Common sense and some experience have already taught you much of what you need to know about production processes. You know what it takes to write a term paper or prepare a dinner. You need money to buy the materials, you need a place to work, and you need to be organized to get the task done. The same is true of the production process in industry. It uses basic inputs to produce outputs (see Figure 9.1). Production adds value, or utility, to materials or processes.

Form utility is the value producers add to materials in the creation of finished goods and services, such as by transforming silicon into computer chips or putting services together to create a vacation package. Form utility can exist at the retail level as well. For example, a butcher can produce a specific cut of beef from a whole cow, or a baker can make a specific type of cake from basic ingredients. We'll be discussing utility in more detail in Chapter 15.

Manufacturers use several different processes to produce goods. Andrew S. Grove, the former chairman of computer chip manufacturer Intel, uses this analogy to explain production:

> Imagine that you're a chef . . . and that your task is to serve a breakfast consisting of a three-minute soft-boiled egg, buttered toast, and coffee. Your job is to prepare and deliver the three items simultaneously, each of them fresh and hot.

Grove says this task encompasses the three basic requirements of production: (1) to build and deliver products in response to the demands of the customer at a scheduled delivery time, (2) to provide an acceptable quality level, and (3) to provide everything at the lowest possible cost.

Let's use the breakfast example to understand process and assembly. **Process manufacturing** physically or chemically changes materials. For example, boiling physically changes the egg. Similarly, process manufacturing turns sand into glass or computer chips. The **assembly process** puts together components (eggs, toast, and coffee) to make a product (breakfast). Cars are made through an assembly process that puts together the frame, engine, and other parts.

Production processes are either continuous or intermittent. A **continuous process** is one in which long production runs turn out finished goods over time. As a chef, you could have a conveyor belt that continuously lowers eggs into boiling water for three minutes and then lifts them out. A three-minute egg would be available whenever you wanted one. A chemical plant, for example, is run on a continuous process.

form utility
The value producers add to materials in the creation of finished goods and services.

process manufacturing
That part of the production process that physically or chemically changes materials.

assembly process
That part of the production process that puts together components.

continuous process
A production process in which long production runs turn out finished goods over time.

FIGURE 9.1 THE PRODUCTION PROCESS
The production process consists of taking the factors of production (land, etc.) and using those inputs to produce goods, services, and ideas. Planning, routing, scheduling, and the other activities are the means to accomplish the objective—output.

It usually makes more sense when responding to specific customer orders to use an **intermittent process**. Here the production run is short (one or two eggs) and the producer adjusts machines frequently to make different products (like the oven in a bakery or the toaster in a diner). Manufacturers of custom-designed furniture would use an intermittent process.

Today many manufacturers use intermittent processes. Computers, robots, and flexible manufacturing processes allow firms to turn out custom-made goods almost as fast as mass-produced goods were once produced. We'll discuss how they do that in more detail in the next few sections as we explore advanced production techniques and technology.

The Need to Improve Production Techniques and Cut Costs

The ultimate goal of operations management is to provide high-quality goods and services instantaneously in response to customer demand. As we stress throughout this book, traditional organizations were simply not designed to be so responsive to the customer. Rather, they were designed to make goods efficiently (inexpensively). The idea behind mass production was to make a large number of a limited variety of products at very low cost.

Over the years, low cost often came at the expense of quality and flexibility. Furthermore, suppliers didn't always deliver when they said they would, so manufacturers had to carry large inventories of raw materials and components to keep producing. Such inefficiencies made U.S. companies vulnerable to foreign competitors who were using more advanced production techniques and less expensive labor.

As a result of new global competition, companies have had to make a wide variety of high-quality custom-designed products at low cost. Clearly, something had to change on the production floor to make that possible. Several major developments have made U.S. companies more competitive: (1) computer-aided design and manufacturing, (2) flexible manufacturing, (3) lean manufacturing, (4) mass customization, and (5) robotics.

Computer-Aided Design and Manufacturing

One development that has changed production techniques is the integration of computers into the design and manufacturing of products. The first thing computers did was help in the design of products, in a process called **computer-aided design (CAD)**. Autodesk makes a fully operational computer-aided design software program called 123 Design that's free and allows individuals to do things that automakers once required mainframe computers to do.[17]

The next step was to bring computers directly into the production process with **computer-aided manufacturing (CAM)**. CAD/CAM, the use of both computer-aided design and computer-aided manufacturing, makes it possible to custom-design products to meet the needs of small markets with very little increase in cost. A manufacturer programs the computer to make a simple design change, and that change is readily incorporated into production. In the clothing industry, a computer program establishes a pattern and cuts the cloth automatically, even adjusting to a specific person's dimensions to create custom-cut clothing at little additional cost. In food service, CAM supports on-site, small-scale, semiautomated, sensor-controlled

---

intermittent process
A production process in which the production run is short and the machines are changed frequently to make different products.

computer-aided design (CAD)
The use of computers in the design of products.

computer-aided manufacturing (CAM)
The use of computers in the manufacturing of products.

Bakers, like Duff Goldman of Charm City Cakes, add form utility to materials by transforming basic ingredients into special customized cakes. Can you see how the production of such cakes involves both process manufacturing and assembly processes?

baking in fresh-baked cookie shops to make consistent quality easy to achieve. Of course, 3D printers are among the latest CAM technology. A product is made layer by layer until it appears, almost by magic, as a finished good.

CAD has doubled productivity in many firms. In the past CAD machines couldn't talk to CAM machines directly. Today, however, software programs unite CAD and CAM: the result is **computer-integrated manufacturing (CIM)**. The software is expensive, but it cuts as much as 80 percent of the time needed to program machines to make parts. The printing company JohnsByrne uses CIM in its Niles, Illinois, plant and has noticed decreased overhead, reduced outlay of resources, and fewer errors. Consult the *International Journal of Computer Integrated Manufacturing* for other examples.

Flexible Manufacturing

Flexible manufacturing means designing machines to do multiple tasks so they can produce a variety of products. Allen-Bradley uses flexible manufacturing to build motor starters. Orders come in daily, and within 24 hours the company's 26 machines and robots manufacture, test, and package the starters—which are untouched by human hands. Allen-Bradley's machines are so flexible that managers can include a special order, even a single item, in the assembly without slowing down the process. Did you notice that these products were made without any labor? One way to compete with cheap overseas labor is to have as few workers as possible.

3-D CAD tools allow designers to create cloth prototypes without a pattern's traditional stages: seaming, trying on, alterations, etc. What advantages might this technology offer to smaller manufacturing companies?

Lean Manufacturing

Lean manufacturing is the production of goods using less of everything than in mass production: less human effort, less manufacturing space, less investment in tools, and less engineering time to develop a new product.[18] A company becomes lean by continuously increasing its capacity to produce high-quality goods while decreasing its need for resources.[19] Here are some characteristics of lean companies:

- They take half the human effort.
- They have half the defects in the finished product or service.
- They require one-third the engineering effort.
- They use half the floor space for the same output.
- They carry 90 percent less inventory.

Technological improvements are largely responsible for the increase in productivity and efficiency of U.S. plants. That technology made labor more productive and made it possible to pay higher wages. On the other hand, employees can get frustrated by innovations (e.g., they must learn new processes), and companies must constantly train and retrain employees to stay competitive. The need for more productivity and efficiency has never been

computer-integrated manufacturing (CIM)
The uniting of computer-aided design with computer-aided manufacturing.

flexible manufacturing
Designing machines to do multiple tasks so that they can produce a variety of products.

lean manufacturing
The production of goods using less of everything compared to mass production.

greater. The solution to growing the economy depends on such innovations. One step in the process is to make products more individualistic. The next section discusses how that happens.

Mass Customization

To *customize* means to make a unique product or provide a specific service to specific individuals. Although it once may have seemed impossible, **mass customization**, which means tailoring products to meet the needs of a large number of individual customers, is now practiced widely. The National Bicycle Industrial Company in Japan makes 18 bicycle models in more than 2 million combinations, each designed to fit the needs of a specific customer. The customer chooses the model, size, color, and design. The retailer takes various measurements from the buyer and faxes the data to the factory, where robots handle the bulk of the assembly.

More and more manufacturers are learning to customize their products. Some colleges, even, are developing promotions for individual students. Some General Nutrition Center (GNC) stores feature machines that enable shoppers to custom-design their own vitamins, shampoo, and lotions. The Custom Foot stores use infrared scanners to precisely measure each foot so that shoes can be made to fit perfectly. Adidas can make each shoe fit perfectly for each customer. You can even buy custom-made M&M's in colors of your choice. See the Spotlight on Small Business box for a unique way of using mass customization.

Mass customization exists in the service sector as well. Capital Protective Insurance (CPI) uses the latest computer software and hardware to sell customized risk-management plans to companies. Health clubs offer unique fitness programs for individuals, travel agencies provide vacation packages that vary according to individual choices, and some colleges allow students to design their own majors. It is much easier to custom-design service programs than to custom-make goods, because there is no fixed tangible good to adapt. Each customer can specify what he or she wants, within the limits of the service organization—limits that seem to be ever-widening.

Not only can you customize the colors of your M&M's, you can also have personal messages and/or images imprinted on them. What other customized products can you think of?

Robotics

Industrial robotics can work 24 hours a day, seven days a week with great precision. Mass customization is no problem for them. At least no one has heard them complain. Of course, robots *do* replace people on the assembly line, but most of those jobs are dirty or so repetitive that robots are necessary, or at least helpful.[20] No doubt you have heard or seen robots that help doctors perform the most delicate of procedures.[21] In other words robots are slowly, but surely either helping people perform better or are replacing them completely. Soon we may be entering what could be known as the robot economy.[22] Most people think that China is so successful because of cheap labor, but China may soon be the world's largest robot market.[23]

Make Your Own Kind of Music

Kevin Tully is the first to admit he's no Jimi Hendrix when it comes to playing a guitar. Still, as a lifelong guitar player he considered his two guitars priceless and true extensions of himself. While studying for the bar exam, he contacted his music-loving friend Dave Barry with an idea about starting a business where fellow guitar players had the opportunity to create their own custom guitars.

After attracting start-up capital of $25,000 from the business incubator at his alma mater Northeastern University, Moniker Guitars was born. While custom-made guitars were not a new idea, the reality was everyday musicians did not have the money or reputation to create their own

signature style guitar. Tully believed that by using mass customization, Moniker could follow Nike's model called NikeiD that lets consumers customize their shoes. By using online design tools and advanced manufacturing techniques, Moniker was able to produce top-quality, personalized guitars for what a guitar player would pay for a generic model.

Today, Moniker's website lets guitar pickers customize their instruments using color and graphics, as well as hardware and pickups. The company is the first in the country to use PPG paint on its guitars—the same paint used by Lamborgini and Ferrari automobiles. If polka dots are your passion, or tiger stripes turn you on, Moniker will deliver. According to Kevin Tully, "Every design is different. You never paint the same guitar twice. Every day is a new project. I love it."

Sources: Sandra Zaragoza, "Boston Duo Starts Customized Guitar Shop in Austin," *Austin Business Journal*, July 23, 2012; and Chris Raymond, "Design Your Own Guitar—This Startup Will Build It," *Popular Mechanics*, February 7, 2014.

Using Sensing, Measurement, and Process Control

Most advanced manufacturing techniques are driven by computers working with vast amounts of data. Such data controls sensors that measure humidity, global positioning trackers (that fix location), or calipers that measure a material's thickness. Products can be tracked from the beginning of production to the point of delivery. The moment anything goes wrong, a sensor can detect it immediately and notify someone to make the needed changes.[24] Companies are also using nanomanufacturing. A nanometer is one-billionth of a meter, so nanomanufacturing means being able to manipulate materials on a molecular or even atomic scale.[25]

- What is form utility?
- Define and differentiate the following: process manufacturing, assembly process, continuous process, and intermittent process.
- What do you call the integration of CAD and CAM?
- What is mass customization?

LO 9–4 Describe operations management planning issues including facility location, facility layout, materials requirement planning, purchasing, just-in-time inventory control, and quality control.

OPERATIONS MANAGEMENT PLANNING

Operations management planning helps solve many of the problems in the service and manufacturing sectors. These include facility location, facility layout, materials requirement planning, purchasing, inventory control, and quality control. The resources used may be different, but the management issues are similar.

Facility Location

facility location
The process of selecting a geographic location for a company's operations.

Facility location is the process of selecting a geographic location for a company's operations. In keeping with the need to focus on customers, one strategy is to find a site that makes it easy for consumers to use the company's services and to communicate about their needs. Flower shops and banks have placed facilities in supermarkets so that their products and services are more accessible than in freestanding facilities. You can find a McDonald's inside some Walmart stores and gas stations. Customers order and pay for their meals at the pumps, and by the time they've filled their tanks, it's time to pick up their food.

The ultimate in convenience is never having to leave home to get services. That's why there is so much interest in Internet banking, Internet shopping, online education, and other services. Internet commerce is now using Facebook and other social media to make transactions even easier. For brick-and-mortar retailers to beat such competition, they have to choose good locations and offer outstanding service. Study the location of service-sector businesses—such as hotels, banks, athletic clubs, and supermarkets—and you'll see that

Facility location is a major decision for manufacturing and other companies. The decision involves taking into account the availability of qualified workers; access to suppliers, customers, and transportation; and local regulations including zoning and taxes. How has the growth of commerce on the Internet affected company location decisions?

the most successful are conveniently located. Google is building large data centers in the United States where states give out tax breaks and cheap electricity is readily available in large quantities. They are also located near bodies of water for cooling their servers.

Facility Location for Manufacturers

Geographic shifts in production sometimes result in pockets of unemployment in some geographic areas and tremendous growth in others. We are witnessing such changes in the United States, as automobile and tractor production has shifted to more southern cities.[26]

Why would companies spend millions of dollars to move their facilities from one location to another? In their decisions they consider labor costs; availability of resources, including labor; access to transportation that can reduce time to market; proximity to suppliers; proximity to customers; crime rates; quality of life for employees; cost of living; and the need to train or retrain the local workforce.

Even though labor is becoming a smaller percentage of total cost in highly automated industries, availability of low-cost labor or the right kind of skilled labor remained a key reason many producers moved their plants to Malaysia, China, India, Mexico, and other countries. In general, however, U.S. manufacturing firms tend to pay more and offer more benefits than local firms elsewhere in the world.

Inexpensive resources are another major reason for moving production facilities. Companies usually need water, electricity, wood, coal, and other basic resources. By moving to areas where these are inexpensive and plentiful, firms can significantly lower not only the cost of buying such resources but also the cost of shipping finished products. Often the most important resource is people, so companies tend to cluster where smart and talented people are. Witness Silicon Valley in California and similar areas in Colorado, Massachusetts, Virginia, Texas, Maryland, and other states.

Time-to-market is another decision-making factor. As manufacturers attempt to compete globally, they need sites that allow products to move quickly, at the lowest costs, so they can be delivered to customers fast. Access to highways, rail lines, waterways, and airports is thus critical.[27] Information technology (IT) is also important to quicken response time, so many firms are seeking countries with the most advanced information systems.

Another way to work closely with suppliers to satisfy customers' needs is to locate production facilities near supplier facilities. That cuts the cost of distribution and makes communication easier.

Many businesses are building factories in foreign countries to get closer to their international customers. That's a major reason the Japanese automaker Honda builds cars in Ohio and the German company Mercedes builds them in Alabama. When U.S. firms select foreign sites, they consider whether they are near airports, waterways, and highways so that raw and finished goods can move quickly and easily.

Businesses also study the quality of life for workers and managers. Are good schools nearby? Is the weather nice? Is the crime rate low? Does the local community welcome new businesses? Do the chief executive and other key managers want to live there? Sometimes a region with a high quality of life is also an expensive one, which complicates the decision. In short, facility location has become a critical issue in operations management. The Making Ethical Decisions box looks at the kinds of decisions companies must make when it comes to locating.

Taking Operations Management to the Internet

Many rapidly growing companies do very little production themselves. Instead, they outsource engineering, design, manufacturing, and other tasks to companies such as Flextronics and Sanmina-SCI that specialize in those functions. They create new relationships with suppliers over the Internet, making operations management an *interfirm* process in which companies work closely together to design, produce, and ship products to customers.

Manufacturing companies are developing Internet-focused strategies that will enable them and others to compete more effectively in the future. These changes are having a dramatic effect on operations managers as they adjust from a one-firm system to an *interfirm* environment and from a relatively stable environment to one that is constantly changing and evolving.

Facility Location in the Future

Information technology (IT)—that is, computers, modems, e-mail, voice mail, text messaging, teleconferencing, etc.—is giving firms and employees increased flexibility to choose locations while staying in the competitive mainstream. **Telecommuting**, working from home via computer, is a major trend in business. Companies that no longer need to locate near sources of labor will be able to move to areas where land is less expensive and the quality of life may be higher. Furthermore, more salespeople are keeping in touch with the company and its customers through videoconferencing, using computers to talk with and show images to others.[28]

One big incentive to locate in a particular city or state is the tax situation there and degree of government support. Some states and local governments have higher taxes than others, yet many compete fiercely by offering companies tax reductions and other support, such as zoning changes and financial aid, so they will locate there. Have you seen, for example, the ads for entrepreneurs to locate in New York State? They are offering no taxes for 10 years. Some people would like the federal government to offer financial incentives—beyond what is already being offered by state and local agencies—to various manufacturing companies to build factories in the United States.

Facility Layout

Facility layout is the physical arrangement of resources, including people, to most efficiently produce goods and provide services for customers. Facility

telecommuting
Working from home via computer.

facility layout
The physical arrangement of resources (including people) in the production process.

materials requirement planning (MRP)
A computer-based operations management system that uses sales forecasts to make sure that needed parts and materials are available at the right time and place.

layout depends greatly on the processes that are to be performed. For services, the layout is usually designed to help the consumer find and buy things, including on the Internet. Some stores have kiosks that enable customers to search for goods online and place orders or make returns and credit payments in the store. In short, the facilities and Internet capabilities of service organizations are becoming more customer-oriented.

Some service-oriented organizations, such as hospitals, use layouts that improve efficiency, just as manufacturers do. For manufacturing plants, facilities layout has become critical because cost savings of efficient layouts are enormous.

Many companies are moving from an *assembly-line layout,* in which workers do only a few tasks at a time, to a *modular layout,* in which teams of workers combine to produce more complex units of the final product. There may have been a dozen or more workstations on an assembly line to complete an automobile engine in the past, but all that work might be done in one module today.

When working on a major project, such as a bridge or an airplane, companies use a *fixed-position layout* that allows workers to congregate around the product to be completed.

A *process layout* is one in which similar equipment and functions are grouped together. The order in which the product visits a function depends on the design of the item. This allows for flexibility. The Igus manufacturing plant in Cologne, Germany, can shrink or expand in a flash. Its flexible design keeps it competitive in a fast-changing market. Because the layout of the plant changes so often, some employees use scooters in order to more efficiently provide needed skills, supplies, and services to multiple workstations. A fast-changing plant needs a fast-moving employee base to achieve maximum productivity. Figure 9.2 illustrates typical layout designs.

Materials Requirement Planning

Materials requirement planning (MRP) is a computer-based operations management system that uses sales forecasts to make sure needed parts and materials are available at the right time and place. **Enterprise resource planning (ERP),** a newer version of MRP, combines the computerized functions of all the divisions and subsidiaries of the firm—such as finance, human resources, and order fulfillment—into a single integrated software program that uses a single database. The result is shorter time between orders and payment, less staff needed to do ordering and order processing, reduced inventories, and better customer service. For example, the customer can place an order, either through a customer service representative or online, and immediately see when the order will be filled and how much it will cost. The representative can instantly see the customer's credit rating and order history, the company's inventory, and the shipping schedule. Everyone else in the company can see the new order as well; thus when one department finishes its portion, the order is automatically routed via the ERP system to the next department. The customer can see exactly where the order is at any point by logging into the system.

At Cisco Systems, work spaces in some offices are fluid and unassigned, so employees with laptops and mobile phones can choose where to sit when they arrive each day. What do you think are some of the advantages of such nontraditional facility layouts? Are there any disadvantages?

enterprise resource planning (ERP)
A newer version of materials requirement planning (MRP) that combines the computerized functions of all the divisions and subsidiaries of the firm—such as finance, human resources, and order fulfillment—into a single integrated software program that uses a single database.

FIGURE 9.2 TYPICAL LAYOUT DESIGNS

PRODUCT LAYOUT (also called Assembly-Line Layout)
Used to produce large quantities of a few types of products.

PROCESS LAYOUT
Frequently used in operations that serve different customers' different needs.

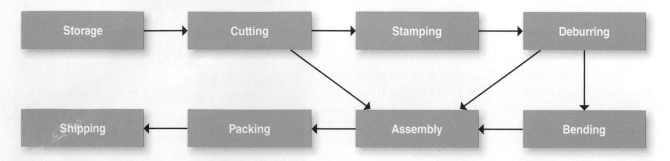

CELLULAR or MODULE LAYOUT
Can accommodate changes in design or customer demand.

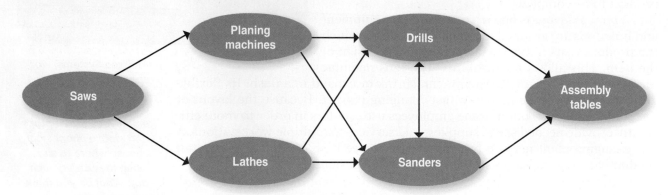

FIXED-POSITION LAYOUT
A major feature of planning is scheduling work operations.

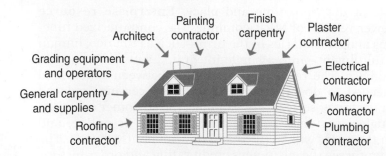

Purchasing

Purchasing is the function that searches for high-quality material resources, finds the best suppliers, and negotiates the best price for quality goods and services. In the past, manufacturers dealt with many suppliers so that if one couldn't deliver, the firm could get materials from someone else. Today, however, manufacturers rely more heavily on just one or two suppliers, because the relationship between suppliers and manufacturers is much closer than before. Producers share so much information that they don't want too many suppliers knowing their business.

The Internet has transformed the purchasing function. A business looking for supplies can contact an Internet-based purchasing service and find the best items at the best price. Similarly, a company wishing to sell supplies can use the Internet to find all the companies looking for such supplies. The time and dollar cost of purchasing items has thus been reduced tremendously.

purchasing
The function in a firm that searches for high-quality material resources, finds the best suppliers, and negotiates the best price for goods and services.

Just-in-Time Inventory Control

One major cost of production is the expense of holding parts, motors, and other items in storage for later use. Storage not only subjects items to obsolescence, pilferage, and damage but also requires construction and maintenance of costly warehouses. To cut such costs, many companies have implemented a concept called **just-in-time (JIT) inventory control**. JIT systems keep a minimum of inventory on the premises—and deliver parts, supplies, and other needs just in time to go on the assembly line. To work effectively, however, the process requires an accurate production schedule (using ERP) and excellent coordination with carefully selected suppliers, who are usually connected electronically so they know what will be needed and when. Sometimes the suppliers build new facilities close to the main producer to minimize distribution time. JIT runs into problems when suppliers are farther away. Weather may delay shipments, for example. You saw the problems that emerged when weather (earthquakes and the resulting tsunami) disrupted the supply chain of materials from Japan to the United States in 2011. JIT systems make sure the right materials are at the right place at the right time at the cheapest cost to meet both customer and production needs. That's a key step in modern production innovation.

just-in-time (JIT) inventory control
A production process in which a minimum of inventory is kept on the premises and parts, supplies, and other needs are delivered just in time to go on the assembly line.

Quality Control

Maintaining **quality** means consistently producing what the customer wants while reducing errors before and after delivery. In the past, firms often conducted quality control at the end of the production line. Products were completed first and then tested for quality. This resulted in several problems:

1. The need to inspect work required extra people and resources.
2. If an error was found, someone had to correct the mistake or scrap the product. This, of course, was costly.
3. If the customer found the mistake, he or she might be dissatisfied and might even buy from another firm thereafter.

quality
Consistently producing what the customer wants while reducing errors before and after delivery to the customer.

Such problems led to the realization that quality is not an outcome; it is a never-ending process of continually improving what a company produces. Quality control should thus be part of the operations management planning process rather than simply an end-of-the-line inspection.

Nestlé Purina was awarded a Baldrige. What's that?

It's like Best in Show, but for businesses.

Nestlé Purina Petcare Company wishes to thank our associates, customers, and business partners for helping us be our best. We are honored to be the first consumer package goods company to receive the Malcolm Baldrige National Quality Award for organizational performance excellence, and share our success with the community.

Malcolm Baldrige National Quality Award 2010 Award Recipient

PURINA.
Your Pet, Our Passion

www.purina.com • www.nestlepurinacareers.com

The Nestlé Purina PetCare Company, headquartered in St. Louis, received the Malcolm Baldrige National Quality Award in the manufacturing category. What quality criteria do you think the award was based on?

Companies have turned to the use of modern quality-control standards such as Six Sigma. **Six Sigma quality**, which sets a benchmark of just 3.4 defects per million opportunities, detects potential problems to prevent their occurrence. That's important to a company that makes 4 million transactions a day, like some banks.

Statistical quality control (SQC) is the process some managers use to continually monitor all phases of the production process and ensure quality is being built into the product from the beginning. **Statistical process control (SPC)** is the process of testing statistical samples of product components at each stage of production and plotting the test results on a graph. Managers can thus see and correct any deviation from quality standards. Making sure products meet standards all along the production process reduces the need for a quality-control inspection at the end because mistakes are caught much earlier in the process. SQC and SPC thus save companies much time and money.

Some companies use a quality-control approach called the Deming cycle (after the late W. Edwards Deming, the father of the movement toward quality). Its steps are Plan, Do, Check, Act (PDCA). Again, the idea is to find potential errors *before* they happen.

U.S. businesses are getting serious about providing top customer service, and many are already doing it. Service organizations are finding it difficult to provide outstanding service every time because the process is so labor-intensive. Physical goods (e.g., a gold ring) can be designed and manufactured to near perfection. However, it is hard to reach such perfection when designing and providing a service experience such as a dance on a cruise ship or a cab drive through New York City.

The Baldrige Awards

A standard was set for overall company quality with the introduction of the Malcolm Baldrige National Quality Awards, named in honor of a former U.S. secretary of commerce. Companies can apply for these awards in each of the following areas: manufacturing, services, small businesses, nonprofit/government, education, and health care.

To qualify, an organization has to show quality in key areas such as leadership, strategic planning, customer and market focus, information and analysis, human resources focus, process management, and business results. Major criteria for earning the award include whether customer wants and needs are being met and whether customer satisfaction ratings are better than those of competitors. As you can see, the focus is shifting away from just making quality goods and services to providing top-quality customer service in all respects.

ISO 9000 and ISO 14000 Standards

The International Organization for Standardization (ISO) is a worldwide federation of national standards bodies from more than 140 countries that set global measures for the quality of individual products. ISO is a

Six Sigma quality
A quality measure that allows only 3.4 defects per million opportunities.

statistical quality control (SQC)
The process some managers use to continually monitor all phases of the production process to ensure that quality is being built into the product from the beginning.

nongovernmental organization established to promote the development of world standards to facilitate the international exchange of goods and services. (ISO is not an acronym. It comes from the Greek word *isos,* meaning "oneness.") **ISO 9000** is the common name given to quality management and assurance standards.

The standards require that a company determine what customer needs are, including regulatory and legal requirements, and make communication arrangements to handle issues such as complaints. Other standards cover process control, product testing, storage, and delivery.

What makes ISO 9000 so important is that the European Union (EU) demands that companies that want to do business with the EU be certified by ISO standards. Some major U.S. companies are also demanding that suppliers meet these standards. Several accreditation agencies in Europe and the United States will certify that a company meets the standards for all phases of its operations, from product development through production and testing to installation.

ISO 14000 is a collection of the best practices for managing an organization's impact on the environment. As an environmental management system, it does not prescribe a performance level. Requirements for certification include having an environmental policy, having specific improvement targets, conducting audits of environmental programs, and maintaining top management review of the processes.

Certification in both ISO 9000 and ISO 14000 would show that a firm has a world-class management system in both quality and environmental standards. In the past, firms assigned employees separately to meet each set of standards. Today, ISO 9000 and 14000 standards have been blended so that an organization can work on both at once. ISO is now compiling social responsibility guidelines to go with the other standards.

statistical process control (SPC)
The process of testing statistical samples of product components at each stage of the production process and plotting those results on a graph. Any variances from quality standards are recognized and can be corrected if beyond the set standards.

ISO 9000
The common name given to quality management and assurance standards.

ISO 14000
A collection of the best practices for managing an organization's impact on the environment.

test prep

- What are the major criteria for facility location?
- What is the difference between MRP and ERP?
- What is just-in-time inventory control?
- What are Six Sigma quality, the Baldrige Award, ISO 9000, and ISO 14000?

LO 9–5   Explain the use of PERT and Gantt charts to control manufacturing processes.

CONTROL PROCEDURES: PERT AND GANTT CHARTS

Operations managers must ensure products are manufactured and delivered on time, on budget, and to specifications. How can managers be sure all will go smoothly and be completed by the required time? One popular technique for monitoring the progress of production was developed in the 1950s for

program evaluation and review technique (PERT)
A method for analyzing the tasks involved in completing a given project, estimating the time needed to complete each task, and identifying the minimum time needed to complete the total project.

critical path
In a PERT network, the sequence of tasks that takes the longest time to complete.

Gantt chart
Bar graph showing production managers what projects are being worked on and what stage they are in at any given time.

constructing nuclear submarines: the **program evaluation and review technique (PERT)**. PERT users analyze the tasks to complete a given project, estimate the time needed to complete each, and compute the minimum time needed to complete the whole project.

The steps used in PERT are (1) analyzing and sequencing tasks that need to be done, (2) estimating the time needed to complete each task, (3) drawing a PERT network illustrating the information from steps 1 and 2, and (4) identifying the critical path. The **critical path** is the sequence of tasks that takes the longest time to complete. We use the word *critical* because a delay anywhere along this path will cause the project or production run to be late.

Figure 9.3 illustrates a PERT chart for producing a music video. The squares indicate completed tasks, and the arrows indicate the time needed to complete each. The path from one completed task to another illustrates the relationships among tasks; the arrow from "set designed" to "set materials purchased" indicates we must design the set before we can purchase the materials. The critical path, indicated by the bold black arrows, shows producing the set takes more time than auditioning dancers, choreographing dances, or designing and making costumes. The project manager now knows it's critical that set construction remain on schedule if the project is to be completed on time, but short delays in dance and costume preparation are unlikely to delay it.

A PERT network can be made up of thousands of events over many months. Today, this complex procedure is done by computer. Another, more basic strategy manufacturers use for measuring production progress is a Gantt chart. A **Gantt chart** (named for its developer, Henry L. Gantt) is a bar graph, now also prepared by computer, that clearly shows what projects are being worked on and how much has been completed at any given time. Figure 9.4, a

FIGURE 9.3 PERT CHART FOR A MUSIC VIDEO

The minimum amount of time it will take to produce this video is 15 weeks. To get that number, you add the week it takes to pick a star and a song to the four weeks to design a set, the two weeks to purchase set materials, the six weeks to construct the set, the week of rehearsals, and the final week when the video is made. That's the critical path. Any delay in that process will delay the final video.

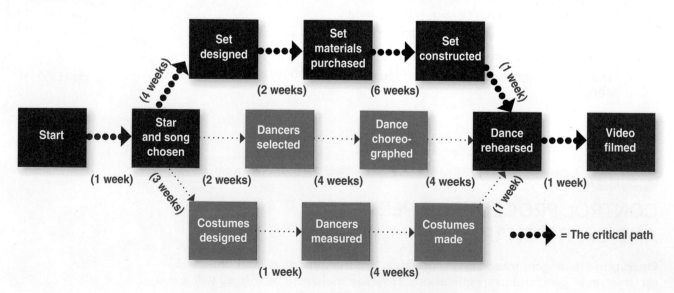

Gantt chart for a doll manufacturer, shows that the dolls' heads and bodies should be completed before the clothing is sewn. It also shows that at the end of week 3, the dolls' bodies are ready, but the heads are about half a week behind. Using a Gantt-like computer program, a manager can trace the production process minute by minute to determine which tasks are on time and which are behind, so that adjustments can be made to allow the company to stay on schedule.

PREPARING FOR THE FUTURE

The United States remains a major industrial country, but competition grows stronger each year. Tremendous opportunities exist for careers in operations management as both manufacturing and service companies fight to stay competitive. Students who can see future trends and have the skills to own or work in tomorrow's highly automated factories and modern service facilities will benefit.

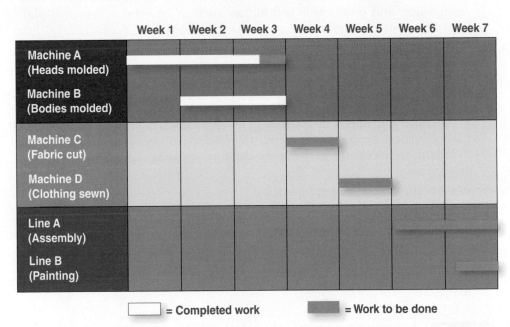

FIGURE 9.4 GANTT CHART FOR A DOLL MANUFACTURER

A Gantt chart enables a production manager to see at a glance when projects are scheduled to be completed and what the status is now. For example, the dolls' heads and bodies should be completed before the clothing is sewn, but they could be a little late as long as everything is ready for assembly in week 6. This chart shows that at the end of week 3, the dolls' bodies are ready, but the heads are about half a week behind.

□ = Completed work   ▬ = Work to be done

- Draw a **PERT** chart for making a breakfast of three-minute eggs, buttered toast, and coffee. Define the critical path.
- How could you use a Gantt chart to keep track of production?

summary

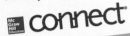

LO 9–1   Describe the current state of U.S. manufacturing and what manufacturers have done to become more competitive.

- **What is the current state of manufacturing in the United States?**
  Activity in the nation's manufacturing sector has declined since its height. The result has been fewer jobs in manufacturing. Even though manufacturing companies offer fewer jobs, they have become more productive, meaning that they need fewer employees to do the same amount of work. Today many manufacturing jobs are coming back to the U.S. as labor costs increase in other countries. Much of this chapter is devoted to showing you what manufacturers and service providers can do to revive the U.S. economy to become world-class competitors.

- **What have U.S. manufacturers done to achieve increased output?**
  U.S. manufacturers have increased output by emphasizing close relationships with suppliers and other companies to satisfy customer needs; continuous improvement; quality; site selection; use of the Internet to unite companies; and production techniques such as enterprise resource planning, computer-integrated manufacturing, flexible manufacturing, lean manufacturing, and robotics.

LO 9–2   Describe the evolution from production to operations management.

- **What is production management?**
  Production management consists of all the activities managers do to help their firms create goods. To reflect the change in importance from manufacturing to services, the term *production* is often replaced by the term *operations*.

- **What is operations management?**
  Operations management is the specialized area in management that converts or transforms resources, including human resources, into goods and services.

- **What kind of firms use operations managers?**
  Firms in both the manufacturing and service sectors use operations managers.

LO 9–3   Identify various production processes and describe techniques that improve productivity, including computer-aided design and manufacturing, flexible manufacturing, lean manufacturing, mass customization, and robotics.

- **What is process manufacturing, and how does it differ from assembly processes?**
  Process manufacturing physically or chemically changes materials. Assembly processes put together components.

- **How do CAD/CAM systems work?**
  Design changes made in computer-aided design (CAD) are instantly incorporated into the computer-aided manufacturing (CAM) process. The linking of CAD and CAM is computer-integrated manufacturing (CIM).

- **What is flexible manufacturing?**
  Flexible manufacturing means designing machines to produce a variety of products.

- **What is lean manufacturing?**
  Lean manufacturing is the production of goods using less of everything than in mass production: less human effort, less manufacturing space, less investment in tools, and less engineering time to develop a new product.

- **What is mass customization?**
  Mass customization means making custom-designed goods and services for a large number of individual customers. Flexible manufacturing makes mass customization possible. Given the exact needs of a customer, flexible machines can produce a customized good as fast as mass-produced goods were once made. Mass customization is also important in service industries.

- **How do robotics help make manufacturers more competitive?**
  Industrial robotics can work 24 hours a day, seven days a week, with great precision. Most of the jobs they replace are dirty or so repetitive that robots are necessary, or at least helpful.

LO 9–4 Describe operations management planning issues including facility location, facility layout, materials requirement planning, purchasing, just-in-time inventory control, and quality control.

- **What is facility location and how does it differ from facility layout?**
  Facility location is the process of selecting a geographic location for a company's operations. Facility layout is the physical arrangement of resources, including people, to produce goods and services effectively and efficiently.

- **How do managers evaluate different sites?**
  Labor costs and land costs are two major criteria for selecting the right sites. Other criteria include whether resources are plentiful and inexpensive, skilled workers are available or are trainable, taxes are low and the local government offers support, energy and water are available, transportation costs are low, and the quality of life and of education are high.

- **What relationship do materials requirement planning (MRP) and enterprise resource planning (ERP) have with the production process?**
  MRP is a computer-based operations management system that uses sales forecasts to make sure the needed parts and materials are available at the right time and place. Enterprise resource planning (ERP), a newer version of MRP, combines the computerized functions of all the divisions and subsidiaries of the firm—such as finance, material requirements planning, human resources, and order fulfillment—into a single integrated software program that uses a single database. The result is shorter time between orders and payment, less staff to do ordering and order processing, reduced inventories, and better customer service for all the firms involved.

- **What is just-in-time (JIT) inventory control?**
  JIT requires suppliers to deliver parts and materials just in time to go on the assembly line so they don't have to be stored in warehouses.

- **What is Six Sigma quality?**
  Six Sigma quality sets standards at just 3.4 defects per million opportunities and detects potential problems before they occur. Statistical quality control (SQC) is the process some managers use to continually monitor all processes in the production process and ensure quality is being built into the product from the beginning. Statistical process control (SPC) tests statistical samples of product components at each stage of the production process and plots the results on a graph so managers can recognize and correct deviations from quality standards.

- **What quality standards do firms use in the United States?**
  To qualify for the Malcolm Baldrige National Quality Award, a company must demonstrate quality in seven key areas: leadership, strategic planning, customer and market focus, information and analysis, human resources focus, process management, and business results. International standards U.S. firms strive to meet include ISO 9000 and ISO 14000. The first is a world standard for quality and the second is a collection of the best practices for managing an organization's impact on the environment.

LO 9–5   Explain the use of PERT and Gantt charts to control manufacturing processes.

- **Is there any relationship between a PERT chart and a Gantt chart?**
  Figure 9.3 shows a PERT chart. Figure 9.4 shows a Gantt chart. Whereas PERT is a tool used for planning, a Gantt chart is a tool used to measure progress.

key terms

assembly process 247

computer-aided design (CAD) 248

computer-aided manufacturing (CAM) 248

computer-integrated manufacturing (CIM) 249

continuous process 247

critical path 260

enterprise resource planning(ERP) 255

facility layout 254

facility location 252

flexible manufacturing 249

form utility 247

Gantt chart 260

intermittent process 248

ISO 14000 259

ISO 9000 259

just-in-time (JIT) inventory control 257

lean manufacturing 249

mass customization 250

materials requirement planning (MRP) 254

operations management 245

process manufacturing 247

production 245

production management 245

program evaluation and review technique (PERT) 260

purchasing 257

quality 257

Six Sigma quality 258

statistical process control (SPC) 259

statistical quality control (SQC) 258

telecommuting 254

critical thinking

1. Workers on the manufacturing floor are being replaced by robots and other machines. On the one hand, this lets companies compete with cheap labor from other countries. On the other hand, automation eliminates many jobs. Are you concerned that automation may increase unemployment or underemployment in the United States and around the world? Why or why not?

2. Computer-integrated manufacturing (CIM) has revolutionized the production process. What will such changes mean for the clothing industry, the shoe industry, and other fashion-related industries? What will they mean for other consumer and industrial goods industries? How will you benefit as a consumer?

3. One way to create new jobs in the United States is to increase innovation among new graduates from engineering and the sciences. How can the United States motivate more students to major in those areas?

developing **workplace skills**

Key: ● **Team**   ★ **Analytic**   ▲ **Communication**   ▣ **Technology**

1. Choosing the right location for a manufacturing plant or a service organization is often critical to its success. Form small groups and have each group member pick one manufacturing plant or one service organization in town and list at least three reasons why its location helps or hinders its success. If its location is not ideal, what would be a better one?   ●★▲

2. In teams of four or five, discuss the need for better operations management in the airline industry. Have the team develop a report listing (a) problems team members have encountered in traveling by air and (b) suggestions for improving operations so such problems won't occur in the future.   ●★▲

3. Discuss some of the advantages and disadvantages of producing goods overseas using inexpensive labor. Summarize the moral and ethical dimensions of this practice.   ★▲

4. Think of any production facility at your school, such as a sandwich shop, library, or copy center, and redesign the layout (make a pencil sketch) to more effectively serve customers and allow employees to be more effective and efficient.   ★▲

5. Think about recent experiences you have had with service organizations and select one in which you had to wait for an unreasonable length of time to get what you wanted. Describe what happens when customers are inconvenienced, and explain how management could make the operation more efficient and customer-oriented.   ★▲

taking it to the **net**

PURPOSE

To illustrate production processes.

EXERCISE

Take a virtual tour of the Hershey Foods Corporation's chocolate factory by going to www.hersheys.com/discover/tour_video.asp.

1. Does Hershey use process manufacturing or the assembly process? Is the production of Hershey's chocolate an intermittent or continuous production process? Justify your answers.

2. What location factors might go into the selection of a manufacturing site for Hershey's chocolate?

video case

KEEPING YOUR EYE ON THE BALL

We sometimes read a newspaper or magazine or listen to a news report and hear about the downfall of U.S. manufacturing and how many people are losing their jobs in manufacturing plants. It sounds depressing but the question is, "Has the United States really fallen that far behind other countries in manufacturing capability?" The answer is no, and this video is meant to highlight just one example of a successful manufacturing company. There are thousands of others that could be discussed in a similar manner.

There is no doubt that U.S. manufacturers are being challenged by companies in Mexico, China, India, Brazil, Indonesia, and all over the world—but that is nothing new. The question is whether or not the United States can respond effectively to such challenges today as it has done in the past. Don't forget that much, if not most, of the machinery and equipment being used in foreign plants was produced in the United States. Note, too, that many companies—like Honda and Toyota—have built manufacturing plants in the United States.

This video features Ball metal beverage containers. You've seen them everywhere. But have you given any thought to how those cans came to be? Have you wondered why Ball has been so successful in the United States that it expanded operations by buying four U.S. manufacturing plants from giant brewer Anheuser-Busch InBev?

The text mentions several things that U.S. manufacturers are doing to stay competitive in today's global markets. They include focusing on customers; maintaining close relationships with suppliers (e.g., using just-in-time inventory control); practicing continuous improvement; focusing on quality; saving on costs through site selection; utilizing the Internet; and adopting new production processes like computer-integrated manufacturing. Foreign businesses are busy copying what we do, so U.S. producers need to do things better and faster and cheaper, if they can. Speaking of cans, you can see and hear what Ball is doing to stay competitive in the video. Note that Ball is using a continuous process. What other processes might the company use?

U.S. companies are using computer-aided design and computer-aided manufacturing, united in computer-integrated manufacturing. They also do flexible manufacturing, which means they can produce a variety of products using the same machinery. It should not surprise you to learn that Ball located its facilities close to its customers. That makes distribution faster, easier, and cheaper.

Of course, quality is a key consideration in any manufacturing plant. Can you imagine trying to open a can and having the opener break off in your fingers or having a can that leaks all over your car? Manufacturers try for zero defects, but often settle for some slightly lower standard such as Six Sigma (only 3.4 defects per million).

Next time you take a cold drink from a can, think about Ball and the other companies that make the United States a major producer of consumer goods. Think, too, of the opportunities that will present themselves to tomorrow's college graduates. Students seem less attracted to manufacturing today, but that means more opportunities tomorrow for those students who see growth in some areas of manufacturing. That includes, of course, companies that produce solar panels, power plants, and more. You only have to look around your home or office to see the many products being made and the many products that will be made using biotechnology, nanotechnology, and so on.

THINKING IT OVER

1. Looking at the future of manufacturing in the United States, do you think U.S. companies like Ball are adapting to the challenges of foreign manufacturers? What is Ball doing to stay competitive?

2. The video mentions the loss of U.S. manufacturing jobs to overseas locations. What is this called? What is the opposite trend that has occurred in the United States with companies like Toyota and Honda?

3. What is meant by Six Sigma?

notes

1. Conor Dougherty, "Unemployment Rises in Every State," *The Wall Street Journal,* January 28, 2009.
2. Carmen M. Reinhart and Kenneth S. Rogoff, "What Other Financial Crises Tell Us," *The Wall Street Journal,* February 3, 2009.
3. Spencer Jakab, "Manufacturing Pause Isn't Cause for Alarm," *The Wall Street Journal,* January 2, 2014.
4. Ro Khanna, "Myths about Manufacturing Jobs," *The Washington Post,* February 17, 2013.
5. Richard Stengel, "Made in America, Again," *Time,* April 22, 2013.
6. Brad Plumer, "Back to 'Made in America'?" *The Washington Post,* May 1, 2013.
7. Michelene Maynard, "Toyota, Mississippi," *Forbes,* July 16, 2012.
8. Thomas A. Kochan, "A Jobs Compact for America's Future," *Harvard Business Review,* March 2012.
9. John Deutch and Edward Steinfeld, "Made in America, and Everywhere Else," *The Wall Street Journal,* March 13, 2013.
10. Emi Kolawole, "It's Not the Jetsons, But," *The Washington Post,* May 1, 2013.
11. James R. Hagerty, "Manufacturers Gain Ground," *The Wall Street Journal,* August 19, 2013.
12. James R. Hagerty, "In World of Big Stuff, The U.S. Still Rules," *The Wall Street Journal,* December 4, 2012.
13. George Halvorson, "The Culture to Cultivate," *Harvard Business Review,* July–August, 2013.
14. Andrea Petersen, "Checking In? Hidden Ways Hotels Court Guests Faster," *The Wall Street Journal,* April 12, 2012.
15. Alina Dizik, "Why All the Locals Are Lounging in the Hotel Lobby," *The Wall Street Journal,* April 19, 2012.
16. H. David Sherman and Joe Zhu, "Analyzing Performance in Service Organizations," *Sloan Management Review,* Summer 2013.
17. John Koten, "What's Hot in Manufacturing Technology," *The Wall Street Journal,* June 11, 2013.
18. Ann C. Logue, "Trimming the Fat," *Entrepreneur,* February 2014.
19. Steve Blank, "'Lean' Is Shaking Up the Entrepreneurial Landscape," *Harvard Business Review,* July–August, 2013.
20. Kevin Kelly, "Better than Human," *Wired,* January 2013.
21. Bill Alpert, "Robots in Search of Added Employment," *Barron's,* January 28, 2013.
22. David Von Drehle, "The Robot Economy," *Time,* September 9, 2013.
23. Dexter Roberts, "The March of Robots into Chinese Factories," *Bloomberg Businessweek,* November 29, 2012.
24. Ibid.
25. Ibid.
26. "Time to Head Home for Some Manufacturers," editorial, *Bloomberg Businessweek,* February 6–12, 2012.
27. David Simchi-Levi, James Paul Peruvankal, Narenda Mulani, Bill Read, and John Ferreira, "Is It Time to Rethink Your Manufacturing Strategy?" *MIT Sloan Management Review,* Winter 2012.
28. Brad Feld, "The Simple Change That's Completely Transformed How I Get Things Done," *Inc.,* December–January 2014.

photo credits

10 Motivating Employees

Learning Objectives

AFTER YOU HAVE READ AND STUDIED THIS CHAPTER, YOU SHOULD BE ABLE TO

LO 10-1 Explain Taylor's theory of scientific management.

LO 10-2 Describe the Hawthorne studies and their significance to management.

LO 10-3 Identify the levels of Maslow's hierarchy of needs and apply them to employee motivation.

LO 10-4 Distinguish between the motivators and hygiene factors identified by Herzberg.

LO 10-5 Differentiate among Theory X, Theory Y, and Theory Z.

LO 10-6 Explain the key principles of goal-setting, expectancy, reinforcement, and equity theories.

LO 10-7 Show how managers put motivation theories into action through such strategies as job enrichment, open communication, and job recognition.

LO 10-8 Show how managers personalize motivation strategies to appeal to employees across the globe and across generations.

Yum! Brands ranks as one of the largest food companies in the world, although there's a good chance that many people have never heard of it. That's because consumers are likely more familiar with the company's stable of famous fast-food chains like Taco Bell, Pizza Hut, and KFC. Thanks to powerful brands like these, Yum! stock has grown double digits every year since 1997. In that span of time, Yum! opened five restaurants per day.

Keeping such a large operation successful requires expert leadership, which Executive Chairman David Novak provides to a remarkable degree. However, he's certainly not the type of person to accept sole credit for a job well done. Novak stresses the importance of teamwork and recognition of customer-focused behavior. Using his own leadership-development program called Taking People with You, Novak teaches how positive personal development can benefit entire companies by bringing people closer together. He shows managers the power of recognition when motivating employees. Not only has Novak's program made him indispensible at Yum!, but he's also an inspiration among the corporate leaders who learn his methods at conferences around the world. "He is a rocket booster on stage," said Kathleen Matthews, an executive vice president at Marriott Hotels. "He has an authentic core and seems to truly believe what he preaches."

After earning a degree in journalism with an advertising emphasis from the University of Missouri, Novak spent a few years in the advertising business before landing a job in marketing at Pizza Hut. He soon rose through the ranks of the fast-food chain and then through PepsiCo, its parent company at the time.

At the time Novak was promoted to run KFC, the company hadn't hit its profit target in many years. The long period of declining business created an environment of animosity in which the company's leadership and the franchisees didn't like or trust each other. Novak believed that a change in culture would improve the company's performance dramatically. "I think business is fun," says Novak. "I think people would much rather work in a fun environment. But people want to win. So I wanted to create a team that was hardworking, very competitive, but we had fun. And I thought the biggest thing I could do was tap into the universal need for recognition." So he created the Rubber Chicken Award as a lighthearted way to recognize employees' accomplishments and motivate them to further greatness.

To Novak, most corporate trophies are awarded too long after the fact to hold any personal importance. That's why he doled out rubber chickens as president of KFC and statues of chattering teeth on legs as CEO of Yum! Brands immediately after a person exceeded expectations. Novak's motivational efforts had an immediate effect on KFC, leading to the brand's turnaround in the 1990s. Novak's success made him the natural choice to lead as president of Yuml Brands—alongside the late Andrall "Andy" Pearson—when it was spun off from PepsiCo in 1997. Since Novak became CEO in 1999 and Chairman in 2001, he has been committed to growing the company by boosting employee morale. "I'm on earth to encourage others, lift lives, help create leaders, inspire people, recognize others," said Novak. "When I'm spending time doing that—those are my best days."

In this chapter, you'll learn about the theories and practices managers like David Novak use in motivating their employees to focus on goals common to them and the organization.

Sources: Geoff Colvin, "Great Job! How Yum! Brands Uses Recognition to Build Teams and Get Results," *Fortune,* July 25, 2013; Shani Magosky, "Heed the Oracle of Kentucky (aka Yum!) Brands CEO David Novak," *The Huffington Post,* April 18, 2013; and Tiffany Hsu, "Yum! CEO David Novak on Rubber Chickens, China and Taco Bell," *Los Angeles Times,* March 30, 2012.

David Novak

- Executive Chairman of Yum! Brands
- Built a fun culture at Pizza Hut, KFC, and PepsiCo
- Created Walk the Talk Award to reward performance

www.yum.com
@yumbrands

name that **company**

Job enlargement combines a series of tasks into one challenging and interesting assignment. This home appliance manufacturer redesigned its washing machine production process so that employees could assemble an entire water pump instead of just adding one part. Name that company. (Find the answer in the chapter.)

intrinsic reward
The personal satisfaction you feel when you perform well and complete goals.

One important type of motivator is intrinsic (inner) rewards, which include the personal satisfaction you feel for a job well done. People who respond to such inner promptings often enjoy their work and share their enthusiasm with others. Are you more strongly motivated by your own desire to do well, or by extrinsic rewards like pay and recognition?

THE VALUE OF MOTIVATION

"If work is such fun, how come the rich don't do it?" quipped comedian Groucho Marx. Well, the rich do work—Bill Gates didn't make his billions playing computer games. And workers can have fun, if managers make the effort to motivate them.

It's difficult to overstate the importance of workers' job satisfaction. Happy workers usually lead to happy customers, and happy customers lead to successful businesses. On the other hand, unhappy workers are likely to leave. When that happens, the company usually loses more than an experienced employee. It can also lose the equivalent of 6 to 18 months' salary to cover the costs of recruiting and training a replacement.[1] The "soft" costs of losing employees are even greater: loss of intellectual capital, decreased morale of remaining workers, increased employee stress, decreased customer service, interrupted product development, and a poor reputation.

While it is costly to recruit and train new workers, it's also expensive to retain those who are disengaged. The word *engagement* is used to describe employees' level of motivation, passion, and commitment. Engaged employees work with passion and feel a connection to their company.[2] Disengaged workers have essentially checked out; they plod through their day putting in time, but not energy. Not only do they act out their unhappiness at work, but disengaged employees undermine the efforts of engaged co-workers. A Gallup survey estimated that the lower productivity of actively disengaged workers costs the U.S. economy between $450 to $550 billion a year.[3]

Motivating the right people to join the organization and stay with it is a key function of managers. Top-performing managers are usually surrounded by top-performing employees. It is no coincidence that geese fly faster in formation than alone. Although the desire to perform well ultimately comes from within, good managers stimulate people and bring out their natural drive to do a good job. People are willing to work, and work hard, if they feel their work makes a difference and is appreciated.[4]

People are motivated by a variety of things, such as recognition, accomplishment, and status. An **intrinsic reward** is the personal satisfaction you feel when you perform well and complete goals. The belief that your work makes a significant contribution to the organization or to society is a form of intrinsic reward. An **extrinsic reward** is given to you by someone else as recognition for good work. Pay increases, praise, and promotions are extrinsic rewards.

This chapter will help you understand the concepts, theories, and practice of motivation. We begin with a look at some traditional theories of motivation. Why should you bother to know about these theories? Because sometimes "new" approaches aren't really new; variations of them have been tried in the past. Knowing what has gone before will help you see what has worked and what hasn't. First, we discuss the Hawthorne studies because they created a new interest in worker satisfaction and motivation. Then we look at some assumptions about employees that come from the traditional theorists. You will see the names of these theorists over and over in business literature and future courses: Taylor, Mayo, Maslow, Herzberg, and McGregor. Finally, we'll introduce modern motivation theories and show you how managers apply them.

extrinsic reward
Something given to you by someone else as recognition for good work; extrinsic rewards include pay increases, praise, and promotions.

scientific management
Studying workers to find the most efficient ways of doing things and then teaching people those techniques.

LO 10–1   Explain Taylor's theory of scientific management.

Frederick Taylor: The Father of Scientific Management

Several 19th-century thinkers presented management principles, but not until the early 20th century did any work with lasting implications appear. *The Principles of Scientific Management* was written by U.S. efficiency engineer Frederick Taylor and published in 1911, earning Taylor the title "father of scientific management." Taylor's goal was to increase worker productivity to benefit both the firm and the worker. The solution, he thought, was to scientifically study the most efficient ways to do things, determine the one "best way" to perform each task, and then teach people those methods. This approach became known as **scientific management**. Three elements were basic to Taylor's approach: time, methods, and rules of work. His most important tools were observation and the stopwatch. Taylor's thinking lies behind today's measures of how many burgers McDonald's expects its cooks to flip.

A classic Taylor story describes his study of men shoveling rice, coal, and iron ore with the same type of shovel. Believing different materials called for different shovels, he proceeded to invent a wide variety of sizes and shapes of shovels and, stopwatch in hand, measured output over time in what were called **time-motion studies**. These were studies of the tasks performed in a job and the time needed for each. Sure enough, an average person could shovel 25 to 35 tons more per day using the most efficient motions and the proper shovel. This finding led to time-motion studies of virtually every factory job. As researchers determined the most efficient ways of doing things, efficiency became the standard for setting goals.

UPS tells drivers how to get out of their trucks, how fast to walk, how many packages to pick up and deliver a day, and even how to hold their keys. Can you see how UPS follows the principles of scientific management by teaching people the one "best way" to perform each task?

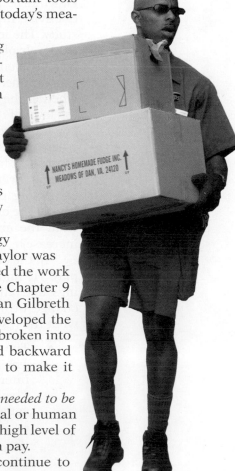

Taylor's scientific management became the dominant strategy for improving productivity in the early 1900s. One follower of Taylor was Henry L. Gantt, who developed charts by which managers plotted the work of employees a day in advance down to the smallest detail. (See Chapter 9 for a discussion of Gantt charts.) U.S. engineers Frank and Lillian Gilbreth used Taylor's ideas in a three-year study of bricklaying. They developed the **principle of motion economy**, showing how every job could be broken into a series of elementary motions called a *therblig* (*Gilbreth* spelled backward with the *t* and *h* transposed). They then analyzed each motion to make it more efficient.

Scientific management viewed people largely as machines that needed to be properly programmed. There was little concern for the psychological or human aspects of work. Taylor believed that workers would perform at a high level of effectiveness—that is, be motivated—if they received high enough pay.

Some of Taylor's ideas are still in use. Some companies continue to emphasize conformity to work rules rather than creativity, flexibility, and

time-motion studies
Studies, begun by Frederick Taylor, of which tasks must be performed to complete a job and the time needed to do each task.

principle of motion economy
Theory developed by Frank and Lillian Gilbreth that every job can be broken down into a series of elementary motions.

responsiveness. For example, United Parcel Service (UPS) tells drivers how to get out of their trucks (with right foot first), how fast to walk (three feet per second), how many packages to pick up and deliver a day (an average of 400), and how to hold their keys (teeth up, third finger). Drivers wear ring scanners, electronic devices on their index fingers wired to a small computer on their wrists. The devices shoot a pattern of photons at a bar code on a package to let a customer check the Internet and know exactly where a package is at any given moment. If a driver is considered slow, a supervisor rides along, prodding the driver with stopwatches and clipboards. UPS has a training center in Landover, Maryland, with simulators that teach employees how to properly lift and load boxes, drive their trucks proficiently, and even lessen the risk of slipping and falling when carrying a package.[5]

The benefits of relying on workers to come up with solutions to productivity problems have long been recognized, as we shall discover next.

LO 10–2 Describe the Hawthorne studies and their significance to management.

Elton Mayo and the Hawthorne Studies

One study, inspired by Frederick Taylor's research, began at the Western Electric Company's Hawthorne plant in Cicero, Illinois, in 1927 and ended six years later. Let's see why it is one of the major studies in management literature.

Elton Mayo and his colleagues from Harvard University came to the Hawthorne plant to test the degree of lighting associated with optimum productivity. In this respect, their study was a traditional scientific management study. The idea was to keep records of the workers' productivity under different levels of illumination. But the initial experiments revealed what seemed to be a problem. The researchers had expected productivity to fall as the lighting was dimmed. Yet the experimental group's productivity went up regardless of whether the lighting was bright or dim, and even when it was reduced to about the level of moonlight.

In a second series of 13 experiments, a separate test room was set up where researchers could manipulate temperature, humidity, and other environmental factors. Productivity went up each time; in fact, it increased by 50 percent overall. When the experimenters repeated the original conditions (expecting productivity to fall to original levels), productivity increased yet again. The experiments were considered a total failure at this point. No matter what the experimenters did, productivity went up. What was causing the increase?

In the end, Mayo guessed that some human or psychological factor was at play. He and his colleagues interviewed the workers, asking about their feelings and attitudes toward the experiment. The answers began a profound change in management thinking that still has repercussions today. Here is what the researchers concluded:

- The workers in the test room thought of themselves as a social group. The atmosphere was informal, they could talk freely, and they interacted regularly with their supervisors and the experimenters. They felt special and worked hard to stay in the group. This motivated them.

- The workers were included in planning the experiments. For example, they rejected one kind of pay schedule and recommended another, which was adopted. They believed their ideas were respected and felt engaged in managerial decision making. This, too, motivated them.

- No matter the physical conditions, the workers enjoyed the atmosphere of their special room and the additional pay for being more productive. Job satisfaction increased dramatically.

Researchers now use the term **Hawthorne effect** to refer to people's tendency to behave differently when they know they're being studied. The Hawthorne study's results encouraged researchers to study human motivation and the managerial styles that lead to higher productivity. Research emphasis shifted from Taylor's scientific management toward Mayo's new human-based management.

Mayo's findings led to completely new assumptions about employees. One was that pay is not the only motivator. In fact, money was found to be a relatively ineffective motivator. New assumptions led to many theories about the human side of motivation. One of the best-known motivation theorists was Abraham Maslow, whose work we discuss next.

Little did Elton Mayo and his research team from Harvard University know they would forever change managers' beliefs about employee motivation. Their research at the Hawthorne plant of Western Electric in Cicero, Illinois (pictured here), gave birth to the concept of human-based motivation by showing that employees behaved differently simply because they were involved in planning and executing the experiments.

LO 10–3 Identify the levels of Maslow's hierarchy of needs and apply them to employee motivation.

MOTIVATION AND MASLOW'S HIERARCHY OF NEEDS

Psychologist Abraham Maslow believed that to understand motivation at work, we must understand human motivation in general. It seemed to him that motivation arises from need. That is, people are motivated to satisfy unmet needs. Needs that have already been satisfied no longer provide motivation.

Figure 10.1 shows **Maslow's hierarchy of needs**, whose levels are:

Physiological needs: Basic survival needs, such as the need for food, water, and shelter.

Safety needs: The need to feel secure at work and at home.

Social needs: The need to feel loved, accepted, and part of the group.

Esteem needs: The need for recognition and acknowledgment from others, as well as self-respect and a sense of status or importance.

Self-actualization needs: The need to develop to one's fullest potential.

When one need is satisfied, another, higher-level need emerges and motivates us to satisfy it. The satisfied need is no longer a motivator. For example, if you just ate a full-course dinner, hunger would not be a motivator (at least for several hours), and your attention might turn to your surroundings (safety needs) or family (social needs). Of course, lower-level needs (perhaps thirst) may reemerge at any time they are not being met and take your attention away from higher-level needs.

To compete successfully, U.S. firms must create a work environment that includes goals such as social contribution, honesty, reliability, service, quality, dependability, and unity—for all levels of employees. Chip Conley, founder of

Hawthorne effect

The tendency for people to behave differently when they know they are being studied.

Maslow's hierarchy of needs

Theory of motivation based on unmet human needs from basic physiological needs to safety, social, and esteem needs to self-actualization needs.

FIGURE 10.1 MASLOW'S HIERARCHY OF NEEDS

Maslow's hierarchy of needs is based on the idea that motivation comes from need. If a need is met, it's no longer a motivator, so a higher-level need becomes the motivator. Higher-level needs demand the support of lower-level needs. This chart shows the various levels of need. Do you know where you are on the chart right now?

 connect

▶ **iSee It!** Need help understanding Maslow's hierarchy? Visit your Connect e-book video tab for a brief animated explanation

Joie de Vivre, a chain of 30 boutique hotels, thinks about higher-level needs such as meaning (self-actualization) for all employees, including lower-level workers. Half his employees are housekeepers who clean toilets all day. How does he help them feel they're doing meaningful work? One technique is what he calls the George Bailey exercise, based on the main character in the movie *It's a Wonderful Life*. Conley asked small groups of housekeepers what would happen if they weren't there every day. Trash would pile up, bathrooms would be full of wet towels, and let's not even think about the toilets. Then he asked them to come up with some other name for housekeeping. They offered suggestions like "serenity keepers," "clutter busters," or "the peace-of-mind police." In the end, these employees had a sense of how the customers' experience wouldn't be the same without them. This gave meaning to their work that helped satisfy higher-level needs.[6]

LO 10–4   Distinguish between the motivators and hygiene factors identified by Herzberg.

HERZBERG'S MOTIVATING FACTORS

Another direction in managerial theory explores what managers can do with the job itself to motivate employees. In other words, some theorists ask: Of all the factors controllable by managers, which are most effective in generating an enthusiastic work effort?

In the mid-1960s, psychologist Frederick Herzberg conducted the most discussed study in this area. Herzberg asked workers to rank various job-related factors in order of importance relative to motivation. The question was: What creates enthusiasm for workers and makes them work to full potential? The most important factors were:

1. Sense of achievement.
2. Earned recognition.
3. Interest in the work itself.
4. Opportunity for growth.
5. Opportunity for advancement.

6. Importance of responsibility.
7. Peer and group relationships.
8. Pay.
9. Supervisor's fairness.
10. Company policies and rules.
11. Status.
12. Job security.
13. Supervisor's friendliness.
14. Working conditions.

Factors receiving the most votes all clustered around job content. Workers like to feel they contribute to the company (sense of achievement was number 1). They want to earn recognition (number 2) and feel their jobs are important (number 6). They want responsibility (which is why learning is so important) and to earn recognition for that responsibility by having a chance for growth and advancement. Of course, workers also want the job to be interesting. Do you feel the same way about your work?

Workers did not consider factors related to job environment to be motivators. It was interesting to find that one of those factors was pay. Workers felt the *absence* of good pay, job security, and friendly supervisors could cause dissatisfaction, but their presence did not motivate employees to work harder; it just provided satisfaction and contentment. Would you work harder if you were paid more?

Herzberg concluded that certain factors, which he called **motivators,** made employees productive and gave them satisfaction. These factors, as you have seen, mostly related to job content. Herzberg called other elements of the job **hygiene factors** (or maintenance factors). These related to the job environment and could cause dissatisfaction if missing but would not necessarily motivate employees if increased. See Figure 10.2 for a list of motivators and hygiene factors.

Herzberg's motivating factors led to this conclusion: The best way to motivate employees is to make their jobs interesting, help them achieve their objectives, and recognize their achievement through advancement and added responsibility.[7] A review of Figure 10.3 shows the similarity between Maslow's hierarchy of needs and Herzberg's theory.

Look at Herzberg's motivating factors, identify those that motivate you, and rank them in order of importance to you. Keep them in mind as you consider jobs and careers. What motivators do your job opportunities offer you? Are they the ones you consider important? Evaluating your job offers in terms of what's really important to you will help you make a wise career choice.

motivators
In Herzberg's theory of motivating factors, job factors that cause employees to be productive and that give them satisfaction.

hygiene factors
In Herzberg's theory of motivating factors, job factors that can cause dissatisfaction if missing but that do not necessarily motivate employees if increased.

Motivators	Hygiene (Maintenance) Factors
(These factors can be used to motivate workers.)	(These factors can cause dissatisfaction, but changing them will have little motivational effect.)
Work itself Achievement Recognition Responsibility Growth and advancement	Company policy and administration Supervision Working conditions Interpersonal relations (co-workers) Salary, status, and job security

FIGURE 10.2 HERZBERG'S MOTIVATORS AND HYGIENE FACTORS
There's some controversy over Herzberg's results. For example, sales managers often use money as a motivator. Recent studies have shown that money can be a motivator if used as part of a recognition program.

FIGURE 10.3 COMPARISON OF MASLOW'S HIERARCHY OF NEEDS AND HERZBERG'S THEORY OF FACTORS

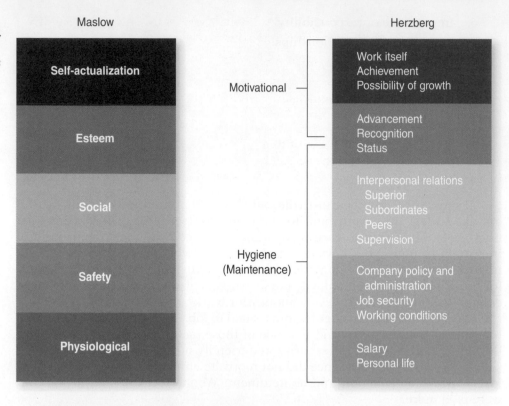

Use LearnSmart to help retain what you have learned. Access your instructor's Connect course to check out LearnSmart, or go to learnsmartadvantage.com for help.

LEARNSMART

test prep

- **What are the similarities and differences between Taylor's time-motion studies and Mayo's Hawthorne studies?**
- **How did Mayo's findings influence scientific management?**
- **Draw a diagram of Maslow's hierarchy of needs. Label and describe the parts.**
- **Explain the distinction between what Herzberg called motivators and hygiene factors.**

LO 10–5   Differentiate among Theory X, Theory Y, and Theory Z.

MCGREGOR'S THEORY X AND THEORY Y

The way managers go about motivating people at work depends greatly on their attitudes toward workers. Management theorist Douglas McGregor observed that managers' attitudes generally fall into one of two entirely different sets of managerial assumptions, which he called Theory X and Theory Y.

Theory X

The assumptions of Theory X management are:

- The average person dislikes work and will avoid it if possible.
- Because of this dislike, workers must be forced, controlled, directed, or threatened with punishment to make them put forth the effort to achieve the organization's goals.

- The average worker prefers to be directed, wishes to avoid responsibility, has relatively little ambition, and wants security.

- Primary motivators are fear and punishment.

The natural consequence of these assumptions is a manager who is very busy and watches people closely, telling them what to do and how to do it. Motivation is more likely to take the form of punishment for bad work than reward for good work. Theory X managers give workers little responsibility, authority, or flexibility. Taylor and other theorists who preceded him would have agreed with Theory X. Time-motion studies calculated the one best way to perform a task and the optimal time to devote to it. Researchers assumed workers needed to be trained and carefully watched to see that they conformed to standards.

Many managers and entrepreneurs still suspect that employees cannot be fully trusted and need to be closely supervised.[8] No doubt you have seen such managers in action. How did they make you feel? Were these managers' assumptions accurate regarding workers' attitudes?

Theory Y

Theory Y makes entirely different assumptions about people:

- Most people like work; it is as natural as play or rest.

- Most people naturally work toward goals to which they are committed.

- The depth of a person's commitment to goals depends on the perceived rewards for achieving them.

- Under certain conditions, most people not only accept but also seek responsibility.

- People are capable of using a relatively high degree of imagination, creativity, and cleverness to solve problems.

- In industry, the average person's intellectual potential is only partially realized.

- People are motivated by a variety of rewards. Each worker is stimulated by a reward unique to him or her (time off, money, recognition, and so on).

Rather than authority, direction, and close supervision, Theory Y managers emphasize a relaxed managerial atmosphere in which workers are free to set objectives, be creative, be flexible, and go beyond the goals set by management. A key technique here is *empowerment*, giving employees authority to make decisions and tools to implement the decisions they make. For empowerment to be a real motivator, management should follow these three steps:

1. Find out what people think the problems in the organization are.

2. Let them design the solutions.

3. Get out of the way and let them put those solutions into action.

Often employees complain that although they're asked to engage in company decision making, their managers fail to actually empower them to make decisions. Have you ever worked in such an atmosphere? How did that make you feel?

Theory X managers don't live to make their employees happy. For example, Charlie Ergen, the founder and chairman of Dish Networks, makes employees work long hours, a whole lot of mandatory overtime, with few paid holidays. Employees describe the Ergen-created company culture as one of condescension and distrust. Yet the company's earnings have consistently beat market expectations. Would you prefer to work for a Theory X or a Theory Y manager?

OUCHI'S THEORY Z

One reason many U.S. companies choose a more flexible managerial style is to meet competition from firms in Japan, China, and the European Union. In the 1980s, Japanese companies seemed to be outperforming U.S. businesses. William Ouchi, management professor at the University of California–Los Angeles, wondered whether the reason was the way Japanese companies managed their workers. The Japanese approach, which Ouchi called Type J, included lifetime employment, consensual decision making, collective responsibility for the outcomes of decisions, slow evaluation and promotion, implied control mechanisms, nonspecialized career paths, and holistic concern for employees. In contrast, the U.S. management approach, which Ouchi called Type A, relied on short-term employment, individual decision making, individual responsibility for the outcomes of decisions, rapid evaluation and promotion, explicit control mechanisms, specialized career paths, and segmented concern for employees.

Type J firms are based on the culture of Japan, which includes a focus on trust and intimacy within the group and family. Conversely, Type A firms are based on American culture, which includes a focus on individual rights and achievements. Ouchi wanted to help U.S. firms adopt successful Japanese strategies, but he realized it wouldn't be practical to expect U.S. managers to accept an approach based on the culture of another country. Judge for yourself. A job for life may sound good until you think of the implications: no chance to change jobs and no opportunity to move quickly through the ranks.

Ouchi recommended a hybrid approach, Theory Z (see Figure 10.4). Theory Z includes long-term employment, collective decision making, individual responsibility for the outcomes of decisions, slow evaluation and promotion, moderately specialized career paths, and holistic concern for employees (including family). Theory Z views the organization as a family that fosters cooperation and organizational values.

In recent years, demographic and social changes, fierce global competition, and the worst recession in their country's history have forced Japanese managers to reevaluate the way they conduct business. The effects of the 2011 earthquake on Japanese businesses reinforced the need to change and become more efficient in order to compete effectively.

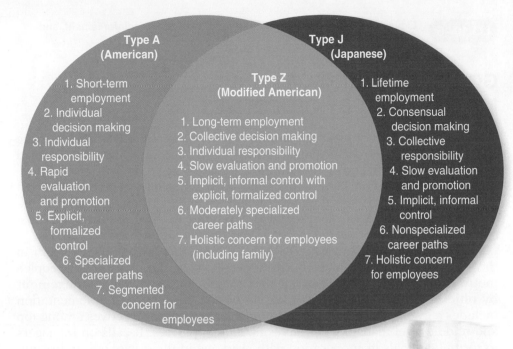

FIGURE 10.4 THEORY Z: A BLEND OF AMERICAN AND JAPANESE MANAGEMENT APPROACHES

Type A (American)
1. Short-term employment
2. Individual decision making
3. Individual responsibility
4. Rapid evaluation and promotion
5. Explicit, formalized control
6. Specialized career paths
7. Segmented concern for employees

Type Z (Modified American)
1. Long-term employment
2. Collective decision making
3. Individual responsibility
4. Slow evaluation and promotion
5. Implicit, informal control with explicit, formalized control
6. Moderately specialized career paths
7. Holistic concern for employees (including family)

Type J (Japanese)
1. Lifetime employment
2. Consensual decision making
3. Collective responsibility
4. Slow evaluation and promotion
5. Implicit, informal control
6. Nonspecialized career paths
7. Holistic concern for employees

Electronics giant Hitachi was the first major Japanese company to quit requiring corporate calisthenics. Having everyone start the day with group exercises had symbolized doing the same thing the same way, and reinforced the cultural belief that employees should not take risks or think for themselves. Many managers think such conformity is what hurt Japanese business. Will Japanese managers move toward the hybrid Theory Z in the future? We'll have to wait and see. An appropriate managerial style matches the culture, situation, and specific needs of the organization and its employees. (See Figure 10.5 for a summary of Theories X, Y, and Z.)

FIGURE 10.5 A COMPARISON OF THEORIES X, Y, AND Z

THEORY X	THEORY Y	THEORY Z
1. Employees dislike work and will try to avoid it.	1. Employees view work as a natural part of life.	1. Employee involvement is the key to increased productivity.
2. Employees prefer to be controlled and directed.	2. Employees prefer limited control and direction.	2. Employee control is implied and informal.
3. Employees seek security, not responsibility.	3. Employees will seek responsibility under proper work conditions.	3. Employees prefer to share responsibility and decision making.
4. Employees must be intimidated by managers to perform.	4. Employees perform better in work environments that are nonintimidating.	4. Employees perform better in environments that foster trust and cooperation.
5. Employees are motivated by financial rewards.	5. Employees are motivated by many different needs.	5. Employees need guaranteed employment and will accept slow evaluations and promotions.

LO 10–6   Explain the key principles of goal-setting, expectancy, reinforcement, and equity theories.

GOAL-SETTING THEORY AND MANAGEMENT BY OBJECTIVES

goal-setting theory
The idea that setting ambitious but attainable goals can motivate workers and improve performance if the goals are accepted, accompanied by feedback, and facilitated by organizational conditions.

Goal-setting theory says setting ambitious but attainable goals can motivate workers and improve performance if the goals are accepted and accompanied by feedback, and if conditions in the organization pave the way for achievement. All organization members should have some basic agreement about both overall goals and specific objectives for each department and individual. Thus there should be a system to engage everyone in the organization in goal setting and implementation.

The late management expert Peter Drucker developed such a system in the 1960s. "Managers cannot motivate people; they can only thwart people's motivation because people motivate themselves," he said. Called **management by objectives (MBO)**, Drucker's system of goal setting and implementation includes a cycle of discussion, review, and evaluation of objectives among top and middle-level managers, supervisors, and employees. It calls on managers to formulate goals in cooperation with everyone in the organization, to commit employees to those goals, and to monitor results and reward accomplishment. Government agencies like the Department of Defense use MBO.

management by objectives (MBO)
A system of goal setting and implementation; it involves a cycle of discussion, review, and evaluation of objectives among top and middle-level managers, supervisors, and employees.

MBO is most effective in relatively stable situations when managers can make long-range plans and implement them with few changes. Managers must also understand the difference between helping and coaching subordinates. *Helping* means working with the subordinate and doing part of the work if necessary. *Coaching* means acting as a resource—teaching, guiding, and recommending—but not participating actively or doing the task. The central idea of MBO is that employees need to motivate themselves.

Employee input and expectations are important.[9] Problems can arise when management uses MBO as a strategy for forcing managers and workers to commit to goals that are not agreed on together, but are instead set by top management.[10]

Victor Vroom identified the importance of employee expectations and developed a process called expectancy theory. Let's examine this concept next.

MEETING EMPLOYEE EXPECTATIONS: EXPECTANCY THEORY

expectancy theory
Victor Vroom's theory that the amount of effort employees exert on a specific task depends on their expectations of the outcome.

According to Victor Vroom's **expectancy theory**, employee expectations can affect motivation. That is, the amount of effort employees exert on a specific task depends on their expectations of the outcome. Vroom contends that employees ask three questions before committing their maximum effort to a task: (1) Can I accomplish the task? (2) If I do accomplish it, what's my reward? (3) Is the reward worth the effort? (See Figure 10.6.)

Think of the effort you might exert in class under the following conditions: Suppose your instructor says that to earn an A in the course, you must achieve an average of 90 percent on coursework plus jump eight feet high. Would you exert maximum effort toward earning an A if you knew you could not possibly jump eight feet high? Suppose your instructor said any student can earn an A in the course, but you know this instructor has not awarded an A in 25 years of teaching. If the reward of an A seems unattainable, would you exert significant effort in the course? Better yet, let's say you read online that businesses prefer

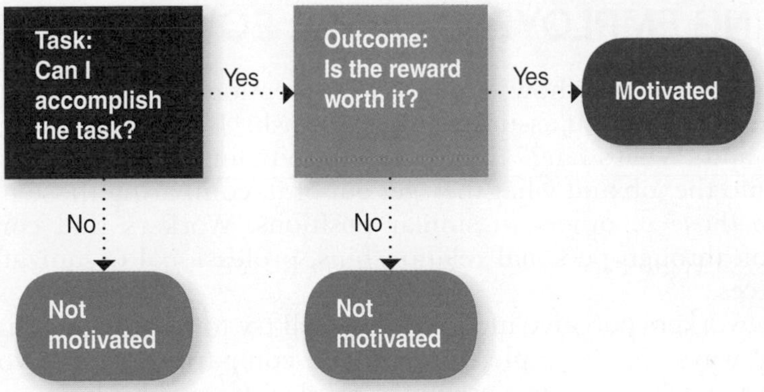

FIGURE 10.6 EXPECTANCY THEORY

The amount of effort employees exert on a task depends on their expectations of the outcome.

hiring C-minus students to A-plus students. Does the reward of an A seem worth it? Now think of similar situations that may occur on the job.

Expectancy theory does note that expectation varies from individual to individual. Employees establish their own views of task difficulty and the value of the reward.[11] Researchers David Nadler and Edward Lawler modified Vroom's theory and suggested that managers follow five steps to improve employee performance:[12]

1. Determine what rewards employees value.
2. Determine each employee's desired performance standard.
3. Ensure that performance standards are attainable.
4. Guarantee rewards tied to performance.
5. Be certain that employees consider the rewards adequate.

REINFORCING EMPLOYEE PERFORMANCE: REINFORCEMENT THEORY

According to **reinforcement theory**, positive reinforcers, negative reinforcers, and punishers motivate a person to behave in certain ways. In other words, motivation is the result of the carrot-and-stick approach: individuals act to receive rewards and avoid punishment. Positive reinforcements are rewards such as praise, recognition, and a pay raise. Punishment includes reprimands, reduced pay, and layoffs or firing. Negative reinforcement occurs when people work to escape the punishers. Escaping the punishment reinforces or rewards the positive behavior. A manager might also try to stop undesirable behavior by not responding to it. This response is called extinction because managers hope the unwanted behavior will become extinct. Figure 10.7 illustrates how a manager can use reinforcement theory to motivate workers.

reinforcement theory
Theory that positive and negative reinforcers motivate a person to behave in certain ways.

	ADD STIMULI	SUBTRACT STIMULI
Increase Behavior	Positive Reinforcement: Jill gets praise (the reinforcement added) for turning in her reports on time (target behavior to increase).	Negative Reinforcement: Jack is on probation (punishment that will be removed) until such time as he can turn in 3 reports on time (target behavior to increase).
Decrease Behavior	Punishment: Jack gets written up (the punisher) for turning in his reports late (target behavior to decrease).	Extinction: Jill does not get praise (reinforcement is removed) when her reports are turned in late (target behavior to decrease), no matter how well done they are.

FIGURE 10.7 REINFORCEMENT THEORY

Managers can either add or subtract stimuli (positive reinforcement, negative reinforcement, or punishers) to increase desired behavior or decrease undesired behavior.

Source: Casey Limmer, MSW, LCSW, Washington University.

TREATING EMPLOYEES FAIRLY: EQUITY THEORY

equity theory
The idea that employees try to maintain equity between inputs and outputs compared to others in similar positions.

Equity theory looks at how employees' perceptions of fairness affect their willingness to perform. It assumes employees ask, "If I do a good job, will it be worth it?" and "What's fair?" Employees try to maintain equity between what they put into the job and what they get out of it, comparing those inputs and outputs to those of others in similar positions. Workers find comparative information through personal relationships, professional organizations, and other sources.

When workers perceive inequity, they will try to reestablish fairness in a number of ways. For example, suppose you compare the grade you earned on a term paper with your classmates' grades. If you think you received a lower grade than someone who put out the same effort as you, you may (1) reduce your effort on future class projects or (2) rationalize the difference by saying, "Grades are overvalued anyway!" If you think your paper received a higher grade than comparable papers, you will probably (1) increase your effort to justify the higher reward in the future or (2) rationalize by saying, "I'm worth it!"

In the workplace, perceived inequity may lead to lower productivity, reduced quality, increased absenteeism, and voluntary resignation.

Remember that equity judgments are based on perception and are therefore subject to error. When workers overestimate their own contributions—as happens often—they feel *any* rewards given out for performance are inequitable.[13] Sometimes organizations try to deal with this by keeping employee salaries secret, but secrecy may make things worse. Employees are likely to overestimate the salaries of others, in addition to overestimating their own contribution. The best remedy is generally clear and frequent communication. Managers must communicate as clearly as possible both the results they expect and the outcomes that will occur.[14]

test prep

- Briefly describe the managerial attitudes behind Theories X, Y, and Z.
- Explain goal-setting theory.
- Evaluate expectancy theory. When could expectancy theory apply to your efforts or lack of effort?
- Explain the principles of equity theory.

LO 10–7   Show how managers put motivation theories into action through such strategies as job enrichment, open communication, and job recognition.

PUTTING THEORY INTO ACTION

Now that you know what a few theorists have to say about motivation, you might be asking yourself "So what? What do all those theories have to do with what really goes on in the workplace today?" Fair question. Let's look at how companies put the theories into action through job enrichment, open communication, and job recognition.

Motivation through Job Enrichment

Managers have extended both Maslow's and Herzberg's theories through **job enrichment**, a strategy that motivates workers through the job itself. Work is assigned so that individuals can complete an identifiable task from beginning to end and are held responsible for successful achievement. Job enrichment is based on Herzberg's higher motivators, such as responsibility, achievement, and recognition.[15] It stands in contrast to *job simplification,* which produces task efficiency by breaking a job into simple steps and assigning people to each. Review Maslow's and Herzberg's work to see how job enrichment grew from those theories.

Those who advocate job enrichment believe that five characteristics of work are important in motivation and performance:[16]

1. *Skill variety.* The extent to which a job demands different skills.
2. *Task identity.* The degree to which the job requires doing a task with a visible outcome from beginning to end.
3. *Task significance.* The degree to which the job has a substantial impact on the lives or work of others in the company.
4. *Autonomy.* The degree of freedom, independence, and discretion in scheduling work and determining procedures.
5. *Feedback.* The amount of direct and clear information given about job performance.

Variety, identity, and significance contribute to the meaningfulness of the job. Autonomy gives people a feeling of responsibility; feedback contributes to a feeling of achievement and recognition.

One type of job enrichment is **job enlargement**, which combines a series of tasks into one challenging and interesting assignment. Maytag, the home appliance manufacturer, redesigned its washing machine production process so that employees could assemble an entire water pump instead of just adding one part. **Job rotation** also makes work more interesting and motivating by moving employees from one job to another. One problem, of course, is the need to train employees to do several different operations. However, the resulting increase in motivation and the value of having flexible, cross-trained employees usually offsets the costs.

Motivating through Open Communication

Communication and information must flow freely throughout the organization when employees are empowered to make decisions—they can't make them in a vacuum. Procedures for encouraging open communication include the following:[17]

- *Create an organizational culture that rewards listening.* Top managers must create places to talk and show employees that talking with superiors counts—by providing feedback, adopting employee suggestions, and rewarding upward communication— even if the discussion is negative. Employees must feel free to say anything they deem appropriate and believe their opinions are valued.
- *Train supervisors and managers to listen.* Most people receive no training in how to

job enrichment
A motivational strategy that emphasizes motivating the worker through the job itself.

job enlargement
A job enrichment strategy that involves combining a series of tasks into one challenging and interesting assignment.

job rotation
A job enrichment strategy that involves moving employees from one job to another.

Here a worker in Baccarat's factory puts the finishing touches on a crystal vase. One of the hallmarks of job enrichment is the worker's ability to perform a complete task from beginning to end. Why do you think this might be more motivating than simply adding a few parts to a product on an assembly line?

listen, in school or anywhere else, so organizations must do such training themselves or hire someone to do it,

- *Use effective questioning techniques.* We get information through questioning. Different kinds of questions yield different kinds of information. Closed questions that generate yes/no answers don't encourage the longer, more thoughtful responses that open questions do. Appropriate personal questions can create a sense of camaraderie between employee and manager.

- *Remove barriers to open communication.* Separate offices, parking areas, bathrooms, and dining rooms for managers only set up barriers. Other barriers are different dress codes and different ways of addressing one another (like calling workers by their first names and managers by their last). Removing such barriers may require imagination and managers' willingness to give up special privileges.

- *Avoid vague and ambiguous communication.* Passive voice appears weak and tentative. Statements such as "Mistakes were made" leave you wondering who made the mistakes. Hedging is another way managers send garbled messages. Terms like *possibly* and *perhaps* sound wishy-washy to employees who need more definitive direction.

- *Make it easy to communicate.* Encouraging organization members to eat together at large lunch tables, allowing employees to gather in conference rooms, having organizational picnics and athletic teams, and so on can help workers at all levels mix with one another.

- *Ask employees what is important to them.* Managers shouldn't wait until the exit interview to ask an employee, "What can I do to keep you?" Then it's too late. Instead they should have frequent *stay interviews* to find out what matters to employees and what they can do to keep them on the job.

The Adapting to Change box discusses how social media might be disruptive in the workplace as well as the dangers of trying to restrict its use on company equipment.

Applying Open Communication in Self-Managed Teams

In the car business nothing works like the "wow" factor. At Ford, the 400-member Team Mustang group was empowered to create the "wow" response for the company's sleek Mustang convertible. The work team, suppliers, company managers, and even customers worked together to make the Mustang a winner in the very competitive automobile market.

Before the recent economic crisis, the auto companies were often cited for good practices. At Ford Motor Company, for example, a group known as Team Mustang set the guidelines for how production teams should be formed. Given the challenge to create a car that would make people dust off their old "Mustang Sally" records and dance into showrooms, the 400-member team was also given the freedom to make decisions without waiting for approval from headquarters. Everyone worked under one roof in an old warehouse where drafting experts sat next to accountants, engineers next to stylists. Budgetary walls between departments were knocked down too as department managers were persuaded to surrender some control over their subordinates on the team. When the resulting Mustang convertible displayed shaking problems, engineers were so motivated to finish on time and under budget that they worked late into the night, sleeping on the floor when necessary. Senior Ford executives were tempted to intervene, but they stuck with their promise not to meddle. Working with suppliers, the team solved the shaking problem and still came in under budget and a couple of months early. The new car was a hit with drivers, and sales soared.[18]

When Is Social Media Too Social?

There's no doubt the work environment has changed drastically over the past few decades. Employees often spend their entire day, or at least a significant part of it, in front of a computer. Social networking sites like Facebook, Twitter, Skype, and LinkedIn are tools as common to today's workers as typewriters, calculators, and copy machines were to workers in the past. The question businesses must face today is, "Should we allow employees to use social networking sites during the workday?"

New York research firm Statista found that one out of five workplaces block access to Facebook on company computers. The most common argument for blocking access is that time spent on Facebook wastes company time. There is also concern that employees could breach confidentialities and leak private company information through a social networking site. Companies also fear they could be vulnerable to hack attacks through social networks.

Proponents of allowing Facebook in the workplace believe that, far from being a distraction at work, social media tools like Facebook enable employees to share information with each other and better deal with customer inquiries. Angelo Kinicki, management professor at Arizona State University, offers four reasons why banning Facebook at work is a bad idea. According to Professor Kinicki,

1. You can alienate younger employees, like Millennials who use social media on a regular basis.

2. Banning social media suggests the business doesn't trust employees.

3. If your policy prohibits social media, employees won't feel supported by management, leading to disengagement and lower productivity.

4. Social media allows employee relaxation from their work situation. Banning it would be like telling employees they cannot talk about sports.

Whether workers who tweet, chat, like, and Skype on the job are productive or time wasters is something each organization has to decide for itself.

Sources: Bernhard Warner, "When Social Media at Work Don't Create Productivity-Killing Distractions," *Bloomberg Businessweek,* April 1, 2013; Stephanie Vozza, "Why Banning Facebook in Your Workplace Is a Stupid Move," *Entrepreneur,* September 30, 2013; and Rick Mulready, "Why It Might Be Time to Ditch Your Facebook Strategy," *Entrepreneur,* January 3, 2014.

To implement such teams, managers at most companies must reinvent work. This means respecting workers, providing interesting work, developing workers' skills, allowing autonomy, decentralizing authority, and rewarding good work. Let's take a look at some of the ways companies recognize and reward good work.

Recognizing a Job Well Done

A recent survey indicated that 79 percent of employees who voluntarily left their jobs did so because of lack of appreciation.[19] Letting people know you appreciate their work is usually more powerful than giving a raise or bonus alone.[20] When 8,000 recent college graduates were asked what was most important to them as they were deciding where to work, salary was not the ultimate motivator. Yes, they needed enough money to cover their basic needs. However, the majority of participants rated career advancement opportunities as well as interesting and challenging work to be the most important things.[21] Clearly, providing advancement opportunity and recognizing achievements are important in attracting and retaining valuable employees.

Promotions aren't the only way to celebrate a job well done. Recognition can be as simple as noticing positive actions out loud, making employees feel their efforts are worthwhile and valued enough to be noticed. For example: "Sarina, you didn't say much in the meeting today. Your ideas are usually so valuable; I missed hearing them." This comment lets Sarina know her ideas are appreciated, and she'll be more apt to participate fully in the next meeting.

Travelocity's Gnomie Award, based on the company's mascot, the traveling gnome, is given to employees nominated by their peers for outstanding performance. Winners receive a $750 travel voucher, a paid day off, recognition at the company's quarterly meeting, and a golden gnome. What part do you think these awards play in motivating the winners to continue their outstanding performance?

Here are just a few examples of ways managers have raised employee spirits without raising paychecks:

- A Los Angeles law firm sent 400 employees and their families to Disneyland for the day. FedEx Office did something similar, but it sent high-achieving employees to Disneyland *and* put the company's top executives in those employees' place while they were gone.

- Give More Media offers perks like Netflix and XM Satellite Radio memberships. It also encourages participation in its Smile and Give program, which gives employees three paid days off to work for a nonprofit of their choice.

- Walt Disney World offers more than 200 employee recognition programs. The Spirit of Fred Award is named after an employee named Fred, who makes each award (a certificate mounted and varnished on a plaque) himself. Fred's name became an acronym for Friendly, Resourceful, Enthusiastic, and Dependable.

- Maritz Inc., in Fenton, Missouri, has a Thanks a Bunch program that gives flowers to a selected employee in appreciation of a job well done. That employee passes the bouquet to someone else who helped. The idea is to see how many people are given the flowers throughout the day. The bouquet comes with thank-you cards that are entered into a drawing for awards like binoculars and jackets.

- Hewlett-Packard (HP) bestows its Golden Banana Award for a job well done. The award started when an engineer burst into his manager's office saying he'd found the solution to a long-standing problem. In his haste to find something to give the employee to show his appreciation, the manager grabbed a banana from his lunch and said, "Well done! Congratulations!" The Golden Banana is now one of the most prestigious honors given to an inventive HP employee.

The Spotlight on Small Business box offers examples of what a number of small businesses have done to motivate employees.

Giving valued employees prime parking spots, more vacation days, or more flexible schedules may help them feel their work is appreciated, but sometimes nothing inspires workers like the prospect of a payout down the road. Companies that offer a small equity stake or stock options often have a good chance of developing loyal employees

The same things don't motivate all employees. Next we'll explore how employees from different cultures and generations are motivated in different ways.

LO 10–8   Show how managers personalize motivation strategies to appeal to employees across the globe and across generations.

PERSONALIZING MOTIVATION

Managers cannot use one motivational formula for all employees. They have to get to know each worker personally and tailor the motivational effort to the individual. This is further complicated by the increase in global business and the fact that managers now work with employees from a variety of cultural backgrounds. Cultural differences also exist between generations raised in the same country. Let's look at how managers personalize their strategies to appeal to employees across the globe and across generations.

Going Up against the Heavyweights

The competition to attract and retain top-notch workers is "job one" for all businesses big or small. But how can small companies compete against the likes of Apple, Amazon, and Google? Wouldn't any talented person choose to work for one of these big-name employers that offer such perks as onsite gourmet meals, putting greens, gymnasiums, and massages?

It's true small businesses cannot offer the money, benefits, or glory of working for one of the corporate heavyweights. But they can offer more intangible benefits such as collaborative management, less bureaucracy, more lifestyle balance, a sense of independence, and sometimes even potential ownership. Many small businesses strive to create an upbeat, relaxed company culture that encourages employees to bond with one another rather

than compete against each other for the next promotion. By instilling the idea that the business's culture belongs to the employees, culture can equal perks, fun, and happiness. Small businesses also can take advantage of motivating

employees with open communication and broad responsibility on the job. Individual workers can have more say in the company and not feel like just another drone in a giant corporate beehive.

This doesn't mean small businesses can't also try their hand at

the innovative perks department. At Sparta Systems employees are invited to step away from their desks and engage in video and board games. Bigcommerce offers employees a weekly boot camp with a certified trainer. Zoosk invites employees to bring their dogs to work. Shift Communications even gives workers outside recess like the good-old days of elementary school. Not only do businesses hope these methods help employees bond with their colleagues, they also hope they become productive workers. Do you think such workplaces might appeal to Millennials? Why?

Sources: Gene Marks, "Startup Perks Wal-Mart and Amazon Can Never Offer," *Entrepreneur*, October 22, 2013; Michael Fertik, "How to Cultivate the Culture That Makes Your Company Succeed," *Inc.*, February 2014; and Laura Garnett, "3 Questions That Will Motivate Your Employees," *Inc.*, February 2014.

Motivating Employees across the Globe

Different cultures experience motivational approaches differently; therefore, managers study and understand these cultural factors in designing a reward system. In a *high-context culture*, workers build personal relationships and develop group trust before focusing on tasks. In a *low-context culture*, workers often view relationship building as a waste of time that diverts attention from the task. Koreans, Thais, and Saudis tend to be high-context workers who often view their U.S. colleagues as insincere due to their need for data and quick decision making.

Dow Chemical solved a cross-cultural problem with a recognition program for its 54,000 employees in over 36 countries who use a wide variety of languages and currencies. Globoforce Ltd. created a web-based program for Dow called Recognition@Dow that automatically adjusts for differences created by cultural preferences, tax laws, and even local standards of living. Thus a U.S. employee might receive a gift certificate for Macy's, whereas a Chinese employee receives one for online retailer Dangdang.com. The system even allows employees to nominate colleagues for recognition using an "award wizard" to help determine the appropriate award.[22]

Understanding motivation in global organizations and building effective global teams are still new tasks for most companies. Developing group leaders who are culturally astute, flexible, and able to deal with ambiguity is a challenge businesses face in the 21st century. See the Reaching Beyond Our Borders box for more about managing culturally diverse employees.

Beyond Just Knowing Cross-Cultural Differences

As companies today become more global and employees more diverse than ever before, managers are well aware of their need to develop cross-cultural competencies. This means not only understanding different languages, but also understanding different food choices, customs, how people want to be addressed, how much space should be between people, and particularly, how employees expect to be managed.

Many companies do a respectable job in developing cultural intelligence in managers before they move to different global assignments. For example, IBM works closely with leaders in business, government, academia, and community organizations before entering a new market. Why then do seasoned managers, who appreciate diversity and are schooled in cross-cultural differences, often have problems motivating employees in their new global environment?

According to Professor Andrew Molinsky, of Brandeis University's International Business School, the problems occur because of what he refers to as "cultural code-switching." This problem appears when managers are aware of how they should approach and deal with global employees, but deep down they lack the ability to adapt their behavior to the situation. When this happens, their behavior seems unauthentic to global employees, and therefore not effective. An example would be an American executive giving feedback to Japanese employees. The American's natural style is to "tell-it-like-it-is," but Japanese workers expect a much more indirect approach. That may be difficult for the American to do. What managers need to develop is "global dexterity," the ability to shift one's own cultural behavior in a way that's effective and appropriate in the global setting. It always helps to know what to do, but it's even more important to know how to do it.

Sources: Andrew Molinsky, Thomas H. Davenport, Bala Iyer, and Cathy Davidson, "Three Skills Every 21st-Century Manager Needs," *Harvard Business Review*, February 2012; Dan Schawbel, "Andy Molinsky: How to Adapt to Cultural Changes in Foreign Countries," *Forbes*, April 10, 2013; and Samuel J. Palmisano, "The Former CEO of IBM on Working at a Global Scale," *Fast Company*, April 10, 2014.

Motivating Employees across Generations

Members of each generation—baby boomers (born between 1946 and 1964), Generation X (born between 1965 and 1980), Generation Y, also known as Millennials or echo boomers (born between 1980 and 1995), Generation Z (born 1995–2009), Generation Alpha (born after 2010)—are linked through experiences they shared in their formative years, usually the first 10 years of life. (Note: The year spans for Gen X, Y, and Z are widely debated so these dates are approximations.) The beliefs you accept as a child affect how you view risk, challenge, authority, technology, relationships, and economics. When you're in a management position, they can even affect whom you hire, fire, or promote.

In general, boomers were raised in families that experienced unprecedented economic prosperity, secure jobs, and optimism about the future. Gen Xers were raised in dual-career families with parents who focused on work. As children, they attended day care or became latchkey kids. Their parents' layoffs added to their insecurity about a lifelong job. Millennials were raised by indulgent parents, and most don't remember a time without cell phones, computers, and electronic entertainment. Gen Zers grew up post 9/11, in the wake of the Great Recession and amid countless reports of school violence.

The main constant in the lives of Gen Xers, Millennials, and Gen Zers is inconstancy. Consider the unprecedented change in the past 20 years in every area (i.e., economic, technological, scientific, social, and political). Gen Xers, Millennials, and Gen Zers expect change. It is the absence of change that they find questionable.

How do generational differences among these groups affect motivation in the workplace? Boomer managers need to be flexible with their younger employees, or they will lose them. Gen X employees need to use their enthusiasm for change and streamlining to their advantage. Although many are unwilling to pay the same price for success their parents and grandparents did, their concern about undue stress and long hours doesn't mean they lack ambition. They want economic security as much as older workers, but they have a different approach to achieving it. Rather than focusing on job security, Gen Xers tend to focus on career security instead and are willing to change jobs to find it.

Many Gen Xers are now managers, responsible for motivating other employees. What kind of managers are they? In general, they are well equipped to motivate people. They usually understand that there is more to life than work, and they think a big part of motivating is letting people know you recognize that fact. Gen X managers tend to focus more on results than on hours in the workplace. They tend to be flexible and good at collaboration and consensus building. They often think in broader terms than their predecessors because the media have exposed them to problems around the world. They also have a big impact on their team members. They are more likely to give them the goals and outlines of the project and leave them alone to do their work.

Perhaps the best asset of Gen X managers is their ability to give employees feedback, especially positive feedback. One reason might be that they expect more of it themselves. One new employee was frustrated because he hadn't received feedback from his boss since he was hired—two weeks earlier. In short, managers need to realize that young workers demand performance reviews and other forms of feedback more than the traditional one or two times a year.

As Millennials entered the job market, they created a workplace four generations deep. As a group, they tend to share a number of characteristics: they're often impatient, skeptical, blunt, expressive, and image-driven. Like any other generation, they can transform their characteristics into unique skills. For example, Millennials tend to be adaptable, tech-savvy, able to grasp new concepts, practiced at multitasking, efficient, and tolerant.[23] Millennials tend to place a higher value on work–life balance, expect their employers to adapt to them (not the other way around), and are more likely to rank fun and stimulation in their top five ideal-job requirements.[24] What do you think are the most effective strategies managers can use to motivate Millennial workers?

Many Millennials haven't rushed to find lifetime careers after graduation. They tend to "job surf" and aren't opposed to living with their parents while they test out jobs. Some of this career postponement isn't by choice as much as a result of the state of the economy. The recession hurt younger workers more deeply than other workers. In fact, today Millennials are less likely to be employed than Gen Xers or boomers were at the same age. The number of young people without a job has risen by 30 percent since 2007.[25] The recession has increased the competition for jobs as younger workers struggle to enter the job market, boomers try to make up lost retirement savings, and Gen Xers fight to pay mortgages and raise families.

As Millennials assume more responsibilities in the workplace, they sometimes must manage and lead others far older than themselves. How can young managers lead others who may have more experience than they do? Perhaps the three most important things to keep in mind are to be confident, be open-minded, and solicit feedback regularly.[26] Just remember that asking for input and advice is different from asking for permission or guidance.

As Gen Zers begin to enter the workplace, they are likely to be more cautious and security-minded, but inspired to improve the world. Since they've seen the effects of the economy firsthand, they are more aware of troubling times. A recent survey of Gen Zers shows that they believe school violence/shootings will have the biggest impact on their generation, overriding the invention of

Millennials tend to be skeptical, outspoken, and image-driven as well as adaptable, tech-savvy employees with a sense of fun and tolerance. It is important for managers of all ages to be aware that employees of different generations communicate differently. How do you think generational differences will affect this manager and employee?

Gary Kelly, CEO of Southwest Airlines, shocked his co-workers the year he showed up at the company Halloween party dressed as Gene Simmons, front man for the rock group KISS. Now each year in his blog he asks Southwest employees to suggest his next costume. How do you think Kelly's Halloween antics help develop happy, productive, and loyal employees?

social networking and the election of the first black president. These events make them resilient and pragmatic; they want to confront rather than hide from their problems.[27]

It is important for managers of all ages to be aware that employees of different generations communicate differently. The traditionalists, the generation that lived through the Great Depression and World War II, prefer to communicate face-to-face. Their second choice is by phone, but recordings often frustrate them. Boomers generally prefer to communicate in meetings or conference calls. Gen Xers generally prefer e-mail and will choose meetings only if there are no other options. Millennials most often use technology to communicate, particularly through social media.[28]

In every generational shift, the older generation tends to say the same thing about the new: "They break the rules." The traditionalists said it of the baby boomers. Boomers look at Gen Xers and say, "Why are they breaking the rules?" And now Gen Xers are looking at Millennials and Gen Zers and saying, "What's wrong with these kids?" And you know Gen X and Z will be saying the same thing about Generation Alpha someday.

One thing in business is likely to remain constant: much motivation will come from the job itself rather than from external punishments or rewards. Managers need to give workers what they require to do a good job: the right tools, the right information, and the right amount of cooperation. Motivation doesn't have to be difficult. It begins with acknowledging a job well done—and especially doing so in front of others. After all, as we said earlier, the best motivator is frequently a sincere "Thanks, I really appreciate what you're doing."

test prep

- What are several steps firms can take to increase internal communications and thus motivation?
- What problems may emerge when firms try to implement participative management?
- Why is it important to adjust motivational styles to individual employees? Are there any general principles of motivation that today's managers should follow?

summary

LO 10–1 Explain Taylor's theory of scientific management.

- **What is Frederick Taylor known for?**
  Human efficiency engineer Frederick Taylor was one of the first people to study management and has been called the father of scientific management. He conducted time-motion studies to learn the most efficient way of doing a job and then trained workers in those procedures. He published his book *The Principles of Scientific Management* in 1911. Henry L. Gantt and Frank and Lillian Gilbreth were followers of Taylor.

LO 10–2 Describe the Hawthorne studies and their significance to management.

- **What led to the more human-based managerial styles?**
  The greatest impact on motivation theory was generated by the Hawthorne studies in the late 1920s and early 1930s. In these studies, Elton Mayo found that human factors such as feelings of involvement and participation led to greater productivity gains than did physical changes in the workplace.

LO 10–3 Identify the levels of Maslow's hierarchy of needs and apply them to employee motivation.

- **What did Abraham Maslow find human motivation to be based on?**
  Maslow studied basic human motivation and found that motivation was based on needs. He said that a person with an unfilled need would be motivated to satisfy it and that a satisfied need no longer served as motivation.

- **What levels of need did Maslow identify?**
  Starting at the bottom of Maslow's hierarchy and going to the top, the levels of need are physiological, safety, social, esteem, and self-actualization.

- **Can managers use Maslow's theory?**
  Yes, they can recognize what unmet needs a person has and design work so that it satisfies those needs.

LO 10–4 Distinguish between the motivators and hygiene factors identified by Herzberg.

- **What is the difference between Frederick Herzberg's motivator and hygiene factors?**
  Herzberg found that while some factors motivate workers (motivators), others cause job dissatisfaction if missing but arc not motivators if present (hygiene or maintenance factors).

- **What are the factors called motivators?**
  The work itself, achievement, recognition, responsibility, growth, and advancement.

- **What are the hygiene (maintenance) factors?**
  Company policies, supervision, working conditions, interpersonal relationships, and salary.

LO 10–5 Differentiate among Theory X, Theory Y, and Theory Z.

- **Who developed Theory X and Theory Y?**
  Douglas McGregor held that managers have one of two opposing attitudes toward employees. He called them Theory X and Theory Y.

- **What is Theory X?**
  Theory X assumes the average person dislikes work and will avoid it if possible. Therefore, people must be forced, controlled, and threatened with punishment to accomplish organizational goals.

- **What is Theory Y?**
  Theory Y assumes people like working and will accept responsibility for achieving goals if rewarded for doing so.

- **What is Theory Z?**
  William Ouchi based Theory Z on Japanese management styles and stresses long-term employment; collective decision making; individual responsibility; slow evaluation and promotion; implicit, informal control with explicit, formalized control; moderately specialized career paths; and a holistic concern for employees (including family).

LO 10–6 Explain the key principles of goal-setting, expectancy, reinforcement, and equity theories.

- **What is goal-setting theory?**
  Goal-setting theory is based on the notion that setting ambitious but attainable goals will lead to high levels of motivation and performance if the goals are accepted and accompanied by feedback, and if conditions in the organization make achievement possible.

- **What is management by objectives (MBO)?**
  MBO is a system of goal setting and implementation; it includes a cycle of discussion, review, and evaluation of objectives among top and middle-level managers, supervisors, and employees.

- **What is the basis of expectancy theory?**
  According to Victor Vroom's expectancy theory, employee expectations can affect an individual's motivation.

- **What are the key elements of expectancy theory?**
  Expectancy theory centers on three questions employees often ask about performance on the job: (1) Can I accomplish the task? (2) If I do accomplish it, what's my reward? and (3) Is the reward worth the effort?

- **What are the variables in reinforcement theory?**
  Positive reinforcers are rewards like praise, recognition, or raises that a worker might strive to receive after performing well. Negative reinforcers are punishments such as reprimands, pay cuts, or firing that a worker might be expected to try to avoid.

- **According to equity theory, employees try to maintain equity between inputs and outputs compared to other employees in similar positions. What happens when employees perceive that their rewards are not equitable?**
  If employees perceive they are under-rewarded, they will either reduce their effort or rationalize that it isn't important. If they perceive that they are over-rewarded, they will either increase their effort to justify the higher reward in the future or rationalize by saying, "I'm worth it!" Inequity leads to lower productivity, reduced quality, increased absenteeism, and voluntary resignation.

LO 10–7 Show how managers put motivation theories into action through such strategies as job enrichment, open communication, and job recognition.

- **What characteristics of work affect motivation and performance?**
  The job characteristics that influence motivation are skill variety, task identity, task significance, autonomy, and feedback.

- **Name two forms of job enrichment that increase motivation.**
  Job enlargement combines a series of tasks into one challenging and interesting assignment. Job rotation makes work more interesting by moving employees from one job to another.

- **How does open communication improve employee motivation?**
  Open communication helps both top managers and employees understand the objectives and work together to achieve them.

- **How can managers encourage open communication?**
  Managers can create an organizational culture that rewards listening, train supervisors and managers to listen, use effective questioning techniques, remove barriers to open communication, avoid vague and ambiguous communication, and actively make it easier for all to communicate.

LO 10–8 Show how managers personalize motivation strategies to appeal to employees across the globe and across generations.

- **What is the difference between high-context and low-context cultures?**
  In high-context cultures, people build personal relationships and develop group trust before focusing on tasks. In low-context cultures, people often view relationship building as a waste of time that diverts attention from the task.

- **How are Generation X managers likely to be different from their baby boomer predecessors?**
  Baby boomers tend to be willing to work long hours to build their careers and often expect their subordinates to do likewise. Gen Xers may strive for a more balanced lifestyle and are likely to focus on results rather than on how many hours their teams work. Gen Xers tend to be better than previous generations at working in teams and providing frequent feedback. They usually are not bound by traditions that may constrain those who have been with an organization for a long time and are willing to try new approaches to solving problems.

- **What are some common characteristics of Millennials?**
  Millennials tend to be adaptable, tech-savvy, able to grasp new concepts, practiced at multitasking, efficient, and tolerant. They often place a higher value on work–life balance, expect their employers to adapt to them, and are more likely to rank fun and stimulation in their top five ideal-job requirements.

key terms

equity theory 282
expectancy theory 280
extrinsic reward 270
goal-setting theory 280
Hawthorne effect 273
hygiene factors 275
intrinsic reward 270

job enlargement 283
job enrichment 283
job rotation 283
management by
  objectives (MBO) 280
Maslow's hierarchy of
  needs 273

motivators 275
principle of motion
  economy 271
reinforcement theory 281
scientific
  management 271
time-motion studies 271

critical thinking

Your job right now is to finish reading this chapter. How strongly would you be motivated to do that if you were sweating in a room at 105 degrees Fahrenheit? Imagine your roommate has turned on the air-conditioning. Once you are more comfortable, are you more likely to read? Look at Maslow's hierarchy of needs to see what need would be motivating you at both times. Can you see how helpful Maslow's theory is in understanding motivation by applying it to your own life?

developing **workplace skills**

Key: ● **Team**   ★ **Analytic**   ▲ **Communication**   ▣ **Technology**

★ ▲   1. Talk with several of your friends about the subject of motivation. What motivates them to work hard or not work hard in school and on the job? How important to them is self-motivation as opposed to external reward?

★   2. Look over Maslow's hierarchy of needs and try to determine where you are right now on the hierarchy. What needs of yours are not being met? How could a company go about meeting those needs and thus motivate you to work more effectively?

★ ▲   3. One recent managerial idea is to let employees work in self-managed teams. There is no reason why such teams could not be formed in colleges as well as businesses. Discuss the benefits and drawbacks of dividing your class into self-managed teams for the purpose of studying, doing cases, and so forth.

★   4. Think of all the groups with which you have been associated over the years—sports groups, friendship groups, and so on—and try to recall how the leaders of those groups motivated the group to action. Did the leaders assume a Theory X or a Theory Y attitude? How often was money a motivator? What other motivational tools were used and to what effect?

★   5. Herzberg concluded that pay was not a motivator. If you were paid to get better grades, would you be motivated to study harder? In your employment experiences, have you ever worked harder to obtain a raise or as a result of receiving a large raise? Do you agree with Herzberg about the effects of pay?

taking it to the **net**

PURPOSE

To assess your personality type using the Jung-Myers-Briggs typology test and to evaluate how well the description of your personality type fits you.

EXERCISE

Sometimes understanding differences in employees' personalities helps managers understand how to motivate them. Find out about your personality by going to the Human Metrics website (www.humanmetrics.com) and take the Jung Typology Test (based on Carl Jung's and Isabel Myers-Briggs's approaches to typology). (Disclaimer: The test, like all other personality tests, is only a rough and preliminary indicator of personality.)

1. After you identify your personality type, read the corresponding personality portrait. How well or how poorly does the identified personality type fit?

2. Sometimes a personality test does not accurately identify your personality, but it may give you a place to start looking for a portrait that fits. After you have read the portraits on the website, ask a good friend or relative which one best describes you.

video case   Mc Graw Hill Education ■ connect

APPLETREE ANSWERS

Service industries strive to relieve their customers' anxieties, but often those stresses are transferred to the service employees. For example, help desk call center workers face so much tension that turnover rates can reach as high as 125 percent per year. That amounts to a loss of every employee plus a quarter of their replacements in a single year. Since finding new people to fill all those positions can be expensive, the savviest companies look for ways to motivate their employees to be productive and happy so that they choose to stick around for a while.

John Ratliff of Appletree Answers, a company that provides call center and receptionist services for other businesses, was able to expand his company from a one-man operation to a thriving business with 650 employees at more than 20 locations. Appletree supports clients ranging from sole proprietors to Fortune 500 companies in every industry imaginable.

Early in its growth, however, Appletree suffered the same high turnover rate that is common in the call center industry. Ratliff decided to restructure the business to focus on employee satisfaction and wellness. First, he developed a new set of company principles that encouraged staffers to "think like a customer" and "take care of each other." In order to accommodate his largely Generation Y employees, Ratliff instituted flexible schedules and arranged for additional training programs. Ratliff also encourages employees to submit ideas regarding the company's projects. A desktop app called Idea Flash lets staffers send their suggestions to executives, further enriching the job experience.

In his quest to turn his company around, Ratliff discovered that some of his employees struggled with problems such as serious illnesses, financial hardships, and even homelessness. To combat these crises, he created the Dream On program to provide personalized motivation that doesn't come in a standard paycheck. Similar to the Make a Wish Foundation, Dream On strives to help make selected employees' "dreams" come true, whether it is a trip to Disney World for a sick child or a luxury honeymoon for a loyal worker.

Working in this newly fulfilling environment had a profound effect on Appletree's staff. No longer just seat-fillers, their personal commitment to the company became an integral part of its goals and culture. Because of all this positive reinforcement, Appletree staffers are not only more willing to stay at their jobs, but they also perform their tasks with more energy and effort. John Ratliff's unique approach gives his company a leg up on the industry while still caring deeply for his employees. That's known as a "win–win."

THINKING IT OVER

1. Why is employee turnover very costly for companies?

2. How did John Ratliff increase employee motivation by understanding and adapting the motivational theories discussed in the chapter? Which theory do you think is most appropriate?

3. How did the Dream On program motivate workers and help build stability within the organization?

notes

1. Suzanne Lucas, "How Much Employee Turnover Really Costs You," *Inc.,* August 30, 2013.

2. Victor Lipman, "Why Are So Many Employees Disengaged?" *Forbes,* January 18, 2014.

3. Victor Lipman, "Most American Workers are Disengaged," *Psychology Today,* October 10, 2013.

4. Jacquelyn Smith, "The Best Companies to Work for in 2014," *Forbes,* December 11, 2013; and "100 Best Companies to Work For," www.fortune.com, accessed March 2014.

5. Devin Leonard, "He'll Make Your Dreams Come True," *Bloomberg Businessweek,* January 5, 2014.

6. Tomio Geron, "Airbnb Hires Joie de Vivre's Chip Conley as Head of Hospitality," *Forbes,* September 17, 2013; Mike Hofman, "The Idea That Saved My Company," *Inc.,* October 2007; and Joie de Vivre Hotels, www.jdvhotels.com, accessed March 2014.

7. Nadia Goodman, "Methods for Building Employee Loyalty," *Entrepreneur,* January 9, 2013.

8. Caleb Hannan, "Management Secrets from the Meanest Company in America," *Bloomberg Businessweek,* January 2, 2013.

9. Steve Denning, "The Golden Age of Management Is Now," *Forbes,* August 5, 2013.

10. Victor Lipman, "Without This Quality, Management Doesn't Work," *Forbes,* October 1, 2013.

11. "The Best Ways to Reward Employees," www.entrepreneur.com, accessed March 2014; Kevin Kruse, "25 Low Cost Ways to Reward Employees," *Forbes,* March 1, 2013; and Peter Economy, "5 Secrets for Rewarding Employees," *Inc.,* September 3, 2013.

12. David Nadler and Edward Lawler, "Motivation—a Diagnostic Approach," *Perspectives on Behavior in Organizations* (New York: McGraw-Hill, 1977).

13. David Nicklaus, "What Price Awards?" *St. Louis Post-Dispatch,* April 19, 2013.

14. Jason Daley, "In It for the Long Haul," *Entrepreneur,* February 2013.

15. "What Makes Employees Unhappy," *Inc.,* February 2013.

16. Rob Goffee, "Creating the Best Workplace on Earth," *Harvard Business Review,* May 2013.

17. Glenn Llopis, "6 Ways Effective Listening Can Make You a Better Leader," *Forbes,* May 20, 2013; Josh Patrick, "Do You Listen to Your Employees?," *The New York Times,* March 7, 2013; Shirley Engelmeier, "As Employees 'Lean In,' Companies Must 'Listen In,'" *Fast Company,* May 10, 2013; and Rajat Paharia, "Your Employees Are Telling You What Motivates Them. Why Aren't You Listening?" *Wired,* September 12, 2013.

18. Alisa Priddle and Chris Woodyard, "Ford Improves the Convertible in New Mustang," *USA Today,* February 27, 2014; and Patrick Rall, "Late Run Rush Pushes Ford Mustang Past Chevrolet Camaro in February Sales," *Torque News,* February 3, 2014.

19. Maria Elana Duran, "How to Boost Morale at Your Business," *U.S. News & World Report,* March 6, 2014.

20. Megan M. Biro, "5 Ways Leaders Rock Employee Recognition," *Forbes,* January 13, 2013.

21. Jacquelyn Smith, "What Employers Need to Know about the Class of 2012," *Forbes,* April 3, 2012; and Tim Logan, "What Makes for a Good Workplace?" *St. Louis Post-Dispatch,* June 23, 2013.

22. Dow Chemical Company, www.dow.com, accessed March 2014.

23. Vineet Nayar, "Handing the Keys to Gen Y," *Harvard Business Review,* May 2013.

24. Christopher Hann, "We're All in This Together," *Entrepreneur,* March 2013.

25. "Generation Jobless," *The Economist,* April 27, 2013.

26. Ryan Inzana, "Your New Office BFFs," *Money,* May 2013.

27. "Generation Z: Rebels with a Cause," *Forbes,* May 28, 2013.

28. Marina Khidekel, "The Misery of Mentoring Millennials," *Bloomberg Businessweek,* March 18–24, 2013.

photo credits

11

Human Resource Management:

Finding and Keeping the Best Employees

Learning Objectives

AFTER YOU HAVE READ AND STUDIED THIS CHAPTER, YOU SHOULD BE ABLE TO

LO 11-1 Explain the importance of human resource management, and describe current issues in managing human resources.

LO 11-2 Illustrate the effects of legislation on human resource management.

LO 11-3 Summarize the five steps in human resource planning.

LO 11-4 Describe methods that companies use to recruit new employees, and explain some of the issues that make recruitment challenging.

LO 11-5 Outline the six steps in selecting employees.

LO 11-6 Illustrate employee training and development methods.

LO 11-7 Trace the six steps in appraising employee performance.

LO 11-8 Summarize the objectives of employee compensation programs, and evaluate pay systems and fringe benefits.

LO 11-9 Demonstrate how managers use scheduling plans to adapt to workers' needs.

LO 11-10 Describe how employees can move through a company: promotion, reassignment, termination, and retirement.

Getting to know **Tony Hsieh**

Although online shopping sites are becoming the dominant force in the retail world, they often fall short of their brick-and-mortar rivals in terms of customer service. At the online shoe vendor Zappos, however, a unique company culture ensures customers don't have to sacrifice quality service for convenience.

When Tony Hsieh joined Zappos as CEO, he wanted to change the corporate work environment for the better. After selling his first company to Microsoft for a whopping $265 million, Hsieh didn't want a job in a gray, cubicle-filled office. "For me, I didn't want to be part of a company where I dreaded going into the office," said Hsieh. To set Zappos apart from other online retailers, he wanted his service representatives to wow customers with their energy and expertise. To do that Hsieh needed upbeat employees who were motivated by the love of their work. He gave his call center staffers remarkable freedom, allowing them to talk to customers for hours at a time or send flowers and thank-you notes on the company's dime.

Not only does this strategy do wonders for customer satisfaction, it also keeps employee morale sky high. In order to succeed at this job, Zappos's service reps must be creative, energetic, generous, and understanding. But this commitment to excellence doesn't end with the company's spirited call center employees. When candidates for departments like marketing or management reach the interview stage, Hsieh starts testing them before they even set foot in the company's Las Vegas headquarters. "A lot of our job candidates are from out of town, and we'll pick them up from the airport in a Zappos shuttle, give them a tour, and then they'll spend the rest of the day interviewing," said Hsieh. "At the end of the day of interviews, the recruiter will circle back to the shuttle driver and ask how he or she was treated. It doesn't matter how well the day of interviews went, if our shuttle driver wasn't treated well, then we won't hire that person." The examination doesn't end once the person lands the job. Regardless of their position, new hires must spend their first month helping customers in the call center. If they can't thrive, they're gone.

Along with creating open and accessible work environments, Hsieh also tries to break down as many barriers between employees and management as possible. Zappos executives are affectionately referred to as "monkeys," and the best view from the company's 10-story Vegas high-rise is reserved for the call center workers. In fact, Hsieh puts so much faith in his staff that in 2014 he announced Zappos would be eliminating most of its traditional managers, corporate titles, and hierarchy entirely. Instead, the company will be replacing its standard chain of command with a "holacracy." This new company structure splits employees into overlapping but mostly self-ruling "circles" that allow them to have a greater voice in how the company is run. Although time will tell whether or not this radical system works, Tony Hsieh's commitment to an offbeat but efficient workplace has already grown Zappos into a $2 billion company. If anybody can pull off such an unorthodox office structure, it's Hsieh.

In this chapter, you'll learn how businesses that succeed like Zappos recruit, manage, and make the most of their employees.

Sources: Jena McGregor, "Zappos Says Goodbye to Bosses," *The Washington Post*, January 3, 2014; Edward Lewine, "Tony Hsieh's Office: Welcome to the Rain Forest," *The New York Times*, December 28, 2013; Max Nisen, "Tony Hsieh's Brilliant Strategy for Hiring Kind People," *Business Insider*, November 22, 2013; Kim Bhasin, "Tony Hsieh: Here's Why I Don't Want My Employees to Work From Home," *Business Insider*, March 6, 2013; and Adam Bryant, "On a Scale of 1 to 10, How Weird Are You?" *The New York Times*, January 9, 2010.

Tony Hsieh
- CEO of Zappos
- Created an offbeat but efficient workplace
- Empowers staffers to wow customers

www.zappos.com

@zappos

This company manages its global workforce of about 100,000 employees and 100,000 subcontractors with a database that matches employee skills, experiences, schedules, and references with jobs available. For example, if a client in Quebec has a monthlong project that needs a consultant who speaks English and French, and has an advanced degree in engineering and experience with Linux programming, the system can quickly find the best-suited person available. Name that company. (Find the answer in the chapter.)

LO 11–1 Explain the importance of human resource management, and describe current issues in managing human resources.

WORKING WITH PEOPLE IS JUST THE BEGINNING

Students often say they want to go into human resource management because they want to "work with people." Human resource managers do work with people, but they are also deeply involved in planning, record keeping, and other administrative duties. To begin a career in human resource management, you need a better reason than "I want to work with people." This chapter will tell you what else human resource management is all about.

human resource management (HRM)
The process of determining human resource needs and then recruiting, selecting, developing, motivating, evaluating, compensating, and scheduling employees to achieve organizational goals.

Human resource management (HRM) is the process of determining human resource needs and then recruiting, selecting, developing, motivating, evaluating, compensating, and scheduling employees to achieve organizational goals (see Figure 11.1). For many years, human resource management was called "personnel" and involved clerical functions such as screening applications, keeping records, processing the payroll, and finding new employees when necessary. The roles and responsibilities of HRM have evolved primarily because of two key factors: (1) organizations' recognition of employees as their ultimate resource and (2) changes in the law that rewrote many traditional practices. Let's explore both.

Developing the Ultimate Resource

One reason human resource management is receiving increased attention now is that the U.S. economy has experienced a major shift—from traditional manufacturing industries to service and high-tech manufacturing industries that require highly technical job skills. This shift means that many workers must be retrained for new, more challenging jobs. They truly are the ultimate resource. People develop the ideas that eventually become products to satisfy consumers' wants and needs. Take away their creative minds, and leading firms such as Disney, Apple, Procter & Gamble, Google, Facebook, and General Electric would be nothing.

In the past, human resources were plentiful, so there was little need to nurture and develop them. If you needed qualified people, you simply hired them. If they didn't work out, you fired them and found others. Most firms assigned the job of recruiting, selecting, training, evaluating, compensating, motivating, and, yes, firing people to the functional departments that employed them, like accounting, manufacturing, and marketing. Today the job of human

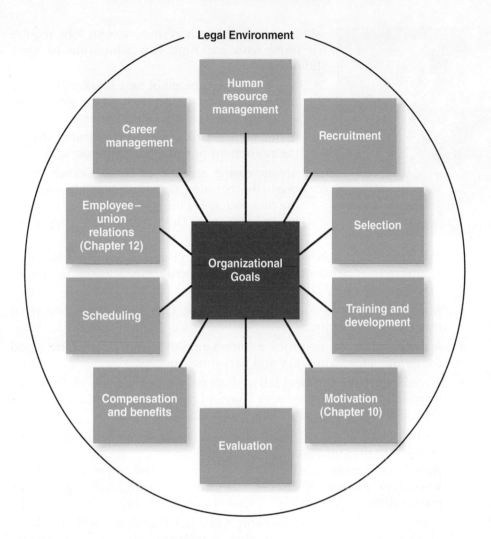

FIGURE 11.1 HUMAN RESOURCE MANAGEMENT
As this figure shows, human resource management is more than hiring and firing personnel. All activities are designed to achieve organizational goals within the laws that affect human resource management. (Note that human resource management includes motivation, as discussed in Chapter 10, and employee–union relations, as discussed in Chapter 12.)

resource management has taken on an increased role in the firm since *qualified* employees are much scarcer, which makes recruiting and retaining people more important and more difficult.[1]

In the future, human resource management may become the firm's most critical function, responsible for dealing with all aspects of a business's most critical resource—people. In fact, the human resource function has become so important that it's no longer the job of just one department; it's a responsibility of *all* managers. What human resource challenges do all managers face? We'll outline a few next.

The Human Resource Challenge

Many of the changes that have had the most dramatic impact on U.S. business are those in the labor force.[2] The ability to compete in global markets depends on new ideas, new products, and new levels of productivity—in other words, on people with good ideas. These are some of the challenges and opportunities in human resources:

- Shortages of trained workers in growth areas, such as computer technology, biotechnology, robotics, green technology, and the sciences.

- Large numbers of skilled and unskilled workers from declining industries, such as steel and automobiles, who are unemployed or underemployed and need retraining. *Underemployed workers* are those who have more

U.S. firms face a shortage of workers skilled in areas like science, green technology, and the development of clean energy sources like these solar panels. What other job markets do you think will grow as companies focus more on environmentally friendly policies? Which ones appeal to you?

skills or knowledge than their current jobs require or those with part-time jobs who want to work full-time.

- A growing percentage of new workers who are undereducated and unprepared for jobs in the contemporary business environment.

- A shortage of workers in skilled trades due to the retirement of aging baby boomers.[3]

- An increasing number of baby boomers who, due to the recession, delay retirement (preventing the promotion of younger workers) or move to lower-level jobs (increasing the supply of workers for such jobs).

- An increasing number of both single-parent and two-income families, resulting in a demand for job sharing, maternity leave, and special career advancement programs for women.

- A shift in employee attitudes toward work. Leisure time has become a much higher priority, as have flextime and a shorter workweek.

- A severe recession that took a toll on employee morale and increased the demand for temporary and part-time workers.[4]

- A challenge from overseas labor pools whose members work for lower wages and are subject to fewer laws and regulations than U.S. workers. This results in many jobs being outsourced overseas.

- An increased demand for benefits tailored to the individual yet cost-effective to the company.

- Growing concerns over health care, elder care, child care, drug testing, workplace violence (all discussed in Chapter 12), and opportunities for people with disabilities.

- Changes through the Affordable Care Act that have added a large number of new regulations that employers must read, interpret, implement, and track.[5]

- A decreased sense of employee loyalty, which increases employee turnover and the cost of replacing lost workers.

Given these issues, you can see why human resource management has taken a central place in management thinking. However, significant changes in laws covering hiring, safety, unionization, equal pay, and affirmative action have also had a major influence. Let's look at their impact on human resource management.

LO 11–2   Illustrate the effects of legislation on human resource management.

LAWS AFFECTING HUMAN RESOURCE MANAGEMENT

Until the 1930s, the U.S. government had little to do with human resource decisions. Since then, legislation and legal decisions have greatly affected all areas of human resource management, from hiring to training to monitoring working conditions (see Figure 11.2). These laws were passed because many businesses did not exercise fair labor practices voluntarily.

One of the more important pieces of social legislation passed by Congress was the Civil Rights Act of 1964. This act generated much debate and was amended 97 times before final passage. Title VII of that act brought the

FIGURE 11.2 GOVERNMENT LEGISLATION AFFECTING HUMAN RESOURCE MANAGEMENT

National Labor Relations Act of 1935. Established collective bargaining in labor–management relations and limited management interference in the right of employees to have a collective bargaining agent.

Fair Labor Standards Act of 1938. Established a minimum wage and overtime pay for employees working more than 40 hours a week. Amendments expanded the classes of workers covered, raised the minimum wage, redefined regular-time work, raised overtime payments, and equalized pay scales for men and women.

Manpower Development and Training Act of 1962. Provided for the training and retraining of unemployed workers.

Equal Pay Act of 1963. Specified that men and women doing equal jobs must be paid the same wage.

Civil Rights Act of 1964. For firms with 15 or more employees, outlawed discrimination in employment based on sex, race, color, religion, or national origin.

Age Discrimination in Employment Act of 1967. Outlawed employment practices that discriminate against people 40 and older. An amendment outlaws requiring retirement by a specific age.

Occupational Safety and Health Act of 1970. Regulated the degree to which employees can be exposed to hazardous substances and specified the safety equipment the employer must provide.

Equal Employment Opportunity Act of 1972. Strengthened the Equal Employment Opportunity Commission (EEOC) and authorized the EEOC to set guidelines for human resource management.

Comprehensive Employment and Training Act of 1973 (CETA). Provided funds for training unemployed workers.

Vocational Rehabilitation Act of 1973. Extended protection to people with any physical or mental disability.

Employee Retirement Income Security Act of 1974 (ERISA). Regulated and insured company retirement plans.

Immigration Reform and Control Act of 1986. Required employers to verify employment eligibility of all new hires including U.S. citizens.

Supreme Court ruling against set-aside programs (affirmative action), 1989. Declared that setting aside 30 percent of contracting jobs for minority businesses was reverse discrimination and unconstitutional.

Older Workers Benefit Protection Act, 1990. Protects older people from signing away their rights to pensions and protection from illegal age discrimination.

Civil Rights Act of 1991. For firms with over 15 employees, extends the right to a jury trial and punitive damages to victims of intentional job discrimination.

Americans with Disabilities Act of 1990 (1992 implementation). Prohibits employers from discriminating against qualified individuals with disabilities in hiring, advancement, or compensation and requires them to adapt the workplace if necessary.

Family and Medical Leave Act of 1993. Businesses with 50 or more employees must provide up to 12 weeks of unpaid leave per year upon birth or adoption of an employee's child or upon serious illness of a parent, spouse, or child.

Americans with Disabilities Amendments Act of 2008 (ADA). Provides broader protection for disabled workers and reverses Supreme Court decisions deemed too restrictive. Adds disabilities such as epilepsy and cancer to ADA coverage.

Lilly Ledbetter Fair Pay Act of 2009. Amends the Civil Rights Act of 1964 by changing the start of the 180-day statute of limitations for filing a discrimination suit from the date of the first discriminatory paycheck to the date of the most recent discriminatory paycheck.

government directly into the operations of human resource management. Title VII prohibits discrimination in hiring, firing, compensation, apprenticeships, training, terms, conditions, or privileges of employment based on race, religion, creed, sex, or national origin. Age was later added to the conditions of the act. The Civil Rights Act of 1964 was expected to stamp out discrimination in the workplace, but specific language in it made enforcement quite difficult. Congress took on the task of amending the law.

In 1972, the Equal Employment Opportunity Act (EEOA) was added as an amendment to Title VII. It strengthened the Equal Employment Opportunity Commission (EEOC), which was created by the Civil Rights Act, by giving it rather broad powers. For example, it permitted the EEOC to issue guidelines for acceptable employer conduct in administering equal employment opportunity. The EEOC also mandated specific record-keeping procedures, and Congress vested it with the power of enforcement to ensure these mandates were carried out. The EEOC became a formidable regulatory force in the administration of human resource management.[6]

affirmative action
Employment activities designed to "right past wrongs" by increasing opportunities for minorities and women.

reverse discrimination
Discrimination against members of a dominant or majority group (e.g., whites or males) usually as a result of policies designed to correct previous discrimination against minority or disadvantaged groups.

Perhaps the most controversial policy enforced by the EEOC involved **affirmative action**, designed to "right past wrongs" by increasing opportunities for minorities and women. Interpretation of the affirmative action law led employers to actively recruit, and in some cases give preference to, women and minority group members. Questions persist about the legality of affirmative action and the effect it may have in creating a sort of reverse discrimination in the workplace. **Reverse discrimination** has been defined as discriminating against members of a dominant or majority group (e.g., whites or males) usually as a result of policies designed to correct previous discrimination. The issue has generated heated debate as well as many lawsuits.

The Civil Rights Act of 1991 expanded the remedies available to victims of discrimination by amending Title VII of the Civil Rights Act of 1964. Now victims of discrimination have the right to a jury trial and punitive damages. Human resource managers must follow court decisions closely to see how the law is enforced.

The Office of Federal Contract Compliance Programs (OFCCP) ensures that employers comply with nondiscrimination and affirmative action laws and regulations when doing business with the federal government.

Laws Protecting Employees with Disabilities and Older Employees

As you read above, laws prohibit discrimination related to race, sex, or age in hiring, firing, and training. The Vocational Rehabilitation Act of 1973 extended protection to people with any physical or mental disability.

The Americans with Disabilities Act of 1990 (ADA) requires employers to give applicants with physical or mental disabilities the same consideration for employment as people without disabilities. The ADA also protects individuals with disabilities from discrimination in public accommodations, transportation, and telecommunications.

The Americans with Disabilities Act guarantees that all U.S. workers have equal opportunity in employment. This legislation requires businesses to make "reasonable accommodations" on the job for people with disabilities. What required accommodations do you think would be reasonable?

The ADA requires making "reasonable accommodations" for employees with disabilities, such as modifying equipment or widening doorways. Most companies have no trouble making structural changes to be accommodating. However, at times such changes can be difficult for some small businesses.[7] Employers used to think that being fair meant treating everyone the same, but *accommodation* in fact means treating people *according to their specific needs.* That can include putting up barriers to isolate people readily distracted by noise, reassigning workers to new tasks, and making changes in supervisors' management styles. Accommodations are not always expensive; an inexpensive headset can allow someone with cerebral palsy to talk on the phone.

In 2008, Congress passed the Americans with Disabilities Amendments Act, which overturned Supreme Court decisions that had reduced protections for certain people with disabilities such as diabetes, epilepsy, heart disease, autism, major depression, and cancer.[8] In 2011, the EEOC issued regulations that widened the range of disabilities covered by the ADA and shifted the burden of proof of disability in labor disputes from employees to business owners. Enforcement of this law promises to be a continuing issue for human resource management.

The Age Discrimination in Employment Act of 1967 (ADEA) protects individuals 40 or older from employment and workplace discrimination in hiring, firing, promotion, layoff, compensation, benefits, job assignments, and training. The ADEA is enforced by the EEOC, applies to employers with 20 or more employees, and protects both employees and job applicants.[9] It also outlaws mandatory retirement in most organizations. It does, however, allow age restrictions for certain job categories such as airline pilot or bus driver if evidence shows that the ability to perform significantly diminishes with age or that age imposes a danger to society.

Effects of Legislation

Clearly, laws ranging from the Social Security Act of 1935 to the 2008 Americans with Disabilities Amendments Act require human resource managers to keep abreast of laws and court decisions to effectively perform their jobs. Choosing a career in human resource management offers a challenge to anyone willing to put forth the effort. Remember:

- Employers must know and act in accordance with the legal rights of their employees or risk costly court cases.

- Legislation affects all areas of human resource management, from hiring and training to compensation.

- Court cases demonstrate that it is sometimes legal to provide special employment (affirmative action) and training to correct discrimination in the past.

- New court cases and legislation change human resource management almost daily; the only way to keep current is to read the business literature and stay familiar with emerging issues.

test prep

- What is human resource management?
- What did Title VII of the Civil Rights Act of 1964 achieve?
- What is the EEOC, and what was the intention of affirmative action?
- What does *accommodations* mean in the Americans with Disabilities Act of 1990?

Use LearnSmart to help retain what you have learned. Access your instructor's Connect course to check out LearnSmart or go to learnsmartadvantage.com for help.

LEARNSMART

LO 11–3 Summarize the five steps in human resource planning.

DETERMINING A FIRM'S HUMAN RESOURCE NEEDS

All management, including human resource management, begins with planning. The five steps in the human resource planning process are:

1. *Preparing a human resource inventory of the organization's employees.* This inventory should include ages, names, education, capabilities, training, specialized skills, and other relevant information (such as

job analysis
A study of what employees do who hold various job titles.

job description
A summary of the objectives of a job, the type of work to be done, the responsibilities and duties, the working conditions, and the relationship of the job to other functions.

job specifications
A written summary of the minimum qualifications required of workers to do a particular job.

languages spoken). It reveals whether the labor force is technically up-to-date and thoroughly trained.[10]

2. *Preparing a job analysis.* A **job analysis** is a study of what employees do who hold various job titles. It's necessary in order to recruit and train employees with the necessary skills to do the job. The results of job analysis are two written statements: job descriptions and job specifications. A **job description** specifies the objectives of the job, the type of work, the responsibilities and duties, working conditions, and the job's relationship to other functions. **Job specifications** are a written summary of the minimal education and skills to do a particular job. In short, job descriptions are about the job, and job specifications are about the person who does the job. Visit the Occupational Information Network (O*NET) at www.onetcenter.org for detailed information about job analyses and job descriptions. See Figure 11.3 for a hypothetical job description and job specifications.

3. *Assessing future human resource demand.* Because technology changes rapidly, effective human resource managers are proactive; that is, they forecast the organization's requirements and train people ahead of time or ensure trained people are available when needed.

4. *Assessing future labor supply.* The labor force is constantly shifting: getting older, becoming more technically oriented, becoming more diverse. Some workers will be scarcer in the future, like biomedical engineers and robotic repair workers, and others will be oversupplied, like assembly-line workers.

5. *Establishing a strategic plan.* The human resource strategic plan must address recruiting, selecting, training, developing, appraising, compensating, and scheduling the labor force. Because the first four steps lead up to this one, we'll focus on them in the rest of the chapter.

FIGURE 11.3 JOB ANALYSIS
A job analysis yields two important statements: job descriptions and job specifications. Here you have a job description and job specifications for a sales representative.

JOB ANALYSIS
Observe current sales representatives doing the job. Discuss job with sales managers. Have current sales reps keep a diary of their activities.

JOB DESCRIPTION	JOB SPECIFICATIONS
Primary objective is to sell company's products to stores in Territory Z. Duties include servicing accounts and maintaining positive relationships with clients. Responsibilities include: • Introducing the new products to store managers in the area. • Helping the store managers estimate the volume to order. • Negotiating prime shelf space. • Explaining sales promotion activities to store managers. • Stocking and maintaining shelves in stores that wish such service.	Characteristics of the person qualifying for this job include: • Two years' sales experience. • Positive attitude. • Well-groomed appearance. • Good communication skills. • High school diploma and two years of college credit.

Some companies use advanced technology to perform the human resource planning process more efficiently. IBM manages its global workforce of about 100,000 employees and 100,000 subcontractors with a database that matches employee skills, experiences, schedules, and references with jobs available. The company also created a cloud-hosted software suite that's designed for automating and improving human resource tasks.[11] For example, if a client in Quebec, Canada, has a monthlong project requiring a consultant who speaks English and French, has an advanced degree in engineering, and experience with Linux programming, IBM can find the best-suited consultant available and put him or her in touch with the client.

LO 11–4   Describe methods that companies use to recruit new employees, and explain some of the issues that make recruitment challenging.

RECRUITING EMPLOYEES FROM A DIVERSE POPULATION

Recruitment is the set of activities for obtaining the right number of qualified people at the right time. Its purpose is to select those who best meet the needs of the organization. You might think a continuous flow of new people into the workforce makes recruiting easy. On the contrary, it's become very challenging for several reasons:

- Some organizations have policies that demand promotions from within, operate under union regulations, or offer low wages, which makes recruiting and keeping employees difficult or subject to outside influence and restrictions.

- An emphasis on corporate culture, teamwork, and participative management makes it important to hire people who not only are skilled but also fit in with the culture and leadership style of the company. Wegmans Food Markets (a member of *Fortune* magazine's list of best companies to work for 17 straight years) encourages employees to do whatever they think is necessary to make a customer happy. The company is currently experimenting with a personal

connect

▶ **iSee It!** Need help understanding the five steps of human resource planning? Visit your Connect e-book video tab for a brief animated explanation.

recruitment
The set of activities used to obtain a sufficient number of the right employees at the right time.

Human resource managers today have the opportunity to recruit people from a wide range of cultural and ethnic backgrounds. What are some of the advantages of a diverse workforce?

shopper service. This service allows customers to create a shopping list on Wegman's website or smartphone app; employees will gather the order and then deliver it to the customer's car when they come to the store.[12]

- Sometimes people with the necessary skills are not available; then workers must be hired and trained internally.[13]

Human resource managers can turn to many sources for recruiting assistance (see Figure 11.4). *Internal sources* include current employees who can be transferred or promoted or who can recommend others to hire. Using internal sources is less expensive than recruiting from outside and helps maintain employee morale. However, it isn't always possible to find qualified workers within the company, so human resource managers also use *external sources* such as advertisements, public and private employment agencies, college placement bureaus, management consultants, Internet sites, professional organizations, referrals, and online and walk-in applications. Management consulting firm McKinsey uses a database of 27,000 former consultants who left the firm in good standing as brand ambassadors and recruiters for the firm.[14]

Recruiting qualified workers may be particularly difficult for small businesses with few staff members and less-than-competitive compensation to attract external sources.[15] CareerBuilder.com, Monster.com, and Indeed.com have helped such firms by attracting more than 80 million visitors per month. The Spotlight on Small Business box offers additional ways small businesses can recruit.

FIGURE 11.4 EMPLOYEE SOURCES

Internal sources are often given first consideration, so it's useful to get a recommendation from a current employee of the firm for which you want to work. College placement offices are also an important source. Be sure to learn about such facilities early so that you can plan a strategy throughout your college career.

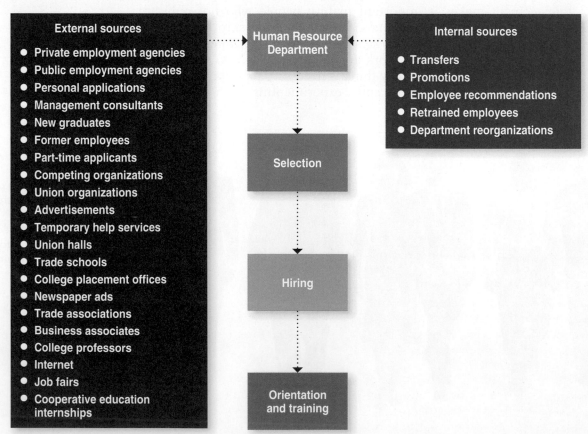

External sources

- Private employment agencies
- Public employment agencies
- Personal applications
- Management consultants
- New graduates
- Former employees
- Part-time applicants
- Competing organizations
- Union organizations
- Advertisements
- Temporary help services
- Union halls
- Trade schools
- College placement offices
- Newspaper ads
- Trade associations
- Business associates
- College professors
- Internet
- Job fairs
- Cooperative education internships

Human Resource Department

Selection

Hiring

Orientation and training

Internal sources

- Transfers
- Promotions
- Employee recommendations
- Retrained employees
- Department reorganizations

Competing for the Cream of the Crop

Most small-business owners would agree that attracting top-quality employees is one of their major challenges. Unfortunately, competing for the cream of the crop is difficult when you can't afford expensive recruiters or pay gold-plated benefits to lure qualified workers. Despite these hurdles, small businesses can compete if they follow certain recruiting recommendations. Here are a few helpful tips:

- *Define who you are as a company.* Instead of describing what skills and experience are required of a prospective employee, start off by explaining what your company does and what its vision is all about. Quite often top-quality candidates will not agree to an interview until they know what the job is all about.
- *Build a strong staff referral program.* The more your current staff is engaged in the search and interview process, the better the chance to find recruits with the right personality and skills. Remember, no recruiter or website knows the organization's culture better than its employees.
- *Have future employees audition for the job.* Hiring workers first on a temporary basis or an internship allows you to test candidates before deciding whether to make an offer of permanent employment.
- *Look at your customers.* Loyal and informed customers can often be a source of potential employees. Build-A-Bear Workshop, for example, often hires customers who come into its stores and exhibit a real interest in the company and its products.
- *Become involved with community organizations.* Many community organizations have top-notch volunteers or employees who may be looking for a new opportunity. Also, don't forget nonprofit organizations or agencies that welcome immigrants new to a region or people in need of a job who may be excellent candidates you can train.
- *Actively seek publicity and word of mouth to create a "buzz" for your company.* Publicity is more believable than advertising; word of mouth is a very effective recruiting tool. Building an image of a dynamic workplace with eager and energetic workers will attract others.
- *Make use of Internet services, social media, and local government agencies.* Recruiting on an online service like Monster.com is very cost-efficient. Government employment services are free and social media creates opportunities to target key employee groups. While not as potent as staff referrals, all provide a source of reaching potential prize employees.

Sources: Raj Sheth, "Small Business Advice: How to Establish a Recruiting Process and Develop a Culture," *The Washington Post*, January 29, 2014; Ritika Puri, "Four Ways Small Businesses Can Recruit Top Talent," *Forbes*, February 18, 2014; and Marc Wayshak, "5 Things You Should Not Do When Hiring for Your Organization," *Entrepreneur*, April 1, 2014.

LO 11–5   Outline the six steps in selecting employees.

SELECTING EMPLOYEES WHO WILL BE PRODUCTIVE

Selection is the process of gathering information and deciding who should be hired, under legal guidelines, to serve the best interests of the individual and the organization. Selecting and training employees are extremely expensive processes in some firms. Just think what's involved: advertising or recruiting agency fees, interview time, medical exams, training costs, unproductive time spent learning the job, possible travel and moving expenses, and more. It can cost one and a half times the employee's annual salary to recruit, process, and train even an entry-level worker, and over six figures for a top manager.[16]

A typical selection process has six steps:

1. *Obtaining complete application forms.* Although equal employment laws limit the kinds of questions that can appear, applications help reveal the applicant's educational background, work experience, career objectives, and other qualifications directly related to the job.

selection
The process of gathering information and deciding who should be hired, under legal guidelines, to serve the best interests of the individual and the organization.

309

Large retail employers like Winn-Dixie and Finish Line make the application process more efficient by using an automated program called Workforce Talent Acquisition.[17] An applicant sits at a computer and answers questions about job experience, time available to work, and personality. The software e-mails a report to the hiring manager recommending whether to interview the applicant and, if so, suggesting questions to ask. Mike Marchetti, executive vice president of store operations for Finish Line, says his company processed 330,000 applications, eliminating 60,000 interview hours and reducing turnover 24 percent.[18]

2. *Conducting initial and follow-up interviews.* A staff member from the human resource department often screens applicants in a first interview. If the interviewer considers the applicant a potential hire, the manager who will supervise the new employee may interview the applicant as well. It's important that managers prepare adequately for the interview to avoid selection decisions they may regret.[19] No matter how innocent the intention, missteps such as asking about pregnancy or child care could later be evidence if the applicant files discrimination charges.

3. *Giving employment tests.* Organizations often use tests to measure basic competency in specific job skills like welding or firefighting, and to help evaluate applicants' personalities and interests. The tests should always be directly related to the job. Employment tests have been legally challenged as potential means of discrimination. Many companies test potential employees in assessment centers where they perform actual job tasks. Such testing can make the selection process more efficient and will generally satisfy legal requirements.

4. *Conducting background investigations.* Most organizations now investigate a candidate's work record, school record, credit history, and references more carefully than in the past to help identify those most likely to succeed. It is simply too costly to hire, train, and motivate people only to lose them and have to start the process over. Services such as LexisNexis allow prospective employers not only to conduct speedy background checks of criminal records, driving records, and credit histories but also to verify work experience and professional and educational credentials.[20] The Adapting to Change box discusses how companies use Facebook and other social media to screen job applicants and weed out those with undesirable traits.

5. *Obtaining results from physical exams.* There are obvious benefits to hiring physically and mentally healthy people. However, according to the Americans with Disabilities Act, medical tests cannot be given just to screen out individuals. In some states, physical exams can be given only after an offer of employment has been accepted. In states that allow pre-employment physical exams, they must be given to everyone applying for the same position. Pre-employment testing to detect drug or alcohol abuse has been controversial, as has screening to detect carriers of HIV, the virus that causes AIDS.

6. *Establishing trial (probationary) periods.* Often an organization will hire an employee conditionally to let the person prove his or her value on the job. After a specified probationary period (perhaps six months or a year), the firm can either permanently hire or discharge that employee on the basis of supervisors' evaluations. Although such systems make it easier to fire inefficient or problem employees, they do not eliminate the high cost of turnover.

Keeping the Right Face on Facebook

Today, the Internet offers companies a gold mine of information concerning potential employees. Estimates are that three out of five organizations use social networking sites such as LinkedIn, Twitter, and of course Facebook to screen prospective hires and evaluate a person's fit with a company's culture. What this means to you is that your social media footprint could be a selling tool in your job search—or could end up costing you a job.

What you do online goes into the virtual world and stays there. The online personality you project reflects to employers who you really are. The growing use of social media background checks has created a new set of candidate disqualifiers. Some of the most flagrant violations that will put you in a company's reject pile include posting:

- Provocative or inappropriate photos
- Information about excessive drinking or using drugs
- Negative comments about a previous employer
- Discriminatory comments related to race, gender, religion, etc.

It's best to use social media to your advantage. Many companies admit to hiring a candidate because of the professional image they conveyed on social media. If you have reservations about posting something on Facebook, the best advice is, don't.

Sources: Kerry Hannon, "Social Media Can Cost You a Job: 6 Solutions," *Forbes,* June 30, 2013; Leslie Kwoh, "Beware: Potential Employers Are Watching You," *The Wall Street Journal,* October 29, 2012; and Ed Zitron, "Social Media Habits of Highly Annoying People," *Inc.,* February 7, 2014.

The selection process is often long and difficult, but it is worth the effort to select new employees carefully because of the high cost of replacing them.[21] Care helps ensure that new employees meet all requirements, including communication skills, education, technical skills, experience, personality, and health.

Hiring Contingent Workers

A company with employment needs that vary—from hour to hour, day to day, week to week, or season to season—may find it cost-effective to hire contingent workers. **Contingent workers** include part-time workers (anyone who works 1 to 34 hours per week), temporary workers (workers paid by temporary employment agencies), seasonal workers, independent contractors, interns, and co-op students.

Companies may also hire contingent workers when full-timers are on some type of leave (such as maternity leave), when there is a peak demand for labor or products (like the holiday shopping season), or when quick service to customers is a priority. Companies also tend to hire more contingent workers in an uncertain economy, particularly when they are available and qualified, and when the jobs require minimal training.

Contingent workers receive few benefits; they are rarely offered health insurance, vacation time, or company pensions. They also tend to earn less than permanent workers do. On the positive side, many on temporary assignments are eventually offered full-time positions. Managers see using temporary workers as a way of weeding out poor workers and finding good hires. Although exact numbers are difficult to gather, the Bureau of Labor Statistics estimates there are approximately 5.7 million contingent workers in the United States, with the majority under age 25.[22] Experts say temps are filling openings in an increasingly broad range of jobs, from unskilled manufacturing and distribution positions to middle management. Increasing numbers of contingent workers are educated professionals such as accountants, attorneys, and engineers.

Many companies include college students in their contingent workforce plan. Working with temporary staffing agencies, companies have easier access

contingent workers
Employees that include part-time workers, temporary workers, seasonal workers, independent contractors, interns, and co-op students.

to workers who have already been screened. Of course, temp agencies benefit college students as well. Once the agencies have assessed the workers, their information is entered into their databases. Then when students are coming back in town for vacations or whatever, they can call the agency and ask them to put their names into the system for work assignments. There is no need to spend time searching for openings or running around town for interviews. Companies such as Randstad USA, a global staffing services giant with over 1,000 branches in the United States, welcomes college students primarily because of their computer skills and familiarity with many of the popular software programs that companies use.[23]

College interns can be considered temporary workers. However, when these internships are unpaid, ethical questions could arise (see the Making Ethical Decisions box).

In an era of rapid change and economic uncertainty, some contingent workers have even found that temping can be more secure than full-time employment.

Seasonal businesses, such as Halloween stores and haunted houses, depend on hiring contingent (temporary) workers to help them through the limited times they are operational. What are the advantages and disadvantages of hiring contingent workers? What are the advantages and disadvantages of being a contingent worker?

test **prep**

- What are the five steps in human resource planning?
- What factors make it difficult to recruit qualified employees?
- What are the six steps in the selection process?
- Who is considered a contingent worker, and why do companies hire such workers?

Use LearnSmart to help retain what you have learned. Access your instructor's Connect course to check out LearnSmart, or go to learnsmartadvantage.com for help.

■LEARNSMART·

LO 11–6   Illustrate employee training and development methods.

TRAINING AND DEVELOPING EMPLOYEES FOR OPTIMUM PERFORMANCE

As technology and other innovations change the workplace, companies must offer training programs that often are quite sophisticated. The term **training and development** includes all attempts to improve productivity by increasing an employee's ability to perform. A well-designed training program often leads to higher retention rates, increased productivity, and greater job satisfaction. Employers in the United States generally find that money for training is well spent. *Training* focuses on short-term skills, whereas *development* focuses on long-term abilities. Both include three steps: (1) assessing organization needs

Intern or Indentured Servant?

Traditionally, unpaid internships have been a great way for young people to transition from college to the workforce. The sacrifice of financial benefits usually pays off in practical experience the interns otherwise would not get in a classroom. Businesses in turn risk nothing financially, but could end up benefiting in the long run if an intern eventually becomes a key paid employee. However, with entry-level positions scarce in today's job market, interns can end up in an unpaid position for as long as six months with no chance of advancement. At that point, interns may wonder if they are improving their chances for a rewarding career or simply performing free services for the company.

In order to distinguish a quality internship from a dead end, simply look at the tasks you're asked to do every day. If your central duties include keeping

the coffee pot full or running errands, chances are that those jobs will not translate into valuable experience down the line. Interns should be taught about the day-to-day duties of a business, not how to be professional gofers. Management must also be sure to outline an intern's responsibilities explicitly and provide regular feedback. Even without a regular paycheck, internships can be beneficial as long as the person is compensated in experience.

Some businesses are quite willing to give interns plenty of professional responsibility. For example, one Toronto newspaper fired all of its paid staff writers and replaced them with unpaid interns.

Is it ethical for companies to use unpaid interns if they know they will not have any jobs to offer at the end of the internships or if the unpaid internships replace paid jobs? Why or why not?

Sources: Knight Kiplinger, "Are Unpaid Interns Exploited by Employers?" *Kiplinger*, April 2011; Bruce Weinstein, "Dos and Don'ts of Unpaid Internships," *Bloomberg Businessweek*, May 28, 2010; and Cathy Vandewater, "Are Unpaid Internships Fair?" Vault Careers, www.vault.com, February 3, 2012.

---

and employee skills to determine training needs; (2) designing training activities to meet identified needs; and (3) evaluating the training's effectiveness. Some common training and development activities are employee orientation, on-the-job training, apprenticeships, off-the-job training, vestibule training, job simulation, and management training.

- **Orientation** is the activity that initiates new employees into the organization; to fellow employees; to their immediate supervisors; and to the policies, practices, and objectives of the firm. Orientation programs range from informal talks to formal activities that last a day or more and often include scheduled visits to various departments and required reading of handbooks. For example, at Zappos every new employee in the online retailer's Henderson, Nevada, headquarters must spend two weeks answering customer calls, two weeks learning in a classroom, and a week shipping boxes in the company's Kentucky fulfillment center.[24]

- **On-the-job training** lets the employee learn by doing, or by watching others for a while and then imitating them, right at the workplace. Salespeople, for example, are often trained by watching experienced salespeople perform (often called *shadowing*). Naturally, this can be either quite effective or disastrous, depending on the skills and habits of the person being observed. On-the-job training is the easiest kind of training to implement when the job is relatively simple (such as clerking in a store) or repetitive (such as collecting refuse, cleaning

training and development
All attempts to improve productivity by increasing an employee's ability to perform. Training focuses on short-term skills, whereas development focuses on long-term abilities.

orientation
The activity that introduces new employees to the organization; to fellow employees; to their immediate supervisors; and to the policies, practices, and objectives of the firm.

on-the-job training
Training at the workplace that lets the employee learn by doing or by watching others for a while and then imitating them.

apprentice programs
Training programs during which a learner works alongside an experienced employee to master the skills and procedures of a craft.

off-the-job training
Internal or external training programs away from the workplace that develop any of a variety of skills or foster personal development.

online training
Training programs in which employees complete classes via the Internet.

vestibule training
Training done in schools where employees are taught on equipment similar to that used on the job.

At FedEx, time is money. That's why the company spends six times more on employee training than the average firm. Does the added expense pay off? You bet. FedEx enjoys a remarkably low 4 percent employee turnover rate. Should other companies follow FedEx's financial commitment to training? Why?

carpets, or mowing lawns). More demanding or intricate jobs require a more intense training effort. Intranets and other forms of technology make cost-effective on-the-job training programs available 24 hours a day. Computer systems can monitor workers' input and give them instructions if they become confused about what to do next.

- In **apprentice programs** a trainee works alongside an experienced employee to master the skills and procedures of a craft. Some apprentice programs include classroom training. Trade unions in skilled crafts, such as bricklaying and plumbing, require a new worker to serve as an apprentice for several years to ensure excellence as well as to limit entry to the union. Workers who successfully complete an apprenticeship earn the classification *journeyman*. As baby boomers retire from skilled trades such as pipefitting, welding, and carpentry, shortages of trained workers are developing. Apprentice programs may be shortened to prepare people for skilled jobs in changing industries such as auto repair and aircraft maintenance that require increased knowledge of computer technology. About 375,000 apprentices are registered with the U.S. Department of Labor.[25]

- **Off-the-job training** occurs away from the workplace and consists of internal or external programs to develop any of a variety of skills or to foster personal development. Training is becoming more sophisticated as jobs become more sophisticated. Furthermore, training is expanding to include education (through the PhD) and personal development. Subjects may include time management, stress management, health and wellness, physical education, nutrition, and even art and languages.

- **Online training** demonstrates how technology is improving the efficiency of many off-the-job training programs. Most colleges and universities now offer a wide variety of online classes, sometimes called *distance learning*, including introductory business courses. Both nonprofit and profit-seeking businesses make extensive use of online training. The Red Cross offers an online tutorial called "Be Red Cross Ready" to help citizens prepare for disasters such as floods, tornadoes, or hurricanes. Technology giants like EMC and large manufacturers like Timken use the online training tool GlobeSmart to teach employees how to operate in different cultures.[26] Online training's key advantage is the ability to provide a large number of employees with consistent content tailored to specific training needs at convenient times.

- **Vestibule training** (or near-the-job training) is done in classrooms with equipment similar to that used on the job so that employees learn proper methods and safety procedures before assuming a specific job assignment. Computer and robotics training is often completed in a vestibule classroom.

- **Job simulation** is the use of equipment that duplicates job conditions and tasks so that trainees can learn skills before attempting them on the job. It differs from vestibule training in that it duplicates the *exact* combination of conditions that occur on the job. This is the kind of training given to astronauts, airline pilots, army tank operators, ship captains, and others who must learn difficult procedures off the job.

Management Development

Managers often need special training. To be good communicators, they need to learn listening skills and empathy. They also need time management, planning, and human relations skills.

Management development, then, is the process of training and educating employees to become good managers, and then monitoring the progress of their managerial skills over time. Management development programs are widespread, especially at colleges, universities, and private management development firms. Managers may participate in role-playing exercises, solve various management cases, and attend films and lectures to improve their skills.

Management development is increasingly being used as a tool to accomplish business objectives. General Electric's and Procter & Gamble's management teams were built with significant investment in their development. Most management training programs include several of the following:

- *On-the-job coaching.* A senior manager assists a lower-level manager by teaching needed skills and providing direction, advice, and helpful feedback. E-coaching is being developed to coach managers electronically, though it will take time and experimentation before firms figure out how to make coaches come to life online.

- *Understudy positions.* Job titles such as *undersecretary* and *assistant* are part of a relatively successful way of developing managers. Selected employees work as assistants to higher-level managers and participate in planning and other managerial functions until they are ready to assume such positions themselves.

- *Job rotation.* So that they can learn about different functions of the organization, managers are often given assignments in a variety of departments. Such job rotation gives them the broad picture of the organization they need to succeed.

- *Off-the-job courses and training.* Managers periodically go to classes or seminars for a week or more to hone technical and human relations skills. Major universities like the University of Michigan, MIT, and the University of Chicago offer specialized short courses to assist managers in performing their jobs more efficiently. McDonald's Corporation has its own Hamburger University. Managers and potential franchisees attend six days of classes and complete a course of study equivalent to 36 hours of college business-school credit.[27]

Networking

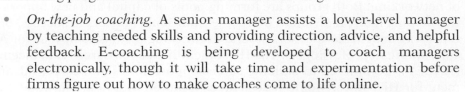

Networking is the process of establishing and maintaining contacts with key managers in your own and other organizations, and using those contacts to weave strong relationships that serve as informal development systems. Of equal or greater importance may be a **mentor**, a corporate manager who supervises, coaches, and guides selected lower-level employees by introducing them to the right people and generally acting as their organizational sponsor.[28] In most organizations informal mentoring occurs as experienced employees assist less experienced workers. However, many organizations formally assign mentors to employees considered to have strong potential.[29]

It's also important to remember that networking and mentoring go beyond the business environment. For example, college is a perfect place to begin networking. Associations you nurture with professors, with local businesspeople through internships, and especially with your classmates can provide a valuable network to turn to for the rest of your career.

NASA's KC-135 aircraft helped astronauts like these train for space missions. After the plane makes a fast and steep ascent, it suddenly free-falls for 20 to 30 seconds enabling the passengers to experience "apparent weightlessness." (For obvious reasons the plane is also known as the Vomit Comet.) Do you think simulation training is effective for jobs like this? Why or why not?

job simulation
The use of equipment that duplicates job conditions and tasks so trainees can learn skills before attempting them on the job.

management development
The process of training and educating employees to become good managers, and then monitoring the progress of their managerial skills over time.

networking
The process of establishing and maintaining contacts with key managers in and outside the organization and using those contacts to weave strong relationships that serve as informal development systems.

mentor
An experienced employee who supervises, coaches, and guides lower-level employees by introducing them to the right people and generally being their organizational sponsor.

Diversity in Management Development

As more women moved into management, they learned the importance of networking and of having mentors. Unfortunately, women often have more difficulty than men in networking or finding mentors, since most senior managers are male. In 1988, women won a major legal victory when the U.S. Supreme Court ruled it illegal to bar women from certain clubs, long open to men only, where business activity flows and contacts are made. This decision allowed more women to enter established networking systems or, in some instances, create their own. Today, women are members of such prestigious clubs such as the Augusta National Golf Club.

Similarly, African American and Hispanic managers learned the value of networking. Both groups are forming pools of capital and new opportunities helping many individuals overcome traditional barriers to success. *Black Enterprise* magazine sponsors several networking forums each year for African American professionals. The Hispanic Alliance for Career Enhancement (HACE) is committed to building career opportunities and career advancement for Hispanics. Monte Jade is an association that helps Taiwanese and Chinese professionals assimilate into U.S. business. Sulekha is an Indian networking group that unites Indians in the United States and around the world.

Companies that take the initiative to develop female and minority managers understand three crucial principles: (1) grooming women and minorities for management positions isn't about legality, morality, or even morale but rather about bringing more talent in the door, the key to long-term profitability; (2) the best women and minorities will become harder to attract and retain, so companies that commit to development early have an edge; and (3) having more women and minorities at all levels lets businesses serve their increasingly female and minority customers better. If you don't have a diversity of people working in the back room, how are you going to satisfy the diversity of people coming in the front door?

LO 11–7   Trace the six steps in appraising employee performance.

APPRAISING EMPLOYEE PERFORMANCE TO GET OPTIMUM RESULTS

performance appraisal
An evaluation that measures employee performance against established standards in order to make decisions about promotions, compensation, training, or termination.

Managers must be able to determine whether their workers are doing an effective and efficient job, with a minimum of errors and disruptions. They do so by using a **performance appraisal**, an evaluation that measures employee performance against established standards in order to make decisions about promotions, compensation, training, or termination. Performance appraisals have six steps:

1. *Establishing performance standards.* This step is crucial. Standards must be understandable, subject to measurement, and reasonable. Both manager and subordinate must accept them.

2. *Communicating those standards.* It's dangerous to assume that employees know what is expected of them. They must be told clearly and precisely what the standards and expectations are, and how to meet them.

3. *Evaluating performance.* If the first two steps are done correctly, performance evaluation is relatively easy. It is a matter of evaluating the employee's behavior to see whether it matches standards.

4. *Discussing results with employees.* Employees often make mistakes and fail to meet expectations at first. It takes time to learn a job and do it well. Discussing an employee's successes and areas that need improvement can provide managers an opportunity to be understanding and helpful and guide the employee to better performance. The performance appraisal can also allow employees to suggest how a task could be done better.

5. *Taking corrective action.* As part of performance appraisal, a manager can take corrective action or provide feedback to help the employee perform better. The key word here is *perform*. The primary purpose of an appraisal is to improve employee performance if possible.[30]

6. *Using the results to make decisions.* Decisions about promotions, compensation, additional training, or firing are all based on performance evaluations. An effective performance appraisal system is also a way of satisfying legal requirements about such decisions.

Managing effectively means getting results through top performance. That's what performance appraisals are for at all levels of the organization, including at the top where managers benefit from reviews by their subordinates and peers.

In the *360-degree review,* management gathers opinions from all around the employee, including those under, above, and on the same level, to get an accurate, comprehensive idea of the worker's abilities. Figure 11.5 illustrates how managers can make performance appraisals more meaningful.

FIGURE 11.5 CONDUCTING EFFECTIVE APPRAISALS AND REVIEWS

DO	DON'T
• **DO** allow sufficient time, without distractions, for appraisal. (Turn off the phone or close the office door.)	• **DON'T** attack the employee personally. Critically evaluate his or her work.
• **DO** include the employee in the process as much as possible. (Let the employee prepare a self-improvement program.)	• **DON'T** make the employee feel uncomfortable or uneasy. Never conduct an appraisal where other employees are present (such as on the shop floor).
• **DO** end the appraisal with positive suggestions for employee improvement.	• **DON'T** wait until the appraisal to address problems with the employee's work that have been developing for some time.

test prep

- Name and describe four training techniques.
- What is the primary purpose of a performance appraisal?
- What are the six steps in a performance appraisal?

LO 11—8   Summarize the objectives of employee compensation programs, and evaluate pay systems and fringe benefits.

COMPENSATING EMPLOYEES: ATTRACTING AND KEEPING THE BEST

Companies don't just compete for customers; they also compete for employees. Compensation is one of the main tools companies use to attract qualified employees, and one of their largest operating costs. The long-term success of a firm—perhaps even its survival—may depend on how well it can control employee costs and optimize employee efficiency. Service organizations like hospitals, hotels, and airlines struggle with high employee costs since these firms are *labor-intensive* (the primary cost of operations is the cost of labor). Manufacturing firms in the auto and steel industries have asked employees to take reductions in wages (called givebacks) to make the firms more competitive. (We discuss this in Chapter 12.) Those are just a few reasons compensation and benefit packages require special attention.[31] In fact, some experts believe determining how best to compensate employees is today's greatest human resources challenge.

A carefully managed and competitive compensation and benefit program can accomplish several objectives:

- Attracting the kinds of people the organization needs, and in sufficient numbers.

- Providing employees with the incentive to work efficiently and productively.

- Keeping valued employees from going to competitors or starting competing firms.

- Maintaining a competitive position in the marketplace by keeping costs low through high productivity from a satisfied workforce.

- Providing employees with some sense of financial security through fringe benefits such as insurance and retirement benefits.

Pay Systems

The way an organization chooses to pay its employees can have a dramatic effect on efficiency and productivity. Managers thus look for a system that compensates employees fairly.

Many companies still use the pay system known as the Hay system, devised by Edward Hay. This plan is based on job tiers, each of which has a strict pay range. The system is set up on a point basis with three key factors considered: know-how, problem solving, and accountability.

Firms like San Francisco–based Skyline Construction let workers pick their own pay system. They can earn a fixed salary or collect a lower salary with potential for a bonus. John Whitney, author of *The Trust Factor*, believes that companies should set pay at the market level or better and then award all employees the same percentage merit raise. Doing so, he says, sends the message that everyone in the company is important. Figure 11.6 outlines some of the most common pay systems. Which do you think is the fairest?

Competitive compensation and benefit programs can have a tremendous impact on employee efficiency and productivity. Sometimes businesses reward exceptional performance by awarding bonuses. Does your instructor ever award bonuses for exceptional performance in class?

FIGURE 11.6 PAY SYSTEMS

Salary

Fixed compensation computed on weekly, biweekly, or monthly pay periods (e.g., $1,600 per month or $400 per week). Salaried employees do not receive additional pay for any extra hours worked.

Hourly wage or daywork

Wage based on number of hours or days worked, used for most blue-collar and clerical workers. Often employees must punch a time clock when they arrive at work and when they leave. Hourly wages vary greatly. The federal minimum wage is $7.25, and top wages go as high as $40 per hour or more for skilled craftspeople. This does not include benefits such as retirement systems, which may add 30 percent or more to the total package.

Piecework system

Wage based on the number of items produced rather than by the hour or day. This type of system creates powerful incentives to work efficiently and productively.

Commission plans

Pay based on some percentage of sales. Often used to compensate salespeople, commission plans resemble piecework systems.

Bonus plans

Extra pay for accomplishing or surpassing certain objectives. There are two types of bonuses: monetary and cashless. Money is always a welcome bonus. Cashless rewards include written thank-you notes, appreciation notes sent to the employee's family, movie tickets, flowers, time off, gift certificates, shopping sprees, and other types of recognition.

Profit-sharing plans

Annual bonuses paid to employees based on the company's profits. The amount paid to each employee is based on a predetermined percentage. Profit sharing is one of the most common forms of performance-based pay.

Gain-sharing plans

Annual bonuses paid to employees based on achieving specific goals such as quality measures, customer satisfaction measures, and production targets.

Stock options

Right to purchase stock in the company at a specific price over a specific period. Often this gives employees the right to buy stock cheaply despite huge increases in the price of the stock. For example, if over the course of his employment a worker received options to buy 10,000 shares of the company stock at $10 each and the price of the stock eventually grows to $100, he can use those options to buy the 10,000 shares (now worth $1 million) for $100,000.

Compensating Teams

Thus far, we've talked about compensating individuals. What about teams? Since you want your teams to be more than simply a group of individuals, would you compensate them like individuals? If you can't answer that question immediately, you're not alone. Most managers believe in using teams, but fewer are sure about how to pay them. Team-based pay programs are not as effective or as fully developed as managers would hope. Measuring and rewarding individual performance on teams, while at the same time rewarding team performance, is tricky—but it can be done. Professional football players, for example, are rewarded as a team when they go to the playoffs and to the Super Bowl, but they are paid individually as well. Companies are now experimenting with and developing similar incentive systems.

Jim Fox, founder and senior partner of compensation and human resource specialist firm Fox Lawson & Associates, insists that setting up the team right in the first place is the key element to designing an appropriate team compensation plan. He believes the pay model to enhance performance will be a natural outcome of the team's development process. Jay Schuster, coauthor of a study of team pay, found that when pay is based strictly on individual performance, it erodes team cohesiveness and makes the team less likely meet its goals as a collaborative effort. Workplace studies indicate over 50 percent of team compensation plans are based on team goals. Skill-based pay and gain-sharing systems are the two most common compensation methods for teams.

Skill-based pay rewards the growth of both the individual and the team. Base pay is raised when team members learn and apply new skills. Baldrige Award winner Eastman Chemical Company rewards its teams for proficiency in technical, social, and business knowledge skills. A cross-functional compensation policy team defines the skills. The drawbacks of skill-based pay are twofold: the system is complex, and it is difficult to relate the acquisition of skills directly to profit gains.

Most *gain-sharing systems* base bonuses on improvements over previous performance.[32] Nucor Steel, one of the largest U.S. steel producers, calculates bonuses on quality—tons of steel that go out the door with no defects. There are no limits on bonuses a team can earn; they usually average around $20,000 per employee each year.[33]

It is important to reward individual team players also. Outstanding team players—who go beyond what is required and make an outstanding individual contribution—should be separately recognized, with cash or noncash rewards. A good way to compensate for uneven team participation is to let the team decide which members get what type of individual award. After all, if you really support the team process, you need to give teams freedom to reward themselves.

Fringe Benefits

Fringe benefits include sick-leave pay, vacation pay, pension plans, and health plans that provide additional compensation to employees beyond base wages. Benefits in recent years grew faster than wages and can't really be considered fringe anymore. In 1929, such benefits accounted for less than 2 percent of payroll; today they can account for about 30 percent. Health care costs have been one of the key reasons for the increase, forcing employees to pay a larger share of their own health insurance bill. Furthermore, it's still unclear exactly what the cost of the Affordable Care Act will be for businesses.[34] Employees often will request more fringe benefits instead of salary, in order to avoid higher taxes. This has resulted in increased debate and government investigation.

Fringe benefits can include recreation facilities, company cars, country club memberships, discounted massages, special home-mortgage rates, paid and unpaid sabbaticals, day care services, and executive dining rooms. Increasingly, employees often want dental care, mental health care, elder care, legal counseling, eye care, and even short workweeks.

fringe benefits
Benefits such as sick-leave pay, vacation pay, pension plans, and health plans that represent additional compensation beyond base wages.

The workers at DreamWorks Studios who helped create Shrek enjoy perks like free breakfast and lunch, afternoon yoga classes, free movie screenings, on-campus art classes, and monthly parties. How might fringe benefits like these affect employee performance?

Cultural Challenges without Conflict

Human resource management of a global workforce begins with an understanding of the customs, laws, and local business needs of every country in which the organization operates. Country-specific cultural and legal standards can affect a variety of human resource functions:

- *Compensation.* Salaries must be converted to and from foreign currencies. Often employees with international assignments receive special allowances for relocation, children's education, housing, travel, and other business-related expenses.
- *Health and pension standards.* There are different social contexts for benefits in other countries. In the Netherlands, the government provides retirement income and health care.

- *Paid time off.* Four weeks of paid vacation is the standard of many European employers. But many other countries lack the short-term and long-term absence policies offered in the

United States, including sick leave, personal leave, and family and medical leave. Global companies need a standard definition of *time off.*
- *Taxation.* Each country has different taxation rules, and the

payroll department must work within each country's regulations.
- *Communication.* When employees leave to work in another country, they often feel disconnected from their home country. Wise companies use their intranet and the Internet to help these faraway employees keep in direct contact.

Human resource policies at home are influenced more and more by conditions and practices in other countries and cultures. Human resource managers need to sensitize themselves and their organizations to overseas cultural and business practices.

Sources: Roy Mauer, "SHRM Identifies Global HR Trends for 2014," *Society for Human Resource Management*, February 3, 2014; and Will Yakowicz, "The Fine Art of Negotiating in Different Cultures," *Inc.,* December 6, 2013.

Understanding that it takes many incentives to attract and retain the best employees, dozens of firms among *Fortune* magazine's "100 Best Companies to Work For" list offer so-called soft benefits. *Soft benefits* help workers maintain the balance between work and family life that is often as important to hardworking employees as the nature of the job itself. These perks include on-site haircuts and shoe repair, concierge services, and free breakfasts. Freeing employees from errands and chores gives them more time for family—and work. Biotechnology firm Genentech even offers doggie day care and Netflix offers employees unlimited vacation days.[35]

At one time, most employees sought benefits that were similar. Today, however, some may seek child care benefits while others prefer attractive pension plans.[36] To address such growing demands, over half of all large firms offer **cafeteria-style fringe benefits**, in which employees can choose the benefits they want up to a certain dollar amount. Such plans let human resource managers equitably and cost-effectively meet employees' individual needs by allowing them choice.

As the cost of administering benefits programs has accelerated, many companies have chosen to outsource this function. Managing benefits can be especially complicated when employees are located in other countries. The Reaching Beyond Our Borders box discusses the human resource challenges faced by global businesses. To put it simply, benefits are often as important to recruiting top talent as salary and may even become more important in the future.

cafeteria-style fringe benefits
Fringe benefits plan that allows employees to choose the benefits they want up to a certain dollar amount.

LO 11–9   Demonstrate how managers use scheduling plans to adapt to workers' needs.

SCHEDULING EMPLOYEES TO MEET ORGANIZATIONAL AND EMPLOYEE NEEDS

Workplace trends and the increasing costs of transportation have led employees to look for scheduling flexibility. Flextime, in-home employment, and job sharing are important benefits employees seek.

Flextime Plans

flextime plan
Work schedule that gives employees some freedom to choose when to work, as long as they work the required number of hours or complete their assigned tasks.

core time
In a flextime plan, the period when all employees are expected to be at their job stations.

A **flextime plan** gives employees some freedom to choose which hours to work, as long as they work the required number of hours or complete their assigned tasks. The most popular plans allow employees to arrive between 7:00 and 9:00 a.m. and leave between 4:00 and 6:00 p.m. Flextime plans generally incorporate core time. **Core time** is the period when all employees are expected to be at their job stations. An organization may designate core time as 9:00 to 11:00 a.m. and 2:00 to 4:00 p.m. During these hours all employees are required to be at work (see Figure 11.7). Flextime allows employees to adjust to work-life demands. Two-income families find them especially helpful. Companies that use flextime say that it boosts employee productivity and morale.[37]

Flextime is not for all organizations, however. It doesn't suit shift work like fast-food or assembly processes like manufacturing, where everyone on a given shift must be at work at the same time. Another disadvantage is that managers often have to work longer days to assist and supervise in organizations that may operate from 6:00 a.m. to 6:00 p.m. Flextime also makes communication more difficult since certain employees may not be there when others need to talk to them. Furthermore, if not carefully supervised, some employees could abuse the system, causing resentment among others.

compressed workweek
Work schedule that allows an employee to work a full number of hours per week but in fewer days.

Another option that about one in four companies uses is a **compressed workweek**. An employee works the full number of hours, but in fewer than the standard number of days. For example, an employee may work four 10-hour days and then enjoy a long weekend, instead of working five 8-hour days with a traditional weekend. There are obvious advantages of compressed

FIGURE 11.7 A FLEXTIME CHART
At this company, employees can start work anytime between 6:30 and 9:30 a.m. They take a half hour for lunch anytime between 11:00 a.m. and 1:30 p.m. and can leave between 3:00 and 6:30 p.m. Everyone works an eight-hour day. The blue arrows show a typical employee's flextime day.

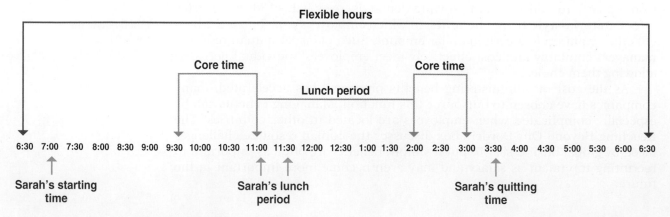

workweeks, but some employees get tired working such long hours, and productivity can decline. Others find the system a great benefit, however, and are enthusiastic about it.[38] Nurses often work compressed weeks.

Home-Based Work

Nearly 13 million U.S. workers now work from home at least once per week.[39] Approximately 12 percent of businesses use some home-based work. Home-based workers can choose their own hours, interrupt work for child care or other tasks, and take time out for personal reasons. Working at home isn't for everyone. It requires discipline to stay focused on the job and not be easily distracted.[40]

Home-based work can also be a cost saver for employers. Estimates are a company can reduce operating costs by almost $6,500 per year for every employee who telecommutes just one day a week.[41] However, home-based work is not for every company either. In 2013, Yahoo! announced that employees would no longer be allowed to work from home. Bank of America also made significant cuts to its popular My Work program that permits employees to work remotely about 60 percent of the time.

Many large companies also offer "hot-desking," or sharing a desk with other employees who work at different times. Companies such as Office Depot have shifted to U.S. home-based call agents and saved 30 or 40 percent on the cost of each call by not providing workspace (or benefits) for its home-based call center workers. Figure 11.8 outlines the benefits and challenges of home-based work to organizations, individuals, and society.

Job-Sharing Plans

Job sharing lets two or more part-time employees share one full-time job. Students and parents with small children, for instance, may work only during school hours, and older workers can work part-time before fully retiring or after retiring. Benefits of job sharing include:

- Employment opportunities for those who cannot or prefer not to work full-time.

job sharing
An arrangement whereby two part-time employees share one full-time job.

FIGURE 11.8 BENEFITS AND CHALLENGES OF HOME-BASED WORK
Home-based work (also known as telecommuting) offers many benefits and challenges to organizations, individuals, and society as a whole.

	BENEFITS	CHALLENGES
To Organization	• Increases productivity due to fewer sick days, fewer absences, higher job satisfaction, and higher work performance ratings • Broadens available talent pool • Reduces costs of providing on-site office space	• Makes it more difficult to appraise job performance • Can negatively affect the social network of the workplace and can make it difficult to promote team cohesiveness • Complicates distribution of tasks (should office files, contact lists, and such be allowed to leave the office?)
To Individual	• Makes more time available for work and family by reducing or eliminating commute time • Reduces expenses of buying and maintaining office clothes • Avoids office politics • Helps balance work and family • Expands employment opportunities for individuals with disabilities	• Can cause feeling of isolation from social network • Can raise concerns regarding promotions and other rewards due to being out of sight, out of mind • May diminish individual's influence within company due to limited opportunity to learn the corporate culture
To Society	• Decreases traffic congestion • Discourages community crime that might otherwise occur in bedroom communities • Increases time available to build community ties	• Increases need to resolve zoning regulations forbidding business deliveries in residential neighborhoods • May reduce ability to interact with other people in a personal, intimate manner

- An enthusiastic and productive workforce.
- Reduced absenteeism and tardiness.
- Ability to schedule part-time workers into peak demand periods (e.g., banks on payday).
- Retention of experienced employees who might otherwise have retired.

Disadvantages include the need to hire, train, motivate, and supervise at least twice as many people and perhaps prorate some fringe benefits. But firms are finding that the advantages generally outweigh the disadvantages.

Lo 11–10   Describe how employees can move through a company: promotion, reassignment, termination, and retirement.

MOVING EMPLOYEES UP, OVER, AND OUT

Employees don't always stay in the position they were hired to fill. They may excel and move up the corporate ladder or fail and move out the door. Employees can also be reassigned or retire. Of course, some choose to move themselves by going to another company.

Promoting and Reassigning Employees

Many companies find that promotion from within the company improves employee morale. It's also cost-effective in that the promoted employees are already familiar with the corporate culture and procedures and don't need to spend valuable time on basic orientation.

In the new, flatter corporate structures (see Chapter 8), there are fewer levels for employees to reach than in the past. Thus they often move *over* to a new position rather than *up*. Such lateral transfers allow employees to develop and display new skills and learn more about the company overall. Reassignment is one way of motivating experienced employees to remain in a company with few advancement opportunities.

Terminating Employees

We've seen that the relentless pressure of global competition, shifts in technology, increasing customer demands for greater value, and uncertain economic conditions have human resource managers struggling to manage layoffs and firings. Even if the economy is booming, many companies are hesitant to hire or rehire workers full-time. Why is that the case? One reason is that the cost of terminating employees is prohibitively high in terms of lost training costs and possible damages and legal fees for wrongful discharge suits. That's why many companies are either using temporary employees or outsourcing certain functions.

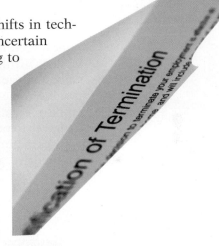

At one time the prevailing employment doctrine in the United States was "employment at will." This meant managers had as much freedom to fire workers as workers had to leave voluntarily. Most states now limit the at-will doctrine to protect employees from wrongful firing. An employer can no longer fire someone for exposing the company's illegal actions or refusing to violate a law. Employees who are members of a minority or other protected group also may have protections under equal employment law. In some cases, workers fired for using illegal drugs have sued on the grounds that they have an illness (addiction) and are therefore protected by laws barring discrimination under the Americans with Disabilities Act (ADA). Well-intended legislation has in some ways restricted management's ability to terminate employees as it increased workers' rights to their jobs. See Figure 11.9 for advice about how to minimize the chance of wrongful discharge lawsuits.

> *During the economic crisis, managers had to terminate a great number of employees. As the economy slowly recovered, have employers rehired full-time workers? Why or why not? What alternatives do employers have?*

FIGURE 11.9 HOW TO AVOID WRONGFUL DISCHARGE LAWSUITS

Sources: "In Economics Old and New, Treatment of Workers Is Paramount," *The Washington Post*, February 11, 2001, p. L1; and U.S. Law, www.uslaw.com.

Consultants offer this advice to minimize the chance of a lawsuit for wrongful discharge:

- Prepare before hiring by requiring recruits to sign a statement that retains management's freedom to terminate at will.
- Don't make unintentional promises by using such terms as *permanent employment*.
- Document reasons before firing and make sure you have an unquestionable business reason for the firing.
- Fire the worst first and be consistent in discipline.
- Buy out bad risk by offering severance pay in exchange for a signed release from any claims.
- Be sure to give employees the true reasons they are being fired. If you do not, you cannot reveal it to a recruiter asking for a reference without risking a defamation lawsuit.
- Disclose the reasons for an employee's dismissal to that person's potential new employers. For example, if you fired an employee for dangerous behavior and you withhold that information from your references, you can be sued if the employee commits a violent act at his or her next job.

Retiring Employees

Companies looking to downsize sometimes offer early retirement benefits to entice older (and more expensive) workers to retire. Such benefits can include one-time cash payments, known in some companies as *golden handshakes*. The advantage early retirement benefits have over layoffs or firing is the increased morale of surviving employees. Retiring senior workers earlier also increases promotion opportunities for younger employees.

Losing Valued Employees

In spite of a company's efforts to retain them, some talented employees will choose to pursue opportunities elsewhere. Knowing their reasons for leaving can be invaluable in preventing the loss of other good people in the future. One way to learn the reasons is to have an outside expert conduct an *exit interview*. Outsiders can provide confidentiality and anonymity that earns more honest feedback than employees are comfortable giving in face-to-face interviews with their bosses. Web-based systems can capture, track, and statistically analyze employee exit interview data to generate reports that identify trouble areas. Such programs can also coordinate exit interview data with employee satisfaction surveys to predict which departments should expect turnover to occur.

Attracting and retaining the best employees is the key to success in the competitive global business environment. Dealing with controversial issues employees have on the job is challenging and never-ending. Chapter 12 discusses such issues.

Use LearnSmart to help retain what you have learned. Access your instructor's Connect course to check out LearnSmart, or go to learnsmartadvantage.com for help.

LEARNSMART

test prep

- Can you name and describe five alternative compensation techniques?
- What advantages do compensation plans such as profit sharing offer an organization?
- What are the benefits and challenges of flextime? Telecommuting? Job sharing?

summary

LO 11–1 Explain the importance of human resource management, and describe current issues in managing human resources.

- **What are current challenges and opportunities in the human resource area?**
Many current challenges and opportunities arise from changing demographics: more women, minorities, immigrants, and older workers in the workforce. Others include a shortage of trained workers and an abundance of unskilled workers, skilled workers in declining industries requiring retraining, changing employee work attitudes, and complex laws and regulations.

LO 11–2   Illustrate the effects of legislation on human resource management.

- **What are some of the key laws?**
  See Figure 11.2 and review the text section on laws.

LO 11–3   Summarize the five steps in human resource planning.

- **What are the steps in human resource planning?**
  The five steps are (1) preparing a human resource inventory of the organization's employees; (2) preparing a job analysis; (3) assessing future demand; (4) assessing future supply; and (5) establishing a plan for recruiting, hiring, educating, appraising, compensating, and scheduling employees.

LO 11–4   Describe methods that companies use to recruit new employees, and explain some of the issues that make recruitment challenging.

- **What methods do human resource managers use to recruit new employees?**
  Recruiting sources are classified as either internal or external. Internal sources include those hired from within (transfers, promotions, reassignments) and employees who recommend others to hire. External recruitment sources include advertisements, public and private employment agencies, college placement bureaus, management consultants, professional organizations, referrals, walk-in applications, and the Internet.
- **Why has recruitment become more difficult?**
  Legal restrictions complicate hiring and firing practices. Finding suitable employees can be more difficult if companies are considered unattractive workplaces.

LO 11–5   Outline the six steps in selecting employees.

- **What are the six steps in the selection process?**
  The steps are (1) obtaining complete application forms, (2) conducting initial and follow-up interviews, (3) giving employment tests, (4) conducting background investigations, (5) obtaining results from physical exams, and (6) establishing a trial period of employment.

LO 11–6   Illustrate employee training and development methods.

- **What are some training activities?**
  Training activities include employee orientation, on- and off-the-job training, apprentice programs, online training, vestibule training, and job simulation.
- **What methods help develop managerial skills?**
  Management development methods include on-the-job coaching, understudy positions, job rotation, and off-the-job courses and training.
- **How does networking fit in this process?**
  Networking is the process of establishing contacts with key managers within and outside the organization to get additional development assistance.

LO 11–7   Trace the six steps in appraising employee performance.

- **How do managers evaluate performance?**
  The steps are (1) establish performance standards; (2) communicate those standards; (3) compare performance to standards; (4) discuss results;

(5) take corrective action when needed; and (6) use the results for decisions about promotions, compensation, additional training, or firing.

LO 11–8   Summarize the objectives of employee compensation programs, and describe various pay systems and fringe benefits.

- **What are common types of compensation systems?**
  They include salary systems, hourly wages, piecework, commission plans, bonus plans, profit-sharing plans, and stock options.

- **What types of compensation are appropriate for teams?**
  The most common are gain-sharing and skill-based compensation programs. Managers also reward outstanding individual performance within teams.

- **What are fringe benefits?**
  Fringe benefits include sick leave, vacation pay, company cars, pension plans, and health plans that provide additional compensation to employees beyond base wages. Cafeteria-style fringe benefits plans let employees choose the benefits they want, up to a certain dollar amount.

LO 11–9   Demonstrate how managers use scheduling plans to adapt to workers' needs.

- **What scheduling plans can adjust work to employees' need for flexibility?**
  Such plans include job sharing, flextime, compressed workweeks, and home-based work.

Access your instructor's Connect course to check out LearnSmart or go to learnsmartadvantage.com for help.

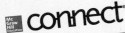

LO 11–10   Describe how employees can move through a company: promotion, reassignment, termination, and retirement.

- **How can employees move within a company?**
  Employees can be moved up (promotion), over (reassignment), or out (termination or retirement) of a company. They can also choose to leave a company to pursue opportunities elsewhere.

---

key terms

affirmative action 304

apprentice programs 314

cafeteria-style fringe benefits 321

compressed workweek 322

contingent workers 311

core time 322

flextime plan 322

fringe benefits 320

human resource management (HRM) 300

job analysis 306

job description 306

job sharing 323

job simulation 314

job specifications 306

management development 315

mentor 315

networking 315

off-the-job training 314

online training 314

on-the-job training 313

orientation 313

performance appraisal 316

recruitment 307

reverse discrimination 304

selection 309

training and development 312

vestibule training 314

critical thinking

1. Does human resource management interest you as a career? What are your experiences working with human resource professionals?

2. What effects have dual-career families had on the human resource function?

3. What problems can arise when family members work together in the same firm?

4. If you were a human resource manager, how would you address the brain drain that occurs as knowledgeable workers retire?

5. Imagine you must fire an employee. What effect might the dismissal have on remaining employees? Explain how you would tell the employee and your other subordinates.

developing workplace skills

Key: ● **Team**   ★ **Analytic**   ▲ **Communication**   ◙ **Technology**

1. Look for job listings online or in your local newspaper and find at least two positions you might like to have when you graduate. List the qualifications specified in each of the ads and identify methods the companies might use to determine how well applicants meet them.   ◙ ★

2. Read several current business periodicals or search online to find information about the latest court rulings on benefits, affirmative action, and other human resource issues. Summarize your findings. Is there a trend in these decisions? If so, what is it, and what will it mean for tomorrow's college graduates?   ◙ ★

3. Recall any on-the-job and off-the-job training sessions you've experienced. Write a brief critique of each. How would you improve them? Share your ideas with the class.   ★ ▲

4. Consider the following occupations: doctor, computer salesperson, computer software developer, teacher, and assembly worker. Identify the method of compensation you think is appropriate for each. Explain your answer.   ★ ▲

5. Choose one of these positions: a human resource manager notifying employees of mandatory drug testing or an employee representative protesting such testing. Write a memorandum supporting your position.   ★ ▲

taking it to the net

PURPOSE

The two purposes here are to illustrate the types of questions managers typically ask during interviews and to practice answering such questions in a safe environment.

EXERCISE

Go to Monster.com and search for the article "100 Potential Interview Questions." This article lists some of the more common questions asked during an interview. Click on the questions for advice about how to best answer the questions. This will give you the opportunity to test your answers so that when you do go on an actual interview you are less likely to fumble for an answer.

---

video case   McGraw Hill Education connect

TEACH FOR AMERICA

There are many critical problems affecting America's public education system, especially the lack of qualified teachers willing to work at troubled inner city schools. The teaching profession's human resource management process may be breaking down in its ability to find and retain the best teachers possible.

The government service program Teach for America tries to solve this problem by training young, highly qualified college grads to teach at underperforming schools. For a two-year period, Teach for America recruits work with students who are dealing with crises like poverty, insufficient nutrition, and low self-esteem. Although most participants use the program as a first step into an education career, others apply the lessons they learn from the program to many different professions.

Ultimately, though, Teach for America's mission is to place more quality teachers into the schools that need them. Many Professional teachers avoid the challenges of inner-city schools, leaving these institutions understaffed. To the human resource managers of many public school systems, Teach for America recruits are an irreplaceable resource. That's because applicants are evaluated rigorously through a lengthy recruitment process. After applicants are interviewed by phone, they must then develop a prospective lesson plan. If they pass that stage, they do an in-person interview, take a written test, and participate in a monitored group discussion with other applicants. In the end, only about 1 applicant in 10 makes it into the popular program.

Once selected, Teach for America recruits go through a structured orientation and off-the-job training program that ends in job simulation

exercises. The intensive five-week summer course prepares volunteers for the challenges and needs of the inner-city classroom. They are then assigned to a school, where they receive additional support and training. Since the job can be extremely challenging, Teach for America's relatively generous compensation package serves as a major motivator. As teachers, recruits earn salaries comparable to other colleagues at their grade level.

Teach for America closely evaluates the performance of its teachers to judge the overall effectiveness of the program. Teach for America alumni perform better than many of their counterparts, including some career teachers with more training and education. And even when performance is about the same, recruits may be filling positions that were otherwise impossible to fill because of lack of candidates and resources.

Despite all the good work it's done so far, Teach for America knows that the American public school system still has a lot to learn about educating disadvantaged children. But with the more than 10,000 recruits it trains each year, Teach for America continues to provide challenged students with a fighting chance to fulfill their untapped potential.

THINKING IT OVER

1. What seems to be the primary reason why Teach for America teachers perform better than many other teachers?

2. What types of training do Teach for America recruits undergo before they are placed in the classroom?

3. Why is a rigorous performance appraisal program a key part of the Teach for America program?

notes

1. "Coming to an Office Near You," *The Economist,* January 18, 2014; and "The Onrushing Wave," *The Economist,* January 18, 2014.
2. Floyd Norris, "Changes in the Labor Force Mask Gains in the Jobs Situation," *The New York Times,* November 1, 2013; Brad Plumer, "Three Reasons the U.S. Labor Force Keeps Shrinking," *The Washington Post,* September 6, 2013; and Victoria Stilwell, "Boomers Turn On, Tune In, Drop Out of U.S. Labor Force, *Bloomberg Businessweek,* February 10, 2014.
3. Joshua Wright, "America's Skilled Trades Dilemma: Shortages Loom as Most-in-Demand Group of Workers Ages," *Forbes,* March 7, 2013.
4. Brad Plumer, "CBO: Expect Slower Growth This Decade—and as a Result Higher Deficits," *The Washington Post,* February 4, 2014.
5. Louise Radnofsky and Damien Paletta, "Health Law to Cut into Labor Force," *The Wall Street Journal,* February 4, 2014.
6. Douglas Ernst, "Some Member of Civil-Rights Panel Accuse EEOC of Overreach on Racism," *The Washington Times,* February 20, 2014; and Jacob Gershman, "EEOC Sues Less, but Tactics Draw Flak," *The Wall Street Journal,* February 9, 2014.
7. Patrick May, "Disabled 'Serial Plaintiffs' Do Legal Battle with Small Businesses over Access Issues," *San Jose Mercury News,* February 18, 2014.
8. Equal Employment Opportunity Commission, www.eeoc.gov, accessed March 2014.
9. Penelope Lemov, "What It Takes to Win an Age Discrimination Case," *Forbes,* April 30, 2013.
10. Julian L. Alssid, "A New Gallup Survey Says Colleges and Employers Disagree about How Workforce-Ready Graduates Are . . . Who's Right?" *Huffington Post,* February 27, 2014.
11. Juan Carlos Perez, "IBM Preps Talent Suite for Human Resources Tasks," *PC World,* January 27, 2014.
12. Bennett J. Louden, "Rochester Grocers Wary of Tech, Adapt Slowly," *Rochester Democrat and Chronicle,* February 28, 2014.
13. Patricia Stilwell, "Report: Economy Will Face Shortage of 20 Million Workers in 2020," *US News & World Report,* July 8, 2013.
14. "Gone But Not Forgotten," *The Economist,* March 1, 2014.
15. Mark Cohen, "Online Hiring Tools Are Changing Recruiting Techniques," *The New York Times,* May 15, 2013; and Raj Sheth, "How to Establish a Recruiting Process and Develop a Culture," *The Washington Post,* January 29, 2014.
16. John Brandon, "The Real Cost of Hiring the Wrong Employee," *Inc.,* September 2013.
17. Kronos, www.kronos.com/hiring-software/hiring.aspx, accessed March 2014.
18. Kronos, www.kronos.ca/Case-Study/Finish-Line.aspx, accessed March 2014.
19. Brandon, "The Real Cost of Hiring the Wrong Employee."
20. "LexisNexis, www.lexisnexis.com, accessed March 2014; and Dave Larsen, "LexisNexis Wins Software Industry Award," *Dayton Daily News,* February 11, 2014.
21. Suzanne Lucas, "How Much Employee Turnover Really Costs You," *Inc.,* August 2013; and Jena MacGregor, "What It Costs to Replace a Twenty-Something," *The Washington Post,* August 6, 2013.
22. U.S. Department of Labor, www.dol.gov, accessed March 2014.
23. RandstadUSA, www.us.randstad.com, accessed March 2014.
24. Scott Levy, "Why Stellar Customer Service Is Key to Building Your Online Brand," *Entrepreneur,* December 23, 2013.
25. U.S. Department of Labor, www.doleta.gov, accessed March 2014.
26. GlobeSmart, www.globesmart.com, accessed March 2014.
27. McDonald's, www.mcdonalds.com, accessed March 2014.
28. Ross McCammon, "Guiding Lights," *Entrepreneur,* March 2013.
29. Jeffrey Dauksevich, "How to Be an Effective Mentor," *Entrepreneur,* December 27, 2013; and John Brandon, "How to Maximize the Benefits of Mentoring," *Inc.,* January 2014.
30. Daniel Bortz, "Ace Your Annual Review," *Money,* March 2014.
31. Sharon Wienbar, "Making Sense Out of Cents: Determining Employee Compensation," *Entrepreneur,* February 13, 2014.
32. Ronald J. Recardo and Diane Pricones, "Is Gainsharing for You?" www.qualitydigest.com, accessed March 2014.
33. Motley Fool Staff, "Q-and-A with Nucor CEO Dan DiMicco," *The Motley Fool,* www.fool.com, January 10, 2011.
34. Chad Terhune, "Health Premiums Expected to Rise for Many Small Firms under Obamacare," *Los Angeles Times,* February 25, 2014; and Joane Weiner, "Experts Disagree about Job Losses and the Moral Status of Obamacare," *The Washington Post,* February 26, 2014.
35. Amanda Greene, "Nine Companies with the Best Perks," www.womansday.com/life-9-companies-the-best-perks, accessed March 2014.
36. Scott Liebs, "You Can Buy Employee Happiness. (But Should You?) Companies That Offer Lavish Benefits Believe There Is a Return on Their Investment. The Challenge: Figuring Out How to Calculate It," *Inc.,* January 2014.
37. Gwen Moran, "Surviving the Open-Floor Plan," *Entrepreneur,* February 13, 2014.
38. Scott Benson, "Why Compressed Workweeks Can Be Great for Employers and Employees," *Huffington Post,* March 5, 2014.
39. Beth Braverman, "Be There—Even When You're Not," *CNNMoney.com,* March 2013.
40. Bill Kolbenschlag, "How to Keep Virtual Teams Connected," *Forbes,* March 5, 2014.
41. Anne Kates Smith, "Make Working at Home Work," *Kiplinger Personal Finance,* January 2013.

photo credits

12

Dealing with Union and Employee–Management Issues

Learning objectives

AFTER YOU HAVE READ AND STUDIED THIS CHAPTER, YOU SHOULD BE ABLE TO

LO 12-1   Trace the history of organized labor in the United States.

LO 12-2   Discuss the major legislation affecting labor unions.

LO 12-3   Outline the objectives of labor unions.

LO 12-4   Describe the tactics used by labor and management during conflicts, and discuss the role of unions in the future.

LO 12-5   Assess some of today's controversial employee–management issues, such as executive compensation, pay equity, sexual harassment, child care and elder care, drug testing, and violence in the workplace.

The relationship between management and employees is a delicate one. While both have a vested interest in seeing their business thrive, the needs and desires of each party can sometimes be wholly different. Few people understand this better than DeMaurice Smith, executive director of the NFL Players Association (NFLPA). In 2011 Smith butted heads with team owners during a labor lockout that would have delayed the next NFL season if not for the last-minute collective bargaining deal he negotiated.

Before he was brokering high-level contracts, Smith spent his childhood in a small Maryland town just outside of Washington, DC. His parents provided plenty of inspiration as he developed the attributes that would serve him so well in his adult life. Smith's father was the son of a sharecropper in the Jim Crow—era South and one of 14 siblings. His mother, meanwhile, had suffered severe burns as a child and had to relearn how to walk. "I'd like to tell you there was some hokey speeches about overcoming adversity and all those things in my parents' house growing up, but there weren't," said Smith. "It was a very quiet confidence that you could talk about anything, you could do anything, and regardless of what happens this family will stick together."

After getting a bachelor's degree in political science from Cedarville University, Smith earned a law degree at the University of Virginia in 1989. He soon landed a job as Assistant United States Attorney in the District of Columbia where he gained a reputation as a tough but dedicated trial lawyer. He spent nine years as a prosecutor before joining a powerful Washington firm that represented senior executives at some of the biggest companies in the nation. The valuable connections Smith developed at these jobs proved to be the deciding factor when the NFLPA elected him as its director in 2009.

Smith didn't have much time to celebrate his new position, though. By then the NFL team owners had decided not to renew the collective bargaining agreement (CBA) that it had struck with players years before. With a $4 billion TV deal soon to take effect, Smith and the NFLPA knew the owners wanted more money before a new CBA would be signed. After failing to find a compromise before the CBA's expiration date, the NFLPA renounced its collective bargaining rights and were "locked out" of work. In the months that followed, Smith took the spotlight as federal mediations failed and an anti-trust suit filed against NFL owners gained steam. Relations between the two parties only became more strained as summer arrived without a new deal in place. Employees and fans began to prepare for the unthinkable: an autumn without NFL football.

The lockout saga finally came to an end when Smith brokered a new CBA in July. Although the deal slightly reduced salaries for rookies, it also introduced new safety rules that extended off-seasons and reduced the amount of rough contact during practice. With the lockout now in his rearview mirror, safety concerns are now Smith's number one priority.

Professional sports, of course, is not the only industry that has problems dealing with labor—management relations, employee compensation, and other work-related issues. This chapter discusses such issues and other employee—management concerns, including executive pay, pay equity, child and elder care, drug testing, and violence in the workplace.

Sources: Jim Trotter, "DeMaurice Smith Chastises NFL for Lack of Player Safety," *Sports Illustrated,* January 31, 2013; Aaron Kuriloff, "Four of Five NFL Players Distrust Team Doctor, Survey Says," *Bloomberg Businessweek,* February 1, 2013; and "Executive Director: DeMaurice Smith," www.nflplayers.com, accessed April 2014.

DeMaurice Smith

- Executive Director of the NFL Players Association
- Faced off with NFL owners during the 2011 players lockout
- Negotiates player/ex-player issues like safety and health care

www.nfl.com

@demauricesmith

The late management consultant Peter Drucker suggested that CEOs should not earn more than 20 times the salary of the company's lowest-paid employee. Most firms ignore his suggestion, but at our company executives' pay is capped at 19 times the average employee's salary. Still, we are one of the fastest-growing companies in the United States. Name that company. (The answer is in the chapter.)

EMPLOYEE–MANAGEMENT ISSUES

union

An employee organization whose main goal is representing its members in employee–management negotiation of job-related issues.

A good starting point in discussing employee–management relations in the United States is a discussion of labor unions. A **union** is an employee organization whose main goal is representing its members in employee–management negotiations over job-related issues. Recently labor unions have been in the news more than they have been for years. For example, the conflicts between players and various professional sports regarding safety concerns is just one issue making headlines.

Another major issue involves dealing with public sector labor unions (those employees who work for governments, such as teachers, firefighters, police officers, etc.). With many states facing serious debt problems, and major cities like Detroit declaring bankruptcy, government officials are trying to cut costs, particularly labor costs.[1] However, states with public sector unions have had limited ability to cut labor costs because of prior agreements with the unions that represent public workers. For now, it is enough to say that public sector labor unions and governments will have challenges going forward due to increasing labor and pension costs to governments. Before we get into such issues, however, let's explore the nature of unions in general and what the issues have been over time.

The relationship between managers and employees isn't always smooth. Management's responsibility to produce a profit by maximizing productivity sometimes necessitates hard decisions, which limit managers' chances to win popularity contests with workers. Labor (the collective term for nonmanagement workers) is interested in fair and competent management, human dignity, and a reasonable share in the wealth its work generates. Like other managerial challenges, employee–management issues require open discussion, goodwill, and compromise.

Workers originally formed unions to protect themselves from intolerable work conditions and unfair treatment, and also to secure some say in the operation of their jobs. As the number of private sector union members grew, workers gained more negotiating power with managers and more political power. For example, labor unions were largely responsible for the establishment of minimum-wage laws, overtime rules, workers' compensation, severance pay, child-labor laws, job safety regulations, and more.[2]

Union strength among private workers, however, has waned as private labor unions have lost the economic and political power they once had, and membership has declined.[3] Economists suggest that increased global competition, shifts from manufacturing to service and high-tech industries that are less heavily unionized, growth in part-time work, and changes in management philosophies are some of the reasons for private labor's decline. Many insist that private unions have seen their brightest days.[4] Let's first look at labor unions and then analyze some key issues affecting employee–management relations.

LO 12–1   Trace the history of organized labor in the United States.

LABOR UNIONS YESTERDAY AND TODAY

Historians generally agree that today's unions are an outgrowth of the economic transition caused by the Industrial Revolution of the 19th and early 20th centuries. Workers who once toiled in the fields, dependent on the mercies of nature for survival, found themselves relying on the continuous roll of factory presses and assembly lines for their living. Making the transition from an agricultural economy to an industrial economy was quite difficult. Over time, workers in businesses learned that strength through unity (unions) could lead to improved job conditions, better wages, and job security.

Today's critics of organized labor maintain that few of the inhuman conditions once dominant in U.S. industry exist in the modern workplace. They argue that labor is an industry in itself, and protecting workers has become secondary.[5] Some workplace analysts maintain that the current legal system and changing management philosophies minimize the possibility that sweatshops (workplaces of the late 19th and early 20th centuries with unsatisfactory, unsafe, or oppressive labor conditions) could reappear in the United States. Let's look at the history of labor unions to see how we got to where we are today.

craft union
An organization of skilled specialists in a particular craft or trade.

While the technological achievement of the Industrial Revolution brought countless new products to market and reduced the need for physical labor in many industries, it also put pressure on workers to achieve higher productivity in factory jobs that called for long hours and low pay. Can you see how these conditions made it possible for labor unions to take hold by the turn of the 20th century?

The History of Organized Labor

Formal labor organizations in the United States date to the time of the American Revolution. As early as 1792, cordwainers (shoemakers) in Philadelphia met to discuss fundamental work issues of pay, hours, conditions, and job security—pretty much the same issues that dominate labor negotiations today. The cordwainers were a **craft union**, an organization of skilled specialists in a particular craft or trade, typically local or regional. Most craft unions were established to achieve some short-range goal, such as curtailing the use of convict labor as an alternative to available free labor. Often, after attaining their goal, the union disbanded. This situation changed dramatically in the late 19th century with the expansion of the Industrial Revolution in the United States. The Industrial Revolution brought enormous productivity increases, gained through mass production and job specialization, that made the United States an economic world power. This growth, however, created problems for workers in terms of productivity expectations, hours of work, wages, job security, and unemployment.

Workers were faced with the reality that productivity was vital. Those who failed to produce, or who stayed home because they were ill or had family problems, lost their jobs. Over time, the increased emphasis on production led firms

to expand the hours of work. The length of the average workweek in 1900 was 60 hours, but an 80-hour week was not uncommon for some industries.[6] Wages were low, and child labor was widespread. Minimum-wage laws and unemployment benefits were nonexistent, which made periods of unemployment hard on families who earned subsistence wages. The nearby Spotlight on Small Business box highlights the severity of these conditions and the tragedy that resulted.

Knights of Labor
The first national labor union; formed in 1869.

The first truly national labor organization was the **Knights of Labor**, formed by Uriah Smith Stephens in 1869. The Knights offered membership to all private working people, *including employers,* and promoted social causes as well as labor and economic issues. By 1886, the organization claimed a membership of 700,000. The Knights' intention was to gain significant *political* power and eventually restructure the U.S. economy. The organization fell from prominence, however, after being blamed for a bomb that killed eight policemen during a labor rally at Haymarket Square in Chicago in 1886.

American Federation of Labor (AFL)
An organization of craft unions that championed fundamental labor issues; founded in 1886.

A rival group, the **American Federation of Labor (AFL)**, was formed that same year. By 1890, the AFL, under the dynamic leadership of Samuel Gompers, stood at the forefront of the labor movement. The AFL was never one big union, but rather an organization of craft unions that championed fundamental labor issues. It intentionally limited membership to skilled workers (craftspeople), assuming they would have better bargaining power than unskilled workers in obtaining concessions from employers. As a federation, its many individual unions can become members yet keep their separate union status.

industrial unions
Labor organizations of unskilled and semiskilled workers in mass-production industries such as automobiles and mining.

Over time, an unauthorized AFL group called the Committee of Industrial Organizations began to organize **industrial unions**, which consisted of unskilled and semiskilled workers in mass-production industries such as automobile manufacturing and mining. John L. Lewis, president of the United Mine Workers, led this committee. His objective was to organize both craftspeople and unskilled workers under one banner.

Congress of Industrial Organizations (CIO)
Union organization of unskilled workers; broke away from the American Federation of Labor (AFL) in 1935 and rejoined it in 1955.

When the AFL rejected his proposal in 1935, Lewis broke away to form the **Congress of Industrial Organizations (CIO)**. The CIO soon rivaled the AFL in membership, partly because of the passage of the National Labor Relations Act (also called the Wagner Act) that same year (see the next section). For 20 years, the two organizations struggled for power. It wasn't until passage of the Taft-Hartley Act in 1947 (see Figure 12.1) that they saw the benefits of a merger. In 1955, the two groups formed the AFL-CIO. The AFL-CIO today maintains affiliations with 56 national and international labor unions and has about 12.5 million members.[7]

Public Sector Union Membership

People typically think of union members as workers in construction and manufacturing in the private sector of the economy. However, 7.2 million of the 14.5 million workers in unions work in the public sector, not the private sector. This means taxpayers pay the cost of union workers' wages and benefits.[8] Union membership in the public sector stands at 35 percent compared to just 6.6 percent in the private sector.[9] Still, public sector membership has fallen by approximately 120,000 since 2013 with much of the loss the result of state and local government revenue shortfalls caused by the economic crisis beginning in 2008. As states and local governments battle with high labor and pension costs, the challenge of dealing with public sector unions is sure to continue.[10] Several states are also challenging mandatory public sector union membership rules called "fair share dues."[11] The Supreme Court is expected to rule on the issue.

The Factory Blaze That Fired Up a Movement

On March 25, 1911, a warm spring day in New York City, hundreds of young women (the youngest 14 years old) were busy at work at the Triangle Shirtwaist Company when the unthinkable happened. A fire raced from the eighth floor to the ninth and then the tenth. As the panic-stricken women tried to race to safety they found that a crucial door was locked, trapping them in the fire. It was suggested at a later trial that the door was kept locked to prevent theft. In the blaze that lasted about 18 minutes, 146 workers were killed. Many of the workers burned to death, while others jumped to their fate holding hands with their clothes burning. The fire became the touchstone for organized labor and raised support for changes in the workplace.

Prior to the tragedy at Triangle Shirtwaist, workers had struck for

higher pay, shorter hours (the average workweek was often 60 hours), and safer workplace conditions. Unfortunately public opinion was strongly against them. After the tragedy, the

International Ladies' Garment Workers' Union (now called Workers United) grew in numbers and in public support. Today labor leaders say that the Triangle fire is evidence of why labor unions are crucial to maintain workplace balance in the United States. At a ceremony in New York City commemorating the 100th anniversary of the fire, labor leaders encouraged workers to not let the modern labor movement die. It's hard to imagine that in the 1950s, unions represented 36 percent of the private sector workers in the United States, compared to just 6.7 percent today.

Sources: "Remembering the 1911 Triangle Factory Fire," *Cornell University, ILR School*, accessed April 2014; Beth Fouhy, "NYC Marks 100th Anniversary of Deadly Factory Fire," *Bloomberg Businessweek*, March 25, 2011; Bureau of Labor Statistics, www.bls.gov, accessed April 2014; and Walter Loeb, "Walmart's Manufacturing Dream Is Just a Dream," *Forbes*, January 31, 2014.

LO 12–2 Discuss the major legislation affecting labor unions

LABOR LEGISLATION AND COLLECTIVE BARGAINING

Much of the growth and influence of organized labor in the United States has depended primarily on two major factors: the law and public opinion. Figure 12.1 outlines five major federal laws with a significant impact on the rights and operations of labor unions. Take a few moments to read it before going on. Note that such laws govern *private* workers.

The Norris-LaGuardia Act paved the way for union growth in the United States. This legislation prohibited employers from using employment contracts that included provisions such as a yellow-dog contract. A **yellow-dog contract** required employees to agree, as a condition of employment, not to join a union. The National Labor Relations Act (or Wagner Act) passed three years later provided labor unions with clear legal justification to pursue key issues that were strongly supported by Samuel Gompers and the AFL. One of these issues, **collective bargaining**, is the process whereby union and management representatives negotiate a contract for workers. The Wagner Act expanded labor's right to collectively bargain by obligating employers to meet

yellow-dog contract
A type of contract that required employees to agree as a condition of employment not to join a union; prohibited by the Norris-LaGuardia Act in 1932.

collective bargaining
The process whereby union and management representatives form a labor–management agreement, or contract, for workers.

FIGURE 12.1 MAJOR LEGISLATION AFFECTING LABOR–MANAGEMENT RELATIONS

Norris-LaGuardia Act, 1932	Prohibited courts from issuing injunctions against nonviolent union activities; outlawed contracts forbidding union activities; outlawed the use of yellow-dog contracts by employers. (Yellow-dog contracts were contractual agreements forced on workers by employers whereby the employee agreed not to join a union as a condition of employment.)
National Labor Relations Act (Wagner Act), 1935	Gave employees the right to form or join labor organizations (or to refuse to form or join); the right to collectively bargain with employers through elected union representatives; and the right to engage in labor activities such as strikes, picketing, and boycotts. Prohibited certain unfair labor practices by the employer and the union, and established the National Labor Relations Board to oversee union election campaigns and investigate labor practices. This act gave great impetus to the union movement.
Fair Labor Standards Act, 1938	Set a minimum wage and maximum basic hours for workers in interstate commerce industries. The first minimum wage set was 25 cents an hour, except for farm and retail workers.
Labor–Management Relations Act (Taft-Hartley Act), 1947	Amended the Wagner Act; permitted states to pass laws prohibiting compulsory union membership (right-to-work laws); set up methods to deal with strikes that affect national health and safety; prohibited secondary boycotts, closed shop agreements, and featherbedding (the requiring of wage payments for work not performed) by unions. This act gave more power to management.
Labor–Management Reporting and Disclosure Act (Landrum-Griffin Act), 1959	Amended the Taft-Hartley Act and the Wagner Act; guaranteed individual rights of union members in dealing with their union, such as the right to nominate candidates for union office, vote in union elections, attend and participate in union meetings, vote on union business, and examine union records and accounts; required annual financial reports to be filed with the U.S. Department of Labor. One goal of this act was to clean up union corruption.

at reasonable times and bargain in good faith with respect to wages, hours, and other terms and conditions of employment.[12]

Collective bargaining in public sector unions is a key issue today. In some states public employees are not given the privilege of collective bargaining. Controversy arises when people perceive that public employees are winning more or better health care, more or better hours of work, and so on than workers in the private sector. If this is the case, some have questioned whether or not collective bargaining in public unions should be allowed to continue. Public and private union members have joined together to fight efforts to take away collective bargaining gains among public employees in states like Wisconsin, Ohio, and California.[13]

Union Organizing Campaigns

The Wagner Act established an administrative agency (discussed in Bonus Chapter A), the National Labor Relations Board (NLRB), to oversee labor–management relations. The NLRB consists of five members appointed by the

U.S. president and is authorized to investigate and remedy unfair labor practices. It also provides workplace guidelines and legal protection to workers seeking to vote on organizing a union to represent them.[14] **Certification** is the formal process whereby the NLRB recognizes a labor union as the authorized bargaining agent for a group of employees. **Decertification** is the process by which workers can take away a union's right to represent them. Figure 12.2 describes the steps in both certification and decertification processes. After an election, both the union and company have five days to contest the results with the NLRB.

certification
Formal process whereby a union is recognized by the National Labor Relations Board (NLRB) as the bargaining agent for a group of employees.

decertification
The process by which workers take away a union's right to represent them.

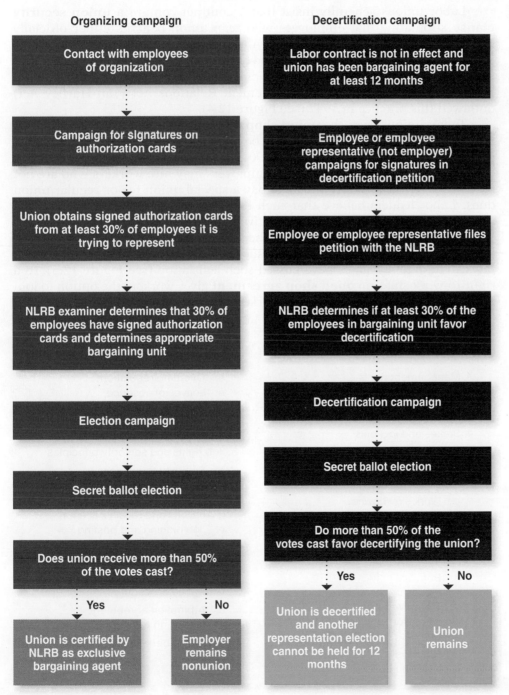

FIGURE 12.2 STEPS IN UNION-ORGANIZING AND DECERTIFICATION CAMPAIGNS
Note that the final vote in each case requires that the union receive over 50 percent of the votes cast. Note, too, that the election is secret.

negotiated labor–management agreement (labor contract)
Agreement that sets the tone and clarifies the terms under which management and labor agree to function over a period of time.

union security clause
Provision in a negotiated labor–management agreement that stipulates that employees who benefit from a union must either officially join or at least pay dues to the union.

closed shop agreement
Clause in a labor–management agreement that specified workers had to be members of a union before being hired (was outlawed by the Taft-Hartley Act in 1947).

union shop agreement
Clause in a labor–management agreement that says workers do not have to be members of a union to be hired, but must agree to join the union within a prescribed period.

agency shop agreement
Clause in a labor–management agreement that says employers may hire nonunion workers; employees are not required to join the union but must pay a union fee.

right-to-work laws
Legislation that gives workers the right, under an open shop agreement, to join or not join a union if it is present.

open shop agreement
Agreement in right-to-work states that gives workers the option to join or not join a union, if one exists in their workplace.

LO 12–3   Outline the objectives of labor unions.

Objectives of Organized Labor over Time

The objectives of labor unions shift with social and economic trends. The **negotiated labor–management agreement**, informally referred to as the labor contract, sets the tone and clarifies the terms and conditions under which management and the union will function over a specific period. Unions attempt to address their most pressing concerns in the labor contract such as job security and offshore outsourcing. Negotiations can cover a wide range of work topics, and it can take a long time to reach an agreement. Figure 12.3 lists topics commonly negotiated by management and labor.

Labor unions generally insist that a contract contain a **union security clause** stipulating that employees who reap union benefits either officially join or at least pay dues to the union. After passage of the Wagner Act, unions sought strict security in the form of the **closed shop agreement**, which specified that workers had to be members of a union before being hired for a job. To labor's dismay, the Labor–Management Relations Act (Taft-Hartley Act) outlawed this practice in 1947 (see Figure 12.4).

Today, unions favor the **union shop agreement**, under which workers do not have to be members of a union to be hired but must agree to join within a prescribed period (usually 30, 60, or 90 days). However, under a contingency called an **agency shop agreement**, employers may hire workers who are not required to join the union but must pay a special union fee or regular union dues. Labor leaders believe that such fees or dues are justified because the union represents all workers in collective bargaining, not just its members.

The Taft-Hartley Act recognized the legality of the union shop but granted individual states the power to outlaw such agreements through **right-to-work laws**.[15] To date, 24 states have passed such legislation (see Figure 12.5). In a right-to-work state, an **open shop agreement** gives workers the option to join or not join a union if one exists. A worker who does not join cannot be forced to pay a fee or dues.[16]

FIGURE 12.3 ISSUES IN A NEGOTIATED LABOR–MANAGEMENT AGREEMENT
Labor and management often meet to discuss and clarify the terms that specify employees' functions within the company. The topics listed in this figure are typically discussed during these meetings.

1. Management rights
2. Union recognition
3. Union security clause
4. Strikes and lockouts
5. Union activities and responsibilities
   a. Dues checkoff
   b. Union bulletin boards
   c. Work slowdowns
6. Wages
   a. Wage structure
   b. Shift differentials
   c. Wage incentives
   d. Bonuses
   e. Piecework conditions
   f. Tiered wage structures
7. Hours of work and time-off policies
   a. Regular hours of work
   b. Holidays
   c. Vacation policies

   d. Overtime regulations
   e. Leaves of absence
   f. Break periods
   g. Flextime
   h. Mealtime allotments
8. Job rights and seniority principles
   a. Seniority regulations
   b. Transfer policies and bumping
   c. Promotions
   d. Layoffs and recall procedures
   e. Job bidding and posting
9. Discharge and discipline
   a. Suspension
   b. Conditions for discharge
10. Grievance procedures
    a. Arbitration agreement
    b. Mediation procedures
11. Employee benefits, health, and welfare

FIGURE 12.4 DIFFERENT FORMS OF UNION AGREEMENTS

Closed shop

The Taft-Hartley Act made this form of agreement illegal. Under this type of labor agreement, employers could hire only current union members for a job.

Union shop

The majority of labor agreements are of this type. In a union shop, the employer can hire anyone, but as a condition of employment, employees hired must join the union to keep their jobs.

Agency shop

Employers may hire anyone. Employees need not join the union, but are required to pay a union fee. A small percentage of labor agreements are of this type.

Open shop

Union membership is voluntary for new and existing employees. Those who don't join the union don't have to pay union dues. Few union contracts are of this type.

Future contract negotiations will likely focus on evolving workplace issues such as child and elder care, worker retraining, two-tiered wage plans, drug testing, and other such work-related issues. Job security will remain a top union priority due to the threat of job losses from offshore outsourcing and free trade agreements. For public union employees, the major issue may be collective bargaining in general as states like Wisconsin try to restrict their power to bargain collectively, thus significantly reducing the unions' value to members.[17]

Unions will continue to support federal changes such as minimum wage increases. Many unions (particularly those in the service, retail, and hospitality industries) have clauses in their contracts that peg pay to a certain percentage above the minimum wage. Any increase in the minimum wage triggers an automatic raise in union wages. Currently the average union worker in these industries earns $22 an hour, whereas the minimum wage is only $7.25. Critics of the recent proposals to raise the minimum wage to $9–$10 say that if it is raised, many low-skilled workers would be priced out of the market and unemployment will increase. In other words, union workers will earn more, while other

FIGURE 12.5 STATES WITH RIGHT-TO-WORK LAWS

= Right-to-work states

workers may lose their jobs.[18] Advocates of the wage increase say that the increase is necessary to protect the "working poor." What do you think?

Resolving Labor–Management Disagreements

The negotiated labor–management agreement becomes a guide to work relations between management and the union. However, it doesn't necessarily end negotiations between them because there are sometimes differences concerning interpretations of the agreement. For example, managers may interpret a certain clause in the agreement to mean they are free to select who works overtime. Union members may interpret the same clause to mean that managers must select employees for overtime on the basis of seniority. If the parties can't resolve such controversies, employees may file a grievance.

A **grievance** is a charge by employees that management is not abiding by or fulfilling the terms of the negotiated labor–management agreement as they perceive it. Overtime rules, promotions, layoffs, transfers, and job assignments are generally sources of employee grievances. Handling them demands a good deal of contact between union officials and managers. Grievances, however, do not imply that a company has broken the law or the labor agreement. In fact, the vast majority of grievances are negotiated and resolved by **shop stewards** (union officials who work permanently in an organization and represent employee interests on a daily basis) and supervisory-level managers. However, if a grievance is not settled at this level, formal grievance procedures will begin. Figure 12.6 illustrates the steps a formal grievance procedure could follow.

grievance
A charge by employees that management is not abiding by the terms of the negotiated labor–management agreement.

shop stewards
Union officials who work permanently in an organization and represent employee interests on a daily basis.

FIGURE 12.6 THE GRIEVANCE RESOLUTION PROCESS
The grievance process may move through several steps before the issue is resolved. At each step, the issue is negotiated between union officials and managers. If no resolution is achieved, an outside arbitrator may be mutually agreed on. If so, the decision by the arbitrator is binding (legally enforceable).

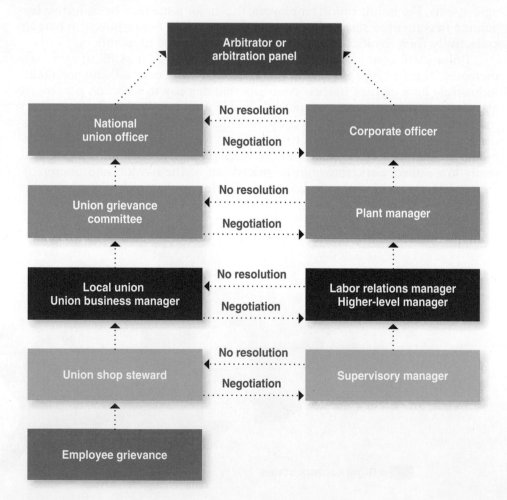

Mediation and Arbitration

During the contract negotiation process, there is generally a **bargaining zone**, which is the range of options between the initial and final offers that each party will consider before negotiations dissolve or reach an impasse. If labor and management negotiators aren't able to agree on alternatives within this bargaining zone, mediation may be necessary.

Mediation is the use of a third party, called a *mediator*, who encourages both sides in a dispute to continue negotiating and often makes suggestions for resolving the matter. Keep in mind that mediators evaluate facts in the dispute and then make suggestions, not decisions. Elected officials (both current and past), attorneys, and college professors often serve as mediators in labor disputes. The National Mediation Board provides federal mediators when requested in a labor dispute. In 2011, the National Football League and the Players Association asked for the assistance of a federal mediator in their attempt to forge a new contract. The National Hockey League made the same request during its labor dispute in 2012.[19]

A more extreme option used to resolve conflicts is **arbitration**—an agreement to bring an impartial third party—a single arbitrator or arbitration panel—to render a binding decision in a labor dispute. The arbitrator(s) must be acceptable to both labor and management. You may have heard of professional baseball players filing for arbitration to resolve a contract dispute with their teams or to contest a penalty imposed by the league.[20] Many negotiated labor–management agreements in the United States call for the use of arbitration to end labor disputes. The nonprofit American Arbitration Association is the dominant organization used in dispute resolution.[21]

bargaining zone
The range of options between the initial and final offer that each party will consider before negotiations dissolve or reach an impasse.

mediation
The use of a third party, called a mediator, who encourages both sides in a dispute to continue negotiating and often makes suggestions for resolving the dispute.

arbitration
The agreement to bring in an impartial third party (a single arbitrator or a panel of arbitrators) to render a binding decision in a labor dispute.

iSee It! Need help understanding mediation vs. arbitration? Visit your Connect e-book video tab for a brief animated explanation.

LO 12–4 Describe the tactics used by labor and management during conflicts, and discuss the role of unions in the future.

TACTICS USED IN LABOR–MANAGEMENT CONFLICTS

If labor and management cannot reach an agreement through collective bargaining, and negotiations break down, either side, or both, may use specific tactics to enhance its negotiating position and perhaps sway public opinion. Unions primarily use strikes and boycotts, as well as pickets and work slowdowns. Management may implement lockouts, injunctions, and even strikebreakers. The following sections explain each tactic briefly.

Union Tactics

A **strike** occurs when workers collectively refuse to go to work. Strikes have been the most potent union tactic. They attract public attention to a labor dispute and can cause operations in a company to slow down or totally cease. Besides refusing to work, strikers may also picket the company, walking around carrying signs and talking with the public and the media about the issues in the dispute. Unions also often use picketing as an informational tool before going on strike. One purpose of picketing is to alert the public to an

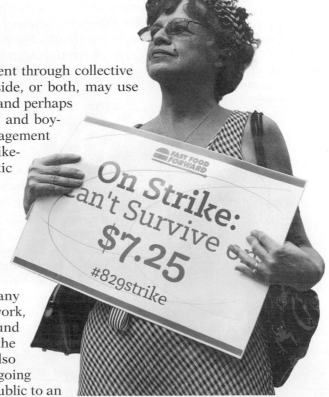

strike

A union strategy in which workers refuse to go to work; the purpose is to further workers' objectives after an impasse in collective bargaining.

cooling-off period

When workers in a critical industry return to their jobs while the union and management continue negotiations.

primary boycott

When a union encourages both its members and the general public not to buy the products of a firm involved in a labor dispute.

secondary boycott

An attempt by labor to convince others to stop doing business with a firm that is the subject of a primary boycott; prohibited by the Taft-Hartley Act.

lockout

An attempt by management to put pressure on unions by temporarily closing the business.

The conflict between NFL players and owners in 2011 resulted in the owners locking the players out of team facilities for many months. How did the lockout affect the 2011–2012 season? What effect did the lockout have on fans?

issue stirring labor unrest, even though a strike has not yet been approved by the union's membership. Strikes sometimes lead to the resolution of a labor dispute; however, they also have generated violence and extended bitterness. Often after a strike is finally settled, labor and management remain openly hostile toward each other and mutual complaints of violations of the negotiated labor–management agreement continue.

The public often realizes how important a worker is when he or she goes on strike. In Chicago, 350,000 students and their parents experienced an unexpected seven-day vacation when Chicago teachers went on strike in 2012. That's why many states prohibit public safety workers (police and firefighters) and teachers from striking, even though they can be unionized. Employees of the federal government, such as postal workers, can unionize but are also denied the right to strike. When strikes are prohibited, however, workers sometimes display their frustrations by engaging in sickouts (often called the *blue flu*). That is, they arrange as a group to be absent from work and claim illness as the reason. In critical industries such as airlines and railroads, under the Taft-Hartley Act, the U.S. president can ask for a **cooling-off period**, during which workers return to their jobs while negotiations continue, to prevent a strike. The cooling-off period can last up to 80 days.

Today, both labor and management seek to avoid strikes. However, as technological change, offshore outsourcing, wage disparities, and reductions in worker benefits continue it's unlikely that strikes will disappear.[22] Strikes in entertainment, health care, transportation, fast food, professional sports, and other industries prove the strike is not dead as a labor tactic.

Unions also attempt boycotts as a means to obtain their objectives in a labor dispute. Boycotts can be classified as primary or secondary. A **primary boycott** occurs when labor encourages both its members and the general public not to buy the products or services of a firm engaged in a labor dispute. A **secondary boycott** is an attempt by labor to convince others to stop doing business with a firm that is the subject of a primary boycott. Labor unions can legally authorize primary boycotts, but the Taft-Hartley Act prohibits using secondary boycotts. For example, a union could not initiate a secondary boycott against a retail chain because its stores carry products of a company that's the target of a primary boycott.

Management Tactics

Like labor unions, management also uses specific tactics to achieve its workplace goals. A **lockout** is an attempt by management to put pressure on union workers by temporarily closing the business. When workers don't work, they don't get paid. Though management rarely uses this tactic, high-profile lockouts such as the National Football League players and lower-profile lockouts like the Minnesota Orchestra, show that this tactic is still used.[23] Management, however, most often uses injunctions and strikebreakers to counter labor demands it sees as excessive.

An **injunction** is a court order directing someone to do something or to refrain from doing something. Management has sought injunctions to order striking workers back to work, limit the number of pickets during a strike, or otherwise deal with any actions that could be detrimental to the public

To Cross or Not to Cross?

The recent economic slowdown has been very difficult. Your wallet is almost empty, and bills for your college expenses, food, and other expenses keep going up. You read last weekend that Shop-Till-You-Drop, a local grocery chain in your town, is looking for workers to replace striking members of United Food and Commercial Workers (UFCW). The workers are striking because of a reduction in health insurance benefits and reduced payment to their pensions.

Several classmates at your college are UFCW members employed at Shop-Till-You-Drop stores, and many other students at your college are supporting the strike. The stores also employ many people from your neighborhood whose families depend on the income and benefits. Shop-Till-You-Drop argues that the company has made a fair offer to the union, but with the increasing cost of health care and other benefits, the workers' demands are excessive and could force the company into bankruptcy.

Shop-Till-You-Drop is offering replacement workers an attractive wage rate and flexible schedules to cross the picket line and work during the strike. The company has suggested the possibility of permanent employment, depending on the results of the strike. As a struggling student, you could use the job and the money for tuition and expenses. Will you cross the picket line and apply? What could be the consequences of your decision? Is your choice ethical?

welfare. For a court to issue an injunction, management must show a just cause, such as the possibility of violence or destruction of private property.

Employers have had the right to replace striking workers since a 1938 Supreme Court ruling, but this tactic was used infrequently until the 1980s. The use of strikebreakers since then has been a particular source of hostility and violence in labor relations. **Strikebreakers** (called scabs by unions) are workers hired to do the jobs of striking employees until the labor dispute is resolved. Be sure to read the nearby Making Ethical Decisions box, which deals with this issue.

injunction
A court order directing someone to do something or to refrain from doing something.

strikebreakers
Workers hired to do the jobs of striking workers until the labor dispute is resolved.

The Future of Unions and Labor–Management Relations

Organized labor is at a crossroads. As noted earlier, less than 7 percent of workers in the private sector are unionized and nearly half of all union members work in the public sector, with union membership varying considerably by state (see Figure 12.7).[24] Once-powerful unions like the United Auto Workers (UAW) have lost three-fourths of their membership since 1979.[25] This loss has occurred despite unions like the UAW granting management concessions, or **givebacks**, of previous gains in attempts to save jobs. Both public and private sector union members now face challenges as they try to maintain remaining wage and fringe benefit gains achieved in past negotiations. Perhaps what's even more concerning to labor unions is that union membership is highest among workers 45–64 years old and lowest among workers 18–25 years old.[26]

Unions in the future will undoubtedly be quite different from those in the past. Today the largest union in the United States is the National Education Association (NEA) with 3.2 million members. The Service Employees International Union (SEIU) with 2.2 million members is second. You might note that the NEA is a public sector union and the SEIU's emphasis is on services. To grow, unions will have to include more white-collar, female, and foreign-born workers than they have traditionally included. The traditional manufacturing base that unions depended on for growth needs to give way to organizing efforts in industries like health care (over 16 million workers) and information

givebacks
Concessions made by union members to management; gains from labor negotiations are given back to management to help employers remain competitive and thereby save jobs.

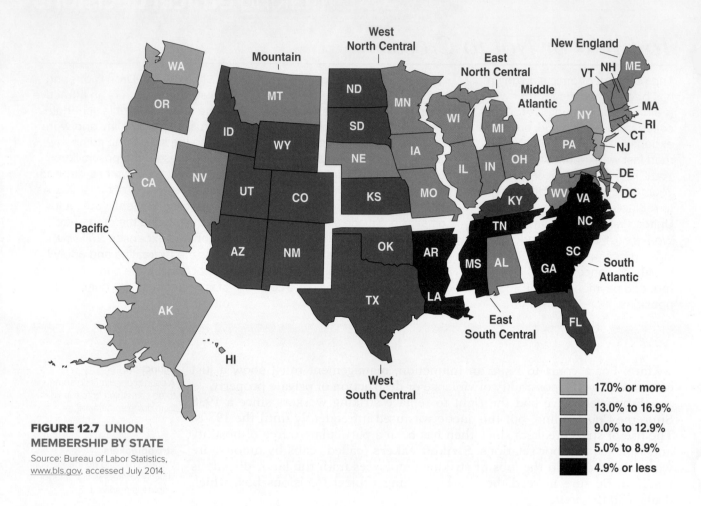

FIGURE 12.7 UNION MEMBERSHIP BY STATE

Source: Bureau of Labor Statistics, www.bls.gov, accessed July 2014.

Legend:
- 17.0% or more
- 13.0% to 16.9%
- 9.0% to 12.9%
- 5.0% to 8.9%
- 4.9% or less

technology (over 4 million workers).[27] Unions will also need to take on a new role in partnering with management in training workers, redesigning jobs, and assimilating the changing workforce to the job requirements of the new service and knowledge-work economy. How organized labor and management handle these challenges may well define the future for labor unions. After the Test Prep, we will look at other issues facing employees and managers in the 21st century.

Use LearnSmart to help retain what you have learned. Access your instructor's Connect course to check out LearnSmart or go to learnsmartadvantage.com for help.

■■LEARNSMART®

test **prep**

- What are the major laws that affected union growth, and what does each one cover?
- How do changes in the economy affect the objectives of unions?
- What are the major tactics used by unions and by management to assert their power in contract negotiations?
- What types of workers do unions need to organize in the future?

LO 12–5 Assess some of today's controversial employee–management issues, such as executive compensation, pay equity, sexual harassment, child care and elder care, drug testing, and violence in the workplace.

CONTROVERSIAL EMPLOYEE–MANAGEMENT ISSUES

This is an interesting time in the history of employee–management relations. Organizations are active in global expansion, offshore outsourcing, and technology change. The U.S. economy is recovering from the worst recession in many decades. The government is taking a more active role in mandating what benefits and assurances businesses must provide to workers. Employees are raising questions of fairness, income inequality, and workplace security. Let's look at several key workplace issues, starting with executive compensation.

Executive Compensation

Kobe Bryant dribbles his way to $62 million a year, Robert Downey Jr. acts his way to $75 million a year, Jennifer Lopez sings her way to $45 million a year, and Ellen DeGeneres talks and jokes her way to over $55 million a year.[28] Is it out of line, then, for Lawrence Ellison, CEO of Oracle, to make $77 million a year?[29] Chapter 2 explained that the U.S. free-market system is built on incentives that allow top executives to make such large amounts—or more. Today, however, the government, boards of directors, stockholders, unions, and employees are challenging this principle and arguing that executive compensation has gotten out of line. In fact, the average total CEO compensation (salary, bonuses, and incentives) at a major company was $12.3 million, compared to just over $35,000 for the average worker.[30] The Adapting to Change box explores the disparity between what college head coaches earn (millions) and what college athletes earn (nothing).

In theory, CEO compensation and bonuses are determined by the firm's profitability or an increase in its stock price. The logic of this assumption was that as the fortunes of a company and its stockholders grew, so would the rewards of the CEO. Today, however, executives generally receive stock options (the ability to buy company stock at a set price at a later date) and restricted stock (stock issued directly to the CEO that can't be sold usually for three or four years) as part of their compensation. Stock options account for over 50 percent of a CEO's compensation, and restricted stock makes up almost 25 percent.

What's even more frustrating to those who question how much chief executives are paid is that CEOs are often rewarded richly even if their company does not meet expectations, or they leave under pressure.[31] Leo Apotheker was entitled to almost $35 million for less than one year's work at Hewlett-Packard during which time the company stock price fell by 46 percent.[32] Ron Johnson was given a $52 million signing bonus from JCPenney and left the company 17 months later after the stock price fell by 50 percent. Many CEOs are also awarded fat retainers, consulting contracts, and lavish perks when they retire.

USA Today *listed Disney as one of the eight U.S. companies that most owed their employees a raise. The average Disney World cast member earned $8.47 an hour in 2013. Meanwhile Disney's CEO Robert Iger enjoyed a total compensation package of $34.3 million. Corporate boards of directors determine executive compensation. Do you think this is a fair system of compensation for CEOs? Do you think workers should have input?*

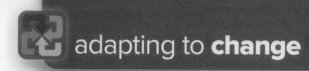
College Athletes: What Are They Worth?

Few would argue that football is a booming profit center for many colleges in the National Collegiate Athletic Association (NCAA) Division I (the highest level of NCAA sports). NCAA basketball is no slacker either. The 2014 NCAA Men's Championship drew a sell-out crowd at AT&T Stadium in Dallas while more than 23 million watched on television. Broadcasting rights for the entire tournament cost CBS $771 million. Regional economies in college towns like Columbia, Missouri; College Station, Texas; and South Bend, Indiana, reap huge revenues on sports weekends. The University of Texas enjoyed revenues of $163 million from athletics in 2014. Coaches are given contracts worth millions. All is good for everyone.

Well, not everyone. There's one group of stakeholders noticeably absent from this payday: the players. College athletes are not allowed to draw a salary or receive any gifts or other compensation for their extracurricular efforts. Of course, some college athletes do receive scholarships that cover part or all of their tuition and room and board. However,

the amount of revenue generated by competitions like basketball's March Madness or football's National Championship have led many to demand that student athletes receive a cut of the action. After all, they believe they invest just as much time with practice and travel as their coaches do.

Northwestern University's football players won a ruling from the National Labor Relations Board (NLRB) that gave them the right to unionize. The players argued they deserved collective bargaining rights, financial coverage for sports-related injuries, an educational trust to help players

graduate, and a team of concussion experts to be placed on the sidelines at games. With football workweeks stretching out to as long as 60 hours, the players believed they deserved compensation to justify the sport's dominance over their lives. Northwestern is appealing, claiming the players have an educational relationship with the school rather than an economic one.

The school also sees Title IX requirements as an obstacle. For instance, if the college began paying its men's football and basketball team, it would need to do the same for its unprofitable athletic programs, regardless of sport or gender. This is a pay issue that could be a game changer. What do you think? Are athletes employees of the school or are they students? Should players be paid for their participation or should they be treated like participants in any other voluntary extracurricular activity?

Sources: Alejandra Cancino, "Northwestern, Football Players Cap Off Arguments in Union Effort," *Chicago Tribune*, March 18, 2014; Ken Badenhausen, "NCAA Tournament 2014: By the Numbers," *Forbes*, March 20, 2014; and Brian Bennett, "Northwestern Players Get Union Vote," *ESPN*, March 26, 2014.

Noted economist Thomas Piketty believes this income inequality is harmful and unnecessary, "When you pay $10 million instead of $1 [million], you don't have necessarily better performance or much higher productivity. . . . So I think there is really very little evidence that we need to pay people 100 times or 200 times the average wage to get them to work. I think you have people who would accept the work for only 10 or 20 times the average wage."[33] Whole Foods is one company that follows the suggestions of Piketty. At Whole Foods, executive pay is capped at 19 times the average employee's salary. Unfortunately, not many companies have placed such limits on executive compensation. Today the average CEO makes over 350 times what the lowest-paid employee earns.[34] Some numbers can be staggering. For example, a custodian earning just over minimum wage at CBS would have to work over 3,200 years to make what CEO Les Moonves earned in 2013 ($62 million).[35]

As global competition intensifies, executive paychecks in Europe have increased, but European CEOs typically earn considerably less than what U.S.

CEOs make. In some European countries, such as Germany, by law workers have a say in company management and are entitled to seats on the board of directors of major firms. Since boards set executive pay, this could be a reason why pay imbalances are less in Germany. This process, called *co-determination*, calls for cooperation between management and workers in decision making. In Japan, few Japanese CEOs take home super-sized paychecks like in the United States.

Today, government and shareholder pressure for full disclosure of executive compensation is putting U.S. boards of directors on notice that they are not there simply to enrich CEOs. The passage of the Dodd-Frank Wall Street Reform and Consumer Protection Act was intended to give shareholders more say in compensation decisions and is requiring more information about executive pay packages. Still, it's important to remember that most U.S. executives are responsible for multibillion-dollar corporations, work 70-plus hours a week, and often travel excessively. Many have turned potential problems at companies into successes and reaped huge benefits for employees and stockholders as well as themselves. Furthermore, there are few seasoned, skilled professionals who can manage large companies, especially troubled companies looking for the right CEO to accomplish a turnaround. There's no easy answer to the question of what is fair compensation for executives, but it's a safe bet the controversy will not go away.

Pay Equity

The Equal Pay Act of 1963 requires companies to give equal pay to men and women who do the same job. For example, it's illegal to pay a female nurse less than a male nurse unless factors such as seniority, merit pay, or performance incentives are involved. But *pay equity* goes beyond the concept of equal pay for equal work; it says people in jobs that require similar levels of education, training, or skills should receive equal pay. Pay equity compares the value of a job like a hair stylist or librarian (traditionally women's jobs) with jobs like a plumber or truck driver (traditionally men's jobs). Such a comparison shows that "women's" jobs tend to pay less— sometimes much less. This disparity caused a brief reconsideration of a 1980s concept called *comparable worth* that suggested people in jobs requiring similar levels of education, training, or skills should receive equal pay. Evidence did not support that comparable worth would lead to better market equilibrium, only more chaos and inequity.

In the United States today, women earn 77 percent of what men earn, although the disparity varies by profession, job experience and tenure, and level of education.[36] In the past, the primary explanation for this disparity was that women worked only 50 to 60 percent of their available years once they left school, whereas men normally worked all those years. This explanation doesn't have much substance today because fewer women leave the workforce for an extended time. Other explanations suggest many women devote more time to their families than men do and thus accept lower-paying jobs with more flexible hours.

Today women are competing financially with men in fields such as health care, biotechnology, information technology, and other knowledge-based jobs. Younger women are faring better than older women financially. Recent reports suggest that young urban women actually earn 8 percent more than their male counterparts due to their higher college graduation rates. Today women earn almost 60 percent of the bachelor's and master's degrees awarded.[37] With more women earning business degrees, the number of women in management and high-paying finance

Women have made important strides in business, politics, and sports. They still, however, are behind when it comes to getting paid. Today women earn only 77 percent of what men earn. Such disparities cause many to support the case for comparable worth and a more equitable workplace. What's your opinion concerning this issue?

jobs has also increased considerably over the past 10 years. Still, Heather Boushey, a senior economist at the Center for American Progress, believes that the government puts too much faith in the idea that education will automatically close the pay gap.[38] She and other critics claim that women, especially women with children, still earn less, are less likely to go into business, and are more likely to live in poverty than men.[39] There is no question that pay equity promises to remain a challenging employee–management issue.

Sexual Harassment

sexual harassment
Unwelcome sexual advances, requests for sexual favors, and other conduct (verbal or physical) of a sexual nature that creates a hostile work environment.

Sexual harassment refers to unwelcome sexual advances, requests for sexual favors, and other verbal or physical conduct of a sexual nature that creates a hostile work environment.[40] The Civil Rights Act of 1991 governs sexual harassment of both men and women. In 1997, the Supreme Court reinforced this fact when it said same-sex harassment also falls within the purview of sexual harassment law. Managers and workers are now much more sensitive to sexual comments and behavior than they were in the past. The number of complaints filed with the Equal Employment Opportunity Commission (EEOC) has declined significantly over the past 20 years yet EEOC statistics show sexual harassment remains a persistent employee complaint.[41] The number of reports of sexual harassment and assault in the military, to both men and women, has risen sharply in recent years.[42] Conduct on the job can be considered illegal under specific conditions:

Unwelcome sexual advances, requests for sexual favors, and other verbal or physical conduct are prohibited under the Civil Rights Act of 1991. While most employees are aware of sexual harassment policies in the workplace, they are often not certain what sexual harassment actually means. Should companies train employees about the dos and don'ts of acceptable sexual conduct on the job?

- An employee's submission to such conduct is explicitly or implicitly made a term or condition of employment, or an employee's submission to or rejection of such conduct is used as the basis for employment decisions affecting the worker's status. A threat like "Go out with me or you're fired" or "Go out with me or you'll never be promoted here" constitutes *quid pro quo sexual harassment.*

- The conduct unreasonably interferes with a worker's job performance or creates an intimidating, hostile, or offensive work environment. This type of harassment is *hostile work environment sexual harassment.*

The Supreme Court broadened the scope of what can be considered a hostile work environment; the key word seemed to be *unwelcome,* a term for behavior that would offend a reasonable person. Companies and individuals have found that the U.S. justice system means business in enforcing sexual harassment laws. In a highly publicized case, the Mayor of San Diego, California, was forced to resign in 2013 after a sexual harassment scandal.[43] Banking giant JPMorgan paid $1.5 million to settle a sexual harassment suit that alleged a hostile work environment for female mortgage bankers. Foreign companies doing business in the United States are also not immune to sexual harassment charges as both Toyota and Nissan discovered.

A key problem is that workers and managers often know a policy concerning sexual harassment exists, but have no idea what it says. To remedy this, some states have taken the lead. California and Connecticut require all companies with 50 employees or more to provide sexual harassment prevention training to supervisors. Maine requires such training for companies with 15 or more employees. Many companies have set up rapid, effective grievance procedures and react promptly to allegations of harassment. Such efforts may save businesses millions of dollars in lawsuits and make the workplace more productive and harmonious. Nonetheless, there is a long way to go before sexual harassment as a key employee–management issue disappears.

Child Care

Today women make up almost half the workforce in the United States. Approximately three-fourths of women with children under 18 (including over 60 percent of mothers with children under age 3) are in the workforce. Such statistics concern employers for two reasons: (1) absences related to child care cost U.S. businesses billions of dollars annually, and (2) the issue of who should pay for employee child care raises a question that often divides employees. Many co-workers oppose child care benefits for parents or single parents, arguing that single workers and single-income families should not subsidize child care. Others contend that employers and the government have the responsibility to create child care systems to assist employees. Unfortunately federal assistance has not increased since passage of the Welfare Reform Act many years ago, and few expect new government spending for child care due to the current federal deficit problems. Thus, child care remains an important workplace issue.

A number of large companies offer child care as an employee benefit. *Working Mother* magazine compiles an annual list of the 100 best companies for working mothers.[44] Both IBM and Johnson & Johnson have been praised as particularly sympathetic and cooperative with working mothers and have made the list every year for the past 25 years. Other large firms with extensive child care programs include American Express, Bristol-Myers Squibb, and Intel, which provide online homework assistance for employees' children. Some additional child care benefits provided by employers include:

- Discount arrangements with national child care chains.
- Vouchers that offer payments toward child care the employee selects.
- Referral services that help identify high-quality child care facilities to employees.

On-site day care is still a relatively uncommon employee benefit in the United States today. Although it is often expensive to operate, it can pay big dividends in employee satisfaction and productivity. Who should pay for employee benefits like child care and elder care, the employee or the company?

- On-site child care centers at which parents can visit children at lunch or during lag times throughout the workday.
- Sick-child centers to care for moderately ill children.

Unfortunately, small businesses with fewer than 100 employees cannot compete with big companies in providing assistance with child care. Some small companies, however, have found that implementing creative child care programs can help them compete with larger organizations in hiring and retaining qualified employees. Haemonetics, located in Braintree, Massachusetts, is a leading company in blood processing technology that believes creating a work–life balance is the key to keeping valued workers. The company operates "Kid's Space at Haemonetics" at its corporate headquarters staffed by highly qualified early childhood educators from Bright Horizons who develop planned and spontaneous daily activities.

Twenty-five years ago, entrepreneurs Roger Brown and Linda Mason recognized the emerging need for child care as a benefit in the workplace. The husband-and-wife team started Bright Horizons Family Solutions Inc. to provide child care at worksites for employers. Today, their company is the leading provider in the corporate-sponsored child care market and runs nearly 700 child care centers for about 400 companies including almost 100 Fortune 500 companies. Increasing numbers of two-income households and the over 13.7 million single-parent households in the United States ensure that child care will remain a key employee–management issue even as businesses face the growing challenge of elder care.[45]

Elder Care

Currently, there are approximately 40.3 million Americans over the age of 65. Over the next 20 years, the number of Americans over 65 is expected to grow to over 70 million; that will be approximately 20 percent of the U.S. population in 2030. The likelihood that an American age 65 will live to age 90 has also increased significantly.[46] What this means is that many workers will be confronted with how to care for older parents and other relatives.[47] Today in the United States, 65.7 million caregivers (constituting 31 percent of U.S. households) are providing some care to an elderly person.[48] According to the National Alliance for Caregiving, such caregiving obligations cause employees to miss approximately 15 million days of work per year. Companies are losing an estimated $35 billion a year in reduced productivity, absenteeism, and turnover from employees responsible for aging relatives.[49] Elder care is becoming a key workplace issue.

The U.S. Office of Personnel Management (OPM) found that employees with elder care responsibilities need information about medical, legal, and insurance issues, as well as the full support of their supervisors and company.[50] The OPM also suggests such caregivers may require flextime, telecommuting, part-time employment, or job sharing. Some firms offer employee assistance programs. DuPont and JPMorgan Chase provide elder care management services that include a needs assessment program for the employee. AAA and UPS offer health-spending accounts in which employees can put aside pretax income for elder care expenses. However, the number of companies offering elder care benefits is small compared to the number offering child care benefits. A Hewitt Associates survey found that only 49 percent of companies either currently had an elder care program or planned to introduce one in the near future. Unfortunately, the government does not provide much relief since both Medicare and Medicaid place heavy financial burdens for care on family caregivers.[51]

According to the American Association of Retired Persons (AARP), as more experienced and high-ranking employees care for older parents and relatives, the costs to companies will rise even higher. This argument makes sense, since older, more experienced workers often hold jobs more critical to a company than those held by younger workers (who are most affected by child care issues). Many firms now face the fact that transfers and promotions are often out of the question for employees whose elderly parents need ongoing care. Unfortunately, as the nation gets older, the elder care situation will grow considerably worse, meaning this employee–management issue will persist well into the future.

Drug abuse costs the U.S. economy hundreds of billions of dollars in lost work, health care costs, crime, traffic accidents, and productivity. It is estimated that each drug abuser can cost an employer approximately $10,000 a year. Today, over 80 percent of major companies drug test new employees and 40 percent conduct random drug testing. Do you think these efforts are successful in reducing drug abuse in the workplace? Why or why not?

Drug Testing

Not long ago, acquired immunodeficiency syndrome (AIDS) caused great concern in the workplace. Many companies called for pre-employment testing for AIDS. Thankfully, the spread of AIDS has declined in the United States—good news for all citizens and for business. However, alcohol and drug abuse are serious workplace issues that touch far more workers and stretch from factory floors to construction sites to the locker rooms of professional sports teams.

Alcohol is the most widely used drug in the workplace, with an estimated 6.5 percent of full-time U.S. employees believed to be heavy drinkers.[52] Approximately 40 percent of industrial injuries and fatalities can be linked to alcohol consumption. According to the Department of Health and Human Services' Substance Abuse & Mental Health Services Association, more than 8 percent of full-time workers ages 18–49 use illegal drugs. In some industries, such as food services and construction, the percentage of workers using illegal drugs is much higher. How do you think the legalization of marijuana in states like Colorado and Washington will affect the workplace?

Individuals who use illegal drugs are three and a half times more likely to be in workplace accidents and five times more likely to file a workers' compensation claim than other employees. According to the National Institute on Drug Abuse, employed drug users cost their employers about twice as much in medical and workers' compensation claims as do their drug-free co-workers. The U.S. Department of Labor projects that over a one-year period, drug abuse costs the U.S. economy $414 billion in lost work, health care costs, crime, traffic accidents, and other expenses, and over $150 billion in lost productivity.[53] The National Institutes of Health estimates each drug abuser can cost an employer approximately $10,000 annually. Drug abusers are associated with 50 percent on-the-job accident rates, 10 percent higher absenteeism, 30 percent more turnover, and more frequent workplace violence incidents. Today, over 80 percent of major companies drug test new employees and 40 percent conduct random drug testing.

Violence in the Workplace

The school shootings at Sandy Hook Elementary School shocked the nation. The tragedy also reminded businesses that even though workplace violence has declined since the 1990s, the threat has in no way disappeared.[54] Employers must be vigilant about potential violence in the workplace. The Bureau of Labor Statistics reports that more than 2 million Americans are impacted by workplace violence annually. The Occupational Safety and Health Administration (OSHA) reports that homicides account for 16 percent of all workplace deaths and are the number one cause of death for women in the workplace. In fact, one in six violent crimes in the United States occurs at work.

Many companies have taken action to prevent problems before they occur. They have held focus groups that invite employee input, hired managers with strong interpersonal skills, and employed skilled consultants to deal with any growing potential for workplace violence. State Farm Insurance and Verizon Wireless are among companies that have initiated policies to deal with this growing threat. At software firm Mindbridge, based in Worcester, Pennsylvania, two company officials must be present whenever an employee is disciplined or fired. In many states employers can seek a temporary restraining order on behalf of workers experiencing threats or harassment.

Some companies believe that the media exaggerates reports of workplace violence. According to the Bureau of Labor Statistics, 70 percent of U.S. workplaces neither provide any formal training for dealing with prevention of violence at work nor have a policy that addresses workplace violence. Unfortunately, organizations such as the U.S. Postal Service, U.S. Military, and Xerox can attest that workplace violence is all too real and is likely to be an issue for the foreseeable future.

Firms that have healthy employee–management relations have a better chance to prosper than those that don't. Taking a proactive approach is the best way to ensure positive employee–management work environments. The proactive manager anticipates potential issues and works toward resolving them before they get out of hand—a good lesson for any manager.

test prep

- How does top-executive pay in the United States compare with top-executive pay in other countries?
- What's the difference between pay equity and equal pay for equal work?
- How is the term *sexual harassment* defined, and when does sexual behavior become illegal?
- What are some of the issues related to child care and elder care, and how are companies addressing those issues?

summary

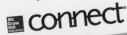
LO 12–1   Trace the history of organized labor in the United States.

- **What was the first union?**
  The cordwainers (shoemakers) organized a craft union of skilled specialists in 1792. The Knights of Labor, formed in 1869, was the first national labor organization.

- **How did the AFL-CIO evolve?**
  The American Federation of Labor (AFL), formed in 1886, was an organization of craft unions. The Congress of Industrial Organizations (CIO), a group of unskilled and semiskilled workers, broke off from the AFL in 1935. Over time, the two organizations saw the benefits of joining and

became the AFL-CIO in 1955. The AFL-CIO is a federation of labor unions, not a national union.

LO 12–2 Discuss the major legislation affecting labor unions.

- **What are the provisions of the major legislation affecting labor unions?**
  See Figure 12.1.

LO 12–3 Outline the objectives of labor unions.

- **What topics typically appear in labor–management agreements?**
  See Figure 12.3.

LO 12–4 Describe the tactics used by labor and management during conflicts, and discuss the role of unions in the future.

- **What are the tactics used by unions and management in conflicts?**
  Unions can use strikes and boycotts. Management can use strikebreakers, injunctions, and lockouts.

- **What will unions have to do to cope with declining membership?**
  Unions are facing a changing workplace. The National Education Associations is now the nation's largest union. The Service Employees International Union (SEIU), with 2.2 million members, is the second largest union. Going forward, unions must adapt to an increasingly white-collar, female, and culturally diverse workforce. To help keep U.S. businesses competitive in global markets, many have taken on a new role in assisting management in training workers, redesigning jobs, and assimilating the changing workforce.

LO 12–5 Assess some of today's controversial employee–management issues, such as executive compensation, pay equity, sexual harassment, child care and elder care, drug testing, and violence in the workplace.

- **What is a fair wage for managers?**
  The market and the businesses in it set managers' salaries. What is fair is open to debate.

- **How are equal pay and pay equity different?**
  The Equal Pay Act of 1963 provides that workers receive equal pay for equal work (with exceptions for seniority, merit, or performance). Pay equity is the demand for equivalent pay for jobs requiring similar levels of education, training, and skills.

- **How are some companies addressing the child care issue?**
  Responsive companies are providing child care on the premises, emergency care when scheduled care is interrupted, discounts with child care chains, vouchers to be used at the employee's chosen care center, and referral services.

- **What is elder care, and what problems do companies face with regard to this growing problem?**
  Workers who need to provide elder care for dependent parents or others are generally more experienced and vital to the mission of the organization than younger workers are. The cost to business is very large and growing.

• **Why are more and more companies now testing workers and job applicants for substance abuse?**
Drug abuse costs the U.S. economy $414 billion in lost work, health care costs, crime, traffic accidents, and other expenses, and over $150 billion in lost productivity. Individuals who use drugs are three and a half times more likely to be in workplace accidents and five times more likely to file a workers' compensation claim than those who do not use drugs.

key terms

agency shop agreement 340	craft union 335	open shop agreement 340
American Federation of Labor (AFL) 336	decertification 339	primary boycott 344
arbitration 343	givebacks 345	right-to-work laws 340
bargaining zone 343	grievance 342	secondary boycott 344
certification 339	industrial unions 336	sexual harassment 350
closed shop agreement 340	injunction 344	shop stewards 342
collective bargaining 337	Knights of Labor 336	strike 343
Congress of Industrial Organizations (CIO) 336	lockout 344	strikebreakers 345
cooling-off period 344	mediation 343	union 334
	negotiated labor–management agreement (labor contract) 340	union security clause 340
		union shop agreement 340
		yellow-dog contract 337

critical thinking

1. Do you believe that union shop agreements are violations of a worker's freedom of choice in the workplace? Do you think open shop agreements unfairly penalize workers who pay dues to unions they have elected to represent them in the workplace?

2. Some college football and basketball coaches earn huge incomes. Should college volleyball and swimming coaches be paid comparably? Should colleges pay their student athletes to play? Should players in the Women's National Basketball Association (WNBA) be paid the same as their male counterparts in the National Basketball Association (NBA)? What role should market forces and government play in determining such wages?

3. If a company provides employer-paid child care services to workers with children, should those who don't have children or don't need child care services be paid extra?

developing workplace skills

Key: ● Team   ★ Analytic   ▲ Communication   ⊡ Technology

★ ⊡   1. Check whether your state supports the right of public employees (police, firefighters, teachers) to unionize and collectively bargain. If not, should it? Should such workers be allowed to strike?

★ ▲   2. Evaluate the following statement: "Labor unions are dinosaurs that have outlived their usefulness in today's knowledge-based economy." After your evaluation, take the position on this statement that differs from your own point of view and defend that position. Be sure to consider such questions as: Do unions serve a purpose in some industries? Do unions make the United States less competitive in global markets?

3. Research federal and state legislation related to child care, parental leave, and elder care benefits for employees. Are specific trends emerging? Should companies be responsible for providing such workplace benefits, or should the government share some responsibility? Why?

4. Compile a list of two or three employee–management issues not covered in the chapter. Compare your list with those of several classmates and see which issues you selected in common and which are unique to each individual. Pick an issue you all agree will be important in the future and discuss its likely effects and outcomes.

5. Do businesses and government agencies have a duty to provide additional benefits to employees beyond fair pay and good working conditions? Propose a system you consider fair and equitable for employees and employers.

taking it to the **net**

PURPOSE

To understand why workers choose to join unions and how unions have made differences in certain industries.

EXERCISE

Visit the AFL-CIO website (www.aflcio.org) and find information about why workers join unions and what the benefits have been.

1. Explain how union membership has affected minorities, women, older workers, and part-time workers.

2. The AFL-CIO site presents the union's perspective on labor issues. Look at the key issues and check sources such as the National Association of Manufacturers (www.nam.org) and the National Right to Work Legal Defense Foundation (www.righttowork.org) that support management's perspectives and compare their positions on these issues.

Video Case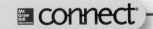

UNITED WE STAND

After reading this chapter, you should be familiar with the history of labor unions. You have learned the tactics that labor uses to demand new benefits from management, and you have learned the tactics that management uses to respond to labor demands. You are also familiar with the various laws that are involved in labor–management disputes. You may get the impression from the media that labor unions are in decline and don't have much clout anymore. In fact, the number of

people in labor unions has declined dramatically, but that doesn't mean that labor unions are not important today or that they have lost their passion for seeking fair treatment by companies.

We are so accustomed to thinking about labor unions in the auto, steel, and other related industries that we tend to overlook some truly key industries where labor unions are very important. No doubt you have heard in passing of the Screen Actors Guild (SAG), the American Federation of

Television and Radio Artists, and the Writers Guild of America. But do you have any idea what issues the membership faces in such unions? Are they the same issues that unions have always had—seniority, pay, benefits, etc.—or are they somehow different?

Many young people dream of becoming a "movie star." They see the glamour, the excitement, the adulation of the fans, and the huge paychecks. What they don't see behind the scenes is the constant fight going on to win and keep certain privileges that past actors have won. Back in the 1930s, actors worked unrestricted hours, had no required meal breaks, and had unbreakable seven-year contracts. The producers tried to control whom you could marry, what political views you expressed, and what your morals should be. The Screen Actors Guild won some concessions for the actors in 1937, but the studios pretty much still "owned" their stars. Eventually the stars won the right to better contracts, to the point where independent studios were formed and actors could control their own careers, even demanding a percentage of the gross for their pay.

Other issues concerned residuals for films shown on TV and in reruns. Contracts had to do with things such as commercials and how the actors would be paid for them. Today's contracts deal with issues like diversity, salary and work conditions, financial assurances, safety considerations, and so on. Stipulations are constantly changing for actors. For example, independent film producers in the United States and around the world have different rules and requirements. TV commercials now appear on cell phones. The Screen Actors Guild keeps up with such changes to ensure fair treatment of its members.

While SAG is for movie actors, the American Federation of Television and Radio Artists is a performer's union for actors, radio and TV announcers, and newspersons, singers, and others who perform on radio and/or TV. It negotiates wages and working conditions much like SAG, including health care and pensions. You can imagine negotiating an issue like equal pay for equal work when dealing with highly paid actors with huge egos.

The Writers Guild of America (WGA) represents writers in the motion picture, broadcast, and news media industries. Like actors, writers have issues dealing with pay, benefits, retirement, etc. The more you think about it, the more it will become clear to you that actors and others in the entertainment industry need unions or some other kind of organization to protect them from unfair practices. You can only imagine what treatment actors and others get from independent companies in other countries if they don't have representation.

Unions today are gathering momentum in nontraditional professions like nursing and teaching (including college teachers). They are also gaining support in low paying jobs like fast food where the push is on for more equitable wages.

THINKING IT OVER

1. What is the general attitude in your class toward labor unions? Are there many union workers in your town? Do you see labor unions gaining strength in the future?

2. One of the primary concerns of traditional labor unions is the treatment of outsourcing. Could the entertainment industry outsource operations? How would this affect SAG and the other unions?

3. The video touches on the era of Senator Joe McCarthy and the House Un-American Activities Committee. How has the government impacted on the growth and stability of labor unions?

notes

1. Alana Semeuls and Michael Muskal, "Bankruptcy Protection Offers Hope for Detroit, Setback for Its Unions," *Los Angeles Times*, December 3, 2013; and "In a Hit to Unions, Detroit Bankruptcy OK'd," *Associated Press*, December 3, 2013.
2. Tom Watson, "Jobs with Justice: New Campaign Takes Aim at Low Wages, Working Poor, Falling Middle Class," *Forbes*, December 30, 2013.
3. Chris Isidore, "Union Membership at Businesses Grows," *CNN Money*, January 27, 2014.
4. Steve Greenhouse, "Share of Workforce in a Union Falls to a 97-Year Low," *The New York Times*, January 23, 2013; and "Union Decline in Public Sector," *The New York Times*, January 24, 2014.
5. Luke Rosiak, "Union Bosses' Salaries Put 'Big' in Big Labor," *Washington Times*, January 11, 2013; and Andrew Doughman, "Union Leaders Salaries Stay High Even in Hard Times," *Las Vegas Sun*, August 19, 2013.
6. Morgan Housal, "50 Reasons Why This Is the Greatest Time Ever," *USA Today*, February 2, 2014.
7. www.aftcio.org, accessed January 2014.
8. Charles Lane, "Public Sector Unions Interfere with the Public Interest," *The Washington Post*, January 27, 2014.
9. www.bls.gov, accessed January 2014.
10. Andrew Harris and Tim Jones, "Illinois Unions Sue to Stop $100 Billion Pension Funding Fix," *Bloomberg Businessweek*, January 29, 2014.

11. David Savage, "Scalia May Be the Swing Vote in Union Fees Case," *Los Angeles Times,* January 21, 2014; and Garrett Epps, "The Supreme Court Case That Could Clobber Public-Sector Unions," *The Atlantic,* January 21, 2014.

12. Drew Sharp, "College Athletes' Fight Not Equal to Unions, But Reform Needed," *The Detroit Free Press,* January 30, 2014.

13. Tim Reid, "Democrats Feud over California Pension Reform Measure," *Chicago Tribune,* February 4, 2014.

14. Sam Hananel, "Labor Board Tries Again to Change Union Rules," *Bloomberg Businessweek,* February 5, 2014.

15. Frank Keating and Brandon Dutcher, "Right-to-Work Laws Help States like Oklahoma Shine," *Forbes,* October 18, 2013.

16. www.carpenters.org, accessed April 2014; and Austin Smith, "What Right-to-Work Would Do for New York," *New York Post,* December 12, 2012.

17. Steven Greenhouse, "Wisconsin's Legacy for Unions," *The New York Times,* February 22, 2014.

18. Richard Berman, "Why Unions Want a Higher Minimum Wage," *The Wall Street Journal,* February 25, 2013.

19. Ira Podell, "NHL Lockout 2012: Mediator Gets League, Union Back Together," *Associated Press,* January 5, 2013; and Mike Brehm and Kevin Allen, "NHL Lockout Ends at 113 Days: A Daily Look Back," *USA Today,* January 6, 2013.

20. Steve Eder, "Arbitrator's Ruling Banishes the Yankee's Alex Rodriguez for a Season," *The New York Times,* January 11, 2014; and Mason Levinson, "Heyward Signs Two Year Contract with Braves to Avoid Arbitration," *Bloomberg Businessweek,* February 4, 2014.

21. www.adr.org, accessed April 2014.

22. Steve Greenhouse, "Wage Strike Planned at Fast Food Outlets," *The New York Times,* December 1, 2013.

23. Kristin Tillotson, "After Bitter Labor Battle, Minnesota Orchestra Seeks Harmony," *Minneapolis Star Tribune,* February 4, 2014; and Michael Cooper, "Minnesota Orchestra Contract Ends Long Labor Lockout," *The New York Times,* January 14, 2014.

24. Amanda Becker, "U.S. Union Membership Steady at 11.3 Percent in 2013," *Reuters,* January 24, 2014; and Melanie Trottman, "Labor Union Membership Rate Stays Steady in 2013," *The Wall Street Journal,* January 24, 2014.

25. Paul A. Eisenstein, "UAW Consider First Dues Hike Since 1967," *CNBC,* December 3, 2013.

26. www.bls.gov, accessed April 2014.

27. Charles Kenny, "Factory Jobs Are Gone; Get over It," *Bloomberg Businessweek,* January 23, 2014.

28. Dorothy Pomerantz, "The Celebrity 100," *Forbes,* July 15, 2013.

29. Christopher Matthews, "Top 10 Highest Paid CEOs," *Time,* December 4, 2013.

30. Jennifer Liberto, "CEOs Earn 354 Times More Than Average Workers," *CNN Money,* April 15, 2013.

31. Jeff Green, "Why Fired CEOs Go Straight to the Bank," *Bloomberg Businessweek,* June 6, 2013.

32. Jeff Green, "Golden Hellos," *Bloomberg Businessweek,* December 8, 2013.

33. Damian Paletta, "5 Takeaways on Wealth and Inequality from Piketty," *The Wall Street Journal,* April 14, 2014.

34. Michael Hiltzak, "CEO-to-Worker Pay Gap Is Obscene: Want to Know How Obscene?" *Los Angeles Times,* October 20, 2013; and Dave Michaels, "CEO-to-Worker Pay Ratio Disclosure Proposed by Divided SEC," *Bloomberg Personal Finance,* September 18, 2013.

35. Elliot Blair Smith and Phil Kuntz, "Disclosed: The Pay Gap Between CEOs and Employees," *Bloomberg Businessweek,* May 2, 2013; and Christopher Matthews, "Top 10 Highest Paid CEOs," *Time,* December 4, 2013.

36. Ben Weber, "Gender Bias by the Numbers," *Bloomberg Businessweek,* January 27, 2014.

37. Anne Fisher, "Boys versus Girls: What's Behind the College Grad Gender Gap?" *Fortune,* March 27, 2013.

38. www.americanprogress.org/boushey, accessed April 2014.

39. www.americanprogress.org, accessed May 2012.

40. www.eeoc.gov, accessed April 2014.

41. Ibid.

42. Jennifer Steinhauer, "Reports of Sexual Assault Rise Sharply," *The New York Times,* November 9, 2014.

43. Robin Abcarian, "Lessons from Ex-San Diego Mayor Filner's Sex Harassment Scandal," *Los Angeles Times,* October 15, 2013; and James Nash, "San Diego Mayor to End Sexual Harassment Case," *Bloomberg Businessweek,* August 22, 2013.

44. www.workingmother.com, accessed April 2014.

45. www.censusbureau.gov, accessed April 2014.

46. Janet Novack, "Essential Numbers for Retirement Planning: Your Personal Life Expectancy," *Forbes,* January 21, 2014.

47. Gary Drevitch, "Welcome to Age 50: Top Caregiving Tips," *Forbes,* January 8, 2014.

48. Kathy Caprino, "7 Ways to Transform Caregiving from Burden to Opportunity," *Forbes,* December 30, 2013.

49. www.caregiving.org, accessed April 2014.

50. Julie Landry Laviolette, "Tips in Caring for Your Aging Parents," *Miami Herald,* February 4, 2014.

51. Ann Carrns, "Assessing the Costs of Caring for an Aging Relative," *The New York Times,* August 28, 2013.

52. www.nih.gov, accessed April 2014.

53. www.dol.gov, accessed April 2014.

54. Kimberly Hefling, "School Shootings Continue Despite Increased Security after Sandy Hook Killings," *Huffington Post,* February 2, 2014.

photo credits

PART 5

13

Marketing: Helping Buyers Buy

Learning Objectives

AFTER YOU HAVE READ AND STUDIED THIS CHAPTER, YOU SHOULD BE ABLE TO

LO 13-1 Define *marketing*, and apply the marketing concept to both for-profit and nonprofit organizations.

LO 13-2 Describe the four Ps of marketing.

LO 13-3 Summarize the marketing research process.

LO 13-4 Show how marketers use environmental scanning to learn about the changing marketing environment.

LO 13-5 Explain how marketers apply the tools of market segmentation, relationship marketing, and the study of consumer behavior.

LO 13-6 Compare the business-to-business market and the consumer market.

In the business world, you don't necessarily have to be the first person to think of a good idea in order for it to become successful. Oftentimes, the entrepreneurs who uniquely market an existing product or service enjoy big returns on their investments.

Daymond John set off on his path to prosperity in 1989 when he began sewing wool hats in his Queens, New York, apartment. For the previous few weeks he had noticed young men in the neighborhood sporting short snowcaps with the tops cut off and cinched together with string. John couldn't believe that department stores were selling the hats for as much as $20. So, with the help of a neighbor, he sewed dozens of hats and sold them for $10 in front of the New York Coliseum. John was astounded when he ended up with $800 after his first day. Knowing he had a great concept on his hands, John threw himself into his new apparel business. As a nod to the do-it-yourself origins of the venture, he named the company FUBU—"For Us By Us."

To go along with his distinctive brand name, John designed a graffiti-inspired logo and sewed it onto sweatshirts, tees, and other sportswear. Despite a strong start, John soon ran into problems. "Like most entrepreneurs, the initial struggle was to go past the point of imagination and make it a point of conception, where I was actually putting together a product and producing it," said John. "Everyone has an idea, but it's taking those first steps toward turning that idea into a reality that are always the toughest." Finding the time to accomplish all this proved difficult. After a day of calling distributors and sewing, John would then trudge off to his night job as a server at Red Lobster. FUBU ended up running out of money three times, causing John to consider abandoning the idea altogether.

But in 1992 he relaunched the brand with the help of three partners and a new business strategy. John knew he certainly wasn't the only talented individual living in Hollis, Queens. The neighborhood had been home to hip-hop legends like Run-DMC, Salt-N-Pepa, and LL Cool J. In order to get FUBU into the public eye, John worked hard to put his clothes into the hands of his famous friends. "I'd give them a shirt to wear on stage, sneak in their trailer, steal it and give it to another rapper," said John. The company's big break came in 1993 when LL Cool J wore a FUBU hat in a commercial for Gap. The retailer pulled the commercial a month later when executives realized they had been unknowingly promoting another brand, but by then the spot had done wonders to raise FUBU's profile. Still, the company wasn't solvent enough to receive approval for a small-business loan. As a result, John and his mother mortgaged their house for $100,000 and bet their future on FUBU's success.

It turned out to be a good decision. John achieved another professional coup when he took the brand to a famous industry trade show in Las Vegas. Despite not having enough money to buy a booth at the event, John and his partners managed to negotiate more than $300,000 worth of orders out of a hotel room. Meanwhile, the brand continued to gain traction with many in the hip-hop community. In 1996 FUBU secured LL Cool J's services as an official celebrity spokesman. "I'm a firm believer in utilizing celebrities because they tap into people on an emotional basis," said John. "When you get behind a celebrity, he'll get behind you." By the end of the 1990s, FUBU was bringing in more than $350 million in annual revenue. Since then, John has used his position as a millionaire mogul to invest in tech start-ups and advise other entrepreneurs, especially in his role as a judge on the TV show *Shark Tank*.

In this chapter you'll learn how master marketers like Daymond John identify their audience and figure out how to reach them. Whether through distribution, advertising, or publicity, successful marketing makes a connection with a customer that they won't soon forget.

Sources: Emily Inverso, "Shark Tank's Daymond John on the Business of Being Broke—And More," *Forbes*, March 6, 2014; Harley Finkelstein, "Daymond John Answers Your Questions," *Huffington Post*, February 10, 2014; and Teri Evans, "Shark Tank's Daymond John on Thinking Big," *Entrepreneur*, October 31, 2012.

Daymond John
- Founder of FUBU
- Started by sewing wool hats in his apartment
- Turned FUBU into a multimillion-dollar lifestyle brand

www.fubu.com

@fubuapparel

This company studies population growth and regional trends as it expands its product line for specific regions of the country. Its research led to the creation of Creole flavors targeted primarily to the South and spicy nacho cheese flavors made especially for Texas and California. Name that company. (The answer can be found in this chapter.)

LO 13–1 Define *marketing*, and apply the marketing concept to both for-profit and nonprofit organizations.

WHAT IS MARKETING?

marketing
The activity, set of institutions, and processes for creating, communicating, delivering, and exchanging offerings that have value for customers, clients, partners, and society at large.

The term *marketing* means different things to different people. Many think of marketing as simply "selling" or "advertising." Yes, selling and advertising are part of marketing, but it's much more. The American Marketing Association has defined **marketing** as the activity, set of institutions, and processes for creating, communicating, delivering, and exchanging offerings that have value for customers, clients, partners, and society at large. We can also think of marketing, more simply, as the activities buyers and sellers perform to facilitate mutually satisfying exchanges.

In the past marketing focused almost entirely on helping the seller sell. That's why many people still think of it as mostly selling, advertising, and distribution from the seller to the buyer. Today, much of marketing is instead about helping the buyer buy.[1] Let's examine a couple of examples.

Today, when people want to buy a new or used car, they often go online first. They go to a website like Cars.com to search for the vehicle they want. At other websites they compare prices and features. By the time they go to the dealer, they may know exactly which car they want and the best price available.

The websites have helped the buyer buy. Not only are customers spared searching one dealership after another to find the best price, but manufacturers and dealers are eager to participate so that they don't lose customers. The future of marketing is doing everything you can to help the buyer buy. The easier a marketer makes the purchase decision process, the more that marketer will sell.[2]

Let's look at another case. In the past, one of the few ways students and parents could find the college with the right "fit" was to travel from campus to campus, a grueling and expensive process. Today, colleges use podcasts, virtual tours, live chats, and other interactive technologies to make on-campus visits less necessary. Such virtual tours help students and their parents buy.

Of course, helping the buyer buy also helps the seller sell. Think about that for a minute. In the vacation market, many people find the trip they want themselves. They go online to find the right spot, and then make choices, sometimes questioning potential sellers. In industries like this, the role of marketing is to make sure that a company's products or services are easily found online, and that the company responds effectively to potential customers. Websites like Expedia, Travelocity, and Priceline allow customers to find the best price or set their own.

These are only a few examples of the marketing trend toward helping buyers buy. Consumers today spend hours searching the Internet for good deals.

Wise marketers provide a wealth of information online and even cultivate customer relationships using blogs and social networking sites such as Facebook and Twitter.[3]

Online communities provide an opportunity to observe people (customers and others) interacting with one another, expressing their own opinions, forming relationships, and commenting on various goods and services. It is important for marketers to track what relevant bloggers are writing by doing blog searches using key terms that define their market. Vendors who have text-mining tools can help companies measure conversations about their products and their personnel. Much of the future of marketing lies in mining such online conversations and responding appropriately. For example, marketers are learning why people shop online, put the goods into a shopping cart, but then end the sale before they give their credit card information.[4] Retailers and other marketers who rely solely on traditional advertising and selling are losing out to new ways of marketing.[5]

The Evolution of Marketing

What marketers do at any particular time depends on what they need to do to fill customers' needs and wants, which continually change. Let's take a brief look at how those changes have influenced the evolution of marketing. Marketing in the United States has passed through four eras: (1) production, (2) selling, (3) marketing concept, and (4) customer relationship. Today, a new era is emerging: mobile/on-demand marketing (see Figure 13.1).

The Production Era   From the time the first European settlers began their struggle to survive in America until the early 1900s, the general philosophy of business was "Produce as much as you can, because there is a limitless market for it." Given the limited production capability and vast demand for products in those days, that production philosophy was both logical and profitable. Business owners were mostly farmers, carpenters, and trade workers. They needed to produce more and more, so their goals centered on production.

The Selling Era   By the 1920s, businesses had developed mass-production techniques (such as automobile assembly lines), and production capacity often exceeded the immediate market demand. Therefore, the business philosophy

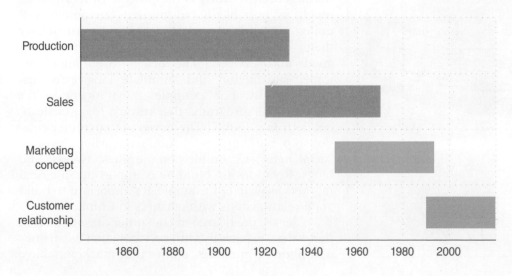

FIGURE 13.1 MARKETING ERAS
The evolution of marketing in the United States involved four eras: (1) production, (2) selling, (3) marketing concept, and (4) customer relationship. Today a new era is emerging: mobile/on-demand marketing.

turned from producing to selling. Most companies emphasized selling and advertising in an effort to persuade consumers to buy existing products; few offered extensive service after the sale.

The Marketing Concept Era   After World War II ended in 1945, returning soldiers starting new careers and beginning families sparked a tremendous demand for goods and services. The postwar years launched the sudden increase in the birthrate that we now call the baby boom, and also a boom in consumer spending. Competition for the consumer's dollar was fierce. Businesses recognized that they needed to be responsive to consumers if they wanted to get their business, and a philosophy emerged in the 1950s called the marketing concept.

The **marketing concept** had three parts:

1. *A customer orientation.* Find out what consumers want and provide it for them. (Note the emphasis on meeting consumer needs rather than on promotion or sales.)

2. *A service orientation.* Make sure everyone in the organization has the same objective: customer satisfaction. This should be a total and integrated organizational effort. That is, everyone from the president of the firm to the delivery people should be customer-oriented. Does that seem to be the norm today?

3. *A profit orientation.* Focus on those goods and services that will earn the most profit and enable the organization to survive and expand to serve more consumer wants and needs.

It took awhile for businesses to implement the marketing concept. The process went slowly during the 1960s and 1970s. During the 1980s, businesses began to apply the marketing concept more aggressively than they had done over the preceding 30 years. That led to a focus on customer relationship management (CRM) that has become very important today. We explore that concept next.

The Customer Relationship Era   In the 1990s and early 2000s, some managers extended the marketing concept by adopting the practice of customer relationship management. **Customer relationship management (CRM)** is the process of learning as much as possible about present customers and doing everything you can over time to satisfy them—or even to exceed their expectations—with goods and services.[6] The idea is to enhance customer satisfaction and stimulate long-term customer loyalty. For example, most airlines offer frequent-flier programs that reward loyal customers with free flights. The newest in customer relationship building, as mentioned earlier, involves social networks, online communities, tweets, and blogs. Relationship building is important in global markets as well. For example, it's important to build good relationships with partners in China.[7]

Clearly, the degree of consumer dissatisfaction that exists, especially with services such as airlines and phone companies, shows that marketers have

---

marketing concept
A three-part business philosophy: (1) a customer orientation, (2) a service orientation, and (3) a profit orientation.

customer relationship management (CRM)
The process of learning as much as possible about customers and doing everything you can to satisfy them—or even exceed their expectations—with goods and services.

In the selling era, the focus of marketing was on selling, with little service afterward and less customization. What economic and social factors made this approach appropriate for the time?

Making Sustainability Just Peachy

We probably all remember enjoying a piping hot bowl of Campbell's soup on a blustery day. As the company slogan said, it was "mmm mmm" good. What you may not know is Campbell Soup is one of only 18 U.S. companies named to the Global 100 Most Sustainable Corporations in the World list. Through its corporate social responsibility program, the company strives to make a positive impact in the markets it serves. Its work with the Food Bank of South New Jersey is a great example of being responsible and promoting sustainability.

The Food Bank of South Jersey learned that local farmers were discarding almost 1 million peaches a year in landfills. The peaches were perfectly fine to eat, but had bruises and other imperfections that made them unacceptable to grocery store produce managers. When the food bank asked if it could have the peaches, the farmers agreed to donate them at no cost. The question of what to do with the peaches was challenging until the Food Bank and Campbell's teamed up and "Just Peachy Salsa" was born.

Campbell's agreed to manufacture the salsa at no cost. In fact, employees donated their time and agreed to label 42,000 jars of "Just Peachy Salsa" by hand. Because of the collaboration, South Jersey farmers did not have the expense of dumping peaches or the negative environmental impact of clogging landfills. The local Food Bank was able to generate close to $100,000 per year to provide additional food products to people in need, and consumers can enjoy a healthy product. When it comes to seeking sustainability, Campbell's really is "mmm mmm" good.

Sources: Kurt Kuehn and Lynnette McIntire, "Sustainability a CFO Can Love," *Harvard Business Review*, April 2014; "Campbell Soup Company Named to Global 100 Sustainability Index," *Reuters*, January 22, 2014; and Campbell Soup Company, www.campbellsoupcompany.com (accessed April 2014).

a long way to go to create customer satisfaction and loyalty. Since many consumers today are interested in green products and protecting the environment, relationship building also means responding to that desire. The Seeking Sustainability box explores sustainability in the food industry.

The Emerging Mobile/On-Demand Marketing Era The digital age is increasing consumers' power and pushing marketing toward being on demand, not just always "on." Consumers are demanding relevant information exactly when they want it, without all the noise of unwanted messages. Search technologies have made product information pervasive. Consumers share, compare, and rate experiences through social media; and mobile devices make it all available 24/7.

Developments such as inexpensive microtransmitters embedded in products will allow consumers to search by image, voice, or gestures. For example, if your friend has a product you like, you will be able to just tap it with your phone and instantly get product reviews, prices, and so on. If you can't decide what color to buy, you can just send the photo to your Facebook friends who can vote for their favorite. After you buy it, you will get special offers from the manufacturer or its partners for similar products or services.

As digital technology continues to grow, consumer demands are likely to rise in four areas:[8]

1. *Now.* Consumers want to interact anywhere, anytime.
2. *Can I?* They want to do new things with different kinds of information in ways that create value for them. For example, a couple wanting to know if they can afford to buy a house they walk by could simply snap a photo and instantly see the sale price and other property information; while at

Kids will spend 11 minutes dressing Spike up like a princess.

How about two minutes to brush their teeth?

Brushing for two minutes now can save your child from severe tooth pain later. Two minutes, twice a day. They have the time. For fun, 2-minute videos to watch while brushing, go to 2min2x.org.

Ad Council   PARTNERSHIP FOR Healthy Mouths Healthy Lives

©2013 Healthy Mouths, Healthy Lives

The Ad Council sponsors many public service ads like this one. The idea is to make the public more aware of various needs that only nonprofit organizations are meeting. The ads then encourage the public to get engaged in the issue somehow, if only by donating money. Have you responded to any Ad Council advertisements?

 connect

 iSee It! Need help understanding the marketing mix? Visit your Connect e-book video tab for a brief animated explanation.

marketing mix
The ingredients that go into a marketing program: product, price, place, and promotion.

the same time the device automatically accesses their financial information, contacts mortgagers, and obtains loan preapproval.

3. *For me.* Consumers expect all data stored about them to be used to personalize what they experience.

4. *Simple.* Consumers expect all interactions to be easy.

Companies will be looking for employees who can improve the business's handling of social media, big data, and customer experiences. Maybe you will be one of them.

Nonprofit Organizations and Marketing

Even though the marketing concept emphasizes a profit orientation, marketing is a critical part of almost all organizations, including nonprofits.[9] Charities use marketing to raise funds for combating world hunger, for instance, or to obtain other resources. The Red Cross uses promotion to encourage people to donate blood when local or national supplies run low. Greenpeace uses marketing to promote ecologically safe technologies. Environmental groups use marketing to try to cut carbon emissions. Churches use marketing to attract new members and raise funds. Politicians use marketing to get votes.

States use marketing to attract new businesses and tourists. Many states, for example, have competed to get automobile companies from other countries to locate plants in their area. Schools use marketing to attract new students. Other organizations, such as arts groups, unions, and social groups, also use marketing. The Ad Council, for example, uses public service ads to create awareness and change attitudes on such issues as drunk driving and fire prevention.

Organizations use marketing, in fact, to promote everything from environmentalism and crime prevention ("Take A Bite Out Of Crime") to social issues ("Friends Don't Let Friends Drive Drunk").

LO 13–2   Describe the four Ps of marketing.

THE MARKETING MIX

We can divide much of what marketing people do into four factors, called the four Ps to make them easy to remember. They are:

1. Product
2. Price
3. Place
4. Promotion

Managing the controllable parts of the marketing process means (1) designing a want-satisfying product, (2) setting a price for the product, (3) putting the product in a place where people will buy it, and (4) promoting the product. These four factors are called the **marketing mix** because businesses blend them together in a well-designed marketing program (see Figure 13.2).

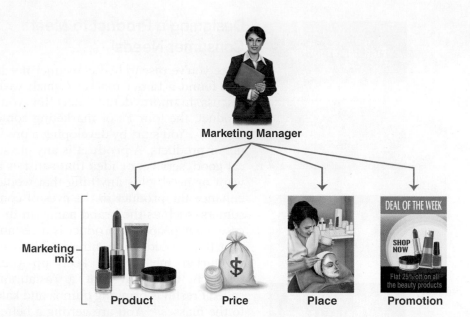

FIGURE 13.2 MARKETING MANAGERS AND THE MARKETING MIX
Marketing managers must choose how to implement the four Ps of the marketing mix: product, price, place, and promotion. The goals are to please customers and make a profit.

Applying the Marketing Process

The four Ps are a convenient way to remember the basics of marketing, but they don't necessarily include everything that goes into the marketing process for all products. One of the best ways to understand the entire marketing process is to take a product or a group of products and follow the process that led to their development and sale (see Figure 13.3).

Imagine, for example, that you and your friends want to start a money-making business near your college. You've noticed a lot of vegetarians among your acquaintances. You do a quick survey in a few dorms, sororities, and fraternities and find many vegetarians—and other students who like to eat vegetarian meals once in a while. Your preliminary research indicates some demand for a vegetarian restaurant nearby. You check the fast-food stores in the area and find that none offer more than one or two vegetarian meals. In fact, most don't have any, except salads and some soups.

You note that haute-vegetarian menus are big in Europe.[10] Why not in the United States? You also note that McDonald's went vegetarian in India in 2013.[11] You find that KFC Canada offers a vegan version of its chicken sandwich in 500 of its 750 outlets. Further research identifies a number of different kinds of vegetarians. Vegans eat neither eggs nor dairy products. Vegan diets took off when Beyonce's 22-day vegan diet was announced. Bill Clinton says he's been vegan since 2009.[12] Such publicity led to the announcement that 2014 was "the year of the vegan."[13]

You conclude that a vegetarian restaurant would have to appeal to all kinds of vegetarians to be a success. Your research identifies vegan farmers who don't use any synthetic chemical fertilizers, pesticides, herbicides, or genetically modified ingredients. You also find that there is a company that is making an egg-like product from vegetables. That would appeal to those vegetarians who don't eat eggs.[14]

You've just performed the first few steps in the marketing process. You noticed an opportunity (a need for vegetarian food, perhaps near campus). You conducted some preliminary research to see whether your idea had any merit. And then you identified groups of people who might be interested in your product. They will be your *target market* (the people you will try to persuade to come to your restaurant).

FIGURE 13.3 THE MARKETING PROCESS WITH THE FOUR PS

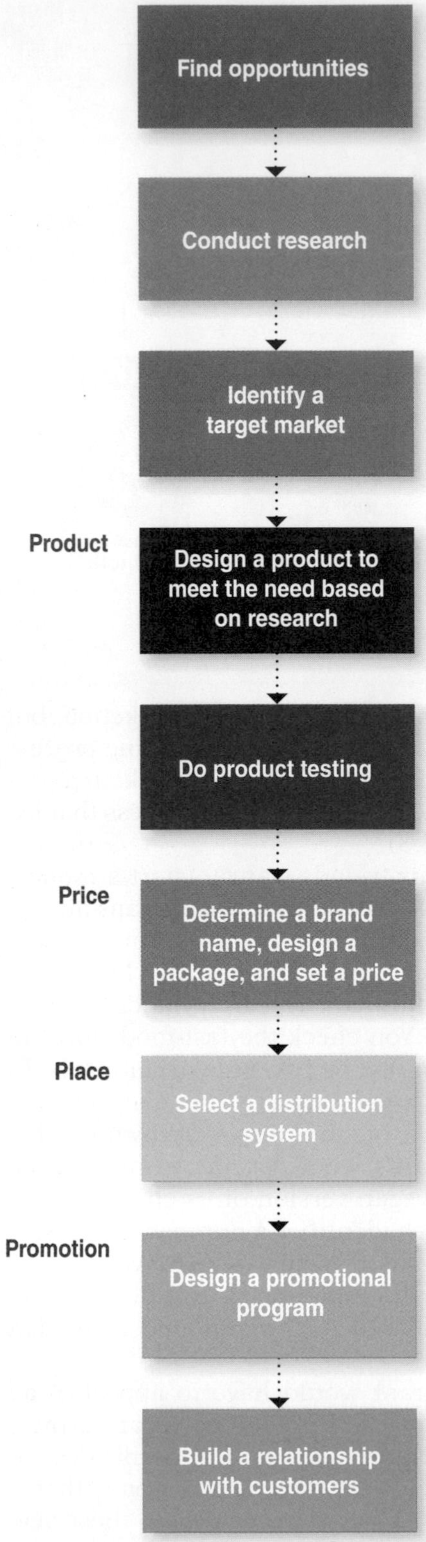

product
Any physical good, service, or idea that satisfies a want or need plus anything that would enhance the product in the eyes of consumers, such as the brand.

test marketing
The process of testing products among potential users.

brand name
A word, letter, or group of words or letters that differentiates one seller's goods and services from those of competitors.

Find opportunities

Conduct research

Identify a target market

Product

Design a product to meet the need based on research

Do product testing

Price

Determine a brand name, design a package, and set a price

Place

Select a distribution system

Promotion

Design a promotional program

Build a relationship with customers

Designing a Product to Meet Consumer Needs

Once you've researched consumer needs and found a target market (which we'll discuss in more detail later) for your product, the four Ps of marketing come into play. You start by developing a product or products. A **product** is any physical good, service, or idea that satisfies a want or need, plus anything that would enhance the product in the eyes of consumers, such as the brand name. In this case, your proposed product is a restaurant that would serve different kinds of vegetarian meals. You keep up your research, and find that a restaurant called Freshii is bringing quinoa and kale to the masses.[15] You are getting a better idea of what your products should be.

It's a good idea at this point to do concept testing. That is, you develop an accurate description of your restaurant and ask people, in person or online, whether the idea of the restaurant and the kind of meals you intend to offer appeals to them. If it does, you might go to a supplier that offers vegetarian products to get the ingredients to prepare samples that you can take to consumers to test their reactions. The process of testing products among potential users is called **test marketing**. For example, you can test market your vegetarian burgers and learn how best to prepare them.[16]

If consumers like the products and agree they would buy them, you have the information you need to find investors and look for a convenient location to open a restaurant. You'll have to think of a catchy name. (For practice, stop for a minute and try to think of one.) We'll use Very Vegetarian in this text, although we're sure you can think of a better name. Meanwhile, let's continue with the discussion of product development.

You may want to offer some well-known brand names to attract people right away. A **brand name** is a word, letter, or group of words or letters that differentiates one seller's goods and services from those of competitors. Brand names of vegetarian products include Tofurky, Mori-Nu, and Yves Veggie Cuisine. We'll discuss the product development process in detail in Chapter 14, and follow the Very Vegetarian case to show you how all marketing and other business decisions tie together. For now, we're simply sketching the whole marketing process to give you an overall picture. So far, we've covered the first P of the marketing mix: product. Next comes price.

Setting an Appropriate Price

After you've decided what products and services you want to offer consumers, you have to set appropriate prices. Those prices depend on a number of factors. In the restaurant business, the price could be close to what other restaurants charge to stay competitive. Or you might charge less to attract business, especially at the beginning. Or you may offer high-quality products for which customers are willing to pay a little more (as Starbucks does). You also have to consider the costs of producing, distributing, and promoting the product, which all influence your price. We'll discuss pricing issues in more detail in Chapter 14.

A vegetarian restaurant might fill a popular need in the neighborhood of many college campuses today. Is there one near your school? What can you tell about its manager's application of the four Ps of marketing—product, price, place, and promotion?

Getting the Product to the Right Place

There are several ways you can serve the market for vegetarian meals. You can have people come in, sit down, and eat at the restaurant, but that's not the only alternative—think of pizza. You could deliver the food to customers' dorms, apartments, and student unions. You may want to sell your products in supermarkets or health-food stores, or through organizations that specialize in distributing food products. Such intermediaries are the middle links in a series of organizations that distribute goods from producers to consumers. (The more traditional word for them is *middlemen*.) Getting the product to consumers when and where they want it is critical to market success. Don't forget to consider the Internet as a way to reach consumers. We'll discuss the importance of marketing intermediaries and distribution in detail in Chapter 15.

Developing an Effective Promotional Strategy

The last of the four Ps of marketing is promotion. **Promotion** consists of all the techniques sellers use to inform people about and motivate them to buy their products or services. Promotion includes advertising; personal selling; public relations; publicity; word of mouth (viral marketing); and various sales promotion efforts, such as coupons, rebates, samples, and cents-off deals. We'll discuss promotion in detail in Chapter 16.

promotion
All the techniques sellers use to inform people about and motivate them to buy their products or services.

Promotion often includes relationship building with customers. Among other activities, that means responding to suggestions consumers make to improve the products or their marketing, including price and packaging. For Very Vegetarian, postpurchase, or after-sale, service may include refusing payment for meals that weren't satisfactory and stocking additional vegetarian products customers say they would like. Listening to customers and responding to their needs is the key to the ongoing process that is marketing.

test prep

- What does it mean to "help the buyer buy"?
- What are the three parts of the marketing concept?
- What are the four Ps of the marketing mix?

Use LearnSmart to help retain what you have learned. Access your instructor's Connect course to check out LearnSmart, or go to learnsmartadvantage.com for help.

LEARNSMART

LO 13–3   Summarize the marketing research process.

PROVIDING MARKETERS WITH INFORMATION

Every decision in the marketing process depends on information. When they conduct **marketing research**, marketers analyze markets to determine opportunities and challenges, and to find the information they need to make good decisions.

Marketing research helps identify what products customers have purchased in the past, and what changes have occurred to alter what they want now and what they're likely to want in the future. Marketers also conduct research on business trends, the ecological impact of their decisions, global trends, and more. Businesses need information to compete effectively, and marketing research is the activity that gathers it. You have learned, for example, how important research is to a person contemplating starting a vegetarian restaurant. Besides listening to customers, marketing researchers also pay attention to what employees, shareholders, dealers, consumer advocates, media representatives, and other stakeholders have to say. As noted earlier, much of that research is now being gathered online through social media. Despite all that research, however, marketers still have difficulty understanding their customers as well as they should.[17]

The Marketing Research Process

A simplified marketing research process consists of at least four key steps:

1. Defining the question (the problem or opportunity) and determining the present situation.
2. Collecting research data.
3. Analyzing the research data.
4. Choosing the best solution and implementing it.

The following sections look at each of these steps.

Defining the Question and Determining the Present Situation   Marketing researchers need the freedom to discover what the present situation is, what the problems or opportunities are, what the alternatives are, what information they need, and how to go about gathering and analyzing data.

Collecting Data   Usable information is vital to the marketing research process. Research can become quite expensive, however, so marketers must often

Personal interviews are one way of collecting primary research data about customers' needs, wants, and buying habits. Perhaps someone has stopped you in a shopping mall recently to ask you some questions about a product or product category you use. What might contribute to the difficulty of collecting information through such interviews, and how can marketers improve the process?

make a trade-off between the need for information and the cost of obtaining it. Normally the least expensive method is to gather information already compiled by others and published in journals and books or made available online.

Such existing data are called **secondary data**, since you aren't the first one to gather them. Figure 13.4 lists the principal sources of secondary marketing research information. Despite its name, *secondary* data is what marketers should gather *first* to avoid incurring unnecessary expense. To find secondary data about vegetarians, go to the website for *Vegetarian Times* (www.vegetariantimes.com) or search other websites on vegetarianism.

FIGURE 13.4 SELECTED SOURCES OF PRIMARY AND SECONDARY INFORMATION

PRIMARY SOURCES	SECONDARY SOURCES		
Interviews Surveys Observation Focus groups Online surveys Questionnaires Customer comments Letters from customers	**Government Publications**		
	Statistical Abstract of the United States *Survey of Current Business* *Census of Retail Trade*	*Census of Transportation* *Annual Survey of Manufacturers*	

Commercial Publications

ACNielsen Company studies on retailing and media
Marketing Research Corporation of America studies on consumer purchases
Selling Areas—Marketing Inc. reports on food sales

Magazines

Entrepreneur	*Journal of Retailing*	*Journal of Advertising Research*
Bloomberg Businessweek	*Journal of Consumer Research*	Trade magazines appropriate to your industry such as *Progressive Grocer*
Fortune	*Journal of Advertising*	
Inc.	*Journal of Marketing Research*	
Advertising Age	*Marketing News*	Reports from various chambers of commerce
Forbes	*Hispanic Business*	
Harvard Business Review	*Black Enterprise*	
Journal of Marketing		

Newspapers

The Wall Street Journal, Barron's, your local newspapers

Internal Sources

Company records	Income statements
Balance sheets	Prior research reports

General Sources

Internet searches	Commercial databases
Google-type searches	

Often, secondary data don't provide all the information managers need for important business decisions. To gather additional in-depth information, marketers must do their own research. The results of such *new studies* are called **primary data**. One way to gather primary data is to conduct a survey.

Telephone surveys, online surveys, mail surveys, and personal interviews are the most common forms of primary data collection. Focus groups (defined below) are another popular method of surveying individuals. What do you think would be the best way to survey students about your potential new restaurant? Would you do a different kind of survey after it had been open a few months? How could you help vegetarians find your restaurant? That is, how could you help your buyers buy? One question researchers pay close attention to is: "Would you recommend this product to a friend?"

A **focus group** is a group of people who meet under the direction of a discussion leader to communicate their opinions about an organization, its products, or other given issues. This textbook is updated periodically using many focus groups made up of faculty and students. They tell us, the authors, what subjects and examples they like and dislike, and the authors follow their suggestions for changes.

Marketers can now gather both secondary and primary data online. The authors of this text, for example, do much research online, but they also gather data from books, articles, interviews, and other sources.

primary data
Data that you gather yourself (not from secondary sources such as books and magazines).

focus group
A small group of people who meet under the direction of a discussion leader to communicate their opinions about an organization, its products, or other given issues.

The authors of this text enjoy the benefits of using focus groups. College faculty and students come to these meetings and tell us how to improve this book and its support material. We listen carefully and make as many changes as we can in response. Suggestions have included adding more descriptive captions to the photos in the book and making the text as user-friendly as possible. How are we doing so far?

Analyzing the Research Data   Marketers must turn the data they collect in the research process into useful information. Careful, honest interpretation of the data can help a company find useful alternatives to specific marketing challenges. For example, by doing primary research, Fresh Italy, a small Italian pizzeria, found that its pizza's taste was rated superior to that of the larger pizza chains. However, the company's sales lagged behind the competition. Secondary research on the industry revealed that free delivery (which Fresh Italy did not offer) was more important to customers than taste. Fresh Italy now delivers—and has increased its market share.

Choosing the Best Solution and Implementing It   After collecting and analyzing data, market researchers determine alternative strategies and make recommendations about which may be best and why. This final step in a research effort also includes following up on actions taken to see whether the results were what was expected. If not, the company can take corrective action and conduct new studies in its ongoing attempt to provide consumer satisfaction at the lowest cost. You can see, then, that marketing research is a continuous process of responding to changes in the marketplace and in consumer preferences.

LO 13–4   Show how marketers use environmental scanning to learn about the changing marketing environment.

THE MARKETING ENVIRONMENT

environmental scanning
The process of identifying the factors that can affect marketing success.

Marketing managers must be aware of the surrounding environment when making marketing mix decisions. **Environmental scanning** is the process of identifying factors that can affect marketing success. As you can see in Figure 13.5, they include global, technological, sociocultural, competitive, and economic influences. We discussed these factors in some detail in Chapter 1, but now let's review them from a strictly marketing perspective.

FIGURE 13.5 THE MARKETING ENVIRONMENT

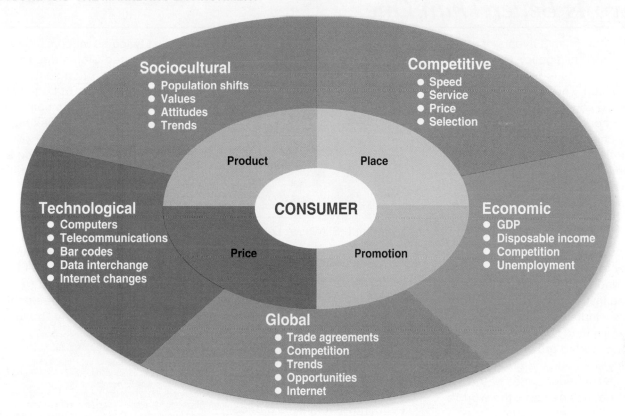

Global Factors

Using the Internet, businesses can reach many of the world's consumers relatively easily and carry on a dialogue with them about the goods and services they want (see the Reaching Beyond Our Borders box). The globalization process puts more pressure on those whose responsibility it is to deliver products to these global customers.

Technological Factors

The most important technological changes also relate to the Internet. Using consumer databases, blogs, social networking, and the like, companies can develop products and services that closely match consumers' needs. As you read in Chapter 9, firms can now produce customized goods and services for about the same price as mass-produced goods. Thus flexible manufacturing and mass customization are also major influences on marketers. You can imagine, for example, using databases to help you devise custom-made fruit mixes and various salads for your customers at Very Vegetarian.

Sociocultural Factors

Marketers must monitor social trends to maintain their close relationship with customers, since population growth and changing demographics can have an effect on sales. One of the fastest-growing segments of the U.S. population in the 21st century is people over 65. The increase in the number of older adults creates growing demand for retirement communities, health care, prescription drugs, recreation, continuing education, and more. Do you see any evidence that older people would enjoy having more vegetarian meals?

Two Is Better Than One

After more than 35 years of a strict one-child policy, China agreed to change the infamous regulation. The new law allows married couples to have two children if one of the spouses is an only child. Besides affecting countless families, the new reform promises to have a big impact on businesses as the policy switch could mean 9.5 million additional babies coming into the Chinese market in the next five years. Producers of everything from baby formula and diapers, to violins and *guzhengs* (a Chinese string instrument) predict a future sales windfall with the new policy.

While many businesses can expect added growth due to the policy shift, one the greatest long-term beneficiaries of the change may be Lego, the world's second largest toymaker. Since the company has little room to

grow in the U.S. (where Lego controls 85 percent of the construction toy market), China is now one of its key target markets. In 2013, Lego enjoyed sales growth in China of 70 percent as parents sought educational toys for their children. Chinese parents are particularly attracted to Lego because they feel the toy helps develop their children's creativity.

Lego, however, faces a price obstacle in China because its

sets cost twice as much as they do in the United States due to import and distribution costs. To reduce the high cost of Legos in China, the company has committed to build a factory in Jiaxing, an industrial town near Shanghai. The cost of building a factory may be a relatively small price to pay since the Asia-Pacific region is predicted to overtake North America as the largest regional toy market sometime in the next few years. With the expected number of Chinese children expected to grow significantly, Lego feels this is a market it can clearly "build on."

Sources: Isabella Steger and Laurie Burkitt, "Chinese Couples—and Investors—Are Pregnant with Anticipation," *The Wall Street Journal,* November 19, 2013; Ted Trautman, "The Year of the Lego," *The New Yorker,* November 11, 2013; and Susan Scutti, "One-Child Policy Is One Big Problem for China," *Newsweek,* January 23, 2014.

Other shifts in the U.S. population are creating new challenges for marketers as they adjust their products to meet the tastes and preferences of Hispanic, Asian, and other growing ethnic groups. To appeal to diverse groups, marketers must listen better and be more responsive to unique ethnic needs. What might you do to appeal to specific ethnic groups with Very Vegetarian?

Competitive Factors

Of course, marketers must pay attention to the dynamic competitive environment. Many brick-and-mortar companies must be aware of new competition from the Internet, including firms that sell automobiles, insurance, music, and clothes. In the book business, Barnes & Noble is still adjusting to the new reality of Amazon.com's huge selection of books at good prices. Borders Books went out of business. What will the challenge from Kindle and other eReaders provide? Now that consumers can literally search the world for the best buys online, marketers must adjust their pricing, delivery, and services accordingly. Can you see any opportunities for Very Vegetarian to make use of the Internet and social media?

Economic Factors

Marketers must pay close attention to the economic environment. As we began the new millennium, the United States was experiencing slow growth, and few customers were eager to buy the most expensive automobiles, watches, and vacations. As the economy slowed, marketers had to adapt by offering products that were less expensive and more tailored to consumers with modest incomes.

What economic changes are occurring around your school that might affect a new vegetarian restaurant? How has the economic crisis or natural disasters, such as floods and drought, affected your area?

TWO DIFFERENT MARKETS: CONSUMER AND BUSINESS-TO-BUSINESS (B2B)

Marketers must know as much as possible about the market they wish to serve. As we defined it in Chapter 6, a market consists of people with unsatisfied wants and needs who have both the resources and the willingness to buy. There are two major markets in business: the *consumer market* and the *business-to-business market*. The **consumer market** consists of all the individuals or households that want goods and services for personal consumption or use and have the resources to buy them.

The **business-to-business (B2B) market** consists of all the individuals and organizations that want goods and services to use in producing other goods and services or to sell, rent, or supply goods to others.[18] Oil-drilling bits, cash registers, display cases, office desks, public accounting audits, and business software are B2B goods and services. Traditionally, they have been known as *industrial* goods and services because they are used in industry.

The important thing to remember is that the buyer's reason for buying—that is, the end use of the product—determines whether a product is a consumer product or a B2B product. A cup of yogurt that a student buys for breakfast is a consumer product. However, when Very Vegetarian purchases the same cup of yogurt to sell to its breakfast customers, it has purchased a B2B product. The following sections outline consumer and B2B markets.

The business-to-business (B2B) market consists of individuals and organizations that sell goods and services to other businesses. A manufacturer, for instance, buys its parts and supplies in the B2B market.

consumer market
All the individuals or households that want goods and services for personal consumption or use.

business-to-business (B2B) market
All the individuals and organizations that want goods and services to use in producing other goods and services or to sell, rent, or supply goods to others.

- What are the four steps in the marketing research process?
- What is environmental scanning?
- What factors are included in environmental scanning?

Use LearnSmart to help retain what you have learned. Access your instructor's Connect course to check out LearnSmart, or go to learnsmartadvantage.com for help.

■|LEARNSMART·

LO 13–5 Explain how marketers apply the tools of market **segmentation**, relationship marketing, and the study of consumer behavior.

THE CONSUMER MARKET

The total potential consumer market consists of the billions of people in global markets. Because consumer groups differ greatly by age, education level, income, and taste, a business usually can't fill the needs of every group. It must decide which groups to serve, and then develop products and services specially tailored to their needs.

Take the Campbell Soup Company, for example. You know Campbell for its traditional soups such as chicken noodle and tomato. You may also have

market segmentation
The process of dividing the total market into groups whose members have similar characteristics.

target marketing
Marketing directed toward those groups (market segments) an organization decides it can serve profitably.

FIGURE 13.6 MARKET SEGMENTATION
This table shows some of the methods marketers use to divide the market. The aim of segmentation is to break the market into smaller units.

noticed that Campbell has expanded its U.S. product line to appeal to a number of different tastes. Aware of population growth in the South and in Latino communities in cities across the nation, it introduced a Creole soup for the southern market and a red bean soup for the Latino market. In Texas and California, where people like their food with a bit of kick, Campbell makes its nacho cheese soup spicier than in other parts of the country. It's just one company that has had some success studying the consumer market, breaking it down into categories, and developing products for separate groups.

The process of dividing the total market into groups with similar characteristics is called **market segmentation**. Selecting which groups or segments an organization can serve profitably is **target marketing**. For example, a shoe store may choose to sell only women's shoes, only children's shoes, or only athletic shoes. The issue is finding the right *target market*—the most profitable segment—to serve.

Segmenting the Consumer Market

A firm can segment the consumer market several ways (see Figure 13.6). Rather than selling your product throughout the United States, you might focus on just

Main Dimension	Sample Variables	Typical Segments
Geographic segmentation	Region	Northeast, Midwest, South, West
	City or county size	Under 5,000; 5,000–10,999; 11,000–19,999; 20,000–49,999; 50,000 and up
	Density	Urban, suburban, rural
Demographic segmentation	Gender	Male, female
	Age	Under 5; 5–10; 11–18; 19–34; 35–49; 50–64; 65 and over
	Education	Some high school or less, high school graduate, some college, college graduate, postgraduate
	Race	Caucasian, African American, Indian, Asian, Hispanic
	Nationality	American, Asian, Eastern European, Japanese
	Life stage	Infant, preschool, child, teenager, collegiate, adult, senior
	Income	Under $15,000; $15,000–$24,999; $25,000–$44,999; $45,000–$74,999; $75,000 and over
	Household size	1; 2; 3–4; 5 or more
	Occupation	Professional, technical, clerical, sales supervisors, farmers, students, home-based business owners, retired, unemployed
Psychographic segmentation	Personality	Gregarious, compulsive, extroverted, aggressive, ambitious
	Values	Actualizers, fulfillers, achievers, experiencers, believers, strivers, makers, strugglers
	Lifestyle	Upscale, moderate
Benefit segmentation	Comfort Convenience Durability Economy Health Luxury Safety Status	(Benefit segmentation divides an already established market into smaller, more homogeneous segments. Those people who desire economy in a car would be an example. The benefit desired varies by product.)
Volume segmentation	Usage	Heavy users, light users, nonusers
	Loyalty status	None, medium, strong

Turning Negatives to Positive

When Amazon invited customers to start posting reviews of products 20 years ago, many thought the online retailer had lost its good sense. Today, market researchers admit that Amazon's move created a monumental change in the consumer decision-making process. A recent Nielsen research report helped confirm this shift. The company surveyed 28,000 Internet users in 56 countries and found that online reviews from sites like Amazon are the second most trusted source of a brand's reliability (second only to the recommendations of friends and family). It's no wonder then that in this digital age, we are overwhelmed with the opinions of others about products, opinions we tend to treat as trustworthy and factual. But exactly how reliable are the ratings assigned by reviewers? Is the trust we place in these ratings misplaced? The best answer might be "maybe."

As human beings we have a "herding" tendency that often causes us to think and act in the same way as people around us. Therefore, if reviewers read other product reviews that lean positively toward a product, there's a good chance they may rate the product favorably even if that was not their original impression. Such behavior may be a major reason why extremely high ratings easily outnumber negative ratings on Amazon. Researchers also believe that online reviewers are more positively predisposed to a product because they voluntarily bought the product and are less likely to criticize it. This is generally referred to as a *selection bias*.

Another problem with the validity of online reviews is that reviewers will sometimes rate products negatively when there are shipping or other ordering problems that have nothing to do with the quality of the products

themselves. Amazon has tried to correct these inherent challenges through the creation of Amazon Vine, an invitation-only program that involves the site's top reviewers. These elite reviewers are sent free merchandise to review. Amazon believes working with the site's most trusted reviewers provides more useful reviews for customers to consider. Still, critics contend that giving products for free might create a bias toward a positive rather than negative rating. However, research has shown that the Vine reviewers actually bestow fewer stars than regular reviewers. Strangely, research has also shown that even a product with only negative reviews sells better than a product with no reviews at all. Go figure.

Sources: Lisa Chow, "Top Reviewers on Amazon Get Tons of Free Stuff," *NPR*, October 30, 2013; Joe Queenan, "Why I'm Hating All That Online Rating," *The Wall Street Journal*, February 21, 2014; and Sinan Aral, "The Problem with Online Ratings," *MIT Sloan Management Review*, Winter 2014.

- *Reference group* is the group an individual uses as a reference point in forming beliefs, attitudes, values, or behavior. A college student who carries a briefcase instead of a backpack may see businesspeople as his or her reference group.

- *Culture* is the set of values, attitudes, and ways of doing things transmitted from one generation to another in a given society. The U.S. culture emphasizes and transmits the values of education, freedom, and diversity.

- *Subculture* is the set of values, attitudes, and ways of doing things that results from belonging to a certain ethnic group, racial group, or other group with which one closely identifies (e.g., teenagers).

- *Cognitive dissonance* is a type of psychological conflict that can occur after a purchase. Consumers who make a major purchase may have doubts about whether they got the best product at the best price. Marketers must reassure such consumers after the sale that they made a good decision. An auto dealer, for example, may send positive press articles about the particular car a consumer purchased, offer product guarantees, and provide certain free services.

Many universities have expanded the marketing curriculum to include courses in business-to-business marketing. As you'll learn below, that market is huge.

LO 13–6   Compare the business-to-business market and the consumer market.

THE BUSINESS-TO-BUSINESS MARKET

Business-to-business (B2B) marketers include manufacturers; intermediaries such as retailers; institutions like hospitals, schools, and charities; and the government. The B2B market is larger than the consumer market because items are often sold and resold several times in the B2B process before they reach the final consumer. B2B marketing strategies also differ from consumer marketing because business buyers have their own decision-making process. Several factors make B2B marketing different, including these:

1. Customers in the B2B market are relatively few; there are just a few large construction firms or mining operations compared to the 80 million or so households in the U.S. consumer market.[21]

2. Business customers are relatively large; that is, big organizations account for most of the employment in the production of various goods and services. Nonetheless, there are many small- to medium-sized firms in the United States that together make an attractive market.

3. B2B markets tend to be geographically concentrated. For example, oilfields are found in the Southwest and Canada. Thus B2B marketers can concentrate their efforts on a particular area and minimize distribution problems by locating warehouses near industrial centers.

4. Business buyers are generally more rational and less emotional than ultimate consumers; they use product specifications to guide buying choices and often more carefully weigh the total product offer, including quality, price, and service.

5. B2B sales tend to be direct, but not always. Tire manufacturers sell directly to auto manufacturers but use intermediaries, such as wholesalers and retailers, to sell to ultimate consumers.

6. Whereas consumer promotions are based more on *advertising*, B2B sales are based on *personal selling*. There are fewer customers and they usually demand more personal service.

Figure 13.7 shows some of the differences between buying behavior in the B2B and consumer markets. B2B buyers also use the Internet to make purchases. You'll learn more about the business-to-business market in advanced marketing courses.

YOUR PROSPECTS IN MARKETING

There is a wider variety of careers in marketing than in most business disciplines. If you major in marketing, an array of career options will be available to you. You could become a manager in a retail store like Saks or Target. You could do marketing research or work in product management. You could go into selling, advertising, sales promotion, or public relations. You could work in transportation, storage, or international distribution. You could design interactive websites. These are just a few of the possibilities. Think, for

FIGURE 13.7 COMPARING BUSINESS-TO-BUSINESS AND CONSUMER BUYING BEHAVIOR

	Business-to-business Market	Consumer Market
Market Structure	Relatively few potential customers	Many potential customers
	Larger purchases	Smaller purchases
	Geographically concentrated	Geographically dispersed
Products	Require technical, complex products	Require less technical products
	Frequently require customization	Sometimes require customization
	Frequently require technical advice, delivery, and after-sale service	Sometimes require technical advice, delivery, and after-sale service
	Buyers are trained	No special training
Buying Procedures	Negotiate details of most purchases	Accept standard terms for most purchases
	Follow objective standards	Use personal judgment
	Formal process involving specific employees	Informal process involving household members
	Closer relationships between marketers and buyers	Impersonal relationships between marketers and consumers
	Often buy from multiple sources	Rarely buy from multiple sources

example, of the many ways to use Facebook, Google, and other new technologies in marketing. As you read through the following marketing chapters, consider whether a marketing career would interest you.

test prep

- Can you define the terms *consumer market* and *business-to-business market*?
- Can you name and describe five ways to segment the consumer market?
- What is niche marketing, and how does it differ from one-to-one marketing?
- What are four key factors that make B2B markets different from consumer markets?

Use LearnSmart to help retain what you have learned. Access your instructor's Connect course to check out LearnSmart, or go to learnsmartadvantage.com for help.

LEARNSMART

summary

LO 13–1 Define *marketing*, and apply the marketing concept to both for-profit and nonprofit organizations.

- What is marketing?
Marketing is the activity, set of institutions, and processes for creating, communicating, delivering, and exchanging offerings that have value for customers, clients, partners, and society at large.

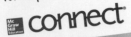

- **How has marketing changed over time?**
  During the *production era*, marketing was largely a distribution function. Emphasis was on producing as many goods as possible and getting them to markets. By the early 1920s, during the *selling era*, the emphasis turned to selling and advertising to persuade customers to buy the existing goods produced by mass production. After World War II, the tremendous demand for goods and services led to the *marketing concept era*, when businesses recognized the need to be responsive to customers' needs. During the 1990s, marketing entered the *customer relationship era*, focusing on enhancing customer satisfaction and stimulating long-term customer loyalty. Today marketers are using mobile/on-demand marketing to engage customers.

- **What are the three parts of the marketing concept?**
  The three parts of the marketing concept are (1) a customer orientation, (2) a service orientation, and (3) a profit orientation (that is, marketing goods and services that will earn a profit and enable the firm to survive and expand).

- **What kinds of organizations are involved in marketing?**
  All kinds of organizations use marketing, including for-profit and nonprofit organizations like states, charities, churches, politicians, and schools.

LO 13–2   Describe the four Ps of marketing.

- **How do marketers implement the four Ps?**
  The idea behind the four Ps is to design a *product* people want, *price* it competitively, *place* it where consumers can find it easily, and *promote* it so consumers know it exists.

LO 13–3   Summarize the marketing research process.

- **What are the steps in conducting marketing research?**
  (1) Define the problem or opportunity and determine the present situation, (2) collect data, (3) analyze the data, and (4) choose the best solution.

LO 13–4   Show how marketers use environmental scanning to learn about the changing marketing environment.

- **What is environmental scanning?**
  Environmental scanning is the process of identifying factors that can affect marketing success. Marketers pay attention to all the environmental factors that create opportunities and threats.

- **What are some of the more important environmental trends in marketing?**
  The most important global and technological change is probably the growth of the Internet and mobile marketing. Another is the growth of consumer databases, with which companies can develop products and services that closely match consumers' needs. Marketers must monitor social trends like population growth and shifts to maintain their close relationship with customers. They must also monitor the dynamic competitive and economic environments.

LO 13–5   Explain how marketers apply the tools of market segmentation, relationship marketing, and the study of consumer behavior.

- **What are some of the ways marketers segment the consumer market?**
  Geographic segmentation means dividing the market into different regions. Segmentation by age, income, and education level is *demographic*

segmentation. We study a group's values, attitudes, and interests using *psychographic segmentation.* Determining which benefits customers prefer and using them to promote a product is *benefit segmentation.* Separating the market by usage is called *volume segmentation.* The best segmentation strategy is to use all the variables to come up with a consumer profile for a target market that's sizable, reachable, and profitable.

• **What is the difference between mass marketing and relationship marketing?**
Mass marketing means developing products and promotions to please large groups of people. Relationship marketing tends to lead away from mass production and toward custom-made goods and services. Its goal is to keep individual customers over time by offering them products or services that meet their needs.

• **What are some of the factors that influence the consumer decision-making process?**
Factors that influence the consumer decision-making process include learning, reference group, culture, subculture, and cognitive dissonance.

LO 13–6 Compare the business-to-business market and the consumer market.

• **What makes the business-to-business market different from the consumer market?**
Customers in the B2B market are relatively few and large. B2B markets tend to be geographically concentrated, and industrial buyers generally are more rational than ultimate consumers in their selection of goods and services. B2B sales tend to be direct, and there is much more emphasis on personal selling than in consumer markets.

key terms

benefit segmentation 377
brand name 368
business-to-business (B2B) market 375
consumer market 375
customer relationship management (CRM) 364
demographic segmentation 377
environmental scanning 372
focus group 371

geographic segmentation 377
marketing 362
marketing concept 364
marketing mix 366
marketing research 370
market segmentation 376
mass marketing 378
niche marketing 377
one-to-one marketing 378
primary data 371

product 368
promotion 369
psychographic segmentation 377
relationship marketing 378
secondary data 370
target marketing 376
test marketing 368
volume (or usage) segmentation 377

critical thinking

1. When businesses buy goods and services from other businesses, they usually buy in large volume. Salespeople in the business-to-business market usually are paid on a commission basis; that is, they earn a certain percentage of each sale they make. Why might B2B sales be a more financially rewarding career area than consumer sales?

2. Industrial companies sell goods such as steel, lumber, computers, engines, parts, and supplies. Name three such companies.

3. What environmental changes are occurring in your community? What was the impact of the recent economic crisis? What environmental changes in marketing are most likely to change your career prospects in the future? How can you learn more about those changes? What might you do to prepare for them?

4. Which of your needs are not being met by businesses and/or nonprofit organizations in your area? Are there enough people with similar needs to attract an organization that would meet those needs? How would you find out?

developing **workplace skills**

Key: ● Team   ★ Analytic   ▲ Communication   ▣ Technology

★▲ 1. Think of an effective marketing mix for a new electric car or a brushless car wash for your neighborhood. Be prepared to discuss your ideas in class.

●★▲ 2. Working in teams of five, think of a product or service your friends want but cannot get on or near campus. You might ask your friends at other schools what's available there. What kind of product would fill that need? Discuss your results in class and how you might go about marketing that new product or service.

★ 3. Business has fallen off greatly at your upscale restaurant because of the slow economy. List four things you can do to win back the loyalty of your past customers.

●★▲ 4. Working in teams of four or five, list as many brand names of pizza as you can, including from pizza shops, restaurants, supermarkets, and so on. Merge your list with the lists from other groups or classmates. Then try to identify the target market for each brand. Do they all seem to be after the same market, or are there different brands for different markets? What are the separate appeals?

★▲ 5. Take a little time to review the concepts in this chapter as they apply to Very Vegetarian, the restaurant we used as an example throughout. Have an open discussion in class about (*a*) a different name for the restaurant, (*b*) a location for the restaurant, (*c*) a promotional program, and (*d*) a way to establish a long-term relationship with customers.

taking it to the **net**

PURPOSE

To demonstrate how the Internet can be used to enhance marketing relationships.

EXERCISE

Nike wants to help its customers add soul to their soles and express their individuality by customizing their own shoes. See for yourself at www.nike.com. Enter "customize" in the search box and build a shoe that fits your style.

1. What if you're in the middle of your shoe design and have questions about what to do next? Where can you go for help?

2. How does Nike's website help the company strengthen its relationships with its stakeholders? Give examples to support your answer.

3. How do the elements of the website reflect Nike's target market?

4. Does Nike invite comments from visitors to its website? If so, how does this affect its attempt to build positive relationships with its customers?

video case   McGraw Hill Education **connect**®

USING THE 4 Ps AT ENERGIZER

The Energizer Bunny is a marketing icon. How many people are not familiar with this marketing campaign? The precursor to the company known today as Energizer was founded by two inventors: the inventor of the battery and the inventor of the flashlight. The synergy should be obvious. This partnership grew into the leading manufacturer and seller of batteries in the world today. Energizer is truly a global company—operating across the globe. Energizer has developed and implemented an outstanding marketing approach to its product lines. In fact, Energizer demonstrates the full range of marketing concepts, including the use of social media and market research in successfully promoting and sustaining a brand.

Advertising Age magazine ranks the brand icon Energizer Bunny as the number five brand icon of the twentieth century. This provides Energizer a competitive advantage in many of its markets. The company is continually involved in new product development through the identification and understanding of consumer needs, including how a person intends to use a battery, in what devices, and the types of users for various products where Energizer batteries can be used.

Energizer has a well-developed and highly effective marketing division that is responsible for helping to ensure the success of current and new products. The video walks the viewer through the four Ps of marketing—product, price, place, and promotion—and shows how Energizer utilizes marketing concepts effectively.

The company views its approach to marketing and selling its product lines as one that is focused on developing, cultivating, and expanding customer relationships. Energizer is a company that has been significantly impacted by the growth of technology and uses this and the growth of the Internet as parts of its overall marketing communications approach to develop strong and lasting relationships with its customers.

The video demonstrates the importance of relationship marketing as a key to Energizer's success. The complexities involved in the marketing mix, marketing research, and new product development are highlighted through specific examples in the video, such as the new product introduced by the company each summer. We see how the company uses qualitative data such as focus groups and secondary data to test market its product, elicit customer feedback, collect demographic and other data, and match its marketing strategy to be consistent with the appropriate segmentation factors.

THINKING IT OVER

1. Identify the elements that must be considered in the marketing environment.

2. Briefly discuss the evolution of marketing at Energizer as described in the video.

3. The Energizer Bunny is considered a marketing icon. What does this mean?

notes

1. Brent Adamson, Matthew Dixon, and Nicholas Toman, "A New Guide to Selling," *Harvard Business Review*, August 2012.
2. Patrick Spenner and Karen Freeman, "To Keep Your Customers, Keep It Simple," *Harvard Business Review*, May 2012.
3. Barbara Giamanco and Kent Gregoire, "Tweet Me, Friend Me, Make Me Buy," *Harvard Business Review*, July–August 2012.
4. Kasey Wehrum, "Their Carts Are Full, So Why Won't They Buy?" *Inc.*, December 2013.
5. J. J. Martin, "The Shopping Social Networks," *The Wall Street Journal*, October 27–28, 2012.
6. Jason Fried, "Marketing Without Marketing," *Inc.*, January 2014.
7. Roy J. Chua, "Building Effective Relationships in China," *Sloan Management Review*, Summer 2012.

8. Peter Dahlström and David Edelman, "The Coming Era of 'On-Demand' Marketing," *McKinsey Quarterly,* April 2013.
9. Vanessa Small, "LinkedIn Connects Members with Volunteer Options," *The Washington Post,* January 21, 2014.
10. Alexander Lobrano, "La Nouvelle Veg," *The Wall Street Journal,* April 20–21, 2013.
11. Annie Gasparro and Juoie Jargon, "McDonald's to Go Vegetarian in India," *The Wall Street Journal,* September 5, 2012.
12. Jenn Harris, "Al Gore Is Now Vegan, Just Like Bill Clinton," *Los Angeles Times,* November 26, 2013.
13. Trupti Rami, "Veganism in Seven Decades," *New York,* January 20–27, 2014.
14. Terence Chea, "San Francisco Startup Seeks Egg Alternatives," *The Washington Times,* December 9, 2013.
15. Dinah Eng, "A Fresh Take on Food," *Fortune,* April 29, 2013.
16. Tim Kraft, "The Trick to Getting NoBull on More Grills," *The Washington Post,* January 20, 2013.
17. Susan Dumenco, "Data, Data Everywhere, and Not an Insight in Sight," *Advertising Age,* March 18, 2013.
18. Mark Henricks, "B2B," *Inc.,* February 2014.
19. Julien Cayla, Robin Beers, and Eric Arnould, "Stories That Deliver Business Insights," *Sloan Management Review,* Winter 2014.
20. Julie Liesse, "How Understanding Consumers' Purchase Cycle Can Help Brands Grow," *Advertising Age,* September 30, 2013.
21. U.S. Census Bureau, www.census.gov, accessed April 2014.

photo credits

14

Developing and Pricing Goods and Services

Learning Objectives

AFTER YOU HAVE READ AND STUDIED THIS CHAPTER, YOU SHOULD BE ABLE TO

LO 14-1   Describe a total product offer.

LO 14-2   Identify the various kinds of consumer and industrial goods.

LO 14-3   Summarize the functions of packaging.

LO 14-4   Contrast *brand*, *brand name*, and *trademark*, and show the value of brand equity.

LO 14-5   Explain the steps in the new-product development process.

LO 14-6   Describe the product life cycle.

LO 14-7   Identify various pricing objectives and strategies.

Getting to Know **Kathy Ireland**

In today's fame-fueled culture, celebrities can make a quick buck by using their names to advertise products. The problem with these endorsement deals, though, is that they last only as long as the spokesperson stays famous. For former supermodel Kathy Ireland, such an unsustainable plan simply would not do.

Ireland caught the entrepreneurial bug early in life. "I was 4 years old, and I sold rocks I painted from my wagon," said Ireland. "It was before mace, so people used them as self-defense." By age 11 she was earning $60 a month delivering newspapers. Five years later Ireland saw her income grow even more when a representative for the Elite Modeling Agency discovered her at finishing school. At 20 she appeared in the *Sports Illustrated* Swimsuit Issue for the first of 13 consecutive appearances. When she finally graced the magazine's cover in 1989, it became *Sports Illustrated*'s best-selling issue ever.

Modeling brought Ireland wealth and fame, but she had the good sense to know that it wouldn't last forever. "The modeling industry was not part of my path or my plan," said Ireland. "In fact, the entire time I worked in the modeling industry, I tried and failed at many businesses." In 1993 she received an offer to model socks, a gig that most jet-setting supermodels would reject outright. Rather than get herself down about such an unglamorous job, Ireland used her experience to turn it into a business opportunity. Instead of acting solely as a spokesperson, she suggested to brand the socks with her name. Ireland ended up striking a deal with the socks' marketer that allowed her a royalty for every product sold. Along with the help of a $50,000 personal loan, Kathy Ireland Worldwide was officially in business.

Once the socks turned out to be a success, Ireland started licensing her name out to other types of apparel like exercise clothes and swimwear. By 1994 she signed an exclusive deal to sell her products at Kmart. The retailer hoped Ireland would do for clothing what Martha Stewart had done for housewares. However, Ireland's plans stretched out far beyond apparel. The legendary

investor and billionaire Warren Buffett once told her that while fashion changes constantly, the home stays relatively the same. Ireland took that advice to heart when her company expanded into furniture by 1998. With this new market, Ireland had finally found a motto for her brand: "Finding solutions for families, especially busy moms." Within a year Kathy Ireland Worldwide expanded into carpets, flooring, and floor tiles. Kmart, on the other hand, had fallen into bankruptcy around the turn of the millennium. Realizing her entire enterprise rested upon one shaky retailer, in 2003 Ireland made the decision to break her relationship with Kmart as well as apparel all together. "When I wanted to make a bold change, people said I was crazy," said Ireland. "They said what I wanted to do had never been done. But 'it's never been done' does not mean it can't be done."

Though her choice seemed risky at the time, Ireland's gamble paid off handsomely in the long run. By attaching a celebrity name to mundane products like replacement windows and area rugs, Ireland created a recognizable, reliable brand that earns $2 billion in annual retail revenue. Kathy Ireland Worldwide itself manages to bring in more than $300 million a year in profit, more than Martha Stewart, thanks to the amazingly low overhead brought on by its licensing model. Although this type of operation requires significant legal and financial expertise, Ireland maintains an active role by working as chief designer for the company's many products. In fact, the designs for each of the company's more than 15,000 products started with an idea from Ireland herself.

Like Kathy Ireland, the companies that command the business world are innovative pioneers. In this chapter you'll learn all about how entrepreneurs develop and price new products and services. You will also learn about packaging, branding, and other elements of a total product offer.

Sources: Eric T. Wagner, "From Bikini to Boardroom: 4 Secrets from Kathy Ireland," *Forbes*, December 10, 2013; "Kathy Ireland: How Did I Get Here?" *Bloomberg Businessweek*, July 25, 2013; and Dorothy Pomerantz, "How Sports Illustrated Swimsuit Model Kathy Ireland Became a $350 Million Mogul," *Forbes*, February 8, 2012.

Kathy Ireland
- CEO of Kathy Ireland Worldwide
- Former supermodel
- Built a $2 billion business empire

www.kathyireland.com

@kathyireland

LO 14–1 Describe a total product offer.

PRODUCT DEVELOPMENT AND THE TOTAL PRODUCT OFFER

value
Good quality at a fair price. When consumers calculate the value of a product, they look at the benefits and then subtract the cost to see if the benefits exceed the costs.

Global managers will be challenging U.S. managers with new products at low prices.[1] The best way to compete is to design and promote better products, meaning products that customers perceive to have the best **value**—good quality at a fair price. One of the American Marketing Association's definitions of marketing says it's "a set of processes for creating, communicating, and delivering *value* to customers." When consumers calculate the value of a product, they look at the benefits and then subtract the cost (price) to see whether the benefits exceed the costs, including the cost of driving to the store (or shipping fees if they buy the product online). You may have noticed that many restaurants pushed "value meals" when the economy slowed. John Mackey of Whole Foods says that Trader Joe's offers customers great *value* every day rather than have frequent sales, as many retailers do.[2]

Whether consumers perceive a product as the best value depends on many factors, including the benefits they seek and the service they receive. To satisfy consumers, marketers must learn to listen better and constantly adapt to changing market demands.[3] See the Adapting to Change box for an example of how one bar uses Facebook and Twitter to let customers decide which craft beers to have on tap.

Marketers have learned that adapting products to new competition and new markets is an ongoing need. We're sure you've noticed menu changes at your local fast-food restaurants over time. An organization can't do a one-time survey of consumer wants and needs, design a group of products to meet those needs, put them in the stores, and then just relax. It must constantly monitor changing consumer wants and needs, and adapt products, policies, and services accordingly. For example, consumers are looking for healthier food choices today than in the past. Did you know that McDonald's now sells as much chicken as beef?

McDonald's and other restaurants are constantly trying new ideas.[4] For example, McDonald's added smoothies and oatmeal with fruit. It also offers a choice of side salad, fruit, or vegetables in place of fries with its value meals. It is trying an all-day breakfast menu. Burger King often follows McDonald's with its offerings.[5] Have you noticed, for example, that Burger King has added lattes and flavored coffee to its menus?[6]

Of course, McD's answers with more new ideas. For example, in Kokomo, Indiana, McDonald's tried waiter service and a more varied menu. In New York, it offered McDonuts to compete with Krispy Kreme. In Atlanta and other cities, McDonald's had computer stations linked to the Internet. In Hawaii, it tried a Spam breakfast platter, and in Columbus, Ohio, a mega-McDonald's had a karaoke booth.

Bellying Up to Social Media

Social media is in a constant state of change. Do businesses have to keep up with it? Absolutely. At least that's how Chris Dilla, owner of Bocktown Beer and Grill, sees it. As she puts it, "The minute I met Twitter, I realized how valuable it would be." Without having the money for advertising, she turned to social media to help make the Pittsburgh gastro pub a staple on the city's craft beer scene. In addition to making maximum use of Twitter and Facebook, Bocktown also optimized its mobile website, making it easier for customers to engage with the brand when they are on the go.

But Dilla's relationship with social media isn't limited to giants like Twitter and Facebook. A few years back Bocktown introduced Tabbedout, a mobile payment app that allows customers to pay straight from their smartphones. Developed by a start-up in Austin, Texas, customers can get started with the service by entering their credit card information on the app. The data are stored on their device and remain encrypted, ensuring that Tabbedout is even safer than dropping off your credit card with a server. Bar patrons at Bocktown can use Tabbedout to immediately open a tab through the app. They can also create a unique five-digit code that tallies their total bill. When they are ready to call it a day or night, all customers need to do to settle their tab is press a button on the app and then walk out the door.

Dilla has no intention of slowing down the Beer and Grill's social media presence. The bar recently added a new app called NoWait which saves customers time by letting them see the restaurant's wait time, add their names to a wait list, check their place in line, and receive a text when their table is ready. It's places like Bocktown that are fueling the tremendous growth of the craft beer industry. Who knows when Bocktown Beer and Grill's relationship with social media will come to a head.

Sources: Brad Tuttle, "7 Signs That the Craft Beer Craze Has Gone Totally Mainstream," *Time*, September 22, 2013; Kim Lyons, "Passionate Owner of Two Suburban Pittsburgh Restaurants Attuned to Social Media," *Pittsburgh Post-Gazette*, March 5, 2014; and Bocktown Beer & Grill, www.bocktown.com, accessed April 2014.

McDonald's is challenging Starbucks and Dunkin' Donuts for the coffee market.[7] What was Starbucks's answer to the new challenges? It began offering more food products. The new menu includes Starbucks's own pastries and juices.[8] Oatmeal has become a huge success there as well. Have you seen the Starbucks displays in your local supermarket? Starbucks is reaching out to many new distributors with its products.

Offerings may differ in various locations, according to the wants of the local community. In Iowa pork tenderloin is big, but in Oklahoma City it's tortilla scramblers. Globally, companies must adapt to local tastes. At Bob's Big Boy in Thailand, you can get Tropical Shrimp; at Carl's Jr. in Mexico, you can order the Machaca Burrito; and at Shakey's Pizza in the Philippines, you can get Cali Shandy, a Filipino beer. Product development, then, is a key activity in any modern business, anywhere in the world.

You can imagine what can happen when your product loses some of its appeal.[9] Zippo lighters, for example, has lost some market as people turn away from smoking cigarettes to using E-Cigarettes.[10] Zippo, therefore, tried offering products such as key holders, tape measures, and belt buckles. They are no

Apple, Samsung, and other smartphone makers are fighting for a greater share of the huge mobile market. Each continues to improve and add features hoping to win customers. What features would a smartphone company have to add to its product offer in order to convince you to switch phones or carriers?

distributed product development
Handing off various parts of your innovation process—often to companies in other countries.

total product offer
Everything that consumers evaluate when deciding whether to buy something; also called a value package.

longer being sold, but Zippo introduced a new men's fragrance and a clothing line that includes hoodies, ball caps, and jeans.

Who would have guessed that Cokes would someday be sold in Keurig-type machines? Watch out SodaStream.[11] And who would have expected watchmakers, like Piaget and Swatch (Omega and Breguet), to push jewelry in their stores?[12] It's all part of a movement across the world to offer consumers new products.

Distributed Product Development

The increase in outsourcing and alliance building has resulted in innovation efforts that often require using multiple organizations separated by cultural, geographic, and legal boundaries. **Distributed product development** is the term used to describe handing off various parts of your innovation process—often to companies in other countries. It is difficult enough to coordinate processes within a firm; it becomes substantially more difficult when trying to coordinate multifirm processes. Great care must be taken to establish goals and procedures and standards before any such commitment is made. One company that has collaborated with many other firms to make innovative products is 3M Company. It has developed some 55,000 products from Scotch tape to Thinsulate, and many of those products are embedded in other products such as the iPhone.

Developing a Total Product Offer   From a strategic marketing viewpoint, a product is more than just the physical good or service. A **total product offer** consists of everything consumers evaluate when deciding whether to buy something. Thus, the basic product or service may be a washing machine, an insurance policy, or a beer, but the total product offer includes some or all of the *value enhancers* in Figure 14.1. You may hear some people call the basic product the "core product" and the total product offer the "augmented product." Can you see how sustainability can be part of the augmented product?[13]

When people buy a product, they may evaluate and compare total product offers on many dimensions. Some are tangible (the product itself and its package); others are intangible (the producer's reputation and the image created by advertising). A successful marketer must begin to think like a consumer and evaluate the total product offer as a collection of impressions created by all the factors listed in Figure 14.1. It is wise to talk with consumers to see which features and benefits are most important to them and which value enhancers they want or don't want in the final offering.[14] Frito-Lay, for example, had to drop biodegradable bags because they were "too noisy." Who would think of such a thing when developing a product?

What questions might you ask consumers when developing the total product offer for Very Vegetarian? (Recall the business idea we introduced in Chapter 13.) Remember, store surroundings are important in the restaurant business, as are the parking lot and the condition of bathrooms.

Sometimes an organization can use low prices to create an attractive total product offer.[15] For example, outlet stores offer brand-name goods for less. Shoppers like getting high-quality goods and low prices, but they must be careful. Outlets also carry lower-quality products with similar but not exactly

FIGURE 14.1 POTENTIAL COMPONENTS OF A TOTAL PRODUCT OFFER

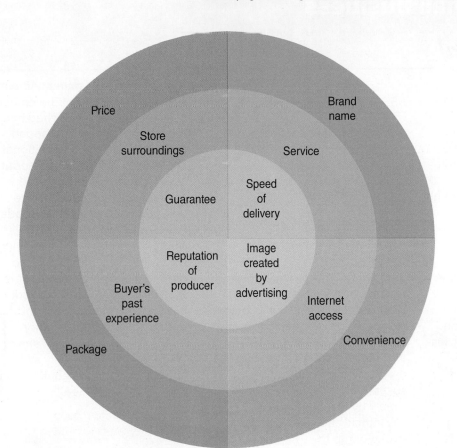

the same features as goods carried in regular stores. Different consumers may want different total product offers, so a company must develop a variety of offerings.

Product Lines and the Product Mix

Companies usually don't sell just one product. A **product line** is a group of products that are physically similar or intended for a similar market. They usually face similar competition. In one product line, there may be several competing brands. Notice, for example, Diet Coke, Diet Coke with Splenda, Coke Zero, Diet Coke with Lemon, Diet Coke with Lime, Diet Vanilla Coke, and Diet Cherry Coke. Now Coca-Cola is creating low-sugar drinks that taste better.[16] Makes it kind of hard to choose, doesn't it? Both Coke and Pepsi have added water and sports drinks to their product lines to meet new consumer tastes.

Procter & Gamble (P&G) has many brands in its laundry detergent product line, including Tide, Era, Downy, and Bold. P&G's product lines together make up its **product mix**, the combination of all product lines offered by a manufacturer. Have you noticed that there are more than 300 distinct types of toothpastes available in stores? Do you think that is too many or not?

Service providers have product lines and product mixes as well. A bank or credit union may offer a variety of services from savings accounts, automated teller machines, and computer banking to money market funds, safe deposit boxes, car loans, mortgages, traveler's checks, online banking, and insurance.[17] AT&T combines services (communications) with goods (phones) in its product mix, with special emphasis on wireless. The Spotlight on Small Business box features a story about how an entrepreneur expanded his company's product mix by adding new products and services.

product line
A group of products that are physically similar or are intended for a similar market.

product mix
The combination of product lines offered by a manufacturer.

Sealing the Deal

As a Navy Seal, Randy Hetrick had to keep his body in the same type of peak physical condition as a professional athlete. But during a training mission in Southeast Asia, Hetrick and his team had to remain undercover in a warehouse for weeks with only enough room for pushups and sit-ups. He remembered a workout that used his body weight as resistance rather than barbells, and created a "gizmo" out of spare parachute harnesses and nylon webbing that he attached to the end of a door. It worked great for him and his seal team. As time passed, his "gizmo" became Hetrick's passion. Along with the help of his fellow Seals, he worked to develop and improve the product.

Although Hetrick had a tough time convincing people that his idea was worth anything, he worked on his product with

conditioning coaches at the school's gym and eventually created a refined prototype. His "gizmo" had evolved into a sophisticated piece of equipment featuring three adjustable straps attached to a metal ring. It allowed users to perform hundreds of different exercises by suspending their legs in the air or simply by leaning forward.

Hetrick's beloved "gizmo" evolved into the TRX Suspension Trainer. As his business grew, Hetrick wondered if it was time

to reevaluate his marketing plan to take advantage of the company's success. He launched Fitness Anywhere and began providing classes, instructional DVDs, and online videos about suspension training. These added services launched the company into profitability. Today, Fitness Anywhere is a $50 million business occupying four floors of a San Francisco office building. The top floor is a 2,500-square-foot gym overlooking the city and kitchens throughout the office offer an array of energy bars and protein shakes. "Working out is not only sanctioned, it almost is required," says the former Navy Seal.

Sources: Brent Gleeson, "Veteran-Owned Businesses: Taking the Country by Storm," *Forbes*, April 3, 2014; and Katie Lobosco, "Vet Turns Military Training into $50 Million Fitness Company," *CNN Money*, November 10, 2013.

LO 14–2   Identify the various kinds of consumer and industrial goods.

PRODUCT DIFFERENTIATION

product differentiation
The creation of real or perceived product differences.

Product differentiation is the creation of real or perceived product differences. Actual product differences are sometimes quite small, so marketers must use a creative mix of branding, pricing, advertising, and packaging (value enhancers) to create a unique, attractive image. Note the positive effect of developing brands like Samsung, Google, and YouTube.[18] Various bottled water companies have successfully attempted product differentiation. The companies made their bottled waters so attractive through branding, pricing, and promotion that now restaurant customers often order water by brand name.

There's no reason why you couldn't create a similar attractive image for Very Vegetarian, your vegetarian restaurant. Small businesses can often win market share with creative product differentiation. One yearbook entrepreneur competes by offering multiple clothing changes, backgrounds, and poses along with special allowances, discounts, and guarantees. His small business has the advantage of being more flexible in adapting to customer needs and wants, and he's able to offer attractive product options. He has been so successful that companies use him as a speaker at photography conventions. How could you respond creatively to the consumer wants of vegetarians? Note the success that companies have had using the term *organic* in their promotions.[19]

Marketing Different Classes of Consumer Goods and Services

One popular classification of consumer goods and services has four general categories—convenience, shopping, specialty, and unsought.

1. **Convenience goods and services** are products the consumer wants to purchase frequently and with a minimum of effort, like candy, gum, milk, snacks, gas, and banking services. One store that sells mostly convenience goods is 7-Eleven. Location, brand awareness, and image are important for marketers of convenience goods and services. The Internet has taken convenience to a whole new level, especially for banks and other service companies.

2. **Shopping goods and services** are products the consumer buys only after comparing value, quality, price, and style from a variety of sellers. Target is one store that sells mostly shopping goods. Because many consumers carefully compare such products, marketers can emphasize price differences, quality differences, or some combination of the two. Think of how the Internet has helped you find the right shopping goods.[20] Think also of how people compare prices at competing wireless carriers.[21]

3. **Specialty goods and services** are consumer products with unique characteristics and brand identity. Because consumers perceive that specialty goods have no reasonable substitute, they put forth a special effort to purchase them. Examples include fine watches, expensive wine, fur coats, jewelry, imported chocolates, and services provided by medical specialists or business consultants. Specialty goods are often marketed through specialty magazines. Specialty skis may be sold through sports magazines and specialty foods through gourmet magazines. Again, the Internet helps buyers find specialty goods. In fact, some specialty goods can be sold exclusively on the Internet.

4. **Unsought goods and services** are products consumers are unaware of, haven't necessarily thought of buying, or suddenly find they need to solve an unexpected problem. They include emergency car-towing services, burial services, and insurance.

The marketing task varies according to the category of product; convenience goods are marketed differently from specialty goods. The best way to promote convenience goods is to make them readily available and create the proper image. Some combination of price, quality, and service is the best appeal for shopping goods. Specialty goods rely on reaching special market segments through advertising. Unsought goods such as life insurance often rely on personal selling. Car towing relies heavily on online directories, such as Yelp.

Whether a good or service falls into a particular class depends on the individual consumer. Coffee can be a shopping good for one consumer, while flavored gourmet roast is a specialty good for another. Some people shop around to compare different dry cleaners, so dry cleaning is a shopping service for them. Others go to the closest store, making it a convenience service. Marketers must carefully monitor their customer base to determine how consumers perceive their products.

When you're in a hurry and need something quickly, convenience stores offer a variety of goods that you can get when you're in a pinch. What convenience goods do you buy, and where do you find them?

convenience goods and services
Products that the consumer wants to purchase frequently and with a minimum of effort.

shopping goods and services
Those products that the consumer buys only after comparing value, quality, price, and style from a variety of sellers.

specialty goods and services
Consumer products with unique characteristics and brand identity. Because these products are perceived as having no reasonable substitute, the consumer puts forth a special effort to purchase them.

unsought goods and services
Products that consumers are unaware of, haven't necessarily thought of buying, or find that they need to solve an unexpected problem.

Many goods could be classified as consumer goods or industrial goods, based on their uses. For example, a computer that a person uses at home for personal use would clearly be a consumer good. But that same computer used in a commercial setting, such as a hospital, would be classified as an industrial good. What difference does it make how a good is classified?

industrial goods
Products used in the production of other products. Sometimes called business goods or B2B goods.

Marketing Industrial Goods and Services

Many goods could be classified as consumer goods or industrial goods, based on their uses. A computer kept at home for personal use is clearly a consumer good. But in a commercial setting, such as an accounting firm or manufacturing plant, the same computer is an industrial good.

Industrial goods (sometimes called business goods or B2B goods) are products used in the production of other products. They are sold in the business-to-business (B2B) market.[22] Some products can be both consumer and industrial goods. We've just mentioned how personal computers fit in both categories. As a consumer good, a computer might be sold through electronics stores or computer magazines. Most of the promotion would be advertising. As an industrial good, personal computers are more likely to be sold through salespeople or on the Internet. Advertising is less of a factor when selling industrial goods.[23] Thus, you can see that classifying goods by user category helps marketers determine the proper marketing mix strategy.[24]

Figure 14.2 shows some categories of both consumer goods and industrial goods and services. *Installations* consist of major capital equipment such as new factories and heavy machinery. *Capital items* are expensive products that last a long time. A new factory building is both a capital item and an installation. *Accessory equipment* consists of capital items that are not quite as long-lasting or expensive as installations—like computers, copy machines, and various tools. Various categories of industrial goods are shown in the figure.

test prep ✔✔

- What value enhancers may be included in a total product offer?
- What's the difference between a product line and a product mix?
- Name the four classes of consumer goods and services, and give examples of each.
- Describe three different types of industrial goods.

FIGURE 14.2 VARIOUS CATEGORIES OF CONSUMER AND INDUSTRIAL GOODS AND SERVICES

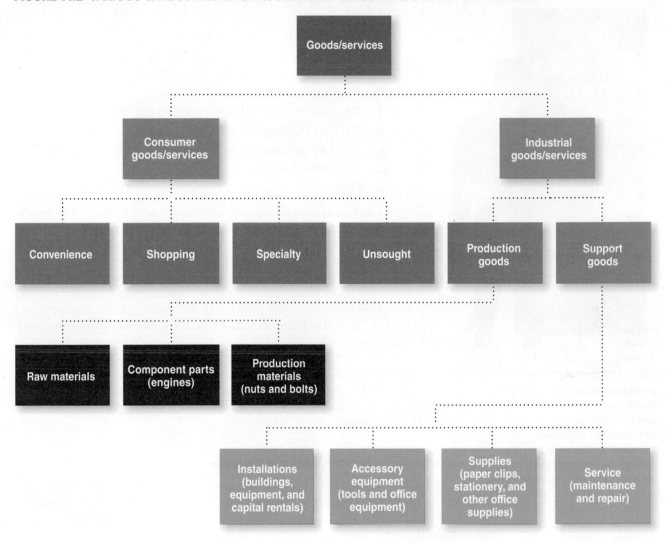

LO 14–3   Summarize the functions of packaging.

PACKAGING CHANGES THE PRODUCT

We've said that consumers evaluate many aspects of the total product offer, including the brand. It's surprising how important packaging can be in such evaluations of various goods. Many companies have used packaging to change and improve their basic product. We have squeezable ketchup bottles that stand upside down; square paint cans with screw tops and integrated handles; plastic bottles for motor oil that eliminate the need for funnels; single-use packets of spices; and so forth. Another interesting innovation is aromatic packaging. Arizona Beverage Company now has aromatic caps on its flavored iced teas.

In each case, the package changed the product in consumers' minds and opened large new markets. Do you sometimes have difficulty opening plastic packaging? Which packaging innovations do you like best? Can you see some market potential in developing better packaging? Packaging has even become a profession. Check out the Michigan State University School of

Even industrial products can benefit from innovative packaging. This foot-tall High-Tech CFO Action Figure is a talking doll created by a design consulting firm in response to a client's request for a written report for business analysts. Long after a report would have been filed, the Chief Financial Officer doll is still sitting on executives' desks. Can you think of other packaging innovations for office products?

bundling
Grouping two or more products together and pricing them as a unit.

brand
A name, symbol, or design (or combination thereof) that identifies the goods or services of one seller or group of sellers and distinguishes them from the goods and services of competitors.

Packaging, for example. Packages must perform the following functions:

1. Attract the buyer's attention.
2. Protect the goods inside, stand up under handling and storage, be tamperproof, and deter theft.
3. Be easy to open and use.
4. Describe and give information about the contents.
5. Explain the benefits of the good inside.
6. Provide information on warranties, warnings, and other consumer matters.
7. Give some indication of price, value, and uses.

Packaging can also make a product more attractive to retailers. The Universal Product Codes (UPCs) on many packages help stores control inventory. They combine a bar code and a preset number that gives the retailer information about the product's price, size, color, and other attributes. In short, packaging changes the product by changing its visibility, usefulness, or attractiveness.

One relatively new packaging technology for tracking products is the radio frequency identification (RFID) chip, especially the ones made with nanoparticle powder. When attached to a product, the chip sends out signals telling a company where the product is at all times. RFID chips carry more information than bar codes, don't have to be read one at a time (whole pallets can be read in an instant), and can be read at a distance. Walmart has been a leader in using RFID technology.

The Growing Importance of Packaging

Packaging has always been an important aspect of the product offer, but today it's carrying more of the promotional burden than in the past. Many products once sold by salespersons are now sold in self-service outlets, and the package has acquired more sales responsibility. The Fair Packaging and Labeling Act was passed to give consumers much more quantity and value information on product packaging.

Packaging may make use of a strategy called **bundling**, which combines goods and/or services for a single price. Virgin Airlines has bundled door-to-door limousine service and in-flight massages in its total product offer. Financial institutions are offering everything from financial advice to help in purchasing insurance, stocks, bonds, mutual funds, and more. When combining goods or services into one package, marketers must not include so much that the price gets too high. It's best to work with customers to develop value enhancers that meet their individual needs.

LO 14–4   Contrast *brand, brand name,* and *trademark,* and show the value of brand equity.

BRANDING AND BRAND EQUITY

A **brand** is a name, symbol, or design (or combination thereof) that identifies the goods or services of one seller or group of sellers and distinguishes them from the goods and services of competitors. The word *brand* includes practically all means of identifying a product. As we noted in Chapter 13, a *brand name* consists of a word, letter, or group of words or letters that differentiates one seller's goods and services from those of competitors. Brand names you may be familiar with include Red Bull, Sony, Del Monte, Campbell, Levi's, Google, Borden, Michelob, and of course many more. Brand names give products a distinction that tends to make them attractive to consumers. Apple and Google now rein as brand champions—we're sure you understand why.[25] The Reaching Beyond Our Borders box discusses product names in more depth.

A **trademark** is a brand that has exclusive legal protection for both its brand name and its design. Trademarks like McDonald's golden arches are widely recognized and help represent the company's reputation and image. McDonald's might sue to prevent a company from selling, say, McDonnel hamburgers. Did you know there are Starsbuck coffee shops in China? (Look closely at that name.)

People are often impressed by certain brand names, even though they say there's no difference between brands in a given product category. For example, even when people say that all aspirin is alike, if you put two aspirin bottles in front of them—one with the Bayer label and one with an unknown name—most choose the one with the well-known brand name. Gasoline buyers often choose a brand name (e.g., Exxon) over price.

For the buyer, a brand name ensures quality, reduces search time, and adds prestige to purchases. For the seller, brand names facilitate new-product introductions, help promotional efforts, add to repeat purchases, and differentiate products so that prices can be set higher. What brand-name products do you prefer?

Brand Categories

Several categories of brands are familiar to you. **Manufacturers' brands** represent manufacturers that distribute products nationally—Xerox, Sony, and Dell, for example.

Dealer (private-label) brands are products that don't carry the manufacturer's name but carry a distributor or retailer's name instead. Kenmore and DieHard are dealer brands sold by Sears. These brands are also known as *house brands* or *distributor brands*.

Many manufacturers fear having their brand names become generic names. A *generic name* is the name for a whole product category. Did you know that aspirin and linoleum were once brand names? So were nylon, escalator, kerosene, and zipper. All those names became so popular, so identified with the product, that they lost their brand status and became generic. (Such issues are decided in the courts.) Their producers then had to come up with new names. The original Aspirin, for example, became Bayer aspirin. Companies working hard to protect their brand names today include Xerox and Rollerblade (in-line skates).

Generic goods are nonbranded products that usually sell at a sizable discount compared to national or private-label brands. They feature basic packaging and are backed with little or no advertising. Some are of poor quality, but many come close to the same quality as the national brand-name goods they copy. There are generic tissues, generic cigarettes, generic drugs, and so on. Consumers today are buying large amounts of generic products because their overall quality has improved so much in recent years. What has been your experience trying generic products?

Knockoff brands are illegal copies of national brand-name goods. If you see an expensive brand-name item such as a Polo shirt or a Rolex watch for sale at a ridiculously low price, you can be pretty sure it's a knockoff. Often the

The Heinz Dip & Squeeze® ketchup package allows restaurant owners to offer their customers a choice of peeling off the lid for dipping or tearing off the top for squeezing. The package contains three times as much ketchup as traditional sachets and uses less packaging. Shaped like the iconic Heinz tomato ketchup glass bottles, the packets reinforce the Heinz Ketchup brand.

trademark
A brand that has exclusive legal protection for both its brand name and its design.

manufacturers' brands
The brand names of manufacturers that distribute products nationally.

dealer (private-label) brands
Products that don't carry the manufacturer's name but carry a distributor or retailer's name instead.

generic goods
Nonbranded products that usually sell at a sizable discount compared to national or private-label brands.

knockoff brands
Illegal copies of national brand-name goods.

Playing the Name Game

So, you've developed a product and you're ready to take it on the market. What should you call it? America's favorite cookie, Oreo, is said to be a great name because the two O's nicely mirror the shape of the cookie itself. Could the name be part of the charm? Think of other names that come to your mind when you think of American products: Coke, Nike, and Häagen-Dazs.

Are you surprised that Häagen-Dazs is an American product? Häagen Dazs was founded in 1961. Company founder Reuben Mattas wanted a name that projected high quality. Being enamored with Dutch/Swedish modern architecture and impressed with the quality of Duncan Hines products, Mattas played around with words until he came up with the name Häagen-Dazs. The name means absolutely nothing but it seemed to project another world

quality he wanted for his premium ice cream. Today, the Häagen-Dazs name resonates around the globe, including nations like Japan where it has just introduced innovative veggie flavors like tomato cherry and carrot orange.

At one time, finding a name like Häagen-Dazs was relatively simple. Now, with a couple hundred countries on the cyber-platform, choosing the right name is a global issue. For example, when Russian gas company Gazprom

formed a joint venture with Nigeria's NNPC, the company was called NiGaz. Not a great name, we'd say. On the other hand, a web development company in New Zealand chose the name hairyLemon. It has been estimated that at least a third of hairyLemon's business was because of its name.

Every once in a while, a successful name is created by accident. Google is a good example. The global search engine was supposed to be called Googol (a scientific name for 1 followed by one hundred zeros). However, the founders made a typo when registering the domain name. The error resulted in a warm, catchy, human-sounding name. Some mistakes turn out to be luckier than others.

Sources: Greg Emerson, "Häagen-Dazs Vegetable Ice Cream Flavors to Debut in Japan," *Newsday*, April 20, 2014; Gwen Moran, "5 Strategies to Build a Global Brand," *Entrepreneur*, May 7, 2013; and Interbrand, www.interbrand.com, accessed April 2014.

brand name is just a little off, too, like Palo (Polo) or Bolex (Rolex). Look carefully. Zippo has taken to calling counterfeit copies "Rippos."

Generating Brand Equity and Loyalty

A major goal of marketers in the future will be to reestablish the notion of brand equity. **Brand equity** is the value of the brand name and associated symbols. Usually, a company cannot know the value of its brand until it sells it to another company. Brand names with high reported brand equity ratings include Reynolds Wrap aluminum foil and Ziploc food bags. What's the most valuable brand name today? It's Apple.[26]

The core of brand equity is **brand loyalty**, the degree to which customers are satisfied, like the brand, and are committed to further purchases. A loyal group of customers represents substantial value to a firm, and that value can be calculated. One way manufacturers are trying to create more brand loyalty is by lowering the carbon footprint of their products.

Companies try to boost their short-term performance by offering coupons and price discounts to move goods quickly. This can erode consumers' commitment to brand names, especially of grocery products. Many consumers complain when companies drop brand names like Astro Pops or Flex shampoo. Such complaints show the power of brand names. Now companies realize the value of brand equity and are trying harder to measure the earning power of strong brand names.[27]

brand equity
The value of the brand name and associated symbols.

brand loyalty
The degree to which customers are satisfied, like the brand, and are committed to further purchases.

Brand awareness refers to how quickly or easily a given brand name comes to mind when someone mentions a product category. Advertising helps build strong brand awareness. Established brands, such as Coca-Cola and Pepsi, are usually among the highest in brand awareness. Sponsorship of events, like football's Orange Bowl and NASCAR's Cup Series, helps improve brand awareness. Simply being there over and over also increases brand awareness. That's one way Google became such a popular brand.

Perceived quality is an important part of brand equity. A product that's perceived as having better quality than its competitors can be priced accordingly. The key to creating a perception of quality is to identify what consumers look for in a high-quality product, and then to use that information in every message the company sends out. Factors influencing the perception of quality include price, appearance, and reputation.

Consumers often develop *brand preference*—that is, they prefer one brand over another—because of such cues. When consumers reach the point of *brand insistence,* the product becomes a specialty good. For example, a consumer may insist on Goodyear tires for his or her car.

It's now so easy to copy a product's benefits that off-brand products can draw consumers away from brand-name goods. Brand-name manufacturers like Intel Corporation have to develop new products and new markets faster and promote their names better than ever before to hold off challenges from competitors.

Creating Brand Associations

The name, symbol, and slogan a company uses can assist greatly in brand recognition for that company's products. **Brand association** is the linking of a brand to other favorable images, like famous product users, a popular celebrity, or a particular geographic area. Note, for example, how ads for Mercedes-Benz associate its company's cars with successful people who live luxurious lives. The person responsible for building brands is known as a brand manager or product manager. We'll discuss that position next.

Brand Management

A **brand manager** (known as a *product manager* in some firms) has direct responsibility for one brand or product line, and manages all the elements of its marketing mix: product, price, place, and promotion. Thus, you might think of the brand manager as the president of a one-product firm.

One reason many large consumer-product companies created this position was to have greater control over new-product development and product promotion. Some companies have brand-management *teams* to bolster the overall effort. In B2B companies, brand managers are often known as product managers.

brand awareness
How quickly or easily a given brand name comes to mind when a product category is mentioned.

brand association
The linking of a brand to other favorable images.

brand manager
A manager who has direct responsibility for one brand or one product line; called a *product manager* in some firms.

test prep

- What seven functions does packaging now perform?
- What's the difference between a brand name and a trademark?
- Can you explain the difference between a manufacturer's brand, a dealer brand, and a generic brand?
- What are the key components of brand equity?

Use LearnSmart to help retain what you have learned. Access your instructor's Connect course to check out LearnSmart, or go to learnsmartadvantage.com for help.

LEARNSMART

LO 14–5   Explain the steps in the new-product development process.

THE NEW-PRODUCT DEVELOPMENT PROCESS

The odds a new product will fail are high. Not delivering what is promised is a leading cause of new-product failure. Other causes include getting ready for marketing too late, poor positioning, too few differences from competitors, and poor packaging. As Figure 14.3 shows, new-product development for producers consists of six stages.

New products continue to pour into the market every year, and their profit potential looks tremendous. Think, for example, of 3D printing, streaming TV, video games and products, smartphones, tablets, and other innovations. Where do these ideas come from? How are they tested? What's the life span for an innovation? Let's look at these issues.

Generating New-Product Ideas

It now takes about seven ideas to generate one commercial product. Most ideas for new industrial products come from employee suggestions rather than research and development. Research and development, nonetheless, is a major source of new products. Employees are a major source for new consumer-goods ideas. Firms should also listen to their suppliers for new-product ideas because suppliers are often exposed to new ideas. Present customers are also a good source for new-product ideas.

Product Screening

Product screening reduces the number of new-product ideas a firm is working on at any one time so it can focus on the most promising. *Screening* applies criteria to determine whether the product fits well with present products, has good profit potential, and is marketable. The company may assign each of these factors a weight and compute a total score for each new product so that it can compare their potentials.

Product Analysis

After product screening comes **product analysis**, or making cost estimates and sales forecasts to get a feeling for the profitability of new-product ideas. Products that don't meet the established criteria are withdrawn from consideration.

Product Development and Testing

If a product passes the screening and analysis phase, the firm begins to develop it further, testing many different product concepts or

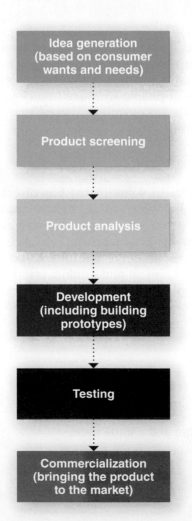

FIGURE 14.3 THE NEW-PRODUCT DEVELOPMENT PROCESS
Product development is a six-stage process. Which stage do you believe to be the most important?

product screening
A process designed to reduce the number of new-product ideas being worked on at any one time.

product analysis
Making cost estimates and sales forecasts to get a feeling for profitability of new-product ideas.

Tom Szaky of TerraCycle makes new products such as plant food planters, pencil cases, and tote bags from discarded products made by other companies. (To see his bags made from drink pouches and Oreo cookie wrappers, go to www.terracycle.net.) Do you own products that are made of recycled material?

alternatives. A firm that makes packaged meat products may develop the concept of a chicken dog—a hot dog made of chicken that tastes like an all-beef hot dog. It will develop a prototype, or sample, so that consumers can try the taste. The Adapting to Change box discusses how one company gets their customers to help them develop new products.

Concept testing takes a product idea to consumers to test their reactions. Do they see the benefits of this new product? How frequently would they buy it? At what price? What features do they like and dislike? What changes in it would they make? The firm tests samples using different packaging, branding, and ingredients until a product emerges that's desirable from both production and marketing perspectives. As you plan for Very Vegetarian, can you see the importance of concept testing for new vegetarian dishes?

concept testing
Taking a product idea to consumers to test their reactions.

Commercialization

Even if a product tests well, it may take quite awhile to achieve success in the market. Take the zipper, for example, the result of one of the longest development efforts on record for a consumer product. After Whitcomb Judson received the first patents for his clothing fastener in the early 1890s, it took more than 15 years to perfect the product—and even then consumers weren't interested. Judson's company suffered numerous financial setbacks, name changes, and relocations before settling in Meadville, Pennsylvania. Finally, the U.S. Navy started using zippers during World War I. Today, Talon Inc. is the leading U.S. maker of zippers, producing some 500 million of them a year.

The example of the zipper shows why the marketing effort must include **commercialization**, which includes (1) promoting the product to distributors and retailers to get wide distribution, and (2) developing strong advertising and sales campaigns to generate and maintain interest in the product among distributors and consumers. New products are now getting rapid exposure to global markets through commercialization on the Internet and social media. Websites enable consumers to view new products, ask questions, and make purchases easily and quickly.

commercialization
Promoting a product to distributors and retailers to get wide distribution, and developing strong advertising and sales campaigns to generate and maintain interest in the product among distributors and consumers.

Making the Right Cut

The fashion industry is a complicated combination of designers, buyers, brands, and media tastemakers who work hard to make fashion exclusive and unpredictable. For ModCloth founders Eric and Susan Gregg Koger, however, fashion is a more democratic endeavor than fashion gurus at *Vogue* let on. The company's website sells the work of more than 600 independent designers. The vintage-style outfits on ModCloth appeal to shoppers looking for funky clothes that don't normally find their way into women's shops or department stores.

For the Kogers, stocking unique merchandise is the key to their success. After all, the Internet is home to thousands of apparel sites, from big-name retailers to small independent vendors. The most successful online operations have a defining characteristic that separates them from the rest of the pack. Customers keep coming back to ModCloth because of the interactivity of the brand.

Floral Dress from ModCloth's Private Label "Myrtlewood," www. modcloth.com/shop/dresses/ spellbinding-ability-dress.

The company is able to retain customer loyalty by continuously trying to engage its customers. For example, the company's clothing design contest, "Make the Cut," invites customers to submit their

own dress sketches. Contest winners have a chance to have their designs produced and sold on the company's website. In the most recent contest, more than 1,900 designs were sent in during the two-week submission period. With the company's "Be the Buyer" program, ModCloth accepts a sample from a designer, puts the photos online, then asks customers if it should produce the item. Any customers who would like the help of a fashion advisor can get help from Modstylists, who are available 24/7. Customers can chat, call, or e-mail an in-house stylist to get advice dealing with questions about fit, sizing, or styling. The company's marketing objective is to be "the fashion company you are friends with." That's why the Kogers continue to look for even more ways to engage customers.

Sources: Marisa Meltzer, "ModCloth Is Selling an Era They Missed Out On," *The New York Times*, September 11, 2013; Barbara Thau, "Retailers Wake Up to Plus-Size Market with Trendier, Tonier Fare," *Forbes*, January 10, 2014; and Alice Truong, "ModCloth Wraps Up a Very Social Year," *Fast Company*, January 17, 2014.

LO 14–6   Describe the product life cycle.

THE PRODUCT LIFE CYCLE

product life cycle
A theoretical model of what happens to sales and profits for a product class over time; the four stages of the cycle are introduction, growth, maturity, and decline.

Once a product has been developed and tested, it goes to market. There it may pass through a **product life cycle** of four stages: introduction, growth, maturity, and decline (see Figure 14.4). This cycle is a *theoretical* model of what happens to sales and profits for a *product class* over time. However, not all individual products follow the life cycle, and particular brands may act differently. For example, while frozen foods as a generic class may go through the entire cycle, onc brand may never get beyond the introduction stage. Some product classes, such as microwave ovens, stay in the introductory stage for years. Some products, like catsup, become classics and never experience decline. Others, such as fad clothing, may go through the entire cycle in a few months. Still others may be withdrawn from the market altogether. Nonetheless, the product life cycle may provide some basis for anticipating future market developments and for planning marketing strategies.

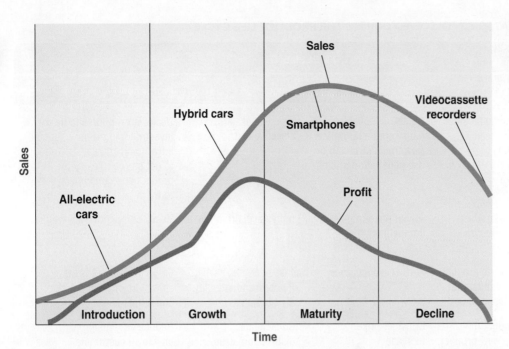

FIGURE 14.4 SALES AND PROFITS DURING THE PRODUCT LIFE CYCLE
Note that profit levels start to fall *before* sales reach their peak. This is due to increasing price competition. When profits and sales start to decline, it's time to come out with a new product or to remodel the old one to maintain interest and profits.

Example of the Product Life Cycle

The product life cycle can give marketers valuable clues to successfully promoting a product over time. Some products, like crayons and sidewalk chalk, have very long product life cycles, change very little, and never seem to go into decline. Crayola has been successfully selling crayons for 100 years! How long do you think the new virtual video games will last?

You can see how the theory works by looking at the product life cycle of instant coffee. When it was introduced, most people didn't like it as well as "regular" coffee, and it took several years for instant coffee to gain general acceptance (introduction stage). At one point, though, instant coffee grew rapidly in popularity, and many brands were introduced (growth stage). After a while, people became attached to one brand and sales leveled off (maturity stage). Sales then went into a slight decline when freeze-dried coffees were introduced (decline stage). Now freeze-dried coffee is, in turn, at the decline stage as consumers are buying bags of coffee from Starbucks and brewing them at home. It's extremely important for marketers to recognize what stage a product is in so that they can make intelligent and efficient marketing decisions about it.

Using the Product Life Cycle

Different stages in the product life cycle call for different marketing strategies. Figure 14.5 outlines the marketing mix decisions you might make. As you go through the figure, you'll see that each stage calls for multiple marketing mix changes. Remember, these concepts are largely theoretical and you should use them only as guidelines. We'll discuss the price strategies mentioned in the figure later in this chapter.

Figure 14.6 shows in theory what happens to sales volume, profits, and competition during the product life cycle. Compare it to Figure 14.4. Both figures show that a product at the mature stage may reach the top in sales growth while profit is decreasing. At that stage, a marketing manager may decide to create a new image for the product to start a new growth cycle. You may have

 connect

iSee It! Need help understanding product life cycle? Visit your Connect e-book video tab for a brief animated explanation.

FIGURE 14.5 SAMPLE STRATEGIES FOLLOWED DURING THE PRODUCT LIFE CYCLE

MARKETING MIX ELEMENTS				
Life Cycle Stage	Product	Price	Place	Promotion
Introduction	Offer market tested product; keep mix small	Go after innovators with high introductory price (skimming strategy) or use penetration pricing	Use wholesalers, selective distribution	Dealer promotion and heavy investment in primary demand advertising and sales promotion to get stores to carry the product and consumers to try it
Growth	Improve product; keep product mix limited	Adjust price to meet competition	Increase distribution	Heavy competitive advertising
Maturity	Differentiate product to satisfy different market segments	Further reduce price	Take over wholesaling function and intensify distribution	Emphasize brand name as well as product benefits and differences
Decline	Cut product mix; develop new product ideas	Consider price increase	Consolidate distribution; drop some outlets	Reduce advertising to only loyal customers

FIGURE 14.6 HOW SALES, PROFITS, AND COMPETITION VARY OVER THE PRODUCT LIFE CYCLE

Life Cycle Stage	Sales	Profits	Competitors
Introduction	Low sales	Losses may occur	Few
Growth	Rapidly rising sales	Very high profits	Growing number
Maturity	Maturity	Declining profits	Stable number, then declining
Decline	Falling sales	Profits may fall to become losses	Declining number

noticed how Arm & Hammer baking soda gets a new image every few years to generate new sales. One year it's positioned as a deodorant for refrigerators and the next as a substitute for harsh chemicals in swimming pools. Knowing what stage in the cycle a product has reached helps marketing managers decide when such strategic changes are needed.

Theoretically, all products go through these stages at various times in their life cycle. What happens to sales as a product matures?

Use LearnSmart to help retain what you have learned. Access your instructor's Connect course to check out LearnSmart, or go to learnsmartadvantage.com for help.

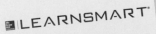

- What are the six steps in the new-product development process?
- What is the difference between product screening and product analysis?
- What are the two steps in commercialization?
- What is the theory of the product life cycle?

LO 14–7   Identify various pricing objectives and strategies.

COMPETITIVE PRICING

Pricing is so important to marketing and the development of total product offers that it has been singled out as one of the four Ps in the marketing mix, along with product, place, and promotion. It's one of the most difficult of the four Ps for a manager to control, however, because price is such a critical ingredient in consumer evaluations of the product. In this section, we'll explore price both as an ingredient of the total product offer and as a strategic marketing tool.

Pricing Objectives

A firm may have several objectives in mind when setting a pricing strategy. When pricing a new vegetarian offering, we may want to promote the product's image. If we price it *high* and use the right promotion, maybe we can make it the BMW of vegetarian meals. We also might price it high to achieve a certain profit objective or return on investment. We could also price our product *lower* than its competitors, because we want low-income people to afford this healthy meal. That is, we could have some social or ethical goal in mind. Low pricing may also discourage competition because it reduces the profit potential, but it may help us capture a larger share of the market.

A firm may have several pricing objectives over time, and it must formulate these objectives clearly before developing an overall pricing strategy. Popular objectives include the following:

1. *Achieving a target return on investment or profit.* Ultimately, the goal of marketing is to make a profit by providing goods and services to others. Naturally, one long-run pricing objective of almost all firms is to optimize profit. One way companies have tried to increase profit is by reducing the amount provided to customers. Thus cereal companies have cut the amount of cereal in a box, toilet paper companies are making their products smaller, and so on. Have you noticed this happening for products you buy?

2. *Building traffic.* Supermarkets often advertise certain products at or below cost to attract people to the store. These products are called *loss leaders.* The long-run objective is to make profits by following the short-run objective of building a customer base.

3. *Achieving greater market share.* One way to capture a larger part of the market is to offer lower prices, low finance rates (like 0 percent financing), low lease rates, or rebates.

4. *Creating an image.* Certain watches, perfumes, and other socially visible products are priced high to give them an image of exclusivity and status.

5. *Furthering social objectives.* A firm may want to price a product low so people with little money can afford it. The government often subsidizes the price of farm products to keep basic necessities affordable.

A firm may have short-run objectives that differ greatly from its long-run objectives. Managers should understand both types at the beginning and put both into their strategic marketing plan. They should also set pricing objectives in the context of other marketing decisions about product design, packaging, branding, distribution, and promotion. All these marketing decisions are interrelated.

Intuition tells us the price charged for a product must bear some relationship to the cost of producing it. Prices usually *are* set somewhere above cost. But as we'll see, price and cost aren't always related. In fact, there are three major approaches to pricing strategy: cost-based, demand-based (target costing), and competition-based.

Cost-Based Pricing

Producers often use cost as a primary basis for setting price. They develop elaborate cost accounting systems to measure production costs (including materials, labor, and overhead), add in a margin of profit, and come up with a price. Picture the process in terms of producing a car. You add up all the various components—engine parts, body, tires, radio, door locks and windows, paint, and labor—add a profit margin, and come up with a price. The question is whether the price will be satisfactory to the market as well. In the long run, the market—not the producer—determines what the price will be (see Chapter 2). Pricing should take into account costs, but it should also include the expected costs of product updates, the marketing objectives for each product, and competitor prices.

Demand-Based Pricing

Unlike cost-based pricing, **target costing** is demand based. That means we design a product so it not only satisfies customers but also meets the profit margins we've set. Target costing makes the final price an *input* to the product development process, not an outcome of it. You first estimate the selling price people would be willing to pay for a product and then subtract your desired profit margin. The result is your target cost of production, or what you can spend to profitably produce the item.

Competition-Based Pricing

Competition-based pricing is a strategy based on what all the other competitors are doing. The price can be at, above, or below competitors' prices. Pricing depends on customer loyalty, perceived differences, and the competitive climate.[28] **Price leadership** is the strategy by which one or more dominant firms set pricing practices all competitors in an industry follow. You may have noticed that practice among oil companies and some fast-food companies.[29]

Break-Even Analysis

Before you begin selling a new vegetarian sandwich, it may be wise to determine how many sandwiches you'd have to sell before making a profit. You'd then determine whether you could reach such a sales goal. **Break-even analysis** is the process used to determine profitability at various levels of sales. The break-even point is the point where revenues from sales equal all costs. The formula for calculating the break-even point is as follows:

$$\text{Break-even point (BEP)} = \frac{\text{Total fixed costs (FC)}}{\text{Price of one unit (P)} - \text{Variable costs (VC) of one unit}}$$

Total fixed costs are all the expenses that remain the same no matter how many products are made or sold. Among the expenses that make up

Shoppers around the world look for bargains, as these consumers in Austria are doing. How many different ways can marketers appeal to shoppers' desires to find the lowest price? Do online retailers adopt different pricing strategies?

target costing
Designing a product so that it satisfies customers and meets the profit margins desired by the firm.

competition-based pricing
A pricing strategy based on what all the other competitors are doing. The price can be set at, above, or below competitors' prices.

price leadership
The strategy by which one or more dominant firms set the pricing practices that all competitors in an industry follow.

break-even analysis
The process used to determine profitability at various levels of sales.

fixed costs are the amount paid to own or rent a factory or warehouse and the amount paid for business insurance. **Variable costs** change according to the level of production. Included are the expenses for the materials used in making products and the direct costs of labor used in making those goods. For producing a specific product, let's say you have a fixed cost of $200,000 (for mortgage interest, real estate taxes, equipment, and so on). Your variable cost (e.g., labor and materials) per item is $2. If you sold the products for $4 each, the break-even point would be 100,000 items. In other words, you wouldn't make any money selling this product unless you sold more than 100,000 of them:

$$\text{BEP} = \frac{\text{FC}}{\text{P} - \text{VC}} = \frac{\$200,000}{\$4.00 - \$2.00} = \frac{\$200,000}{\$2.00} = 100,000 \text{ boxes}$$

Other Pricing Strategies

Let's say a firm has just developed a new line of products, such as 3D printers. The firm has to decide how to price these units at the introductory stage of the product life cycle. A **skimming price strategy** prices a new product high to recover research and development costs and make as much profit as possible while there's little competition. Of course, those large profits will eventually attract new competitors.

A second strategy is to price the new products low. Low prices will attract more buyers and discourage other companies from making similar products because profits are slim. This **penetration strategy** enables the firm to penetrate or capture a large share of the market quickly.[30]

Retailers use several pricing strategies. **Everyday low pricing (EDLP)** is the choice of Home Depot and Walmart. They set prices lower than competitors and don't usually have special sales. The idea is to bring consumers to the store whenever they want a bargain rather than having them wait until there is a sale.

Department stores and some other retailers most often use a **high–low pricing strategy.** Regular prices are higher than at stores using EDLP, but during special sales they're lower. The problem with such pricing is that it encourages consumers to wait for sales, thus cutting into profits. One store that tried such pricing was JCPenney. When the store moved away from that strategy, sales fell off dramatically and may never recover, even though the store has since returned to that strategy. As online shopping continues to grow, you may see fewer stores with a high–low strategy because consumers will be able to find better prices online.[31]

Retailers can use price as a major determinant of the goods they carry. Some promote goods that sell for only 99 cents, or for less than $5.00. Some of those 99-cent stores have raised their prices to over a dollar because of rising costs. On the other hand, Family Dollar Store is learning that, for low-income buyers, even $1.00 may be too expensive.[32]

Psychological pricing means pricing goods and services at price points that make the product appear less expensive than it is. A house might be priced at $299,000 because that sounds like a lot less than $300,000. Gas stations almost always use psychological pricing.

How Market Forces Affect Pricing

Recognizing that different consumers may be willing to pay different prices, marketers sometimes price on the basis of consumer demand rather than cost or some other calculation. That's called *demand-oriented pricing,* and you can observe it at movie theaters with low rates for children and drugstores with discounts for senior citizens.

total fixed costs
All the expenses that remain the same no matter how many products are made or sold.

variable costs
Costs that change according to the level of production.

skimming price strategy
Strategy in which a new product is priced high to make optimum profit while there's little competition.

penetration strategy
Strategy in which a product is priced low to attract many customers and discourage competition.

everyday low pricing (EDLP)
Setting prices lower than competitors and then not having any special sales.

high–low pricing strategy
Setting prices that are higher than EDLP stores, but having many special sales where the prices are lower than competitors' prices.

Some products are priced high to create a high-status image of exclusivity and desirability. Jimmy Choo shoes fall into this category. What is the total product offer for a product like this?

psychological pricing
Pricing goods and services at price points that make the product appear less expensive than it is.

Today, marketers are facing a pricing problem: Most customers compare prices of goods and services online. Priceline.com introduced consumers to a "demand collection system," in which buyers post the prices they are willing to pay and invite sellers to accept or decline the price. Consumers can get great prices on airlines, hotels, and other products by naming their price. They can also get used goods online at places like Craigslist. Clearly, price competition is going to heat up as consumers have more access to price information from all around the world. As a result, nonprice competition is likely to increase.

NONPRICE COMPETITION

Marketers often compete on product attributes other than price. You may have noted that price differences are small for products like gasoline, candy bars, and even major products such as compact cars and private colleges.

You won't typically see price as a major promotional appeal on television. Instead, marketers tend to stress product images and consumer benefits such as comfort, style, convenience, and durability.

Many small organizations promote the services that accompany basic products rather than price in order to compete with bigger firms. Good service will enhance a relatively homogeneous product. Danny O'Neill, for example, is a small wholesaler who sells gourmet coffee to upscale restaurants. He has to watch competitors' prices *and* the services they offer so that he can charge the premium prices he wants. To charge high prices, he has to offer and then provide superior service. Larger companies often do the same thing. Some airlines stress friendliness, large "sleeping" seats, promptness, abundant flights, and other such services. Many hotels stress "no surprises," business services, health clubs, and other extras.

Use LearnSmart to help retain what you have learned. Access your instructor's Connect course to check out LearnSmart, or go to learnsmartadvantage.com for help.

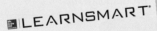

- Can you list two short-term and two long-term pricing objectives? Can the two be compatible?
- What are the limitations of a cost-based pricing strategy?
- What is psychological pricing?

summary

Access your instructor's Connect course to check out LearnSmart or go to learnsmartadvantage.com for help.

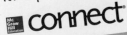

LO 14–1   Describe a total product offer.

- **What's included in a total product offer?**
  A total product offer consists of everything consumers evaluate when deciding whether to buy something. It includes price, brand name, and satisfaction in use.

- **What's the difference between a product line and a product mix?**
  A product line is a group of physically similar products with similar competitors. A product line of gum may include bubble gum and sugarless gum. A product mix is a company's combination of product lines. A

manufacturer may offer lines of gum, candy bars, and breath mints in its product mix.

- **How do marketers create product differentiation for their goods and services?**
  Marketers use a combination of pricing, advertising, and packaging to make their products seem unique and attractive.

LO 14–2   Identify the various kinds of consumer and industrial goods.

- **What are consumer goods?**
  Consumer goods are sold to ultimate consumers like you and me for personal use.

- **What are the four classifications of consumer goods and services, and how are they marketed?**
  There are convenience goods and services (requiring minimum shopping effort); shopping goods and services (for which people search and compare price and quality); specialty goods and services (which consumers go out of their way to get, and for which they often demand specific brands); and unsought goods and services (products consumers are unaware of, haven't thought of buying, or need to solve an unexpected problem). Convenience goods and services are best promoted by location, shopping goods and services by some price/quality appeal, and specialty goods and services by specialty magazines and interactive websites.

- **What are industrial goods, and how are they marketed differently from consumer goods?**
  Industrial goods are products sold in the business-to-business (B2B) market and used in the production of other products. They're sold largely through salespeople and rely less on advertising.

LO 14–3   Summarize the functions of packaging.

- **What are the seven functions of packaging?**
  Packaging must (1) attract the buyer's attention; (2) protect the goods inside, stand up under handling and storage, be tamperproof, and deter theft; (3) be easy to open and use; (4) describe the contents; (5) explain the benefits of the good inside; (6) provide information about warranties, warnings, and other consumer matters; and (7) indicate price, value, and uses. Bundling means grouping two or more products into a unit, through packaging, and charging one price for them.

LO 14–4   Contrast *brand, brand name,* and *trademark,* and show the value of brand equity.

- **Can you define brand, brand name, and trademark?**
  A *brand* is a name, symbol, or design (or combination thereof) that identifies the goods or services of one seller or group of sellers and distinguishes them from the goods and services of competitors. The word *brand* includes all means of identifying a product. A *brand name* consists of a word, letter, or group of words or letters that differentiates one seller's goods and services from those of competitors. A *trademark* is a brand that has exclusive legal protection for both its brand name and design.

- **What is brand equity, and how do managers create brand associations?**
  Brand equity is the value of a brand name and associated symbols. Brand association is the linking of a brand to other favorable images such as product users, a popular celebrity, or a geographic area.

- **What do brand managers do?**
  Brand managers coordinate product, price, place, and promotion decisions for a particular product.

LO 14–5 Explain the steps in the new-product development process.

- **What are the six steps of the product development process?**
  The steps of product development are (1) generation of new-product ideas, (2) product screening, (3) product analysis, (4) development, (5) testing, and (6) commercialization.

LO 14–6 Describe the product life cycle.

- **What is the product life cycle?**
  The product life cycle is a theoretical model of what happens to sales and profits for a product class over time.

- **What are the four stages in the product life cycle?**
  The four product life cycle stages are introduction, growth, maturity, and decline.

LO 14–7 Identify various pricing objectives and strategies.

- **What are pricing objectives?**
  Pricing objectives include achieving a target profit, building traffic, increasing market share, creating an image, and meeting social goals.

- **What strategies can marketers use to determine a product's price?**
  A skimming strategy prices the product high to make big profits while there's little competition. A penetration strategy uses low price to attract more customers and discourage competitors. Demand-oriented pricing starts with consumer demand rather than cost. Competition-oriented pricing is based on all competitors' prices. Price leadership occurs when all competitors follow the pricing practice of one or more dominant companies.

- **What is break-even analysis?**
  Break-even analysis is the process used to determine profitability at various levels of sales. The break-even point is the point where revenues from sales equal all costs.

- **Why do companies use nonprice strategies?**
  Pricing is one of the easiest marketing strategies to copy. It's often not a good long-run competitive tool.

---

key terms

brand 398
brand association 401
brand awareness 401
brand equity 400
brand loyalty 400
brand manager 401
break-even analysis 408
bundling 398
commercialization 403

competition-based pricing 408
concept testing 403
convenience goods and services 395
dealer (private-label) brands 399
distributed product development 392

everyday low pricing (EDLP) 409
generic goods 399
high–low pricing strategy 409
industrial goods 396
knockoff brands 399
manufacturers' brands 399

critical thinking

1. What value enhancers affected your choice of the school you attend? Did you consider size, location, price, reputation, WiFi services, library and research services, sports, and courses offered? What factors were most important? Why? What schools were your alternatives? Why didn't you choose them?

2. What could you do to enhance the product offer of Very Vegetarian, other than changing the menu from time to time?

3. How could you use psychological pricing when making up the menu at Very Vegetarian?

4. Are you impressed by the use of celebrities in product advertisements? What celebrity could you use to promote Very Vegetarian?

developing workplace skills

Key: ● Team   ★ Analytic   ▲ Communication   ▣ Technology

1. Look around your classroom and notice the different types of shoes students are wearing. What product qualities were they looking for when they chose their shoes? How important were price, style, brand name, and color? Describe the product offerings you would feature in a new shoe store designed to appeal to college students. ★ ▲

2. A total product offer consists of everything consumers evaluate when choosing among products, including price, package, service, and reputation. Working in teams, compose a list of factors consumers might consider when evaluating the total product offer of a vacation resort, a smartphone, and a rental apartment. ● ★ ▲

3. How important is price to you when buying the following: clothes, milk, computers, haircuts, rental cars? What nonprice factors, if any, are more important than price? How much time do you spend evaluating factors other than price when making such purchases? ★

4. Go through several local stores of different types and note how often they use psychological pricing. Discuss the practice with the class to see whether students recognize the influence psychological pricing has upon them. ★ ▲

taking it to the **net**

PURPOSE

To assess how consumers can use the Internet to shop for various goods.

EXERCISE

Shopbots are Internet sites for finding the best prices on goods you need. No shopbot searches the entire Internet, so it's a good idea to use more than one to get the best deals. Furthermore, not all shopbots quote shipping and handling costs. Here are some to try: MySimon.com, PriceGrabber.com, PriceSCAN. com, and YahooShopping.com.

1. Which of the shopbots offers the most goods and the most information? How helpful are the consumer reviews? The product descriptions?

2. Which shopbot is easiest to use? The hardest? Why?

3. Write down some of the prices you find on the Internet and then go to a local store, such as Walmart or Target, and compare prices. Does either source (online or brick-and-mortar) consistently offer the best price?

4. Compare shopping on the Internet to shopping in stores. What are the advantages and disadvantages of each? Which has the best total product offer?

video case

McGraw Hill Education **connect**

DREAM DINNERS FOOD-TO-GO

Dream Dinners is a Washington-based, innovative food-to-go concept. The company is franchised around the country and collectively sells over 700,000 servings each month. At Dream Dinners, customers are able to put together a variety of meals that can be taken home and prepared in minutes. This approach provides a nutritious meal, saves customers time, and is convenient, while also helping families reestablish "dinner time" as an important social event. The value proposition in this product includes saving time, while providing convenient, nutritional family meals for customers. The Dream Dinners concept demonstrates the process of the total product offering and each of the steps in the process.

This business concept evolved from the experiences of a group of friends who met monthly to cook dinners to place in freezers to help each other out. The group did this for about seven years before launching the business model. The driving force behind the concept is to reemphasize the value of family time at dinner. Providing customers the ability to assemble a month's worth of dinners would save tremendous time at home and would allow for more quality time to be spent with family members. The company describes its core demographic as women with school-age children.

Dream Dinners seeks to influence how its customers value its product. The company discovered that its best marketing promotion comes from social media and word of mouth of customers who are in the stores—a satisfied customer tells her friends and so on. Customers perceive value from a product by weighing the benefits they expect from the product and the cost of receiving those goods. The importance of listening to the customer is critical to success in today's competitive marketplace. The video explains how Dream Dinners engages in the product development process through growing its markets by offering environmentally friendly products. To this end, Dream Dinners provides 3–4 new dinner options each month. The company gauges its business success through a pricing model that is based on a cost-plus margin.

Success is defined as an average dollar ticket that consists of a customer spending a minimum of $150 per month by assembling 6 full-size dinners or 12 small-size dinners. The company has four key principles that it uses to assess its overall effectiveness. These principles are (1) that the meals are easy, wonderful, and delicious; (2) that customers have a great experience in the store assembling meals; (3) that the menu items are easy for the store owner to provide; and (4) that the menu items are acceptable to the home office. The key differentiator for Dream Dinners is the quality of the food when compared with competitors.

THINKING IT OVER

1. In what classification of consumer products would you consider Dream Dinners? Why did you select that category?

2. What are the steps in the new-product development process?

3. What stage of the product life cycle is Dream Dinners currently in? Why did you make that choice?

notes

1. Timothy Appel, "A Crib for Baby: Made in China or Made in U.S.A.," *The Wall Street Journal,* May 22, 2012.

2. John Mackey and Raj Sisodia, *Conscious Capitalism* (Boston, MA: Harvard Business Review Press, 2013).

3. Dana Mattioli and Miguel Bustillo, "Can Texting Save Stores?" *The Wall Street Journal,* May 9, 2012.

4. Annie Gasparro and Melodie Warner, "New Menu Boosts McDonalds," *The Wall Street Journal,* June 11, 2013; Maureen Morrison, "The Breakfast Club: Restaurant Marketers Wake Up to $50 Billion Opportunity," *Advertising Age,* May 13, 2013; Julie Jargon, "McDonald's Pledges to Offer Veggies," *The Wall Street Journal,* September 27, 2013; and editorial in *Nutrition Action Newsletter,* January/February 2014.

5. Maureen Morrison, "Did Someone Say McCopycat? BK Emulates McD's Menu," *Advertising Age,* December 2, 2013.

6. Annie Gasparro, "Burger King Steps Up Its Coffee Offerings," *The Wall Street Journal,* February 13, 2013.

7. Maureen Morrison and E. J. Schultz, "McD's Looking to Clean Up in the Coffee Aisle," *Advertising Age,* November 11, 2013.

8. Julie Jargon, "Evolution of Starbucks Food," *The Wall Street Journal,* October 2, 2013.

9. "E-Cig Ad Fires Across Bow of Traditional Tobacco Companies," editorial, *Advertising Age,* January 6, 2014.

10. Lauren Weber and Mike Esterl, "E-Cigarette Rise Poses Quandary for Employers," *The Wall Street Journal,* January 16, 2014.

11. Annie Gasparro and Mike Esterl, "Secret to Homemade Coke: Instant Cold, No Canisters," *The Wall Street Journal,* February 7, 2014.

12. John Revill, "From Swiss Watches to Necklaces," *The Wall Street Journal,* January 23, 2014.

13. Knut Haanaes, David Michael, Jeremy Jurgens, and Subramanian Ragan, "Making Sustainability Profitable," *Harvard Business Review,* March 2013.

14. Emma K. Macdonald, Hugh N. Wilson, and Umut Konus, "Better Customer Insight—In Real Time," *Harvard Business Review,* September 2012.

15. Serena Ng, "At P&G, New Tide Comes In, Old Price Goes Up," *The Wall Street Journal,* February 11, 2014.

16. E. J. Schultz, "How Pepsico and Coca-Cola Are Creating the Cola of the Future," *Advertising Age,* December 2, 2013.

17. Ismat Sarah Mangla, "Credit Unions' Homey Image Starts to Fray," *Money,* April 6, 2013.

18. "World's Top Brands," editorial in *Time,* February 3, 2014.

19. Sarah Nassauer, "Organic Tries to Grow Up," *The Wall Street Journal,* January 23, 2014.

20. Miriam Gottfried, "Amazon: It's Not Just for Christmas," *The Wall Street Journal,* February 1–2, 2014.

21. Victor Luckerson, "Service Charge," *Time,* January 27, 2014.

22. Mark Henricks, "Business to Business & Service Concepts Lead Franchising Growth," *Inc.,* February 2014.

23. Linda McGovern, "B-To-B Player USG Looks to Rebrand with Olympic Sponsorship," *Advertising Age,* January 6, 2014.

24. Richard Ettenson, Eduardo Conrado, and Jonathan Knowles, "Rethinking the 4 P's," *Harvard Business Review,* January–February 2013.

25. Vauhini Vara, "The Cycle of Brand Backlash," *This Week,* October 11, 2013.

26. "The World's Most Valuable Brands," *Forbes,* www.forbes .com, accessed April 2014.

27. Marine Cole, "Lemkau Chases What Matters—Brand Image," *Advertising Age,* January 20, 2014.

28. Geoffrey A. Fowler, "Price Check: Do Online Grocers Beat Supermarkets?" *The Wall Street Journal,* January 8, 2014.

29. Anne Gasparro, "McDonald's, Wendy's in Price Fight," *The Wall Street Journal,* May 9, 2013.

30. Judith Ohikuare, "New Year, No Excuses," *Inc.,* February 2013.

31. Kerri Anne Renzulli, "People Who Shop on the Web . . . At the Store," *Money,* December 2013.

32. Paul Ziobro and Suzanne Kapner, "Last Cent: Dollar Store Is Getting Too Expensive," *The Wall Street Journal,* January 10, 2014.

photo credits

15

Distributing Products

Learning Objectives

AFTER YOU HAVE READ AND STUDIED THIS CHAPTER, YOU SHOULD BE ABLE TO

LO 15-1 Explain the concept of marketing channels and their value.

LO 15-2 Demonstrate how intermediaries perform the six marketing utilities.

LO 15-3 Identify the types of wholesale intermediaries in the distribution system.

LO 15-4 Compare the distribution strategies retailers use.

LO 15-5 Explain the various kinds of nonstore retailing.

LO 15-6 Explain the various ways to build cooperation in channel systems.

LO 15-7 Describe logistics and outline how intermediaries manage the transportation and storage of goods.

When it comes to executing a corporate comeback, there's nobody quite like Netflix CEO Reed Hastings. He's faced critics repeatedly in his career, beginning with those who doubted that his DVD-by-mail company could compete against traditional video stores. After almost singlehandedly ending the era of brick-and-mortar video distribution, Hastings nearly lost it all when he split Netflix's Internet streaming and DVD delivery services into two separate entities. But the brand bounced back in a big way thanks to Hastings's commitment to his company's instant streaming capabilities. In fact, now on any given weeknight Netflix is responsible for more than a third of all Internet traffic.

Even before he entered the business world, Hastings had an eye for disrupting standard procedures in order to improve efficiency. While studying mathematics at Bowdoin College, he spent his summers training with the Marines and continued his service after graduation. Although Hastings was dedicated to serving his country, his inquiring mind didn't work well in a military environment. "I found myself questioning how we packed our backpacks and how we made our beds," said Hastings. "My questioning wasn't particularly encouraged, and I realized I might be better off in the Peace Corps." The Marines granted his transfer, and soon Hastings found himself in Swaziland teaching geometry and algebra to high school students. Three years in the impoverished African nation taught Hastings a great deal about the world around him and his own role within it. "Once you have hitchhiked across Africa with 10 bucks in your pocket, starting a business doesn't seem too intimidating," said Hastings.

Hastings returned to the U.S. in the late 1980s and earned his Master's degree in computer engineering from Stanford. A few years later he founded his first company, a troubleshooting and debugging developer called Pure Software. A larger tech firm soon purchased the profitable start-up from Hastings, giving him the opportunity and the capital to pursue his riskiest venture yet—Netflix. Hastings came up with the idea after he racked up a $40 late fee at a video rental store for a VHS copy of *Apollo 13*. "I had misplaced the cassette," said Hastings. "I didn't want to tell my wife about it. And I said to myself, 'I'm going to compromise the integrity of my marriage over a late fee?'" Netflix's concept connected with consumers quickly: for a monthly fee they could receive and return DVDs through the mail with no risk of late fees.

Despite its success, Hastings saw limits to the DVD-mailing game. He knew the instant access offered by streaming video would eventually put him out of business. "Back when we were just mailing DVDs, we were thinking, 'Can we be ready for the transformation to streaming?'" said Hastings. "'Can we know our subscribers well enough to show them what they want?'" So he and his team worked tirelessly to acquire TV and film licenses while also developing technology to stream video on a mass scale. Netflix rolled out its streaming service in the late 2000s to great interest, attracting millions of subscribers within a few years. However, Hastings made a mistake in 2011 when he tried to spin off Netflix's DVD-mailing into an entirely different company called Qwikster. He backed down following a customer revolt, but the brand suffered for months. But with original, critically acclaimed programs like *House of Cards* now streaming on Netflix, there's no doubt that Hastings has changed the ways many people enjoy entertainment.

The four Ps of marketing are product, place, promotion, and price. This chapter is all about place. The place function goes by many other names as well, including shipping, warehousing, distribution, logistics, and supply-chain management. We'll explore all these concepts in this chapter. At the end, you will have a much better understanding of the many steps required to get products from the producer to the consumer.

Sources: Michael J. de la Merced, "Netflix Says It Opposes Comcast's Merge Bid," *The New York Times*, April 21, 2014; Amy Zipkin, "Out of Africa, Onto the Web," *The New York Times*, December 17, 2006; Nancy Hass, "And the Award for the Next HBO Goes to . . ." *GQ*, February 2013; Kevin Spacey, "The 2011 Time 100: Reed Hastings," *Time*, April 21, 2011; and Ashlee Vance, "Netflix, Reed Hastings Survive Missteps to Join Silicon Valley's Elite," *Bloomberg Businessweek*, May 9, 2013.

Reed Hastings

- CEO of Netflix
- Transformed Netflix from DVD delivery service to king of streaming video

www.netflix.com

@netflix

name that **company**

This U.S. company is known for having low prices all the time. One way it keeps prices low is by eliminating as many wholesalers as possible and doing the wholesale function itself. Name that company? (Find the answer in this chapter.)

marketing intermediaries
Organizations that assist in moving goods and services from producers to businesses (B2B) and from businesses to consumers (B2C).

channel of distribution
A whole set of marketing intermediaries, such as agents, brokers, wholesalers, and retailers, that join together to transport and store goods in their path (or channel) from producers to consumers.

agents/brokers
Marketing intermediaries who bring buyers and sellers together and assist in negotiating an exchange but don't take title to the goods.

Distribution warehouses, such as Amazon's distribution center in Phoenix, Arizona, store goods until they are needed. Have you ever thought about the benefits of having food, furniture, clothing, and other needed goods close at hand?

LO 15–1 Explain the concept of marketing channels and their value.

THE EMERGENCE OF MARKETING INTERMEDIARIES

It's easy to overlook distribution and storage in marketing, where the focus is often on advertising, selling, marketing research, and other functions. But it doesn't take much to realize how important distribution is. Imagine the challenge Timberland faces of getting raw materials together, making millions of pairs of shoes, and then distributing those shoes to stores throughout the world. That's what thousands of manufacturing firms—making everything from automobiles to furniture and toys—have to deal with every day.[1] Imagine further that there has been a major volcano eruption or tsunami that has caused a disruption in the supply of goods. Such issues are commonplace for distribution managers.[2]

Fortunately there are hundreds of thousands of companies and individuals whose job it is to help move goods from the raw-material state to producers, and then on to consumers. Then, as is often the case, the products are sent from consumers to recyclers and back to manufacturers or assemblers.[3] Did you know that 75 percent of the waste in the U.S. is recyclable, but only 30 percent of it makes into the recycling system?[4] See the Seeking Sustainability box for more on sustainability and the distribution process.

Managing the flow of goods has become one of the most important managerial functions for many organizations. Let's look at how this function is carried out.

Marketing intermediaries (once called *middlemen*) are organizations that assist in moving goods and services from producers to businesses (B2B) and from businesses to consumers (B2C). They're called intermediaries because they're in the middle of a series of organizations that join together to help distribute goods from producers to consumers. A **channel of distribution** consists of a whole set of marketing intermediaries, such as agents, brokers, wholesalers, and retailers, that join together to transport and store goods in their path (or channel) from producers to consumers. **Agents/brokers** are marketing intermediaries who bring buyers and sellers together and assist in negotiating an exchange but don't take title to the goods—that is, at no point do they own the goods. Think of real estate agents as an example.

A **wholesaler** is a marketing intermediary that sells to other organizations, such as retailers, manufacturers, and hospitals.[5] Wholesalers are part of the B2B system. Because of high distribution

Answer May Be Blowing in the Wind

When IKEA, the world's largest furniture and home-furnishings retailer, introduced its "People and Planet Positive" program, it pledged to do its part to take care of the environment. The company's recent Sustainability Report shows that it is keeping that pledge.

One example is the wind-energy investment the company is making in the United States. IKEA recently announced to a congressional task force on climate change that it plans to construct a wind farm in Illinois with 49 wind turbines that will generate enough electricity for 34,000 homes. Interestingly, the wind farm will not supply any energy to IKEA's 38 stores in North America. It's part of the company's goal to be energy neutral—that is, not using any more energy at its stores than it's able to produce.

Its interest in renewable energy sources is only one example of IKEA's sustainability efforts. The company continuously focuses on how it uses resources and ways to make better use of them. For example, in the shipping world, almost everything ends up stacked on a wooden pallet. After years of research, IKEA developed a type of pallet that's lighter and cheaper than its wooden equivalent. Made of paper, the pallet is 90 percent lighter than wood and weighs just five and a half pounds. Still, IKEA officials aren't satisfied and are already at work seeking a better alternative than paper. Chief Sustainability Officer Steve Howard makes it clear that sustainability will be a decisive factor in determining which businesses will still be here 30 years from now. IKEA is committed to "future proofing" the company and being around in the 2040s and beyond.

Sources: Julie Wernau, "IKEA Invests in Wind Farm in Illinois," *Chicago Tribune*, April 11, 2014; Peter Kelly-Detweiler, "IKEA's Aggressive Approach to Sustainability Creates Enormous Business Opportunities," *Forbes*, February 7, 2014; and Andria Cheng, "IKEA Assembles a Sustainability Program," *The Wall Street Journal*, April 15, 2014.

costs, Walmart has been trying to eliminate independent wholesalers from its system and do the job itself. That is, Walmart provides its own warehouses and has its own trucks. It has over 120 distribution centers and 53,000 trailers to distribute goods to its stores. Finally, a **retailer** is an organization that sells to ultimate consumers (people like you and me).

Channels of distribution help ensure communication flows *and* the flow of money and title to goods. They also help ensure that the right quantity and assortment of goods will be available when and where needed. Figure 15.1 shows selected channels of distribution for both consumer and industrial goods.

You can see the distribution system in the United States at work when you drive down any highway and see the thousands of trucks and trains moving goods from here to there. Less visible, however, are the many distribution warehouses that store goods until they are needed. Have you ever thought about the benefits of having food, furniture, and other needed goods close at hand? Have you seen distribution warehouses along the road as you drive from town to town?

Why Marketing Needs Intermediaries

Figure 15.1 shows that some manufacturers sell directly to consumers. So why have marketing intermediaries at all? The answer is that intermediaries perform certain marketing tasks—such as transporting, storing, selling, advertising, and relationship building—faster and more cheaply than most manufacturers could. Here's a simple analogy: You could personally deliver packages to people anywhere in the world, but usually you don't. Why not? Because it's generally cheaper and faster to have them delivered by the U.S. Postal Service or a private firm such as UPS.

Similarly, you could sell your home by yourself or buy stock directly from individual companies, but you probably wouldn't. Why? Again, because agents

wholesaler
A marketing intermediary that sells to other organizations.

retailer
An organization that sells to ultimate consumers.

FIGURE 15.1 SELECTED CHANNELS OF DISTRIBUTION FOR CONSUMER AND INDUSTRIAL GOODS AND SERVICES

Channels for consumer goods						Channels for industrial goods	
This channel is used by craftspeople and small farmers.	This channel is used for cars, furniture, and clothing.	This channel is the most common channel for consumer goods such as groceries, drugs, and cosmetics.	This is a common channel for food items such as produce.	This is a common channel for consumer services such as real estate, stocks and bonds, insurance, and nonprofit theater groups.	This is a common channel for nonprofit organizations that want to raise funds. Included are museums, government services, and zoos.	This is the common channel for industrial products such as glass, tires, and paint for automobiles.	This is the way that lower-cost items such as supplies are distributed. The wholesaler is called an industrial distributor.

and brokers are marketing intermediaries who make the exchange process easier and more efficient and profitable. In the next section, we'll explore how intermediaries improve the efficiency of various exchanges.

How Intermediaries Create Exchange Efficiency

Here is an easy way to see the benefits of using marketing intermediaries. Suppose five manufacturers of various food products each tried to sell directly to five retailers. The number of exchange relationships needed to create this market is 5 times 5, or 25.

But picture what happens when a wholesaler enters the system. The five manufacturers each contact the wholesaler, establishing five exchange relationships. The wholesaler then establishes contact with the five retailers, creating five more exchange relationships. The wholesaler's existence reduces the number of exchanges from 25 to only 10. Figure 15.2 shows this process.

Some economists have said that intermediaries add *costs* and should be eliminated. Marketers say intermediaries add *value,* and that the *value greatly exceeds the cost.* Let's explore this debate and see what value intermediaries provide.

The Value versus the Cost of Intermediaries

The public has often viewed marketing intermediaries with a degree of suspicion. Some surveys show about half the cost of what we buy is marketing costs that go largely to pay for the work of intermediaries. If we could only get rid of intermediaries, people reason, we could greatly reduce the cost of everything we buy. Sounds good, but is the solution really that simple?

Take a box of cereal that sells for $4. How could we, as consumers, get the cereal for less? Well, we could all drive to Michigan, where some cereal is produced, and save shipping costs. But imagine millions of people getting in their cars and driving to Michigan just to buy cereal. No, it doesn't make sense. It's much cheaper to have intermediaries bring the cereal to major cities. That might make transportation and warehousing by wholesalers necessary. These steps add cost, don't they? Yes, but they add value as well—the value of not having to drive to Michigan.

The cereal is now in a warehouse somewhere on the outskirts of the city. We could all drive down to the wholesaler and pick it up. But that still isn't the most economical way to buy cereal. If we figure in the cost of gas and time, the cereal will again be too expensive. Instead, we prefer to have someone move the cereal from the warehouse to a truck, drive it to the corner supermarket, unload it, unpack it, price it, shelve it, and wait for us to come in to

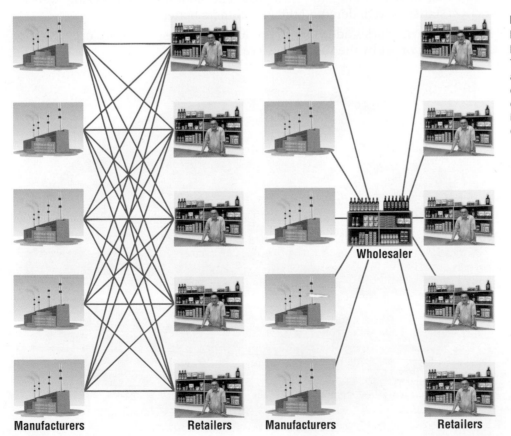

FIGURE 15.2 HOW INTERMEDIARIES CREATE EXCHANGE EFFICIENCY
This figure shows that adding a wholesaler to the channel of distribution cuts the number of contacts from 25 to 10. This improves the efficiency of distribution.

Manufacturers   **Retailers**   **Manufacturers**   **Retailers**

buy it. To make it even more convenient, the supermarket may stay open for 24 hours a day, seven days a week. Think of the costs. But think also of the value! For $4, we can get a box of cereal *when* we want it, and with little effort.

If we were to get rid of the retailer, we could buy a box of cereal for slightly less, but we'd have to drive farther and spend time in the warehouse looking through rows of cereals. If we got rid of the wholesaler, we could save a little more money, not counting our drive to Michigan. But a few cents here and there add up—to the point where distribution (marketing) may add up to 75 cents for every 25 cents in manufacturing costs. Figure 15.3 shows where your money goes in the distribution process. The largest percentage goes to people who drive trucks and work in wholesale and retail organizations. Note that only 3.5 cents goes to profit.

Here are three basic points about intermediaries:

1. Marketing intermediaries can be eliminated, but their activities can't; that is, you can eliminate some wholesalers and retailers, but then consumers or someone else would have to perform the intermediaries' tasks, including transporting and storing goods, finding suppliers, and establishing communication with suppliers. Not all organizations use all the intermediaries. Ringling Barnum and Bailey Circus, for example, have their own train. They need such a train because they have to move 120 human performers, about 60 animals, and a crew of over 100 people. The train is more than a mile long.[6] That doesn't mean that the circus doesn't use intermediaries, such as retailers; it just means that some intermediary functions can be done in-house.

2. Intermediary organizations have survived because they perform marketing functions faster and more cheaply than others can. To maintain their competitive position in the channel, they now must adopt the latest technology. That includes search engine optimization, social networking (on sites like Facebook), and analyzing website statistics to understand their customers better.

3. Intermediaries add costs to products, but these costs are usually more than offset by the values they create.

FIGURE 15.3
DISTRIBUTION'S EFFECT ON YOUR FOOD DOLLAR
Note that the farmer gets only 25 cents of your food dollar. The bulk of your money goes to intermediaries to pay distribution costs. Their biggest cost is labor (truck drivers, clerks), followed by warehouses and storage.

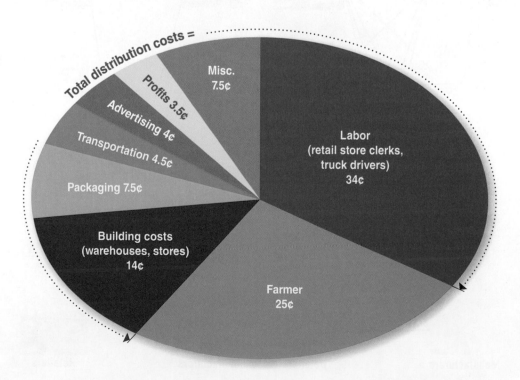

LO 15–2   Demonstrate how intermediaries perform the six marketing utilities.

THE UTILITIES CREATED BY INTERMEDIARIES

Utility, in economics, is the want-satisfying ability, or value, that organizations add to goods or services by making them more useful or accessible to consumers than they were before. The six kinds of utility are form, time, place, possession, information, and service. Although producers provide some utilities, marketing intermediaries provide most. Let's look at how.

Form Utility

Traditionally, producers rather than intermediaries have provided form utility (see Chapter 9) by changing raw materials into useful products. Thus, a farmer who separates the wheat from the chaff and the processor who turns the wheat into flour are creating form utility. Retailers and other marketers sometimes provide form utility as well. For example, retail butchers cut pork chops from a larger piece of meat and trim off the fat. The baristas at Starbucks make coffee just the way you want it.

Time Utility

Intermediaries, such as retailers, add **time utility** to products by making them available when consumers need them. Devar Tennent lives in Boston. One winter evening while watching TV with his brother, Tennent suddenly got the urge for a hot dog and a Coke. The problem was there were no hot dogs or Cokes in the house.

Devar ran down to the corner delicatessen and bought some hot dogs, buns, Cokes, and potato chips. He also bought some frozen strawberries and ice cream. Devar was able to get these groceries at midnight because the local deli was open 24 hours a day. That's time utility. You can buy goods at any time on the Internet, but you can't beat having them available right around the corner *when you want them*. On the other hand, note the value an Internet company provides by staying accessible 24 hours a day.

Place Utility

Intermediaries add **place utility** to products by placing them *where* people want them. While traveling through the badlands of South Dakota, Juanita Ruiz got hungry and thirsty. There are no stores for miles in this part of the country, but Juanita saw signs along the road saying a 7-Eleven was ahead. Following the signs, she stopped at the store for refreshments. She also bought some sunglasses and souvenir items there. The goods and services provided by 7-Eleven are in a convenient place for vacationers.

Throughout the United States, 7-Eleven stores remain popular because they are usually in easy-to-reach locations. They provide place utility. As more and more sales become global, place utility will grow in importance. Grocery stores are now adding pickup services, so that customers can order online and then pick up their food at a convenient time and place. This is just one more example of place utility.[7]

utility
In economics, the want-satisfying ability, or value, that organizations add to goods or services.

time utility
Adding value to products by making them available when they're needed.

place utility
Adding value to products by having them where people want them.

Think of how many stores provide time utility by making goods and services available to you 24 hours a day, seven days a week. Have you ever needed to renew a prescription late at night or needed a late-night snack? Can you see how time utility offers added value?

Service after the sale is one of the contributing factors to Apple's success. Customers can call to make an appointment with an Apple Genius who will help them learn how to use their computers, iPhones, or iPads. How does this service add value to Apple's products?

possession utility
Doing whatever is necessary to transfer ownership from one party to another, including providing credit, delivery, installation, guarantees, and follow-up service.

information utility
Adding value to products by opening two-way flows of information between marketing participants.

service utility
Adding value by providing fast, friendly service during and after the sale and by teaching customers how to best use products over time.

Possession Utility

Intermediaries add **possession utility** by doing whatever is necessary to transfer ownership from one party to another, including providing credit. Activities associated with possession utility include delivery, installation, guarantees, and follow-up service. Larry Rosenberg wanted to buy a nice home in the suburbs. He found just what he wanted, but he didn't have the money he needed. So he went with the real estate broker to a local savings and loan and borrowed money to buy the home. Both the real estate broker and the savings and loan are marketing intermediaries that provide possession utility. For those who don't want to own goods, possession utility makes it possible for them to use goods through renting or leasing.

Information Utility

Intermediaries add **information utility** by opening two-way flows of information between marketing participants. Jerome Washington couldn't decide what kind of TV set to buy. He looked at various ads in the newspaper, talked to salespeople at several stores, read material at the library and on the Internet, and tweeted his friends. Newspapers, salespeople, libraries, websites, and government publications are all information sources made available by intermediaries. They provide information utility.

Service Utility

Intermediaries add **service utility** by providing fast, friendly service during and after the sale and by teaching customers how to best use products over time. Sze Leung bought a Mac from Apple for his home office. The Apple store Leung used continues to offer help whenever he needs it. He also gets software updates to keep his computer up-to-date. What attracted Leung to Apple in the first place was the helpful, friendly service he received from the salesperson in the store and the service from the techies at the Genius Bar. Service utility is rapidly becoming the most important utility for many retailers, because without it they would lose business to direct marketing (e.g., marketing by catalog or online). Can you see how the Internet can provide some forms of service utility?

test **prep**

- What is a channel of distribution, and what intermediaries participate in it?
- Why do we need intermediaries? Illustrate how intermediaries create exchange efficiency.
- How would you defend intermediaries to someone who said getting rid of them would save consumers millions of dollars?
- Can you give examples of the utilities intermediaries create and how they provide them?

LO 15–3   Identify the types of wholesale intermediaries in the distribution system.

WHOLESALE INTERMEDIARIES

Let's stop for a minute and distinguish wholesaling from retailing and clearly define the functions of each. Some producers deal only with wholesalers and won't sell directly to retailers or to end users (consumers). Some producers deal with both wholesalers and retailers, but give wholesalers a bigger discount. In turn, some wholesalers sell to both retailers and consumers. The office superstore Staples is a good example. It sells office supplies to small businesses and to consumers as well. Warehouse clubs such as Sam's Club and Costco are other companies with both wholesale and retail functions.

The difference is this: A *retail sale* is the sale of goods and services to consumers *for their own use.* A *wholesale sale* is the sale of goods and services to businesses and institutions, like schools or hospitals, *for use in the business,* or to wholesalers or retailers *for resale.*

Wholesalers make business-to-business sales. Most people are not as familiar with the various kinds of wholesalers as they are with retailers. So, let's explore some of these helpful wholesale intermediaries. Most of them provide a lot of marketing jobs and offer you a good opportunity.

Merchant Wholesalers

Merchant wholesalers are independently owned firms that take title to the goods they handle. About 80 percent of wholesalers fall in this category. There are two types of merchant wholesalers: full-service and limited-function. *Full-service wholesalers* perform all the distribution functions (see Figure 15.4). *Limited-function wholesalers* perform only selected functions, but try to do them especially well. Three common types of limited-function wholesalers are rack jobbers, cash-and-carry wholesalers, and drop shippers.

merchant wholesalers
Independently owned firms that take title to the goods they handle.

FIGURE 15.4 A FULL-SERVICE WHOLESALER

A FULL-SERVICE WHOLESALER WILL:	THE WHOLESALER MAY PERFORM THE FOLLOWING SERVICES FOR CUSTOMERS:
1. Provide a sales force to sell the goods to retailers and other buyers.	1. Buy goods the end market will desire and make them available to customers.
2. Communicate manufacturers' advertising deals and plans.	2. Maintain inventory, thus reducing customers' costs.
3. Maintain inventory, thus reducing the level of the inventory suppliers have to carry.	3. Transport goods to customers quickly.
4. Arrange or undertake transportation.	4. Provide market information and business consulting services.
5. Provide capital by paying cash or making quick payments for goods.	5. Provide financing through granting credit, which is especially critical to small retailers.
6. Provide suppliers with market information they can't afford or can't obtain themselves.	6. Order goods in the types and quantities customers desire.
7. Undertake credit risk by granting credit to customers and absorbing any bad debts, thus relieving the supplier of this burden.	
8. Assume the risk for the product by taking title.	

Source: Thomas C. Kinnear, *Principles of Marketing,* 4th ed., © 1995, p. 394. Reprinted by permission of Pearson Education, Inc., Upper Saddle River, NJ.

rack jobbers
Wholesalers that furnish racks or shelves full of merchandise to retailers, display products, and sell on consignment.

cash-and-carry wholesalers
Wholesalers that serve mostly smaller retailers with a limited assortment of products.

drop shippers
Wholesalers that solicit orders from retailers and other wholesalers and have the merchandise shipped directly from a producer to a buyer.

Rack jobbers furnish racks or shelves full of merchandise, like music, toys, hosiery, and health and beauty aids, to retailers. They display the products and sell them on consignment, meaning they keep title to the goods until they're sold and then share the profits with the retailer. Have you seen shelves at the supermarket full of magazines and related items? Rack jobbers likely put them there.

Cash-and-carry wholesalers serve mostly smaller retailers with a limited assortment of products. Traditionally, retailers went to such wholesalers, paid cash, and carried the goods back to their stores—thus the term *cash-and-carry*. Today, stores such as Staples allow retailers and others to use credit cards for wholesale purchases. Thus the term *cash-and-carry* is becoming obsolete for wholesalers.

Drop shippers solicit orders from retailers and other wholesalers and have the merchandise shipped directly from a producer to a buyer. They own the merchandise but don't handle, stock, or deliver it. That's done by the producer. Drop shippers tend to handle bulky products such as coal, lumber, and chemicals.

Agents and Brokers

Agents and brokers bring buyers and sellers together and assist in negotiating an exchange. However, unlike merchant wholesalers, agents and brokers never own the products they distribute. Usually they do not carry inventory, provide credit, or assume risks. While merchant wholesalers earn a profit from the sale of goods, agents and brokers earn commissions or fees based on a percentage of the sales revenues. Agents often maintain long-term relationships with the people they represent, whereas brokers are usually hired on a temporary basis.

Agents who represent producers are either *manufacturer's agents* or *sales agents*. As long as they do not carry competing products, manufacturer's agents may represent several manufacturers in a specific territory. They often work in the automotive supply, footwear, and fabricated steel industries. Sales agents represent a single producer in a typically larger territory.

Brokers have no continuous relationship with the buyer or seller. Once they negotiate a contract between the parties, their relationship ends. Producers of seasonal products like fruits and vegetables often use brokers, as does the real estate industry.

Agents and brokers are a familiar type of intermediary. Typically they don't take possession of the goods they sell. A real estate broker, for instance, facilitates the transaction between seller and buyer but never holds title to the house. What functions does a realtor provide in a home sale?

 LO 15–4   Compare the distribution strategies retailers use.

RETAIL INTERMEDIARIES

A retailer, remember, is a marketing intermediary, like a supermarket, that sells to ultimate consumers. The United States boasts more than 2 million retail stores, not including retail websites. Retail organizations employ more than 5 million people and are one of the major employers of marketing graduates.[8] The recent recession has affected retailers, forcing many to cut back on employees. No doubt you're aware of the intense competition between retail stores

FIGURE 15.5 TYPES OF RETAIL STORES

TYPE	DESCRIPTION	EXAMPLE
Department store	Sells a wide variety of products (clothes, furniture, housewares) in separate departments	Sears, JCPenney, Nordstrom
Discount store	Sells many different products at prices generally below those of department stores	Walmart, Target
Supermarket	Sells mostly food with other nonfood products such as detergent and paper products	Safeway, Kroger, Albertson's
Warehouse club	Sells food and general merchandise in facilities that are usually larger than supermarkets and offer discount prices; membership may be required	Costco, Sam's Club
Convenience store	Sells food and other often-needed items at convenient locations; may stay open all night	7-Eleven
Category killer	Sells a huge variety of one type of product to dominate that category of goods	Toys "R" Us, Bass Pro Shops, Office Depot
Outlet store	Sells general merchandise directly from the manufacturer at a discount; items may be discontinued or have flaws ("seconds")	Nordstrom Rack, Liz Claiborne, Nike, TJ Maxx
Specialty store	Sells a wide selection of goods in one category	Jewelry stores, shoe stores, bicycle shops

and Amazon. Retail stores are fighting back, but some say that Amazon will win in the end.[9] If so, what effect will Amazon's success have on the number of retail jobs?

Figure 15.5 lists, describes, and gives examples of various kinds of retailers. Have you shopped in each kind of store? What seem to be the advantages of each? Would you enjoy working in a retail store of some kind? Some retailers seem to compete mostly on price, but others, such as specialty stores, use variety as a competitive tool. The Adapting to Change box describes how mobile food services compete using place and social media. Marketers use several strategies for retail distribution. We explain them next.

Retail Distribution Strategy

Because different products call for different retail distribution strategies, a major decision marketers must make is selecting the right retailers to sell their products. There are three categories of retail distribution: intensive, selective, and exclusive.

Intensive distribution puts products into as many retail outlets as possible, including vending machines. Products that need intensive distribution include convenience goods such as candy, gum, and popular magazines.

Selective distribution uses only a preferred group of the available retailers in an area. Such selection helps ensure producers of quality sales and service. Manufacturers of appliances, furniture, and clothing (shopping goods) use selective distribution.

Exclusive distribution is the use of only one retail outlet in a given geographic area. The retailer has exclusive rights to sell the product and is therefore likely to carry a large inventory, give exceptional service, and pay more attention to this brand than to others. Luxury auto manufacturers often use exclusive distribution, as do producers of specialty goods such as skydiving equipment.

intensive distribution
Distribution that puts products into as many retail outlets as possible.

selective distribution
Distribution that sends products to only a preferred group of retailers in an area.

exclusive distribution
Distribution that sends products to only one retail outlet in a given geographic area.

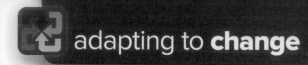

adapting to change

Truckin' On with Social Media

It's a typical hectic lunch hour in New York City, and people of all ages are lined up for one of the city's favorite lunch fares. You're probably thinking the eager diners are waiting for a table at one of New York's famous restaurants like Delmonico's. You might be surprised to learn the line is for Korilla BBQ food truck's Korean-style burritos. The worker's pace at Korilla's is constant until the word goes out "That's a wrap" meaning the truck is sold out. As the truck makes its exit, Korilla's chef pulls out his iPhone and sends a tweet to the truck's 22,000 followers: Korilla @116th & Amsterdam open for dinner at 5:00 p.m.

The food truck craze swept cities like New York just about the same time that Twitter and

Facebook began their market surge. Food truck vendors now use Twitter and other social media to reveal their current locations and build customer relationships. Special food truck app TruxMap Lite is active in 24 U.S. cities and tells you exactly where gourmet trucks nearest to you are. In other instances, customers who enjoy the thrill of the chase use social media to track their favorite food trucks as they move about the city.

Today, the over 3 million food trucks cruising around the United States have also advanced from the days of strictly hawking hot dogs and other traditional foods. Ambitious young chefs prepare cuisine such as specialty crepes, kimchi pork fries, osso bucco, French rotisserie RoliRoti, Vietnamese banh mi and Gruyère grilled cheese. If you haven't already done so, take a look online for a food truck near you. Say, how about a Very Vegetarian truck?

Sources: Kim LaChance Shandrow, "Lunch Seekers: 3 Free Apps to Help You Locate Gourmet Food Trucks," *Entrepreneur*, February 27, 2014; Jane Seo, "The New Cool Kid on the Block: How Food Trucks Evolved From Roach Coaches to Cultural Phenomena," *Huffington Post*, August 8, 2013; and Karsten Strauss, "Food Trucks: 25 of the Coolest," *Forbes*, November 18, 2013.

test prep

- Describe the activities of rack jobbers and drop shippers.
- What kinds of products would call for each of the different distribution strategies: intensive, selective, and exclusive?

LO 15–5   Explain the various kinds of nonstore retailing.

NONSTORE RETAILING

Nothing else in retailing has received more attention recently than electronic retailing. Internet retailing (e.g., Amazon) is just one form of nonstore retailing. Other categories include telemarketing; vending machines, kiosks, and carts; direct selling; multilevel marketing; and direct marketing. Small businesses can use nonstore retailing to open up new channels of distribution for their products.

Electronic Retailing

electronic retailing
Selling goods and services to ultimate customers (e.g., you and me) over the Internet.

social commerce
A form of electronic commerce that involves using social media, online media that supports social interaction, and user contributions to assist in the online buying and selling of products and services.

Electronic retailing consists of selling goods and services to ultimate consumers online. **Social commerce** is a form of electronic commerce that involves using social media, online media that supports social interaction, and user contributions to assist in the online buying and sell-ing of products and services (see Figure 15.6 for a list of different types of social commerce).

Thanks to website improvements and discounting, online retail sales have risen dramatically over the last few years.[10] But getting customers is only half the battle. The other half is delivering the goods, providing helpful service, and keeping your customers. When electronic retailers lack sufficient inventory or fail to deliver goods on time (especially at holidays and other busy periods), customers often give up and go back to brick-and-mortar stores.

Most online retailers offer e-mail order confirmation. But sometimes they are not as good as stores at handling complaints, accepting returns, and pro-viding personal help. Some online sellers are improving customer service by adding help buttons that lead customers to real-time online assistance from a human employee.

Old brick-and-mortar stores that add online outlets are sometimes called brick-and-click stores. They allow customers to choose which shopping tech-nique suits them best. Most companies that want to compete in the future will probably need both a real store and an online presence to provide consumers with all the options they want.

Traditional retailers like Sears have learned that selling online calls for a new kind of distribution. Sears's warehouses were accustomed to deliver-ing truckloads of goods to the company's retail outlets. But they were not prepared to deliver to individual consumers, except for large orders like fur-niture and appliances. It turns out, therefore, that both traditional and online retailers have to develop new distribution systems to meet the demands of today's Internet-savvy shoppers. It's often easy to sell goods and services on eBay, but there is always the need to distribute those goods. Most people outsource that function to FedEx or UPS, which have the needed expertise.

FIGURE 15.6 TYPES OF SOCIAL COMMERCE

Social commerce denotes a wide range of shopping, recommending, and selling behaviors. As these models are tested and proven to increase sales and customer satisfaction, more will be introduced.

1. **Peer-to-peer sales platforms** (eBay, Etsy, Amazon Marketplace): Community-based marketplaces, or bazaars, where individuals communicate and sell directly to other individuals.

2. **Social network–driven sales** (Facebook, Pinterest, Twitter): Sales driven by refer-rals from established social networks.

3. **Group buying** (Groupon, LivingSocial): Products and services offered at a reduced rate.

4. **Peer recommendations** (Amazon, Yelp, JustBoughtIt): Sites that aggregate prod-uct or service reviews, recommend products based on others' purchasing history.

5. **User-curated shopping** (The Fancy, Lyst, Svpply): Shopping-focused sites where users create and share lists of products and services where others can shop.

6. **Participatory commerce** (Threadless, Kickstarter, CutOnYourBias): Consumers become involved directly in the production process through voting, funding and collaboratively designing products.

7. **Social shopping** (Motilo, Fashism, GoTryItOn): Sites that attempt to replicate shop-ping offline with friends by including chat and forum features for exchanging advice and opinions.

Source: Lauren Indvik, "The Seven Species of Social Commerce," *Mashable*, www.mashable.com, accessed April 2014.

Telemarketing

Telemarketing is the sale of goods and services by telephone. Many companies use it to supplement or replace in-store selling and complement online selling. Many send a catalog to consumers, who order by calling a toll-free number. Many electronic retailers provide a help feature online that serves the same function.

Vending Machines, Kiosks, and Carts

Vending machines dispense convenience goods when consumers deposit sufficient money. They carry the benefit of location—they're found in airports, office buildings, schools, service stations, and other areas where people want convenience items. In Japan, they sell everything from bandages and face cloths to salads and spiced seafood. Vending by machine will be an interesting area to watch as more innovations are introduced in the United States. U.S. vending machines are already selling iPods, Bose headphones, sneakers, digital cameras, and DVD movies. You can even find earthworms or Chardonnay in some vending machines. An ATM in Abu Dhabi dispenses gold.

Carts and kiosks have lower overhead costs than stores do, so they can offer lower prices on items such as T-shirts, purses, watches, and cell phones. You often see vending carts outside stores or along walkways in malls. Some mall owners love them because they're colorful and create a marketplace atmosphere. Kiosk workers often dispense coupons and helpful product information. You may have noticed airlines are using kiosks to speed the process of getting on the plane. Most provide a boarding pass and allow you to change your seat. Many kiosks serve as gateways to the Internet, so in one place consumers can shop at a store and still have access to all the products available on the Internet. What's your reaction to such kiosks?

Direct Selling

Direct selling reaches consumers in their homes or workplaces. Many businesses use direct selling to sell cosmetics, household goods, lingerie, artwork, and candles at house parties they sponsor. Because so many men and women work outside the home and aren't in during the day, companies that use direct selling are sponsoring parties at workplaces or at home on evenings and weekends. Some companies, however, such as those in encyclopedia sales, have dropped most of their direct selling efforts in favor of online selling.

Would you like a pizzeria that never closes? Let's Pizza vending machines bake fresh pizza from scratch in less than three minutes 24/7. The process starts as soon as a customer inserts payment and chooses from the four varieties available. The machine mixes the flour and water, kneads the dough, rolls it out, adds the toppings and bakes while you watch. To see it in action, just do a YouTube search.

Multilevel Marketing

Many companies have had success using multilevel marketing (MLM) and salespeople who work as independent contractors. Some of the best known MLM companies include Avon, Amway, and Herbalife.[11] Salespeople earn commissions on their own sales, create commissions for the "upliners" who recruited them, and receive commissions from any "downliners" they recruit to sell. When you have hundreds of downliners—people recruited by the people you recruit—your commissions can be sizable. Some people make tens of thousands of dollars a month this way. The main attraction of multilevel marketing for employees, other than the potential for making money, is the low cost of entry. For a small investment, the average person can get started and begin recruiting others.

That doesn't mean you should get involved with such schemes. Many people question MLM because some companies using it have acted unethically. More often than not, people at the bottom buy the products themselves and sell a bare minimum, if anything, to others. In other words, be careful of multilevel schemes as a seller and as a buyer. But do not dismiss them out of hand, because some are successful. Potential employees must be very careful to examine the practices of such firms.

Direct Marketing

Direct marketing includes any activity that directly links manufacturers or intermediaries with the ultimate consumer. It includes direct mail, catalog sales, and telemarketing as well as online marketing. Popular consumer catalog companies that use direct marketing include L.L.Bean and Lands' End. Direct marketing has created tremendous competition in some high-tech areas as well.

Direct marketing has become popular because shopping from home or work is more convenient for consumers than going to stores. Instead of driving to a mall, people can shop online. Or they can browse catalogs and advertising supplements in the newspaper and magazines and then buy by phone, mail, or online. Interactive online selling provides increasing competition for retail stores. For example, L.L.Bean put pressure on rivals by eliminating shipping charges. That made L.L.Bean even more attractive to people who like to shop by catalog or online.

Direct marketing took on a new dimension with interactive video. Companies that use interactive video have become major competitors for those who market through static paper catalogs. For example, customers watching a video of a model moving and turning around in a dress get a much better idea of the look and feel of the outfit than simply seeing it in a printed photo.

To offer consumers the maximum benefit, marketing intermediaries must work together to ensure a smooth flow of goods and services. There hasn't always been total harmony in the channel of distribution. As a result, channel members have created systems to make the flows more efficient. We'll discuss those next.

direct marketing
Any activity that directly links manufacturers or intermediaries with the ultimate consumer.

LO 15–6   Explain the various ways to build cooperation in channel systems.

BUILDING COOPERATION IN CHANNEL SYSTEMS

One way traditional retailers can compete with online retailers is to be so efficient that online retailers can't beat them on cost—given the need for customers to pay for delivery. That means manufacturers, wholesalers, and retailers must work closely to form a unified system. How can manufacturers get wholesalers and retailers to cooperate in such a system? One way is to link the firms in a formal relationship. Four systems have emerged to tie firms together: corporate systems, contractual systems, administered systems, and supply chains.

Corporate Distribution Systems

In a **corporate distribution system** one firm owns all the organizations in the channel of distribution. If the manufacturer owns the retail firm, clearly it can maintain a great deal of control over its operations. Sherwin Williams, for example, owns its own retail stores and coordinates everything: display, pricing, promotion, inventory control, and so on.

Contractual Distribution Systems

If a manufacturer can't buy retail stores, it can try to get retailers to sign a contract to cooperate with it. In a **contractual distribution system** members are bound to cooperate through contractual agreements. There are three forms of contractual systems:

1. *Franchise systems* such as McDonald's, KFC, Baskin-Robbins, and AAMCO. The franchisee agrees to all the rules, regulations, and procedures established by the franchisor. This results in the consistent quality and level of service you find in most franchised organizations.

2. *Wholesaler-sponsored chains* such as Ace Hardware and IGA food stores. Each store signs an agreement to use the same name, participate in chain promotions, and cooperate as a unified system of stores, even though each is independently owned and managed.

3. *Retail cooperatives* such as Associated Grocers. This arrangement is much like a wholesaler-sponsored chain except it is initiated by the retailers. The same degree of cooperation exists, and the stores remain independent. Normally in such a system, retailers agree to focus their purchases on one wholesaler, but cooperative retailers could also purchase a wholesale organization to ensure better service.

Franchisors like Chocolate Chocolate Chocolate Company use a contractual distribution system that requires franchisees to follow the franchisors' rules and procedures. How does such a system ensure consistent quality and level of service?

Administered Distribution Systems

If you were a producer, what would you do if you couldn't get retailers to sign an agreement to cooperate? You might manage all the marketing functions yourself, including display, inventory control, pricing, and promotion. A system in which producers manage all the marketing functions at the retail level is called an **administered distribution system**. Kraft does that for its cheeses. Scott does it for its seed and other lawn care products. Retailers cooperate with producers in such systems because they get a great deal of free help. All the retailer has to do is ring up the sale.

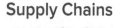

Supply Chains

A **supply chain (or value chain)** consists of all the linked activities various organizations must perform to move goods and services from the sources of raw materials to ultimate consumers. A supply chain is longer than a channel of distribution because it includes links from suppliers to manufacturers, whereas the channel of distribution begins with manufacturers. Channels of distribution are part of the overall supply chain (see Figure 15.7).

FIGURE 15.7 THE SUPPLY CHAIN

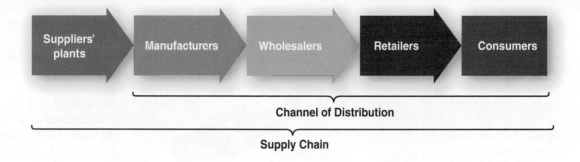

Included in the supply chain are farmers, miners, suppliers of all kinds (parts, equipment, supplies), manufacturers, wholesalers, and retailers. **Supply-chain management** is the process of managing the movement of raw materials, parts, work in progress, finished goods, and related information through all the organizations in the supply chain; managing the return of such goods if necessary; and recycling materials when appropriate.[12] A key issue today is making the supply chain sustainable because so much of what affects the environment is caused by distribution.[13]

One complex supply chain is that for the automaker Kia's Sorento model. The Sorento is assembled in South Korea and made of over 30,000 components from all over the world. The shock and front-loading system is from AF Sachs AG, the front-wheel drive is from BorgWarner, and the tires are from Michelin. Air bags are sometimes flown in from Swedish company Autoliv Inc., which makes them in Utah. As you can see, supply-chain management is interfirm and international.

Companies like SAP, i2, and Oracle have developed software to coordinate the movement of goods and information so that producers can translate consumer wants into products with the least amount of materials, inventory, and time. Firms can move parts and information so smoothly, they look like one firm.[14] Naturally, the software systems are quite complex and expensive, but they can pay for themselves in the long run because of inventory savings, customer service improvement, and responsiveness to market changes. Because such systems are so effective and efficient, they are sometimes called *value chains* instead of supply chains.

Not all supply chains are as efficient as they can be. Some companies have struggled with high distribution costs, including the cost of disruptions, inefficient truck routes, and excess inventory. The complexity of supply-chain management often leads firms to outsource the whole process to experts that know how to integrate it. Imagine a company that does business in 125 countries with 37 different currencies. It may use services such as Oracle's PeopleSoft Supply Chain Management and Financial Management solutions. PeopleSoft provides financial help, making it easier and less expensive to ship goods anywhere in the world and be sure of payment.

Outsourcing supply-chain management is on the rise as more firms realize how complex distribution is. Outsourcing this function can have serious consequences, as companies learned when they found lead paint in toys and contaminants in the drug heparin. The Reaching Beyond Our Borders box discusses how the supply is only as strong as its weakest link.

supply-chain management
The process of managing the movement of raw materials, parts, work in progress, finished goods, and related information through all the organizations involved in the supply chain; managing the return of such goods, if necessary; and recycling materials when appropriate.

Weak Links Can Break a Chain

For companies around the globe, carefully constructed supply chains can cut costs significantly. For example, you can imagine components traveling from Thailand, the Philippines, Malaysia, and Taiwan to a factory in China where they are assembled before being sold as iPhones or iPads in an Apple store in New York. When nothing goes wrong, supply chains can be a smashing success; costs are reduced, supplies uninterrupted, and all is well. But in this imperfect world, anything can happen and sometimes things do go wrong.

Natural disasters can wreak economic havoc on supply chains. Catastrophes like the floods in Thailand in 2013 devastated the region causing billions of dollars in damage. The flooding also resulted in Honda having to cut

the operating hours of its Ohio factory in half when the raging water overwhelmed its overseas suppliers. As Honda and other companies found out, supply chains may be great at keeping overhead low, but those savings could be moot if an unforeseen disaster brings the entire business grinding to a halt.

Managing the integrity of products throughout the entire supply chain is also a major concern. According to the Bureau of

Industry and Security of the U.S. Department of Commerce, counterfeit products are making their way through supply chains across a number of industry sectors. Aston Martin, a British luxury sports carmaker, was forced to recall 5,000 cars because of problems caused by counterfeit throttle pedal arms from China. As you may have guessed, the company is moving manufacturing of the pedal arms back to England.

Businesses must devise ways to make their supply chains more robust and not just more cost effective. Let's hope they spot the weak links before the supply chain breaks.

Sources: Christina Larson, "James Bond's Sports Car Has China Supply Chain Problems," *Bloomberg Businessweek*, February 5, 2014; and Suzanne Kapner and Ben Fox Rubin, "Supply-Chain Problems Dog Lululemon," *The Wall Street Journal*, January 13, 2014.

LO 15–7 Describe logistics and outline how intermediaries manage the transportation and storage of goods.

LOGISTICS: GETTING GOODS TO CONSUMERS EFFICIENTLY

Shipping costs have risen dramatically in recent years. It has been estimated that distribution makes up almost 10 percent of GDP.[15] When shipping from country to country, it is often impossible to use trucks or trains because the goods have to travel over water. Shipping by air is often prohibitively expensive, which sometimes narrows the choice to moving goods by ship. But how do you get the goods to the ship—and from the ship to the buyer? How do you keep costs low enough to make exchanges beneficial for you and your customers?[16] And how do you handle foreign trade duties and taxes? Distributing goods globally is complicated. As transportation and distribution have grown more complex, marketers have responded by developing more sophisticated systems.

To better manage customs problems, for instance, many turn to web-based trade compliance systems. Firms like TradePoint and Xporta determine what paperwork is needed, cross-checking their databases for information about foreign trade duties and taxes, U.S. labor law restrictions, and federal regulations from the Food and Drug Administration or the Bureau of Alcohol, Tobacco, Firearms and Explosives. In other words, they manage logistics.

Logistics is the planning, implementing, and controlling of the physical flow of materials, final goods, and related information from points of origin to points of consumption to meet customer requirements at a profit. Logistics describes how companies perform the 7 Rs: getting the right product to the right place, to the right customer, at the right time, in the right quantity, in the right condition, and at the right price.[17] **Inbound logistics** brings raw materials, packaging, other goods and services, and information from suppliers to producers.

Materials handling is the movement of goods within a warehouse, from warehouses to the factory floor, and from the factory floor to various workstations. *Factory processes* change raw materials and parts and other inputs into outputs, such as finished goods like shoes, cars, and clothes.

Outbound logistics manages the flow of finished products and information to business buyers and ultimately to consumers like you and me. What do you think of Amazon's idea of using drones to deliver goods to your home? Even if the company does follow through, widespread use of delivery drones is probably a long way into the future.[18] **Reverse logistics** brings goods back to the manufacturer because of defects or for recycling materials.[19]

Logistics is as much about the movement of *information* as it is about the movement of goods. Customer wants and needs must flow through the system all the way to suppliers and must do so in real time. Information must also flow down through the system with no delay. That, of course, demands sophisticated hardware and software.

Third-party logistics is the use of outside firms to help move goods from here to there. It is part of the trend to outsource functions your firm cannot do more efficiently than outside firms. The 3PLs (third-party logistics providers) that have superior capability in business intelligence and are proactively sharing that knowledge are the ones who will grow in the future.

How do you get products to people around the world after the sale? What are your options? You could send goods by truck, train, ship, or pipeline. You could use a shipping specialist, such as UPS, FedEx, or the U.S. Postal Service, but often that is expensive, especially for large items. Nonetheless, some of the most sophisticated marketers outsource the distribution process to such specialists. All transportation modes can be evaluated on basic service criteria: cost, speed, dependability, flexibility, frequency, and reach. Figure 15.8 compares the various transportation modes on these criteria.

logistics
The marketing activity that involves planning, implementing, and controlling the physical flow of materials, final goods, and related information from points of origin to points of consumption to meet customer requirements at a profit.

inbound logistics
The area of logistics that involves bringing raw materials, packaging, other goods and services, and information from suppliers to producers.

materials handling
The movement of goods within a warehouse, from warehouses to the factory floor, and from the factory floor to various workstations.

outbound logistics
The area of logistics that involves managing the flow of finished products and information to business buyers and ultimate consumers (people like you and me).

reverse logistics
The area of logistics that involves bringing goods back to the manufacturer because of defects or for recycling materials.

How do you move heavy raw materials like timber from one country to another? This photo shows some of the firms engaged in the logistics process. A trucking firm brings the logs to a dock where huge cranes lift them into the hold of a ship. The ship must be unloaded and the logs put on another truck to travel to a processing plant. Why is managing the logistics process a key to survival in some industries?

FIGURE 15.8 COMPARING TRANSPORTATION MODES

Combining trucks with railroads lowers cost and increases the number of locations reached. The same is true when combining trucks with ships. Combining trucks with airlines speeds goods over long distances and gets them to almost any location.

MODE	COST	SPEED	ON-TIME DEPENDABILITY	FLEXIBILITY HANDLING PRODUCTS	FREQUENCY OF SHIPMENTS	REACH
Railroads	Medium	Slow	Medium	High	Low	High
Trucks	High	Fast	High	Medium	High	Highest
Pipelines	Low	Medium	Highest	Lowest	Highest	Lowest
Ships (water)	Lowest	Slowest	Lowest	Highest	Lowest	Low
Airplanes	Highest	Fastest	Low	Low	Medium	Medium

Trains Are Great for Large Shipments

The largest percentage of goods in the United States (by volume) is shipped by rail.[20] Railroad shipment is best for bulky items such as coal, wheat, automobiles, and heavy equipment; and it is quickly becoming an alternative for transporting oil.[21]

Railroads should continue to hold their own in competition with other modes of transportation.[22] They offer a relatively energy-efficient way to move goods and could experience significant gains if fuel prices climb. This is true in China as well as the United States.[23] Even short-line railroads (those that connect local branches of track to larger lines) will be growing.[24]

A company may not ship enough goods to think of using a railroad. Such smaller manufacturers or marketers can get good rates and service by using a **freight forwarder**, which puts many small shipments together to create a single large one that can be transported cost-effectively by truck or train. Such shipments are known as less-than-carload (LCL) shipments.[25] Some

freight forwarder
An organization that puts many small shipments together to create a single large shipment that can be transported cost-effectively to the final destination.

Railroads carry over a third of all goods shipped within the United States, and are expected to remain a dominant transportation mode. What are some of the advantages of shipping by rail, for both large and small producers?

freight forwarders also offer warehousing, customs assistance, and other services along with pickup and delivery. You can see the benefits of such a company to a smaller seller. A freight forwarder is just one of many distribution specialists that have emerged to help marketers move goods from one place to another.

Trucks Are Good for Small Shipments to Remote Locations

The second-largest surface transportation mode is motor vehicles (trucks and vans). As Figure 15.8 shows, trucks reach more locations than trains and can deliver almost any commodity door-to-door.

You could buy your own truck to make deliveries, but for widespread delivery you can't beat trucking specialists. Like freight forwarders, they have emerged to supply one important marketing function—transporting goods.

When fuel prices rise, trucking companies look for ways to cut costs. The newest measure of transportation from farm to consumer is the *carbon cost*. Some argue that the fewer miles food travels, the better for the environment, but that may not always be true.

Water Transportation Is Inexpensive but Slow

When sending goods overseas, often the least expensive way is by ship. Obviously, ships are slower than ground or air transportation, so water transportation isn't appropriate for goods that need to be delivered quickly. Water transport is local as well as international.[26] If you live near the Mississippi River, you've likely seen towboats hauling as many as 30 barges at a time, with a cargo of up to 45,000 tons. On smaller rivers, towboats can haul about eight barges, carrying up to 20,000 tons—that's the equivalent of four 100-car railroad trains. Add to that Great Lakes shipping, shipping from coast to coast and along the coasts, and international shipments, and water transportation takes on a new dimension as a key transportation mode.

Pipelines Are Fast and Efficient

One transportation mode we don't often observe is pipelines. Pipelines primarily transport water, petroleum, and petroleum products—but a lot more products than you may imagine are shipped by pipelines. For example, coal can be sent by pipeline by first crushing it and mixing it with water. Today, there is a lot of discussion about shipping natural gas by pipeline. Much shale oil is now being shipped by rail, but recent accidents are leading companies to move to pipelines.[27] The battle between railroads and pipelines is going to be a huge one.[28]

Air Transportation Is Fast but Expensive

Today, only a small proportion of shipping goes by air.[29] Nonetheless, air transportation is a critical factor in many industries, carrying everything from small packages to luxury cars and elephants. Its primary benefit is speed. No firms know this better than FedEx and UPS. As just two of several competitors vying for the fast-delivery market, FedEx and UPS have used air transport to expand into global markets.

The air freight industry is starting to focus on global distribution. Emery, now part of UPS, has been an industry pioneer in establishing specialized sales and operations teams aimed at serving the distribution needs of specific industries. KLM Royal Dutch Airlines has cargo/passenger planes that handle high-profit items such as diplomatic pouches and medical supplies. Specializing in such cargo has enabled KLM to compete with FedEx, TNT, and DHL.

Intermodal Shipping

intermodal shipping
The use of multiple modes of transportation to complete a single long-distance movement of freight.

Intermodal shipping uses multiple modes of transportation—highway, air, water, rail—to complete a single long-distance movement of freight. Services that specialize in intermodal shipping are known as intermodal marketing companies.[30] Today, railroads are merging with each other and with other transportation companies to offer intermodal distribution.[31]

Railroads joined with trucking firms to create a shipping process called *piggybacking.* A truck trailer is detached from the cab, loaded onto a railroad flatcar, and taken to a destination where it is offloaded, attached to a truck, and driven to the customer's plant. Sometimes two truck trailers are stacked together to form a 20-foot-high railroad car, called a double stack. When truck trailers are placed on ships to travel long distances at lower rates, it's called *fishyback.* When they are placed in airplanes, that's *birdyback.*

Picture an automobile made in Japan for sale in the United States. It's shipped by truck to a loading dock, and from there moved by ship to a port in the United States. It may be placed on another truck and then taken to a railroad station for loading on a train that will take it across the country, to again be loaded on a truck for delivery to a local dealer. Now imagine that one integrated shipping firm handled all that movement. That's what intermodal shipping is all about.

The Storage Function

The preceding sections detailed the various ways of shipping goods once the company has sold them. But that's only the first step in understanding the system that moves goods from one point to another. Another important part of a complex logistics system is storage.

Buyers want goods delivered quickly. That means marketers must have goods available in various parts of the country ready to be shipped locally when ordered. Macy's is building warehouses all across the country in order to get goods to consumers faster.[32] A good percentage of the total cost of logistics is for storage. This includes the cost of the storage warehouse (distribution facility) and its operation, plus movement of goods within the warehouse.

There are two major kinds of warehouses: storage and distribution. A *storage warehouse* holds products for a relatively long time. Seasonal goods such as lawn mowers are kept in such a warehouse. *Distribution warehouses* are facilities used to gather and redistribute products. You can picture a distribution warehouse for FedEx or UPS handling thousands of packages in a very short time. The packages are picked up at places throughout

RFID tags are being used in all kinds of situations, from the movement of goods to the tracking of livestock. RFID tags in products like these clothes help retailers and producers track products from the suppliers' docks through the retailers' doors. How can RFID tags help you avoid losing your luggage, car keys, and other things?

the country and then processed for reshipment at these centers. General Electric's combination storage and distribution facility in San Gabriel Valley, California, gives you a feel for how large such buildings can be. It is nearly half a mile long and 465 feet wide—that's enough to hold almost 27 football fields.

Tracking Goods

How do producers keep track of where their goods are at any given time? As we noted in Chapter 14, some companies use Universal Product Codes—the familiar black-and-white bar codes and a preset number—to keep track of inventory. Bar codes got a big lift when camera phone apps made it possible to compare prices and read reviews about products from different suppliers.

Radio frequency identification (RFID), which we also mentioned earlier, tags merchandise so that it can be tracked from its arrival on the supplier's docks to its exit through the retailer's door.[33] Walmart, Target, and other organizations all plan to require suppliers to use RFID. The U.S. uses RFID codes to track military equipment.[34]

Few companies are more interested in tracking items than UPS, which now uses a mix of Bluetooth's short-range radio capability and wireless receivers to track merchandise. It claims the system is even better than RFID. The U.S. State Department offers an electronic passport card as a substitute for passport books for use by U.S. citizens who travel often to Canada, Mexico, and the Caribbean. It uses an RFID chip to provide data about the user and is more convenient and less expensive than a passport book. The card is very controversial, however, because some people believe it can be easily altered.

WHAT ALL THIS MEANS TO YOU

The life or death of a firm often depends on its ability to take orders, process orders, keep customers informed about the progress of their orders, get the goods out to customers quickly, handle returns, and manage any recycling issues. Some of the most exciting firms in the marketplace are those that assist in some aspect of supply-chain management.

What all this means to you is that many new jobs are becoming available in the exciting area of supply-chain management. These include jobs in distribution: trains, airplanes, trucks, ships, and pipelines. It also means jobs handling information flows between and among companies, including website development. Other jobs include processing orders, keeping track of inventory, following the path of products as they move from seller to buyer and back, recycling goods, and much more.

test prep ✓✓

- What four systems have evolved to tie together members of the channel of distribution?
- How does logistics differ from distribution?
- What are inbound logistics, outbound logistics, and reverse logistics?

summary

LO 15–1   Explain the concept of marketing channels and their value.

- **What is a channel of distribution?**
  A channel of distribution consists of a whole set of marketing intermediaries, such as agents, brokers, wholesalers, and retailers, that join together to transport and store goods in their path (or channel) from producers to consumers.

- **How do marketing intermediaries add value?**
  Intermediaries perform certain marketing tasks—such as transporting, storing, selling, advertising, and relationship building—faster and more cheaply than most manufacturers could. Channels of distribution ensure communication flows and the flow of money and title to goods. They also help ensure that the right quantity and assortment of goods will be available when and where needed.

- **What are the principles behind the use of such intermediaries?**
  Marketing intermediaries can be eliminated, but their activities can't. Without wholesalers and retailers, consumers would have to perform the tasks of transporting and storing goods, finding suppliers, and establishing communication with them. Intermediaries add costs to products, but these costs are usually more than offset by the values they create.

LO 15–2   Demonstrate how intermediaries perform the six marketing utilities.

- **How do intermediaries perform the six marketing utilities?**
  A retail grocer may cut or trim meat, providing some form utility. But marketers are more often responsible for the five other utilities. They provide time utility by having goods available *when* people want them, and place utility by having goods *where* people want them. Possession utility makes it possible for people to own things and includes credit, delivery, installation, guarantees, and anything else that completes the sale. Marketers also inform consumers of the availability of goods and services with advertising, publicity, and other means. That provides information utility. Finally, marketers provide fast, friendly, and efficient service during and after the sale (service utility).

LO 15–3   Identify the types of wholesale intermediaries in the distribution system.

- **What is a wholesaler?**
  A wholesaler is a marketing intermediary that sells to organizations and individuals, but not to final consumers.

- **What are some wholesale organizations that assist in the movement of goods from manufacturers to consumers?**
  Merchant wholesalers are independently owned firms that take title to the goods they handle. *Rack jobbers* furnish racks or shelves full of merchandise to retailers, display products, and sell on consignment. *Cash-and-carry wholesalers* serve mostly small retailers with a limited assortment of products. *Drop shippers* solicit orders from retailers and other wholesalers and have the merchandise shipped directly from a producer to a buyer.

LO 15–4 Compare the distribution strategies retailers use.

- **What is a retailer?**
A retailer is an organization that sells to ultimate consumers. Marketers develop several strategies based on retailing.

- **What are three distribution strategies marketers use?**
Marketers use three basic distribution strategies: intensive (putting products in as many places as possible), selective (choosing only a few stores in a chosen market), and exclusive (using only one store in each market area).

LO 15–5 Explain the various kinds of nonstore retailing.

- **What are some of the forms of nonstore retailing?**
Nonstore retailing includes electronic retailing; telemarketing (marketing by phone); vending machines, kiosks, and carts (marketing by putting products in convenient locations, such as in the halls of shopping centers); direct selling (marketing by approaching consumers in their homes or places of work); multilevel marketing (marketing by setting up a system of salespeople who recruit other salespeople and help them to sell directly to customers); and direct marketing (direct mail and catalog sales). Telemarketing and online marketing are also forms of direct marketing.

LO 15–6 Explain the various ways to build cooperation in channel systems.

- **What are the four types of distribution systems?**
The four distribution systems that tie firms together are (1) *corporate systems,* in which all organizations in the channel are owned by one firm; (2) *contractual systems,* in which members are bound to cooperate through contractual agreements; (3) *administered systems,* in which all marketing functions at the retail level are managed by manufacturers; and (4) *supply chains,* in which the various firms in the supply chain are linked electronically to provide the most efficient movement of information and goods possible.

LO 15–7 Describe logistics and outline how intermediaries manage the transportation and storage of goods.

- **What is logistics?**
Logistics includes planning, implementing, and controlling the physical flow of materials, final goods, and related information from points of origin to points of consumption to meet customer requirements at a profit.

- **What is the difference between logistics and distribution?**
Distribution generally means transportation. Logistics is more complex. *Inbound logistics* brings raw materials, packaging, other goods and services, and information from suppliers to producers. *Materials handling* is the moving of goods from warehouses to the factory floor and to various workstations. *Outbound logistics* manages the flow of finished products and information to business buyers and ultimate consumers (people like you and me). *Reverse logistics* brings goods back to the manufacturer because of defects or for recycling materials.

• **What are the various transportation modes?**
Transportation modes include rail (for heavy shipments within the country or between bordering countries); trucks (for getting goods directly to consumers); ships (for slow, inexpensive movement of goods, often internationally); pipelines (for moving water, oil, and other such goods); and airplanes (for shipping goods quickly).

• **What is intermodal shipping?**
Intermodal shipping uses multiple modes of transportation—highway, air, water, rail—to complete a single long-distance movement of freight.

• **What are the different kinds of warehouses?**
A storage warehouse stores products for a relatively long time. Distribution warehouses are used to gather and redistribute products.

key terms

administered distribution system 432
agents/brokers 418
cash-and-carry wholesalers 426
channel of distribution 418
contractual distribution system 432
corporate distribution system 432
direct marketing 431
direct selling 430
drop shippers 426
electronic retailing 428
exclusive distribution 427

freight forwarder 436
inbound logistics 435
information utility 424
intensive distribution 427
intermodal shipping 438
logistics 435
marketing intermediaries 418
materials handling 435
merchant wholesalers 425
outbound logistics 435
place utility 423
possession utility 424

rack jobbers 426
retailer 419
reverse logistics 435
selective distribution 427
service utility 424
social commerce 428
supply chain (value chain) 432
supply-chain management 433
telemarketing 430
time utility 423
utility 423
wholesaler 418

critical thinking

1. Imagine that we have eliminated marketing intermediaries, and you need groceries and shoes. How would you find out where the shoes and groceries are? How far would you have to travel to get them? How much money do you think you'd save for your time and effort?

2. Which intermediary do you think is most important today and why? What changes are happening to companies in that area?

3. One scarce item in the future will be water. If you could think of an inexpensive way to get water from places of abundance to places where it is needed for drinking, farming, and other uses, such as fracking, you could become a wealthy marketing intermediary. Pipelines are an alternative, but could you also freeze the water and ship it by train or truck? Could you use ships to tow icebergs to warmer climates? What other means of transporting water might there be?

developing **workplace skills**

Key: ● **Team**   ★ **Analytic**   ▲ **Communication**   ▣ **Technology**

1. The six utilities of marketing are form, time, place, possession, information, and service. Give examples of organizations in your area that perform each of these functions. ★

2. Form small groups and diagram how Dole might get pineapples from a field in Thailand to a canning plant in California to a store near your college. Include the intermediaries and the forms of transportation each one might use. ▲★●

3. Compare the merits of buying and selling goods in brick-and-mortar stores and on online. What advantages do physical stores have? Has anyone in the class tried to sell anything online? How did he or she ship the product? ★

4. In class, discuss the differences between wholesaling and retailing and why retailing has more appeal for students considering jobs. Since fewer students seek jobs in wholesaling than in retailing, do you think wholesaling jobs may be easier to get? ▲★

5. One part of retailing is using auction sites like eBay to sell new and used merchandise. Form small groups and discuss group members' experiences using eBay. What tips have they learned? How do eBay users minimize the problems associated with shipping? ▲★●

taking it to the **net**

PURPOSE

To examine how small businesses can learn to use the Internet to distribute their products directly to customers.

EXERCISE

Many small-business owners have no idea how to begin selling goods online. Several free websites have been developed to help them get started with tasks from setting up their site to doing online marketing, handling credit purchases, and more. Go to Homestead.com or BlueVoda.com and listen to the presentations they make. Search the web to find other sources of help in designing your own website. Then answer the following questions:

1. How long do the websites say that it takes to get started?

2. Does the process seem easier or harder than you imagined?

3. Do you have questions that the websites did not answer?

4. What help are you given, if any, in planning how to ship your goods?

video case

FEDEX

FedEx is the world's largest express delivery company. Every year the Memphis-based freighter moves more than 4 million packages to 220 countries. All told, the company's annual payload weighs in at a gargantuan 11 million pounds. By getting products to businesses and consumers quickly, FedEx thrives in its role as a marketing intermediary.

Despite its success, FedEx isn't as self-sufficient as it might appear. After all, much of FedEx's income is dependent on other businesses using the freighter to ship their wares. If these clients become big enough, though, they could start to look for ways to consolidate their business. Oftentimes that means getting rid of intermediaries like FedEx. Once these outside ties are cut, the companies are then free to establish their own in-house distribution systems.

However, companies like FedEx provide businesses with more than just delivery services. Although marketing intermediaries do not create stand-alone value for their clients, they add vital utility to existing products and services. In fact, many companies find that they're better off improving their current services with the help of outside firms rather than build their own departments from scratch.

For instance, a shipping company that specializes in transporting massive loads of raw materials may try to cut costs by taking control of its small-scale shipping as well. Items on the large-scale side of the supply chain are normally freighted by trains or cargo ships, which are a far cry from the small, individually driven trucks that FedEx uses. Because of this huge difference in operations, even the most efficient freighters would be hard pressed to juggle both large- and small-scale shipping successfully. In this way, FedEx's ability to ship lots of smaller volume orders quickly makes it an ideal partner.

A typical transaction works like this: Manufacturers purchase a label from FedEx's website and place it on their shipment, which can be anything from a single box to a whole palette full of products. A company driver then picks up the delivery at a scheduled time and scans it into a tracking system. She then takes it to the nearest FedEx processing center to be flown to a transport hub. The hub sends the package to another airport, which sends it to another FedEx processing center. From there, it's put on a truck and delivered to the wholesaler who ordered it. The process is so efficient that a product ordered in the evening may be at the wholesaler's door by the next morning. And throughout the process, the package's location can be tracked, the shipment insured, and the time of delivery predictably guaranteed and protected by a requirement of face-to-face delivery.

This fast-acting infrastructure is FedEx's greatest asset. Because of its speed, its retail clients don't need to waste precious sales floor space by overstocking products. What's more, FedEx can keep its prices below what it would cost the wholesaler to maintain its own fleet of delivery vehicles. That's because FedEx controls each step of the process from pickup to dropoff. Through its strong commitment to logistics, FedEx stands to be successful for a long time.

THINKING IT OVER

1. Why would companies choose to use an intermediary like FedEx instead of taking on distribution responsibilities themselves?

2. Significant numbers of consumers are choosing to do their shopping online. Will this decision most likely hurt or help FedEx's business?

3. What utilities does FedEx provide for its customers? Which utility is probably the most important to its customers?

notes

1. Jens Hansegard and Niclas Rolander, "For IKEA, Online Isn't the Main Showroom," *The Wall Street Journal,* January 29, 2014.
2. David Gould, "Risk Gets Sophisticated," *Bloomberg Businessweek,* March 4–March 10, 2013.
3. Patrick Burnson, "Reverse Logistics: Closing the Global Supply Chain Loop," *Logistics Management,* February 2013.
4. "CSU Students Favor a Plastic Ban," *Rocky Mountain Collegian,* April 3, 2014.
5. Norm Brodsky, "The Wholesalers Dilemma," *Inc.,* October 2012.
6. Catherine Dunn, "Travel with a Trunk," *Fortune,* February 3, 2014.
7. Christopher Matthews, "It's in the Bag," *Time,* February 3, 2014.
8. Bureau of Labor Statistics, www.bis.gov, accessed April 2014.
9. Shelly Banjo, "Wal-Mart's E-Stumble," *The Wall Street Journal,* June 19, 2013.
10. James K. Glassman, "Top Dogs in E-tailing," *Kiplinger's Personal Finance,* June 2012.
11. "The Bottom Line," *The Economist,* January 5, 2013.
12. *Fortune,* advertisement, April 8, 2013.
13. David Beederman, "Charting Sustainability," *The Journal of Commerce,* September 2, 2013.
14. Richard Kauffeld, Adam Michaels, and Curt Michaels, "Designing the Right Supply Chain," *Strategy + Business,* Spring 2013.
15. John D. Schultz, "New Order, New Opportunities on the Rise," *Logistics Management,* July 2013.
16. Margaret Littman, "Get It Out There," *Entrepreneur,* August 2012.
17. C. Shane Hunt and John E. Mello, *Marketing* (New York: McGraw-Hill Education, 2015).
18. Joe Queenan, "Give a Drone an Inch, and It'll Fly a Mile," *The Wall Street Journal,* January 25–26, 2014.
19. Dale S. Rogers, Ron Lambke, and John Benardino, "Taking Control of Reverse Logistics," *Logistics Management,* May 2013.
20. Jeff Berman, "Rail," *Logistics Management,* July 2013.
21. Steven Mufson and Juliet Eilperin, "Railroads Emerge as Alternative to Transport Canadian Oil Sands," *The Washington Post,* March 2013.
22. Betsy Morris, "Boom Times on the Tracks: Rail Capacity, Spending Soar," *The Wall Street Journal,* March 27, 2013.
23. Dexter Roberts, Henry Meyer, and Dorothee Tschampa, "When It Doesn't Have to Be There Overnight," *Bloomberg Businessweek,* December 24–January 6, 2013.
24. Teresa Rivas, "Ride on This Rail," *Barron's,* January 27, 2014.
25. William B. Cassidy, "Smaller or Smarter?" *The Journal of Commerce,* July 8, 2013.
26. Inti Landauro, "Meet the World's Largest Cargo Ships," *The Wall Street Journal,* January 8, 2013.
27. Patrice Hill, "Rail Accidents Fuel Pipeline Push," *The Washington Times,* January 27, 2014.
28. Matthew Philips and Asjylyn Loder, "All Aboard the Crude Express," *Bloomberg Businessweek,* June 17–June 23, 2013.
29. Patrick Burnson, "Air—Marginal Growth, Freight Volumes Stagnant," *Logistics Management,* July, 2013.
30. Brooks Bentz and Scott Fata, "Getting Serious about Multi-Modal," *Logistics Management,* October, 2013.
31. Mary C. Holcomb and Karl B. Manrodt, "Masters Co-Create Value," *Logistics Management,* September, 2013.
32. Dana Mattioli, "Macy's Regroups in Warehouse Wars," *The Wall Street Journal,* May 15, 2012.
33. Maida Napolitano, "RFID Settles In," *Logistics Management,* April, 2013.
34. Marjorie Censer, "Branching Out beyond Military Work," *The Washington Post,* August 19, 2013.

photo credits

16

Using Effective Promotions

Learning Objectives

AFTER YOU HAVE READ AND STUDIED THIS CHAPTER, YOU SHOULD BE ABLE TO

LO 16-1 Identify the new and traditional tools that make up the promotion mix.

LO 16-2 Contrast the advantages and disadvantages of various advertising media, including the Internet and social media.

LO 16-3 Illustrate the steps of the B2B and B2C selling processes.

LO 16-4 Describe the role of the public relations department, and show how publicity fits in that role.

LO 16-5 Assess the effectiveness of various forms of sales promotion, including sampling.

LO 16-6 Show how word of mouth, viral marketing, blogging, podcasting, e-mail marketing, and mobile marketing work.

In the digital age, savvy self-promotion is often the key to success. But with so much new content added online every day, it can be difficult to tell if your hard work will ever pay off with a viral hit. Few people understand this better than Chris Hardwick, comedian and co-founder of the media company Nerdist Industries. After years of diminishing returns in show business, Hardwick started a blog and a podcast that served as an outlet for his geeky passions. Over the span of just a few months, "The Nerdist" did more to launch Hardwick's career than a decade's worth of stand-up comedy and TV hosting gigs.

After graduating from UCLA with a degree in philosophy, Hardwick first broke into the entertainment industry as a radio DJ. His energetic presence and strong sense of humor brought him to the attention of MTV, who hired Hardwick to host the dating show *Singled Out* in 1995. Although the hit show gave him national exposure, it didn't lead to the kind of Hollywood opportunities that Hardwick hoped for. In between hosting various TV shows and acting in low-budget movies, Hardwick honed his stand-up skills in comedy clubs across the country.

In order to put his career back into his own hands, Hardwick realized he needed to explore the subjects that really interested him. He was a lifelong fan of comic books and science fiction. Hardwick couldn't focus on these nerdy pursuits when he was playing it cool in front of the MTV cameras. Demand for geeky media hit an all-time high as previously niche products like computers and gadgets became mainstream. "If you were a nerd when I was growing up, in the 80s, you were socially ostracized," said Hardwick. "But now everything's so readily available everywhere, all the time. People don't necessarily have to be into just one or two things anymore." So in 2008 Hardwick launched a blog and Twitter account called *The Nerdist* as a way to discuss his interests as well as promote his stand-up dates. He updated the blog with posts covering everything from the latest iPhone rumors to news about *Star Trek*. As his following grew steadily, he started recording a podcast with two comedian friends. Within a year the show was averaging 75,000 downloads per episode while *The Nerdist*

Twitter account boasted more than 1.4 million followers.

All this buzz brought Hardwick into contact with Peter Levin, an entrepreneur and former entertainment executive who ran a successful e-mail newsletter called *GeekChicDaily*. The two recognized how Levin's business acumen could complement Hardwick's personality and fan base. They entered a partnership in 2011 and formed Nerdist Industries with Levin as CEO and Hardwick as chief creative officer. The pair brought in other writers and podcasters under the Nerdist banner, while generating revenue through advertising. By 2013, the Nerdist had accumulated more than 4.5 million followers across its associated accounts. The company also began to move into television, including the Hardwick-hosted, social media–driven game show *@midnite*. The brand's success brought it to the attention of Legendary Entertainment, the production company responsible for the *Dark Knight* and *Hangover* franchises. Legendary purchased Nerdist Industries for an undisclosed sum, but kept the company's founders in charge of the multi-million-dollar operation.

Sometimes the only thing keeping a good idea from being a successful idea is promotional expertise. In this chapter we explore all the traditional and newer elements of promotion. We'll explain how marketers use different media and the advantages and disadvantages of each. We'll also take a look at the role of public relations as well as the differences between B2C and B2B promotions. Finally, throughout the chapter we'll pay particular attention to the promotional uses of Chris Hardwick's areas of expertise: electronic media like blogging, social networking, and podcasts.

Sources: John Patrick Pullen, "Inside Nerdist's Media Empire for the Internet Age," *Entrepreneur,* August 21, 2013; Joel Warner, "Nerd Inc.: CEO Peter Levin Takes Nerdist Industries Mainstream," *Bloomberg Businessweek,* July 11, 2013; Grace Bello, "Talking to The Nerdist's Chris Hardwick," *The Awl,* January 13, 2012; and Michael Ventre, "Chris Hardwick on Becoming TV's Nerd Icon," *Esquire,* October 22, 2013.

Chris Hardwick
- Co-founder of Nerdist Industries
- Comedian
- Used his self-promotion skills to build a nerdy media empire

www.nerdist.com

@nerdist

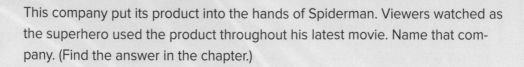

name that **company**

This company put its product into the hands of Spiderman. Viewers watched as the superhero used the product throughout his latest movie. Name that company. (Find the answer in the chapter.)

LO 16–1 Identify the new and traditional tools that make up the promotion mix.

PROMOTION AND THE PROMOTION MIX

Promotion is one of the four Ps of marketing. As noted in Chapter 13, promotion consists of all the techniques sellers use to motivate people to buy their products or services. Both profit-making and nonprofit organizations use promotional techniques to communicate with people in their target markets about goods and services, and to persuade them to participate in a marketing exchange.[1] Marketers use many different tools to promote their products. Traditionally, those tools were advertising, personal selling, public relations, and sales promotion. Today they also include e-mail promotions, mobile promotions, social networking, blogging, podcasting, tweets, and more.[2]

The combination of promotional tools an organization uses is called its **promotion mix**; see Figure 16.1. We show the product in the middle of the figure to illustrate that the product itself can also be a promotional tool, such as when marketers give away free samples.

Integrated marketing communication (IMC) combines the promotional tools into one comprehensive, unified promotional strategy.[3] With IMC, marketers can create a positive brand image, meet the needs of the consumer, and meet the strategic marketing and promotional goals of the firm. Emphasis today is on integrating traditional media, like TV, with social media, or integrating print media with online sites.[4]

Figure 16.2 shows the six steps in a typical promotional campaign. Let's begin exploring promotional tools by looking at advertising—the most visible tool.

promotion mix
The combination of promotional tools an organization uses.

integrated marketing communication (IMC)
A technique that combines all the promotional tools into one comprehensive, unified promotional strategy.

 connect

▶ **iSee It!** Need help understanding integrated marketing communication? Visit your Connect e-book video tab for a brief animated explanation.

FIGURE 16.1 THE TRADITIONAL PROMOTION MIX

FIGURE 16.2 STEPS IN A PROMOTIONAL CAMPAIGN

1. Identify a target market. (Refer back to Chapter 13 for a discussion of segmentation and target marketing.)

2. Define the objectives for each element of the promotion mix. Goals should be clear and measurable.

3. Determine a promotional budget. The budgeting process will clarify how much can be spent on advertising, personal selling, and other promotional efforts.

4. Develop a unifying message. The goal of an integrated promotional program is to have one clear message communicated by advertising, public relations, sales, and every other promotional effort.

5. Implement the plan. Advertisements, blogs, and other promotional efforts must be scheduled to complement efforts being made by public relations and sales promotion. Salespeople should have access to all materials to optimize the total effort.

6. Evaluate effectiveness. Measuring results depends greatly on clear objectives. Each element of the promotional mix should be evaluated separately, and an overall measure should be taken as well. It is important to learn what is working and what is not.

 LO 16–2   Contrast the advantages and disadvantages of various advertising media, including the Internet and social media.

ADVERTISING: INFORMING, PERSUADING, AND REMINDING

Advertising is paid, nonpersonal communication through various media by organizations and individuals who are in some way *identified in the message.* Identification of the sender separates advertising from *propaganda,* which is nonpersonal communication that *does not have an identified sponsor.* Figure 16.3 lists various categories of advertising. Take a minute to look it over; you'll see there's a lot more to advertising than just television commercials.

advertising
Paid, nonpersonal communication through various media by organizations and individuals who are in some way identified in the advertising message.

FIGURE 16.3 MAJOR CATEGORIES OF ADVERTISING

Different kinds of advertising are used by various organizations to reach different market targets.

- *Retail advertising*—advertising to consumers by various retail stores such as supermarkets and shoe stores.

- *Trade advertising*—advertising to wholesalers and retailers by manufacturers to encourage them to carry their products.

- *Business-to-business advertising*—advertising from manufacturers to other manufacturers. A firm selling motors to auto companies would use business-to-business advertising.

- *Institutional advertising*—advertising designed to create an attractive image for an organization rather than for a product. "We Care about You" at Giant Food is an example. "Virginia Is for Lovers" and "I ❤ New York" were two institutional campaigns by government agencies.

- *Product advertising*—advertising for a good or service to create interest among consumer, commercial, and industrial buyers.

- *Advocacy advertising*—advertising that supports a particular view of an issue (e.g., an ad in support of gun control or against nuclear power plants). Such advertising is also known as cause advertising.

- *Comparison advertising*—advertising that compares competitive products. For example, an ad that compares two different cold care products' speed and benefits is a comparative ad.

- *Interactive advertising*—customer-oriented communication that enables customers to choose the information they receive, such as interactive video catalogs that let customers select which items to view.

- *Online advertising*—advertising messages that appear on computers as people visit different websites.

- Mobile advertising—advertising that reaches people on their smartphones.

FIGURE 16.4 ESTIMATED U.S. ADVERTISING SPENDING IN 2013 BY MEDIUM (IN BILLIONS OF DOLLARS)

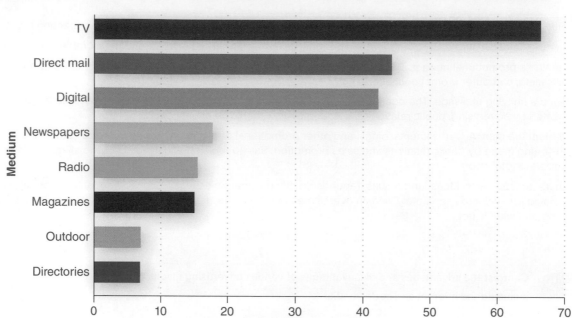

It's also easy to appreciate the impact of advertising spending on the U.S. economy; see Figure 16.4. Total ad volume was estimated to be about $215 billion for 2013. Note that TV is the number one medium, with expenditures of about $66 billion.

How do we, as consumers, benefit from these advertising expenditures? Ads are informative. Direct mail is full of information about products, prices, features, store policies, and more; so is newspaper advertising. Newspaper advertising is down because more and more people are getting their news on mobile devices. While many people look at the ads on mobile devices, the ads are often too small to be very effective.[5] Nonetheless, mobile advertising is growing very, very fast.[6]

Advertising seems to be everywhere as we go about our daily lives. How many advertisements can you spot in this photo? Can the noise created by so many ads interfere with the messages the advertisers are trying to communicate?

Not only does advertising inform us, but the money advertisers spend for commercial time pays the production costs of TV and radio programs. Advertising also helps cover the major costs of producing newspapers and magazines. Subscriptions and newsstand revenues may cover only mailing and promotional costs. Figure 16.5 compares the advantages and disadvantages for marketers of various advertising media. Notice that newspapers, radio, and directories are especially attractive to local advertisers.

Marketers must choose which media will best reach the audience they desire. Radio advertising, for example, is less expensive than TV advertising and often reaches people when they have few other distractions, such as while they're driving. Recent research has revealed the effectiveness of radio as a traditional medium.[7] Radio is especially effective at selling services people don't usually read about in print media—banking, mortgages, continuing education, and brokerage services, to name a few. On the other hand, radio has become so commercial-ridden that many people pay to switch to commercial-free satellite radio. Marketers also search for other places to put advertising, such as on video screens mounted in elevators. Have you noticed ads on park benches and grocery carts? You've certainly seen them on websites you visit.

FIGURE 16.5 ADVANTAGES AND DISADVANTAGES OF VARIOUS ADVERTISING MEDIA

The most effective media are often very expensive. The inexpensive media may not reach your market. The goal is to use the medium that can reach your desired market most effectively and efficiently.

Medium	Advantages	Disadvantages
Newspapers	Good coverage of local markets; ads can be placed quickly; high consumer acceptance; ads can be clipped and saved.	Ads compete with other features in paper; poor color; ads get thrown away with paper (short life span).
Television	Uses sight, sound, and motion; reaches all audiences; high attention with no competition from other material.	High cost; short exposure time; takes time to prepare ads. Digital video recorders skip over ads.
Radio	Low cost; can target specific audiences; very flexible; good for local marketing.	People may not listen to ads; depends on one sense (hearing); short exposure time; audience can't keep ads.
Magazines	Can target specific audiences; good use of color; long life of ads; ads can be clipped and saved.	Inflexible; ads often must be placed weeks before publication; cost is relatively high.
Outdoor	High visibility and repeat exposures; low cost; local market focus.	Limited message; low selectivity of audience.
Direct mail	Best for targeting specific markets; very flexible; ads can be saved.	High cost; consumers may reject ads as junk mail; must conform to post office regulations.
Directories (Yellow Pages–type print and online advertising)	Great coverage of local markets; widely used by consumers.	Competition with other ads; cost may be too high for very small businesses.
Internet	Inexpensive global coverage; available at any time; interactive.	Customers may leave the site before buying.
Mobile advertising	Great reach among younger shoppers.	Easy to ignore, avoid.
Social media	Wonderful communication tools.	Time drain.

Mobile marketing via smartphones started out mostly as text messages, but now stores like Starbucks can send signals to your phone as you approach the store, reminding you to stop in for a latte. Kraft Foods developed the iPhone Assistant, an iPhone application that serves up recipes for users—recipes made with Kraft products. Other retailers use e-mail advertisements to build brand awareness and drive people to their stores or websites. Social media in general are growing so fast that some marketers can hardly keep up. In the next sections, we'll look in more depth at traditional advertising media.

Television Advertising

Television offers many advantages to national advertisers, but it's expensive. Thirty seconds of advertising during the Super Bowl telecast can cost $4 million.[8] That's not including the production costs of the ads. How many bottles of beer or automobiles must a company sell to pay for such commercials? A lot, but few media besides television allow advertisers to reach so many people with such impact, although not all ads are equally effective.[9] Were you disappointed with some of the TV ads during the last Super Bowl? Of course, advertisers can book cheaper airtime on other TV shows. For example, 30 seconds on *America's Funniest Home Videos* costs just over $63,000 or on *CSI* just over $113,000.[10]

Despite what you may read about the growth of alternative promotional tools, TV advertising is still a dominant medium; sometimes that means local (spot) TV.[11] There are even TV ads within TV ads. Did you see, for example, the ad for TaylorMade inside a BMW ad?[12] Of course, TV is helped by the fact that many people tweet about what they have seen on TV, making Twitter a "force multiplier" for TV.[13] DVRs enable consumers to skip the ads on TV. This may make TV less attractive to advertisers unless commercials get so much better that people *want* to watch them. Program delivery systems, such as video on demand, make it even more difficult for TV advertisers to catch consumers' eyes. Thus marketers are demanding better and more accurate

Product placement is often subtle. You can see products like the ones shown on the table in movies and on TV shows. The goal is to influence you to want that product yourself. What product placements have you noticed in your favorite TV shows and movies?

measurements of the effectiveness of TV advertising, and many are switching to social media as a result. After all, more than half of U.S. consumers now have smartphones.[14]

Product Placement

TV advertising isn't limited to traditional commercials; sometimes the products appear in the programs themselves. With **product placement**, advertisers pay to put their products into TV shows and movies where the audience will see them. One classic example of product placement is the trail of Reese's Pieces in the movie *E.T.* Many placements are subtler, like the wheeled luggage from ZÜCA Inc. that appeared on the TV show *CSI.* In *The Amazing Spider-man*, the superhero uses a Sony Experia mini pro smartphone to make calls to his girlfriend, check voice mail, and listen to a police radio broadcast. He also plays a game on the phone screen.[15]

In addition to TV and movies, product placement is also used in video games. If you're a gamer, you've seen in-game ads, like ads around the court in basketball games. Technology allows vending machines in racing games to be branded and rebranded over time, depending on whether Coke, Pepsi, Exxon, or Shell has purchased ad time. Do you think people are influenced by such exposure?

Infomercials

An **infomercial** is a full-length TV program devoted exclusively to promoting a particular good or service. Infomercials have been successful because they show the product and how it works in great detail. They are the equivalent of sending your very best salespeople to a person's home and having them use all of their techniques to make the sale: drama, demonstration, testimonials, graphics, and more.

Products that have earned over $1 billion in sales through infomercials include Proactiv (acne cream), Soloflex, Total Gym, Bowflex (exercise machines), the George Foreman Grill, and Ron Popeil's Rotisserie and Grill. Some products, such as personal development seminars, real estate programs, and workout tapes, are hard to sell without showing people a sample of their contents and using testimonials. Have you purchased any products that you saw in an infomercial?

Online Advertising

When marketers advertise on an online search engine such as Google or Bing, they can reach the people they most want to reach—consumers looking for information about specific products.[16] One goal of online advertising is to get potential customers to a website where they can learn more about the company and its products—and the company can learn more about them.[17] If users click through an ad to get to the website, the company has an opportunity to gather their names, addresses, opinions, and preferences. Online advertising thus brings customers and companies together. Another advantage is that it enables advertisers to see just how many people have clicked on an ad and how much of it each potential customer has read or watched. It is one of the fastest-growing parts of advertising.

product placement
Putting products into TV shows, movies, and other media where they will be seen.

infomercial
A full-length TV program devoted exclusively to promoting goods or services.

Online advertising is the fastest-growing type of advertising and can offer more than just a list of products and their features. For example, Obsessive Ink's website allows users to upload a photo of themselves and designs they might like to have etched into their skin. They can experiment with size and placement and use social media to gather opinions of friends and family before making a lifelong decision.

Pay-per-Tweet

In the world of Twitter, not all tweets are created equal. Anyone can join the social network for free, leading to a user base ranging from students to celebrities. It's these high-profile personalities, however, that can really make the most of their 140-character statements.

By teaming up with special marketing companies, people like Justin Bieber and Kim Kardashian earn thousands of dollars simply by mentioning a product in their tweets. Bieber, for instance, urged his millions of followers to send Mother's Day flowers through 1-800-Flowers.com. Celebrities get paid on a sliding scale depending on how many users "follow" their Twitter account. That means a celebrity like Khloe Kardashian, who boasts more than 9 million followers, can earn as much as $13,000 per endorsement of Sugar Bear. In some cases celebrities don't even

need to worry about writing the tweets themselves. Media marketers like Ad.ly or IZEA will compose the spots themselves in order to maximize the message's effectiveness.

Of course, celebrities don't want their followers to know that,

and will hide the fact that these are ads within their many hashtags. The personal touch that many Twitter users love could be lost if more people discover that the famous figures they admire are only using the service to shill for other companies. On the other hand, it's not like the idea of a celebrity spokesperson is a brand-new concept developed by Twitter. People in the public eye will always leverage their fame to make money. In the end, fans will need to be wary about what to believe in their Twitter feeds. Do you think it is ethical for celebrities to get paid to tweet prewritten ads that appear to be their own personal comments without using #ad?

Sources: Liat Kornowski, "Celebrity Sponsored Tweets: What the Stars Get Paid for Advertising in 140 Characters," *Huffington Post,* May 30, 2013; Bryanna Cappadonna, "Celebrities Are Paid How Much to Tweet?! Not at Unreal Candy," *Boston Magazine,* June 11, 2013; and Melinda Emerson, "When Celebrities Tweet about Your Business," *Huffington Post,* January 24, 2014.

interactive promotion
Promotion process that allows marketers to go beyond a monologue, where sellers try to persuade buyers to buy things, to a dialogue in which buyers and sellers work together to create mutually beneficial exchange relationships.

E-mail marketing is a big component of online advertising. However, advertisers have to be careful not to overuse it because many customers don't like to see too much promotional e-mail in their in-boxes. Thus some companies use e-mail as an alert to send users to other social media such as Facebook and Twitter. The Making Ethical Decisions box discusses how some businesses pay celebrities to tweet prewritten ads.

Interactive promotion allows marketers to go beyond a *monologue,* in which sellers try to persuade buyers to buy things, to a *dialogue,* in which buyers and sellers work together to create mutually beneficial exchange relationships. Technology has greatly improved customer communications and has fundamentally changed the way marketers work with customers. Notice we said *working with* rather than *promoting to*. Marketers now want to *build relationships* with customers over time. That means carefully listening to what consumers want, tracking their purchases, providing them with excellent service, and giving them access to a full range of information.

Using Social Media to Monitor Ad Effectiveness

Dr Pepper has millions of fans on Facebook. The company can track and test users who "like" the soft drink. The company can measure how many times a message is reviewed, how many times it is shared, and what the fan response is. Social media have made it possible for organizations to test ads before airing them on traditional media, like TV, and to listen to the reasons why people like and dislike messages.

It is best, if a company wants to establish a base with customers, to include top managers in the dialogue. For example, Richard Branson of Virgin Group Ltd. and Tony Hsieh of Zappos tweet their customers. Sherry Chris of Better Homes & Gardens Real Estate LLC spends two hours each day reading and contributing to Twitter, Facebook, LinkedIn, and Foursquare. Such involvement with customers has become a major part of many companies' listening strategy. It may take time, but there is not a better way to learn about what customers are thinking and saying about your firm.

Global Advertising

Global advertising requires the marketer to develop a single product and promotional strategy it can implement worldwide. Certainly global advertising that's the same everywhere can save companies money in research and design. In some cases, however, promotions tailored to specific countries or regions may be more successful since each country or region has its own culture, language, and buying habits.

Some problems do arise when marketers use one campaign in all countries. When a Japanese company tried to use English words to name a popular drink, it came up with Pocari Sweat, not a good image for most English-speaking people. In England, the Ford Probe didn't go over too well because the word *probe* made people think of doctors' waiting rooms and medical examinations. People in the United States may have difficulty with Krapp toilet paper from Sweden. But perhaps worse was the translation of Coors's slogan "Turn it loose," which became "Suffer from diarrhea." Clairol introduced its curling iron, the Mist Stick, to the German market, not realizing *mist* in German can mean "manure." As you can see, getting the words right in international advertising is tricky and critical. So is understanding the culture, which calls for researching each country, designing appropriate ads, and testing them. The Reaching Beyond Our Borders box discusses how a well-known company promotes products in foreign markets.

Many marketers today are moving from globalism (one ad for everyone in the world) to regionalism (specific ads for each country or for specific groups within a country). In the future, marketers will prepare more custom-designed promotions to reach even smaller audiences—audiences as small as one person.

This ad is designed for African American women. There are many ads directed toward the Latina and Asian markets as well. What other groups are attractive candidates for targeted ads?

What's in Your Oreo?

For more than 100 years, to Americans an Oreo was just an Oreo: two layers of crunchy cookie sandwiching a creamy vanilla center. For many years, Kraft Foods, the maker of Oreos, followed the old adage "If it ain't broke, don't fix it." Today, however, if you visit the cookie aisle in your local supermarket, you find variations of Oreos such as cookie dough, marshmallow crispy, even birthday cake. Kraft knew to keep the brand vibrant and to reach different segments of the market, expanding its flavors was a good option.

It also knew it was a good decision to expand Oreos into global markets. Today, you can find Oreos in more than 100 countries across the globe. However, Kraft understood that globally consumer tastes vary just like in the United States. What some people consider mouthwatering in one country will be frowned upon somewhere else. So with Oreos spanning the globe, additional variations on the original cookie-and-creme formula became even more extreme. China, for instance, prefers green tea–flavored Oreos. In Indonesia, consumers prefer Blueberry Ice Cream and Orange Ice Cream–flavored Oreos. Argentines like their Oreos stuffed with banana and *dulce de leche,* a type of candied milk.

Sources: Samantha Grossman, "Oreo Launches Two New Flavors, and They're Both Delicious," *Time,* January 23, 2014; and Gina Pace, "Oreo to Launch Two New Cookie Flavors," *The New York Daily News,* January 24, 2014.

LO 16–3   Illustrate the steps of the B2B and B2C selling processes.

PERSONAL SELLING: PROVIDING PERSONAL ATTENTION

personal selling
The face-to-face presentation and promotion of goods and services.

Personal selling is the face-to-face presentation and promotion of goods and services, including the salesperson's search for new prospects and follow-up service after the sale. Effective selling isn't simply a matter of persuading others to buy. In fact, it's more accurately described today as helping others satisfy their wants and needs (again, helping the buyer buy).

Given that perspective, you can see why salespeople use smartphones, tablets, laptops and other technology to help customers search for information, design custom-made products, look over prices, and generally do everything it takes to complete the order. The benefit of personal selling is having a person help you complete a transaction. The salesperson should listen to your needs, help you reach a solution, and do everything possible to make accomplishing it smoother and easier.

It's costly for firms to provide customers with personal attention, so those companies that retain salespeople must train them to be especially effective, efficient, and helpful. To attract new salespeople, companies are paying them quite well. The average cost of a single sales call to a potential business-to-business (B2B) buyer is about $500.[18] Surely no firm would pay that much to send anyone but a skillful and highly trained professional salesperson and consultant.

Steps in the Selling Process

The best way to understand personal selling is to go through the selling process. Imagine you are a software salesperson whose job is to show business users the advantages of various products your firm markets. One product critically important to establishing long-term relationships with customers is customer relationship management (CRM) software, particularly social CRM that integrates social media to create a community-based relationship with customers. Let's go through the seven steps of the selling process to see what you can do to sell social CRM software.

Although this is a business-to-business (B2B) example, the process in consumer selling is similar, but less complex. In both cases the salesperson must have deep product knowledge—that is, he or she must know the product—and competitors' products—thoroughly.

1. Prospect and Qualify   The first step in the selling process is **prospecting**, researching potential buyers and choosing those most likely to buy. The selection process is called **qualifying**. To qualify people means to make sure they have a need for the product, the authority to buy, and the willingness to listen to a sales message. Some people call prospecting and qualifying the process of *lead generation*.

A person who meets the qualifying criteria is called a **prospect**. Salespeople often meet prospects at trade shows, where they come to booths sponsored by manufacturers and ask questions. Others may visit your website seeking information. But often the best prospects are people recommended to you by others who use or know about your product. Salespeople often e-mail prospects with proposals to see whether there is any interest before making a formal visit.

2. Preapproach   The selling process may take a long time, and gathering information before you approach the customer is crucial. Before making a sales call, you must do some further research. In the preapproach phase, you learn as much as possible about customers and their wants and needs.[19] Before you try to sell the social CRM software, you'll want to know which people in the company are most likely to buy or use it. What kind of customers do they deal with? What kind of relationship strategies are they using now? How is their system set up, and what kind of improvements are they looking for? All that information should be in a database so that, if one representative leaves the firm, the company can carry information about customers to the new salesperson.

3. Approach   "You don't have a second chance to make a good first impression." That's why the approach is so important. When you call on a customer for the first time, you want to give an impression of friendly professionalism, create rapport, build credibility, and start a business relationship. Often a company's decision to use a new software package is based on the buyer's perception of reliable service from the salesperson. In selling social CRM products, you can make it known from the start that you'll be available to help your customer train its employees and to upgrade the package when necessary.

You're familiar with all kinds of situations in which people do personal selling. They work in local department stores and sell all kinds of goods and services like automobiles, insurance, and real estate. What could they do to be more helpful to you, the customer?

prospecting
Researching potential buyers and choosing those most likely to buy.

qualifying
In the selling process, making sure that people have a need for the product, the authority to buy, and the willingness to listen to a sales message.

prospect
A person with the means to buy a product, the authority to buy, and the willingness to listen to a sales message.

Making the sale isn't the end of the salesperson's relationship with the customer. The salesperson should follow up on the sale to make sure the customer is happy and perhaps suggest something to complement what the customer purchased. Have salespeople been able to sell you more because they used effective follow-up procedures? How did they do it?

trial close
A step in the selling process that consists of a question or statement that moves the selling process toward the actual close.

4. Make a Presentation   In your actual presentation of the software, you'll match the benefits of your value package to the client's needs. Since you've done your homework and know the prospect's wants and needs, you can tailor your sales presentation accordingly. The presentation is a great time to use testimonials, showing potential buyers that they're joining leaders in other firms who are using the product.

5. Answer Objections   Salespeople should anticipate any objections the prospect may raise and determine the proper responses. They should think of questions as opportunities for creating better relationships, not as challenges to what they're saying. Customers may have legitimate doubts, and salespeople are there to resolve them. Successfully and honestly working with others helps build relationships based on trust. Often salespeople can introduce the customer to others in the firm who can answer their questions and provide them with anything they need. Using a laptop or other mobile device, salespeople may set up a virtual meeting in which the customer can chat with company colleagues and begin building a relationship.

6. Close the Sale   After a salesperson has answered questions and objections, he or she may present a **trial close**, a question or statement that moves the selling process toward the actual purchase. A salesperson might ask, "When would be the best time to train your staff to use the new software?" The final step is to ask for the order and show the client where to sign. Once a relationship is established, the goal of the sales call may be to get a testimonial from the customer.

7. Follow Up   The selling process isn't over until the order is approved and the customer is happy. Salespeople need to be providers of solutions for their customers and to think about what happens after the sale. The follow-up step includes handling customer complaints, making sure the customer's questions are answered, and quickly supplying what the customer wants. Often, customer service is as important to the sale as the product itself. That's why most manufacturers have websites where customers can find information and get questions answered. You can see why we describe selling as a process of establishing relationships, not just exchanging goods or services. The sales relationship may continue for years as the salesperson responds to new requests for information and provides new services.

The selling process varies somewhat among different goods and services, but the general idea stays the same. The goals of a salesperson are to help the buyer buy and make sure the buyer is satisfied after the sale.

The Business-to-Consumer Sales Process

Most sales to consumers take place in retail stores, where the role of the salesperson differs somewhat from that in B2B selling. In both cases, knowing the product comes first. However, in business-to-consumer (B2C) sales, the salesperson does not have to do much prospecting or qualifying. The seller assumes most people who come to the store are qualified to buy the merchandise (except in sales of expensive products, such as automobiles and furniture,

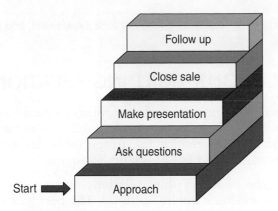

FIGURE 16.6 STEPS IN THE BUSINESS-TO-CONSUMER (B2C) SELLING PROCESS

during which salespeople may have to ask a few questions to qualify prospective customers before spending too much time with them).

Similarly, retail salespeople don't usually have to go through a preapproach step, although they should understand as much as possible about the type of people who shop at a given store. Often the people who come to a store have already done some research online and know exactly what they want.[20] The salesperson does need to focus on the customer and refrain from talking to fellow salespeople—or, worse, to friends on the phone. Have you ever experienced such rude behavior from salespeople? What did you think?

The first formal step in the B2C sales process is the approach. Too many salespeople begin with a line like "May I help you?" but the answer too often is "No." A better approach is "How can I help you?" or, simply, "Welcome to our store." The idea is to show the customer you are there to help and are friendly and knowledgeable.[21]

Discover what the customer wants first, and then make a presentation. Salespeople should show customers how the company's products meet their needs and answer questions that help customers choose the right products for them.

As in B2B selling, it is important to make a trial close, like "Would you like me to put that on hold?" or "Will you be paying for that with your store credit card?" Selling is an art, and a salesperson must learn how to walk the fine line between being helpful and being pushy. Often individual buyers need some time alone to think about the purchase. The salesperson must respect that need but still be clearly available when needed.

After-sale follow-up is an important but often neglected step in B2C sales. If the product is to be delivered, the salesperson should follow up to be sure it is delivered on time. The same is true if the product has to be installed. There is often a chance to sell more merchandise when a salesperson follows up on a sale. Figure 16.6 shows the whole B2C selling process. Compare it to the seven-step process we outlined earlier for B2B selling.

test prep ✓✓

- What are the four traditional elements of the promotion mix?
- What are the three most important advertising media in order of dollars spent?
- What are the seven steps in the B2B selling process? How does it differ from the B2C selling process?

Use LearnSmart to help retain what you have learned. Access your instructor's Connect course to check out LearnSmart, or go to learnsmartadvantage.com for help.

LEARNSMART

LO 16-4   Describe the role of the public relations department, and show how publicity fits in that role.

PUBLIC RELATIONS: BUILDING RELATIONSHIPS

public relations (PR)
The function that evaluates public attitudes, changes policies and procedures in response to the public's requests, and executes a program of action and information to earn public understanding and acceptance.

Public relations (PR) is the function that evaluates public attitudes, changes policies and procedures in response to the public's requests, and executes a program of action and information to earn public understanding and acceptance. In other words, a good public relations program has three steps:

1. *Listen to the public.* Public relations starts with good marketing research to evaluate public attitudes. The best way to learn what the public wants is to listen to people often—in different forums, including on social media. For example, General Mills learned that consumers were concerned about genetically modified organisms (GMOs) in the products they bought when it noticed the tens of thousands of Facebook posts supporting the efforts of an anti-GMO activist group.[22]

2. *Change policies and procedures.* Businesses earn understanding not by bombarding the public with propaganda but by creating programs and practices in the public interest. For example, General Mills responded to the anti-GMO concerns by removing GMOs from original-flavored Cheerios.

3. *Inform people you're responsive to their needs.* It's not enough to simply have programs in the public interest. You have to *tell* the public about those programs. Public relations has more power to influence consumers than other corporate communications because the message comes via the media, a source usually perceived as trustworthy. That's exactly what General Mills did by placing a GMO-free label on its new Cheerios box.[23]

Recent events have emphasized the need for good public relations. Such events include GM's safety problems, Japan's nuclear power problems, and the issues surrounding some politicians, key actors, and sports personalities.[24]

The PR department maintains close ties with company stakeholders (customers, media, community leaders, government officials, and other corporate stakeholders). Marketers are looking for alternatives to advertising. Public relations is a good alternative. As newspapers cut back on their reporting staff, people are looking for other sources of news information, including publicity releases. Linking up with bloggers has become an important way to keep company names in the news. Public relations is so important to some firms that everyone in other departments beyond the PR department are participating as well.[25]

Publicity: The Talking Arm of PR

Publicity is the talking arm of public relations and one of the major functions of almost all organizations. Here's how it works: Suppose you want to introduce your store, Very Vegetarian, to consumers, but you have little money to promote it. You need to get some initial sales to generate funds. One effective way to reach the public is through publicity.

publicity
Any information about an individual, product, or organization that's distributed to the public through the media and that's not paid for or controlled by the seller.

Publicity is any information about an individual, product, or organization that's distributed to the public through the media and is not paid for or controlled by the seller. It takes skill to write interesting or newsworthy press releases that the media will want to publish. You may need to write different stories for different media.[26] One story may introduce the new owners. Another may describe the unusual product offerings. If the stories are published, news about your store will reach many potential consumers (and investors, distributors, and dealers) and you may be on your way to becoming a successful marketer.[27] John D. Rockefeller once remarked, "Next to doing the right thing, the most important thing is to *let people know* that you are doing the right thing." What might Very Vegetarian do to help the community and thus create more publicity?

Besides being free, publicity has several further advantages over other promotional tools like advertising. It may reach people who wouldn't read an ad. It may appear on the front page of a newspaper or in some other prominent position, or be given air time on a television news show. Perhaps the greatest advantage of publicity is its believability. When a newspaper or magazine publishes a story as news, the reader treats that story as news—and news is more believable than advertising.

Publicity has several disadvantages as well. For example, marketers have no control over whether, how, and when the media will use the story. The media aren't obligated to use a publicity release, most of which are thrown away. Furthermore, the media may alter the story so that it's not positive. There's good publicity (customers camp out all night to buy your products) and bad publicity (defective products are recalled). Also, once a story has run, it's not likely to be repeated. Advertising, in contrast, can be repeated as often as needed. One way to see that the media handle your publicity well is to establish a friendly relationship with media representatives and be open with them.

Some companies will race to extremes to generate publicity. This streaker avoided Super Bowl XXXVIII security to show off a tattooed message for Internet casino GoldenPalace .com. Which do you think attracts more attention for a firm, an appealing news story or a paid ad?

LO 16–5 Assess the effectiveness of various forms of sales promotion, including sampling.

SALES PROMOTION: GIVING BUYERS INCENTIVES

Sales promotion is the promotional tool that stimulates consumer purchasing and dealer interest by means of short-term activities. These activities include such things as displays, trade shows and exhibitions, event sponsorships, and contests. Figure 16.7 lists some B2B sales promotion techniques.

For consumer sales promotion activities, think of those free samples you get in the mail, cents-off coupons you clip from newspapers, contests that various retail stores sponsor, and prizes in cereal boxes (see Figure 16.7). Some experts caution not to give too much away during such promotions.[28] You can stimulate sales at Very Vegetarian by putting half-off coupons in the school paper and home mailers. Do you see any problems that might emerge by using Groupon to bring in customers?

Sales promotion programs are designed to supplement personal selling, advertising, public relations, and other promotional efforts by creating enthusiasm for the overall promotional program. Sales promotion can take place both within and outside the company. The most important

sales promotion
The promotional tool that stimulates consumer purchasing and dealer interest by means of short-term activities.

FIGURE 16.7 SALES PROMOTION TECHNIQUES

B2B	• Trade shows • Portfolios for salespeople • Deals (price reductions)	• Catalogs • Conventions

B2C	• Coupons • Cents-off promotions • Sampling • Premiums • Sweepstakes • Contests	• Bonuses (buy one, get one free) • Catalogs • Demonstrations • Special events • Lotteries • In-store displays

internal sales promotion efforts are directed at salespeople and other customer-contact people, such as customer service representatives and clerks. Internal sales promotion efforts include (1) sales training; (2) the development of sales aids such as flip charts, portable audiovisual displays, and videos; and (3) participation in trade shows where salespeople can get leads. Other employees who deal with the public may also receive special training to improve their awareness of the company's offerings and make them an integral part of the total promotional effort.

After generating enthusiasm internally, marketers want to make distributors and dealers eager to help promote the product. Trade shows allow marketing intermediaries to see products from many different sellers and make comparisons among them. Today, virtual trade shows on the Internet, called webinars, enable buyers to see many products without leaving the office. Such promotions are usually interactive, so buyers can ask questions, and the information is available 24 hours a day, seven days a week.

The International Manufacturing Trade Show in Chicago featured more than 2,000 booths, giving buyers for other businesses thousands of new products to explore and purchase. Can you see why trade shows in many industries are an efficient and necessary way to stay abreast of the latest developments, competitors, and consumer reactions and needs?

After the company's employees and intermediaries have been motivated with sales promotion efforts, the next step is to promote to final consumers using samples, coupons, cents-off deals, displays, store demonstrations, premiums, contests, rebates, and so on. Sales promotion is an ongoing effort to maintain enthusiasm, so sellers use different strategies over time to keep the ideas fresh. You could put food displays in your Very Vegetarian store to show customers how attractive the products look. You could also sponsor in-store cooking demonstrations to attract new vegetarians.

One popular sales promotion tool is **sampling**—letting consumers have a small sample of the product for no charge. Because many consumers won't buy a new product unless they've had a chance to see it or try it, grocery stores often have people standing in the aisles handing out small portions of food and beverage products. Sampling is a quick, effective way of demonstrating a product's superiority when consumers are making a purchase decision. Standing outside Very Vegetarian and giving out samples would surely attract attention.

Event marketing involves sponsoring events such as rock concerts or being at various events to promote products. When Pepsi introduced its SoBe (herbal fortified drinks) product line, it used a combination of sampling, event marketing, and a new website. Pepsi first sent samples to beach cities during spring break where students got samples of the drinks. Sampling and event marketing can be effective promotional tools used to introduce new products.

test prep

- What are the three steps in setting up a public relations program?
- What are the sales promotion techniques used to reach consumers?
- What sales promotion techniques are used to reach businesses?

Everyone likes a free sample. Sampling is a promotional strategy that lets people try a new product, often in a situation when they can buy it right away if they like it. What are some advantages of sampling food products that advertising can't duplicate?

LO 16–6   Show how word of mouth, viral marketing, blogging, podcasting, e-mail marketing, and mobile marketing work.

WORD OF MOUTH AND OTHER PROMOTIONAL TOOLS

Although word of mouth was not traditionally listed as one of the major promotional efforts (it was not considered to be manageable), it is now one of the most effective, especially on the Internet.[29] In **word-of-mouth promotion**, people tell other people about products they've purchased. We've already discussed the role of social media in spreading word of mouth. Beyond word of mouth is customer participation, that is, getting customers to provide constructive suggestions and share their ideas on how to shape product and service offerings.[30]

Anything that encourages people to talk favorably about an organization can be effective word of mouth.[31] Notice, for example, how stores use clowns, banners, music, fairs, and other attention-getting devices to create word of mouth. Clever commercials can also generate word of mouth. The more that

Use LearnSmart to help retain what you have learned. Access your instructor's Connect course to check out LearnSmart, or go to learnsmartadvantage.com for help.

LEARNSMART

sampling
A promotional tool in which a company lets consumers have a small sample of a product for no charge.

word-of-mouth promotion
A promotional tool that involves people telling other people about products they've purchased.

What Are Companies Yelping About?

Restaurants, carpet cleaning services, and car repair services are businesses that truly benefit from the power of word-of-mouth promotion. In fact, word of mouth is perhaps the most important promotional tool small businesses have. That's why businesses from bakeries to barbershops were happy to greet the introduction of Yelp.com in the early 2000s. At Yelp, users can log on and review their experiences with a business and hopefully spread some love that will help the business grow. Unfortunately, many businesses that live and die by these online reviews are now questioning the methodology and ethics of Yelp.

The Federal Trade Commission has received more than 2,046 complaints filed about Yelp since 2008. The majority of the complaints are from small businesses that claim to have received unfair or fraudulent reviews after turning down an offer to advertise on Yelp. Consumer review websites, like Yelp and Angie's List, are protected against liability for defamation claims that stem from user comments under the Communications Decency Act passed in 1996. This protection riles business owners who say the system is stacked against them.

Yelp agrees that fake reviews are not fair, and boasts that it has fought against such reviews since its inception. The company maintains its "review filter" is the most efficient and sophisticated in the industry. Yet it will not explain exactly how the filter works. Ultimately, Yelp is going to have to answer three key questions: Is it punishing small or midsized businesses that do not purchase advertising on the site? Is it effective at removing fake reviews? Is it providing bad reviews for competitors of paying advertisers?

New York's attorney general Eric Schneiderman says the process of posting false reviews online is "the 21st century's version of false advertising." His department recently completed a sting operation that caught 19 different companies that were hired to write fake reviews. The companies were fined varying amounts that totaled $350,000.

Sources: Daniel Roberts, "Yelp's Fake Review Problem," *CNN Money*, September 26, 2013; Angus Loten, "Yelp Reviews Brew a Fight over Free Speech vs. Fairness," *The Wall Street Journal*, April 2, 2014; and Brian Nichols, "Yelp: Will Smoke Lead to a Stock Fire?" *The Motley Fool*, April 4, 2014.

---

people talk about your products and your brand name, the more easily customers remember them when they shop.

One especially effective strategy for spreading positive word of mouth is to send testimonials to current customers. Most companies use these only in promoting to new customers, but testimonials are also effective in confirming customers' belief that they chose the right company. Therefore, some companies make it a habit to ask customers for referrals.

Word of mouth is so powerful that negative word of mouth can hurt a firm badly. Criticism of a product or company can spread through online forums, social media, and websites (see the Adapting to Change box). Addressing consumer complaints quickly and effectively is one of the best ways to reduce the effects of negative word of mouth.

You may enjoy brainstorming strategies for creating word of mouth about Very Vegetarian. If your efforts are great, your message may "go viral" and be seen by millions of consumers.[32] **Viral marketing** includes any strategy that encourages people to pass on a marketing message to others, creating exponential growth in the message's influence as the message reaches thousands, to millions.[33] Many viral marketing programs give away free products or services, often in exchange for valuable e-mail addresses. Free attracts attention; once you have consumers' attention they can see other products or services you offer and buy those.

viral marketing
Any strategy that encourages people to pass on a marketing message to others, creating exponential growth in the message's influence as the message reaches thousands, to millions.

Blogging

There are hundreds of millions of blogs online. How do blogs affect marketing? Creating a blog is great way to interact with the customers. Business can attract new customers when they coordinate their social media profiles with their blogs. As people click to a company's blog through the social media profile, it helps improve the company's website ranking. People love to share content they find relevant. In order for a blog to succeed, a business must take time to post and respond to the customers that leave comments. They can use some of the comments to help create new posts. They have to post consistently in order to be recognized by the search engines, and to keep customers coming back to the blog for new information. If the blog isn't kept updated, it will lose traffic and, therefore, its power as a promotional tool.

Podcasting

Podcasting is a means of distributing multimedia digital files on the Internet for downloading to a portable media player. Podcasts are important because they are a great way to capture your existing and prospective customers' attention for an extended period of time by giving them something of value that is easy for them to understand.[34] Of course, many companies have also found success in creating videos for YouTube.

E-Mail Promotions

Armstrong, the flooring manufacturer, has an e-mail marketing program designed to increase brand awareness among commercial suppliers. At one time it sent out monthly e-mails to announce new products and product updates and to keep people loyal to the brand. Over time, however, those e-mails lost their power. Armstrong then turned to an e-mail service provider that completely revamped the program. The provider divided the market into four separate segments and tracked the success of the e-mails much more closely.

Mobile Marketing

Most marketers make sure their media are viewable on mobile devices like tablets and smartphones. One key to success, therefore, is to keep the message brief, because mobile users don't want to read through much text. With mobile media, marketers can use text messaging to promote sweepstakes, send customers news or sports alerts, and give them company information. Companies can determine where you are and send you messages about restaurants and other services in your vicinity.

MANAGING THE PROMOTION MIX: PUTTING IT ALL TOGETHER

Each target group calls for a separate promotion mix. Advertising is most efficient for reaching large groups of consumers whose members share similar traits. Personal selling is best for selling to large organizations. To motivate people to buy now rather than later, marketers use sales promotions like sampling, coupons, discounts, special displays, and premiums. Publicity supports other efforts and can create a good impression among all consumers. Word of mouth is often the most powerful promotional tool. Generate it by listening, being responsive, and creating an impression worth passing on to others that you spread through blogging, podcasting, and tweeting.

Mobile media allow marketers to reach customers through text messaging. Have you received such promotional messages? For which products are they most effective?

podcasting
A means of distributing multimedia digital files on the Internet for downloading to a portable media player.

> *Ads in bus shelters are nothing new, but Kraft pumped hot air into 10 Chicago bus stops to promote its Stove Top stuffing mix. The idea was to remind consumers of the warm feeling they got when eating the product. Do you think giving consumers experiences (like warmth on a cold day) is an effective way to remind them of a product?*

Promotional Strategies

How do producers move products to consumers? In a **push strategy**, the producer uses advertising, personal selling, sales promotion, and all other promotional tools to convince wholesalers and retailers to stock and sell merchandise, *pushing* it through the distribution system to the stores. If the push strategy works, consumers will walk into a store, see the product, and buy it.

A **pull strategy** directs heavy advertising and sales promotion efforts toward *consumers*. If the pull strategy works, consumers will go to the store and ask for the products. The store owner will order them from the wholesaler, who in turn will order them from the producer. Products are thus *pulled* through the distribution system.

It has been important to make promotion part of a total systems approach to marketing. That is, promotion was part of supply-chain management. In such cases, retailers would work with producers and distributors to make the supply chain as efficient as possible. Then a promotional plan would be developed for the *whole system*. The idea would be to develop a total product offer that would appeal to everyone: manufacturers, distributors, retailers, and consumers.

push strategy
Promotional strategy in which the producer uses advertising, personal selling, sales promotion, and all other promotional tools to convince wholesalers and retailers to stock and sell merchandise.

pull strategy
Promotional strategy in which heavy advertising and sales promotion efforts are directed toward consumers so that they'll request the products from retailers.

Use LearnSmart to help retain what you have learned. Access your instructor's Connect course to check out LearnSmart, or go to learnsmartadvantage.com for help.

LEARNSMART

test prep

- What is viral marketing?
- What are blogging and podcasting?
- Describe a push strategy and a pull strategy.

summary

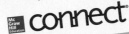
LO 16–1 Identify the new and traditional tools that make up the promotion mix.

- **What is promotion?**
Promotion is an effort by marketers to inform and remind people in the target market about products and to persuade them to participate in an exchange.

- **What are the four traditional promotional tools that make up the promotion mix?**
The four traditional promotional tools are advertising, personal selling, public relations, and sales promotion. The product itself can also be a promotional tool—that's why it is shown in the middle of Figure 16.1.

LO 16–2 Contrast the advantages and disadvantages of various advertising media, including the Internet and social media.

- **What is advertising?**
Advertising is limited to paid, nonpersonal (not face-to-face) communication through various media by organizations and individuals who are in some way identified in the advertising message.

- **What are the advantages of using the various media?**
Review the advantages and disadvantages of the various advertising media in Figure 16.5.

- **Why the growing use of infomercials?**
Infomercials are growing in importance because they show products in use and present testimonials to help sell goods and services.

LO 16–3 Illustrate the steps of the B2B and B2C selling processes.

- **What is personal selling?**
Personal selling is the face-to-face presentation and promotion of products and services. It includes the search for new prospects and follow-up service after the sale.

- **What are the seven steps of the B2B selling process?**
The steps of the selling process are (1) prospect and qualify, (2) preapproach, (3) approach, (4) make presentation, (5) answer objections, (6) close sale, and (7) follow up.

- **What are the steps in the B2C selling process?**
The steps are the approach, which includes asking questions; the presentation, which includes answering questions; the close; and the follow-up.

LO 16–4 Describe the role of the public relations department, and show how publicity fits in that role.

- **What is public relations?**
Public relations (PR) is the function that evaluates public attitudes, changes policies and procedures in response to the public's requests, and executes a program of action and information to earn public understanding and acceptance.

- **What are the three major steps in a good public relations program?**
(1) Listen to the public, (2) develop policies and procedures in the public interest, and (3) tell people you're being responsive to their needs.

* **What is publicity?**

  Publicity is the talking part of sales promotion; it is information distributed by the media that's not paid for, or controlled by, the seller. Publicity's greatest advantage is its believability.

LO 16–5   Assess the effectiveness of various forms of sales promotion, including sampling.

* **How are sales promotion activities used both within and outside the organization?**

  Internal sales promotion efforts are directed at salespeople and other customer-contact people to keep them enthusiastic about the company. Internal sales promotion activities include sales training, sales aids, audio-visual displays, and trade shows. External sales promotions to consumers rely on samples, coupons, cents-off deals, displays, store demonstrators, premiums, and other incentives.

LO 16–6   Show how word of mouth, viral marketing, blogging, podcasting, e-mail marketing, and mobile marketing work.

* **Is word of mouth a major promotional tool?**

  Word of mouth was not one of the traditional forms of promotion because it was not considered to be manageable, but it has always been an effective way of promoting goods and services.

* **How is word of mouth used in promotion today?**

  The goal of word of mouth is to get the company's message to as many people as possible. Viral marketing includes any strategy that encourages people to pass on a marketing message to others, creating exponential growth in the message's influence as the message reaches thousands, to millions. Many viral marketing programs give away free products or services, often in exchange for valuable e-mail addresses.

* **What other promotional tools can marketers use to promote products?**

  Other promotional tools include blogging, podcasting, e-mail promotions, and mobile marketing.

* **What are the major promotional strategies?**

  In a *push strategy*, the producer uses advertising, personal selling, sales promotion, and all other promotional tools to convince wholesalers and retailers to stock and sell merchandise. In a *pull strategy*, heavy advertising and sales promotion efforts are directed toward consumers so they'll request the products from retailers.

key terms

advertising 449	podcasting 465	push strategy 466
infomercial 453	product placement 453	qualifying 457
integrated marketing communication (IMC) 448	promotion mix 448	sales promotion 461
	prospect 457	sampling 463
	prospecting 457	trial close 458
interactive promotion 454	publicity 460	viral marketing 464
personal selling 456	public relations (PR) 460	word-of-mouth promotion 463
	pull strategy 466	

1. What kinds of problems can emerge if a firm doesn't communicate with environmentalists, the news media, and the local community? Do you know of any firms that aren't responsive to your community? What are the consequences?

2. How often do you buy online? If you don't actually buy, do you use the Internet to compare goods and prices? Do you or your friends take advantage of low prices on used goods on eBay or other online sites like Craigslist? Do you look at ads on the Internet? Do they seem to be effective?

3. As interactive communications between companies and customers grow, do you think traditional advertising will grow or decline? What will be the effect of growth or decline on the price we pay for TV programs, newspapers, and magazines?

4. How have blogging, podcasting, and social media affected other media you use, like newspapers or television? Do you read print newspapers now or do you get your news some other way? Do you watch programs on TV or on other devices? How has the move away from print and network television affected advertising?

developing **workplace skills**

Key: ● **Team**   ★ **Analytic**   ▲ **Communication**   ▣ **Technology**

1. Using at least two different media—a newspaper, magazine, television, radio, the Internet—choose two ads you consider effective and two you find ineffective. Be prepared to explain your choices. ★ ▲

2. Scan your local newspaper or search online for examples of publicity (stories about new products) and sales promotion (coupons, contests, sweepstakes). Share your examples and discuss the effectiveness of such promotional efforts with the class. ▲ ★ ▣

3. Many students shy away from careers in selling, often because they think they are not outgoing enough or that salespeople are dishonest or pushy. Prepare a one-page document about your experience with salespeople and what you think of selling as a career. ▲ ★

4. In small groups, discuss whether you are purchasing more goods using catalogs and/or the Internet and why. Do you look up information online before buying goods and services? How helpful are such searches? Present your findings to the class. ▲ ★ ●

5. In small groups, list six goods and services most students own or use and discuss promotional techniques that prompt you to buy them: advertising, personal selling, social media, publicity, sales promotion, or word of mouth. Which seems most effective for your group? Why? ▲ ★ ●

taking it to the **net**

PURPOSE

To learn about business blogs.

EXERCISE

Go to www.google.com/blogger to learn how easy it is to start your own blog. Then go to the following business-oriented blogs: VentureBlog.com (www.ventureblog.com) and PatentPending.blogs.com (http://patentpending.blogs.com).

1. What kind of subjects are covered in each blog?

2. What are the advantages and disadvantages of reading such blogs?

3. Would you like to see a blog for this course? For your school?

video case   ■McGraw Hill Education connect

SXSW

South by Southwest (SXSW) is an annual music, film, and technology festival held in Austin, Texas. For 10 days in March, the city welcomes thousands of concertgoers, film buffs, and industry insiders. Part trade show and part mega-concert, this enormous event not only makes fans of hip art happy; it also serves as a meeting point for new artists and potential managers, collaborators, and industry executives.

The music portion of the most recent SXSW featured more than 2,000 acts playing for tens of thousands of roving guests. With so many people in attendance, the event presents ample opportunity for promotions of all types. Each year the festival teams up with corporate sponsors like Doritos, AT&T, and Chevrolet to advertise at the event. These business-to-business (B2B) relationships benefit both parties by giving SXSW crucial operating income while providing the companies with a presence at a cool event.

SXSW also features several business-to-consumer (B2C) promotions. For a lower price, attendees can choose to access just a single event, like the film festival. But buying a higher-priced badge not only gets the attendees into all events, but grants them access to VIP keynote speakers, parties, and workshops. These types of deals represent the lifeblood of the event and the main source of the festival's income.

With so much to do and see, SXSW naturally generates a lot of publicity. Radio stations and magazines run dozens of stories in the run-up to the festival because they consider the event to be news. Each of those stories ends up becoming free publicity for SXSW, giving organizers an incentive to create as much buzz as possible. To accomplish this goal, a public relations team hired by the festival actively seeks publicity from interested stakeholders. This includes the city of Austin itself, which is more than happy to let SXSW fly banners over the streets. As the largest revenue-generating event in Austin, the city's cooperation with the festival makes a lot of sense.

Music is a product that benefits from a personal touch, so many bands that attend SXSW rely on "street teams" to get the word out. These dedicated fans work for free to promote the band and, by proxy, the event. The fans are more than happy to hand out fliers or talk about the event at local record stores and coffee shops in order to make people aware of their favorite performers. All of this personal selling benefits not only the bands, but the event as well. After all, these street teams consist of thousands of people *volunteering* to talk about the festival. You can't buy promotion like that.

That kind of grass-roots publicity is some of the most effective and least expensive available. Every time a music fan tweets about the event, mentions it in a YouTube video or podcast, or blogs about the great time he or she had at the last SXSW, that positive message spreads to several new people. And in today's social media–driven world, a dependable word-of-mouth recommendation might be the most important type of promotion. Still, it's impossible to completely control the things that people say about you or your company. That's why SXSW employs a number of different promotional strategies in its quest to stay cool.

THINKING IT OVER

1. What are the critical differences between publicity and advertising?

2. Identify the four elements of the promotion mix.

3. On which of the four elements of the promotion mix does SXSW rely most?

notes

1. Julie Liesse, "15 on 15: Council Founders Share Industry Highlights," *Advertising Age,* Special Advertising Section, November 11, 2013.
2. Caitlin Laluza, "The Explosion of Mobile Audiences: What It Means for Public Relations," *The Public Relations Strategist,* Fall 2013.
3. "Coke: Buzz Doesn't Work, but Social Is Crucial," *Advertising Age,* editorial, March 25, 2013.
4. Wes Nichols, "The Future of Advertising," *Harvard Business Review,* March 2013.
5. Sunil Gupta, "For Mobile Devices, Think Apps, Not Ads," *Harvard Business Review,* March 2013.
6. Miguel Helft, "Selling Brands on Facebook," *Fortune,* March 18, 2013.
7. Benjamin Palmer, "Why Modern Marketers and Creatives Need to Reevaluate Radio, the World's Most Popular Medium," *Advertising Age,* September 30, 2013.
8. Suzanne Vranica, "And Now, Ads for the Super Bowl Ads," *The Wall Street Journal,* January 27, 2014.
9. Jack Neff, "80% of Super Bowl Ads Flop: Study," *Advertising Age,* January 6, 2014.
10. You can find data on the cost of various 30-second spots in *Advertising Age,* October 21, 2013.
11. Jack Neff, "Walmart Takes TV Fight Local," *Advertising Age,* April 8, 2013.
12. Michael McCarthy, "BMW Teams Up with TaylorMade for Ad within Ad," *Advertising Age,* July 15, 2013.
13. Jeff Bercovici, "Can Twitter Save TV?" *Forbes,* October 28, 2013.
14. *Advertising Age,* August 19, 2013.
15. Mark Milian and Michael White, "Sony's Scene-Stealing Product Placements," *Bloomberg Businessweek,* July 16–July 22, 2012.
16. Amal Sharma, Shalini Ramachandran, and Don Clark, "Amazon Joins the TV Crush," *The Wall Street Journal,* January 22, 2014.
17. Ralph Anderson, Srinvason Swaminathan, and Rajiv Metha, "How to Drive Customer Satisfaction," *Sloan Management Review,* Summer 2013.
18. Russ Hill, "What Is the Cost of a B2B Sales Call?" *CRM Insights,* www.crm-insights.com, November 4, 2013.
19. Brent Adamson, Matthew Dixon, and Nicholas Toman, "The End of Solution Sales," *Harvard Business Review,* July–August 2012.
20. James Farley, "How to Sell to Customers Who Know Everything," *Harvard Business Review,* July–August 2012.
21. Katrina Pugh and Laurance Prusak, ""Designing Effective Knowledge Networks," *Sloan Management Review,* Fall 2013.
22. "General Mills Notches PR Win with GMO-Free Cheerios (But Activists Want More)," editorial, *Advertising Age,* January 6, 2014.
23. Ibid.
24. Stephen Dupont, "Understanding the Language of Economics Is Critical to Communicating Effectively," *The Public Relations Strategist,* Winter 2013.
25. Todd Henneman, "Is HR at Its Breaking Point?" *Workforce Management,* April 2013.
26. Lisa Ward, "What to Do after Your 15 Minutes of Fame," *The Wall Street Journal,* December 2, 2013.
27. Ibid.
28. V. Kumar and Bharath Rajan, "The Perils of Social Coupon Campaigns," *Sloan Management Review,* Summer 2012.
29. Rakesh Niraj, "Just How Much Is Word of Mouth Worth?" *Weatherhead Collection,* Fall 2013.
30. Michael McCarthy, "Tesla Generates Small Sales, Huge Buzz Without Paid Ads," *Advertising Age,* June 10, 2013; and Omar Merlo, Andreas B. Eisingerich, and Seigyoung Auh, "Why Customer Participation Matters," *Sloan Management Review,* Winter 2014.
31. "Get 'Em Talking," *Entrepreneur,* editorial, August 2012.
32. Michael Fitzgerald, "The Myth about Viral Marketing," *Sloan Management Review,* Spring 2013.
33. Ralph F. Wilson, "The Six Simple Principles of Viral Marketing," *Web Marketing Today,* www.webmarketingtoday.com, May 12, 2012.
34. Kim Garst, "Social Media Marketing World 2014," *Huffington Post,* www.huffingtonpost, April 9, 2014.

photo credits

PART 6

17

Understanding Accounting and Financial Information

Learning Objectives

AFTER YOU HAVE READ AND STUDIED THIS CHAPTER, YOU SHOULD BE ABLE TO

LO 17-1 Demonstrate the role that accounting and financial information play for a business and its stakeholders.

LO 17-2 Identify the different disciplines within the accounting profession.

LO 17-3 List the steps in the accounting cycle, distinguish between accounting and bookkeeping, and explain how computers are used in accounting.

LO 17-4 Explain how the major financial statements differ.

LO 17-5 Demonstrate the application of ratio analysis in reporting financial information.

Getting to know **John Raftery**

After John Raftery was sworn into the United States Marine Corps in 1999, he served in the infantry and then in a reconnaissance battalion. He was deployed to the Middle East and was one of many Marines who took part in Operation Iraqi Freedom, helping liberate Baghdad in 2003. After his discharge from the Marine Corps, Raftery faced the same challenge as many of his fellow veterans: how to transfer what he learned in the military to the business world. He chose to take advantage of his GI Bill educational benefits to go to Dallas Baptist University (DBU). John studied accounting and served as vice president of the DBU Accounting Society and as the campus representative for the Becker CPA Review. He learned that accounting offered solid career opportunities.

After earning his degree in accounting, Raftery went to work at a health care firm as an accounting assistant. He worked hard learning the ins-and-outs of public accounting, but soon realized that a career as an accountant wasn't for him. Raftery's real aspiration was to be an entrepreneur. He applied for admission to a program called the Entrepreneurship Boot Camp for Veterans with Disabilities. The weeklong intensive training course was specifically designed for vets with disabilities interested in starting their own businesses. John was one of the first veterans accepted into the program.

After completing the entrepreneurship program, John felt confident enough to launch his own business, Patriot Contractors, in Red Oak, Texas. The company "accessorizes" buildings in the commercial and government sector—building out interior space with cabinets, countertops, railings and other items. *Inc.* magazine ranked Patriot Contractors as one of the fastest-growing private companies in America. The company also received special recognition from President Obama, who invited Raftery to Washington to attend his speech to Congress introducing the Jumpstart Our Business Startups Act (JOBS Act). Patriot Contractors was cited by the president as an example of the potential of veteran entrepreneurship.

As Patriot Contractors adds employees and increases revenues, Raftery credits two key personal accomplishments for his company's success. One was his experience as part of a military recon team that helped him understand the importance of applying the capabilities and limitations of his team members to complete a mission successfully. He also credits his knowledge of accounting for helping him develop into a businessperson who can speak the language of business. John readily admits, "Not a day goes by in running my company that I don't leverage some part of my accounting knowledge."

Controlling costs, managing cash flows, understanding profit margins and taxes, and reporting finances accurately are keys to survival for both growing organizations like Patriot Contractors and large corporations. This chapter will introduce you to the accounting fundamentals and financial information critical to business success. The chapter also briefly explores the financial ratios that are essential in measuring business performance in a large or small business.

Sources: Patriot Contractors, www.patriot.com, accessed May 2014; Gwen Moran, "How Military Veterans Are Finding Success in Small Business," *Entrepreneur,* February 20, 2012; and an interview with John Raftery, April 2014.

John Raftery
- Founder of Patriot Contractors
- Used accounting knowledge and military experience to start own business

www.patriotcontractorsinc.com

@RafteryJ

473

name that **company**

Accounting software makes financial information available whenever the organization needs it. We specialize in software that addresses the accounting needs of small businesses that are often very different from major corporations. Name that company. (Find the answer in the chapter.)

LO 17–1 Demonstrate the role that accounting and financial information play for a business and for its stakeholders.

THE ROLE OF ACCOUNTING INFORMATION

Small and large businesses often survive or fail according to how well they handle financial procedures. Financial management is the heartbeat of competitive businesses, and accounting information helps keep the heartbeat stable.

Accounting reports and financial statements reveal as much about a business's health as pulse and blood pressure readings tell us about a person's health. Thus, you have to know something about accounting if you want to succeed in business. It's almost impossible to understand business operations without being able to read, understand, and analyze accounting reports and financial statements.

By the end of the chapter, you should have a good idea what accounting is, how it works, and the value it offers businesses. You should also know some accounting terms and understand the purpose of accounting statements. Your new understanding will pay off as you become more active in business, or will help you in simply understanding what's going on in the world of business and finance.

What Is Accounting?

accounting

The recording, classifying, summarizing, and interpreting of financial events and transactions to provide management and other interested parties the information they need to make good decisions.

Accounting is the recording, classifying, summarizing, and interpreting of financial events and transactions in an organization to provide management and other interested parties the financial information they need to make good decisions about its operation. Financial transactions include buying and selling goods and services, acquiring insurance, paying employees, and using supplies. Usually we group all purchases together, and all sales transactions together. The method we use to record and summarize accounting data into reports is an *accounting system* (see Figure 17.1).

A major purpose of accounting is to help managers make well-informed decisions. Another is to report financial information about the firm to interested stakeholders, such as employees, owners, creditors, suppliers, unions, community activists, investors, and the government (for tax purposes) (see Figure 17.2). Accounting is divided into several major disciplines. Let's look at those next.

FIGURE 17.1 THE ACCOUNTING SYSTEM
The inputs to an accounting system include sales documents and other documents. The data are recorded, classified, and summarized. They're then put into summary financial statements such as the income statement and balance sheet and statement of cash flows.

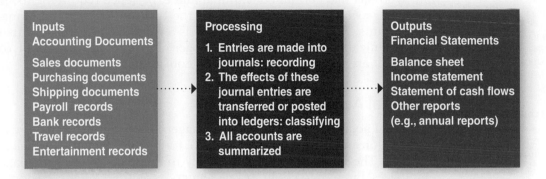

Inputs
Accounting Documents

Sales documents
Purchasing documents
Shipping documents
Payroll records
Bank records
Travel records
Entertainment records

Processing

1. Entries are made into journals: recording
2. The effects of these journal entries are transferred or posted into ledgers: classifying
3. All accounts are summarized

Outputs
Financial Statements

Balance sheet
Income statement
Statement of cash flows
Other reports
(e.g., annual reports)

LO 17–2   Identify the different disciplines within the accounting profession.

ACCOUNTING DISCIPLINES

You may think accounting is only for profit-seeking firms. Nothing could be further from the truth. Accounting, often called the language of business, allows us to report financial information about nonprofit organizations such as churches, schools, hospitals, fraternities, and government agencies.[1] The accounting profession is divided into five key working areas: managerial accounting, financial accounting, auditing, tax accounting, and governmental and not-for-profit accounting. All five are important, and all create career opportunities.[2] Let's explore each.

Managerial Accounting

Managerial accounting provides information and analysis to managers *inside* the organization to assist them in decision making. Managerial accounting is concerned with measuring and reporting costs of production, marketing, and other functions; preparing budgets (planning); checking whether or not units are staying within their budgets (controlling); and designing strategies to minimize taxes.

managerial accounting
Accounting used to provide information and analyses to managers inside the organization to assist them in decision making.

FIGURE 17.2 USERS OF ACCOUNTING INFORMATION AND THE REQUIRED REPORTS
Many types of organizations use accounting information to make business decisions. The reports need to vary according to the information each user requires. An accountant must prepare the appropriate forms.

USERS	TYPE OF REPORT
• Government taxing authorities (e.g., the Internal Revenue Service)	• Tax returns
• Government regulatory agencies	• Required reports
• People interested in the organization's income and financial position (e.g., owners, creditors, financial analysts, suppliers)	• Financial statements found in annual reports (e.g., income statement, balance sheet, statement of cash flows)
• Managers of the firm	• Financial statements and various internally distributed financial reports

certified management accountant (CMA)
A professional accountant who has met certain educational and experience requirements, passed a qualifying exam, and been certified by the Institute of Certified Management Accountants.

financial accounting
Accounting information and analyses prepared for people outside the organization.

annual report
A yearly statement of the financial condition, progress, and expectations of an organization.

private accountant
An accountant who works for a single firm, government agency, or nonprofit organization.

public accountant
An accountant who provides accounting services to individuals or businesses on a fee basis.

Assembling an aircraft engine requires many tools, parts, raw materials, and other components as well as labor costs. Keeping these costs at a minimum and setting realistic production schedules is critical to a business's survival. What other internal departments must management accountants team with to ensure company competitiveness?

If you are a business major, you'll probably take a course in managerial accounting. You may even pursue a career as a certified management accountant. **A certified management accountant (CMA)** is a professional accountant who has met certain educational and experience requirements, passed a qualifying exam, and been certified by the Institute of Certified Management Accountants.[3] With the growing emphasis on global competition, outsourcing, and organizational cost-cutting, managerial accounting is one of the most important areas you may study in your college career.[4]

Financial Accounting

Financial accounting differs from managerial accounting in that the financial information and analyses it generates are for people primarily *outside* the organization. The information goes not only to company owners, managers, and employees, but also to creditors and lenders, employee unions, customers, suppliers, government agencies, and the general public. External users are interested in questions like: Is the organization profitable? Is it able to pay its bills? How much debt does it owe? These questions and others are often answered in the company's **annual report**, a yearly statement of the financial condition, progress, and expectations of an organization. As pressure from stakeholders for detailed financial information has grown, companies are seeking to reduce cost by putting the annual report on the firm's website and making better use of the Form 10-K that is required by the Securities and Exchange Commission.[5]

It's critical for firms to keep accurate financial information. Therefore, many organizations employ a **private accountant** who works for a single firm, government agency, or nonprofit organization. However, not all firms or nonprofit organizations want or need a full-time accountant. Fortunately, thousands of accounting firms in the United States provide the accounting services an organization needs through public accountants.

For a fee, a **public accountant** provides accounting services to individuals or businesses. Such services can include designing an accounting system, helping select the correct software to run the system, and analyzing an organization's financial performance. An accountant who passes a series of examinations established by the American Institute of Certified Public Accountants (AICPA) and meets the state's requirement for education and experience is recognized as a **certified public accountant (CPA)**. CPAs find careers as private or public accountants and are often sought to fill other financial positions within organizations. Today, there are over 645,000 CPAs in the United States, 386,000 of whom are members of the AICPA.[6]

Accountants know it's vital for users of a firm's accounting information to be assured the information is accurate. The independent Financial Accounting Standards Board (FASB) defines the *generally accepted accounting principles (GAAP)* that accountants must follow.[7] If accounting reports are prepared in accordance with GAAP, users can expect the information to meet standards upon which accounting professionals have agreed.

Unfortunately, the accounting profession suffered a dark period in the early 2000s when accounting scandals at WorldCom, Enron, and Tyco raised public suspicions about the profession and corporate integrity in general. Arthur Andersen, one of the nation's leading accounting firms, was forced out of business after being convicted of obstruction of justice for shredding records in the Enron case (the conviction was later overturned by the U.S. Supreme Court).[8]

Scrutiny of the accounting industry intensified, and resulted in the U.S. Congress's passage of the

few of the many government agencies that offer career possibilities to accountants seeking to work in government accounting.

Not-for-profit organizations often require accounting professionals. Charities like the Salvation Army, Red Cross, museums, and hospitals all hire accountants to show contributors how their money is spent. In fact, their need for trained accountants is growing since donors to nonprofits usually want to see exactly how and where the funds they contribute are being spent. During the recent recession, many businesses and individuals cut back on donations, making it more important than ever to account for every dollar contributed.[18]

As you can see, managerial and financial accounting, auditing, tax accounting, and governmental and not-for-profit accounting each require specific training and skill. After the Test Prep, we will clarify the difference between accounting and bookkeeping.

test prep

- What is the key difference between managerial and financial accounting?
- How is the job of a private accountant different from that of a public accountant?
- What is the job of an auditor? What's an independent audit?

LO 17–3   List the steps in the accounting cycle, distinguish between accounting and bookkeeping, and explain how computers are used in accounting.

THE ACCOUNTING CYCLE

The **accounting cycle** is a six-step procedure that results in the preparation and analysis of the major financial statements (see Figure 17.4). It relies on the work of both a bookkeeper and an accountant. **Bookkeeping**, the recording of business transactions, is a basic part of financial reporting. Accounting, however, goes far beyond the mere recording of financial information. Accountants classify and summarize financial data provided by bookkeepers, and then interpret the data and report the information to management. They also suggest strategies for improving the firm's financial condition and prepare financial analyses and income tax returns.

A bookkeeper's first task is to divide all the firm's transactions into meaningful categories, such as sales documents, purchasing receipts, and shipping documents, being very careful to keep the information organized and manageable. Bookkeepers then record financial data from the original transaction documents (sales slips and so forth) into a record book or computer program called a **journal**. The word *journal* comes from the French word *jour*, which means "day." Therefore, a journal is where the day's transactions are kept.

It's quite possible to make a mistake when recording financial transactions, like entering $10.98 as $10.89. That's why bookkeepers record all transactions in two places, so they can check one list of transactions against the other to make sure both add up to the same amount. If the amounts are not

Use LearnSmart to help retain what you have learned. Access your instructor's Connect course to check out LearnSmart, or go to learnsmartadvantage.com for help.

LEARNSMART

 connect

iSee It! Need help understanding the accounting cycle? Visit your Connect e-book video tab for a brief animated explanation.

FIGURE 17.4 STEPS IN THE ACCOUNTING CYCLE

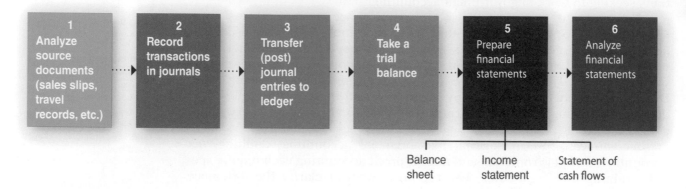

1	2	3	4	5	6
Analyze source documents (sales slips, travel records, etc.)	Record transactions in journals	Transfer (post) journal entries to ledger	Take a trial balance	Prepare financial statements	Analyze financial statements

Balance sheet   Income statement   Statement of cash flows

double-entry bookkeeping
The practice of writing every business transaction in two places.

ledger
A specialized accounting book or computer program in which information from accounting journals is accumulated into specific categories and posted so that managers can find all the information about one account in the same place.

trial balance
A summary of all the financial data in the account ledgers that ensures the figures are correct and balanced.

equal, the bookkeeper knows there is a mistake. The practice of writing every transaction in two places is called **double-entry bookkeeping**. It requires two entries in the journal and in the ledgers (discussed next) for each transaction.

Suppose a business wanted to determine how much it paid for office supplies in the first quarter of the year. Without a specific bookkeeping tool, that would be difficult—even with accurate accounting journals. Therefore, bookkeepers use a specialized accounting book or computer program called a **ledger**. In the ledger, they transfer (or post) information from accounting journals into specific categories so managers can find all the information about a single account, like office supplies or cash, in one place.

The next step in the accounting cycle is to prepare a **trial balance**, a summary of all the financial data in the account ledgers that ensures the figures are correct and balanced. If the information in the account ledgers is not accurate, the accountant must correct it before preparing the firm's financial statements. Using the correct information, the accountant then prepares the firm's financial statements—including a balance sheet, an income statement, and a statement of cash flows—according to GAAP.

Using Technology in Accounting

A long while ago, accountants and bookkeepers needed to enter all of a firm's financial information by hand. The advent of adding machines and calculators made the job a bit simpler, but still generally required a paper entry. Toward the end of the 20th century, technology simplified the accounting process considerably. Today, computerized accounting programs can post information from journals instantaneously from remote locations to encrypted laptops or cell phones, making financial information available whenever the organization needs it. The company's sensitive financial information is safe and secure, but is in the accountant's hands when needed. Such assistance frees accountants' time for more important tasks such as financial analysis and financial forecasting.

Computerized accounting programs are also particularly helpful to small-business owners, who don't often have the variety of accounting personnel within their companies that larger firms enjoy. Accounting software—such as Intuit's QuickBooks—addresses the specific needs of small businesses that are often significantly different from the needs of a major corporation.[19] Small-business owners, however, need to understand exactly which programs are best suited for their particular company needs. That's one reason why entrepreneurs planning to start a business should either hire or consult with an accountant to identify the particular needs of their firm.[20] They can then develop a specific accounting system that works with the accounting software they've chosen.

With sophisticated accounting software available and technology capabilities growing, you might wonder why you need to study and understand accounting. Without question technology has greatly assisted businesspeople and certainly helped ease the monotony of bookkeeping and accounting work. Unfortunately the work of an accountant requires training and very specific competencies that computers are not programmed to handle. It's the partnership of technology and an accountant's knowledge that helps a firm make the right financial decisions. After the Test Prep, we'll explore the balance sheet, income statement, and statement of cash flows. It's from the information contained in these financial statements that the accountant analyzes and evaluates the financial condition of the firm.

test prep

- How is the job of the bookkeeper different from that of an accountant?
- What's the purpose of accounting journals and of a ledger?
- Why does a bookkeeper prepare a trial balance?
- How has computer software helped businesses in maintaining and compiling accounting information?

Use LearnSmart to help retain what you have learned. Access your instructor's Connect course to check out LearnSmart, or go to learnsmartadvantage.com for help.

LEARNSMART

LO 17–4   Explain how the major financial statements differ.

UNDERSTANDING KEY FINANCIAL STATEMENTS

An accounting year is either a calendar or fiscal year. A calendar year begins January 1 and ends December 31. A fiscal year can begin at any date designated by the business. A **financial statement** is a summary of all the financial transactions that have occurred over a particular period. Financial statements indicate a firm's financial health and stability, and are key factors in management decision making.[21] That's why stockholders (the owners of the firm), bondholders and banks (people and institutions that lend money to the firm), labor unions, employees, and the Internal Revenue Service are all interested in a firm's financial statements. The key financial statements of a business are:

financial statement
A summary of all the financial transactions that have occurred over a particular period.

1. The *balance sheet*, which reports the firm's financial condition *on a specific date*.

2. The *income statement*, which summarizes revenues, cost of goods, and expenses (including taxes), for a specific period and highlights the total profit or loss the firm experienced *during that period*.

3. The *statement of cash flows*, which provides a summary of money coming into and going out of the firm. It tracks a company's cash receipts and cash payments.

The differences among the financial statements can best be summarized this way: The balance sheet details what the company owns and owes on a certain day; the income statement shows the revenue a firm earned selling its products compared to its selling costs (profit or loss) over a specific period of time; and the statement of cash flows highlights the difference between cash coming in and cash going out of a business. To fully understand this important financial information, you need to know the purpose of an organization's financial statements. To help with this task, we'll explain each statement in more detail next.

The Fundamental Accounting Equation

Imagine you don't owe anybody money. That is, you have no liabilities (debts). In this case, your assets (cash and so forth) are equal to what you *own* (your equity). However, if you borrow some money from a friend, you have incurred a liability. Your assets are now equal to what you *owe* plus what you own. Translated into business terms, Assets = Liabilities + Owners' equity.

In accounting, this equation must always be balanced. For example, suppose you have $50,000 in cash and decide to use that money to open a small coffee shop. Your business has assets of $50,000 and no debts. The accounting equation would look like this:

$$\text{Assets} = \text{Liabilities} + \text{Owner's equity}$$
$$\$50,000 = \$0 \qquad + \$50,000$$

You have $50,000 cash and $50,000 owners' equity (the amount of your investment in the business—sometimes referred to as net worth). However, before opening the business, you borrow $30,000 from a local bank; now the equation changes. You have $30,000 of additional cash, but you also have a debt (liability) of $30,000. (Remember, in double-entry bookkeeping we record each business transaction in two places.)

Your financial position within the business has changed. The equation is still balanced, but we change it to reflect the borrowing transaction:

$$\text{Assets} = \text{Liabilities} + \text{Owner's equity}$$
$$\$80,000 = \$30,000 \quad + \$50,000$$

This **fundamental accounting equation** is the basis for the balance sheet.

The Balance Sheet

A **balance sheet** is the financial statement that reports a firm's financial condition at a specific time. As highlighted in the sample balance sheet in Figure 17.5 (for our hypothetical vegetarian restaurant, Very Vegetarian, introduced in Chapter 13), assets are listed in a separate column from liabilities and owners' (or stockholders') equity. The assets are equal to, or *balanced* with, the liabilities and owners' (or stockholders') equity. The balance sheet is that simple.

Let's say you want to know what your financial condition is at a given time. Maybe you want to buy a house or car and therefore need to calculate your available resources. One of the best measuring sticks is your balance sheet. First, add up everything you own—cash, property, and money owed you. These are your assets. Subtract from that the money you owe others—credit card debt, IOUs, car loan, student loans and the like. These are your liabilities. The resulting figure is your net worth, or equity. This is fundamentally what companies do in preparing a balance sheet: they follow the procedures set in the fundamental accounting equation. In that preparation, any company that is publicly traded is required by the Securities and Exchange Commission (discussed in depth in Chapter 19) to follow GAAP.[22]

VERY VEGETARIAN
Balance Sheet
December 31, 2015

Assets

① Current assets

Cash	$ 15,000	
Accounts receivable	200,000	
Notes receivable	50,000	
Inventory	335,000	
Total current assets		$600,000

② Fixed assets

Land		$ 40,000	
Building and improvements	$200,000		
Less: Accumulated depreciation	−90,000		
		110,000	
Equipment and vehicles	$ 120,000		
Less: Accumulated depreciation	−80,000		
		40,000	
Furniture and fixtures	$ 26,000		
Less: Accumulated depreciation	−10,000		
		16,000	
Total fixed assets			206,000

③ Intangible assets

Goodwill	$ 20,000	
Total intangible assets		20,000
Total assets		$826,000

Liabilities and Owners' Equity

④ Current liabilities

Accounts payable	$ 40,000	
Notes payable (due June 2016)	8.000	
Accrued taxes	150,000	
Accrued salaries	90,000	
Total current liabilities		$288,000

⑤ Long-term liabilities

Notes payable (due Mar. 2020)	$ 35,000	
Bonds payable (due Dec. 2025)	290,000	
Total long-term liabilities		325,000
Total liabilities		$ 613,000

⑥ Owners' equity

Common stock (1,000,000 shares)	$100,000	
Retained earnings	113,000	
Total owners' equity		213,000
Total liabilities & owners' equity		$826,000

FIGURE 17.5 SAMPLE VERY VEGETARIAN BALANCE SHEET

① Current assets: Items that can be converted to cash within one year.

② Fixed assets: Items such as land, buildings, and equipment that are relatively permanent.

③ Intangible assets: Items of value such as patents and copyrights that don't have a physical form.

④ Current liabilities: Payments that are due in one year or less.

⑤ Long-term liabilities: Payments that are not due for one year or longer.

⑥ Owners' equity: The value of what stockholders own in a firm (also called stockholders' equity).

Since it's critical that you understand the financial information on the balance sheet, let's take a closer look at what is in a business's asset account and what is in its liabilities and owners' equity accounts.

Classifying Assets

Assets are economic resources (things of value) owned by a firm. Assets include productive, tangible items such as equipment, buildings, land, furniture, and motor vehicles that help generate income, as well as intangible items

assets
Economic resources (things of value) owned by a firm.

with value like patents, trademarks, copyrights, and goodwill. Goodwill represents the value attached to factors such as a firm's reputation, location, and superior products. Goodwill is included on a balance sheet when one firm acquires another and pays more for it than the value of its tangible assets. Intangible assets like brand names can be among the firm's most valuable resources. Think of the value of brand names such as Starbucks, Coca-Cola, McDonald's, and Apple. Not all companies, however, list intangible assets on their balance sheets.

Accountants list assets on the firm's balance sheet in order of their **liquidity**, or the ease with which they can convert them to cash. Speedier conversion means higher liquidity. For example, an *account receivable* is an amount of money owed to the firm that it expects to receive within one year. It is considered a liquid asset because it can be quickly converted to cash. Land, however, is not considered a liquid asset because it takes time, effort, and paperwork to sell. It is considered as a fixed or long-term asset. Assets are thus divided into three categories, according to how quickly they can be turned into cash:

1. **Current assets** are items that can or will be converted into cash within one year. They include cash, accounts receivable, and inventory.

2. **Fixed assets** are long-term assets that are relatively permanent such as land, buildings, and equipment. (On the balance sheet we can also refer to these as property, plant, and equipment.)

3. **Intangible assets** are long-term assets that have no physical form but do have value. Patents, trademarks, copyrights, and goodwill are intangible assets.

Liabilities and Owners' Equity Accounts

Liabilities are what the business owes to others—its debts. *Current liabilities* are debts due in one year or less. *Long-term liabilities* are debts not due for one year or more. The following are common liability accounts recorded on a balance sheet (look at Figure 17.5 again):

1. **Accounts payable** are current liabilities or bills the company owes others for merchandise or services it purchased on credit but has not yet paid for.

2. **Notes payable** can be short-term or long-term liabilities (like loans from banks) that a business promises to repay by a certain date.

3. **Bonds payable** are long-term liabilities; money lent to the firm that it must pay back. (We discuss bonds in depth in Chapters 18 and 19.)

As you saw in the fundamental accounting equation, the value of things you own (assets) minus the amount of money you owe others (liabilities) is called *equity*. The value of what stockholders own in a firm (minus liabilities) is called *stockholders' equity* or *shareholders' equity*. Because stockholders are the owners of a firm, we also call stockholders' equity **owners' equity**, or the amount of the business that belongs to the owners, minus any liabilities the business owes. The formula for owners' equity, then, is assets minus liabilities.

The owners' equity account will differ according to the type of organization. For sole proprietors and partners, owners' equity means the value of everything owned by the business minus any liabilities of the owner(s), such as bank loans. Owners' equity in these firms is called the *capital account*.

For corporations, the owners' equity account records the owners' claims to funds they have invested in the firm (such as stock), as well as retained

---

liquidity
The ease with which an asset can be converted into cash.

current assets
Items that can or will be converted into cash within one year.

fixed assets
Assets that are relatively permanent, such as land, buildings, and equipment.

intangible assets
Long-term assets (e.g., patents, trademarks, copyrights) that have no real physical form but do have value.

liabilities
What the business owes to others (debts).

accounts payable
Current liabilities or bills the company owes to others for merchandise or services purchased on credit but not yet paid for.

notes payable
Short-term or long-term liabilities that a business promises to repay by a certain date.

bonds payable
Long-term liabilities that represent money lent to the firm that must be paid back.

owners' equity
The amount of the business that belongs to the owners minus any liabilities owed by the business.

ASSETS		LIABILITIES	
Cash	$ _____	Installment loans & interest	$ _____
Savings account	_____	Other loans & interest	_____
Checking account	_____	Credit card accounts	_____
Home	_____	Mortgage	_____
Stocks & bonds	_____	Taxes	_____
Automobile	_____	Cell phone service	_____
IRA or Keogh	_____		
Personal property	_____		
Other assets	_____		
Total assets	$ _____	Total liabilities	$ _____

Determine your net worth:

Total assets	$ _____
Total liabilities	− _____
Net worth	$ _____

FIGURE 17.6 YOU INCORPORATED
How do you think You Inc. stacks up financially? Let's take a little time to find out. You may be pleasantly surprised, or you may realize that you need to think hard about planning your financial future. Remember, your net worth is nothing more than the difference between what you own (assets) and what you owe (liabilities). Be honest, and do your best to give a fair evaluation of your private property's value.

retained earnings
The accumulated earnings from a firm's profitable operations that were reinvested in the business and not paid out to stockholders in dividends.

income statement
The financial statement that shows a firm's profit after costs, expenses, and taxes; it summarizes all of the resources that have come into the firm (revenue), all the resources that have left the firm (expenses), and the resulting net income or net loss.

earnings. **Retained earnings** are accumulated earnings from the firm's profitable operations that are reinvested in the business and not paid out to stockholders in distributions of company profits. (Distributions of profits, called dividends, are discussed in Chapter 19.) Take a few moments to look again at Figure 17.5 and see what facts you can determine about the vegetarian restaurant, Very Vegetarian, from its balance sheet. After the Test Prep, have some fun and estimate your own personal net worth, following the directions in Figure 17.6.

test **prep**

- What do we call the formula for the balance sheet? What three accounts does it include?
- What does it mean to list assets according to liquidity?
- What's the difference between long-term and short-term liabilities on the balance sheet?
- What is owners' equity, and how is it determined?

Use LearnSmart to help retain what you have learned. Access your instructor's Connect course to check out LearnSmart, or go to learnsmartadvantage.com for help.

LEARNSMART

The Income Statement

The financial statement that shows a firm's bottom line—that is, its profit after costs, expenses, and taxes—is the **income statement**. The income statement summarizes all the resources, called *revenue*, that have come into the firm from operating activities, money resources the firm used up, expenses it incurred in doing business, and resources it has left after paying all costs and expenses, including taxes. The resources (revenue) left over or depleted are referred to as **net income or net loss** (see Figure 17.7).

net income or net loss
Revenue left over or depleted after all costs and expenses, including taxes, are paid.

FIGURE 17.7 SAMPLE VERY VEGETARIAN INCOME STATEMENT

① Revenues: Value of what's received from goods sold, services rendered, and other financial sources.

② Cost of goods sold: Cost of merchandise sold or cost of raw materials or parts used for producing items for resale.

③ Gross profit: How much the firm earned by buying or selling merchandise.

④ Operating expenses: Cost incurred in operating a business.

⑤ Net income after taxes: Profit or loss over a specific period after subtracting all costs and expenses, including taxes.

VERY VEGETARIAN
Income Statement
For the Year Ended December 31, 2015

① **Revenues**				
Gross sales			$ 720,000	
Less: Sales returns and allowances	$ 12,000			
Sales discounts	8,000		− 20,000	
Net sales				$700,000
② **Cost of goods sold**				
Beginning inventory, Jan. 1			$ 200,000	
Merchandise purchases	$400,000			
Freight	40,000			
Net purchases			440,000	
Cost of goods available for sale	$640,000			
Less ending inventory, Dec. 31			−230,000	
Cost of goods sold				−410,000
③ **Gross profit**				$290,000
④ **Operating expenses**				
Selling expenses				
Salaries for salespeople	$ 90,000			
Advertising	18,000			
Supplies	2,000			
Total selling expenses			$ 110,000	
General expenses				
Office salaries	$ 67,000			
Depreciation	1,500			
Insurance	1,500			
Rent	28,000			
Light, heat, and power	12,000			
Miscellaneous	2,000			
			112,000	
Total operating expenses				222,000
Net income before taxes				$ 68,000
Less: Income tax expense				19,000
⑤ **Net income after taxes**				$ 49,000

The income statement reports the firm's financial operations over a particular period of time, usually a year, a quarter of a year, or a month. It's the financial statement that reveals whether the business is actually earning a profit or losing money. The income statement includes valuable financial information for stockholders, lenders, potential investors, employees, and, of course, the government. Because it's so valuable, let's take a quick look at how to compile the income statement. Then we will discuss what each element in it means.

        Revenue
 −   Cost of goods sold
 −   Gross profit (gross margin)
 −   Operating expenses
 =   Net income before taxes
 −   Taxes
 =   Net income or loss

Revenue

Revenue is the monetary value of what a firm received for goods sold, services rendered, and other payments (such as rents received, money paid to the firm for use of its patents, interest earned, etc.). Be sure not to confuse the terms *revenue* and *sales;* they are not the same thing. True, most revenue the firm earns does come from sales, but companies can also have other sources of revenue. Also, a quick glance at the income statement shows you that *gross sales* refers to the total of all sales the firm completed. *Net sales* are gross sales minus returns, discounts, and allowances.

Cost of Goods Sold

The **cost of goods sold (or cost of goods manufactured)** measures the cost of merchandise the firm sells or the cost of raw materials and supplies it used in producing items for resale. It makes sense to compare how much a business earned by selling merchandise and how much it spent to make or buy the merchandise. The cost of goods sold includes the purchase price plus any freight charges paid to transport goods, plus any costs associated with storing the goods.

In financial reporting, it doesn't matter when a firm places a particular item in its inventory, but it does matter how an accountant records the cost of the item when the firm sells it. To find out why, read the Spotlight on Small Business box about two different inventory valuation methods.

When we subtract the cost of goods sold from net sales, we get gross profit or gross margin. **Gross profit (or gross margin)** is how much a firm earned by buying (or making) and selling merchandise. In a service firm, there may be no cost of goods sold; therefore, gross profit could *equal* net sales. Gross profit does not tell you everything you need to know about the firm's financial performance. To get that, you must also subtract the business's expenses.

Operating Expenses

In selling goods or services, a business incurs certain **operating expenses** such as rent, salaries, supplies, utilities, and insurance. Other operating expenses that appear on an income statement, like depreciation, are a bit more complex. For example, have you ever heard that a new car depreciates in market value as soon as you drive it off the dealer's lot? The same principle holds true for assets such as equipment and machinery. **Depreciation** is the systematic write-off of the cost of a tangible asset over its estimated useful life. Under accounting rules set by GAAP and the Internal Revenue Service (which are beyond the scope of this chapter), companies are permitted to recapture the cost of these assets over time by using depreciation as an operating expense.

We can classify operating expenses as either selling or general expenses. *Selling expenses* are related to the marketing and distribution of the firm's goods or services, such as advertising, salespeople's salaries, and supplies. *General expenses* are administrative expenses of the firm such as office salaries, depreciation, insurance, and rent. Accountants are trained to help you record all applicable expenses and find other relevant expenses you can deduct from your taxable income as a part of doing business.

Jennifer Behar runs a small bakery that sells products like chocolate biscotti and rosemary flatbread to high-end retailers like Whole Foods Market and Dean & DeLuca. Behar began her business with borrowed funds and doubled revenues in one year. What is the difference between revenue and sales?

The Ins and Outs of Valuing Inventory

Generally accepted accounting principles (GAAP) sometimes permit an accountant to use different methods of accounting for a firm's inventory. Two of the most popular treatments are called FIFO and LIFO.

Let's look at a simple example. Say your college bookstore buys 100 copies of a particular textbook in July at $100 a copy. When classes begin in mid-August, the bookstore sells 50 copies of the text to students at $120 each. Since the same book will be used again next term, the bookstore places the 50 copies it did not sell in its inventory until then.

In late December, the bookstore orders 50 additional copies of the text to sell for the coming term. However, the publisher's price has increased to $120 a copy due to inflation and other increased production and distribution costs. The bookstore now has in its inventory 100 copies of the

same textbook, purchased during different buying cycles. If it sells 50 copies to students at $140 each at the beginning of the new term in January, what's the bookstore's cost of the book for accounting purposes? Actually, it depends.

The books sold are identical, but the accounting treatment could be different. If the bookstore uses a method called first in, first out (FIFO), the cost of goods sold is $100 for each textbook, because the textbook the store bought first—the *first in*—cost $100. The bookstore could use another method, however. Under last in, first out (LIFO), its *last* purchase of the textbooks, at $120 each, determines the cost of each of the 50 textbooks sold.

If the book sells for $140, what is the difference in gross profit (margin) between using FIFO and using LIFO? As you can see, the inventory valuation method used makes a difference.

depreciation
The systematic write-off of the cost of a tangible asset over its estimated useful life.

Net Profit or Loss

After deducting all expenses, we can determine the firm's net income before taxes, also referred to as net earnings or net profit (see Figure 17.7 again). After allocating for taxes, we get to the *bottom line,* which is the net income (or perhaps net loss) the firm incurred from revenue minus sales returns, costs, expenses, and taxes over a period of time. We can now answer the question, "Did the business earn or lose money in the specific reporting period?"

As you can see, the basic principles of the balance sheet and income statement are already familiar to you. You know how to keep track of costs and expenses when you prepare your own budget. If your rent and utilities exceed your earnings, you know you're in trouble. If you need more money, you may need to sell some of the things you own to meet your expenses. The same is true in business. Companies need to keep track of how much money they earn and spend, and how much cash they have on hand. The only difference is that they tend to have more complex problems and a good deal more information to record than you do.

Users of financial statements are interested in how a firm handles the flow of cash coming into a business and the cash flowing out of the business. Cash flow problems can plague both businesses and individuals. Keep this in mind as we look at the statement of cash flows next.

The Statement of Cash Flows

The **statement of cash flows** reports cash receipts and cash disbursements related to the three major activities of a firm:

- *Operations* are cash transactions associated with running the business.

- *Investments* are cash used in or provided by the firm's investment activities.

- *Financing* is cash raised by taking on new debt, or equity capital or cash used to pay business expenses, past debts, or company dividends.

Accountants analyze all changes in the firm's cash that have occurred from operating, investing, and financing in order to determine the firm's net cash position. The statement of cash flows also gives the firm some insight into how to handle cash better so that no cash flow problems occur—such as having no cash on hand for immediate expenses.[23]

Figure 17.8 shows a sample statement of cash flows, again using the example of Very Vegetarian. As you can see, the statement of cash flows answers such questions as: How much cash came into the business from current operations, such as buying and selling goods and services? Did the firm use cash to buy stocks, bonds, or other investments? Did it sell some investments that brought in cash? How much money did the firm take in from issuing stock?

We analyze these and other financial transactions to see their effect on the firm's cash position. Managing cash flow can mean success or failure of any business, which is why we analyze it in more depth in the next section.

Most businesses incur operating expenses including rent, salaries, utilities, supplies, and insurance. What are some of the likely operating expenses for companies like Starbucks?

statement of cash flows

Financial statement that reports cash receipts and disbursements related to a firm's three major activities: operations, investments, and financing.

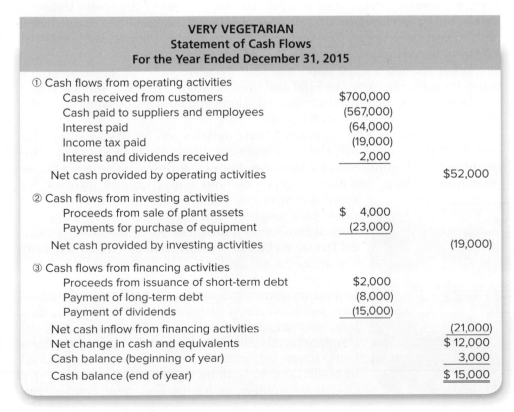

VERY VEGETARIAN		
Statement of Cash Flows		
For the Year Ended December 31, 2015		
① Cash flows from operating activities		
Cash received from customers	$700,000	
Cash paid to suppliers and employees	(567,000)	
Interest paid	(64,000)	
Income tax paid	(19,000)	
Interest and dividends received	2,000	
Net cash provided by operating activities		$52,000
② Cash flows from investing activities		
Proceeds from sale of plant assets	$ 4,000	
Payments for purchase of equipment	(23,000)	
Net cash provided by investing activities		(19,000)
③ Cash flows from financing activities		
Proceeds from issuance of short-term debt	$2,000	
Payment of long-term debt	(8,000)	
Payment of dividends	(15,000)	
Net cash inflow from financing activities		(21,000)
Net change in cash and equivalents		$ 12,000
Cash balance (beginning of year)		3,000
Cash balance (end of year)		$ 15,000

FIGURE 17.8 SAMPLE VERY VEGETARIAN STATEMENT OF CASH FLOWS

① Cash receipts from sales, commissions, fees, interest, and dividends. Cash payments for salaries, inventories, operating expenses, interest, and taxes.

② Includes cash flows that are generated through a company's purchase or sale of long-term operational assets, investments in other companies, and its lending activities.

③ Cash inflows and outflows associated with the company's own equity transactions or its borrowing activities.

Would You Cook the Books?

The recent recession hit small manufacturers very hard. Many did not survive the downturn. You are the lone accountant employed by Keegan's Feast, a small producer of premium dog food that sells directly online. Many of the company's customers became cost-conscious during the downturn and purchased lower-cost brands. Fortunately, with the economy recovering, many of the firm's old customers are returning and things are looking up. The problem is the company's cash flow suffered during the recession, and the firm needs immediate funding to continue to pay its bills. You know the CEO has prepared a proposal to a local bank asking for short-term financing. Unfortunately, you are aware that Keegan's financial statements for the past year will not show good results. Your expectation is the bank will not approve the loan on the basis of the financial information, even though the firm seems to be coming back.

Before you close the books for the end of the year, the CEO suggests you might "improve" the company's financial statements by treating the sales made at the beginning of January of the current year as if they were made in December of the past year. He is confident the company auditors will not discover the discrepancy.

You know this is against the rules of the Financial Accounting Standards Board (FASB), and you refuse to alter the information. The CEO warns that without the bank loan, the business is likely to close, meaning you and everyone else will be out of a job. You know he's probably right, and also know it's unlikely the firm's employees will find new jobs. What are your alternatives? What are the likely consequences of each? What will you do?

---

cash flow
The difference between cash coming in and cash going out of a business.

Cash flow is the difference between money coming into and going out of a business. Careful cash flow management is a must for a business of any size, but it's particularly important for small businesses and for seasonal businesses like ski resorts. Have you read of any firms that were forced into bankruptcy because of cash flow problems?

The Need for Cash Flow Analysis

Cash flow, if not properly managed, can cause a business much concern.[24] Understanding cash flow analysis is important and not difficult to understand. Let's say you borrow $100 from a friend to buy a used bike and agree to pay her back at the end of the week. You then sell the bike for $150 to someone else, who also agrees to pay you by the end of the week. Unfortunately, by the weekend your buyer does not have the money as promised, and says he will have to pay you next month. Meanwhile, your friend wants the $100 you agreed to pay her by the end of the week!

What seemed a great opportunity to make an easy $50 profit is now a cause for concern. You owe $100 and have no cash. What do you do? If you were a business, you might default on the loan and possibly go bankrupt, even though you had the potential for profit.

It's possible for a business to increase its sales and profits yet still suffer cash flow problems. **Cash flow** is simply the difference between cash coming in and cash going out of a business. Poor cash flow constitutes a major operating problem for many companies, and is particularly difficult for small and seasonal businesses.[25] Accountants sometimes face tough ethical challenges in reporting the flow of funds into a business. Read the Making Ethical Decisions box to see how such an ethical dilemma can arise.

How do cash flow problems start? Often in order to meet the growing demands of customers, a business buys goods on credit (using no cash). If it then sells a large number of goods on credit (getting no cash), the company needs more credit from a lender (usually a bank) to pay its immediate bills. If a firm has reached its credit limit and can borrow no more, it has a severe cash flow problem. It has cash coming in at a later date, but no cash to pay current expenses. That problem could, unfortunately, force the firm into bankruptcy, even though sales may be strong—all because no cash was available when it was most needed. Cash flow analysis shows that a business's relationship with its lenders is critical to preventing cash flow problems. Accountants can provide valuable insight and advice to businesses in managing cash flow, suggesting whether they need cash and how much. After the Test Prep, we will see how accountants analyze financial statements using ratios.

test prep

- What are the key steps in preparing an income statement?
- What's the difference between revenue and income on the income statement?
- Why is the statement of cash flows important in evaluating a firm's operations?

LO 17–5   Demonstrate the application of ratio analysis in reporting financial information.

ANALYZING FINANCIAL PERFORMANCE USING RATIOS

The firm's financial statements—its balance sheet, income statement, and statement of cash flows—form the basis for financial analyses performed by accountants inside and outside the firm. **Ratio analysis** is the assessment of a firm's financial condition, using calculations and financial ratios developed from the firm's financial statements. Financial ratios are especially useful in comparing the company's performance to its financial objectives and to the performance of other firms in its industry. You probably are already familiar with the use of ratios. For example, in basketball, we express the number of shots made from the foul line with a ratio: shots made to shots attempted. A player who shoots 85 percent from the foul line is considered an outstanding foul shooter; you don't want to foul this player in a close game.

    Whether ratios measure an athlete's performance or the financial health of a business, they provide valuable information. Financial ratios provide key insights into how a firm compares to other firms in its industry on liquidity, amount of debt, profitability, and overall business activity. Understanding and interpreting business ratios is important to sound financial analysis. Let's look briefly at four key types of ratios businesses use to measure financial performance.

ratio analysis
The assessment of a firm's financial condition using calculations and interpretations of financial ratios developed from the firm's financial statements.

Liquidity Ratios

We've discussed that *liquidity* refers to how fast an asset can be converted to cash. Liquidity ratios measure a company's ability to turn assets into cash to pay its short-term debts (liabilities that must be repaid within one year). These short-term debts are of particular importance to the firm's lenders who expect to be paid on time. Two key liquidity ratios are the current ratio and the acid-test ratio.

The *current ratio* is the ratio of a firm's current assets to its current liabilities. This information appears on the firm's balance sheet. Look back at Figure 17.5, which details Very Vegetarian's balance sheet. The company lists current assets of $600,000 and current liabilities of $288,000, yielding a current ratio of 2.08, which means Very Vegetarian has $2.08 of current assets for every $1 of current liabilities. See the following calculation:

$$\text{Current ratio} = \frac{\text{Current assets}}{\text{Current liabilities}} = \frac{\$600,000}{\$288,000} = \$2.08$$

The question the current ratio attempts to answer is: Is Very Vegetarian financially secure for the short term (less than one year)? It depends! Usually a company with a current ratio of 2 or better is considered a safe risk for lenders granting short-term credit, since it appears to be performing in line with market expectations. However, lenders will also compare Very Vegetarian's current ratio to that of competing firms in its industry and to its current ratio from the previous year to note any significant changes.

Another key liquidity ratio, called the *acid-test* or *quick ratio,* measures the cash, marketable securities (such as stocks and bonds), and receivables of a firm, compared to its current liabilities. Again, this information is on a firm's balance sheet.

$$\text{Acid-test ratio} = \frac{\text{Cash} + \text{Accounts receivable} + \text{Marketable securities}}{\text{Current liabilities}}$$

$$= \frac{\$265,000}{\$288,000} = 0.92$$

This ratio is particularly important to firms with difficulty converting inventory into quick cash. It helps answer such questions as: What if sales drop off and we can't sell our inventory? Can we still pay our short-term debt? Though ratios vary among industries, an acid-test ratio between 0.50 and 1.0 is usually considered satisfactory, but bordering on cash flow problems. Therefore, Very Vegetarian's acid-test ratio of 0.92 could raise concerns that perhaps the firm may not meet its short-term debt and may have to go to a high-cost lender for financial assistance.

Leverage (Debt) Ratios

Leverage (debt) ratios measure the degree to which a firm relies on borrowed funds in its operations. A firm that takes on too much debt could experience problems repaying lenders or meeting promises made to stockholders. The *debt to owners' equity ratio* measures the degree to which the company is financed by borrowed funds that it must repay. Again, let's use Figure 17.5 to measure Very Vegetarian's level of debt:

$$\text{Debt to owners' equity ratio} = \frac{\text{Total liabilities}}{\text{Owners' equity}} = \frac{\$613,000}{\$213,000} = 288\%$$

Anything above 100 percent shows a firm has more debt than equity. With a ratio of 288 percent, Very Vegetarian has a rather high degree of debt compared to its equity, which implies that lenders and investors may perceive the firm to be quite risky. However, again *it's important to compare a firm's debt ratios to those of other firms in its industry,* because debt financing is more acceptable in some industries than in others. Comparisons with the same firm's past debt ratios can also identify possible trends within the firm or industry.

Profitability (Performance) Ratios

Profitability (performance) ratios measure how effectively a firm's managers are using its various resources to achieve profits. Three of the more important ratios are earnings per share (EPS), return on sales, and return on equity.

EPS is a revealing ratio because earnings help stimulate the firm's growth and provide for stockholders' dividends. The Financial Accounting Standards Board requires companies to report their quarterly EPS in two ways: basic and diluted. The *basic earnings per share (basic EPS) ratio* helps determine the amount of profit a company earned for each share of outstanding common stock. The *diluted earnings per share (diluted EPS) ratio* measures the amount of profit earned for each share of outstanding common stock, but also considers stock options, warrants, preferred stock, and convertible debt securities the firm can convert into common stock. For simplicity's sake, we will compute only the basic EPS for Very Vegetarian:

$$\text{Basic earnings per share} = \frac{\text{Net income after taxes}}{\text{Number of common stock shares outstanding}}$$

$$= \frac{\$49,000}{\$1,000,000 \text{ shares}} = \$0.049 \text{ per share}$$

Another reliable indicator of performance is *return on sales,* which tells us whether the firm is doing as well as its competitors in generating income from sales. We calculate it by comparing net income to total sales. Very Vegetarian's return on sales is 7 percent, a figure we must measure

Building luxury hotels, like the Cosmopolitan and Vdara hotels in Las Vegas generally requires taking on a high degree of debt before the hotel ever earns its first dollar. Once opened, the companies incur heavy expenses daily just to keep the business functioning efficiently. Would monitoring the four key accounting ratios be a major part of the accountants' jobs at the new hotels?

Inventory turnover is critical to just about any business, particularly restaurants that serve perishable items and that must turn over tables to keep the flow of food moving and profits up. Can you think of other businesses that need to watch their inventory turnover closely?

FIGURE 17.9 ACCOUNTS IN THE BALANCE SHEET AND INCOME STATEMENT

BALANCE SHEET ACCOUNTS			INCOME STATEMENT ACCOUNTS			
Assets	**Liabilities**	**Owners' Equity**	**Revenues**	**Cost of Goods Sold**	**Expenses**	
Cash	Accounts payable	Capital stock	Sales revenue	Cost of buying goods	Wages	Interest
Accounts receivable	Notes payable	Retained earnings	Rental revenue	Cost of storing goods	Rent	Donations
Inventory	Bonds payable	Common stock	Commissions revenue		Repairs	Licenses
Investments	Taxes payable	Treasury stock	Royalty revenue		Travel	Fees
Equipment						
Land					Insurance	Supplies
Buildings					Utilities	Advertising
Motor vehicles					Entertainment	Taxes
Goodwill					Storage	

against similar numbers for competing firms to judge Very Vegetarian's performance:

$$\text{Return on sales} = \frac{\text{Net income}}{\text{Net sales}} = \frac{\$49,000}{\$700,000} = 7\%$$

The higher the risk of failure or loss in an industry, the higher the return investors expect on their investment; they expect to be well compensated for shouldering such odds. *Return on equity* indirectly measures risk by telling us how much a firm earned for each dollar invested by its owners. We calculate it by comparing a company's net income to its total owners' equity. Very Vegetarian's return on equity looks reasonably sound since some believe anything over 15 percent is considered a reasonable return:

$$\text{Return on equity} = \frac{\text{Net income after tax}}{\text{Total owners' equity}} = \frac{\$49,000}{\$213,000} = 23\%$$

Remember that profits help companies like Very Vegetarian grow. That's why profitability ratios are such closely watched measurements of company growth and management performance.

Activity Ratios

Converting the firm's inventory to profits is a key function of management. Activity ratios tell us how effectively management is turning over inventory.

The *inventory turnover ratio* measures the speed with which inventory moves through the firm and gets converted into sales. Idle inventory sitting in a warehouse earns nothing and costs money. The more efficiently a firm sells or turns over its inventory, the higher its revenue. We can measure the inventory turnover ratio for Very Vegetarian as follows:

$$\text{Inventory turnover} = \frac{\text{Costs of goods sold}}{\text{Average inventory}} = \frac{\$410,000}{\$215,000} = 1.9 \text{ times}$$

A lower-than-average inventory turnover ratio often indicates obsolete merchandise on hand or poor buying practices. Managers need to be aware

Speaking a Universal Accounting Language

Throughout this text you've read about the tremendous impact the global market has on business. U.S. companies like Coca-Cola earn the majority of their revenues from global markets, which helps their profitability. However, this also creates considerable accounting headaches. Since no global accounting system exists, multinationals like Coca-Cola must adapt their accounting procedures to different countries' rules. Fortunately, help may be on the way. The Financial Accounting Standards Board (FASB) in the United States and the London-based International Accounting Standards Board (IASB) hope that situation will change.

With over 100 countries using the International Financial Reporting Standards (IFRS), the governing bodies of the accounting profession in the United States proposed the integration of the U.S. accounting code with the IFRS used around the world. The U.S. Securities and Exchange Commission (SEC) seemed to support such a change, and even suggested the IFRS might replace the long-standing generally accepted accounting principles (GAAP). However, the financial crisis shifted the agency's priorities to the financial rule making required by the Dodd-Frank Act and away from IFRS. The SEC's strategic plan, extending through 2018, does not offer a strong endorsement of moving to one global accounting standard. The agency also noted a lack of strong support for the adoption of IFRS in the United States.

Nonetheless many accountants continue to support the shift to global standards for accounting. James Quigley, former chief executive officer of Deloitte Touche Tohmatsu, one of the Big Four U.S. accounting firms, believes that since we have global capital markets, we need global standards for accounting. Still, it appears that IFRS is coming later rather than sooner to an accounting department near you.

Sources: Emily Chasan, "SEC's New Strategic Plan Backs Away from IFRS," *The Wall Street Journal,* February 4, 2014; Michael Cohn, "NASBA Questions FAF Funding of IFRS Foundation," *Accounting Today,* February 20, 2014; and Securities and Exchange Commission, www.sec.gov, accessed March 2014.

of proper inventory control and anticipated inventory turnover to ensure proper performance. For example, have you ever worked as a food server in a restaurant like Very Vegetarian? How many times did your employer expect you to *turn over* a table (keep changing customers at the table) in an evening? The more times a table turns, the higher the return to the owner. Of course, like other ratios, rates of inventory turnover vary from industry to industry.

Accountants and other finance professionals use several other specific ratios, in addition to the ones we've discussed. To review where the accounting information in ratio analysis comes from, see Figure 17.9 for a quick reference. Remember, financial analysis begins where the accounting financial statements end.

Like other business disciplines, accounting is subject to change. The accounting profession is feeling the impact of the global market. The Reaching Beyond Our Borders box discusses a movement to globalize accounting procedures. It's something that accountants will be following closely. Before leaving this chapter, it's worth saying once more that, as the language of business, accounting is a worthwhile language to learn.

test **prep**

- What is the primary purpose of performing ratio analysis using the firm's financial statements?
- What are the four main categories of financial ratios?

summary

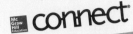
LO 17–1 Demonstrate the role that accounting and financial information play for a business and for its stakeholders.

- **What is accounting?**
Accounting is the recording, classifying, summarizing, and interpreting of financial events and transactions that affect an organization. The methods we use to record and summarize accounting data into reports are called an accounting system.

LO 17–2 Identify the different disciplines within the accounting profession.

- **How does managerial accounting differ from financial accounting?**
Managerial accounting provides information and analyses to managers within the firm to assist them in decision making. Financial accounting provides information and analyses to external users of data such as creditors and lenders.

- **What is the job of an auditor?**
Auditors review and evaluate the standards used to prepare a company's financial statements. An independent audit is conducted by a public accountant and is an evaluation and unbiased opinion about the accuracy of a company's financial statements.

- **What is the difference between a private accountant and a public accountant?**
A public accountant provides services for a fee to a variety of companies, whereas a private accountant works for a single company. Private and public accountants do essentially the same things with the exception of independent audits. Private accountants do perform internal audits, but only public accountants supply independent audits.

LO 17–3 List the steps in the accounting cycle, distinguish between accounting and bookkeeping, and explain how computers are used in accounting.

- **What are the six steps of the accounting cycle?**
The six steps of the accounting cycle are (1) analyzing documents; (2) recording information into journals; (3) posting that information into ledgers; (4) developing a trial balance; (5) preparing financial statements—the balance sheet, income statement, and statement of cash flows; and (6) analyzing financial statements.

- **What is the difference between bookkeeping and accounting?**
Bookkeeping is part of accounting and includes the systematic recording of data. Accounting includes classifying, summarizing, interpreting, and reporting data to management.

- **What are journals and ledgers?**
Journals are the first place bookkeepers record transactions. Bookkeepers then summarize journal entries by posting them to ledgers. Ledgers are specialized accounting books that arrange the transactions by homogeneous groups (accounts).

- **How do computers help accountants?**
Computers can record and analyze data and provide financial reports. Software can continuously analyze and test accounting systems to be sure they are functioning correctly. Computers can help decision making by providing appropriate information, but they cannot themselves make good

financial decisions. Accounting applications and creativity are still human functions.

LO 17–4 Explain how the major financial statements differ.

- **What is a balance sheet?**
A balance sheet reports the financial position of a firm on a particular day. The fundamental accounting equation used to prepare the balance sheet is Assets = Liabilities + Owners' equity.

- **What are the major accounts of the balance sheet?**
Assets are economic resources owned by the firm, such as buildings and machinery. Liabilities are amounts the firm owes to creditors, bondholders, and others. Owners' equity is the value of everything the firm owns—its assets—minus any liabilities; thus, Owners' equity = Assets − Liabilities.

- **What is an income statement?**
An income statement reports revenues, costs, and expenses for a specific period of time (say, the year ended December 31, 2015). The formulas we use in preparing the income statement are:

  - **Revenue** − **Cost of goods sold** = **Gross margin**
  - **Gross margin** **Operating expenses** = **Net income before taxes**
  - **Net income before taxes** − **Taxes** = **Net income (or net loss)**
    Net income or loss is also called the bottom line.

- **What is a statement of cash flows?**
Cash flow is the difference between cash receipts (money coming in) and cash disbursements (money going out). The statement of cash flows reports cash receipts and disbursements related to the firm's major activities: operations, investments, and financing.

LO 17–5 Demonstrate the application of ratio analysis in reporting financial information.

- **What are the four key categories of ratios?**
The four key categories of ratios are liquidity ratios, leverage (debt) ratios, profitability (performance) ratios, and activity ratios.

- **What is the major value of ratio analysis to the firm?**
Ratio analysis provides the firm with information about its financial position in key areas *for comparison to other firms in its industry and its own past performance.*

key terms

critical thinking

1. As a potential investor in a firm or perhaps the buyer of a particular business, would it be advisable for you to evaluate the company's financial statements? Why or why not? What key information would you seek from a firm's financial statements?

2. Why must accounting reports be prepared according to specific procedures (GAAP)? Should we allow businesses some flexibility or creativity in preparing financial statements? Why or why not?

3. What value do financial ratios offer investors in reviewing the financial performance of a firm?

4. Why is it important to remember financial ratios can differ from industry to industry?

developing workplace skills

Key: ● Team   ★ Analytic   ▲ Communication   ▣ Technology

1. Contact a CPA at a firm in your area, or talk with a CPA in your college's business department. Ask what challenges, changes, and opportunities he or she foresees in the accounting profession in the next five years. List the CPA's forecasts on a sheet of paper and then compare them with the information in this chapter.

2. Go to the websites of the American Institute of Certified Public Accountants (www.aicpa.org) and the Institute of Management Accountants (www.imanet.org). Browse the sites and find the requirements for becoming a certified public accountant (CPA) and a certified management accountant (CMA). Compare the requirements of the programs and decide which program is more appealing to you.

3. Suppose you are a new board member for an emerging not-for-profit organization hoping to attract new donors. Contributors want to know how efficiently not-for-profit organizations use their donations. Unfortunately, your fellow board members see little value in financial reporting and analysis and believe the good works of the organization speak for themselves. Prepare a fact sheet convincing the board of the need for effective financial reporting with arguments about why it helps the organization's fund-raising goals.

4. Obtain a recent annual report for a company of your choice. (Hints: *The Wall Street Journal* has a free annual reports service, and virtually all major companies post their annual reports on their websites.) Look over the firm's financial statements and see whether they match the information in

this chapter. Read the auditor's opinion (usually at the end of the report) and evaluate what you think are the most important conclusions of the auditors.

5. Obtain a recent annual report for a company of your choice (see the hints in exercise 4) and try your hand at computing financial ratios. Compute the current ratio, debt to owners' equity ratio, and basic earnings per share ratio. Then request an annual report from one of the firm's major competitors and compute the same ratios for that company. What did you find?

taking it to the **net**

PURPOSE

To calculate and analyze the current and quick (acid-test) ratios of different businesses.

EXERCISE

Potz and Pans, a small gift shop, has current assets of $45,000 (including inventory valued at $30,000) and $9,000 in current liabilities. WannaBees, a specialty clothing store, has current assets of $150,000 (including inventory valued at $125,000) and $85,000 in current liabilities. Both businesses have applied for loans. Click the Calculators box on the toolbar at www.bankrate.com and then click on Small Business to answer the following questions:

1. Calculate the current ratio for each company. Which company is more likely to get the loan? Why?

2. The acid-test ratio subtracts the value of the firm's inventory from its total current assets. Because inventory is often difficult to sell, this ratio is considered an even more reliable measure of a business's ability to repay loans than the current ratio. Calculate the acid-test ratio for each business and decide whether you would give either the loan. Why or why not?

video case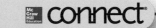

THE ACCOUNTING FUNCTION AT GOODWILL INDUSTRIES

Goodwill Industries is a major charitable organization that relies primarily on financial and nonfinancial donations and grants. It has retail operations that help sustain its financial operations so as to fulfill its mission to help train, support, and employ disadvantaged individuals and those with disabilities.

The video introduces the accounting function and the specific steps involved in the accounting cycle. The similarities and differences between for-profit and not-for-profit entities are discussed in detail. The importance of accounting in providing financial information and analysis is featured. Emphasis is placed on financial statements as

well as ratio analysis in helping gauge the financial health of the organization.

Accounting is crucial for all organizations, whether they are a small business, large corporation, or a governmental or not-for-profit organization. The different types of accounting are discussed, including managerial, financial, tax, auditing, governmental, and not-for-profit. Balance sheets, income statements, and statements of cash flows provide important information for managers and others in the organization, helping to demonstrate whether the organization is on budget or whether there are variances between projected and actual revenues. Costs and expenses have to be kept in line and are carefully monitored and analyzed by the accounting function.

Sufficient cash flow is critical to the sustainability of any organization, particularly the not-for-profit organization; in this case, Goodwill. Not-for-profit organizations utilize performance ratio analysis to gauge their overall financial performance. The results of these analyses help management assess the organization's performance against its plan or budget. They also help develop strategic plans for the future as well as benchmark against other similar companies.

THINKING IT OVER

1. What's the difference between assets and liabilities? Which of the key financial statements features these categories prominently?

2. Identify the six steps in the accounting cycle.

3. What are the key reasons that firms do ratio analysis?

notes

1. Eric Sobota, "Doing Business with the Government: Administrative Challenges Faced by Nonprofits," *Nonprofit Quarterly,* January 14, 2014; and John A Byrne, "The GMAT: An Exam with Greater Profit Margins Than Apple," *Fortune,* February 17, 2014.

2. Evan Taylor, "Best Jobs: Accountant," *U.S. News and World Report,* January 22, 2014.

3. www.imanet.org/certification, accessed May 2014.

4. Michael Cohn, "AICPA and CIMA Propose Management Accounting Framework," *Accounting Today,* February 10, 2014.

5. Nellie S. Huang, "Make the Most of an Annual Report," *Kiplinger's Personal Finance,* March 2014.

6. www.aicpa.org, accessed May 2014.

7. Mariella Segarra, "FASB Issues New Private Company Accounting Alternatives," *CFO,* January 20, 2014.

8. Jerry Markon and Alice Crites, "Accenture, Hired to Help Fix HealthCare.gov, Has Had a Series of Stumbles," *The Washington Post,* February 9, 2014; and Sam Fleming, "Accountants PwC, Deloitte, KPMG, and EY Face Taming Moves," *Financial Times,* February 12, 2014.

9. "Shining a Light on the Auditors," *The Economist,* December 7, 2013.

10. Stephanie Armour, "Lew Says Reforms Making Financial System Safer," *The Wall Street Journal,* December 5, 2013.

11. Karen Weise, "Will Dodd-Frank Ever Be Finished?" *Bloomberg Businessweek,* August 20, 2013.

12. Michael Rapoport, "Audit Reports Add Beef," *The Wall Street Journal,* August 13, 2013; and Nellie Huang, "7 Clues for Investors to Look for Within Annual Reports," *Kiplinger's Personal Finance,* March 2014.

13. Michael Rapoport, "KPMG to Pay $8.2 Million to Settle SEC Charges," *The Wall Street Journal,* January 24, 2014.

14. Kathy Hoffelder, "Top Audit Deficiency: Evidence Collection," *CFO,* May 10, 2013.

15. www.thiia.org/certification, accessed May 2014.

16. Amrick Randhawa, "Don't Have a Tax Pro Yet? Time to Get Moving," *Entrepreneur,* February 12, 2014; and Pamela Yip, "Be Picky When Choosing a Tax Preparer," *Dallas Morning News,* January 26, 2014.

17. www.gasb.org, accessed May 2014.

18. Colleen O'Connor, "More Than Half of Nonprofits Haven't Recovered Recession Losses," *The Denver Post,* December 10, 2013.

19. Michael Cohn, "Wave Adds Bank Reconciliation to Online Accounting Software," *Accounting Today,* February 11, 2014; and Pedro Hernandez, "Plan for Small Business Success," *Small Business Computing,* February 14, 2014.

20. Tom Taulli, "Xero: Taking Aim at the Intuit Goliath," *Forbes,* January 26, 2014.

21. Mary Ellen Biery, "What Are Your Financial Statements Telling You?" *Forbes,* December 22, 2013.

22. Catherine Clifford, "New Accounting Framework to Ease Burdens for Small Business," *Entrepreneur,* June 10, 2013.

23. Jonathan Lack, "How to Manage Your Cash Flow Better in 2014," *Houston Business Journal,* January 23, 2014.

24. Jill Hamburg-Conlon, "Don't Run Out of Cash: 3 Growth Company Case Studies," *Inc.,* January 2014.

25. Joe Worth, "How Much Cash On Hand Is Too Much? And What Should I Do with It?" *Entrepreneur,* January 2014.

photo credits

18

Financial Management

Learning Objectives

AFTER YOU HAVE READ AND STUDIED THIS CHAPTER, YOU SHOULD BE ABLE TO

LO 18-1   Explain the role and responsibilities of financial managers.

LO 18-2   Outline the financial planning process, and explain the three key budgets in the financial plan.

LO 18-3   Explain why firms need operating funds.

LO 18-4   Identify and describe different sources of short-term financing.

LO 18-5   Identify and describe different sources of long-term financing.

Getting to know **Sabrina Simmons**

As chief financial officer (CFO) of Gap, Sabrina Simmons knows a thing or two about keeping current with trends. Fashion is a volatile industry that can shift suddenly on the whims of consumers. Companies that lose their "cool" factor can quickly disappear from the market if they fail to rebuild their brand. Gap was in the middle of a crisis of this scale when Simmons joined as treasurer in 2001. Besides being stuck in a creative rut, a series of poor capital market investments had hurt the company's finances. In her first act on the job, Simmons balanced the books and made executives swear that the company would never rely on risky investments to drive revenue again. It's an accomplishment that she remains proud of to this day. "Nobody is coming through this recession unscathed, but it feels great to sleep at night knowing our balance sheet is rock solid," said Simmons.

Before making a splash at Gap, Simmons earned her bachelor's degree in finance from University of California, Berkeley, and her MBA from UCLA. A certified public accountant, Simmons spent her post-grad years in various bookkeeping jobs at companies like Hewlett-Packard and Ford subsidiary USL Capital. She took her first foray into fashion as an assistant treasurer at Levi Strauss. Her performance at the iconic blue jean maker caught the eye of British genetics firm Sygen International, which hired Simmons as its CFO in the late 1990s. However, the slow world of science made Simmons miss the apparel business. When a treasurer position at Gap opened up, she seized the opportunity to get back into fashion.

While her handling of the company's early-2000s identity crisis put her in the spotlight, Simmons didn't have time to celebrate. Soon Gap began investing millions in an offshoot store called Forth & Towne. Unlike the company's collection of youthful brands, like Old Navy and Banana Republic, Forth & Towne was meant to appeal to older shoppers who had lost touch with

Gap over the years. Unfortunately, the retailer's heavily hyped launch did little to generate interest among its target market. "After investing tens of millions of dollars, we made the difficult decision to cut our losses and shut it down after two years," said Simmons. "The silver lining is we learned many tough lessons. And this failure, though very public, didn't stop us from taking those lessons learned and investing in other good ideas."

One of those good ideas was Piperlime.com, an accessories brand that launched a year after Forth & Towne's failure. The online boutique quickly developed a customer base and continues to grow. In recognition of her accomplishments with the company, Gap appointed Simmons CFO in 2008. She's had to put out a number of fires since then, including the closing of hundreds of stores in 2012. Nevertheless, Simmons is steadfast in her commitment to never accept defeat. "Take intelligent risks and accept sensible failures," said Simmons. "Tenacity and persistence are great traits. And don't be afraid to fail. It's a great way to learn."

Risk and uncertainty clearly define the role of financial management. In this chapter, you'll explore the role of finance in business. We'll discuss the challenges and the tools top managers like Sabrina Simmons use to attain financial stability and growth.

Sources: Paul Quintaro, "Gap Offers Details on Advances in Omni-Channel Retailing, Global Growth," *Benzinga,* April 16, 2014; Sabrina Simmons, "Commencement Address 2010: Berkeley-Haas Undergraduate Program," www.Haas.Berkeley.edu, May 19 2010; and Susan Berfield, "Can Rebekka Bay Fix the Gap?" *Bloomberg Businessweek,* March 20, 2014.

Sabrina Simmons

- CFO of Gap
- Balanced the company's books
- Accepted and learned from failures

www.gap.com

@Gap

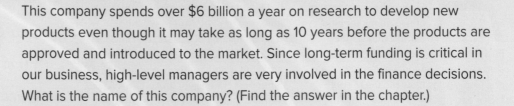
This company spends over $6 billion a year on research to develop new products even though it may take as long as 10 years before the products are approved and introduced to the market. Since long-term funding is critical in our business, high-level managers are very involved in the finance decisions. What is the name of this company? (Find the answer in the chapter.)

LO 18–1 Explain the role and responsibilities of financial managers.

THE ROLE OF FINANCE AND FINANCIAL MANAGERS

finance

The function in a business that acquires funds for the firm and manages those funds within the firm.

financial management

The job of managing a firm's resources so it can meet its goals and objectives.

financial managers

Managers who examine financial data prepared by accountants and recommend strategies for improving the financial performance of the firm.

The goal of this chapter is to answer two major questions: "What is finance?" and "What do financial managers do?" **Finance** is the function in a business that acquires funds for the firm and manages them within the firm. Finance activities include preparing budgets; doing cash flow analysis; and planning for the expenditure of funds on such assets as plant, equipment, and machinery. **Financial management** is the job of managing a firm's resources to meet its goals and objectives. Without a carefully calculated financial plan and sound financial management, a firm has little chance for survival, regardless of its product or marketing effectiveness. Let's briefly review the roles of accountants and financial managers.

We can compare an accountant to a skilled laboratory technician who takes blood samples and other measures of a person's health and writes the findings on a health report (in business, this process is the preparation of financial statements). A financial manager is like the doctor who interprets the report and makes recommendations that will improve the patient's health. In short, **financial managers** examine financial data prepared by accountants and recommend strategies for improving the financial performance of the firm.

Clearly financial managers can make sound financial decisions only if they understand accounting information. That's why we examined accounting in Chapter 17. Similarly, a good accountant needs to understand finance. Accounting and finance go together like peanut butter and jelly. In large and medium-sized organizations, both the accounting and finance functions are generally under the control of a chief financial officer (CFO). A CFO is generally the second highest paid person in an organization and CFOs often advance to the top job of CEO.[1] However, financial management could also be in the hands of a person who serves as company treasurer or vice president of finance. A comptroller is the chief *accounting* officer.

Figure 18.1 highlights a financial manager's tasks. As you can see, two key responsibilities are to obtain funds and to effectively control the use of those funds. Controlling funds includes managing the firm's cash, credit accounts (accounts receivable), and inventory. Finance is a critical activity in both profit-seeking and nonprofit organizations.[2]

Finance is important, no matter what the firm's size. As you may remember from Chapter 6, financing a small business is essential if the firm expects to survive its important first five years. But the need for careful financial management remains a challenge that any business, large or small, must face throughout its existence. This is a lesson many U.S. businesses learned the hard way when the recent financial crisis threatened the economy.[3]

FIGURE 18.1 WHAT FINANCIAL MANAGERS DO

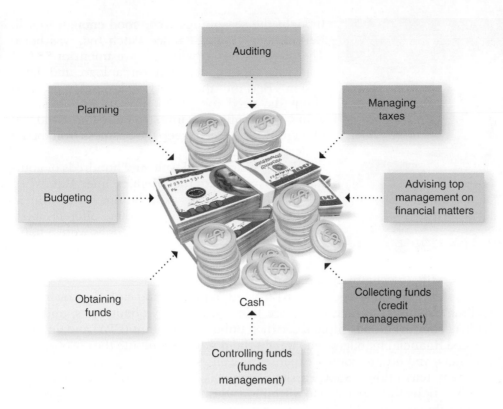

General Motors (GM), once the world's dominant automaker, faced extinction in 2009 because of severe financial problems. The company survived due to a direct government loan of $7 billion and an additional $43 billion in bailout funds from the U.S. Treasury.[4] The $43 billion in bailout funds gave the government 60 percent ownership in the company. (The government sold its last share of GM in 2013 for a total loss of about $10 billion.)[5] The government also approved an $85 billion loan to save insurance giant American International Group (AIG) from collapse and passed the $700 billion Troubled Assets Relief Program (TARP) to help restore confidence and stability in the U.S. financial system. Today, many small banks are still struggling to repay the TARP funds.[6]

The Value of Understanding Finance

Three of the most common reasons a firm fails financially are:

1. Undercapitalization (insufficient funds to start the business).
2. Poor control over cash flow.
3. Inadequate expense control.

You can see all three in the following classic story:

Two friends, Elizabeth Bertani and Pat Sherwood, started a company called Parsley Patch on what can best be described as a shoestring budget. It began when Bertani prepared salt-free seasonings for her husband, who was on a no-salt diet. Her friend Sherwood

Michael Miller overhauled the underperforming Goodwill Industries operation in Portland, Oregon, by treating the nonprofit like a for-profit business. He trimmed operating expenses comparing sales by store, closing weak outlets and opening new ones in better locations, and cutting distribution costs. Sales soared from $4 million to over $135 million, eliminating the need for outside funding.

thought the seasonings were good enough to sell. Bertani agreed, and Parsley Patch Inc. was born. The business began with an investment of $5,000 that was rapidly depleted on a logo and label design. Bertani and Sherwood quickly learned about the need for capital in getting a business going. Eventually, they invested more than $100,000 of their own money to keep the business from being undercapitalized.

Everything started well, and hundreds of gourmet shops adopted the product line. But when sales failed to meet expectations, the women decided the health-food market offered more potential because salt-free seasonings were a natural for people with restricted diets. The choice was a good one. Sales soared, approaching $30,000 a month. Still, the company earned no profits.

Bertani and Sherwood weren't trained in monitoring cash flow or in controlling expenses. In fact, they were told not to worry about costs, and they hadn't. They eventually hired a certified public accountant (CPA) and an experienced financial manager, who taught them how to compute the costs of their products, and how to control expenses as well as cash moving in and out of the company (cash flow). Soon Parsley Patch was earning a comfortable margin on operations that ran close to $1 million a year. Luckily, the owners were able to turn things around before it was too late. Eventually, they sold the firm to spice and seasonings giant McCormick.[7]

If Bertani and Sherwood had understood finance before starting their business, they might have been able to avoid the problems they encountered. The key word here is *understood*. You do not have to pursue finance as a career to understand it. Financial understanding is important to anyone who wants to start a small business, invest in stocks and bonds, or plan a retirement fund. In short, finance and accounting are two areas everyone in business should study. Since we discussed accounting in Chapter 17, let's look more closely at what financial management is all about.

What Is Financial Management?

Financial managers are responsible for paying the company's bills at the appropriate time, and for collecting overdue payments to make sure the company does not lose too much money to bad debts (people or firms that don't pay their bills). Therefore, finance functions, such as buying merchandise on credit (accounts payable) and collecting payment from customers (accounts receivable), are key components of the financial manager's job. While these functions are vital to all types of businesses, they are particularly critical to small and medium-sized businesses, which typically have smaller cash or credit cushions than large corporations.[8]

It's also essential that financial managers stay abreast of changes or opportunities in finance, such as changes in tax law, since taxes represent an outflow of cash from the business.[9] Financial managers must also analyze the tax implications of managerial decisions to minimize the taxes the business must pay. Usually a member of the firm's finance department, the internal auditor, also checks the journals, ledgers, and financial statements the accounting department prepares, to make sure all transactions are in accordance with generally accepted accounting principles (GAAP). Without such audits, accounting statements would be less reliable.[10] Therefore, it is important that internal auditors be objective and critical of any improprieties or deficiencies noted in their evaluation.[11] Thorough internal audits assist the firm in financial planning, which we'll look at next.

LO 18–2 Outline the financial planning process, and explain the three key budgets in the financial plan.

FINANCIAL PLANNING

Financial planning means analyzing short-term and long-term money flows to and from the firm. Its overall objective is to optimize the firm's profitability and make the best use of its money. It has three steps: (1) forecasting the firm's short-term and long-term financial needs, (2) developing budgets to meet those needs, and (3) establishing financial controls to see whether the company is achieving its goals (see Figure 18.2). Let's look at each step and the role it plays in improving the organization's financial health.

Forecasting Financial Needs

Forecasting is an important part of any firm's financial plan. A **short-term forecast** predicts revenues, costs, and expenses for a period of one year or less. Part of the short-term forecast may be a **cash flow forecast**, which predicts the cash inflows and outflows in future periods, usually months or quarters. The inflows and outflows of cash recorded in the cash flow forecast are based on expected sales revenues and various costs and expenses incurred, as well as when they are due for payment. The company's sales forecast estimates projected sales for a particular period. A business often uses its past financial statements as a basis for projecting expected sales and various costs and expenses.

A **long-term forecast** predicts revenues, costs, and expenses for a period longer than 1 year, sometimes as long as 5 or 10 years. This forecast plays a

short-term forecast
Forecast that predicts revenues, costs, and expenses for a period of one year or less.

cash flow forecast
Forecast that predicts the cash inflows and outflows in future periods, usually months or quarters.

long-term forecast
Forecast that predicts revenues, costs, and expenses for a period longer than 1 year, and sometimes as far as 5 or 10 years into the future.

FIGURE 18.2 FINANCIAL PLANNING
Note the close link between financial planning and budgeting.

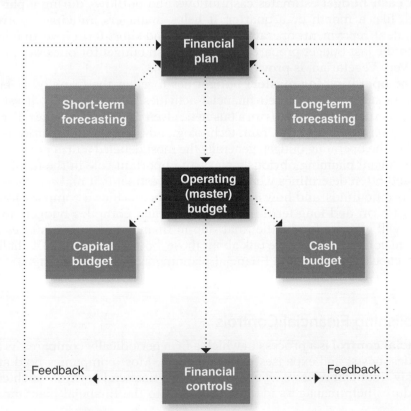

crucial part in the company's long-term strategic plan, which asks questions such as: What business are we in? Should we be in it five years from now? How much money should we invest in technology and new plant and equipment over the next decade? Will we have cash available to meet long-term obligations? Innovations in web-based software help financial managers address these long-term forecasting questions.

The long-term financial forecast gives top management, as well as operations managers, some sense of the income or profit potential of different strategic plans.[12] It also helps in preparing company budgets.

Working with the Budget Process

budget
A financial plan that sets forth management's expectations and, on the basis of those expectations, allocates the use of specific resources throughout the firm.

A **budget** sets forth management's expectations for revenues and, on the basis of those expectations, allocates the use of specific resources throughout the firm. As a financial plan, it depends heavily on the accuracy of the firm's balance sheet, income statement, statement of cash flows, and short-term and long-term financial forecasts, which all need to be as accurate as possible. To effectively prepare budgets, financial managers must take their forecasting responsibilities seriously.[13] A budget becomes the primary guide for the firm's financial operations and expected financial needs.

There are usually several types of budgets in a firm's financial plan:

- A capital budget.
- A cash budget.
- An operating or master budget.

Let's look at each.

capital budget
A budget that highlights a firm's spending plans for major asset purchases that often require large sums of money.

A **capital budget** highlights a firm's spending plans for major asset purchases that often require large sums of money, like property, buildings, and equipment.

cash budget
A budget that estimates cash inflows and outflows during a particular period like a month or a quarter.

A **cash budget** estimates cash inflows and outflows during a particular period, like a month or a quarter. It helps managers anticipate borrowing needs, debt repayment, operating expenses, and short-term investments, and is often the last budget prepared. A sample cash budget for our example company, Very Vegetarian, is provided in Figure 18.3.

operating (or master) budget
The budget that ties together the firm's other budgets and summarizes its proposed financial activities.

The **operating (or master) budget** ties together the firm's other budgets and summarizes its proposed financial activities. More formally, it estimates costs and expenses needed to run a business, given projected revenues. The firm's spending on supplies, travel, rent, technology, advertising, and salaries is determined in the operating budget, generally the most detailed a firm prepares.

Financial planning obviously plays an important role in the firm's operations and often determines what long-term investments it makes, when it will need specific funds, and how it will generate them. Once a company forecasts its short-term and long-term financial needs and compiles budgets to show how it will allocate funds, the final step in financial planning is to establish financial controls. Before we talk about those, however, Figure 18.4 challenges you to check your personal financial planning skill by developing a monthly budget for "You Incorporated."

Establishing Financial Controls

financial control
A process in which a firm periodically compares its actual revenues, costs, and expenses with its budget.

Financial control is a process in which a firm periodically compares its actual revenues, costs, and expenses with its budget. Most companies hold at least monthly financial reviews as a way to ensure financial control. Such control procedures help managers identify variances to the financial plan and allow

| VERY VEGETARIAN | | | |
| Monthly Cash Budget | | | |
	JANUARY	FEBRUARY	MARCH
Sales forecast	$50,000	$45,000	$40,000
Collections			
Cash sales (20%)		$ 9,000	$ 8,000
Credit sales (80% of past month)		$40,000	$36,000
Monthly cash collection		$49,000	$44,000
Payments schedule			
Supplies and material		$ 11,000	$ 10,000
Salaries		12,000	12,000
Direct labor		9,000	9,000
Taxes		3,000	3,000
Other expenses		7,000	5,000
Monthly cash payments		$42,000	$39,000
Cash budget			
Cash flow		$ 7,000	$ 5,000
Beginning cash		−1,000	6,000
Total cash		$ 6,000	$ 11,000
Less minimum cash balance		−6,000	−6,000
Excess cash to market securities		$ 0	$ 5,000
Loans needed for minimum balance		0	0

FIGURE 18.3 A SAMPLE CASH BUDGET FOR VERY VEGETARIAN

them to take corrective action if necessary. Financial controls also help reveal which specific accounts, departments, and people are varying from the financial plan. Finance managers can judge whether these variances are legitimate and thereby merit adjustments to the plan. Shifts in the economy or unexpected global events can also alter financial plans. For example, currency problems in emerging markets or a slowdown in the Chinese economy can cause many companies to consider adjusting their financial plans.[14] After the Test Prep, we'll see why firms need readily available funds.

test prep

- Name three finance functions important to the firm's overall operations and performance.
- What three primary financial problems cause firms to fail?
- How do short-term and long-term financial forecasts differ?
- What is the purpose of preparing budgets in an organization? Can you identify three different types of budgets?

FIGURE 18.4 YOU INCORPORATED MONTHLY BUDGET
In Chapter 17, you compiled a sample balance sheet for You Inc. Now, let's develop a monthly budget for You Inc. Be honest and think of everything that needs to be included for an accurate monthly budget for You!

	EXPECTED	ACTUAL	DIFFERENCE
Monthly income			
Wages (net pay after taxes)	_____	_____	_____
Savings account withdrawal	_____	_____	_____
Family support	_____	_____	_____
Loans	_____	_____	_____
Other sources	_____	_____	_____
Total monthly income	_____	_____	_____
Monthly expenses			
Fixed expenses	_____	_____	_____
Rent or mortgage	_____	_____	_____
Car payment	_____	_____	_____
Health insurance	_____	_____	_____
Life insurance	_____	_____	_____
Tuition or fees	_____	_____	_____
Other fixed expenses	_____	_____	_____
Subtotal of fixed expenses	_____	_____	_____
Variable expenses	_____	_____	_____
Food	_____	_____	_____
Clothing	_____	_____	_____
Entertainment	_____	_____	_____
Transportation	_____	_____	_____
Phone	_____	_____	_____
Utilities	_____	_____	_____
Publications	_____	_____	_____
Internet connection	_____	_____	_____
Cable television	_____	_____	_____
Other expenses	_____	_____	_____
Subtotal of variable expenses	_____	_____	_____
Total expenses	_____	_____	_____
Total income − Total expenses = Cash on hand/(Cash deficit)	_____	_____	_____

LO 18–3   Explain why firms need operating funds.

THE NEED FOR OPERATING FUNDS

In business, the need for operating funds never seems to end. That's why sound financial management is essential to all businesses. And like our personal financial needs, the capital needs of a business change over time. Remember the example of Parsley Patch to see why a small business's financial requirements can shift considerably. The same is true for large corporations such as Apple, Johnson & Johnson, and Nike when they venture into new-product areas or new markets. Virtually all organizations have operational needs for which they need funds. Key areas include:

- Managing day-by-day needs of the business.
- Controlling credit operations.
- Acquiring needed inventory.
- Making capital expenditures.

Let's look carefully at the financial needs of these key areas, which affect both the smallest and the largest of businesses.

Managing Day-by-Day Needs of the Business

If workers expect to be paid on Friday, they don't want to wait until Monday for their paychecks. If tax payments are due on the 15th of the month, the government expects the money on time. If the interest payment on a business loan is due on the 30th of this month, the lender doesn't mean the 1st of next month. As you can see, funds have to be available to meet the daily operational costs of the business.

Financial managers must ensure that funds are available to meet daily cash needs without compromising the firm's opportunities to invest money for its future. Money has a *time value*.[15] In other words, if someone offered to give you $200 either today or one year from today, you would benefit by taking the $200 today. Why? It's very simple. You could invest the $200 you receive today and over a year's time it would grow. The same is true in business; the interest a firm gains on its investments is important in maximizing the profit it will gain. That's why financial managers often try to minimize cash expenditures to free up funds for investment in interest-bearing accounts. They suggest the company pay its bills as late as possible (unless a cash discount is available for early payment). They also advise companies to try to collect what's owed them as fast as possible, to maximize the investment potential of the firm's funds. Unfortunately, collecting funds as fast as possible can be particularly challenging. This was especially true during the Great Recession.[16] Efficient cash management is particularly important to small firms since their access to capital is much more limited than larger businesses.[17]

Controlling Credit Operations

Financial managers know that in today's highly competitive business environment, making credit available helps keep current customers happy and helps attract new ones. Credit for customers can be especially important during tough financial times like the recession that began in 2008 when lenders were hesitant to make loans.

The problem with selling on credit is that as much as 25 percent of the business's assets could be tied up in its credit accounts (accounts receivable). This forces the firm to use its own funds to pay for goods or services sold to customers who bought on credit. Financial managers in such firms often develop efficient collection procedures, like offering cash or quantity discounts to buyers who pay their accounts by a certain time. They also scrutinize old and new credit customers to see whether they have a history of meeting credit obligations on time.

It's difficult to think of a business that doesn't make credit available to its customers. However, collecting accounts receivable can be time-consuming and expensive. Accepting credit cards such as Visa, MasterCard, and American Express can simplify transactions for sellers and guarantee payment. What types of products do you regularly purchase with a credit card?

Good Finance or Bad Medicine?

Imagine that you have just earned your business degree and have been hired as a hospital administrator at a small hospital that, like many others, is experiencing financial problems. Having studied finance, you know that efficient cash management is important to all firms in all industries to meet the day-by-day operations of the firm. One way to ensure such efficiency is to use a carefully planned and managed inventory control system that can reduce the amount of cash an organization has tied up in inventory. Being familiar with just-in-time inventory, you know it is a proven system that helps reduce the costs of managing inventory.

At a meeting of the hospital's executive committee, you recommend that the hospital save money by using a just-in-time inventory system to manage its drug supply. You suggest discontinuing the hospital's large stockpile of drugs, especially expensive cancer treatment drugs that tie up a great deal of the hospital's cash, and shift to ordering them just when they are needed. Several members seem to like the idea, but the doctors in charge of practicing medicine and oncology are outraged, claiming you are sacrificing patients' well-being for cash. After debate, the committee says the decision is up to you. What will you do? What could result from your decision?

One convenient way to decrease the time and expense of collecting accounts receivable is to accept bank credit cards such as MasterCard or Visa. The banks that issue these cards have already established the customer's creditworthiness, which reduces the business's risk. Businesses must pay a fee to accept credit cards, but the costs are usually offset by the benefits.[18] In an effort to reduce those credit card costs as well as speed up the transaction process, many businesses today accept mobile payments through services like Square and Level Up.[19] For example, Chipotle, Starbucks, and Dunkin Donuts have invested in mobile payment systems.[20] Mobile payment systems not only make transactions quick and simple, the processors usually charge lower fees than traditional credit card companies.[21]

Acquiring Needed Inventory

As we saw in Chapter 13, effective marketing requires focusing on the customer and providing high-quality service and readily available goods. A carefully constructed inventory policy helps manage the firm's available funds and maximize profitability. Doozle's, an ice cream parlor in St. Louis, Missouri, deliberately ties up fewer funds in its inventory of ice cream in winter. It's obvious why: demand for ice cream is lower in winter.

Just-in-time inventory control (see Chapter 9) and other such methods can reduce the funds a firm must tie up in inventory. Carefully evaluating its inventory turnover ratio (see Chapter 17) can also help a firm control the outflow of cash for inventory. A business of any size must understand that poorly managed inventory can seriously affect cash flow and drain its finances dry. The nearby Making Ethical Decisions box raises an interesting question about sound financial management and inventory control in a critical industry.

Making Capital Expenditures

capital expenditures

Major investments in either tangible long-term assets such as land, buildings, and equipment or intangible assets such as patents, trademarks, and copyrights.

Capital expenditures are major investments in either tangible long-term assets such as land, buildings, and equipment, or intangible assets such as patents, trademarks, and copyrights. In many organizations the purchase of major assets—such as land for future expansion, manufacturing plants to increase production capabilities, research to develop new-product ideas, and

FIGURE 18.5 WHY FIRMS NEED FUNDS

SHORT-TERM FUNDS	LONG-TERM FUNDS
Monthly expenses	New-product development
Unanticipated emergencies	Replacement of capital equipment
Cash flow problems	Mergers or acquisitions
Expansion of current inventory	Expansion into new markets (domestic or global)
Temporary promotional programs	New facilities

equipment to maintain or exceed current levels of output—is essential. Expanding into new markets can be expensive with no guarantee of success. Therefore, it's critical that companies weigh all possible options before committing a large portion of available resources.

Consider a firm that needs to expand its production capabilities due to increased customer demand. It could buy land and build a new plant, purchase an existing plant, or rent space. Can you think of financial and accounting considerations at play in this decision?

The need for operating funds raises several questions for financial managers: How does the firm obtain funds to finance operations and other business needs? Will it require specific funds in the long or the short term? How much will it cost (i.e., interest) to obtain these funds? Will they come from internal or external sources? We address these questions next.

Alternative Sources of Funds

We described finance earlier as the function in a business responsible for acquiring and managing funds. Sound financial management determines the amount of money needed and the most appropriate sources from which to obtain it. A firm can raise needed capital by borrowing money (debt), selling ownership (equity), or earning profits (retained earnings). **Debt financing** refers to funds raised through various forms of borrowing that must be repaid. **Equity financing** is money raised from within the firm, from operations or through the sale of ownership in the firm (stock). Firms can borrow funds either short-term or long-term. **Short-term financing** refers to funds needed for a year or less. **Long-term financing** covers funds needed for more than a year (usually 2 to 10 years). Figure 18.5 highlights reasons why firms may need short-term and long-term funds.

We'll explore the different sources of short- and long-term financing next. Let's first pause to check your understanding by doing the Test Prep.

iSee It! Need help understanding equity financing and debt financing? Visit your Connect e-book video tab for a brief animated explanation.

debt financing
Funds raised through various forms of borrowing that must be repaid.

equity financing
Money raised from within the firm, from operations or through the sale of ownership in the firm (stock or venture capital).

short-term financing
Funds needed for a year or less.

long-term financing
Funds needed for more than a year (usually 2 to 10 years).

test prep

- Money has time value. What does this mean?
- Why is accounts receivable a financial concern to the firm?
- What's the primary reason an organization spends a good deal of its available funds on inventory and capital expenditures?
- What's the difference between debt and equity financing?

OBTAINING SHORT-TERM FINANCING

The bulk of a finance manager's job does not relate to obtaining long-term funds. In small businesses, for example, long-term financing is often out of the question.[22] Instead, day-to-day operations call for the careful management of *short-term* financial needs. Firms may need to borrow short-term funds for purchasing additional inventory or for meeting bills that come due unexpectedly. Like an individual, a business, especially a small business, sometimes needs to secure short-term funds when its cash reserves are low. Let's see how it does so.

trade credit
The practice of buying goods and services now and paying for them later.

promissory note
A written contract with a promise to pay a supplier a specific sum of money at a definite time.

One thing you can never have too much of is cash. Financial managers must make certain there is enough cash available to meet daily financial needs and still have funds to invest in its future. What does it mean when we say cash has a time value?

Trade Credit

Trade credit is the practice of buying goods or services now and paying for them later. It is the most widely used source of short-term funding, the least expensive, and the most convenient. Small businesses rely heavily on trade credit from firms such as United Parcel Service, as do large firms such as Kmart or Macy's. When a firm buys merchandise, it receives an invoice (a bill) much like the one you receive when you buy something with a credit card. As you'll see, however, the terms businesses receive are often different from those on your monthly statement.

Business invoices often contain terms such as *2/10, net 30*. This means the buyer can take a 2 percent discount for paying the invoice within 10 days. Otherwise the total bill (net) is due in 30 days. Finance managers pay close attention to such discounts because they create opportunities to reduce the firm's costs. Think about it for a moment: If the terms are 2/10, net 30, the customer will pay 2 percent more by waiting an extra 20 days to pay the invoice. If the firm *can* pay its bill within 10 days, it is needlessly increasing its costs by not doing so.

Some suppliers hesitate to give trade credit to an organization with a poor credit rating, no credit history, or a history of slow payment. They may insist the customer sign a **promissory note**, a written contract with a promise to pay a supplier a specific sum of money at a definite time. Promissory notes are negotiable. The supplier can sell them to a bank at a discount (the amount of the promissory note less a fee for the bank's services in collecting the amount due), and the business is then responsible for paying the bank.

Family and Friends

As we discussed in Chapter 17, firms often have several bills coming due at the same time with no sources of funds to pay them. Many small firms obtain short-term funds by borrowing money from family and friends. Such loans can create problems, however, if all parties do not understand cash flow. That's why it's sometimes better, when possible, to go to a commercial bank that fully understands the business's risk and can help analyze its future financial needs rather than borrow from friends or relatives.[23]

Entrepreneurs appear to be listening to this advice. According to the National Federation of Independent Business, entrepreneurs today are relying less on family and friends as a source of borrowed funds than they have in the past.[24] If an entrepreneur decides to ask family or friends for financial assistance, it's important that both parties (1) agree to specific loan terms, (2) put the agreement in writing, and (3) arrange for repayment in the same way they would for a bank loan. Such actions help keep family relationships and friendships intact.

Commercial Banks

Banks, being sensitive to risk, generally prefer to lend short-term money to larger, established businesses. Imagine the different types of businesspeople who go to banks for a loan, and you'll get a better idea of the requests bankers evaluate. Picture, for example, a farmer going to the bank in spring to borrow funds for seed, fertilizer, equipment, and other needs that will be repaid after the fall harvest. Or consider a local toy store buying merchandise for Christmas sales. The store borrows the money for such purchases in the summer and plans to pay it back after Christmas. Restaurants often borrow funds at the beginning of the month and pay at the end of the month.

How much a business borrows and for how long depends on the kind of business it is, and how quickly it can resell the merchandise it purchases with a bank loan or use it to generate funds. In a large business, specialists in a company's finance and accounting departments do a cash flow forecast. Small-business owners generally lack such specialists and must monitor cash flow themselves.

The Great Recession severely curtailed bank lending to small businesses. It was difficult for even a promising and well-organized small business to obtain a bank loan. Fortunately, the situation seems to be changing as the economy is improving. The Consumer Finance Protection Bureau is even said to be considering investigating loans to small businesses as part of its job.[25] What's important for a small firm to remember is if it gets a bank loan, the owner or person in charge of finance should keep in close touch with the bank and send regular financial statements to keep the bank up-to-date on its operations. The bank may spot cash flow problems early or be more willing to lend money in a crisis if the business has established a strong relationship built on trust and sound management. The Adapting to Change box discusses how changing its strategy helped one business attract investors.

Did you ever wonder how retail stores get the money to buy all the treasures we splurge on during the holidays? Department stores and other large retailers make extensive use of commercial banks and other lenders to borrow the funds they need to buy merchandise and stock their shelves. How do the stores benefit from using this type of financing?

Threading the Financial Needle

Coming up with a great idea is only the first step in starting a business. Entrepreneurs need money to turn their ideas into reality. Luckily, a number of potential investors are willing to open their wallets for what they think is going to be the next big thing. But to attract these "angel investors," entrepreneurs must be sure their business concepts have been carefully planned. James Reinhart, CEO of the clothing exchange website thredUP, knows this about as well as anyone.

While attending college, Reinhart and his roommate realized that they owned too many clothes. After gathering start-up funds of $70,000 from family, friends, and personal savings, Reinhart and his partners launched thredUP, a website where people could buy and sell used clothing cheaply. Within three months the site drew in more than 10,000 members.

Reinhart soon discovered that the market for used children's

clothes was much larger than the adult market since children grow out of their clothes every three to six months. So the site changed its focus to targeting parents looking to "trade up" their kids' wardrobes. Parents send in clothes that are assessed by professional buyers to judge quality and the firm's ability to resell them. The higher the quality, the more money the company pays the sender. The company then resells the clothing on its website.

Reinhart was able to improve the site thanks to a $250,000 angel investor who loved thredUP's new strategy. Soon thredUP attracted $1.4 million more in investment, which it used to phase out the site's original service entirely to focus solely on the children's clothing. The next year, the company secured a round of venture capital funding, this time topping out at a whopping $50 million. With the new investment, Reinhart could have expanded thredUP into other areas. Instead he focused on spending the money to improve the current business model. "As an entrepreneur, you're always thinking about the adjacent things to do, but we have the opportunity to build a really big, important business in the market," Reinhart said. "That's what we're going to do."

Sources: thredUP, www.thredUP.com, accessed April 2014; Philip Levinson, "thredUP's HBS Founders Master the Art of the Pivot," *The Harbus*, March 7, 2012; and "thredUP.com Releases Second Annual Clothing Resale Report," *The Providence Journal*, February 26, 2014.

Different Forms of Short-Term Loans

secured loan
A loan backed by collateral, something valuable such as property.

Commercial banks offer different types of short-term loans. A **secured loan** is backed by *collateral*, something valuable such as property. If the borrower fails to pay the loan, the lender may take possession of the collateral. An automobile loan is a secured loan. If the borrower doesn't repay it, the lender will repossess the car. Inventory of raw materials like coal, copper, and steel often serve as collateral for business loans. Collateral removes some of the bank's risk in lending the money.

Accounts receivable are company assets often used as collateral for a loan; this process is called *pledging* and works as follows: A percentage of the value of a firm's accounts receivable pledged (usually about 75 percent) is advanced to the borrowing firm. As customers pay off their accounts, the funds received are forwarded to the lender in repayment of the funds that were advanced.

unsecured loan
A loan that doesn't require any collateral.

An **unsecured loan** is more difficult to obtain because it doesn't require any collateral. Normally, lenders give unsecured loans only to highly regarded customers—long-standing businesses or those considered financially stable.

line of credit
A given amount of unsecured short-term funds a bank will lend to a business, provided the funds are readily available.

If a business develops a strong relationship with a bank, the bank may open a **line of credit** for the firm, a given amount of unsecured short-term

A secured loan is backed by collateral, a tangible item of value. A car loan, for instance, is a secured loan in which the car itself is the collateral. What is the collateral in a mortgage loan?

funds a bank will lend to a business, provided the funds are readily available. A line of credit is *not* guaranteed to a business. However, it speeds up the borrowing process since a firm does not have to apply for a new loan every time it needs funds.[26] As a business matures and becomes more financially secure, banks will often increase its line of credit. Some even offer a **revolving credit agreement**, a line of credit that's guaranteed but usually comes with a fee. Both lines of credit and revolving credit agreements are particularly good sources of funds for unexpected cash needs.

revolving credit agreement
A line of credit that's guaranteed but usually comes with a fee.

If a business is unable to secure a short-term loan from a bank, the financial manager may seek short-term funds from **commercial finance companies**. These non-deposit-type organizations make short-term loans to borrowers who offer tangible assets like property, plant, and equipment as collateral. Commercial finance companies will often make loans to businesses that cannot get short-term funds elsewhere. Since commercial finance companies assume higher degrees of risk than commercial banks, they usually charge higher interest rates. General Electric Capital is one of the world's largest commercial finance companies, with $584 billion in assets and operations in over 50 countries around the world.[27]

commercial finance companies
Organizations that make short-term loans to borrowers who offer tangible assets as collateral.

Factoring Accounts Receivable

One relatively expensive source of short-term funds for a firm is **factoring**, the process of selling accounts receivable for cash. Factoring dates as far back as 4,000 years, during the days of ancient Babylon. Here's how it works: Let's say a firm sells many of its products on credit to consumers and other businesses, creating a number of accounts receivable. Some buyers may be slow in paying their bills, so a large amount of money is due the firm. A *factor* is a market intermediary (usually a financial institution or a commercial bank) that agrees to buy the firm's accounts receivable, at a discount, for cash. The discount depends on the age of the accounts receivable, the nature of the business, and the condition of the economy. When it collects the accounts receivable that were originally owed to the firm, the factor keeps them.

factoring
The process of selling accounts receivable for cash.

While factors charge more than banks' loan rates, remember many small businesses cannot qualify for a loan. So even though factoring is an expensive way of raising short-term funds, it is popular among small businesses. A company can often reduce its factoring cost if it agrees to reimburse the factor for slow-paying accounts, or to assume the risk for customers who don't pay at all. Remember, factoring is not a loan; it is the sale of a firm's asset (accounts receivable). Factoring is common in the textile and furniture businesses, and in growing numbers of global trade ventures.

Commercial Paper

commercial paper

Unsecured promissory notes of $100,000 and up that mature (come due) in 270 days or less.

Often a corporation needs funds for just a few months and prefers not to have to negotiate with a commercial bank. One strategy available to larger firms is to sell commercial paper. **Commercial paper** consists of *unsecured* promissory notes, in amounts of $100,000 and up, that mature or come due in 270 days or less. Commercial paper states a fixed amount of money the business agrees to repay to the lender (investor) on a specific date at a specified rate of interest.

Because commercial paper is unsecured, only financially stable firms (mainly large corporations with excellent credit reputations) are able to sell it. Commercial paper can be a quick path to short-term funds at lower interest than charged by commercial banks. Even very stable firms like General Electric, however, had trouble selling commercial paper during the Great Recession. The Federal Reserve had to step in and assist many companies with their short-term financing by purchasing their short-term commercial paper. Since most commercial paper matures in 30 to 90 days, it can be an investment opportunity for buyers who can afford to put up cash for short periods to earn some interest on their money.[28]

Credit Cards

According to the National Small Business Association (NSBA), nearly one-third of all small firms now use credit cards to finance their businesses.[29] Even though more businesses are turning to credit cards for financing, two-thirds believe the terms of their cards are getting worse and it's very likely they are correct. The Credit Card Responsibility Accountability and Disclosure Act reduced consumer interest rates and approved many protections for consumers against card-company abuses. Unfortunately rates for small-business and corporate credit cards did not fall under the protection of the law. Still, with many traditional financing options closed to them, entrepreneurs are often forced to finance their firms with credit cards.

Credit cards provide a readily available line of credit that can save time and the likely embarrassment of being rejected for a bank loan. Of course, in contrast to the convenience they offer, credit cards are extremely risky and costly. Interest rates can be exorbitant, and there can be considerable penalties if users fail to make their payments on time. Savvy businesspersons study the perks that are offered with many cards and determine which might be the most beneficial to their companies. Joe Speiser, of pet-food distributor Petflow.com, found a cash-back card that helped put additional dollars back into his business.[30] Still, when dealing with credit cards, remember it's an expensive way to borrow money and credit cards are probably best used as a last resort.

After the Test Prep questions, we'll look into long-term financing options.

test prep

- What does an invoice containing the terms *2/10, net 30* mean?
- What's the difference between trade credit and a line of credit?
- What's the key difference between a secured and an unsecured loan?
- What is factoring? What are some of the considerations factors consider in establishing their discount rate?

LO 18–5 Identify and describe different sources of long-term financing.

OBTAINING LONG-TERM FINANCING

In a financial plan, forecasting determines the amount of funding the firm will need over various periods and the most appropriate sources for obtaining those funds. In setting long-term financing objectives, financial managers generally ask three questions:

1. What are our organization's long-term goals and objectives?
2. What funds do we need to achieve the firm's long-term goals and objectives?
3. What sources of long-term funding (capital) are available, and which will best fit our needs?

Firms need long-term capital to purchase expensive assets such as plant and equipment, to develop new products, or perhaps finance their expansion. In major corporations, the board of directors and top management usually make decisions about long-term financing, along with finance and accounting executives. Pfizer, one of the world's largest research-based biomedical and pharmaceutical companies, spends over $6 billion a year researching and developing new products.[31] The development of a single new drug could take 10 years and cost the firm over $1 billion before it brings in any profit. Plus the company loses its patent protection on a drug after 20 years.[32] It's easy to see why high-level managers make the long-term financing decisions at Pfizer. Owners of small and medium-sized businesses are almost always actively engaged in analyzing their long-term financing decisions.

As we noted earlier, long-term funding comes from two major sources, debt financing and equity financing. Let's look at these sources next. But first check out the Reaching Beyond Our Borders box to learn why a source of long-term funding is raising eyebrows in the financial community.

Debt Financing

Debt financing is borrowing money the company has a legal obligation to repay. Firms can borrow by either getting a loan from a lending institution or issuing bonds.

Debt Financing by Borrowing from Lending Institutions Long-term loans are usually due within 3 to 7 years but may extend to 15 or 20 years. A **term-loan agreement** is a promissory note that requires the borrower to repay the loan

term-loan agreement
A promissory note that requires the borrower to repay the loan in specified installments.

Are They Heroes or Hustlers?

Sovereign wealth funds (SWFs) are large investment companies that are owned by governments. They have been a part of global financial markets for decades and today are currently valued at over $6 trillion. The largest SWFs are operated by Norway, United Arab Emirates, Saudi Arabia, China, Kuwait, and Singapore. During the recent financial crisis, SWFs were hailed as heroes and saviors in the U.S. financial community because of the billions of dollars they invested in U.S. companies that were struggling to survive. Although SWFs provide distressed companies with much-needed capital when it is needed, the presence of foreign governments in the U.S. business world makes some people nervous. This is especially true with SWFs controlled by nations that the United States sometimes has shaky relationships with in global affairs.

Time Warner's Manhattan headquarters found ready buyers from the SWFs of Abu Dhabi and Singapore. New foreign investors from China's SWF are making their debut in the U. S. economy. Such activity has caused some politicians and business executives to question the motives and intentions of these government-operated investment funds.

Fortunately, the facts don't seem to support the suspicions about SWFs. Although purchases like Time Warner's headquarters raise questions about U.S. real estate being taken over by foreign governments, in reality foreign investment in the United States accounted for only 10 percent of the total real estate purchases in 2013. SWFs also face significant investigation by the U.S. government if they attempt to purchase more than 10 percent of a U.S.-based company. It seems that SWFs provide more advantages for the U.S. economy than serious threats. However, it's always safe to be prudent when inviting investments from foreign governments. For the moment, though, foreign governments seem more focused on addressing their own problems rather than causing a stir here.

Sources: Eliot Brown, "Time Warner Nears Deal to Sell Headquarters," *The Wall Street Journal*, January 15, 2014; Ashley Stahl, "The Promise and Perils of Sovereign Wealth Funds," *Forbes*, December 19, 2013; and John Aziz, "Does the United States Need a Sovereign Wealth Fund?" *The Week*, January 20, 2014.

---

with interest in specified monthly or annual installments. A major advantage is that the loan interest is tax-deductible.

Long-term loans are both larger and more expensive to the firm than short-term loans. Since the repayment period can be quite long, lenders assume more risk and usually require collateral, which may be real estate, machinery, equipment, company stock, or other items of value. Lenders may also require certain restrictions to force the firm to act responsibly. The interest rate is based on the adequacy of collateral, the firm's credit rating, and the general level of market interest rates. The greater the risk a lender takes in making a loan, the higher the rate of interest. This principle is known as the **risk/return trade-off**.

risk/return trade-off
The principle that the greater the risk a lender takes in making a loan, the higher the interest rate required.

Debt Financing by Issuing Bonds   If an organization is unable to obtain its long-term financing needs by getting a loan from a lending institution such as a bank, it may try to issue bonds. To put it simply, a bond is like an IOU with a promise to repay the amount borrowed, with interest, on a certain date. The terms of the agreement in a bond issue are the **indenture terms**. The types of organizations that can issue bonds include federal, state, and local governments; federal government agencies; foreign governments; and corporations.

indenture terms
The terms of agreement in a bond issue.

You may already be familiar with bonds. You may own investments like U.S. government savings bonds, or perhaps you volunteered your time to help a local school district pass a bond issue. If your community is building a new stadium or cultural center, it may sell bonds to finance the project. Businesses and governments compete when issuing bonds. Potential investors (individuals and institutions) measure the risk of purchasing a bond against the return the bond promises to pay—the interest—and the issuer's ability to repay when promised.

Like other forms of long-term debt, bonds can be secured or unsecured. A **secured bond** is issued with some form of collateral, such as real estate, equipment, or other pledged assets. If the bond's indenture terms are violated (e.g., not paying interest payments), the bondholder can issue a claim on the collateral. An **unsecured bond**, called a debenture bond, is backed only by the reputation of the issuer. Investors in such bonds simply trust that the organization issuing the bond will make good on its financial commitments.

Bonds are a key means of long-term financing for many organizations. They can also be valuable investments for private individuals or institutions. Given this importance, we will discuss bonds in depth in Chapter 19.

Equity Financing

If a firm cannot obtain a long-term loan from a lending institution or is unable to sell bonds to investors, it may seek equity financing. Equity financing makes funds available when the owners of the firm sell shares of ownership to outside investors in the form of stock, when they reinvest company earnings in the business, or when they obtain funds from venture capitalists.

Equity Financing by Selling Stock   The key thing to remember about stock is that stockholders become owners in the organization. Generally, the corporation's board of directors decides the number of shares of stock that will be offered to investors for purchase. The first time a company offers to sell its stock to the general public is called an *initial public offering (IPO)*. Selling stock to the public to obtain funds is by no means easy or automatic. U.S. companies can issue stock for public purchase only if they meet requirements set by the U.S. Securities and Exchange Commission (SEC) and various state agencies.[33] They can offer different types of stock such as common and preferred. We'll discuss IPOs and common and preferred stock in depth in Chapter 19.

Equity Financing from Retained Earnings   You probably remember from Chapter 17 that the profits the company keeps and reinvests in the firm are called *retained earnings*. Retained earnings often are a major source of

secured bond
A bond issued with some form of collateral.

unsecured bond
A bond backed only by the reputation of the issuer; also called a debenture bond.

When credit grew tight in the recent financial crisis, John Mickey, who makes promotional items with corporate logos, tapped his retirement funds to obtain start-up money for his new venture. Why is this financing strategy considered risky?

long-term funds, especially for small businesses since they often have fewer financing alternatives, such as selling stock or bonds, than large businesses do. However, large corporations also depend on retained earnings for needed long-term funding. In fact, retained earnings are usually the most favored source of meeting long-term capital needs. A company that uses them saves interest payments, dividends (payments for investing in stock), and any possible underwriting fees for issuing bonds or stock. Retained earnings also create no new ownership in the firm, as stock does.

Suppose you wanted to buy an expensive personal asset such as a new car. Ideally you would go to your personal savings account and take out the necessary cash. No hassle! No interest! Unfortunately, few people have such large amounts of cash available. Most businesses are no different. Even though they would like to finance long-term needs from operations (retained earnings), few have the resources available to accomplish this.

Equity Financing from Venture Capital   The hardest time for a business to raise money is when it is starting up or just beginning to expand.[34] A start-up business typically has few assets and no market track record, so the chances of borrowing significant amounts of money from a bank are slim. **Venture capital** is money invested in new or emerging companies that some investors—venture capitalists—believe have great profit potential. Venture capital helped firms like Intel, Apple, and Cisco Systems get started and helped Facebook and Google expand and grow. Venture capitalists invest in a company in return for part ownership of the business. They expect higher-than-average returns and competent management performance for their investment.

The venture capital industry originally began as an alternative investment vehicle for wealthy families. The Rockefeller family, for example (whose vast fortune came from John D. Rockefeller's Standard Oil Company, started in the 19th century), financed Sanford McDonnell when he was operating his company from an airplane hangar. That small venture eventually grew into McDonnell Douglas, a large aerospace and defense contractor that merged with Boeing Corporation in 1997. The venture capital industry grew significantly in

venture capital
Money that is invested in new or emerging companies that are perceived as having great profit potential.

the 1990s, especially in high-tech centers like California's Silicon Valley, where venture capitalists concentrated on Internet-related companies. Problems in the technology industry and a slowdown in the economy in the early 2000s reduced venture capital expenditures. The Great Recession caused venture capital spending to drop to new lows. Today, as the economy recovers from the recession, venture capital is slowly rising again.

Comparing Debt and Equity Financing

Figure 18.6 compares debt and equity financing options. Raising funds through borrowing to increase the firm's rate of return is referred to as **leverage**. Though debt increases risk because it creates a financial obligation that must be repaid, it also enhances the firm's ability to increase profits. Recall that two key jobs of the financial manager or CFO are forecasting the firm's need for borrowed funds and planning how to manage these funds once they are obtained.

leverage
Raising needed funds through borrowing to increase a firm's rate of return.

Firms are very concerned with the cost of capital. **Cost of capital** is the rate of return a company must earn in order to meet the demands of its lenders and expectations of its equity holders (stockholders or venture capitalists). If the firm's earnings are larger than the interest payments on borrowed funds, business owners can realize a higher rate of return than if they used equity financing. Figure 18.7 describes an example, again involving our vegetarian restaurant, Very Vegetarian (introduced in Chapter 13). If Very Vegetarian needed $200,000 in new financing, it could consider debt by selling bonds or equity through offering stock. Comparing the two options in this situation, you can see that Very Vegetarian would benefit by selling bonds since the company's earnings are greater than the interest paid on borrowed funds (bonds). However, if the firm's earnings were less than the interest paid on borrowed funds (bonds), Very Vegetarian could lose money. It's also important to remember that bonds, like all debt, have to be repaid at a specific time.

cost of capital
The rate of return a company must earn in order to meet the demands of its lenders and expectations of its equity holders.

Individual firms must determine exactly how to balance debt and equity financing by comparing the costs and benefits of each. Leverage ratios (discussed in Chapter 17) can also give companies an industry standard for this balance, to which they can compare themselves. Still debt varies considerably among major companies and industries. Tech leader Apple, for example, has modest long-term debt of $16 billion even though it has more than $140 billion in cash available. Automaker Ford Motor Company has almost $110

FIGURE 18.6 DIFFERENCES BETWEEN DEBT AND EQUITY FINANCING

	Type of Financing	
Conditions	**Debt**	**Equity**
Management influence	There's usually none unless special conditions have been agreed on.	Common stockholders have voting rights.
Repayment	Debt has a maturity date.	Stock has no maturity date.
	Principal must be repaid.	The company is never required to repay equity.
Yearly obligations	Payment of interest is a contractual obligation.	The firm isn't legally liable to pay dividends.
Tax benefits	Interest is tax-deductible.	Dividends are paid from after-tax income and aren't deductible.

Additional Debt		Additional Equity	
Stockholders' equity	$500,000	Stockholders' equity	$500,000
Additional equity	—	Additional equity	$200,000
Total equity	$500,000	Total equity	$700,000
Bond @ 8% interest	200,000	Bond interest	—
Total shareholder equity	$500,000	Total shareholder equity	$700,000
Year-End Earnings			
Gross profit	$100,000	Gross profit	$100,000
Less bond interest	−16,000	Less interest	—
Operating profit	$ 84,000	Operating profit	$100,000
Return on equity	16.8%	Return on equity	14.3%
($84,000 ÷ $500,000 = 16.8%)		($100,000 ÷ $700,000 = 14.3%)	

billion of debt on its balance sheet, mild compared to General Electric, which has over $360 billion of debt on its balance sheet. According to Standard & Poor's and Moody's Investors Service (firms that provide corporate and financial research), the debt of large industrial corporations and utilities typically ranges between 30 and 35 percent of its total assets. The amount of small-business debt obviously varies considerably from firm to firm.

Lessons Learned from the Recent Financial Crisis

The financial crisis that started in 2008 caused financial markets to suffer their worst fall since the Great Depression of the 1920s and 1930s. The collapse of financial markets could be laid at the feet of financial managers for failing to do their job effectively. Poor investment decisions and risky financial dealings (especially in real estate) caused long-standing financial firms such as Lehman Brothers to close their doors. The multibillion-dollar Ponzi scheme of once-respected "financial manager" Bernie Madoff further caused the public's trust in financial managers to disappear. Unfortunately, it also caused many investors' funds to disappear as well.

The financial meltdown led the U.S. Congress to pass sweeping financial regulatory reform. The Dodd-Frank Wall Street Reform and Consumer Protection Act affects almost every aspect of the U.S. financial services industry. As the government increases its involvement and intervention in financial markets, the requirements of financial institutions and financial managers have become more stringent.[35] This means that the job of the financial manager promises to become even more challenging. The events in the late 2000s questioned the integrity and good judgment of financial managers much like events in the early 2000s questioned the integrity and judgment of the accounting industry (see Chapter 17). Without a doubt, financial managers have a long road back to earning the trust of the public.

Chapter 19 takes a close look at securities markets as a source of securing long-term financing for businesses and as a base for investment options for private investors. You will learn how securities exchanges work, how firms issue stocks and bonds, how to choose the right investment strategy, how to buy and sell stock, where to find up-to-date information about stocks and bonds, and more. Finance takes on a new dimension when you see how you can participate in financial markets yourself.

- What are the two major forms of debt financing available to a firm?
- How does debt financing differ from equity financing?
- What are the three major forms of equity financing available to a firm?
- What is leverage, and why do firms choose to use it?

summary

LO 18–1   Explain the role and responsibilities of financial managers.

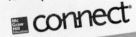

- **What are the most common ways firms fail financially?**
The most common financial problems are (1) undercapitalization, (2) poor control over cash flow, and (3) inadequate expense control.

- **What do financial managers do?**
Financial managers plan, budget, control funds, obtain funds, collect funds, conduct audits, manage taxes, and advise top management on financial matters.

LO 18–2   Outline the financial planning process, and explain the three key budgets in the financial plan.

- **What are the three budgets in a financial plan?**
The capital budget is the spending plan for expensive assets such as property, plant, and equipment. The cash budget is the projected cash balance at the end of a given period. The operating (master) budget summarizes the information in the other two budgets. It projects dollar allocations to various costs and expenses given various revenues.

LO 18–3   Explain why firms need operating funds.

- **What are firms' major financial needs?**
Businesses need financing for four major tasks: (1) managing day-by-day operations, (2) controlling credit operations, (3) acquiring needed inventory, and (4) making capital expenditures.

- **What's the difference between debt financing and equity financing?**
Debt financing raises funds by borrowing. Equity financing raises funds from within the firm through investment of retained earnings, sale of stock to investors, or sale of part ownership to venture capitalists.

- **What's the difference between short-term and long-term financing?**
Short-term financing raises funds to be repaid in less than a year, whereas long-term financing raises funds to be repaid over a longer period.

LO 18–4   Identify and describe different sources of short-term financing.

- **Why should businesses use trade credit?**
Trade credit is the least expensive and most convenient form of short-term financing. Businesses can buy goods today and pay for them sometime in the future.

- **What is meant by a line of credit and a revolving credit agreement?**
  A line of credit is an agreement by a bank to lend a specified amount of money to the business at any time, if the money is available. A revolving credit agreement is a line of credit that guarantees a loan will be available—for a fee.

- **What's the difference between a secured loan and an unsecured loan?**
  An unsecured loan has no collateral backing it. Secured loans have collateral backed by assets such as accounts receivable, inventory, or other property of value.

- **Is factoring a form of secured loan?**
  No, factoring means selling accounts receivable at a discounted rate to a factor (an intermediary that pays cash for those accounts and keeps the funds it collects on them).

- **What's commercial paper?**
  Commercial paper is a corporation's unsecured promissory note maturing in 270 days or less.

LO 18–5   Identify and describe different sources of long-term financing.

- **What are the major sources of long-term financing?**
  Debt financing is the sale of bonds to investors and long-term loans from banks and other financial institutions. Equity financing is obtained through the sale of company stock, from the firm's retained earnings, or from venture capital firms.

- **What are the two major forms of debt financing?**
  Debt financing comes from two sources: selling bonds and borrowing from individuals, banks, and other financial institutions. Bonds can be secured by some form of collateral or unsecured. The same is true of loans.

- **What's leverage, and how do firms use it?**
  Leverage is borrowing funds to invest in expansion, major asset purchases, or research and development. Firms measure the risk of borrowing against the potential for higher profits.

key terms

budget 508	**finance** 504	**revolving credit agreement** 517
capital budget 508	**financial control** 508	**risk/return trade-off** 520
capital expenditures 512	**financial management** 504	**secured bond** 521
cash budget 508	**financial managers** 504	**secured loan** 516
cash flow forecast 507	**indenture terms** 520	**short-term financing** 513
commercial finance companies 517	**leverage** 523	**short-term forecast** 507
commercial paper 518	**line of credit** 516	**term-loan agreement** 519
cost of capital 523	**long-term financing** 513	**trade credit** 514
debt financing 513	**long-term forecast** 507	**unsecured bond** 521
equity financing 513	**operating (or master) budget** 508	**unsecured loan** 516
factoring 517	**promissory note** 514	**venture capital** 522

1. What are the primary sources of short-term funds for new business owners? What are their major sources of long-term funds?

2. Why does a finance manager need to understand accounting information if the firm has a trained accountant on its staff?

3. Why do firms generally prefer to borrow funds to obtain long-term financing rather than issue shares of stock?

developing **workplace skills**

Key: ● **Team**   ★ **Analytic**   ▲ **Communication**   ▣ **Technology**

1. Go to your college's website and see whether its operating budget is online. If not, go to the campus library and see whether the reference librarian has a copy of your college's operating budget for the current year. Try to identify major capital expenditures your college has planned for the future. ▣★

2. One of the most difficult concepts to get across to small-business owners is the need to take all the trade credit they can get. For example, the credit terms 2/10, net 30 can save businesses money if they pay their bills in the first 10 days. Work with a group of classmates to build a convincing financial argument for using trade credit. ★▲●

3. Go online and check the capitalization required to open a franchise of your choice, like Subway or McDonald's. Does the franchisor offer financial assistance to prospective franchisees? Evaluate the cost of the franchise versus its business potential using the risk/return trade-off discussed in the chapter. ▣★

4. Contact a lending officer at a local bank in your community, or visit the bank's website, to check the bank's policies on providing a business a line of credit and a revolving line of credit. Evaluate the chances that this bank will give a small business either form of short-term loan. ▣★

5. Factoring accounts receivable is a form of financing used since the days of Babylonian King Hammurabi 4,000 years ago. Today it's still a source of short-term funds used by small businesses. Visit www.21stfinancialsolutions.com to get more in-depth information about factoring and be prepared to discuss the pros and cons of factoring to the class. ▣★▲

taking it to the **net**

PURPOSE

To identify which types of companies qualify for financing through the Small Business Administration.

EXERCISE

Many small-business owners have a difficult time finding financing to start or expand their business. The Small Business Administration is one potential source of financing for many types of small businesses, but there are also some businesses that do not qualify for SBA loans. Go to www.sba.gov/content/businesses-eligible-ineligible-sba-assistance and see whether the following businesses are eligible to apply for SBA financing:

1. Growing Like a Weed is a lawn care business that needs funding to buy additional equipment in order to expand. Does it meet SBA criteria? Why or why not?

2. Glamour Galore is a cosmetic company that pays sales commissions based on a system that depends upon salespeople recruiting additional salespeople. It needs funding to build a marketing campaign. Does it meet SBA criteria? Why or why not?

3. Glory Days is an old-time pinball and jukebox refurbishing company. Its founding partners need funding to buy inventory. Do they meet SBA criteria? Why or why not?

4. Lettuce Entertain U is a company needing funding to remodel an old warehouse to house its latest vegan restaurant. Does it meet SBA criteria? Why or why not?

video case

Mc Graw Hill Education **connect**

STARTING UP: TOM AND EDDIE'S

This video features the start-up company called Tom and Eddie's, an upscale hamburger restaurant in the Chicago area. Started in 2009 at the height of the great recession, the partners had a difficult time securing bank financing. As a result, they financed the operation themselves with the help of a third partner, Vince Nocarando. The partners both had long and successful careers as executives with McDonald's. Tom was executive vice president for new locations and Eddie was the president and CEO of North American operations.

Both partners, as a result of their experience at McDonald's, are well suited for the restaurant business. One of the most challenging and important elements of a successful start-up, like Tom and Eddie's, is a talented financial manager. Recognizing the importance of the financial function, they hired another former McDonald's executive, Brian Gordon, as CFO. Gordon explains that cash flow is the most important element in starting up a restaurant. In fact, cash flow is more important than profits in the first and perhaps second year of operation. Second to cash flow in terms of importance for sustainability is the management and control of inventory.

Cash flow is important, according to the CFO, because of the "known" costs, such as rent, payroll, inventory, taxes, and utilities. These are "known" costs because they are recurring and the relative costs are known on a weekly or monthly basis. CFO Gordon explains that cash flow is important in managing these known costs because of the significant "unknown" factor, which is sales.

Tom and Eddie's uses a very technology-intensive inventory management and control system because of the perishable nature of foodstuffs associated with the restaurant business. According to CFO Gordon, the restaurant has "net 14" terms with its food vendors. This means that the invoice is paid 14 days after the receipt of the goods. This is a form of financing, according to the CFO, that allows the company to turn that inventory once or twice during the 14-day period.

At the time of the video, Tom and Eddie's was in its fifteenth month of operation with three restaurants in the Chicago area. According to one of the partners, Eddie, the goal is to grow to 10 stores and then look at franchising the operation. When considering where to open a new operation, Eddie indicates that careful consideration is given to the demographics of the area, including the average income level of those working and living in the area to be served, the age of the population, the square footage of the surrounding commercial space, and ease of access to the location. Equipment is purchased rather than financed by the partners.

According to the partners, entrepreneurs think in terms of opportunities, not in terms of potential failure. With 15 months of successful operation, capital will be easier to raise from traditional sources of financing, such as banks, to expand the operation. Who knows, maybe a franchised Tom and Eddie's will be opening soon in a location near you.

THINKING IT OVER

1. What are the three factors associated with operating funds, according to the video?

2. What is meant by the term "front of the house"?

3. Why, according to the video, was bank financing unavailable for Tom and Eddie's start-up?

notes

1. Karen Weise, "Big Paydays for CFOs," *Bloomberg Businessweek,* May 19, 2013; and Emily Coyle, "Meet the Five Highest Paid CFOs in the S&P 500," *The Week,* July 8, 2013.
2. Mariella Segarra and David M. Katz, "What's It Like to Be a Nonprofit CFO?" *CFO.com,* November 27, 2013.
3. Jake Grouvm, "2008 Financial Crisis Impact Still Hurting States," *USA Today,* September 15, 2013.
4. Tim Higgins, Ian Katz, and Kasia Kimasinaska, "GM Bailout Ends as U.S. Sells Last of 'Government Motors,'" *Bloomberg Personal Finance,* December 9, 2013; and Bill Vlasic and Anne Lowery, "U.S. Ends Bailout of G.M., Selling Last Shares of Stock," *The New York Times,* December 9, 2013.
5. Ibid.
6. Saabria Chaudhuri, Michael Rapoport, and Alan Zibel, "Small Banks Face TARP Hit," *The Wall Street Journal,* February 7, 2014.
7. McCormick, www.mccormick.com, accessed February 2014.
8. Amy Haimerl, "15 Costly Mistakes Startups Make," *Crain's Detroit Business,* February 10, 2014.
9. Glenn Kessler, "Senator Scott's Claim That the Medical Device Tax Will Cost Small Business $29 Billion," *The Washington Post,* February 4, 2014.
10. Kathy Hoffelder, "Poor Internal Control Tests Hurt Financial Statement Audits," *CFO,* October 13, 2013.
11. Kathy Hoffelder, "Internal Audit Shines Brighter with Boards," *CFO,* March 22, 2013.
12. Bill Conerly, "Long-Term Economic Forecast: Key Issues and Business Strategy Implications," *Forbes,* January 12, 2014.
13. Russ Banham, "May the Field Be with You," *CFO,* October 9, 2013.
14. Keith Bradsher, "As China's Economy Slows, the Pain Hits Home," *The New York Times,* January 29, 2014; and Steve Shafer, "Why Panic-Prone Emerging Markets Are Breaking Down in 2014," *Forbes,* February 3, 2014.
15. Khan Academy, www.khanacademy.org, accessed February 2014.
16. Edward Teach, "Calm, Cool, and Collecting," *CFO,* October 15, 2013; and Jennifer Smith, "Law Firms Press to Get Bill Paid by Year End," *The Wall Street Journal,* December 22, 2013.
17. Scott Liebs, "4 Money Mistakes That Entrepreneurs Must Avoid," *Inc.,* February 2014.
18. T. J. McCue, "Why Don't More Small Businesses Accept Credit Cards?" *Forbes,* August 8, 2013; and "What You May Not Know about Your Credit Card Processor," *Milwaukee Journal Sentinal,* February 3, 2014.
19. Scott Kirsner, "Startups Offer Tech to Change the Way You Pay," *The Boston Globe,* February 9, 2014.
20. Venessa Wong, "Chipotle Wants to Speed Up with Mobile Payments," *Bloomberg Businessweek,* February 3, 2014.
21. J. J. Colao, "Interchange Fees Are for Suckers: LevelUp Hints at the Future of Mobile Payments," *Forbes,* March 21, 2013.
22. Ty Kisel, "Small Business Financing Is Available, Just Not Where You're Looking," *Forbes,* September 24, 2013.
23. Karen Haywood Queen, "Borrowing from Friends and Family," *MSN Money,* September 3, 2013.
24. National Federation of Independent Business, www.nfib.com, accessed February 2014.
25. "Consumer Finance Protection Bureau," *The Economist,* February 1, 2014.
26. Stephen D. Simpson, CFA, "The Basics of Lines of Credit," *Forbes.com,* August 6, 2013.
27. www.gecapital.com, accessed February 2014; and Chanella Bessette, "At GE, a Push for Innovation Through Partnerships," *Fortune,* February 7, 2014.
28. John Parry, "U.S. Commercial Paper Contracts to Lowest Level Since September," *Bloomberg Businessweek,* January 23, 2014.
29. Catherine Clifford, "Best Credit Cards for Small Business Owners in 2013," *Entrepreneur,* June 7, 2013; and National Small Business Advocate, www.nsba.biz, accessed February 2014.
30. Annamaria Andriotis, "The Return of Small-Business Credit Cards," *The Wall Street Journal,* January 16, 2012; "American Express OPEN Revamps Simple Cash (R) Business Credit Card by Giving Small Business Owners the Ability to Customize Their Cash Back Rewards," *The Wall Street Journal,* January 28, 2014; and "Petflow.com Continues Dominant Rise to Become Highest-Trafficked Online Pet Property in North America," *Business Wire,* February 13, 2014.
31. Jonathan D. Rockoff and Tess Stynes, "Pfizer Is Upbeat about Breast Cancer Drug, Pneumonia Vaccine," *The Wall Street Journal,* January 28, 2014.
32. Dan Carroll, "Pfizer Beats Falling Profit as the Dow Bounces Back from Recent Lows," *The Motley Fool,* January 28, 2014; and Johanna Bennett, "Pfizer's Finally a Buy," *Barron's,* February 12, 2014.
33. Ryan C. Fuhrman, "The Road to Creating an IPO," *Forbes,* August 28, 2013; and David Gelles and Michael J. de la Merced, "New IPO Rules Promise a Lot Less Information," *Boston Globe,* February 10, 2014.
34. Sam Hogg, "Why So Many Startups Never Reach Their Second Funding Round," *Entrepreneur,* February 8, 2014.
35. Abha Bhattarai and Catherine Ho, "Four Years into Dodd-Frank, Local Banks Say This Is the Year They'll Feel the Most Impact," *The Washington Post,* February 7, 2014.

19

Using Securities Markets for Financing and Investing Opportunities

Learning Objectives

I n some ways, making a stock trade in the modern age has become easy. Anybody with an e-mail address and a bank account can sign up with an online brokerage like E*Trade or Schwab and instantly start trading stocks from around the globe. However, having the ability to make *wise* trades is another matter.

Many people, hoping to understand investing, turn to experts like Mellody Hobson. As president of Ariel Investments, Hobson oversees assets of more than $9 billion. Hobson is interested in more than just her company's bottom line. As a staunch advocate for economic literacy and investor education, Hobson regularly contributes financial advice on radio, TV, and a column in *Black Enterprise Magazine*. She sits on the boards of prominent companies like DreamWorks Animation, Starbucks, and Estee Lauder. As a result, Hobson is considered to be one of the most intelligent and capable financial advisors in the industry. "She is the Picasso of questions," said DreamWorks CEO Jeff Katzenberg. "She can ask a question like nobody else. You have to find in yourself the answer to it. There's a real art to that."

Hobson was born the youngest of six children to a single mom in Chicago. She developed a strong work ethic, and was the first person in her family to attend college, graduating from Princeton University in 1991. She interned at Ariel Investments while in college and returned there to accept an entry-level position when she finished school. On her first day, Hobson received a crucial bit of advice from CEO John Rogers that still sticks with her: "John informed me that I would frequently find myself in the company of rich and successful people with big titles, lots of degrees and lots of experience," said Hobson. "And yet, my ideas could still be as good or even better."

Rogers's words encouraged Hobson as she rose through the ranks at Ariel. By 2000 she was appointed company president, placing her among the most prominent African American women in business. Under her watch Ariel Investments has grown to become the largest minority-owned mutual fund in the world.

Hobson has often said that her odds-defying rise to the top would not have been possible without a patient attitude. In fact, patience lies at the heart of Hobson's investment strategy at Ariel. True to its turtle logo, the company focuses on stocks and equity funds that will perform well in the long term, as opposed to risky but potentially lucrative short-term options. "For 30 years, we have been underscoring this idea of patient investing," said Hobson. "However, patience is not just our investment strategy but also how we build our business. Ariel is the only job I have ever had, and I have worked here more than 22 years. We live these values."

Expert investors like Mellody Hobson value sound judgment over just about anything else. But to be a successful investor, you need a little education on other important topics as well. In this chapter you'll learn about the many ways that money can be invested in securities markets.

Sources: Ben Lillie, "Be Color Brave, Not Color Blind: Mellody Hobson at TED2014," *TED Blog,* March 20, 2014; Mellody Hobson and Jeffrey Katzenberg, "The Best Advice I Ever Got," *Fortune,* November 1, 2013; Mellody Hobson, "Lean In Stories: Mellody Hobson on the Difference Between Assertive and Abrasive," *Blue Sky–Chicago Tribune,* December 7, 2013; and "Patient Investing: An Interview with Mellody Hobson," *Leaders Magazine,* January 2014.

Mellody Hobson
- President of Ariel Investments
- Expert investor
- Financial educator

www.arielinvestments.com/

@ArielFunds

531

name that **company**

If someone had bought 100 shares in this company when it was first available to the public in 1965, it would have cost $2,250. If he or she held on to the stock, the number of shares the person would have today would be 74,360 (after 12 stock splits) with a value of approximately $7.4 million. What is the name of this company? (Find the answer in the chapter.)

initial public offering (IPO)
The first public offering of a corporation's stock.

David and Tom Gardner, the Motley Fools, are passionate about spreading the message that securities markets can provide opportunities for all. The brothers have built their careers on providing high-quality financial information to investors regardless of education or income. Visit their website at www.fool. com for more information.

LO 19–1 Describe the role of securities markets and of investment bankers.

THE FUNCTION OF SECURITIES MARKETS

Securities markets—financial marketplaces for stocks, bonds, and other investments—serve two major functions. First, they assist businesses in finding long-term funding to finance capital needs, such as expanding operations, developing new products, or buying major goods and services. Second, they provide private investors a place to buy and sell securities (investments), such as stocks and bonds, that can help them build their financial future. In this chapter, we look at securities markets first from the perspective of funding for businesses and second as markets for private investors to buy and trade investments.

Securities markets are divided into primary and secondary markets. *Primary markets* handle the sale of *new* securities. This is an important point to understand. Corporations make money on the sale of their securities (stock) only once—when they sell it on the primary market. The first public offering of a corporation's stock is called an **initial public offering (IPO)**. After that, the *secondary market* handles the trading of these securities between investors, with the proceeds of the sale going to the investor selling the stock, not to the corporation whose stock is sold. For example, imagine your vegetarian restaurant, Very Vegetarian, has grown into a chain and your products are available in many retail stores throughout the country. You want to raise additional funds to expand further. If you offer 1 million shares of stock in your company at $10 a share, you can raise $10 million at this initial offering. However, after the initial sale, if Shareholder Jones decides to sell 100 shares of her Very Vegetarian stock to Investor Smith, Very Vegetarian collects nothing from that transaction. Smith buys the stock from Jones, not from Very Vegetarian. It is possible, however, for companies like Very Vegetarian to offer additional shares of stock for sale to raise additional capital.

As mentioned in Chapter 18, we can't overemphasize the importance of long-term funding to businesses. Given a choice, businesses normally prefer to meet their long-term financial needs by using retained earnings or borrowing funds either from a lending institution (bank, pension fund, insurance company) or corporate bond issue. However, if long-term funds are not available from retained earnings or lenders, a company may be able to raise capital by issuing corporate stock. (Recall from Chapter 18 that selling stock in the corporation is a form of *equity financing* and issuing corporate bonds is a form of *debt financing.*) Social networking giant Facebook's IPO in 2012 raised $16 billion for the company.[1] Visa, however, remains the largest U.S. IPO of the past 25 years raising $18 billion from its IPO in 2008. These sources of equity and bond financing are not available to all companies, especially small businesses.

Let's imagine you need further long-term financing to *expand* operations at Very Vegetarian. Your chief financial officer (CFO) says the company lacks sufficient retained earnings and she doesn't think it can secure the needed funds from a lending institution. She suggests that you offer shares of stock or issue corporate bonds to private investors to secure the funding. She warns, however, that issuing shares of stock or corporate bonds is not simple or automatic. To get approval for stock or bond issues you must make extensive financial disclosures and undergo detailed scrutiny by the U.S. Securities and Exchange Commission (SEC). Because of these requirements, your CFO recommends that the company turn to an investment banker for assistance. Let's see why.

The Role of Investment Bankers

Investment bankers are specialists who assist in the issue and sale of new securities. These large financial firms can help companies like Very Vegetarian prepare the extensive financial analyses necessary to gain SEC approval for bond or stock issues. Investment bankers can also *underwrite* new issues of stocks or bonds. That is, the investment banking firm buys the entire stock or bond issue at an agreed-on discount, which can be quite sizable, and then sells the issue to private or institutional investors at full price.

Institutional investors are large organizations—such as pension funds, mutual funds, and insurance companies—that invest their own funds or the funds of others. Because of their vast buying power, institutional investors are a powerful force in securities markets.

Before we look at stocks and bonds as long-term financing and investment opportunities in more depth, it's important to understand stock exchanges—the places where stocks and bonds are traded.

> **investment bankers**
> Specialists who assist in the issue and sale of new securities.

> **institutional investors**
> Large organizations—such as pension funds, mutual funds, and insurance companies—that invest their own funds or the funds of others.

LO 19–2   Identify the stock exchanges where securities are traded.

STOCK EXCHANGES

As the name implies, a **stock exchange** is an organization whose members can buy and sell (exchange) securities on behalf of companies and individual investors. The New York Stock Exchange (NYSE) was founded in 1792 and was then primarily a floor-based exchange, which means trades physically took place on the floor of the stock exchange. Things changed in 2005 when the NYSE merged with Archipelago, a securities trading company that specialized in electronic trades. Two years later, it merged with Europe's Euronext exchange, and became the NYSE Euronext. In 2013, the Intercontinental Exchange (ICE) located in Atlanta purchased the NYSE Euronext for $8.2 billion.[2]

Today, the once active floor of the NYSE Euronext is now largely symbolic.[3] Most trading takes place on computers that can transact thousands of stock trades within seconds. In fact, trading stocks has become a very small part of the exchange's revenue.[4] The bulk of the company's revenue comes from selling complex financial contracts and market information to companies like Yahoo and Google that offer stock quotes as a service on their websites. They also earn revenue from fees paid by over 8,000 companies listed on the NYSE Euronext.[5]

> **stock exchange**
> An organization whose members can buy and sell (exchange) securities for companies and individual investors.

The NYSE Euronext was the largest floor-based exchange, where stock trades were made on the crowded floor of the exchange. Today stocks are bought and sold primarily on electronic networks. The illustration (on the right) of the exchange floor today seems deserted compared to the old days.

over-the-counter (OTC) market
Exchange that provides a means to trade stocks not listed on the national exchanges.

NASDAQ
A nationwide electronic system that links dealers across the nation so that they can buy and sell securities electronically.

Securities and Exchange Commission (SEC)
The federal agency that has responsibility for regulating the various stock exchanges.

Not all securities are traded on registered stock exchanges. The **over-the-counter (OTC) market** provides companies and investors with a means to trade stocks not listed on the large securities exchanges. The OTC market is a network of several thousand brokers who maintain contact with one another and buy and sell securities through a nationwide electronic system. Trading is conducted between two parties directly, instead of through an exchange like the NYSE Euronext.

The **NASDAQ** (originally known as the National Association of Securities Dealers Automated Quotations) was the world's first electronic stock market. It evolved from the OTC market but is no longer part of it. The NASDAQ is an electronic-based network that links dealers so they can buy and sell securities electronically rather than in person. In 2007, the NASDAQ purchased the Swedish OMX Group and is now the NASDAQ OMX Group. It is the largest U.S. electronic stock trading market and has more trading volume than any electronic exchange in the world. The NASDAQ originally dealt mostly with smaller firms, but today well-known companies such as Facebook, Microsoft, Intel, Google, and Starbucks trade their stock on the NASDAQ. The NASDAQ also handles federal, state, and city government bonds and lists approximately 3,300 companies with a market value over $8 trillion.[6]

Adding a company to an exchange is a highly competitive undertaking, and the battle between the stock exchanges for a stock listing is often fierce.[7] If a company fails to meet the requirements of an exchange, the stock can be delisted from the exchange.[8] You can find the requirements for registering (listing) stocks on the NYSE Euronext and NASDAQ on their websites at www.nyx.com and www.nasdaqomx.com. The Spotlight on Small Business box discusses how the JOBS Act now gives small businesses access to public securities markets.

Securities Regulations and the Securities and Exchange Commission

The **Securities and Exchange Commission (SEC)** is the federal agency responsible for regulating the various stock exchanges. The Securities Act of 1933 helps protect investors by requiring full disclosure of financial information by firms selling bonds or stock. The U.S. Congress passed this legislation to deal with the free-for-all atmosphere that existed in the securities markets during the 1920s and the early 1930s that helped cause the Great Depression. The Securities and Exchange Act of 1934 created the SEC.

Companies trading on the national exchanges must register with the SEC and provide it with annual updates. The 1934 act also established specific guidelines that companies must follow when issuing financial securities, such as stocks or bonds. For example, before issuing either stocks or bonds for sale to the public, a company must file a detailed registration statement with the

Giving Small Business a Jump on Funding

The most frequent complaint from small businesses is the lack of available financing. This scarcity of funding often thwarts any expansion or hiring plans small businesses may be considering. The goal of the Jumpstart Our Business Startups Act (JOBS Act) is to ease small business financing problems. In the JOBS Act, securities rules are streamlined to give small firms access to public securities markets. The Securities and Exchange Commission (SEC) was charged with adopting rules on general solicitations and equity crowdfunding.

The SEC altered securities laws in a number of ways. A brief summary includes:

- Raised from 500 to 2,000 the number of shareholders a company could have before it's required to register its stock with the SEC.

- Allows private companies to advertise to investors, but permits companies to accept funds only from individuals who earn more than $200,000 a year or have personal assets in excess of $1 million.

- Exempts emerging growth companies with gross revenues less than $1 billion from some of the stringent financial reporting rules of the Sarbanes-Oxley Act (see Chapter 17).

- Allows *equity* crowdfunding through investment brokers or portals, but limits the amount individuals with modest incomes or net worth can invest to a percentage of their annual income or assets.

- Expanded the ability of private companies to raise capital through limited stock offerings.

Many in the investment community have cheered the act's passage as a tremendous means for small businesses to generate needed funds. However, many investment analysts see major problems. One problem is the high number of small businesses that fail every year. Another is how investors will be able to resell stock when there is no broker or exchange to facilitate the sale. Still others have blasted the law as ripe for investment fraud. Time will tell if the JOBS Act is a boom or bust for many small businesses and investors.

Sources: Kathy Kristof, "Investor Beware," *Kiplinger's Personal Finance*, February 2014; Eric T. Wagner, "Equity Crowdfunding 101: Is It Right for Your Startup?" *Forbes*, March 18, 2014; and Kendall Almerico, "The JOBS Act Provision That Could Change IPOs Forever," *Entrepreneur*, February 21, 2014.

SEC that includes extensive economic and financial information. The condensed version of that registration document—called a **prospectus**—must be sent to prospective investors.

The 1934 act also established guidelines to prevent insiders within the company from taking advantage of privileged information they may have. *Insider trading* is using knowledge or information that individuals gain through their position that allows them to benefit unfairly from fluctuations in security prices. The key words here are *benefit unfairly*. Insiders within a firm are permitted to buy and sell stock in the company they work for, so long as they do not take unfair advantage of information unknown to the public.

Originally, the SEC defined the term *insider* rather narrowly as covering a company's directors and employees and their relatives. Today the term has been broadened to include just about anyone with securities information not available to the general public. Let's say the CFO of Very Vegetarian tells her next-door neighbor she is finalizing paperwork to sell the company to a large corporation, and the neighbor buys the stock based on this information. A court may well consider the purchase an insider trade. Penalties for insider trading can include fines or imprisonment.[9] For example, billionaire hedge fund manager Raj Rajaratnam was convicted of insider trading in a high-profile case in 2011. SAC Capital portfolio manager Matthew Martoma was convicted in 2014 in the largest insider-trading scheme ever, and could face 15 to 20 years in prison. The company paid $1.5 billion in fines.[10] Look at Figure 19.1 and test your skill in identifying insider trading.

prospectus
A condensed version of economic and financial information that a company must file with the SEC before issuing stock; the prospectus must be sent to prospective investors.

FIGURE 19.1 IS IT INSIDER TRADING OR NOT?

Insider trading involves buying or selling a stock on the basis of company information not available to the investing public. These hypothetical examples will give you an idea of what's legal and what's illegal. The answers are at the bottom of the box.

1. You work in research and development at a large company and have been involved in a major effort that should lead to a blockbuster new product coming to the market. News about the product is not public, and very few other workers even know about it. Can you purchase stock in the company?

2. Pertaining to the above situation, you are in a local coffee bar and mention to a friend about what's going on at the company. Another customer seated at an adjoining table overhears your discussion. Can this person legally buy stock in the company before the public announcement?

3. You work as an executive secretary at a major investment banking firm. You are asked to copy documents that detail a major merger about to happen that will keenly benefit the company being taken over. Can you buy stock in the company before the announcement is made public?

4. Your stockbroker recommends that you buy shares in a little-known company. The broker seems to have some inside information, but you don't ask any questions about his source. Can you buy stock in this company?

5. You work as a cleaning person at a major securities firm. At your job you come across information from the trash cans and computer printers of employees of the firm that provide detailed information about several upcoming deals the firm will be handling. Can you buy stock in the companies involved?

Answers: 1. No; 2. Yes; 3. No; 4. Yes; 5. No.

Foreign Stock Exchanges

Thanks to expanded communications and the relaxation of many legal barriers, investors can buy securities from companies almost anywhere in the world. If you uncover a foreign company you feel has great potential for growth, you can purchase shares of its stock with little difficulty from U.S. brokers who have access to foreign stock exchanges. Foreign investors can also invest in U.S. securities, and large foreign stock exchanges, like those in London and Tokyo, trade large amounts of U.S. securities daily. In addition to the London and Tokyo exchanges, other major stock exchanges are located in Shanghai, Sydney, Hong Kong, São Paolo, and Toronto. Stock exchanges have become active in Africa as well.[11]

Raising long-term funds using equity financing by issuing stock is an option many companies pursue. After the Test Prep, let's look in more depth at how firms raise capital by issuing stock.

Use LearnSmart to help retain what you have learned. Access your instructor's Connect course to check out LearnSmart, or go to learnsmartadvantage.com for help.

 LEARNSMART

 test **prep**

- **What is the primary purpose of a securities exchange?**
- **What does NASDAQ stand for? How does this exchange work?**

Compare the advantages and disadvantages of equity financing by issuing stock, and detail the differences between common and preferred stock.

HOW BUSINESSES RAISE CAPITAL BY SELLING STOCK

Stocks are shares of ownership in a company. A **stock certificate** represents stock ownership. It specifies the name of the company, the number of shares owned, and the type of stock it represents. Companies, however, are not required to issue paper stock certificates to owners since stock is generally held electronically.

Stock certificates sometimes indicate a stock's *par value,* which is a dollar amount assigned to each share of stock by the corporation's charter. Today, since par values do not reflect the market value of the stock (what the stock is actually worth), most companies issue stock with a very low par value or no par value. **Dividends** are part of a firm's profits that the firm may (but is not required to) distribute to stockholders as either cash payments or additional shares of stock.[12] Dividends are declared by a corporation's board of directors and are generally paid quarterly.

Advantages and Disadvantages of Issuing Stock

Some advantages to a firm of issuing stock include:

- As owners of the business, stockholders never have to be repaid their investment.
- There's no legal obligation to pay dividends to stockholders; therefore, the firm can reinvest income (retained earnings) to finance future needs.
- Selling stock can improve the condition of a firm's balance sheet since issuing stock creates no debt. (A corporation may also buy back its stock to improve its balance sheet and make the company appear stronger financially.)[13]

Disadvantages of issuing stock include:

- As owners, stockholders (usually only common stockholders) have the right to vote for the company's board of directors. (Typically, one vote is granted for each share of stock.) Issuing new shares of stock can thus alter the control of the firm.
- Dividends are paid from profit after taxes and are not tax-deductible.
- The need to keep stockholders happy can affect managers' decisions.

Companies can issue two classes of stock: common and preferred. Let's see how these two forms of equity financing differ.

Issuing Shares of Common Stock

Common stock is the most basic form of ownership in a firm. In fact, if a company issues only one type of stock, by law it must be common stock. Holders of common stock have the right to (1) elect members of the company's board of directors and vote on important issues affecting the company and (2) share in the firm's profits through dividends, if approved by the firm's board of directors. Having voting rights in a corporation allows common stockholders to

stocks
Shares of ownership in a company.

stock certificate
Evidence of stock ownership that specifies the name of the company, the number of shares it represents, and the type of stock being issued.

dividends
Part of a firm's profits that the firm may distribute to stockholders as either cash payments or additional shares of stock.

common stock
The most basic form of ownership in a firm; it confers voting rights and the right to share in the firm's profits through dividends, if approved by the firm's board of directors.

When Twitter issued its initial public offering (IPO), the company raised more than $2.1 billion from the sale. Can you see why issuing stock can be an appealing option for financing a company's growth?

influence corporate policy because the board members they elect choose the firm's top management and make major policy decisions. Common stockholders also have a *preemptive right* to purchase new shares of common stock before anyone else. This allows common stockholders to maintain their proportional share of ownership in the company.

Issuing Shares of Preferred Stock

preferred stock
Stock that gives its owners preference in the payment of dividends and an earlier claim on assets than common stockholders if the company is forced out of business and its assets sold.

Owners of **preferred stock** are given preference in the payment of company dividends and must be paid their dividends in full before any common stock dividends can be distributed (hence the term *preferred*). They also have a prior claim on company assets if the firm is forced out of business and its assets sold. Normally, however, preferred stockholders do not get voting rights in the firm.

Preferred stock may be issued with a par value that becomes the base for a fixed dividend the firm is willing to pay. For example, if a preferred stock's par value is $50 a share and its dividend rate is 4 percent, the dividend is $2 a share. An owner of 100 preferred shares receives a fixed yearly dividend of $200 if dividends are declared by the board of directors.

Preferred stock can have other special features that common stock doesn't have.[14] For example it can be *callable*, which means preferred stockholders could be required to sell their shares back to the corporation. Preferred stock can also be converted to shares of common stock (but not the other way around), and it can be *cumulative*. That is, if one or more dividends are not paid when promised, they accumulate and the corporation must pay them in full at a later date before it can distribute any common stock dividends.[15]

Companies often prefer to raise capital by debt financing. One debt funding option frequently used by larger firms is issuing corporate bonds. Let's look at what's involved with issuing corporate bonds and how they differ from issuing stock.

- Name at least two advantages and two disadvantages of a company's issuing stock as a form of equity financing.
- What are the major differences between common stock and preferred stock?

 LO 19—4 Compare the advantages and disadvantages of obtaining debt financing by issuing bonds, and identify the classes and features of bonds.

HOW BUSINESSES RAISE CAPITAL BY ISSUING BONDS

A **bond** is a corporate certificate indicating that an investor has lent money to a firm (or a government). An organization that issues bonds has a legal obligation to make regular interest payments to investors and to repay the entire bond principal amount at a prescribed time. Let's further explore the language of bonds so you understand exactly how they work.

Learning the Language of Bonds

Corporate bonds are usually issued in units of $1,000 (government bonds can be in much larger amounts). The *principal* is the face value (dollar value) of a bond, which the issuing company is legally bound to repay in full to the bondholder on the **maturity date**. **Interest** is the payment the bond issuer makes to the bondholders to compensate them for the use of their money. If Very Vegetarian issues a $1,000 bond with an interest rate of 5 percent and a maturity date of 2025, it is agreeing to pay the bondholder a total of $50 interest each year until a specified date in 2025, when it must repay the full $1,000. Maturity dates can vary. Firms such as Disney, IBM, and Coca-Cola have issued so-called century bonds with 100-year maturity dates.[16]

Bond interest is sometimes called the *coupon rate,* a term that dates back to when bonds were issued as *bearer* bonds. The holder, or bearer, was considered the bond's owner. Back then, the company issuing the bond kept no record of changes in ownership. Bond interest was paid to whoever clipped coupons attached to the bond and sent them to the issuing company for payment. Today, bonds are registered to specific owners and changes in ownership are recorded electronically.

The interest rate paid by U.S. government bonds influences the bond interest rate businesses must pay. U.S. government bonds are considered safe investments, so they can pay lower interest. Figure 19.2 describes several types of government bonds that compete with U.S. corporate bonds in securities markets. Bond interest rates also vary according to the state of the economy, the reputation of the issuing company, and the interest rate for bonds of similar companies. Though bond interest is quoted for an entire year, it is usually paid in two installments, and the rate generally cannot be changed.

Bond rating organizations assess the creditworthiness of a corporation's bond issues. Independent rating firms such as Standard & Poor's, Moody's Investors Service, and Fitch Ratings rate bonds according to their degree of

bond
A corporate certificate indicating that a person has lent money to a firm (or a government).

maturity date
The exact date the issuer of a bond must pay the principal to the bondholder.

interest
The payment the issuer of the bond makes to the bondholders for use of the borrowed money.

FIGURE 19.2 TYPES OF GOVERNMENT SECURITIES THAT COMPETE WITH CORPORATE BONDS

U.S. government bond

Issued by the federal government; considered the safest type of bond investment

Treasury bill (T-bill)

Matures in less than a year; issued with a minimum denomination of $1,000

Treasury note

Matures in 10 years or less; sold in denominations of $1,000 up to $1,000,000

Treasury bond

Matures in 25 years or more; sold in denominations of $1,000 up to $1,000,000

Municipal bond

Issued by states, cities, counties, and other state and local government agencies; usually exempt from federal taxes

Yankee bond

Issued by a foreign government; payable in U.S. dollars

risk. Bonds can range from the highest quality to junk bonds (which we discuss later in this chapter). Figure 19.3 gives an example of the range of bond ratings issued by the ratings agencies.

Advantages and Disadvantages of Issuing Bonds

Bonds offer long-term financing advantages to an organization:

- Bondholders are creditors of the firm, not owners. They seldom vote on corporate matters; thus, management maintains control over the firm's operations.
- Bond interest is a business expense and tax-deductible to the firm (see Chapter 17).
- Bonds are a temporary source of funding. They're eventually repaid and the debt obligation is eliminated.
- Bonds can be repaid before the maturity date if they are *callable*. Bonds can also be converted to common stock. (We discuss both features below.)

Bonds also have financing drawbacks:

- Bonds increase debt (long-term liabilities) and may adversely affect the market's perception of the firm.
- Paying interest on bonds is a legal obligation. If interest is not paid, bondholders can take legal action to force payment.
- The face value of the bond must be repaid on the maturity date. Without careful planning, this obligation can cause cash flow problems when the repayment comes due.

Different Classes of Bonds

debenture bonds
Bonds that are unsecured (i.e., not backed by any collateral such as equipment).

Corporations can issue two different classes of corporate bonds. *Unsecured bonds,* usually called **debenture bonds**, are not backed by any specific collateral (such as land or equipment). Only firms with excellent reputations

Bond Rating Agencies			
Moody's	Standard & Poor's	Fitch Ratings	Descriptions
Aaa	AAA	AAA	Highest quality (lowest default risk)
Aa	AA	AA	High quality
A	A	A	Upper medium grade
Baa	BBB	BBB	Medium grade
Ba	BB	BB	Lower medium grade
B	B	B	Speculative
Caa	CCC, CC	CCC	Poor (high default risk)
Ca	C	DDD	Highly speculative
C	D	D	Lowest grade

FIGURE 19.3 BOND RATINGS: MOODY'S INVESTORS SERVICE, STANDARD & POOR'S INVESTOR SERVICE, AND FITCH RATINGS

and credit ratings can issue debenture bonds, due to the lack of security they provide investors. *Secured bonds,* sometimes called mortgage bonds, are backed by collateral such as land or buildings that is pledged to bondholders if interest or principal isn't paid when promised. A corporate bond issuer can choose to include different bond features. Let's look at some special features.

Special Bond Features

By now you should understand that bonds are issued with an interest rate, are unsecured or secured by some type of collateral, and must be repaid at their maturity date. This repayment requirement often leads companies (or governments) to establish a reserve account called a **sinking fund**. Its primary purpose is to ensure that enough money will be available to repay bondholders on the bond's maturity date. Firms issuing sinking-fund bonds periodically *retire* (set aside) some part of the principal prior to maturity so that enough funds will accumulate by the maturity date to pay off the bond. Sinking funds are generally attractive to both issuing firms and investors for several reasons:

sinking fund
A reserve account in which the issuer of a bond periodically retires some part of the bond principal prior to maturity so that enough capital will be accumulated by the maturity date to pay off the bond.

- They provide for an orderly retirement (repayment) of a bond issue.
- They reduce the risk the bond will not be repaid.
- They support the market price of the bond because they reduce the risk the bond will not be repaid.

A *callable bond* permits the bond issuer to pay off the bond's principal before its maturity date. This gives companies some discretion in their long-term forecasting. Suppose Very Vegetarian issued $10 million in 20-year bonds at 10 percent interest. Its yearly interest expense is $1 million ($10 million times 10 percent). If market conditions change and bonds of the same quality now pay only 7 percent, Very Vegetarian will be paying 3 percent, or $300,000 ($10 million times 3 percent), in excess interest yearly. The company could benefit by calling in (paying off) the old bonds and issuing new bonds at the lower rate. If a company calls a bond before maturity, it often pays investors a price above the bond's face value.

Investors can convert *convertible bonds* into shares of common stock in the issuing company. This can be an incentive for an investor because common stock value tends to grow faster than a bond. Therefore, if the value of the firm's common stock grows sizably over time, bondholders can compare the value of continued bond interest earned with the potential profit of a specified number of shares of common stock into which the bonds can be converted.[17]

Now that you understand the advantages and disadvantages of stocks and bonds as a financing tool from a company's perspective, let's explore the opportunities stocks and bonds provide for *investors*. First, though, check your progress with the Test Prep questions.

test prep

- Why are bonds considered a form of debt financing?
- What does it mean if a firm issues a 9 percent debenture bond due in 2025?
- Explain the difference between an unsecured and a secured bond.
- Why are convertible bonds attractive to investors?

Lo 19–5   Explain how to invest in securities markets and set investment objectives such as long-term growth, income, cash, and protection from inflation.

HOW INVESTORS BUY SECURITIES

Investing in stocks and bonds is not difficult. First, you decide what stock or bond you want to buy. After that, you find a brokerage firm authorized to trade securities to execute your order. A **stockbroker** is a registered representative who works for a brokerage firm as a market intermediary to buy and sell securities for clients. Stockbrokers place an order and negotiate a price. After the transaction is completed, the trade is reported to your broker, who notifies you. Today, large brokerage firms maintain automated order systems that allow brokers to enter your order the instant you make it. The order can be confirmed in seconds.

stockbroker
A registered representative who works as a market intermediary to buy and sell securities for clients.

Online brokers like TD Ameritrade, Scottrade, and E*Trade specialize in providing information for investors. What are some of the features of this website that are designed to provide investment information?

Money Going Up in Smoke

You recently received news that your Uncle Alex passed away after a long battle with lung cancer. To your surprise, he left you $25,000 in his will, saying you were his favorite nephew. You remember your uncle as a hard-working man who loved baseball and liked nothing better than to watch you pitch for your college team. Unfortunately, your uncle started smoking as a young man and eventually became a heavy chain-smoker. His doctors said that smoking was the primary cause of his lung cancer.

After receiving the inheritance, you wonder where to invest the money. Your old teammate, Jack, who is now a financial advisor, recommends that you buy stock in a well-known multinational firm that offers a good dividend and has solid global growth potential. He tells you the firm's primary product is tobacco, but assures you it produces many other products as well. You know Jack has your best interests at heart. You also believe Uncle Alex would like to see the money he left you grow. However, you wonder if a company that markets tobacco is an appropriate place to invest the inheritance from Uncle Alex. What are the ethical alternatives in this situation? What are the consequences of the alternatives? What will you do?

A stockbroker can also be a source of information about what stocks or bonds would best meet your financial objectives, but it's still important to learn about stocks and bonds on your own.[18] Investment analysts' advice may not always meet your specific expectations and needs.

Investing through Online Brokers

Investors can also choose from multiple online trading services to buy and sell stocks and bonds. TD Ameritrade, E*Trade, Charles Schwab, and Fidelity are among the leaders.[19] Investors who trade online are willing to do their own research and make investment decisions without the direct assistance of a broker. This allows online brokers the ability to charge much lower trading fees than traditional stockbrokers. The leading online services do provide important market information, such as company financial data, price histories of a stock, and analysts' reports. Often the level of information services you receive depends on the size of your account and your level of trading.

Whether you decide to use an online broker or to invest through a traditional stockbroker, remember that investing means committing your money with the hope of making a profit. The dot-com bubble in the early 2000s and the financial crisis that began in 2008 proved again that investing is a risky business.[20] Therefore, the first step in any investment program is to analyze your level of risk tolerance. Other factors to consider include your desired income, cash requirements, and need to hedge against inflation, along with the investment's growth prospects. The Making Ethical Decisions box describes an interesting stock investment decision.

You are never too young or too old to invest, but you should first ask questions and consider investment alternatives. Let's take a look at several strategies.

Choosing the Right Investment Strategy

Investment objectives change over the course of a person's life. A young person can better afford to invest in high-risk investment options, such as stocks, than can a person nearing retirement. Younger investors generally look for significant growth in the value of their investments over time. If stocks go into a tailspin and decrease in value, as they did in 2008, a younger person has time to wait for stock values to rise again. Older people, perhaps on a fixed income, lack the luxury of waiting and may be more inclined to invest in bonds that offer a steady return as a protection against inflation.

Global Stocks: Love Them or Leave Them

Concerns about the ups and downs of U.S. stocks may keep you from even thinking about investing in global stocks. If you also read the news about conflicts in Eastern Europe and the Middle East and natural disasters in Japan and Indonesia, the thought of investing globally may grow even less attractive. Your inclination is to forget about global stocks and play it safe with what may seem to be relatively secure U.S. securities. However, financial analysts generally recommend investing in some global stocks in order to diversify your investments.

Let's consider a few market facts that support their suggestion. If you research respected U.S. blue-chip stocks like Coca-Cola, IBM, and McDonald's, you will find they earn a large portion of their revenue from global markets. It's also important to note, at one time the United States accounted for over half of the global economy; today it accounts for about one-fourth. Economists also project developing economies in areas such as Asia and Africa will grow at a much faster pace than the United States.

Given the potential return, you would be remiss to not at least explore the opportunities that exist in global markets. However, like any investments, set your long-term financial goals and stay abreast of the daily news. Keep the following suggestions in mind as you consider global investments:

- Invest in familiar global companies with a solid reputation and record of performance. Companies like Honda (Japan), Nestlé (Switzerland), Samsung (South Korea), and Siemens (Germany) come to mind.
- Invest in only global stocks listed on U.S. exchanges. These companies must comply with U.S. accounting standards and rules of the SEC. American Depository Receipts (ADRs) are global stocks traded on U.S. exchanges and represent a set number of shares in a foreign company that are held on deposit at a U.S. bank.
- Invest in mutual and exchange-traded funds (ETFs), which offer a wide range of global opportunities. Many funds and ETFs have a mix of U.S. and foreign stocks. Others may focus strictly on specific countries such as China, on entire regions such as Africa, Asia, Europe, or Latin America, or on the entire world.
- Avoid Investing in stocks from countries with a history of currency problems or political instability.

Sources: Selena Maranjian, "Foreign Stocks with Dividends," *The Motley Fool*, January 2, 2014; Robert Schmansky, "How Much Should You Invest in International Stock Mutual Funds?" *Forbes*, August 8, 2013; and John Waggoner, "Investing: Simplify Life, Go Global, with Funds," *USA Today*, March 14, 2013.

Consider five key criteria when selecting investment options:

1. *Investment risk.* The chance that an investment will be worth less at some future time than it's worth now.
2. *Yield.* The expected return on an investment, such as interest or dividends, usually over a period of one year.
3. *Duration.* The length of time your money is committed to an investment.
4. *Liquidity.* How quickly you can get back your invested funds in cash if you want or need them.
5. *Tax consequences.* How the investment will affect your tax situation.

What's important in any investment strategy is the risk/return trade-off. Setting investment objectives such as *growth* (choosing stocks you believe will increase in price) or *income* (choosing bonds that pay consistent interest) should set the tone for your investment strategy.

Reducing Risk by Diversifying Investments

diversification
Buying several different investment alternatives to spread the risk of investing.

Diversification involves buying several different types of investments to spread the risk of investing. An investor may put 25 percent of his or her money into U.S. stocks that have relatively high risk but strong growth potential, another 25 percent in conservative government bonds, 25 percent in dividend-paying stocks that provide income, 10 percent in an international mutual fund (discussed later), and the rest in the bank for emergencies and other possible investment opportunities. By diversifying with such a *portfolio strategy* or *allocation model*, investors decrease the chance of losing everything they have invested.[21]

Both stockbrokers and certified financial planners (CFPs) are trained to give advice about the investment portfolio that would best fit each client's financial objectives. However, the more investors themselves read and study the market, the higher their potential for gain. A short course in investments can also be useful. Stocks and bonds are investment opportunities individuals can use to enhance their financial future. The Reaching Beyond Our Borders box discusses growing opportunities investors can find in global stocks. Before we look at stocks and bonds in depth, let's check your understanding with the Test Prep.

capital gains
The positive difference between the purchase price of a stock and its sale price.

Use LearnSmart to help retain what you have learned. Access your instructor's Connect course to check out LearnSmart, or go to *learnsmartadvantage.com* for help.

test prep

- What is the key advantage of investing through online brokers? What is the key disadvantage?
- What is the primary purpose of diversifying investments?

LO 19–6   Analyze the opportunities stocks offer as investments.

INVESTING IN STOCKS

Buying stock makes investors part owners of a company. This means that as stockholders they can participate in its success. Unfortunately, they can also lose money if a company does not do well or the overall stock market declines.

Stock investors are often called bulls or bears according to their perceptions of the market. *Bulls* believe that stock prices are going to rise; they buy stock in anticipation of the increase. A bull market is when overall stock prices are rising. *Bears* expect stock prices to decline and sell their stocks in anticipation of falling prices. That's why, when stock prices are declining, the market is called a bear market.

The market price and growth potential of most stock depends heavily on how well the corporation is meeting its business objectives. A company that achieves its objectives offers great potential for **capital gains**, the positive difference between the price at which you bought a stock and what you sell it for. For example, an investment of $2,250 in 100 shares of McDonald's when the company first offered its stock to the public in 1965 would have grown to 74,360 shares (after the company's 12 stock splits) worth approximately $7.4 million as of year-end market close on December 31, 2013.[22] Now that's a lot of Big Macs!

Investors often select stocks depending on their investment strategy. Stocks issued by higher-quality companies such as Coca-Cola, Johnson & Johnson, and IBM are referred to as *blue-chip stocks* (a term derived from poker where the highest value chip was the blue chip). These stocks

It's fun to stop and enjoy a Dairy Queen sundae, especially if you own the company. Warren Buffett, America's most successful investor, built his fortune through prudent investing and is the second wealthiest person (after Bill Gates) in the United States. Rather than waiting until after his death, Buffett began giving the bulk of his fortune to the Gates Foundation in 2006. His annual donation is approximately $2 billion.

generally pay regular dividends and experience consistent price appreciation.

Stocks of corporations in emerging fields such as technology, biotechnology, or Internet-related firms, whose earnings are expected to grow at a faster rate than other stocks, are referred to as *growth stocks*. While riskier, growth stocks may offer the potential for higher returns. Stocks of public utilities are considered *income stocks* because they usually offer investors a high dividend yield that generally keeps pace with inflation. There are even *penny stocks*, representing ownership in companies that compete in high-risk industries like oil exploration. Penny stocks sell for less than $2 (some analysts say less than $5) and are considered risky investments.[23]

When purchasing stock, investors have choices when placing buy orders. A *market order* tells a broker to buy or sell a stock immediately at the best price available. A *limit order* tells the broker to buy or sell a stock at a specific price, if that price becomes available. Let's say a stock is selling for $40 a share. You believe the price will eventually go higher but could drop to $36 first. You can place a limit order at $36, so your broker will buy the stock at $36 if it drops to that price. If the stock never falls to $36, the broker will not purchase it for you.

Stock Splits

Brokers prefer stock purchases in *round lots* of 100 shares at a time. Investors, however, often cannot afford to buy 100 shares, and therefore often buy in *odd lots,* or fewer than 100 shares at a time. High per-share prices can induce companies to declare **stock splits**, in which they issue two or more shares for every one that's outstanding. If Very Vegetarian stock were selling for $100 a share, the firm could declare a two-for-one stock split. Investors who owned one share of Very Vegetarian would now own two, each worth only $50 (half as much as before the split).

Stock splits cause no change in the firm's ownership structure and no immediate change in the investment's value. Investors generally approve of stock splits, however, because they believe demand for a stock may be greater at $50 than at $100, and the price may then go up in the near future. A company cannot be forced to split its stock, and today stock splits are becoming less common.[24] Legendary investor Warren Buffett's firm, Berkshire Hathaway, has never split its Class A stock even when its per-share price surpassed $150,000. Google, however, decided to split its stock two-for-one after the stock price exceeded $1,000 per share, and credit card giant MasterCard split its stock ten-for-one as its stock price neared $900 per share.[25]

Buying Stock on Margin

Buying stock on margin means borrowing some of the stocks' purchase cost from the brokerage firm. The margin is the portion of the stocks' purchase price that investors must pay with their own money. The board of governors of the Federal Reserve System sets *margin rates* in the U.S. market. Briefly, if the margin rate is 50 percent, an investor who qualifies for a margin account may borrow up to 50 percent of the stock's purchase price from the broker.

Although buying on margin sounds like an easy way to buy more stocks, the downside is that investors must repay the credit extended by the broker, plus interest. If the investor's account goes down in value, the broker may issue a *margin call*, requiring the investor to come up with funds to cover the

If you stroll through Times Square in New York City, you never have to wonder how stocks on the NASDAQ exchange are performing. The NASDAQ price wall continuously updates prices and the number of shares being traded. Originally, the NASDAQ dealt primarily with small companies; today, it competes with the NYSE Euronext for new stock listings.

stock splits
An action by a company that gives stockholders two or more shares of stock for each one they own.

buying stock on margin
Purchasing stocks by borrowing some of the purchase cost from the brokerage firm.

losses the account has suffered.[26] If the investor is unable to fulfill the margin call, the broker can legally sell off shares of the investor's stock to reduce the broker's chance of loss. Margin calls can force an investor to repay a significant portion of his or her account's loss within days or even hours. Buying on margin is thus a risky way to invest in stocks.

Understanding Stock Quotations

Publications like *The Wall Street Journal, Barron's,* and *Investor's Business Daily* carry a wealth of information concerning stocks and other investments. Your local newspaper may carry similar information as well. Financial websites like MSN Money, Yahoo! Finance, and CNBC carry up-to-the-minute information about companies that is much more detailed and only a click away. Take a look at Figure 19.4 to see an example of a stock quote from MSN Money for Microsoft. Microsoft trades on the NASDAQ exchange under the symbol MSFT. Preferred stock is identified by the letters *pf* following the company symbol. Remember, corporations can have several different preferred stock issues.

The information provided in the quote is easy to understand. It includes the highest and lowest price the stock traded for that day, the stock's high and low over the past 52 weeks, the dividend paid (if any), the stock's dividend yield (annual dividend as a percentage of the stock's price per share), important ratios like the price/earnings (P/E) ratio (the price of the stock divided by the firm's per-share earnings), and the earnings per share. Investors can also see the number of shares traded (volume) and the total market capitalization of the firm. More technical features, such as the stock's beta (which measures the degree of the stock's risk), may also appear. Figure 19.4 illustrates the stock's intraday trading (trading throughout the current day), but you can also click to see charts for different time periods. Similar information about bonds, mutual funds, and other investments is also available online.

You might want to follow the market behavior of specific stocks that catch your interest, even if you lack the money to invest in them. Many successful investors started in college by building hypothetical portfolios of stocks and tracking their performance. The more you know about investing before you

FIGURE 19.4 UNDERSTANDING STOCK QUOTATIONS

Microsoft Corporation (MSFT) - NasdaqGS ★ Follow

45.22 ↑0.27 (0.60%) 4:00PM EDT

After Hours : **45.20** ↓0.02 (0.04%) 5:59PM EDT

Prev Close:	44.95	Day's Range:	44.83 - 45.25
Open:	44.88	52wk Range:	30.95 - 45.71
Bid:	45.18 x 600	Volume:	22,272,025
Ask:	45.20 x 100	Avg Vol (3m):	28,677,000
1y Target Est:	47.00	Market Cap:	372.61B
Beta:	0.68	P/E (ttm):	16.94
Earnings Date:	Oct 22 - Oct 27 (Est.)	EPS (ttm):	2.67
		Div & Yield:	1.12 (2.70%)

actually risk your money, the better. (The Developing Workplace Skills and Taking It to the Net exercises at the end of this chapter have exercises you can use for practice.)

LO 19–7   Analyze the opportunities bonds offer as investments.

INVESTING IN BONDS

Investors looking for guaranteed income and limited risk often turn to U.S. government bonds for a secure investment. These bonds have the financial backing and full faith and credit of the federal government. Municipal bonds are offered by local governments and often have advantages such as tax-free interest. Some may even be insured. Corporate bonds are a bit riskier and more challenging.

First-time corporate bond investors often ask two questions. The first is, "If I purchase a corporate bond, do I have to hold it until the maturity date?" No, you do not. Bonds are bought and sold daily on major securities exchanges (the secondary market we discussed earlier). However, if you decide to sell your bond to another investor before its maturity date, you may not get its face value. If your bond does not have features that make it attractive to other investors, like a high interest rate or early maturity, you may have to sell at a *discount*, that is, a price less than the bond's face value. But if other investors do highly value it, you may be able to sell your bond at a *premium*, a price above its face value. Bond prices generally fluctuate inversely with current market interest rates. This means *as interest rates go up, bond prices fall, and vice versa.* Like all investments, however, bonds have a degree of risk.

The second question is, "How can I evaluate the investment risk of a particular bond issue?" Standard & Poor's, Moody's Investors Service, and Fitch Ratings rate the risk of many corporate and government bonds (look back at Figure 19.3). In evaluating the ratings, recall the risk/return trade-off: The higher the risk of a bond, the higher the interest rate the issuer must offer. Investors will invest in a bond considered risky only if the potential return (interest) is high enough. In fact, some will invest in bonds considered junk.

Investing in High-Risk (Junk) Bonds

junk bonds
High-risk, high-interest bonds.

Although bonds are considered relatively safe investments, some investors look for higher returns through riskier high-yield bonds called **junk bonds**. Standard & Poor's, Moody's Investors Service, and Fitch Ratings define junk bonds as those with high risk *and* high default rates.[27] Junk bonds pay investors interest as long as the value of the company's assets remains high and its cash flow stays strong. Although the interest rates are attractive and often tempting, if the company can't pay off the bond, the investor is left with an investment that isn't worth more than the paper it's written on—in other words, junk.

Understanding Bond Quotations

Bond prices are quoted as a percentage of $1,000, and their interest rate is often followed by an *s* for easier pronunciation. For example, 9 percent bonds due in 2025 are called 9s of 25. Figure 19.5 is an example of a bond quote for Goldman Sachs from Yahoo! Finance. The quote highlights the bond's interest rate (coupon rate), maturity date, rating, current price, and whether it's callable. The more you know about bonds, the better prepared you will be to discuss your financial objectives with investment advisors and brokers and be sure their advice is consistent with your best interests and objectives.

GOLDMAN SACHS GROUP INC

FIGURE 19.5
UNDERSTANDING BOND
QUOTATIONS

OVERVIEW	
Price:	100.74
Coupon (%):	5.000
Maturity Date:	1-Oct-2014
Yield to Maturity (%):	-11.265
Current Yield (%):	4.963
Fitch Ratings:	A
Coupon Payment Frequency:	Semi-Annual
First Coupon Date:	1-Apr-2005
Type:	Corporate
Callable:	No

OFFERING INFORMATION	
Quantity Available:	13
Minimum Trade Qty:	1
Dated Date:	29-Sep-2004
Settlement Date:	15-Sep-2014

LO 19–8   Explain the investment opportunities in mutual funds and exchange-traded funds (ETFs).

INVESTING IN MUTUAL FUNDS AND EXCHANGE-TRADED FUNDS

A **mutual fund** buys stocks, bonds, and other investments and then sells shares in those securities to the public. A mutual fund is like an investment company that pools investors' money and then buys stocks or bonds (for example) in many companies in accordance with the fund's specific purpose. Mutual fund managers are specialists who pick what they consider to be the best stocks and bonds available and help investors diversify their investments.

Mutual funds range from very conservative funds that invest only in government securities to others that specialize in emerging biotechnology firms, Internet companies, foreign companies, precious metals, and other investments with greater risk. Some funds will have a mix of investments like stocks and bonds. The number of mutual funds available today is staggering. For example, there were over 4,600 mutual funds investing in U.S. stocks in 2013.[28] Investors have invested over $13 trillion in mutual funds. Figure 19.6 gives you a list of some mutual fund investment options.

Young or new investors are often advised to buy shares in *index funds* that invest in a certain kind of stocks or bonds or in the market as a whole.[29] An index fund may focus on large companies, small companies, emerging countries, or real estate (real estate investment trusts, or REITs). One way to diversify your investments is by investing in a variety of index funds. A stockbroker, certified financial planner (CFP), or banker can help you find the option that best fits your investment objectives. The *Morningstar Investor* newsletter is an excellent resource for evaluating mutual funds, as are business publications such as *Bloomberg Businessweek, The Wall Street Journal, Money, Forbes, Investor's Business Daily,* and many others.

With mutual funds it's simple to change your investment objectives if your financial objectives change. For example, moving your money from a bond fund to a stock fund is no more difficult than making a phone call, clicking a mouse, or tapping your cellphone. Another advantage of mutual funds is that you can generally buy directly from the fund and avoid broker fees or

mutual fund
An organization that buys stocks and bonds and other investments, then sells shares in those securities to the public.

FIGURE 19.6 MUTUAL FUND OBJECTIVES

Mutual funds have a wide array of investment categories. They range from low-risk, conservative funds to others that invest in high-risk industries. Listed here are abbreviations of funds and what these abbreviations stand for.

AB	Investment-grade corporate bonds	MP	Stock and bond fund
AU	Gold oriented	MT	Mortgage securities
BL	Balanced	MV	Mid-cap value
EI	Equity income	NM	Insured municipal bonds
EM	Emerging markets	NR	Natural resources
EU	European region	PR	Pacific region
GL	Global	SB	Short-term corporate bonds
GM	General municipal bond	SC	Small-cap core
GT	General taxable bonds	SE	Sector funds
HB	Health/biotech	SG	Small-cap growth
HC	High-yield bonds	SM	Short-term municipal bonds
HM	High-yield municipal bonds	SP	S&P 500
IB	Intermediate-term corporate bonds	SQ	Specialty
IG	Intermediate-term government bonds	SS	Single-state municipal bonds
IL	International	SU	Short-term government bonds
IM	Intermediate-term municipal bonds	SV	Small-cap value
LC	Large-cap core	TK	Science & technology
LG	Large-cap growth	UN	Unassigned
LT	Latin America	UT	Utility
LU	Long-term U.S. bonds	WB	World bonds
LV	Large-cap value	XC	Multi-cap core
MC	Mid-cap core	XG	Multi-cap growth
MG	Mid-cap growth	XV	Multi-cap value

Sources: *The Wall Street Journal* and *Investor's Business Daily.*

commissions. However, check for fees and charges of the mutual fund because they can differ significantly. A *load fund,* for example, charges investors a commission to buy or sell its shares; a *no-load fund* charges no commission.[30]

It's important to check the long-term performance of the fund's managers; the more consistent the performance of the fund's management, the better. Mutual funds called *open-end funds* will accept the investments of any interested investors. *Closed-end funds,* however, limit the number of shares; once the fund reaches its target number, no new investors can buy into the fund.[31]

Exchange-traded funds (ETFs) resemble both stocks and mutual funds. They are collections of stocks, bonds, and other investments that are traded on securities exchanges, but are traded more like individual stocks than like mutual funds. Mutual funds, for example, permit investors to buy and sell shares only at the close of the trading day. ETFs can be purchased or sold at any time during the trading day just like individual stocks. Investors have invested over $1.6 trillion in ETFs.

The key points to remember about mutual funds and ETFs is that they offer small investors a way to spread the risk of stock and bond ownership and have their investments managed by a financial specialist for a fee. Financial advisors put mutual funds and ETFs high on the list of recommended investments, particularly for small or first-time investors.[32]

exchange-traded funds (ETFs)
Collections of stocks, bonds, and other investments that are traded on exchanges but are traded more like individual stocks than like mutual funds.

Understanding Mutual Fund Quotations

You can investigate the specifics of various mutual funds by contacting a broker or contacting the fund directly by phone or through its website. Business publications and online sources also provide information about mutual funds.

Look at the example of the Pimco High Income fund from Yahoo! Finance in Figure 19.7. The fund's name is listed in large letters. The quotation includes the price of the fund, as well as the previous day's closing price and the opening price. The chart also shows the 52-week range, the daily and average volumes, the earnings per share, and the dividend/yield.

Figure 19.8 evaluates bonds, stocks, mutual funds, and ETFs according to risk, income, and possible investment growth (capital gain).

Pimco High Income Fund Pimco Hi (PHK) - NYSE ★ Follow

13.01 ↑0.01 (0.08%)   4:05PM EDT

Prev Close:	**13.00**	Day's Range:	**12.95 - 13.02**
Open:	**12.99**	52wk Range:	**11.47 - 13.75**
Bid:	**12.94** x 1000	Volume:	**527,469**
Ask:	**13.01** x 200	Avg Vol (3m):	**639,641**
1y Target Est:	**N/A**	Market Cap:	**N/A**
Beta:	**N/A**	P/E (ttm):	**N/A**
Next Earnings Date:	**N/A**	EPS (ttm):	**-0.12**
		Div & Yield:	**1.06 (7.70%)**

FIGURE 19.7
UNDERSTANDING MUTUAL FUND QUOTATIONS

Investment	Degree of risk	Expected income	Possible growth (capital gain)
Bonds	Low	Secure	Little
Preferred stock	Medium	Steady	Little
Common stock	High	Variable	Good
Mutual funds	Medium	Variable	Good
ETFs	Medium	Variable	Good

FIGURE 19.8
COMPARING INVESTMENTS

 **test prep** ✓✓

- What is a stock split? Why do companies sometimes split their stock?
- What does buying stock on margin mean?
- What are mutual funds and ETFs?
- What is the key benefit to investors in investing in a mutual fund or ETF?

Use LearnSmart to help retain what you have learned. Access your instructor's Connect course to check out LearnSmart, or go to learnsmartadvantage.com for help.

■■ LEARNSMART®

LO 19–9   Describe how indicators like the Dow Jones Industrial Average affect the market.

UNDERSTANDING STOCK MARKET INDICATORS

Investors today have an enormous wealth of investment information available to them. Newspapers like *The Wall Street Journal, Barron's,* and *Investor's Business Daily* provide vast amounts of information about companies and global markets. Television networks like MSNBC and CNBC offer daily investment analysis and different viewpoints to assist investors. Websites like MSN Money and Yahoo! Finance offer financial information to investors free of charge that not long ago was available only to brokers for a hefty fee. But keep in mind that investing is an inexact science. Every time someone sells a stock, believing it will fall, someone else is buying it, believing its price will go higher.

You often hear business news reports include a comment like, "The Dow was up 90 points today in active trading." Ever wonder what that's all about? The **Dow Jones Industrial Average (the Dow)** is the average cost of 30 selected industrial stocks. The financial industry uses it to give an indication of the direction (up or down) of the stock market over time. Charles Dow began the practice of measuring stock averages in 1884, using the prices of 12 key stocks. In 1982, the Dow was broadened to include 30 stocks. The 12 original and the 30 current stocks in the Dow are illustrated in Figure 19.9. Do you recognize any of the 12 original companies?

Today, Dow Jones & Company substitutes new stocks in the Dow when it's deemed appropriate. In 1991, Disney was added to reflect the increased economic importance of the service sector. In 1999, the Dow added Home Depot and SBC Communications along with its first NASDAQ stocks, Intel and Microsoft. In 2013, Visa, Goldman Sachs, and Nike replaced Alcoa, Bank of America, and Hewlett-Packard.[33]

Critics argue that the 30-company Dow sample is too small to get a good statistical representation of the direction of the market over time. Many investors and analysts prefer to follow stock indexes like the Standard & Poor's 500 (S&P 500), which tracks the performance of 400 industrial, 40 financial, 40 public utility, and 20 transportation stocks. Investors also closely follow the NASDAQ average, which is quoted each trading day to show trends in this important exchange.

Staying abreast of the market will help you decide what investments seem most appropriate to your needs and objectives. Remember two key investment realities: Your personal financial objectives and needs change over time, and markets can be volatile. Let's look at market volatility and the challenges that present investors with new risks and opportunities.

Dow Jones Industrial Average (the Dow)
The average cost of 30 selected industrial stocks, used to give an indication of the direction (up or down) of the stock market over time.

FIGURE 19.9 THE ORIGINAL DOW AND CURRENT DOW

THE ORIGINAL DOW 12	THE 30 CURRENT DOW COMPANIES	
American Cotton Oil	American Express	JPMorgan Chase
American Sugar Refining Co.	AT&T	McDonald's
American Tobacco	Boeing	Merck
Chicago Gas	Caterpillar	Microsoft
Distilling & Cattle Feeding Co.	Chevron	3M
General Electric Co.	Cisco	Nike
Laclede Gas Light Co.	Coca-Cola	Pfizer
National Lead	DuPont	Procter & Gamble
North American Co.	ExxonMobil	Travelers
Tennessee Coal, Iron & Railroad Co.	General Electric	United Health Group
U.S. Leather	Goldman Sachs	United Technologies
U.S. Rubber Co.	Home Depot	Verizon
	IBM	Visa
	Intel	Wal-Mart Stores
	Johnson & Johnson	Walt Disney

Riding the Market's Roller Coaster

Throughout the 1900s, the stock market had its ups and downs, spiced with several major tremors. The first major crash occurred on Tuesday, October 29, 1929 (called Black Tuesday), when the stock market lost almost 13 percent of its value in a single day. This day, and the deep depression that followed, reinforced the reality of market volatility, especially to those who bought stocks heavily on margin. On October 19, 1987, the stock market suffered the largest one-day drop in its history, losing over 22 percent of its value. On October 27, 1997, investors again felt the market's fury. Fears of an impending economic crisis in Asia caused panic and widespread losses. Luckily, the market regained its strength after a short downturn.

After regaining strength in the late 1990s, the market again suffered misfortune in the early 2000s. All told, investors lost $7 trillion in market value from 2000 through 2002 due to the burst of the tech stock bubble. A recovery that started in the mid-2000s was cut short in 2008, when the financial crisis fueled a massive exodus from the stock market, resulting in record losses.

What caused the market turmoil of 1987, 1997, 2000–2002, and 2008? In 1987, many analysts agreed it was **program trading**, in which investors give their computers instructions to sell automatically to avoid potential losses, if the price of their stock dips to a certain point. On October 19, 1987, computers' sell orders caused many stocks to fall to unbelievable depths. The crash prompted the U.S. exchanges to create mechanisms called *curbs* and *circuit breakers* to restrict program trading whenever the market moves up or down by a large number of points in a trading day. A key computer is turned off and program trading is halted. If you watch programming on CNBC or MSNBC, you'll see the phrase *curbs in* appear on the screen.

Circuit breakers are more drastic than curbs and are triggered when the Dow falls 10, 20, or 30 percent in a day. That happened on October 27, 1997, when the market suffered an approximate 7 percent decline and the market closed for the day at 3:30 p.m. instead of 4:00. Many believe the 1997 market drop (caused by the financial crisis in Asia) could have been much worse without the trading restrictions. Depending on the rate of decline and the time of day, circuit breakers will halt trading for half an hour to two hours so traders have time to assess the situation.

program trading
Giving instructions to computers to automatically sell if the price of a stock dips to a certain point to avoid potential losses.

Investing in the stock market has never been for the faint of heart. The market seems to have continuous steep climbs and sharp falls. Do you have the risk tolerance to survive the wild market swings?

Huge swings in the market cause much anguish among Wall Street workers and people in general. What have we learned from market bubbles like those in technology and real estate?

In the late 1990s the stock market reached unparalleled heights only to collapse into a deep decline in 2000–2002. The bursting of the dot-com bubble was the primary reason. A bubble is caused when too many investors drive the price of something (in this case dot-com stocks) unrealistically high.

The dot-com crash was, unfortunately, accompanied by disclosures of financial fraud at companies such as WorldCom, Enron, and Tyco. Investors had trusted that the real value of these companies was fairly reflected in their financial statements. This trust was shattered when they found investment analysts often provided clients with wildly optimistic evaluations and recommendations about companies they knew were not worth their current prices.

After the financial downturn caused by the dot-com bubble, the stock market surged in the mid-2000s and set a new high. The market's growth was dramatic, especially in the real estate sector. From 2000 to 2006 prices of existing homes rose 50 percent; however, between 2006 and 2011, housing values fell $6.3 trillion. The real estate bubble was like the dot-com bubble before it: Investors believed that home prices would increase forever. Financial institutions reduced their lending requirements for buyers, homebuilders overbuilt, and buyers overspent, all sharing blame for the crisis. The government also contributed to the problem by requiring more mortgages be given to low- and moderate-income buyers, many with weak credit scores or no verification of income or assets. These *subprime* loans were pooled together and repackaged as mortgage-backed securities that were sold to investors (discussed in Chapter 20). What followed were huge numbers of foreclosures, the failure of government-sponsored mortgage giants Fannie Mae and Freddie Mac, and more than 350 bank failures.

The collapse of the real estate market caused the economy a combined loss of $8 trillion in housing and commercial property. Financial institutions, like Lehman Brothers, went out of business and Wall Street icon Merrill Lynch was purchased by Bank of America. With financial markets in the worst condition since the Great Depression and the economy in a deep recession, the federal government took action. Congress passed a $700 billion financial package called the Troubled Asset Relief Program (TARP) that allowed the Treasury Department to purchase or insure "troubled assets" to bolster banks and bail out the automotive industry and insurer American International Group (AIG). Unfortunately, in 2009 the economy continued to decline and unemployment grew to double digits, causing President Obama to encourage passage of an $800 billion economic stimulus package—a blend of tax cuts and increased government spending—that was intended to reduce unemployment and provide a "significant boost" to the crippled economy.

Since 2009, the economy has slowly recovered. Unfortunately, unemployment has remained high and consumers remain skeptical about the nation's economic future. Also, of the 5 million Americans who suffered foreclosure on their homes due to the financial crisis, many do not see owning another home as part of the "American Dream."[34] On the positive side, the amount of TARP funds the government spent did not approximate the $700 billion that was appropriated. The troubled banks repaid most of the money they received through TARP (with interest) and AIG repaid the government in full. The government did lose $10 billion when it sold its final shares of General Motors. Since then, the stock market has experienced growth and again moved to new highs.[35] What the future of the stock market will be remains to be seen.

FIGURE 19.10 CLEANING
UP THE STREET
Key Provisions of the Dodd-
Frank Wall Street Reform and
Consumer Protection Act

Key Dodd-Frank Provisions

• Gave the government power to seize and shutter large financial institutions on the verge of collapse.

• Put derivatives and complicated financial deals (including those that packaged subprime mortgages) under strict governmental oversight.

• Required hedge funds to register with the SEC and provide information about trades and portfolio holdings.

• Created the Consumer Financial Protection Bureau to watch over the interests of American consumers by reviewing and enforcing federal financial laws.

Investing Challenges in the 21st-Century Market

As you can see from the previous section, in the stock market, what goes up may also go down. Financial markets will likely experience changes in the future that will only heighten investor risk. The financial crisis also reinforced the fact that the world's economies are closely linked. The United States was not the only nation affected by the financial crisis; financial markets in Europe, Asia, and South America felt the pain as well. Persistent challenges and even political and social change promise to make securities markets exciting but not stable places to be in the 21st century. Figure 19.10 highlights new government regulations designed to address some of these challenges.

Remember to diversify your investments, and be mindful of the risks of investing. Taking a long-term perspective is also a wise idea. There's no such thing as easy money or a sure thing. If you carefully research companies and industries, keep up with the news, and make use of investment resources—such as newspapers, magazines, newsletters, the Internet, TV programs, and college classes—the payoff can be rewarding over time.

test prep

• What does the Dow Jones Industrial Average measure? Why is it important?

• Why do the 30 companies comprising the Dow change periodically?

• Explain program trading and the problems it can create.

Use LearnSmart to help retain what you have learned. Access your instructor's Connect course to check out LearnSmart, or go to learnsmartadvantage.com for help.

LEARNSMART

summary

LO 19–1   Describe the role of securities markets and of investment bankers.

• **What opportunities do securities markets provide businesses and individual investors?**
By issuing securities businesses are able to raise much-needed funding to help finance their major expenses. Individual investors can share in the success and growth of emerging or established firms by investing in them.

Access your instructor's Connect course to check out LearnSmart or go to learnsmartadvantage.com for help.

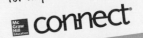

• **What role do investment bankers play in securities markets?**
Investment bankers are specialists who assist in the issue and sale of new securities.

LO 19–2   Identify the stock exchanges where securities are traded.

• **What are stock exchanges?**
Stock exchanges are securities markets whose members are engaged in buying and selling securities such as stocks and bonds.

• **What are the different exchanges?**
The NYSE Euronext lists the stock of over 8,000 companies. The NASDAQ is a telecommunications network that links dealers across the nation so that they can buy and sell securities electronically rather than in person. It is the largest U.S. electronic stock trading market. There are stock exchanges all over the world.

• **What is the over-the-counter (OTC) market?**
The OTC market is a system for exchanging stocks not listed on the national exchanges.

• **How are securities exchanges regulated?**
The Securities and Exchange Commission (SEC) regulates securities exchanges and requires companies that intend to sell bonds or stocks to provide a prospectus to potential investors.

• **What is insider trading?**
Insider trading is the use of information or knowledge that individuals gain that allows them to benefit unfairly from fluctuations in security prices.

LO 19–3   Compare the advantages and disadvantages of equity financing by issuing stock, and detail the differences between common and preferred stock.

• **What are the advantages and disadvantages to a firm of selling stock?**
The advantages of selling stock include the following: (1) the stock price never has to be repaid to stockholders, since they become owners in the company; (2) there is no legal obligation to pay stock dividends; and (3) the company incurs no debt, so it may appear financially stronger. Disadvantages of selling stock include the following: (1) stockholders become owners of the firm and can affect its management by voting for the board of directors; (2) it is more costly to pay dividends since they are paid in after-tax profits; and (3) managers may be tempted to make stockholders happy in the short term rather than plan for long-term needs.

• **What are the differences between common and preferred stock?**
Holders of common stock have voting rights in the company. In exchange for having no voting rights, preferred stockholders receive a fixed dividend that must be paid in full before common stockholders receive a dividend. Preferred stockholders are also paid back their investment before common stockholders if the company is forced out of business.

LO 19–4   Compare the advantages and disadvantages of obtaining debt financing by issuing bonds, and identify the classes and features of bonds.

• **What are the advantages and disadvantages of issuing bonds?**
The advantages of issuing bonds include the following: (1) management retains control since bondholders cannot vote; (2) interest paid on bonds is

tax-deductible; (3) bonds are only a temporary source of financing, and after they are paid off the debt is eliminated; (4) bonds can be paid back early if they are callable; and (5) sometimes bonds can be converted to common stock. The disadvantages of bonds include the following: (1) because bonds are an increase in debt, they may adversely affect the market's perception of the company; (2) the firm must pay interest on its bonds; and (3) the firm must repay the bond's face value on the maturity date.

- **What are the different types of bonds?**
  Unsecured (debenture) bonds are not supported by collateral, whereas secured bonds are backed by tangible assets such as mortgages, buildings, and equipment.

LO 19–5   Explain how to invest in securities markets and set investment objectives such as long-term growth, income, cash, and protection from inflation.

- **How do investors normally make purchases in securities markets?**
  Investors can purchase investments through market intermediaries called stockbrokers, who provide many different services. Online investing, however, has become extremely popular.

- **What are the criteria for selecting investments?**
  Investors should determine their overall financial objectives and evaluate investments according to (1) risk, (2) yield, (3) duration, (4) liquidity, and (5) tax consequences.

- **What is diversification?**
  Diversification means buying several different types of investments (government bonds, corporate bonds, preferred stock, common stock, global stock) with different degrees of risk. The purpose is to reduce the overall risk an investor would assume by investing in just one type of security.

LO 19–6   Analyze the opportunities stocks offer as investments.

- **What is a market order?**
  A market order tells a broker to buy or sell a security immediately at the best price available.

- **A limit order?**
  A limit order tells the broker to buy or sell if the stock reaches a specific price.

- **What does it mean when a stock splits?**
  When a stock splits, stockholders receive two (or more) shares of stock for each share they own. Each is worth half (or less) of the original share, so while the number of the shares increases, the total value of stockholders' holdings stays the same. Stockholders hope the lower per-share price that results may increase demand for the stock.

- **What does buying on margin mean?**
  An investor buying on margin borrows part (the percentage allowed to be borrowed is set by the Federal Reserve) of the cost of a stock from the broker to get shares of stock without immediately paying the full price.

- **What type of information do stock quotations give you?**
  Stock quotations provide the highest and lowest price in the last 52 weeks; the dividend yield; the price/earnings ratio; the total shares traded that day; and the closing price and net change in price from the previous day.

LO 19–7   Analyze the opportunities bonds offer as investments.

- **What is the difference between a bond selling at a discount and a bond selling at a premium?**
  In the secondary market a bond selling at a premium is priced above its face value. A bond selling at a discount sells below its face value.

- **What is a junk bond?**
  Junk bonds are high-risk (rated BB or below), high-interest debenture bonds that speculative investors often find attractive.

- **What information does a bond quotation give you?**
  A bond quotation gives the bond's interest rate (coupon rate), maturity date, rating, current price, and whether it's callable.

LO 19–8   Explain the investment opportunities in mutual funds and exchange-traded funds (ETFs).

- **How can mutual funds help individuals diversify their investments?**
  A mutual fund is an organization that buys stocks and bonds and then sells shares in those securities to the public, enabling individuals to invest in many more companies than they could otherwise afford.

- **What are ETFs?**
  Like mutual funds, ETFs are collections of stocks that are traded on securities exchanges, but they are traded more like individual stocks.

LO 19–9   Describe how indicators like the Dow Jones Industrial Average affect the market.

- **What is the Dow Jones Industrial Average?**
  The Dow Jones Industrial Average is the average price of 30 specific stocks that analysts use to track the direction (up or down) of the stock market.

key terms

bond 539	**initial public offering (IPO)** 532	**preferred stock** 538
buying stock on margin 546	**institutional investors** 533	**program trading** 553
capital gains 545	**interest** 539	**prospectus** 535
common stock 537	**investment bankers** 533	**Securities and Exchange Commission (SEC)** 534
debenture bonds 540	**junk bonds** 548	**sinking fund** 541
diversification 544	**maturity date** 539	**stockbroker** 542
dividends 537	**mutual fund** 549	**stock certificate** 537
Dow Jones Industrial Average (the Dow) 552	**NASDAQ** 534	**stock exchange** 533
exchange-traded funds (ETFs) 550	**over-the-counter (OTC) market** 534	**stocks** 537
		stock splits 546

critical thinking

1. Imagine you inherited $50,000 and you want to invest it to meet two financial goals: (*a*) to save for your wedding, which you plan to have in two years, and (*b*) to save for your retirement a few decades from now. How would you invest the money? Explain your answer.

2. If you are considering investing in the bond market, how could information provided by Standard & Poor's, Moody's Investors Service, and Fitch Ratings help you?

3. Why do companies like callable bonds? Why are investors generally not very fond of them?

4. If you were thinking about investing in the securities market, would you prefer individual stocks, mutual funds, or ETFs? Explain your choice by comparing the advantages and disadvantages of each.

5. Consider the companies added and subtracted from the Dow Jones Industrial Average over the past five years. (Go to www.djaverages.com, then proceed to Dow Jones Learning Center to learn more about these companies.) What types of companies were added and deleted? Why do you think the changes were made? Do you think new changes will be made in the next five years? Why?

developing **workplace skills**

Key: ● **Team**   ★ **Analytic**   ▲ **Communication**   ▣ **Technology**

1. Go to the websites of Charles Schwab (www.schwab.com), E*Trade (www.etrade.com), and TD Ameritrade (www.tdameritrade.com). Investigate each of these brokerage companies to compare their fees and what they offer in terms of research and advice. Which firm seems most appropriate to your investment objectives? Be prepared to defend your choice to the class.   ▣ ★ ▲

2. Visit MSN Money or Yahoo! Finance and select six stocks for your portfolio—three from the NYSE and three from the NASDAQ. Track the stocks daily for three weeks using the graphs provided on the websites to see how market trends and information affected your stock's performance. Report your observations.   ▣ ★ ▲

3. U.S. government bonds compete with corporations for investors' dollars. Check out the different types of bonds the federal government offers and list the types most appealing to you. (Hint: See www.treasurydirect.gov.) Be sure to check out TIPs.   ▣ ★ ▲

4. See whether anyone in class is interested in forming an investment group. If so, each member should choose one stock and one mutual fund or ETF. Record each student's selections and the corresponding prices. In two weeks measure the percentage of change in the investments and discuss the results.   ● ▣ ★ ▲

5. Go to the websites of Charles Schwab (www.schwab.com), E*Trade (www.etrade.com), or TD Ameritrade (www.tdameritrade.com) and find two IPOs offered in the past year or so. Track the performance of each from its introduction to its present market price. Report your observations.   ▣ ★ ▲

taking it to the **net**

PURPOSE

To evaluate and understand the advantages and disadvantages of ETFs.

EXERCISE

Exchange-traded funds (ETFs) are a low-cost, flexible way to diversify a portfolio. To learn more, go to Yahoo! Finance (www.finance.yahoo.com) and click on investing, then on the ETFs tab.

1. What are the pros and cons of investing in ETFs?

2. What are the five most actively traded ETFs?

3. Which ETFs grew the most in the last three years?

4. In which industry sectors or countries do these high-growth ETFs specialize?

video case   Mc Graw Hill Education connect®

WHERE DID ALL MY MONEY GO?

We all hear about the importance of investing, but how do you know what the best investments are? Is there an objective source you can use to get investment advice? The answer is, yes, you can get much helpful and unbiased information from a company called Morningstar.

Most people choose between stocks and bonds. When you buy stocks, you buy part ownership of a firm. You can choose from large firms like AT&T and Microsoft or smaller firms. Morningstar can help you choose from the thousands of firms available.

One way to spread the risk of investing in stock is to diversify. That is, you can buy stock in a variety of firms in a variety of sectors. For example, you can buy stock in firms from other countries, in service firms, manufacturing firms, health care firms, and so on. One easy way to diversify is to buy mutual funds. Such funds buy a whole range of stocks and then sell you a portion of that fund. ETFs, or exchange-traded funds, are much like mutual funds, but you buy and sell them through stock exchanges much like you would buy individual shares of stock.

In the long run, most investment advisors recommend investing in stock. Yes, the stock market goes up and down, but they say, in the long run, stocks usually go up. Since young people can wait for years to sell their stock, investment advisors

like Morningstar would usually recommend stock (or mutual funds) to them.

Would Morningstar also be likely to recommend bonds? Sure. When you buy a bond, you are actually lending a company, the government, or some government agency money. The company (or the government) promises to return the money to you, plus interest. If the interest is high enough, such an investment makes sense. Of course, some companies are riskier than others, so the interest paid on bonds varies. Morningstar will help you choose bonds that are appropriate for you and your situation.

Almost everyone needs some investment advice. Morningstar has earned a reputation for being objective and helpful. This video is meant to reveal the benefits and drawbacks of investing. But stocks and bonds can earn you a nice return on your investment if you know what you are doing. If you don't know what you are doing, you can lose your savings rather quickly. Morningstar is just one source of information. You should explore as many sources as possible to learn about investing. Such sources include your textbook, your local newspaper, magazines such as *Money* and *Personal Finance*, and TV shows featuring financial news.

Everyone should have some money set aside (e.g., in a bank) for emergencies. Everyone should diversify their investments among stocks, bonds, real estate, and other investments, depending on their income and their willingness to assume risk.

Morningstar and other sources of advice are very important to your financial health. You have seen how some people believed that real estate could do nothing but go up. The recent real estate crash proved them wrong. The same is true of stocks, bonds, gold, oil, and other investments. They all involve risk, and expert advice is often wrong; but in any case, it pays to have the best, unbiased advice you can get, like that from Morningstar. It also helps to have several other sources of advice, including your own knowledge, gathered carefully over time.

THINKING IT OVER

1. Are you confident about investing in stocks, bonds, mutual funds, ETFs, and other investments? What sources of information would you use to make a decision about investments?

2. Should you totally rely on Morningstar or any other investment advice service or should you search out several sources of advice? How can you know what advice is best?

3. Given what you've read in this text and from other sources, would you recommend that your fellow students' first investment be in stocks, bonds, mutual funds, ETFs, real estate, or some other investments? Why?

notes

1. Katie Roof, "Big Tech IPOs for 2014," *Forbes,* December 23, 2013.
2. Nandini Sukumar, "BME May Evaluate NYSE Technology Units, Won't Buy Euronext Stake," *Bloomberg Businessweek,* February 24, 2014; and Steven M. Sears, "Master of the Markets," *Barron's,* February 10, 2014.
3. "The End of the Street," *The Economist,* November 16, 2013.
4. Bradley Hope and Keiko Morris, "NYSE's New York City Footprint May Shrink," *The Wall Street Journal,* February 17, 2014.
5. NYSE Euronext, www.nyx.com, accessed May 2014.
6. NASDAQ OMX, www.nasdaqomx.com, accessed May 2014.
7. Chris Dieterich, "Big Board Scores One for Humans," *The Wall Street Journal,* January 5, 2014; and Sam Mamudi and Ari Levy, "NASDAQ Offers an IPO Alternative," *Bloomberg Businessweek,* February 13, 2014.
8. Dan Stumpf, "U.S. Public Companies Rise Again," *The Wall Street Journal,* February 5, 2014.
9. Peter J. Henning, "Paying the Price for Insider Trading Profits," *The New York Times,* February 24, 2014.
10. Christopher M. Matthews, "Prosecutors Tell Jury to Convict Martoma, As Insider Trading Trial Nears End," *The Wall Street Journal,* February 3, 2014; and Michelle Celarier, "Ex-SAC Martoma Asks Judge to Toss Guilty Verdict," *New York Post,* February 24, 2014.
11. "Bull Runs Free in African Stock Markets," *USA Today,* May 27, 2013.
12. Shirley A. Lazo, "Global Payouts Hit $1 Trillion," *Barron's,* March 1, 2014.
13. Kopin Tan, "Buyback Bonbons," *Barron's,* January 6, 2014.
14. "Common and Preferred Stock: What's the Difference," *The Motley Fool,* February 23, 2014.
15. Tom Konrad, "Power REIT's Preferred Stock Offering: A Hedge That Pays 7.75%," *Forbes,* February 7, 2014.
16. Katy Burne, "Bankers Pitch 100-Year Bonds," *The Wall Street Journal,* August 23, 2010; Vivianne Sander, Michael Mackenzie, and Henny Sander, "Verizon Eyes Maturities of 100 Years for Bonds," *Financial Times,* September 7, 2013; and Katie Linsell, "EDF's Borrowing Exceeds $12 Billion This Week with 100-Year Bond," *Bloomberg News,* January 17, 2014.
17. William Baldwin, "Six Ways to Inflation-Proof Your Bonds," *Forbes,* March 2, 2011; and 4 Ways Bonds Can Fit into Your Portfolio," *Forbes,* February 9, 2012.
18. Kevin Harlan, "The Changing Broker Scene Offers Options for Traders," *Investor's Business Daily,* April 25, 2011; and Eve Kaplan, "The Difference between a Stockbroker, Financial Advisor and Planner Explained," *Forbes,* March 15, 2012.
19. Selena Maranjian, "How to Find the Best Online Brokers," *The Motley Fool,* June 25, 2013; and Ken Hoover and Donald Gold, "Research, Stock Trading Tools Sharpen at Top Brokers," November 25, 2013.
20. Carolyn Bigda, "Happy Fifth Birthday, Mr. Bull," *Kiplinger's Personal Finance,* March 2014.
21. Ryan Caldbeck, "Successful Venture Investing: The Importance of Understanding Risks, and Diversification," *Forbes,* February 19, 2014.
22. McDonald's www.mcdonalds.com/aboutmcdonalds/ stocksplit, accessed May 2014.
23. Andrew Tangel, "'Massive Trading Suspensions' Highlight Threat of Penny Stock Fraud," *Los Angeles Times,* February 3, 2014.
24. Ben Levisohn, "Splits Dive; Cheap Stocks Thrive," *Barron's,* January 6, 2014.
25. Dakin Campbell and Elizabeth Dexheimer, "MasterCard Boosts Dividend 83%, Announces 10 for 1 Stock Split," *Bloomberg Personal Finance,* December 10, 2013; and Alistar Barr, "Google Hits Record on Revenue Gain, Stock Split," *USA Today,* January 30, 2014.
26. "Motley Fool—Buying on Margin Is a Tightrope Deal," *The Columbus Dispatch,* February 2, 2014.
27. Michael Aneiro, "Junk Yields: Too Low for Comfort," *Barron's,* January 6, 2014; and Vivianne Rodrigues, "Taper Time-Bomb Hits High U.S. Yield Debt," *Financial Times,* February 10, 2014.
28. Rob Silverblatt, "Are There Too Many Mutual Funds?" *U.S. News & World Report,* June 10, 2013.
29. Jia Lynn Yung, "Warren Buffett Reveals the One Stock Fund You Need to Invest In," *The Washington Post,* February 24, 2014.
30. Jeff Sommer, "Give Fees an Inch and They'll Take a Mile," *The New York Times,* March 1, 2014.

31. Andrew Bary, "The Case for Closed-End Funds," *Barron's*, December 23, 2013.

32. Patrick Graham, "Wealth Advisor: Embracing ETFs Over Index Mutual Funds," *The Wall Street Journal*, February 21, 2014; and David Ning, "Signs Index Funds Aren't for You," *U.S. News & World Report*, February 26, 2014.

33. Jeffrey R. Kosnett, "The Dow Loves Dividends," *Kiplinger's Personal Finance*, December 2013; and Rodney Brooks, John Waggoner, and Matt Krantz, "Dow 30 Adds Goldman Sachs, Nike, and Visa," *USA Today*, September 10, 2013.

34. V. Dionne Hayes, Peyton Craighill, and Scott Clement, "For More People, the American Dream Does Not Include a Home of Their Own," *The Washington Post*, March 1, 2014.

35. Stan Choe, "Five Years into Bull Market, Returns Can Be Deceiving," *The Boston Globe*, March 2, 2014.

photo credits

20

Money, Financial Institutions, and the Federal Reserve

Learning Objectives

AFTER YOU HAVE READ AND STUDIED THIS CHAPTER, YOU SHOULD BE ABLE TO

LO 20-1 Explain what money is and what makes money useful.

LO 20-2 Describe how the Federal Reserve controls the money supply.

LO 20-3 Trace the history of banking and the Federal Reserve System.

LO 20-4 Classify the various institutions in the U.S. banking system.

LO 20-5 Briefly trace the causes of the banking crisis, and explain how the government protects your funds during such crises.

LO 20-6 Describe how technology helps make banking more efficient.

LO 20-7 Evaluate the role and importance of international banking, the World Bank, and the International Monetary Fund.

Getting to know **Janet Yellen**

Janet Yellen is the head of the Federal Reserve, the agency in charge of the nation's monetary policy. At the Fed, she manages the money supply and interest rates, which keeps her constantly in the public eye. But Yellen's economic responsibilities aren't the only reason she attracts attention: she is also the first woman to chair the Fed in the institution's 100-year history.

Growing up in Brooklyn, Yellen was an overachiever at a young age. In high school she served as editor in chief of the newspaper and earned the title of class scholar while holding prominent positions in the booster, history, and psychology clubs. Yellen was named valedictorian and winner of multiple scholastic awards. She continued this commitment to excellence at Brown University where she was one of the first women to major in economics. Yellen was inspired to study the subject after attending a lecture by James Tobin, a prominent professor and devotee of the famous economist John Maynard Keynes. After getting her undergrad degree, she moved on to Yale University to earn a doctorate in economics, where Tobin served as her advisor.

After completing her education, Yellen switched to the other side of the classroom and began teaching at the University of California–Berkeley's Haas School of Business. She used her time in the academic world to make major advances in economics, particularly in regard to unemployment. As a pioneering thinker on "efficiency wage" unemployment, Yellen discovered that not only do employees become less productive when their pay is cut, but they're also far more likely to quit. She has been committed to reducing the effects of unemployment ever since. "These are not just statistics to me," said Yellen. "We know that long-term unemployment is devastating to workers and their families. The toll is simply terrible on the mental and physical health of workers."

Yellen's passion for her work and unrivaled expertise brought her to the attention of President Clinton, who appointed her to the Federal Reserve Board of Governors. Although Yellen was new to government service, she was never afraid to disagree with her superiors. In one famous instance, Yellen publicly debated former Fed chair Alan Greenspan about rising inflation. While Greenspan wanted to drive inflation down to zero, Yellen argued that a small amount of inflation would actually help to reduce the frequency of recessions. Her use of scholarship and research to back up her claims earned her many admirers as well as detractors, who felt she should have stuck closer to the party line. Despite these critics, Yellen continued to rise through the ranks. After leading the White House Council of Economic Advisers, Yellen was appointed president of the Federal Reserve Bank of San Francisco. Her presence turned around the ailing branch almost immediately. "People became much more ambitious when she got there," said economist Justin Wolfers. Yellen's San Francisco success made her a natural candidate to become vice chair of the Fed in 2010 and then chair in 2014. Only time will tell if success will follow Yellen yet again as she tackles her biggest challenge yet.

You will learn more about the Federal Reserve and the banking system in general in this chapter. Using that information, you can better understand Yellen's decisions. Keep up with what she is doing by reading the business press and listening to business reports. Her successes and failures will be making headlines for a long time.

Sources: Sheelah Kolhatkar and Matthew Philips, "Who Is Janet Yellen? A Look at the Frontrunner for the Next Fed Chairman," *Bloomberg Businessweek*, September 19, 2013; Binyamin Appelbaum, "Possible Fed Successor Has Admirers and Foes," *The New York Times*, April 24, 2013; and Dylan Matthews, "Nine Amazing Facts about Janet Yellen, Our Next Fed Chair," *The Washington Post*, October 9, 2013.

Janet Yellen
- First female chair of the Federal Reserve
- Economist
- Passionate about reducing unemployment

www.federalreserve.gov

@The_Yellen

name that **company**

This company recently opened an online store using a new form of money. What is the name of this company and what currency does it use? (You can find the answer in this chapter.)

LO 20–1 Explain what money is and what makes money useful.

WHY MONEY IS IMPORTANT

The Federal Reserve, or the Fed, is the organization in charge of money in the United States. You will be hearing a lot about it and its head, Janet Yellen, in the coming years. That is why we chose her to be the subject of the Getting to Know feature for this chapter. Once you have some understanding of the Federal Reserve, our goal in this chapter is to introduce you to the world of banking.

Two of the most critical issues in the United States today, economic growth and the creation of jobs, depend on the ready availability of money. Money is so important to the economy that many institutions have evolved to manage it and make it available when you need it. Today you can get cash from an automated teller machine (ATM) almost anywhere in the world, and most organizations will also accept a check, credit card, debit card, or smart card for purchases. Some businesses will even accept Bitcoins, an online version of money.[1] We shall talk about Bitcoins later in the chapter. Behind the scenes is a complex system of banking that makes the free flow of money possible. Each day, about $4 trillion is exchanged in the world's currency markets. Therefore, what happens to any major country's economy has an effect on the U.S. economy and vice versa.

Let's start at the beginning by discussing exactly what the word *money* means and how the supply of money affects the prices you pay for goods and services.

What Is Money?

money
Anything that people generally accept as payment for goods and services.

Money is anything people generally accept as payment for goods and services. In the past, objects as diverse as salt, feathers, fur pelts, stones, rare shells, tea, and horses have served as money. In fact, until the 1880s, cowrie shells were one of the world's most popular currencies.

Newer engraved bills make counterfeiting much more difficult than in the past. The bills look a little different from older ones and are different colors. If you owned a store, what would you do to make sure employees wouldn't accept counterfeit bills?

Barter is the direct trading of goods or services for other goods or services.[2] Though barter may sound like something from the past, many people have discovered the benefits of bartering online.[3] One entrepreneur describes his bartering experience as follows: "Last year we bartered the creation of a full-color graphic novel in exchange for a new website design. . . . The value of the trade was $50,000. We provided three months of writing services to provide the graphic novel story line . . . and then five months of illustration. In exchange, they helped us to define, design and then program our new website."[4]

Some people barter goods and services the old-fashioned way. In Siberia, for example, people have bought movie tickets with two eggs, and in Ukraine people have paid their energy bills with sausages and milk. Today you can go to a *barter exchange* where you can put goods or services into the system and get trade credits for other goods and services that you need. The barter exchange makes it easier to barter because you don't have to find people with whom to barter. The exchange does that for you.

The problem with traditional barter is that eggs and milk are difficult to carry around. Most people need some object that's portable, divisible, durable, and stable so that they can trade goods and services without carrying the actual goods around with them. One solution is coins and paper bills. The five standards for a useful form of money are:

- *Portability.* Coins and paper money are a lot easier to take to market than pigs or other heavy products.

- *Divisibility.* Different-sized coins and bills can represent different values. Prior to 1963, a U.S. quarter had half as much silver content as a half-dollar coin, and a dollar had four times the silver of a quarter. Because silver is now too expensive, today's coins are made of other metals, but the accepted values remain.

- *Stability.* When everybody agrees on the value of coins, the value of money is relatively stable. In fact, U.S. money has become so stable that much of the world has used the U.S. dollar as the measure of value. If the value of the dollar fluctuates too rapidly, the world may turn to some other form of money, such as the euro, for the measure of value.

- *Durability.* Coins last for thousands of years, even when they've sunk to the bottom of the ocean, as you've seen when divers find old coins in sunken ships.

- *Uniqueness.* It's hard to counterfeit, or copy, elaborately designed and minted coins. With the latest color copiers, people are able to duplicate the look of paper money relatively easily. Thus, the government has had to go to extra lengths to make sure *real* dollars are readily identifiable. That's why you have newer paper money with the picture slightly off center and with invisible lines that quickly show up when reviewed by banks and stores. On the new $100 bill, for example, Ben Franklin shares space with colorful illustrations, hidden text, and pictographs that reveal themselves only when they are lit from behind or exposed to ultraviolet light.[5] Coins and paper money simplified exchanges. Most countries have their own currencies, and they're all about equally portable, divisible, and durable. However, they're not always equally stable.

Electronic cash (e-cash) is one of the newest forms of money. You can make online payments using Quicken or Microsoft Money or e-mail e-cash

Although people have long used barter to exchange goods without money, one problem is that objects like chickens and eggs are harder to carry around than a ten-dollar bill. What other drawbacks does bartering have?

barter
The direct trading of goods or services for other goods or services.

The Bitcoin Is in the Mail

It's difficult to imagine a currency being called cool or trendy. But these terms are often used when describing Bitcoin, a form of digital currency created in 2008. Bitcoin is accepted at online operations ranging from tech-savvy retailers, to pizza parlors, to shady gambling sites.

Bitcoin is attractive to many users because there's no central authority that regulates the currency. Transactions involve two people anywhere in the world with no intermediaries (banks), government regulations, or transaction fees involved. In fact, you do not even have to give your name. Bitcoins are stored in a digital wallet that serves as a virtual bank account or on a user's computer. Several marketplaces, called "Bitcoin exchanges," are available for consumers to buy Bitcoins using different currencies. MtGox was once the largest Bitcoin exchange. (Claiming it had been hacked, MtGox lost around $412.5 million belonging to customers

and over $55 million of its own money, and filed for bankruptcy in 2014.)

So just how much is a Bitcoin worth? That's a very good question. Bitcoin's volatility stems from its decentralized valuation system. Value is based on demand, as transactions run across a peer-to-peer network of personal computers. Since Bitcoins are not managed from a central bank like typical currencies, an arsenal of algorithms constantly recalculates the

currency's value. This system has caused the value of Bitcoins to spike wildly—then fall in value almost as fast. The value of Bitcoins has fluctuated from $13 in 2012 to $1,200 in December of 2013. This unpredictability has given skeptics plenty of reasons to question Bitcoin's practicality. Governments are concerned about illegal activities being conducted through Bitcoin transactions. They are also considering taxation issues.

Bitcoin is just one of many digital currencies that have hit the market. Whether these currencies achieve a level of stability or just become interesting financial case studies for the digital age remains to be seen.

Sources: Sunny Freeman, "What Is Bitcoin? 11 Things You Need to Know About the Digital Currency," *Huffington Post,* January 26, 2014; Jose Pagliary, "New IRS Rules Make Using Bitcoins a Fiasco," *CNN Money,* March 31, 2014; Ashley Vance and Brad Stone, "The Bitcoin-Mining Arms Race Heats Up," *Bloomberg Businessweek,* January 9, 2014; and Ryan Derousseau, "Boom in Virtual Money Mints Real Gains and Losses," *Money,* January–February 2014.

using PayPal. Recipients can choose automatic deposit to their bank, e-dollars for spending online, or a traditional check in the mail. Bitcoin is a digital version of money that is tougher to forge, cuts across international boundaries, and can be stored on your hard drive instead of in a bank. However, the Bitcoin is not yet generally accepted.[6] Nonetheless, efforts will be made in the future to create a cashless society using some other form of currency than the bills and coins we now use. Cryptocurrencies like Bitcoin are too new to know their value, but many competitors have arisen in recent years. They include Litecoin, Peercoin, NXT, and Dogcoin.[7] Bitcoin, however, now has its own online store called Bitcoin Shop Inc.[8] See the Adapting to Change box for more about Bitcoin.

No one knows which of the cryptocurrencies will succeed. On the other hand, no one can be sure of the future of the nickel or the penny either. The U.S. Mint is examining different metals and alloys to bring down the production costs of the nickel, dime, and quarter. It now costs 1.8 cents to make a penny and 9.4 cents to make a nickel.[9] Someday you may find that your nickels and pennies are lighter and a different color.

LO 20–2   Describe how the Federal Reserve controls the money supply.

What Is the Money Supply?

As Fed chairperson, Janet Yellen is in control of the U.S. money supply. Two questions emerge from that sentence. What is the money supply? Why does it need to be controlled?

The **money supply** is the amount of money the Federal Reserve makes available for people to buy goods and services. And, yes, the Federal Reserve, in tandem with the U.S. Treasury, can create more money if it is needed. For example, some of the trillions of dollars that were being spent over the last few years to get the economy moving again were printed with authorization from the Federal Reserve. The terms QE 1 and QE 2 mean quantitative easing one and two, but the real meaning was that the Fed was creating more money ($85 billion a month) because it believed that money was needed to get the economy moving again. Before he left office, former Fed chairperson Ben Bernanke announced that the Fed was cutting back its support for the economy from $85 billion a month to $75 billion.[10] It did that by cutting back $5 billion each on the purchase of mortgage and Treasury bond purchases.[11] Yellen is continuing the process of cutting back on the creation of new money. We'll see if that slows the economy or not.

Recently, Yellen announced further cutbacks. That was not good news for banks because they had been paying very low interest rates and lending at much higher rates.[12] It was not good news for young people who have to borrow money to buy homes either.

There are several ways of referring to the U.S. money supply. They're called M-1, M-2, and M-3. The M stands for money, and the 1, 2, and 3 stand for different definitions of the money supply. **M-1** includes coins and paper bills, money that's available by writing checks (demand deposits and share drafts), and money held in traveler's checks—that is, money that can be accessed quickly and easily. **M-2** includes everything in M-1 plus money in savings accounts, and money in money market accounts, mutual funds, certificates of deposit, and the like—that is, money that may take a little more time to obtain than coins and paper bills. M-2 is the most commonly used definition of money. **M-3** is M-2 plus big deposits like institutional money market funds.

Managing Inflation and the Money Supply

Imagine what would happen if governments (or in the case of the United States, the Federal Reserve, a nongovernmental organization) were to generate twice as much money as exists now (that wouldn't be too hard to imagine if the Fed kept pumping $75 billion a month into the economy.) There would be twice as much money available, but still the same amount of goods and services. What would happen to prices? (Hint: Remember the laws of supply and demand from Chapter 2.) Prices would go *up*, because more people would try to buy goods and services with their money and bid up the price to get what they wanted. This rise in price is called *inflation*, which some people call "too much money chasing too few goods."

Now think about the opposite: What would happen if the Fed took money out of the economy, or put less money in? Prices would go down because there would be an oversupply of goods and services compared to the money available to buy them; this decrease in prices is called *deflation*.

Now we come to our second question about the money supply: Why does it need to be controlled? The reason is that doing so allows us to manage,

money supply
The amount of money the Federal Reserve Bank makes available for people to buy goods and services.

M-1
Money that can be accessed quickly and easily (coins and paper money, checks, traveler's checks, etc.).

M-2
Money included in M-1 plus money that may take a little more time to obtain (savings accounts, money market accounts, mutual funds, certificates of deposit, etc.).

M-3
M-2 plus big deposits like institutional money market funds.

somewhat, the prices of goods and services. The size of the money supply also affects *employment* and *economic growth* or decline. That's why the Fed and Janet Yellen are so important.[13]

The European Central Bank (ECB) may also do quantitative easing (increase the money supply), and has seriously considered doing so.[14] At this point, it is good for you to know that the global money supply is controlled by *central banks* like the Federal Reserve, and what central banks do affects the economies of the world.

The Global Exchange of Money

A *falling dollar value* means that the amount of goods and services you can buy with a dollar decreases. A *rising dollar value* means that the amount of goods and services you can buy with a dollar goes up. Thus, the price in euros you pay for a German car will be lower if the U.S. dollar rises relative to the euro. However, if the euro rises relative to the dollar, the cost of cars from Germany will go up and U.S. consumers may buy fewer German cars.

What makes the dollar weak (falling value) or strong (rising value) is the position of the U.S. economy relative to other economies. When the economy is strong, the demand for dollars is high, and the value of the dollar rises. When the economy is perceived as weakening, however, the demand for dollars declines and the value of the dollar falls. The value of the dollar thus depends on a relatively strong economy. (See Chapter 3 for further discussion of effects of changes in currency values or exchange rates.) In the following section, we'll discuss in more detail the money supply and how it's managed. Then we'll explore the U.S. banking system and how it lends money to businesses and individuals, like you and me.

CONTROL OF THE MONEY SUPPLY

Theoretically, with the proper monetary policy in place to control the money supply, one can keep the economy growing without causing inflation. (See Chapter 2 to review monetary policy.) Again, the organization in charge of monetary policy is the Federal Reserve.

Basics about the Federal Reserve

The Federal Reserve System consists of five major parts: (1) the board of governors; (2) the Federal Open Market Committee (FOMC); (3) 12 Federal Reserve banks; (4) three advisory councils; and (5) the member banks of the system. Figure 20.1 shows where the 12 Federal Reserve banks are located. (You should know that the Federal Reserve is *not* a part of the U.S. government, despite its name. It is a private firm.)

The board of governors administers and supervises the 12 Federal Reserve banks. The seven members of the board are appointed by the president and confirmed by the senate. The board's primary function is to set monetary policy. The Federal Open Market Committee (FOMC) has 12 voting members and is the policy-making body. The committee is made up of the seven-member board of governors plus the president of the New York reserve bank and four members who rotate in from the other reserve banks. The advisory councils represent the various banking districts, consumers, and member institutions, including banks, savings and loan institutions, and credit unions. They offer suggestions to the board and to the FOMC.

The Fed buys and sells foreign currencies, regulates various types of credit, supervises banks, and collects data on the money supply and other

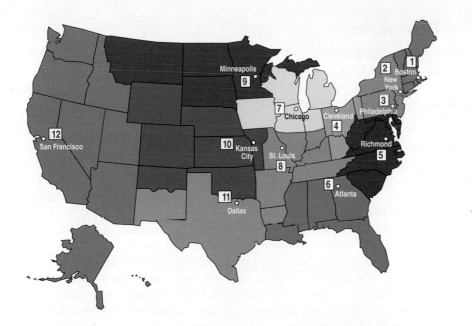

FIGURE 20.1 THE 12 FEDERAL RESERVE DISTRICT BANKS

economic activity. As part of monetary policy, the Fed determines the reserve requirement, that is, the level of reserve funds all financial institutions must keep at one of the 12 Federal Reserve banks. It buys and sells government securities in *open-market operations*. Finally, it lends money to member banks at an interest rate called the *discount rate*.

As noted, the three basic tools the Fed uses to manage the money supply are reserve requirements, open-market operations, and the discount rate (see Figure 20.2). Let's explore how it administers each. Note how each move the Fed makes affects the economy.

FIGURE 20.2 HOW THE FEDERAL RESERVE CONTROLS THE MONEY SUPPLY

Reserve Requirements

Control Method	Immediate Result	Long-Term Effect
A. Increase.	Banks put more money into the Fed, reducing money supply; thus, there is less money available to lend to customers.	Economy slows.
B. Decrease.	Banks put less money into the Fed, increasing the money supply; thus, there is more money available to lend to customers.	Economy speeds up.

Open-Market Operations

Control Method	Immediate Result	Long-Term Effect
A. Fed sells bonds.	Money flows from the economy to the Fed.	Economy slows.
B. Fed buys bonds.	Money flows into the economy from the Fed.	Economy speeds up.

Managing the Discount Rate

Control Method	Immediate Result	Long-Term Effect
A. Rate increases.	Banks borrow less from the Fed; thus, there is less money to lend.	Economy slows.
B. Rate decreases.	Banks borrow more from the Fed; thus, there is more money to lend.	Economy speeds up.

reserve requirement
A percentage of commercial banks' checking and savings accounts that must be physically kept in the bank.

open-market operations
The buying and selling of U.S. government bonds by the Fed with the goal of regulating the money supply.

discount rate
The interest rate that the Fed charges for loans to member banks.

The Reserve Requirement

The **reserve requirement** is a percentage of commercial banks' checking and savings accounts they must keep in the bank (as cash in the vault) or in a non-interest-bearing deposit at the local Federal Reserve district bank. The reserve requirement is one of the Fed's tools. When it increases the reserve requirement, money becomes scarcer, which in the long run tends to reduce inflation. For instance, if Omaha Security Bank holds deposits of $100 million and the reserve requirement is, say, 10 percent, then the bank must keep $10 million on reserve. If the Fed were to increase the reserve requirement to 11 percent, then the bank would have to put an additional $1 million on reserve, *reducing the amount it could lend out*. Since this increase in the reserve requirement would affect all banks, the money supply would be reduced and prices would likely fall.

A decrease of the reserve requirement, in contrast, *increases* the funds available to banks for loans, so they can make more loans, and money tends to become more readily available. An increase in the money supply can *stimulate the economy* to achieve higher growth rates, but it can also create inflationary pressures. That is, the prices of goods and services may go up. Can you see why the Fed may want to decrease the reserve requirement when the economy is in a recession? Can you also see the danger of inflation?

Open-Market Operations

Open-market operations consist of the buying and selling of government bonds. To decrease the money supply, the federal government sells U.S. government bonds to the public. The money it gets as payment is no longer in circulation, decreasing the money supply. If the Fed wants to increase the money supply, it buys government bonds back from individuals, corporations, or organizations that are willing to sell. The money the Fed pays for these securities enters circulation, increasing the money supply. That's why the Fed bought bonds during the recent recession. The idea was to get the economy growing again, though it wasn't as successful as hoped.[15]

The Discount Rate

The Fed has often been called the bankers' bank, because member banks can borrow money from the Fed and pass it on to their customers in the form of loans. The **discount rate** is the interest rate the Fed charges for loans to member banks. An increase in the discount rate discourages banks from borrowing and reduces the number of available loans, decreasing the money supply. In contrast, lowering the discount rate encourages member banks to borrow money and increases the funds they have available for loans, which is supposed to increase the money supply. For many months, the Fed lowered the discount rate to almost zero, hoping to increase bank lending. Nonetheless, many banks still seemed reluctant to make loans.

The discount rate is one of two interest rates the Fed controls. The other is the rate banks charge each other, called the *federal funds rate*.[16]

The Federal Reserve's Check-Clearing Role

If you write a check to a local retailer that uses the same bank you do, it is a simple matter to reduce your account by the amount of the check and increase the amount in the retailer's account. But what happens if you write a check to a retailer in another state? That's where the Fed's check-clearing function comes into play.

That retailer will take the check to its bank. That bank will deposit the check for credit in the closest Federal Reserve bank. That bank will send the check to your local Federal Reserve bank for collection. The check will then be sent to your bank and the amount of the check will be withdrawn. Your bank will authorize the Federal Reserve bank in your area to deduct the amount of the check. That bank will pay the Federal Reserve bank that began the process in the first place. It will then credit the deposit account in the bank where the retailer has its account. That bank will then credit the account of the retailer. (See Figure 20.3 for a diagram of such an interstate transaction.) This long and involved process is a costly one for the Fed; therefore, banks have taken many measures to lessen the use of checks. Such efforts include the use of credit cards, debit cards, and other electronic transfers of money.

As you can see, the whole economy is affected by the Federal Reserve System's actions. Next we'll briefly discuss the history of banking to give you some background about why the Fed came into existence about 100 years ago.[17] Then we'll explore what's happening in banking today.

Suppose Mr. Brown, a farmer from Quince Orchard, Maryland, purchases a tractor from a dealer in Austin, Texas.

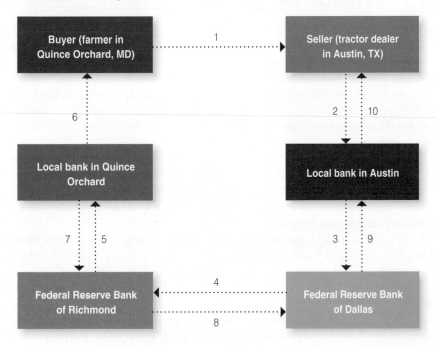

FIGURE 20.3 CHECK-CLEARING PROCESS THROUGH THE FEDERAL RESERVE BANK SYSTEM

1. Mr. Brown sends his check to the tractor dealer.
2. The dealer deposits the check in his account at a local bank in Austin.
3. The Austin bank deposits the check for credit in its account at the Federal Reserve Bank of Dallas.
4. The Federal Reserve Bank of Dallas sends the check to the Federal Reserve Bank of Richmond for collection.
5. The Federal Reserve Bank of Richmond forwards the check to the local bank in Quince Orchard, where Mr. Brown has his account.
6. The local bank in Quince Orchard deducts the check amount from Mr. Brown's account.
7. The Quince Orchard bank authorizes the Federal Reserve Bank of Richmond to deduct the check amount from its deposit account with the Federal Reserve Bank.
8. The Federal Reserve Bank of Richmond pays the Federal Reserve Bank of Dallas.
9. The Federal Reserve Bank of Dallas credits the Austin bank's deposit account.
10. The Austin bank credits the tractor dealer's account.

test prep ✔✔✔

- What is money?
- What are the five characteristics of useful money?
- What are "Bitcoins"?
- What is the money supply, and why is it important?
- How does the Federal Reserve control the money supply?
- What are the major functions of the Federal Reserve? What other functions does it perform?

LO 20–3 Trace the history of banking and the Federal Reserve System.

THE HISTORY OF BANKING AND THE NEED FOR THE FED

There was a time when there were no banks in the United States. Strict laws in Europe limited the number of coins people could bring to the colonies in the New World. Thus, colonists were forced to *barter* for goods; for example, they might trade cotton and tobacco for shoes and lumber.

The demand for money was so great that Massachusetts issued its own paper money in 1690, and other colonies soon followed suit. But continental money, the first paper money printed in the United States, became worthless after a few years because people didn't trust its value.

Land banks were established to lend money to farmers. But Great Britain, still in charge of the colonies at that point, ended land banks by 1741. The colonies rebelled against these and other restrictions on their freedom, and a new bank was formed in Pennsylvania during the American Revolution to finance the war against England.

In 1791, after the United States gained independence, Alexander Hamilton persuaded Congress to form a *central bank* (a bank at which other banks could keep their funds and borrow funds if needed). This first version of a federal bank closed in 1811, only to be replaced in 1816 because state-chartered banks couldn't support the War of 1812. The battle between the Second (Central) Bank of the United States and state banks got hot in the 1830s. Several banks in Tennessee were hurt by pressure from the Central Bank. The fight ended when the Central Bank was closed in 1836. You can see that there was great resistance to a central bank, like the Federal Reserve, through much of U.S. history.

By the time of the Civil War, the U.S. banking system was a mess.[18] Different banks issued different kinds of currencies. People hoarded gold and silver coins because they were worth more as precious metal than as money. That may be happening again today. In any case, the chaos continued long after the war ended, reaching something of a climax in 1907, when many banks failed. People got nervous about the safety of banks and, in a run on the banks, attempted to withdraw their funds. Soon the cash was depleted and some banks had to refuse money to depositors. This caused people to distrust the banking system in general.

Despite the long history of opposition to a central bank, the cash shortage problems of 1907 led to the formation of an organization that could lend money to banks—the Federal Reserve System. It was to be a "lender of last

The Federal Reserve System was designed in 1913 to prevent the kind of run on banks that had occurred in 1907. Yet the stock market crash of 1929 caused depositors to make another run on their banks and take big withdrawals. Federal deposit insurance was established in 1933 to protect depositors' money. Do you think that these protections are enough?

resort" in such emergencies. Under the Federal Reserve Act of 1913, all feder-ally chartered banks had to join the Federal Reserve. State banks could also join. The Federal Reserve became the bankers' bank. If banks had excess funds, they could deposit them in the Fed; if they needed extra money, they could borrow from the Fed. The Federal Reserve System has been intimately related to banking ever since, but never more than now.[19]

Banking and the Great Depression

The Federal Reserve System was designed to prevent a repeat of the 1907 panic. Nevertheless, the stock market crash of 1929 led to bank failures in the early 1930s. When the stock market began tumbling, people hurried to banks to with-draw cash. In spite of the Federal Reserve System, the banks ran out of money, and states were forced to close them. President Franklin D. Roosevelt extended the period of bank closings in 1933 to gain time to come up with a solution to the problem. In 1933 and 1935, Congress passed legislation to strengthen the banking system. The most important move was to establish federal deposit insurance to further protect the public from bank failures. As you can see, bank crises are nothing new; they often occur during a recession. From 1945 to 2009, the United States experienced 11 recessions. The average duration was 10 months; the longest recession (2008–2009) was 18 months. Now that you know something about the Federal Reserve, let's turn our attention to U.S. banks.

LO 20–4   Classify the various institutions in the U.S. banking system.

THE U.S. BANKING SYSTEM

The U.S. banking system consists of commercial banks, savings and loan asso-ciations, and credit unions. In addition, there are various financial organiza-tions, or nonbanks, that accept no deposits but offer many of the services of regular banks. Let's discuss the activities and services of each, starting with commercial banks.

Commercial Banks

The banks that are probably the most familiar to you are commercial banks. A **commercial bank** is a profit-seeking organization that receives deposits from individuals and corporations in the form of checking and savings accounts, and uses these funds to make loans. It has two types of customers—depositors and borrowers—and is equally responsible to both. A commercial bank makes a profit by efficiently using depositors' funds as inputs (on which it pays interest) to invest in interest-bearing loans to other customers. If the revenue generated by loans exceeds the interest paid to depositors plus operating expenses, the bank makes a profit.

commercial bank
A profit-seeking organization that receives deposits from individuals and corporations in the form of checking and savings accounts and then uses some of these funds to make loans.

Services Provided by Commercial Banks

Individuals and corporations that deposit money in a checking account can write personal checks to pay for almost any purchase or transaction. The technical name for a checking account is a **demand deposit** because the money is available on demand from the depositor. Some banks impose a service charge for check-writing privileges or demand a minimum deposit. They might also charge a small handling fee for each check written.[20] For corporate depositors, the amount of the service charge often depends on the average daily balance in the checking account, the number of checks written, and the firm's credit rating and credit history.

demand deposit
The technical name for a checking account; the money in a demand deposit can be withdrawn anytime on demand from the depositor.

In the past, checking accounts paid no interest to depositors, but interest-bearing checking accounts have experienced phenomenal growth in recent years. Commercial banks also offer a variety of savings account options. A savings account is technically a **time deposit** because the bank can require a prior notice before you make a withdrawal. It would be wise for you to compare online and neighborhood banks to find where your money can earn the most interest. (In most cases, you won't earn much interest in any bank today.)

time deposit
The technical name for a savings account; the bank can require prior notice before the owner withdraws money from a time deposit.

A **certificate of deposit (CD)** is a time-deposit (savings) account that earns interest, to be delivered on the certificate's maturity date. The depositor agrees not to withdraw any of the funds until then. CDs are now available for periods of months to years; usually the longer the period, the higher the interest rate. The interest rates also depend on economic conditions. At the present time, interest rates are very low because the economy is not robust.

certificate of deposit (CD)
A time-deposit (savings) account that earns interest to be delivered at the end of the certificate's maturity date.

Commercial banks may also offer credit cards to creditworthy customers, life insurance, inexpensive brokerage services, financial counseling, automatic payment of bills, safe-deposit boxes, individual retirement accounts (IRAs), traveler's checks, trust departments, automated teller machines, and overdraft checking account privileges. The latter means preferred customers can automatically get loans when they've written checks exceeding their account balance.

Services to Borrowers

Commercial banks offer a variety of services to individuals and corporations in need of a loan. Generally, loans are given on the basis of the recipient's creditworthiness, although the recent real estate collapse was partially due to banks ignoring that rule.[21] Banks want to manage their funds effectively, and are supposed to screen loan applicants carefully to ensure that the loan plus interest will be paid back on time. Clearly banks failed to do that in the period leading up to the banking crisis. We will discuss why that happened later in the chapter. The Making Ethical Decisions box explores a more minor issue that could occur in your banking efforts.

Would You Tell the Teller?

You are at the teller window of your bank making a withdrawal. The teller counts out your money and says: "OK, here's your $300." You count the money and see the teller has given you $320 by mistake. When you point this out, the teller replies indignantly, "I don't think so. I counted the money in front of you."

You are upset by her quick denial of a mistake and her attitude. You have to decide whether or not to give her back the overpayment of $20. What are your alternatives? What would you do? Is that the ethical thing to do?

Meanwhile, it is good to know that banks are doing their best to adapt to mobile users.[22] Coin, for example, is a credit card–size device that digitally stores up to eight credit, debit, gift, or membership cards, which you can toggle between using your mobile phone.[23] Nearly two-thirds of the country's biggest banks now let customers make a deposit by taking a photo of the check.

Savings and Loan Associations (S&Ls)

A **savings and loan association (S&L)** is a financial institution that accepts both savings and checking deposits, and provides home mortgage loans. S&Ls are often known as thrift institutions because their original purpose (starting in 1831) was to promote consumer thrift and home ownership. To help them encourage home ownership, thrifts were permitted for many years to offer slightly higher interest rates on savings deposits than banks. Those rates attracted a large pool of funds, which S&Ls used to offer long-term fixed-rate mortgages.

Between 1986 and 1995, nearly 1,300 S&Ls failed. Reasons for the failures included the inflation of the 1970s, deregulation, regulatory failure (regulators allowed insolvent thrifts to stay open while their situations worsened), and fraud.[24] Today, S&Ls no longer offer better rates than banks because of changes in government laws, and many S&Ls have become banks. According to the FDIC, there are now about 934 savings and loan companies in the United States.

savings and loan association (S&L)
A financial institution that accepts both savings and checking deposits and provides home mortgage loans.

Credit Unions

Credit unions are nonprofit, member-owned financial cooperatives that offer the full variety of banking services to their members—interest-bearing checking accounts at relatively high rates, short-term loans at relatively low rates, financial counseling, life insurance policies, and a limited number of home mortgage loans. They are organized by government agencies, corporations, unions, and professional associations. Today, credit unions are growing in popularity.[25]

As nonprofit institutions, credit unions enjoy an exemption from federal income taxes.[26] You might want to visit a local credit union to see whether you are eligible to belong, and then compare the rates to those at local banks. Credit unions often have fewer branches than banks and less access to ATMs. It's best to determine what services you need, and then compare those services to the same services offered by banks. It is good to know that the money in credit union accounts is also insured for $250,000—as it is in your local bank.

credit unions
Nonprofit, member-owned financial cooperatives that offer the full variety of banking services to their members.

Credit unions are member-owned financial cooperatives that offer their members a wide range of banking services and, because they are nonprofits, are exempt from federal income tax. Do you belong to a credit union?

Other Financial Institutions (Nonbanks)

nonbanks
Financial organizations that accept no deposits but offer many of the services provided by regular banks (pension funds, insurance companies, commercial finance companies, consumer finance companies, and brokerage houses).

Nonbanks are financial organizations that accept no deposits but offer many of the services provided by regular banks. Nonbanks include life insurance companies, pension funds, brokerage firms, commercial finance companies, and corporate financial services (like GE Capital).

As competition between banks and nonbanks has increased, the dividing line between them has become less apparent. This is equally true in Europe, where U.S. companies compete with European banks. The diversity of financial services and investment alternatives nonbanks offer has led banks to expand their own services. In fact, many banks have merged with brokerage firms to offer full-service financial assistance.

Life insurance companies provide financial protection for policyholders, who periodically pay premiums. In addition, insurers invest the funds they receive from policyholders in corporate and government bonds. In recent years, more insurance companies have begun to provide long-term financing for real estate development projects. Do you think that was a wise decision?

pension funds
Amounts of money put aside by corporations, nonprofit organizations, or unions to cover part of the financial needs of members when they retire.

Pension funds are monies put aside by corporations, nonprofit organizations, or unions to help fund their members' financial needs when they retire. Contributions to pension funds are made by employees, employers, or both. To generate additional income, pension funds typically invest in low-return but safe corporate stocks or other conservative investments, such as government securities and corporate bonds.

Many financial services organizations that provide retirement and health benefits, such as TIAA-CREF, are becoming a major force in U.S. financial markets. They also lend money directly to corporations.

Brokerage firms have traditionally offered investment services in stock exchanges in the United States and abroad. They have also made serious

Taking a Bite Out of the Sharks

Ivan Rincon was convinced his online swimwear shop could float if he could just get needed capital. Unfortunately, banks rejected him because he didn't have collateral. This caused him to do what many small businesses have to do; he turned to a nonbank lender called a merchant cash advance provider. He obtained a cash advance of $200,000, but soon realized he was paying an annual interest rate of more than 50%. Fortunately, he was able to pay back the loan before things got desperate. He then heard about Dealstruck.

Dealstruck is an example of a new type of alternative, nonbank lender. The company provides a middle ground between banks that lend to only very creditworthy small businesses and merchant

cash advance lenders that have lower criteria for lending, but much higher interest rates. Dealstruck, like competitors Funding Circle and Fundation, uses a peer-to-peer model where wealthy investors provide the capital for the loans. The loans are secured by the owner's personal guarantees or business assets. Dealstruck's interest rates range

from 8 to 24 percent for loans up to $250,000, and can stretch over a period of three years. Ethan Senturia, CEO of Dealstruck, promises, "Our loans are not always cheap, but we tell you what we are charging and why."

The peer-to-peer lending model has played an active role in *individual* lending for a while, with Lending Club a pioneer in this area. As Dealstruck and its competitors grow and heat up the market for peer-to-peer small-business lending, Lending Club has decided to become one of the newest competitors in small-business lending and offer peer-to-peer loans to small businesses too.

Sources: Patrick Clark, "A U.K. Peer-to-Peer Lender Wants U.S. Businesses to Forget Banks," *Bloomberg Businessweek,* October 24, 2013; and Amy Cortese, "Can't Get a Bank Loan? The Alternatives Are Expanding," *The New York Times,* March 5, 2014.

inroads into regular banks' domain by offering high-yield combination savings and checking accounts. In addition, they offer money market accounts with check-writing privileges and allow investors to borrow, using their securities as collateral.

Commercial and consumer finance companies sometimes offer short-term loans to those who cannot meet the credit requirements of regular banks, such as new businesses, or who have exceeded their credit limit and need more funds. Be careful when borrowing from such institutions, however, because their interest rates can be quite high. The Spotlight on Small Business box offers an example of a newer type of nonbank that offers a way for small business owners to raise the funds they need to start or expand their businesses.

test **prep**

- Why did the United States need a Federal Reserve Bank?
- What are the differences among banks, savings and loan associations, and credit unions?
- What is a consumer finance company?

Use LearnSmart to help retain what you have learned. Access your instructor's Connect course to check out LearnSmart, or go to learnsmartadvantage.com for help.

▤LEARNSMART

THE BANKING CRISIS AND HOW THE GOVERNMENT PROTECTS YOUR MONEY

What led to the banking crisis that occurred a few years ago? There is no simple answer. Some people believe the Federal Reserve is partly responsible because it kept the cost of borrowing so low that people were tempted to borrow more than they could afford to pay back. Congress, very interested in creating more "affordable housing," prodded banks to lend to people with minimal assets. The Community Reinvestment Act further encouraged loans to families with questionable ability to repay. You get the idea that banks were partially responsible for the crisis when you hear that JPMorgan Chase agreed to pay $13 billion for its role in the crisis.[27]

Other organizations pressured banks, normally quite risk-averse, to make risky loans. Banks learned they could avoid much of the risk by dividing their portfolios of mortgages up and selling the mortgage-backed securities (MBSs) to other banks and other organizations all over the world. These securities seemed quite safe because they were backed by the homes that were mortgaged. Fannie Mae and Freddie Mac are both quasi-government agencies that seemed to guarantee the value of MBSs. Banks sold more and more of such seemingly safe securities, hoping to make lots of money. Bankers were then accused of pushing loans onto naive consumers.

Meanwhile, the Federal Reserve and the Securities and Exchange Commission failed to issue sufficient warnings. That is, it failed in its regulatory duties. When the value of homes began to decline, people began defaulting on their loans (not paying them) and turned the properties back over to the banks. Almost 5 million households have suffered through housing foreclosures since the housing bubble burst in 2007. Since the banks owned the mortgages on those homes, their profits declined dramatically, leading to a banking crisis—and the need for the government and the Fed to help the banks out. Not doing so was considered too risky because the whole economy might fail otherwise. The long-term effects of that process are not yet known. There is much in the newspapers and on TV about the rise in housing prices and how the crisis is over, but such optimism may be overdone. As of May 2014, there were still almost 10 million households (one-fifth of those with mortgages) that owed more on their homes than the houses were worth. Thus far, the government's Home Affordable Modification Program has helped only one-quarter of the 4 million homeowners it was intended to serve.[28]

The bursting of the housing bubble forced a sharp decline in home values. When homeowners discovered they owed more on their mortgages than their homes were worth, many stopped paying off their loans, and the banks foreclosed on their homes. While home prices have since risen in many areas of the country, as of 2014 one-fifth of the households with mortgages still owed more than the homes were worth.

So whom do we blame for the banking crisis? The answer is that we could blame the Fed for suppressing interest rates, Congress for promoting questionable loans, the banks for making such loans and creating mortgage-backed securities that were not nearly as safe as promoted, government regulatory agencies for not doing their job, and people who took advantage of low interest rates to borrow money they couldn't reasonably hope to repay. No matter who was to blame, the crisis still needed to be solved.

Toward the end of George W. Bush's presidency, the Treasury Department proposed a $700 billion "bailout" package, known as the Troubled Asset Relief Program (TARP). The program was

enacted in October 2008. President Barack Obama, who took office in January 2009, proposed over $800 billion in additional government spending plus a stimulus package. The economy responded, but very slowly.

Protecting Your Funds

The recent banking crisis is nothing new. The government had seen similar problems during the Great Depression of the 1930s. To prevent investors from ever again being completely wiped out during an economic downturn, it created three major organizations to protect your money: the Federal Deposit Insurance Corporation (FDIC); the Savings Association Insurance Fund (SAIF); and the National Credit Union Administration (NCUA). All three insure deposits in individual accounts up to a certain amount. Because these organizations are so important to the safety of your money, let's explore them individually in more depth.

The Federal Deposit Insurance Corporation (FDIC)

The **Federal Deposit Insurance Corporation (FDIC)** is an independent agency of the U.S. government that insures bank deposits. If a bank were to fail, the FDIC would arrange to have that bank's accounts transferred to another bank or reimburse depositors up to $250,000 per account. The FDIC covers many institutions, mostly commercial banks. Of course, one problem is that the government doesn't have unlimited money to cover all losses if too many banks should fail.

Federal Deposit Insurance Corporation (FDIC)
An independent agency of the U.S. government that insures bank deposits.

The Savings Association Insurance Fund (SAIF)

The **Savings Association Insurance Fund (SAIF)** insures holders of accounts in savings and loan associations. A brief history will show why it was created. Some 1,700 bank and thrift institutions had failed during the early 1930s, and people were losing confidence in them. The FDIC and the Federal Savings and Loan Insurance Corporation (FSLIC) were designed (in 1933 and 1934, respectively) to create more confidence in banking institutions by protecting people's savings from loss. Recently, to get more control over the banking system in general, the government placed the FSLIC under the FDIC and gave it a new name: the Savings Association Insurance Fund (SAIF).

Savings Association Insurance Fund (SAIF)
The part of the FDIC that insures holders of accounts in savings and loan associations.

The National Credit Union Administration (NCUA)

The National Credit Union Administration (NCUA) provides up to $250,000 coverage per individual depositor per institution. This coverage includes all accounts—checking accounts, savings accounts, money market accounts, and certificates of deposit. Depositors qualify for additional protection by holding accounts jointly or in trust. Individual retirement accounts (IRAs) are also separately insured up to $250,000. Credit unions, like banks, suffered from the banking crisis, and got money from the federal government to make more loans.

LO 20–6   Describe how technology helps make banking more efficient.

USING TECHNOLOGY TO MAKE BANKING MORE EFFICIENT

Imagine the cost to a bank of approving a written check, physically processing it through the banking system, and mailing it back to you. It's expensive. Bankers have long looked for ways to make the system more efficient.

electronic funds transfer (EFT) system

A computerized system that electronically performs financial transactions such as making purchases, paying bills, and receiving paychecks.

debit card

An electronic funds transfer tool that serves the same function as checks: it withdraws funds from a checking account.

smart card

An electronic funds transfer tool that is a combination credit card, debit card, phone card, driver's license card, and more.

One solution was to issue credit cards to reduce the flow of checks, but they too have their costs: there's still paper to process. Accepting credit cards costs retailers about 2 percent of the amount charged. In the future we'll see much more electronic rather than physical exchange of money, because it is the most efficient way to transfer funds.

If you must use a credit card, be sure to search for one that offers the best deal for you. Some offer cash back, others offer free travel, and so forth.[29] Don't just sign up for whatever card is offering free T-shirts on campus. Do your research.

In an **electronic funds transfer (EFT) system**, messages about a transaction are sent from one computer to another. Thus, organizations can transfer funds more quickly and economically than with paper checks. EFT tools include electronic check conversion, debit cards, smart cards, direct deposits, and direct payments.

A **debit card** serves the same function as a check—it withdraws funds from a checking account. When the sale is recorded, the debit card sends an electronic signal to the bank, automatically transferring funds from your account to the seller's. A record of transactions immediately appears online. Debit transactions surpassed credit years ago and continue to grow.

Payroll debit cards are an efficient way for some firms to pay their workers, and are an alternative to cash for those who don't qualify for a credit or debit card— the so-called unbanked.[30] Employees can access funds in their accounts immediately after they are posted, withdraw them from an ATM, pay bills online, or transfer funds to another cardholder. The system is much cheaper for companies than issuing checks, and more convenient for employees. On the other hand, debit cards don't offer the same protection as credit cards. If someone steals your credit card, you are liable only for a certain amount. You are liable for everything when someone steals your debit card.[31]

A **smart card** is an electronic funds transfer tool that combines a credit card, debit card, phone card, driver's license card, and more. Smart cards replace the typical magnetic strip on a credit or debit card with a microprocessor. The card can then store a variety of information, including the holder's bank balance. Merchants can use this information to check the card's validity and spending limits, and transactions can debit up to the amount on the card.

Some smart cards have embedded radio frequency identification (RFID) chips that make it possible to enter buildings and secure areas and to buy gas and other items with a swipe of the card. A biometric function lets you use your fingerprint to boot up your computer. Students are using smart cards to open locked doors to dorms and identify themselves to retailers near campus and online. The cards also serve as ATM cards.

For many, the ultimate convenience in banking is automatic transactions such as direct deposit and direct payments. A *direct deposit* is a credit made directly to a checking or savings account in place of a paycheck. The employer contacts the bank and orders it to transfer funds from the employer's account to the worker's account. Individuals can use direct deposits to transfer funds to other accounts, such as from a checking account to a savings or retirement account.

A *direct payment* is a preauthorized electronic payment. Customers sign a separate form for each company whose bill they would like to automatically pay from their checking or savings account on a specified date. The customer's bank completes each transaction and records it on the customer's monthly statement.

Online Banking

Almost all top U.S. retail banks allow customers to access their accounts online, and most have bill-paying capacity. Thus, you can complete all your financial transactions from home, using your telephone, computer, or mobile device to transfer funds from one account to another, pay your bills, and check the balance in each of your accounts. You can apply for a car loan or mortgage and get a response while you wait. Buying and selling stocks and bonds is equally easy.

Internet banks such as E*Trade Bank offer online banking only, not physical branches. They can offer customers slightly higher interest rates and lower fees because they do not have the overhead costs traditional banks have. While many consumers are pleased with the savings and convenience, not all are happy with the service. Why? Some are nervous about security. People fear putting their financial information into cyberspace, where others may see it despite all the assurances of privacy.

 LO 20–7 Evaluate the role and importance of international banking, the World Bank, and the International Monetary Fund.

INTERNATIONAL BANKING AND BANKING SERVICES

Smartphone apps, such as PayPal's, allow users to pay for purchases with their phones. What problems could there be with such capabilities?

Banks help companies conduct business in other countries by providing three services: letters of credit, banker's acceptances, and money exchange. If a U.S. company wants to buy a product from Germany, the company could pay a bank to issue a letter of credit. A **letter of credit** is a promise by the bank to pay the seller a given amount if certain conditions are met. For example, the German company may not be paid until the goods have arrived at the U.S. company's warehouse. A **banker's acceptance** promises that the bank will pay some specified amount at a particular time. No conditions are imposed. Finally, a company can go to a bank and exchange U.S. dollars for euros to use in Germany; that's called *currency* or *money exchange*.

Banks are making it easier than ever for travelers and businesspeople to buy goods and services overseas. Automated teller machines now provide yen, euros, and other foreign currencies through your personal Visa, MasterCard, Cirrus, or American Express card.

Leaders in International Banking

It would be shortsighted to discuss the U.S. economy apart from the world economy. If the Federal Reserve decides to lower interest rates, within minutes foreign investors can withdraw their money from the United States and put it in countries with higher rates. Of course, the Fed's increasing of interest rates can draw money to the United States equally quickly.

Today's money markets thus form a global market system of which the United States is just a part. International bankers make investments in any country where they can get a maximum return for their money at a reasonable risk. About $4 trillion is traded daily! The net result of international banking and finance has been to link the economies of the world into one interrelated system with no regulatory control. U.S. firms must compete for funds with firms all over the world. An efficient firm in London or Tokyo is more likely to

letter of credit
A promise by the bank to pay the seller a given amount if certain conditions are met.

banker's acceptance
A promise that the bank will pay some specified amount at a particular time.

World Bank
The bank primarily responsible for financing economic development; also known as the International Bank for Reconstruction and Development.

International Monetary Fund (IMF)
Organization that assists the smooth flow of money among nations.

get international financing than a less efficient firm in Detroit or Chicago. Global markets mean that banks do not necessarily keep their money in their own countries. They make investments where they get the maximum return.

What this means for you is that banking is no longer a domestic issue; it's a global one. To understand the U.S. financial system, you must learn about the global financial system, including foreign central banks.[32] To understand the state of the U.S. economy, you need to learn about the economic condition of countries throughout the world. In the new world economy financed by international banks, the United States is just one player. To be a winner, it must stay financially secure and its businesses must stay competitive in world markets. Recently, some countries have restricted the free flow of money among nations. The future of such movements is yet to be determined.[33]

The World Bank and the International Monetary Fund (IMF)

The bank primarily responsible for financing economic development is the International Bank for Reconstruction and Development, or the **World Bank**. After World War II, it lent money to countries in Western Europe so they could rebuild. Today, it lends most of its money to developing nations to improve their productivity and help raise standards of living and quality of life. That includes working to eliminate diseases that kill millions of people each year.

The World Bank has faced considerable criticism and protests around the world. Environmentalists charge that it finances projects damaging to the ecosystem. Human rights activists and unionists say the bank supports countries that restrict religious freedoms and tolerate sweatshops. AIDS activists complain that it does not do enough to get low-cost AIDS drugs to developing nations.

The World Bank and the International Monetary Fund (IMF) are intergovernmental organizations that help support the global banking community. Both draw protests for their actions. Why?

Despite its efforts to improve, the World Bank still has many critics. Some want it to forgive the debts of developing countries and others want it to stop making such loans until the countries institute free markets and the right to own property. Some changes in World Bank policy may lie ahead.

In contrast to the World Bank, the **International Monetary Fund (IMF)** was established to foster cooperative monetary policies that stabilize the exchange of one national currency for another. About 188 countries are voluntary members of the IMF and allow their money to be freely exchanged for foreign money, keep the IMF informed about changes in monetary policy, and modify those policies on the advice of the IMF to accommodate the needs of the entire membership.[34]

The IMF is designed to oversee member countries' monetary and exchange rate policies. Its goal is to maintain a global monetary system that works best for all nations and enhances world trade.[35] While it is not primarily a lending institution like the World Bank, its members do contribute funds according to their ability, and those funds are available to countries in financial difficulty. The Reaching Beyond Our Borders box discusses what is happening today at the World Bank and the IMF.

New Day, New Issues across the Globe

Things certainly look brighter today than they did before the annual meeting of the IMF/World Bank six years ago. Back then the fall of Lehman Brothers and the extreme vulnerability of the global financial system had shocked financial officials around the world. Trade was plummeting, economic confidence had reached bottom, and high unemployment seemed inevitable. Fortunately, the global financial system is no longer a dark threat to the world economy. Still, the global economy today is far from healthy, which means the World Bank and the IMF have new challenges to face throughout the world.

Christine Lagarde, the managing director of the IMF, has promoted a gradual change in the 188-member organization's culture and role in global finance. Under her direction, the IMF provides policy advice to member countries when requested. The organization has also spoken out on issues such as climate change and income inequality. The IMF has also initiated research on the link between job creation, labor market policies, and unemployment.

One of Ms. Lagarde's major fears is that the financial crisis did lasting harm to the potential pace of growth in many economies across the globe. This means the global economy risks years of sluggish growth unless aggressive steps are taken by central bankers and lawmakers in both advanced and emerging countries to make their economies more competitive. The IMF and the World Bank are both trying to come up with answers to key global issues before there is another serious crisis.

Sources: Ian Talley, "IMF's Lagarde: Global Economy May Face Years of Slow, Subpar Growth," *The Wall Street Journal*, April 2, 2014; Mohammed El-Erian, "What We Need from the IMF/World Bank Meetings," *Financial Times*, October 6, 2013; and David Wessel, "The Likely Buzz at the IMF/World Bank Meetings," *The Wall Street Journal*, April 9, 2014.

test **prep**

- What are some of the causes for the banking crisis that began in 2008?
- What is the role of the FDIC?
- How does a debit card differ from a credit card?
- What is the World Bank and what does it do?
- What is the IMF and what does it do?

Use LearnSmart to help retain what you have learned. Access your instructor's Connect course to check out LearnSmart, or go to learnsmartadvantage.com for help.

LEARNSMART

summary

LO 20–1 Explain what money is and what makes money useful.

- **What is money?**
  Money is anything people generally accept as payment for goods and services.
- **What are the five standards for a useful form of money?**
  The five standards for a useful form of money are portability, divisibility, stability, durability, and uniqueness.
- **What are "Bitcoins," and can you buy things online with them?**
  Bitcoins are a form of online money. Bitcoin has an online store that accepts the currency.

Access your instructor's Connect course to check out LearnSmart or go to learnsmartadvantage.com for help.

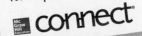

LO 20–2   Describe how the Federal Reserve controls the money supply.

- **How does the Federal Reserve control the money supply?**
  The Federal Reserve makes financial institutions keep funds in the Federal Reserve System (reserve requirement), buys and sells government securities (open-market operations), and lends money to banks (the discount rate). To increase the money supply, the Fed can cut the reserve requirement, buy government bonds, and lower the discount rate.

LO 20–3   Trace the history of banking and the Federal Reserve System.

- **How did banking evolve in the United States?**
  Massachusetts issued its own paper money in 1690; other colonies followed suit. British land banks lent money to farmers but ended such loans by 1741. After the American Revolution, there was much debate about the role of banking, and heated battles between the Central Bank of the United States and state banks. Eventually, a federally chartered and state-chartered system was established, but chaos continued until many banks failed in 1907. The system was revived by the Federal Reserve only to fail again during the Great Depression. There have been 11 recessions since then, including the recent one.

LO 20–4   Classify the various institutions in the U.S. banking system.

- **What institutions make up the banking system?**
  Savings and loans, commercial banks, and credit unions are all part of the banking system.

- **How do they differ from one another?**
  Before deregulation in 1980, commercial banks were unique in that they handled both deposits and checking accounts. At that time, savings and loans couldn't offer checking services; their main function was to encourage thrift and home ownership by offering high interest rates on savings accounts and providing home mortgages. Deregulation closed the gaps between banks and S&Ls, and they now offer similar services.

- **What kinds of services do they offer?**
  Banks and thrifts offer such services as savings accounts, checking accounts, certificates of deposit, loans, individual retirement accounts (IRAs), safe-deposit boxes, online banking, life insurance, brokerage services, and traveler's checks.

- **What is a credit union?**
  A credit union is a member-owned cooperative that offers everything a bank does—it takes deposits, allows you to write checks, and makes loans. It also may sell life insurance and offer mortgages. Credit union interest rates are sometimes higher than those from banks, and loan rates are often lower.

- **What are some of the other financial institutions that make loans and perform banklike operations?**
  Nonbanks include life insurance companies that lend out their funds, pension funds that invest in stocks and bonds and make loans, brokerage firms that offer investment services, and commercial finance companies.

LO 20–5 Briefly trace the causes of the banking crisis, and explain how the government protects your funds during such crises.

- **What caused the banking crisis?**
  The goal was to have affordable housing, so the government urged banks to make loans to some who could not afford to repay. The banks wanted to minimize the risk of such loans, so they created mortgage-backed securities and sold them to other banks and organizations throughout the world. The government did not regulate these transactions well, and many banks failed because housing values fell and people defaulted on their loans. Many have been blamed for the loss: the Fed, Congress, bank managers, Fannie Mae, and Freddie Mac, among them.

- **What agencies insure the money you put into a bank, S&L, or credit union?**
  Money deposited in banks is insured by the Federal Deposit Insurance Corporation (FDIC). Money in S&Ls is insured by another agency connected to the FDIC, the Savings Association Insurance Fund (SAIF). Money in credit unions is insured by the National Credit Union Administration (NCUA). Accounts are now insured to $250,000.

LO 20–6 Describe how technology helps make banking more efficient.

- **What are debit cards and smart cards?**
  A debit card looks like a credit card but withdraws money that is already in your account. When the sale is recorded, the debit card sends an electronic signal to the bank, automatically transferring funds from your account to the seller's. A smart card is an electronic funds transfer tool that combines a credit card, debit card, phone card, driver's license card, and more. Smart cards replace the typical magnetic strip on a credit or debit card with a microprocessor.

- **What is the benefit of automatic transactions and online banking?**
  A *direct deposit* is a credit made directly to a checking or savings account in place of a paycheck. A *direct payment* is a preauthorized electronic payment. Customers sign a separate form for each company whose bill they would like to automatically pay from their checking or savings account on a specified date. The customer's bank completes each transaction and records it on the customer's monthly statement. All top U.S. retail banks now allow customers to access their accounts online, and most have bill-paying capacity.

LO 20–7 Evaluate the role and importance of international banking, the World Bank, and the International Monetary Fund.

- **What do we mean by global markets?**
  Global markets mean that banks do not necessarily keep their money in their own countries. They make investments where they get the maximum return. What this means for you is that banking is no longer a domestic issue; it's a global one.

- **What roles do the World Bank and the IMF play?**
  The World Bank (also called the International Bank for Reconstruction and Development) is primarily responsible for financing economic development. The International Monetary Fund (IMF), in contrast, was established to assist the smooth flow of money among nations. It requires members (who join voluntarily) to allow their own money to be exchanged for foreign money freely, to keep the IMF informed about changes in monetary policy, and to modify those policies on the advice of the IMF to accommodate the needs of the entire membership.

key terms

banker's acceptance 583
barter 567
certificate of deposit (CD) 576
commercial bank 576
credit unions 577
debit card 582
demand deposit 576
discount rate 572
electronic funds transfer (EFT) system 582

Federal Deposit Insurance Corporation (FDIC) 581
International Monetary Fund (IMF) 584
letter of credit 583
M-1 569
M-2 569
M-3 569
money 566
money supply 569
nonbanks 578

open-market operations 572
pension funds 578
reserve requirement 572
savings and loan association (S&L) 577
Savings Association Insurance Fund (SAIF) 581
smart card 582
time deposit 576
World Bank 584

critical thinking

1. If you were chairperson of the Federal Reserve, what economic figures might you use to determine how well you were doing? What role did Ben Bernanke, the previous head of the Fed, play in the recent banking crisis?

2. How much cash do you usually carry with you? What other means do you use to pay for items at the store or on the Internet? What trends do you see in such payments? How might those trends make your purchase experience more satisfactory?

3. If the value of the dollar declines relative to the euro, what will happen to the price of French wine sold in U.S. stores? Will people in France be more or less likely to buy a U.S.-made car? Why?

4. Do you keep your savings in a bank, an S&L, a credit union, or some combination? Have you compared the benefits you could receive from each? Where would you expect to find the best loan values?

developing workplace skills

Key: ● Team   ★ Analytic   ▲ Communication   ▣ Technology

●★▣▲ 1. In a small group, discuss the following: What services do you use from banks and S&Ls? Does anyone use online banking? What seem to be its pluses and minuses? Use this opportunity to go online to compare the rates and services of various local banks and S&Ls.

★▲ 2. Poll the class to see who uses a bank and who uses a credit union. Have class members compare the services at each (interest rates on savings accounts, services available, loan rates). If anyone uses an online service, see how those rates compare. If no one uses a credit union or online bank, discuss the reasons.

●★▲ 3. One role of the Federal Reserve is to help process your checks. In small groups discuss when and where you use checks, credit cards, debit cards, and cash. Do you often write checks for small amounts? Would you stop if you calculated how much it costs to process such checks? Have you switched to debit cards as a result? Discuss your findings with the class.

4. Form several smaller groups and discuss the recent banking crisis. How has it affected the people in the class? What has happened to banks and the economy in general since the start of the banking crisis? What have been the political implications of recent economic changes?

5. Write a one-page paper on the role of the World Bank and the International Monetary Fund in providing loans to countries. Is it important for U.S. citizens to lend money to people in other countries through such organizations? Why or why not? Be prepared to debate the value of these organizations in class.

taking it to the **net**

PURPOSE

To learn more about the banking crisis that began in 2008 and what has happened since.

EXERCISE

1. Do an Internet search to find the latest articles on the global financial crisis. What has happened to banking in the United States and around the world since 2009? What role has the Fed played in trying to end the crisis in the United States?

2. How many search items have appeared covering this issue? What does the number of articles tell you about the importance of this issue?

3. Develop your own story about the causes of the banking crisis. Talk to others in the class and compare stories. What organizations share the blame for the crisis?

video case

THE FINANCIAL CRISIS

Looking back a few years ago in 2011, millions had lost homes, businesses had failed, foreclosures were at an all-time record high, and unemployment remained very high at 9 percent. These outcomes were due, in large part, to the financial crisis of 2006–2010.

In the year 2000, the tech stock bubble burst, which sent markets plummeting around the globe. Around the same time, ethics violations surfaced for major companies including Enron, WorldCom, Global Crossing, and Tyco. With the economy in a slump, the government wanted to stimulate consumer spending and business investment. To do this, the Federal Reserve lowered the prime interest rate from 6.5 percent to 1 percent. This ease of credit made mortgages, credit cards, and other consumer loans easy to get. In fact, the average household debt to disposable income in 2007 was 127 percent.

The U.S. Congress, through the 2010 financial crisis investigating committee, determined that the crisis was avoidable. Some of the factors identified as leading to the crisis included the proliferation of subprime mortgages that, in the period between 2004 and 2006, comprised about 20 percent of all mortgages. This was a twofold increase in subprime loans.

The SEC lowered the leverage requirements for investment banks, leading banks to borrow significantly more than they had in reserves. During this period of time, mortgage-backed securities (MBSs) were bundled and sold to investors. These MBS products included subprime mortgages, as well. During this same period of time, the major financial rating agencies such as Moody's and Standard and Poor's continued to provide AAA ratings (the highest rating) for MBS products, assuring investors of their value.

In 2007, the housing bubble burst, with housing prices tumbling and the value of MBS products falling, in some cases, to worthless status. Many people found themselves "underwater," meaning that they owed more on their houses than they were worth. These folks and many who had subprime mortgages defaulted on their obligations. As the MBS declined in value, investment banks and other financial firms began to fail, as their debt was higher than the value of their assets.

This financial crisis had global consequences. The failure of very large (or "too big to fail") investment banks could not be allowed to stand; thus, the federal government intervened with a $700 billion bailout for banks called the Troubled Asset Relief Program (TARP), designed to bail out troubled banks and prevent further failures. In 2009, the president signed an $800 billion stimulus designed to help stimulate the economy, help businesses borrow and invest, and as a result, create jobs.

The global crisis of confidence described in the video represents the largest economic failure since the Great Depression of the 1930s. The long-term effects of the financial crisis are yet to be completely determined.

THINKING IT OVER

1. Describe how the Federal Reserve can use its authority to attempt to stimulate the economy.

2. One of the major problems that led to the financial crisis was the housing bubble. What is meant by the "housing bubble"?

3. Name and explain two of the reasons the Congressional committee identified for the recent financial crisis.

notes

1. Brian Wesbury, "How Much Does That Burger Cost in Bitcoins?" *The Wall Street Journal,* December 16, 2013.
2. Christina Le Beau, "Rules of the Trade," *Entrepreneur,* February 2014.
3. Norm Brodsky, "Don't Worry; Grow Happy," *Inc.,* May 2013.
4. J. D. Harrison, "When Cashflow Is Tight, Some Businesses Barter," *The Washington Post,* March 17, 2013.
5. Nomann Merchant, "$100 Bill Undergoes Major Makeover," *The Washington Times,* September 26, 2013.
6. Mohana Ravidranath, "In D.C., Bitcoin Starting to Gain Currency," *The Washington Post,* December 23, 2013.
7. *Tomorrow in Review,* January 16, 2014, tomorrowinreview@ Agorafinancial.com, accessed May 2014.
8. Joe Light, "New Perch in Markets for Bitcoin," *The Wall Street Journal,* February 7, 2014.
9. Jeffrey Sparshott, "Change for a Nickel? Mint Considers It," *The Wall Street Journal,* January 17, 2014.
10. Ira Iosebishvili, "Signs Point to Year of the Dollar's Ascent," *The Wall Street Journal,* December 27, 2013.
11. Ylan Q. Mui, "Fed Will Begin Easing Stimulus," *The Washington Post,* December 19, 2013.
12. Francesco Guerrera, "Tallying Winners, Losers in 'QE' Era," *The Wall Street Journal,* January 14, 2014.
13. Zachary Karabell, "Maybe the All-Powerful Federal Reserve Isn't," *The Washington Post,* November 24, 2013.
14. Jonathan Buck, "ECB Will Boost Support If Euro Zone Stumbles," *Barron's,* January 13, 2014.
15. Thomas V. DiBacco, "Federal Reserve's Woeful Century," *The Washington Times,* December 23, 2013.
16. Patrice Hill, "Markets Reel as the Fed Cuts Back Stimulus," *The Washington Times,* January 30, 2014.
17. Robert E. Grady, "The Fed Celebrates Its 100th Birthday," *The Wall Street Journal,* December 23, 2013.
18. To read more about this era, see John Steele Gordon, "How the Civil War United Our Money," *Barron's,* January 21, 2013.
19. Patrice Hill, "Markets Reel as the Fed Cuts Back Stimulus," *The Washington Times,* January 30, 2014.
20. Anna Maria Andriotis and Saabira Chaudhuri, "Free Checks Go Way of Free Lunch," *The Wall Street Journal,* February 6, 2014.
21. Sheila Bair, "When It Comes to the New Banking Rules, More Isn't Always Better," *Fortune,* February 3, 2014.
22. *Fortune,* advertisement, January 13, 2014.
23. Hanah Cho, quoted in "Banking: Meeting the Mobile Challenge," *The Week,* December 27, 2013.
24. Federal Deposit Insurance Corporation, www.fdic.gov, accessed May 2014.
25. Lisa Brown, "Credit Unions Promote, Gain Share," *St. Louis Post-Dispatch,* August, 30, 2013.
26. Brendan Greeley, "Have Credit Unions Become Stealth Banks?" *Bloomberg Businessweek,* May 20–26, 2013.
27. *World,* editorial, December 14, 2013.
28. Peter Dreier, "What Housing Recovery?" *The New York Times,* May 8, 2014.
29. Lisa Gerstner, "Pick the Best Credit Card for You," *Kiplinger's Personal Finance,* February 2013.
30. Danielle Douglas, "Rise in Prepaid Debit Cards Entices Banks to Sponsor Them," *The Washington Post,* January 24, 2014.
31. Danielle Douglas, "When It Comes to Plastic, Credit and Debit Not Created Equally," *The Washington Post,* February 7, 2014.
32. Brian Blackstone and Todd Buell, "Europe Central Banks Ready for New Stimulus," *The Wall Street Journal,* February 7, 2014.
33. Rana Foroohar, "The End of Easy Money," *Time,* April 15, 2013.
34. Martin Crutsinger, "IMF Raises Outlook for Global and U.S. Economic Growth," *The Washington Times,* January 22, 2014; and the International Monetary Fund, www.imf.org, accessed May 2014.
35. Howard Schneider, "After Financial Crisis, IMF Pauses to Take Stock of Policies," *The Washington Post,* April 17, 2013.

A

Working within the Legal Environment

Learning Objectives

AFTER YOU HAVE READ AND STUDIED THIS BONUS CHAPTER, YOU SHOULD BE ABLE TO

A-1 Define *business law,* distinguish between statutory and common law, and explain the role of administrative agencies.

A-2 Define *tort law* and explain the role of product liability in tort law.

A-3 Identify the purposes and conditions of patents, copyrights, and trademarks.

A-4 Describe warranties and negotiable instruments as covered in the Uniform Commercial Code.

A-5 List and describe the conditions necessary to make a legally enforceable contract, and describe the possible consequences if such a contract is violated.

A-6 Summarize several laws that regulate competition and protect consumers in the United States.

A-7 Explain the role of tax laws in generating income for the government and as a method of discouraging or encouraging certain behaviors among taxpayers.

A-8 Distinguish among the various types of bankruptcy as outlined by the Bankruptcy Code.

A-9 Explain the role of deregulation as a tool to encourage competition.

L e Bron James is considered by many to be one of the NBA's most valuable players. He was the mainstay of the two-time league champion Miami Heat before moving back to the Cleveland Cavaliers. As familiar as you may be with players like LeBron, it's unlikely you're familiar with another valuable member of the Miami Heat team: Eve Wright Taylor. That's because Taylor doesn't make her mark shooting three-pointers. She serves as vice president and associate general counsel of the Miami Heat and the AmericanAirlines Arena.

Taylor received her undergraduate degree from DePauw University and went on to law school at the University of Indiana. After graduation, she worked in a corporate law firm in Minneapolis before deciding to embark on a new challenge. She became legal counsel and senior director of business affairs for the Ladies Professional Golf Association (LPGA). At the LPGA, Taylor was involved with many legal and business parts of the organization including tournament contracts, licensing agreements, corporate sponsorships, trademark management, television broadcast rights, and other duties. After six successful years at the LPGA, Taylor was offered a new opportunity in one of the most male-dominated industries in the world, the National Basketball Association (NBA).

When she joined the Heat, Taylor quickly found that not only was the Heat one of the hottest teams in basketball, her job was also a hot spot. It seemed that no two days were alike and her job touched every aspect of the organization. She quickly found there was a legal component to virtually everything that involved the team including the AmericanAirlines Arena that the Heat called home. On a particular day Taylor may be asked for legal advice on issues involving marketing and promotions, arena concerts and events, corporate sales, merchandising initiatives, and player-related matters, such as obtaining visas for foreign players on the team.

It's doubtful Taylor will ever reach the fame of LeBron James or be inducted into the NBA Hall of Fame, but that doesn't mean the Heat doesn't appreciate her efforts. Besides having two rings celebrating the Heat's NBA Championships, Taylor, who is Vice President and Associate General Counsel of the team, is also a sought-after speaker who regularly presents seminars on sports business, licensing, sponsorship, and other legal issues. She recently published her first book, *Life at the Speed of Passion,* and promises more to come. When it comes to Eve Wright Taylor, there's no doubt about it, life is a full-court press.

Professional sports, of course, is not the only industry where legal issues affect almost every area of the business. The United States has more lawyers than any nation and is the world's most litigious society. In this chapter, we briefly discuss the history and structure of the U.S. legal system. Then we'll take a look at key areas of business law such as torts, patents, copyrights, and trademarks as well as sales law, contract law, laws to protect competition and consumers, tax law, and bankruptcy law. We also discuss the controversial topic of deregulation. You probably won't be ready for a game of one-on-one with Eve Wright Taylor after reading this chapter, but if you use it as a foundation to the study of law, who knows what your future may be?

Sources: "Forty Under 40," *Sports Business Journal,* March 12, 2012; Sonja D. Mack, "40 Rising Stars 40 & Under," *Black Enterprise,* February 2012; and "Calculated Risk Taker," National Black Law Students Association, www.nblsa.com, accessed May 2014.

Eve Wright Taylor

- Vice president & associate general counsel for Miami Heat

- Deals with every legal issue that involves the team, including the arena

www.nba.com/heat

@EveWrightExec

name that **company**

As a key federal government agency, we have a key role in mergers and acquisitions in the U.S. business community. Without our approval, mergers or acquisitions can be rejected. For example, we approved the merger of American Airlines with U.S. Airways, but rejected a merger between AT&T and T-Mobile. Name our organization. (Find the answer in this chapter.)

LO A–1 Define *business law*, distinguish between statutory and common law, and explain the role of administrative agencies.

THE CASE FOR LAWS

Imagine a society without laws. Just think: no speed limits, no age restrictions on the consumption of alcohol, no limitations on who can practice law or medicine—a society where people are free to do whatever they choose, with no interference. Obviously, the more we consider this possibility, the more unrealistic we realize it is. Laws are an essential part of a civilized nation. Over time, though, the depth and scope of the body of laws must change to continue reflecting the needs of society. The **judiciary** is the branch of government chosen to oversee the legal system through a system of courts.

The U.S. court system is organized at the federal, state, and local levels. At both the federal and state levels, trial courts hear cases involving criminal and civil law. *Criminal law* defines crimes, establishes punishments, and regulates the investigation and prosecution of people accused of committing crimes. *Civil law* proceedings cover noncriminal acts—marriage, personal injury suits, and so on. Both federal and state systems have appellate courts that hear appeals from the losing party about decisions made at the trial-court level. Appellate courts can review and overturn these decisions.

The judiciary also governs the activities and operations of business, including hiring and firing practices, unpaid leave for family emergencies, environmental protection, worker safety, freedom from sexual harassment at work, and more. As you may suspect, businesspeople prefer to set their own standards of behavior and often complain that the government is overstepping its bounds in governing business. Unfortunately, the economic crisis highlighted that the U.S. business community did not implement acceptable standards—particularly in financial markets—causing the government to expand its control and enforcement procedures.[1] This chapter will look at specific laws and regulations and how they affect businesses.

Business law refers to the rules, statutes, codes, and regulations that provide a legal framework for the conduct of business and that are enforceable by court action. A businessperson must be familiar with laws regarding product liability, sales, contracts, fair competition, consumer protection, taxes, and bankruptcy. Let's start by briefly discussing the foundations of law and what the legal system is all about.

Statutory and Common Law

Two major fields of law are important to businesspeople: statutory law and common law.

---

judiciary
The branch of government chosen to oversee the legal system through a system of courts.

business law
The rules, statutes, codes, and regulations that provide a legal framework for the conduct of business and that are enforceable by court action.

Statutory law includes state and federal constitutions, legislative enactments, treaties of the federal government, and ordinances—in short, written law. You can read the statutes that make up this body of law, but they are often written in language whose meaning must be determined in court. With over 1.2 million licensed lawyers, the United States has more lawyers per citizen than any country in the world.[2]

Common law is the body of law that comes from decisions handed down by courts. We often call it *unwritten law* because it does not appear in any legislative enactment, treaty, or other written document. Under common law principles, what judges have decided in previous cases is very important in deciding today's cases. Such decisions are called **precedent**, and they guide judges in the handling of new cases. Common law evolves through decisions made in trial courts, appellate courts, and special courts (e.g., probate courts or bankruptcy courts). Lower courts (trial courts) must abide by the precedents set by higher courts (e.g., appellate courts) such as the U.S. Supreme Court.

Administrative Agencies

Administrative agencies are federal or state institutions and other government organizations created by Congress or state legislatures with delegated power to create rules and regulations within their given area of authority.

Legislative bodies can create administrative agencies and also terminate them. Some administrative agencies hold quasi-legislative, quasi-executive, and quasi-judicial powers. This means that an agency is allowed to pass rules and regulations within its area of authority, conduct investigations in cases of suspected rules violations, and hold hearings if it feels rules and regulations have been violated.

Administrative agencies issue more rulings affecting business and settle more business disputes than courts do. Such agencies include the Securities and Exchange Commission (SEC), the Federal Communications Commission, and the Equal Employment Opportunity Commission (EEOC). Figure A.1 lists and describes the powers and functions of several administrative agencies at the federal, state, and local levels of government.

statutory law
State and federal constitutions, legislative enactments, treaties of the federal government, and ordinances—in short, written law.

common law
The body of law that comes from decisions handed down by courts; also referred to as unwritten law.

precedent
Decisions judges have made in earlier cases that guide the handling of new cases.

administrative agencies
Federal or state institutions and other government organizations created by Congress or state legislatures with delegated power to create rules and regulations within their mandated area of authority.

FIGURE A.1 EXAMPLES OF FEDERAL, STATE, AND LOCAL ADMINISTRATIVE AGENCIES

Federal Agencies

Examples	Powers and Functions
Federal Trade Commission	Enforces laws and guidelines regarding unfair business practices and acts to stop false and deceptive advertising and labeling.
Food and Drug Administration	Enforces laws and regulations to prevent distribution of adulterated or misbranded foods, drugs, medical devices, cosmetics, and veterinary products, as well as any hazardous consumer products.

State Agencies

Examples	Powers and Functions
Public utility commissions	Set rates that can be charged by various public utilities to prevent unfair pricing by regulated monopolies (e.g., natural gas, electric power companies).
State licensing boards	License various trades and professions within a state (e.g., state cosmetology board, state real estate commission).

Local Agencies

Examples	Powers and Functions
Maricopa County Planning Commission	Oversees land-use proposals, long-term development objectives, and other long-range issues in Maricopa County, Arizona.
City of Chesterfield Zoning Board	Recommends policy regarding zoning of commercial and residential property in the city of Chesterfield, Missouri.

test prep

- What is business law?
- What's the difference between statutory and common law?
- What is an administrative agency?

LO A–2   Define *tort law* and explain the role of product liability in tort law.

TORT LAW

tort
A wrongful act that causes injury to another person's body, property, or reputation.

A **tort** is a wrongful act that causes injury to another person's body, property, or reputation. Although torts often are noncriminal acts, courts can award victims compensation if the conduct that caused the harm is considered intentional. Legally, an *intentional* tort is a willful act that results in injury. The question of intent was a major factor in the lawsuits against the U.S. tobacco industry. Courts had to decide whether tobacco makers intentionally withheld information from the public about the harmful effects of their products.

negligence
In tort law, behavior that causes unintentional harm or injury.

Negligence, in tort law, describes behavior that causes *unintentional* harm or injury. A court's finding of negligence can lead to huge judgments against businesses. In another classic case, McDonald's lost a lawsuit to an elderly woman severely burned by hot coffee bought at a drive-through window. The jury felt that McDonald's failed to provide an adequate warning on the cup. Product liability is a controversial area of tort law, so let's take a closer look at this issue.

Product Liability

Few issues in business law raise as much debate as product liability. Critics believe product liability laws have gone too far; others feel these laws should be expanded. **Product liability** holds businesses liable for harm that results from the production, design, or inadequate warnings of products they market.[3] The average product liability case can cost businesses millions, including defense costs, out-of-court settlements, and jury awards.

At one time the legal standard for measuring product liability was whether a producer knowingly placed a hazardous product on the market. Today, many states have extended product liability to the level of **strict product liability**—legally meaning liability without regard to fault. That is, a company that places a defective product on the market can be held liable for damages—a monetary settlement awarded to a person injured by another's actions—even if the company did not know of the defect at the time of sale.

Strict product liability is a major concern for businesses. More than 70 companies have been forced into bankruptcy due to asbestos litigation and the issue is not yet closed.[4] About 2,000 new cases of mesothelioma (a cancer linked to asbestos exposure) are diagnosed every year according to the Mesothelioma Center, keeping the legal docket busy.[5] Lead-based paint producers continue to face expensive lawsuits even though lead-based paint has been banned in the United States since 1978.[6] Mattel was forced in the mid-2000s to recall over 9 million toys produced in China due to lead paint concerns. In 2014, Toyota Motors quickly issued stop-sale orders for its Camry and Corolla models after finding seat material did not comply with U.S. fire safety standards.[7] The company was forced to recall 8.1 million cars beginning in 2009 due to sudden acceleration incidents, and in 2014 reached a $1.2 billion settlement with the U.S. government admitting that it misled U.S. consumers by making deceptive statements about safety issues.[8] At the time of this writing, GM is undergoing congressional investigation of why it took the company years to recall vehicles with known defects linked to 13 deaths.[9]

Some product liability cases have raised intriguing questions about responsibility. Handgun manufacturers were unsuccessfully sued by cities including Chicago and Miami for the costs of police work and medical care necessitated by gun violence. McDonald's faced a product liability suit (later dismissed) claiming that its food caused obesity, diabetes, and other health problems in children. Some communities, however, have reacted by banning trans fats in food, regulating menu information, and eliminating toys in children's products like McDonald's Happy Meals. New York City even attempted to place a ban on large sugary soft drinks sold at restaurants, sports arenas, and other venues.[10] The ban was later ruled unconstitutional. Many schools, however, are replacing soft drinks in vending machines with fruit juice and water.

Tort and product liability reform remains a key objective of business. Congress took action with passage of the Class Action Fairness Act in 2005, which expanded federal jurisdiction over many large class-action lawsuits. The legislation has been beneficial to some businesses since their cases were brought to federal court rather than state courts where awards were typically much higher. Still, businesses and insurance companies argue that more needs to be done to assist companies with product liability.[11] Consumer protection groups disagree and feel not enough is being done to protect consumers. Figure A.2 highlights a brief history of several major product liability awards that have cost companies dearly.

product liability
Part of tort law that holds businesses liable for harm that results from the production, design, or use of products they market.

strict product liability
Legal responsibility for harm or injury caused by a product regardless of fault.

FIGURE A.2 MAJOR PRODUCT LIABILITY CASES

Company	Year	Settlement
Ford Motor Company	1978	$125 million in punitive damages awarded in the case of a 13-year-old boy severely burned in a rear-end collision involving a Ford Pinto
A. H. Robins	1987	Dalkon Shield intrauterine birth-control devices recalled after eight separate punitive-damage awards
Playtex Company	1988	Considered liable and suffered a $10 million damage award in the case of a toxic shock syndrome fatality in Kansas; removed certain types of tampons from the market
Jack in the Box	1993	Assessed large damages after a two-year-old child who ate at Jack in the Box died of *E. coli* poisoning and others became ill
Sara Lee Corporation	1998	Costly company recall necessitated when tainted hot dogs caused food poisoning death of 15 people
General Motors	1999	Suffered $4.8 billion punitive award in a faulty fuel-tank case
Major Tobacco Firms	2004	$130 billion sought by the federal government for smoking cessation programs (settled for $10 billion)

Sources: U.S. Department of Justice and American Trial Lawyers Association.

(**LO A-3**)   Identify the purposes and conditions of patents, copyrights, and trademarks.

LEGALLY PROTECTING IDEAS: PATENTS, COPYRIGHTS, AND TRADEMARKS

patent
A document that gives inventors exclusive rights to their inventions for 20 years.

Have you ever invented a product you think may have commercial value? Many people have, and to protect their ideas they took the next step and applied for a patent. A **patent** is a document that gives inventors exclusive rights to their inventions for 20 years from the date they file the patent applications.

Patent applicants must make sure a product is truly unique and should seek the advice of an attorney; in fact, fewer than 2 percent of product inventors file on their own. How good are your chances of receiving a patent if you file for one? About 50 percent of patent applications received by the U.S. Patent and Trademarks Office (USPTO) are approved, with fees that vary according to the complexity of the patent. A patent dealing with complex technology can cost anywhere from $10,000 to $30,000, whereas a patent dealing with simpler concepts (like a better mousetrap) will cost the inventor about $5,000 to $10,000.[12]

Patent owners have the right to sell or license the use of their patent to others. Foreign companies are also eligible to file for U.S. patents. They account for nearly half the U.S. patents issued. Penalties for violating a patent (patent infringement) can be costly. Dr. Gary Michelson received a settlement of $1.35 billion from Medtronic Inc. to end litigation and license patents covering a range of back-surgery products.[13] The USPTO does not take action on behalf of patent holders if patent infringement occurs. The defense of patent rights is solely the job of the patent holder.

The American Inventors Protection Act was passed to require that patent applications be made public after 18 months regardless of whether a patent has been awarded. This law was passed in part to address critics who argued that some inventors intentionally delayed or dragged out a patent application because they expected others to eventually develop similar products or technology. Then when someone (usually a large company) filed for a similar patent, the inventor surfaced to claim the patent—referred to as a *submarine patent*—and demanded large royalties (fees) for its use. The late engineer Jerome Lemelson reportedly collected more than $1.3 billion in patent royalties for a series of long-delayed patents—including forerunners of the fax machine, industrial robots, and the bar-code scanner—from auto, computer, retail, and electronics companies.[14]

Technology companies like Apple and Google have been the subject of lawsuits filed by "patent trolls" that license patents (or buy the licensed patents) and file infringement lawsuits against companies that often cost millions of dollars.[15] The trolls never intend to use the patents; their only intention is to file the lawsuits in the hopes of a financial settlement.[16] Apple, Google, and other companies have asked for assistance from the U.S. Supreme Court, which is expected to rule on this issue.[17] Verizon, Google, and Cisco took action to defend themselves against patent infringement suits by joining Allied Security Trust, a not-for-profit firm that acquires intellectual property of interest to its members. The idea is to buy up patents that could impact their companies before they fall into the hands of others (mainly patent trolls) looking to pursue settlements or legal damages against the tech firms.[18]

Just as a patent protects an inventor's right to a product or process, a **copyright** protects a creator's rights to materials such as books, articles, photos, paintings, and cartoons. Copyrights are filed with the Library of Congress and require a minimum of paperwork. They last for the lifetime of the author or artist plus 70 years and can be passed on to the creator's heirs. The Copyright Act of 1978, however, gives a special term of 75 years from publication to works published before January 1, 1978, whose copyrights had not expired by that date. The holder of a copyright can either prevent anyone from using the copyrighted material or charge a fee for using it. Author J. K. Rowling won a copyright violation suit against a fan who wanted to publish an unauthorized Harry Potter encyclopedia. If a work is created by an employee in the normal course of a job, the copyright belongs to the employer and lasts 95 years from publication or 120 years from creation, whichever comes first.

A *trademark* is a legally protected name, symbol, or design (or combination of these) that identifies the goods or services of one seller and distinguishes them from those of competitors. Trademarks generally belong to the owner forever, as long as they are properly registered and renewed every 10 years. Some well-known trademarks include the Aflac duck, Disney's Mickey Mouse, the Nike swoosh, and the golden arches of McDonald's. Like a patent, a trademark is protected against infringement. Businesses fight hard to protect trademarks, especially in global markets where trademark pirating can be extensive. (Chapter 14 discusses trademarks in more detail.)

Viacom filed a lawsuit against YouTube (now owned by Google) for allowing users to upload its content to the video-sharing website. After a seven-year copyright violation battle costing Google more than $100 million, the two finally reached an out-of-court settlement in 2014. Viacom was seeking $1 billion in damages, but the terms of the final agreement were not disclosed.

copyright
A document that protects a creator's rights to materials such as books, articles, photos, paintings, and cartoons.

test **prep**

- What is tort law?
- What is product liability? What is strict product liability?
- How many years is a patent protected from infringement?
- What is a copyright?

Use LearnSmart to help retain what you have learned. Access your instructor's Connect course to check out LearnSmart, or go to learnsmartadvantage.com for help.

LEARNSMART

LO A–4   Describe warranties and negotiable instruments as covered in the Uniform Commercial Code.

Uniform Commercial Code (UCC)
A comprehensive commercial law adopted by every state in the United States that covers sales laws and other commercial laws.

Would you buy a new car if the dealer offered no warranty? How about an iPhone or a major kitchen appliance with no guarantee of performance? Warranties are an important part of a product and are generally of major concern to purchasers. It's important to check whether a product's warranty is full or limited. Should colleges offer students warranties with their degree programs?

SALES LAW: THE UNIFORM COMMERCIAL CODE

At one time, laws governing businesses varied from state to state, making interstate trade extremely complicated. Today, all states have adopted the same commercial law. The **Uniform Commercial Code (UCC)** is a comprehensive commercial law that covers sales laws and other commercial laws. Since all 50 states have adopted the law (although it does not apply in certain sections of Louisiana), the UCC simplifies commercial transactions across state lines.

The UCC has 11 articles, which contain laws covering sales; commercial paper such as promissory notes and checks; bank deposits and collections; letters of credit; bulk transfers; warehouse receipts, bills of lading, and other documents of title; investment securities; and secured transactions. We do not have space in this text to discuss all 11 articles, but we will discuss two: Article 2, which regulates warranties, and Article 3, which covers negotiable instruments.

Warranties

A *warranty* guarantees that the product sold will be acceptable for the purpose for which the buyer intends to use it. There are two types of warranties. **Express warranties** are specific representations by sellers that buyers rely on regarding the goods they purchase. The warranty you receive in the box with an iPad or a toaster is an express warranty.

Implied warranties are legally imposed on the seller, specifying that a product will conform to the customary standards of the trade or industry in which it competes. An implied warranty entitles you to expect that a toaster will toast your bread to your desired degree (light, medium, dark) or that food you buy for consumption off an establishment's premises is fit to eat.

Warranties can be either full or limited. A full warranty requires a seller to replace or repair a product at no charge if the product is not functioning or defective, whereas a limited warranty typically limits the defects or mechanical problems the seller covers. Companies often offer extended warranties that provide more coverage, but for a price, of course.[19] Many of the rights of buyers, including the right to accept or reject goods, are spelled out in Article 2 of the UCC.

Negotiable Instruments

Negotiable instruments are forms of commercial paper (such as checks) that are transferable among businesses and individuals; they represent a promise to pay a specified amount. Article 3 of the Uniform Commercial Code requires negotiable instruments to follow four conditions. They must

(1) be written and signed by the maker or drawer, (2) be made payable on demand or at a certain time, (3) be made payable to the bearer (the person holding the instrument) or to specific order, and (4) contain an unconditional promise to pay a specified amount of money. Checks or other forms of negotiable instruments are transferred (negotiated for payment) when the payee signs the back. The payee's signature is called an *endorsement*.

LO A–5   List and describe the conditions necessary to make a legally enforceable contract, and describe the possible consequences if such a contract is violated.

CONTRACT LAW

If I offer to sell you my bike for $50 and later change my mind, can you force me to sell the bike by saying we had a contract? If I lose $120 to you in a poker game, can you sue in court to get your money? If I agree to sing at your wedding for free and back out at the last minute, can you claim I violated a contract? These are the kinds of questions contract law answers.

A **contract** is a legally enforceable agreement between two or more parties. **Contract law** specifies what constitutes a legally enforceable agreement. Basically, a contract is legally binding if the following conditions are met:

1. *An offer is made.* An offer to do something or sell something can be oral or written. If I agree to sell you my bike for $50, I have made an offer. That offer is not legally binding, however, until the following other conditions are met.

2. *There is a voluntary acceptance of the offer.* The principle of *mutual acceptance* means that both parties to a contract must agree on the terms. If I use duress—coercion through force or threat of force—in getting you to agree to buy my bike, the contract will not be legal. You couldn't use duress to get me to sell my bike, either. Even if we both agree, though, the contract is still not legally binding without the next four conditions.

3. *Both parties give consideration.* **Consideration** means something of value. If I agree to sell you my bike for $50, the bike and the $50 are consideration, and we have a legally binding contract. If I agree to sing at your wedding and you do not give me anything in return (consideration), we have no contract.

4. *Both parties are competent.* A person under the influence of alcohol or drugs, or a person of unsound mind (one who has been legally declared incompetent), cannot be held to a contract. In many cases, a minor may not be held to a contract either. If a 15-year-old agrees to pay $10,000 for a car, the seller will not be able to enforce the contract due to the buyer's lack of competence.

5. *The contract covers a legal act.* A contract covering the sale of illegal drugs or stolen merchandise is unenforceable since such sales are violations of criminal law. (If gambling is prohibited by state law in your state, you cannot sue to collect the poker debt.)

6. *The contract is in proper form.* An agreement for the sale of goods worth $500 or more must be in writing. Contracts that cannot be fulfilled within one year also must be put in writing. Contracts regarding real property (land and everything attached to it) must be in writing.

express warranties
Specific representations by the seller that buyers rely on regarding the goods they purchase.

implied warranties
Guarantees concerning products legally imposed on the seller.

negotiable instruments
Forms of commercial paper (such as checks) that are transferable among businesses and individuals and represent a promise to pay a specified amount.

contract
A legally enforceable agreement between two or more parties.

contract law
Set of laws that specify what constitutes a legally enforceable agreement.

consideration
Something of value; consideration is one of the requirements of a legal contract.

Breach of Contract

Both parties in a contract may voluntarily choose to end the agreement. **Breach of contract** occurs when one party fails to follow the terms of a contract.[20] If that happens the following may occur:

1. *Specific performance.* The party who violated the contract may be required to live up to the agreement if money damages would not be adequate. If I legally offered to sell you a rare painting, I would have to sell you that painting.

2. *Payment of damages.* If I fail to live up to a contract, you can sue me for **damages**, usually the amount you would lose from my nonperformance. If we had a legally binding contract for me to sing at your wedding, for example, and I failed to come, you could sue me for the cost of hiring a new singer.

3. *Discharge of obligation.* If I fail to live up to my end of a contract, you can agree to drop the matter. Generally you would not have to live up to your end of the agreement either.

Lawyers would not be paid so handsomely if contract law were as simple as implied in these rules. That's why it's always best to put a contract in writing even though oral contracts can be enforceable under contract law. The contract should clearly specify the offer and consideration, and the parties to the contract should sign and date it. A contract does not have to be complicated as long as (1) it is in writing, (2) it specifies mutual consideration, and (3) it contains a clear offer and agreement.

- What is the purpose of the Universal Commercial Code (UCC)?
- Compare express and implied warranties.
- What are the four elements of a negotiable instrument specified in the UCC?
- What are the six conditions for a legally binding contract? What can happen if a contract is breached?

LO A–6 Summarize several laws that regulate competition and protect consumers in the United States.

PROMOTING FAIR AND COMPETITIVE BUSINESS PRACTICES

Competition is a cornerstone of the free-market system (see Chapter 2). A key responsibility of legislators is to pass laws that ensure a competitive atmosphere among businesses and promote fair business practices. The U.S. Justice Department's antitrust division and other government agencies serve as watchdogs to guarantee competition in markets flows freely and new competitors have open access to the market. The government's power here is broad. The Justice Department's antitrust division has investigated the competitive practices of market giants such as Microsoft, Apple, Visa, and Google. Figure A.3 highlights several high-profile antitrust cases.

Antitrust oversight was not always the rule, however. Big businesses were once able to force smaller competitors out of business with little government resistance. The following brief history details how government responded to past problems. We'll also look at new challenges government regulators face today.

The History of Antitrust Legislation

In the late 19th century, big oil companies, railroads, steel companies, and other industrial firms dominated the U.S. economy. Some feared that such large and powerful companies would be able to crush any competitors and then charge high prices. In that atmosphere, Congress passed the Sherman Antitrust Act in 1890 to prevent large organizations from stifling the competition of smaller or newer firms. The Sherman Act forbids (1) contracts, combinations, or conspiracies in restraint of trade, and (2) the creation of actual monopolies or attempts to monopolize any part of trade or commerce.

Because some of the language in the Sherman Act was vague, there was doubt about just what practices it prohibited. To clarify its intentions Congress enacted the following laws.

- *The Clayton Act of 1914.* The Clayton Act prohibits exclusive dealing, tying contracts, and interlocking directorates. It also prohibits buying large amounts of stock in competing corporations. *Exclusive dealing* is selling goods with the condition that the buyer will not buy from a competitor (when the effect lessens competition). A *tying contract* requires a buyer to purchase unwanted items in order to purchase desired ones. Let's say I wanted to purchase 20 cases of Pepsi-Cola per week to sell in my restaurant. Pepsi, however, says it will sell me the 20 cases only if I also agree to buy 10 cases each of its Mountain Dew and Diet Pepsi products. My purchase of Pepsi-Cola would be *tied* to the purchase of the other two products. An *interlocking directorate* occurs when a company's board of directors includes members of the boards of competing corporations.

- *The Federal Trade Commission Act of 1914.* The Federal Trade Commission Act prohibits unfair methods of competition in commerce. This

FIGURE A.3 HISTORY OF HIGH-PROFILE ANTITRUST CASES

Case	Outcome
United States v. *Standard Oil* 1911	Standard Oil broken up into 34 companies; Amoco, Chevron, and ExxonMobil are results of the breakup
United States v. *American Tobacco* 1911	American Tobacco split into 16 companies; British Tobacco and R.J.Reynolds are results of the breakup
United States v. *E. I. du Pont de Nemours* 1961	DuPont ordered to divest its 23 percent ownership stake in General Motors
United States v. *AT&T* 1982	Settled after Ma Bell agreed to spin off its local telephone operations into seven regional operating companies
United States v. *Microsoft* 2000	Microsoft ordered to halt prior anticompetitive practices

Source: U.S. Department of Justice.

legislation set up the five-member Federal Trade Commission (FTC) to enforce compliance with the act. The FTC deals with a wide range of competitive issues—everything from preventing companies from making misleading "Made in the USA" claims to insisting funeral providers give consumers accurate, itemized price information about funeral goods and services. It has the added responsibility for overseeing mergers and acquisitions (Chapter 5) in health care, defense, scientific, industrial, and technology industries.[21] For example, the FTC approved the American Airlines and U.S. Airways merger, but rejected the merger of AT&T and T-Mobile.[22] The Wheeler-Lea Amendment of 1938 also gave the FTC additional jurisdiction over false or misleading advertising, along with the power to increase fines if its requirements are not met within 60 days.

- *The Robinson-Patman Act of 1936.* The Robinson-Patman Act prohibits price discrimination and applies to both sellers and buyers who knowingly induce or receive price discrimination. Certain types of price cutting are criminal offenses punishable by fine and imprisonment. That includes price differences that "substantially" weaken competition unless they can be justified by lower selling costs associated with larger purchases. The law also prohibits advertising and promotional allowances unless they are offered to all retailers, large and small. Remember that this legislation applies to business-to-business transactions and not to business-to-consumer transactions.

The change in U.S. business from manufacturing to knowledge-based technology has created new regulatory challenges for federal agencies. In the early 2000s, Microsoft's competitive practices were the focus of an intense antitrust investigation by the Justice Department. The government charged that Microsoft hindered competition by refusing to sell its Windows operating system to computer manufacturers that refused to sell Windows-based computers exclusively. The case ended with a settlement between the Justice Department and Microsoft that expired in 2011. The Federal Trade Commission reached an agreement with Google a year later that avoided a long investigation after the company agreed to change some of its business practices.[23] Many antitrust advocates believe these cases broadened the definition of anticompetitive behavior and proved the government's resolve in enforcing antitrust laws. The FTC's decision involving Comcast's $45 billion offer for Time Warner's cable business will be an interesting case to follow.[24] It's safe to conclude antitrust issues will persist well into the future.

LAWS TO PROTECT CONSUMERS

consumerism
A social movement that seeks to increase and strengthen the rights and powers of buyers in relation to sellers.

Although Vibram denied any wrongdoing, it offered refunds to buyers of its FiveFinger shoes in order to settle a class action lawsuit. The lawsuit claimed the company misrepresented health research by advertising that its shoes (which are designed to mimic barefoot running) improved posture, strengthened muscles and reduced injuries. Both Reebok and Skechers had to pay $25 to $40 million to settle similar suits.

Consumerism is a social movement that seeks to increase and strengthen the rights and powers of buyers in relationship to sellers. It is the people's way of getting a fair share and equitable treatment in marketing exchanges. The Public Company Accounting Reform and Investor Protection Act (better known as the Sarbanes-Oxley Act) was passed to allay concerns about falsified financial statements from companies like Enron and WorldCom in the early 2000s. The financial crisis again fueled consumer anger, this time against the Treasury Department, Federal Reserve, and Securities and Exchange Commission (SEC) for their lack of oversight of the financial markets. The collapse of the real estate market, crisis in the banking industry, and failure of quasi-governmental mortgage agencies such as Fannie Mae and Freddie Mac led to passage of the Dodd-Frank Wall Street Reform and Consumer Protection Act. This legislation created the Consumer Financial Protection Bureau that provides government oversight involving consumers in areas such as online banking, home mortgage loans, and high-interest payday loans.[25] Figure A.4 lists other major consumer protection laws.

FIGURE A.4 CONSUMER PROTECTION LAWS

Fair Packaging and Labeling Act (1966)	Makes unfair or deceptive packaging or labeling of certain consumer commodities illegal.
Child Protection Act (1966)	Removes from sale potentially harmful toys and allows the FDA to pull dangerous products from the market.
Truth-in-Lending Act (1968)	Requires full disclosure of all finance charges on consumer credit agreements and in advertisements of credit plans.
Child Protection and Toy Safety Act (1969)	Protects children from toys and other products that contain thermal, electrical, or mechanical hazards.
Fair Credit Reporting Act (1970)	Requires that consumer credit reports contain only accurate, relevant, and recent information and are confidential unless a proper party requests them for an appropriate reason.
Consumer Product Safety Act (1972)	Created an independent agency to protect consumers from unreasonable risk of injury arising from consumer products and to set safety standards.
Magnuson-Moss Warranty–Federal Trade Commission Improvement Act (1975)	Provides for minimum disclosure standards for written consumer product warranties and allows the FTC to prescribe interpretive rules and policy statements regarding unfair or deceptive practices.
Alcohol Labeling Legislation (1988)	Provides for warning labels on liquor saying that women shouldn't drink when pregnant and that alcohol impairs a person's abilities.
Nutrition Labeling and Education Act (1990)	Requires truthful and uniform nutritional labeling on every food the FDA regulates.
Consumer Credit Reporting Reform Act (1997)	Increases responsibility of credit issuers for accurate credit data and requires creditors to verify that disputed data are accurate. Consumer notification is necessary before reinstating the data.
Children's Online Privacy Protection Act (2000)	Gives parents control over what information is collected online from their children under age 13; requires website operators to maintain the confidentiality, security, and integrity of the personal information collected from children.
Country of Origin Labeling Law (2009)	Requires that the product label on most food products sold in U.S. supermarkets gives the product's country of origin.
Credit Card Accountability, Responsibility, and Disclosure (CARD) Act (2009)	Designed to protect consumers from unfair credit card practices.

LO A–7   Explain the role of tax laws in generating income for the government and as a method of discouraging or encouraging certain behaviors among taxpayers.

TAX LAWS

taxes
How the government (federal, state, and local) raises money.

Mention taxes and most people frown. **Taxes** are the way federal, state, and local governments raise money. They affect almost every individual and business in the United States.

Governments primarily use taxes as a source of funding for their operations and programs. Taxes can also help discourage or encourage certain behaviors among taxpayers. If the government wishes to reduce consumer use of certain classes of products like cigarettes or liquor, it can pass *sin taxes* on them to raise their cost. Since the Great Recession, increasing sin taxes (i.e., taxes on things like liquor and cigarettes) has become a popular way for cash-starved states to raise revenue.[26] Colorado and Washington are the only two states that have legalized recreational marijuana. Both have levied taxes they believe will help their economies.[27] In fact, Colorado expects to bring in approximately $100 million a year in taxes on marijuana sales.[28] In other situations, the government may encourage businesses to hire new employees or purchase new equipment by offering a *tax credit,* an amount firms can deduct from their tax bill.

Taxes are levied from a variety of sources. Income taxes (personal and business), sales taxes, and property taxes are the major bases of tax revenue. The federal government receives its largest share of taxes from income. States and local communities make extensive use of sales taxes. School districts generally depend on property taxes.

The tax policies of states and cities are important considerations when businesses seek to locate operations. They also affect personal decisions such as retirement. As government revenues at all levels have decreased, new tax issues were debated. One such issue involved taxing Internet sales. Many states claimed they were losing billions in sales taxes by not collecting from Internet sales transactions. Large states like California, New York, and Illinois have already taken action on Internet sales taxes, as have many smaller states. New York, for example, passed a law that requires out-of-state online companies to collect sales taxes from New York shoppers. Other states are petitioning Congress to pass a law permitting them to collect sales taxes from e-commerce transactions. The European Union levies certain Internet taxes, so expect the U.S. debate to intensify. Figure A.5 highlights the primary types of taxes levied on individuals and businesses.

FIGURE A.5 TYPES OF TAXES

Types of Taxes	
Type	**Purpose**
Income taxes	Taxes paid on the income received by businesses and individuals. Income taxes are the largest source of tax income received by the federal government.
Property taxes	Taxes paid on real and personal property. *Real property* is real estate owned by individuals and businesses. *Personal property* is a broader category that includes any movable property such as tangible items (wedding rings, equipment, etc.) or intangible items (stocks, checks, mortgages, etc.). Taxes are based on their assessed value.
Sales taxes	Taxes paid on merchandise sold at the retail level.
Excise taxes	Taxes paid on selected items such as tobacco, alcoholic beverages, airline travel, gasoline, and firearms. These are often referred to as *sin taxes*. Income generated from the tax goes toward a specifically designated purpose. For example, gasoline taxes often help the federal government and state governments pay for highway construction or improvements.

LO A–8   Distinguish among the various types of bankruptcy as outlined by the Bankruptcy Code.

BANKRUPTCY LAWS

Bankruptcy is the legal process by which a person, business, or government entity, unable to meet financial obligations, is relieved of those debts by a court. Courts divide any of the debtor's assets among creditors, allowing them to recover at least part of their money and freeing the debtor to begin anew. The U.S. Constitution gives Congress the power to establish bankruptcy laws, and legislation has existed since the 1890s. Major amendments to the bankruptcy code include the Bankruptcy Amendments and Federal Judgeship Act of 1984, the Bankruptcy Reform Act of 1994, and the Bankruptcy Abuse Prevention and Consumer Protection Act of 2005.

The 1984 law allows a person who is bankrupt to keep part of the equity (ownership) in a house and car, and some other personal property. The 1994 Act amended more than 45 sections of the bankruptcy code and created reforms to speed up and simplify the process. The Bankruptcy Abuse Prevention and Consumer Protection Act of 2005 was passed to reduce the total number of bankruptcy filings and to eliminate the perceived ease of filing for bankruptcy. The legislation increased the cost of filing and made it difficult for people (especially those with high incomes) to escape overwhelming debt from credit cards, medical bills, student loans, or other loans not secured through a home or other asset. It also requires debtors to receive credit counseling.

Bankruptcies started growing in the late 1980s and have increased tremendously since. Many attribute the increase to a lessening of the stigma of bankruptcy, an increase in understanding of bankruptcy law and its protections, and increased advertising by bankruptcy attorneys. Some suggest that the ease with which certain consumers could get credit contributed to the number of filings by allowing people to readily overspend. The 2005 reform helped reduce the annual number of bankruptcy filings to 600,000 from an average of 1.5 million between 2001 and 2004. However, the financial crisis pushed the number of bankruptcies again to over a million. As the economy continues to come back slowly, bankruptcies reached 1.03 million in 2013.[29] Although high-profile bankruptcies of businesses—such as Blockbuster, Circuit City, Borders, and the City of Detroit—tend to dominate the news, over 90 percent of bankruptcy filings each year are by individuals.[30]

Bankruptcy can be either voluntary or involuntary. In **voluntary bankruptcy**, the debtor applies for bankruptcy; in **involuntary bankruptcy**, the creditors start legal action against the debtor. Most bankruptcies are voluntary, since creditors usually wait in hopes they will be paid all the money due them rather than settle for only part of it.

Bankruptcy procedures begin when a petition is filed with the court under one of the following sections of the Bankruptcy Code:

- Chapter 7—"straight bankruptcy" or liquidation (used by businesses and individuals).
- Chapter 11—reorganization (used almost exclusively by businesses).
- Chapter 13—repayment (used by individuals).

Chapter 7 is the most popular form of bankruptcy among individuals; it requires the sale of nonexempt assets. Under federal exemption statutes, a debtor may be able to retain (exempt) up to $22,975 of equity in a home; up to $3,675 of equity in an automobile; up to $12,250 in household furnishings,

bankruptcy
The legal process by which a person, business, or government entity, unable to meet financial obligations, is relieved of those obligations by a court that divides any assets among creditors, allowing creditors to get at least part of their money and freeing the debtor to begin anew.

voluntary bankruptcy
Legal procedures initiated by a debtor.

involuntary bankruptcy
Bankruptcy procedures filed by a debtor's creditors.

apparel, and musical instruments; and up to $1,550 in jewelry.[31] States can choose different exemption statutes. When the sale of assets is over, creditors, including the government if taxes are owed, divide the remaining cash as stipulated by law. First, creditors with secured claims receive the collateral for their claims or repossess the claimed asset (such as an automobile or home); then unsecured claims (backed by no asset) are paid in this order:

1. Costs of the bankruptcy case.
2. Any business costs incurred after bankruptcy was filed.
3. Wages, salaries, or commissions owed (limited to $2,000 per creditor).
4. Contributions to employee benefit plans.
5. Refunds to consumers who paid for products that weren't delivered (limited to $900 per claimant).
6. Federal and state taxes.

Figure A.6 outlines the steps used in liquidating assets under Chapter 7.

In Chapter 11 bankruptcy, a company sued by creditors continues to operate under court protection while it tries to work out a plan for paying off its debts. Under certain conditions it may sell assets, borrow money, and change company officers to strengthen its market position. A court-appointed trustee supervises the proceedings and protects the creditors' interests.

A company does not have to be insolvent to file for relief under Chapter 11. In theory, it is a way for sick companies to recover, designed to help both debtors and creditors find the best solution. In reality, however, less than one-third of Chapter 11 companies survive—usually those with lots of cash available.[32] The Bankruptcy Reform Act of 1994 provides a fast-track procedure for small businesses filing under Chapter 11. Individuals can also file under Chapter 11, but it's uncommon.

FIGURE A.6 HOW ASSETS ARE DIVIDED IN BANKRUPTCY

This figure shows that the creditor (the person owed money) selects the trustee (the person or organization that handles the sale of assets). Note that the process may be started by the debtor or the creditors.

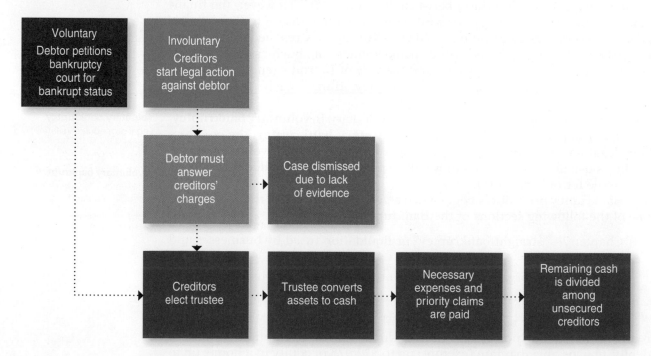

Chapter 13 permits individuals, including small-business owners, to pay back creditors over three to five years. Chapter 13 proceedings are less complicated and less expensive than Chapter 7 proceedings. The debtor files a proposed plan with the court for paying off debts. If the plan is approved, the debtor pays a court-appointed trustee in monthly installments as agreed on in the repayment plan. The trustee then pays each creditor.

LO A–9   Explain the role of deregulation as a tool to encourage competition.

DEREGULATION VERSUS REGULATION

Under Article I, Section 8, Clause 3 of the U.S. Constitution, the Commerce Clause gives Congress the right "to regulate commerce." The debate concerning the degree of regulation, however, has been a source of disagreement for many years. At one time, the United States had laws and regulations covering almost every aspect of business. Some felt there were too many laws and regulations, costing the public too much money (see Figure A.7). A movement toward deregulation took hold. **Deregulation** means that the government withdraws certain laws and regulations that seem to hinder competition. The most publicized examples of deregulation first occurred in the airline and telecommunications industries.

Consumers clearly benefited from the Airline Deregulation Act of 1978 that ended federal control of commercial airlines. Before passage of the act, the government restricted where airlines could land and fly. When the restrictions were lifted, airlines began competing for different routes and charging lower prices. The skies were also opened to new competitors, such as Southwest, to take advantage of new opportunities. Today some believe the airline industry could use more government intervention since passenger services have decreased, delays and flight cancellations have increased, direct flights have decreased, and charges, such as bag fees, have become common.

deregulation
Government withdrawal of certain laws and regulations that seem to hinder competition.

FIGURE A.7 HAMBURGER REGULATIONS

Does this amount of regulation seem just right, too little, or too much for you?

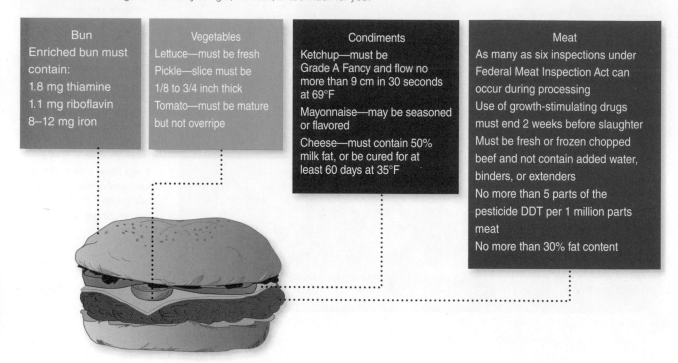

Bun
Enriched bun must contain:
1.8 mg thiamine
1.1 mg riboflavin
8–12 mg iron

Vegetables
Lettuce—must be fresh
Pickle—slice must be 1/8 to 3/4 inch thick
Tomato—must be mature but not overripe

Condiments
Ketchup—must be Grade A Fancy and flow no more than 9 cm in 30 seconds at 69°F
Mayonnaise—may be seasoned or flavored
Cheese—must contain 50% milk fat, or be cured for at least 60 days at 35°F

Meat
As many as six inspections under Federal Meat Inspection Act can occur during processing
Use of growth-stimulating drugs must end 2 weeks before slaughter
Must be fresh or frozen chopped beef and not contain added water, binders, or extenders
No more than 5 parts of the pesticide DDT per 1 million parts meat
No more than 30% fat content

Passage of the Telecommunications Act in 1996 brought similar deregulation to telecommunications and gave consumers a flood of options in local telephone service markets. There was also a significant increase in retail video competition. In the past, most homes received only four TV channels (the three major networks—NBC, CBS, and ABC—and public broadcasting). Today most households receive a dozen or more over-the-air stations and hundreds more on cable, satellite, and the Internet.

Deregulation efforts have also been attempted in the electric power industry. Twenty-four states have passed utility deregulation laws intended to increase competition and provide consumers with lower price options. California became the first state to deregulate electric power in the late 1990s and experienced significant problems, especially with large-scale blackouts (loss of power). Blackouts also occurred on the East Coast. Still, some utility deregulation programs have been somewhat successful.[33] Time will tell whether utility deregulation will survive and prosper across the United States.

The financial market crisis reopened the question of how much deregulation is too much. Deregulation in the banking and investments industries had changed the nature of financial and mortgage markets and created huge problems. For example, the Federal Reserve System's reluctance to toughen mortgage regulations and the government's insistence on providing more home loans to high-risk borrowers contributed to the collapse in the real estate market. The financial crisis that followed led to passage of the most sweeping regulation of financial markets since the Great Depression.

In 2010, the U.S. Congress passed the Patient Protection and Affordable Care Act (PPACA), also known as Obamacare. The new law was implemented in 2013, and introduced a comprehensive system of mandated health insurance for Americans not covered under an insurance plan. The law also provides for increased government regulation of the insurance industry. While the Patient Protection and Affordable Care Act is to be phased in over a four-year period, proposed adjustments to the legislation promise to keep the PPACA in the news.[34]

Most agree some regulation of business seems necessary to ensure fair and honest dealings with the public. Corporate scandals in the early 2000s and the financial crisis led consumers and investors to call for increased government regulation in the financial sector. While the final implementation of the health care law is still evolving, it's almost certain that businesses will need to deal with some form of health care regulation. With increasing global competition, U.S. business will need to work with government to create a competitive environment that is fair and open and accepts responsibilities to all stakeholders.

test prep

- What is the primary purpose of antitrust law?
- Describe the different bankruptcy provisions under Chapters 7, 11, and 13.
- What is deregulation? Give examples of successful and unsuccessful deregulation.

Use LearnSmart to help retain what you have learned. Access your instructor's Connect course to check out LearnSmart, or go to learnsmartadvantage.com for help.

LEARNSMART

summary

Access your instructor's Connect course to check out LearnSmart or go to learnsmartadvantage.com for help.

connect

LO A–1   Define *business law*, distinguish between statutory and common law, and explain the role of administrative agencies.

- **What is the difference between statutory law and common law?**
  Statutory law includes state and federal constitutions, legislative enactments, treaties of the federal government, and ordinances—in short, written law. Common law is the body of unwritten law that comes from decisions handed down by judges.

- **What are administrative agencies?**
  Administrative agencies are federal or state institutions and other government organizations created by Congress or state legislatures with power to create rules and regulations within their area of authority.

LO A–2   Define *tort law* and explain the role of product liability in tort law.

- **What is an intentional tort?**
  An intentional tort is a willful act that results in injury.

- **What is negligence?**
  Negligence, in tort law, is behavior that causes *unintentional* harm or injury. Findings of negligence can lead to huge judgments against businesses.

LO A–3   Identify the purposes and conditions of patents, copyrights, and trademarks.

- **What are patents and copyrights?**
  A patent is a document that gives inventors exclusive rights to their inventions for 20 years from the date they file the patent applications. A copyright protects a creator's rights to materials such as books, articles, photos, paintings, and cartoons.

- **What is a trademark?**
A trademark is a legally protected name, symbol, or design (or combination of these) that identifies the goods or services of one seller and distinguishes them from those of competitors.

LO A–4   Describe warranties and negotiable instruments as covered in the Uniform Commercial Code.

- **What does Article 2 of the UCC cover?**
Article 2 contains laws regarding warranties. Express warranties are guarantees made by the seller, whereas implied warranties are guarantees imposed on the seller by law.

- **What does Article 3 of the UCC cover?**
Article 3 covers negotiable instruments such as checks. A negotiable instrument must (1) be written and signed by the maker or drawer, (2) be made payable on demand or at a certain time, (3) be made payable to the bearer (the person holding the instrument) or to specific order, and (4) contain an unconditional promise to pay a specified amount of money.

LO A–5   List and describe the conditions necessary to make a legally enforceable contract, and describe the possible consequences if such a contract is violated.

- **What makes a contract enforceable under the law?**
An enforceable contract must meet six conditions: (1) an offer must be made, (2) the offer must be voluntarily accepted, (3) both parties must give consideration, (4) both parties must be competent, (5) the contract must be legal, and (6) the contract must be in proper form.

- **What are the possible consequences if a contract is violated?**
If a contract is violated, one of the following may be required: (1) specific performance, (2) payment of damages, or (3) discharge of obligation.

LO A–6   Summarize several laws that regulate competition and protect consumers in the United States.

- **What does the Sherman Act cover?**
The Sherman Act forbids contracts, combinations, or conspiracies in restraint of trade and actual monopolies or attempts to monopolize any part of trade or commerce.

- **What does the Clayton Act add?**
The Clayton Act prohibits exclusive dealing, tying contracts, interlocking directorates, and buying large amounts of stock in competing corporations.

- **Which act regulates false and deceptive advertising?**
The Federal Trade Commission Act prohibits unfair methods of competition in commerce, including deceptive advertising.

- **Which act prohibits price discrimination and demands proportional promotional allowances?**
The Robinson-Patman Act applies to both sellers and buyers who knowingly induce or receive an unlawful discrimination in price.

LO A–7   Explain the role of tax laws in generating income for the government and as a method of discouraging or encouraging certain behaviors among taxpayers.

- **How does the government use taxes to encourage or discourage certain behavior among taxpayers?**

If the government wishes to change citizens' behavior, it can reduce their use of certain classes of products (cigarettes, liquor) by passing *sin taxes* to raise their cost. In other situations, the government may offer tax credits to encourage businesses to hire new employees or purchase new equipment.

LO A–8 Distinguish among the various types of bankruptcy as outlined by the Bankruptcy Code.

- **What are the bankruptcy laws?**
  Chapter 7 calls for straight bankruptcy, in which all assets are divided among creditors after exemptions. Chapter 11 allows a firm to reorganize and continue operation after paying only a limited portion of its debts. Chapter 13 allows individuals to pay their creditors over an extended period of time.

LO A–9 Explain the role of deregulation as a tool to encourage competition.

- **What are a few of the most publicized examples of deregulation?**
  Perhaps the most publicized examples of deregulation have been those in the airline and telecommunications industries. Some states have attempted deregulation of utilities.

---

key terms

administrative agencies 3	damages 10	patent 6
bankruptcy 15	deregulation 17	precedent 3
breach of contract 10	express warranties 8	product liability 5
business law 2	implied warranties 8	statutory law 3
common law 3	involuntary	strict product liability 5
consideration 9	bankruptcy 15	taxes 14
consumerism 12	judiciary 2	tort 4
contract 9	negligence 4	Uniform Commercial
contract law 9	negotiable	Code (UCC) 8
copyright 7	instruments 8	voluntary bankruptcy 15

critical thinking

1. Supporters of tort reform say it's unfair that plaintiffs (the parties bringing lawsuits) don't have to pay damages to the defendants (the parties subject to the lawsuits) if they lose the case. Should plaintiffs pay damages if they lose a case? Why or why not?

2. Go to the website of the U.S. Patent and Trademark Office (www.uspto. gov) and view the information about obtaining a patent. See whether you can estimate how long the process will take and what your cost will be.

3. Call your local real estate board or visit a realtor and obtain a copy of a real estate contract. Read it carefully to see how it meets the six requirements stated in the chapter for a contract to be legal and binding.

4. Twenty-four states have implemented utility deregulation. Has your state or a neighboring state implemented utility deregulation? How does it seem to be working?

developing **workplace skills**

Key: • **Team**   ★ **Analytic**   ▲ **Communication**   ▣ **Technology**

★ ▲ 1. Do you think the laws that promote fair and competitive practices are effective in the United States? Why or why not? Provide evidence for your view.

★ 2. Increasing numbers of individuals file for bankruptcy each year. Do you think the U.S. Congress was correct in toughening the bankruptcy laws?

• ★ ▲ 3. Divide the class into teams to debate the question: Should government action to deal with deceptive business practices increase, or should we count on business to regulate itself to prevent deceptive practices? Which solution is better for society and business in the long run?

• ★ ▲ 4. Go online to find the answers to the following questions. Does your state have an income tax? What percentage of your income do you have to pay in state income tax? What about property taxes and sales taxes? How do these taxes in your area compare to those in three other states and communities of your choice?

• ★ ▲ 5. In 2005, Congress passed bankruptcy reform legislation that makes it more difficult for individuals to file for bankruptcy under Chapter 7 and limits certain debts that cannot now be eliminated. Research the law online and offer reasons why you support or oppose it. You might want to go to www.bankruptcyaction.com for help.

taking it to the **net**

PURPOSE

You and several of your musician friends decide to start a band you want to call the Individual Mandates. You want to protect the band name and the new songs you've written so that other groups can't use them. Go to the U.S. Patent and Trademark Office's website (www.uspto.gov) to find out how to get the protection you seek.

EXERCISE

1. Do you need to apply for patents, copyrights, or trademarks, or some combination of these to protect your band name and songs?

2. When can you use the trademark symbols™ and ®?

3. How can you secure a copyright for your songs?

4. What are the advantages of registering copyrights?

notes

1. Charles W. Calomiris and Allen H. Meltzer, "How Dodd-Frank Doubles Down on 'Too Big to Fail,'" *The Wall Street Journal,* February 12, 2014.
2. American Bar Association Market Research Department, www.americanbar.org, accessed May 2014.
3. Peter Loftus, "Merck to Settle Contraceptive Product Liability Lawsuits," *The Wall Street Journal,* February 7, 2014.
4. Henry C. Jackson, "House Votes to Increase Asbestos Claim Disclosure," *Bloomberg Businessweek,* November 13, 2013; and "W.R. Grace Emerges from Bankruptcy," *Bloomberg Businessweek,* February 3, 2014.

5. Mesothelioma Center, www.asbestos.com, accessed May 2014.

6. James R. Hagerty and Dionne Searcy, "Long Time Seen for Lead-Paint Ruling," *The Wall Street Journal,* December 17, 2013; and Daniel Fisher, "Slumlords Are the Big Winners in California Judge's $1 Billion Lead-Paint Ruling," *Forbes,* December 17, 2013.

7. Joann Muller, "Toyota Halts Sales of Popular Models to Fix Seat Heaters," *Forbes,* January 30, 2014; and Ben Klayman, "Toyota Tells U.S. Agency Seat Issue Could Lead to Recall," *Chicago Tribune,* January 30, 2014.

8. Shaya Tayefe Mohajir, "Toyota Settlement: Orange County to Receive $16 Million over Acceleration, Braking Issues," *Huffington Post,* April 5, 2013; Jerry Hirsch, "NHTSA Opens Probe into Brake Failures of Toyota Camry Hybrid Sedan," *Los Angeles Times,* January 27, 2014; and Chris Woodward and Kevin Johnson, "Toyota to Pay $1.2 Billion to Settle Criminal Probe," *USA Today,* March 20, 2014.

9. Jeff Plungis, "GM Investigated over Ignition Recall Linked to 13 Deaths," *Bloomberg Businessweek,* February 27, 2014.

10. Gary Strauss and Rebecca Castagna, "NYC Ban on Large Sugary Drinks Fizzles Again," *USA Today,* July 30, 2013.

11. Dimitra Kessenides, "The Case against Class Actions, Sort Of," *Bloomberg Businessweek,* January 19, 2014.

12. Christopher Hann, "Protect Your Brilliant Idea," *Entrepreneur,* June 2013; and United States Patent and Trademark Office, www.USPTO.gov, accessed May 2014.

13. Larry Gordon, "Surgeon and Inventor Gives $50 Million for USC Building," *Los Angeles Times,* January 13, 2014.

14. Laura Braverman, "Patent Law Changes Alter Entrepreneurs' Planning," *USA Today,* September 19, 2013; "Can You Keep a Secret?" *The Economist,* March 16, 2013; and Issie Lapowsky, "Patents: The Race Now Goes to the Swiftest," *Inc.,* June 2013.

15. Greg Stohr and Susan Decker, "The Supreme Court Takes on Patent Trolls," *Bloomberg Businessweek,* February 13, 2014.

16. Jeremy Quittner, "Is This the Beginning of the End for Patent Trolls? Let's Hope So," *Inc.,* January 2014; and Bill McClellan, "A Patent Attorney Steals the Spotlight," *St. Louis Post Dispatch,* May 16, 2014.

17. Susan Decker, "Google's Giant $1 Patent Victory," *Bloomberg Businessweek,* February 6, 2014.

18. Rachel Abrams, "Market for Patents Was Softer in 2013, Firms Say," *The New York Times,* February 4, 2014.

19. Rachel Rothman, "Worth It or Not: Extended Warranties," *Good Housekeeping,* February 1, 2014.

20. Eric Markowitz, "When Kickstarter Investors Want Their Money Back," *Inc.,* January 2013.

21. Federal Trade Commission, www.ftc.gov/about-ftc/bureaus-offices, accessed May 2014.

22. Ben Metzabaugh, "First U.S. Airways Plane Flies with the New American Livery," *USA Today,* January 30, 2014; and Terry Maxon, "American Airlines, U.S. Airways Tie Their Route Networks Together," *Dallas Morning News,* February 5, 2014.

23. Sharon Gaudin, "Antitrust Deal Leaves Google Unscathed," *Computerworld,* February 6, 2014.

24. Cecilia Kang, "Comcast, Time Warner Cable Agree to Merge in $45 Billion Deal," *The Washington Post,* February 12, 2014.

25. "Caveat Vendor: A New Regulator Takes an Expansive View of Its Remit," *The Economist,* February 1, 2014.

26. Jay Miller, "Will Support Be on Display for Another Sin Tax—One Supporting Arts in 2015?" *Crain's Cleveland Business,* February 18, 2014.

27. B. Shane Scott, "Why Colorado and Washington Were Wise to Legalize Pot," *Entrepreneur,* January 20, 2014; and Brian Bremner and Vincent Del Guidice, "Legal Weed's Strange Economics in Colorado," *Bloomberg Businessweek,* January 9, 2014.

28. Jolie Lee, "Colorado Makes $3.5 in Pot Revenue in January," *USA Today,* March 11, 2014.

29. Tom Hals, "U.S. Business Bankruptcies Dropped by 24 Percent in 2013," *Reuters,* January 6, 2014.

30. Matt Helms and Nathan Bomey, "Detroit's Bankruptcy Blueprint: Here's What to Expect," *USA Today,* February 18, 2014.

31. Nolo, www.nolo.com, accessed May 2014.

32. Andy McDonald, "8 Companies You Didn't Know Went Bankrupt," *Huffington Post,* July 11, 2013.

33. William Pentland, "After Decades of Doubt, Deregulation Delivers Lower Electricity Prices," *Forbes,* October 13, 2013.

34. "At the Obamacare Improv," *The Wall Street Journal,* February 14, 2014; Jennifer Rubin, "Obamacare Delay, Instant Ridicule," *The Washington Post,* February 11, 2014; and Noam M. Levey, "U.S. to Further Delay Employer Care Mandate," *Los Angeles Times,* February 10, 2014.

photo credits

B

Using Technology to Manage Information

Learning Objectives

AFTER YOU HAVE READ AND STUDIED THIS BONUS CHAPTER, YOU SHOULD BE ABLE TO

B-1 Outline the changing role of business technology.

B-2 List the types of business information, identify the characteristics of useful information, and discuss how data are stored and analyzed.

B-3 Compare the scope of the Internet, intranets, extranets, and virtual private networks and explain how broadband technology enabled the evolution to Web 2.0 and 3.0.

B-4 Explain virtual networking and discuss the benefits and drawbacks for cloud computing.

B-5 Evaluate the human resource, security, privacy, and stability issues affected by information technology.

Getting to know **Jack Dorsey**

Technology innovators strive to change the ways we communicate and manage information through hardware, software, and the Internet. Today's tech experts often move from company to company, hoping that one of their new ventures turns into "the next big thing."

Programmer and entrepreneur Jack Dorsey discovered a way to make "the next big thing"—twice. In 2006 he co-founded the microblogging site Twitter. He also launched Square, a service that allows businesses to accept debit and credit card payments through mobile devices. These revolutionary enterprises made Dorsey a billionaire by the time he turned 35.

Before he took the tech world by storm, Dorsey was just a data-obsessed kid from St. Louis, Missouri. Using his father's CB radio and a police scanner, he would spend hours tracking the city's police and emergency personnel. Dorsey's dad bought him a computer so he could record and analyze the movements further. After learning a coding language, Dorsey constructed a program that graphically showed the movements of all the vehicles. Dorsey devoted his full attention to the hypnotizing program. "It's a rush," said Dorsey. "You forget to sleep. You forget to eat. I just felt so great, because, Oh, I can actually build something that enables me to see the city." But Dorsey knew that an important element was missing from the program: people. "I could see ambulances, I could see black cars, but I was missing the individuals," said Dorsey.

Transferring the real world into a virtual landscape became Dorsey's ultimate goal. He explored the idea further as a computer science and math student at the Missouri University of Science and Technology. Meanwhile, the car-tracking software he created as a kid got the attention of a bike-messenger start-up in New York. Dorsey left the Midwest in his junior year to join the company while going to New York University. He eventually moved to San Francisco to start his own web-based taxi dispatching service, but the dot-com bust of the late-1990s ended that dream.

Dorsey spent the next few years coding at various companies. He also trained as a massage therapist,

developed a secure ticketing system for the tourist ferry to Alcatraz Island, and even briefly studied fashion design. No matter what he did, though, Dorsey couldn't stop thinking about his people-free mapping program. By the mid-2000s, his obsession with SMS text messaging and the growing influence of social media had finally given him a solution to his problem. One day when he was sitting with two friends, Dorsey asked, "What if we used SMS to report what you're doing, and also to receive news of what everyone else is doing?" The trio soon set to work on a messaging service that could keep people connected through small bursts of information. They named the service Twitter after the way a cell phone vibrates when receiving a message. At first many people wondered why they would want to limit their communication to just 140 characters. As the years went by, however, hundreds of millions were drawn to Twitter's ability to plug into an international conversation with other users, companies, and celebrities.

Despite the social network's runaway success, Dorsey wasn't finished disrupting things. His mobile-payment company Square recently struck a deal with Starbucks, which will soon use the service in its more than 7,000 American stores. In fact, as developers like Jack Dorsey and tech companies continue to change the face of the digital landscape, it's possible that even the most entrenched technologies could become obsolete in a few years. In this bonus chapter you'll learn about how this ever-changing tech world affects business.

Sources: D. T. Max, "Two-Hit Wonder," *The New Yorker,* October 21, 2013; Seth Stevenson, "Simplicity and Order For All," *The Wall Street Journal,* October 26, 2012; Jake Tapper and Sherisse Pham, "Jack Dorsey on His Desire to Be Mayor of New York City, Steve Jobs, and Being a Bachelor," *CNN,* March 21, 2013; Tim Bradshaw, "Jack Dorsey: Twitter Star Seeking Investors," *Financial Times,* October 4, 2013.

Jack Dorsey

- Co-founder of Twitter
- Founder of Square
- Programmer, pioneer

www.twitter.com

@jack

name that **company**

This company used social media to build its business. Its customers design new products, name them, and enter them in the company's database. Customers may even make YouTube commercials that are featured on the company's video wall. If other customers buy the new product, the creator gets a small store credit. Name that company. (Find the answer in the chapter.)

LO B–1 Outline the changing role of business technology.

THE ROLE OF INFORMATION TECHNOLOGY

The importance of business knowledge is nothing new—what is newer is the recognition of the need to manage it like any other asset. To manage knowledge, a company needs to share information efficiently throughout the organization and to implement systems for creating new knowledge. This need is constantly leading to new technologies that support the exchange of information among staff, suppliers, and customers. Studies have shown that data-driven decision making (i.e., collecting data, analyzing it, and using it to make crucial decisions, like whether to create a new product or service) lifts productivity 5 percent higher than decision making based on experience and intuition.[1]

Evolution from Data Processing to Business Intelligence

To understand technology today, it is helpful to review how we got here.

data processing (DP)
Name for business technology in the 1970s; included technology that supported an existing business and was primarily used to improve the flow of financial information.

- In the 1970s, business technology was known as **data processing (DP)**. (Although many people use the words *data* and *information* interchangeably, they mean different things. *Data* are raw, unanalyzed, and unorganized facts and figures. *Information* is processed and organized data that managers can use for decision making.) The primary purpose of data processing was to improve the flow of financial information. Data processing employees were support staff who rarely came in contact with customers.

information systems (IS)
Technology that helps companies do business; includes such tools as automated teller machines (ATMs) and voice mail.

- In the 1980s, business technology became known as **information systems (IS)** when it moved out of the back room and into the center of the business. Its role changed from *supporting* the business to *doing* business. Customers began to interact with a wide array of technological tools, from automated teller machines (ATMs) to voice mail. As business increased its use of information systems, it became more dependent on them.

- Until the late 1980s, business technology was just an addition to the existing way of doing business. Keeping up-to-date was a matter of using new technology on old methods. But things started to change when businesses applied new technology to new methods. Business technology then became known as **information technology (IT)**, and its role became to *change* business by storing, retrieving, and sending information efficiently.

information technology (IT)
Technology used to store, retrieve, and send information efficiently.

- In the 1990s, the introduction of the World Wide Web changed the way that people interacted with one another and information. Online services such as Google offered a new way of accessing information. In addition, bluetooth technology created conveniences by providing wireless communication systems to replace cables that typically connected devices, thus freeing people to access information wherever they wanted.

- In the 2000s, as this technology became more sophisticated, it became better known as **business intelligence (BI) or analytics**. BI refers to a variety of software applications used to analyze an organization's raw data and derive useful insights from it. BI activities include data mining (which we discuss later in this chapter), online analytical processes, querying, and reporting.[2] Knowledge is information charged with enough intelligence to make it relevant and useful. Knowledge technology adds a layer of intelligence to filter appropriate information and deliver it when it is needed.

BI changes the traditional flow of information. Instead of an individual going to the database, the database comes to the individual. Managers can put a new employee at a workstation using BI training software and let the system take over everything from laying out a checklist of the tasks required on a shift to providing answers and insights that once would have taken up a supervisor's time.

BI helps businesspeople focus on what's important: deciding how to react to problems and opportunities. For example, imagine you're a sales rep who just closed a big deal. While you celebrate your success, the finance department is upset because your customer never pays on time, which costs the company a lot of money. BI could provide you that insight so that you could negotiate different payment terms with the customer, thus connecting sales activity to financial requirements in a seamless process.

Technology changes react with one another to create more change. Maintaining the flexibility to successfully integrate these changes is crucial to business survival. Packard Bell and Kodak once dominated their industries, but failed to compete effectively and lost market share. In the case of Kodak, even though it invented the first digital camera, the company was concerned that digital photography would eat into its traditional film business. So Kodak decided to continue to focus on film rather than digital cameras, a decision that eventually led to the company's bankruptcy.[3] Both Packard Bell and Kodak had size and money, but not flexibility.

Knowledge sharing is at the heart of keeping pace with change. Of course, it can be difficult to predict which new technologies will be successful. For a fun look at the worst tech predictions of all time, see Figure B.1.

Obviously, the role of the IT staff has changed as technology itself has improved and evolved. The chief information officer (CIO) has moved out of the back room and into the boardroom, and now spends less time worrying about keeping systems running and more time finding ways to boost business by applying technology to purchasing decisions, operational strategy, and marketing and sales. Today the role of the CIO is to help the business use technology to communicate better with others, while offering better service and lower costs.[4]

How Information Technology Changes Business

Time and place have always been at the center of business. Customers once had to go to the business during certain hours to satisfy their needs. For example, people went to the store to buy clothes. They went to the bank to arrange for a loan. Businesses decided when and where they did business with them. Today, IT allows businesses to deliver goods and services whenever and wherever the customer wants them. You can order books and clothes, arrange a home mortgage loan, and buy music or a car online, anytime you choose.

The Fire Phone, Amazon's first entry into the smartphone market, offers a unique feature called Firefly. Imagine noticing your friend sporting a cool new headset. With just a click of a button, Firefly will identify the headset and show you all the purchasing info you need—including reviews, of course. Another click and it's on the way to your home—all before you've had a chance to reconsider whether you really need that headset. Can you see how Firefly helps buyers buy?

business intelligence (BI) or analytics
The use of data analytic tools to analyze an organization's raw data and derive useful insights from it.

FIGURE B.1 THE WORST TECH PREDICTIONS OF ALL TIME
You can't be right all the time. Here are a few quotes from technology leaders who got it wrong—*way* wrong.

FIGURE B.1 THE WORST TECH PREDICTIONS OF ALL TIME
You can't be right all the time. Here are a few quotes from technology leaders who got it wrong—*way* wrong.

"Television won't be able to hold onto any market it captures after the first six months. People will soon get tired of staring at a plywood box every night."
—Darryl Zanuck, Executive at 20th Century Fox, 1946

"I predict the Internet will soon go spectacularly supernova and in 1996 catastrophically collapse."
—Robert Metcalfe, founder of 3Com, 1995

"Inventions have long since reached their limit, and I see no hope for further developments."
—Roman engineer Julius Sextus Frontinus, 10 A.D.

"This 'telephone' has too many shortcomings to be seriously considered as a means of communication."
— Western Union internal memo, 1876

"I think there is a world market for maybe five computers."
—Thomas Watson, president of IBM, 1943

"Do not bother to sell your gas shares. The electric light has no future."
—Professor John Henry Pepper, scientist, 1870s

"Who the hell wants to hear actors talk?"
—H. M. Warner, Warner Brothers, 1927

"There is no reason anyone would want a computer in their home."
—Ken Olsen, founder of Digital Equipment Corporation, 1977

"Remote shopping, while entirely feasible, will flop."
—*Time*, 1966

Sources: David Zeiler, "The 10 Worst Tech Predictions of All Time," *Money Morning*, www.moneymorning.com, accessed June 2014; and Mark Spoonauer, "10 Worst Tech Predictions of All Time," *Labtop*, August 7, 2013.

Consider how IT has changed the entertainment industry. Forty-five years ago, you had to go to a movie theater if you wanted to see a movie. Forty years ago, you could wait for it to be on television. Thirty years ago, you could wait for it to be on cable television. Twenty-five years ago, you could go to a video store and rent it. Now you can order video on demand by satellite, cable, or WiFi or download it to watch on your TV, computer, smartphone, iPad, or other device whenever and wherever you wish.

As IT broke time and location barriers, it created new organizations and services that are independent of location. For example, NASDAQ is an electronic stock exchange without trading floors where buyers and sellers make trades by computer. Smartphones, laptops, and tablets allow you access to people and information as if you were in the office. That independence brings work to people instead of people to work.

The way people do business drastically changes when companies increase their technological capabilities. Electronic communications can provide substantial time savings. E-mail and texting have put an end to tedious games of telephone tag and are far faster than paper-based correspondence. Internet and intranet communications using shared documents and other methods allow contributors to work on a common document without time-consuming meetings. See Figure B.2 for other examples of how information technology is changing business.

FIGURE B.2 HOW INFORMATION TECHNOLOGY IS CHANGING BUSINESS
This table shows a few ways that information technology is changing businesses, their employees, suppliers, and customers.

Organization

Technology is breaking down corporate barriers, allowing functional departments or product groups (including factory workers) to share critical information instantly.

Operations

Technology shrinks cycle times, reduces defects, and cuts waste. Service companies use technology to streamline ordering and communication with suppliers and customers.

Staffing

Technology eliminates layers of management and cuts the number of employees. Companies use computers and telecommunication equipment to create "virtual offices" with employees in various locations.

New products

Information technology cuts development cycles by feeding customer and marketing comments to product development teams quickly so that they can revive products and target specific customers.

Customer relations

Customer service representatives can solve customers' problems instantly by using company-wide databases to complete tasks from changing addresses to adjusting bills. Information gathered from customer service interactions can further strengthen customer relationships.

New markets

Since it is no longer necessary for customers to walk down the street to get to stores, online businesses can attract customers to whom they wouldn't otherwise have access.

test prep

- How has the role of information technology changed since the days when it was known as data processing?
- How has information technology changed the way we do business?

LO B–2   List the types of business information, identify the characteristics of useful information, and discuss how data are stored and analyzed.

TYPES OF INFORMATION

Today, information flows into and through an organization from many different directions. The types of information available to businesses today include:

- *Business process information.* This includes all transaction data gathered at the point of sale as well as information gained through operations like enterprise resource planning, supply chain management, and customer relationship management systems.
- *Physical-world observations.* These result from the use of radio frequency identification (RFID) devices, miniature cameras, wireless access, global positioning systems, and sensor technology—all of which have to do with where people or items are located and what they are doing.

Advances in retinal scanning technology allow companies like Kimberly Clark to track how many seconds a person spends looking at different packaging designs for paper towels. Retinal scanning simulations aid marketers in determining what will attract customers the most. What other ways can you think of for businesses to make use of biometric technology?

Computer chips cost pennies apiece and can be found in a wide range of products, including credit cards, printer ink cartridges, baseballs, tire valves, running shoes, vacuum cleaners, and even beer mugs. That's right—Mitsubishi has produced a "smart" beer mug that senses when it is time for a refill and sends a signal to the bartender.

- *Biological data.* Forms of identification include improved fingerprinting technology and biometric devices that scan retinas, recognize faces and voices, and analyze DNA. Although such information usually serves security purposes, it can also be used to customize products and services by tracking shoppers' eyes in stores.[5]

- *Public data.* Free and accessible, public data include the electronic traces we leave when posting to the Internet, sending e-mail, and using instant messaging. More and more, public data are being stored, shared, or sold.

- *Data that indicate personal preferences or intentions.* Online shoppers leave a trail of information that can reveal personal likes and dislikes.

The volume and complexity of all these data and information are staggering. Computing systems can search through text, numbers, audio, and video—and identify, categorize, and refine relevant opinions on any topic imaginable.

Managing Information

Even before the use of computers, managers had to sift through mountains of information to find what they needed to help them make decisions. Today, businesspeople are faced with *infoglut,* an overabundance of data. Have you seen the classic episode of TV's *I Love Lucy* with Lucy and Ethel working in a factory on the candy line? Everything was going OK until the candy started coming too fast for them. Then mayhem broke loose. That's what's happening to many managers today, with information instead of candy. Too much information can confuse issues rather than clarify them.

How can managers keep from getting buried in the infoglut? Stepping back to gain perspective is the key. It is important to identify the four or five key goals you wish to reach, and eliminate information not related to them. That can cut the information flow by half. As we were gathering information for this chapter, we collected hundreds of print journal articles and found thousands more online. Feeling the pressure of information overload, we identified the objectives we wanted the chapter to help you accomplish and eliminated all the articles that didn't address those objectives. As we further refined our objectives, the huge file gradually dropped to a manageable size.

Obviously, not all the information that ends up on your desk will be useful. The usefulness of management information depends on four characteristics:

1. *Quality.* Quality means that the information is accurate and reliable. When the clerk at a fast-food restaurant enters your order into the cash register, it may be automatically fed to a computer that calculates the day's sales and profits as soon as the store closes. The sales and expense data must be accurate, or the rest of the calculations will be wrong. Quality can be a real problem when a large number of calculations are based on questionable sales forecasts rather than actual sales.

2. *Completeness.* There must be enough information to allow you to make a decision, but not so much as to confuse the issue. Today, as we have noted, the problem is often too much information rather than too little.

3. *Timeliness.* Information must reach managers quickly. E-mail and texting can let marketing, engineering, and production know about a problem with a product the same day the salesperson hears about it, so customer complaints can be handled instantly if possible, or certainly within a day. Product changes can be made on the spot using computer-integrated manufacturing, as discussed in Chapter 9.

4. *Relevance.* Different managers have different information needs. Since information systems often provide too much data, managers must learn which questions to ask to get the answers they seek.

Remember, though, that you can never read everything available. Set objectives for yourself, and do the best you can.

Organizing E-Mail and Electronic Files

Even though many businesspeople communicate through real-time technology, such as instant messaging, videoconferencing, or Internet relay chats, e-mail is still a dominant method of communication, particularly when sending attached electronic files. Today's information management tools make it easier than ever for individuals and small businesses to organize information. Here are some tips for sorting e-mail and electronic files so that you can find what you need easily and quickly:[6]

1. *Use your e-mail program's organizing tools.* Most e-mail programs allow you to create folders for specific topics, projects, or clients. As you work through your in-box, move the messages you want to keep to the appropriate folders. Archive your old e-mail monthly. Figure B.3 offers suggestions for ways to reduce the number of distractions caused by sending and receiving e-mail.

2. *Use consistent file names.* Save related materials across multiple software programs under the same name, and file them together. Perhaps you've been assigned to work with a team of other students to create a sample business plan for this course. You could save all files (whether e-mail, spreadsheets, PowerPoint, or Word documents) with a file name that begins "Business Plan Project" and store them in one folder in "My Documents."

- Turn off all electronic alerts.
- Limit the number of times you check e-mail to no more than a few times a day.
- Delete garbage messages (i.e., spam, junk mail, etc.) first.
- Reply immediately only to urgent alerts and messages that take less than 2 minutes to write a response and save the rest for later.
- Set a specific time (i.e., at the end of the workday) to respond to remaining messages.
- Limit use of the reply-all button.
- Use an automatic out-of-office message such as "I will be offline until after 5 p.m. Please call me if you have an urgent message." This will give you time to focus on work while letting others know not to expect a reply soon.
- Don't limit your communication to e-mail or texting. Communicating by phone or in person can sometimes save time and build relationships.

Sources: Joanna Stern, "Cellphone Users Check Phones 150x/Day and Other Internet Fun Facts," *ABC News*, www.abcnews.com, May 29, 2013; "Get More Done by Only Checking Email Twice a Day," *Time Management Ninja*, www.timemanagementninja.com, accessed June 2014; and Bob Sullivan and Hugh Thomas, "Brain Interrupted," *The New York Times*, May 3, 2013.

FIGURE B.3 TAMING ELECTRONIC COMMUNICATION INTERRUPTIONS
Typical office workers are interrupted every 11 minutes, and it takes them about 25 minutes to return to the original task. Studies show that people don't really multitask, but rather toggle rapidly between tasks, and there are costs involved in doing so. So much interruption undermines workers' attention spans, increases stress, and decreases job satisfaction and creativity. Here are a few hints to reduce the number of electronic distractions.

3. *Use online backup services.* Backup, backup, backup—we've all heard how important it is to back up our files, but we often forget to follow through. Don't risk an avoidable loss. As the cost of online storage continues to drop, backing up files to online services such as Dropbox can be a very cost-effective way to protect your files.

4. *Use desktop search software.* Finding files can be easier with a desktop search software program like Google Desktop or Windows Live Search. Google Desktop has an enterprise version for midsize companies. Larger companies also have access to Google but may need to pay for additional tech support.

Big Data and Data Analytics

Chances are that some program is keeping track of every click you make online, every movement you make as you shop in stores, every restaurant you go to for lunch—even what you eat. Collecting such data isn't enough; you have to derive meaning from it. And when you collect more data, you need more storage. How do businesses store and organize a data glut so that it eventually becomes useful information? The answer for many companies is data analytics. **Data analytics** is the process of collecting, organizing, storing, and analyzing large sets of data ("big data") in order to identify patterns and other information that is most useful to the business now and for making future decisions.[7]

One part of data analytics is *data mining,* a technique for looking for hidden patterns and previously unknown relationships among the data. The legendary example is a study by a retail chain that revealed a spike in beer sales coinciding with a spike in diaper sales on weekdays between 5:00 and 7:00 p.m. The conclusion that thirsty dads pick up diapers on the way home from work prompted store managers to consider moving the diapers next to the beer to boost sales. The retailer never did pair the Heineken with the Huggies, but the story led to a new science of tracking what's selling where and who's buying it. For example, because data mining showed Walmart that U.S. consumers like to buy Pop-Tarts (particularly strawberry) just before a hurricane hits, the company makes sure they're available in the right place at the right time.

The lesson here is that companies can gain a competitive advantage with high-quality data that support management decisions. Companies can better target their goods and service, attract new customers, and adjust prices. Figure B.4 offers a few examples of sectors that benefit from big data and data analytics.

Of course, when so much data and such powerful analytic tools are used by so many companies, mistakes are bound to happen. For example, an out-of-print book was recently listed on Amazon as having 17 copies available: 15 used from $35.54 and two new from $23,698,655.93 (plus $3.99 shipping). The astronomical price was the result of two sellers' automated programs that each raised the book price based on the other's price. While the only thing these two sellers lost in this automated bidding war was a book sale, another Amazon seller, a T-shirt company called Solid Gold Bomb, didn't fare so well.

Solid Gold Bomb uses a program that takes libraries of words that are used in popular phrases, such as "Keep Calm and Carry On," and automatically mixes them with other popular words. It then designs a T-shirt emblazoned with the new phrase (it doesn't actually print the shirt until someone orders it) and automatically posts it on Amazon. You can imagine the public relations nightmare when the shirt "Keep Calm and Rape a Lot" was posted for sale. Since it was all done automatically, no one at Solid Gold Bomb had actually seen the listing until the complaints poured in. The company's reputation was damaged by a T-shirt that never actually existed. The lesson to be learned is that companies must make certain that the applications they use to analyze data are not flawed.[8]

Data analytics
The process of collecting, organizing, storing, and analyzing large sets of data ("big data") in order to identify patterns and other information that is most useful to the business now and for making future decisions.

FIGURE B.4 EXAMPLES OF SECTORS THAT BENEFIT FROM BIG DATA AND DATA ANALYTICS

E-commerce

Online sellers can analyze cart data to change prices for people who leave items behind in order to attract them back to the site and follow through on the purchase.

Retail

Stores such as Target can tell from a woman's previous purchases that she's pregnant. It can then send her coupons and other promotions for baby products. It can analyze the data a little more and promote similar products to the grandparents-to-be.

Real estate

Beach house rental agents can target vacation promotions to people who buy sunscreen frequently.

Law enforcement

Video cameras in light fixtures collect and feed data to software that can spot long lines, recognize license plates, and even identify suspicious activity, sending alerts to the appropriate staff. Sensors in the fixtures can pinpoint a gunshot, sense an earthquake or dangerous gas, or spot a person stopping at various cars in a parking lot.

Health care

Smartphones with motion sensors can detect early signs of Parkinson's disease.

Sources: Adam Tanner, "How Much Did You Pay for That Lipstick?" *Forbes*, April 14, 2014; "Dynamic Data," *Fortune*, October 7, 2013; Diane Cardwell, "At Newark Airport the Lights Are On, and They're Watching You," *The New York Times*, February 17, 2014; Philip Atiba Goff, "Can Big Data Transform Social Justice," *CNN*, www.cnn.com, May 2, 2014; and "Tech," *The Kiplinger Letter*, May 23, 2014.

test prep

- What types of information are available to businesses today?
- What are the four characteristics of information that make it useful?
- What is data mining and how do businesses use it?

Use LearnSmart to help retain what you have learned. Access your instructor's Connect course to check out LearnSmart, or go to learnsmartadvantage.com for help.

LEARNSMART

LO B–3 Compare the scope of the Internet, intranets, extranets, and virtual private networks and explain how broadband technology enabled the evolution to Web 2.0 and 3.0.

THE HEART OF KNOWLEDGE MANAGEMENT: THE INTERNET

You already know the Internet is a network of computer networks that evolved from a one-to-one communications tool to a one-to-many broadcast communication tool. Today it is the *heart of knowledge management*. Internet users can point and click their way from site to site with complete freedom. But what if you don't want just anybody to have access to your website? You might create an intranet, extranet, or virtual private network.

Intranets An **intranet** is a companywide network, closed to public access, that uses Internet-type technology. To prevent unauthorized outsiders (particularly

intranet
A companywide network, closed to public access, that uses Internet-type technology.

the competition) from accessing their sites, companies can construct a firewall between themselves and the outside world. A firewall can consist of hardware, software, or both. Firewalls allow only authorized users to access the intranet. Some companies use intranets only to publish employee phone lists and policy manuals, while others create interactive applications that fully exploit the technology's possibilities. They allow employees to update their addresses or submit company forms such as supply requisitions, time sheets, or payroll forms online, eliminating paper handling and speeding decision making.[9]

Extranets   Many businesses choose to open their intranets to other, selected companies and even customers, through the use of extranets. An **extranet** is a semiprivate network that lets more than one company access the same information or allows people on different servers to collaborate. Now almost all companies can use extranets for electronic data interchange (EDI) functions like sharing data and processing orders, specifications, invoices, and payments.

Notice that we described an extranet as a semiprivate network. This means that outsiders cannot access the network easily, but since an extranet does use public lines, knowledgeable hackers can gain unauthorized access. Most companies want a network as private and secure as possible, so they use dedicated lines (lines reserved solely for the network).

Dedicated lines are expensive, however, and they limit extranet use only to computers directly linked to those lines. What if your company needs to link securely with another firm or an individual for just a short time? Installing dedicated lines in this case would be too expensive and time-consuming. Virtual private networks are a solution.

Virtual Private Networks   A **virtual private network (VPN)** is a private data network that creates secure connections, or "tunnels," over regular Internet lines. It gives users the same capabilities as an extranet at much lower cost by using shared public resources rather than private ones. Just as phone companies provide secure shared resources for voice messages, VPNs provide the same secure sharing of public resources for data. This allows for on-demand networking: An authorized user can join the network for any desired function at any time, for any length of time, while keeping the corporate network secure. You probably use a VPN when you log on to your school's website. VPNs are commonplace in schools across the country that want to allow only affiliated students and faculty access to accounts like Blackboard (an online tool used to enhance teaching and learning, share course documentation and register for courses). If you don't have access to a corporate VPN, you can easily set up an account at a public VPN provider like WiTopia, StrongVPN, or Hotspot Shield.[10]

How do users log on to an organization's network? They do so through an *enterprise portal* that centralizes information and transactions and serves as an entry point to a variety of resources, such as e-mail, financial records, schedules, and employment and benefits files. Portals can even include streaming video of the company's day care center. They are more than simply web pages with links. They identify users and allow them access to areas of the intranet according to their roles: customers, suppliers, employees, and so on. They make information available in one place so that users don't have to deal with a dozen different web interfaces.

The challenge to the chief information officer (CIO) is to integrate resources, information, reports, and so on—all of which may be in a variety of places—so that they appear seamless to the user.

Broadband Technology

The more traffic on the Internet, the slower connections become. Tools to unlock these traffic jams include **broadband technology**, a continuous connection to the Internet that allows users to send and receive mammoth video, voice, and data

---

extranet
A semiprivate network that uses Internet technology and allows more than one company to access the same information or allows people on different servers to collaborate.

virtual private network (VPN)
A private data network that creates secure connections, or "tunnels," over regular Internet lines.

broadband technology
Technology that offers users a continuous connection to the Internet and allows them to send and receive mammoth files that include voice, video, and data much faster than ever before.

files faster than ever before. Even though broadband in the United States is dramatically faster than old dial-up connections, its average speed of 9.8 megabits per second is snail-like compared to the 22.1 and 13.3 averages of South Korea and Japan, respectively.[11] President Obama has made improving and expanding broadband technology a priority of his administration.[12] As people use more and more bandwidth to stream videos on services like Netflix or music on apps like Pandora, Internet service providers have begun to place caps on the amount of broadband consumers can use. Right now this isn't a problem for most users since average usage is well below the current caps, but as more mobile devices and services come online, the more likely broadband will become a consumption-based service (i.e., you pay for the broadband you use).

Net Neutrality   Today there is plenty of debate about "net neutrality" and the Federal Communication Commission's (FCC) role in regulating it.[13] One issue is defining what net neutrality even is. Some say it is treating all traffic on the Internet the same, whether it's e-mail from your mom or web page traffic on Google. Others say net neutrality is treating all the same type of content the same way, whether it's a video of frolicking kittens or a video of an ongoing surgery. Still others say net neutrality is nothing more than forbidding ISPs from blocking specific websites or services.[14] As video streaming services like Netflix and Amazon increasingly hog the lines, the debate over how the existing broadband should be distributed and who should regulate the distribution should go on for quite some time. What does this mean to you? If ISPs can charge for speed, deep-pocketed companies like Netflix and Amazon can pay the fees (passing them on to you, the customer, of course); and low-budget and start-up sites are likely to lose customers unwilling to travel at slower speeds, reducing competition and innovation. It is also possible that ISPs can begin charging people to go to certain websites; the more money you're willing to pay, the more sites you'll have access to. Rich customers and poor customers will get two different webs.[15]

Meanwhile new services like Google Fiber, a high-speed fiber network up to 100 times faster than average connections, give us hope that broader pipes may be on the horizon.[16]

Internet2   Even with broadband technology, scientists and other scholars who access, transmit, and manipulate complex mathematical models, data sets, and other digital elements need a faster solution. Their answer? Create a private Internet reserved for research purposes only. **Internet2** runs more than 22,000 times faster than today's public infrastructure, and supports heavy-duty applications such as videoconferencing, collaborative research, distance education, digital libraries, and full-body simulations known as tele-immersion.[17] A key element of Internet2 is a network called very-high-speed backbone network service (vBNS), which was set up in 1995 as a way to link government supercomputer centers and a select group of universities. The power of Internet2 makes it possible for a remote medical specialist to assist in a medical operation over the Internet without having the connection deteriorate as, say, home users watch *House of Cards*.

Internet2 became available to only a few select organizations in late 1997, but there are now more than 500 member universities, government agencies, corporations, and laboratories in over 100 countries.[18] Whereas the public Internet divides bandwidth equally among users (if there are 100 users, they each get to use 1 percent of the available bandwidth), Internet2 is more capitalistic. Users who are willing to pay more can use more bandwidth.

How the existing broadband should be distributed and who should regulate the distribution are major concerns today. Why does it matter how broadband is divided and distributed? Some people are concerned that ISPs will charge customers to go to certain websites: the more money you're willing to pay, the more and better sites you'll have access to. Rich customers and poor customers could get two different webs. Other people say that it's only fair that whoever uses the most broadband should pay the most. What do you think?

Internet2
The private Internet system that links government supercomputer centers and a select group of universities; it runs more than 22,000 times faster than today's public infrastructure and supports heavy-duty applications.

Some fear that Internet2 may soon be overrun by undergrads engaged in video streaming and other resource-hogging pursuits. But the designers of Internet2 are thinking ahead. Not only do they expect Internet history to repeat itself; they are counting on it. They are planning to filter Internet2 technology out to the wider Internet community in such a way that there is plenty of room on the road for all of us—at a price, of course.

Social Media and Web 2.0

For businesses, social media provide an array of opportunities and challenges. They are an inexpensive way to gain exposure. Most important, they give businesses tools to collaborate with consumers on product development, service enhancement, and promotion. Until now, using social media has been optional for most businesses. However, many believe that businesses that do not have a social media presence will not survive. We're not talking just about a Facebook page with an occasional update. Successful businesses will have a social media ecosystem and comprehensive strategy where every part of the organization collaborates and where customers are part of the conversation instantly.

Adam Kidron, co-founder of Manhattan hamburger restaurant 4food, says he wouldn't be in business if it were not for social media. The restaurant is based on customization. Customers choose the type of bun (i.e., bagel, multigrain, brioche, pumpernickel, etc.), donut-shaped burger (i.e., beef, lamb, egg, turkey, salmon, veggie, sausage, etc.), "scoop" to fill the donut hole (i.e., avocado and chili mango, potato and chorizo hash, etc.), and then finally the cheese and condiments. Social media become part of the fundamental product when a customer creates a new product and they use their own mobile device or one of the iPads placed around the restaurant to create a name for

FIGURE B.5 TIPS FOR USING SOCIAL MEDIA TO PARTNER WITH CUSTOMERS
Using social media is about trusting your brand and identity to your customers, partners, and the world at large. The world is going to do things with your brand, whether or not you participate in the process. Here are some tips to keep in mind.

- **If your competition is using social media, you had better be using it too.** More than 50 percent of Twitter users say that they follow companies, brands, or products on social networks.

- **Let the network mature and develop a comprehensive social media strategy.** Don't just set up a network and immediately begin exploiting it. For example, when the list of online supporters started to grow, the Obama fund-raisers wanted to immediately tap them for contributions. They were persuaded to wait until his e-mail team created an environment that let people know they were part of the campaign.

- **Take customers' comments seriously and establish two-way communication.** People expect to be listened to. If you respond, they'll keep coming back. Post questions and surveys.

- **Ask your customers to answer common questions.** Asking your most active fans and advocates to answer common questions is an effective way of acknowledging the value of loyal customers while adding credibility to information about your product or service.

- **Be authentic.** You have to talk directly with your customers, not just make an announcement as you would in a press release. Keep it authentic and you'll build a personality around your company and your brand.

- **Make your corporate site social.** Provide social sharing opportunities by offering share buttons, tweet widgets, and Facebook like buttons to make it easier to share across social networks.

Sources: Stephanie Frasco, "100 Facts about Twitter, and Why They Matter to Your Business," *Social Media Today*, www.socialmediatoday.com, September 26, 2013; "Effective Social Media Strategies—Four Tips, Four Benefits," Oracle, www.oracle.com, accessed June 2014; and Cindy King, "10 Social Media Tips to Enhance Your Marketing," *Social Media Examiner*, www.socialmediaexaminer.com, March 12, 2014.

their burger and save it in 4food's database. If they like the burger, they can post their creation directly to Twitter or Facebook. If they *really* like the burger, they can create a YouTube commercial that is shown on the restaurant's giant video wall along with Twitter feeds. If another customer buys the burger, the creator gets a 25-cent credit on his or her 4food account.[19]

It is inevitable that at some point a company is going to suffer some negative social media buzz. For example, when McDonald's introduced its new Happy Meal mascot, Happy, the company was hit with a storm of social media criticism about the weird-looking guy. What did McDonald's do? Well, it just acknowledged it and tweeted back with an image of Happy reading all the negative comments on his laptop. After the image was sent to McDonald's 2.5 million Twitter followers and 31 million Facebook friends, a social media monitoring tool showed that there were 190 positive comments to every one negative comment about Happy. Soon there were no comments at all. The lesson to be learned here is that all businesses and organizations should monitor and respond quickly to social chatter. When bad buzz happens, a company should identify the source and nature of the buzz and develop a quick response to contain it.[20]

Figure B.5 offers suggestions to consider when using social media in business. The most important thing to remember is that the social media have to serve a unique purpose and not be just gimmicky add-ons.

Social networking is the best example of what tech publisher Tim O'Reilly dubbed "Web 2.0." **Web 2.0** is the set of tools that allow people to build social and business connections, share information, and collaborate on projects online with user-generated sites like blogs, wikis, social networking sites and other online communities, and virtual worlds. (In this context, *Web 1.0* refers to corporate-generated sites like Google and Amazon.) YouTube and the microblogging site Twitter are among the largest Web 2.0 businesses, where ordinary people create all the content.

Web 2.0
The set of tools that allow people to build social and business connections, share information, and collaborate on projects online (including blogs, wikis, social networking sites and other online communities, and virtual worlds).

Web 3.0

Another generation of web innovators has expanded the utility of the web so that it enables an unprecedented level of intelligence in almost all applications. The objective is to pull data in real time, as needed. As you pull data, the system learns about you and your interests and pushes information it "thinks" you might like toward you.[21] Known as Web 3.0, this technology represents a shift in how people interact with the web, and vice versa.[22] Those who describe Web 1.0 as the Static Web and Web 2.0 as the Social Web, describe Web 3.0 as the Personal Web. You could think of Web 3.0 as Web 2.0 with a brain. **Web 3.0** technology is made up of three basic components: semantic web, mobile web, and immersive Internet, which are all leading to what many call the Internet of Things.[23]

Web 3.0
A combination of technologies that adds intelligence and changes how people interact with the web, and vice versa (consists of the semantic web, mobile web, and immersive Internet).

Semantic Web The semantic web refers to powerful intelligent decision-making applications.[24] For example, Amdocs is a company that interacts with customers on behalf of its clients in service industries such as telecom, health care, utilities, and insurance. This requires the Amdocs representatives to have real-time knowledge from internal sources—such as service disruptions and policy management—and external forces, such as social trends and competitive offers. Using Web 3.0 semantic technologies, Amdocs combines information from a variety of sources in real time to anticipate the reason for a customer's call. Responses can be made 30 percent faster, which makes customers happy.[25]

Mobile Web The mobile web allows users to use the web as they move from one device to another and one location to another. Location-based services are tied to devices that can track a user's whereabouts and suggest

Wearable technology such as Google Glass, smart watches and other hands-free technology may change the way we communicate, and how we work and play. Some Google Glass Explorers (as the first adopters are called) have encountered negative reactions from other people. For example, some people want them to leave or take the glasses off, since the wearers could be taking photos or videos of them. What do you think the benefits and drawbacks of Google Glass are?

places, like restaurants or shops, in the area. You can get a message from Starbucks offering you a discount on a latte as you walk by the door. If you do drop in the store, you can use an app on your smartphone to pay for your drink. Because so many customers use multiple devices throughout the day, it is important that a business uses the same design in apps for all types of computers, phones, and tablets. Then users will be able to rely on consistent, high-quality access no matter what type of device they're using. Users can be frustrated or annoyed when they can't find what they need or where they were earlier.[26]

Immersive Internet   The immersive Internet includes virtual worlds, augmented reality, and 3D environments. The use of virtual worlds, simulations, augmented reality, and multiplayer gaming technologies is expected to increase dramatically for learning in the next few years. For example, Intel's Real Sense technology recognizes gestures and facial features, which allows it to understand movement and emotions. It recognizes foregrounds and backgrounds, which allows it to enhance interactive reality; and it can scan items in three dimensions. The use of gestures, voice, and touch encourages children to become more active participants in learning games. In a game based on Scholastic's Clifford the Big Red Dog, kids can use arm and hand motions, talk, and touch to move within the game and learn core literacy skills while playing. For us bigger kids, Intel is working with DreamWorks animation to bring users new experiences with characters and content. The Real Sense technology is also expected to bring 3D scanning and printing to mainstream users, allowing them to easily and affordably create 3D items.[27]

Internet of Things   The Internet connects more people faster than ever before, and mobile devices let people be online all of the time. However, it's not just phones and tablets that connect us to the Internet. There are so many other things that connect us that the term the "Internet of Things (IoT) has become popular in mainstream media. IoT refers to technology that enables ordinary objects to be connected to the Internet by using sensors, cameras, software, databases, and massive data centers.[28] There are WiFi-based home automation networks that automatically cool or heat your home, turn the lights on and off, and change the controls on your garage doors, from your smartphone or computer. A technology called Echo can monitor your home's water, gas, and electricity consumption and reward you for conserving. Wearables such as smart watches or conductive fibers woven into the fabric of your workout clothes can monitor your breathing and heart rate, count your steps, and send the information to your phone.[29]

Soon every part of our lives will be quantifiable and we could be even more accountable for our decisions. For example, skipping the gym too many times may prompt your gym shoes to auto tweet to your health insurance network, which may decide to increase your premiums. While this may seem futuristic, there are many companies today that get measurable results by analyzing data collected from networked things. For example, John Deere can do remote, wireless diagnostics of tractors and combines, saving farmers days of down time. Union Pacific reduced the number of train derailments caused by failed bearings by 75 percent using near-real-time analysis of data collected by sensors along the tracks.[30]

Who's the "Boss" of the Internet?

The U.S. Defense Department created the first computer network in the late 1960s; and Tim Berners-Lee, a software engineer in a physics lab in Switzerland, invented the World Wide Web in 1990.[31] But who controls the Internet now? Well, the U.S. Commerce Department controls the root server for the domain name system, a digital directory that tells your computer where to go when you type in a web address, including ".gov" or ".edu." This gives the U.S. hazy ownership rights to the Internet. The U.S. created the Internet Corporation for Assigned Names and Numbers (ICANN) in 1998 to keep the management of networks in the hands of a private sector system of committees representing multiple stakeholders including companies, academics, and governments.

The U.S. government agreed to work with ICANN to give away all of its ownership of the Internet to the private sector by sometime in 2015. Some people believe that the U.S. giving up Internet ownership will give countries like Russia and China the ability to convince other countries to add regulatory power that would limit access to certain sites as they tried to do in 2013.[32] Others believe the opposite is true, that giving up U.S. ownership weakens Russia's and China's argument that the Internet is controlled by one country.[33] To date, the U.S. has been successful in building a coalition of nations that agrees the Internet should be free of government regulations or restrictions on free speech.[34] What does this mean to you? It could mean that someday the Internet would be very different than it is today; you may not be free to go where you want or say what you want on the Internet. On the other hand, the coalition may remain strong enough to keep the Internet open to everyone. We'll have to wait and see.

test prep

- How do computer networks change the way employees gather information?
- What is the Internet of Things?

LO B–4   Explain virtual networking and discuss the benefits and drawbacks for cloud computing.

VIRTUAL NETWORKING AND CLOUD COMPUTING

Computers can be networked a couple of ways: by hardware (i.e., cables, switches, etc.) or by software. For every computer a company has in its hardware-based network, an array of potential problems lurks in the shadows, from time-wasting crashes to crippling viruses. To remedy this, many companies have turned to **virtual networking**, a process that allows software-based networked computers to run multiple operating systems and programs, and share storage. Virtual networking can be either external or internal. *External networking* treats the network as a single pool of resources that can all be accessed regardless of its physical components (i.e., networked computers share the resources of all the other computers on the network). *Internal networking*

virtual networking
A process that allows software-based networked computers to run multiple operating systems and programs, and share storage.

Cloud computing changes the way people and businesses use technology. Since their data are stored in the cloud rather than locked on their computers, users are free to access the data from anywhere with any device rather than only from their own personal computers. How has cloud computing changed the way you access your programs and files?

cloud computing
A form of virtualization in which a company's data and applications are stored at offsite data centers that are accessed over the Internet (the cloud).

Use LearnSmart to help retain what you have learned. Access your instructor's Connect course to check out LearnSmart, or go to learnsmartadvantage.com for help.

▣ LEARNSMART®

shares the resources of one central computer with all the networked computers.[35] You might think of external networking as being decentralized and internal networking as being centralized.

Companies that want to virtualize but not to store all those data in their own offices need only look to the sky for a solution called **cloud computing**. This technology stores a company's data and applications at offsite data centers, accessed over the Internet.[36] The data aren't necessarily stored in a single data center; portions could be in a series of centers anywhere in the world. The data are easily accessible from any computer with an Internet connection. Vendors like Amazon, Google, Apple, and IBM offer cloud computing for a monthly pay-as-you-go fee.[37]

There are three types of cloud computing: (1) *private* clouds (wholly behind a firewall), *public* clouds (run on remote computers), and (3) *hybrid* clouds (consist of a private cloud for essential tasks, but use a public cloud as needed).[38]

The advantages of cloud computing include:[39]

1. **Reduced software costs.** Most software is free because the service provider supplies it. No more paying for upgrades or spending time installing all those patches since they're installed in the cloud.

2. **Improved security.** Offsite centers provide full and regular backups of data, etc., which is something many small businesses fail to do regularly.

3. **Flexible capacity.** Sometimes businesses need large chunks of capacity during peak demand periods, but much less at other times. Cloud computing allows the company to rent only what it needs when it needs it. If its needs increase, it just rents more. This is especially important to growing businesses that don't know what their needs will be.

4. **Lower equipment costs.** Since applications run in the cloud and not on your desk, you don't need to buy expensive equipment.

5. **Easier access.** Since you access all of your documents in the cloud via the Internet, it is much easier to share documents and make sure that everyone is working with the latest version.

Of course, cloud computing has its disadvantages as well. Primarily these involve concerns about security, stability, and control of data.[40] (We'll discuss these issues in more detail later in the chapter.) Popular cloud-storage service Dropbox suffered a 3-hour outage in early 2014 and another outage a few months later. Its 100 million customers were temporarily locked out of their files.[41] Dropbox was also accused of misleading users about the security and privacy of their files.[42] VMware provides a service that lets IT managers control the data on private and public clouds so that they can enjoy the cost savings and flexibility of cloud services, but still maintain control over security.

- How do computer networks change the way employees manage information?
- What are the benefits and drawbacks of cloud computing?

Evaluate the human resource, security, privacy, and stability issues affected by information technology.

EFFECTS OF INFORMATION TECHNOLOGY ON MANAGEMENT

The increase of information technology has affected management greatly and will continue to do so. Four major issues today are human resource changes, security threats, privacy concerns, and stability.

Human Resource Issues

We talked in Chapter 8 about tall versus flat organization structures. Computers often eliminate middle-management functions and thus flatten organization structures.

Human resource managers need to recruit employees who know how to use the new technology or train those who already work in the company. The speed at which technology has advanced has created a generational divide in terms of tech skills among different-aged workers. This creates greater challenges when it comes to recruitment and training. Companies often hire consultants instead of internal staff to address these concerns. Outsourcing technical training allows them to concentrate on their core businesses.

Perhaps the most revolutionary effect of computers and the Internet is telecommuting. Using computers linked to the company's network, mobile employees can transmit their work to the office from anywhere as easily as they can walk to the boss's office. Naturally, that decreases travel time and overall costs, and often increases productivity. Having fewer employees in the office also means that a company can get by with smaller, and therefore less expensive, office space than before.

Telecommuting enables men and women to work while staying home with small children or elders. It has also been a tremendous boon for workers with disabilities. Employees who can work after hours on their home computers, rather than staying late at the office, report lowered stress and improved morale. Telecommuting is most successful among people who are self-starters, who don't have home distractions, and whose work doesn't require face-to-face interaction with co-workers.

Electronic communication can never replace face-to-face communication for creating enthusiasm and team spirit, however. Even as telecommuting has grown in popularity, some telecommuters report that a consistent diet of long-distance work leaves them feeling dislocated or left out of the loop. Some miss the energy of social interaction or dislike the intrusion of work into what is normally a personal setting. Often people working from home don't know when to turn the work off. Some companies are therefore using telecommuting only as a part-time alternative. In fact, industry now defines telecommuting as working at home a minimum of two days a week.

Figure B.6 illustrates how information technology changes the way managers and workers interact. For additional information about telecommuting and home-based workers, review Chapters 6 and 11.

Telecommuting is one of the biggest human resource boons of the wireless age, but some employees are better suited to its demands than others. Do you have what it takes?

FIGURE B.6 WHEN
INFORMATION
TECHNOLOGY ALTERS
THE WORKPLACE

MANAGERS MUST	WORKERS MUST
• Instill commitment in subordinates rather than rule by command and control.	• Become initiators, able to act without management direction.
• Become coaches, training workers in necessary job skills, making sure they have resources to accomplish objectives, and explaining links between a job and what happens elsewhere in the company.	• Become financially literate so that they can understand the business implications of what they do and changes they suggest.
• Give greater authority to workers over scheduling, priority setting, and even compensation.	• Learn group interaction skills, including how to resolve disputes within their work group and how to work with other functions across the company.
• Use new information technologies to measure workers' performance, possibly based on customer satisfaction or the accomplishment of specific objectives.	• Develop new math, technical, and analytical skills to use newly available information on their jobs.

Security Issues

"Secure" information may be at risk from hackers who break into companies' networks; from employees who steal it; or from companies' own incompetence, poor gatekeeping, or sloppy procedures. Computer security is more complicated today than ever, as smartphones and the networks they run on, social networks and online games, and USB storage devices (flash drives and memory cards) become hackers' targets. When information was processed on mainframes, the single data center was easier to control because there was limited access to it. Today, however, computers are accessible not only in all areas within the company but also in all areas of other companies with which the firm does business.

virus
A piece of programming code inserted into other programming to cause some unexpected and, for the victim, usually undesirable event.

Viruses An ongoing security threat is the spread of computer viruses over the Internet. A **virus** is a piece of programming code inserted into other programming that usually lies dormant until triggered to cause some unexpected and, for the victim, usually undesirable event. Users pick up viruses by unknowingly downloading infected programming over the Internet or sharing an infected USB storage device. Often the source of the infected file is unaware of the virus. Some viruses are playful messages ("Kilroy was here!"), but some can be quite harmful, erasing data or causing your hard drive to crash. Programs such as Norton AntiVirus inoculate your computer so that it doesn't catch a known virus. But because new viruses are being developed constantly, antivirus programs may have only limited success. Thus it is important to keep your antivirus protection up-to-date and, more important, practice safe computing by not downloading files from unknown sources.

Hackers If a business stores customer data, it is subject to laws and regulations regarding the proper protection of these data. Many smaller businesses that don't have the manpower to handle security concerns might consider hiring a managed security services provider (MSSP) like Alert Logic or Perimeter E-Security.[43] MSSPs can install and manage firewalls, virtual private networks, web filtering and antispam programs, security intelligence services, and wireless and mobile functions. Even with all of this security protection, it is still possible that hackers can get through. Perhaps you were one of the tens of millions who had to get new credit or debit cards and monitor their credit reports when hackers breached Target's system and stole credit and debit card numbers. Target is now offering new credit cards with chip-and-pin technology to prevent further fraud.[44]

Some security experts advise businesses to assume that their systems have been breached and take the fight to the hackers. They recommend using methods that will frustrate the hackers and drive up their cost in order to deter them from future hacking. These methods include planting false information on their systems to mislead data thieves, and creating decoys that gather information about intruders. CloudFare offers a service called Maze, which it describes as "a virtual labyrinth of gibberish and gobbledygook."[45] Bottom line is that businesses that store data will need stronger and smarter tools to protect themselves from hackers.

Phishing   *Phishing* is another type of online security threat. A scammer will embellish an e-mail message with a stolen logo for a well-recognized brand such as eBay, PayPal, or Citibank that makes the message look authentic. Phishing messages often state something like "Account activation required" or "Your account will be canceled if you do not verify." When the victims click the link contained in the message, they are sent to a phony website that takes their personal information and uses it to commit fraud. The best way to avoid a phishing scam is never to access a website through a link in an e-mail message. Instead, open a new window and go to the home page of the company's website directly.

As more people log on to the Internet, the number of legal issues surrounding its use will likely increase. Today, copyright and pornography laws are entering into the virtual world. Other legal questions relate to intellectual property and contract disputes, online sexual and racial harassment, and the use of electronic communication to promote crooked sales schemes. Cybercrimes cost the United States billions of dollars a year.[46]

Cyberterrorism   Until September 11, 2001, corporate and government security officials worried mostly about online theft, credit card fraud, and hackers. Today, however, they are most concerned about *cyberterrorism*. Terrorist hackers could shut down the entire communications, money supply, electricity, and transportation systems. Recently hackers tried to get control of the CIA's main computer, and there were a string of denial of service attacks on other government computers. Although these sophisticated cyberattacks inconvenienced governmental agencies and had little impact on day-to-day public life, many are increasingly worried about an attack on the energy sector. In fact, the most sophisticated cyberthreat yet, called the Mask, was detected by an Internet security company in 2014 and has taken over thousands of IP addresses in dozens of countries. Its most likely target is oil and natural gas companies.[47]

The Critical Infrastructure Protection Board, a part of the U.S. Department of Homeland Security, was created after September 11, 2001, to devise a plan for improving the security of the United States' critical infrastructure. The agency needs the cooperation of businesses across the country, because 85 percent of the system it needs to protect is in the private sector. Companies have been reluctant to file reports about security breaches, however,

Were you one of the tens of millions who had to get a new credit or debit card when hackers breached Target's system and stole credit and debit card numbers? What can you do to protect yourself from loss when someone steals your vital information from a third party? How did the hacking affect Target's relationship with you and other customers? How did it affect the company's finances?

How many of the online and mobile apps that you use track your whereabouts (both your physical location and where you go online) and share that information with third parties? Probably more than you think.

for fear the public will lose faith in their ability to protect their assets. To encourage the sharing of such information, Congress passed the Critical Infrastructure Information Act of 2002, assuring businesses that any information they provide the Department of Homeland Security will remain secret through an exemption from the Freedom of Information Act. This is only a start on what is likely to be a long effort to improve security technologies.

Privacy Issues

The increasing use of technology creates major concerns about privacy. In 2013, Edward Snowden leaked classified documents to the media regarding NSA's tactics in tracking U.S. citizens, international governments, and companies. Snowden's revelations changed the public conversation about privacy and security.[48]

You don't need to be the target of a criminal investigation to have your e-mail or phone calls snooped, and you're being watched by many more entities than the government. Of course, we've already talked about how your online clicks are monitored by private industry.[49] In addition, many U.S. companies scan employee e-mail regularly, and it's legal. They look for trade secrets, non-work-related traffic, harassing messages, and conflicts of interest. Any hacker with a desire to read your thoughts can also trap and read your messages, most of which are unencrypted. Some e-mail systems, such as Lotus Notes, can encrypt e-mail to keep corporate messages private. If you use browser-based e-mail, you can obtain a certificate that has an encryption key from a company such as VeriSign. Legitimate users who want to decrypt your mail need to get an unlocking key.

The Internet presents increasing threats to your privacy, as more personal information is stored in computers and more people are able to access it, legally or not. Some websites allow people to search for vehicle ownership from a license number or to find other individuals' real estate property records. One key question in the debate over protecting our privacy is "Isn't this personal information already public anyway?" Civil libertarians have long fought to keep certain kinds of information available to the public. If access to such data is restricted on the Internet, wouldn't we have to reevaluate our policies on all public records? Privacy advocates don't think so. After all, the difference is that the Internet makes obtaining personal information *too* easy. Would your neighbors or friends even consider going to the appropriate local agency and sorting through public documents for hours to find your driving records or to see your divorce settlement? Probably not. But they might dig into your background if all it takes is a few clicks of a button.

Many web servers track the online movements of users willing to swap such personal details for free access to online information. Site owners can share your data with others without your permission. Websites also often send **cookies** to your computer that stay on your hard drive. These are pieces of information such as registration data (name and password) or user preferences that the browser sends back to the server whenever you return to that website. Some software, known as spyware, can be installed on your computer without your knowledge. The spyware can then infect your system with viruses and track your online behavior.

Do you mind someone watching over your shoulder while you're on the web? Tim Berners-Lee, the researcher who invented the World Wide Web, led

cookies
Pieces of information, such as registration data or user preferences, sent by a website over the Internet to a web browser that the browser software is expected to save and send back to the server whenever the user returns to that website.

the development of a way to prevent you from receiving cookies without your permission. His Platform for Privacy Preferences, or P3, allows a website to automatically send information on its privacy policies.[50] With P3 you can set up your web browser to communicate only with those websites that meet certain criteria. You need to decide how much information about yourself you are willing to give away. Remember, we are living in an information economy, and information is a commodity—that is, an economic good with a measurable value.[51]

Stability Issues

Although technology can provide significant increases in productivity and efficiency, instability has a significant impact on business. Candy maker Hershey discovered the Halloween trick was on it one year when the company couldn't get its treats to stores on time. Failure of its new $115 million computer system disrupted shipments, and retailers were forced to order Halloween candy from other companies, leaving Hershey with a 12 percent decrease in sales that quarter.

What's to blame? Experts say it is a combination of computer error; human error; malfunctioning software; and an overly complex marriage of software, hardware, and networking equipment. Some systems are launched too quickly to be bug-proof, and some executives don't have the technical knowledge to challenge computer specialists. As critical as technology is to business, some of it is not built for rigorous engineering, and some people aren't properly trained to use it. As things get more complex, we will probably be prone to more errors.

TECHNOLOGY AND YOU

If you're beginning to think being computer illiterate may be occupational suicide, you're getting the point. As information technology eliminates old jobs while creating new ones, it will be up to you to learn and maintain the skills you need to be certain you aren't left behind. And, who knows, maybe you can find a job like Gabi Gregg did. MTV appreciated so much the trust and passion she shared with her many Twitter followers that it offered her a job. It made her MTV first "TJ" in order to help "amplify the voice of our audience as part of the global conversation." She loves her new job, and the $100,000 a year salary isn't bad either!

test **prep**

- How has information technology changed the way people work?
- What management issues have been affected by the growth of information technology?

Use LearnSmart to help retain what you have learned. Access your instructor's Connect course to check out LearnSmart, or go to learnsmartadvantage.com for help.

■LEARNSMART

summary

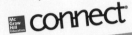

LO B–1   Outline the changing role of business technology.

- **What have been the various names and roles of business technology since 1970?**
  In the 1970s, business technology was called data processing (DP) and its role was to support existing business. In the 1980s, its name became information systems (IS) and its role changed to doing business. In the 1990s, business technology became information technology (IT) and its role now is to change business. As technology became more sophisticated in the 2000s, it became known as business intelligence (or analytics) and includes data mining, online analytical processes, querying, and reporting.

- **How does information technology change business?**
  Information technology has minimized the importance of time and place to businesses. Firms that are independent of time and location can deliver products and services whenever and wherever convenient for the customer. See Figure B.6 for examples of how information technology changes business.

- **What is business intelligence?**
  Business intelligence refers to a variety of software applications that analyze an organization's raw data and take out useful insights from it.

LO B–2   List the types of business information, identify the characteristics of useful information, and discuss how data are stored and analyzed.

- **What types of information are available to businesses today?**
  The types of information available to businesses today include (1) business process information, (2) physical-world observations, (3) biological data, (4) public data, and (5) data that indicate personal preferences or intentions.

- **How can you deal with information overload?**
  The most important step in dealing with information overload is to identify your four or five key goals. Eliminate information that will not help you meet them.

- **What makes information useful?**
  The usefulness of management information depends on four characteristics: quality, completeness, timeliness, and relevance.

- **What is big data and data analytics?**
  Data analytics is the process of collecting, organizing, storing, and analyzing large sets of data ("big data") in order to identify patterns and other information that is most useful to the business now and for making future decisions. Data mining is the part of data analytics that involves looking for hidden patterns and previously unknown relationships among the data.

LO B–3   Compare the scope of the Internet, intranets, extranets, and virtual private networks and explain how broadband technology enabled the evolution to Web 2.0 and 3.0.

- **What information technology is available to help business manage information?**
  The heart of information technology involves the Internet, intranets, extranets, and virtual private networks. The Internet is a massive network of thousands of smaller networks open to everyone with a computer and a modem.

An intranet is a companywide network protected from unauthorized entry by outsiders. An extranet is a semiprivate network that allows more than one company to access the same information. A virtual private network is a private data network that creates secure connections, or "tunnels," over regular Internet lines.

- **What is Web 2.0?**
  Web 2.0 is the set of tools that allows people to build social and business connections, share information, and collaborate on projects online with user-generated sites like blogs, wikis, social networking sites and other online communities, and virtual worlds. YouTube and Twitter are among the largest Web 2.0 businesses, where ordinary people create all the content.

- **What is Web 3.0?**
  Web 3.0 is technology that adds a level of intelligence to interacting with the Web. It could be described as the Personal Web, whereas Web 1.0 can be thought of as the Static Web and Web 2.0 as the Social Web. Web 3.0 is made up of three basic components: the semantic web, the mobile web, and the immersive Internet, which are all leading to what many call the Internet of Things.

- **What is the Internet of Things?**
  Internet of Things refers to technology that enables ordinary objects to be connected to the Internet by using sensors, cameras, software, databases, and massive data centers.

 LO B–4   Explain virtual networking and discuss the benefits and drawbacks for cloud computing.

- **What is virtual networking?**
  Virtual networking is a process that allows software-based networked computers to run multiple operating systems and programs, and share storage. Virtual networking can be either external or internal. *External networking* treats the network as a single pool of resources that can all be accessed regardless of its physical components (i.e., networked computers share the resources of all the other computers on the network). *Internal networking* shares the resources of one central computer with all the networked computers.

- **What is cloud computing and what are its benefits and drawbacks?**
  Cloud computing is technology that stores a company's data and applications at offsite data centers, accessed over the Internet. Its benefits are reduced software costs, improved security, flexible capacity, lower equipment costs, and easier access. The drawbacks of cloud computing are concerns about security, stability, and control of data.

 LO B–5   Evaluate the human resource, security, privacy, and stability issues affected by information technology.

- **What effect has information technology had on business management?**
  Computers eliminate some middle management functions and thus flatten organization structures. Computers also allow employees to work from their own homes. On the negative side, computers sometimes allow information to fall into the wrong hands. Concern for privacy is an issue affected by the vast store of information available on the Internet. Finding the balance between freedom to access private information and individuals' right to maintain privacy will require continued debate.

key terms

broadband technology 10
business intelligence (BI) or analytics 3
cloud computing 16
cookies 20
data analytics 8
data processing (DP) 2

extranet 10
information systems (IS) 2
information technology (IT) 2
Internet2 11
intranet 9

virtual networking 15
virtual private network (VPN) 10
virus 18
Web 2.0 13
Web 3.0 13

critical thinking

1. What information, either for your personal life or for your job, would you like to receive exactly when and where you need it?

2. What are the implications for world trade given the ability firms and government organizations now have to communicate across borders so easily?

3. How will the introduction and integration of more and more devices into the Internet of Things affect your life? Do you think they will widen or narrow the gap between the haves and have-nots (rich and poor people)?

developing workplace skills

Key: ● Team   ★ Analytic   ▲ Communication   ◉ Technology

● ◉ ▲ ★ 1. Imagine you have $2,000 to buy or upgrade a computer system. Research hardware and software in computer magazines and on websites such as ZDNet (www.zdnet.com). Visit a computer store or shop online to find the best value. List what you would buy, and write a summary explaining your choices.

◉ ▲ ★ 2. Interview someone who bought a computer to use in his or her business. Ask why he or she bought that specific computer and how it is used. Ask about any problems that occurred during the purchase process or in installing and using the system. What would the buyer do differently next time? What software does he or she find especially useful?

◉ ▲ ★ 3. Describe one computer glitch you've experienced and what you did to resolve it. Discuss the consequences of the interruption (lost data, decreased productivity, increased stress). What steps have you taken to prevent a recurrence of the problem you faced?

● ◉ ★ 4. Choose a topic that interests you and use two search engines to find information about it online. Narrow your search using the tips offered by the search engine. Did both search engines find the same websites? If not, how were their results different? Which engine found the most appropriate information?

5. How has technology changed your relationship with specific businesses or organizations such as your bank, your school, and your favorite places to shop? Has it strengthened or weakened your relationship? Has technology affected your relationship with your family, friends, and community? Take a sheet of paper and write down how technology has helped build your business and personal relationships on one side. On the other side, list how technology has weakened those relationships. What can you and others do to use technology more effectively to reduce any negative impact?

taking it to the **net**

PURPOSE

To identify how the Internet of Things (IoT) uses connected devices to gather and analyze data to provide information useful to both businesses and individuals.

EXERCISE

Go to http://postscapes.com/what-exactly-is-the-internet-of-things-infographic and scroll through the infographic "What Exactly Is the Internet of Things?"

1. IoT is driven by a combination of what three components? Give three examples of each of them.

2. List three smart devices and applications created by the interaction of the three components of IoT identified in question 1.

3. How is IoT impacting business?

notes

1. John Naughton, "We're All Being Mined for Data—but Who Are the Real Winners?" *The Guardian,* June 7, 2014.
2. Ryan Mulcahy, "Business Intelligence Definition and Solutions," *CIO,* www.cio.com, accessed June 2014.
3. "Kodak Files for Bankruptcy, No More Kodak Moments," *Business Today,* www.businesstoday.com, accessed June 2014.
4. Ernest von Simson, "The New Role of the CIO," *Bloomberg Businessweek,* May 22, 2013; and Shane O'Neill, "Digital Business Skills: Most Wanted List," *InformationWeek,* May 1, 2014.
5. Scott Young, "Bringing Eye-Tracking to the Stores," *Perception Research Services,* www.prservices.com, accessed June 2014.
6. Jilly Duffy, "Get Organized: How to Clean Out Your Inbox," *PCMagazine,* September 23, 2013; and Jennifer Forker, "Tips to Organize Your Email and Other Digital Clutter," *Huffington Post,* March 5, 2013.
7. Brady Dale, "In Brooklyn, a Grasp at Giving 'Big Data' Meaning," *CNN Money,* April 28, 2014; Irving Wladawsky-Berger, "Data-Driven Decision Making: Promises and Limits," *The Wall Street Journal,* September 27, 2013; and Katherine Noyes, "IBM Stakes Its Claim in 'Scale-Out' Storage for Big Data," *CNN Money,* May 14, 2014.
8. Joshua Klein, "When Big Data Goes Bad," *CNN Money,* November 5, 2013.
9. Juan Carlos Perez, "Badgeville Aims to Make Child's Play Out of Software Deployment," *PC World,* June 10, 2014.
10. Roland Waddilove, "How to Set Up a VPN Service to Surf the Web Anonymously," *PC World,* May 19, 2014.
11. Emil Protalinski, "Akamai: Average Internet Speed Grew 29% Year-over-Year to 3.6 Mbps," *The Next Web,* www.tnw.com, accessed June 2014.
12. National Broadband Plan, www.broadband.gov, accessed June 2014.
13. David Nicklaus, Todd Shields, and Chris Strohm, "FCC Advances Fast Lane Rules," *St. Louis Post-Dispatch,* May 16, 2014.
14. Nancy Scola, "Five Myths about Net Neutrality," *The Washington Post,"* June 12, 2014.
15. Betsy Issacson, "Web 3.0: What the Web Could Look Like without Net Neutrality," *Huffington Post,* January 25. 2014.
16. Fiber Google, www.fiber.google.com, accessed June 2014.
17. Jim Clayman, "Internet2 CIO to Discuss the Emerging Higher Education Community Cloud at Three Rivers Systems' Annual Global Users Conference," *St. Louis Post-Dispatch,* June 8, 2014.
18. Internet2, www.internet2.edu, accessed June 2014.
19. 4food, www.4food.com, accessed June 2014.
20. *Randy Hlavac,* "Because We're Happy: Using Social Media to Turn Audiences Around," *Forbes,* June 3, 2014.

21. Anjana Ahuja, "Thinking Machines Are Ripe for a World Take-over," *Financial Times,* June 10, 2014.
22. Trish Winters, "Web 3.0," *Bitcoin Magazine,* www.bitcoinmagazine.com, April 25, 2014; and Harry Siegel, "Humanity, We Had a Good Run," *The New York Daily News,* June 9, 2014.
23. Anthony Wing Cosner, "Famo.us Part I: New Concepts Will Increase the Flow of Highly Dynamic Web 3.0 Apps," *Forbes,* May 27, 2014.
24. World Wide Web Consortium, www.w3c.org, accessed June 2014.
25. *PR Newswire,* "Amdocs Announces Self-Optimizing Networks Solution for Customer Experience-Driven Network Automation," *Web 2.0 Journal,* web2.sys-con.com, February 10, 2014.
26. George Glover, "Why Responsive Web Design Is the Cornerstone to Any Mobile Strategy," *Business 2 Community,* www.business2community.com, June 2, 2014.
27. "Intel Brings Immersive, Human Interaction to Devices in 2014," *The Wall Street Journal,* January 6, 2014; Bob Tita, "How 3-D Printing Works," *The Wall Street Journal,* June 11, 2013; and Mark Jenkins, "3-D Printing Can Make Everyone a Designer," *Washington Post,* March 15, 2013.
28. Lori Kozlowski, "Everthing Is Connected: What "The 'Internet of Things' Means Now," *Forbes,* April 23, 2014; and Stuart Dredge, "10 Things We Learned from Pew Research's Internet of Things Report," *The Guardian,* May 14, 2014.
29. "An Uncommon Thread," *The Economist,*" March 8., 2014.
30. Chris Murphy, "Internet of Things: What's Holding Us Back," *InformationWeek,* www.informationweek.com, May 5, 2014.
31. "Who Invented the Internet?" *History,* www.history.com, December 18, 2013; and *World Wide Web Foundation,* www.webfoundation.org, accessed June 2014.
32. Todd Shields, "House Republicans Question U.S. Plan to Give Up Internet Control," *Bloomberg Businessweek,* April 2, 2014; and Brendan Greeley, "The U.S. Gives Up Its Control of the Free Speech Internet," *Bloomberg Businessweek,* March 17, 2014.
33. Emma Woollacott, "U.S. Government Cedes Control of the Internet," *Forbes,* March 15, 2014.
34. Tom Risen, "The U.S. Gives the Internet to the World," *U.S. News & World Report,* March 17, 2014.
35. Network Virtualization, *Webopedia,* www.webopedia.com, accessed June 2014; and Kurt Marko, "Network Virtualization: The Final Piece of the Private Cloud," *Forbes,* March 25, 2014.
36. Quentin Hardy, "Cloud Computing, in Translation," *The New York Times,* June 11, 2014.
37. David Kramer, "A Layman's Guide to Cloud Computing," *Huffington Post,* June 12, 2014.
38. Quentin Hardy, "The Era of Cloud Computing," *The New York Times,* June 11, 2014; and "Migration: A Planned, Structured Cloud Approach," *CIO.,* www.cio.com, June 11, 2014.
39. Joe McKendrick, "5 Benefits of Cloud Computing You Aren't Likely to See in a SalesBrochure," *Forbes,* July 12, 2013; Ian Stone, "Cloud Computing Enables Businesses to Discover Their Entrepreneurial Spirit," *The Guardian,* April 15, 2014; and "Cloud Computing Industry Analysis and Infographic: Companies Overspend on Infrastructure by 30% or More," *PRWeb,* www.prweb.com, June 3, 2014.
40. Archana Venkatraman, "Advantages and Disadvantages of Cloud Computing," *ComputerWeekly,* www.computerweekly.com, accessed June 2014; and Mikal E. Belicove, "Will the Cloud Rain on My Parade?," *Entrepreneur,* August 2013.
41. Zack Whittaker, "Dropbox Hit by Outage; File Sync Busted," *ZDNet,* www.zdnet.com, March 14, 2014.
42. Warwick Ashford, "Dropbox Can Be Hacked, Say Security Researchers," *ComputerWeekly,* www.computerweekly.com, August 29, 2014.
43. C. J. Ariottta, "Top Emerging Managed Security Service Providers," *MSPMentor,* www.mspmentor.com, January 14, 2013.
44. Shan Li, "Target Hires New Security Chief from General Motors after Security Breach," *Los Angeles Times,* June 11, 2014.
45. "Firewalls and Firefights," *The Economist,* August 10, 2013.
46. "SIRF's Up," *The Economist,* November 30, 2014.
47. Christopher Harress, "Obama Says Cyberterrorism Is the Country's Biggest Threat, U.S. Government Assembles 'Cyber Warriors,'" *International Business Times,* February 18, 2014.
48. Daniel Terdiman, "The Most Anticipated SXSW Talk in Years, Snowden Fires Up Austin," *CNet,* www.cnet.com, March 10, 2014.
49. Josh Gerstein and Stephanie Simon, "Who Watches the Watchers? Big Data Goes Unchecked," *Politico,* www.politico.com, May 14, 2014.
50. Platform for Privacy Preferences, www.w3.org/P3P, accessed June 2014.
51. "Hiding from Big Data," *The Economist,* June 7, 2014.

photo credits

C

Managing Risk

Learning Objectives

AFTER YOU HAVE READ AND STUDIED THIS BONUS CHAPTER, YOU SHOULD BE ABLE TO

C-1   Identify the environmental changes that have made risk management important.

C-2   Explain the four ways of managing risk, and distinguish between insurable and uninsurable risk.

C-3   Define insurance policies, and explain the law of large numbers and the rule of indemnity.

C-4   Discuss the various types of insurance businesses can buy to manage risk.

Getting to know **Dan Amos**

t may seem a bit strange that a multinational company would credit its existence to three brothers, an idea, and a duck; yet that's how one of the giants of the insurance industry describes its company history. Sixty years ago, John, Paul, and Bill Amos did not claim to be insurance experts, but they knew people in the U.S. wanted financial protection against the risk of an accident or illness. The brothers created the American Family Life Assurance Company with a firm promise to be there when policyholders needed them. In 1989, the company changed its name to the acronym Aflac. Dan Amos, son of co-founder Paul Amos, has been CEO of Aflac for over a quarter of a century.

Today, Aflac is the largest provider of supplemental health insurance in the United States. Supplemental insurance helps pay for expenses that normal health insurance doesn't cover when accidents or illness occur. Generally, benefits are paid directly to a person to help with out-of-pocket medical expenses or lost wages. CEO Amos sees growing opportunities for Aflac as the United States appears to be moving toward national health care under the Patient Protection and Affordable Care Act (also called Obamacare). Amos predicts the company will find more opportunities to grow, especially among smaller employers. Amos speculates the company may decide to offer major medical insurance in the future.

Aflac decided to limit its operations to two countries, the United States and Japan. The company in fact has a long-standing presence in Japan. John Amos, Aflac's first CEO, visited the Osaka World's Fair in 1970 and observed that fairgoers were all wearing surgical masks. He reasoned that if people would buy surgical masks to protect themselves from getting sick, they probably would buy health insurance to protect themselves financially if they did get sick. Today, approximately 75 percent of the company's revenue is from Japan. Aflac is the number one life insurance company in terms of individual policies in Japan, and almost 90 percent of the companies listed on the Tokyo Stock Exchange offer Aflac products to employees.

Aflac was named one of the 100 best U.S. companies to work for. Amos says he owes a great deal of credit for this success to a duck. The Aflac Duck made his television debut in 2000 and has appeared in many commercials with a host of celebrities. He even appeared in a series of commercial spots where he fractured his beak and needed supplemental insurance. The message was, "If the Aflac duck can get hurt, anyone can get hurt. That's why you need Aflac." The duck has been enshrined on Madison Avenue's Walk of Fame as one of America's favorite advertising icons.

In this bonus chapter, you will learn something about risk management. The industry is so large and there is so much to learn that we only scratch the surface. Nonetheless, risk management has become such a huge part of every manager's responsibilities that you need to know the basics of risk management before you become involved in any kind of business. The best advice we can offer to you is: Don't duck this chapter.

Dan Amos

- CEO of Aflac
- Limits operations to two countries, U.S. and Japan

www.aflac.com

@AFLAC

Sources: Chuck Williams, "Sunday Interview with Aflac CEO Dan Amos," *Columbus Ledger Enquirer,* March 1, 2014; Tim Nudd, " The Spot: Lame Duck," *Ad Week,* February 13, 2013; and Aflac, www.aflac.com, accessed May 2014.

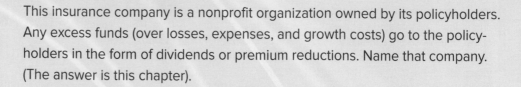

name that **company**

LO C–1 Identify the environmental changes that have made risk management important.

UNDERSTANDING BUSINESS RISKS

No one knows better than Dan Amos at Aflac that managing risk is a challenge for businesses throughout the world. Almost every day we hear of a tornado, hurricane, earthquake, flood, fire, airplane crash, terrorist threat, or car accident that destroyed property or injured or killed someone. The Insurance Institute for Business & Home Safety says that one out of four small businesses is forced to permanently close after a disaster.[1]

Hackers and viruses are an increasing threat to computers, and identity theft is commonplace. Theft and fraud can destroy a small business. Business lawsuits in recent years have covered everything from job-related accidents to product liability.

Such reports are so much a part of the news that we tend to accept these events as part of everyday life. But the losses of property, equipment, transportation, communications, security, energy, and other resources mean a great deal to the people and organizations injured by them. In some states, insurance against such loss is not available or is too expensive for high-risk businesses. New legislation in some areas aims to lessen some of these risks so that companies can obtain insurance coverage again at a reasonable price.

Edward Snowden, former technical assistant for the CIA, leaked classified documents to the media regarding NSA's tactics in tracking U.S. citizens, international governments, and companies. What strategies can help firms and even governments protect themselves against this type of pure risk?

A recent report found that 80 percent of organizations either have or are in the process of developing an ERM (Enterprise Risk Management) program.[2] An ERM program usually has a few well-defined goals, such as defining (1) which risks the program will manage; (2) what risk management processes, technologies, and investments will be required; and (3) how risk management efforts will be coordinated across the firm.[3]

How Rapid Change Affects Risk Management

Risk goes beyond the obvious dangers of fire, theft, or accident. It is inherent in every decision a manager makes, and the prudent company assesses its exposure in all of them. Risk managers are expanding their expertise into human resources, information technology, security, legal, site construction, and more. Change is occurring so fast that it is difficult to identify new risks until they are upon us. Who can evaluate the risks of buying or selling products online? How will currencies fluctuate in the next financial crisis, and how will their daily ups and downs affect the profits of global trade?[4] How will climate change affect farms, cattle, and the price of food?[5] What would happen to the economy if there were a new terrorist attack or a flu epidemic? What can we do to manage the risks of financial failure at home and social unrest abroad?[6] Let's explore how companies go about managing risk. We'll begin by going over a few key terms.

 LO C–2   Explain the four ways of managing risk, and distinguish between insurable and uninsurable risk.

MANAGING RISK

Risk is the chance of loss, the degree of probability of loss, and the amount of possible loss. There are two different kinds of risk:

- **Speculative risk** can result in *either* profit or loss. A firm takes on speculative risk by buying new machinery, acquiring more inventory or a new plant, and making other potentially profitable decisions in which the probability of loss may be relatively low and the amount of loss known. An entrepreneur's chance to make a profit is a speculative risk. Banks that bought mortgage-backed securities were taking a speculative risk.

- **Pure risk** is the threat of loss with *no* chance for profit, such as the threat of fire, accident, or theft. If such events occur, a company loses money, but if they don't, the company gains nothing.

The risk that most concerns businesspeople is pure risk. It threatens the very existence of some firms. Once they identify pure risks, firms have several options:

1. Reduce the risk.
2. Avoid the risk.
3. Self-insure against the risk.
4. Buy insurance against the risk.

We'll discuss the option of buying insurance in detail later in this chapter. First we'll discuss each of the other alternatives for managing risk, which reduce the need for outside insurance.

risk
The chance of loss, the degree of probability of loss, and the amount of possible loss.

speculative risk
A chance of either profit or loss.

pure risk
The threat of loss with no chance for profit.

Reducing Risk

A firm can reduce risk by establishing loss-prevention programs such as fire drills, health education, safety inspections, equipment maintenance, accident prevention programs, and so on. Many retail stores use mirrors, video cameras, and other devices to prevent shoplifting. Water sprinklers and smoke detectors help minimize fire loss. Most industrial machines have safety devices to protect workers' fingers, eyes, and so on.

Employees as well as managers can reduce risk. Truck drivers can wear seat belts to minimize injuries from accidents, operators of loud machinery can wear earplugs to reduce the chance of hearing loss, and those who lift heavy objects can wear back braces. The beginning of an effective risk management strategy is a good loss-prevention program.[7] However, high insurance rates have forced some firms to go beyond merely preventing risks to avoiding them, in extreme cases by going out of business. Avoiding accidents is critical to the survival of the firm and its workers.[8]

Avoiding Risk

We can't avoid every risk. There is always the chance of fire, theft, accident, or injury. But some companies are avoiding risk by not accepting hazardous jobs and by outsourcing shipping and other functions. The threat of lawsuits has driven some drug companies to stop manufacturing vaccines, and some consulting engineers refuse to work on hazardous sites. Some companies are losing outside members of their boards of directors who don't have liability coverage protecting them from legal action against the firms they represent. Many companies have cut back on their investments to avoid the risk of financial losses.

Self-Insurance

self-insurance
The practice of setting aside money to cover routine claims and buying only "catastrophe" policies to cover big losses.

Self-insurance is the practice of setting aside money to cover routine claims, and buying only "catastrophe" insurance policies to cover big losses. It is most appropriate when a firm has several widely distributed facilities. Firms with a single huge facility, in which a major fire or earthquake could destroy the entire operation, usually turn to insurance companies to cover the risk of loss.

This is what remained of a car repair shop after a tornado passed through Revere, Massachusetts, in 2014. Businesses cannot accurately estimate damage from natural disasters like tornadoes beforehand. That's the reason for having insurance. Do you think this car repair shop's insurance covered most of the damage caused by the storm?

One of the riskier self-insurance strategies is for a company to "go bare," paying claims from its operating budget instead of from a special fund. The whole firm could go bankrupt over one claim if the damages are high enough. A less risky alternative is to form group-insurance pools that share similar risks.

Buying Insurance to Cover Risk

Although well-designed and enforced risk-prevention programs reduce the probability of claims, accidents do happen. Insurance is the armor individuals, businesses, and nonprofit organizations use to protect themselves from various financial risks. Together they spend about 10 percent of gross domestic product (GDP) on insurance premiums. The federal government provides some insurance protection (see Figure C.1), but individuals and businesses must cover most on their own.

To reduce the cost of insurance, some companies buy a business ownership policy (BOP)—a package that includes property and liability insurance. We will continue our discussion of insurance by identifying the types of risks that are uninsurable and insurable.

What Risks Are Uninsurable?

Not all risks are insurable. An **uninsurable risk** is one that no insurance company will cover. Examples of things that you cannot insure include market risks (e.g., losses that occur because of price changes, style changes, or new products that make your product obsolete); political risks (e.g., losses from war or government restrictions on trade); some personal risks (such as loss of a job); and some risks of operation (e.g., strikes or inefficient machinery).

uninsurable risk
A risk that no insurance company will cover.

Unemployment Compensation
Provides financial benefits, job counseling, and placement services for unemployed workers.

Social Security
Provides retirement benefits, life insurance, health insurance, and disability income insurance.

Federal Housing Administration (FHA)
Provides mortgage insurance to lenders to protect against default by home buyers.

National Flood Insurance Association
Provides compensation for damage caused by flooding and mudslides to properties located in flood-prone areas.

Federal Crime Insurance
Provides insurance to property owners in high-crime areas.

Federal Crop Insurance
Provides compensation for damaged crops.

Pension Benefit Guaranty Corporation
Insures pension plans to prevent loss to employees if the company declares bankruptcy or goes out of business.

FIGURE C.1 PUBLIC INSURANCE
State or federal government agencies that provide insurance protection.

What Risks Are Insurable?

An **insurable risk** is one the typical insurance company will cover, using the following guidelines:

1. The policyholder must have an **insurable interest**, which means the policyholder is the one at risk to suffer a loss. You cannot buy fire insurance on your neighbor's house and collect if it burns down.

2. The loss must be measurable.

3. The chance of loss must be measurable.

4. The loss must be accidental.

5. The insurance company's risk should be dispersed; that is, spread among different geographical areas so a flood or other natural disaster in one area will not bankrupt the insurance company.

6. The insurance company must be able to set standards for accepting the risk.

test prep

- Why are companies more aware now of the need to manage risk?
- What is the difference between pure risk and speculative risk?
- What are the four major options for handling risk?
- What are some examples of uninsurable risk?

LO C–3   Define insurance policies, and explain the law of large numbers and the rule of indemnity.

UNDERSTANDING INSURANCE POLICIES

An **insurance policy** is a written contract between the insured, whether an individual or organization, and an insurance company that promises to pay for all or part of a loss by the insured. A **premium** is the fee the insurance company charges, the cost of the policy to the insured. A **claim** is a statement of loss that the insured sends to the insurance company to request payment.

Like all private businesses, insurance companies are designed to make a profit. They therefore gather data to determine the extent of various risks. What makes it possible for insurance companies to accept risk and profit is the law of large numbers.

The **law of large numbers** says that if a large number of people or organizations are exposed to the same risk, a predictable number of losses will occur during a given period of time. (For your information, the figures for homes are as follows: Over the course of a 30-year mortgage, a home has a 9 percent chance of catching fire and a 26 percent chance of flooding.) Once the insurance company predicts the number of losses likely to occur, it can determine the appropriate premiums for each policy it issues against that loss. The premium will be high enough to cover expected losses and yet earn a profit for the firm and its stockholders. Today, many insurance companies are charging high premiums not for expected losses but for the costs they anticipate from the increasing number of court cases and high damage awards.

Almost everyone who drives is exposed to the risk of having an accident at some point. Insurance companies use the law of large numbers to predict the losses such accidents will cause and set their policy premiums high enough to cover the losses while earning a profit. How much do you pay for your auto policy?

Rule of Indemnity

The **rule of indemnity** says an insured person or organization cannot collect more than the actual loss from an insurable risk. Nor can you buy two insurance policies, even from two insurance companies, and collect from both for the same loss. You cannot gain from risk management; you can only minimize losses.

rule of indemnity
Rule saying that an insured person or organization cannot collect more than the actual loss from an insurable risk.

Types of Insurance Companies

There are two major types of insurance companies. A **stock insurance company** is owned by stockholders, just like any other investor-owned company. A **mutual insurance company** is an organization owned by its policyholders. It is a nonprofit organization, and any excess funds (over losses, expenses, and growth costs) go to the policyholders in the form of dividends or premium reductions. New York Life is the largest mutual insurance company in the U.S.

stock insurance company
A type of insurance company owned by stockholders.

mutual insurance company
A type of insurance company owned by its policyholders.

 ✓✓

- What is the law of large numbers?
- What is the rule of indemnity?

Use LearnSmart to help retain what you have learned. Access your instructor's Connect course to check out LearnSmart, or go to learnsmartadvantage.com for help.

LEARNSMART

LO C–4   Discuss the various types of insurance businesses can buy to manage risk.

INSURANCE COVERAGE FOR VARIOUS KINDS OF RISK

There are many types of insurance to cover various losses: property and liability insurance, health insurance, and life insurance. Property losses result from fires, accidents, theft, or other perils. Liability losses result from property damage or injuries suffered by others for which the policyholder is held responsible. Figure C.2 lists the types of insurance available. Let's begin our exploration of insurance by looking at health insurance.

FIGURE C.2 PRIVATE INSURANCE

Property and Liability

Fire	Covers losses to buildings and their contents from fire.
Automobile	Covers property damage, bodily injury, collision, fire, theft, vandalism, and other related vehicle losses.
Homeowner's	Covers the home, other structures on the premises, home contents, expenses if forced from the home because of an insured peril, third-party liability, and medical payments to others.
Computer coverage	Covers loss of equipment from fire, theft, and sometimes spills, power surges, and accidents.
Professional liability	Protects from suits stemming from mistakes made or bad advice given in a professional context.
Business interruption	Provides compensation for loss due to fire, theft, or similar disasters that close a business. Covers lost income, continuing expenses, and utility expenses.
Nonperformance loss protection	Protects from failure of a contractor, supplier, or other person to fulfill an obligation.
Criminal loss protection	Protects from loss due to theft, burglary, or robbery.
Commercial credit insurance	Protects manufacturers and wholesalers from credit losses due to insolvency or default.
Public liability insurance	Provides protection for businesses and individuals against losses resulting from personal injuries or damage to the property of others for which the insured is responsible.
Extended product liability insurance	Covers potentially toxic substances in products; environmental liability; and, for corporations, director and officer liability.
Fidelity bond	Protects employers from employee dishonesty.
Surety bond	Covers losses resulting from a second party's failure to fulfill a contract.
Title insurance	Protects buyers from losses resulting from a defect in title to property.
Cyber attack insurance	Helps protect companies from hackers.

Health Insurance

Basic health insurance	Covers losses due to sickness or accidents.
Major medical insurance	Protects against catastrophic losses by covering expenses beyond the limits of basic policies
Hospitalization insurance	Pays for most hospital expenses.
Surgical and medical insurance	Pays costs of surgery and doctor's care while recuperating in a hospital.
Dental insurance	Pays a percentage of dental expenses.
Disability income insurance	Pays income while the insured is disabled as a result of accident or illness.

Life Insurance

Group life insurance	Covers all the employees of a firm or members of a group.
Owner or key executive insurance	Enables businesses of sole proprietors or partnerships to pay bills and continue operating, saving jobs for the employees. Enables corporations to hire and train or relocate another manager with no loss to the firm.
Retirement and pension plans	Provides employees with supplemental retirement and pension plans.
Credit life insurance	Pays the amount due on a loan if the debtor dies.

Health Insurance

The United States is going through a period of major changes in health insurance. Recent legislation, such as the Affordable Care Act (Obamacare), has the government much more involved in the health insurance process. Because it is so important to your future, you should keep up with these changes. We are likely to see many variations of health coverage in the future. Some companies have decided to self-insure against health care costs.

Health Savings Accounts

Health savings accounts (HSAs) (formerly called medical savings accounts) are tax-deferred savings accounts linked to low-cost, high-deductible health insurance policies. The idea is for your employer (or you) to take the money currently spent on high-cost, low-deductible health insurance and deposit it into a health savings account. You would use the money only for needed health care services. At the end of the year, you get to keep the money you don't spend in the account for future medical coverage. One major benefit to you is that the money grows tax-free until you take it out. There are likely to be other such plans proposed to compete with the comprehensive national health care system now being offered.

health savings accounts (HSAs)
Tax-deferred savings accounts linked to low-cost, high-deductible health insurance policies.

Disability Insurance

Disability insurance replaces part of your income—usually 50 to 70 percent—if you become disabled and unable to work. You must usually be disabled for a certain period, such as 60 days, before you can begin collecting. Insurance experts recommend getting disability insurance if your employer does not offer it, because the chances of becoming disabled by a disease or accident when you are young are much higher than the chance of dying. The premiums for disability insurance vary according to age, occupation, and income.

An employee with a work-related illness or injury can get workers' compensation benefits regardless of who was at fault. In exchange for these benefits, employees usually do not have the right to sue the employer for damages related to those injuries.

Workers' Compensation

Workers' compensation insurance guarantees payment of wages, medical care, and rehabilitation services, such as retraining, for employees injured on the job. Employers in every state are required to provide this insurance. It also pays benefits to the survivors of those who die as a result of work-related injuries. The cost of workers' compensation varies by the company's safety record, the size of its payroll, and the types of hazards its workers face. It costs more to insure a steelworker than an accountant because the risk of injury is greater.

Liability Insurance

Professional liability insurance covers people found liable for professional negligence. If a lawyer gives advice carelessly and the client loses money, the client may sue the lawyer for an amount equal to that lost, and liability insurance will cover the lawyer's loss. Professional liability insurance is also known as *malpractice insurance.* That term may bring doctors and dentists to mind, but many other professionals, including mortgage brokers and real estate appraisers, are buying professional liability insurance because of large lawsuits their colleagues have faced.

Product liability insurance covers liability arising out of products sold. A person injured by, say, a ladder or some other household good may sue the manufacturer for damages. Insurance usually covers such losses.

Life Insurance for Businesses

Regardless of how careful we are, we all face the prospect of death. To ensure that those left behind will be able to continue the business, entrepreneurs often buy life insurance that will pay partners and others what they need to keep the firm going.[9] The best kind of insurance to cover executives in the firm is term insurance, but dozens of new policies with interesting features are now available.[10]

Insurance Coverage for Home-Based Businesses

Homeowner's policies usually don't have adequate protection for a home-based business.[11] For example, they may have a limit for business equipment. For more coverage, you may need to add an endorsement, sometimes called a *rider,* to your homeowner's policy. If clients visit your office or if you receive deliveries regularly, you may need home-office insurance. It protects you from slip-and-fall lawsuits and other risks associated with visitors. For more elaborate businesses, such as custom cabinetry shops and other types of manufacturing or inventory-keeping businesses, you may need a business-owner policy. Unless you are an expert on insurance, you will need to consult an insurance agent about the best insurance for your home-based business needs.

The Risk of Damaging the Environment

Risk management now goes far beyond the protection of individuals, businesses, and nonprofit organizations from known risks. It means the evaluation of worldwide risks with many unknowns, such as climate change.[12] It also means prioritizing these risks so that international funds can be spent where they can do the most good. No insurance company can protect humanity from all such risks. These risks are the concern of businesses and governments throughout the world, with the assistance of the international scientific community. They should also be your concern as you study risk management in all its dimensions. For example, think of the risks that accompany the search for natural gas using fracking. Now that such a search has gone global, companies throughout the world are examining the risks involved.[13] That means more jobs and more interest in risk management in general.

Protection from Cyber Attacks

Often you will see articles in newspapers about a company being hacked by some outside (or inside) individuals or groups that steal your private information, such as social security numbers, address, and so on. Cyber risk insurance can help a business prepare for the worst. For example, it will cover a company should its employees or customers decide to file against them in the event that their information is leaked.[14]

test prep

- Why should someone buy disability insurance?
- How many different kinds of private insurance can you name?

Use LearnSmart to help retain what you have learned. Access your instructor's Connect course to check out LearnSmart, or go to learnsmartadvantage.com for help.

LEARNSMART

summary

 LO C–1 Identify the environmental changes that have made risk management important.

- **What changes have made risk management more important?**
  Hurricanes, floods, terrorist threats, identity theft, and an unstable economy have all contributed to additional risk and the need for more risk management.

Access your instructor's Connect course to check out LearnSmart or go to learnsmartadvantage.com for help.

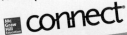 **connect**

LO C–2 Explain the four ways of managing risk, and distinguish between insurable and uninsurable risk.

- **What are the four major ways of managing risk?**
  The major ways of managing risk are (1) reduce risk, (2) avoid risk, (3) self-insure, and (4) buy insurance.

- **What's the difference between insurable and uninsurable risk?**
  Uninsurable risk is risk that no insurance company will cover. Examples of things that you cannot insure include market risks, political risks, some personal risks (such as loss of a job), and some risks of operation (e.g., strikes or inefficient machinery).

  An insurable risk is one the typical insurance company will cover. Generally, insurance companies use the following guidelines when evaluating whether a risk is insurable: (1) the policyholder must have an insurable interest, (2) the amount of loss should be measurable, (3) the chance of loss should be measurable, (4) the loss should be accidental, (5) the risk should be dispersed, and (6) the insurance company can set standards for accepting risks.

LO C–3   Define insurance policies, and explain the law of large numbers and the rule of indemnity.

- **What is the rule of indemnity?**
The rule of indemnity says an insured person or organization cannot collect more than the actual loss from an insurable risk.

LO C–4   Discuss the various types of insurance businesses can buy to manage risk.

- **What are the two kinds of insurance companies?**
A stock insurance company is owned by stockholders, just like any other investor-owned company. A mutual insurance company is owned by its policyholders.

- **What kind of policies cover health risks?**
The United States is going through a period where government involvement with health care is being debated and tested in the courts. It is too early to tell what the final outcome will be. Health savings accounts (HSAs) enable you to pay for your doctors from a tax-deferred savings account and buy insurance for catastrophes.

- **What is workers' compensation insurance?**
Workers' compensation insurance guarantees payment of wages, medical care, and rehabilitation services like retraining for employees injured on the job. Employers in every state are required to provide this insurance. Professional liability insurance covers people found liable for professional negligence. Product liability insurance provides coverage against liability arising out of products sold. Most businesses also have some kind of life insurance for their executives. Serving as a director on a corporate board carries with it great standing—and great risk of liability. If you conduct business from home, you should also have some form of home-office insurance to cover liabilities.

- **What are businesses doing to cover the risks of harming the environment?**
Many businesses are doing what they can to minimize damage to the environment. Such risks, however, are often beyond what businesses can manage. They are also the concern of governments around the world.

key terms

claim 6	law of large numbers 6	rule of indemnity 7
health savings accounts (HSAs) 9	mutual insurance company 7	self-insurance 4
insurable interest 6	premium 6	speculative risk 3
insurable risk 6	pure risk 3	stock insurance company 7
insurance policy 6	risk 3	uninsurable risk 5

critical thinking

1. Are you self-insuring your residence and your assets? What have you done to reduce your risk? Have you done anything to avoid risk? How much would it cost to buy insurance for your dwelling and the contents?

2. What risks do you take that insurance cannot cover?

3. What actions have you taken to avoid risk?

4. What can you do to lower your personal risk of loss from natural disasters such as floods, hurricanes, and tornadoes?

developing **workplace skills**

Key: ● **Team**   ★ **Analytic**   ▲ **Communication**   ▣ **Technology**

1. Write a one-page paper about ways you could reduce risk in your life (such as not driving above the speed limit). Form small groups and share what you have written. Which of your classmates' suggestions can you adopt in your life?   ★ ▲

2. You cannot insure yourself against speculative risk. However, you can minimize the risks you take when investing. Compare and contrast the risks of investing in stocks versus investing in bonds for the long term.   ★

3. Much of risk management consists of reducing risky behavior. What kinds of risky behavior have you observed among fellow college students? How can college students learn about and minimize these risks? Are they doing so? Discuss the merits of having a risk manager for education facilities.   ★ ▲

4. Form small groups and discuss liability insurance, automobile insurance, health insurance (i.e., Obamacare), renter's insurance, life insurance, and disability insurance. Develop a list of questions to discuss openly in class so that everyone is more informed about these issues. Do your fellow students understand all of these types of insurance?   ● ★ ▲

5. Write a two-page essay on the risks of a terrorist attack, a natural disaster, climate change, or a major health disaster. Which risk do you perceive as most likely? Most dangerous? Discuss what you could do to warn others of such risks and motivate them to do something about them.   ★ ▲

taking it to the **net**

PURPOSE

To learn about insurance for your dwelling and property, and to examine the issue of liability.

EXERCISE

Go to the Information Insurance Institute's website (www.iii.org). Explore the site and then answer the following questions:

1. What is homeowner's insurance?

2. What is in a standard policy?

3. What different types of homeowner's policies are there?

4. What is renter's insurance?

5. Is an umbrella policy a wise purchase? Why or why not?

notes

1. Jeffrey McKinney, "Before Disaster Strikes," *Black Enterprise,* May 2013.

2. David Gould, "The Root of Risk," *Bloomberg Businessweek,* October 7–13, 2013.

3. A special advertisement in *Bloomberg Businessweek,* March 10, 2013.

4. Rachel Ensign and Ari I. Weinberg, "Now Let's All Raise Our Glasses to Risk-Modeling and Optimization," *The Wall Street Journal,* March 4, 2013.

5. Evan Rothman, "Strategic Security, " *Bloomberg Businessweek,* February 4, 2013.

6. A special advertisement in *Bloomberg Businessweek,* March 4—10, 2013.

7. Ensign and Weinberg, "Now Let's All Raise Our Glasses to Risk Modeling and Optimization."

8. Gregory J. Millman and Samuel Rubenfeld, "For Corporate America, Risk Is Big Business," *The Wall Street Journal,* January 16, 2014.

9. Bill Harris, "Irreplaceable You," *Inc.,* February 2013.

10. Charles Passy, "Outliving Expectations," *Smart Money,* March, 2012; and Russ Banham, "Protecting the Corporate Executive," *The Wall Street Journal,* May 21, 2013.

11. Lisa Gibbs, "Covered? Don't Be So Sure," *Money,* April 2013.

12. David Deming, "Another Year of Global Cooling," *The Washington Times,* January 17, 2014.

13. Brian Swint, "Shale Goes Global," *Bloomberg Businessweek,* November 18, 2013–January 2, 2014.

14. Lisa Gerstner, "Why Chip Cards Are a Safer Bet," *Kiplinger's Personal Finance,"* April 2014.

photo credits

D

Managing Personal Finances

Learning Objectives

AFTER YOU HAVE READ AND STUDIED THIS BONUS CHAPTER, YOU SHOULD BE ABLE TO

D-1 Outline the six steps for controlling your assets.

D-2 Explain how to build a financial base, including investing in real estate, saving money, and managing credit.

D-3 Explain how buying the appropriate insurance can protect your financial base.

D-4 Outline a strategy for retiring with enough money to last a lifetime.

It is important for all of us to keep our personal finances in order. The recent financial crisis proved to us just how volatile the economy can be.

Many who did not plan responsibly during the good times found themselves in trouble when the economy turned sour.

Few people understand the importance of financial planning better than Alexa von Tobel, a certified financial planner (CFP) and founder and CEO of LearnVest, a personal financial planning website. A graduate of Harvard College, von Tobel worked at Morgan Stanley before becoming head of business development at former file sharing service Drop.io. From there, she attended Harvard Business School until she took a leave of absence to start LearnVest with the hope of bringing financial planning to the masses.

Research showed that people in the U.S. are poor financial planners and poor savers. Only 30 percent had a long-term savings plan and only 10 percent had ever spoken to a financial planner. One obvious reason why consumers failed to contact a financial planner was the cost. Traditional financial plans typically are priced in the range of $3,000–$5,000, and often require minimum balances. Von Tobel believed the cost structure of the industry was way out of the reach of most consumers. LearnVest offers financial planning services with reasonable flat rates that vary with the customer's financial needs. The company charges no percentage fees and does not require minimum balances.

The original mission of LearnVest was to help female consumers to plan for their financial future. Today, men make up approximately 25 percent of the site's users. Von Tobel proposes a simple 50/20/30 plan that anyone can follow to help build a firm financial future. The 50/20/30 formula suggests that 50 percent of your take-home pay goes to pay for essentials (rent/mortgage, utilities, groceries, transportation); 20 percent goes to your future (savings for emergencies, debt repayment, retirement funds); and 30 percent goes to your lifestyle (travel, shopping, restaurants, etc.). She warns younger people, particularly in their 20s and 30s, to not make big mistakes like accumulating too much credit card debt and paying bills late. It helps to remember her words, "Money is a tool that allows you to live your richest life. And remember, you can take out a loan for college, but you can't take out a loan for retirement."

Alexa von Tobel doesn't suggest how you should live and what you should buy; she only wants to help you to think about why you are buying something and its financial ramifications. Her new book *Financially Fearless* sounds like a good investment. In this chapter we'll take a look at all the ways that will help you keep your finances in order.

Sources: Claire Suddath, "Your Women's Financial Planning: Alexa von Tobel's Advice," *Bloomberg Businessweek,* December 19, 2013; Meghan Casserly, "LearnVest's Planning $16.5 Million Cash Infusion," *Forbes,* June 26, 2013; Dan Schwabel, "Alexa von Tobel: How to Be the Master of Your Personal Future," *Forbes,* January 20, 2014; and Janet Novack and Samantha Sharf, "The Recession Generation," *Forbes,* August 18, 2014.

Alexa von Tobel

- Founder and CEO of LearnVest
- Certified financial planner
- Named "One of the Coolest Young Entrepreneurs" by Inc. magazine

www.learnvest.com

@alexavontobel

name that **company**

One way to save money is to use your credit cards wisely. There are organizations that can help you compare credit cards to get the most out of them. What is the name of one of those organizations? (You can find the answer in this bonus chapter.)

LO D–1 Outline the six steps for controlling your assets.

THE NEED FOR PERSONAL FINANCIAL PLANNING

The United States is largely a capitalist country. It follows, then, that the secret to success in such a country is to have capital, or money. With capital, you can take nice vacations, raise a family, invest in stocks and bonds, buy the goods and services you want, give generously to others, and retire with enough money to see you through. Money management, however, is not easy. You have to earn the money in the first place. Your chances of becoming wealthy are much greater if you choose to become an entrepreneur. That's one of the reasons why we have put so much emphasis on entrepreneurship throughout the text, including a whole chapter on the subject. Of course, there are risks in starting a business, but the best time to take risks is when you are young. Would it help you to be more motivated if you knew that there are over a thousand billionaires in the world and they average some $4.5 billion in wealth? Not all billionaires are in the United States, For example, there are 55 billionaires in Africa.[1]

After you earn so much money, you have to learn to spend it wisely, save some, and insure yourself against the risks of serious accidents, illness, or death. With a little bit of luck, you may be one of the millionaires or billionaires discussed in this book.

You'll likely need some help. Recently high school seniors averaged a grade of less than 50 percent on questions having to do with financial concepts. Another report found that college students are also poorly educated about financial matters such as IRAs and 401(k) plans.[2] Even people who are retired are finding that they don't know enough about such plans. This bonus chapter will give you the basics so that you'll be ahead of the game. Financial management is so important to your fiscal health that you may enjoy taking an entire class on it.[3] Check your school to see what is available.

Financial Planning Begins with Making Money

You already know that one of the secrets to finding a good-paying job is having a good education. That is still true, although what you major in does matter.[4] Throughout history, an investment in business education has paid off regardless of the state of the economy or political ups and downs. Benjamin Franklin said, "If a man empties his purse into his head, no one can take it away from him. An investment in knowledge always pays the best interest." Education has become even more important since we entered the information age. One way to start to become a millionaire, therefore, is to finish college. Make sure you investigate all the financial help available to you.

Making money is one thing; saving, investing, and spending it wisely is something else. Following the advice in the next section will help you become one of those with enough to live in comfort throughout your life.[5]

Six Steps to Controlling Your Assets

The only way to save enough money to do all the things you want to do in life is to spend less than you make. Although you may find it difficult to save today, it is not only possible but also imperative if you want to accumulate enough to be financially secure. Fewer than 1 in 10 U.S. adults has accumulated enough money by retirement age to live comfortably, and 1 in 4 U.S. households does not have a retirement account at all.[6] Don't become one of them. The following are six steps you can take today to get control of your finances.

Step 1: Take an Inventory of Your Financial Assets   To take inventory, you need to develop a balance sheet for yourself, like the one in Chapter 17. Remember, a balance sheet starts with the fundamental accounting equation: Assets = Liabilities + Owners' equity. List your tangible assets (such as big-screen TV, DVR player, iPad, computer, cell phone, bicycle, car, jewelry, clothes, and savings account) on one side, and your liabilities (including mortgage, credit card debt, and auto and education loans) on the other.

Assign a dollar figure to each of your assets, based on its current value, not what you originally paid for it. If you have debts, subtract them from your assets to get your net worth. If you have no debts, your assets equal your net worth. If your liabilities exceed the value of your assets, you are not on the path to financial security. You may need more financial discipline in your life.

Let's also create an income statement for you. At the top of the statement is revenue (all the money you take in from your job, investments, and so on). Subtract all your costs and expenses (rent or mortgage, credit card and other loan payments, utilities, commuting costs, and so on) to get your net income or profit. Software programs like Quicken and websites like Dinkytown.net have a variety of tools that can easily help you with these calculations.

Now is also an excellent time to think about how much money you will need to accomplish all your goals. The more clearly you can visualize your goals, the easier it is to begin saving for them.

Step 2: Keep Track of All Your Expenses Do you occasionally find yourself running out of cash? If you experience a cash flow problem, the only way to trace where the money is going is to keep track of every cent you spend. Keeping records of your expenses can be tedious, but it's a necessary step if you want to learn discipline. Actually, it could turn out to be enjoyable because it gives you such a feeling of control.

Here's what to do: List *everything* you spend as you go through the day. That list is your journal.

It might take a little time to balance your income with your expenses to make sure you have money left to save and invest, but the effort is worth it. People who don't take this step can reach retirement without enough funds to live on. How could you cut back your expenses?

At the end of the week, transfer your journal entries into a record book or computerized accounting program.

Develop spending categories (accounts) to make your task easier and more informative. You can have a category called "Food" for all food you bought from the grocery or convenience store during the week. You might want a separate account for meals eaten away from home, because you can dramatically cut these costs if you make your meals at home.

Other accounts could include rent, insurance, automobile repairs and gasoline, clothing, utilities, toiletries, entertainment, and donations to charity. Most people also like to have a category called "Miscellaneous" for impulse items like latte and candy. You won't believe how much you fritter away on miscellaneous items unless you keep a *detailed* record for at least a couple of months.

Develop your accounts on the basis of what's most important to you or where you spend the most money. Once you have recorded all your expenses for a few months, you'll easily see where you are spending too much and what you have to do to save more. A venti mocha frappuccino at a coffee specialty shop may cost about $4.25. If you cut back from five to one a week, you'll save $17 a week, or over $850 a year. Over 10 years, that could mean an extra $12,000 for retirement, if you invest the money wisely.

Step 3: Prepare a Budget   Once you know your financial situation and your sources of revenue and expenses, you're ready to make a personal budget. Remember, budgets are financial plans. A household budget includes mortgage or rent, utilities, food, clothing, vehicles, furniture, life insurance, car insurance, medical care, and taxes.

You'll need to choose how much to allow for such expenses as eating out, entertainment, cell phone use, and so on. Keep in mind that what you spend now reduces what you can save later. Spending $5 or more a day for cigarettes or coffee adds up to about $35 a week, $140 a month, $1,700 a year. If you can save $5 a day, you'll have about $1,700 saved by the end of the year. Keep this up during four years of college and you'll have about $7,000 by graduation. And that's before adding any interest your money will earn. If you would invest the savings in a mutual fund earning 6 percent compounded annually, you would double your money every 12 years. The Rule of 72 says that your money doubles every 12 years at 6%. You do that calculation by dividing the percentage earned into 72 (72 divided by 6 = 12). Cost-saving choices you might consider to reach this goal are listed in Figure D.1.

Running a household is similar to running a small business. It takes the same careful record keeping, the same budget processes and forecasting, and the same control procedures. Sometimes it also creates the same need to borrow funds or rely on a credit card and become familiar with interest rates. The time you spend practicing budgeting techniques will benefit you throughout your life. You might start by going online to Mint.com. It will help you with your budgeting needs.

Step 4: Pay Off Your Debts   The first thing to do with the money remaining after you pay your monthly bills is to pay off your debts, starting with those carrying the highest interest rates. Credit card debt may be costing you 18 percent or more a year. A survey of 100 campuses found that over one-fourth of college students said they had been charged a fee for a late payment. It's better to pay off a debt that costs 18 percent than put the money in a bank account that earns, say, 2 percent or less.[7] Check credit card statements and other mailings carefully to make certain the charges are accurate.

FIGURE D.1 POSSIBLE COST-SAVING CHOICES
The choices you make today can have a dramatic impact on your financial future. Compare the differences these few choices you can make now would mean to your future net worth. If you would make the lower-cost choices five days a week during your four years of college, you'd have more than $8,300 by graduation. (*Note that the figures in this chart are based on 20 weekdays per month.*)

First Choice Cost per Month	Alternate Choice Cost per Month	Savings per Month
Starbucks tall caffè latte $3.00 for 20 days = $60.00	Service station cappuccino $0.70 for 20 days = $14.00	$ 46.00
Fast-food lunch of burger, fries, and soft drink $5.00 for 20 days = $100.00	Lunch brought from home $2 for 20 days = $40.00	60.00
Bottled water $1.50 for 20 days = $30.00	Refill water bottle $0 for 20 days = $0	30.00
Download album = $10.00	Listen to your old albums = $0.00	10.00
Banana Republic T-shirt = $40.00	Old Navy T-shirt = $12.00	28.00
	Total savings per month	$174.00
		× 48 months
	Total savings through 4 years of college	$8,352.00

Step 5: Start a Savings Plan   It's important to save some money each month in a separate account for large purchases you're likely to make (such as a car or house). Then, when it comes time to make that purchase, you'll have the needed cash. Save at least enough for a significant down payment so that you can reduce the finance charges you'll pay to borrow the rest.

The best way to save money is to *pay yourself first*. When you get your paycheck, first take out money for savings and then plan what to do with the rest. You can arrange with your bank or mutual fund to deduct a certain amount for savings every month. You'll be pleasantly surprised when the money starts accumulating and earning interest over time. With some discipline, you can eventually reach your goal of becoming a millionaire. It's not as difficult as you may think. Figure D.2 shows how $5,000 grows over various periods at different rates of return. If you start saving at age 40, you'll have 25 years in by the time you reach 65.

Step 6: Borrow Only to Buy Assets That Increase in Value or Generate Income   Don't borrow money for ordinary expenses; you'll only get into more debt that way. If you have budgeted for emergencies, such as car repairs and

ANNUAL RATE OF RETURN				
Time	2%	5%	8%	11%
5 years	$5,520	$ 6,381	$ 7,347	$ 8,425
10 years	6,095	8,144	10,795	14,197
15 years	6,729	10,395	15,861	23,923
20 years	7,430	13,266	23,305	40,312
25 years	8,203	16,932	34,242	67,927

FIGURE D.2 HOW MONEY GROWS
This chart illustrates how $5,000 would grow at various rates of return. Recent savings account interest rates were very low (less than 2 percent), but in earlier years they've been over 5 percent.

health care costs, you should be able to stay financially secure. Most financial experts advise saving about six months of earnings for contingencies. Keep this money in highly liquid accounts, such as a bank account or money market fund.

Only the most unexpected of expenses should cause you to borrow. It is hard to wait until you have enough money to buy what you want, but learning to wait is a critical part of self-discipline. Of course, you can always try to produce more income by working overtime or by working on the side for extra revenue.

If you follow these six steps, not only will you have money for investment, but you'll have developed most of the financial techniques needed to become financially secure. If you find it hard to live within a budget at first, remember the payoff is well worth the effort.

LO D–2 Explain how to build a financial base, including investing in real estate, saving money, and managing credit.

BUILDING YOUR FINANCIAL BASE

The path to success in a capitalist system is to have capital to invest, yet many students today graduate with debt. As you've read, accumulating capital takes discipline and careful planning. With the money you save, however, you can become an entrepreneur, one of the fastest ways to wealth.

Living frugally is extremely difficult for the average person. Most people are eager to spend their money on a new car, furniture, electronics, clothes, entertainment, and the like. They look for a fancy apartment with all the amenities. A capital-generating strategy may require forgoing most (though not all) of these purchases to accumulate investment money. It might mean living like a frugal college student, in a relatively inexpensive apartment furnished in hand-me-downs from parents, friends, Craigslist, and resale shops.

For five or six years, you can manage with the old sound system, a used car, and a few nice clothes. The strategy is sacrifice, not luxury. It's important not to feel burdened by this plan; instead, feel happy knowing your financial future will be more secure. That's the way the majority of millionaires got their money. If living frugally seems too restrictive for you, you can still save at least a little. It's better to save a smaller amount than not to save at all.

It's wise to plan your financial future with the same excitement and dedication you bring to other aspects of your life. If you get married, for example, it is important to discuss financial issues with your spouse. Conflicts over money are a major cause of divorce, so agreeing on a financial strategy before marriage is very important.

A great strategy for couples is to try to live on one income and to save the other. The longer you wait to marry, the more likely it will be that one of you can be earning enough to do that—as a college graduate. If the second spouse makes $35,000 a year after taxes, saving that income for five years quickly adds up to $175,000 (plus interest).

What do you do with the money you accumulate? Your first investment might be a low-priced home. Why? The purpose of this investment is to lock in payments for your shelter at a fixed amount. Through the years, home ownership has been a wise investment, unlike renting, but that may be changing.[8]

Many people take huge risks by buying too much home for their income. Furthermore people sometimes take out interest-only or other loans that are very risky, as recent headlines have shown. The old rule of thumb "Don't buy a home that costs more than two and a half times your annual income" still stands. Buy for the long term, and stay within your means. What has happened to housing prices in your area over the last couple of years? Lower prices may mean opportunity if the market gains strength.

Real Estate: Historically, a Relatively Secure Investment

The real estate bust that began in 2008 was a relatively uncommon occurrence. House prices had risen dramatically, causing a bubble that burst. Prices fell sharply until the spring of 2012 when prices began to rise again. While prices aren't back to their peak in most areas, real estate is likely to continue to provide several investment benefits. First, a home is the one investment that you can live in. Second, once you buy a home, your mortgage payments are relatively fixed (though taxes and utilities may go up). As your income rises, mortgage payments get easier to make, but renters often find that rents go up at least as fast as income. On the other hand, the changes in home prices have made it more important than ever for you to check whether it is better to own or rent.[9] How deeply particular cities were affected by the falling housing prices varies greatly from region to region.

Paying for a home has historically been a good way of forcing yourself to save. You must make the payments every month. Those payments are an investment that can prove to be very rewarding over time. A home is also a good asset to use when applying for a business loan.

Some couples have used the seed money accumulated from saving one income (in the strategy outlined above) to buy two attached homes so that they can live in one part and rent out the other. The rent they earn covers a good part of the payments for both homes, so the couple can live comfortably, yet inexpensively, while their investment in a home appreciates. In this way they accumulate capital, and, as they grow older, they pull far ahead of their peers in terms of financial security. As capital accumulates and values rise, they can sell and buy an even larger apartment building or a single-family home. Many have made fortunes in real estate in just this way.

Buying a home has usually been a very good and safe investment. But sometimes housing prices can rise fast, as they did between 2000 and 2007, and then fall, as they did between 2008 and 2012. Housing prices have been recovering since then in many areas. What has happened to housing prices in your area over the last few years?

FIGURE D.3 HOW MUCH HOUSE CAN YOU AFFORD?

Monthly mortgage payments—including interest, principal, real estate taxes, and insurance—generally shouldn't amount to more than 28 percent of your monthly income. Here's how much people in various income categories can afford to pay for a home if they use a 30-year mortgage and make a 10 percent down payment.

		INTEREST RATES			
Income	Monthly Payment	5%	6%	7%	15%
$ 30,000	$ 700	$106,263	$ 98,303	$ 91,252	$ 56,870
50,000	1,167	180,291	167,081	155,376	98,606
80,000	1,867	287,213	266,056	247,308	155,916
100,000	2,333	361,240	334,832	311,433	198,013

Source: Federal Housing Finance Board.

Many people are making an income by renting unused space on Airbnb.[10] Of course, it all depends on how valuable your space is. A double in New York City may bring in some real income if you rent it while away. Such rentals may be part of a "shared economy" that is emerging. That is, people are learning to share cars, homes, bicycles, driveways, and tools as a way of saving some money.[11]

Once you understand the benefits of home ownership versus renting, you can decide whether those same principles apply to owning the premises where you set up your own business—or owning your own equipment, vehicles, and the like. Figure D.3 will give you some idea of how expensive a house you can afford, given your income. You can find current mortgage interest rates and mortgage calculators at Interest.com.

Tax Deductions and Home Ownership

Buying a home is likely to be the largest and perhaps the most important investment you'll make. It's nice to know that the federal government is willing to help you with it. Here's how: Interest on your home mortgage payments is tax deductible. So are your real estate taxes. Since virtually all your mortgage payments during the first few years are applied to the interest on your loan, almost all the early payments are tax deductible—a tremendous benefit. If your payments are $1,000 a month and your income is in a 25 percent tax bracket, during the early years of your mortgage the government will, in effect, give you credit for about $250 of your payment, lowering your real cost. This makes home ownership much more competitive with renting than it may appear.

It is said that there are three keys to getting the optimal return on a home or any real estate investment: location, location, and location. A home in the best part of town, near good schools, shopping, and work, is usually a sound financial investment. Less expensive homes may appreciate in value more slowly than homes in the city or town center. It's usually better, from a financial viewpoint, to buy a smaller home in a great location than a large home in a not-so-great setting.

Where to Put Your Savings

Where are some other good places to save your money? For a young person, one of the *worst* places to keep long-term investments is a bank or savings and loan. It is important to have savings equivalent to about six months of living expenses in the bank for emergencies, but the bank is not the best place to invest. Internet banks pay higher interest than your local bank, but even their rates are relatively low.

One of the best places to invest over time has been the stock market. The stock market does tend to go up and down, but over a longer period of time it has proved to be one of the best investments. About half of U.S. households own stock and mutual funds. Most financial experts believe the stock market will grow more slowly in the future than it has over the last 50 years, but the U.S. economy has always managed to rise up after a crisis, like the stock market fall of recent years.

The future always looks gloomy during a financial crisis, but that doesn't mean you shouldn't take risks. Remember, the greater the risk, usually the greater the return. When stock prices are low, that's the time to *buy*. When stocks collapse, it's an opportunity to get into the stock market, not avoid it. The average investor buys when the market is high and sells when it's low. Clearly, that's not a good idea. It takes courage to buy when everyone else is selling. In the long run, however, this **contrarian approach** to investing is the way the rich get richer.[12]

Chapter 19 gave you a foundation for starting an investment program. That chapter also talked about bonds, but bonds have traditionally lagged behind stocks as a long-term investment.

contrarian approach
Buying stock when everyone else is selling or vice versa.

Learning to Manage Credit

Credit cards are an important element in your personal financial system, even if you rarely use them. First, you may have to own a credit card to buy certain goods or even rent a car, because some businesses require one for identification and to ensure payment. Second, you can use a credit card to keep track of purchases. A gasoline credit card gives you records of purchases over time for your income tax returns (if you drive for work) and financial planning purposes. Third, a credit card is more convenient than cash or checks. You can carry less cash and easily cancel a stolen card to protect your account. Not all credit cards are alike, however. One card, called Coin, stores data for your credit, debit, loyalty, membership, and gift cards.[13] You can decide which card is best for you by comparing them at CardRatings.com or CreditCards.com. The most secure cards will be PIN and chip cards, since such cards are much less prone to identity theft.[14]

Credit card companies like Visa often encourage young people to apply for credit cards—even during halftime as they're doing here at a Purdue basketball game. Why are such companies so willing to give you a credit card?

College credit card debt is on the rise. Half of college students have four or more cards and only 17 percent report regularly paying off their balance. If you do use a credit card, pay the balance in full during the period when no interest is charged. Finance charges on credit card purchases usually amount to 12 to 26 percent annually. Some credit card companies will reward you for paying on time. If you finance a TV, home appliances, or other purchases with a credit card, you may end up spending much more than if you pay with cash. Not having to pay 18 percent or more in interest is as good as earning 18 percent tax-free. You may want to choose a card that pays you back in cash or offers credits toward the purchase of a car or frequent-flier miles. The value of these "givebacks" can be as high as 6 percent.[15] Some cards have no annual fees; others have lower interest rates.

The danger of a credit card is the flip side of its convenience. It's too easy to buy things you wouldn't buy if you had to pay cash, or to pile up debts you can't repay. If you aren't the type who can stick to a financial plan or household budget, *it may be better not to have a credit card at all.* Imagine a customer who has a $10,000 balance on his or her credit card with a 16 percent interest rate and pays the minimum 4 percent monthly payment. How long will it take to pay off the debt, and what would the cost for interest be? The answers: 14 years and nearly $5,000—and that's without using the card again to purchase so much as a candy bar. Prior to 2006, the minimum payment was 2 percent. The lower minimum payment may have been enticing for the short term, but over time that same $10,000 balance would have taken over 30 years to repay and cost over $18,000 in interest if only the 2 percent minimum was paid.

Another danger of credit cards is the issue of hacking. Stores like Target, Neiman Marcus, and Michael's have had credit card numbers stolen.[16] This identity theft results in people getting access to your e-mail addresses, names, and account numbers. The newer credit cards use both a chip embedded in the card and a customer PIN. Time will tell if these cards will cut down on the losses due to stolen credit card numbers.[17]

Some people would be better off with a *debit* card only. Debit cards don't allow you to spend more than what you have in the bank, a great benefit for those who are not as careful with their spending as they should be.[18] Furthermore, there are no interest payments or annual fees.

Of the debtors seeking help at the National Consumer Counseling Service, more than half were between 18 and 32. A recent credit card law created new consumer credit card protections. The new law allows card issuers to increase interest rates for only a limited number of reasons and restricts increasing rates at all during the first year of a new card account. People must be at least 21 years old or get an adult to co-sign with them if they want new credit cards on their own. The Consumer Financial Protection Bureau regulates financial products and services, including mortgages, credit cards, student loans, and debt collection. You would be wise to explore what is available to you.

Use LearnSmart to help retain what you have learned. Access your instructor's Connect course to check out LearnSmart, or go to learnsmartadvantage.com for help.

ILEARNSMART°

test **prep**

- What are the six steps you can take to control your finances?
- What steps should a person follow to build capital?
- Why is real estate a good investment?

LO D–3 Explain how buying the appropriate insurance can protect your financial base.

PROTECTING YOUR FINANCIAL BASE: BUYING INSURANCE

One of the last things young people think about is the idea that they may become sick, get injured, or die. It is not a pleasant thought, but the unexpected does happen every day. To protect your loved ones from the loss of your income, you should buy life insurance.[19] Nearly a third of U.S. households have no life insurance coverage. This is one sign of how the financial pressures of today have affected families.

The simplest and least expensive form of life insurance is **term insurance**. It is pure insurance protection for a given number of years that typically costs less the younger you buy it (see Figure D.4). Every few years, you might have to renew the policy, and the premium can then rise. Check prices through a service like InsWeb.com or use one of Quicken's personal finance software packages.

How much insurance do you need? *Newsweek* posed this question: We just had our first baby; how much life insurance should we have? Answer: Seven times your family income plus $100,000 for college. Apportion your coverage so that a spouse earning 60 percent of the income carries 60 percent of the insurance.

Multiyear level-premium insurance guarantees that you'll pay the same premium for the life of the policy. Recently, 40 percent of new term policies guaranteed a set rate for 20 years or more. Some companies allow you to switch your term policy for a more expensive whole or universal life policy.

Whole life insurance combines pure insurance and savings, so you are buying both insurance and a savings plan. This may be a good idea for those people who have trouble saving money. A universal life policy lets you choose how much of your payment should go to insurance and how much to investments. The investments in such plans traditionally are very conservative but pay a steady interest rate.

Variable life insurance is a form of whole life insurance that invests the cash value of the policy in stocks or other high-yielding securities. Death benefits may thus vary, reflecting the performance of the investments.

Life insurance companies recognized people's desire to earn higher returns on their insurance (and to protect themselves against running out of money before they die) and began selling annuities. An **annuity** is a contract to make regular payments to a person for life or for a fixed period. With an

term insurance
Pure insurance protection for a given number of years.

whole life insurance
Life insurance that combines pure insurance and savings.

variable life insurance
Whole life insurance that invests the cash value of the policy in stocks or other high-yielding securities.

annuity
A contract to make regular payments to a person for life or for a fixed period.

INSURANCE NEEDS IN EARLY YEARS ARE HIGH	INSURANCE NEEDS DECLINE AS YOU GROW OLDER
1. Children are young and need money for education.	1. Children are grown.
2. Mortgage is high relative to income.	2. Mortgage is low or completely paid off.
3. Often there are auto payments and other bills to pay.	3. Debts are paid off.
4. Loss of income would be disastrous.	4. Insurance needs are few.
	5. Retirement income is needed.

FIGURE D.4 WHY BUY TERM INSURANCE?

annuity, you are guaranteed to have an income until you die (or for the agreed upon period).

There are two kinds of annuities: fixed and variable. *Fixed annuities* are investments that pay the policyholder a specified interest rate. They are not as popular as *variable annuities,* which provide investment choices identical to mutual funds. Such annuities are becoming more popular than term or whole life insurance. But buyers must be careful in selecting an insurance company and choosing the investments made with their money.

Consult a financial advisor who is not an insurance agent and who can help you make the wisest decision about insurance. You can also check out the insurance company through a rating service such as A.M. Best (www.ambest .com) or Moody's Investors Service (www.moodys.com).

Health Insurance

The law called the Patient Protection and Affordable Care Act (PPACA) requires nonexempt individuals to maintain a minimum level of health insurance or pay a tax penalty. The Supreme Court ruled that this highly controversial law (often called Obamacare) was constitutional in that it was within Congress's power to tax. It is important that you follow the changes as the new law is implemented because almost everything to do with your health care could be affected.

You may already have health insurance coverage through your employer. If not, you can buy health insurance through the government's health care Marketplace at healthcare.gov or directly from insurance companies like United Healthcare or Blue Cross/Blue Shield. One of the more popular health insurance alternatives is a health savings account (HSA), a tax-deferred savings account linked to a low-cost, high-deductible health insurance policy. The idea is to use the money that would have been spent on high-cost, low-deductible health insurance and deposit it in a health savings account. You can use the money in the HSA only for needed health care services. One major benefit to you is that the money grows tax-free until you take it out.

Disability Insurance

disability insurance
Insurance that pays part of the cost of a long-term sickness or an accident.

Your chances of becoming disabled at an early age are much higher than your chances of dying in an accident. It's dangerous financially not to have any health insurance. Hospital costs are simply too high to risk financial ruin by going uninsured. It is often a good idea to supplement health insurance policies with **disability insurance** that pays part of the cost of a long-term sickness or an accident. Disability insurance replaces part of your lost income, and, in some cases, pays disability related costs not covered by health insurance. Call an insurance agent or check online for possible costs of such insurance. The cost is relatively low to protect yourself from losing your income for an extended period.

Homeowner's or Renter's Insurance

You may be surprised how much it would cost to replace all the things you own. As you begin to accumulate possessions, you may want to have apartment or homeowner's insurance that covers their loss. Specify that you want *guaranteed replacement cost.* That means the insurance company will give you whatever it costs to buy all those things *new.* It costs a little more than a policy without guaranteed replacement, but you will get a lot more if you have a loss.[20]

The other option is insurance that covers the *depreciated cost* of the items. A sofa you bought five years ago for $600 may be worth only $150 now. That current value is what your insurance would pay you, not the $700 or more to buy a brand-new sofa. If your computer is stolen, you might get only a couple hundred dollars rather than its replacement cost.

Most policies don't cover expensive items like engagement and wedding rings. You can buy a *rider* to your policy to cover them at a reasonable cost.

Other Insurance

Most states require drivers to have automobile insurance; if your state doesn't, it's a good idea to buy it anyway. Be sure to insure against losses from uninsured motorists. Consider accepting a large deductible to keep the premiums low, and pay for small damages yourself.

You'll also need liability insurance to protect yourself against being sued by someone you accidentally injure. Often you can get a discount by buying all your insurance (life, health, homeowner's, automobile) with one company. This is called an **umbrella policy**. Look for other discounts such as for safe driving, good grades, and more.

umbrella policy
A broadly based insurance policy that saves you money because you buy all your insurance from one company.

LO D–4 Outline a strategy for retiring with enough money to last a lifetime.

PLANNING YOUR RETIREMENT

It may seem a bit early to be planning your retirement; however, not doing so would be a big mistake. Successful financial planning means long-range planning, and retirement is a critical phase of life. What you do now could make a world of difference in your quality of life after age 65, or whenever you retire. Presently, only 58 percent of workers say they or their spouses are currently saving for later life. Over 65 percent of workers say they are behind schedule in planning and saving for retirement.[21] As you can see, many people *never* get around to saving enough money for retirement. [22]

One purpose of planning your personal finances is to have enough money for retirement. If you plan to relax and travel when you retire, you need to begin saving now. What are your retirement goals, and what resources will you need to accomplish them?

Social Security

Social Security is the Old-Age, Survivors, and Disability Insurance Program established by the Social Security Act of 1935. It consists not of a fund of money but of a continuous flow of contributions in and payments out. The Social Security money you'll begin to receive when you retire will come directly from the Social Security taxes being paid by workers at that time. However, the number of people retiring and living longer is increasing dramatically, while the number paying into Social Security is declining. Maintaining Social Security may thus require reducing benefits, encouraging people to retire later, limiting cost-of-living adjustments (COLAs) made to benefits over time, and increasing Social Security taxes.[23]

Social Security will not provide you with ample funds for retirement. Plan now to save your own funds for your nonworking years. The government has established incentives to encourage you. Here are some specifics.

Individual Retirement Accounts (IRAs)

Traditionally, an **individual retirement account (IRA)** has been a tax-deferred investment plan that enables you (and your spouse, if you are married) to save part of your income for retirement. A traditional IRA allows people who qualify to deduct from their reported income the money they put into an account. **Tax-deferred contributions** are those for which you pay no current taxes, but the earnings gained in the IRA are taxed as income when they are withdrawn from your IRA after retirement.

Let's see why a traditional IRA is a good deal for an investor. The tremendous benefit is the fact that the invested money is not taxed. That means faster and higher returns for you. Say you put $5,500 into an IRA each year. (The maximum IRA contribution was $5,500 in 2014. If you're 50 or older, you can make an additional $1,000 "catch-up" contribution.) Normally you'd pay taxes on that $5,500 when you receive it as income. But because you put it into an IRA, you won't. If you're in the 25 percent tax bracket, that means you'll save $1,375 in taxes! Put another way, the $5,500 you save costs you only $4,125—a huge bargain.

The earlier you start saving, the better—because your money has a chance to double and double again. If you save $5,500 a year for 35 years in an IRA and earn 10 percent a year, you'll accumulate savings of more than $1.6 million. If you start when you're just out of school, you'll be a millionaire by the time you're 50. All you have to do is save $5,500 a year and earn 10 percent. You may be wise to use a Roth IRA instead (see the following).

If you increase your contribution to the maximum allowable each time it is raised, you can reach your million-dollar goal even earlier. The actual rate of return depends on the type of investments you choose. No one can predict future rates of return with certainty, and investments with higher rates of return also have higher risk. The actual rate of return on investments can vary widely over time (from the highest gain of 61 percent in 1983 to the lowest loss of −43 percent in 2008), but the average annual gain for the S&P 500 between 1970 and 2013 was 10.6 percent.[24] Some analysts expect it to be lower in the coming years, so you may need to save more to reach the same goals.

The earlier you start saving, the better. Consider this: If you were to start contributing $5,500 to an IRA earning 10 percent when you're 22 years old and do so for only five years, you'd have about $37,000 by the time you're 27. Even if you *never added another penny* to the IRA, by the time you're 65 you'd have almost $1.4 million. If you waited until you were 30 to start saving, you would need to save $5,500 every year for 32 years to have the same nest egg.

And what would you have if you started saving at 22 *and* continued nonstop every year until 65? More than $3.5 million! Can you see why investment advisors often say that an IRA is the best way to invest in your retirement?

A second kind of IRA is the **Roth IRA**. You don't get up-front deductions from your taxes as with a traditional IRA, but earnings grow tax-free and are tax-free when withdrawn. *This is often the best deal for college-age students.* You can transfer money from a traditional IRA into a Roth IRA. You will have to pay taxes first, but the long-term benefits often make this exchange worthwhile if you believe your tax rate will be higher when you retire than it is now.

Both types of IRA have advantages and disadvantages, so ask a financial advisor which is best for you. You may decide to have both.

You can't take money from either type of IRA until you are 59½ years old without paying a 10 percent penalty. That's a benefit for you, because it can keep you from tapping into your IRA in an emergency or when you're tempted to make a large impulse purchase. But the money is there if a real need or emergency arises. The government now allows you to take out some funds to invest in an education or a first home. But check the rules; they change over time.

Your local bank, savings and loan, and credit union all have different types of IRAs. Insurance companies offer them too. If you're looking for a higher return (and more risk), you can put your IRA funds into U.S. and international stocks, bonds, mutual funds, exchange-traded funds, or precious metals. You can switch from fund to fund or from investment to investment. You can even open several different IRAs as long as the total doesn't exceed the government's limit. Consider contributing to an IRA through payroll deductions to ensure that you invest the money before you're tempted to spend it.

Roth IRA
An IRA where you don't get up-front deductions on your taxes as you would with a traditional IRA, but the earnings grow tax-free and are also tax-free when they are withdrawn.

If the value of your retirement account plunges, you may have to defer your dream of an early retirement. If you have already started to save for your retirement, is your portfolio well diversified?

Simple IRAs

Companies with 100 or fewer workers can provide them with a simple IRA. Employees can contribute a larger part of their income annually than with a regular IRA (up to $12,000 versus $5,500), and the company matches their contribution. This plan enables people to save much more money over time and can help small companies compete for available workers.

MyIRAs

In 2014, President Obama announced a new a Roth IRA–type retirement savings plan called myIRA for low- and middle-income individuals. Simple and Roth IRAs typically require a $2,000 deposit to open and $500 thereafter, and banks or brokerages often charge fees to maintain accounts with lower balances. With a myIRA, households earning less than $191,000 can open an account with as little as $25, with additional contributions as low as $5, and there are no fees. Savers invest after-tax dollars and can withdraw the money in retirement tax-free.

Unlike other IRAs, myIra funds can only be invested in government savings bonds. Since the bonds are backed by the government, savers will never lose their principal investment. However, the accounts won't grow very quickly since the interest rates on these bonds are usually low. There is no penalty if the principal is withdrawn early; but

there is a penalty for early interest withdrawal. The account balance can be rolled over to a Roth at any time, but must be rolled over when it reaches $15,000.[25] You obviously won't become a millionaire with a myIRA, but if you have extremely limited funds this may be at least a start toward saving for retirement. The myIRA is currently a pilot program, so it may be awhile before we know how successful this new type of retirement account is.

401(k) Plans

401(k) plan
A savings plan that allows you to deposit pretax dollars and whose earnings compound tax-free until withdrawal, when the money is taxed at ordinary income tax rates.

A **401(k) plan** is an employer-sponsored savings plan that allows you to deposit a set amount of pretax dollars and collect compounded earnings tax-free until withdrawal, when the money is taxed at ordinary income tax rates. These or similar plans are the only pension many people have, but only about 70 percent of eligible employees make any contributions, and many companies are discontinuing their benefits. As a result, there have been several proposals for how to improve 401(k) plans.[26] Private equity firms, like the Blackstone Group, are eager to get people to sign up for their own 401(k) plans because so much money is involved.[27] Meanwhile, firms like IBM are actually cutting back on the amount they pay out from 401(k) plans by making only end-of-the-year payments to the fund rather than periodic contributions. All such actions can only add to the woes of future retirees.[28]

The plans have three benefits: (1) your contributions reduce your present taxable income, (2) tax is deferred on the earnings, and (3) many employers will match your contributions, sometimes 50 cents on a dollar. No investment will give you a better deal than an instant 50 percent return on your money. Not all companies have equally good programs, so be sure to check out what is available to you.

You should deposit at least as much as your employer matches, often up to 15 percent of your salary. You can usually select how the money in a 401(k) plan is invested: stocks, bonds, and in some cases real estate. Be careful not to invest all your money in the company where you work. It's always best to diversify your funds among different companies and among stocks, bonds, and real estate investment trusts.

Your financial assets can protect your children and even your grandchildren far into the future, if you have taken the right steps through estate planning. What can you do now in order to make sure your assets are divided the way you would like them to be when you're gone?

Like the simple IRA, there is a simple 401(k) plan for those firms that employ 100 or fewer employees. Employees again are allowed to invest an amount (maximum of $17,500 in 2014) that is matched by the employer. This is a rather new program, but it should also prove popular among small businesses in attracting new workers.

Keogh Plans

Millions of small-business owners don't have the benefit of a corporate retirement system. Such people can contribute to an IRA, but the amount they can invest is limited. The alternative for all those doctors, lawyers, real estate agents, artists, writers, and other self-employed people is to establish their own Keogh plan. It's like an IRA for entrepreneurs. You can also look into simplified employee pension (SEP) plans, the best types of IRAs for sole proprietors.

The advantage of Keogh plans is that participants can invest up to $52,000 per year. Like simple IRAs, Keogh funds aren't taxed until they are withdrawn, nor are the returns the funds earn. Thus, a person in the 25 percent tax bracket who invests $10,000 yearly in a Keogh saves $2,500 in taxes. That means, in essence, that the government is financing 25 percent of his or her retirement fund. As with an IRA, this is an excellent deal.

As with an IRA, there's a 10 percent penalty for early withdrawal. Also like an IRA, funds may be withdrawn in a lump sum or spread out over the years. However, the key decision is the one you make now—to begin early to put funds into an IRA, a Keogh plan, or both so that the "magic" of compounding can turn that money into a sizable retirement fund.

Financial Planners

If the idea of developing a comprehensive financial plan for yourself or your business seems overwhelming, relax; help is available from financial planners. Be careful, though—anybody can claim to be a financial planner today. It's often best to find a certified financial planner (CFP), that is, a professional with a bachelor's degree who has completed a curriculum in personal financial planning, passed a 10-hour examination, and has at least three years of experience in financial planning.[29] Unfortunately, many so-called financial planners are simply insurance salespeople.

In the past few years, there has been an explosion in the number of companies offering other businesses financial services, sometimes called one-stop financial centers or financial supermarkets because they provide a variety of financial services, ranging from banking service to mutual funds, insurance, tax assistance, stocks, bonds, and real estate. It pays to shop around for financial advice. Find someone who understands your business and is willing to spend some time with you.

Financial planning covers all aspects of investing, from life and health insurance all the way to retirement and death. Financial planners can advise you on the proper mix of IRAs, stocks, bonds, real estate, and so on.

Estate Planning

Your retirement may be far away, but it is never too early to begin thinking about estate planning, or making financial arrangements for those who will inherit from you. You may even help your parents or others to do such planning. An important first step is to select a guardian for your minor children. That person should have a genuine concern for your children as well as a parental style and moral beliefs you endorse.

Also ensure that you leave sufficient resources to rear your children, not only for living expenses but also for medical bills, college, and other major expenses. Often life insurance is a good way to ensure such a fund. Be sure to discuss all these issues with the guardian, and choose a contingent guardian in case the first choice is unable to perform the needed functions.

A second step is to prepare a **will**, a document that names the guardian for your children, states how you want your assets distributed, and names the executor for your estate. An **executor** assembles and values your estate, files income and other taxes, and distributes assets.

A third step is to prepare a durable power of attorney. This document gives an individual you name the power to take over your finances if you become incapacitated. A *durable power of attorney for health care* delegates power to a person you name to make health care decisions for you if you are unable to make such decisions yourself.

Other steps to follow are beyond the scope of this text. You may need to contact a financial planner/attorney to help you do the paperwork and planning to preserve and protect your investments for your children and spouse and others. But it all begins with a strong financial base.

will
A document that names the guardian for your children, states how you want your assets distributed, and names the executor for your estate.

executor
A person who assembles and values your estate, files income and other taxes, and distributes assets.

Use LearnSmart to help retain what you have learned. Access your instructor's Connect course to check out LearnSmart, or go to learnsmartadvantage.com for help.

LEARNSMART®

test prep

- What are three advantages of using a credit card?
- What kind of life insurance is recommended for most people?
- What are the advantages of investing through an IRA? A Keogh account? A 401(k) account?
- What are the main steps in estate planning?

summary

LO D–1   Outline the six steps for controlling your assets.

- **What are the six steps to managing personal assets?**
(1) Take an inventory of your financial assets by developing a balance sheet for yourself with the fundamental accounting equation: Assets = Liabilities + Owners' equity; (2) keep track of all your expenses; (3) prepare a budget; (4) pay off your debts; (5) start a savings plan (the best way is to pay yourself first); and (6) if you must borrow, borrow only for assets that can increase in value or generate income.

LO D–2   Explain how to build a financial base, including investing in real estate, saving money, and managing credit.

- **How can I accumulate funds?**
First, find a job. Try to live as frugally as possible. Invest your savings to generate even more capital. One such investment is a duplex home where the renter helps the owner pay the mortgage.

- **Why is real estate such a good investment?**
First, a home is the one investment you can live in. Second, once you buy a home, the payments are relatively fixed (though taxes and utilities may

go up). As your income rises, the house payments get easier to make, while rents tend to go up at least as fast as income.

- **How does the government help you buy real estate?**
  The government allows you to deduct interest payments on the mortgage, which lets you buy more home for the money.

- **Where is the best place to keep savings?**
  It is best, in the long run, to invest in stocks. Although they go up and down in value, in the long run stocks earn more than most other investments. Diversify among mutual funds and other investments.

- **What is a good way to handle credit cards?**
  Pay the balance in full during the period when no interest is charged. Not having to pay 16 percent interest is as good as earning 16 percent tax-free. Often a debit card is better than a credit card because it limits your spending to the amount you have in the bank.

 Explain how buying the appropriate insurance can protect your financial base.

- **What is the role of insurance in protecting capital?**
  Insurance protects you from loss. If you were to die, your heirs would lose the income you would have earned. You can buy life insurance to make up for some or all of that loss.

- **Why is term insurance preferred?**
  Term insurance is pure insurance protection for a given number of years. You can buy much more term insurance than whole life insurance for the same amount of money.

- **Do I need other insurance?**
  It is important to have health insurance to protect against large medical bills. You also need car insurance (get a high deductible) and liability insurance in case you injure someone. You should also have homeowner's or renter's insurance. Often an umbrella policy will provide all your insurance protection for a lower cost.

 Outline a strategy for retiring with enough money to last a lifetime.

- **Can I rely on Social Security to cover my retirement expenses?**
  Social Security depends on payments from current workers to cover the needs of retired people. Fewer workers are paying into the system, so you cannot rely on it to cover all your retirement expenses.

- **What are the basics of saving for retirement?**
  Supplement Social Security with savings plans of your own. Everyone should have an IRA or some other retirement account. A Roth IRA is especially good for young people because your money grows tax-free and is tax-free when you withdraw it. For entrepreneurs, a Keogh plan or simplified employee pension (SEP) plan is wise. If you work for someone else, check out the 401(k) plan. Find a financial advisor who can recommend the best savings plan and help you make other investments.

- **What are the basics of estate planning?**
  You need to choose a guardian for your children, prepare a will, and assign an executor for your estate. Sign a durable power of attorney to enable someone else to handle your finances if you are not capable. The same

applies to a health durable power of attorney. Estate planning is complex and often calls for the aid of a financial planner/attorney, but the money is well spent to protect your assets.

key terms

annuity 11	individual retirement account (IRA) 14	term insurance 11
contrarian approach 9	Roth IRA 15	umbrella policy 13
disability insurance 12	Social Security 14	variable life insurance 11
executor 18	tax-deferred contributions 14	whole life insurance 11
401(k) plan 16		will 18

critical thinking

1. Have you given any thought to becoming an entrepreneur? Do the statistics about millionaires in this chapter give you some courage to pursue such a venture?

2. Housing prices in many parts of the United States are falling. What is the situation where you live? Would you encourage a college graduate in your area to buy a home or rent?

3. What kinds of questions must a person ask before considering the purchase of a home?

4. What insurance coverage do you have? What type of insurance do you need to buy next?

developing workplace skills

Key: ● Team   ★ Analytic   ▲ Communication   ◙ Technology

★ ◙ ▲ 1. Check your local paper or use an online realtor to gather information regarding the cost to rent a two-bedroom apartment and to buy a two-bedroom condominium in your area. Go to Dinkytown.net and use the site's "rent-versus-buy calculator" to compare these costs. Discuss your findings in small groups.

★ ▲ 2. Talk with someone you know who has invested in a family home. What appreciation has he or she gained on the purchase price? (Or, conversely, how has the value depreciated?) What other benefits has the home brought? Draw up a list of the benefits and drawbacks of owning a home and real estate in general as an investment. Be prepared to give a one-minute presentation on what you learned.

★ ◙ ▲ 3. Go online and find out the cost of major medical/hospital treatments in your area. Ask some older friends or acquaintances about medical insurance and whether they have ever gone without any. What types of insurance do they recommend? Discuss your results with the class.

4. The best time to start saving for the future is *now*. To prove this point to yourself, find a savings calculator online and calculate how much you will have at age 65 if you begin saving $100 a month now, and $100 a month 10 years from now.

5. Go online and check out the benefits and drawbacks of both traditional and Roth IRAs. Be prepared to make a two-minute presentation about each and to discuss your findings in class.

taking it to the **net**

PURPOSE

To use online resources to make smart personal finance decisions.

EXERCISE

Use the calculators at Dinkytown.net to answer the following questions:

1. You need $5,000 for a trip to Europe in two years. How much would you have to deposit monthly in a savings account paying 1 percent in order to meet your goal?

2. Investing $1,000 at 6 percent for five years, what is the difference in purchasing power of your savings if inflation increases by 2 percent annually during that time? By 4 percent?

3. Starting today, how much would you need to save each month in order to become a millionaire before you retire?

4. You need a new car. What car can you afford if you have $1,500 for a down payment, can make monthly payments of $300, and get $1,000 for trading in your old clunker?

5. How much house can you afford if you earn $36,000 a year and have $10,000 savings for a down payment, a $6,000 car loan balance, and no credit card debts?

notes

1. "Africa's Billionaires Club," *Time,* October 21, 2013.
2. Kelly Greene, "How to Fine-Tune Your 401 (k)," *The Wall Street Journal,* January 25–26, 2014.
3. Veronica Dagher, "Wanted: Ideas to Teach Teenagers about Money," *The Wall Street Journal,* February 4, 2014.
4. Alexandra Wolfe, "Drew Faust" (President of Harvard), *The Wall Street Journal,* February 1–2, 2014.
5. Anne Tergesen, "Seven Resolutions to Get Your Nest Egg in Shape," *The Wall Street Journal,* January 14, 2013.
6. Marketwatch, "1 in 4 Americans Aren't Saving for Retirement," *New York Post,* May 23, 2014.
7. Elizabeth Dwoskin and Frank Bass, "Who's Complaining about Your Bank," *Bloomberg Businessweek,* April 8–14, 2013.
8. "Signs You Should Keep Renting," *The Week,* May 9, 2014.
9. Carol Hymowitz, "The Buy/Rent Balance Shifts," *Bloomberg Businessweek,* January 6–12, 2014.
10. Emily Belz, "A Room of One's Own," *World,* December 14, 2013.
11. Tomio Geron, "The Share Economy," *Forbes,* February 11, 2013.
12. Anne Kates Smith, "Where to Put Your Money Now," *Kiplinger's Personal Finance,* July 2014.
13. Lisa Gerstner, "One Card That Claims to Do It All," *Kiplinger's Personal Finance,* March 2014.
14. Meredith Derby Berg, "Seven Ways Retailers Are Embracing Tech," *Advertising Age,* February 3, 2014.
15. Odysseas Papadimitriou, "Best Credit Cards for 2014," *Bottom Line Personal,* February 1, 2014.
16. Charles Levinson and Danny Yadron, "Card-Theft Code Grew in the Net's Dark Alleys," *The Wall Street Journal,* January 22, 2014.
17. Bill Saporito, "Plastic Surgery," *Time,* February 10, 2014.

18. Lisa Gerstner, "Credit or Debit: Pick Your Plastic," *Kiplinger's Personal Finance,* August 2013.
19. Peter Katt, "Life Insurance Cash Value: A Practical Discussion," *AAII Journal,* January 2014.
20. An editorial in *AAA World,* November/December 2013.
21. Tergesen, "Seven Resolutions to Get Your Nest Egg in Shape."
22. Michael A. Fletcher, "Future Retirees at Greater Fiscal Risk," *The Washington Post,* February 17, 2013.
23. Ezra Klein, "Entitlements Are the Problem? Maybe They're the Answer," *The Washington Post,* April 7, 2013.
24. www.standardandpoors.com, accessed May 2014.
25. Michael A. Fletcher, "New Retirement Savings Option Is Seen as a Moderate First Step," *The Washington Post,* January 20, 2014; Lydia DePillis, "Bit by Bit to Build a Nest Egg," *The Washington Post,* February 2, 2014; an editorial in *The Washington Times,* February 3, 2014; and "Nine Things to Know about Obama's myIRA Accounts," *The Wall Street Journal,* January 29, 2014.
26. Knight Kiplinger, "A Bold 401(k) Overhaul," *Kiplinger's Personal Finance,* June 2013.
27. Margaret Collins and Devin Banerjee, "Would You Like Some PE in Your 401(k)?" *Bloomberg Businessweek,* April 8–14, 2013.
28. Anjelica Tan, "IBM Sets a Stingier 401(k) Standard," *Kiplinger's Personal Finance,* March 2013.
29. Certified Financial Planner Board of Certification, www.cfp.net, accessed May 2014.

photo credits

Getting the Job You Want

We hope that as you've read the text, you've developed an idea of the type of career you'd like to build for yourself. If so, how will you go about getting a job you want in your chosen field? That is what this Epilogue is all about. Good luck—we hope you find a job doing something you love!

- Job Search Strategy
- Search for Jobs Online
- Job Search Resources
- Writing Your Résumé
- Putting Your Résumé Online
- Writing a Cover Letter
- Preparing for Job Interviews
- Be Prepared to Change Careers

One of the most important goals of this book is to help you get the job you want. First, you have to decide what you want to do. So far we've helped you explore this decision by explaining what people do in the various business functions: human resource management, marketing, accounting, finance, and so on. There are many good books about finding the job you want, so we can only introduce the subject here.

If you are a returning student, you have both blessings and handicaps that younger students do not have. First, you may have had a full-time job already. Second, you are more likely to know what kind of job you don't want. That is a real advantage. By exploring the various business careers in depth, you should be able to choose a career path that will meet your objectives.

If you have a full-time job right now, you already know that working while going to school requires juggling school and work responsibilities. Many older students must also balance family responsibilities in addition to those of school and work. But take heart. You have also acquired many skills from these experiences. Even if they were acquired in unrelated fields, these skills will be invaluable as you enter your new career. You can compete with younger students because you have the focus that comes with experience. Instructors enjoy having both kinds of students in class because they have different perspectives.

So, whether you're beginning your first career or your latest career, it's time to develop a strategy for finding and getting a personally satisfying job.

Do you look forward to saying, "I got the job!" after your years of college study? Job fairs are among the many resources that can help you find the right job for you. Is it ever too early to start thinking about your career?

JOB SEARCH STRATEGY

It is never too early to begin thinking about a future career or careers. The following strategies will give you some guidance in that pursuit:

1. **Begin with self-analysis.** You might begin your career quest by completing a self-analysis inventory. You can refer to Figure E.1 for a sample of a simple assessment.

2. **Search for jobs you would enjoy.** Begin at your college's career planning office or website, if your school has one. Talk to people in various careers, even after you've found a job. Career progress demands continuous research.

3. **Begin the networking process.** Networking remains the number one way for new job seekers to get their foot in the door. You can start with your fellow students, family, relatives, neighbors, friends, professors, and local businesspeople. Be sure to keep a record of names, addresses, and phone numbers of contacts, including where they work, the person who recommended them to you, and the relationship between the source person and the contact. A great way to build contacts and make a good impression on employers is to do part-time work and summer internships for firms you find interesting.

4. **Use social media for help.** Many professionals use online social networking sites, like Facebook, Twitter, and LinkedIn, to expand their networks and share industry news. If you haven't already, start profiles with these sites and start making connections. Don't sign up for a profile if you won't use it; employers will only think you don't finish

FIGURE E.1 A PERSONAL ASSESSMENT

Interests

1. How do I like to spend my time?
2. Do I enjoy being with people?
3. Do I like working with mechanical things?
4. Do I enjoy working with numbers?
5. Am I a member of many organizations?
6. Do I enjoy physical activities?
7. Do I like to read?

Abilities

1. Am I adept at working with numbers?
2. Am I adept at working with mechanical things?
3. Do I have good verbal and written communication skills?
4. What special talents do I have?
5. In which abilities do I wish I were more adept?

Education

1. Have I taken certain courses that have prepared me for a particular job?
2. In which subjects did I perform the best? The worst?
3. Which subjects did I enjoy the most? The least?
4. How have my extracurricular activities prepared me for a particular job?
5. Is my GPA an accurate picture of my academic ability? Why?
6. Do I want a graduate degree? Do I want to earn it before beginning my job?
7. Why did I choose my major?

Experience

1. What previous jobs have I held? What were my responsibilities in each?
2. Were any of my jobs applicable to positions I may be seeking? How?
3. What did I like the most about my previous jobs? Like the least?
4. Why did I work in the jobs I did?
5. If I had to do it over again, would I work in these jobs? Why?

Personality

1. What are my good and bad traits?
2. Am I competitive?
3. Do I work well with others?
4. Am I outspoken?
5. Am I a leader or a follower?
6. Do I work well under pressure?
7. Do I work quickly, or am I methodical?
8. Do I get along well with others?
9. Am I ambitious?
10. Do I work well independently of others?

Desired job environment

1. Am I willing to relocate? Why?
2. Do I have a geographic preference? Why?
3. Would I mind traveling in my job?
4. Do I have to work for a large, nationally known firm to be satisfied?
5. Must I have a job that initially offers a high salary?
6. Must the job I assume offer rapid promotion opportunities?
7. In what kind of job environment would I feel most comfortable?
8. If I could design my own job, what characteristics would it have?

Personal goals

1. What are my short- and long-term goals? Why?
2. Am I career-oriented, or do I have broader interests?
3. What are my career goals?
4. What jobs are likely to help me achieve my goals?
5. What do I hope to be doing in 5 years? In 10 years?
6. What do I want out of life?

what you start. When posting to these websites, be careful to include only information you would want a potential hiring agent to see and not something that might hurt your chances for landing a job.

5. **Prepare a good cover letter and résumé.** Once you know what you want to do and where you would like to work, you need to develop a good résumé and cover letter. Your résumé lists your education, work experience, and activities. We'll talk about these key job search tools in more detail. We'll also give you a list of resources you can use.

6. **Develop interviewing skills.** Interviewers will be checking your appearance (clothes, haircut, fingernails, shoes); your attitude (friendly, engaged); your verbal ability (speaking clearly); and your motivation

(enthusiasm, passion). Note also that interviewers want you to have been active outside of school and to have set goals. Have someone evaluate you on these qualities now to see if you have any weak points. You can then work on those weaknesses before you have any actual job interviews. We'll give you some clues on how to do this later.

7. **Follow up.** Write a thank-you e-mail after interviews, even if you think they didn't go well. You have a chance to make a lasting impression with a follow-up note. If you are interviewed by a group of people, ask for their business cards at the interview and e-mail them each separately. Let the company know you are still interested and indicate your willingness to travel to be interviewed. Get to know people in the company and learn from them whom to contact and what qualifications to emphasize.

Professional interview behavior includes writing a follow-up letter to thank the person or persons you met. What are your goals in writing such a letter?

SEARCHING FOR JOBS ONLINE

Social networking has become a powerful force in the job search. This should be no surprise; networking has always been the best way to hear about job leads, and networking online only makes it easier to connect and communicate with the people who could one day hire you.

Employers can use your online profiles to find your previous employers, learn more about your personality and interests, and gauge if you'd match the company's needs. Employers can also find red flags that can keep you from being hired, such as provocative photos, evidence of excessive drinking or drug use, bad-mouthing of previous employers, or discriminatory comments about race, age, gender, or other topics. The key is to build a professional yet genuine personality online, one you won't mind showing to your future boss.

You can be sure that a future employer will check out your social media personality before hiring you. Here are a few social media sites you should be on:

- Facebook—"Like" the company's page on Facebook and look through its posts, photos, and comments to get a sense for what the company does.

- Twitter—Follow people who work in the industries and positions you are applying for. Share links to interesting articles or updates, and "re-tweet," or repeat, interesting stories from other professionals.

- LinkedIn—Companies have always relied on current employees to find their best new employees, and LinkedIn makes finding those connections easier. Using LinkedIn, you may find out that your high school friend's old college roommate is hiring, and that connection could be enough to get you the job.

- Google1: Organize your business contacts into "circles" and consider reaching out to them in "hangouts" to discuss industry news and find job openings.

- Pinterest: Share photos or videos that showcase your skills, especially if your experiences are creative or visual. Or, just show employers your personality by sharing images you enjoy.

- YouTube: Show off your communication skills and personality by posting videos. If you don't have videos from your previous work experiences, consider starting a video blog where you share your opinions on topics relevant to your business.

- Blog/Personal Website: While you should be careful about posting any personal information that could lead to identity theft on a public website, consider the value of writing regularly about a topic related to your career interests. A well-written blog can attract the attention of employers. However, if you create a blog, remember to proofread everything you post. Be sure to call attention to your blog posts by using Twitter and LinkedIn updates with links to what you write.

JOB SEARCH RESOURCES

Your school placement bureau's office and website are good places to begin learning about potential employers. On-campus interviewing is often a great source of jobs (see Figure E.2). Your library and the Internet may have annual reports that will give you even more information about your selected companies.

Other good sources of jobs include the want ads, job fairs, summer and other internship programs, placement bureaus, and sometimes walking into firms that appeal to you and asking for an interview. The *Occupational Outlook Quarterly*, produced by the U.S. Department of Labor, says this about job hunting:

> The skills that make a person employable are not so much the ones needed on the job as the ones needed to get the job, skills like the ability to find a job opening, complete an application, prepare the résumé, and survive an interview.

Here are a few printed sources you can use for finding out about jobs, writing résumés and cover letters, and other career information:

1. U.S. Department of Labor, "Occupational Outlook Handbook," 2013–2014
2. Carole Martin, *What to Say in Every Job Interview* (McGraw-Hill, 2014)
3. Martin Yate, *Knock 'em Dead 2014: The Ultimate Job Search Guide* (Adams Media Corporation, 2014)
4. Damien Birket, *The Job Search Checklist* (AMACON, 2013)

FIGURE E.2 WHERE COLLEGE STUDENTS FIND JOBS

SOURCE OF JOB	
Online searches	College faculty/staff referrals
On-campus interviewing	Internship programs
Write-ins	High-demand major programs
Current employee referrals	Minority career programs
Job listings with placement office	Part-time employment
Responses from want ads	Unsolicited referrals from placement
Walk-ins	Women's career programs
Cooperative education programs	Job listings with employment agencies
Summer employment	Referrals from campus organizations

5. Richard N. Bolles, *What Color Is Your Parachute? 2014: A Practical Manual for Job-Hunters and Career-Changers* (Ten Speed Press, 2014)

6. Paul D. Tieger, Barbara Barron, and Kelly Tieger, *Do What You Are: Discover the Perfect Career for You Through the Secrets of Personality Type* (Little, Brown, and Company, 2014)

7. Nicolas Lore, *The Pathfinder: How to Choose or Change Your Career for a Lifetime of Satisfaction and Success* (Touchstone Books, 2012)

8. Gwenn Wilson, *100% Job Search Success* (Cengage Learning, 2014)

9. Fred Koon, *Leveraging LinkedIn: For Job Success in 2014* (Create Space Independent Publishing Platform, 2014)

To find information about careers or internships online, try these sites (though keep in mind that addresses on the Internet are subject to sudden and frequent change):

- www.CareerBuilder.com
- www.Monster.com
- www.JobSearch.about.com
- www.Indeed.com
- www.GlassDoor.com
- www.TweetMyJobs.com

It's never too early in your career to begin designing a résumé and thinking of cover letters. A quality résumé is both deep and wide: deep, meaning you had a deep commitment to your activities (leadership roles, responsibilities, long-term commitments), and wide, meaning you were active in several, varied areas (jobs, internships, clubs, volunteering).

By preparing a résumé now, you may find gaps that need to be filled before you can land the job you want. For example, if you discover that you haven't been involved in enough outside activities to impress an employer, join a club or volunteer your time. If you are weak on job experience, seek an internship or part-time job to fill in that gap.

It's never too soon to prepare a résumé, so let's discuss how.

WRITING YOUR RÉSUMÉ

A résumé is a one-page document that lists information an employer would need to evaluate whether you qualify for that company's job opening. A résumé explains your immediate goals and career objectives as well as your educational background, experience, interests, and other relevant data. For example, experience working with teams is important to many companies. If you don't show an employer you have experience working with teams on your résumé, how can that employer decide if you should get an interview? Employers don't *read* résumés—they *scan* them, so use action words like those listed in Figure E.3 to grab an employer's attention quickly. You must be comprehensive and clear in your résumé if you are to communicate all your attributes.

Your résumé is an advertisement for yourself. If your ad is better than the other person's ad, you're more likely to get the interview. In this case, *better* means that your ad highlights your attributes more attractively. In discussing your education, for example, be sure to highlight your extracurricular activities such as part-time jobs, sports, and clubs. If you did well in school, include your grades. Be sure to describe your previous jobs, including your responsibilities, achievements, and special projects. If you include an interests section, don't just list your hobbies, but describe how deeply you are involved. If you organized the club, volunteered your

Administered	Directed	Investigated	Scheduled
Budgeted	Established	Managed	Served
Conducted	Handled	Operated	Supervised
Coordinated	Implemented	Organized	Teamed
Designed	Improved	Planned	Trained
Developed	Increased	Produced	Wrote

time, or participated in an organization, make sure to say so in the résumé. The idea is to make yourself look as good on paper as you are in reality.

Here are some hints on preparing your résumé:

- Keep it simple. Put a summary of your skills and your objective at the top so that the reader can capture as much as possible in the first 30 seconds.

- If you e-mail your résumé, send it in the text of the message; don't just send it as an attachment. It takes too long for the receiver to open an attachment.

- Customize each mailing to that specific company. You may use a standard résumé, but add data to customize it and to introduce it.

- Use any advertised job title as the subject of your e-mail message, including any relevant job numbers.

See Figure E.4 for a sample résumé. Most companies prefer that you keep your résumé to one page unless you have many years of experience.

PUTTING YOUR RÉSUMÉ ONLINE

Many larger firms seek candidates on the Internet, and online tools can help you expand your résumé into a portfolio complete with links, work samples, and even video. An online résumé can thus allow you to reach the greatest number of potential employers with the least amount of effort.

But remember, thousands of other eager job hunters send résumés online, and the volume can overwhelm recruiters. That doesn't mean you shouldn't post your résumé online, but you can't just send a few hundred résumés into cyberspace and then sit back and wait for the phone to ring. Include online résumés as a tool in your job search process, but continue to use the more traditional tools, such as networking.

If you are sending a résumé through a career listing site like Monster.com, the company may be using a computer program to scan your résumé for keywords before actual humans get their hands on it. Computer programs look at résumés much differently than people do, so some people's perfectly executed, beautifully worded résumés don't pass the computer's test. If you are submitting a résumé online, you must understand what the computer is programmed to look for. While scannable résumés are on their way out, you may still find value in creating an online résumé that will pass the computer scan with flying colors. Here are five ways to write an online résumé that will get you past the computer evaluation stage:

- Include as many of the keywords in the company's job description as possible. If you are applying for a sales management position, use the words "sales," "managed," and "manager" often in your résumé.

- Visit the employer's website. Are there any words they use to describe their corporate culture? If so, include those adjectives in your résumé as well.

Yann Ng
345 Big Bend Boulevard
Kirkwood, MO, 63122
314-555-5385
yng@stilnet.com

Job objective: Sales representative in business-to-business marketing

Education: Earned 100 percent of college expenses working 35 hours per week

A.A. in Business, May 2013
St. Louis Community College at Meramec
Grade Point Average: 3.6

B.S. in Business, Marketing Major, expected May 2015
University of Missouri, St. Louis
Grade Point Average: 3.2 overall, 3.5 in major
Dean's List for two semesters

Experience

Schnuck's Supermarket, Des Peres, MO, 5/11 – present

- Responded to customer requests quickly as evening and weekend checkout cashier
- Trained new hires to build customer retention, loyalty, and service
- Learned on-the-job principles behind brand management, retail sales, and consumer product marketing

Mary Tuttle's Flowers, Kirkwood, MO, Summer 2009 and Summer 2010

- Created flower arrangements to customer specifications, managed sales transactions, and acted as an assistant to the manager
- Developed skills in customer relationship management
- Created window displays to enhance visual merchandising and retail marketing to consumers

Student Leadership

SLCC Student Representative Board: Created action plan for fundraising drive, which resulted in our largest donations ever to Habitat for Humanity
UMSL Student American Marketing Association: Ran team-building and recruitment activities, which resulted in a 10 percent increase in membership
UMSL Student Government Association: Ran focus groups to help prioritize goals, helping us target changes in the way we allocate student fees

Language Skills: Fluent in English, Vietnamese, and French

Computer Skills: Microsoft Office, Photoshop, and HTML/Web Publishing

- Developed own website (www.yng@stilnet.com)
- Created effective PowerPoint slides using Photoshop for Consumer Behavior class

- Keep your formatting simple and streamlined. Avoid underlining, italics, and boxes. You don't want to confuse the computer with fancy designs. Keep it simple and save your formatted résumé for the next stages in the process.
- List all the universities or colleges you've attended, even if it was just for a class or a semester. Some computer programs assign higher point values to prestigious universities.
- Don't ever lie, exaggerate, or cheat the system. You'll get caught, and you won't get the job.

Figure E.5 offers a sample online résumé, but you should consult the latest résumé handbook to see what the newer résumés should look like.

Posting résumés to online job sites can cause privacy nightmares for job seekers, who fear everything from identity theft to losing their current job when employers find out that they are looking for new jobs. Sometimes posted résumés are sold to other sites or individuals willing to pay for them. Scam artists posing as recruiters can download all the résumés they want and do virtually whatever they want with them. At worst, online résumés can give identity thieves a starting point to steal personal information.

FIGURE E.5 SAMPLE ONLINE RÉSUMÉ

Yann Ng
345 Big Bend Boulevard
Kirkwood, MO, 63122
314-555-5385
yng@stilnet.com

Job objective: Sales representative in business-to-business marketing

Education:
A.A. in Business, May 2013
St. Louis Community College at Meramec
Grade point average: 3.6

B.S. in Business, Marketing major, expected May 2015
University of Missouri, St. Louis
Grade point average: 3.2 overall, 3.5 in major
Dean's List for two semesters

Experience:
Schnuck's Supermarket, Des Peres, MO, 5/11 – present Responded to customer requests quickly as evening and weekend checkout cashier. Trained new hires to build customer retention, loyalty, and service. Learned on-the-job principles behind brand management, retail sales, and consumer product marketing.

Mary Tuttle's Flowers, Kirkwood, MO, Summer 2009 and Summer 2010 Created flower arrangements to customer specifications, managed sales transactions, and acted as an assistant to the manager. Developed skills in customer relationship management. Created window displays to enhance visual merchandising and retail marketing to consumers.

Student Leadership
SLCC Student Representative Board: Created action plan for fundraising drive
UMSL Student American Marketing Association: Ran team-building and recruitment activities UMSL Student Government Association: Ran focus groups to help prioritize goals.

Language Skills
English
Vietnamese
French

Computer Skills
Microsoft Office
Photoshop
HTML/Web Publishing

Here are tips to protect your résumé and your identity:

- *Never* include highly private information, such as Social Security numbers and birthdays.
- Check job boards' privacy policies to see how information is used and resold.
- Post résumés directly to employers if possible.
- Date résumés and remove them promptly after finding a job.
- If possible, withhold confidential information such as telephone numbers and your name and use temporary e-mail addresses for contacts.

Some companies take résumés via Twitter before accepting full-page résumés by e-mail. Find a creative way to shorten your career objectives, experience, and interests to under 140 characters and share it with your connections.

WRITING A COVER LETTER

A cover letter is used to announce your availability and to introduce the résumé, but it also showcases your personality to an employer, often for the first time. The cover letter is probably one of the most important advertisements anyone will write in a lifetime—so it should be done right.

First, the cover letter should indicate that you've researched the organization and are interested in a job there. Let the organization know what sources you used and what you know in the first paragraph to get the attention of the reader and show your interest.

You may have heard people say, "What counts is not what you know, but whom you know." If you don't know anyone, *get* to know someone. You can do this by calling the organization, visiting the offices, or reaching out on social media to talk to people who already have the kind of job you're hoping to get. Then, at the beginning of your cover letter, mention that you've talked with some of the firm's employees, showing the letter reader that you "know someone," if only casually, and that you're interested enough to actively pursue the organization. This is all part of networking.

Describe yourself in the next paragraph of your cover letter. Be sure to show how your experiences will benefit the organization. For example, don't just say, "I will be graduating with a degree in marketing." Say, "You will find that my college training in marketing and marketing research has prepared me to learn your marketing system quickly and begin making a contribution right away." The sample cover letter in Figure E.6 will give you a better feel for how this looks.

Use the last paragraph of your cover letter to say you are available for an interview at a time and place convenient for the interviewer. Offer to follow up with a phone call or e-mail if you don't hear from the employer after some time. Again, see the sample cover letter in Figure E.6 for guidance. Notice in this letter how the writer subtly shows that she reads business publications and draws attention to her résumé.

Principles to follow in writing a cover letter and preparing your résumé include:

- Be confident. List all your good qualities and attributes.
- Don't be apologetic or negative. Write as one professional to another, not as a humble student begging for a job.
- Describe how your experience and education can add value to the organization.

FIGURE E.6 SAMPLE
COVER LETTER

345 Big Bend Blvd.
Kirkwood, MO 63122
October 10, 2015

Mr. Carl Karlinski
Premier Designs
45 Apple Court
Chicago, IL 60536

Dear Mr. Karlinski: (Address the letter to a real person whenever possible.)

Recent articles in *Inc.* and *Success* praised your company for its innovative products and strong customer orientation. Having used your creative display materials at Mary Tuttle's Flowers, I'm familiar with your visually stimulating designs. Christie Bouchard, your local sales representative, told me all about your products and your sales training program at Premier Designs. Having talked with her about the kind of salespeople you are seeking, I believe I have the motivation and people skills to be successful.

Proven Sales Ability: For two summers, I created and sold flower arrangements at Mary Tuttle's Flowers, developing a loyal customer base. Also, for four years, I've practiced personable customer relations, based on the excellent customer-oriented training program that Schnuck's Supermarket delivers in the St. Louis region. I know our regular customers by name; they've told me that they first look for my station when they are checking out. I would bring this same attention to developing relationships in a business-to-business sales position.

Self-Motivation: I've worked 35 hours per week and every summer during my college years and have paid for 100 percent of my expenses. In addition, I've paid for trips to Asia, Europe, and the Americas.

Leadership: I've served actively in student governance both on the Student Representative Board at St. Louis Community College and as a part of the student government at the University of Missouri. I've always gotten to know other students to find out how I could make a difference through my student government work. I would take the initiative to not only serve customers well but also to help other new salespeople.

I will be in the Chicago area the week of January 4–9 and would appreciate the opportunity to meet with you to learn more about Premier's sales opportunities. I will phone your administrative assistant to check on your availability. Thank you for considering my application. I would work hard to maintain and expand the business-to-business relationships that have made Premier Designs so successful.

Sincerely,

Yann Ng

- Research every prospective employer thoroughly before writing anything. Use a rifle approach rather than a shotgun approach. That is, write effective marketing-oriented letters to a few select companies rather than general letters to a long list.
- Have your materials prepared by an experienced keyboarder if you are not highly skilled yourself. Use printing services like FedEx Office if you do not have access to a good-quality printer.
- Have someone edit your materials for spelling, grammar, and style. Don't be like the student who sent out a second résumé to correct "some mixtakes." Or another who said, "I am acurite with numbers."
- Don't send the names of references until asked.

PREPARING FOR JOB INTERVIEWS

Companies use interviews to decide which qualified candidates are the best match for the job, so be prepared for your interviews. There are five stages of interview preparation:

1. **Do research about the prospective employers.** Learn what industry the firm is in, its competitors, the products or services it produces and their acceptance in the market, and the title of your desired position. You can find such information in the firm's annual reports, in Standard & Poor's, Hoover's, Moody's manuals, and various business publications such as *Fortune, Bloomberg Businessweek,* and *Forbes.* Ask your librarian for help or search the Internet. You can look in the *Reader's Guide to Business Literature* to locate the company name and to look for articles about it. This important first step shows you have initiative and interest in the firm.

2. **Practice the interview.** Figure E.7 lists some of the more frequently asked questions in an interview. Practice answering these questions at the placement office and with your roommate, parents, or friends. Don't memorize your answers, but do be prepared—know what you're going to say. Interviewers will be impressed if you prepare questions for them about the products, job, company culture, and so on. Figure E.8 shows sample questions you might ask. Be sure you know whom to contact, and write down the names of everyone you meet. Review the action words in Figure E.3 and try to fit them into your answers.

FIGURE E.7 FREQUENTLY ASKED QUESTIONS

- How would you describe yourself?
- What are your greatest strengths and weaknesses?
- How did you choose this company?
- What do you know about the company?
- What are your long-range career goals?
- What courses did you like best? Least?
- What are your hobbies?
- Do you prefer a specific geographic location?
- Are you willing to travel (or move)?
- Which accomplishments have given you the most satisfaction?
- What things are most important to you in a job?
- Why should I hire you?
- What experience have you had in this type of work?
- How much do you expect to earn?

FIGURE E.8 SAMPLE QUESTIONS TO ASK THE INTERVIEWER

- Who are your major competitors, and how would you rate their products and marketing relative to yours?
- How long does the training program last, and what is included?
- How soon after school would I be expected to start?
- What are the advantages of working for this firm?
- How much travel is normally expected?
- What managerial style should I expect in my area?
- How would you describe the working environment in my area?
- How would I be evaluated?
- What is the company's promotion policy?
- What is the corporate culture?
- What is the next step in the selection procedures?
- How soon should I expect to hear from you?
- What other information would you like about my background, experience, or education?
- What is your highest priority in the next six months and how could someone like me help?

3. **Be professional during the interview.** You should look and sound professional throughout the interview. Dress appropriately. When you meet the interviewers, greet them by name, smile, and maintain good eye contact. Sit up straight in your chair and be alert and enthusiastic. If you have practiced, you should be able to relax and be confident. Other than that, be yourself, answer questions, and be friendly and responsive. (You learned about what types of questions job interviewers are legally allowed to ask you in Chapter 11.) Remember, the interview is not one-way communication; don't forget to ask the questions you've prepared before the interview. Do *not* ask about salary, however, until you've been offered a job. When you leave, thank the interviewers and, if you're still interested in the job, tell them so. If they don't tell you, ask them what the next step is. Maintain a positive attitude. Figures E.9 and E.10 outline what the interviewers will be evaluating.

4. **Follow up on the interview.** First, write down what you can remember from the interview: names of the interviewers and their titles, dates for training, and so forth, so you can send a follow-up letter, a letter of

FIGURE E.9 TRAITS RECRUITERS SEEK IN JOB PROSPECTS

1. **Ability to communicate.** Do you have the ability to organize your thoughts and ideas effectively? Can you express them clearly when speaking or writing? Can you present your ideas to others in a persuasive way?

2. **Intelligence.** Do you have the ability to understand the job assignment? Learn the details of operation? Contribute original ideas to your work?

3. **Self-confidence.** Do you demonstrate a sense of maturity that enables you to deal positively and effectively with situations and people?

4. **Willingness to accept responsibility.** Are you someone who recognizes what needs to be done and is willing to do it?

5. **Initiative.** Do you have the ability to identify the purpose of work and to take action?

6. **Leadership.** Can you guide and direct others to obtain the recognized objectives?

7. **Energy level.** Do you demonstrate a forcefulness and capacity to make things move ahead? Can you maintain your work effort at an above-average rate?

8. **Imagination.** Can you confront and deal with problems that may not have standard solutions?

9. **Flexibility.** Are you capable of changing and being receptive to new situations and ideas?

10. **Interpersonal skills.** Can you bring out the best efforts of individuals so they become effective, enthusiastic members of a team?

11. **Self-knowledge.** Can you realistically assess your own capabilities? See yourself as others see you? Clearly recognize your strengths and weaknesses?

12. **Ability to handle conflict.** Can you successfully contend with stress situations and antagonism?

13. **Competitiveness.** Do you have the capacity to compete with others and the willingness to be measured by your performance in relation to that of others?

14. **Goal achievement.** Do you have the ability to identify and work toward specific goals? Do such goals challenge your abilities?

15. **Vocational skills.** Do you possess the positive combination of education and skills required for the position you are seeking?

16. **Direction.** Have you defined your basic personal needs? Have you determined what type of position will satisfy your knowledge, skills, and goals?

Source: "So You're Looking for a Job?" The College Placement Council.

Candidate: "For each characteristic listed below there is a rating scale of 1 through 7, where '1' is generally the most unfavorable rating of the characteristic and '7' the most favorable. Rate each characteristic by *circling* just one number to represent the impression you gave in the interview that you have just completed."

Name of Candidate _____

1. Appearance

| Sloppy | 1 | 2 | 3 | 4 | 5 | 6 | 7 | Neat |

2. Attitude

| Unfriendly | 1 | 2 | 3 | 4 | 5 | 6 | 7 | Friendly |

3. Assertiveness/Verbal Ability

a. Responded completely to questions asked

| Poor | 1 | 2 | 3 | 4 | 5 | 6 | 7 | Excellent |

b. Clarified personal background and related it to job opening and description

| Poor | 1 | 2 | 3 | 4 | 5 | 6 | 7 | Excellent |

c. Able to explain and sell job abilities

| Poor | 1 | 2 | 3 | 4 | 5 | 6 | 7 | Excellent |

d. Initiated questions regarding position and firm

| Poor | 1 | 2 | 3 | 4 | 5 | 6 | 7 | Excellent |

e. Expressed thorough knowledge of personal goals and abilities

| Poor | 1 | 2 | 3 | 4 | 5 | 6 | 7 | Excellent |

4. Motivation

| Poor | 1 | 2 | 3 | 4 | 5 | 6 | 7 | High |

5. Subject/Academic Knowledge

| Poor | 1 | 2 | 3 | 4 | 5 | 6 | 7 | Good |

6. Stability

| Poor | 1 | 2 | 3 | 4 | 5 | 6 | 7 | Good |

7. Composure

| Ill at ease | 1 | 2 | 3 | 4 | 5 | 6 | 7 | Relaxed |

8. Personal Involvement/Activities, Clubs, Etc.

| Low | 1 | 2 | 3 | 4 | 5 | 6 | 7 | Very high |

9. Mental Impression

| Dull | 1 | 2 | 3 | 4 | 5 | 6 | 7 | Alert |

10. Adaptability

| Poor | 1 | 2 | 3 | 4 | 5 | 6 | 7 | Good |

11. Speech Pronunciation

| Poor | 1 | 2 | 3 | 4 | 5 | 6 | 7 | Good |

12. Overall Impression

| Unsatisfactory | 1 | 2 | 3 | 4 | 5 | 6 | 7 | Highly satisfactory |

13. Would you hire this individual if you were permitted to make a decision right now?

Yes   No

recommendation, or some other information to keep their interest. Your enthusiasm for working for the company could be a major factor in them hiring you.

5. **Be prepared to act.** Know what you want to say if you do get a job offer. You may not want the job once you know all the information. Don't expect to receive a job offer from everyone you meet, but do expect to learn something from every interview. With some practice and persistence, you should find a rewarding and challenging job.

BE PREPARED TO CHANGE CAREERS

If you're like most people, you'll follow several different career paths over your lifetime. This enables you to try different jobs and to stay fresh and enthusiastic. The key to moving forward and finding personal satisfaction in your career is a willingness to change and grow. This means that you'll have to write many cover letters and résumés and go through many interviews. Each time you change jobs, go through the steps in this section of the Epilogue to be sure you're fully prepared. Good luck!

All your efforts pay off when you land the job you want and take the first big step in your career. Go for it!

photo credits

A

absolute advantage (p. 64) The advantage that exists when a country has a monopoly on producing a specific product or is able to produce it more efficiently than all other countries.

accounting (p. 474) The recording, classifying, summarizing, and interpreting of financial events and transactions to provide management and other interested parties the information they need to make good decisions.

accounting cycle (p. 479) A six-step procedure that results in the preparation and analysis of the major financial statements.

accounts payable (p. 484) Current liabilities involving money owed to others for merchandise or services purchased on credit but not yet paid for.

acquisition (p. 135) One company's purchase of the property and obligations of another company.

administered distribution system (p. 432) A distribution system in which producers manage all of the marketing functions at the retail level.

administrative agencies (p. A-3) Federal or state institutions and other government organizations created by Congress or state legislatures with delegated power to pass rules and regulations within their mandated area of authority.

advertising (p. 449) Paid, nonpersonal communication through various media by organizations and individuals who are in some way identified in the advertising message.

affiliate marketing (p. 159) An Internet-based marketing strategy in which a business rewards individuals or other businesses (affiliates) for each visitor or customer the affiliate sends to its website.

affirmative action (p. 304) Employment activities designed to "right past wrongs" by increasing opportunities for minorities and women.

agency shop agreement (p. 340) Clause in a labor–management agreement that says employers may hire nonunion workers; employees are not required to join the union but must pay a union fee.

agents/brokers (p. 418) Marketing intermediaries who bring buyers and sellers together and assist in negotiating an exchange but don't take title to the goods.

American Federation of Labor (AFL) (p. 336) An organization of craft unions that championed fundamental labor issues; founded in 1886.

annual report (p. 476) A yearly statement of the financial condition, progress, and expectations of an organization.

annuity (p. D-11) A contract to make regular payments to a person for life or for a fixed period.

apprentice programs (p. 314) Training programs involving a period during which a learner works alongside an experienced employee to master the skills and procedures of a craft.

arbitration (p. 343) The agreement to bring in an impartial third party (a single arbitrator or a panel of arbitrators) to render a binding decision in a labor dispute.

assembly process (p. 247) That part of the production process that puts together components.

assets (p. 483) Economic resources (things of value) owned by a firm.

auditing (p. 477) The job of reviewing and evaluating the information used to prepare a company's financial statements.

autocratic leadership (p. 197) Leadership style that involves making managerial decisions without consulting others.

B

balance of payments (p. 66) The difference between money coming into a country (from exports) and money leaving the country (for imports) plus money flows from other factors such as tourism, foreign aid, military expenditures, and foreign investment.

balance of trade (p. 66) The total value of a nation's exports compared to its imports over a particular period.

balance sheet (p. 482) Financial statement that reports a firm's financial condition at a specific time and is composed of three major accounts: assets, liabilities, and owners' equity.

ballyhooed *Talked about in an exaggerated way.*

banker's acceptance (p. 583) A promise that the bank will pay some specified amount at a particular time.

Note: Terms and definitions printed in italics are considered business slang, or jargon.

bankruptcy (p. A-15) The legal process by which a person, business, or government entity unable to meet financial obligations is relieved of those obligations by a court that divides any assets among creditors, allowing creditors to get at least part of their money and freeing the debtor to begin anew.

bargaining zone (p. 343) The range of options between the initial and final offer that each party will consider before negotiations dissolve or reach an impasse.

barter (p. 567) The direct trading of goods or services for other goods or services.

bear market *Situation where the stock market is declining in value and investors feel it will continue to decline.*

been there, done that *Prior experience.*

benchmarking (p. 228) Comparing an organization's practices, processes, and products against the world's best.

benefit segmentation (p. 377) Dividing the market by determining which benefits of the product to talk about.

bond (p. 539) A corporate certificate indicating that a person has lent money to a firm.

bonds payable (p. 484) Long-term liabilities that represent money lent to the firm that must be paid back.

bookkeeping (p. 479) The recording of business transactions.

bottom line *The last line in a profit and loss statement; it refers to net profit or loss.*

brain drain (p. 41) The loss of the best and brightest people to other countries.

brainstorming (p. 192) Coming up with as many solutions to a problem as possible in a short period of time with no censoring of ideas.

brand (p. 398) A name, symbol, or design (or combination thereof) that identifies the goods or services of one seller or group of sellers and distinguishes them from the goods and services of competitors.

brand association (p. 401) The linking of a brand to other favorable images.

brand awareness (p. 401) How quickly or easily a given brand name comes to mind when a product category is mentioned.

brand equity (p. 400) The value of the brand name and associated symbols.

brand loyalty (p. 400) The degree to which customers are satisfied, like the brand, and are committed to further purchases.

brand manager (p. 401) A manager who has direct responsibility for one brand or one product line; called a product manager in some firms.

brand name (p. 368) A word, letter, or group of words or letters that differentiates one seller's goods and services from those of competitors.

breach of contract (p. A-10) When one party fails to follow the terms of a contract.

break-even analysis (p. 408) The process used to determine profitability at various levels of sales.

brightest days *The best of times for a person or organization.*

broadband technology (p. B-10) Technology that offers users a continuous connection to the Internet and allows them to send and receive mammoth files that include voice, video, and data much faster than ever before.

budget (p. 508) A financial plan that sets forth management's expectations, and, on the basis of those expectations, allocates the use of specific resources throughout the firm.

bull market *Situation where the stock market is increasing in value and investors feel it will continue to grow.*

bundling (p. 398) Grouping two or more products together and pricing them as a unit.

bureaucracy (p. 217) An organization with many layers of managers who set rules and regulations and oversee all decisions.

business (p. 4) Any activity that seeks to provide goods and services to others while operating at a profit.

business cycles (p. 49) The periodic rises and falls that occur in economies over time.

business environment (p. 11) The surrounding factors that either help or hinder the development of businesses.

business intelligence (BI) (or analytics) (p. B-3) The use of data analytic tools to analyze an organization's raw data and derive useful insights from them.

business law (p. A-2) Rules, statutes, codes, and regulations that are established to provide a legal framework within which business may be conducted and that are enforceable by court action.

business plan (p. 167) A detailed written statement that describes the nature of the business, the target market, the advantages the business will have in relation to competition, and the resources and qualifications of the owner(s).

business-to-business (B2B) market (p. 375) All the individuals and organizations that want goods and services to use in producing other goods and services or to sell, rent, or supply goods to others.

buying stock on margin (p. 546) Purchasing stocks by borrowing some of the purchase cost from the brokerage firm.

C

cafeteria-style fringe benefits (p. 321) Fringe benefits plan that allows employees to choose the benefits they want up to a certain dollar amount.

cannibalize a business *One franchise pulls business away from another franchise, for example.*

capital budget (p. 508) A budget that highlights a firm's spending plans for major asset purchases that often require large sums of money.

capital expenditures (p. 512) Major investments in either tangible long-term assets such as land, buildings, and equipment or intangible assets such as patents, trademarks, and copyrights.

capital gains (p. 545) The positive difference between the purchase price of a stock and its sale price.

capitalism (p. 34) An economic system in which all or most of the factors of production and distribution are privately owned and operated for profit.

cash-and-carry wholesalers (p. 426) Wholesalers that serve mostly smaller retailers with a limited assortment of products.

cash budget (p. 508) A budget that estimates cash inflows and outflows during a particular period like a month or a quarter.

cash flow (p. 490) The difference between cash coming in and cash going out of a business.

cash flow forecast (p. 507) Forecast that predicts the cash inflows and outflows in future periods, usually months or quarters.

center stage *A very important position.*

centralized authority (p. 218) An organization structure in which decision-making authority is maintained at the top level of management at the company's headquarters.

certificate of deposit (CD) (p. 576) A time-deposit (savings) account that earns interest to be delivered at the end of the certificate's maturity date.

certification (p. 339) Formal process whereby a union is recognized by the National Labor Relations Board (NLRB) as the bargaining agent for a group of employees.

certified internal auditor (CIA) (p. 477) An accountant who has a bachelor's degree and two years of experience in internal auditing, and who has passed an exam administered by the Institute of Internal Auditors.

certified management accountant (CMA) (p. 476) A professional accountant who has met certain educational and experience requirements, passed a qualifying exam in the field, and been certified by the Institute of Certified Management Accountants.

certified public accountant (CPA) (p. 476) An accountant who passes a series of examinations established by the American Institute of Certified Public Accountants (AICPA).

chain of command (p. 216) The line of authority that moves from the top of a hierarchy to the lowest level.

channel of distribution (p. 418) A whole set of marketing intermediaries, such as agents, brokers, wholesalers, and retailers, that join together to transport and store goods in their path (or channel) from producers to consumers.

claim (p. C-6) A statement of loss that the insured sends to the insurance company to request payment.

climate change (p. 19) The movement of the temperature of the planet up or down over time.

climbed the ladder *Promoted to higher-level jobs.*

closed shop agreement (p. 340) Clause in a labor–management agreement that specified workers had to be members of a union before being hired (was outlawed by the Taft-Hartley Act in 1947).

cloud computing (p. B-16) A form of virtualization in which a company's data and applications are stored at offsite data centers that are accessed over the Internet (the cloud).

collective bargaining (p. 337) The process whereby union and management representatives form a labor–management agreement, or contract, for workers.

command economies (p. 42) Economic systems in which the government largely decides what goods and services will be produced, who will get them, and how the economy will grow.

commercial bank (p. 576) A profit-seeking organization that receives deposits from individuals and corporations in the form of checking and savings accounts and then uses some of these funds to make loans.

commercial finance companies (p. 517) Organizations that make short-term loans to borrowers who offer tangible assets as collateral.

commercialization (p. 403) Promoting a product to distributors and retailers to get wide distribution, and developing strong advertising and sales campaigns to generate and maintain interest in the product among distributors and consumers.

commercial paper (p. 518) Unsecured promissory notes of $100,000 and up that mature (come due) in 270 days or less.

common law (p. A-3) The body of law that comes from decisions handed down by judges; also referred to as unwritten law.

common market (p. 79) A regional group of countries that have a common external tariff, no internal tariffs, and a coordination of laws to facilitate exchange; also called a *trading bloc*. An example is the European Union.

common stock (p. 537) The most basic form of ownership in a firm; it confers voting rights and the right to share in the firm's profits through dividends, if offered by the firm's board of directors.

communism (p. 42) An economic and political system in which the government makes almost all economic decisions and owns almost all the major factors of production.

comparative advantage theory (p. 64) Theory that states that a country should sell to other countries those products that it produces most effectively and efficiently, and buy from other countries those products that it cannot produce as effectively or efficiently.

competition-based pricing (p. 408) A pricing strategy based on what all the other competitors are doing. The price can be set at, above, or below competitors' prices.

compliance-based ethics codes (p. 100) Ethical standards that emphasize preventing unlawful behavior by increasing control and by penalizing wrongdoers.

compressed workweek (p. 322) Work schedule that allows an employee to work a full number of hours per week but in fewer days.

computer-aided design (CAD) (p. 248) The use of computers in the design of products.

computer-aided manufacturing (CAM) (p. 248) The use of computers in the manufacturing of products.

computer-integrated manufacturing (CIM) (p. 249) The uniting of computer-aided design with computer-aided manufacturing.

concept testing (p. 403) Taking a product idea to consumers to test their reactions.

conceptual skills (p. 194) Skills that involve the ability to picture the organization as a whole and the relationship among its various parts.

conglomerate merger (p. 135) The joining of firms in completely unrelated industries.

Congress of Industrial Organizations (CIO) (p. 336) Union organization of unskilled workers; broke away from the American Federation of Labor (AFL) in 1935 and rejoined it in 1955.

consideration (p. A-9) Something of value; consideration is one of the requirements of a legal contract.

consumerism (p. A-12) A social movement that seeks to increase and strengthen the rights and powers of buyers in relation to sellers.

consumer market (p. 375) All the individuals or households that want goods and services for personal consumption or use.

consumer price index (CPI) (p. 48) Monthly statistics that measure the pace of inflation or deflation.

contingency planning (p. 191) The process of preparing alternative courses of action that may be used if the primary plans don't achieve the organization's objectives.

contingent workers (p. 311) Workers who do not have the expectation of regular, full-time employment.

continuous process (p. 247) A production process in which long production runs turn out finished goods over time.

contract (p. A-9) A legally enforceable agreement between two or more parties.

contract law (p. A-9) Set of laws that specify what constitutes a legally enforceable agreement.

contract manufacturing (p. 69) A foreign country's production of private-label goods to which a domestic company then attaches its brand name or trademark; part of the broad category of *outsourcing.*

contractual distribution system (p. 432) A distribution system in which members are bound to cooperate through contractual agreements.

contrarian approach (p. D-9) Buying stock when everyone else is selling or vice versa.

controlling (p. 188) A management function that involves establishing clear standards to determine whether or not an organization is progressing toward its goals and objectives, rewarding people for doing a good job, and taking corrective action if they are not.

convenience goods and services (p. 395) Products that the consumer wants to purchase frequently and with a minimum of effort.

conventional (C) corporation (p. 127) A state-chartered legal entity with authority to act and have liability separate from its owners.

cookies (p. B-20) Pieces of information, such as registration data or user preferences, sent by a website over the Internet to a web browser that the browser software is expected to save and send back to the server whenever the user returns to that website.

cooking the books *Making accounting information look better than it actually is to outside observers and users of financial information of a company.*

cooling-off period (p. 344) When workers in a critical industry return to their jobs while the union and management continue negotiations.

cooperative (p. 143) A business owned and controlled by the people who use it—producers, consumers, or workers with similar needs who pool their resources for mutual gain.

copyright (p. A-7) A document that protects a creator's rights to materials such as books, articles, photos, and cartoons.

core competencies (p. 229) Those functions that the organization can do as well as or better than any other organization in the world.

core inflation (p. 48) CPI minus food and energy costs.

core time (p. 322) In a flextime plan, the period when all employees are expected to be at their job stations.

corporate distribution system (p. 432) A distribution system in which all of the organizations in the channel of distribution are owned by one firm.

corporate philanthropy (p. 103) The dimension of social responsibility that includes charitable donations.

corporate policy (p. 104) The dimension of social responsibility that refers to the position a firm takes on social and political issues.

corporate responsibility (p. 104) The dimension of social responsibility that includes everything from hiring minority workers to making safe products.

corporate social initiatives (p. 104) Enhanced forms of corporate philanthropy directly related to the company's competencies.

corporate social responsibility (CSR) (p. 102) A business's concern for the welfare of society.

corporation (p. 120) A legal entity with authority to act and have liability separate from its owners.

cost of capital (p. 523) The rate of return a company must earn in order to meet the demands of its lenders and expectations of its equity holders.

cost of goods sold (or cost of goods manufactured) (p. 487) A measure of the cost of merchandise sold or cost of raw materials and supplies used for producing items for resale.

couch potatoes *People who sit and watch TV for hours at a time.*

countertrading (p. 76) A complex form of bartering in which several countries may be involved, each trading goods for goods or services for services.

counting on it *Expecting it.*

craft union (p. 335) An organization of skilled specialists in a particular craft or trade.

credit unions (p. 577) Nonprofit, member-owned financial cooperatives that offer the full variety of banking services to their members.

critical path (p. 260) In a PERT network, the sequence of tasks that takes the longest time to complete.

cross-functional self-managed teams (p. 226) Groups of employees from different departments who work together on a long-term basis.

current assets (p. 484) Items that can or will be converted into cash within one year.

customer relationship management (CRM) (p. 364) The process of learning as much as possible about customers and doing everything you can over time to satisfy them—or even exceed their expectations—with goods and services.

D

damages (p. A-10) The monetary settlement awarded to a person who is injured by a breach of contract.

data analytics (p. B-8) The process of collecting, organizing, storing, and analyzing large sets of data ("big data") in order to identify patterns and other information that is most useful to the business now and for making future decisions.

database (p. 15) An electronic storage file for information.

data processing (DP) (p. B-2) Name for business technology in the 1970s; included technology that supported an existing business and was primarily used to improve the flow of financial information.

dealer (private-label) brands (p. 399) Products that don't carry the manufacturer's name but carry a distributor or retailer's name instead.

debenture bonds (p. 540) Bonds that are unsecured (i.e., not backed by any collateral such as equipment).

debit card (p. 582) An electronic funds transfer tool that serves the same function as checks: it withdraws funds from a checking account.

debt financing (p. 513) Funds raised through various forms of borrowing that must be repaid.

decentralized authority (p. 218) An organization structure in which decision-making authority is delegated to lower-level managers more familiar with local conditions than headquarters management could be.

decertification (p. 339) The process by which workers take away a union's right to represent them.

decision making (p. 192) Choosing among two or more alternatives.

deflation (p. 48) A situation in which prices are declining.

demand (p. 37) The quantity of products that people are willing to buy at different prices at a specific time.

demand deposit (p. 576) The technical name for a checking account; the money in a demand deposit can be withdrawn anytime on demand from the depositor.

demographic segmentation (p. 377) Dividing the market by age, income, and education level.

demography (p. 17) The statistical study of the human population with regard to its size, density, and other characteristics such as age, race, gender, and income.

departmentalization (p. 220) The dividing of organizational functions into separate units.

depreciation (p. 487) The systematic write-off of the cost of a tangible asset over its estimated useful life.

depression (p. 49) A severe recession, usually accompanied by deflation.

deregulation (p. A-17) Government withdrawal of certain laws and regulations that seem to hinder competition.

devaluation (p. 76) Lowering the value of a nation's currency relative to other currencies.

digital natives (p. 229) Young people who have grown up using the Internet and social networking.

direct marketing (p. 431) Any activity that directly links manufacturers or intermediaries with the ultimate consumer.

direct selling (p. 430) Selling to consumers in their homes or where they work.

disability insurance (p. D-12) Insurance that pays part of the cost of a long-term sickness or an accident.

discount rate (p. 572) The interest rate that the Fed charges for loans to member banks.

disinflation (p. 48) A situation in which price increases are slowing (the inflation rate is declining).

distributed product development (p. 392) Handing off various parts of your innovation process—often to companies in other countries.

diversification (p. 544) Buying several different investment alternatives to spread the risk of investing.

dividends (p. 537) Part of a firm's profits that the firm may distribute to stockholders as either cash payments or additional shares of stock.

double-entry bookkeeping (p. 480) The practice of writing every business transaction in two places.

Dow Jones Industrial Average (the Dow) (p. 552) The average cost of 30 selected industrial stocks, used to give an indication of the direction (up or down) of the stock market over time.

drop shippers (p. 426) Wholesalers that solicit orders from retailers and other wholesalers and have the merchandise shipped directly from a producer to a buyer.

dumping (p. 67) Selling products in a foreign country at lower prices than those charged in the producing country.

E

e-commerce (p. 14) The buying and selling of goods over the Internet.

economic pie *The money available in the economy.*

economics (p. 30) The study of how society chooses to employ resources to produce goods and services and distribute them for consumption among various competing groups and individuals.

economies of scale (p. 214) The situation in which companies can reduce their production costs if they can purchase raw materials in bulk; the average cost of goods goes down as production levels increase.

electronic funds transfer (EFT) system (p. 582) A computerized system that electronically performs financial transactions such as making purchases, paying bills, and receiving paychecks.

electronic retailing (p. 428) Selling goods and services to ultimate customers (e.g., you and me) over the Internet.

e-mail snooped *When someone other than the addressee reads e-mail messages.*

embargo (p. 78) A complete ban on the import or export of a certain product, or the stopping of all trade with a particular country.

empowerment (p. 16) Giving frontline workers the responsibility, authority, freedom, training, and equipment they need to respond quickly to customer requests.

enabling (p. 199) Giving workers the education and tools they need to make decisions.

enterprise resource planning (ERP) (p. 255) A newer version of materials requirement planning (MRP) that combines the computerized functions of all the divisions and subsidiaries of the firm—such as finance, human resources, and order fulfillment—into a single integrated software program that uses a single database.

enterprise zones (p. 161) Specific geographic areas to which governments try to attract private business investment by offering lower taxes and other government support.

entrepreneur (p. 4) A person who risks time and money to start and manage a business.

entrepreneurial team (p. 157) A group of experienced people from different areas of business who join together to form a managerial team with the skills needed to develop, make, and market a new product.

entrepreneurship (p. 152) Accepting the risk of starting and running a business.

environmental scanning (p. 372) The process of identifying the factors that can affect marketing success.

equity financing (p. 513) Money raised from within the firm, from operations or through the sale of ownership in the firm (stock or venture capital).

equity theory (p. 282) The idea that employees try to maintain equity between inputs and outputs compared to others in similar positions.

ethics (p. 96) Standards of moral behavior, that is, behavior accepted by society as right versus wrong.

everyday low pricing (EDLP) (p. 409) Setting prices lower than competitors and then not having any special sales.

exchange rate (p. 75) The value of one nation's currency relative to the currencies of other countries.

exchange-traded funds (ETFs) (p. 550) Collections of stocks that are traded on exchanges but are traded more like individual stocks than like mutual funds.

exclusive distribution (p. 427) Distribution that sends products to only one retail outlet in a given geographic area.

executor (p. D-18) A person who assembles and values your estate, files income and other taxes, and distributes assets.

expectancy theory (p. 280) Victor Vroom's theory that the amount of effort employees exert on a specific task depends on their expectations of the outcome.

exporting (p. 63) Selling products to another country.

express warranties (p. A-8) Specific representations by the seller that buyers rely on regarding the goods they purchase.

external customers (p. 202) Dealers, who buy products to sell to others, and ultimate customers (or end users), who buy products for their own personal use.

extranet (p. B-10) A semiprivate network that uses Internet technology and allows more than one company to access the same information or allows people on different servers to collaborate.

extrinsic reward (p. 270) Something given to you by someone else as recognition for good work; extrinsic rewards include pay increases, praise, and promotions.

F

facility layout (p. 254) The physical arrangement of resources (including people) in the production process.

facility location (p. 252) The process of selecting a geographic location for a company's operations.

factoring (p. 517) The process of selling accounts receivable for cash.

factors of production (p. 10) The resources used to create wealth: land, labor, capital, entrepreneurship, and knowledge.

Federal Deposit Insurance Corporation (FDIC) (p. 581) An independent agency of the U.S. government that insures bank deposits.

finance (p. 504) The function in a business that acquires funds for the firm and manages those funds within the firm.

financial accounting (p. 476) Accounting information and analyses prepared for people outside the organization.

financial control (p. 508) A process in which a firm periodically compares its actual revenues, costs, and expenses with its budget.

financial management (p. 504) The job of managing a firm's resources so it can meet its goals and objectives.

financial managers (p. 504) Managers who examine financial data prepared by accountants and recommend strategies for improving the financial performance of the firm.

financial statement (p. 481) A summary of all the transactions that have occurred over a particular period.

fiscal policy (p. 49) The federal government's efforts to keep the economy stable by increasing or decreasing taxes or government spending.

fixed assets (p. 484) Assets that are relatively permanent, such as land, buildings, and equipment.

flat organization structure (p. 219) An organization structure that has few layers of management and a broad span of control.

flexible manufacturing (p. 249) Designing machines to do multiple tasks so that they can produce a variety of products.

flextime plan (p. 322) Work schedule that gives employees some freedom to choose when to work, as long as they work the required number of hours.

focus group (p. 371) A small group of people who meet under the direction of a discussion leader to communicate their opinions about an organization, its products, or other given issues.

foreign direct investment (FDI) (p. 71) The buying of permanent property and businesses in foreign nations.

foreign subsidiary (p. 71) A company owned in a foreign country by another company, called the *parent company.*

formal organization (p. 232) The structure that details lines of responsibility, authority, and position; that is, the structure shown on organization charts.

form utility (p. 247) The value producers add to materials in the creation of finished goods and services.

401(k) plan (p. D-16) A savings plan that allows you to deposit pretax dollars and whose earnings compound tax free until withdrawal, when the money is taxed at ordinary income tax rates.

franchise (p. 136) The right to use a specific business's name and sell its products or services in a given territory.

franchise agreement (p. 136) An arrangement whereby someone with a good idea for a business sells the rights to use the business name and sell a product or service to others in a given territory.

franchisee (p. 136) A person who buys a franchise.

franchisor (p. 136)   A company that develops a product concept and sells others the rights to make and sell the products.

free-for-all atmosphere   *A situation where all order seems to be lost in conducting business.*

free-market economies (p. 42)   Economic systems in which the market largely determines what goods and services get produced, who gets them, and how the economy grows.

free-rein leadership (p. 198)   Leadership style that involves managers setting objectives and employees being relatively free to do whatever it takes to accomplish those objectives.

free trade (p. 63)   The movement of goods and services among nations without political or economic barriers.

freight forwarder (p. 436)   An organization that puts many small shipments together to create a single large shipment that can be transported cost-effectively to the final destination.

fringe benefits (p. 320)   Benefits such as sick-leave pay, vacation pay, pension plans, and health plans that represent additional compensation to employees beyond base wages.

from scratch   *From the beginning.*

fundamental accounting equation (p. 482)   Assets = Liabilities + Owners' equity; this is the basis for the balance sheet.

G

Gantt chart (p. 261)   Bar graph showing production managers what projects are being worked on and what stage they are in at any given time.

General Agreement on Tariffs and Trade (GATT) (p. 79)   A 1948 agreement that established an international forum for negotiating mutual reductions in trade restrictions.

general partner (p. 123)   An owner (partner) who has unlimited liability and is active in managing the firm.

general partnership (p. 123)   A partnership in which all owners share in operating the business and in assuming liability for the business's debts.

generic goods (p. 399)   Nonbranded products that usually sell at a sizable discount compared to national or private-label brands.

geographic segmentation (p. 377)   Dividing the market by cities, counties, states, or regions.

get in on the dough   *Take the opportunity to make some money.*

givebacks (p. 345)   Concessions made by union members to management; gains from labor negotiations are given back to management to help employers remain competitive and thereby save jobs.

goals (p. 189)   The broad, long-term accomplishments an organization wishes to attain.

goal-setting theory (p. 280)   The idea that setting ambitious but attainable goals can motivate workers and improve performance if the goals are accepted, accompanied by feedback, and facilitated by organizational conditions.

go for the gold   *To work to be the very best (figuratively winning a gold medal).*

go out with me   *Go with me to dinner or to a movie or some other entertainment.*

gone off the deep end   *Doing something risky, almost crazy—like jumping into the deep end of a swimming pool when you can't swim.*

goods (p. 4)   Tangible products such as computers, food, clothing, cars, and appliances.

goofing off   *Doing things at work not associated with the job, such as talking with others at the drinking fountain.*

government and not-for-profit accounting (p. 478)   Accounting system for organizations whose purpose is not generating a profit but serving ratepayers, taxpayers, and others according to a duly approved budget.

greening (p. 19)   The trend toward saving energy and producing products that cause less harm to the environment.

grievance (p. 342)   A charge by employees that management is not abiding by the terms of the negotiated labor–management agreement.

gross domestic product (GDP) (p. 46)   The total value of final goods and services produced in a country in a given year.

gross output (GO) (p. 46)   A measure of total sales volume at all stages of production.

gross profit (or gross margin) (p. 487)   How much a firm earned by buying (or making) and selling merchandise.

H

hand over the keys   *Give access to others.*

hard copy   *Copy printed on paper.*

Hawthorne effect (p. 273)   The tendency for people to behave differently when they know they are being studied.

health savings accounts (HSAs) (p. C-9) Tax-deferred savings accounts linked to low-cost, high-deductible health insurance policies.

heart The most important part of something; the central force or idea.

hierarchy (p. 216) A system in which one person is at the top of the organization and there is a ranked or sequential ordering from the top down of managers who are responsible to that person.

high–low pricing strategy (p. 409) Setting prices that are higher than EDLP stores, but having many special sales where the prices are lower than competitors'.

horizontal merger (p. 135) The joining of two firms in the same industry.

hot second Immediately.

human relations skills (p. 194) Skills that involve communication and motivation; they enable managers to work through and with people.

human resource management (HRM) (p. 300) The process of determining human resource needs and then recruiting, selecting, developing, motivating, evaluating, compensating, and scheduling employees to achieve organizational goals.

hygiene factors (p. 275) In Herzberg's theory of motivating factors, job factors that can cause dissatisfaction if missing but that do not necessarily motivate employees if increased.

I

identity theft (p. 16) The obtaining of individuals' personal information, such as Social Security and credit card numbers, for illegal purposes.

If it isn't broken, don't fix it Don't risk making things worse by changing things that don't need to be changed.

implied warranties (p. A-8) Guarantees legally imposed on the seller.

importing (p. 63) Buying products from another country.

import quota (p. 78) A limit on the number of products in certain categories that a nation can import.

inbound logistics (p. 435) The area of logistics that involves bringing raw materials, packaging, other goods and services, and information from suppliers to producers.

income statement (p. 485) The financial statement that shows a firm's profit after costs, expenses, and taxes; it summarizes all of the resources that have come into the firm (revenue), all the resources that have left the firm, expenses, and the resulting net income or net loss.

incubators (p. 161) Centers that offer new businesses low-cost offices with basic business services.

indenture terms (p. 520) The terms of agreement in a bond issue.

independent audit (p. 477) An evaluation and unbiased opinion about the accuracy of a company's financial statements.

individual retirement account (IRA) (p. D-14) A tax-deferred investment plan that enables you (and your spouse, if you are married) to save part of your income for retirement; a traditional IRA allows people who qualify to deduct from their reported income the money they put into an account.

industrial goods (p. 396) Products used in the production of other products. Sometimes called business goods or B2B goods.

industrial unions (p. 336) Labor organizations of unskilled and semiskilled workers in mass-production industries such as automobiles and mining.

inflation (p. 47) A general rise in the prices of goods and services over time.

infomercial (p. 453) A full-length TV program devoted exclusively to promoting goods or services.

informal organization (p. 225) The system that develops spontaneously as employees meet and form cliques, relationships, and lines of authority outside the formal organization; that is, the human side of the organization that does not appear on any organization chart.

information systems (IS) (p. B-2) Technology that helps companies do business; includes such tools as automated teller machines (ATMs) and voice mail.

information technology (IT) (p. B-2) Technology used to store, retrieve, and send information efficiently.

information utility (p. 424) Adding value to products by opening two-way flows of information between marketing participants.

initial public offering (IPO) (p. 532) The first public offering of a corporation's stock.

injunction (p. 344) A court order directing someone to do something or to refrain from doing something.

insider trading (p. 105) An unethical activity in which insiders use private company information to further their own fortunes or those of their family and friends.

institutional investors (p. 533) Large organizations—such as pension funds, mutual funds, and insurance companies—that invest their own funds or the funds of others.

insurable interest (p. C-6) The possibility of the policyholder to suffer a loss.

insurable risk (p. C-6) A risk that the typical insurance company will cover.

insurance policy (p. C-6) A written contract between the insured and an insurance company that promises to pay for all or part of a loss.

intangible assets (p. 484) Long-term assets (e.g., patents, trademarks, copyrights) that have no real physical form but do have value.

integrated marketing communication (IMC) (p. 448) A technique that combines all the promotional tools into one comprehensive and unified promotional strategy.

integrity-based ethics codes (p. 100) Ethical standards that define the organization's guiding values, create an environment that supports ethically sound behavior, and stress a shared accountability among employees.

intensive distribution (p. 427) Distribution that puts products into as many retail outlets as possible.

interactive promotion (p. 454) Promotion process that allows marketers to go beyond a monologue, where sellers try to persuade buyers to buy things, to a dialogue in which buyers and sellers work together to create mutually beneficial exchange relationships.

interest (p. 539) The payment the issuer of the bond makes to the bondholders for use of the borrowed money.

intermittent process (p. 248) A production process in which the production run is short and the machines are changed frequently to make different products.

intermodal shipping (p. 438) The use of multiple modes of transportation to complete a single long-distance movement of freight.

internal customers (p. 202) Individuals and units within the firm that receive services from other individuals or units.

International Monetary Fund (IMF) (p. 584) Organization that assists the smooth flow of money among nations.

Internet2 (p. B-11) The private Internet system that links government supercomputer centers and a select group of universities; it runs more than 22,000 times faster than today's public infrastructure and supports heavy-duty applications.

intranet (p. B-9) A companywide network, closed to public access, that uses Internet-type technology.

intrapreneurs (p. 160) Creative people who work as entrepreneurs within corporations.

intrinsic reward (p. 270) The personal satisfaction you feel when you perform well and complete goals.

inverted organization (p. 230) An organization that has contact people at the top and the chief executive officer at the bottom of the organization chart.

investment bankers (p. 533) Specialists who assist in the issue and sale of new securities.

invisible hand (p. 33) A phrase coined by Adam Smith to describe the process that turns self-directed gain into social and economic benefits for all.

involuntary bankruptcy (p. A-15) Bankruptcy procedures filed by a debtor's creditors.

IOU *Debt; abbreviation for "I owe you."*

ISO 14000 (p. 259) A collection of the best practices for managing an organization's impact on the environment.

ISO 9000 (p. 259) The common name given to quality management and assurance standards.

J

job analysis (p. 306) A study of what is done by employees who hold various job titles.

job description (p. 306) A summary of the objectives of a job, the type of work to be done, the responsibilities and duties, the working conditions, and the relationship of the job to other functions.

job enlargement (p. 283) A job enrichment strategy that involves combining a series of tasks into one challenging and interesting assignment.

job enrichment (p. 283) A motivational strategy that emphasizes motivating the worker through the job itself.

job rotation (p. 283) A job enrichment strategy that involves moving employees from one job to another.

job sharing (p. 323) An arrangement whereby two part-time employees share one full-time job.

job simulation (p. 314) The use of equipment that duplicates job conditions and tasks so that trainees can learn skills before attempting them on the job.

job specifications (p. 306) A written summary of the minimum qualifications required of workers to do a particular job.

joint venture (p. 70) A partnership in which two or more companies (often from different countries) join to undertake a major project.

journal (p. 479) The record book or computer program where accounting data are first entered.

judiciary (p. A-2) The branch of government chosen to oversee the legal system through the court system.

jumped headfirst *Began quickly and eagerly without hesitation.*

junk bonds (p. 548) High-risk, high-interest bonds.

just-in-time (JIT) inventory control (p. 257) A production process in which a minimum of inventory is kept on the premises and parts, supplies, and other needs are delivered just in time to go on the assembly line.

K

Keynesian economic theory (p. 51) The theory that a government policy of increasing spending and cutting taxes could stimulate the economy in a recession.

key player *Important participant.*

kick back and relax *To take a rest.*

Knights of Labor (p. 336) The first national labor union; formed in 1869.

knockoff brands (p. 399) Illegal copies of national brand-name goods.

know-how *A level of specific expertise.*

knowledge management (p. 199) Finding the right information, keeping the information in a readily accessible place, and making the information known to everyone in the firm.

L

latchkey kids *School-age children who come home to empty houses since all of the adults are at work.*

law of large numbers (p. C-6) Principle that if a large number of people are exposed to the same risk, a predictable number of losses will occur during a given period of time.

leading (p. 188) Creating a vision for the organization and guiding, training, coaching, and motivating others to work effectively to achieve the organization's goals and objectives.

lean manufacturing (p. 249) The production of goods using less of everything compared to mass production.

ledger (p. 480) A specialized accounting book or computer program in which information from accounting journals is accumulated into specific categories and posted so that managers can find all the information about one account in the same place.

letter of credit (p. 583) A promise by the bank to pay the seller a given amount if certain conditions are met.

level playing field *Treating everyone equally.*

leverage (p. 523) Raising needed funds through borrowing to increase a firm's rate of return.

leveraged buyout (LBO) (p. 136) An attempt by employees, management, or a group of investors to purchase an organization primarily through borrowing.

liabilities (p. 484) What the business owes to others (debts).

licensing (p. 68) A global strategy in which a firm (the licensor) allows a foreign company (the licensee) to produce its product in exchange for a fee (a royalty).

limited liability (p. 123) The responsibility of a business's owners for losses only up to the amount they invest; limited partners and shareholders have limited liability.

limited liability company (LLC) (p. 132) A company similar to an S corporation but without the special eligibility requirements.

limited liability partnership (LLP) (p. 123) A partnership that limits partners' risk of losing their personal assets to only their own acts and omissions and to the acts and omissions of people under their supervision.

limited partner (p. 123) An owner who invests money in the business but does not have any management responsibility or liability for losses beyond the investment.

limited partnership (p. 123) A partnership with one or more general partners and one or more limited partners.

line of credit (p. 516) A given amount of unsecured short-term funds a bank will lend to a business, provided the funds are readily available.

line organization (p. 223) An organization that has direct two-way lines of responsibility, authority, and communication running from the top to the bottom of the organization, with all people reporting to only one supervisor.

line personnel (p. 223) Employees who are part of the chain of command that is responsible for achieving organizational goals.

liquidity (p. 484) The ease with which an asset can be converted into cash.

lockout (p. 344) An attempt by management to put pressure on unions by temporarily closing the business.

logistics (p. 435) The marketing activity that involves planning, implementing, and controlling the physical flow of materials, final goods, and related information from points of origin to points of consumption to meet customer requirements at a profit.

long-term financing (p. 513) Funds needed for more than a year (usually 2 to 10 years).

long-term forecast (p. 507) Forecast that predicts revenues, costs, and expenses for a period longer than 1 year, and sometimes as far as 5 or 10 years into the future.

loss (p. 4) When a business's expenses are more than its revenues.

M

M-1 (p. 569) Money that can be accessed quickly and easily (coins and paper money, checks, traveler's checks, etc.).

M-2 (p. 569) Money included in M-1 plus money that may take a little more time to obtain (savings accounts, money market accounts, mutual funds, certificates of deposit, etc.).

M-3 (p. 569) M-2 plus big deposits like institutional money market funds.

Ma Bell Telecommunication giant AT&T.

macroeconomics (p. 30) The part of economics study that looks at the operation of a nation's economy as a whole.

management (p. 187) The process used to accomplish organizational goals through planning, organizing, leading, and controlling people and other organizational resources.

management by objectives (MBO) (p. 280) Peter Drucker's system of goal setting and implementation; it involves a cycle of discussion, review, and evaluation of objectives among top and middle-level managers, supervisors, and employees.

management development (p. 315) The process of training and educating employees to become good managers and then monitoring the progress of their managerial skills over time.

managerial accounting (p. 475) Accounting used to provide information and analyses to managers within the organization to assist them in decision making.

manufacturers' brands (p. 399) The brand names of manufacturers that distribute products nationally.

market (p. 172) People with unsatisfied wants and needs who have both the resources and the willingness to buy.

marketing (p. 362) The activity, set of institutions, and processes for creating, communicating, delivering, and exchanging offerings that have value for customers, clients, partners, and society at large.

marketing concept (p. 364) A three-part business philosophy: (1) a customer orientation, (2) a service orientation, and (3) a profit orientation.

marketing intermediaries (p. 418) Organizations that assist in moving goods and services from producers to businesses (B2B) and from businesses to consumers (B2C).

marketing mix (p. 366) The ingredients that go into a marketing program: product, price, place, and promotion.

marketing research (p. 370) The analysis of markets to determine opportunities and challenges, and to find the information needed to make good decisions.

market price (p. 37) The price determined by supply and demand.

market segmentation (p. 376) The process of dividing the total market into groups whose members have similar characteristics.

marriage of software, hardware, etc. Combination of various technologies.

Maslow's hierarchy of needs (p. 273) Theory of motivation based on unmet human needs from basic physiological needs to safety, social, and esteem needs to self-actualization needs.

mass customization (p. 250) Tailoring products to meet the needs of individual customers.

mass marketing (p. 378) Developing products and promotions to please large groups of people.

master limited partnership (MLP) (p. 123) A partnership that looks much like a corporation (in that it acts like a corporation and is traded on a stock exchange) but is taxed like a partnership and thus avoids the corporate income tax.

materials handling (p. 435) The movement of goods within a warehouse, from warehouses to the factory floor, and from the factory floor to various workstations.

materials requirement planning (MRP) (p. 255) A computer-based operations management system that uses sales forecasts to make sure that needed parts and materials are available at the right time and place.

matrix organization (p. 224) An organization in which specialists from different parts of the organization are brought together to work on specific projects but still remain part of a line-and-staff structure.

maturity date (p. 539) The exact date the issuer of a bond must pay the principal to the bondholder.

measuring stick Tool used to evaluate or compare something.

mediation (p. 343) The use of a third party, called a mediator, who encourages both sides in a dispute to continue negotiating and often makes suggestions for resolving the dispute.

mentor (p. 315) An experienced employee who supervises, coaches, and guides lower-level employees by introducing them to the right people and generally being their organizational sponsor.

merchant wholesalers (p. 425) Independently owned firms that take title to the goods they handle.

merger (p. 135) The result of two firms forming one company.

Mickey D's Nickname for McDonald's.

microeconomics (p. 30) The part of economics study that looks at the behavior of people and organizations in particular markets.

micropreneurs (p. 157) Entrepreneurs willing to accept the risk of starting and managing the type of business that remains small, lets them do the kind of work they want to do, and offers them a balanced lifestyle.

middle management (p. 194) The level of management that includes general managers, division managers, and branch and plant managers who are responsible for tactical planning and controlling.

mine the knowledge Make maximum use of the knowledge employees have.

mission statement (p. 189) An outline of the fundamental purposes of an organization.

mixed economies (p. 43) Economic systems in which some allocation of resources is made by the market and some by the government.

monetary policy (p. 51) The management of the money supply and interest rates by the Federal Reserve Bank.

money (p. 566) Anything that people generally accept as payment for goods and services.

money supply (p. 569) The amount of money the Federal Reserve Bank makes available for people to buy goods and services.

monopolistic competition (p. 39) The degree of competition in which a large number of sellers produce very similar products that buyers nevertheless perceive as different.

monopoly (p. 39) A degree of competition in which only one seller controls the total supply of a product or service, and sets the price.

more than meets the eye More than one can see with his or her own eyes; much is happening that is not visible.

motivators (p. 275) In Herzberg's theory of motivating factors, job factors that cause employees to be productive and that give them satisfaction.

mouse-click away Ease of doing something by using the computer or Internet.

muddy the water *Making things even more difficult than they currently are.*

multinational corporation (p. 71) An organization that manufactures and markets products in many different countries and has multinational stock ownership and multinational management.

mutual fund (p. 549) An organization that buys stocks and bonds and then sells shares in those securities to the public.

mutual insurance company (p. C-7) A type of insurance company owned by its policyholders.

N

NASDAQ (p. 534) A nationwide electronic system that communicates over-the-counter trades to brokers.

national debt (p. 50) The sum of government deficits over time.

negligence (p. A-4) In tort law, behavior that causes unintentional harm or injury.

negotiable instruments (p. A-8) Forms of commercial paper (such as checks) that are transferable among businesses and individuals and represent a promise to pay a specified amount.

negotiated labor–management agreement (labor contract) (p. 340) Agreement that sets the tone and clarifies the terms under which management and labor agree to function over a period of time.

net income or net loss (p. 485) Revenue left over after all costs and expenses, including taxes, are paid.

networking (pp. 226, 315) The process of establishing and maintaining contacts with key managers in one's own organization and other organizations and using those contacts to weave strong relationships that serve as informal development systems.

niche marketing (p. 377) The process of finding small but profitable market segments and designing or finding products for them.

nonbanks (p. 578) Financial organizations that accept no deposits but offer many of the services provided by regular banks (pension funds, insurance companies, commercial finance companies, consumer finance companies, and brokerage houses).

nonprofit organization (p. 7) An organization whose goals do not include making a personal profit for its owners or organizers.

North American Free Trade Agreement (NAFTA) (p. 80) Agreement that created a free-trade area among the United States, Canada, and Mexico.

notes payable (p. 484) Short-term or long-term liabilities that a business promises to repay by a certain date.

O

objectives (p. 189) Specific, short-term statements detailing how to achieve the organization's goals.

off-the-job training (p. 314) Training that occurs away from the workplace and consists of internal or external programs to develop any of a variety of skills or to foster personal development.

oligopoly (p. 39) A degree of competition in which just a few sellers dominate the market.

one-to-one marketing (p. 378) Developing a unique mix of goods and services for each individual customer.

online training (p. 314) Training programs in which employees complete classes via the Internet.

on-the-job training (p. 313) Training at the workplace that lets the employee learn by doing or by watching others for a while and then imitating them.

open-market operations (p. 572) The buying and selling of U.S. government bonds by the Fed with the goal of regulating the money supply.

open shop agreement (p. 340) Agreement in right-to-work states that gives workers the option to join or not join a union, if one exists in their workplace.

operating (or master) budget (p. 508) The budget that ties together the firm's other budgets and summarizes its proposed financial activities.

operating expenses (p. 487) Costs involved in operating a business, such as rent, utilities, and salaries.

operational planning (p. 190) The process of setting work standards and schedules necessary to implement the company's tactical objectives.

operations management (p. 245) A specialized area in management that converts or transforms resources (including human resources) into goods and services.

organizational (or corporate) culture (p. 231) Widely shared values within an organization that provide unity and cooperation to achieve common goals.

organization chart (p. 216) A visual device that shows relationships among people and divides the organization's work; it shows who is accountable for the completion of specific work and who reports to whom.

organizing (p. 188) A management function that includes designing the structure of the organization and creating conditions and systems in which everyone and everything work together to achieve the organization's goals and objectives.

orientation (p. 313) The activity that introduces new employees to the organization; to fellow employees; to their immediate supervisors; and to the policies, practices, and objectives of the firm.

other side of the tracks *The area where people with less money live.*

outbound logistics (p. 435) The area of logistics that involves managing the flow of finished products and information to business buyers and ultimate consumers (people like you and me).

out of the office loop *Out of the line of communication that occurs in the workplace.*

outsourcing (p. 6) Contracting with other companies (often in other countries) to do some or all of the functions of a firm, like its production or accounting tasks.

over-the-counter (OTC) market (p. 534) Exchange that provides a means to trade stocks not listed on the national exchanges.

owners' equity (p. 484) The amount of the business that belongs to the owners minus any liabilities owed by the business.

P

participative (democratic) leadership (p. 198) Leadership style that consists of managers and employees working together to make decisions.

partnership (p. 120) A legal form of business with two or more owners.

patent (p. A-6) A document that gives inventors exclusive rights to their inventions for 20 years.

pave the way *Process of making a task easier.*

peanut butter and jelly *Popular combination for sandwich; the two are seen as perfect complementary products.*

penetration strategy (p. 409) Strategy in which a product is priced low to attract many customers and discourage competition.

pension funds (p. 578) Amounts of money put aside by corporations, nonprofit organizations, or unions to cover part of the financial needs of members when they retire.

perks *Short for* perquisites; *compensation in addition to salary, such as day care or a company car.*

perfect competition (p. 38) The degree of competition in which there are many sellers in a market and none is large enough to dictate the price of a product.

performance appraisal (p. 316) An evaluation that measures employee performance against established standards in order to make decisions about promotions, compensation, training, or termination.

personal selling (p. 456) The face-to-face presentation and promotion of goods and services.

piece of the action *A share in the opportunity.*

pink slip *A notice that you've lost your job.*

pitch in *To help as needed.*

place utility (p. 423) Adding value to products by having them where people want them.

planning (p. 188) A management function that includes anticipating trends and determining the best strategies and tactics to achieve organizational goals and objectives.

PMI (p. 192) Listing all the pluses for a solution in one column, all the minuses in another, and the implications in a third column.

podcasting (p. 465) A means of distributing audio and video programs via the Internet that lets users subscribe to a number of files, also known as feeds, and then hear or view the material at the time they choose.

possession utility (p. 424) Doing whatever is necessary to transfer ownership from one party to another, including providing credit, delivery, installation, guarantees, and follow-up service.

poster child *Best example.*

precedent (p. A-3) Decisions judges have made in earlier cases that guide the handling of new cases.

preferred stock (p. 538) Stock that gives its owners preference in the payment of dividends and an earlier claim on assets than common stockholders if the company is forced out of business and its assets sold.

premium (p. C-6) The fee charged by an insurance company for an insurance policy.

price leadership (p. 408) The strategy by which one or more dominant firms set the pricing practices that all competitors in an industry follow.

primary boycott (p. 344) When a union encourages both its members and the general public not to buy the products of a firm involved in a labor dispute.

primary data (p. 371) Data that you gather yourself (not from secondary sources such as books and magazines).

principle of motion economy (p. 271) Theory developed by Frank and Lillian Gilbreth that every job can be broken down into a series of elementary motions.

private accountant (p. 476) An accountant who works for a single firm, government agency, or nonprofit organization.

problem solving (p. 192) The process of solving the everyday problems that occur. Problem solving is less formal than decision making and usually calls for quicker action.

process manufacturing (p. 247) That part of the production process that physically or chemically changes materials.

producer price index (PPI) (p. 48) An index that measures prices at the wholesale level.

product (p. 368) Any physical good, service, or idea that satisfies a want or need plus anything that would enhance the product in the eyes of consumers, such as the brand name.

product analysis (p. 402) Making cost estimates and sales forecasts to get a feeling for profitability of new-product ideas.

product differentiation (p. 394) The creation of real or perceived product differences.

production (p. 245) The creation of finished goods and services using the factors of production: land, labor, capital, entrepreneurship, and knowledge.

production management (p. 245) The term used to describe all the activities managers do to help their firms create goods.

productivity (p. 14) The amount of output you generate given the amount of input (e.g., hours worked).

product liability (p. A-5) Part of tort law that holds businesses liable for harm that results from the production, design, sale, or use of products they market.

product life cycle (p. 404) A theoretical model of what happens to sales and profits for a product class over time; the four stages of the cycle are introduction, growth, maturity, and decline.

product line (p. 393) A group of products that are physically similar or are intended for a similar market.

product mix (p. 393) The combination of product lines offered by a manufacturer.

product placement (p. 453) Putting products into TV shows and movies where they will be seen.

product screening (p. 402) A process designed to reduce the number of new-product ideas being worked on at any one time.

profit (p. 4) The amount of money a business earns above and beyond what it spends for salaries and other expenses.

program evaluation and review technique (PERT) (p. 260) A method for analyzing the tasks involved in completing a given project, estimating the time needed to complete each task, and identifying the minimum time needed to complete the total project.

program trading (p. 553) Giving instructions to computers to automatically sell if the price of a stock dips to a certain point to avoid potential losses.

promissory note (p. 514) A written contract with a promise to pay a supplier a specific sum of money at a definite time.

promotion (p. 369) All the techniques sellers use to inform people about and motivate them to buy their products or services.

promotion mix (p. 448) The combination of promotional tools an organization uses.

pros and cons *Arguments for and against something.*

prospect (p. 457) A person with the means to buy a product, the authority to buy, and the willingness to listen to a sales message.

prospecting (p. 457) Researching potential buyers and choosing those most likely to buy.

prospectus (p. 535) A condensed version of economic and financial information that a company must file with the SEC before issuing stock; the prospectus must be sent to prospective investors.

psychographic segmentation (p. 377) Dividing the market using the group's values, attitudes, and interests.

psychological pricing (p. 409) Pricing goods and services at price points that make the product appear less expensive than it is.

public accountant (p. 476) An accountant who provides accounting services to individuals or businesses on a fee basis.

public domain software (or freeware) (p. B-16) Software that is free for the taking.

publicity (p. 460) Any information about an individual, product, or organization that's distributed to the public through the media and that's not paid for or controlled by the seller.

public relations (PR) (p. 460) The management function that evaluates public attitudes, changes policies and procedures in response to the public's requests, and executes a program of action and information to earn public understanding and acceptance.

pull strategy (p. 466) Promotional strategy in which heavy advertising and sales promotion efforts are directed toward consumers so that they'll request the products from retailers.

pump up the profits *Making profits in a company appear larger than they actually are under recognized accounting rules.*

purchasing (p. 257) The function in a firm that searches for quality material resources, finds the best suppliers, and negotiates the best price for goods and services.

pure risk (p. C-3) The threat of loss with no chance for profit.

push strategy (p. 466) Promotional strategy in which the producer uses advertising, personal selling, sales promotion, and all other promotional tools to convince wholesalers and retailers to stock and sell merchandise.

Q

qualifying (p. 457) In the selling process, making sure that people have a need for the product, the authority to buy, and the willingness to listen to a sales message.

quality (p. 257) Consistently producing what the customer wants while reducing errors before and after delivery to the customer.

quality of life (p. 6) The general well-being of a society in terms of its political freedom, natural environment, education, health care, safety, amount of leisure, and rewards that add to the satisfaction and joy that other goods and services provide.

quid pro quo *Latin phrase meaning "something given in return for something else."*

quite a stir *Something that causes a feeling of concern.*

R

rack jobbers (p. 426) Wholesalers that furnish racks or shelves full of merchandise to retailers, display products, and sell on consignment.

ratio analysis (p. 491) The assessment of a firm's financial condition using calculations and interpretations of financial ratios developed from the firm's financial statements.

real time (p. 227) The present moment or the actual time in which something takes place.

recession (p. 49) Two or more consecutive quarters of decline in the GDP.

recruitment (p. 307) The set of activities used to obtain a sufficient number of the right people at the right time.

reinforcement theory (p. 281) Theory that positive and negative reinforcers motivate a person to behave in certain ways.

relationship marketing (p. 378) Marketing strategy with the goal of keeping individual customers over time by offering them products that exactly meet their requirements.

reserve requirement (p. 572) A percentage of commercial banks' checking and savings accounts that must be physically kept in the bank.

resource development (p. 31) The study of how to increase resources and to create the conditions that will make better use of those resources.

restructuring (p. 230) Redesigning an organization so that it can more effectively and efficiently serve its customers.

retailer (p. 419) An organization that sells to ultimate consumers.

retained earnings (p. 485) The accumulated earnings from a firm's profitable operations that were reinvested in the business and not paid out to stockholders in dividends.

revenue (p. 4) The total amount of money a business takes in during a given period by selling goods and services.

reverse discrimination (p. 304) Discrimination against whites or males in hiring or promoting.

reverse logistics (p. 435) The area of logistics that involves bringing goods back to the manufacturer because of defects or for recycling materials.

revolving credit agreement (p. 517) A line of credit that is guaranteed but usually comes with a fee.

right-to-work laws (p. 340) Legislation that gives workers the right, under an open shop, to join or not join a union if it is present.

risk/return trade-off (p. 520) The principle that the greater the risk a lender takes in making a loan, the higher the interest rate required.

Roth IRA (p. D-15) An IRA where you don't get upfront deductions on your taxes as you would with a traditional IRA, but the earnings grow tax-free and are also tax-free when they are withdrawn.

rule of indemnity (p. C-7) Rule saying that an insured person or organization cannot collect more than the actual loss from an insurable risk.

rules-of-the-road orientation *Introduction to the proper procedures within an organization.*

S

sales promotion (p. 461) The promotional tool that stimulates consumer purchasing and dealer interest by means of short-term activities.

sampling (p. 463) A promotional tool in which a company lets consumers have a small sample of a product for no charge.

savings and loan association (S&L) (p. 577) A financial institution that accepts both savings and checking deposits and provides home mortgage loans.

Savings Association Insurance Fund (SAIF) (p. 581) The part of the FDIC that insures holders of accounts in savings and loan associations.

scientific management (p. 271) Studying workers to find the most efficient ways of doing things and then teaching people those techniques.

S corporation (p. 132) A unique government creation that looks like a corporation but is taxed like sole proprietorships and partnerships.

sea of information *Lots of information, often too much to process.*

secondary boycott (p. 344) An attempt by labor to convince others to stop doing business with a firm that is the subject of a primary boycott; prohibited by the Taft-Hartley Act.

secondary data (p. 370) Information that has already been compiled by others and published in journals and books or made available online.

secured bond (p. 521) A bond issued with some form of collateral.

secured loan (p. 516) A loan backed by collateral (something valuable, such as property).

Securities and Exchange Commission (SEC) (p. 534) Federal agency that has responsibility for regulating the various exchanges.

selection (p. 309) The process of gathering information and deciding who should be hired, under legal guidelines, for the best interests of the individual and the organization.

selective distribution (p. 427) Distribution that sends products to only a preferred group of retailers in an area.

self-insurance (p. C-4) The practice of setting aside money to cover routine claims and buying only "catastrophe" policies to cover big losses.

Service Corps of Retired Executives (SCORE) (p. 175) An SBA office with volunteers from industry, trade associations, and education who counsel small businesses at no cost (except for expenses).

services (p. 4) Intangible products (i.e., products that can't be held in your hand) such as education, health care, insurance, recreation, and travel and tourism.

service utility (p. 424) Adding value by providing fast, friendly service during and after the sale and by teaching customers how to best use products over time.

sexual harassment (p. 350) Unwelcome sexual advances, requests for sexual favors, and other conduct (verbal or physical) of a sexual nature that creates a hostile work environment.

shaky ground *Idea that possible problems lie ahead.*

Sherlock Holmes *A famous fictional detective who was particularly adept at uncovering information to solve very difficult mysteries.*

shoestring budget *A budget that implies the company is short on funds and includes only a minimal amount of financial expenditures (i.e., it's as thin as a shoestring).*

shopping goods and services (p. 395) Those products that the consumer buys only after comparing value, quality, price, and style from a variety of sellers.

shop stewards (p. 342) Union officials who work permanently in an organization and represent employee interests on a daily basis.

short-term financing (p. 513) Funds needed for a year or less.

short-term forecast (p. 507) Forecast that predicts revenues, costs, and expenses for a period of one year or less.

sift through mountains of information *Sort through large volumes of information.*

sinking fund (p. 541) A reserve account in which the issuer of a bond periodically retires some part of the bond principal prior to maturity so that enough capital will be accumulated by the maturity date to pay off the bond.

sin taxes *Taxes used to discourage the use of goods like liquor or cigarettes.*

Six Sigma quality (p. 258) A quality measure that allows only 3.4 defects per million opportunities.

skimming price strategy (p. 409) Strategy in which a new product is priced high to make optimum profit while there's little competition.

small business (p. 162) A business that is independently owned and operated, is not dominant in its field of operation, and meets certain standards of size (set by the Small Business Administration) in terms of employees or annual receipts.

Small Business Administration (SBA) (p. 171) A U.S. government agency that advises and assists small businesses by providing management training and financial advice and loans.

Small Business Investment Company (SBIC) Program (p. 172) A program through which private investment companies licensed by the Small Business Administration lend money to small businesses.

smart card (p. 582) An electronic funds transfer tool that is a combination credit card, debit card, phone card, driver's license card, and more.

smoking gun *An issue or other disclosure that could prove a person or organization has done something wrong.*

social audit (p. 108) A systematic evaluation of an organization's progress toward implementing socially responsible and responsive programs.

social commerce (p. 428) A form of electronic commerce that involves using social media, online media that supports social interaction, and user contributions to assist in the online buying and selling of products and services.

socialism (p. 41) An economic system based on the premise that some, if not most, basic businesses should be owned by the government so that profits can be more evenly distributed among the people.

Social Security (p. D-14) The term used to describe the Old-Age, Survivors, and Disability Insurance Program established by the Social Security Act of 1935.

sole proprietorship (p. 120) A business that is owned, and usually managed, by one person.

sovereign wealth funds (SWFs) (p. 72) Investment funds controlled by governments holding large stakes in foreign companies.

span of control (p. 219) The optimum number of subordinates a manager supervises or should supervise.

specialty goods and services (p. 395) Consumer products with unique characteristics and brand identity. Because these products are perceived as having no reasonable substitute, the consumer puts forth a special effort to purchase them.

speculative risk (p. C-3) A chance of either profit or loss.

squeezing franchisees' profits *Tightening or reducing profits.*

staffing (p. 195) A management function that includes hiring, motivating, and retaining the best people available to accomplish the company's objectives.

staff personnel (p. 223) Employees who advise and assist line personnel in meeting their goals.

stagflation (p. 48) A situation when the economy is slowing but prices are going up anyhow.

stakeholders (p. 6) All the people who stand to gain or lose by the policies and activities of a business and whose concerns the business needs to address.

standard of living (p. 5) The amount of goods and services people can buy with the money they have.

state capitalism (p. 35) A combination of freer markets and some government control.

statement of cash flows (p. 489) Financial statement that reports cash receipts and disbursements related to a firm's three major activities: operations, investments, and financing.

state-of-the-art *The most modern type available.*

statistical process control (SPC) (p. 258) The process of taking statistical samples of product components at each stage of the production process and plotting those results on a graph. Any variances from quality standards are recognized and can be corrected if beyond the set standards.

statistical quality control (SQC) (p. 258) The process some managers use to continually monitor all phases of the production process to assure that quality is being built into the product from the beginning.

statutory law (p. A-3) State and federal constitutions, legislative enactments, treaties of the federal government, and ordinances—in short, written law.

staying afloat *Staying in business during tough times.*

stockbroker (p. 542) A registered representative who works as a market intermediary to buy and sell securities for clients.

stock certificate (p. 537) Evidence of stock ownership that specifies the name of the company, the number of shares it represents, and the type of stock being issued.

stock exchange (p. 533) An organization whose members can buy and sell (exchange) securities for companies and investors.

stock insurance company (p. C-7) A type of insurance company owned by stockholders.

stocks (p. 537) Shares of ownership in a company.

stock splits (p. 546) An action by a company that gives stockholders two or more shares of stock for each one they own.

strategic alliance (p. 71) A long-term partnership between two or more companies established to help each company build competitive market advantages.

strategic planning (p. 190) The process of determining the major goals of the organization and the policies and strategies for obtaining and using resources to achieve those goals.

strict product liability (p. A-5) Legal responsibility for harm or injury caused by a product regardless of fault.

strike (p. 343) A union strategy in which workers refuse to go to work; the purpose is to further workers' objectives after an impasse in collective bargaining.

strikebreakers (p. 345) Workers hired to do the jobs of striking workers until the labor dispute is resolved.

supervisory management (p. 194) Managers who are directly responsible for supervising workers and evaluating their daily performance.

supply (p. 37) The quantity of products that manufacturers or owners are willing to sell at different prices at a specific time.

supply chain (or value chain) (p. 432) The sequence of linked activities that must be performed by various organizations to move goods from the sources of raw materials to ultimate consumers.

supply-chain management (p. 433) The process of managing the movement of raw materials, parts, work in progress, finished goods, and related information through all the organizations involved in the supply chain; managing the return of such goods, if necessary; and recycling materials when appropriate.

SWOT analysis (p. 189) A planning tool used to analyze an organization's strengths, weaknesses, opportunities, and threats.

T

tactical planning (p. 190) The process of developing detailed, short-term statements about what is to be done, who is to do it, and how it is to be done.

tall organization structure (p. 219) An organizational structure in which the pyramidal organization chart would be quite tall because of the various levels of management.

target costing (p. 408) Designing a product so that it satisfies customers and meets the profit margins desired by the firm.

target marketing (p. 376) Marketing directed toward those groups (market segments) an organization decides it can serve profitably.

tariff (p. 78) A tax imposed on imports.

tax accountant (p. 478) An accountant trained in tax law and responsible for preparing tax returns or developing tax strategies.

tax-deferred contributions (p. D-14) Retirement account deposits for which you pay no current taxes, but the earnings gained are taxed as regular income when they are withdrawn at retirement.

taxes (p. A-14) How the government (federal, state, and local) raises money.

technical skills (p. 194) Skills that involve the ability to perform tasks in a specific discipline or department.

technology (p. 14) Everything from phones and copiers to computers, medical imaging devices, personal digital assistants, and the various software programs that make business processes more effective, efficient, and productive.

telecom *Short for telecommunications.*

telecommuting (p. 254) Working from home via computer and modem.

telemarketing (p. 430) The sale of goods and services by telephone.

telephone tag *To leave a telephone message when you attempt to return a message left for you.*

term insurance (p. D-11) Pure insurance protection for a given number of years.

term-loan agreement (p. 519) A promissory note that requires the borrower to repay the loan in specified installments.

test marketing (p. 368) The process of testing products among potential users.

thorny issue *An issue that can cause pain or difficulty (as a thorn on a rose bush may).*

through the grapevine *Informal information communication; stories told by one person to the next.*

time deposit (p. 576) The technical name for a savings account; the bank can require prior notice before the owner withdraws money from a time deposit.

time in the trenches *Working with the other employees and experiencing what they contend with as opposed to managing from an office and relying solely on reports about what is happening in the workplace.*

time-motion studies (p. 271) Studies, begun by Frederick Taylor, of which tasks must be performed to complete a job and the time needed to do each task.

time utility (p. 423) Adding value to products by making them available when they're needed.

top management (p. 193) Highest level of management, consisting of the president and other key company executives who develop strategic plans.

to take a break *To slow down and do something besides work.*

tort (p. A-4) A wrongful act that causes injury to another person's body, property, or reputation.

total fixed costs (p. 408) All the expenses that remain the same no matter how many products are made or sold.

total product offer (p. 392) Everything that consumers evaluate when deciding whether to buy something; also called a *value package.*

trade credit (p. 514) The practice of buying goods and services now and paying for them later.

trade deficit (p. 66) An unfavorable balance of trade; occurs when the value of a country's imports exceeds that of its exports.

trademark (p. 399) A brand that has exclusive legal protection for both its brand name and its design.

trade protectionism (p. 77) The use of government regulations to limit the import of goods and services.

trade surplus (p. 66) A favorable balance of trade; occurs when the value of a country's exports exceeds that of its imports.

training and development (p. 312) All attempts to improve productivity by increasing an employee's ability to perform. Training focuses on short-term skills, whereas development focuses on long-term abilities.

transparency (p. 196) The presentation of a company's facts and figures in a way that is clear and apparent to all stakeholders.

trial balance (p. 480)   A summary of all the financial data in the account ledgers that ensures the figures are correct and balanced.

trial close (p. 458)   A step in the selling process that consists of a question or statement that moves the selling process toward the actual close.

trigger-happy   *Term that refers to people reacting too fast to the circumstances facing them in a difficult situation.*

turn a blind eye   *Ignore something of importance.*

turn the work off   *Stop working.*

U

umbrella policy (p. D-13)   A broadly based insurance policy that saves you money because you buy all your insurance from one company.

unemployment rate (p. 46)   The number of civilians at least 16 years old who are unemployed and tried to find a job within the prior four weeks.

Uniform Commercial Code (UCC) (p. A-8)   A comprehensive commercial law, adopted by every state in the United States, that covers sales laws and other commercial laws.

uninsurable risk (p. C-5)   A risk that no insurance company will cover.

union (p. 334)   An employee organization that has the main goal of representing members in employee–management bargaining over job-related issues.

union security clause (p. 340)   Provision in a negotiated labor–management agreement that stipulates that employees who benefit from a union must either officially join or at least pay dues to the union.

union shop agreement (p. 340)   Clause in a labor–management agreement that says workers do not have to be members of a union to be hired, but must agree to join the union within a prescribed period.

unlimited liability (p. 121)   The responsibility of business owners for all of the debts of the business.

unsecured bond (p. 521)   A bond backed only by the reputation of the issuer; also called a debenture bond.

unsecured loan (p. 516)   A loan that doesn't require any collateral.

unsought goods and services (p. 395)   Products that consumers are unaware of, haven't necessarily thought of buying, or find that they need to solve an unexpected problem.

utility (p. 423)   In economics, the want-satisfying ability, or value, that organizations add to goods or services when the products are made more useful or accessible to consumers than they were before.

V

value (p. 390)   Good quality at a fair price. When consumers calculate the value of a product, they look at the benefits and then subtract the cost to see if the benefits exceed the costs.

variable costs (p. 409)   Costs that change according to the level of production.

variable life insurance (p. D-11)   Whole life insurance that invests the cash value of the policy in stocks or other high-yielding securities.

venture capital (p. 522)   Money that is invested in new or emerging companies that are perceived as having great profit potential.

venture capitalists (p. 170)   Individuals or companies that invest in new businesses in exchange for partial ownership of those businesses.

vertical merger (p. 135)   The joining of two companies involved in different stages of related businesses.

vestibule training (p. 314)   Training done in schools where employees are taught on equipment similar to that used on the job.

viral marketing (p. 464)   The term now used to describe everything from paying customers to say positive things on the Internet to setting up multilevel selling schemes whereby consumers get commissions for directing friends to specific websites.

virtual corporation (p. 227)   A temporary networked organization made up of replaceable firms that join and leave as needed.

virtual networking (p. B-15)   A process that allows software-based networked computers to run multiple operating systems and programs, and share storage.

virtual private network (VPN) (p. B-10)   A private data network that creates secure connections, or "tunnels," over regular Internet lines.

virus (p. B-18) A piece of programming code inserted into other programming to cause some unexpected and, for the victim, usually undesirable event.

vision (p. 189) An encompassing explanation of why the organization exists and where it's trying to head.

volume (or usage) segmentation (p. 377) Dividing the market by usage (volume of use).

voluntary bankruptcy (p. A-15) Legal procedures initiated by a debtor.

W

walk out the door *Leave the company; quit your job.*

watching over your shoulder *Looking at everything you do.*

Web 2.0 (p. B-13) The set of tools that allow people to build social and business connections, share information, and collaborate on projects online (including blogs, wikis, social networking sites and other online communities, and virtual worlds).

Web 3.0 (p. B-13) A combination of technologies that adds intelligence and changes how people interact with the web, and vice versa (consists of the semantic web, mobile web, and immersive Internet).

whistleblowers (p. 101) Insiders who report illegal or unethical behavior.

whole life insurance (p. D-11) Life insurance that stays in effect until age 100.

wholesaler (p. 418) A marketing intermediary that sells to other organizations.

will (p. D-18) A document that names the guardian for your children, states how you want your assets distributed, and names the executor for your estate.

word-of-mouth promotion (p. 463) A promotional tool that involves people telling other people about products they've purchased.

World Bank (p. 584) The bank primarily responsible for financing economic development; also known as the International Bank for Reconstruction and Development.

World Trade Organization (WTO) (p. 79) The international organization that replaced the General Agreement on Tariffs and Trade, and was assigned the duty to mediate trade disputes among nations.

Y

yellow-dog contract (p. 337) A type of contract that required employees to agree as a condition of employment not to join a union; prohibited by the Norris-LaGuardia Act in 1932.